OXFORD HISTORY OF MODERN EUROPE

General Editors

LORD BULLOCK *and* SIR WILLIAM DEAKIN

Oxford History of Modern Europe

THE STRUGGLE FOR MASTERY IN
EUROPE 1848–1918   *Available in paperback*
A. J. P. TAYLOR

THE RUSSIAN EMPIRE 1801–1917
Available in paperback
HUGH SETON-WATSON

A HISTORY OF FRENCH PASSIONS
Available in paperback in two volumes
AMBITION, LOVE, AND POLITICS
INTELLECT, TASTE, AND ANXIETY
THEODORE ZELDIN

GERMANY 1866–1945   *Available in paperback*
GORDON A. CRAIG

THE LOW COUNTRIES 1780–1940
E. H. KOSSMANN

SPAIN 1808–1975   *Available in paperback*
RAYMOND CARR

GERMAN HISTORY 1770–1866   *Available in paperback*
JAMES J. SHEEHAN

A PEOPLE APART: A POLITICAL HISTORY OF THE
JEWS IN EUROPE 1789–1939
Available in paperback
DAVID VITAL

THE TRANSFORMATION OF EUROPEAN
POLITICS 1763–1848   *Available in paperback*
PAUL W. SCHROEDER

THE LIGHTS
THAT FAILED

EUROPEAN
INTERNATIONAL HISTORY
1919–1933

ZARA STEINER

OXFORD
UNIVERSITY PRESS

OXFORD

UNIVERSITY PRESS

Great Clarendon Street, Oxford OX2 6DP

Oxford University Press is a department of the University of Oxford.
It furthers the University's objective of excellence in research, scholarship,
and education by publishing worldwide in

Oxford New York

Auckland Cape Town Dar es Salaam Hong Kong Karachi Kuala Lumpur
Madrid Melbourne Mexico City Nairobi New Delhi
Shanghai Taipei Toronto

With offices in

Argentina Austria Brazil Chile Czech Republic France Greece
Guatemala Hungary Italy Japan South Korea Poland Portugal
Singapore Switzerland Thailand Turkey Ukraine Vietnam

Published in the United States
by Oxford University Press Inc., New York

British Library Cataloguing in Publication Data

Data available

Library of Congress Cataloging in Publication Data

Data available

ISBN 0-19-822114-2

1 3 5 7 9 10 8 6 4 2

Typeset by Kolam Information Services Pvt. Ltd, Pondicherry, India
Printed in Great Britain
on acid-free paper by
Biddles Ltd
King's Lynn, Norfolk

PREFACE

This book has been a long time in the making. Too many years have elapsed since I accepted Lord Bullock's invitation to write about European international relations between the two world wars. I started with the intention of trying to understand the tangled international history of the years that led to the crushing of hopes and illusions about the forward progress of European civilization. At the time I believed that it would also be possible and useful to review the literature on the inter-war period and update accounts that were in general use some twenty years ago. I hoped to move away from the existing emphasis on western Europe and look at the growing monographic literature on eastern Europe in order to provide a more complete and balanced picture of what was, in my view, a single continent with shared as well as distinct histories. I believed that post-war eras can have distinctive characters of their own and that the 1920s should be treated as a decade which followed an earlier world war, the focus of my previous historical research, rather than, as was common, the precursor of the war that followed. I also wanted to look at some of the questions resulting from the expansion of the field of international history beyond the confines of traditional diplomatic history.

So much has happened during the course of my writing that I have been forced to rethink and rewrite sections of this book. First, the Cold War came to an end and a new epoch in the history of international relations began. The ending came, moreover, without another great war between the two superpowers or an intra-European war of major proportions. Consciously or unconsciously, these contemporary events were bound to affect my perception of the period with which I was dealing. It was only as I was completing this study that I realized how far my own life was marked by the Second World War rather than the events which followed. During the course of my writing I have become acutely conscious of the chronological 'mental maps' that almost all historians carry with them. Reading new books on the 1919–39 period, I can almost recognize when their authors came to maturity, whether before or during the Second World War, or in the Cold War or post-Cold War years. Secondly, the enormous number of relevant books that has appeared has meant that no single person can canvas the field across in the major European languages, not to speak of the others. It is not that the older books have become dated; on the contrary, many have improved with the passage of time, and one is astonished at how often their conclusions are confirmed by newer research. New sources, however, have been opened. Even the Soviet archives, so long closed to historians, are beginning— admittedly in a frustratingly slow and irregular manner—to reveal their contents to researchers. Secondary accounts of the inter-war years can make use of east European sources that were unavailable even ten years ago. The intelligence services of some countries have also opened their records, allowing historians to explore the 'missing dimension' in the histories of national foreign and security policies. Quite apart from the availability of new sources, the geographic map of historical enquiry has expanded beyond recognition, adding to the number of questions which present-day students of international history must examine. One consequence of this vast explosion of the field has been the increasing number of collective works that have appeared in almost every language. The technological revolution may well alter the way international history will be studied in the very near future. The computer-illiterate student of the field, like myself, may come to be regarded as a dinosaur.

This book represents a journey in self-education. I hope that something of what I have learned will be communicated to its readers. It also rests on the highly unfashionable premise that history is more than a simple expression of opinion about the past, dependent on the personality and viewpoint of the person who writes it. Though total objectivity is obviously impossible and no one can really reproduce the story of the past freed from his or her own presumptions, I believe that it is possible to illuminate the thinking and the actions of the major players in this drama without gross distortions, and that one can describe the outlines of the worlds, real and imagined, within which they operated. I have tried to put together the many pieces of the European puzzle in a meaningful manner. While there will never be one common or accepted interpretation of these events, all approaches are not equally valid. It is in the hope of explaining as well as I can the course of events that led to one of the most tragic and inhumane periods in European history that I have written this book.

This will be a two-volume study of the inter-war years. The separation underlines my conviction that the 1920s should be seen in the light of the Great War and the peace treaties rather than as the prologue to what happened in the Hitler era. This first volume falls into two parts. Part I shows how the peacemakers and their successors dealt with the problems of a shattered Europe. The war had fundamentally altered both the internal structures of many of the European states and transformed the traditional international order. Differently from most historians, I have shown that the management of the European state system in the decade after 1919, while in some ways resembling that of the past, assumed a shape that distinguished it both from the pre-war decades and the post-1933 period. In handling the problems of war and peace, reconstruction and stabilization, Europe's statesmen were forced to fashion new methods of addressing problems that were no longer suitable for traditional treatment. What evolved was an international regime run by those who still viewed Europe as the centre of the world and who looked backward as well as forward, but who also experimented with new forms of international discourse, some of which survived their subsequent destruction and reappeared after 1945. The multifarious nature of European international relations at this time dictates a somewhat non-sequential approach, as I have tried to untangle the many threads, both internal and external, which constituted the differing national approaches to foreign affairs. At the same time I have tried to convey the simultaneity and overlapping nature of the reconstruction occuring in western and eastern Europe, in fascist Italy and the Soviet Union, which marked the emergence of a very fragile international regime.

Part II covers the 'hinge years', 1929 to 1933; both starting and closing dates are only bookmarks of convenience. These were the years in which many of the experiments in internationalism came to be tested and their weaknesses revealed. Many of the difficulties stemmed from the enveloping economic depression, but there were other blows to the international regime which shook its foundations. The way was open to the movements towards étatism, autarcy, virulent nationalism, and expansionism which characterized the post-1933 European scene. The events of these years were critical to both Hitler's challenge to the European status quo and the reactions of the European statesmen to his assault on what remained of an international system.

The second volume will deal with the years 1933–9, again divided into two unequal periods, 1933–8 and from 1938 to the outbreak of war. An epilogue will take the story down to 1941. Hitler is at the centre of this account. While I have few doubts about his ultimate intentions, I will show how far the achievement of his long-range objectives were due to the active support and compliance of the majority of Germans and the reaction of the other European powers, both large and small. While Hitler posed an exceptional challenge to the international system, the policies of other statesmen dictated the course of the 'twisted road to war'. I cannot hope to explain why Hitler succeeded in a politically sophisticated and culturally rich nation like Germany, a problem which continues to trouble historians, but I can examine the ideological assumptions, perceptions of power, past experiences, and domestic pressures that explain the actions taken by the main European players. The second section dealing with the last months of peace challenges the realist or neo-realist explanations of the outbreak of war. The point is made that recently opened archives and the new questions raised by contemporary international historians warrant the re-examination of the Hitler period, despite the vast literature on the origins of the Second World War. The epilogue, too, will look in brief at new interpretations of the transformation of a limited European conflict into a world war that radically changed both the existing and future configurations of global power and influence. Though the two books are parts of a single argument, they can be read separately without detracting from their central theme. There was no straight line from the peace settlements of 1919 to the outbreak and spread of the European conflict, though the Great War set in motion the shock waves that led to the loss of European predominance.

This book is based primarily on printed and secondary sources, although I have worked in the archives of four countries in order to get a feel for the main actors in this complex story. Each chapter is followed by a bibliography giving some indication of the books and articles relevant to the chapter. The final bibliography lists primary sources, public and private, used in this first volume. Footnotes, which I have used sparingly, refer mainly to material from the sources. Wherever possible, I have tried to cite this material in its published form.

If I were to acknowledge the many men and women in Britain, France, Germany, Italy, Romania, Russia, Switzerland, Canada, and the United States who have either answered my queries or looked up papers I have needed, this paragraph would look like a *Who's Who* in the field of International History. I can only say that no one whom I approached failed to assist me, and that the generosity of my fellow historians has been quite amazing. I am truly grateful, and hope that this general acknowledgement will prove acceptable. Archivists in Paris, Bonn, Geneva, Birmingham University, Churchill College, the Bodleian at Oxford, and the University Library at Cambridge have been uniformly helpful in the research for this volume. Like all researchers, I found the facilities at the Public Record Office at Kew a real boost for morale. I must record my deep indebtedness to my many research students, coming from a variety of countries, most of whose Ph.D. theses, now appearing as books, are cited during the course of this volume. They have assisted me in a multitude of ways, extending from dog-walking to the identification and often translations of articles and books that I otherwise would have missed. As I have never had a university post, my main debt to Cambridge has been the opportunity to have such students and to act as examiner for other Ph.D. candidates, most of whom have kept me abreast of the latest work in a swiftly changing field. I must single out two of my former research students, Dr Felicity von Peters, who did yeoman service in trying to impose order on my many files in the early stages of my research, and Dr Andrew Webster, without whose labours the manuscript for this volume would never have emerged from the computer. I owe too a special debt to Dr Niall Johnson, who prepared the final copy of this book for the Oxford University Press. Individual members of the History Faculty and the Centre of International Studies have provided intellectual stimulation and the opportunity to try out ideas.

New Hall has been my academic home throughout my academic career in Cambridge, offering companionship, a much-needed room of my own, and the chance to supervise undergraduates both from the college and elsewhere. Without my New Hall salary, I might have become a more popular author! I owe a debt of gratitude to the Leverhulme Trust, the Nuffield Foundation Small Grants Scheme, the John D. and Catherine T. MacArthur Foundation, and the John Simon Guggenheim Memorial Foundation for grants that enabled me to travel to archives in Britain as well as abroad, to employ a research student to work in Moscow, and for support during the final preparations of this book for publication. The Leverhulme funding also allowed me to secure the services of a historian and statistician, Dr Declan Reilly, who compiled, with the assistance of others cited elsewhere, the statistical charts included in this book. I am grateful for his patience, perseverance, and above all for his explanations of what statistics can or cannot prove. I wish to thank my two editors at Oxford University Press, Ruth Parr and Anne Gelling, for their encouragement and particularly Kay Rogers for her help in preparing the manuscript for publication. Finally, I must mention my indebtedness to the three anonymous readers of the manuscripts of both these volumes. They have gone far beyond the bounds of their duties, to the surprise and gratitude of my editors at the Oxford University Press. Their extensive and detailed reports were of the greatest use. They are not responsible for the stubbornness of the writer in rejecting some of their general recommendations that would have resulted in a better but a very different book.

I have two special debts to acknowledge. The first is to the late Lord Bullock, the general editor of the Oxford History of Modern Europe. Throughout these many years, he never faltered in his support for my work or in his belief that this book would finally see the light of day. His comments, even when critical, were always encouraging and have opened and not closed doors. My final debt is to my husband, George Steiner, who will not believe that this book is really finished until he actually holds the printed volume in his hand. I know that he will enjoy the final product far more than the weeks, months, and years that were spent on writing it. Whether he will find the book worthy of the effort remains to be seen.

Zara Steiner

CONTENTS

LIST OF MAPS AND FIGURES

LIST OF MAPS

LIST OF FIGURES

LIST OF TABLES

PROLOGUE

The Great War was like a terrible volcanic eruption that left immeasurable destruction in its wake. Millions were killed or maimed; countless others were displaced by the hostilities and their aftermath. Billions were spent on the fighting; land and industries were destroyed and all the customary channels of global communication, trade, and finance were seriously disrupted. The raising of armies and the mobilization of civilian populations on such an unprecedented scale by the belligerent states reshaped their domestic landscapes. Many aspects of the former world escaped obliteration and were even left intact, but there was little that was not marked in some way by this manmade catastrophe. The war was both conduit and catalyst, 'the great transformer through which the currents of history emerged with newly determined strengths and directions'.[1] The war did more; it set in motion new ideas and movements whose tremors were felt throughout Europe and beyond. Even where the old elites remained in power, they faced a fundamentally altered environment both at home and abroad that required an expanded armoury of responses. While many of the traditional modes of diplomacy remained in place, new techniques and institutions were needed to deal with the vast expansion of the international map and agenda. The very concept of a 'European system of international relations' was shattered by the Russian revolutions and American participation in the war. The power positions of victors and vanquished were altered by the length of the war and its human and material costs. Many of the world's financial and commercial structures were swept away, along with some of the necessary conditions for their re-establishment. Wartime actions fed national loyalties and evoked heightened nationalism in all its myriad forms. Nationalist demands and economic and social grievances unleashed by the breakdown of traditional structures created revolutionary movements in many parts of Europe. The heady brew of self-determination reached

---

[1] Gerald Feldman, 'Mobilising Economies for War', in Jay Winter, Geoffrey Parker, and Mary R. Habeck (eds.), *The Great War and the Twentieth Century* (New Haven, Conn., 2000), 168.

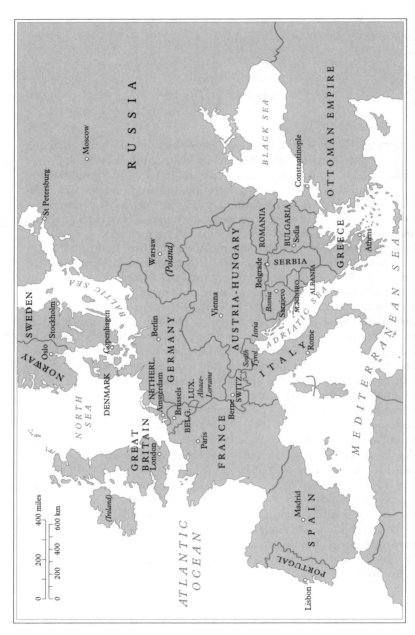

Map 1. Europe in 1914

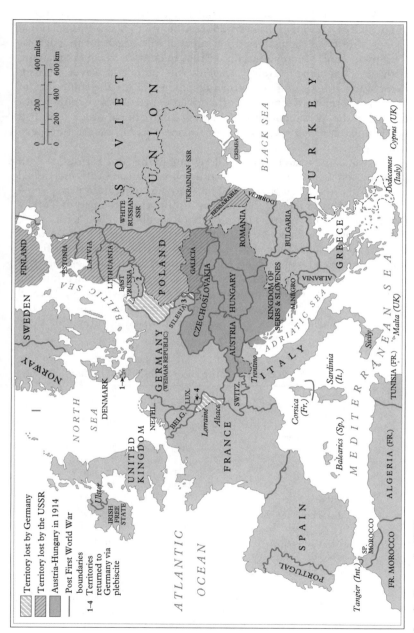

Map 2. Europe in 1919

the Middle East, Central Asia, China, and South-East Asia. Once opened, this Pandora's box could not be shut. Victorious national groups who freed themselves from imperial rule began turning against their own ethnic and religious minorities. In contrast to, and coinciding with, the heightened hostility towards the 'other', however defined, there was a longing for the return of peace and for the fulfilment of wartime promises of a better world, given expression in Leninist doctrines and the Wilsonian vision of a new international order. This had been an extraordinary war that left permanent gashes on the European landscape.

The war came to an end with the signing of the Allied armistice with Germany on 11 November 1918. Bulgaria capitulated first and signed an armistice on 29 September. The German appeal for peace on 4 October 1918 was rapidly followed by armistices on the part of Turkey (30 October) and Austria-Hungary (3 November). The victors were jubilant. The Allied and Associated powers had crushed Prussian militarism and suddenly won that victory which had eluded them for so long. But there was quiet only on the western front. Though the guns fell silent in the west, peace had not yet returned to continental Europe. New armies were on the move in the east seeking to establish national boundaries before the peacemakers met. The break-up of the Habsburg empire and the civil wars in Russia meant that the futures of these

TABLE 1. War Expenditure and Deaths, 1914–1918

	Expenditure $bn.	Dead
Britain	43.8	723,000
British empire	5.8	198,000
France	28.2	1,398,000
Russia	16.3	1,811,000
Italy	14.7	578,000
USA	36.2	114,000
Other	2.0	599,000
Total Entente/Allied	147.0	5,421,000
Germany	47.0	2,037,000
Austria-Hungary	13.4	1,100,000
Bulgaria–Turkey	1.1	892,000
Total Central Powers	61.5	4,029,000
Grand Total	208.5	9,450,000

Sources: Gerd Hardach, *First World War* (Harmondsworth, 1987), 153; J. Winter, *The Great War and The British People* (Basingstoke, 1985), 75.

regions were still unsettled. Influenza swept the globe, causing more deaths than the war itself. Millions of people were displaced by the conflict, and shortages of food, coal, and shelter compounded the miseries of daily life produced by the wartime upheavals. The collapse or overthrow of traditional authorities meant that the governments which had to wrestle with the immediate problems of dislocation and disruption were often new and weak.

Four great empires disappeared, with their ruling dynasties either exiled or killed. In Germany a republic was declared on 9 November. The kaiser was forced to abdicate and the rule of the Hohenzollerns was ended. The disintegration of the Habsburg empire during the latter half of October had little to do with direct Allied action, for the subject nationalities freed themselves before the armistice was concluded. A South Slav state was established on 17 October, and on 1 December the state of the Serbs, Croats, and Slovenes came into being (the name 'Yugoslavia' was not used until 1929). Republics were created in Poland (5 November), Austria (12 November), Czechoslovakia (14 November), and Hungary (16 November). The Emperor Karl went into exile on 12 November and the Habsburg dynasty disappeared as quickly as that of the Hohenzollerns. In Turkey, though the state and Sultanate at first survived, a new government concluded the armistice at Mudros acknowledging the loss of much of its former domain. Constantinople, already occupied by Allied troops, was to be governed by a High Commission with British, French, and Italian members. The Arab lands were withdrawn from Ottoman control and placed under British and French administration. The Greeks were given a zone in the Izmir area and occupied all of Thrace. In Eastern Anatolia, Armenian and Kurdish leaders laid plans for independent states. Meanwhile, British wartime agreements gave hope to Arabs and Zionists alike that their national aspirations would be recognized at the peace conference. Tsarist Russia and the Romanov dynasty had already vanished in the revolutions of 1917, with the tsar and his family murdered on 17 July 1918. The provisional government, dominated by liberals, that had taken power in March 1917 continued to fight the war, only, after a series of military defeats, to be overthrown by the Bolsheviks in November 1917.[2] A Russian–German armistice was followed by formal peace talks in December 1917, that culminated in the draconian settlement of the Treaty of Brest-Litovsk, signed on 3 March 1918. The Russians lost one-fourth of their pre-war European empire, including the Ukraine, Baltic, Finnish, and Polish territories, and 40 per cent of their

---

[2] Western or Gregorian dating is used throughout, rather than the Julian calendar followed by the Russians until 1 February 1918 which was fourteen days earlier.

European population. Lands in the Caucasus were given to the Ottoman Turks. Following the German defeat in the west, the Bolsheviks emerged as the main contender for control of the former Russian lands. By the end of 1918 the new regime was engulfed in a series of murderous civil wars, as it fought internal foes and a variety of foreign armies. Polish, Czech, Finnish, and Ukrainian soldiers were in the field, as were military detachments from Britain, France, the United States, and Japan. Despite mounting fears among Allied leaders about the consequences of the November 1917 revolution, many in the west still hoped that a liberal democratic regime might emerge in Russia. There was a good deal of confusion about the Bolshevik success; concern and condemnation in the victor states coincided with sympathy and goodwill in European labour and socialist circles. Relations between the Allied victors and the new Russian government were highly ambiguous, as the Allies coupled support for the 'White Russians' opposed to the socialist revolution with assurances to the Bolshevik 'Reds' that they were not concerned with Russian domestic affairs. If for some the Bolshevik message of class struggle and world revolution was one of promise, for others the revolutionary movements in Germany, Hungary, and Switzerland were frightening reminders of what might happen if the Bolshevik revolution spread beyond the Russian borders. It was not at all clear in that bitterly cold winter of 1918–19 where the 'red wave' would stop. Along the Russian borders new states had already emerged. The provisional government had recognized national aspirations in Poland, Finland, and Estonia, and these changes were confirmed by the Bolsheviks. The Bolshevik leader, Vladimir Ilyich Lenin, in his 'Decree on Peace' of 8 November 1917, held out the promise of self-determination for all nations, though subsequent actions in Finland and the Ukraine did not coincide with his words. The Allied interventions and the German armistice made it unlikely that the Bolsheviks would be able to reimpose Russian rule without a major military effort.

The experience of war brought more than changes to the states and to the international system of the pre-1914 period. The war introduced profound economic and social effects that, with differing degrees of intensity and importance, were to reverberate throughout the decade and beyond. The war had to be paid for, and distributional questions about the burden of payment affected both domestic and foreign politics. The war had brought new interest groups into the political arena, and gave greater power to those who had formerly been excluded from the ruling elites or whose influence had been muted in the presence of older social groups. It was unlikely that, having tasted power, industrialists and businessmen would not demand a larger voice in the political process than they had enjoyed earlier. The war, moreover, had caused tumultuous changes to the conditions of labour in Europe. Even the peasantry of eastern Europe, most of whom had hitherto lived in static and self-contained communities, was touched by the experience of military service and the wartime demands for their labour. Demobilization brought occupations and land seizures. Rural peasant parties mushroomed and expanded. News of the Russian revolutions spread and had a major impact on the Balkan peasantry. The pressure for land reform became so intense throughout the region that almost all the states instituted land reforms in the post-war period. The ferment in the cities in western as in eastern Europe was equally, if not more, marked. Labour militancy reached a wartime peak in 1917–18, and the unrest continued well beyond the armistice. With labour in short supply during the war, the state's failure to respond to working-class discontent had provoked demonstrations, prolonged strikes, and revolutionary action. The politicization and radicalization of the labour movements varied considerably from country to country, according to their past histories and the respective responses of the belligerent governments. Working-class consciousness increased and unions and socialist parties grew in membership and importance. Though successful revolutions outside of Russia were rare, the divisions in the labour movement created by the Russian example changed both working-class politics and the attitudes of those in political and economic power. In some states, as in Weimar Germany and fascist Italy, corporate solutions were sought, but almost everywhere class conflicts and divisions altered the content and even the forms of political conflict. Even the forces on the left were divided; labour movements and unions had to respond to the new challenge of the Communist parties. In all parts of Europe the possibilities of social revolutions and the establishment of Bolshevik regimes, whether real or imagined, gave an importance to Bolshevik Russia well beyond its immediate threat.

It was inevitable that wartime governments would become more powerful and interventionist as people and resources were called to the service of the state on an unprecedented scale. The challenges from the left provoked strong reactions from the right, accelerating the war-induced changes in political alignments. Though some of the many transformations in political and socio-economic attitudes proved short-lived, others survived to profoundly affect the peace settlements and the shape of the post-war political and social scene. In order to enlist the support of the population and maintain the loyalty of mass armies, governments beat the nationalist drum. New techniques and instruments of propaganda were directed at maintaining morale at home and at the front. One result was that, in the post-war period, politicians in every state had to respond to popular pressures on a scale not seen before

1914. Another effect was to arouse popular feelings that were highly destructive of order and compromise. Ethnic nationalism, whether in the victorious or defeated countries, above all in eastern Europe, was heightened in the scramble for territory that followed the armistice and during the negotiation of the peace. Moreover, the war resulted in the mass movements of people on an unimagined scale, not just from the cities to the countryside, but across national borders. The term 'refugee' took on a new meaning with the forced exchanges of population, and with the flood of men, women, and children from what had been the tsarist empire. Those fleeing or expelled became one of the first problems that the infant international body, the League of Nations, had to face. With their new immigration laws of the 1920s, the Americans blocked the previous flow of immigrants from Italy and the states of central and south-eastern Europe, increasing the pressures on national governments to find alternative solutions to the problems of overpopulation and unemployment.

The public declarations during 1918 of the British prime minister, David Lloyd George, and the American president, Woodrow Wilson, provoked in part by the Bolshevik revolution and Lenin's speeches, encouraged war-weary populations to think of a brave new world. Lloyd George's speech at the Trades Union Congress of 5 January 1918 spoke of a new Europe based on 'reason and justice' and on 'government with the consent of the governed'.[3] While the prime minister's speech had been prepared through lengthy consultation, its American counterpart had not. The celebrated 'Fourteen Points', presented unannounced by Wilson to Congress three days later, unilaterally defined 'the only possible program' for world peace. His points fell into two categories, general principles and territorial adjustments. The former included, as the first four points: 'open covenants of peace, openly arrived at', 'absolute freedom of navigation upon the seas', 'the removal, so far as possible, of all economic barriers', and the promise that 'national armaments will be reduced to the lowest point consistent with domestic safety'. The fourteenth point was for Wilson the most important of all: 'A general association of nations must be formed under specific covenants for the purpose of affording mutual guarantees of political independence and territorial integrity to great and small states alike.' Territorial stipulations were outlined concerning Russia, Belgium, France, Italy, Austria-Hungary, Serbia, Romania, Ottoman Turkey, and Poland. Critically, in these points Wilson employed the language of nationality and self-determination, stating that various borders ought

[3] The full text of the speech is in David Lloyd George, *The War Memoirs of Lloyd George* (London, 1936–8), ii. 1510–17.

to be adjusted according to 'historically established lines of allegiance and nationality', with the peoples within larger empires to be given 'the freest opportunity to autonomous development'.[4] Lenin had called for a 'peace without annexations or indemnities'; the American president held out the prospect of a new political and economic international order that would preserve the future peace. Animated discussions followed Wilson's message, which was variously interpreted. For many in Europe it offered hope for a better world at a time when peace was still remote and the struggle undecided.

The end of the war came unexpectedly. It was General Erich von Ludendorff of the German Supreme Command who first demanded an armistice, and though the German military objected to its actual terms, its political power was now eroded and it was the last imperial government, the reform cabinet of Prince Max of Baden, that asked President Wilson for an armistice based on the Fourteen Points. Despite its decisive military defeat, the German army was still on French territory when the armistice was concluded on 11 November, and the vanquished did not feel crushed when their army marched back to Germany. Until the end of September, German policy-makers had stuck to the belief that they could hold on to most of their territorial conquests. In accepting the armistice terms, the leaders of the newly created republic spoke of a 'just peace' and the promise of participation in the new world system which Wilson proclaimed. They intended that the president should mediate between the republic and the Allies so that Germany, regardless of its defeat, would retain its great-power status and play its part in the reconstituted world order. The significance of the Germans seeking armistice terms from an American president was not lost on either side of the Atlantic. The armistice conditions were stern and non-negotiable: German evacuation of all occupied territories in the west and east (though not until the Allies should so require); the delivery of armaments and rolling stock; Allied occupation of the left bank of the Rhine, along with key bridgeheads and the establishment of a 'neutral zone' on the right bank; the surrender of all submarines and a major part of the surface fleet; and the continuation of the naval blockade until all these conditions were met. Even the initial German disappointment over the terms of the armistice, far harsher than expected and in keeping with Allied aims, failed to shatter German illusions about the role Wilson would play in Paris. The post-revolutionary German government would enter the 'dreamland of the Armistice period', the telling phrase of Ernst Troeltsch, the German theologian.

[4] Wilson, speech to Joint Session of Congress, 8 Jan. 1918, in Arthur Link (ed.), *Collected Papers of Woodrow Wilson* (Princeton, 1984), xlv. 534–9.

Critical for Germany, the peace settlement, and the future of Europe, a constitutional republic was established in Germany and the radical revolutionaries defeated. The disappearance of the imperial regime in Germany in November 1918 was the work of the old elites; it was accompanied by widespread disorders and the creation of workers' and soldiers' councils. The two moderate socialist parties seized the initiative, determined that Germany should be a parliamentary democracy and that order should be restored. Elections held on 19 January 1919 resulted in a victory for the moderate republican parties, the Social Democrats, the Centre Party, and the liberal-left German Democratic Party, who together constituted the 'Weimar coalition'. Five days later the representatives of heavy industry and the trade-union representatives concluded an agreement (the Stinnes–Legien Agreement) which opened the prospect of a corporatist socio-economic settlement and reinforced the unwillingness of the Social Democratic Party leaders to countenance any attack on property. With President Friedrich Ebert's approval, the army and Free Corps volunteers (mercenary bands of ex-soldiers) moved against the radical left. The street fighting in Berlin (10–15 January) culminated in the attack on an ill-considered and chaotic demonstration of extreme left socialists and communists and the deaths of the Communist party leaders, Karl Liebnecht and Rosa Luxembourg, on 15 January. The crushing of the so-called 'Spartacus revolt', in no way deserving of the name, and the 'white terror' that followed was a shattering defeat for the left-wing radicals. Strikes and armed conflicts took place in February and March, and for a brief period, 4 April–1 May, a Soviet republic was established in Bavaria. All were suppressed. The most radical sections of the working class turned to the Communist party, creating an unbridgeable divide between moderates and extremists. Many of the sponsors of the new republic favoured extensive political, economic, and social change, but all rejected the radical transformation of either the state or society. Basic to the compromises on which the Weimar republic was based was a working alliance between the constitutionally minded sections of the middle and working classes. It was an uneasy partnership repeatedly threatened from both the right and the left. The republic was, from the start, a fragile creation.

The Weimar coalition used the promise of a Wilsonian peace as a means of courting mass support. At the same time, the threat that the government might fall to the Bolsheviks was intended to influence Allied opinion. Lloyd George's 'Fontainebleau memorandum' of 25 March 1919, and the beginning of American food shipments to Germany at the end of March, encouraged optimism that the tactic would work. The argument that food shortages would lead to revolution was not without effect. Without the March riots and supposed threats of the communists to the position of the government, it is doubtful whether the British would have joined the Americans who, for a mixture of selfish (there was a glut of American agricultural supplies immediately after the war) and humane reasons, wanted to end the blockade. Most Germans were shocked by the defeat and could not come to terms with the outcome of the war. Germany had not been invaded; in both the west and east German troops still stood on foreign soil when the fighting stopped. President Ebert reflected prevailing opinion when he greeted the troops returning from France: 'I salute you, who return unvanquished from the field of battle.'[5] The majority of Germans refused to accept the reality of the military disaster and, having never experienced war on their own soil, hardly needed convincing that there had been a 'stab in the back'.

It was against a changing and volatile background that the peace would have to be concluded. There would be no breathing space nor moment of repose while the maps were rearranged. The statesmen had to deal with inherited and new situations that limited their freedom of decision. The problems to be resolved were more numerous and far more complex than those faced at the Congress of Vienna in 1815. The process of reconstruction had to take into account a war of extraordinary ferocity that had extended beyond the frontiers of Europe and destroyed, temporarily at least, much of the framework of normal life. The prominence of the United States and the uncertain impact of the revolution and civil war in Russia had to be considered by war leaders unaccustomed to the presence of the former and fearful of the latter. There was no way of judging what further changes were to come. The 'Great War' had begun as a struggle between states who were participants in a well-established European system of international relations; it ended with that system shattered. Europe's leaders were men of the pre-war world, statesmen who looked backwards as well as forward. They would have to reassemble the continental pieces, in quite different ways, if the fruits of victory were to be preserved. The memory of an illusory golden age still suffused the pages of Anthony Eden's (Lord Avon) most moving book, *Another World, 1897–1917*, published in 1976, but however attractive it might have appeared to some who had survived the ordeal of war, there was no possible return to the old order. The disruptions were too many and the effects too widespread. It was a changed world in which the rulers of Europe now operated.

---

[5] Quoted in Harold James, *A German Identity* (London, 1989), 116.

PART I

The Reconstruction of Europe, 1918–1929

1

The Hall of Mirrors: Peacemaking in the West

I

The Paris peace conference was formally opened on 18 January 1919. The place and date, which marked the anniversary of the founding of the German empire in the Hall of Mirrors at the French royal palace of Versailles in 1871, were chosen by the French. The long wait following the armistice resulted from elections in the United States and Britain, and from the time delegates from the far corners of the world needed to arrive: it would take two months for the Japanese delegation to reach Paris. In any case Georges Clemenceau, the French premier, counselled delay until the political situation in the former enemy states was clarified and governments in place were able to discuss peace terms. Once opened, it would be another five months before the conference was ready to present the defeated Germans, in the form of the representatives of the newly formed Weimar republic, with their non-negotiable terms of peace. These peace terms, the muddled and lengthy process by which they were drafted, as well as the personalities and motivations of the men who drafted them, have been fiercely and continually maligned since the very moment of their presentation. The war's final crime, it could still be declared in 1999, was a peace treaty 'whose harsh terms would ensure a second war'.[1] Such simplistic assessments, which view 1919 solely in the light of 1939, take no account of what was actually created at Paris and why. The magnitude of the task confronted by the leaders of the victor powers staggers the imagination. They faced the unresolved problems of pre-1914 Europe as well as the situations created by the war. None of the war leaders, now peacemakers, was blind to the changes wrought by the conflict. Yet the events were too close and experiences too fresh to assess the full nature of these transformations. The best that could be done was to grapple with their most immediate and most pressing consequences. The statesmen met in Paris at a moment of high dislocation in the international order. It was a

[1] *Economist*, 31 Dec. 1999.

time of systemic change, when it was possible to contemplate a new international regime to replace the one that had so spectacularly collapsed. Yet despite the popular hopes roused by President Wilson's proclaimed vision of 'liberal internationalism', the treaties of Paris did not represent the victory of principle and morality over national interest. If the treaties incorporated the principles of democracy, collective security (a term not yet in use), and self-determination, they also reflected the claims of state sovereignty and individual and often conflicting national requirements. The Treaty of Versailles was unquestionably flawed, but the treaty in itself did not shatter the peace that it established.

Neither the conditions in Europe nor in Paris were conducive to rational peacemaking, and the chaotic methods of the three main architects of the German treaty, Georges Clemenceau, David Lloyd George, and Woodrow Wilson, did not help. Paris was scarcely the best venue for a peace conference; the heated atmosphere, fanned by the excesses of the Parisian press, was hardly conducive to reasoned deliberations. Geneva had been suggested but was rejected by Clemenceau and the French. 'I never wanted to hold the Conference in his bloody capital,' Lloyd George complained, 'but the old man wept and protested so much that we gave way.'[2] Little could be done to prepare for a gathering of unprecedented size in a city suffering from an acute shortage of accommodation, fuel, and food. Administrative chaos during the conference left tempers short, and men whose energies should have been directed to questions of high policy found themselves engaged in sorting out housekeeping problems of the most petty kind. Though the precedents of 1815 were studied in detail, there was little resemblance between the Congress of Vienna and the gathering at Paris. In 1815 the peace was made by five powers; in 1919 twenty-seven allied states were represented. Lord Castlereagh, the British foreign secretary, came to Vienna with a staff of fourteen; in 1919 the British delegation, not the largest, consisted of 207 persons backed by a considerable supporting staff of typists, messengers, printers, chauffeurs, chefs, and waiters. Representatives arrived not only from Europe but from all continents, and from small states as well as large. The hotel corridors were crowded with petitioners, some from states or would-be states, others from organizations of all sizes, types, and concerns. Private individuals clamoured to be received by 'men of influence'. The defeated nations—Germany, Austria, Hungary, Bulgaria, and Turkey— did not attend, nor were the Russians invited to the deliberations.

---

[2] Lloyd George, in Sir William Wiseman's peace conference diary, 19 Jan. 1919; quoted in Margaret MacMillan, *Peacemakers: The Paris Conference of 1919 and Its Attempt to End War* (paperback edn., London, 2002), 35.

The number of states represented and the variety of people demanding to be heard were the inevitable result of the expansion of the diplomatic map, both geographically and in the subjects of international concern. The future architects of the peace remained sensitive to the public mood. Unlike those who met at Vienna a century before, the leaders of the four main victor states were elected representatives, responsive and responsible to mass electorates. There were many who believed that, for the first time in Europe's history, the peoples' voices would be heard in the corridors of power. Well over 500 press correspondents eager for news added to the confusion. None of the official delegations had given thought to the problem of satisfying the media's thirst for information. Though President Wilson's Fourteen Points had demanded, in the first point, that 'there shall be no private international understandings of any kind but diplomacy shall proceed always frankly and in the public view', this principle was rapidly discarded in favour of private meetings. It was hardly surprising that the massive American press corps howled in protest. These were not problems that had troubled the peacemakers of 1815.

There had been little discussion about how the peace conference was to be organized. It was at first expected that the victors would decide the terms between themselves in a preliminary conference, and then negotiate with the defeated powers. Drafting the German treaty took so much time and energy, however, that the 'preliminary conference' soon became the peace conference itself. The shape of the conference evolved as the representatives of the great powers steadily took command. From 18 January until 24 March a Council of Ten, consisting of two delegates each from Britain, France, Italy, the United States, and Japan, met in the French foreign minister's beautifully appointed *ancien régime* room in the Quai d'Orsay (the French foreign ministry) under Clemenceau's chairmanship. The smaller states were permitted to present their views to the Council, and did so, often at considerable length and with great vehemence. Their representatives were present when the Council reported back to the full plenary sessions of the Conference but the latter were few and far between and were of little importance. There were interruptions: President Wilson returned to the United States on 15 February, not to return until 14 March; Lloyd George was away in London from 8 February until 14 March; and Clemenceau was forced to withdraw temporarily as the result of an assassination attempt by a young anarchist on 19 February. Discussions continued in their absence, but nothing of importance could be settled. The Japanese ceased to attend meetings on a regular basis. As in every twentieth-century peace conference, the essential decisions were made by the very few. When the chief negotiators reassembled in mid-March it was decided to turn the

Council of Ten into a Council of Four, with Clemenceau, Lloyd George, Wilson, and Vittorio Orlando meeting informally, usually in the American's private residence. Orlando, the Italian prime minister, was never treated as an equal and took only a minor part in the drafting of the treaty with Germany. Lord Riddell, Lloyd George's publicity agent, rightly noted that 'no four kings or emperors could have conducted the conference on more autocratic lines'.[3] In late April, baulked of his demands, Orlando walked out and decision-making rested in the hands of the remaining 'big three'. Clemenceau, Lloyd George, and Wilson debated every clause, sometimes every word, of the articles which concerned them. Their proceedings were informal, chaotic, and often acrimonious. At one point Lloyd George jumped up and seized Clemenceau by the scruff of the neck, forcing Wilson to separate the two men. It was not until Maurice Hankey, the experienced secretary to the British delegation, came into attendance from 19 April that agendas were created and proper minutes kept. Even then there was little order in the way the great men proceeded, whom they conferred with, what they decided, or indeed whom they informed of their decisions. The 'big three' consulted those they trusted and bypassed traditional advisers, excluding them from discussions and keeping them in the dark about the conclusions reached. The professional diplomats long used to dominating the European conferences of the past found themselves shut out, outnumbered, and overwhelmed. In part, the war itself and the Leninist and Wilsonian attacks on the 'old diplomacy' had tarnished their reputations; but war is rarely kind to diplomats, and the foreign ministries in all the belligerent powers were eclipsed during the fighting. The multiplicity and complexity of the issues now raised gave roles of far greater significance than ever before to the 'experts', the men in the British Political Intelligence Department or the American 'Enquiry', both in the preparations for the peace and in Paris itself.

The main inter-Allied conflicts over the German settlement were not fully resolved until mid-April and quarrels with the Italians and Japanese further slowed the rate of progress. Much of the detailed work was handled by the fifty-two commissions or committees created by the Council of Ten. Three different commissions dealt with financial issues. Territorial questions were discussed in committees working independently of each other and often in ignorance of what was being discussed elsewhere. Though it was assumed that the committee decisions would be reviewed by the Council of Four, given the pressure of time most of

---

[3] William R. Keylor, 'Versailles and International Diplomacy', in Manfred F. Boemeke, Gerald D. Feldman, and Elisabeth Glaser (eds.), *The Treaty of Versailles: A Reassessment after 75 Years* (Washington, DC and Cambridge, 1998), 483.

the territorial recommendations, many of which were only ready for presentation in late March, were accepted without further consideration. Only a few, such as over the Polish borders, produced long and acrimonious debates. The pace became increasingly hectic during the last weeks of April, and there were well-founded fears that the draft treaty would not be ready in time. As time began to run out there was also increasing uneasiness in the Allied camp about the German response. The German delegation had already been waiting at the gloomy Hôtel des Réservoirs in Versailles for a week when the final text was sent to the printers. The chaos in the process of peacemaking could hardly have failed to affect its substance. In the end, the last-minute rush of work overwhelmed the co-ordinating committee created to check through the whole draft treaty, a document of over 200 pages with 440 articles, which consequently failed to eliminate the inevitable inconsistencies. The Council of Four never reviewed the draft treaty in its entirety. Members of the victor delegations saw the text only a few hours before it was given to the Germans, and it was only then that the harshness of its terms was recognized. The Germans ended up being presented on 7 May with a draft treaty to which they were given fifteen days to make a written response. Any change of substance, it was feared, could unravel the whole treaty. The peacemakers' difficulties were far from over.

II

It was obvious from the start that the settlement with Germany would be of primary and overriding importance in Paris. In his speeches during 1918 Wilson had stressed that this settlement would be a 'just peace', and that there would be no annexations or punitive damages imposed. Nonetheless, the president's messages, however interpreted in Berlin, in no way qualified the jointly held belief of the three Allied leaders that the Germans were responsible for the war and that justice did not preclude punishment for 'the very great offence against civilisation which the German State committed'.[4] A 'just peace', both Wilson and Lloyd George agreed, did not imply a 'soft peace'. While insisting on German guilt, the 'big three' never considered the destruction of Bismarck's creation. Germany was to be preserved as a unified nation, but prevented from returning to those paths of aggression that had resulted in a European catastrophe. It was over the questions of how this was to be done that the Allied leaders disagreed. The problem of

[4] Quoted in Anthony Lentin, *Lloyd George, Woodrow Wilson and the Guilt of Germany* (Leicester, 1984), 102.

how to deal with Germany meant different things to different leaders. United in war only by the need to defeat Germany, it was hardly surprising that the dominant personages at Paris should soon fall out as differences in national interests could not be disguised.

In every sense, the 'German problem' weighed most heavily on France. They had, as they repeatedly reminded their friends, paid the highest price of all for victory. Of all the belligerents, France had suffered most in terms of her active male population; France had lost 1.3 million soldiers, over a quarter of all men aged between 18 and 27, and incurred 700,000 wounded. The ten northern and eastern departments of the country had provided, along with parts of Belgium, the main battlefields of the war in the west. Much of the industrial heartland of France had been devastated. Neither its allies nor its chief enemy had been similarly affected. Germany had proved, once again, more powerful than France, which achieved victory only as a member of a coalition. France emerged from the fighting more damaged in human and material terms than its defeated enemy, and with much of its adult population suffering from a psychic shock that proved as deep and more long-lasting than the German preoccupation with defeat. For the French, reconstruction meant the constitution of a new political, economic, and strategic order in which France was protected from renewed German attempts at domination. French leaders remained throughout the 1920s obsessed with the fear of German power. France had a security problem that the other victor powers did not share. Only she had to live next to Germany.

Few men in France had made a more realistic appraisal of their country's position in the post-war world, or were more anxious to secure its future, than its premier, Georges Clemenceau, known as 'the Tiger'. The 78-year-old Clemenceau may have seemed a man of the past, and his square-tailed coats, shapeless hats, thick, buckled boots, and suede gloves (worn because of his eczema) accentuated this impression. To Clemenceau, the problem of the peace settlement was the problem of French security: how to protect France against another German aggression, something which all of France believed was possible. In his relentless search for the means to enhance French security, Clemenceau operated on the assumption that neither military defeat nor the fall of the Kaiser would permanently weaken Germany nor curb her continental ambitions. Germany would have to be disarmed, but this would hardly be sufficient for future safety. Even as he savoured the victory that was won at such high cost to France, Clemenceau understood how easily the peace could be lost. Stripped to its essentials, French security required the support of allies and military, territorial, and economic changes that would restrict Germany's capacity to again invade France. Neither the Rhineland nor Belgium was to become a platform for future German attacks. Clemenceau intended, too, that the peace settlements would provide opportunities to redress the unequal balance of economic strength between the two neighbouring nations that the war had not altered. While Clemenceau did not rule out the future possibility of Franco-German economic co-operation, already canvassed in the summer of 1919, it was only a possibility and had to be on terms that would promote French industrial interests.

The direction of French policy lay in Clemenceau's hands. *Père-la-Victoire* dominated his cabinet and enjoyed a strong position in the French Chamber of Deputies. He was to win a striking vote of confidence from the Chamber on 29 December 1918, 386 votes to 89, when he outlined the conditions of peace in general terms and stressed the need to preserve Allied unity. He was not totally free from domestic concerns; there were differences with his old and hated rival the French president, Raymond Poincaré (the feelings were mutual), and fierce clashes with Marshal Foch, infuriated not to be named as a French delegate to the peace conference. There were difficulties, too, with territorially greedy generals and ambitious subordinates in the Rhineland. For the most part, however, the premier overcame opposition to his policies and played his own hand. With few domestic commitments, he came to the peace table free of obligations. He purposely refused to reveal his diplomatic intentions to any but his most intimate advisers, of whom André Tardieu, the former French high commissioner in the United States, and Louis Loucheur, the minister of industrial reconstruction, were the most important. The foreign minister, Stephen Pichon, figured hardly at all. With the young, intellectual Tardieu as Clemenceau's closest confidante, the Quai d'Orsay lost power and handled only matters of secondary importance.

Clemenceau never underestimated the difficulties of peacemaking. As he confided to Poincaré: 'We will not perhaps have the peace that you and I would like. France will have to make sacrifices, not to Germany but to her allies.'[5] A tenacious and stubborn fighter, the Tiger was also a flexible negotiator, almost as skilful as Lloyd George in finding ways out of difficult situations. His talents would be sorely tested. Among Clemenceau's peace aims, his chief goal was always to secure a permanent alliance with Britain and the United States, not just because of common ideological sympathies but because only such an alliance would safeguard France. Clemenceau had a far deeper appreciation of France's weakness and its need for allies than those who, in the relief and self-congratulation of the end of the war, thought that France

---

[5] Quoted in Anthony Adamthwaite, *Grandeur and Misery* (London, 1995), 39.

could stand alone and still achieve those wide-ranging war aims that would redress the pre-war balance between France and Germany. The pre-conference exchanges with Lloyd George had not been encouraging; it proved difficult to pin down France's slippery ally, yet Lloyd George's support was essential for France. It must still have seemed easier to deal with the mercurial and elusive British prime minister than with the stubborn and self-assured American president. France needed the United States, both for immediate relief and for her post-war financial and economic plans. While he made every effort to court him, Clemenceau distrusted Wilson, deplored the vagueness of the Fourteen Points ('the good Lord himself had been satisfied with only ten'), and had little interest in 'Utopian theorists' and their proposed League of Nations except as a means of securing American underwriting for France. The French premier's views were in harmony with the prevailing winds of domestic opinion to which he both contributed and responded. Socialist and labour groups in France had welcomed Wilson's call for a new international order, but popular enthusiasm for the president began to ebb in February 1919 and Clemenceau could treat the League of Nations scheme as a matter of secondary importance, to be dealt with by Léon Bourgeois, a former premier and member of the international court of arbitration.

If the preservation of the wartime alliances took priority of place in Clemenceau's peace aims, the projected territorial changes that would enhance French power and block future German attacks on France absorbed the greater part of his attention and energy. He insisted on the return of Alsace-Lorraine, with its 1814–15 frontiers which included the salients around Saarbrücken and Landau, without a plebiscite. He favoured the annexation of the Saar for strategic and economic reasons; the military wanted a strategic border north of the Saar basin, while French industrialists believed that possession of the Saar mines would help to relieve France's serious coal deficit. Even the addition of the Saar coalfields would leave France short, and coal deliveries from Germany would be high on the list of economic reparations. When forced to give way on annexation, the French still hoped that, through the ownership of the mines, they would succeed in converting the Saarlanders to the advantages of joining France.

Clemenceau was as determined as Marshal Foch on the subject of the Rhine frontier and the detachment of the Rhineland from Germany The French claims, as presented by André Tardieu in a memorandum of 25 February, prepared in consultation with Clemenceau, included demands for the termination of German sovereignty over the territories of the Reich west of the Rhine and an indefinite Allied occupation of the left bank and the Rhine bridgeheads. Except for Alsace-Lorraine, these

German territories would be divided into one or more independent states that would be neutral and disarmed and included in a 'Western European customs zone'. France, Tardieu insisted, had not the slightest interest in annexing any part of the Rhineland, but he said nothing about how they were to be governed. Clemenceau favoured the creation of an independent buffer state, a goal he was forced to abandon at the end of March. He still continued to hope that the local autonomist movements in the Rhineland might succeed, and implicitly permitted, or at the least did not stop, the efforts of the French army of occupation to encourage the separatist movements. Admittedly, he gave no clear lead and was often surprised by the actions of his own officials; there were confused and conflicting policies followed both in Paris and in the Rhineland. While Clemenceau repudiated General Charles Mangin's open support for the abortive coup of the extremist, Hans Dorten, on 1 June 1919—a critical point in the Paris negotiations—he was not unsympathetic towards more moderate and realizable autonomy proposals, such as the mayor of Cologne, Konrad Adenauer's, scheme for creating a separate autonomous state, freed from the control of the Prussian state but within the Reich. Efforts to win the sympathies of the Rhinelanders through propaganda and economic carrots were intensified in the summer and autumn of 1919.

In the north-east, for geo-strategic reasons, Clemenceau favoured the restoration of an independent Belgium freed from the neutrality restrictions imposed by the treaties of 1831, with adjustments to its borders at the expense of the Dutch, who would be compensated in Germany. As in the case of the Rhineland, the intention was to block one of the historic invasion routes into France. In essence, the French wanted to dominate Belgium; there were hopes that any future war would be fought on Belgian and not French soil. Clemenceau wanted to bring Luxembourg within France's political and economic orbit, despite Belgium's own ambitions in the Grand Duchy and intentions to create their own economic union. The new arrangements were expected to strengthen France's western security system and fulfil long-held goals of improving its economic position at German expense.

Clemenceau was hardly likely to ignore the problem of Germany's eastern borders. France had to face the problem of the deficit left in its security by the Russian revolutions. Even British and American 'guarantees' of the western frontiers would not compensate for the disappearance of the vast Russian army on the German border. The French had already begun in 1917 to think of creating 'an eastern barrier' in east-central Europe as a counterweight to Germany. It was mainly with this in mind that they took the lead in publicly supporting Polish independence and in recognizing the extensive territorial claims of the

Polish National Committee, that included Danzig and a corridor to the Baltic. It was with similar hopes that the French backed claims for an independent Czechoslovakia that would include the German speakers of the Sudetan, and favoured an enlarged Serbia and Romania. Clemenceau felt few compunctions about ignoring the principles of self-determination; he sought independent, strong, and viable states that would work together and provide a buttress against German expansion and a barrier between Germany and Russia. It was assumed that the new successor states would fall within the French sphere of influence, and there were extensive plans for their economic penetration.

The French had given considerable thought since the early stages of the conflict to their economic war aims and the possibilities of changing the Franco-German economic equation in France's favour. France suffered from acute shortages of grain and coal, problems that would continue into the post-war period. These shortages had been relieved when America entered the war, and a number of pooling agreements on food, raw materials, and shipping were concluded that were carried out by inter-Allied agencies. However, all French attempts to press for the extension of these wartime arrangements in order to combat a post-war German economic offensive, including plans during 1918 by the then finance minister, Étienne Clémental, to expand France's industrial base and create a customs union with Belgium and an independent Rhineland to isolate and weaken Germany economically, fell on deaf ears. American officials were determined to dismantle the wartime inter-Allied agencies as rapidly as possible and return to normal trading patterns. They considered the most-favoured-nation principle as sacrosanct, disliked the whole idea of inter-Allied co-operation, especially in any institutionalized form, and continued to warn the Allies against any kind of discriminatory measures against Germany. The British, despite favouring some degree of post-war inter-Allied co-operation, opposed the abolition of the most-favoured-nation principle and would not make any commitment to a post-war economic union. Nor would they back the French in the face of strong American opposition. Paris and London anticipated that the Americans would either pool all war costs or consider a cancellation or redistribution of Allied war debts in order to equalize the burdens of the war on the respective belligerents. Such illusions, fuelled by the growing public demand that Germany should make restitution in kind and cash for the destruction it had wrought, had soon to be abandoned. For many Frenchmen, the desire to make the Germans suffer in a concrete way was probably as strong a motive as the demand for reparations.

For his part, Clemenceau focused only on the need to repair the physical damage done to France. His chief criticism of the draft armistice

TABLE 2. Inter-Allied War Debts, 1914–1918 (US$m Current Prices)

Borrowing country	From USA	From UK	From France	Total
Belgium	172	422	535	1,129
France	1,970	1,683	–	3,653
United Kingdom	3,696	–	–	3,696
Greece	–	90	155	245
Italy	1,031	1,885	75	2,991
Serbia (Yugoslavia)	11	92	297	400
Portugal	–	78	220	298
Russia	187	2,472	955	3,614
Total	7,067	6,722	2,237	15,996

Source: H. G. Moulton and L. Pasvolsky, *War Debts and World Prosperity* (Washington, DC, 1932), 426.

terms was directed at the omission of any reference to Germany's obligation to repair the damage she had inflicted. Though the term 'réparation des dommages' was inserted at his request, he did not intend to claim total war costs, which he believed would only reduce France's share of reparations. While not interested in the details of economic policy and notoriously inept when it came to financial matters, Clemenceau had a shrewd appreciation of France's economic interests. He was not consistently well served by his advisers. Even before the peace conference opened, Louis-Lucien Klotz, France's fatuous finance minister, saw in the promise of German reparations a way out of the struggle to conceal the inflationary methods used to cover France's snowballing budget deficit. Without stating a sum, he nevertheless implied that the Germans could pay for the whole cost of the war. There were others whose advice carried far more weight with Clemenceau than the incompetent Klotz. Clémentel, now minister of commerce, knowing by the time of the armistice that he would not get American backing for his pooling arrangements and other plans, shifted his attention to getting maximum Allied support for French reconstruction through the deliveries of coal and raw materials as well as cash payments. Unlike Klotz, however, Clémentel feared the effects of a flood of German marks into France which would fuel inflation and make French exports less competitive. Clémentel and subsequently Louis Loucheur, Clemenceau's chief economic adviser, were prepared to use the demand for high reparations as a bargaining counter with the Americans, but they continued to insist that reparations in kind were far preferable to cash transfers with all their attendant problems.

It was mainly the failure to elicit a positive American response to the French initiatives on continuing economic co-operation that shifted attention to reparations as the chief means to achieve France's economic goals. Because the French were unable to rely on the United States and Britain for future assistance, they focused on reparations for their immediate reconstruction needs and for the fulfilment of longer-term goals. Reparations could provide the means for institutionalizing international economic control of Germany and could be used to redress the economic imbalance between Germany and France. In all these debates, as he sought support for France, Clemenceau had also to prevent the emergence of an Anglo-American combination in opposition to his territorial and economic goals. 'We have won the war: now we have to win the peace', he warned General Henri Mordacq, his military *chef de cabinet*, 'and it may be more difficult.'[6] Lloyd George, in particular, had to be convinced of the need to weaken Germany and strengthen France in the interests of the future peace of Europe.

The position of Britain on the eve of the peace conference was both less and more complex than that of France. In 1914 Britain had been the pre-eminent great power, although even then she was not strong enough to remain neutral in the European struggle. As in the past, the British fought a coalition war against Germany, but the costs of intervention in the Great War, above all in human terms, were far higher than anyone expected. More than 500,000 of her 700,000 British dead were lost on the western front. The shock was all the greater because few had thought in terms of a continental engagement. The closeness of the margin of victory and its human toll encouraged some to speak of isolation or withdrawal from Europe as soon as it became practicable. Withdrawal proved impossible, however attractive the option might have seemed, but there was a general conviction that the costs of intervention had been far too high to ever be repeated. Britain nevertheless emerged from the war in a powerful position. It had put a huge and formidable army in the field, kept the sea lanes open, instituted an apparently effective blockade of Germany, and mobilized its economy effectively—many believed more effectively than any other European nation. The empire had come to its assistance, if at considerable constitutional cost and in some cases with less enthusiasm than was popularly imagined. There were some grounds for concern. The slower pace of Britain's industrial growth and the American and German threat to its share of the world's industrial production had already created alarm before 1914. If the staple industries had over-expanded during the war

<hr>

[6] Quoted in D. R. Watson, *Georges Clemenceau: A Political Biography* (London, 1974), 327.

TABLE 3. British War Loans to Dominions and Allies, Outstanding at the End of the Financial Year (£m)

	1914–15	1915–16	1916–17	1917–18	1918–19	1919–20
Australia	6.3	29.8	49.1	48.6	49.1	51.6
Canada	12.6	28.4	59.5	103.0	72.4	19.4
New Zealand	5.8	11.3	18.2	23.0	29.6	29.6
South Africa	11.7	17.9	17.7	16.7	16.6	15.8
Colonies	3.1	3.8	2.3	3.1	3.2	3.2
Total British empire	39.5	91.2	146.8	194.4	170.9	119.6
France		20.3	191.3	373.0	434.5	514.8
Russia		174.2	400.6	571.2	568.0	568.0
Italy		49.5	157.0	282.8	412.5	457.4
Other Allies	14.2	44.5	78.1	106.2	152.8	180.8
Total Allies	14.2	288.5	827.0	1,333.2	1,567.8	1,721.0
Loans for relief and reconstruction			0.9	2.3	2.5	11.6
Total	53.7	379.7	974.7	1,529.9	1,741.2	1,852.2

Source: E. V. Morgan, *Studies in British Financial Policy 1921–25* (London, 1952), 317.

(their decline would be much sharper than before 1914), the new industries, fostered by the conflict, could be expected to grow quickly in the post-war world. If Europe recovered, British industry would again flourish. More worrying was the fact that, though still a world creditor, Britain now owed the Americans $4.7 billion. The pre-war financial relationship between the two countries was dramatically reversed. The war, moreover, had destroyed the international exchange system that had provided Britain with a positive balance of payments and made London the financial centre of the world. Britain's leaders were convinced that this position could be restored through careful husbandry and American co-operation. As the war ended, too, there were difficulties in Ireland, India, and Egypt that were overtaxing Britain's contracting military resources. The British navy was still the largest in the world, but the United States was emerging as a powerful rival, with plans to build a 'navy second to none'. Britain was great by virtue of its empire alone.

There was a cacophony of voices as Britain's political leaders considered what role the country should play in reconstructing the post-war world. 'Atlanticists' believed that an Anglo-American combination would sustain and nourish the new world order. 'Europeanists' claimed that British pre-eminence would depend on the restoration of a stable and prosperous Europe, in which Germany would take its place.

Imperialists looked to an enlarged and reconstructed empire as a source of investment and trade, and argued that its imperial strength would enable Britain to pursue a policy independent of the United States, its main potential rival. Still others argued for a shift of attention from continental brawls to the more pressing needs of the recently enlarged electorate at home. Though the influence of these different and often overlapping groups varied, their diversity reflected the complexities of the British situation. British power and influence in 1919 was fully comparable to that enjoyed before the war, but she was also more vulnerable to the consequences of the more atomized world resulting from the breakdown of the pre-war international order. There could be no return to the Pax Britannica.

The prime minister, David Lloyd George, looked forward to his sojourn in Paris. The 'Welsh Wizard' was a master negotiator, quick, ingenious, and persuasive. He thrived on difficulties. His abundant energies and rapid changes of direction both amused and infuriated Clemenceau and Wilson. 'Figaro here, Figaro there', muttered Clemenceau during a performance of *The Barber of Seville*, 'he's a kind of Lloyd George.'[7] The 'Khaki election' of 14 December 1918 had shown a swing to the right amid a dramatic outburst of nationalist and anti-German fervour, sentiments encouraged during the latter half of 1918 by the government to combat civilian fatigue, and fanned by sections of the press. Lloyd George had already spoken of a 'sternly just, relentlessly just' peace. On 5 December he demanded that the 'arch-criminal' Kaiser be tried for 'high treason against humanity'.[8] Though the League of Nations idea had warm support in all parties, the demand for retribution and restitution swept the country. Every candidate opposing a harsh peace was defeated. The wartime Coalition government was returned with a large margin, and the election was seen as a personal triumph for Lloyd George. It was, in fact, a sweeping victory for his government's Conservative wing. The prime minister, highly sensitive to shifts in popular mood, had to deal with the Conservative backbenchers in the House of Commons, over whom he had only limited control. While their demands taxed his considerable oratorical and tactical powers, he proved infinitely resourceful in disarming critics and maintaining his supremacy over both colleagues and Commons. It proved the same with his control over the British delegation. Foreign Office officials, and even the foreign secretary himself, Arthur Balfour, both already demoted in importance by Lloyd George during the war, had to work through the prime minister's confidant Philip Kerr, editor

[7] Lentin, *Lloyd George, Woodrow Wilson, and the Guilt of Germany*, 122.
[8] Ibid. 25.

of the influential journal supporting closer imperial union, the *Round Table*, to secure information or even to reach the prime minister at all. The Treasury and Board of Trade, the service departments, special cabinet committees, with imperial as well as British ministers, all considered British policy and further diminished the role of the professional diplomats.

Lloyd George, never short of self-confidence, saw himself as the 'honest broker' at the peace table and the conciliator of men and nations. The problem of how to deal with Germany was, for him, the problem of how to punish Germany and yet preserve a stable and economically healthy Europe. A successful peace settlement, in his view, would require German acquiescence and French self-control. Like Wilson, Lloyd George believed the peace treaty should be just and harsh. He had no doubts about German guilt. In 1918, out of personal inclination as well as for reasons of political expediency, he favoured a peace that would teach the Germans 'an unforgettable lesson'. Germany had to be punished, constrained, and deterred. Yet he knew that the defeated enemy could not permanently be held in a subordinate position. It was not in Europe's nor in Britain's interest to leave her thirsting for revenge. Any future 'Alsace-Lorraines' would serve only to inflame the spirit of German nationalism. The prime minister wanted a treaty that the Germans would accept as the price of their defeat. He looked forward to the construction of a stable Europe that would include a chastened Germany and operate a self-regulating mechanism to keep the peace that would not require outside intervention. Britain would retain her influence as the pivotal state in this newly created equilibrium, but at the lowest cost possible. There was a strong desire in the British cabinet, which Lloyd George fully shared, to return to those traditional policies of peace, stability, and trade that had so long served Britain's national interests. Something more was needed, however, than the restitution of the old system of the 'balance of power', though this did not mean the substitution of the Wilsonian League of Nations for the pre-war mechanisms of great-power diplomacy. If Europe settled down to peace, the British could look to their imperial interests.

With a display of adroitness that few could match, the prime minister managed to secure most of Britain's war aims either before or during the first weeks of the peace conference. The armistice left the country in possession of the greater part of the German fleet, until it was scuttled by the Germans at Scapa Flow on 21 June. She would soon receive the bulk of the German merchant fleet. By the time the war ended the German colonial empire was mainly in British or British empire hands. With the disappearance of the German naval and imperial threat, Britain could afford to take a more detached view of continental affairs. As Clemenceau outlined the French demands in London during a visit in December 1918, it became clear that the two prime ministers put a different weight on their twin objectives—security and stability. The British had no territorial demands in Europe. They would insist on the restoration of Belgium, the ostensible if not the real reason for their original intervention, and support France's claim to Alsace and Lorraine. Lloyd George's military advisers were sympathetic to a French military frontier on the Rhine, but the prime minister, suspecting French annexationist ambitions, resolutely opposed detaching the Rhineland from Germany and rejected the idea of an Allied military presence on the Rhine. He had an open mind about the Saar. He thought that Germany should be disarmed, though this only became a British war aim at the end of 1918 as a means of satisfying the widespread demand for the demobilization of the British armies and the ending of conscription. Lloyd George viewed Clemenceau's territorial objectives with considerable suspicion: he had no intention of substituting France for Germany as the hegemonic power in Europe. Though the prime minister accepted the French need for security, he had no wish to become France's underwriter if its European insurance policy failed.

Like the Americans, the British thought they would be the 'honest brokers' in determining the dispositions in the east of Europe. There was considerable sympathy for the principles of self-determination, particularly within parts of the Foreign Office, where officials argued that peace would be best secured if based on the principles of nationality and self-determination. Lloyd George came late to the idea of the dissolution of the Habsburg monarchy, and followed the French in taking up the cause of Polish independence, which he accepted without enthusiasm, and in his recognition of Bohemian and south Slav aspirations. There was, however, no agreement in London among the British experts about the size and borders of a restored Poland, and uncertainty about the future frontiers of Czechoslovakia and the Kingdom of the Serbs, Croats, and Slovenes. Whereas the French thought of Poland as a barrier against Germany as well as against Bolshevik Russia if the 'Whites' were defeated, Lloyd George became more concerned with the problems of instability created by the likely inclusion of large numbers of Germans in Poland and its potential for future conflicts. There were varying degrees of support for ideas such as an Austro-German union, which officials believed was inevitable, or a Balkan Federation in south-eastern Europe, which would promote stability and provide welcome opportunities for British finance and trade. It was not only the French who harboured extensive economic ambitions in the region.

The question of German liability for the costs of war must be seen, as in the case of France, against the background of fears about a post-war German economic offensive. During the war British planners had also considered a package of discriminatory trade measures against the Central Powers, but the proposals were dropped in the face of American opposition and a negative response in liberal and labour circles at home. At the heart of the debate over German liabilities was the distinction between making restitution only for the damage and destruction wrought by the war in the Allied countries versus paying the far larger overall costs the Allies had incurred in fighting the war. Concern over Britain's post-war position coloured Treasury views about reparations and indemnities: the Treasury wished to keep Germany's liabilities at a level that would not disturb the normal terms of trade nor depend upon Germany creating an export surplus that would hurt British trade and industry. While John Maynard Keynes, the Treasury spokesman, calculated a total figure of £3,000 million, which would not even cover Allied material damage, the Treasury ultimately concluded that Britain's interests would be best served if the Germans paid a reparation bill of only £2,000 million. These were not the figures produced by the Cabinet Committee on indemnity which met in November–December 1918, under the chairmanship of the Australian prime minister William Hughes, a leading anti-German spokesman and champion of high reparations. The committee's members supported a huge indemnity (£24,000 million was the figure mentioned). Their final report recommended that the Germans be required 'to make good the destruction of property and to indemnify the Allies for the cost of the war'.[9] Despite divisions in the cabinet on almost every aspect of reparations policy, the majority agreed that the Germans should be pressed for the highest indemnity possible short of one requiring an army of occupation. Behind this conclusion was not only the upsurge of anti-German feeling during the election campaign, but Britain's own financial weakness and Dominion demands for compensation. Until the eve of the election Lloyd George had taken a cautious approach to the question, but his underlying commitment to securing war costs for Britain pre-dated the election campaign. The cabinet decision to adopt the Hughes Committee report and the appointments of Hughes, Lord Sumner, and Lord Cunliffe, known hardliners, to the Inter-Allied Commission on Reparation, were indications that the British negotiators in Paris would demand a figure far in excess of what the Treasury thought possible or wise. The Germans had lost the war and should pay for it.

[9] Robert E. Bunselmeyer, *Cost of the War, 1914–1919: British Economic War Aims and the Origins of Reparations* (Hamden, Conn., 1975), 103.

Any demand going beyond compensation for material damage suffered was bound to lead to conflict with the Americans. The 'Lansing Note', the pre-armistice agreement of 5 November which the Germans had accepted as part of the armistice terms, specified that compensation should be paid for all damage done to the civilian populations and their property 'by the aggression of Germany by land, by sea and from the air'.[10] Though the Foreign Office and Treasury argued that this precluded any claim for the costs of the war, this was not the view of the prime minister nor the majority of his cabinet. In election campaign speeches voters were encouraged to believe that the government would demand that Germany should pay the whole cost of the war. Lloyd George refused to retreat even when Wilson arrived in London in December insisting that there should be no indemnity against Germany. Still supremely careful about the critical relationship with the American president, the issue was not pressed at the time.

The idea of a League of Nations had been under discussion in Britain since 1917. Lloyd George, more concerned with winning the war, was not unsympathetic and allowed examination of the League idea to go ahead. On 20 March 1918 the Phillimore Committee, composed of Foreign Office officials and historical experts, proposed an alliance of victor states pledged not to go to war without submitting disputes to arbitration or to a conference of member states that would make recommendations for peaceful settlement. Sanctions would be imposed on non-complying countries. Though criticized by some, notably Philip Kerr and Jan Smuts, the influential South African premier, as too cautious, by the time the war ended it was agreed that British planning should move along the committee's lines rather than in a more radical direction. The subject was again debated after the armistice negotiations when, in the weeks before the arrival of the American president in Europe, the cabinet took up the question of British strategy at the forthcoming peace talks. There appeared to be two possible negotiating options: either a partnership with the French and the support of a strengthened France as proposed by Clemenceau, or co-operation with the Americans and the acceptance of Wilson's alternative international order. Opinion grouped decisively around the latter position. The cabinet was by now under strong pressure to go well beyond lip service and to consider seriously the form and role of the new international body. In November 1918 the League of Nations Union was founded, with a large and impressive list of members of all political persuasions, to provide a single focus for pro-League agitation. Because

---

[10] Alan Sharp, *The Versailles Settlement: Peacemaking in Paris, 1919* (Basingstoke and London, 1991), 80.

of its wide membership and close links with each of the political parties, the new organization could not be ignored. In late November Lord Robert Cecil, the former minister of blockade, was appointed to head a new League of Nations section in the Foreign Office and asked to produce draft proposals for the League. Submitted on 17 December, the 'Cecil plan' followed the Phillimore Committee's recommendations: the League was to be a great-power conference system with a permanent secretariat and a structure for the settlement of disputes and the imposition of sanctions. Meanwhile, General Smuts, who was preparing the British brief for the peace conference and strongly supported the American orientation, took up the idea in submissions to the war cabinet and in an influential pamphlet, *The League of Nations: A Practical Suggestion*, also published in December. He argued the case for a strong international organization in the most persuasive and moving language. Only an effective international body, Smuts insisted, would keep the peace, attack the problem of armies and armaments, and protect and nurture those peoples left in the wake of the collapse of the Russian, Austrian, and Turkish empires. Herein lay the origins of the mandates system which, after a considerable Anglo-American debate in Paris, was extended to the German colonies as well. Smuts outlined plans for an executive council of great powers with sweeping authority and minority representation of the middle and small powers, along with a general conference and permanent secretariat. Forced to consider the questions that Lloyd George would discuss with the president, there was a full-scale debate on the League in the Imperial War Cabinet on 24 December. The cabinet rejected the 'guarantees of peace' (the term 'collective security' was not used until the 1930s) and the automatic sanctions embodied in the Phillimore, Cecil, and Smuts proposals. It opted for a less formal international body, modelled along the lines of either the Supreme Council or the Imperial War Cabinet, that would provide a mechanism for international discussion but would leave national sovereignty unimpaired.

Wilson's triumphal visit to London at the end of the month was critical for Lloyd George's approach to the League. The prime minister believed that by backing the new institution he would gain American support on other questions still dividing the two nations, and win American underwriting for the future stability of Europe. The earlier meetings with Foch and Clemenceau had not been reassuring; the League of Nations was an acceptable price for effecting an Anglo-American entente. At the same time, Lloyd George would satisfy the highly vocal supporters of the 'new diplomacy'. Lloyd George was intent on creating a partnership with Wilson, and started with certain advantages over Clemenceau. There was a common interest in the future stability of Europe and a strong preference for a policy of non-intervention in continental conflicts. Though their security situations were clearly different, Wilson and Lloyd George had far less to fear from a revived Germany and more to gain. Anglo-American contacts had been forged and expanded during the war, above all in financial circles, pointing to a post-war partnership that would marginalize France. A shared tradition of moral liberalism found expression in the British population's warm response to Wilson's vision of a new international order. Nevertheless, the prime minister moved cautiously; co-operation with Wilson was not without risks. Britain would stay in close contact with France in case the American partnership proved abortive or the president failed to carry his programme at home. 'After all,' minuted Eyre Crowe, one of the most insightful officials in the Foreign Office, 'we must remember that our friend America lives a long way off. France sits at our door.'[11] In fact, co-operation with Wilson lasted only until Lloyd George had achieved his immediate aims during the early weeks of the conference. The subsequent atomization of the negotiations precluded permanent partnerships, and co-operation tended to be issue specific.

When President Woodrow Wilson, the first serving president to visit the continent, came to Europe in December 1918, he was greeted with wild acclaim. There were cheering crowds and flowers to mark his progress; streets, squares, and bridges were renamed in his honour. Yet neither in his own country nor in the victor states was the upsurge of idealism sustained. Wilson's popularity and negotiating power was at its peak during October 1918; it would diminish once the president crossed the Atlantic, and plummet after his return to Paris in mid-March 1919. The changing domestic political atmosphere had a critical impact on the peace treaty. A Democratic president re-elected in 1916 pledging to keep America out of the war, Wilson's appeal for a Democratic Congress was rejected, and instead, in the Congressional elections of 5 November 1918, the Republicans gained control of both Houses of Congress, and the president's personal and political foe, Henry Cabot Lodge, became chairman of the all-important Senate Foreign Relations Committee. Wilson was aware of his political weakness at home and of the rising tide of militancy but, caught up in the emotional response to his arrival in Europe which bolstered his self-confidence, he believed that he could win the support of 'the people' for his new vision of a peaceful post-war world. The tragic figure of the Paris drama was to suffer the ignominy of misjudgement.

---

[11] Minute by Crowe, 7 Dec. 1918, in M. L. Dockrill, 'Britain, the United States and France and the German Settlement, 1918–1920', in B. J. C. McKercher and D. J. Moss (eds.), *Shadow and Substance in British Foreign Policy, 1895–1939* (Edmonton, 1984), 218.

For the first time in European history, an American president was the central figure in the disposition of continental affairs. American power, real and potential, would have to be considered in the reconstruction of Europe. The president was well aware of the critical difference that American intervention had made to the Allies. He was equally cognizant of the unique position of the United States as the leading financial and economic power, at a time when all the European states were suffering from the effects of war. American participation in the struggle was predicated on the assumption that the defeat of German militarism would give the United States the major voice in shaping the peace. Just as before 1917 he had hoped that the United States might mediate between the belligerents, after America's entry he saw his nation as the arbiter of Europe, the only truly disinterested power in the conflict. To Wilson, the real issue at hand was how to use the opportunity presented by the end of the war and peacemaking to refashion a new world order. The problem went beyond the settlement with Germany itself, and perhaps this is why he would be the most disillusioned of the 'big three' with the ultimate results of the Paris conference. Wilson's appeals for a 'peace of justice' and a 'new world order' created reverberations in the Allied countries and in the enemy camp as well. It was this vision of a future without war, as well as the realities of American power, that explains the wave of enthusiasm that greeted the president when he came to Europe.

The tall, prim, ex-Princeton University president, inclined to ser-monize and to appeal to higher laws, arrived with the highest of expectations. America's mission, he told Congress, was 'to redeem the world and make it fit for free men like ourselves to live in'.[12] Like so many of his countrymen, he was convinced that the United States, through providence and design, had escaped the cycles of war and repression which had marked European history. Other nations could learn and profit from the singular American experience. The European conflict confirmed Wilson's belief that the balance of power and the alliance systems of the past were bankrupt, and that it had been the irresponsibility of the European leaders which led the continent to its catastrophic war. The 'stern Protestant preacher' demanded that his fellow Americans should show the way to a new conception of inter-national relations that would allow men to live in peace and harmony. His was a statement of a new liberal internationalism intended to meet the challenge of the bankrupt Europe and the new Bolshevik creed. The idea of American uniqueness and European depravity had a long history;

---

[12] Woodrow Wilson, *Presidential Messages, Addresses and Public Papers*, vol. 11, ed. R. S. Baker and W. E. Dodd (New York, 1927), 14.

in the past these ideas had nourished American isolationism. Menaced by none, Wilson's calls for American intervention and a leading role in shaping the new world order represented sharp departures from traditional policy.

Wilson's vision of this post-war world was never spelled out in any detail. As with the other two Allied leaders, he excluded all but a few close associates, including the secretary of state, Robert Lansing, from his thinking about the peace. Wilson instead used his closest confidant, Colonel Edward House, as his chief adviser and substitute until the colonel fell from favour after the president's return from the United States in mid-March. With Wilson's tendency to keep his own counsel and to avoid pre-conference planning, there was little personal contact during his voyage to Europe on the SS *George Washington* between him and the many American experts brought along to advise the delegation, though they may well have been cheered by the president's statement, 'You tell me what's right and I'll fight for it'.[13] Wilson purposely discouraged public discussion about the League, and came to Europe with only the vaguest ideas about its organization. The Fourteenth Point declared that 'a general association of nations must be formed under specific covenants for the purpose of affording mutual guarantees of political independence and territorial integrity to great and small states alike'. The very use of the word 'covenants' stressed the spiritual base of the new social contract that was to replace the old system that had failed so catastrophically. In some of his early speeches Wilson called for a general guarantee of political independence and territorial integrity by all states and for all states. In August 1918 he pressed for a universal system of compulsory arbitration and general disarmament. At no point, however, before or after Wilson came to Europe, did he say how this new system was to be organized. The Fourteen Points made no specific mention of 'self-determination', a concept which was to be honoured far more in the breach than the observance both in the German and later in the eastern settlements. The concept was first publicly aired by Wilson to a joint session of Congress on 11 February 1918 called to consider the Central Powers' reply to Wilson's peace terms. The four 'principles', to be added to the Fourteen Points, stressed the need to consider the interests and nationalist aspirations of those concerned and to warn against treating 'people and provinces' as if they were 'mere chattels and pawns in a game, even the great game, now forever discredited, of the balance of power'.[14] Even here, the endorsement of

---

[13] MacMillan, *Peacemakers*, 16.
[14] A. S. Link (ed.), *Collected Papers of Woodrow Wilson*, vols. 45–8 (Princeton, 1965–85), xlvi. 322–3.

self-determination was a general one that could be variously interpreted. Equally vague was the promise of autonomous development for the peoples of Austria-Hungary and the readjustment of the frontiers of Italy. The evacuation and restoration of Belgium was a *sine qua non*, but those of the Fourteen Points referring to the return of Alsace-Lorraine and the restoration of an independent Poland with free and secure access to the sea left many questions unsettled. It was only in the talks with Lloyd George en route to Paris that Wilson made clear that he would oppose the French demands for an enlarged Alsace-Lorraine or the inclusion of the Saar basin within the French domain. This vagueness was equally true of the Wilsonian demands for 'the removal, as far as possible of all economic barriers and the establishment of an equality of trade conditions' (Point 2), and for no indemnities and low reparations. The president looked to a new and secure world order that would foster American economic goals; security and prosperity were inexorably linked. A capitalist free-trade economy, he believed, would be equally beneficial for all states. Like the Gladstonians, Wilson assumed that free competition, an open-door policy, and an end to intrusive government controls would contribute to world peace and prosperity. The president had not considered how his country's new economic power might be utilized. As with so many other issues, beyond general principles there were no specific war aims.

The main aim of the economic peace, from the American viewpoint, was that the Europeans should be encouraged to reconstruct their economies and restore world trade as quickly as possible, so that there would be sufficient sums to pay back their debts to the United States and to buy American exports. If Germany was crippled financially, such a return to normality would be delayed. With the reconstruction of Germany and return to sound financial practices, Europe would re-cover, pay off the costs of the war, and prosper. In Paris Wilson assembled an impressive group of financial and economic experts, including Norman Davis, the assistant secretary of the Treasury and his chief financial adviser, already in close contact with Keynes, and Thomas Lamont from J. P. Morgan & Co., the largest American overseas investment house, but it was to prove a far more difficult scenario to implement than the experts anticipated. American officials and financial and business leaders agreed that restrictive trade arrange-ments of the kind proposed by the French and British would delay world recovery and adversely affect American interests. Wilson's aides quickly pulled out of existing inter-Allied councils and vetoed attempts to prolong wartime pooling arrangements. To some extent, this rejec-tion of economic co-operation was reinforced by a shared conviction that the management of economic affairs should be returned to private

TABLE 4. US Dollar Loans, 1915–1919 ($m current prices)

	Jan. 1915–Apr. 1917	1917–19 (Liberty Act)
Allies		
France and Britain	2,102	7,157
Russia and Italy	75	1,809
Canada and Australia	405	[*]
Germany	8	0
European neutrals	12	344[†]
Other	72	126
Total	2,674	9,436

Notes: *Included in 'Other'; [†]Greece and Belgium.

Source: Barry Eichengreen, *Golden Fetters: The Gold Standard and the Great Depression*, pbk. edn. (1992), 84.

hands in the interests of maximum efficiency and international peace. Nor did the Americans wish to continue arrangements which might give the British a greater direction in economic affairs. Herbert Hoover, in charge of relief operations, was deeply suspicious of the intentions of the Europeans and opposed any programme that prompted inter-Allied control of American resources. He agreed to a temporary scheme of inter-Allied food control only when it was accepted that he should direct relief operations.

Wilson, like the American Treasury and the overwhelming majority of the American people, also took the view that the massive debts incurred by the Allied governments to the United States in fighting the war would have to be paid. As a later president, Calvin Coolidge, was to comment in one of his pithy epigrams: 'They hired the money, didn't they?' The Treasury intended to use the funds to control inflation and to reduce the national debt, which had risen from $123,000 million in 1916 to over double this figure in 1919. There was a widespread view that no connection should be made between Allied war debts and German reparations. The financial experts agreed that there should be compensation for war damages but not for war costs. They wanted a fixed and reasonable sum to be paid within thirty years. Norman Davis, Wilson's chief financial adviser, spoke in early January of a figure between $10,000–$20,000 million. The Treasury was not indifferent to the European plight or to the interconnection between the restoration of international trade and the prosperity of the United States. It considered making long-term loans to American exporters and providing small amounts of credit to the Europeans for a transitional period. But it would be up to private bankers to smooth out whatever difficulties might accompany the return to normal trade. The American refusal to link war debts and reparations was based, too, on assumptions about the possibilities of European recovery through self-effort and private endeavours which Europeans felt underestimated the destructiveness of the war. Having been thwarted in their earlier efforts to extend inter-Allied co-operation, the French and the British continued to press for such a linkage. In his much-quoted letter written to Colonel House in July 1917, President Wilson pointed to a time when the war was over, when 'we can force them [the Allies] to our way of thinking, because by that time they will, among other things be financially in our hands; but we cannot force them now'.[15] But the financial weapon was a blunt instrument, and American policy would not be so stern. Demanding payment for war debts and stopping the flow of credits to allies would only create the hostility and disunity that Wilson hoped to avoid. Nor would such actions be in the American interest. Given the marked differences between the American and Allied economic aims, the economic peace, like so much of the rest of the Versailles treaty, had to be a compromise if it was to be concluded at all.

Wilson's idealism was not naive. It was always combined with a shrewd appreciation of the practicalities of his situation. No one becomes president of the United States with his head in the clouds. He knew that his grandiose plans would arouse opposition. He knew, too, that Britain and France were bound by wartime treaties affecting territorial settlements to which the United States was not a partner and that could compromise the president's position. There would have to be a bargaining process if the presidential promises were to be fulfilled. Wilson's linkage of intervention in the war with his vision of a peaceful future was aimed at courting a politically influential section of the American electorate. Similarly, his turn to the Allies and the modifications of the armistice terms must be seen in terms of practical politics. He had to take into account both the changing political scene at home and the need to secure agreement with the Allied leaders in Paris. The defeat of the Democratic Party in the November 1918 elections contributed to the president's tougher line towards the Germans after his arrival. Knowing the difficulties over the League that he would face in the Senate, the president decided that the Covenant, the heart of his peace programme, should be part of the German treaty. Though he was to grossly mishandle the League fight in the Senate itself, he knew, as he

---

[15] Stephen A. Schuker, 'Origins of American Stabilization Policy in Europe: The Financial Dimension, 1918–1924', in Hans-Jürgen Schröder (ed.), *Confrontation and Cooperation: Germany and the United States in the Era of World War I, 1900–1924* (Oxford, 1993), 380.

bargained in Paris, that the German treaty had to satisfy the majority party and voters who had turned against a lenient peace. Even if he won his domestic battles, Wilson would be dependent on his fellow peace-makers to defend the peace settlement. The president's carrots and sticks proved far less effective than he expected. This was, in part, because he was restricted in what he could do by the nature of his own non-interventionist principles and belief in a liberal trading system. Both the forthcoming battle in the Senate and the need to have the support of the Allies meant a presidential retreat from the statements of principles sketched before he came to Paris. His own belief in the need to chastize the Germans meant that the often purposely inflated hopes of the German leaders were dangerously misplaced. The German government never appreciated Wilson's situation nor understood his attitude towards Germany. Like his European colleagues, the president believed that Germany was the 'guilty party', whose leaders had to be punished and which would have to prove itself worthy before it could be admitted into the new international system. He never gave his full support to the German government created by the November revolution, and con-tinued to demonstrate a certain ambivalence towards its leaders throughout the spring of 1919.

Ultimately, American disinterestedness proved a liability and not an asset. Clemenceau and Lloyd George were powerful enough to shape the peace in a European image. There is little question that the battles in Paris left Wilson drained psychologically as well as physically. He clung to the hope that the League of Nations would correct the mistakes of the peacemakers. The president could not impose his ideal treaty on men concerned with the practicalities of peacemaking. In the end, it was only in regard to the League that the president's wishes appeared fulfilled.

III

The League of Nations was a radical departure from past international practice. Its weaknesses arose from the attempt to restrict the behaviour of member states which, by their very definition, acknowledged no superior secular authority. There were those in the Anglo–American political elites who had their doubts about the new institution. The Allied leaders were warned, in the first instance by Henry Cabot Lodge, that the president's idea would meet formidable domestic opposition. Lord Robert Cecil, the main British spokesman, knew that the pro-jected League was a more powerful institution than the British cabinet wanted. The French representatives were unenthusiastic for the oppos-ite reasons. Their hopes for a powerful Allied institution to enforce the treaty were blocked by the Anglo–American partnership. The question of the League was taken up, as had been Wilson's intention, at the very start of the conference. The British and American delegates met privately and worked out a joint proposal which the president, as chairman of the Commission on the League of Nations, accepted as a working draft. The Hurst–Miller plan reflected the work done earlier in London, and though there were some moments of conflict between Wilson and Cecil, the Covenant was very much the product of this Anglo-American partnership. The structure of the League incorporated Smuts's proposals: an executive Council of the great powers (Britain, France, Italy, Japan, and the United States), an Assembly where all states would be represented, and a permanent secretariat. The states at the peace conference would be members; the admission of others would require a two-thirds vote. Pressure from the smaller powers on the commission led by Belgium resulted in a redrafting of the Council article to admit minority representation on the Council for the smaller states. Four other states would be appointed to the Council on a rotating basis, beginning with Belgium, Brazil, Spain, and Greece. Decisions in the Council would be taken by unanimous vote, guaranteeing the control of the major powers over its decisions. There was no question that Wilson and Cecil intended that the Council should be the effective heart of the League, and that its actions would depend on the agreement of the great powers. While there was to be an International Court of Justice (Article 14), building on the precedents of the pre-war Hague conferences, Wilson was less than enthusiastic about the loose and admittedly weak system so favoured by American jurists, and saw the Court as only one part of the far more radical structure constructed at Paris.

The president's key contribution to the League draft was Article 10, which obligated member states 'to respect and preserve as against external aggression the territorial integrity and existing political independence of all members of the League'. Cecil, well aware of the opposition in the British cabinet to binding obligations, tried to modify this unconditional guarantee or make it less rigid, but the president remained adamant. This represented the heart of his new system. It would make the League something more than a debating society or an enlarged concert of Europe. As it stood, however, any change in the status quo could be interpreted as a threat to a member nation. The best that Cecil could achieve was Article 19, which stated that the 'Assembly may from time to time advise the reconsideration by members of the League of treaties which have become inapplicable and the consideration of international conditions whose continuance might endanger the peace of the world'. This was the only provision in the Covenant providing for peaceful change. Its physical separation from Article 10, and the limitations on what the Assembly could do, reflected Wilson's unwillingness to weaken the Covenant. He was supported by the French, who looked to the League to enforce rather than to revise the peace settlement. In practice, Article 10 was effectively nullified by the Council's unanimity requirement on all substantive questions. Article 11 provided a less absolute conception of the League's purpose. 'Any war or threat of war,' it stated, 'whether immediately affecting any of the members of the League or not, is hereby declared a matter of concern to the whole League, and the League shall take any action that may be deemed wise and effectual to safeguard the peace of nations.' This allowed for the widest variety of possible reactions. The League would be enabled to fulfil its functions as a body for conciliation.

In dealing with the settlement of disputes, Wilson followed the British procedures worked out in the Phillimore Committee. Articles 12, 13, and 15 of the Covenant provided that member states had to submit 'any dispute likely to lead to a rupture' to arbitration, judicial settlement, or consideration by the League Council, and that there must be a three-month delay after any decision before a 'resort to war'. Members agreed not to go to war against any state which complied with the arbitrator's award or with a unanimous Council decision. There were no enforcement provisions. While members agreed that they would carry out 'in full good faith' any arbitral award, refusal to do so would merely lead to a recommendation on action by the Council. In the case of disputes referred to examination by the Council, if no unanimous decision was reached then member states were free to act as they saw necessary 'for the maintenance of right and justice'. Under Article 16, it was to be disregard of these provisions for conflict resolution (it did not refer to Article 10) which would invoke the application of sanctions: 'Should any member of the League resort to war in disregard of its covenants under Articles 12, 13, or 15, it shall *ipso facto* be deemed to have committed an act of war against all other members of the League.' The sanctions provided for by Article 16 stipulated an absolute and immediate economic, financial, and diplomatic boycott, wartime experiences with the blockade weapon having strengthened belief in its efficacy. If non-military deterrents failed, the Council could recommend to the states what military forces they might supply 'to protect the covenants of the League'. In a series of proposals which deliberately challenged the whole Anglo-American conception, the French delegate, Léon Bourgeois, demanded an extended system of compulsory arbitration and an executive council backed by an international army. The British and Americans successfully blocked these French and Belgian efforts. Contrary to French hopes, the Council would have no armed forces of its own and could do no more than request members to supply them when needed. At most, there would be a permanent commission to advise the Council (Article 9) on armaments of new members, disarmament plans, and military, naval, and air questions generally. Nevertheless, the sanctions clauses still went further than the Lloyd George government thought wise. Here again was an uneasy compromise between the absolute freedom of the sovereign state and the wish for collective action to restrain offending states.

In essence, the French idea was an enlarged defensive alliance against a revived Germany. Bourgeois proposed that only a thoroughly reformed and disarmed Germany could be admitted to the League. The Covenant also included a provision (Article 8) making the Council responsible for reducing armaments 'to the lowest point consistent with national safety', fulfilling one of Wilson's pledges in the Fourteen Points. The obligatory disarmament of Germany was linked elsewhere in the peace treaty with the encouragement of the general disarmament of all. Though it was commonly accepted that the arms race had been a major cause of the recent war, the references in the Covenant to disarmament were relatively few and innocuous. It was a question left for future deliberation. What emerged from the conference deliberations was not what the French wanted but, as Cecil warned them, it was as much as they could expect. They had no choice but to agree. Clemenceau remained highly sceptical about the League's utility. Without armed forces at its disposal, the League had no ultimate weapon of enforcement but would be dependent on the goodwill of its members. The French premier sought other safeguards for the security of France.

The president achieved his League goals because of British cooperation. He paid a price for this support. In Point 5 of his Fourteen Points Wilson had spoken of an 'impartial adjustment of colonial claims' which would take into account both the interests of the colonial powers and 'the interests of the populations concerned'. The president refused to sanction the annexationist demands of the Dominions and Japan, whose Pacific ambitions had already raised considerable unease in Washington. The British, despite the shifting fortunes of war, had placed the partition of the German and Turkish empires high on their list of priorities. They were pledged, moreover, to support the annexationist claims of Australia, New Zealand, and South Africa as well as those of Japan. In attempting to bridge the gap, General Smuts extended his original proposals for international oversight of colonial territories into a far more elaborate 'mandate' system under League supervision to cover all new European colonies. The colonies, depending on their stage of development, would be divided into 'A', 'B', and 'C' categories. 'A' mandates, later restricted to the Turkish territories, would be given only administrative advice and assistance before achieving independence. 'B' mandates would come under the direct rule of the mandatory power, and 'C' mandates would be administered as 'integral portions' of the mandatory power's territories. It was only after considerable pressure that William Hughes, the Australian prime minister, was convinced that 'C' mandates were little more than annexed territories by another name. The League would see to it that the prohibitions against slavery, armaments, and fortifications in the 'B' and 'C' mandates were observed. With regard to 'B' mandates, the League would ensure that an open-door policy was preserved with regard to the trade of all League members. Lloyd George pressed this mandate proposal on the president as early as 24 January. Incensed by Hughes's opposition, and still hoping that the system of international supervision over Germany's former colonies could be strengthened, Wilson postponed the assignment of the mandates until early May. The delay was mainly for appearance's sake, for the territories already had been informally allocated. Ultimately, Wilson was less concerned with colonial problems than with the rights of nationalities in Europe. In principle, the president won his case; in practice, the division of the spoils between Britain, France, South Africa, New Zealand, Australia, Japan, and Belgium generally followed the lines of military occupation (Lebanon and Syria were among the exceptions), and confirmed the colonial bargains struck during the war. Italy received no mandates, adding further fuel to Italian discontents. Lloyd George's success was made easier because of Clemenceau's abstention from the arguments between the president and the Dominion representatives. Clemenceau cared little about colonial issues: he took small interest in the disposition of the German colonies or the Anglo-American debate over mandates. Yet the French did not come away with empty hands; they received 60 per cent of the Togoland and the bulk of the Cameroons, easily yielded by the British whose interests lay in East Africa, and would be allowed to conscript troops within these 'C' mandates. They would later get Syria and Lebanon, both recognized as mandates, in the division of Turkey's Arab lands. The new system reflected pre-war attitudes and the new mood of liberal internationalism. It institutionalized the system of colonialism, maintaining the distinctions between advanced and backward people and between colonial rulers and native populations. According to Article 22, the 'tutelage' of those peoples 'not yet able to stand by themselves under the strenuous conditions of the modern world . . . should be entrusted to advanced nations who by reason of their resources, their experience or their geographical position can best undertake this responsibility'. Yet it also introduced, admittedly in a very limited form, new concepts of state accountability to an international body.

It is true that Wilson proposed that the League's Covenant should require all new states and League members to bestow equality of treatment on 'all racial or national minorities', and to provide guarantees against interference or discrimination against any creed or belief which was not actually inconsistent with public order or public morals. His proposals, however, met with considerable opposition, even in the American delegation, on the grounds of violating state sovereignty and because of the practical problems of defining and enforcing a freedom-of-religion clause. Traditional attitudes and domestic purities also coloured the treatment of the Japanese recommendation in April that the Covenant be amended to include the recognition of 'the principle of equality among nations and the just treatment of their nationals'. A number of states, in particular Australia and the United States, fearing that this might affect their ability to control foreign immigration, vetoed the Japanese clause. Wilson believed that the acceptance of a racial-equality clause would lead to Senate rejection of the treaty. For Americans, Australians, and South Africans, racial equality was a highly emotive issue. Liberal, internationally minded Japanese were deeply offended by the absence of a racial-equality clause, and the check by the 'so-called civilized world' was not forgotten. Japan was given a share of the victor's spoils. It acquired the former German Pacific islands north of the Equator as 'C' mandates (Wilson opposed outright possession, despite Japanese occupation and the recognition of its claims by the British, French, and Italians in 1917). There were realistic American fears at the time, shared by Australia and New Zealand, that Japan would fortify the islands and exclude foreign trade. Japan also demanded Kiaochow and other key points on the Shantung peninsula, which the Chinese had leased to Germany in 1897 and which the Japanese seized at the start of the war. American and Chinese objections received only limited support from the British who, along with the French and tsarist Russians, had already recognized the Japanese position and who, in view of their own multiple concessions in the Yangtse, could not accept the presidential proposal that all foreign concessions in China be internationalized. In the end, engaged in a fierce contest with the Italians over Fiume and fearful that the Japanese would abandon the treaty negotiations and even reject the League, Wilson yielded. The Chinese, unmollified by the face-saving stipulation won by Wilson that Kiaochow was to revert to China at some unspecified date, were outraged. They left the conference and refused to sign the Versailles treaty. The Japanese victory was seen generally as a striking presidential defeat on the issue of self-determination. In China, fury over the Paris negotiations mobilized Chinese students; on 4 May 3,000 demonstrators converged on Tiananmen Square, in a massive rally that marked a new stage in the development of Chinese nationalism. Disillusionment with the west and disappointments with their own brand of western-style democracy led some to look to the new Bolshevik government in Russia as a role model, particularly when the latter promised to give up all the earlier tsarists' conquests and concessions. A year after the peace conference a small Chinese Communist Party was formed. The Bolshevik promise was not kept.

These were not the only presidential retreats at Paris. When Wilson returned to Washington after the Covenant was presented to the conference on 14 February, it was clear that, if it was to be accepted by the Senate, he would need at the least a clause explicitly preserving American rights under the 'Monroe Doctrine', the warning by President James Monroe in 1823 against European intervention in the affairs of the American continents. Lloyd George now demanded his pound of flesh, insisting on an Anglo-American naval agreement which would restrict the completion of the American naval building programme proposed in 1918. Admittedly, the House–Cecil agreement of 10 April represented only a partial victory for the British. The Americans agreed to delay the completion of the 1916 programme only until after the peace treaty was signed, and then to reconsider the implementation of the 1918 schedule. In return, Cecil pledged British support for the American amendment. Article 21 consequently specifically exempted the Monroe Doctrine and other such 'regional understandings' from the application of the Covenant. Wilson, nonetheless, felt that he had steered the Covenant to the end he wanted. The League would be the guardian of the peace settlements as a whole: where they needed fixing, 'one by one the mistakes can be brought to the League for readjustment, and the League will act as a permanent clearinghouse where every nation can come, the small as well as the great'.[16] The final draft of the Covenant was presented to the plenary conference on 21 April. It was adopted, as Wilson had demanded, as Part I of the peace treaty. In this case the 'special relationship' between London and Washington functioned well. But this partnership was not extended to the rest of the treaty terms.

IV

It was only after the terms of the Covenant of the League of Nations were settled that the 'big three' could turn to the multitude of other questions that had appeared on the agenda. The first of these was what the French considered to be the heart of the peace treaty, the military, territorial, and economic safeguards for France. The French proposals

[16] S. P. Tillman, *Anglo-American Relations at the Paris Peace Conference of 1919* (Princeton, 1961), 133.

Map 3. The Western European Territorial Settlements

for the disarmament of Germany caused little dissension, except insofar as they were connected with the Rhineland compromise. Conscription and the general staff were abolished, with the Germans restricted to an army of 100,000 men serving not less than twelve years (officers for twenty-five) and dedicated exclusively to the purpose of 'the maintenance of order within the territory and to the control of the frontiers'. Lloyd George won his point that it should be a volunteer force rather than, as Foch wanted, a conscript army. The French would have accepted a larger army with shorter terms of enlistment. Restrictive maximum limits were set on the amounts of artillery, machine-guns, rifles, and ammunition which the army could possess. Germany was forbidden to have an air force, to possess tanks, armoured cars, or submarines, or to manufacture such weapons for others. The German navy was drastically curtailed, with a maximum of six heavy cruisers and six light cruisers subject to upper limits of 10,000 tons and 6,000 tons displacement respectively. Compliance would be monitored by an Inter-Allied Military Control Commission. The defeated enemy was to dismantle many of its fortifications, including all those within 50 kilometres east of the Rhine and those on the island of Heligoland which guarded the entrance to the Elbe and Weser rivers on which Hamburg and Bremen were located. The Kiel Canal was to be opened to all vessels and German rivers internationalized. Ominously for the future, the preamble to the military clauses (Part V of the treaty) stated that the restrictions on Germany were imposed 'in order to render possible the initiation of a general limitation of the armaments of all nations'.

As was anticipated, there were fierce battles with the British and the Americans over the Rhineland question. Clemenceau mistakenly assumed that Lloyd George would support his demands for a permanent end to German sovereignty west of the river and the creation of buffer states. He was forced to retreat. Lloyd George would accept neither the detachment of the Rhineland nor its military occupation, and was backed by Wilson. The Americans were insistent: the League and not the Rhineland would solve France's security problems. As House put it, 'if after establishing the League, we are so stupid as to let Germany train and arm a large army and again become a menace to the world, we would deserve the fate which such folly would bring upon us'.[17] The British prime minister broke the deadlock by offering France, as soon as Wilson returned from America in mid-March, a military guarantee of immediate aid against German aggression. It was a sensational offer, and seemingly strengthened by Lloyd George's promise to authorize the building of a Channel tunnel, already under discussion (though ultimately to be rejected) in London, so that British troops could be quickly dispatched to France. By means of a last-minute sleight-of-hand, he made the British guarantee dependent on the Senate ratification of a parallel but separate American guarantee that he had persuaded Wilson, who minimized its

[17] House diary, 9 Feb. 1919, quoted in MacMillan, *Peacemakers*, 182.

importance, to offer. The possibility of an alliance proved irresistible. Clemenceau was clearly aware of the risks, even if he overlooked the fine print of the agreement which further qualified the offer of support. In return, Clemenceau abandoned his demand for the separation of the Rhineland and permanent occupation of the left bank. Yet, in what has been called by the American historian, Stephen Shuker, 'the diplomatic equivalent of trench warfare', Clemenceau demanded and won further concessions. The left bank of the Rhine and a 50-kilometre strip on the right would be permanently demilitarized: the Germans were forbidden to send soldiers or maintain any military installations in that zone. Further, any German violation of this was stipulated to mean that 'she shall be regarded as committing a hostile act against the Powers signatory of the present Treaty and as calculated to disturb the peace of the world' (Article 44). The provisions meant that Germany was precluded from constructing defences around the Rhine–Ruhr area, the centre of its industrial strength. The French leader had to be content, after a battle with Wilson in Lloyd George's absence, with a fifteen-year occupation of the Rhineland and the river bridgeheads (at Cologne, Coblenz, Mainz, and Kehl), with phased withdrawals at five-year intervals if Germany observed the terms of the treaty. Lloyd George was furious at Wilson's surrender to Clemenceau's demands. With the ending of conscription, British troops would be in short supply and needed for imperial policing duties, and should not be required to stand on the Rhine. Clemenceau's Rhineland compromise was further eased by the promise that, if the guarantee treaties did not materialize and the securities against German aggression were unsatisfactory, the occupation could be prolonged. After some hesitation, Clemenceau also insisted on the adoption of a French Finance Ministry proposal that linked the fulfilment of the reparation clause with the threat of immediate reoccupation (Article 430), giving the reparation settlement an important security aspect. There was much argument in later years whether Article 431, promising the withdrawal of the occupying forces before the fifteen-year limit if Germany fulfilled her undertakings, referred to reparations only or to the whole treaty as was understood at the time. These safeguards did not satisfy Marshal Foch or President Poincaré. Foch's attempt to head a revolt against Clemenceau's leadership fizzled out, however, when, at the crucial Council of Ministers on 25 April, Poincaré remained silent out of fear of provoking a political crisis and the ministers unanimously approved the draft treaty terms. The French premier understood the risks of his bargain, but judged that only an agreement of the three powers, not just in the present but in the future, could guarantee the future peace.

The dispute over the Saar between Clemenceau and Wilson proved to be more bitter than over the barrier on the Rhine. Clemenceau called the president pro-German, and the latter threatened to go home. Lloyd George called in the experts, who found an acceptable compromise. The prime minister was less opposed to the Saarland annexation than Wilson, who insisted that the French claims to the loyalties of the Saarlanders were totally spurious. The French were given the Saar coalfields for fifteen years and, pending a plebiscite at the end of that time, could occupy the territory. Wilson demanded, however, that the Saar should remain under German sovereignty until the vote was taken, and backed the recommendation that the territory should be governed in the interval by a League of Nations commission. If reunited with Germany, the Germans could buy back the mines. Wilson had to be satisfied with a victory that left open the future disposition of the Saar and gave the League a role to play, but which allowed the French the chance to meddle in the region's domestic affairs. When forced to give way on outright annexation, the French still hoped to succeed in converting the Saarlanders to the advantages of joining France. As early as July 1919, a committee was created under the supervision of Clemenceau and Tardieu to encourage a positive result in the eventual plebiscite.

The rectification of borders with Belgium and Denmark clearly favoured French strategic interests. There was good reason for the Belgians—who played a poor hand at Paris, and were less strongly supported by the British than they had expected—to suspect the French of hegemonic ambitions. Belgium was restored as an independent state and given the tiny former German territories of Eupen, Malmédy, and Moresnet. A plebiscite in Luxembourg, held on 28 September 1919, while French troops were in occupation, resulted in an overwhelming vote for the Grand Duchess and for economic union with France. The French position in Luxembourg was later used as bait to secure Belgian adhesion to a military alliance, but France, in any case, was able to secure and retain control over the duchy's railway system which contained vital parts of Europe's rail network, most significantly three lines from Germany to the Paris basin formerly under German control. Plebiscites were to be held in northern and central Schleswig in July 1920; northern Schleswig became part of Denmark, the rest went back to Germany. The divisions followed the nationality lines.

The clash between Clemenceau's hopes for a contained Germany and Lloyd George's concern for the future stability of Europe was central to the Allied decisions on Poland. Clemenceau's interest was to use Poland as a check to Germany and a barrier against the spread of Bolshevism. Lloyd George, and in some measure Wilson, came to believe that a compact Poland restricted to its ethnic core would prove a more stable influence in Europe than the more powerful and ethnically extended state favoured by the French. In the territorial committees considering Germany's eastern borders and the claims of the new states, the French representatives argued the case for their future client and generally succeeded in winning generous terms. Though there were disputes, the British and American experts, intent on assuring the economic and strategic viability of the new states, retreated from the strict application of self-determination principles. As a result, German territorial losses in the east were considerable and the Poles, as the French intended, were the main beneficiaries. The Commission on Polish Affairs was sympathetic to the Poles. The Germans surrendered almost the entire province of Poznan, a large part of West Prussia, an enlarged 'corridor' to the Baltic sea which split East Prussia from the rest of Germany, and, as a main port, the predominately German Hanseatic city of Danzig. It must be remembered that, Danzig aside, most of these territories were heavily Polish so that the division, in reversing the pre-war situation, favoured the dominant nationality. The important coalfield and industrial area of Upper Silesia was also assigned to Poland. Despite objections from the British experts, there was also to be a plebiscite in Allenstein, the area of East Prussia nearest Poland. Over 2 million Germans now came under Polish rule. In 1919 many in Britain believed that the Polish settlement was a gross violation of Wilsonian principles, though it is more likely that the American president was caught up in the difficulties of applying the doctrines of self-determination to the actual situation in central Europe and to the multiplicity of goals that the peacemakers had in mind. Wilson relied on the League of Nations to right whatever wrongs were committed.

It was Lloyd George who led the opposition to the Polish Commission's recommendations. 'Poland was drunk with the new wine of liberty supplied to her by the Allies', Lloyd George believed, and 'fancied herself as the resistless mistress of Central Europe'.[18] He repeatedly clashed with the Poles, not only over the Polish–German border but over their conduct in Galicia and the Ukraine. Lloyd George rightly perceived that Germany would find the loss of its territory to Poland and the inclusion of German citizens in a Polish state as one of the treaty's most intolerable parts. 'My conclusion', he told the Council of Four on 27 March, 'is that we must not create a Poland alienated from the time of its birth by an unforgettable quarrel from its most civilized neighbour.'[19] He secured, after Wilson's return in mid-March, the backing of the president, who had previously accepted the advice of his pro-Polish

[18] Norman Davies, *God's Playground: A History of Poland* (Oxford, 1981), ii. 393.
[19] P. Mantoux, *The Deliberations of the Council of Four*, ed. and trans. A. S. Link, 2 vols. (Princeton, 1992), i. 33–4.

advisers, Robert Lord and Isaiah Bowman, on the need for an enlarged Poland with access to the Baltic. Wilson's change of attitude had as much to do with his exasperation with the French—over the Rhineland, the Saar, their demands on German territory for Poland, and also André Tardieu's secret exchanges with key American Republicans—as with Poland itself. In addition, the quarrel with the Italians over Fiume made him more sensitive to the clashes of nationality claims. Both Lloyd George and Woodrow Wilson were admittedly increasingly irritated by the behaviour of Roman Dmowski, the Polish delegate in Paris, and outraged by the excessive appetites of a weak and divided government. The sharp differences between Dmowski and Józef Piłsudski, the Polish military leader, over Poland's relations with her eastern neighbours fed Anglo-American suspicions about its annexationist ambitions. Whether the Poles would have fared better had Dmowski been less abrasive and the Polish representatives presented a united front remains an open question, but larger issues than the questions of Polish internal debates were involved in the setting of the country's western frontier. Taking new advice, with Clemenceau pressed heavily by Lloyd George and Wilson, the Council of Four agreed that the mainly German-speaking Danzig and its environs should be made a free city under the jurisdiction of the League. The Poles would control the railways, bring the city within the Polish customs union, and conduct its foreign relations. Again due to Lloyd George, there would be a plebiscite in Marienwerder, which contained the vital Danzig–Warsaw railway but had a predominately German population. The demand for plebiscites, as well as later compromise over Upper Silesia, while satisfying Wilsonian principles, were attempts to meet the most pressing German grievances.

Even with these modifications, many of which were due to coalition politics, Poland emerged as a major power in the centre of Europe, with the French as its most loyal backers. Given its geographic situation, between Germany and a still unsettled and unrecognized Bolshevik Russia, Poland's future was bound to be fraught with difficulties. There could be no 'just' solution of the Polish question according to the principles of self-determination. By its very nature Poland was a multinational state, reconstituted from the inhabitants of three former empires who, even in their pre-war situations, did not represent homogeneous ethnic blocs. Poland had not existed as an independent state for over a century. Given the circumstances of its birth, it is almost surprising that the boundaries of the Polish state survived intact until the Fourth Partition of 1939—and that the eastern frontier, settled by the Poles and the Russians in 1921, should have conformed more closely to what Dmowski's supporters demanded than what the British and the Americans had thought desirable. In this respect, far more was owed to the efforts of the Poles themselves than to the assistance of the treaty-makers.

The borders of Czechoslovakia and the future status of Austria, set by experts sitting in separate territorial committees, offended even more strongly against the principle of self-determination. The Czechoslovak borders were established by the different peace treaties concluded in Paris, and were eventually delimited by boundary commissions under each treaty. Those drawn at the expense of the German-speaking populations aroused the most internal opposition. They did not produce, however, major disputes among the peacemakers, nor provoke German protests. Edvard Beneš, the Czech foreign minister, was a more attractive and adroit statesman than Dmowski and a more effective supplicant at Paris. Lloyd George was one of the few who disliked him and found the Czech claims excessive. The French, with whom Beneš had excellent contacts, were determined to establish a state with industrial resources and defensible borders; the commission on Czechoslovak affairs provided the Czechs with both. The Czechs were awarded part of Upper Silesia and the German–Austrian areas of Bohemia with their important coal and industrial resources. Protests from the Bohemian Germans (who were not Germans but Austrians) were discounted. The American delegates argued for modifications, but Clemenceau swept aside such troublesome details and opted for the simple solution of following the pre-war border between Germany and Bohemia. When the Council of Four, where Colonel House was deputizing for the ailing American president, discussed the Commission's report, the matter was quickly and almost casually settled. Beset by controversies over the western and eastern frontiers of Germany, the Council accepted Clemenceau's suggestion, with the Italians supporting France. Neither Lloyd George nor House raised any objections to the inclusion of 3 million German-speakers in the new Czechoslovakia, and there was no talk of future 'Alsace-Lorraines' in Europe. The president backed his representative. Only the Austrians protested strongly against the Allied action when the treaty was in its final stages, and their opposition counted for little. The ban on *Anschluss* (unification with Germany) represented a clear break with the principle of national self-determination. With good reason, Clemenceau insisted that union would dangerously increase German power, and convinced Wilson and Lloyd George to support his view. It was the president who, unwilling to establish a permanent veto on union, found the acceptable formula that made Austrian independence inalienable unless the League of Nations decided otherwise. This satisfied Wilson's conscience while still preserving the French right to prevent future changes in Austria's status. Lloyd George played almost no role in this decision. The French were backed by the Italians and by the Czechs, who had a vested interest in preserving an independent and separate Austria. The opinions of the Austrians who massively supported union were disregarded.

Whereas the League resulted from an Anglo-American initiative and represented a Wilsonian victory, the territorial clauses of the Versailles treaty bore the imprint of France's security needs but also the impact of Polish and Czech nationalism, and the efforts of their respective wartime émigrés who successfully lobbied for support in the victor countries. Clemenceau sacrificed the strategic frontier on the Rhine (the occupation represented an important, if temporary, victory) for the Anglo-American guarantee which, unfortunately for France, would prove to be an unredeemable cheque. Even allowing for this not entirely unanticipated disaster, he did not go away empty-handed. He had combined the promise of future Anglo-American support with a series of physical guarantees. He won a demilitarized Rhineland and a fifteen-year occupation that could be shortened but also prolonged. He lost the battle for sovereignty over the Saar but, as in the Rhineland, the way was left open for an extension of French influence. While he had accepted limits to Polish ambitions in Danzig and Upper Silesia, Clemenceau could take satisfaction from the creation of a large Poland and an economically and strategically viable Czechoslovak state. Contrary to what his French critics claimed, he probably won as much as he could in Paris without sacrificing the inter-Allied solidarity so essential for France, if she was to reverse the process of pre-war decline in order to face a country with a larger population and greater industrial potential.

Germany lost some 27,000 square miles of territory and between 6.5 and 7 million people. Her losses included over 10 per cent of her pre-war resources and an estimated 13.5 per cent of her economic potential.[20] This involved the loss of raw materials for industry as well as agricultural lands, leaving Germany more heavily dependent on its industry and industrial exports than before the war. Its territorial losses included Alsace-Lorraine, and many of the people lost were French or Polish. Given the shared view of German culpability for the Great War and the terms of the German treaty imposed on Russia at Brest-Litovsk, the territorial demands, while considerable, were neither unduly nor unprecedentedly harsh. Germany was left intact. Its basic unity was preserved, as was its ability not just to sustain itself but to recover much of its former economic status. Unlike later settlements, the Versailles territorial changes did not involve the disposition and forced removal of millions of people. If ideals over self-determination were

---

[20] Figures from Sharp, *The Versailles Settlement*, 127–8.

compromised, as was inevitable when the principle was applied in practice, territorial, strategic, and economic realities were incorporated in the drawing of borders, at least, inasmuch as the Allied powers could impose their will.

V

There was no reparation settlement as such. The only decision reached was an agreement to create a Reparations Commission which would determine by May 1921 what sums the Germans were to pay. The only concrete demands made were for a preliminary payment of 20,000 million gold marks and certain designated reparations in goods. Few anticipated such a postponement of this vexatious question. The diplomats had been content to leave the issue to the financial experts, the Commission on Reparations and the Supreme Council (by the end of March, the Council of Four), advised by a small group of specialists. The reparation problem was thus not only discussed in isolation from the territorial issues but separately from the other financial and economic parts of the treaty. Why did the subject become so contentious that it had to be taken up at the highest political levels, and why did such an evasive conclusion emerge?

Part of the answer lay in the public domain. Few questions connected with the peace aroused more popular feeling. In France and Britain, as well as in Italy and Belgium, the reparations question was politicized before the start of the peace conference. A combination of anti-German feeling and the hope that the burden of paying for the war could be shifted onto German shoulders coloured the political landscape. In April 1919 over 300 deputies in the French Chamber supported a manifesto insisting that Germany pay for the whole cost of the war and not just for damage done. It was not a matter of restitution but a claim for retribution against the enemy. In Britain the election promises of 1918 were not forgotten. The *Daily Mail*, first in December 1918 and again in late March 1919, when rumours of compromise circulated in London, initiated a campaign against any reduction in reparation claims. On 8 April, 233 Unionist MPs signed a telegram of protest to Lloyd George, and the prime minister was forced to return to London to defend his policy before the Commons. Whatever was decided in private had to be defended in public. The second problem was that neither between nor within the main delegations was there any agreement on what Germany could or should be expected to pay, or on how the receipts should be allocated. John Foster Dulles, a young lawyer and member of the American group, insisted that Germany's liability as defined by the Lansing Note should be limited to compensation for damage done to the civilian populations of the Allies and their property, and should exclude the costs of waging the war. The American team failed to speak with a united voice, however: Lamont and Davis quarrelled, and Bernard Baruch, a Wall Street banker and adviser to Wilson, could hardly stand working with Lamont. The French, who with the Belgians had the strongest case for reparations as defined in the Lansing Note, could move in the American direction as long as their claim to priority in payments would be maintained. Loucheur, once he replaced Clémental as Clemenceau's chief financial adviser, was prepared to reduce French demands in return for a priority of payment to cover France's material needs. Yet in French political and financial circles there was no consensus even as to whether reparations were the most suitable instrument for remedying France's financial problems. The British were the most divided. The few Treasury experts in Paris, led by Keynes, continued to warn of the dangers of too high a reparations bill, but failed to convince the British representatives on the Reparation Commission. Led by Hughes, the Australian prime minister and chief advocate of extensive reparations, the latter tried to establish a connection between German 'aggression' (the word used in the Lansing Note) and the absolute right of the victors to demand payment for war costs. They needed an inflated bill if Britain was to get its share of the German payments. The prime minister's own political agenda favoured this view. He had insisted during the election campaign that 'Germany must pay the costs of the war up to the limit of her capacity', and that 'you will find that the capacity will go a pretty long way'.[21] British representatives sought an arrangement of payments that would provide as large a share of the reparation bill as possible, as much as a third of any future sum set, and contested French claims for priority. Such clashes did not make the negotiating process any easier. Even when the various experts did concur, their advice was not necessarily accepted by their political masters.

The final explanation for the unsatisfactory outcome must be found in Wilson's unwillingness to use the financial weapons at his command to secure the reparation solution he wanted. Both the British and French hoped that Americans would become the benefactors of Europe, but the Americans refused to assume this role. They argued that debts contracted should be paid. Without the full use of America's financial power and dedicated to the creation of a liberal economic order, Wilson found himself in a relatively weak position. Whether because of concessions made to settle Franco-British clashes or concessions made in the face of a

---

[21] Election address at Bristol, 11 Dec. 1918, in David Lloyd George, *The Truth About the Peace Treaties* (London, 1938), 463, 465.

Franco-British united front, Wilson steadily gave way on most of the reparation points that he considered most essential.

From the start, problems arose over the size of the reparations bill. Little progress was made by the end of February in calculating Allied claims. The first subcommittee (valuation of damage) became so involved in disputes over the question of admissible claims that they ended up with a list which included every conceivable item. Nor was any progress made on setting a provisional sum that the Germans could afford to pay. There were genuine difficulties, but also the wish not to disappoint home electorates with unrealistic expectations. No one knew what Germany could actually afford. There was the danger that the German government might fall if the sum demanded was too high and the treaty too harsh. The French and Americans finally reached a compromise, setting a maximum figure of £8,000 million, but Lord Cunliffe insisted on a far higher sum, completely out of line with what his own Treasury experts considered possible. In mid-March, in order to break the deadlock, the matter was sent to the Council of Four, which referred the question to an informal committee of three—Davis, Loucheur, and Edwin Montagu, the former financial secretary to the British Treasury. The experts, all moderates, recommended that the Germans pay a fixed sum of £6,000 million over a thirty-year period, while admitting privately that the utmost Germany could pay was £3,000 million. Lloyd George vacillated infuriatingly. He rejected this compromise, blaming the state of British public opinion, yet in his 'Fontainebleau memorandum' of 25 March, prepared at a time when the possibility of a harsh peace posed the spectre of a Bolshevized Germany, he warned that 'we cannot both cripple her [Germany] and expect her to pay' and admitted that each amount being considered 'greatly exceeds what, on any calculation, Germany is capable of paying'.[22] His warnings, however, were not followed by any perceptible lowering of the British figures. The American president found the sums being discussed wildly inflated and the ever-growing list of claims for compensation totally unacceptable. But he contested the proposed solution, first suggested by Lamont, of postponing a decision until after the peace conference. On 28 March Klotz, the French finance minister, formally suggested that the final figures be settled by an Inter-Allied Reparation Commission meeting after the peacemakers disbanded. Lloyd George, who had previously favoured a fixed sum to be incorporated in the treaty, was not adverse to the delay, which he thought might lead to saner figures. Though by this time he did not

---

[22] Michael L. Dockrill and J. Douglas Goold, *Peace Without Promise: Britain and the Peace Conferences, 1919–1923* (London, 1981), 51.

want a big reparations bill, he still pressed for a hefty British share of the final total. To secure this, Lloyd George had cleverly combined two British proposals. The first was a formula suggested by Smuts which separated claims for war damage into two categories, damages to persons and damages to property. Smuts expected that these enumerated claims would in fact limit the overall total and not exceed Germany's restricted capacity to pay. Secondly, Lloyd George backed Lord Sumner's demands that pensions and separation allowances be included as war damage. The prime minister then argued that, though the Allies were entitled to compensation for all war costs, the Germans could not remit such astronomical accounts. It was more reasonable to restrict the sums demanded to Smuts's two categories of damage, including, of course, pensions and allowances. By this device Britain's share of any sum ultimately paid by Germany was greatly increased. The prime minister won French acceptance of this formula; the question of priorities remained unsettled. In the end, Belgium got a priority but France did not.

Wilson fought hard against the abandonment of a fixed sum and argued that the postponement of a decision would leave the door open to inflated and punitive demands. He also took umbrage at the British extension of their claims against Germany. The British and French closed ranks; Lloyd George threatened to leave the conference if his demands were not met. The president, worn down by his battles over the Rhineland and Saar, pressed by the prime minister, and cajoled by Smuts, capitulated on both fronts on 1 April. There was a further American retreat on 5 April, when Colonel House was deputizing for the sick president, whose health was collapsing under the strain of the negotiations. Both the expert committee of three and Smuts had suggested the establishment of a permanent commission which could vary Germany's annual payments according to their assessment of its ability to pay. House agreed to allow this Reparation Commission the right to prolong German payments beyond thirty years, thereby relaxing the time limit the Americans had always demanded. Two days later the Council of Four decided that Germany's debt could not be reduced without the consent of all the members of the Reparation Commission. There was a further clash between the French and the British when Klotz demanded that the Reparation Commission base its future calculations on the total sum owed to the Allies rather than on Germany's capacity to pay. At this point Wilson lost his patience, and on 7 April summoned the *George Washington* to Brest. This time Clemenceau climbed down; the issue could be fought out later in the Reparation Commission itself. The French negotiators carefully drafted the terms of reference for the commission, and their precautions paid high dividends when the United States, which was intended to chair the commission, refused to ratify the treaty. Once Wilson announced that the Americans would be represented, Lloyd George believed that an Anglo-American combination on the commission could be used against the French. Confrontation was again postponed. Wilson's intention that there should be no indemnity and that Germany's reparations should be narrowly restricted had been thwarted. These presidential defeats were in danger of being multiplied when the three leaders began to debate the form in which Germany's liability should appear in the treaty. Wilson proposed a repetition of the terms of the Lansing Note; Clemenceau and Lloyd George were insistent that there should be an unequivocal statement of Germany's total liability, to satisfy their respective publics. Clemenceau demanded that it be clearly stated that it was the Allies and not the Germans who were qualifying their unlimited right to compensation on the grounds of practicability. Again, it was House, anxious to end the haggling, who proposed a compromise based on a suggestion of Norman Davis that distinguished between Germany's complete moral responsibility for the war and its consequences and its limited legal liability for reparations. This would meet British and French political objectives, while preserving the categories of liability found in the Lansing Note. Article 231, the so-called 'war guilt' clause, became the first reparation clause and the prologue to the actual enumeration of the Allied claims against Germany. Dulles, who had worked on its wording, thought that he had both established German liability and limited it. In a very brief space of time this article, intended to bridge the gap between what was politically desirable and what was practically possible, became the symbolic representation of the 'unjust peace' for the Germans and their sympathizers.

It was only towards the end of April, after the draft of the reparation section had been completed, that Lloyd George again argued that the Germans would not accept the treaty. It may have been these fears that prompted the prime minister on 24 April to present the president with a radical scheme by Keynes for European reconstruction: a bond issue by the former Central Powers and the eastern European successor states, with interest rates guaranteed by the Americans, the main Allied powers, and the neutral states. One-fifth of the proceeds would be used by the defeated states to purchase food and raw materials; the rest would be distributed among the Allies as a first reparation payment. Wilson rejected Keynes's politically unrealistic proposal: it depended on bringing American capital into Europe, out of which a considerable share would go back into Allied pockets in the form of reparations. The bonds would be used by the participating countries to pay off their war debts. As most of the money would be raised in the United States, the burden of what was in effect an unsecured loan would rest on American investors. The net effect of the scheme was to shift the burden of paying for the war from European onto American shoulders, something which neither Congress nor the electorate would allow. The American Treasury offered a three-year moratorium on the servicing and amortization of Allied war debts, but would not consider the Keynes proposal.

Though an American alternative was proposed, the president was unwilling to reopen the reparation question. American and British experts, after private consultations with their German counterparts, were convinced that the Germans could not pay even the interim amounts demanded (£1,000 million), and argued that the effort would place an intolerable burden on the German economy. They found the German counter-proposal of £5,000 million in reparations, prepared by the Hamburg bankers, including Carl Melchior and Max Warburg, worth considering. Despite his own misgivings, Lloyd George refused to give way. He was determined not to accept a figure that might be lower than what the Germans could be made to pay. By the time the new Reparations Commission met, the prime minister predicted, public tempers would have cooled and the Allies could agree on a reasonable sum which the Germans would then pay. The enemy would be punished, Britain and its empire compensated, and, better still from his standpoint, the French would not walk away with overfull pockets at Britain's expense. Nor were the French dissatisfied with the outcome. A late intervention by Klotz assured France of some payments in cash and kind before the Reparation Commission met. By postponing the decision on a fixed sum, Clemenceau had safeguarded France's position with regard to both the amount and timing of German repayments and had gained the possibility of sanctions against default. The French premier did not actually believe that the Germans could raise the sums being discussed in Paris, but any realistic figure would have created political difficulties in the Chamber. He preferred the Reparation Commission to make the necessary adjustments. In the absence of direct assistance, apart from loans, from the Americans and the British, France would have to look to Germany to get her due. This solution to her problems would depend on Britain's backing in the absence of the Americans and German compliance.

The reparation clauses of the treaty, Articles 231 through 244, began with the statement of the responsibility of Germany and her allies (the same clause was included in the other peace treaties) for Allied loss and damage. Article 232 narrowed the actual scope of German financial liability, and an annex defined the categories to be included. In effect, the Americans were able to restrict claims to an enlarged version of those enumerated in the Lansing Note. Article 233 left the setting of the reparation sum to a Reparation Commission consisting of the four major powers and delegates from Belgium on German, Yugoslavia on eastern, and Japan on naval questions. The commission was to reach agreement on a figure by May 1921 and draw up a schedule of payments for thirty years. It could postpone payments after hearing German representations and take into consideration Germany's capacity to pay. It could not cancel any part of the reparation agreement without specific authorization from the member states. In the interim, Germany was to pay 20,000 million gold marks in cash and kind, including deliveries of coal for ten years and shipments of livestock and chemicals.

The treaty imposed other economic and financial restrictions on Germany. The drafting of the general economic clauses took place before the main decisions were reached on what became the far more important territorial and reparation questions. The 'big three' focused their attention on these and paid scant regard to what was being decided in the economic commission and subcommissions. Little was done to integrate the different sections of the treaty dealing with financial, commercial, and economic matters. The economic clauses, nonetheless, also represented a compromise between Wilson's hopes for a world economy based on 'open door' principles and free trade, and the Anglo-French wish to maintain some form of Allied oversight over the post-war economic order and to check any new German bid to re-establish its economic primacy on the continent. The British hoped to limit Germany's export capacity in order to protect their own overseas trade, but, conscious of the connections between the revival of German strength and British prosperity, were unwilling to see Germany excessively damaged. The French, though increasingly looking to reparations as the way to readjust the Franco-German economic balance in their own favour, sought ways to transfer German economic resources to France and to protect herself and the new successor states from German economic domination. Along with its colonies, Germany's foreign financial holdings were to be confiscated and all German merchant ships above 16,000 tons and smaller vessels surrendered, reducing the German merchant marine to one-tenth its pre-war size. The treaty contained discriminatory measures restricting Germany's freedom to trade, including the suppression of its tariff freedom for at least eighteen months and the granting of most-favoured-nation treatment to the Allies and Associated Powers without reciprocity for five years. There were special economic safeguards for the Rhineland and the surrender of the Saar coalfields to the French. By the time the territorial transfers were completed in 1921, Germany had lost 80 per cent of its 1913 iron-ore output, most of it in Lorraine, and 30 per cent of steel production, with all the former capacity and much of the latter going to France. If

German economic power was cut, much of what was won in Paris by way of the economic clauses gave the French, Poles, and Czechs only temporary protection against Germany and a short head-start period. It is doubtful whether the American president would have agreed to any longer period of interference with German trade and the establishment of the liberal trading regime. Germany was left, as Wilson intended, with its basic industrial capacity intact and in a position to return on equal terms to that regime in the not-too-distant future. The final balance sheet would depend on the degree to which the French could capitalize on their neighbour's momentary weakness and on the decisions of the future Reparation Commission.

VI

The Allied draft was presented to the Germans on 7 May at the Trianon Palace in Versailles. The Germans were given fifteen days to reply in writing, though the deadline was later extended to 29 May. The treaty was a shock both to the German delegation and to their countrymen, the latter shaken first by the unexpected military defeat and then by the shattering of hopes deliberately raised by the Weimar government. Though they had been given a good deal of information about the progress of the negotiations, the German government still believed it could negotiate a 'Wilsonian' treaty. From January 1919, when the foreign minister, Ulrich von Brockdorff-Rantzau, a figure from the old imperial Wilhelmstrasse (Foreign Ministry), prepared the first draft peace plans, until the last version of the 'Guide Lines for the German Peace Negotiators' dated 21 April 1919, the Germans looked to a lenient treaty based on their interpretation of the Fourteen Points. There were warnings that this optimistic reading of their future was misplaced. The first blow came with the release of the League of Nations draft on 14 February and the news that Germany would be excluded from the very body which was to be its means of returning to great-power status. Philipp Scheidemann's government in Berlin responded by drafting a proposal for a more radical and democratic League to demonstrate their loyalty to the new idealism. This, it was believed, would pacify domestic public opinion and convince Wilson that the new Germany had cut its links with the past. Similarly, the threat that, if pressed too hard, the republic might fall and a Bolshevik regime be established was intended to influence Allied opinion. If Wilson and Lloyd George were more concerned than Clemenceau about a left-wing reaction in Germany, the president's fears diminished after the failure of the weak March revolutionary movements. Nor, as some German leaders hoped, would he take the lead in an anti-

Bolshevik campaign in which the Germans could join. The Scheide-mann coalition (majority Socialists, Centre party, and Democrats) never enlisted his full confidence. The anti-Bolshevik argument proved to be a double-edged sword. Colonel House, in Wilson's absence, was suffi-ciently worried that he opted for a speedy conclusion to the negotiations even at the cost of concessions to Clemenceau.

The Germans refused to believe that the American president would not listen sympathetically to their demands for revision. The tactics of the German government were misdirected, as they tried to play the United States off against its associates and return the victors to the Fourteen Points. They again raised the spectre of a Bolshevik revolution in Germany and attacked the moral and legal basis of Germany's exclu-sion from the League and the territorial and reparation clauses. The bitterest criticism was directed against the eastern frontier changes, above all Upper Silesia, important for its industrial assets, West Prussia, and Danzig. In the west, the Germans objected to the Saar arrangement and the territorial cessions to Belgium. Counter-proposals were made for the evacuation of the Rhineland within six months of the treaty being signed. The 'war guilt' clause was also strongly condemned. The German counter-proposal on reparations offered 100 billion gold marks, with the demand that Germany should maintain its territorial integrity as of 1914. The 'Observations of the German Delegation on the Condi-tions of Peace' presented on 29 May were in a volume of over 100 pages. The preface, prepared by a scholar of international law, dealt with the differences between the treaty and the Fourteen Points. The Germans demanded membership of the League of Nations and the retention of Upper Silesia, the Saar, Danzig, and Memel. The central theme, however, was the 'utter destruction of German economic life'.[23] A supplement outlined the disastrous consequences of reparations; Warburg wanted to show that the economic consequences of the peace would require its future revision. The German case was presented in a manner calculated neither to win Wilson's support nor to move the Allies.

It was not Wilson but Lloyd George who proved willing to meet some of the German objections. The British prime minister was genu-inely worried that the Germans would reject the treaty, and that military action, already being considered by Marshal Foch, or the reimposition of the blockade might prove necessary. He was under strong pressure for revision throughout April and May from the members of his delegation who condemned the financial and economic clauses of the treaty as far

[23] Niall Ferguson, *Paper and Iron: Hamburg Business and German Politics in the Era of Inflation, 1897–1927* (Cambridge, 1995), 219.

too harsh and in contradiction of the armistice terms. Keynes, worn out and on the verge of breakdown, insisted that the reparation clauses were morally unjustified and financially unworkable. There was a chorus of hostile criticism at the end of May, led by General Smuts as well as cabinet ministers summoned from London to consider the treaty terms. Though Lloyd George refused to reopen the reparations question, he was more sympathetically inclined towards demands for changes in the Polish settlement, preferring for the most part to leave to Germany the areas that were undoubtedly German and holding plebiscites where the loyalties of the local population might be in question. He agreed, too, to ask for modifications in the cost, length, and nature of the occupation regime in the Rhineland and to hasten the date of German entry into the League if she fulfilled the treaty obligations. When the delegation pressed for more radical proposals on 2 June, the exasperated prime minister turned on his critics. He pointed out that no one present, not even Smuts, who subsequently spoke of the treaty's 'poisonous spirit of revenge', was willing to forgo its colonial and financial benefits.

It was not a propitious moment to reopen the earlier debates. The negotiators were tired and nerves were overstretched. Everyone wanted to go home. The atmosphere in Paris was tense. Alarmed by an outbreak of mutinies in the army, the French military chiefs brought troops back to the capital. Striking workers paraded the boulevards, waving red banners. Lloyd George found Clemenceau in no mood to accept even modest changes, despite threats that Britain would not participate in a renewed war or in a reimposed blockade. Clemenceau did not believe the Germans could reject the treaty. The 'Tiger' had won his victory in the cabinet, but his support in the country had diminished. The treaty terms were the minimum that he could get through the Chamber. He was, as a consequence, particularly infuriated by Lloyd George's last-minute demands for revision. Wilson shared his contempt for what appeared to be a domestic political manoeuvre on the prime minister's part. Wilson had been incensed by the arrogant speech attacking the morality of the treaty given by the seated Rantzau-Brockdorff when given the peace terms on 7 May. During May the president grew increasingly stubborn in his defence of the treaty, despite the opposition of almost the whole American delegation to its terms. On 3 June, at a hostile meeting of the American delegation—its only general gathering during the whole peace conference—the president insisted that justice had been done. There could be no concessions merely to get the Germans to sign the treaty. Irritated by the German demands, the underlying though rarely dominant punitive streak in Wilson's attitude towards Germany came to the foreground. Germany could not be readmitted to the ranks of civilized nations until she had been properly chastized and had admitted her guilt. 'The treaty is undoubtedly very severe indeed,' the president admitted, but it was not 'on the whole unjust . . . [given] the very great offence against civilization which the German state committed'.[24] Behind Wilson's obstinacy lay his concern to preserve the fragile unity between the victors that still remained. He feared the divisive effect of reopening contentious issues. There was, too, the inescapable fact that President Wilson would have to defend the treaty in the Senate. He could not further compromise his position before he returned. Except on the question of reparations, where he initiated one more unsuccessful attempt to establish a fixed sum (he suggested 120 billion gold marks), the president did not use the Anglo-French quarrels to propose substantive changes. On the Polish issue, he found himself more in opposition to the British than to the French. Throughout the negotiations Wilson had seen himself as the impartial judge, punishing the wrongdoers and assisting the victors. In this sense, he was consistent to the end.

Lloyd George demanded a plebiscite in Upper Silesia and changes in the Polish–German frontier. The president at first refused to consider a vote in an area that was clearly Polish, and, backed by Clemenceau, engaged in a fierce debate with the prime minister. But the latter brilliantly forced the president to concede point after point, and the case for a plebiscite for Upper Silesia was won. This was one of the few substantive concessions to the Germans. A newly established Commission on the Eastern Frontiers of Germany worked out the details of the plebiscite and new territorial and economic modifications of the earlier settlement. The Polish prime minister, the great pianist Ignacy Paderewski, reluctantly agreed to the new arrangements. No other major concessions were offered, though the League of Nations was now to supervise popular consultations in Eupen and Malmédy, and German transit rights across the 'Polish Corridor' were strengthened. On the Rhineland issue, Clemenceau gave way to Lloyd George on the question of occupation costs and the protection of civilian life against military interference. He would successfully resist, however, the British demand for a reduction in the length of occupation. Wilson acted as intermediary between the two disputants. Discussions between the main British and French delegates produced an agreement that the occupation could be terminated before the fifteen-year limit if Germany fulfilled her treaty obligations. The French premier, backed by Wilson, was equally adamant in his opposition to Germany's immediate admission to the League. The formula accepted barely altered the original draft.

[24] Klaus Schwabe, *Woodrow Wilson, Revolutionary Germany and Peacemaking, 1918–1919* (Chapel Hill, NC, 1985), 342.

Lloyd George, as Smuts feared, did not demand the revision of the reparation clauses. With Clemenceau, he blocked Wilson's one effort to re-examine the question of Germany's total liability. Nor was the president amenable to new discussions on this subject. He insisted that Germany was the guilty party and must, in principle, agree to full restitution. Wilson reminded Lloyd George that he had been repeatedly thwarted in his own efforts to achieve a fixed sum, and would not now consider changes in clauses that he had never wanted to accept. The Council agreed that the reparation clauses should remain unchanged unless, as Lloyd George had suggested, the Germans made an offer of an acceptable fixed sum within four months of signing the treaty. None of these last-minute alterations touched the substantive interests of the 'big three'. Wilson's resistance to revision gave added weight to Clemenceau's opposition to change. None of the statesmen was willing to undo what had been so laboriously constructed.

The revised treaty, its alterations marked in red ink, was presented to the Germans on 16 June, with a five-day ultimatum. The German delegation found the revised treaty unjust, dishonouring, and unworkable; they advised rejection, despite knowing there was no alternative to acceptance. Already, on its way back from Versailles to Weimar, the German delegation train had been stoned. No one wanted to take responsibility for signing such an unpopular peace. While the Scheidemann cabinet debated in Berlin, the Allies approved General Foch's plans for a military advance on the German capital. The German leaders and their parties, with the exception of the Independent Socialists, found the treaty unacceptable but were divided on the question of rejection. The Centrist politician, Matthias Erzberger, knowing that Germany could not fight, and anxious to preserve national unity, convinced his Catholic Centre party to accept the treaty with two reservations, the 'war guilt' clause and the surrender of Germans accused of war crimes. With his cabinet deadlocked, Scheidemann resigned on 20 June, three days before the Allied deadline. A new government, put together by President Ebert who had been persuaded to stay in office, headed by Gustav Bauer and based on the Socialist and Centre parties, took office. The new cabinet convinced the National Assembly to authorize the signing of the treaty, with the Erzberger caveats. The Council of Four rejected the German reservations. President Wilson composed the twenty-four-hour ultimatum. Advised that the Reichswehr was too weak to face an Allied advance, the Bauer government capitulated. The German cabinet signed the treaty under protest, and without abandoning its condemnation of the 'unheard of injustice' of the conditions of peace. Hatred of the Treaty of Versailles, and particularly its reparations provisions, though of varying importance during the life of the Weimar republic, would be the one tie that bound the deeply divided nation together. The final ceremony, staged to celebrate the French triumph and underline the enemy's humiliation, took place in the Hall of Mirrors at Versailles on 28 June 1919.

VII

The Treaty of Versailles has been repeatedly pilloried, most famously in John Maynard Keynes's pernicious but brilliant *The Economic Consequences of the Peace*, published at the end of 1919 and still the argument found underpinning too many current textbooks. It was Smuts who, during June 1919, suggested to Keynes, who had already resigned from the British Peace Delegation in protest, that he should write an account of the financial clauses and their consequences. Though Smuts repented of his advice, Keynes wrote his highly influential account, deftly portraying Wilson's alleged defeat and craven surrender to the Welsh wizard and the wily Tiger. Keynes's powerful but slanted critique of the reparation clauses became the source of the much broader revisionist case against the 'unjust treaty' in Britain. The German opponents of reparations won a delayed victory. The reverberations of Keynes's arguments were still to be heard after Hitler took power. They are still heard today.

The Treaty of Versailles was not a 'Carthaginian peace'. Germany was not destroyed. Nor was it reduced to a power of the second rank or permanently prevented from returning to great-power status. Outside of Russia, it remained the most populous state in Europe. With the disintegration of Austria-Hungary and the fall of Tsarist Russia, the application of the nationality principle left Germany in a stronger strategic position than before the war. It was now surrounded on almost all its borders by small and weak states, none of which, including Poland, posed a danger to its existence. Heightened claims to national independence would impede, if not block, any moves towards combination and effective containment of Germany. The Russian defeat and Bolshevik revolution freed Germany from one of its foremost rivals and from the threat from any other major power in the Balkans. Germany's productive capacity and industrial potential were left intact. Despite the loss of Saar coal and Lorraine iron ore, Germany remained Europe's 'industrial power-house', able, in a remarkably short time, to dominate the trade of the central and eastern European states.[25] Even in the short

[25] Sally Marks, 'Smoke and Mirrors', in Boemeke, Feldman, and Glaser (eds.), *The Treaty of Versailles*, 360.

term, the Versailles treaty did not leave Germany prostrate; on the contrary, German industry revived, and some historians believe that stabilization might have come earlier had the political structure been less fractured. It has even been argued that stabilization was delayed in order to obtain a reduction in reparations. Many of the restrictions on German economic recovery were of a short-term nature and would lapse in 1925, the longest breathing space that Clemenceau could win for a country that had suffered more in both human and material terms that its defeated enemy. Reparations did not cripple Germany, despite the sometimes hysterical debates that ensued; the terms in the treaty were less onerous than the Germans (and their Anglo-American sympathizers) proclaimed. The problem of payment, when a sum was set, was always a political rather than an economic question. German complaints over their harsh treatment under the terms of the Versailles treaty should be measured against what the draconian Brest-Litovsk treaty with Russia had demonstrated about their own ideas on peace settlements.

The Versailles treaty was, nonetheless, a flawed treaty. There is a good deal of truth in the charge of Clemenceau's nationalist critic, Jacques Bainville, that the treaty 'was too gentle for what is in it that is harsh'.[26] It failed to solve the problem of both punishing and conciliating a country that remained a great power despite the four years of fighting and its military defeat. It could hardly have been otherwise, given the very different aims of the peacemakers, not to speak of the multiplicity of problems that they faced, many well beyond their competence or control. Little beyond the common wish to defeat the Germans had kept the war coalition together; apart from a shared belief in Germany's responsibility for the war, there was even less consensus among the treaty-drafters in Paris. The settlement was further weakened by the way the treaty was drafted and by the erratic methods of its creators. It was never reviewed in its entirety, and compromise or postponed solutions contributed to its incoherence and inconsistency. It is no surprise that the Treaty of Versailles was a bundle of compromises that fully satisfied none of the three peacemakers. The ambiguities, real and imagined, of the military victory in 1918 were as critical and distorting for the deliberations as the pressures of popular politics. Even Henry Kissinger, a fierce critic of the treaty, admits that 'having considered the prewar world too confining, Germany was not likely to be satisfied with *any* terms available after defeat'.[27] The widespread German unwillingness to accept the reality

[26] Pierre Miquel, *La Paix de Versailles et l'opinion publique française* (Paris, 1972), 404.
[27] Henry Kissinger, *Diplomacy* (London, 1994), 242; emphasis in original.

of that defeat would make it even more difficult to establish the treaty's legitimacy. This was a very different world from that of 1815, or of 1944–5.

The Versailles treaty was indeed a victor's peace, framed to punish and constrain the Germans and to vindicate the Allied sacrifices. This was what President Wilson meant when he claimed that, though this was a harsh treaty, it was a just one. But it was also meant to create a legitimate post-war order that the defeated as well as the victor nations could accept. The establishment of the League of Nations, whatever the reservations of the victor powers, held out the promise of a more just international regime which the excluded could one day join. The principle of self-determination, never clearly defined, was not universally applied, for there were few clear-cut ethnic boundaries in east-central Europe. Borders could not be drawn with only ethnic considerations in mind; political, strategic, and economic factors had to be considered. The principle was not applied to Germany; other priorities had to take precedence. Wilson hoped that some of the difficulties could be settled within the framework of the League of Nations. The Germans particularly resented the territorial losses in the east; Germans had long ruled over Poles, even where the latter were the majority, and the reversal of positions was intolerable. The Germans were hardly likely to welcome the creation of an independent Poland, whatever its shape or size. It was, however, the gap between what had been promised and what was done that most troubled those in the Anglo-American peace delegations who looked to Paris for the start of a new chapter in the history of Europe.

The treaty represented an amalgam of realism and idealism; the traditional means of securing peace after victory were combined with new proposals for managing inter-state relations. Less haste and a more methodical approach might well have produced a more internally consistent treaty, but would not have fundamentally affected its substance with regard to the treatment of Germany. While there was no question of dismantling Bismarck's creation, Clemenceau managed to wrest much from his fellow peacemakers to compensate for France's wartime sacrifices and its uniquely exposed position. The drastic cuts in Germany's military power and its territorial, financial, and commercial losses gave France a considerable measure of protection and an opportunity, if limited in time, to compensate for the population gap between France and Germany and for the remaining differentials in their industrial power. France could not, however, sustain her treaty position without the support of allies. Much in the Versailles treaty was left undecided and would depend on the manner of its enforcement. Clemenceau was right when he claimed that it was 'not even a beginning, but the beginning of a beginning'.[28] The treaty terms could have been enforced if the British and French had stood united after the American withdrawal. In this event, there would have been room for revision but it would have taken place within agreed and clearly defined limits. The omens at the Paris peace conference were hardly encouraging in this direction.

The fairest assessment of the peace conference and its results may have been that of Clemenceau: 'In the end, it is what it is; above all else it is the work of human beings and, as a result, it is not perfect. We all did what we could to work fast and well.'[29] The 'captains and the kings' departed. Their underlings were left to pick up the pieces and to get on with the unfinished business of peacemaking. The treaties with Austria, Hungary, and Bulgaria had to be concluded and that with Ottoman Turkey still drafted as the victors pondered and fought over the distribution of the spoils. There was no quiet on the eastern fronts and, like Banquo's ghost, the absent Russians cast their shadows over the peacemakers' attempted mapmaking.

Books

The Armistice
CARSTEN, F. L., *Revolution in Central Europe, 1918–1919* (Berkeley, 1972).
LOWRY, BULLITT, *Armistice 1918* (Kent, Ohio and London, 1996).
RUDIN, HARRY R., *Armistice 1918* (New Haven, Conn., 1944).
SCHULTZ, G., *Revolutions and Peace Treaties, 1917–1920* (London, 1972).
WALWORTH, ARTHUR, *America's Moment, 1918: American Diplomacy at the End of World War I* (New York, 1977).
WATT, RICHARD M., *The Kings Depart: The German Revolution and the Treaty of Versailles, 1918–1919* (Harmondsworth, 1973).

General
BESSEL, RICHARD, *Germany After the First World War* (Oxford, 1993).
BOEMEKE, MANFRED L., FELDMAN, GERALD D., and GLASER, ELISABETH (eds.), *The Treaty of Versailles: A Reassessment after 75 Years* (Washington, DC and Cambridge, 1998). All the chapters are relevant and have excellent bibliographies. For this chapter, see those by Manfred F. Boemeke, Niall Ferguson, Elisabeth Glaser, William R. Keylor, Stephen A. Shuker, and Piotr S. Wandycz.
CARLIER, CLAUDE and SOUTOU, GEORGES-HENRI, *1918–1925: Comment faire la paix?* (Paris, 2001). For this chapter see contributions cited under articles.
DOCKRILL, M. and GOOLD, D., *Peace Without Promise: Britain and the Peace Conference, 1919–1923* (London, 1981).

---

[28] Jean-Baptiste Duroselle, *Clemenceau* (Paris, 1988), 773.
[29] Clemenceau, cited in MacMillan, *Peacemakers*, 469.

—— and FISHER, JOHN, (eds.), *The Paris Peace Conference, 1919: Peace Without Victory* (Basingstoke, Hampshire, 2001). For this chapter, see chapters by Ruth Henig, Alan Sharp, and Zara Steiner.

ELCOCK, GEORGE W., *Portrait of a Decision: The Council of Four and the Treaty of Versailles* (London, 1972).

LENTIN, ANTHONY, *Lloyd George, Woodrow Wilson, and the Guilt of Germany: An Essay in the Prehistory of Appeasement* (Leicester, 1984).

—— *Lloyd George and the Lost Peace* (London, 2001).

LOVIN, CLIFFORD R., *A School For Diplomats: The Paris Peace Conference of 1919* (Lanham, Md., 1997).

MACMILLAN, MARGARET, *The Peacemakers: The Paris Peace Conference of 1919 and its Attempt To End War* (London, 2001).

MARSTON, FRANK S., *The Peace Conference of 1919: Organization and Procedure* (London, 1944).

MAYER, ARNO J., *The Political Origins of the New Diplomacy, 1917–1918* (New Haven, Conn., 1959).

—— *Politics and Diplomacy of Peacemaking: Containment and Counterrevolution at Versailles, 1918–1919* (London, 1967).

NELSON, HAROLD I., *Land and Power: British and Allied Policy on Germany's Frontiers, 1916–1919* (London, 1963).

NICOLSON, HAROLD, *Peacemaking, 1919* (London, 1933).

SACHAR, HOWARD M., *Dreamland: Europeans and Jews in the Aftermath of the Great War* (New York, 2002).

SCHMIDT-HARTMAN, E. and WINTER, S. B. (eds.), *Great Britain, the United States and the Bohemian Lands, 1848–1938* (Munich, 1991). Esp. chapters by Mark Cornwall, Peter Hanak, Yeshayahu Jelinek, and Paul Latawski.

SCHRÖDER, HANS-JÜRGEN (ed.), *Confrontation and Cooperation: Germany and the United States in the Era of World I, 1900–1924* (Providence, RI and Oxford, 1993). Parts III–V.

SHARP, ALAN, *The Versailles Settlement: Peacemaking in Paris, 1919* (Basingstoke, 1991).

SHIMAZU, NAOKO, *Japan, Race and Equality: The Racial Equality Proposal of 1919* (London, 1998).

SILVERMAN, DAN P., *Reconstructing Europe After the Great War* (Cambridge, Mass., 1982).

STEVENSON, DAVID, *The First World War and International Politics* (Oxford, 1988).

SUGAR, PETER F. and LEDERER, IVO J. (eds.), *Nationalism in Eastern Europe* (Seattle, 1969).

WELLS, SAMUEL F. Jr. and SMITH, PAULA BAILEY (eds.), *New European Orders, 1919 and 1991* (Washington, DC, 1996).

War Debts and Reparations

ARTAUD, DENISE, *La Question des dettes interalliés et la reconstruction de l'Europe, 1917–1929*, 2 vols. (Lille, 1978).

BUNSELMEYER, ROBERT E., *Cost of the War, 1914–1919: British Economic War Aims and the Origins of Reparations* (Hamden, Conn., 1975).

BURK, KATHERINE, *Britain, America and the Sinews of War, 1914–1918* (Boston, 1985).

FELDMAN, GERALD D., *The Great Disorder: Politics, Inflation, and Society in the German Inflation, 1914–1924* (New York, 1996).

HOLTFRERICH, CARL-LUDWIG, *Die Deutsche Inflation, 1914–1923: Ursachen und Folgen in Internationaler Perspektive* (Berlin, 1980). English translation by Theo Balderston, *The German Inflation, 1914–1923: Causes and Effects in International Perspective* (Berlin and New York, 1986).

KENT, BRUCE, *The Spoils of War: The Politics, Economics, and Diplomacy of Reparations, 1918–1932* (Oxford, 1989).

KEYNES, JOHN MAYNARD, *The Economic Consequences of the Peace* (London, 1920).

KRÜGER, PETER, *Deutschland und die Reparationen, 1918–19: die Genesis des Reparationsproblems in Deutschland zwischen Waffenstillstand und Versailler Friedensschluss* (Stuttgart, 1973).

MANTOUX, ÉTIENNE, *The Carthaginian Peace or the Economic Consequences of Mr. Keynes* (New York, 1952).

SCHUKER, STEPHEN A., *American 'Reparations' to Germany, 1919–1933: Implications For the Third-World Debt Crisis* (Princeton, 1988).

TRACHTENBURG, MARC, *Reparation in World Politics: France and European Economic Diplomacy, 1916–1923* (New York, 1980).

TURNER, ARTHUR, *The Cost of War: British Policy on French War Debts, 1918–1932* (Brighton, 1998).

League of Nations: Origins

BARIÉTY, JACQUES and FLEURY, ANTOINE (eds.), *Peace Movements and Initiatives in International Policy, 1867–1928* (Berne, 1987).

BIRN, DONALD S., *The League of Nations Union 1918–1945* (Oxford, 1981).

EGERTON, GEORGE W., *Great Britain and the Creation of the League of Nations: Strategy, Politics, and International Organization, 1914–1919* (Chapel Hill, NC, 1978).

GELFAND, LAWRENCE E., *The Inquiry: American Preparations For Peace, 1917–1919* (New Haven, Conn., 1963).

HINSLEY, FRANCIS HARRY, *Power and the Pursuit of Peace: Theory and Practice in the History of Relations Between States* (Cambridge, 1963). Chapter 14.

WALTERS, FRANCIS PAUL, *A History of the League of Nations* (London, 1952).

Austria

ALMOND, NINA and LUTZ, RALPH H. (eds.), *The Treaty of St. Germain: A Documentary History of its Territorial and Political Causes, With a Survey of the Documents of the Supreme Council of the Paris Peace Conference* (Stanford and London, 1935).

CARSTEN, FRANCIS L., *The First Austrian Republic, 1918–1938: A Study Based on British and Austrian Documents* (Aldershot, 1986).

JELAVICH, BARBARA, *Modern Austria: Empire and Republic, 1815–1986* (Cambridge, 1987).

Low, Alfred D., *The Anschluss Movement, 1918–19, and the Paris Peace Conference* (Philadelphia, 1974).

Ormos, Mária, *From Padua to the Trianon, 1918–1920*, trans. Miklós Uszkay (Boulder, Col., 1990).

Suval, Stanley, *The Anschluss Question in the Weimar Era: A Study of Nationalism in Germany and Austria, 1918–1932* (Baltimore, Md., 1974).

Belgium

Johansson, Rune, *Small State in Boundary Conflict: Belgium and the Belgian–German Border 1914–1919* (Lund, 1988).

Marks, Sally, *Innocent Abroad: Belgium at the Peace Conference of 1919* (Chapel Hill, NC, 1981).

Britain

Dockrill, Michael L. and Gould, J. Douglas, *Peace Without Promise: Britain and the Peace Conferences, 1919–1923* (London, 1981).

Goldstein, Erik, *Winning the Peace: British Diplomatic Strategy, Peace Planning, and the Paris Peace Conference, 1916–1920* (Oxford, 1991).

Jaffe, Lorna S., *The Decision to Disarm Germany: British Policy Towards Postwar German Disarmament, 1914–1919* (London, 1985).

Morgan, Kenneth, *Consensus and Disunity: The Lloyd George Coalition Government, 1918–1922* (Oxford, 1979).

Newton, Douglas J., *British Policy and the Weimar Republic, 1918–1919* (Oxford, 1997).

Robbins, Keith, *The Abolition of War: The 'Peace Movement' in Britain 1914–1919* (Cardiff, 1976).

Rothwell, Victor H., *British War Aims and Peace Diplomacy, 1914–1918* (Oxford, 1971).

Wilson, Keith, *Channel Tunnel Visions, 1850–1945: Dreams and Nightmares* (London, 1994).

Czechoslovakia

Frage, Reiner, *London und Prag: Materialien zum Problem eines multinationalen Nationalstaates, 1919–1938* (Munich, 1981).

Mamatey, Victor S. and Luza, Radomir (eds.), *A History of the Czechoslovak Republic, 1918–1948* (Princeton, 1973). See contribution by Victor S. Mamatey.

Perman, D., *The Shaping of the Czechoslovak State* (Leiden, 1962).

Unterberger, Betty Miller, *The United States, Revolutionary Russia and the Rise of Czechoslovakia* (Chapel Hill, NC, 1989).

France

Andrew, Christopher and Kanya-Forstner, Alexander S., *France Overseas: The Great War and the Climax of French Imperial Expansion* (London, 1981).

Bariéty, Jacques, *Les Relations franco-allemandes après la Première Guerre Mondiale, 11 novembre 1918–10 janvier 1925: de l'exécution à la négociation* (Paris, 1975).

BARIÉTY, JACQUES and POIDEVIN, RAYMOND, *Les Relations franco-allemandes, 1815–1975* (Paris, 1977).

HOVI, KARLEVO, *Cordon sanitaire ou barrière de l'est? The Emergence of the French East European Alliance Policy, 1917–1919* (Turku, 1975).

KING, JERE C., *Foch versus Clemenceau: France and German Dismemberment, 1918– 1919* (Cambridge, Mass., 1960).

KOHLER, HENNING, *Novemberrevolution und Frankreich: Die französische Deutschlandpolitik, 1918–1919* (Düsseldorf, 1980).

MCDOUGALL, WALTER A., *France's Rhineland Diplomacy, 1914–1924: The Last Bid For a Balance of Power in Europe* (Princeton, 1978).

MIQUEL, PIERRE, *La Paix de Versailles et l'opinion publique française* (Paris, 1972)

SOUTOU, GEORGES-HENRI, *L'Or et le sang: les buts de guerre économiques de la Première Guerre Mondiale* (Paris, 1989).

STEINMAYER, GITTA, *Die Grundlagen der französischen Deutschlandpolitik, 1917– 19* (Stuttgart, 1979).

STEVENSON, DAVID, *French War Aims Against Germany, 1914–1919* (Oxford, 1982).

WANDYCZ, PIOTR S., *France and Her Eastern Allies, 1919–1925: French–Czecho- slovak–Polish Relations from the Paris Peace Conference to Locarno* (Minneapolis, 1962).

Germany

BRACHER, KARL DIETRICH, FUNKE, MANFRED, and JACOBSEN, HANS-ADOLF (eds.), *Die Weimarer Republik 1918–1933: Politik, Wirtschaft, Gesellschaft* (Düsseldorf, 1987).

FERGUSON, NIALL, *Paper and Iron: Hamburg Business and German Politics in the Era of Inflation, 1897–1927* (Cambridge, 1995).

—— *The Pity of War* (London, 1998).

GRUPP, PETER, *Deutsche Außenpolitik im Schatten von Versailles, 1918–20: Zur Politik des Auswärtigen Amtes von Ende des Ersten Weltkrieges und der November- revolution bis zum Inkrafttreten des Versailler Vertrags (Paderborn, 1988).*

KRÜGER, PETER, *Deutschland und die Reparationen, 1918–19; Die Genesis des Reparationsproblems in Deutschland zwischen Waffenstillstand und Versailler Friedensschluss* (Stuttgart, 1973).

—— *Versailles: Deutsche Außenpolitik zwischen Revisionismus und Friedenssicherung* (Munich, 1986).

LUCKAU, ALMA, *The German Delegation at the Paris Peace Conference* (New York, 1941).

SCHWABE, KLAUS, *Deutsche Revolution und Wilson-Frieden: Die amerikanische und die deutsche Friedensstrategie zwischen Ideologie und Machtpolitik, 1918–1919* (Düsseldorf, 1971). Translated but with differences, as *Woodrow Wilson, Revolutionary Germany, and Peacemaking, 1918–1919: Missionary Diplomacy and the Realities of Power* (Chapel Hill, NC, 1985).

WENGST, UDO, *Graf Brockdorff-Rantzau und die außenpolitischen Anfänge der Weimarer Republik* (Frankfurt a.M., 1973).

Greece

PETSALES-DIOMEDES, N., *Greece at the Paris Peace Conference, 1919* (Thessaloniki, 1978).

SMITH, MICHAEL LLEWELLYN, *Ionian Vision: Greece in Asia Minor, 1919–1922*, 2nd edn. (London, 1998).

Italy

ALBRECHT-CARRIÉ, RENÉ, *Italy at the Paris Peace Conference* (New York, 1938).

BURGWYN, H. JAMES, *The Legend of the Mutilated Victory: Italy, the Great War, and the Paris Peace Conference, 1915–1919* (Westport, Conn. and London, 1993).

ROSSINI, DANIELA, *L'America riscopere l'Italia; L'Inquiry di Wilson e l'origini della questione adriatica, 1917–1919* (Rome, 1992).

Poland

CIENCIALA, ANNA M. and KOMARNICKI, TITUS, *From Versailles to Locarno: Keys to Polish Foreign Policy, 1919–1925* (Lawrence, Kan., 1984).

KOMARNICKI, TITUS, *Rebirth of the Polish Republic: A Study in the Diplomatic History of Europe, 1914–1920* (London, 1957).

LATAWSKI, PAUL (ed.), *The Reconstruction of Poland, 1914–1923* (London, 1993). See contributions of Anna M. Cienciala, Paul Latawski, and Piotr S. Wandycz.

LUNDGREEN-NIELSON, KAY, *The Polish Problem at the Paris Peace Conference: A Study of the Policies of the Great Powers and the Poles, 1918–1919* (Odense, 1979).

SIERPOWSKI, STANISLAW, *L'Italia e la ricostituzione del nuovo stato polacco, 1915–1921* (Warsaw, 1979).

Romania

SPECTOR, SHERMAN DAVID, *Rumania at the Paris Peace Conference: A Study of the Diplomacy of Ioan I. C. Brătianu* (New York, 1962).

United States

AMBROSIUS, LLOYD E., *Woodrow Wilson and the American Diplomatic Tradition: The Treaty Fight in Perspective* (Cambridge, 1987).

FIFIELD, RUSSELL H., *Woodrow Wilson and the Far East: The Diplomacy of the Shantung Question* (New York, 1952).

FLOTO, INGA, *Colonel House in Paris: A Study of American Policy at the Paris Peace Conference, 1919* (Aarhus, 1973).

GARDNER, LLOYD C., *Safe for Democracy: The Anglo-American Response to Revolution, 1913–1923* (New York, 1984).

GELFAND, LAWRENCE E., *The Inquiry* (New Haven, Conn., 1963).

KNOCK, THOMAS J., *To End All Wars: Woodrow Wilson and the Quest for a New World Order* (New York, 1992).

LINK, ARTHUR S., *The Higher Realism of Woodrow Wilson and Other Essays* (Nashville, Tenn., 1971).

LINK, ARTHUR S., *Wilson's Diplomacy: An International Symposium* (Cambridge, Mass., 1973).

—— *Woodrow Wilson and a Revolutionary World, 1913–1921* (Chapel Hill, NC, 1982).

—— (ed.), *Wilson, the Diplomatist: A Look at His Major Foreign Policies* (Baltimore, 1957).

MARTIN, LAURENCE, *Peace Without Victory: Woodrow Wilson and the British Liberals* (New Haven, Conn., 1958).

NINKOVICH, FRANK, *The Wilsonian Century: United State Foreign Policy Since 1900* (Chicago, 1999).

PARRINI, CARL P., *Heir to Empire: United States Economic Diplomacy, 1916–1923* (Pittsburgh, 1969).

SCHWABE, KLAUS, *Woodrow Wilson, Revolutionary Germany, and Peacemaking, 1918–1919: Missionary Diplomacy and the Realities of Power* (Chapel Hill, NC, 1985). See above under *Germany*.

SMITH, DANIEL M., *The Great Departure: The United States and World War I, 1914–1920* (New York, 1965).

THOMPSON, JOHN A., *Woodrow Wilson* (London, 2000).

WALWORTH, ARTHUR, *America's Moment, 1918: American Diplomacy at the End of World War I* (New York, 1977).

—— *Wilson and his Peacemakers: American Diplomacy at the Paris Peace Conference, 1919* (London and New York, 1986).

Yugoslavia

LEDERER, IVO J., *Yugoslavia at the Paris Peace Conference: A Study in Frontiermaking* (New Haven, Conn., 1963).

Articles

BARIÉTY, JACQUES, 'La France et l'Allemagne d'une guerre mondiale a l'autre', in R. Poidevin and Jacques Bariéty (eds.), *Les Relations franco-allemandes 1815–1975* (Paris, 1977).

CIENCIALA, ANNA M., 'The Battle of Danzig and the Polish Corridor at the Paris Peace Conference of 1919', in Paul Latawski (ed.), *The Reconstruction of Poland, 1914–1923* (London, 1992).

COOGAN, JOHN W., 'Wilsonian Diplomacy in War and Peace', in Gordon Martel (ed.), *American Foreign Relations Reconsidered 1890–1933* (London, 1994).

CROUZET, FRANÇOIS, 'Réactions françaises devant les *Consequences Économiques de Paix* de Keynes', *Revue d'Histoire Moderne et Contemporaine*, 19: 1 (1972).

DZIEWANOWSKI, M. K., 'Joseph Piłsudski, the Bolshevik Revolution and Eastern Europe', in Thaddeus V. Gromada (ed.), *Essays on Poland's Foreign Policy, 1919–1939* (New York, 1970).

EGERTON, GEORGE W., ' "Britain and the Great Betrayal": Anglo-American Relations and the Struggle for United States Ratification of the Treaty of Versailles, 1919–1920', *Historical Journal*, 21: 4 (1978).

—— 'Conservative Internationalism: British Approaches to International Organization and the League of Nations', *Diplomacy and Statecraft*, 5: 1 (1994).

FELLNER, FRITZ, 'Der Vertrag von St. Germain', in E. Weinzierl and K. Skalnik (eds.), Österreich 1918–38, Bd. 1 (Vienna, 1983).

GARDNER, LLOYD C., 'The United States, the German Peril, and a Revolutionary World: The Inconsistencies of World Order and National Self-Determination', in Hans-Jürgen Schröder (ed.), Confrontation and Cooperation: Germany and the United States in the Era of World War I, 1900–1924 (Providence, RI, 1994).

GLASER-SCHMIDT, ELISABETH, 'German and American Concepts to Restore a Liberal World Trading System after World War I', in Hans-Jürgen Schröder (ed.), Confrontation and Cooperation: Germany and the United States in the Era of World War I, 1900–1924 (Providence, RI, 1994).

HILLGRUBER, A., 'Unter den Schatten von Versailles', in K. D. Erdman and H. Schulz (eds.), Weimar, Selbstpreisgabe einer Demokratie (Düsseldorf, 1980).

KANYA-FORSTNER, ALEXANDER S., 'The War, Imperialism and Decolonization', in Jay M. Winter, Geoffrey Parker, and Mary R. Habeck (eds.), The Great War and the Twentieth Century (New Haven, Conn., 2000).

KRÜGER, PETER, 'German Disappointment and Anti-Western Resentment, 1918–1919', in Hans-Jürgen Schröder (ed.), Confrontation and Cooperation: Germany and the United States in the Era of World War I, 1900–1924 (Providence, RI, 1994).

LENTIN, ANTHONY, 'What Really Happened at Paris?', Diplomacy and Statecraft, 1: 2 (1990).

—— 'The Treaty That Never Was: Lloyd George and the Abortive Anglo-French Alliance of 1919', in Judith Loades (ed.), The Life and Times of David Lloyd George (Bangor, 1991).

—— 'Several Types of Ambiguity: Lloyd George at the Paris Peace Conference', Diplomacy and Statecraft, 6: 1 (1995).

—— '"Une aberration inexplicable"? Clemenceau and the Abortive Anglo-French Guarantee Treaty of 1919', Diplomacy and Statecraft, 8: 2 (1997).

LEVENE, MARK, 'Nationalism and its Alternatives in the International Arena: The Jewish Question at Paris, 1919', Journal of Contemporary History, 28 (1993).

LINK, WERNER, 'Zum Problem der Kontinuität der amerikanischen Deutschlandpolitik im 20. Jahrhundert', in M. Knapp (ed.), Die deutsch–amerikanischen Beziehungen nach 1945 (Frankfurt and New York, 1975).

MARKS, SALLY, 'Behind the Scenes at the Paris Peace Conference of 1919', Journal of British Studies, 9 (1970).

—— '1918 and After: The Postwar Era', in Gordon Martel (ed.), Origins of the Second World War Reconsidered: The A. J. P. Taylor Debate After Twenty-Five Years (London, 1986).

MAYER, ARNO J., 'Post War Nationalisms, 1918–1919', Past and Present, 34 (1966).

MICHEL, BERNARD, 'La Tchécoslovaquie et la paix', in C. Carlier and G.-H. Soutou (eds.), 1918–1925: Comment faire la paix? (Paris, 2001).

NINKOVICH, FRANK A., 'Woodrow Wilson and the Historical Necessity of Idealism', in id. (ed.), Modernity and Power: A History of the Domino Theory in the Twentieth Century (Chicago, 1994).

PIETRI, NICOLE, 'L'Autriche, 1918–1925: une stabilisation précaire', in C. Carlier and G.-H. Soutou (eds.), *1918–1925: Comment faire la paix?* (Paris, 2001).

SCHUKER, STEPHEN A., 'Finance and Foreign Policy in the Era of German Inflation', in Otto Büsch and Gerald D. Feldmann (eds.), *Historische Prozesse der deutschen Inflation, 1914–1924* (Berlin, 1978).

—— 'The End of Versailles', in Gordon Martel (ed.), *Origins of the Second World War Reconsidered: The A. J. P. Taylor Debate After Twenty-Five Years* (London, 1986).

—— 'Origins of American Stabilization Policy in Europe: The Financial Dimension, 1918–1924', in Hans-Jürgen Schröder (ed.), *Confrontation and Cooperation: Germany and the United States in the Era of World War I, 1900–1924* (Providence, RI, 1994).

SETON-WATSON, CHRISTOPHER, '1919 and the Persistence of Nationalist Aspirations', *Review of International Studies*, 15 (1989).

SOUTOU, GEORGES-HENRI, 'La France et les marches de l'est, 1914–1919', *Revue historique*, 578 (1978).

—— 'La France et l'Allemagne en 1919', in J. M. Valentin, J. Bariéty, and A. Guth (eds.) *La France et l'Allemagne entre les deux guerres mondiales* (Nancy, 1987).

—— 'L' Ordre européen de Versailles à Locarno', in C. Carlier and G.-H. Soutou (eds.), *1918–1925: Comment faire la paix?* (Paris, 2001).

STEIGERWALD, MARK, 'Historiography: The Reclamation of Woodrow Wilson?', *Diplomatic History*, 23: 1 (1999).

STEINER, ZARA, 'Foreign Office Views, Germany and the Great War', in R. J. Bullen, H. Pogge von Strandmann, and A. Polansky (eds.), *Ideas into Politics: Aspects of European History, 1880–1950* (London and Sydney, 1984).

STEVENSON, DAVID, 'France at the Paris Peace Conference: Addressing the Dilemmas of Security', in Robert Boyce (ed.), *Nation and Narration* (London, 1990).

TRACHTENBURG, MARC, 'Versailles After Sixty Years', *Journal of Contemporary History*, 17 (1982).

UNTERBERGER, BETTY MILLER, 'Woodrow Wilson and the Bolsheviks: The "Acid Test" of Soviet–American Relations', *Diplomatic History*, 11: 2 (1987).

WANDYCZ, PIOTR S., 'The Treaty of Riga: Its Significance for Interwar Polish Foreign Policy', in Thaddeus V. Gromada (ed.), *Essays on Poland's Foreign Policy, 1918–1939* (New York, 1970).

WEINBERG, GERHARD L., 'The Defeat of Germany in 1918 and the European Balance of Power', *Central European History*, 2 (1969).

YEARWOOD, PETER, '"On the Safe and Right Lines"; The Lloyd George Government and the Origins of the League of Nations, 1916–1918', *Historical Journal*, 32 (1989).

—— 'Real Securities Against New Wars: Official British Thinking and the Origins of the League of Nations', *Diplomacy and Strategy*, 9: 3 (1998).

Theses

GIRARD, JOYLON PITT, 'Bridge on the Rhine: American Diplomacy and the Rhineland, 1919–23'. Ph.D. dissertation, University of Maryland (1973).

HEMERY, JOHN ANTHONY, 'The Emergence of Treasury Influence in British Foreign Policy', Ph.D. thesis, Cambridge University (1988).

2

Distant Frontiers:
Peacemaking in the East

I

The peace treaties with the other defeated belligerents, each signed in a different Paris suburb, were slowly but steadily concluded over the succeeding months: with Austria (St-Germain), Hungary (Trianon), Bulgaria (Neuilly), and Turkey (Sèvres). While for the 'big three' the German treaty was the centre of major interest, the pre-war map of eastern Europe was even more drastically altered in terms of states and boundaries. Austria–Hungary ceased to exist. New states emerged at the expense of the defeated Habsburg, Hohenzollern, and tsarist empires. The treaties changed the domestic composition as well as the geographic lines of the older Balkan countries. Poland was resurrected and Czechoslovakia created; Serbia was transformed into the Kingdom of the Serbs, Croats, and Slovenes. Romania doubled in population and size, a 'crescent rubbed into a full moon'. Greece should have made substantial territorial gains; Albania was left in its state of anarchy. The result in the Balkan peninsula was to heighten the sense of difference between the winners and losers from the war. Turkey, if the Sèvres settlement had proved lasting, would have been reduced to a mere fragment of its former self. All the settlements were reached in the absence of Russia, at a time when Allied troops were in Russian territory and when there were still hopes that Lenin's government might be overthrown.

The destruction of Austria-Hungary was not exclusively the work of the victors. The Allies had wavered through 1917–18 between hopes for a separate peace with Vienna and support for nationalist independence movements. The restitution of Poland became a French war aim soon after the Russian revolution, but Polish independence would have been compatible with either strategy. President Wilson's reference to the subject peoples of Austria-Hungary who 'should be accorded the freest opportunity of autonomous developments' was far more loosely phrased than his promise of Polish independence in the Fourteen Points.[1] It was only after the possibility of a separate peace with

---

[1] A. S. Link (ed.), *Collected Papers of Woodrow Wilson* (Princeton, 1984), xlv. 527.

Map 4. The Eastern European Territorial Settlements

Austria-Hungary faded from the diplomatic agenda in the spring of 1918 that the three major powers opted for the nationalist solution. Polish and Czech representatives, as well as Romanians campaigning for a large share of eastern Hungary, had been at work in the Allied capitals. The South Slav leaders, too, found western—though not Italian—support for a new state along and north of the Adriatic coast. By the time the armistice was concluded the old empire had all but dissolved from within, and even those who had fought fiercely for the Habsburgs looked to their respective national committees for leadership. The would-be successor states declared their independence before the peace conference opened. As there were only token Allied armies in south-eastern Europe when the war ended, the Italians and Romanians quickly moved to establish new military positions in disputed territories. Each of the successor states seized as much land as possible along necessarily vague frontiers. It was against this background, complicated further in Hungary by the success of Béla Kun's Bolshevik revolution in Budapest in March 1919, that the eastern treaties were concluded. The peacemakers had neither the will nor the military force available to alter in any significant way the locally determined balance of power. Unlike the German treaty, these settlements and the details of the frontiers of the new or enlarged states were mainly negotiated by the foreign ministers and the experts in the territorial committees, where the French or British views tended to prevail. There was little guidance from above. Most of the issues raised by the treaties with Austria, Hungary, and Bulgaria did not demand the attention of the 'big three'; the prolonged and bitter clash with the Italians over their extensive claims for compensation was the exception.

No one—and this is clear from reading the committee discussions—understood the full complexity of the task at hand, despite the preliminary work done by officials before the peace conference assembled. The complications of the local situation, even its geography, would have taxed any group of experts, quite apart from questions of national interest. Statistics were unreliable and maps inaccurate. Ethnic lines were so confused, above all in border areas, that no simple ethnic solution was possible. Strategic and economic considerations clashed or took precedence over claims of nationality. The use of plebiscites made little sense in the emotionally charged atmosphere of the times, though they were used in a number of disputed cases. The organization of the commissions and committees dealing with these states made the experts' tasks no simpler. Overlapping but separate committees handled identical problems in different contexts. Decisions made by the experts on the Romanian commission helped to shape the boundaries not just of Romania but of Yugoslavia, Greece, and Bulgaria as well. With the

exception of Poland, most of the territorial commission recommendations were accepted by the 'big three', who had neither the time nor
competence to review their experts' work. Central and eastern Europe
was largely *terra incognita*; this was not the moment for basic geography
lessons. Those representing the new or expanding states lobbied inces-
santly for the satisfaction of their territorial demands. It was inevitable
that overworked and tired officials were influenced by the personalities
of those representing the disputing claimants. The Czechs were particularly fortunate in this respect, above all in comparison with the Poles.
Edvard Beneš, that 'intelligent, young, plausible, little man', in Harold
Nicolson's words, was well received and his claims sympathetically
reviewed by most, even where the principles of self-determination
were clearly violated.[2] He had the advantage of strong support from
the pro-Czech lobby in London, skilfully mobilized by the well-liked
Tomáš Masaryk and by the influential official and writer R. W. Seton-
Watson and journalist Henry Wickham Steed. Lloyd George, by contrast, believed Beneš little more than a French pawn and found his
territorial demands exorbitant. Eleutherios Venizelos, the Greek prime
minister, on the contrary, was greatly favoured by Lloyd George, and
even the normally sharp-sighted and level-headed Foreign Office official Eyre Crowe admired the Cretan charmer.

As had been promised by President Wilson, though in the vaguest
terms, the creation of new states was to conform to the principles of
'self-determination'. Admittedly, at the time and still today it proved
almost impossible to give an exact meaning of the concept. In 1919 the
American secretary of state, Robert Lansing, asked himself: 'When the
President talks of "self-determination" what unit has he in mind? Does
he mean a race, a territorial area, or a community?'[3] Even the four
principles announced to Congress on 11 February 1918 provided only a
general endorsement of self-determination that could be variously interpreted. Though the president linked the principle with popular sovereignty, the implications were barely grasped. Wilson was surprised and
upset by the number of claimants in Paris, and wished that he had never
used the term. Many in the Anglo-American peace delegations were
alarmed by the possible consequences of its application, for the echoes of
this highly popular idea reverberated far beyond the boundaries of
Europe.

As might have been expected, each claimant wanted self-determination
for itself but not for its neighbours. In a sense, those responsible for

---

[2] Harold Nicolson, *Peacemaking 1919* (London, 1933), 240.
[3] Robert Lansing, *The Peace Negotiations: A Personal Narrative* (Boston and New York,
1921), 97–8, cited in MacMillan, *Peacemakers*, 19.

re-drawing the territorial maps were faced with a fait accompli in eastern Europe and could only deal with the consequences. The leaders of the nationality movements had already laid claim to statehood and troops crossed frontiers to establish national claims. Insofar as ethnic principles were applied, the makers of the peace were adapting the international system to the realities of the European situation. The 'national principle', which had been gaining legitimacy and popularity throughout the previous century, was given international endorsement, and ethnicity and other forms of linguistic and cultural commonality were recognized as the basis for state-building. Wilson believed the principle's identification with democracy made it a better guarantee of peace than the old principles of legitimacy. While many of the nationalist movements proved ephemeral and some of the newly created states enjoyed only the briefest of lives, for the successful the peace treaties provided the stamp of international recognition. The recognition of the national principle's legitimacy marked one of the major seismic shifts in the international order established in 1919.

The principle could only be applied irregularly and was often ignored. It was violated or compromised when the strategic interests of the victor states were engaged, and was neither applied to the defeated, nor to the colonies of the victorious European powers. It was much modified in practice when new boundaries were drawn. Clemenceau told the Council of Four, 'the conference has decided to call to life a certain number of new states. Without committing an injustice, may it sacrifice them by imposing on them unacceptable frontiers toward

TABLE 5. Territory and Population Changes in Eastern Europe, 1914–1930

	Area (sq. km.)		Population (000)		
	1914	1921	1914	1921	1930
Austro-Hungarian Monarchy	676,443		51,390		
Austria		85,553		6,536	6,722
Hungary		92,607		7,600	8,684
Czechoslovakia		140,394		13,613	14,726
Bulgaria	111,800	103,146	4,753	4,910	5,944
Poland		388,279		27,184	
Romania	137,903	304,244	7,516	17,594	18,025
Serbia	87,300		4,548		
Yugoslavia		248,987		12,017	13,930

Sources: I. P. Berend and G. Ranki, 'The Economic Problems of the "Danube Region" at the Breakup of the Austro-Hungarian Monarchy', *Journal of Contemporary History 4* (1969); *League of Nations Statistical Yearbooks 1920–1940*; Steven Morewood and Derek H. Aldcroft, *Economic Change in Eastern Europe Since 1918* (Aldershot, 1995).

Germany?'[4] The territorial commissions, anxious to create durable and viable nations, considered strategic, economic, geographic and other such factors when drawing up the new frontiers. Rival states, basing their demands on the principles of nationality, laid claim to the same territories; the Banat, the bone of fierce contention between Romania and Yugoslavia, was such a rich mixture of nationalities and languages that no purely ethnic division was possible. Nonetheless, as a result of the peace treaties the number of people in eastern and central Europe living under alien governments was reduced by half, and the boundaries drawn in 1919 conformed more closely to the linguistic frontiers in Europe than at any time before.

Unfortunately, in freeing the old minorities the peace settlements created new ones. The irregularities of the ethnographic map of Europe left many national minorities, some long at odds with their new political masters, exposed to a danger that was magnified by the granting of self-determination to some but not all national groups. Belatedly, the peacemakers realized that these latter groups had to be protected. The Jews were a special case. There were pogroms in Poland immediately after the armistice and during the peace conference itself. Pressure from Jewish and other minority organizations forced the 'big three' to take up the issue on 1 May 1919. A Committee on New States was created and drafted the Polish minorities treaty, signed at the same time as the Versailles treaty, which became the model for the minority-protection clauses included in the other three treaties. The peacemakers agreed to offer some form of legal protection to national minorities, not just for their political and judicial rights but also for the free exercise of their religious, linguistic, educational, and cultural practices, but they proved unwilling to consider Wilson's original idea of a universal minority-protection clause to be included within the Covenant of the League of Nations. The minority-protection system recognized the destructive and destabilizing consequences of the self-determination principle, but the system was applied only to a special category of states and within narrowly drawn limits. The list of countries required to sign the minority-protection treaties was extended to cover other new, expanded and defeated states, most situated in eastern Europe, whom the victors thought insufficiently advanced to protect their minorities without some form of oversight. Almost all bitterly resented being singled out in this fashion. 'Minority rights', a highly sophisticated concept, was hardly applied in practice even in well-established democratic states. The 'big three' wanted unitary states and hoped for peaceful

[4] D. Perman, *The Shaping of the Czechoslovak State: A Diplomatic History of the Boundaries of Czechoslovakia* (Leiden, 1962), 132.

assimilation. There were to be no 'states within states' and no direct appeals from minority groups to the League. Minorities had to find a state sponsor, after which the Council of the League could call attention to infractions of the treaties. Disputes could be referred to the Permanent Court of International Justice and, depending on the ruling, the Council could initiate sanctions against the offending state. It was a cumbersome process. The representatives of minority groups were left dissatisfied while the governments that had to sign the treaties remained bitter and resentful. Nonetheless, the attempt to provide some sort of international protection for minorities through the League, however qualified, flawed, or inadequate, was an attempt to expand the existing fabric of internationalism. Like so many parts of the treaties, self-determination and the minority treaties combined moral principles and the dictates of *realpolitik* at a time when the international system favoured sovereign states in general and the great powers in particular.

II

The Italians entered the peace conference with extensive territorial demands already recognized by Britain and France in the secret Treaty of London (26 April 1915). Of the main Allied powers, only Italy was more concerned with the settlements with Germany's allies than with Germany itself, as the promises made to Italy in 1915 could only be fulfilled in the Adriatic and in the former territories of the Habsburg and Turkish empires. Italy was promised possession of the Tyrol to the Brenner Pass (the Trentino and South Tyrol), Trieste, Gorizia (Gorz)–Gradisca, a large part of Istria and the offshore islands, the northern part of Dalmatia with adjacent islands, and a protectorate over Albania, though other claimants would have to be considered. The bribes were sufficient to secure the Italian frontiers, though not enough to turn the Adriatic into an Italian lake. Italy was also offered various colonial pickings, though these were less precise. It was promised undefined 'equitable compensation' in the zone of Adalia should the Ottoman empire collapse, and given the right to compensation in Africa if Britain and France secured a share of the former German colonies. The Treaty of St-Jean de Maurienne (April 1917), promising the province of Adalia as well as recognition of full Italian sovereignty over the Dodecanese islands, occupied after the Italo–Turkish War of 1912, was denounced on the grounds that Russia never ratified the agreement.

These old-fashioned territorial promises, used to secure Italy's entrance into the war, were not compatible with Woodrow Wilson's Fourteen Points, and the American president took up the battle of principle in Paris. The president thought he had won the hearts of the battered Italians and that they would be strong supporters of a Wilsonian peace. In fact the Italian leaders more accurately gauged the public mood. The fourth of the 'big four', Vittorio Orlando, prime minister of Italy since October 1917, came to Paris with the weakest hand to play. He and his complex, dour, and strongly nationalist foreign minister, Sidney Sonnino, were under intense domestic pressure to produce the fruits of victory promised as rewards for entering the war. Territorial acquisitions were the only possible compensation for the terrible battering suffered by the Italian forces in their war against the Austrians. The ignominy of the Italian defeat at Caporetto, when the Italian army had collapsed, had lasting effects. The costs of the war and the economic and social upheaval it created served to undermine a weak economy and an already shaky parliamentary system. By the time the war ended Italy was in political turmoil, its economy in a state of chaos and its industrial workers in a revolutionary mood. The Italian leaders' irredentist hopes were caught up in a much wider nationalist and counter-revolutionary explosion. The Nationalist case for a vast colonial empire and the mastery of the Balkans acquired wide appeal. Right-wing militants, including Benito Mussolini's new fascist forces and the equally aggressive anarcho-syndicalists, took up the cry for the city of Fiume during the last months of the war. The Italians had a more defensible claim to the Adriatic port than to the mainly Slav Dalmatian coast promised in the Treaty of London. The centre of Fiume was Italian; the suburb, Susak, was Slav. But Fiume had been excluded, with Italian consent, from the 1915 agreement as it was Hungary's only port and no one expected the Habsburg monarchy to collapse. It was later promised to Croatia, expected to be an independent state, and subsequently included in the Serbo-Croat-Slovene kingdom (Yugoslavia). Prime Minister Orlando, dependent on the nationalist right and concerned about the position of his beleaguered government, demanded Fiume as well as the 1915 line in Dalmatia, which remained Sonnino's chief concern. Following the armistice with Austria-Hungary, Orlando authorized the occupation of the port in mid-November even before the public agitation spread. Italian troops occupied the city and took up positions in Austrian territory well beyond the agreed London treaty boundaries.

There was little question that Italy's security position had markedly improved after the disintegration of the Habsburg monarchy, and that she could make further gains if her leaders proved adroit negotiators. But Orlando and Sonnino overplayed their hands. The difficulties began on 19 April when the Italian case was presented to the Council of Four. The general belief in Allied circles that Italy was a 'greedy beggar' pre-dated the peace conference and underlined the difficulties faced by the 'least of the great powers' trying to capitalize on what had been a highly expensive intervention. The Italian performance, in the Allied view, added little to the credit side of the war ledger, and though Britain and France felt bound to honour the terms of the Treaty of London, neither wanted to pay the price Orlando demanded. By expanding the Italian claims beyond the 1915 agreement the prime minister jeopardized, as Sonnino feared, his original negotiating position. While the latter tried to ignore Fiume and concentrated on the promises made in the London pact, Orlando appeared to be demanding both the rewards of 1915 and Fiume, though he was not adverse to some concessions in Dalmatia. The creation of Yugoslavia, represented at the peace conference by Serbia, led to a major Italian campaign against the newly created state, which was only constituted on 1 December 1918 and had neither clear borders nor a constitutional framework. The Americans were the first to recognize the new state in February 1919; Britain and France, with some reluctance, did so only when the Versailles treaty was almost ready. The Italians never anticipated the emergence of a unitary Slav state. For Sonnino, the new state inherited the mantle of the Habsburgs and had to be suffocated or contained at birth. Throughout the peace conference he and Orlando disputed its creation, fought against its recognition, supported Montenegrin separatism, and tried to stifle the infant Yugoslav economy through blockade. Right after the armistice with Austria-Hungary the Italian army had rushed troops into Dalmatia, occupying territories inhabited mainly by South Slavs while their troops in Albania fought off the Yugoslav and Greek claimants to that tiny pre-war state. Orlando looked for allies against Yugoslavia and tried each of Italy's recent enemies in turn. The French had to balance their interest in conciliating Italy with hopes for a strong Yugoslavia allied to France. They pressed the Italians, as did the pro-Yugoslav British delegation, to compromise.

It was Fiume, the so-called jewel of the Adriatic, that became the focal point in the open battle between Orlando and Wilson. It rapidly became a burning question of Italian honour and fanned expectations at home. It hardly helped the Italian cause that Sonnino proved to be as inflexible as the American president, making clear his aversion to Wilsonian principles and assuming rigid positions over the deadlock in the Adriatic when compromise should have been the order of the day. President Wilson had already given way to the Italians when he agreed to the Brenner frontier and the annexation of the German-speaking Tyrol. He soon showed the more obstinate side to his nature and refused to consider Orlando's demands, even when the prime minister offered to trade Dalmatia for Fiume. Determined not to give way, the president rejected both the Allied promises of 1915 and the continuing Italian occupation of the contested port, which the Yugoslavs believed essential for Croatia's economic future. The Italians were infuriated but there was little Orlando could do against the president's absolute veto. As the French and British tried to find a way out for the Italian prime minister, Wilson appealed directly to the Italian people (he had enjoyed a tumultuous reception in Rome during his state visit in January 1919) in a statement published in *Le Temps* on 24 April, completely misjudging the popular mood. His public manifesto resulted in the Italian leaders' departure from Paris. Caught between the Italians and the Americans, the French and British backed Wilson. The Italians were told that the Allies would continue to abide by the 1915 terms, but that Wilson's arguments against the Dalmatian claims should be considered and the claim to Fiume abandoned. Orlando and Sonnino arrived back in Italy to a magnificent but short-lived welcome. The Italian walkout accomplished little either in Rome or in Paris.

During Orlando's absence the Italians were punished further when the 'Big Three' approved the Greek occupation of Smyrna and allowed them to occupy a part of the Turkish area allotted to Italy at St-Jean de Maurienne. Italy was also excluded from the division of the former German colonies. Anglo-French threats to deny the Treaty of London if the Italians did not return before the draft treaty was presented to the Germans had their effect. Orlando and Sonnino quietly came back to Paris on 9 May, but the deadlock remained unresolved as Wilson continued to block French efforts to settle the dispute. Failing in Paris and faced with a new wave of strikes and a parliamentary crisis in Rome, Orlando and Sonnino resigned on 19 June. The way to a solution of the Yugoslav dispute had been suggested before the fall of the Orlando government and the departure of Lloyd George and Wilson from the peace conference after the signing of the Versailles treaty. The Italians were to give up most of the Dalmatian mainland and accept a free state in Fiume. On 12 September 1919 Gabriele d'Annunzio, the ageing and financially strapped nationalist poet and veteran of the Italian air force, seized the port with 300 supporters and made himself dictator. His actions won the applause of the nationalists, some disgruntled military leaders, and those industrialists who wanted to keep the army on a wartime footing. Orlando's successor, Francisco Nitti, doubtful about the loyalty of the government troops, remained inactive while waiting for the storm to abate. His authority in Rome survived the attempt to spread the revolution from Fiume to Italy, and d'Annunzio, while an ardent supporter of Mussolini's fascists, began to fade as a political force and had no impact on the November 1919 elections. The events in Fiume made it difficult to convince the British and French that the Nitti government was anxious to compromise over its differences with the Yugoslavs, but once Wilson's political impotence was confirmed direct talks were opened between Nitti and Ante Trumbic, the Yugoslav leader. The rhetorical and inflated Italian demands made in Paris had a bitter aftermath in Italy. There was a popular campaign against the 'mutilated victory' (la vittoria mutilata)—d'Annunzio's term—and the nationalist energies expended in 1919 served to undermine the increasingly threatened and divided liberal forces in Rome. The elections of November 1919, which made the Italian socialists the largest party, exposed the fragility of the inherited political structure.

III

It was not only the Italians who had claims against their former allies. The Romanians, too, had been promised a share of the spoils, and though the Greeks were offered no specific territories, the British felt that Venizelos, the Greek prime minister, should be properly rewarded for his pro-Allied sympathies throughout the war. The Romanians played an exceedingly clever game at the peace conference. The self-important, highly polished, and diplomatically supple Ion Brătianu came away with almost all that he wanted, despite Romania's poor wartime performance. Originally neutral and even loosely allied with Austria-Hungary, the Romanians claimed the territories promised in August 1916 (the Treaty of Bucharest) when the country, having waited for the most favourable bid, finally entered the war on the Allied side. These claims included Transylvania with the approaches to the Hungarian Alfold, and extended as far south as the Banat with the town of Szeged (a territory which went beyond the ethnic border into Hungarian lands), most of the Bukovina, and full participation in any future peace conference. In May 1918, after a successful Bulgarian invasion and a massive German onslaught that almost resulted in the occupation of Bucharest, the Romanians concluded an armistice with the Central Powers. A month earlier, in response to Bolshevik activity, the council of the Romanian-speaking province of Bessarabia voted for conditional union with Romania. The union became unconditional in December 1918, but the Soviet Union never recognized Romanian sovereignty. To enforce her claims under the original Treaty of Bucharest, Romania re-entered the war on the Allied side on 9 November 1918, one week after the Austro-Hungarian surrender and two days before the German armistice. Little was left to chance; the Romanian army was in occupation of most of the disputed territories before the peace was made. Bratianu could count on the support of the French, who looked to Romania as part of an 'eastern barrier' to be constructed against both Germany and the Soviet Union. In the ensuing struggle with Hungary the Romanians were able to exploit the Allied fear of Bolshevism and the indecisive western response to the creation of the Bolshevik Béla Kun government in Hungary. The peace treaties doubled the size (to 305,000 square kilometres) and population (over 17 million) of Romania, making it the second largest state in eastern Europe. The Romanian population, formerly constituting 92 per cent of the pre-war state, now formed only 70 per cent of the total.

British hopes to satisfy the Greeks further complicated the peacemaking process with Bulgaria and Turkey as well as Italy. Venizelos, prime minister of only a notionally united government in Athens, presented a formidable list of demands for having committed Greek troops to the Allied cause. It included northern Epirus from Albania, western Thrace from Bulgaria, and eastern Thrace, the islands, and territories on the Aegean coast of Asia Minor from Turkey. Above all, Venizelos was determined to have Smyrna (Izmir) and its hinterland, with its mixed Greek and Turkish population. Quite apart from his personal friendship with Venizelos, Lloyd George wanted a staunch ally in the eastern Mediterranean, where British interests were engaged but where Britain lacked the resources to defend them. There was a sharp clash with President Wilson over the Greek claim to all of Thrace, and the question was not settled until after the American rejection of the Versailles treaty. Incensed by news of unauthorized Italian landings along the Turkish coast, and suspecting that they were about to launch a major expedition to Asia Minor, Wilson proved more co-operative with regard to Greek claims on Smyrna. An agreement was reached in Paris one day before the Italians returned. There was to be a temporary occupation of Smyrna by an inter-Allied though mainly Greek army, supposedly to prevent the Turks from perpetrating a massacre. It was intended, in fact, that the Greeks should occupy the port. Lloyd George took the initiative; Clemenceau was only marginally interested, and Wilson, out to punish the Italians and influenced by stories of Turkish atrocities against Greeks, was enthusiastic and defended the decision on ethnic grounds. The occupation of Smyrna on 15 May 1920 proved a disaster for Greece; the atrocities which took place there galvanized the Turkish nationalists into action. The Greeks were soon engaged in a punishing and unsuccessful war with the newly created Turkish Nationalist army which resulted in the collapse of all their Turkish ambitions.

IV

The treaties with Austria, Hungary, and Bulgaria (as well as the first treaty with Turkey) followed the German model. Each contained the League Covenant and the Labour Charter. Each included the demand for the surrender of war criminals and contained disarmament clauses, differing in the size of permitted armies but equally punitive in effect. Each treaty contained a reparations section and war-guilt clauses similar to those found in the Versailles treaty. All three settlements imposed similar financial and economic restrictions and applied Versailles principles to ports, international waterways, and rail transit. Each of the Central Powers was required to give priority to the payment of occupation and commission costs. The treaties were concluded without any reference to the principles of self-determination. In the case of Austria, the wishes of the population in the shrunken state for *Anschluss* were deliberately ignored.

The Treaty of St-Germain, signed in the great hall of the old royal chateau on the outskirts of Paris on 10 September 1919, left Austria a tiny, truncated state with no access to the sea and in a precarious economic and financial position. It was treated as an ex-enemy state and not as a new entity. *Anschluss* was forbidden. The central territorial committee recommended that the frontier with Germany should follow pre-war lines. Elsewhere, the claims of Czechoslovakia, Poland, Yugoslavia, and Italy were settled at the expense of the former Austrian part of the Dual Monarchy. An earlier decision by the Council of Four confirming the historic borders of Bohemia and Moravia had given the Sudetenland to Czechoslovakia and the eastern portion of the province of Galicia to Poland. The Austrians, backed by the Italians, protested the transfer of the Klagenfurt basin to the Yugoslavs, who occupied the territory at the end of May 1919 after heavy fighting. The council of four decided that Klagenfurt's fate should be decided by plebiscites. If Yugoslavia won in the southern areas, which had a Slovene majority, there would be a second plebiscite in the northern German zone. The first plebiscite resulted in an Austrian victory so no second vote was held. The Klagenfurt basin remained Austrian. The Austrians, too, claimed the Burgenland in west Hungary, both on ethnic and economic grounds. After first rejecting this demand, the Council of Four, worried by the Béla Kun government in Hungary, reversed itself and modified the frontier in Vienna's favour. The Italians secured the Brenner frontier promised in 1915, though Wilson later regretted his decision, which placed some 230,000 Austrian Germans in the South Tyrol under Italian rule and was clearly a violation of the nationalist principle that provoked local resistance.

It was argued by the leaders of the republic that Austria could not exist in its truncated form, and that neither its banks nor industries would recover from the disintegration of the Dual Monarchy. British Treasury spokesmen argued that the country could not pay reparations or its share of the Monarchy's pre-war debts. But neither James Headlam-Morley, the British representative on the New States

Committee, nor John Maynard Keynes, the Treasury official, both early critics of the Austrian settlement, could overcome opposition from their own nationals as well as from the French. Little was done to protect Austria from the economic effects of the political fragmentation of the empire, though substantial food relief was given to save the population from starvation. British experts favoured some kind of central European and Balkan confederation which could eventually merge. When this was rejected, they proposed the formation of an exclusively economic federation to cross the new national lines. But the peace treaties only stipulated that the ex-enemy states should not discriminate against the Allied powers by granting more favourable tariffs to other nations. There were Austrian protests and proposals by the Supreme Allied Economic Council for linking the territories of the old Monarchy. These, too, proved unacceptable to one or more of the powers concerned. The Supreme Economic Council was not prepared to go beyond a limited arrangement which would permit Austria, Czechoslovakia, and Hungary to grant preferential customs treatment to each other for a three-year period. The new republic of barely 7 million people faced a difficult and impecunious future. The country was considered too small to live but too large to die.

V

It had been planned to present the Austrian and Hungarian treaties together to the 'twin heirs' of the Habsburg monarchy, but the negotiations with Budapest were delayed because of the revolution of March 1919. Mihaly Karolyi, the last prime minister of the old Monarchy and the head of the infant Hungarian republic, was overthrown by a newly formed Bolshevik party under the leadership of Béla Kun. It was a signal for Romanian troops to move beyond the Allied demarcation line drawn to separate the Romanian and Hungarian forces. The Council of Ten, lacking other alternatives, adopted Marshal Foch's plan to stabilize the frontier by establishing a neutral zone which meant a Hungarian withdrawal. Károlyi's failure to win concessions from the Allies, and widespread strikes and land seizures in Hungary, led to his resignation on 21 March, opening the way for Béla Kun's government of socialists and communists. The communist takeover was due, in part, to Hungarian opposition to Allied policy. The ranks of the newly formed Hungarian Red Army were filled by former Austro-Hungarian officers, who would never have participated in revolutionary action otherwise. The peacemakers were at a loss about what to do. None had military forces available to intervene, and despite Foch's urging, Clemenceau wisely held back. Meanwhile, the expert committee on

Romanian and Yugoslav affairs concluded its work, recommending that Romania should obtain all of Transylvania but not the Tisza border on the east Hungarian plain, as had been promised in 1916. The Allied leaders and the Americans, preoccupied with German affairs, accepted the new frontiers without discussion. On 12 May Ion Brătianu, the chief Romanian negotiator, demanded the 1916 line and refused to withdraw his force beyond the Tisza river. This would have meant the Romanian annexation of indisputably Hungarian territories. Wilson and Lloyd George were furious and considered the expulsion of Romania from the conference, but Clemenceau, conscious of the strong pro-Romanian feeling in the Chamber of Deputies and future hopes of including Romania among its eastern allies, checked this demonstration of Allied disapproval.

If, however, the Allies would not countenance military intervention in Budapest, neither were they willing to negotiate with Béla Kun as Hungary's legitimate leader. The western powers were appalled by his ascent to power, and feared that Bolshevism would spread from Budapest to Vienna, the rest of central Europe, and even into the west. Apart from reimposing the blockade there was little that they could do, and the victor leaders drifted along without a policy. By April Wilson, backed by Clemenceau and Lloyd George, decided to send General Smuts on a fact-finding mission to Budapest. He was not to discuss terms, but to offer to lift the Allied blockade if the Hungarians would accept a favourable rectification of the demarcation line in eastern Hungary. Never leaving his train carriage, Smuts stayed only two days (4–5 April 1919). When Kun attempted to secure further concessions, Smuts ordered the train to leave Budapest. Back in Paris, he recommended that the blockade be lifted and that all the successor states be asked to come to discuss an economic reconstruction programme. Neither suggestion found favour. The 'big four' continued without a policy. As a consequence, the Hungarian Soviet Republic, as it was called, launched an attempt to recover Slovakia for Hungary. Its army penetrated deep into central Slovakia and overran all of eastern Slovakia. With Hungarian assistance, a Slovak Soviet Republic was set up. On 13 June the Allies presented to the Hungarians the country's new borders with Czechoslovakia and Romania, hoping to remove the uncertainties in the region. In spite of this, the Czech–Hungarian standoff continued, allowing Marshal Foch to revive his plans for intervention. He presented a twenty-four-hour ultimatum to Béla Kun on 23 June, the day after the work on the German peace treaty had been concluded and when Lloyd George and Wilson were preparing to leave Paris. Kun knew that the French government and military, as well as the remaining British Foreign Office delegation, would allow him little leeway. In return for the promise of a Hungarian

withdrawal, he requested that the Romanians should simultaneously
retire from the Tisza line to the newly announced international border.
Even in the face of the Allied demands the Romanians refused to comply.
On 30 June Kun's forces completed their withdrawal from Slovakia,
where the Soviet regime collapsed, having lasted all of two weeks.

Once Wilson and Lloyd George left Paris Allied policy changed.
Arthur Balfour, the British foreign secretary, was more willing than
Lloyd George to see the Romanians bring down the Bolshevik regime.
Their successful counter-offensive ended on 3 August with the occupation of Budapest. Béla Kun fled first to Vienna and eventually to
Moscow; he died as a victim of the Stalinist purges in 1939. Once
established, the Romanian occupiers refused to leave and began to
strip the country of its industrial and agricultural assets, as well as any
personal objects that could be carried away. Despite mounting Allied
pressure for withdrawal so that a credible government could be formed
and a treaty concluded with Hungary, the Romanians refused to budge.
In the meantime, Czechoslovak forces from the north and Yugoslavs in
the south moved beyond their frontiers. The highly volatile situation
was exploited by the emerging strong man of Hungary, Rear-Admiral
Miklós Horthy, commander of the former Austro–Hungarian navy. He
and his counter-revolutionary forces began to assert control over the
western and central parts of the country, ironically often with Romanian
assistance. In the turmoil, armed gangs of all descriptions began to take
arbitrary reprisals against alleged supporters of the former Bolshevik
system. Resentment against the 'red regime' and Jews ran high; Kun
was Jewish, as were many of the other leaders of the government. The
Supreme Council dispatched a commission of four Allied generals to
sort out Hungary's problems, but without substantial armed backing the
generals proved helpless. In the end, the Paris peace conference sent a
senior British diplomat, Sir George Clerk, a man much influenced by
the nationality principles of the 'New Europe' group led by R. W.
Seton-Watson, to Budapest to conclude a settlement. Backed by a firm
Allied threat to break off relations with Romania, Clerk helped to
secure its withdrawal from Budapest. On 25 November 1919 Clerk
recognized the new Hungarian coalition government and put his faith
in Admiral Horthy as a possible future head of state. The diplomat's
intervention proved critical both for Horthy and for Hungary.

A newly constituted Hungarian assembly, elected, in accordance with
Clerk's wishes, on a democratic franchise, chose Horthy as the country's
head of state. The 'white terror' was in full swing when the general
elections were held, and the election of Horthy took place in the
intimidating presence of the admiral's soldiers in the parliament building. The socialists refused to participate and the forces of the right were

swept into power. The Allies, nonetheless, judged the regime fit enough to sign the peace treaty. The Hungarian delegation which arrived in Neuilly in early 1920 submitted an eloquent plea for the mitigation of the territorial, military, and reparation clauses of the treaty, but to no avail. Nor, despite Italian support and some sympathy in Britain, were the Hungarians successful when they pressed for plebiscites in areas of mixed nationality. Lloyd George took little interest in the negotiations and followed the French lead. This left only the Italians to champion the Hungarian cause. The Hungarian delegation resigned in protest, but Budapest had no choice but to accept the Allied terms. The final treaty, signed at the Trianon Palace near Versailles on 4 June 1920, contained only the most modest concessions. The frontier delimitation commission would look at the mixed areas and some adjustments were made to the reparations bill.

This was a real victors' peace. The Hungarians lost two-thirds of their territory and the populations they had ruled under the Dual Monarchy. Admittedly, the majority among those who were assigned to the new states were ethnically non-Hungarian. Many had been subjected to a harsh and oppressive regime by their former rulers. In Slovakia, a new border gave the Czechs access to the Danube, transferring a relatively compact Magyar population to the newly created nation. The Czechs also acquired Ruthenia, an area populated by Ruthenes, or Little Russians, which might have gone to Russia had the Bolsheviks not been in power. The Yugoslavs, too, benefited from the Hungarian losses, getting a third of the Banat (the rest going to Romania) where the nationalities were impossible to separate, and Croatia, which had enjoyed considerable autonomy within the old Hungary. There was a sizeable Hungarian population between Szeged and Belgrade, in a region called the Vojvodina, which, with the exception of a small enclave around Szeged itself that the Americans insisted the Hungarians should keep, was also awarded to Belgrade. The Hungarians had to surrender Fiume, their one remaining outlet to the sea, though the battle continued to be waged in Paris as to its eventual heir.

The Romanians benefited most from the Treaty of Trianon. Some 1.7 million Magyars of a total 3 million now outside the Hungarian borders lived under Romanian rule in the West Banat, the eastern edge of the plain, and in Transylvania and Bukovina. The new additions to the Romanian state were not all positive gains. Romania was a multinational state; some 5 million of its 17 million inhabitants were not ethnic Romanians. Most of these national groups were small and some, like the Germans and Jews, made their peace with their new rulers. But the largest minority group were the Hungarians, and the chief area of unrest was Transylvania, where the Hungarian minority never accepted the reversal of traditional authority roles. Nor did the Romanian authorities improve the situation by treating the Hungarians as 'foreigners' who had no right to settle in their own former lands. Hungarian revanchism remained a factor in central and south-east European politics throughout the inter-war period. Most of the borders established by Trianon, with the exception of the Burgenland and some changes on the Romanian side, had been settled before the Béla Kun revolution took place and represented, insofar as they contradicted the principle of self-determination, the costs of defeat. Though Hungary was left in possession of its fertile plain and was more economically viable than Austria, it too suffered from the post-war dislocations and, like Austria in 1921, had to be rescued by the League in 1924.

VI

The Treaty of Neuilly with the Bulgarians, signed on 27 November 1919, was again mainly the work of the Allied foreign ministers and the territorial committees. British pro-Hellenism and French wishes to build up Yugoslavia and Romania as future bulwarks of French interests in the Balkans set the contours to the settlement. In Paris the Italians, who, to French and British annoyance, supported Bulgaria as a counterweight to Yugoslavia, and the Americans championed Bulgaria's claims in Thrace. Venizelos demanded both western Thrace, where the Greeks were the largest ethnic group, and eastern Thrace, where the Turks were in the majority. The British strongly backed his claims lest their wartime supporter return home 'absolutely empty handed'. The Italians objected to the eastern Thrace solution on ethnic and economic grounds and convinced the Americans to support their point of view. In July Wilson suggested that Thrace be made part of a new internationalized state centred on Constantinople. The Neuilly treaty awarded eastern Thrace to the Greeks and postponed a solution to the rest of the province. But at the meeting at San Remo in 1920, with the Americans represented only by an observer, the British had a freer hand and the Greeks were given the whole province.

Elsewhere the Bulgarians lost relatively little territory. Greece and Yugoslavia were confirmed in their possession of Macedonia, which they had won from the Turks in 1913, though the Bulgarians outnumbered the Greeks. The British and French fell back on the view that they should not interfere with borders established in this part of the Balkans before 1914, whatever the rights and wrongs of those settlements. There was also the problem of southern Dobruja, which Bulgaria had lost to Romania during the Second Balkan War in 1913 and where there were more Turks, Bulgars, and Tartars than Romanians. This, too, stayed in Romanian hands, in disregard of the fears that this would become an area of Balkan contention. There was a sharp clash between ethnic principles and strategic considerations when Bulgaria's frontiers with Yugoslavia came to be drawn. Serbia's pre-war eastern frontier had made her vulnerable to the Bulgarian attack in 1915, and the British wished to rectify this frontier line in the Yugoslav favour. In the end, American and Italian protests were disregarded and most of the Bulgarian mountain salients were given to Yugoslavia. The Greeks gained eastern Thrace and later, at the San Remo conference in April 1920, western Thrace as well, cutting Bulgaria off from the Aegean Sea. The Turks constituted the majority of the population, but there was no question of an ethnic settlement within the region. Greeks, Romanians, and Yugoslavs all benefited from the Bulgarian losses.

The Bulgarian treaty was unique in the fact that an actual sum for reparations was included. The sum required, 2.25 billion gold francs (about £90 million at 5 per cent interest) to be paid over thirty-eight years, constituted about a quarter of the national wealth; specified payments in kind included a list of enumerated livestock. Bulgaria was more fortunate than Austria and Hungary, but hardly escaped lightly. The Allies maintained their opposition to conscription despite the Bulgarian plea, echoed by the Hungarians, that in an agricultural country it was impossible to raise an army on a volunteer basis. Bulgaria was allowed only a small army of 20,000 troops and an additional 13,000 for border guards and gendarmes. Between September 1918 and March 1920, the major conflict in Bulgaria was between the agrarian and communist parties reflecting the strong pre-war socialist movements (the largest and oldest in the Balkans despite the very weak industrial base) in the country. Famine conditions and the flu epidemic ravaged the urban population and many townspeople were initially kept alive by American relief aid. The agrarians, led by the extremely able Aleksandur Stamboliiski, created and maintained the elected government in March 1920 by using the traditional political tactic of declaring invalid the election of their opponents.

The situation of the Albanians was left largely unremedied at Paris. Independent Albania owed its existence to decisions made at the London Conference of Ambassadors of 1911 convened after the First Balkan War. Disputes between the powers led to a compromise solution that left as many Albanians outside Albania as within it. They were found on adjacent territories in Montenegro, the Kosovo region of Serbia, and in Macedonia, which itself was divided, with a Slav-speaking part in Serbia (later Yugoslavia) and a Greek-speaking part in Greece. The large Kosovo region had been home to Serbs in the Middle Ages but by the twentieth century had become almost entirely Albanian.

Albania had received the least fertile agricultural land and a German prince as ruler, who left the country for good six months after his arrival. The war made the country a parade ground for virtually all of Europe's armies and destroyed the vestiges of indigenous authority. At the Paris peace conference Albania's very survival was in the balance. Without President Wilson's personal intercession the country would have been carved up, according to an Anglo-French-Italian plan, among its neighbours. The Italians had backed a national congress in December 1919 that produced a provisional government. In January 1920 Albanian leaders opposed to Italian patronage held a national congress in Lushnje. The strong man in its newly created government was the still very young Ahmet Bey Zogolli, who had achieved a considerable influence before and during the war. Throughout 1920 the Albanians, struggling for their independence, were involved in skirmishes with Greek and Yugoslav troops. By the end of the year, after the assassination of one of the contenders for the leadership of Albania and the forced retreat of both the Yugoslav and Italian occupying forces, Albania, with its Muslim majority and illiterate population, embarked on a new phase of its precarious national existence. Despite an appeal to the League Council, the question of the Greek and Yugoslav territorial claims was left for the Conference of Ambassadors, a new organization of Allied ambassadors meeting in Paris that assumed some of the functions of the peace conference during and after its last stages and was made responsible for the execution of parts of the treaties. The conference decision in November 1921 generally reaffirmed Albania's 1913 boundaries, with small alterations in favour of Yugoslavia, but recognized Italy's paramount interest in the defence of the country's integrity and independence, an opportunity later exploited by Mussolini.

The treaties with Austria, Hungary, and Bulgaria were far harsher and more vindictive than the one with Germany. The Austrian and Hungarian settlements were punitive in the extreme; the former was left in a perilous economic state, and the latter, if economically viable, was so stripped of territories and people as to guarantee its revisionist status. If the Bulgarian peace treaty was less severe, this was mainly because of that state's poverty and geographic position rather than from any generosity on the part of the Allies. To the critics of the financial clauses, above all of the Austrian treaty, the Anglo-French leaders argued that neither their own electorates nor the people of the successor states would allow the defeated countries to get away with more. In the case of all three treaties, Allied policy was shaped by the exigencies of coalition politics and the hope of securing future allies in central and south-east Europe, rather than by any consideration of the future of the defeated states.

VII

The Treaty of Sèvres, signed with the Turkish Sultanate on 10 August 1920, turned out to be the most complex and severe but also the most short-lived of the peace treaties. From the start Allied peacemaking reflected both wartime commitments that could not be implemented to the satisfaction of the parties concerned and traditional European attitudes towards the Turks. Lloyd George dismissed the Turks 'as a human cancer, a creeping agony in the flesh of the lands that they misgovern, rotting away every fibre of life'.[5] In the aftermath of the war the Turkish settlements showed the degree to which the European powers continued to think of empire as integral to their great-power status. The war had underlined the practical importance of colonies as sources of manpower and strategic commodities. The result was a peace treaty that was little more than a traditional imperial squabble for territory between the European powers. From well before the war's end the British attempted to grab as much as possible of the former Turkish Middle East empire at French expense, using promises of self-determination to both Arabs and Zionists to gain support. Turkish self-determination was never mentioned and the proposed carve-up of the Turkish heartland itself was even more blatant. The subsequent history of the eastern treaty demonstrated that the imperial powers could not totally ignore the new currents unleashed by the war and that there were limits on their ability to impose settlements at will. The conflicting British and French appetites in the region proved as divisive and destructive of their relationship as their disputes over the German question.

Britain and France became unequal competitors in the Middle East when the withdrawal of Russia opened the way to a bilateral partition of the Turkish empire. The eastern phase of the Great War had been very much a British show. British empire troops conquered Palestine and Mesopotamia and advanced deep into Syria. As its military involvement in the east expanded, so did Britain's imperial ambitions. Already in 1915, intent on retaining her key strategic position in the eastern Mediterranean and above all in the Persian Gulf, vital for communications with India, Britain looked to a protectorate in Mesopotamia, the old Ottoman provinces of Mosul, Baghdad, and Basra. Lloyd George, as well as Lord Curzon and Lord Milner, two ardent expansionists, harboured hopes of including Palestine as well as Mesopotamia within the

---

[5] Quoted in Misha Glenny, *The Balkans, 1804–1999: Nationalism, War and the Great Powers* (paperback edn., London, 2000), 363.

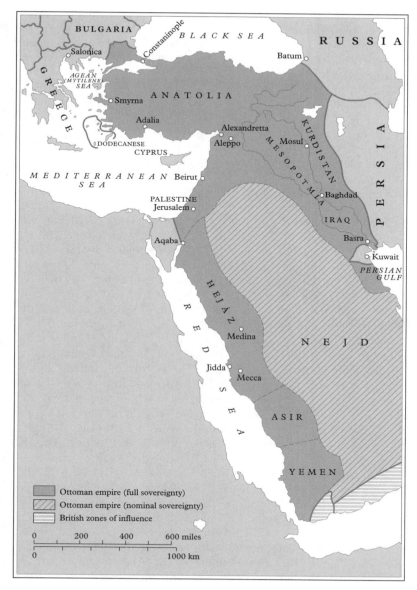

Map 5. The Ottoman Empire in 1914

empire. In the last year of the war the oil supplies of Asiatic Turkey became an important factor in British war aims; the hope to secure oil for the navy and the revenue needed to pay for future development and transportation resulted in further disputes with France over the reputedly oil-rich territory of Mosul.

The British expected to write their own ticket in the Middle East. Unfortunately for their hopes, wartime promises produced a spiral of conflicting obligations that threatened their freedom of action. The British had encouraged the launching of an Arab rebellion against the Turks in 1916 with promises of a future Arab state to Hussain ibn Ali, head of the Hashemite family (claiming direct descent from the prophet Muhammad), and the Sherif of Mecca, despite warnings from the Government of India and the India Office in London of the possible danger to Britain's future position in the region. Badly drafted and full of ambiguities, the letters exchanged between Sir Henry McMahon, the British high commissioner at Cairo, and Hussain in October 1915 have remained the subject of intense controversy. McMahon appears to have confirmed the promise of Arab independence and recognized Hussain's claims to a vast kingdom, including most of the Levant. To safeguard British and French interests, McMahon indicated that the districts of Mersina and Alexandretta (areas along the north-eastern corner of the Mediterranean) and those regions lying to the west of the districts of Damascus, Homs, Hama, and Aleppo should be excluded and that the Mesopotamian *vilayets* (districts) of Basra and Baghdad would require 'special administrative arrangements'. The British undertaking, moreover, was limited to regions where Britain was free to act without detriment to the interests of France, with whom negotiations had already begun. The agreement depended on an Arab uprising against the Turks. One of the most contentious issues, which plagued Anglo-Arab relations for a generation, was the position of Palestine. Though still contested, the Arabs claimed that Palestine did not lie to the west of the four named towns in the McMahon letter and so fell within the area of promised Arab independence. The British promise of what one official called Hussain's 'castle in the sky' may well have been made on the assumption that, once the Arab rebellion took place, the promises would not have to be fulfilled. Whether the McMahon letters carried any legal or moral authority was almost beside the point, as was the question whether the narrow limits of the Arab rebellion actually fulfilled the McMahon quid pro quo. The Arabs could rightly claim that Britain had promised to support Arab independence and that Hussain had launched a revolt against Turkey.

There was a clash in spirit, if not in actual substance, between the McMahon promises to the Arabs and Britain's secret agreement with

France concluded in April 1916 between Sir Mark Sykes and François Georges Picot. French interests in the Levant were explicitly recognized in the Sykes–Picot agreement, concluded at a time when Britain needed French consent to open a 'sideshow' in the east. The agreement recognized the independence of the Arab states while carving out areas for direct Anglo-French control as well as future spheres of influence. France would be predominant in the Syrian and Lebanese coastal areas and in south-eastern Turkey (Cilicia), Britain would have central and southern Mesopotamia and Acre and Haifa in Palestine. The rest of the 'Holy Land' would come under an 'international administration'. A huge area, including the Syrian and Jordanian interiors and northern Mesopotamia, was to become an independent Arab state or a confederation of Arabs divided into northern and southern areas which would come under French and British influence. There was no mention of these spheres of influence in the independent Arab state promised to Hussain. There was a 'profound difference in spirit' between Sykes–Picot and the Hussain–McMahon exchange; the former was an old-fashioned colonial bargain while the latter, without conscious intent, 'imported concepts of nationalism and anticipated principles of self-determination that were to be articulated in 1918'.[6] Hussain was told in general terms of the agreement in May 1917, but the full contents were only revealed when the Bolsheviks published the secret treaties at the end of 1917.

Almost as soon as the Sykes–Picot bargain was struck, the British had second thoughts. As the war ended it was the British, with the only army in the field, who were in actual possession. Lloyd George felt that he could afford to take a strong line and disregard the Sykes–Picot agreement. When British troops moved into Syria the Arabs were allowed to operate in areas promised to France. On 1 October 1918 the forces of Prince Faisal, third son of Hussain, led by T. E. Lawrence, the legendary 'Lawrence of Arabia', along with British empire troops (the Australians did most of the fighting, though the credit went to Faisal) took Damascus, the heart of an ancient Arab empire. The city became the centre of Faisal's administration, covering the areas of Syria that the French intended to control. The British position hardened; there seemed no reason to abide by the terms of the Sykes–Picot agreement with regard to Syria, particularly as Faisal appeared willing to accept British control.

The occupation of Palestine and the decision to underwrite the Zionists created a further contradiction between the wartime deals. There were a number of British cabinet members, including Lloyd George, who were sympathetically inclined to the spreading Zionist

[6] John Paris, *Britain, the Hashemites and Arab Rule, 1920–1925* (London, 2003), 35.

cause and to its persuasive spokesman in London, Chaim Weizmann, a chemist who had invented a much-needed method for the production of cordite during the war. Weizmann became the chief lobbyist for the Zionist movement in political and official circles. Apart from personal predilections, the decision to support the Zionists was dictated by both strategic and diplomatic motives. An internationalized Holy Land was fraught with danger, for Palestine, as Curzon put it, was the military gate to Egypt and the Suez Canal and had to be kept free from outside interference. Recognition of Zionist aspirations was also a diplomatic move intended to block German initiatives and to influence American and Russian Jews, whose power over their respective governments was grossly exaggerated. On 2 November 1917 the foreign secretary, Arthur Balfour, wrote to Lord Rothschild, the main spokesman for the British Zionists: 'His Majesty's Government view with favour the establishment in Palestine of a national home for the Jewish people.' Cabinet members knew that the Zionists were thinking in terms of a state but, by speaking only of a national home and including an assurance that nothing would be done to 'prejudice the civil and religious rights of existing non-Jewish communities in Palestine', they believed it possible to fulfil Britain's pledges to both Arabs and Jews.[7] Warnings from Lord Curzon and Edwin Montagu, the secretary of state for India and an anti-Zionist Jew, of the troubles to come were disregarded. Soon after the 'Balfour declaration' was issued, Hussain received new British assurances, the 'Hogarth message' (from David Hogarth of the Arab Bureau in Cairo) of 4 January 1918, that the return of the Jews to Palestine would not compromise the political and economic rights of the 'existing inhabitants', 90 per cent of whom were Muslim Arabs. As patrons of both the Hashemite dynasty and the Zionists, the British believed they could appear as the spokesman for the new nationalities without incurring the charge of harbouring imperial ambitions. In both cases, the apparent offer of British backing for self-determination was less than forthright.

The twelfth of President Wilson's Fourteen Points promised that the nationalities under Turkish rule should be assured 'an absolutely un-molested opportunity to autonomous development'. On 7 November 1918, in order to allay Arab fears regarding Sykes–Picot and American suspicions regarding their imperialistic designs, an Anglo-French dec-laration proclaimed that France and Britain were 'at one' in wanting to establish 'national governments and administrations deriving their au-thority from the initiative and free choice of the indigenous population'. The declaration went on to state that London and Paris were 'only concerned to ensure by their support and by adequate assistance the

---

[7] Leonard Stein, *The Balfour Declaration* (London, 1961), 548.

regular working of Governments and administrations freely chosen by the populations themselves'.[8] The declaration was enthusiastically received by the Arabs; few took in the meaning of the terms 'support' and 'adequate assistance'. Neither Britain nor France intended establishing 'national governments' based on free choice; at most they were prepared to sanction the creation of an Arab state in the remote Arabian desert. Nonetheless, the notions of self-determination and their own declarations to the Arabs meant that new approaches to imperial control were necessary. By adopting the mandates system suggested by the South African premier Jan Smuts, Britain and France were able to bridge the gap between their own national interests and the claims of the new internationalism. The ex-Turkish communities were to be treated as 'A' mandates, their independence provisionally recognized, subject to a limited period of 'administrative advice and assistance' until able to stand on their own feet. A Permanent Mandates Commission, consisting of experts in colonial administration, would receive and examine annual reports from the mandatory powers, and advise the Council on all such matters. This semblance of international control allowed the British and French to protect their newly acquired positions without incurring American charges of imperialism. For the British, in particular, the mandate system had the additional advantage of undermining the Sykes–Picot arrangements.

The fighting in the Middle East came to an end with Britain's unilateral negotiation of an armistice with the Turks at Mudros on 30 October 1918. In the subsequent Supreme Council meeting, Clemenceau and Lloyd George harangued each other; such an open disregard of French interests forced Clemenceau, a reluctant imperialist, to defend them. French influence in Syria dated to the mid-seventeenth century and was as much cultural and religious (France was the protector of the Christian populace in Syria and Lebanon) as economic. The Comité de l'Asie Française, demanding French control of Cilicia and 'la Syrie intégrale', a wide area extending from the Taurus Mountains to the Sinai, was a relatively small but highly influential imperial lobby with support in the Quai d'Orsay. The Syrian party had not taken kindly to the expanded appetites of the British coalition government and its decision to extend military operations from Mesopotamia into Palestine in early 1917. The French imperialists were worried that Clemenceau, the arch-'westerner', without war aims in the Middle East, might sacrifice French ambitions in Syria for victory on the western front. Their fears seem confirmed when, despite his anger over the armistice,

---

[8] An English translation of the French text of the Anglo-French declaration is given in *Parliamentary Debates, 5th Series, House of Commons*, vol. 145, col. 36.

Clemenceau seemed more concerned about the French future in Europe than with the division of spoils in the Middle East. An unrecorded bargain concluded in London during December 1918 came apart amid claims of bad faith. Clemenceau asserted, and Lloyd George denied, that in return for French acceptance of Britain's rights to Palestine and Mosul, formerly ceded to France, Lloyd George had agreed to accept the remainder of the French claims under Sykes–Picot, to give France an equal share of Mosul oil, and, of critical importance to the French premier, to guarantee British support on the Rhine in case of an unprovoked German attack. Contrary to the fears of the imperialists, Clemenceau was to fight hard to maintain the French position against Lloyd George's vaulting ambitions and diplomatic manoeuvring. There were many confrontations during the sixteen months that elapsed between the de facto division of the mandates in January 1919 and their formal assignment at San Remo in April 1920.

As agreed shortly after the Paris peace conference opened, Armenia, Kurdistan, Syria, Mesopotamia, Palestine, and Arabia were designated 'A' mandates, an unscrupulous though not unexpected use of the mandate concept confirming the special British role in the Middle East. At the so-called request of the populations concerned, Britain would become the mandatory for Mesopotamia and Palestine, and France the mandatory for the whole of Syria, where she was to 'assist' a native Arab government. It was hoped that the Americans would take on the Armenian mandate, a headache that nobody wanted but which was still under consideration in June 1920 when the American Senate rejected the proposal. Clemenceau, preoccupied with the German treaty, agreed to these terms and postponed further discussions of the Near East to avoid confrontation with Britain. It was Lloyd George's subsequent attempts in mid-February, during Wilson's absence in America, to deprive France of her promised rewards in Syria that infuriated the French premier. 'I won't give way on anything more', Clemenceau assured President Poincaré. 'Lloyd George is a cheat. He has managed to turn me into a "Syrian".'[9] When the 'big three' reassembled in Paris in mid-March there was a real danger of an Anglo-French break-up. While the French tried to negotiate with Faisal over the future arrangements for Syria, the British gave the Amir their support for a virtually independent state. The heated arguments between the two prime ministers led to President Wilson's intervention and his suggestion that a joint commission be sent to Syria, still occupied by British troops, and, at Clemenceau's insistence, to Palestine and

---

[9] Quoted in Christopher M. Andrew and Alexander S. Kanya-Forstner, *France Overseas: The Great War and the Climax of French Imperial Expansion* (London, 1981), 189.

Mesopotamia to test local public opinion. Fiercely at odds with one another, but both concluding that the commission was a bad idea, Clemenceau and Lloyd George stalled about naming their representatives, and the two American commissioners, Henry King and Charles Crane, went out to the Middle East without them. The King–Crane report, issued at the end of August 1919, accurately assessed native opinion in the Middle East and Armenia. The Syrians were strongly opposed to any form of French control and the Palestinians rejected the Zionist programme and wanted the future of Palestine decided on the basis of self-determination. The report, not actually published until 1922 though its contents were generally known, had no effect on the Syrian negotiations and only stirred false Arab hopes by the solicitation of their views. No one in London, with Lloyd George's possible exception, actually contemplated ousting the French from Syria, whatever their pleasure in Arab Francophobia, and none of the leading peacemakers was prepared to retract the commitment to the Jewish Zionists.

The Turkish treaty hung fire during the whole summer of 1919. While waiting to hear whether the Americans would assume any mandate in the Middle East, Anglo-French relations deteriorated further. The public campaign mounted by the Syrian party in Paris abetted by the Quai d'Orsay finally alerted the British to the seriousness of the Middle Eastern imbroglio and the dangers of further quarrels with France to the European settlements. The situation became even more confused when the Allies had to deal with conflicting Greek and Italian ambitions in Turkey. The French were not slow to point out that, while both these countries were allowed to occupy territory in Asia Minor, the British continued to block the French military occupation of Syria. The British found themselves seriously overextended as they faced simultaneous challenges in Ireland, India, Egypt, and Mesopotamia. Sir Henry Wilson, the chief of the Imperial General Staff, warned the cabinet that the country lacked the military strength to face unrest at home, and the troubles in Ireland and in other various parts of the empire. Mesopotamia came at the bottom of his list of priorities. Common sense dictated a policy of British withdrawal from Syria and a settlement with France. In September 1919 Lloyd George reversed his policy and agreed to remove the British troops from Syria, Cilicia, and Armenia and accept their replacement by French and Arab forces. Clemenceau agreed to the British evacuation but, intent on having a mandate for the whole of Syria, would not countenance the presence of Arab troops. The British withdrawal opened the way for a bargain at Arab expense. Emir Faisal saw the British desertion as a repudiation of what had been promised to his father and all the subsequent assurances given to the Arabs. Without Britain's backing, he had no choice but to accept the French terms which turned Syria into a French protectorate. He also gave way to the French demand for a separate Lebanon, previously a part of Syria, and a special regime for Alexandretta. The Arabs were sacrificed to the needs of the Entente.

A meeting in London on 11 December 1919 settled the Allied accounts. The British left Syria; the French recognized Faisal as head of an autonomous state under a French mandate and agreed to a truncated Syria, far smaller than the colonial party wanted but sufficient for Clemenceau. Lebanon was promised an autonomous government and independent national status. The British were to have Palestine and Mosul pending a satisfactory oil arrangement. An oil accord, the Greenwood–Berenger agreement of 21 December 1919, was quickly concluded: the French secured a 25 per cent share of the British-controlled Turkish Petroleum Company while conceding to the British two pipelines and railways to transport oil from Mesopotamia and Persia to the Mediterranean. The unresolved difficulties over the Syrian–Palestine frontier were settled in February 1920 when the French agreed to yield territory wanted by the Zionists to make the Palestine mandate more economically viable. In return, Britain accepted the French-proposed boundary between Syria and Turkey.

The Syrians refused to accept Faisal's capitulation, and it was with British help that the French contained the Arab backlash. In March 1920 an elected assembly convoked by Faisal proclaimed the independence of Syria, including Lebanon and Palestine, and made Faisal king. Shortly afterwards a congress of anti-British Mesopotamian officers sitting in Damascus declared the independence of Iraq under King Abdullah, Faisal's older brother, and its union with Syria. The British and French closed ranks. Faisal's claims would be considered only if he accepted the special position of France in Syria and Lebanon and the British position in Palestine. Rejecting these claims, Faisal refused to attend the conference at San Remo in April–May 1920 where the terms of the Treaty of Sèvres were concluded.

The treaty negotiated at San Remo, without either the Turks or Arabs present, largely confirmed the decisions reached at the conference in London held earlier in the year. The form and boundaries of the mandates were decided by the British and French and would be submitted to the League of Nations for acceptance. Under the treaty's terms, the central coastal region of the Arabian peninsula, called the Hejaz (now part of Saudi Arabia), became an independent kingdom. Britain was to have the mandates for Iraq (Mesopotamia) and Palestine, a larger area than assigned her under the Sykes–Picot agreement. The French were made the mandatory power for Syria and Lebanon. The agreement left France free to settle with Faisal without

British intervention. The French attacked and routed the Syrian forces in a single engagement on 24 July 1920 and occupied Damascus. Faisal and his family were exiled. With much of Mesopotamia in revolt, the British decided to restore order by making Faisal the king of Iraq in August 1921, much to the annoyance of the Quai d'Orsay. In 1921, too, in order to satisfy his ambitions and further calm the disturbed region, the British made Abdullah head of the small state of Transjordan, a totally artificial creation with links to Palestine.

The Treaty of Sèvres represented the high point of Allied success. It marked the ending of Ottoman rule in the Middle East, leaving only its European and Anatolian rump as subjects of further controversy. The Turks were left in their capital, but an international commission would control the Straits, which were to be open to all ships in peace and war. Steps were taken to reassure allies and reward friends. The British–French–Italian Tripartite pact, signed concurrently with the Sèvres treaty, recognized Italy's special interest in southern Anatolia and French interests in Cilicia and western Kurdistan. Italian sovereignty over the Dodecanese islands and Rhodes was confirmed. Owing to Lloyd George's continuing support, Venizelos won his case and the Greeks remained in Smyrna. The city and environs were to remain under Turkish sovereignty but would be administered by the Greeks for five years, after which a plebiscite would determine whether the population wished to be under Turkish or Greek rule. Given Greek behaviour in the area, the main question was whether there would be any Turks left to vote. Again due to the adroit tactics of Lloyd George, Greece was awarded the whole of Thrace as well as islands in the Aegean. The British and French argued over the control of the Turkish finances and compromised on a three-power (Italy was included) financial commission to supervise Turkey's revenues and expenditures. A requirement that the Turkish government guarantee the civil and political rights of its minorities reflected the general Allied view of Ottoman behaviour before and during the recent war. The massacre of hundreds of thousands, if not millions, of Armenians in Eastern Anatolia in 1915 confirmed Allied assumptions about Turkish barbarism. The Turkish army was restricted to 50,700 men and its navy drastically reduced. The treaty recognized the independence of Armenia, established as a separate state in 1918, and of Kurdistan, a Kurdish state without borders or definable national identity. Neither promise had any substance.

VIII

If the final settlement reached at San Remo was a division of the spoils with little or no regard for the wishes of the native populations, the

attempt to do the same with the Turkish heartland produced a profoundly different outcome. It had been thought that the division would
involve only the balancing of the claims of the victorious powers
without concern for the beaten foe. Allied policy-makers reckoned
without the appearance of an effective and aggressive Turkish nationalist
movement. For the first six months after the Mudros armistice the
Paris peace conference concerned itself with the conflicting demands
of Italy and Greece to large portions of Asia Minor. The Greek occupation of Smyrna on 15 May 1920 was to change the whole post-war
situation in the Near East by kindling the embers of Turkish nationalism. What was even worse than the Allied decision to sanction the
landing was the actual Greek occupation of the port. Greek soldiers and
civilians living in Smyrna attacked the Turkish community, killing,
maiming, raping, and looting. The Smyrna landings and a series of
subsequent Allied decisions during the ensuing interminable Allied
negotiations convinced the Turkish nationalists that their country
would be almost totally destroyed and that action was essential. The
revival of Turkish nationalism owed its success to Mustapha Kemal, a
38-year-old general who had defeated the British and Russians during
the war and who possessed military and political skills of the highest
order. A strong advocate of an independent Turkey, in contrast to those
who looked to British or American protection, Kemal gathered about
him an ever-increasing number of like-minded nationalists who became
the focal point of opposition both to the Greeks and to the weak
Istanbul government that many still served. Disregarding the armistice
terms, Kemal formulated with his supporters a series of minimal demands, known as the National Covenant, which, while abandoning
Ottoman imperial ambitions and Pan-Turkish irredentism, concentrated on the creation of a sovereign and independent state based on
areas 'inhabited by an Ottoman Muslim majority, united in religion, in
race and, in aim'.[10] Kemal sought the independence of the Anatolian
heartland, the retention of Smyrna with its hinterland, a Thracian
frontier in Europe, and, of course, Constantinople. Given the divisions
among the European powers and the dilatory proceedings in Paris, his
entirely realistic and limited goals proved to be well within Kemal's
military power to achieve. During the summer of 1919 Kemal moved
through Anatolia, recruiting the forces who would fight the Greeks.
Instead of dealing with the new Turkish leader, one of the most brilliant
of the new men whom the war brought to power, the Allies proceeded
to negotiate the peace terms with the enfeebled and malleable sultan.
Slowly becoming aware of the growing Kemalist influence in Anatolia

[10] Quoted in Dockrill and Goold, *Peace Without Promise*, 203.

and determined to assert their position in the Middle East, the British, followed by the hesitant French and Italians, occupied Constantinople on 16 March 1920, despite a previous decision, reached after intense debate among the British policy-makers, to leave the Turks in possession of their capital, mainly to avoid offending the millions of Muslims in British India. The British move left Kemal free to open at Ankara, his new capital in Anatolia, the first Grand National Assembly of Turkey on 23 July 1920. He was made Turkey's first president and prime minister.

The Allies continued to watch the growth of the Kemalist forces but failed to take full measure of the new movement. The terms of the Treaty of Sèvres deprived the Sultanate of what little prestige it still retained. Though the sultan delayed signing the treaty until 10 August 1920, this humiliating peace eroded his authority and strengthened Kemal's hand in Anatolia. The real struggle in Turkey was about to begin. Kemal was a shrewd diplomatist and was soon engaged in dividing his opponents. He courted the Italians, who, having been deprived of their 'just' rewards first by the Allies and then by the Greeks, were willing to settle for the proffered economic concessions. Costly nationalist uprisings against the French in Cilicia resulted in a ceasefire agreement in May. Locked in conflicts with the Armenians and Georgians, Kemal, despite his strong anti-Bolshevism, combined military power and negotiations with the Leninists to settle their border conflicts.

In mid-June 1920 the Nationalists launched an offensive, attacking British troops in the Ismid peninsula and threatening the Straits. Without any other available reinforcements the British cabinet turned to Venizelos, and in return for Greek assistance sanctioned, with reluctant French and Italian consent, a limited advance from Smyrna. There had been warnings from the Foreign Office and the British general staff, as well as from Marshal Foch that Lloyd George's confidence in the strength of the Greek army was seriously misplaced, but the prime minister closed his ears and followed his own course. He believed in Turkish incompetence and grossly exaggerated the number and quality of Venizelos's Greek forces. There was no way that the Allies could have imposed their peace terms except by defeating the Kemalists in the field. Instead, they relied on the Greek army to do their fighting for them. Lloyd George was rewarded at first by a series of Greek military successes in the Straits region. Unfortunately for his inflated hopes, the freakish death of the Greek King Alexander from an infected monkey bite in October 1920, and the unexpected election defeat of Venizelos, led to the return of the exiled pro-German and anti-Allied King Constantine. This provided the catalyst for changes in both French and Italian policies; both governments, particularly the French, who hated Constantine, were prepared to desert Athens, revise Sèvres, and conclude terms with the Kemalists. Neither was prepared to march to the British tune and neither shared Lloyd George's inflated opinion of Greek military prowess. The new Greek government was determined on a forward policy in Asia Minor and the British, partly due to Lloyd George's continuing pro-Hellenism, though refusing to recognize King Constantine, were drawn in its wake.

The sultan's government lost all credibility, while Kemal grew in power and strength with each passing month. Exploiting the newly established ties with the Bolshevik forces in the Caucasus in 1920, the Nationalists regained in the Treaty of Alexandropol (20 December 1920) their territories in Armenia and the strategic areas of Kars and Ardahan lost to Russia in 1878. The weak foundation of the Kemalist–Bolshevik partnership was exposed when quarrels later occurred in both Armenia and Georgia, but the threat of British control over the Straits and the Black Sea, of strategic importance to both, was sufficient to prevent their fragile coalition from collapsing. Once the Caucasian borders were firmly established, the Turkish nationalists could concentrate their forces on the Greek army in Anatolia. The prospect of an alliance between the Bolsheviks and Turks spread alarm throughout Whitehall, and a formidable array of policy-makers urged Lloyd George to seek a new settlement. In February and March 1921 representatives of the Greeks, the sultan, and the Turkish nationalists met in London, but without result. The French premier, Aristide Briand, used the opportunity to negotiate a separate agreement with the Nationalist foreign minister, evacuating Cilicia and rectifying the Syrian border in Turkey's favour in return for economic concessions. The Italians, too, agreed to abandon their claim on the Turkish mainland and to withdraw their forces from Adalia in exchange for Turkish recognition of their right to Tripoli, the Dodecanese islands, and Rhodes. The British now remained the sole great-power defenders of Sèvres. The Greeks were already planning a new offensive. While Lloyd George could not offer concrete assistance, he encouraged the Constantine government to launch its campaign in March 1921, which developed into a major push against Ankara. The Greek army was only 50 kilometres from the Turkish capital when it was stopped in September at the Sakarya river. The twenty-two-day battle left both sides exhausted, but a Kemalist counter-offensive on 8 October forced the Greeks to retreat. It was the final turning point in the Turco-Greek War.

Kemal again proved to be an astute statesman with a sharp Bismarckian sense of the possible. The French still had 80,000 men at risk in Cilicia. Henry Franklin-Bouillon, a strong Turcophile politician whom the British thoroughly disliked, negotiated a new settlement

(20 October 1921) recognizing the Ankara government and withdrawing French forces from Cilicia in return for Turkish recognition of the Syrian mandate and economic concessions. This French 'betrayal' (picked up by British intelligence) infuriated Lord Curzon, the British foreign secretary. Despite his own doubts about Lloyd George's Greek policies, this example of French perfidy confirmed Curzon's view of the faithless Briand. Worse was to follow when Briand fell from power and was replaced by the already detested Raymond Poincaré in January 1922. Realizing that disaster could be postponed but not avoided, Curzon sought the impossible, a negotiated settlement that would involve a Greek retreat but not a surrender to Mustapha Kemal. His attempts at Allied mediation found little sympathy from Poincaré. The latter warned Curzon that his peace proposals were unlikely to be accepted by the nationalists, whom the French refused to coerce. In what proved to be one of the last concerted attempts at Allied mediation, the British, French, and Italian foreign ministers met in Paris on 22 March 1922 and hammered out a compromise, following Curzon's draft proposals. There was to be an armistice; Turkey would receive Constantinople and Anatolia but lose half of its European territories, including Adrianople, to Greece. Most of Thrace and the Asiatic shores of the Dardanelles would be demilitarized, and a small Allied garrison would stay on the Gallipoli peninsula to maintain the 'freedom of the Straits'. The Turks insisted that the evacuation of the Greek forces from Asia Minor should coincide with the ending of hostilities, a condition that the Allies refused to accept. Disputes between the Allies blocked any further progress towards a mediated settlement during the summer months.

The prospects for success were not improved by Lloyd George's continued support for Greece, despite the opposition of almost all of his colleagues, who refused to sanction giving any material assistance to Athens. In a desperate bid for military victory, the Greeks moved two divisions from Anatolia to Thrace with the intention of attacking Constantinople. The Allied governments quickly acted to block the move. In this context Lloyd George's parliamentary speech on 5 August, eulogizing the Greeks and castigating the Turks, sent out all the wrong signals. In Ankara the decision was taken to launch a new offensive on 26 August 1922. This proved to be the final campaign of the war. The Nationalists forced the depleted Greek army out of Smyrna and the rest of Anatolia and advanced into Thrace. Terrible atrocities were committed by both sides, as the Greek armies, accompanied by thousands of Greek civilians who had lived in the Anatolian towns, were forced back to the sea. After occupying Smyrna on 9 September, Kemal allowed most of the Greeks to leave provided that they were evacuated by the beginning of October. These events left permanent scars on the historical memories of both Greeks and Turks that are still unhealed today. The Armenians of Smyrna had nowhere to go, and the entire Armenian quarter, with 300,000 people, was put to the torch.

The Greek defeat undermined Britain's policies. The latter had hoped for an indefinite stalemate in Anatolia that would have provided an opportunity to broker a modest revision of the terms of the Treaty of Sèvres in keeping with Britain's interests. A section of the cabinet feared that the victorious Nationalist armies would threaten the Straits and try to cross into Europe to seize Constantinople (Istanbul). This was the prelude to the Chanak crisis when Britain came close to a war which it would have fought alone and which might have involved a conflict with the Soviet Union. Due to the pioneering work of the Canadian historian, John Ferris, who has reconstructed the intelligence background to the Chanak crisis, far more is now known about its development. Ferris shows how and why differences developed between the policy-makers in London (Lloyd George and a small group of ministers including Curzon, Churchill, Birkenhead, and Austen Chamberlain) and those in Constantinople (General Sir Charles Hartington, commander-in-chief of the occupation forces, Sir Horace Rumbold, the British high commissioner, and Sir Osmond Brock, commander-in-chief of the Mediterranean fleet). Each group had access to multiple but different sources of intelligence which played a critical part in their respective decision-making.[11] It was General Hartington, backed by his own intelligence structure, who became 'the architect' of the 'high risk strategy of bluff and deterrence' which the British followed at Chanak.[12]

The British authorities in London and Istanbul were slow to appreciate the scale of the Turkish victory and the dangers it posed to Britain's position at the Straits. It was not until mid-September that the seriousness of the military situation was recognized. There were difficulties, despite the excellent intelligence reaching London from a variety of sources, in estimating Turkish military strength in Anatolia and the number of Turkish troops that could be deployed near the Dardenelles and the Bosporus. It was even more difficult to judge how many forces the Turks could muster against Chanak or Constantinople, the two most

---

[11] My abbreviated account is drawn largely from John Ferris's material, which updates previous treatments of the Chanak crisis: John R. Ferris, ' "Far Too Dangerous a Gamble"? British Intelligence and Policy during the Chanak Crisis, September–October 1922', in Erik Goldstein and B. J. C. McKercher, *Power and Stability: British Foreign Policy, 1865–1965* (London and Portland, Oreg., 2003); ' "Between Military and Political" British Power and Diplomacy From the Chanak Crisis to the Lausanne Conference, 1922', *Proceedings of the Joint Turkish–Israeli Military History Conference* (Istanbul, 2000). I am most grateful to Dr Ferris for copies of early drafts of these and other as yet unpublished articles.

[12] Ferris, 'Far Too Dangerous a Gamble?', 152.

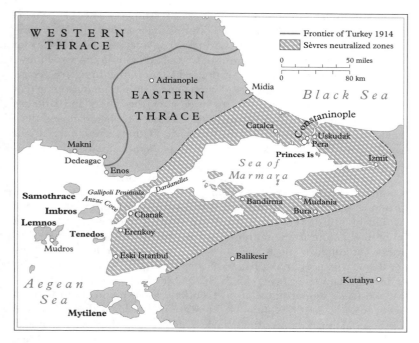

Map 6. The Chanak Crisis

obvious flashpoints, where the Allies had only small forces. The British thought it essential to maintain the existing positions in Constantinople, Chanak, the Ismid peninsula, and Gallipoli if they were to negotiate with Kemal from a position of strength. They did not, however, have the forces necessary for their defence. The Greek army in Thrace was of uncertain value; the French and Italians, according to intelligence reports, already had concluded private deals with Kemal. On 10 September the War Office decided that the Allies could not withstand a Turkish attack and wanted to recall all the British forces to Gallipoli. Ministers agreed that British troops should be evacuated from Chanak and the Ismid peninsula, both located in the neutral zone on the Asiatic side of the Straits. General Hartington rejected this advice. He was convinced that if the British acted boldly, united the Allies, and committed men and prestige to Chanak, the Turks would be deterred from launching an attack. Even weak forces at Chanak and Ismid would provide the coverage needed, along with offers of concessions, to bring the Nationalists to the bargaining table. If Chanak was attacked in strength, Hartington intended to withdraw his forces to Gallipoli. In

Constantinople, citing secret intelligence, Hartington was able to convince the French and Italian high commissioners to have their governments send reinforcements to Chanak. The success of his policy of deterrence depended on a demonstration of Allied unity in which few, not even Hartington, and least of all Lord Curzon, the foreign secretary, believed. Yet Curzon went along with Hartington's strategy, hoping that by following a resolute policy towards both the Turks and Britain's undependable allies, Turkey would be convinced to negotiate and Britain left in a position to control the peace negotiations, though this might mean conceding the Turkish demands in the National Covenant.

The stakes were high, and became even higher during the course of the month. In a flamboyant manifesto, which horrified Lord Curzon, Churchill, a constant critic of Lloyd George's Greek policies, and a small group of other ministers insisted that a Turkish incursion into Europe would nullify the effects of the Great War. Their call to action was published before the Dominions had deciphered the cabinet appeal to them for support. With the exception of Newfoundland and New Zealand, which offered a battalion, the Dominion response was cool. The Canadians sent a firm refusal. None of the Balkan countries solicited for assistance would move against Turkey. Even before Lord Curzon went to Paris on 19 September, Poincaré had ordered the withdrawal of the French troops sent to Chanak. Curzon's meetings with Poincaré and Count Sforza were heated in the extreme. Poincaré explained that the French and Italians had overruled the 'dangerous offers' of their high commissioners at Constantinople and would withdraw their forces from the Asiatic side of the Straits. On the 22nd, Curzon accused France of 'abandonment' and 'desertion'; Poincaré lost his temper and poured out 'torrents of abuse' at the foreign secretary, who collapsed in a nearby room. The meeting was one of the nadir points in Anglo-French relations and coloured relations long after the Chanak crisis was over. Nonetheless, despite the acrimony the three foreign ministers agreed to invite Kemal to attend a conference to negotiate a new treaty. They promised to favourably view Turkish claims to Thrace and to eventually restore Constantinople to Turkey. In return, the Turks were to keep out of the zones designated as neutral and promise not to cross the Straits. On the 23rd, the day the invitation went to Kemal, 1,000 Turks entered the neutral zone south of Chanak with orders not to open fire.

The British already knew from their intelligence sources before the Paris meetings that neither France nor Italy would oppose the Anatolian offensive and that the French had promised aid for the attack. They knew, too, that Italy would follow France and that both would pursue anti-British policies in return for commercial concessions. Such information obviously enraged the British and explains Curzon's accusations of treachery at his Paris meeting with Poincaré. While having ample confirmation of their allies' dealings with the Nationalists, the British also knew from intercepts and agents that neither France nor Italy wanted to see the crisis escalate, and that both were strongly advising the Turks not to attack Britain but to wait for the conference where Britain would have to meet their basic demands. There was also admittedly contradictory intelligence from Turkish and Soviet sources indicating that the two states had a military agreement and that the Soviets had pledged naval assistance, particularly submarines, to Ankara for their war with the Greeks. Viewed against their generally negative view of Soviet intentions, the British concluded that that in any Anglo-Turkish war the USSR would attack British ships. On 18 September ministers decided that if any Soviet warship or submarine approached British ships during the crisis it should be destroyed. In case of war with Turkey, Britain would take action against Russian ships in the Baltic and Black seas. It was at the time of the Chanak crisis, that SIS (the Secret Intelligence Service), which had been moving slowly from reporting that Turkey was a Soviet pawn to suggesting that the two countries were drifting apart, crossed the interpretive divide, but ministers in London were still reacting to the earlier assessments. In the face of confusing intelligence, the British prepared for the worst.

Betweeen 20 and 27 September the British authorities realized that they were facing a major crisis that could well result in war. Britain's allies were supporting the Kemalists; intelligence sources indicated that Kemal was preparing to attack; and reports reaching London and Constantinople provided proof that the Bolsheviks were pushing Turkey to go to war. Many in London believed that a Turkish ultimatum or war was imminent. The British were prepared to make a stand at Chanak, where their troops would fight alone. It was here that Britain had to demonstrate its resolve if it were not to suffer a devastating loss of face throughout the Middle Eastern and Indian empire. The British did not want war with Turkey, but they would not step back. The Turks, too, wished to avoid a conflict, particularly as they had already been promised much of Thrace, but equally they feared the loss of prestige that withdrawal from the neutral zone would entail. British military weaknesss undoubtedly made Chanak a tempting target, and British threats of war might be bluff. With prestige engaged on both sides, there was only a thin line between war and peace.

There were two groups, the Foreign Office in London and the decision-makers in Constantinople, who did not believe that the Nationalists would attack Chanak. Lord Curzon, despite his bitter encounter with Poincaré, was convinced that the French would deter the Kemalists from launching an attack. The Foreign Office interpreted

the incoming intelligence as favourable to peace. As he did not antici-
pate Turkish action, Curzon was prepared to wait out the war of nerves
until the right moment before granting the Turkish request for a
meeting. In Constantinople Hartington was playing a highly complicated game which he never fully explained to his superiors. He thought
that war could be avoided, but if it came he was convinced that he could
hold Chanak and withdraw his other forces to safety. His chief aim was
to convince Kemal that Britain was not bluffing and would resort to war
unless the Nationalists withdrew their troops. At the same time he
sought to reassure them that they would achieve their objectives
through negotiation. On 24, 27, and 28 September Hartington told
his troops to be ready to open fire (which he was prepared to do). He
repeated his threat later, when the Mudania conference appeared on the
brink of breakdown. Though it proved successful, his was a highly
dangerous game.

What is now clear is that Hartington and his associates were making
the essential political decisions and that their warnings that force might
have to be used unnerved and misled their superiors in London. Hartington was the man on the spot; his intelligence was accurate and
focused on the immediate situation, which he considered less immediately dangerous than London was led to believe. Though the generals
and politicians in London were serviced by a number of intelligence
sources covering a much broader range of issues, some of the information was inaccurate and confusing and was read within the context of an
anticipated Kemalist attack. There were ministerial differences over
interpretation and political and personal disputes. Though they tried
to micromanage the Chanak affair, the distance and the time-lag in
communications between London and Constantinople put them at a
disadvantage. Hartington, admittedly under extreme pressure, failed to
keep his superiors fully informed about the nature of his policies and
actions. This failure led to the confusion of 28–9 September, when
London, reacting to Hartington's telegrams over the previous two days,
thought that the general believed that Chanak was in immediate danger
and wanted permission to open hostilities. Hartington was instructed to
tell the Turks that unless they withdraw at once from the neutral zone
around Chanak, his forces would open fire. Hartington did not fear an
imminent attack and was prepared to wait and see if threats of force
would permit the opening of negotiations. He wanted permission to
shoot in order to maintain the peace, but only if it was absolutely
necessary. Lord Curzon, after a meeting with the Turkish representative
in London, Mustapha Reschid, during which the latter agreed to warn
Kemal by wireless to dissociate himself from any 'regretable collision' in
order to avoid giving the British grounds for a declaration of war,

proposed waiting another twenty-four hours before dispatching the ultimatum, but ministers stuck to their original decision. Before Reschid's message had reached Kemal, Hartington, after consultions with Sir Horace Rumbold, had decided not to issue the ultimatum which would have started the war that he hoped to avoid. His decision on 29 September was based on intelligence not yet available to London, and to his own appreciation of the improved prospects for peace. His next step was to warn Kemal's agent in Constantinople, with whom he was in daily contact, that the Turks must commit themselves immediately to armistice talks or face war. On 1 October Mustapha Kemal agreed to open negotiations at Mudania and ordered the cessation of all troop movements. The Chanak crisis was over.

Under the armistice terms negotiated on 11 October the Turks received virtually all that they wanted, without firing a shot. They would have to wait until a formal peace treaty was negotiated to secure their gains. The British outlined the terms of the armistice and convinced Poincaré to support them. The Greeks were to leave eastern Thrace within fifteen days; within thirty days a Turkish civil administration would be installed. An inter-Allied mission would supervise affairs in the interim. The Turks would promise not to move troops into Constantinople, Gallipoli, or Ismid until a peace conference determined their fate. In the aftermath of the rout of the Greek armies in September, a military junta seized power in Greece and forced King Constantine to abdicate. Lloyd George, weakened by the debacle that had brought Britain so close to an unnecessary war, resigned after an adverse vote of the Conservative bloc in the Coalition government at the Carlton Club on 19 October 1922. On 1 November 1922 the Turkish national parliament voted to abolish the Sultanate. The Allied invitation to the Turkish Nationalists to attend a peace conference may well have sealed the Sultanate's fate as the Ottoman grand vizier suggested sending a joint delegation to negotiate the peace. Kemal was not interested. Mohamet VI, the last sultan of a dynasty which dated back to the thirteenth century, left Turkey on 17 November 1922 on a British warship.

Britain almost went to war over Chanak. No government was to take a similar risk until September 1938. It was a dangerous gamble. Due to General Hartington's last-minute action the peace was preserved, but he carried much of the responsibility for the crisis. If the stand at Chanak restored British prestige, Kemal's victory over Greece determined the outcome of the peace negotiations. British hopes to dominate the Aegean had to be abandoned. That this check to their ambitions should come at the hands of the Turks was doubly damaging. Alan Leeper, a Foreign Office official and member of the British delegation at

Lausanne, complained: 'The Turks are so completely unsatisfactory to negotiate with, that I am not hopeful about the result. It is a terrible tragedy that, owing to French treachery, we have to allow them back into Europe at all.'[13] The peace had still to be negotiated; and the final stages of the negotiations coincided with the Anglo-French clash over German reparations. If, for the British, the Turkish settlement was of paramount importance, for the French it was a secondary matter.

There were two conferences at Lausanne, the first extending from 20 November 1922 until 4 February 1923, and the second from 23 April to 24 July 1923, when the Treaty of Lausanne was signed. The proceedings were dominated by Lord George Nathaniel Curzon, ex-viceroy of India and the very embodiment of the old pre-war diplomat. The Middle East was the stage on which he was most at home and where his knowledge and diplomatic skills could be fully utilized. If Curzon can be blamed for some of the decisions that led to the disasters in the Near East, in the difficult bargaining with Ismet Pasha, the head of the Turkish delegation, the foreign secretary secured for Britain the substance of her requirements without turning Turkey into a permanent enemy or a revisionist power. On the Turkish side, Mustapha Kemal had achieved a Greek withdrawal without fighting Britain. Kemal's realism and restraint and Ismet's adroitness and obstinacy paid high dividends. The Turkish leader made no effort to regain the non-Turkish territories of the old Ottoman empire. He sought and won recognition of an independent and defensible state, freed from most of the vestiges of great-power control and without incurring obligations to any other foreign nation, west or east.

The terms of the National Covenant were fulfilled. Allied plans for partitioning Anatolia were permanently frustrated. Turkey regained eastern Thrace, Adrianople (Edirne) was confirmed as a Turkish possession, as was Smyrna (Izmir) and some of the Aegean islands. Constantinople and Gallipoli were to remain in Turkish hands. The Turks were relieved of all reparations, and the hated capitulations, the special legal privileges enjoyed by westerners, were abolished. No guarantees were given to the international bondholders of the Ottoman public debt. With regard to the minority clauses incorporated in the treaty, Curzon's unchanged view of the Turks as oppressive rulers clashed with the demand of the nationalists for complete sovereignty, with no opportunities provided for foreign interference on humanitarian grounds. The clauses were weaker than Curzon wanted, but, contrary to his expectations, the treatment of the minorities within Turkey's

[13] A. W. A. Leeper to his father, 14 Nov. 1922, quoted in Erik Goldstein, 'The British Offical Mind and the Lausanne Conference, 1922–23', in Goldstein and McKercher, *Power and Stability*, 192.

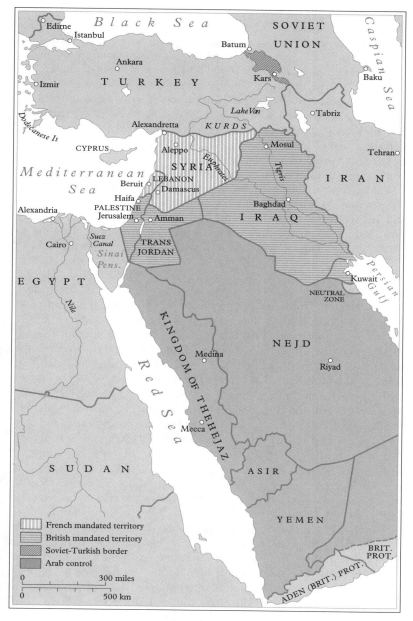

Map 7. Turkish Peace Settlement, 1923

boundaries compared favourably with that of the successor states in Europe. Less satisfactory was the Turco-Greek settlement providing for an obligatory exchange of populations based on religious affiliation. Some 1.3 million adherents of the Orthodox faith would be expelled from Turkey, while nearly 800,000 Muslims were settled there. The absorption of the displaced Greeks, many of whom were not Greek-speakers, almost drove Greece to bankruptcy. Appeals for loans from the League of Nations went unheeded, and it was the Red Cross, particularly its American Committee, which organized relief relying on voluntary contributions. Over the oil-rich vilayet of Mosul, strategically and economically so important to the British, Curzon resisted pressure to seek a compromise both from Ismet and from the new prime minister, Andrew Bonar Law, who, faced with the French occupation of the Ruhr, could ill afford a new crisis in the Middle East. Despite every sign that the French and Italians were supporting Turkish resistance, the foreign secretary prevailed and won acceptance for his proposal to submit the issue to the League of Nations, which indeed in 1925 awarded Mosul to Iraq.

Turkey retained full sovereignty over the Straits, which were to be demilitarized. This was the main area of concern for the British, for it revived the age-old contest with the Russians in the eastern Mediterranean. The Russians had forced acceptance of their participation at Lausanne, though they were allowed only to contribute to the discussions on the status of the Straits. Posing as the defenders of Turkish sovereignty, the Bolsheviks demanded that the question of passage through the Straits should be left to the states bordering the Black Sea. Kemal was far too shrewd to barter away the possibility of reconciliation with Britain for the embrace of the Bolshevik bear. Ismet walked warily between Curzon and Georgy Chicherin, the chief Russian delegate. He finally accepted the British position in order to avoid undue dependence on Moscow and Russian domination of the Black Sea. It was agreed that, in peacetime, the Straits were to be open to all ships. In wartime, if Turkey was neutral, there was to be complete freedom of passage; if it was a belligerent, only neutral ships would be allowed passage. Despite strong Russian objections, demilitarized zones were created on both the European and Asiatic shores of the Straits under an international commission head by a Turkish president. The Straits Convention, signed in Rome on 14 August 1923, was the first multilateral treaty signed by the Soviet government. Ismet's overall success at Lausanne gave Kemal the thrust he needed to complete his revolution at home. On 6 October 1923 Turkish forces reoccupied Constantinople (Istanbul), following a hasty evacuation by the Allies. At the end of October the Grand National Assembly formally declared Turkey a republic. The Treaty of Lausanne, the last of the peace treaties, proved to be the most successful and durable of all the post-war settlements. It was modified only once, and then peacefully, at Montreux in July 1936.

IX

The very severity of the peace settlements with Austria, Hungary, and Bulgaria contributed to their duration. The victor powers in the region were not only strengthened in terms of population and territory, but the weaker states were deprived of the means of revision. The local allies of the western powers, in fear of their wartime opponents (often their former imperial masters), insisted on the strict enforcement of the military and financial terms of the treaties. The harshness of the financial clauses were such that the vanquished states could not fulfil them. The experts correctly predicted that the victors would have to waive or defer payment and even to provide assistance before they could expect reparations or debt repayments. The relief that came was mainly due to British-inspired League action through its financial committee and international financial loans. Such assistance was often rendered in the face of opposition from the smaller victor states.

The peacemakers did not have a free hand in east-central Europe. Much had been settled before the treaties were concluded and signed. Many of the borders resulted from military actions over which the Allies had no control. Where the Allied officials were responsible for the new frontiers, the principles of self-determination were but one factor in their efforts to create enduring and defensible states. The post-war governments in the region had to tackle the problems of new territories, new boundaries, and the absorption of the ethnic minorities from the defeated states. They all faced high inflation and the disruption of traditional trade, as new frontiers meant new customs barriers. Traditional national enmities persisted along with the new ones created by the peace treaties. Many of the states in the region were forced to sign minority treaties, but the League system was weak and yet to be tested. The treaties were deeply resented by those who were required to accept them. The subsequent interventions of the western powers, particularly France and Britain, described in a later chapter, were intermittent, competitive, and divisive but rarely decisive in determining the internal ordering of the new states. France became the dominant diplomatic player; after an initial burst of activity, the British withdrew from east European affairs. Neither Germany nor Soviet Russia challenged the settlements; the former had neither the determination nor the means, and the latter, in the throes of civil wars, had far more pressing priorities. The three treaty settlements had a surprisingly long life. Not only did they survive intact until Hitler's first successful assault in 1938, but the states lasted, in most of their essentials, beyond 1945 despite war, conquest, occupation, and Soviet domination.

Central Europe and the Balkans were left in a fragmented condition. This was the heritage of the disappearance of the dynastic empires, but also the consequence of past histories. The settlements undoubtedly discouraged regional consolidation, though this was not the Allied intention. British and French hopes for economic federation proved illusory. The heightened sense of nationality and the divisions between winners and losers discouraged integration, even of the most modest scope. There was no practical alternative to the creation of the new states, once the leaders of the subject nationalities seized the initiative. The Allied victors could only endorse what had been accomplished and modify borders. Tomáš Masaryk's vision of a union of small nations extending from the North Cape to Cape Matapan, or the Hungarian democrat and exile Oskar Jászi's dream of a Danubian federation covering the territories of the old Dual Monarchy but extended to include the rest of Poland and Romania, were concepts that had no real historical, ideological, or even economic basis. Even the descriptive geographic terms commonly used by historians to group these nations together have provoked debate. The history of all the countries in eastern Europe remained that of individual states.

X

The Turkish settlement had been shaped almost entirely by the old adage 'to the victors go the spoils'. Both in Britain and in France the Great War brought a revival of imperial enthusiasm, and the Treaty of Sèvres represented an old-fashioned imperial feast for the British with a good meal for France. Despite subsequent disturbances and revolts, the two nations held on to what they had taken. Fundamentally, the British did not have the troops needed to implement the Sèvres treaty in Turkey itself and Lloyd George's decision to use the Greeks as a surrogate power proved disastrous for both parties. The crisis at Chanak, which could well have produced a military confrontation between London and Ankara, not only contributed to Lloyd George's downfall but soured British relations with France in Europe.

The possession of empire made powers great. The divison of the Turkish spoils brought the British and French empires to their peak. It was a source of British influence in Europe; it gave weight to French claims to great-power status. From the beginning these powers treated the new mandates as colonies. Leaders and boundaries were imposed arbitrarily, with scant attention to the wishes of the local inhabitants. Even in the short term, however, these acquisitions were a mixed blessing. Both mandatory powers faced unrest that required military intervention and unwanted expenditure. In 1920 and 1922 there were anti-British riots in Palestine and Iraq. In the latter case the British found that aerial bombing of turbulent tribes was much cheaper than sending military expeditions. French troubles in Syria continued long after Faisal was exiled. A rebellion among the Druse, a breakaway Islamic sect, in 1925 was joined by nationalists in Damascus and spread through much of Syria and Lebanon. Superior military strength and a policy of conciliation brought the revolt to an end in late 1926, but the French failed to establish a solid regime in the mandate. The quarrels over Syria left a lasting stain on the Anglo-French relations. The French accused the British of going back on the Sykes–Picot agreement; the British saw the Franklin-Bouillon agreement and the withdrawal of troops from Chanak as examples of French disloyalty. These conflicts poisoned relations between London and Paris long beyond their expiry dates.

Turkey was the success story of the Near East. A secular and modernizing state based on the national principle, it became, apart from the problem of its Kurdish minority, a force for regional stability. Much of the Nationalists' success was due to Kemal's military prowess and to his realism and diplomatic cunning. He eschewed both Pan-Islamic and Pan-Turkish movements, and fought only for what was practicable at the conference at Lausanne. Although he showed no tolerance towards his domestic communists, he cultivated the Soviet Union, which remained a relatively peaceful and benign neighbour. The peace treaty of 1922 with Turkey was considered one of the major achievements of the young Soviet regime.

The revision of the punitive peace of Sèvres and the rise of Arab and Zionist nationalism underlined the changing relationship between the European powers and the peoples they had long considered weak and backward. If the Treaty of Sèvres highlighted the continuity of pre-1914 attitudes, Turkey's successful revision of its terms and the continued simmering of both Zionists and Arab nationalism pointed to a new world in the making.

The Treaties of St-Germain, Neuilly, and Trianon*

Books

ÁDÁM, MAGDA, *The Little Entente and Europe, 1920–1929*, trans. Mátyás Esterházy (Budapest, 1993).

*Also refer to the select Bibliography for Chapter 1, as there is considerable overlap in these two chapters.

ALMOND, NINA and LUTZ, RALPH (eds.), *The Treaty of St Germain* (Stanford, Cal. and London, 1935).

BRUBAKER, ROGER, *Nationalism Reframed: Nationalism and the National Question in the New Europe* (Cambridge, 1996).

CRAMPTON, R. J., *A Concise History of Bulgaria* (Cambridge, 1997).

DEÁK, FRANCIS, *Hungary at the Paris Peace Conference: The Diplomatic History of the Treaty of Trianon* (New York, 1942).

HANAK, PETER and FRANK, TIBOR (eds.), *A History of Hungary* (Bloomington, Ind., 1990).

JELAVICH, BARBARA, *History of the Balkans*, vol. 2 (Cambridge, 1983).

JELAVICH, CHARLES and BARBARA, *The Establishment of the Balkan National States, 1804–1920* (Seattle and London, 1977).

KIRÁLY, BÉLA, PASTOR, PETER, and SANDERS, IVAN (eds.), *War and Society in East Central Europe* (Cambridge, 1996), Vol. 6: *Essays on World War I: Total War and Peacemaking, a Case Study on Trianon* (New York, 1982). Esp. the chapters by Thomas C. Sakmyster and Hugh Seton-Watson.

KLEMPERER, KLEMENS VON, *Ignaz Seipel: Christian Statesman in a Time of Crisis* (Princeton, 1972).

KONTLER, LÁSZLÓ, *Millennium in Central Europe: A History of Hungary* (Budapest, 1999).

LAMPE, JOHN R., *Yugoslavia As History: Twice There Was a Country* (Cambridge, 1996).

LEDERER, IVO J., *Yugoslavia at the Paris Peace Conference: A Study in Frontiermaking* (New Haven, Conn., 1963).

LOW, ALFRED D., *The Anschluss Movement, 1918–19 and the Paris Peace Conference* (Philadelphia, 1974).

MACARTNEY, C. A., *Hungary and Her Successors: The Treaty of Trianon and its Consequences, 1919–1937* (London, 1937; rev. edn. 1965).

—— *National States and National Minorities* (London, 1934; rev. edn. New York, 1968).

SETON-WATSON, HUGH and CHRISTOPHER, *The Making of a New Europe: R. W. Seton-Watson and the Last Years of Austria-Hungary* (London, 1981).

SPECTOR, SHERMAN D., *Rumania at the Paris Peace Conference: A Study of the Diplomacy of Ioan C. Bratianu* (New York, 1962).

SUPPAN, ARNOLD, *Yugoslavien und Österreich 1918–1938; Bilaterale Aussenpolitik im europäischen Umfeld* (Munich, 1996).

TOWLE, PHILIP, *Enforced Disarmament: From the Napolionic Campaigns to the Gulf War* (Oxford 1997), chapter 5.

Articles

FELLNER, FRITZ, 'Der Vertrag von St. Germain', in E. Weinzierl and K. Skalnik (eds.), *Österreich 1918–1939*, Bd. 1 (Vienna, 1983).

PIETRI, NICOLE, 'L' Autriche, 1918–1925; une stabilisation précaire', in C. Carlier and G.-H. Soutou (eds.), *1918–1925: Comment faire la paix?* (Paris, 2001).

The Treaties of Sèvres and Lausanne

Books

AHMAD, FEROZ, *The Making of Modern Turkey* (London and New York, 1993).

ANDREW, CHRISTOPHER M. and KANYA-FORSTNER, ALEXANDER S., *France Overseas: The Great War and the Climax of French Imperial Expansion* (London, 1981).

BENNETT, G. H., *British Foreign Policy During the Curzon Period, 1919–1924* (New York and Basingstoke, 1995).

BULLARD, READER WILLIAM, Sir, *Britain and the Middle East from Earliest Times to 1963* (London, 1964).

BUSCH, BRITON COOPER, *Britain, India and the Arabs, 1914–1921* (Berkeley, Cal., 1971)

—— *Mudros to Lausanne: Britain's Frontier in West Asia, 1918–1923* (Albany, NY, 1976).

COHEN, MICHAEL J., *The Origins and Evolution of the Arab–Zionist Conflict* (Berkeley, Cal., 1987).

CRISS, NUR BILGE, *Istanbul Under Allied Occupation, 1918–1923* (London, 1999).

DANN, URIEL (ed.), *The Great Powers in the Middle East, 1919–1939* (New York, 1988). Esp. chapters by Christopher M. Andrew, Haggai Erlich, and Claudio G. Segrè.

DARWIN, JOHN GARETH, *Britain, Egypt and the Middle East: Imperial Policy in the Aftermath of War 1918–1922* (London, 1981).

DONTAS, DOMNA, *Greece and Turkey: The Regime of the Straits, Lemnos and Samothrace* (Athens, 1987).

DUMONT, PAUL and BACQUÉ-GRAMMONT, JEAN-LOUIS, *La Turquie et la France a l'epoque d'Ataturk* (Paris, 1981).

EVANS, L., *United States Policy and the Partition of Turkey, 1914–1924* (Baltimore, Md., 1965).

EVANS, STEPHEN F., *The Slow Rapprochement: Britain and Turkey in the Age of Kemal Atatürk* (Beverly, 1982).

FISHER, JOHN, *Curzon and British Imperialism in the Middle East, 1915–1919* (London, 1999)

FRIEDMAN, ISAIAH, *The Question of Palestine, 1914–1918: British–Jewish–Arab Relations* (New York, 1973).

—— *Palestine: A Twice-promised Land? The British, the Arabs and Zionism, 1915–1920* (New Brunswick, NJ, 2000).

FROMKIN, DAVID, *A Peace To End All Peace: Creating the Modern Middle East, 1914–1922* (London, 1989).

GÖKAY, BÜLENT, *A Clash of Empires: Turkey Between Russian Bolshevism and British Imperialism, 1918–1923* (London, 1997).

HALE, WILLIAM M., *Turkish Foreign Policy, 1774–2000* (London, 2000).

KAPUR, H., *Soviet Russia and Asia, 1917–1927: A Study of Soviet Policy Towards Turkey, Iran and Afghanistan* (London, 1966).

KAZANCIGIL, ALI and OZBUDUN, ERGUN (eds.), *Ataturk: Founder of a Modern State* (Hamden, Conn., 1991).

KEDOURIE, ELIE, *England and the Middle East: The Destruction of the Ottoman Empire, 1914–1921* (London, 1956).

—— *In the Anglo-Arab Labyrinth: The McMahon–Husayn Correspondence and its Interpretations, 1914–1939* (Cambridge, 1976).

KENT, MARIAN, *The Great Powers and the End of the Ottoman Empire* (London, 1984).

—— *Moguls and Mandarins: Oil, Imperialism, and the Middle East in British Foreign Policy, 1900–1940* (London, 1993).

LEWIS, B., *The Emergence of Modern Turkey* (London, 1961).

LEWIS, G., *Modern Turkey* (New York, 1974).

MACFIE, A. L., *The End of the Ottoman Empire, 1908–1923* (London, 1998).

MANGO, ANDREW, *Atatürk*, 2nd edn. (London, 2001; 1st edn. 1999).

MANSFIELD, PETER, *The Ottoman Empire and Its Successors* (London, 1973).

—— *A History of the Middle East* (London, 1991).

MONROE, ELIZABETH, *Britain's Moment in the Middle East, 1914–1971*, new and rev. edn. (London, 1981).

MORRIS, BENNY, *Righteous Victims: A History of the Zionist-Arab Conflict, 1881–1999* (New York, 1999).

NEVAKIVI, JUKKA, *Britain, France and the Arab Middle East 1914–1920* (London, 1969).

ORGA, I., *Phoenix Ascendant: The Rise of Modern Turkey* (London, 1958).

SACHER, HOWARD M., *Europe Leaves the Middle East* (London, 1972)

SANDERS, RONALD, *The High Walls of Jerusalem: A History of the Balfour Declaration and the Birth of the British Mandate for Palestine* (New York, 1984).

SHAW, S. and E. K., *History of the Ottoman Empire and Modern Turkey*, vol. 2 (Cambridge, 1976).

SHLAIM, AVI, *The Politics of Partition: King Abdullah, the Zionists and Palestine 1921–1951* (Oxford, 1990).

—— *War and Peace in the Middle East: A Concise History* (London, 1995).

SONYEL, S. R., *Turkish Diplomacy, 1918–1923: Mustafa Kemal and the Turkish National Movement* (London, 1975).

TIBAWI, ABDUL LATIF, *Anglo-Arab Relations and the Question of Palestine, 1914–1921* (London, 1977).

VITAL, DAVID, *Zionism: The Crucial Phase* (Oxford, 1987).

WALDER, D., *The Chanak Affair* (London, 1969).

YAPP, MALCOLM E., *The Making of the Modern Near East, 1792–1923* (London, 1988).

—— *The Near East Since the First World War* (London, 1991).

YERGIN, DANIEL, *The Prize: The Epic Quest for Oil, Money, and Power* (New York, 1991).

ZÜRCHER, ERIK J., *Turkey: A Modern History* (London, 1994).

Articles

AHMAD, FEROZ, 'Politics and Islam in Modern Turkey', *Middle Eastern Studies*, 27 (1991).

AKBABA, I., 'The Peace Treaty of Lausanne', *Revue Internationale d'Histoire Militaire*, 40 (1980).

DANILOV, VLADIMIR I., 'Kemalism and World Peace', in Ali Kazancigil and Ergun Ozbudun (eds.), *Ataturk; Founder of a Modern State* (Hamden, Conn., 1991).

DARWIN, J. G., 'The Chanak Crisis and the British Cabinet', *History*, 65 (1980).

DAVIDSON, R. H., 'Middle East Nationalism: Lausanne Thirty Years After', *Middle East Journal*, 7: 3 (1953).

DYER, G., 'The Turkish Armistice of 1918: 1. The Turkish Decision for a Separate Peace in Autumn, 1918', *Middle Eastern Studies*, 8 (1972).

——— 'The Turkish Armistice of 1918: 2. Lost Opportunity: The Negotiations of Moudros', *Middle Eastern Studies*, 8 (1972).

FERRIS, JOHN R., ' "Between Military and Political": British Power and Diplomacy from the Chanak Crisis to the Lausanne Conference, 1922', *Proceedings of the Joint Turkish–Israeli History Conference*, 1, Turkish Army General Staff, Istanbul (2000).

——— ' "Far Too Dangerous a Gamble"? British Intelligence and Policy during the Chanak Crisis, September–October 1922', *Diplomacy and Statecraft*, 14 (2003).

FRIEDMAN, ISAIAH, 'The McMahon–Hussain Correspondence', *Journal of Contemporary History*, 5 (1970).

GAWRYCH, G., 'Kemal Atatürk's Politico-Military Strategy in the Turkish War of Independence, 1919–1922: From Guerrilla Warfare to the Decisive Battle', *Journal of Strategic Studies*, 11: 3 (1988).

GÖKAY, BÜLENT, 'Historiography of the Post-War Turkish Settlement', *New Perspectives on Turkey*, 8: 3 (1992).

——— 'From Western Perceptions to Turkish Self-Perceptions', *Journal of Mediterranean Studies*, 5: 2 (1995).

——— 'Turkish Settlement and the Caucasus, 1918–20', *Middle Eastern Studies*, 32: 2 (1996).

GOLDSTEIN, ERIK, 'British Peace Aims and the Eastern Question: The Political Intelligence Department and the Eastern Committee, 1928', *Middle Eastern Studies*, 24: 4 (1987).

——— 'Great Britain and Greater Greece, 1917–1920', *Historical Journal*, 32: 2 (1989).

——— 'The Eastern Question: The Last Phase', in M. Dockrill and John Fisher (eds.), *The Paris Peace Conference, 1919: Peace Without Victory?* (Basingstoke, 2001).

HOVANNISIAN, R. G., 'Armenia and the Caucasus in the Genesis of the Soviet–Turkish Entente', *International Journal of Middle Eastern Studies*, 4: 2 (1973).

KENT, MARIAN, 'British Policy, International Diplomacy and the Turkish Revolution', *International Journal of Turkish Studies*, 3: 2 (1985/6).

KENT, MARIAN, 'Guarding the Bandwagon: Great Britain, Italy, and Middle Eastern Oil, 1920– 1923', in Edward Ingram (ed.), *National and International Politics in the Middle East: Essays in Honour of Elie Kedourie* (London, 1986).

MACFIE, A. L., 'The Chanak Affair (September–October, 1922)', *Balkan Studies*, 20: 2 (1979).

—— 'British Intelligence and the Causes of Unrest in Mesopotamia 1919–1921', *Middle Eastern Studies*, 35: 1 (1999).

3

The Missing Party: The Soviet Union and the Post-War Settlements

I

The great outcasts of the post-war world were the Bolsheviks, the new and still very much provisional rulers of the vast Russian state. None of the Allied powers welcomed their seizure of power on 7 November 1917. Fernand Grenard, a former French consul-general in Moscow, described the new regime as 'an unlimited despotism...more contrary to a peaceful and healthy organisation of Europe than Prussian despotism',[1] while Winston Churchill, the British secretary of state for war, could still proclaim two years later that:

all the harm and misery in Russia has arisen out of the wickedness and folly of the Bolsheviks, and...there will be no recovery of any kind in Russia or in eastern Europe while these wicked men, this vile group of cosmopolitan fanatics, hold the Russian nation by the hair of its head and tyrannizes over its great population. The policy I will always advocate is the overthrow and destruction of that criminal regime.[2]

Though by 1923 the renamed 'Union of Soviet Socialist Republics' would be an established, if hardly accepted, member of the international community, it had been an open question in the years following the revolution whether the new regime would survive. A draconian peace settlement with Germany in the Treaty of Brest-Litovsk in March 1918 was followed by civil wars against internal opponents and external enemies as the Bolsheviks retreated within the borders of Greater Russia. Yet the revolutionary government emerged victorious from the conflicts, and through the adoption of a more pragmatic foreign policy than the Bolshevik leaders had anticipated began to navigate in the capitalist waters without abandoning their ultimate goals. The failure of the immediate world revolution made it imperative to safeguard the

---

[1] Grenard, quoted in Richard K. Debo, *Survival and Consolidation: The Foreign Policy of Soviet Russia, 1918–1921* (Montreal and Kingston, 1992), 5.
[2] Churchill speech to the Oxford Union, 18 Nov. 1920, quoted in David Carlton, *Churchill and the Soviet Union* (Manchester, 2000), 26.

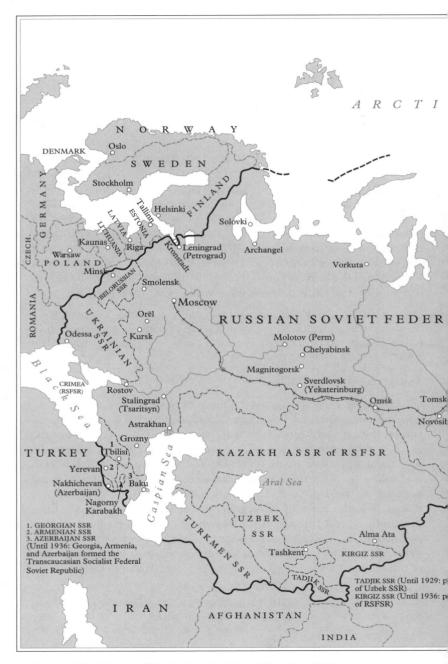

Map 8. The Union of Soviet Socialist Republics after 1922

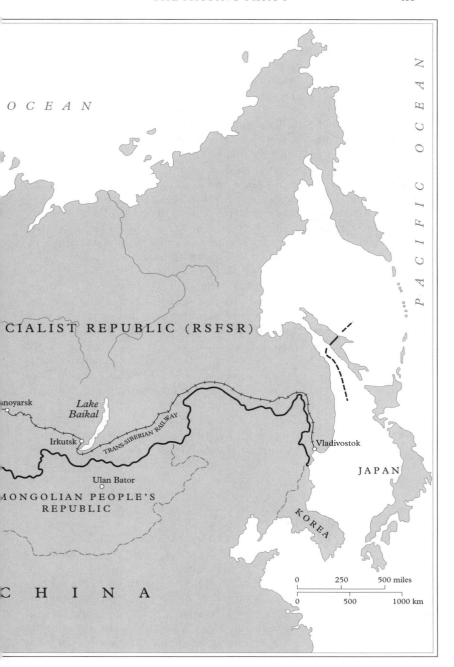

OCEAN

PACIFIC OCEAN

CIALIST REPUBLIC (RSFSR)

noyarsk

Lake Baikal

Irkutsk

TRANS-SIBERIAN RAILWAY

Vladivostok

Ulan Bator

MONGOLIAN PEOPLE'S REPUBLIC

JAPAN

KOREA

CHINA

| 0 | 250 | 500 miles |
| 0 | 500 | 1000 km |

revolution at home, first by concluding peace with Germany and later by opening diplomatic relations with the west and concluding trading agreements with the capitalist powers. The pursuit of revolutionary action and world revolution went hand in hand with the policies of compromise and accommodation. The twin strategies of 'revolution' and 'diplomacy' characterized Russian diplomacy throughout the 1920s. Under these conditions, there was little likelihood that the Bolsheviks would contribute to the stability of a post-war international regime that its leaders were pledged to destroy. Russian revisionism, both ideological and territorial, marked it as a 'rogue state' in the eyes of opponents, yet the predicted conflict between the Bolsheviks and the capitalist states failed to take place, and an uneasy truce, based on mutual suspicion and apprehension, was established and maintained.

Both for ideological and strategic reasons, it seemed far more likely that some form of conflict between the western allies and the infant Bolshevik state would occur. The analysis of international relations by the principal Bolshevik leader and master theoretician, Vladimir Ilyich Lenin, in *Imperialism, the Highest Stage of Capitalism* (1916), had placed at centre stage the struggle between the capitalist powers in the international arena during the last phase of capitalist evolution. With the drying up of domestic investment opportunities, he argued, the most advanced capitalist countries would engage in a fierce global competition for labour, raw materials, and markets. Once the less developed areas of the world were divided and absorbed, the imperialist states would be forced to engage in a war of redistribution, seizing from each other the world resources, markets, and investments they required. The crisis of capitalist development would not be confined to the contradictions in domestic economies, as Karl Marx had predicted, but would result from imperialist rivalries that would eventually destroy the existing system. Lenin also altered Marx's focus of revolutionary action. Since monopoly capitalism would proceed at a different pace in each country, socialist revolutions would not start simultaneously in all states but would occur at different times in one or more separate countries. Socialists could seize power in less advanced countries, but the survival of the revolution would depend on the support of revolutionaries in the more advanced industrialized states. In the non-industrialized or semi-industrialized countries, Lenin argued that revolutionaries should appeal to the class interests of the peasants, and in colonial areas should ally with the nationalist opposition to the imperialists, however socially reactionary they might be. Lenin's pre-revolutionary theories on the international behaviour of the imperialist states in the last phase of finance capitalism played a key role in the party debates over foreign and economic policy in his lifetime. In his thinking, the

Russian revolution made sense only in terms of a general European upheaval, and its success lay in its ability to act as a catalyst for the 'world revolution'. Bolshevik Russia's survival depended on the rising of the peoples of Europe; if imperialism was not crushed, the capitalist powers would turn on the Bolshevik state. This was the meaning of Leon Trotsky's famous statement that 'I will issue a few revolutionary proclamations to the peoples of the world and then shut up shop', when he reluctantly accepted the position of commissar for foreign affairs in November 1917.[3] With the revolution, there would be no need for the institutions (Trotsky visited his new Commissariat only once) and tools of traditional diplomacy.

As no world revolution took place, the Bolsheviks were compelled in order to preserve the revolution, to turn to conventional diplomacy and to sign a pact with one of the capitalist-imperialist powers—a peace treaty with Germany. By the time Trotsky returned from Brest-Litovsk in February 1918 with the harsh German peace terms in hand, Lenin had reconsidered the situation. Though the anticipated world revolution would happen, it might not occur in the immediate future. It was necessary to win a respite for Russia, a 'breathing space' or 'peace break', by playing the capitalist states against each other even at the cost of accepting a peace which meant a betrayal of his ideological convictions. In the debate that followed, only a small minority of Bolsheviks supported Lenin. It was the German military leaders, with their renewal of offensive operations on 18 February, who put an effective end to Trotsky's 'no war, no peace' formula, and it was at Lenin's insistence that the Bolsheviks agreed to accept the ruthless German terms. The Treaty of Brest-Litovsk, signed on 3 March 1918, was a punitive peace. The Russians lost almost one-third of their population and their Ukrainian, Baltic, Finnish, and Polish territories. Lands in the Caucasus were given to the Ottoman Turks. In return, the Russians had won a 'breathing space' which in the absence of world revolution kept stretching out in time.

The breathing space was used to enlarge the Bolshevik party, restructure the state, and build a new 'Red Army'. Both party and state were highly centralized, with Lenin directing the executive political bureau ('Politburo') and the Council of People's Commissars, giving him great, though not unlimited, authority in the revolutionary regime. By the end of 1918 party and state were primarily concerned with the regime's defence. Germany's subsequent defeat by the Allied powers revived hopes that the international revolutionary moment was at hand. The waves of unrest in the lands of the collapsed Dual Monarchy and in

[3] Leon Trotsky, *My Life: An Attempt at an Autobiography* (New York, 1930), 341.

Germany after the armistice warranted such optimism. From Moscow, where the Bolsheviks had moved their capital from Petrograd (formerly St Petersburg) in March 1918, national communist parties were established, mainly recruited from ex-prisoners of war. In Germany, Lenin extended his links with the far left socialists and encouraged the formation of a German Communist party. The failure of the attempted far-left uprising in January 1919 incurred fiery ideological polemics from Lenin, who accused the German majority socialists of a betrayal of the working classes. 'Red' socialist forces supported local Bolsheviks in the Baltic (Estonia, Latvia, and Lithuania) and in the Ukraine, where short-lived Soviet ('workers') republics were created. On 2 March 1919 the 'Comintern' or Third International was founded to co-ordinate the worldwide socialist revolution, a hastily convened assembly (invitations went out on the wireless) of about thirty-five delegates in Moscow, consisting mainly of the Bolshevik leaders and foreign exiles. It was intended to pre-empt the re-establishment of the western European dominated Second International as the active centre of world socialism, and to lay the basis for a worldwide communist movement. German was the common language of the meeting. Delegates made clear their hostility to orthodox social democracy and to the traditional socialist parties. While the emphasis was on the revolution in Europe, the final declaration included an appeal to the 'colonial slaves of Africa and Asia'. Britain and its empire were the main targets; the British were seen as the leaders of the capitalist nations and in the forefront of the rivalry between them. Despite these revolutionary goals, Lenin's 'peace break', in the continuing absence of a successful revolution outside Russia, lengthened. The failure of the German revolutionary actions convinced Lenin that the Bolsheviks now had to consider a settlement with the Allies if the revolution in Russia was to be safeguarded. By the time the civil wars were over, the Bolshevik leader was speaking of 'a new and lengthy period of development'.[4]

II

Before any diplomatic engagement with the victorious imperialist powers could begin, it was necessary to fight for the very survival of the revolution in Russia. Local civil wars broke out in central Russia and in the borderlands of the Tsarist empire. As important were the military interventions by the Allies, begun before their triumph over the Central Powers. These inept incursions, originally intended to reconstitute an

---

[4] Jon Jacobson, *When the Soviet Union Entered World Politics* (Berkeley, Los Angeles, and London, 1994), 19.

eastern front and to protect Allied war materials already stockpiled in Russia, involved Allied military expeditions and the subsidizing of anti-Bolshevik Russian forces. They were sporadic, ill-planned, and poorly co-ordinated, but left a permanent mark on relations between the Bolshevik government and the capitalist states, compounding their ideological and practical divisions. The Allies did not expect the Bolshevik regime to survive but had to take notice of its success and authority over much of central Russia. Though they refused to recognize the new government, Allied representatives nonetheless opened unofficial talks in Petrograd in an effort to convince the Bolsheviks to stay in the war. The talks failed, and when the Treaty of Brest-Litovsk was concluded in March 1918, the pace of Allied activity in Russia was accelerated. The British and French had already agreed to a division of spheres of operation in December 1917, though this proved highly artificial and Allied rivalries in Russia aggravated the conflicts between contending forces in the field prepared to exploit the Anglo-French differences.

British military intervention began in Murmansk in March 1918 and in Archangel in the summer of 1918. Two further interventions took place during the last month of the war, both in Central Asia. The first began as a way of stopping the Turkish advance through Caucasia and ended, with the Turkish armistice, with British military control of the Caucasus and a military 'cordon' from the Black Sea to the Caspian. The second, on the eastern side of the Caspian, saw the British commander in Persia respond to an appeal from local anti-Bolsheviks who, with British assistance, took Merv. In December 1918 the French sent a mixed force of French, Greek, and Polish troops to the Black Sea port of Odessa to safeguard the area for the anti-Bolsheviks during the German withdrawal. The expedition became involved in an incredibly confused local situation, caught up in the fighting between five mutually hostile groups. Other groups became involved in the chaotic conflicts. In mid-May 1918, after a series of misunderstandings and changes of destination, the 'Czech Legion', formed from ex-prisoners of war who had defected from the Austro-Hungarian army, came into conflict with local Bolshevik forces as it moved eastwards along the Trans-Siberian railway towards Vladivostok. Unable to fight the Central Powers in Russia, as was intended, the Legion was trying to get out of Russia in order to reach France and join the battle there. The Legion, consisting of some 42,000 troops, strung out along the whole length of the Trans-Siberian railway from the Urals to Vladivostok, rapidly became the best-organized anti-Bolshevik force in this vast and turbulent region. While Clemenceau wanted the Czechs brought out of Russia to reinforce the Allied troops on the western front, the British nursed the far-fetched idea that the Czechs, supported by the Japanese, might open a new front in Siberia and relieve the German pressure on the Allied armies. The 'rescue' of the Czech Legion, which was well able to look after itself, provided the excuse for the Japanese and American interventions in Siberia. After Brest-Litovsk the Japanese, fearing the spread of Bolshevik influence east of the Urals, but mainly anxious to protect their recently established and profitable economic stake in eastern Siberia against both the Bolsheviks and Americans, endlessly debated the possibility of sending an expedition to the region. In July 1918 the American government, after considerable prodding from the Allied powers, reversed its policy of non-intervention and invited Japan to join in a limited expedition in Siberia. In August a massive landing of Japanese troops took place. Some 70,000 men were committed to eastern Siberia, instead of the small force which the Americans and the British anticipated. The Japanese mainly fought local partisans; they avoided direct confrontation with the Red Army and were only half-hearted allies of the White Russian armies in Siberia under Admiral Aleksandr Kolchak, the self-designated 'Supreme Ruler of Russia', who had established a 'White' government in Omsk.

President Wilson's very hesitant decision in the summer of 1918 to send troops both to Vladivostok and Archangel, though taken mainly in the interests of preserving Allied unity and for the humanitarian purpose of rescuing the Czech Legion, was also intended to constrain Japan. Wilson was understandably wary of American involvement in what, after Trotsky had reorganized the Red Army in the summer of 1918, was clearly an open civil war. All the pressures in Washington were for getting the troops home as soon as the Germans were beaten, and there was no popular support at all for the opening of a new military front in Russia.

With the defeat of the Central Powers the main *raison d'être* for the Allied expeditions had vanished, but the troops stationed on Russian soil became engaged in the many local wars being fought in all the border territories of the old Tsarist empire. There were a multitude of reasons, ideological, financial, and strategic, why the British and French, who lacked the resources to intervene effectively, continued their anti-Bolshevik activity even after the German armistice was concluded. Both Allied governments viewed Bolshevism as a dangerous and destructive creed and feared its spread among their own troops and working classes, quite apart from the danger it posed to central and south-eastern Europe and Islamic Asia. The French had a major financial stake in Russia to protect. Over 80 per cent of their pre-war foreign investment was in tsarist Russia; bonds were held by many thousands of private investors scattered throughout France. Money was also owed to the British and

French governments for wartime loans and purchases of war materials. In Britain, where anti-Bolshevism was often combined with traditional Russophobia, the long-standing concern with the Russian threat to the gateways to India made it likely that the more imperially minded ministers would try to take advantage of Britain's victory over Turkey and the troubled conditions in southern Russia to achieve domination over an area of vital strategic interest. Lord Curzon, lord president in Lloyd George's cabinet until October 1919 when he became foreign secretary, had a clear vision of a new empire in the eastern Mediterranean and south-west Asia buttressed by the creation of a 'chain of friendly states stretching from the confines of Europe to the frontier of the Indian Empire'.[5] The British sought to maintain their influence in the Caucasus, where Georgia, Azerbaijan, and Armenia declared their independence in May 1918, and backed the anti-Bolshevik secessionist movements in Central Asia. The wartime occupation of Persia, Mesopotamia, and Turkish Armenia provided a unique opportunity to extend British influence over the Persian government and to permanently exclude the Russians from northern Persia.

The British attitude was important, for they were the chief underwriters of the White armies in Russia. The French sent only very small numbers of soldiers to Russia and were able to offer the anti-Bolshevik forces only minimal military aid. There were sharp disagreements in the British cabinet about the establishment of the new empire in the east, and a fierce debate over how far the government should commit troops and supplies to achieve it. Both with regard to Turkey and to Russia—and the two problems were linked by Curzon and his supporters—no final decisions were reached and no clear orders were given to the local British commanders who were caught up in the regional fighting. The prime minister, Lloyd George, backed by Austen Chamberlain, the chancellor of the Exchequer, wanted to end the military interventions in Russia and begin negotiations with the Bolsheviks. Lloyd George believed that the Bolsheviks would triumph but that they could be tamed, and that a weakened Russian state would better serve Britain's imperial interests. He and Chamberlain insisted that there were no British troops to spare and, with a pressing need for financial economies, no funds for Russian adventures. The Treasury repeatedly dragged its feet over appropriations, and strongly and successfully opposed new military operations. Curzon, an ex-viceroy of India traditionally anti-Russian and strongly anti-Bolshevik, backed continued and expanded support for the White armies. His views were shared, as

---

[5] Bulent Gokay, 'Turkish Settlement and the Caucasus, 1918–20', *Middle Eastern Studies*, 32: 2 (Apr. 1996), 49.

far as Russia was concerned, by Edwin Montagu, the secretary of state for India, and by Winston Churchill, the imperially minded and virulently anti-Bolshevik secretary of state for war in 1919, who argued for increased subsidies to the anti-Bolshevik armies. Contrary to Lloyd George and Chamberlain, Churchill believed that a major military intervention in Russia would turn the tide in the White favour. Public opinion was divided. Though not decisive in shaping the government's attitude, the Labour party, the more militant Trades Union Congress (TUC), and certain key trade unions all opposed giving aid to the Whites or any form of interference in Russia's civil war. Basil Thomson, director of intelligence at the Home Office, reported to the cabinet in the spring of 1919 that 'every section of the workers' appeared to be against conscription and intervention in Russia.[6] At the same time, when Lloyd George raised the possibility of negotiations with the Bolsheviks, there was a strong negative reaction among the Conservatives in his Coalition party and in the predominantly Conservative press.

The other victorious leaders proved to be equally equivocal when any real decisions had to be taken at the peace conference in Paris. Clemenceau was resolutely opposed to negotiations with the Bolsheviks and was supported in his refusal by a majority of the Chamber of Deputies, though the left and far left were even more hostile to offering assistance to the Whites than in Britain. However fiercely Clemenceau might wax against the Bolsheviks, he was far too realistic to sanction projects that France could not afford. Marshal Foch's grand schemes for a massive military campaign, supported in mid-March 1919 by Churchill, proved unacceptable to the Council of Ten. A similar proposal resurfaced at the end of the month and was similarly rejected. Clemenceau's enthusiasm for anti-Bolshevik campaigns increased when others—the Germans in the Baltic, the Romanians in Hungary, or the Poles in eastern Galicia and in Belorussia—would do the fighting. He preferred to 'let the Russians stew in their own juice', to refuse to negotiate, and to wait on events.[7]

The situation in Washington was as muddled as in London. President Wilson tended to listen to others on the Russian question, and failed to come to any definite conclusions on how the Bolsheviks should be treated. He shared the general feeling in official circles that economic means, particularly the distribution of relief supplies, was a far better way to influence the civil wars in Russia and prevent the spread of Bolshevism than the commitment of troops. Within months of the American landings, limited though they were, there were pressures for

---

[6] Stephen White, *Britain and the Bolshevik Revolution* (London and Basingstoke, 1979), 31.
[7] Watson, *Clemenceau*, 373.

withdrawal. In mid-March 1919 a Senate resolution favouring the evacuation of all American troops was defeated only with the casting of the vice-presidential vote. Wilson was reluctant, nevertheless, to open negotiations with the Bolsheviks for fear that any move towards recognition would intensify Republican opposition to the presidential peacemaking.

A hand-to-mouth policy was adopted at the peace conference that was no policy at all. Approaches were made to the Bolsheviks and Allied withdrawals of their expeditions began, yet support for the main White leaders in Russia, Admiral Kolchak in Siberia, General Anton Denikin in south Russia, and General Nikolai Yudenich in the Baltic, actually increased. In January 1919 the Council of Ten proposed a ceasefire and a conference between all the Russian contenders and the Allies on Prinkipo Island in the Sea of Marmara on 15 February. The Bolsheviks accepted, offering reasonable terms though not a ceasefire. Their willingness to negotiate was the direct result of the absence of revolution in Germany. The Prinkipo project was killed when the joint body representing the Whites of Siberia, north Russia, and the Ukraine, encouraged by the French and by Churchill, refused to participate. In mid-February 1919, while Lloyd George and Wilson were both absent from Paris, Foch and Churchill launched the first of several unsuccessful attempts to secure assent for a military expedition to be sent to Russia. Clemenceau refused to support Foch's schemes either then or later, and Lloyd George reined in the eager Churchill. A second effort at a settlement with the Bolsheviks came against the background of the March strikes and armed clashes in Germany, followed by the creation of the short-lived Bavarian Soviet republic in early April. The Béla Kun Bolshevik government took power in Budapest on 21 March. Strikes and disorders spread in Holland; the Berne government faced a revolutionary situation in Switzerland. Admittedly, the German government overplayed the revolutionary danger: though Lloyd George feared for a 'bolshevised' Germany if the peace treaty was too harsh, Clemenceau never believed in the danger and Wilson ceased to worry during April and even took umbrage at the German warnings of the spectre of revolution. There was, nonetheless, considerable unease in the Allied delegations about the absence of any clear policy in eastern Europe and its effects on the peace treaties. William Bullitt, a junior member of the American delegation, was sent to Moscow on 8 March and began conversations with the Bolshevik leaders. The latter, exceedingly hard pressed and convinced that assistance from the capitalist powers accounted for the survival of the White armies, agreed to accept a temporary division of Russia along existing lines if the Allies would withdraw their troops and cease their aid to the Whites. Bullitt thought

that he had a deal, but was swiftly disillusioned; no one in Paris wanted
to hear about his mission. The proposals found little favour in the
delegations and the discussions were aborted. One partially successful
initiative resulted from the reports of widespread famine and epidemics
in Russia. In mid-April the Council of Four took up the suggestion of
Herbert Hoover, the American chief of the Allied relief administration,
that a neutral commission under Fridtjof Nansen, the famous Norwegian
explorer, should distribute food and offer loans to the Bolsheviks in
return for a ceasefire. Humanitarian in form, acceptance of the plan
would have frozen the existing situation in Russia and was intended to
reduce the Bolshevik appeal by relieving the suffering of the Russian
masses. The ceasefire was rejected, but the Bolsheviks were very anxious
to secure relief assistance and discussions eventually resulted in a major
relief programme under Hoover's auspices.

Parallel with these initiatives which put the possibility of talks with
the Bolsheviks on the Paris agenda, there was a strong movement for the
withdrawal of the Allied forces. By the end of March 1919, with the
British taking the lead, it was agreed that all foreign contingents should
be withdrawn from Russian soil. Many of the Allied troops were in
isolated places, on the defensive and having little effect on the outcome
of the civil war. The evacuation timetable was long drawn out. During
the winter of 1918–19 morale among the French troops in Odessa
plummeted, and in April they were abruptly withdrawn. Mutinies
broke out in the French Black Sea fleet. In separate actions, the British
agreed to withdraw their forces from the Caucasus by the end of 1919,
with the exception of the garrison at Batum, which only departed in
July 1920. While the British were still dealing with the Ottoman Turks,
it would be easier to maintain British influence in south Russia through
control over the Straits and Black Sea than by fighting the Bolsheviks. It
was agreed that northern Russia would have to be evacuated before the
next winter freeze; the Americans left Archangel in June and, after a
final engagement with the Bolshevik forces, the last British troops
were withdrawn from Archangel on 27 September 1920 and from
Murmansk a fortnight later. The Siberian evacuation was slower because
of the Japanese. The Americans sailed from Vladivostok in April 1920.
The Japanese occupation, which brought 'little profit and no fame',
became highly unpopular at home and, in the face of constant American
prodding, the last troops were finally evacuated in 1922.

During the course of 1919 each of the White armies took the
offensive. In March Admiral Kolchak launched an attack against
the Red Army from his Siberian headquarters at Omsk. On 27 April
the Council of Four agreed to send volunteers and munitions to his
army, though they stopped short of full recognition of the Omsk

government. The Red Army soon checked Kolchak's forces, and during the summer months of 1919 they were forced to move back into Siberia. Hordes of refugees, as well as the men of the Czech Legion, fled eastward by train and on foot ahead of the retreating army, hoping to reach Vladivostok. Kolchak himself was captured and shot on 7 February 1920. In the Caucasus, General Denikin launched an offensive north and west through the Ukraine, capturing Kharkov in late June 1919 and Kiev and Kursk in August. When the British decided to pull out of the Caucasus at the end of the year, they agreed to provide Denikin with war materials and attached a small military mission to his army as a form of compensation. It was typical of the vagaries of Allied policy that British assistance should have been withdrawn when Denikin's forces were only 300 kilometres from Moscow and preparing for a rapid advance into central Russia. The Denikin offensive was also checked by the Red Army; his demoralized force suffered a series of defeats in the winter of 1919–20 and was pushed towards the Crimea. Adding to the confusion were territorial and ethnic disputes, both within and between the new Transcaucasian republics and between the republics and the forces of General Denikin, who believed in 'Great Russia, One and Indivisible' and strongly opposed the separatist, nationalist movements even where they were anti-Bolshevik. In March 1920 a portion of his broken army was taken in Allied ships to the Crimea, where in April General Baron Peter Wrangel succeeded to Denikin's command. He would launch the last serious White offensive in the summer of 1920, when the Russo-Polish war was reaching its climax. The anti-Bolsheviks had more success in the Baltic where, with the aid of British naval squadrons, the communist governments of Estonia and Latvia were soon overthrown and new governments established in January and May 1919. In October, at the time of the Denikin challenge to Moscow, a small White army under General Yudenich, fighting on the Estonian frontier, took the offensive and launched an assault on Petrograd. Hastily assembled Red forces under Trotsky's command defeated Yudenich and in mid-November pushed his troops back into Estonia. Angered by Yudenich's Great Russian nationalism, and fearing Bolshevik Russian reprisals, the Estonian government disarmed his army. By the end of 1919 the three main White armies had been decisively defeated. The Bolsheviks, with the support of the Kemalists, regained control of Transcaucasia and, after agreements with the Turks and with the assistance of local nationalists, were able to reconquer and 'sovietize' the independent republics in Central Asia in the winter of 1920–1.

The interventionists were beaten. Had the Allied governments been united and determined, the outcome of the civil war might have been different. Instead, they suffered from a lack of clear purpose and an almost total absence of co-ordinated action. Their erratic and confused attempts to defeat the Bolsheviks using minimal means accomplished nothing. Owing to their vacillation and indecisiveness, as well as to the ineptitude of the White leaders, the Allies were left in an entirely disadvantageous position. They had not intervened in sufficient strength to make any difference to the civil war, but by sending troops and by underwriting the White armies they had missed any opportunity for a temporary settlement when the Bolsheviks were weak and prepared to make concessions. Their bungled interventions instilled in the Bolsheviks the continuing fear that the capitalist world would do its utmost to annihilate the revolutionary regime by force. This apprehension was to colour Soviet policy throughout the inter-war period. The Allied governments were unwilling and unable to countenance a major intervention after just emerging from a punishing war. The Treaty of Versailles noted only that future treaties between the Allies and Russia, or any parts of it, must be recognized. One clause left open the possibility of Russia claiming reparations. The Allied blockade was finally abandoned in January 1921.

III

With the withdrawal of the Allied forces and the defeat of the White armies, the Bolshevik Russian republic turned to the stabilization of its frontiers. By the end of 1919 the Red Army had been pushed out of the Baltic by local volunteer armies, aided by a combination of Germans, White Russians, and Poles. A peace treaty was signed with Estonia on 2 February 1920: Lenin referred to its conclusion as an event of 'gigantic historical significance', and Georgy Chicherin, Trotsky's successor in 1918 as commissar for foreign affairs, called it 'the first experiment in peaceful co-existence with bourgeois states'.[8] Peace treaties were concluded with Lithuania and Latvia on 12 July and 11 August 1920 respectively, with the Russians recognizing the former's claims against Poland to the Vilna region. Finnish independence was already recognized in January 1918. The Finns, who had no love for the Whites who might threaten their independence, took no part in attacks on the Bolsheviks, despite their abiding fear of Russian aggression (the Russian–Finnish border was only 32 kilometres from Leningrad) and fiercely anti-Russian attitude. There was, however, a continuing 'red' against 'white' internal struggle in Finland that went on for years. While still convinced that the revolution would spread, the realistic leaders of Bolshevik Russia engaged in treaty-making where it was feasible. The

---

[8] Jacobson, *Soviet Union*, 18.

Map 9. The Russo–Polish War

frontier disputes between the Poles and Russians developed into an undeclared war and the brief flowering of Bolshevik revolutionary hopes for a rising in Poland that would spread to Germany and beyond.

The actual origins of the Russo-Polish war are still a subject of debate. There is general agreement, however, that the Poles were anxious to extend their borders in the east and were prepared to exploit the weaknesses of the Bolshevik republic in its frontier territories. Józef Piłsudski, the Polish chief of state and commander-in-chief, knew Russia well, having spent several years in Siberia as a political deportee, and recognized the danger of the re-emergence of a strong Russia, whether White or Red. He believed, moreover, that whereas in the west Poland was dependent on the support of the Entente powers for any additional territories she might gain, in the east she had an opportunity to create her own fait accompli. Piłsudski was thinking in terms of a federation under Polish leadership that would include Ukraine, Belorussia, and Lithuania freed from Russian domination, which could play a major role in central Europe. Unable to act until he had reassembled the scattered Polish forces in early 1919, he subsequently sent part of his army north to Vilna, where it easily evicted the weak Bolshevik forces, and then attacked Galicia, seizing control of Lvov. By the summer of 1919 the Polish army had occupied the whole of eastern Galicia. There was not much that the Allies could do, though they knew of the hatred between the Ukrainians and Poles and the possibilities of continued warfare in the east. On 25 June they 'authorized' Poland to occupy East Galicia and to set up a civilian administration. The Poles continued their advance into the Ukraine, where a highly complicated situation existed in which the Ukrainian armies, already divided between anti-Polish and anti-Russian factions which had started fighting the Bolsheviks, ended up fighting against Denikin who had begun his offensive towards Moscow. The Allied powers hoped that the Poles would co-ordinate their efforts with the White general, but Piłsudski had no such intention. Denikin's victory would be of little use to Poland and might even be dangerous to its independence. Piłsudski preferred to deal with the Bolsheviks on his own. The Polish army extended its sphere of influence over most of White Ruthenia and over the western Ukraine. The Reds concentrated on Denikin; once he was defeated and Kiev retaken in December, they were prepared to negotiate with the Poles. On 28 January 1920 they made a concrete offer. They were willing to recognize Polish independence, and to promise not to cross the existing boundary lines between the two countries either in Belorussia or in the Ukraine, and not to conclude any treaty or agreement with Germany or any other country harmful to Poland. It was an attractive offer, and Roman Dmowski, Piłsudski's great rival, and his powerful National Democrats party, urged acceptance, as did the Allied governments. There was strong opposition from Dmowski, as well as from some of the Ukrainian leaders, to Piłsudski's plan for an alliance with the anti-Bolshevik Ukrainians and a joint attack on the Red Army. Piłsudski, always suspicious of Bolshevik intentions toward Poland, preferred not to conclude a peace treaty until the Poles had won a decisive victory over the Russians. While the Poles were secretly discussing their reply to the Russian terms for a peace treaty, he ordered a brief probing attack east of Minsk and was surprised at the weakness of the Red forces. The Polish answer to the Russian offer was sent in late March. They demanded the renunciation of all territories taken from Poland under the eighteenth-century partitions and the right to determine the status of the areas west of the 1772 frontiers. There was no possibility of dialogue on such terms.

Neither the French nor the British favoured a Polish offensive, though the former, who were supplying arms and credits to the Polish government during 1919, were more sympathetic to Piłsudski's aspirations, so important for their own security, than Lloyd George, whose anti-Polish sentiments were strong and who was already considering trade talks with the Bolsheviks. To the Poles, Lloyd George was evasive. He told their representative that Britain would not support a Polish attack on Russia, but promised assistance if Russia attacked Poland within her 'legitimate frontiers'. Anxious about the economic downturn in Britain, the prime minister invited Leonin Krasin, a successful pre-revolutionary businessman, who as Lenin's close collaborator was the Bolshevik republic's chief diplomatic and economic negotiator, to come to London in March 1920. The Lloyd George–Krasin talks began on 31 May. (Lord Curzon had to be shamed into shaking hands with Krasin: 'Curzon!', Lloyd George exclaimed. 'Be a gentleman.'[9]) The negotiations were difficult. Mainly but not solely at Curzon's insistence, the British wanted a comprehensive agreement that would include such demands as the return of British prisoners in Russia, the cessation of Bolshevik propaganda, plotting, and hostile acts in the east, and the recognition of Russian debts to private creditors, in exchange for the resumption of Anglo-Russian trade. With Polish troops advancing into Russia, the cabinet thought it could drive a hard bargain with Moscow. Lloyd George faced strong opposition to any agreement with the Bolsheviks. Conservative backbenchers could see no reason to trade with 'thieves', and the French premier, Alexandre Millerand, refused to join any talks that would give the Bolsheviks political credibility. Worse still for the prospect of success, the British learned through intelligence intercepts that Chicherin was opposing the talks. He thought Krasin far too yielding in the face of British blackmail diplomacy, and angrily denounced the British demands. Knowing of Chicherin's opposition,

[9] Richard H. Ullman, *The Anglo-Soviet Accord* (Princeton, 1972), 97.

Lloyd George stopped the conversations and presented Krasin with an ultimatum. The latter, anxious that the talks should succeed and prepared to return to Moscow to put his case, went off to Russia in early July aboard the flagship of a British destroyer flotilla that Lloyd George put at his disposal. By the time Krasin returned to London in August the Russo-Polish military scene had been totally changed.

The Polish and Ukrainian offensive was launched on 25 April 1920. By 7 May Kiev was in Polish hands. A month later, in a totally separate action, Baron Wrangel's army broke out of the Crimea and advanced to the lower Dnieper. Concentrating almost entirely on the Polish war, the Red Army regrouped in May and began a steadily accelerating counterattack that brought the Russian troops to the gates of Warsaw in August. The summer victories revived hopes in Moscow that the revolution was imminent. The jubilant leaders of the Third International, meeting in their second World Congress during the second half of July—now more genuinely representative, with 169 delegates drawn from forty-one parties—prepared for future revolutionary action. A large map, hung in the conference hall, recorded the progress of the Red armies. General Mikhail Tukhachevsky, the 27-year-old commander of the infantry forces in Poland, wrote to Grigory Zinoviev, who chaired the congress and became president of the 'Comintern', pledging that the Red Army would bring Bolshevik power to Poland and begin 'a world offensive of all the armed forces of the proletariat against the arms of world capitalism'.[10] In a mood of considerable optimism, delegates approved the 'Twenty-one Conditions of Admission into the Communist International' which all national parties would have to accept. To distinguish those parties aligned to the Comintern from the social democratic parties of the Second International, the former were to adopt the name 'communist' and were to disassociate themselves from all bourgeois expedients for the improvement of working-class conditions. Russian leadership of the Comintern was reaffirmed and its control over the national communist parties tightened. In the euphoria created by the victories in Poland, some Bolshevik leaders and Red Army commanders predicted a revolutionary war that would lead to a communist Poland and provide a bridge to Germany. Cooler heads, including that of Trotsky, dismissed the operation as militarily impossible, and Karl Radek, the chief Comintern tactician who knew the Polish situation well, warned that Polish workers would never welcome Russian invaders.

---

[10] R. Craig Nation, *Black Earth, Red Star: A History of Soviet Security Policy, 1917–1991* (Ithaca, NY, 1992), 29.

At their conference at Spa, on 10 July 1920, the Allied leaders responded to the Polish cries of alarm. Lloyd George raised the possibility of sending advisers and equipment to Poland. He may well have been relieved, for he was no enthusiast for intervention, when Marshal Foch claimed that France could do nothing. Having received a telegram from Chicherin agreeing to the 'principles' contained in Lloyd George's aide-memoire and demanding that the trade negotiations begin at once, the British prime minister, with hesitant French agreement, replied by proposing peace talks between Poland and Russia. The Poles were desperate and appealed for Allied help; the Polish premier Władysław Grabski came to Spa to plead the Polish case. Lloyd George, after demanding that Poland abandon its annexationist ambitions and maintain its independence within its own ethnographic frontiers, agreed to consider what could be done to induce the Russians to make peace and, should they refuse, what steps might be taken to assist Poland. Grabski had no choice but to accept the proposed armistice terms. Russian troops were to withdraw 50 kilometres east of the line fixed by the Supreme Council on 8 December 1919 that ran from East Prussia in the north to eastern Galicia in the south; Vilna was to be handed over to Lithuania and, in eastern Galicia, the troops were to stand on the line reached by the time of the prospective armistice. The terms were also sent to Moscow, though, possibly due to carelessness (Lloyd George was handling Russian policy with very little reference to the Foreign Office), it contained a different and more favourable line in East Galicia, that had been adopted by the Allies in November 1919 when Poland was offered a mandate over East Galicia, an offer that she contemptuously rejected. Lord Curzon's note of 11 July, telegraphed to Chicherin, proposing a demarcation line (and so referred to as the 'Curzon line') and a peace conference in London, contained a threat of intervention if Russia rejected the proposed terms. In a bitter and sarcastic reply, the Bolsheviks turned the offer down, correctly surmising that the British threat was little more than bluff. The only immediate action was the sending of separate British and French military missions to Warsaw, mainly, as Millerand instructed its head, to determine what moral and material support could be given Poland in defence of 'frontiers encircling land indisputably Polish'.[11]

Despite a Polish appeal for a ceasefire and the designation of a place for a meeting, the Red Army continued to advance. Trotsky's advice that the Russians should stop at the 'Curzon line', roughly the ethnographic frontier of Poland, and make an offer of peace was rejected by the Politburo. Even Lenin was tempted by the opportunity to carry the

[11] Ullman, *Anglo-Soviet Accord*, 175–6.

revolution to the borders of Germany and possibly to Germany itself. Bolshevik ambitions were buoyed by the strikes called by the strongly anti-Polish German workers in Danzig, and by the actions of Czech railway workers who held up wagons destined for Poland. Assuming that the Red Army would soon enter Warsaw, the Bolsheviks offered to open bilateral talks with the Poles and to attend a London conference with all the powers formerly hostile to Russia. Lloyd George seized on this sign of moderation. He convinced Millerand, who continued to oppose direct Allied–Bolshevik negotiations, that he should attend the conference. In the interim Lloyd George, who had suspended the trade talks until an armistice was concluded, asked Krasin and Lev Kamenev, a representative of the Politburo and chairman of the 'special peace delegation', to return to Britain. Even as the talks in London began, the Red Army continued its advance, and the Russians displayed no haste in opening talks with the Poles. In early August, fearing the fall of Warsaw and the installation of a communist government in Poland, Lloyd George threatened that unless the advance was immediately stopped there would be no conference or trade agreement and that he would order the reimposition of the blockade and the renewal of assistance to Wrangel in the Crimea. In a deeply pessimistic mood, Lloyd George and Millerand reviewed the Polish situation at meetings on 8 and 9 August. Neither of the Entente powers was prepared to send troops to Poland or to make funds available for the Polish war effort. If the Russians refused to negotiate, they could blockade the Russian ports, provide advisers and limited supplies to the Poles, and give naval support to Wrangel's forces in the Crimea. In practical terms, the Poles were offered very little material assistance, and on conditions which reflected the Allied distrust of Piłsudski. The Russian terms, relayed by Kamenev to Lloyd George and to the *Daily Herald* on 2 August, before their meeting with the Poles, were not, in the prime minister's view, ungenerous. On Lenin's insistence, Chicherin offered a frontier boundary more favourable to Poland than the 'Curzon line' and, while making substantial demands, appeared willing to respect Polish independence within her ethnographic borders. Lloyd George recommended their acceptance as a basis for negotiation. The terms, however, included a provision for the formation of a working-class 'civil militia' in Poland that was unacceptable to the Poles. Poland proceeded to provide for its own salvation.

The Red Army began its attack on Warsaw on 13 August. It was repulsed in a pitched battle on the River Vistula. Three days later the Polish troops mounted a successful counter-attack. Tukhachevsky's armies were encircled and routed. Those Russian soldiers who survived and escaped capture retreated eastwards in total disarray. The 'miracle of the Vistula' saved Lloyd George from having to take any action to relieve the Poles. The 'hands off Russia' movement in Britain had spread; more than 300 Councils of Action (groups created by local Trades Councils or the Labour party) were formed, covering the most important industrial centres. Whatever the intentions of their leaders, the rank-and-file opposition was a response to the threat of war rather than to the possibility of an attack on Russia. Further worker action was threatened to protest against intervention and the supply of men and munitions to Poland. A national conference of local trade-union and party branches was called for 13 August; by the time it assembled the Kamenev peace terms had been published and Lloyd George had solicited labour assistance in keeping the Russian government to its offer. The prime minister's promises to the French that he would do something, if not a great deal, to assist the Poles had less to do with saving Poland from disaster than stopping the westward spread of Bolshevism. Lloyd George thought that even if the Poles were defeated by the Russians, as seemed probable, it would still be possible to negotiate terms with Moscow. He was more willing than Millerand to accept changes in the Versailles status quo, whether they involved Germany or Bolshevik Russia. Millerand was far more apprehensive. For him, the idea of a Bolshevik victory over Poland was a catastrophe that would seriously undermine French security. The French, however, were not prepared to act unilaterally because they felt dependent on Britain, and so in the end gave very little concrete assistance to Poland. In a symbolic gesture, Millerand recognized General Wrangel's government at Sevastopol, but he was in no position to provide assistance.

As the tide turned in the Polish favour, Lloyd George began to plan for the renewal of the trade talks with Russia. There was no such move in Paris. The French, like the Belgians, who were also major creditors, were resolutely opposed to any rapprochement with Moscow until the tsarist debt question was settled. With the opening of the Polish counter-offensive and the news of Wrangel's summer success, the French began to talk of a Bolshevik collapse. Piłsudski inflicted defeat after defeat on the retreating Red Army, and by the end of September the Russians had been driven back over the Niemen. In his moment of triumph the rather arrogant Polish leader showed that he had learned the lessons of his earlier failure. On 12 October he concluded an armistice with the Bolsheviks without advancing further into Russian territory. Negotiations for a definitive peace began at once. The Polish–Russian frontier was established without Allied participation. On 18 March 1921, two days after the Bolsheviks concluded their trade agreement with the British, the Poles and Russians signed a formal peace treaty at Riga. Though Poland did not get her 1772 border, the eastern frontier was far more favourable than that of the 'Curzon line'. She gained a large tract of predominately Belorussian territory: some 3 million people of other than Polish nationality, mostly Ukrainians and Belorussians, became Polish subjects. The Russians renounced all claims on Galicia and declared their disinterest in the Polish–Lithuanian dispute. Both sides agreed to refrain from intervention in each other's internal affairs, to abstain from propaganda, and not to harbour organizations hostile to the other country.

Without being anyone else's pawn, but also without the necessary resources to play an independent role in central Europe, Poland's pivotal position depended on the continuing weakness of her two most important neighbours, Russia and Germany, and the avoidance of any agreement between them. Similarly, the extension of Poland's borders in both the east and west beyond their ethnographic limits left her vulnerable to continuing disputes. The boundaries lasted until 1939, when the balance established by the Treaty of Riga was destroyed by the Nazi–Soviet pact. The 'Curzon line', not actually drawn by Curzon, would resurface during the Second World War when Stalin insisted that it was the proper frontier between the Soviet Union and Poland.

Within their own territories, the Bolsheviks were more successful than in Poland. General Wrangel's forces were soon in retreat; the Red Army moved into his last strongholds and took Sevastopol on 14 November 1920. The Bolsheviks had won, and the dreaded foreign intervention was being abandoned. They had to face, however, the question of the Polish defeat, and to consider the failure of the Polish proletariat to respond to revolutionary appeals and the seeming unwillingness of the Russian peasant army to fight for the revolution beyond the borders of Russia. The Bolshevik leadership would have to reassess the international position of communist Russia.

IV

Following the struggle for survival of 1919–20, Bolshevik foreign policy continued to show two faces to the world. Lenin summed up the situation in his speech of 21 November 1920:

We are in the position of not having gained an international victory, which for us is the only sure victory, but of having won conditions enabling us to co-exist with capitalist powers who are now compelled to enter into commercial relations with us. In the course of the struggle we have won the right to an independent existence . . . [It] will be clear that we have won more than a breathing space—we have entered a new period in which we have . . . won the right to our international existence in the network of capitalist states . . .

Today we have to speak, not merely of a breathing space, but of there being a serious chance of a new and lengthy period of development.[12]

The Bolshevik leader used the term 'peaceful coexistence' to mean the maintenance of diplomatic relations with the capitalist states; but in the words of a Bolshevik military hero of the Central Asian wars, Mikhail Frunze, 'the class war of the workers against the class rulers of the old world' would continue.[13] The Russians intended to pursue both their pragmatic and revolutionary aims without sacrificing either. In the years that followed the emphasis would shift according to changing circumstances. A dual policy gradually emerged until the crises in the late twenties when it become necessary to set priorities. A dual policy gradually emerged until the crisis in the late twenties, when it became necessary to set priorities. For relations with two key powers, Britain and Germany, 1921 would be a pivotal year, bringing the conclusion of trade agreements with both.

Though Russia had survived the civil war and the Allied interventions, the country was still faced with economic disaster, poor harvests, closed factories, a transport and communication system reduced to chaos, and rising peasant discontent. The introduction of the New Economic Policy (NEP) in 1921 and an accommodation with the capitalist world were reactions to economic distress and the impossibility of prolonging wartime policies, as well as realism in the face of a stubborn status quo. The retreat from the economic radicalism of the war years and the class war against the peasantry had its foreign-policy equivalent in the temporary co-operation with international capitalism and the return to normal diplomacy in the search for foreign capital, development, and trade in order to restore the shattered economy. Lenin argued that the country had to attract western capital to accelerate the process of Russian industrialization, and was prepared to invite foreign concessionaires to restore the Baku oilfields. Not all of the other Bolshevik leaders agreed either with the NEP or with the search for foreign capital and investment. The influential Trotsky, Karl Radek, and Nikolai Bukharin, one of the Comintern leaders and the editor of *Pravda*, preferred to rely on domestic capital formation rather than on foreign investment to finance industrial expansion until the outbreak of the global revolution. There was a continuous debate in Moscow on the ideological premises of the regime, which played its own role in the

---

[12] Teddy J. Uldricks, 'Russia and Europe: Diplomacy, Revolution, and Economic Development in the 1920s', *International History Review*, 1: 1 (Jan. 1979), 61.
[13] Dale Terence Lahey, 'Soviet Ideological Development of Co-existence, 1917–1927', *Canadian Slavonic Papers*, 87.

formulation of Russian foreign policy. From 1921 on a more accommodationist policy slowly emerged, along with a move towards conventional diplomacy, though there was no clear-cut shift towards 'peaceful coexistence'. The leadership saw no contradiction between safeguarding the security of the Bolshevik state through normal diplomatic channels and promoting the international proletarian revolution.

The Bolsheviks made good use of the distinction between the activities of the 'independent' Comintern and the Russian state. A famous caricature depicted Chicherin, commissar for foreign affairs, tearing his hair while Grigory Zinoviev, the chairman of the Comintern's executive, delivered one of his flamboyant speeches. This was Bolshevik propaganda aimed at confusing western observers. In fact, Chicherin was as much a revolutionary as Zinoviev, though there were debates in each of their respective institutions as to how Russia's aims could be best advanced. The two men were very different in character and they headed institutions of very different kinds. Chicherin was an ex-Menshevik, a brilliant linguist fluent in both European and non-European languages who had lived abroad as an exile, with broad intellectual interests, including a deep love of music. His book on opera was not published until the 1960s because it started with a statement that, while there may be important ideologies and ideas, the sublime music of Mozart reigns above all. Though not a member of the Politburo, he was a convinced Bolshevik and entirely loyal to Lenin. Having spent an apprenticeship in the archives section of the tsarist foreign ministry, he had acquired a deep knowledge of the policies of Alexander Gorchakov, Tsar Alexander II's foreign minister after the Crimean War, who had tried to counterbalance British pressure over the Eastern Question by increasing Russian influence in Central Asia. Chicherin argued for the pursuit of a similar policy in 1919. Britain remained the enemy: it was the old imperial rivalry dressed in ideological clothes. He preferred to orient Russian policy towards Germany. While Chicherin and Curzon genuinely loathed each other, both politically and personally, the commissar enjoyed a special relationship with Count Ulrich von Brockdorff-Rantzau, the German ambassador in Moscow from 1922 until his death in 1928. Both men felt that their countries had been badly treated by the victorious Allied powers, and particularly disliked and distrusted the British. The Commissariat of Foreign Affairs, almost three-quarters of whose officials were middle class (the remainder tried to obscure their aristocratic backgrounds), favoured a traditional approach to foreign affairs. Chicherin used the techniques of the new diplomacy, including open pronouncements, appeals, and denunciations, but also more conventional means in dealing with the capitalist world, even if this meant distancing the diplomats from the activities of the Comintern agents.

Zinoviev, on the other hand, was a Bolshevik of long standing, a member of the Politburo and personally very close to Lenin. He was committed to the view of an inexorable clash between the capitalist and socialist worlds and the triumph of the latter under Bolshevik leadership. Zinoviev saw the developing network of communist and workers' movements in the west and east as the motive force for the future overthrow of the capitalist states. Though he and Chicherin differed on the tactics to be used to further communist interests, not too much should be made of their differences. The Comintern, which claimed to be independent of the Russian state, placed its emphasis on propaganda, agitation, and insurrection and sought to capitalize on the role of the Russian Communist party as the vanguard of the world revolution, since it alone had successfully carried out its historical mission. In practice, the two approaches were not always compatible, and their coexistence could prove counter-productive. But Lenin and his associates believed that both were necessary if the Bolshevik state was to survive and the 'world revolutionary process' brought to its conclusion with the ending of the imperialist world order that alone would guarantee the socialist future. If Zinoviev had the more powerful personality and made his influence felt in the Politburo, in the absence of any successful European revolution Russia's immediate needs favoured Chicherin. Gradually the Comintern came to serve Soviet diplomatic aims, and Zinoviev collaborated with Lenin and later with Stalin in this direction.

Despite his deteriorating health, Lenin maintained the initiative in shaping Russian foreign policy during 1921 and 1922. He was convinced that he could exploit the divisions in the west to secure the much-needed foreign assistance without endangering the survival of socialism in Russia. The Comintern was forced to tailor its policies to fit the Leninist coat. At its third congress, in June–July 1921, a note of caution and self restraint was sounded; communist parties abroad would have to face a prolonged period of preparation for revolution. Even Trotsky defended the 'strategy of temporary retreat' and denied that the interests of the revolutionary world proletariat were being sacrificed to the national interests of Bolshevik Russia. In Moscow, Lenin steered a careful course between the 'integrationists' and the 'leftists' who still preferred revolutionary action abroad and an isolationist economic policy at home. Lenin's protégés among the 'integrationists', Chicherin, Krasin, and Grigory Sokolnikov, an enthusiastic supporter of foreign co-operation who became finance minister in 1922, were encouraged to test the international waters.

When Lloyd George had suggested the resumption of trade talks in 1920, the Bolsheviks quickly responded. The Polish crisis, however, delayed further discussions, as did the endless wrangling over an

Anglo-Soviet exchange of prisoners. Kamenev left England in September. He would have been expelled if he had not been leaving in any case, and would not be permitted to return. Lloyd George accused him of deliberate deception over the peace terms offered to the Poles, and charged him with offering subsidies to the *Daily Herald* and intriguing with the Council of Action. The rapid increase in the number of the insured population out of work in Britain, however, was a powerful incentive to take up Krasin's bid in early November for a renewal of the talks. Lloyd George had considerable difficulty in persuading his cabinet colleagues, above all Curzon and Churchill, to go along with the negotiations. Curzon was obsessed with the Russian threat to the British empire in the east. He had fought hard, if unsuccessfully, to prevent the evacuation of British troops from Batum and north Persia, and had watched with deepest apprehension the development of the Russian–Turkish partnership in Transcaucasia and Asia Minor and the growth of Bolshevik influence in Afghanistan and Persia in the summer of 1920. Curzon's only interest in any agreement with the Bolsheviks was to force them to stop their propaganda and hostile actions in the east. A steady stream of intercepts and intelligence reports, some far from accurate, arrived on his desk, giving substance to the charges of Russian plotting against the British empire. The foreign secretary refused to have anything to do with the trade negotiations, and the Foreign Office example of strict non-involvement was followed by other departments. There were objections, too, from those outside the government who insisted on the Bolshevik recognition of the tsarist debts before embarking on talks. It was only Lloyd George's perseverance that brought the treaty to fruition. He used the British unemployment figures and the promise of some £10 million-worth of Russian orders to win the grudging acquiescence of the cabinet. Even before the agreement was signed, Krasin was going about the country discussing or placing orders for textiles, shoes, and machinery, all industries that were hard hit by the post-war slump.

On the Russian side, the economic motive was paramount. The Anglo-Russian trade agreement was signed on 16 March 1921, just one week after Lenin had announced the tax in kind on agricultural products which introduced the New Economic Policy. This major shift in economic policy made the Soviet regime extremely anxious to bring the negotiations to a successful end. The March agreement was a limited and provisional treaty; there was no general treaty according full *de jure* recognition for another three years. For the Russians, however, it represented a first key step towards diplomatic respectability and the status needed for future commercial agreements. As a consequence of the agreement, British imports from Russia nearly quadrupled in 1922 and exports rose more than 20 per cent. In 1921–2 Russia took nearly half of her imports from Britain and sent back almost a third of her exports. While these figures constituted only a tiny percentage of the pre-war trade between the two states, it was a major breakthrough for Soviet Russia. The Soviet republic, as Lenin remarked, had 'forced open a window', and similar trade agreements followed with other European countries during the course of the year. France and the United States kept their windows officially shut, despite a considerable private trade between the Americans and Russians.

There were hopes in London, as Karl Radek complained, that Manchester trousers and shirts might make the Bolsheviks reasonable and Sheffield razors might, 'if not cut their throats, at least turn them into gentlemen'.[14] Lloyd George, in charge of Russian affairs during this period, believed that the establishment of diplomatic and commercial relations with the capitalist powers would lead the Bolsheviks to soften their policies and even to abandon them. He argued that the conclusion of the trade agreement would strengthen the hand of the moderates, among whom he included Lenin, and curtail the influence of the revolutionary propagandists in Moscow. As his actions at Genoa in 1922 would show, the prime minister had a broader vision of international relations in mind. He was convinced that the opening of the vast Russian market to western goods would not only serve British

TABLE 6. f. Source of Russian/Soviet Imports 1913–1934 (in % of total for each year)

	France	Germany	UK	USA	Others
1913	7.3	47.5	12.6	5.8	26.8
1921/2	0.1	30.9	19.6	16.2	33.2
1922/3	0.4	41.3	25.0	3.0	30.3
1923/4	6.5	19.4	21.0	21.8	31.3
1924/5	3.1	14.2	15.3	27.9	39.5
1925/6	5.3	23.2	17.1	16.2	38.2
1927/8	4.3	26.3	5.0	19.9	44.5
1929	4.8	22.2	6.2	20.1	46.7
1930	4.2	23.7	7.6	25	39.6
1931	3.5	50.2	9	28.1	9.3
1932	4.1	46.5	13.1	4.5	31.8
1933	6.6	42.5	8.8	4.8	37.4
1934	9.4	12.4	13.5	7.7	57

Source: R. W. Davies, Mark Harrison, S. G. Wheatcroft (eds.), *The Economic Transformation of the Soviet Union, 1913–1945* (Cambridge, Cambridge University Press, 1994), 319.

[14] White, *Britain and the Bolshevik Revolution*, 26.

interests but would promote European prosperity and peace. Lloyd George's appeasement policies, whether with regard to Bolshevik Russia or Germany, reflected the traditional Liberal party beliefs in the beneficent effects of trade between nations.

Due to pressure from the British side, the preamble to the trade agreement stated that both countries would refrain from any official propaganda against their respective institutions. The final signing of the treaty was shadowed by British complaints, backed by intelligence reports, about Russia's revolutionary agitation and propaganda in Afghanistan and India. Bolshevik activities in Central Asia continued to unsettle Curzon, and strengthened his conviction that one could not have normal diplomatic relations with a revolutionary state. A letter sent to Krasin, accompanying the treaty and containing these accusations listed the conditions on which continued Anglo-Soviet trade depended. Chicherin, whose continued hostility to any agreement was revealed by the intercepts, rejected the charges of interference and accused Britain of 'irreconcilable hostility' and anti-Bolshevik activity in Europe and beyond. The Bolshevik government's refusal to accept responsibility for the actions of the Comintern particularly infuriated the foreign secretary. Consistent with their continuing belief in nurturing world revolution, the Bolsheviks had indeed been organizing subversion within the British empire. After establishing control over the Central Asian territories, they stepped up their activities in Afghanistan and Persia and established a school at Tashkent under M. N. Roy, a leading member of the Central Asian Bureau of the Comintern, to organize an Indian revolutionary army.

Russian enthusiasm for confrontation with the British reached its peak at the Congress of the People of the East at Baku, the capital of Azerbaijan, in September 1920. In an undisciplined and unsophisticated gathering, some 2,000 delegates from twenty-nine nationalities (half of them from the Caucasus) heard Zinoviev call for a 'holy war' against British imperialism. As it proved difficult to radicalize existing nationalist movements or to establish strong communist parties in Central Asia, the Bolshevik government opted for agreements with existing 'anti-imperial' national governments, whatever their attitudes towards local communist parties. Treaties were negotiated with Persia, Afghanistan, and Turkey in February and March 1921. Each involved the official abandonment of Russian interference in the internal affairs of the countries concerned in return for the normalization of relations. There was a diminution in revolutionary activities in Afghanistan, the school in Tashkent was closed, and, at Chicherin's request, the Communist party of Azerbaijan, the spearhead of the Soviet revolution in northern Persia, was disbanded. Nonetheless, in the summer of 1921

Soviet subversion in India and on India's borders appeared to Curzon, at least, as a major threat to the empire. Though assured by the Indian government that the Bolshevik campaign had been checkmated, British charges and Soviet denials continued to be exchanged. Intelligence based on forged documents supplied by the Secret Intelligence Service led Curzon to send an official protest to Moscow in September 1921, from which he had to backtrack in a most awkward fashion. It was, in fact, only in the spring of 1922 that the Soviet government and the Comintern renewed their support for revolutionary action in India, again with minimal results.

V

In Europe, Zinoviev and the leaders of the Comintern continued to look to the German proletariat to fulfil their predetermined role. Zinoviev worked assiduously to compose the differences between the different German factions, and at the Halle Congress in October 1920 the left wing of the Independent Socialists (USPD) united with the Communists (KPD), producing a single Communist party (KPD) with a strengthened base in the working classes. The KPD became affiliated with the Comintern. Following the German example, national communist parties were formed in France and Italy on the basis of the 'twenty-one conditions' and subordination to the Russian-dominated Comintern. Sizeable parties were created in Bulgaria, Norway, Czechoslovakia, and in Yugoslavia (later declared illegal), but none were of the same importance as that of Germany. The general view of Germany as the next revolutionary homeland coloured Bolshevik thinking, even after the failure of the KPD's 'March operation' in 1921 intended to spearhead an attack on the parliamentary system. Zinoviev and Bukharin, the Comintern leaders, openly encouraged the German communists, and Lenin himself appears to have supported the revolutionary efforts. The rebellion was suppressed in a few days by the Prussian police. The failed action raised vexing questions. If the KPD, the strongest Communist party outside Russia, could not capitalize on domestic unrest, could any other Communist party in western Europe succeed? Lenin, Kamenev, and even Trotsky were prepared to call for a temporary retreat; Zinoviev and others associated with the Comintern still adhered to the 'revolutionary offensive' policy. While the debate continued, members of the 'accommodationist' faction began to think in terms of a rapprochement with the German government. The failure of the 'March operation' and Lenin's abandonment of the idea of a successful proletarian revolution within a 'brief interval' undermined objections to an economic arrangement with Berlin. A trade agreement

would encourage divisions in the capitalist camp, while providing
Bolshevik Russia with the material and technical assistance from
German heavy industry so badly needed to back the NEP. Germany
had been Russia's best pre-war customer, and the eastern orientation in
German foreign policy had a long history dating back to Bismarck.
German motivations for seeking agreement and co-operation with
Bolshevik Russia were both strategic and economic. The failure of the
'Kapp putsch' of March 1920, an attempt of right-wing militarists to seize
power in Berlin that had resulted in the temporary flight of President
Ebert and the government from the capital, meant the abandonment of
extremists' hopes of overturning the Weimar republic and defeating
Bolshevik Russia. German trade-union action broke up the attempted
coup; their successful general strike was backed by a fragile combination
of social democrats and communists. In this struggle the German army,
the Reichswehr, remained neutral and then demanded a price from the
Weimar government for its neutrality. General von Seeckt was made
head of a camouflaged general staff, known as the *Truppenamt*, and the
Reichswehr was allowed to crush the pro-republican and anti-militarist
strikes in the Ruhr. The alliance of the left was rapidly and easily
shattered and the weakness and indecisiveness of the KPD ruthlessly
exposed. If General von Seeckt was determined to wipe out Bolshevism
inside Germany, he nevertheless understood what could be gained for
the infant German republic from a temporary alliance with Bolshevik
Russia. The Reichswehr command was not alone in seeing the usefulness of such an accommodation. In late 1919 and early 1920 the powerful
German industrialist and wartime head of the raw materials division of
the German ministry of war, Walther Rathenau, as well as other businessmen and financiers visited Karl Radek in his Berlin cell, where he
was imprisoned for his participation in the abortive Spartacist uprising
and was awaiting deportation to Russia. Rathenau and Radek discussed
the possibilities of increased German–Russian trade. Ideologically opposed to Bolshevism, Rathenau was interested in the Bolshevik experiment and quick to see the possibilities for Germany. The Russo-Polish
war, too, aroused considerable interest in official German circles.
Though anti-Polish feeling ran high, the German government, in contrast to the Allies, declared its 'neutrality' in the conflict and placed a ban
on the transit of arms through Germany. In July 1920, at the height of
Russian success, the German foreign minister held out to Moscow the
hope of *de jure* recognition and the resumption of full diplomatic relations; the price would be Russian recognition of Germany's pre-war
boundaries. But hopes for a new partition of Poland proved premature,
and there was a momentary chill in German–Russian relations before
both governments returned to the possibilities of rapprochement. Victor

Kopp, the Russian representative in Berlin, wrote to Chicherin, Lenin, and Trotsky on 7 September 1920: 'As a result of our failures on the Polish front and the pending peace with Poland . . . the idea of eastern orientation [in Germany] even if not completely disappeared, in any case, got blurred. The rightist nationalist circles, which linked this idea with the dreams of a military attack, jointly with Soviet Russia against France, now call for its complete abandonment.'[15]

Even during the period of coolness, those Germans who were thinking in terms of an eastern strategy remained active. Talks were opened between Victor Kopp and German military officers (a special section devoted to Russian affairs, *Sondergruppe R*, was established in the war ministry in early 1921) and industrialists interested in rebuilding the Russian armaments industry. Strict secrecy was necessary, as such plans violated the disarmament terms of the Treaty of Versailles. In April 1921 projects for manufacturing aeroplanes, submarines, guns, and shells were secretly discussed in Moscow and Berlin. In the early summer a German mission of military experts visited Russia, and this was followed, despite pessimistic reports and the abandonment of proposed joint ventures, by the foundation of a company (GEFU) to act as a cover for the Reichswehr and the German firms involved in arms transactions.

A provisional Russo-German trade agreement was signed on 6 May 1921, placing relations on a new and more stable basis. German industrialists, fearful that they would be excluded from the Russian market after the conclusion of the Anglo-German trade treaty, had increased their pressure on the foreign ministry. Entente threats to take 50 per cent of German export proceeds as reparation payments provided a further incentive to look to Russia, as did the presentation of the London ultimatum (5 May 1921) setting the schedule of reparation payments. The Russians won a German promise to recognize the Bolshevik mission as the sole Russian representative in Germany, despite the strong preference of German firms for individual contracts. During 1922–3 Germany temporarily replaced Britain as Russia's major source of imports, though Britain proved the better long-term customer, particularly for the wood and agricultural products which constituted so large a proportion of Russian exports. The German trade figures, nonetheless, remained significant, and the German share of the Russian market, though never reaching pre-1914 proportions, continued to grow. Both governments used the possibility of future agreements as carrots and sticks in their dealings with the British and French.

---

[15] Sergei Gorlov, *Sovershenno Sekretno: Alians Moskva–Berlin, 1920–1933 gg (Voenno-politicheskie otnoshenia SSSR–Germania)* (Moscow, 2001), 47.

The new provisional trade agreement, like the Anglo-Soviet trade treaty, represented a further step in the Soviet pursuit of diplomatic recognition. It was followed in the German case with further talks on three levels: economic, military, and political. Conversations between Krasin and the Reichswehr representatives in Berlin gathered pace in the aftermath of the autumn crisis over Upper Silesia. Separate military negotiations involving Seeckt and Junkers, the aircraft producers, ran parallel with the political and economic exchanges, and continued until mid-February 1922. At the end of 1921 Radek, one of the leading Russian supporters of the Berlin–Moscow alliance, was invited to Berlin. Talks were conducted with Chancellor Joseph Wirth, Felix Deutsch of the German electrical cartel AEG, the iron-and-steel magnate Hugo Stinnes, Walther Rathenau, and Baron Ago von Maltzan, a diplomat sympathetic to a Russian understanding whom Wirth had recalled from Athens to head the eastern department of the German foreign ministry. German trade agreements with Moscow could be pursued either on a bilateral basis or as part of a more far-reaching financial and economic arrangement involving Britain, France, Italy, and possibly even the United States. The Wirth government was willing to move in either direction; even Rathenau, who became foreign minister in January 1922, though a strong supporter of the consortium idea, was not averse to separate private arrangements with the Russians.

The possibility of an international consortium for the reconstruction of Russia was raised in conversations between a group of German industrialists and a Soviet delegation led by Krasin in Berlin in May 1921. The subject was again explored in a series of meetings which Rathenau and Stinnes held with interested British and French parties in late December 1921. According to the latter's scheme, the Germans would rebuild the entire Russian railway system, with the financial backing of Britain, France, and possibly the United States. It would be possible, as Rathenau indicated, that part of Germany's profits from her participation in the consortium could be used to pay reparations, an idea that strongly appealed to the British prime minister. Lloyd George took up the proposals for establishing an international consortium that would use the financial resources of the west for the development of the Soviet economy under Anglo-German leadership; he considered Chicherin's proposal in October to call an international conference to discuss Russian and European reconstruction.

Renewed Russian overtures to other capitalist states in mid-1921 coincided with widespread crop failures in the Volga region. The massive Russian famine mobilized world sympathy and action. Efforts were led by the American Relief Administration, a mixed private-public body headed by Hoover, now US secretary of commerce, and by the Red Cross through Nansen, who had played a major part in the repatriation of Russian prisoners of war and had gained the trust of the Bolshevik authorities. In October the Supreme Council called for a meeting of the interested parties in Brussels. Both governments tried to extract as much as possible from Moscow as the price for Allied aid. Lloyd George, finally freed from his Irish preoccupations, seized the initiative at Brussels to secure support for a major credit operation that would link famine-plagued Russia and the capitalist states on terms dictated by the latter, acting (with the exception of the United States) as a single body. Chicherin's response, strengthened by Lenin, was to accept the Brussels demand for the recognition of tsarist pre-war debts, though not, as actually demanded, existing debts, but he also outlined the reciprocal concessions required from the west. The Russians wanted substantial aid and investment, *de jure* recognition, an international conference to mediate reciprocal financial claims, and a final peace treaty. They were unwilling to compromise their position without a substantial return. The Allies were decidedly overconfident that Lenin would see the errors of the Bolshevik ways.

The Bolsheviks felt that they had good cards to play. Knowing of the economic difficulties of the western states, and convinced that the capitalist powers needed the Russian market, they tried during the autumn of 1921 to conclude bargains with individual foreign firms and to promote competitive bids for concessions in the oilfields. British firms were particularly anxious to take up foreign concessions whose legal status was still in doubt. Such activities did not go unnoticed; the French and Americans were unwilling to allow the British sole rights to exploit the Russian market. The Russians remained highly suspicious about doing business with any western bloc of commercial interests, and worried about the quid pro quo the capitalist powers might demand in return for credit and concessions. Though in serious need of capital and technology, Moscow worked out its own proposals for economic reconstruction to be put forward at the future international conference proposed by Chicherin, who went so far as to suggest that Russia might make concessions with regard to the tsarist debt in order to facilitate a general understanding if the Allies offered 'special conditions and facilities which will enable it to carry out this undertaking'.[16] It was Lenin who plotted the strategies pursued at the forthcoming Genoa conference (10 April–19 May 1922), Lloyd George's grand design for the reconstruction of Europe.

---

[16] Quoted in Robert Himmer, 'Rathenau, Russia and Rapallo', *Central European History*, 9 (1976), 160.

VI

The path to Genoa was a bumpy one; the French had little liking for the conference, and the Americans declined to come. The Russian representatives refused to accept the resolutions adopted at the Cannes conference in January 1922 establishing the Supreme Council's terms for Russian participation, though Lenin was in fact anxious that an international conference should be held. The Russians particularly disliked the special protections provided for foreign investors. Lenin assured his domestic critics that the Soviet delegation would go to Genoa as merchants looking for the most economically and politically suitable terms they could secure, and not as supplicants. He took a close personal interest in the proceedings. He recruited the members of the delegation, which included Chicherin, Maxim Litvinov, the deputy chief of the Commissariat of Foreign Affairs, and Krasin, and had special secure lines of communication established so that he could keep in constant contact with them. Policy was given careful consideration. The October 1921 offer to pay back the tsarist loans contracted before 1914 was only the opening move in a far more elaborate chess game. The Narkomindel (People's Commissariat of Foreign Affairs) was asked to formulate a 'broad pacifist programme' outlining the terms for 'peaceful coexistence'. They included the cancellation of all war debts, diplomatic recognition, the promise of non-interference in each other's affairs, an agreement to settle disputes by peaceful means, and a proposal for general disarmament. If the capitalist powers rejected this highly revisionist programme, Lenin was prepared to exploit the differences among them to get the best trade and loan agreements possible.

The first steps in this direction were taken already in the run-up to the conference. Though the Russians welcomed the invitation to Genoa, they had no liking for the proposed international consortium and looked to a separate agreement with Germany as the best means to disrupt it. The Russians used the Anglo-French talks begun in October 1921, supposedly about settling the Russian reparation claims under Article 116 of the Versailles treaty, to intimidate the Germans. Rathenau dismissed the Russian threat of separate agreements with the Entente powers as pure bluff, but Chancellor Wirth and Maltzan initiated preliminary talks with the Russian representatives to discover what terms were required for a separate understanding. Following an invitation from Maltzan, Radek arrived in Berlin in mid-January; month-long discussions followed, but no agreement was reached either on an economic or political treaty. The Russians would not consider giving special rights to a German syndicate composed of Stinnes, Krupp, and

AEG that included the admission of other firms without the approval of the Russian government. Sharp differences over the consortium, as well as Rathenau's refusal to accept a nationalization settlement without most-favoured-nation treatment of German claims, blocked a political settlement. With the exclusion of reparations from the Genoa agenda and a letter from the Reparation Commission on 22 March imposing rigorous conditions for a provisional moratorium, the Germans grew anxious and Maltzan was allowed to resume conversations with Radek and Bukharin, though again with no positive results. It was in the hope of strengthening their negotiating hand that Chicherin and Litvinov stopped in Berlin on the way to Genoa. Somewhat surprisingly, although no treaty was concluded, the Russians and Germans reached agreement on all but two issues and both delegations went to Genoa with a Russian draft treaty in hand. It was almost identical with the one signed two weeks later. At the last moment in Berlin, Rathenau, a complex and imaginative man, a Jew who was very much an outsider in his own foreign ministry and in the government, drew back. He feared the French reaction and still intended, despite adverse signs, to work with Lloyd George and even to act as an arbiter between the Allies and Russia at Genoa. For the same reasons that Chicherin wanted the treaty signed before going to Genoa, Rathenau preferred to wait. Though Chicherin failed in his immediate purpose, he sensed Rathenau's uneasiness about Germany's position and knew that the divided German delegation might prove amenable to Russian persuasion.

The Germans found it difficult to agree on a conference strategy. Reparations had been excluded from discussion at Genoa at French insistence. The memorandum issued by the Allied experts, meeting in London in March to decide how foreign labour and capital could be used for the reconstruction of Russia, not only suggested that Germany would be denied equality of status in any international consortium, but reaffirmed the Russian right to claim reparations under Article 116 of the Versailles treaty. At home, the minority Wirth government was under intense nationalist pressure as it struggled to implement a partial stabilization programme. The Genoa conference could well leave Germany more isolated in Europe than before. In many ways the Russians were in a stronger negotiating position than the Germans.

Chicherin's opening speech at the Genoa conference, first in French and then in English, was brilliantly calculated to deepen the rift between Britain and France and to court the Germans. While dwelling on the riches of the untapped Russian resources waiting to be developed, the commissar raised the possibility of a new peace settlement based on equality between victors and vanquished and a general reduction of armaments. Despite French objections, the German and Russian delegations were given places on all four Genoa commissions; the two Versailles outcasts were brought in from the cold. It was at Lloyd George's villa, however, with the Germans absent, that the Allied leaders discussed with the Russian representatives possible approaches to the problems of war debts, pre-war private and public debts, and the Bolshevik nationalization of foreign concerns. There was no meeting of minds, and the Russians broke off the talks. What happened next is much debated. It may be that Rathenau took alarm at Lloyd George's courting of the Russians or that Maltzan, who knew that the meetings with the Russians had ended in deadlock, thought this was the moment to 'gain freedom of action for Germany' to pursue its interests with the fewest restraints possible.[17] The 'easterner', supported by Wirth from Berlin, played on Rathenau's fears that a settlement would leave Germany isolated and convinced the already nervous foreign minister to take the plunge. Rathenau, fearing an Allied–Russian settlement without German participation, might well have wanted to strike his own bargain first. The treaty signed at the nearby seaside resort of Rapallo on 10 April, Easter Sunday, provided for the establishment of full diplomatic relations, mutual renunciation of claims (relieving the Germans of the nightmare of revived Russian claims for reparations), and for the extension of most-favoured-nation treatment in commercial matters. There was a hint of an accompanying military accord, but the military convention between the Reichswehr and Red Army was signed only on 11 August 1922, with Wirth's knowledge.[18]

The Treaty of Rapallo was a 'bombshell'. Lloyd George was not forewarned, either by Sir Robert Hodgson, the head of the British commercial mission in Moscow, or by Lord D'Abernon, the ambassador in Berlin, who actually knew that the Russian and German delegations were going to Genoa with a draft treaty in hand. The Foreign Office was appalled by D'Abernon's apparent inattentiveness. For William Tyrrell, an assistant under-secretary at the Foreign Office, the pact was 'the most important event which has taken place since the Armistice, but this is not a view which our Embassy at Berlin apparently

---

[17] Peter Krüger, 'The Rapallo Treaty and German Foreign Policy', in Carole Fink, Axel Frohn, and Jürgen Heideking, *Genoa, Rapallo, and European Reconstruction in 1922* (Cambridge, 1991), 59. Compare this with the treatment by Hartmut Pogge von Strandmann, 'Rapallo-Strategy in Preventive Diplomacy: New Sources and New Interpretations', in Volker R. Berghahn and Martin Kitchen (eds.), *Germany in the Age of Total War* (London, 1981).

[18] This information comes from Stephanie C. Salzman, *Britain, Germany and the Soviet Union: Rapallo and After, 1992–1934* (London, 2003), 27, citing a Russian publication: Y. L. Dyakov and T. S. Bushueva (eds.), *Phashistskii Mech Kovalsya v SSSR, Krasnaya Armiya i Reikhsver Tainoye Sotrudnichestvo 1922–1933, Neizvestniye dokumenty* (Moscow, 1992), 15.

take'.[19] The French and eastern European governments expressed extreme alarm. The partnership between Berlin and Moscow confirmed their worst nightmares; the two great powers were in a position to stifle the successor states should they so wish. The challenge to the French security system was palpable; the threat to both Versailles and France's eastern alliances could hardly have been clearer. The German action confirmed Premier Poincaré's view of the untrustworthy *Boche* and highlighted the dangers to France of Lloyd George's great scheme. The Welshman's subsequent diplomatic acrobatics outraged the French premier, and Louis Barthou, his chief representative at Genoa, was subjected to a stream of indignant telegrams from Paris. Despite his anger, Lloyd George, anxious above all to save his conference, worked rapidly and deftly to defuse the situation for fear that a negative reaction would drive the signatories out of Genoa. His exercise in damage-limitation prolonged the life of the conference for another fruitless month.

The Russian coup did not produce a victory at Genoa. There was little possibility that either this conference or its postscript at the Hague would result either in the *de jure* recognition of Bolshevik Russia or the foreign investments and credits the Russians wanted, except on terms that Lenin would not accept. Russian tactics backfired. The contents, probably leaked by the Russians, of a non-existent treaty giving the Royal Dutch Shell group a monopoly over the production and sale of Russian petroleum, as well as a vast concession in the Baku and Grosny areas, infuriated the American, French, and Belgian oil-company representatives who had gathered at Genoa to compete for Russian favours. The American government issued a denunciation of any Russian scheme that violated the 'open door' principle, and the French repudiated their bargain over payments for the expropriation of their citizens' holdings. Lenin, who had already taken a strong stand against concessions to capitalism before the conference assembled, refused to bargain except on conditions of equality. The western powers would not offer the substantial loans and full recognition that were the minimum price for Russian debt repayment and the restoration of foreign commercial rights. Undoubtedly encouraged by the Rapallo treaty, Lenin complained of the 'unspeakably shameful and *dangerous* vacillations of Chicherin and *Litvinov* (not to speak of Krasin)', and sent off a series of reprimands and instructions to the Russian delegation in late April and early May, warning against being coerced or panicked into an agreement.[20] Despite a brilliant diplomatic performance at the Hague

[19] Tyrrell to Lord Curzon, 24 Apr. 1922, Curzon Papers, India Office Library, London, mss. Eur F 112/227.

[20] Jacobson, *Soviet Union*, 96 (emphasis in original).

in July 1922, Maxim Litvinov, the chief Russian delegate, sympathetic to compromise, accomplished nothing. The Allies refused to consider direct loans or government guarantees of private investment unless the Russians made far-reaching concessions to former bondholders. Taking up the Russian hint of a deal with Royal Dutch Shell, a Franco-Belgian group combined with the company to check Russian efforts to promote a concession race. The break-up of the Hague conference ended the first real effort at detente in Bolshevik Russian relations with the west. Lenin was not unduly upset with the break-up of the conference. It had revealed the divisions between the capitalist powers and the willingness of some to 'do business with the Russians'. If necessary, the country could survive without western underwriting. He was fully prepared, however, to abandon the principle of collective agreements in favour of bilateral arrangements for which Rapallo could serve as a model. The Russians concluded a commercial treaty, without recognition, but on an equal footing, at Genoa, with Edvard Beneš of Czechoslovakia. Signed in Prague in June 1922, it governed Czech–Soviet relations for the next thirteen years. Efforts were also made to extend the 1921 preliminary commercial pact with the Italians, though the Chicherin–Giannini treaty concluded on 24 May 1922 did not go far, due to opposition in both countries. Lenin's belief that Italy could be drawn into the Rapallo front was not totally without substance. Mussolini, like his pre-fascist predecessors, found good reasons, in terms of his anti-French policies and Italy's need for Russian grain, metals, and oil imports in exchange for her machines and industrial equipment, to overlook his ideological anti-Bolshevism. Contrary to Lenin's hopes, however, Rapallo had no successor, nor did it prove a useful device for preventing a German settlement with the western European countries.

During the months after the Hague conference the Russian government kept a low profile in Europe. In late May Lenin had suffered his first stroke and was left incapacitated for the next four months, temporarily recovering in time to prepare for the Lausanne conference (November 1922–July 1923). Lloyd George's downfall in October 1922 and Poincaré's continued domination of French diplomacy hardly augured well for further talks with the Allies. Moscow looked to Berlin to cement the new economic arrangements and the secret military projects. Chicherin, deprived of Lenin's active support, spent the summer and autumn in Berlin, conducting negotiations but really marking time until the Moscow situation cleared. In November 1922 Brockdorff-Rantzau, the first German ambassador in four years, arrived in Moscow and soon proved himself a strong supporter of Germany's eastern policy. Berlin after Genoa was entirely caught up in the reparations crisis. With Lenin suffering a further series of strokes that left him physically incapacitated until his death on 21 January 1924, the Soviet leadership would have to cope with the 'German problem' without their master.

VII

The Union of Soviet Socialist Republics (USSR) was formed on 30 December 1922. The country had survived the famine; there was a good harvest in 1922 and NEP was beginning to produce some positive results. The country's internal administrative reorganization was almost complete. The policy of 'peaceful coexistence' paid important dividends. The actual Soviet presence at Genoa at the invitations of the allies was already a step towards respectability, and as such was much disliked by Poincaré and the French. The Rapallo treaty, an equal bargain between two sovereign states, further improved the diplomatic status of the Soviet Union. The treaty indicated that both signatories, the two pariahs of Europe, had an alternative to European reconstruction on Allied terms. The Soviets hoped that the treaty would prevent Germany from playing the balance-of-power game of the pre-1914 period. Even if the west returned to the policy of boycott and ostracism, the Soviet leadership believed that the treaty with Germany would prevent the conclusion of a united anti-Soviet bloc. The Moscow–Berlin link, with its implicit threat to Poland, could considerably weaken France's security system. The Bolsheviks had found a way to enhance their position during a difficult and dangerous, if temporary, phase in their development.

The difficulty was that the Rapallo treaty was the USSR's only real link to the capitalist west, and Germany alone could hardly provide the capital and investment needed for Russian industrialization. 'Peaceful coexistence' began as a tactic to gain time, but there were hopes in Moscow that new bilateral treaties would bring the credits, trade, and technical assistance that the Soviet Union had failed to get at Genoa. The most concerted effort was made with the British, but Chicherin had to deal with Lord Curzon, who was now free to pursue his own stridently anti-Soviet line. On 8 May 1923 the Foreign Office sent a long memorandum, the so-called 'Curzon ultimatum', rehearsing the subversive activities of the USSR in India and Central Asia and demanding the settlement of British claims under the threat of denouncing the 1921 trade agreement. It was a typical Curzon performance; the foreign secretary, well primed by intelligence sources, thought that the unruly Bolsheviks should be taught good international manners. Soviet apprehensions were increased when General Foch paid a visit to Warsaw, and the Soviet observer sent to the Lausanne economic conference was assassinated by a white Russian émigré. The Swiss government denied all responsibility for the protection of their Bolshevik guest and a prolonged diplomatic contretemps followed. There were strident anti-British speeches and demonstrations in Moscow but Chicherin was intent on an agreement. Once again, Krasin was sent to London to calm the troubled waters. The British proposed and the Soviets accepted a new formula about the much disputed propaganda issue and promised that the over-energetic Soviet representative in Kabul would be recalled. No further talks followed and Krasin was dispatched to Paris to break the deadlock there. Any discussions in Paris were bound to be complicated by the large number of individual French holders of tsarist bonds and the unwillingness of the Soviets to offer compensation.

The Soviet Union was still very much on the periphery of European affairs when the reparations crisis and the French occupation of the Ruhr in January 1923 posed a whole series of problems for Lenin's deputies. With Lenin terminally ill, the battle for the succession had already begun and the regime was going through a period of extreme domestic difficulty. The Ruhr crisis found both the Comintern and the German Communist party (KPD) without any clear line of policy. Some members of the Politburo were more worried by the possible defeat of their Rapallo partner and the prospect of an over-powerful France than by the fate of the German revolutionary movement. Nevertheless, throughout 1923 Karl Radek, the veteran Comintern agitator, commuted between Moscow and Germany working up support for the revolution. The old concept of 'national Bolshevism' was revived in the hope of attracting supporters from the extreme right-wing nationalist parties into the Bolshevik camp. Arguments both in Berlin and in Moscow about Soviet intervention were still going on when the Cuno government collapsed in Germany and Stresemann was appointed chancellor in August. Among the Soviet leaders, Trotsky was the most optimistic about the possibility of a German revolution. He was backed by Bukharin and Zinoviev and opposed by Chicherin, probably Kamenev, and Stalin, who during the summer of 1923 warned against the pursuit of illusory revolutionary wars. The Politburo was cautious, but in late August agreed that the Comintern should plan for the anticipated uprising. It appears that it was only when Germany was on the brink of disintegration into separate states that the KPD was told to join with the left-wing socialists in Saxony and Thuringia in preparation for a general strike and workers' revolution. Military advisers were dispatched and small groups, the 'Red hundreds', prepared for armed action. The Red Army did not mobilise, but preparations were made to strengthen the military forces on the western front to bring pressure on Latvia and Lithuania to open a corridor to Germany and to prevent Polish intervention in German affairs. Preventative steps were taken to safeguard any future Soviet Germany from strangulation at birth. The experienced Victor Kopp was sent to the Baltic states and to Poland to secure assurances of non-intervention and to assure future rights of transit. It was hoped to purchase Polish agreement with an offer to support Warsaw's claim to East Prussia, but the talks lapsed when the German revolution collapsed. The ineptitude of the KPD and the unwillingness of the SPD and the non-communist workers to engage in civil war ended whatever hopes there had been for success. The planned insurrection was called off on 21 October 1923. One Hamburg unit, in ignorance of the decision, rebelled and was quickly crushed by the local police and the Reichswehr on its way to Dresden to depose the revolutionary government. The German revolution was over before it began.

It took some time for the Soviet leaders to abandon their hopes for a successful revolution in Germany and to absorb the lesson of its failure. It was becoming clear, though there were important lapses, that it was difficult to pursue outwardly contradictory policies and that a failure on the revolutionary front was bound to have unfortunate repercussions on the diplomatic side. Even as help was being given to the KPD, the German ambassador, Brockdorff-Rantzau, was in Moscow cultivating his excellent relations with Chicherin. The two men had far more in common that their backgrounds and love of cats. Each believed that the Rapallo relationship was in the best interests of both their countries. It is interesting, too, that the Stresemann cabinet chose to accept the fiction that the Soviet government had nothing to do with the activities of the Comintern and KPD. Soviet–German arrangements for military and economic co-operation continued. In Moscow, the Ruhr failure became part of the intra-party debate as the political struggle between Trotsky and Stalin, Zinoviev, and Kamenev continued and intensified.

There was also a parallel Comintern defeat in Bulgaria when the Bulgarian communists, prodded by Zinoviev, staged an uprising with some peasant support on 22 September 1923 against the right-wing government that had succeeded in unseating the Stamboliisky peasant government and murdering its head. The result was a total defeat for the communists, the crushing of the party, and the unleashing of a White terror by the triumphant Tsankov government. There was a curious postscript to these events. In part because of the favoured role of the peasants in NEP, but also because of events in Bulgaria and Poland, Zinoviev and Bukharin backed the creation of a Peasant International. Its first and last congress was held in Moscow in October 1923. Almost nothing productive came of this initiative.

Soviet attention during the latter half of 1923 and 1924 was focused on the intra-party struggle for Lenin's succession between the triumvirate (Stalin, Kamenev, and Zinoviev) and Trotsky, with Stalin determined to discredit his major rival. Despite the political uncertainties, some progress was made on the international front. Both the Italians and British had economic reasons for considering *de jure* recognition, and the installation of a Labour government in London in January 1924 opened the door to talks. In fact, Mussolini had already taken the initiative in a speech on 30 November 1923, and hoped that Italy would be the first victor state to recognize the USSR. The Soviets were more interested in London and used the Italian offer to prod the MacDonald government. On 1 February the British offered *de jure* recognition and the promise of a general treaty to follow. The Soviet–Italian treaty followed a week later. Other countries—Austria, Greece, Norway, and Sweden—later followed suit. The Herriot cabinet, formed in June 1924, recognized the USSR in October. The American government, despite a campaign for recognition, resolutely refused to

TABLE 7. Soviet Exports and Imports, 1913–1938 (1913=100)

	Exports	Imports
1918[a]	0.0	0.1
1919[a]	0.0	0.0
1920[a]	0.0	0.0
1921 (Jan.–Sept.)	0.0	0.1
1921/2	0.1	0.2
1922/3	0.1	0.1
1923/4	27.7	23.3
1924/5	25.9	42.5
1925/6	34.0	51.4
1926/7	40.0	53.9
1927/8	41.2	70.6
1929	54.1	68.0
1930	80.1	88.6
1931	90.1	111.0
1932	74.0	77.8
1933	71.0	52.9
1934	67.3	51.8
1935	59.9	54.8
1936	47.3	54.8
1937	46.3	50.9
1938	39.1	56.5

Note: [a] Figures relating to USSR pre-1939 territory.
Sources: R. W. Davies, M. Harrison, and S. G. Wheatcraft, *The Economic Transformation of the Soviet Union 1913–1945* (Cambridge, Cambridge University Press, 1994) 318; M. R. Dohan and E. Hewett, *Two Studies in Soviet Tressury Trade, 1918–1970* (1973) 24, 27.

consider political action. Private exporters, however, entered the Russian market and, using a joint negotiating agent, concluded an agreement with the Soviet foreign trade monopoly. The Chase National Bank provided a 2 million dollar loan, part of which the Soviets used for cotton purchases.

Many of the Soviet achievements during this period were due to the outcome of their manipulation of the solidarity movements abroad, mostly among the rank and file of the trade unions. This manipulative policy brought about both unconditional recognition and the MacDonald government's acceptance of *de jure* recognition. At the same time, the Russians were able to present their special relationship with the labour movements as an ideological justification for their straightforward diplomatic activities. This was the essence of the NEP policies of attempting a dual approach of compromising with the west while maintaining the Bolshevik ideological principles. It was this duality of approach that would misfire in 1927 after the British general strike, and in China, where similar united front tactics were employed.

Even at this time there were limits to what could be accomplished. The successful negotiations with the Labour government aroused considerable hostility in Conservative, Liberal, and City of London circles. The bankers set conditions for loans that the Russians would not consider. The British wanted payment, at least in part, of the tsarist debts and refused to offer a loan guarantee unless these claims were settled. The talks broke down in August 1924. Some left-wing Labour backbenchers negotiated a compromise. A commercial treaty was to be concluded, but only later would there be a treaty settling the Russian debts and then a guaranteed loan. The opposition was preparing to attack the treaty when parliament reassembled after its recess.

It was not just the question of tsarist debts that blocked progress but the persistent suspicion of Soviet subversive intentions. The Campbell affair (J. R. Campbell, a communist, was charged with inciting soldiers to mutiny, but the Labour attorney-general, pressed by MacDonald, dropped the prosecution to the fury of the Conservatives) and the furore over the 'Zinoviev letter' contributed to the size of the Labour defeat in October 1924. The letter, probably a forgery, purported to be an instruction from the Third International to the British Communist party to promote sedition in the armed services and revolt in the colonies. It was reminiscent of many other previous communications that had been intercepted by the British, which suggested that the communists intended to stir up trouble in India and that Zinoviev intended to extend the Comintern campaign to Britain. The premature publication of the letter, meant to show MacDonald's hostility towards Soviet interference in British affairs, was used by the Tory leadership to prove that Labour was soft on Bolshevism. It seems highly likely that members of the intelligence community had deliberately leaked the letter to the Conservatives and to the *Daily Mail* which published it. Zinoviev insisted that it was a forgery, but the damage was done.

In London, the incoming Conservative cabinet took steps to restrict the circulation of both intelligence intercepts and the regular Special Branch reports, but the continued flow of intelligence alerted the new foreign secretary, Austen Chamberlain, and the smaller group of ministerial recipients to the hostile activities of the Bolsheviks in the east. Chamberlain, while fully aware of the extent of Soviet subversion, was anxious to avoid a break with the Russians on the eve of new negotiations with France and Germany. He was unwilling to follow the lead of the extremists in his cabinet who wanted to expel the Soviets from Britain and break off all relations with the USSR. Chamberlain preferred a 'wait and see' policy towards Moscow. The Russians tried to revive negotiations for a loan, but the foreign secretary proved unresponsive. The growing force of the anti-Bolshevik chorus in London and the conflicts in China raised fears that the British might lead an anti-Soviet bloc.

It was during these months that the conflict between Stalin and his associates against Trotsky took on a sharper ideological edge. In an article that appeared both in *Pravda* and *Izvestiya* on 20 April 1924, 'October and Comrade Trotsky's Theory of Permanent Revolution', Stalin contrasted his own doctrine of 'socialism in one country' with Trotsky's 'permanent revolution'. The revolutionary failure in Germany had led to discussions among the leadership regarding the 'stabilization of capitalism', and what the USSR could do without revolutionary success in western Europe. It was at this point that Stalin's expansion of Lenin's arguments for coexistence was injected into the party debate. It was conceived as a theoretical debating point against Trotsky, but it was also intended to provide a positive response to the failure of world revolution by encouraging hopes that NEP, which Trotsky was already criticizing, could lead to socialism in a peasant economy without outside support. Very roughly summarized, Stalin argued that Russia could proceed to full communism without the aid of revolutionary movements abroad, while Trotsky, whose views remained consistent with those he first expressed in 1906 and then in his numerous writings on the 'Permanent Revolution', insisted that foreign proletarian support was necessary if communist Russia was not to be overwhelmed by the forces of bourgeois reaction. As the power struggle moved in Stalin's direction, 'peaceful coexistence' became an accepted part of his 'socialism in one country' argument. During the next winter Stalin returned to the charge, when the triumvirate split up and Stalin engaged in an open battle for the leadership of the party with Zinoviev, Kamenev, and the Leningrad opposition. He justified the Russian withdrawal from foreign revolutionary action by claiming that both the capitalist and socialist camps had entered a period of stabilization, and that there existed a temporary equilibrium between the two opposing systems. Trotsky argued that unless the class war was carried into the capitalist countries, they would join in an attack on the Soviet Union. Stalin maintained that the imperialist states were sufficiently disorganized by socialist success as to make such a war impossible. The breathing space already won was creating a new period of stability, though the contradictions between the two systems remained and would develop further.

From the Soviet point of view the European situation was deteriorating in 1924–5, for the balance of power was shifting in an adverse direction. The difficulties with Britain were compounded by clear signs that Germany might be moving into the western camp. Already at the end of December 1924, the Russians offered the Germans a new pact to forestall the possibility of their participation in an anti-Soviet bloc. The negotiations that followed the adoption of the Dawes plan and the London agreements and that led to the Locarno settlements represented a major defeat for the Soviet Rapallo policy.

Books

ANDREW, CHRISTOPHER M., *Secret Service: The Making of the British Intelligence Community* (London, 1985).

ARMSTRONG, JAMES DAVID, *Revolution and World Order: The Revolutionary State in International Society* (Oxford, 1993).

BENNETT, GILL, *'A Most Extraordinary and Mysterious Business': The Zinoviev Letter of 1924* (London, 1999).

BERSTEIN, SERGE and BECKER, JEAN-JACQUES, *Histoire de l'anticommunisme en France, 1917–1940* (Paris, 1987).

BORKENAU, VOLKER R., *World Communism: A History of the Communist International* (Ann Arbor, Mich., 1962).

CARLEY, MICHAEL JABARA, *Revolution and Intervention: The French Government and the Russian Civil War, 1917–1919* (Kingston and Montreal, 1983).

CARR, E. H., *The Bolshevik Revolution, 1917–1923*, 3 vols. (London, 1950–3).

—— *German–Soviet Relations Between the Two World Wars, 1919–1939* (Baltimore, 1951).

—— *The Interregnum, 1923–1924* (New York, 1954).

—— *Socialism in One Country, 1924–1926*, 3 vols. (London, 1958–64).

CHESTER, LEWIS, FAY, STEPHEN, and YOUNG, HUGO, *The Zinoviev Letter* (London, 1967).

CHUBARIAN, A. O., *Peaceful Coexistence: The Origin of the Notion* (New York, 1976).

CLAUDÍN, FERNANDO, *The Communist Movement: From Comintern to Cominform*, trans. Brian Pearce and Francis MacDonagh (Harmondsworth, 1975).

COEURE, SOPHIE, *La Grande Lueur à l'est*. *Les Français et l'Union soviétique, 1917–1939* (Paris, 1999).

COHEN, STEPHEN F., *Bukharin and the Bolshevik Revolution: A Political Biography, 1888–1938* (New York, 1973).

—— *Rethinking the Soviet Experience: Politics and History Since 1917* (New York, 1985).

COURTOIS, STÉPHAN, *et al.* (eds.), *Le Livre noir du communisme: crimes, terreurs et répression* (Paris, 1997).

DATTA GUPTA, SOBHANLAL, *Comintern and the Colonial Question, 1920–1937* (Calcutta, 1980).

DAVIES, NORMAN, *White Eagle, Red Star: The Polish–Soviet War, 1919–20* (London, 1972).

DAVIES, R. W., *Soviet Economic Development from Lenin to Khrushchev* (Cambridge, 1998).

DEBO, RICHARD K., *Revolution and Survival: The Foreign Policy of Soviet Russia, 1917–1918* (Toronto, 1979).

—— *Survival and Consolidation: The Foreign Policy of Soviet Russia, 1918–1921* (Montreal, 1992).

DEGRAS, JANE (ed.), *The Communist International, 1919–43* (London, 1956–65).

DYCK, HARVEY L., *Weimar Germany and Soviet Russia, 1926–1933: A Study of Diplomatic Instability* (New York, 1966).

ERICKSON, JOHN, *The Soviet High Command: A Military-Political History, 1918–1941* (New York, 1962).

FIDDICK, THOMAS C., *Russia's Retreat from Poland, 1920: From Permanent Revolution to Peaceful Coexistence* (London, 1990).

FILENE, PETER G., *Americans and the Soviet Experiment, 1917–1933* (Cambridge, Mass., 1967).

FINK, CAROLE, *The Genoa Conference: European Diplomacy, 1921–1922* (Chapel Hill, NC, 1984).

—— FROHN, AXEL, and HEIDEKING, JÜRGEN (eds.), *Genoa, Rapallo and European Reconstruction in 1922* (Cambridge, 1991). Esp. the chapters by Anne Hogenhuis-Seliverstoff, Peter Krüger, Giorgio Petracchi, and Andrew Williams.

FISCHER, LOUIS, *The Soviets in World Affairs: A History of the Relations between the Soviet Union and the Rest of the World, 1917–1929*, 2 vols. (Princeton, 1951).

GEYER, DIETRICH (ed.), *Sowjetunion: Außenpolitik, 1917–1955*, Bd. 1 (Cologne, 1972).

GOLDBACH, MARIE-LUISE, *Karl Radek und die deutsch-sowjetischen Beziehungen, 1918–1923* (Bonn, 1973).

GORLOV, SERGEI, *Sovershenno Sekretno: Alians Moskva–Berlin, 1920–1933 gg (Voenno–Politicheski otnoshenia SSSR–Germania)* [Top Secret: The Moscow–Berlin Alliance, 1920–1933: Military–Political Relations, USSR–Germany] (Moscow, 2001). My thanks go to El'vis Beytullayev who translated parts of the text.

GORODETSKY, GABRIEL (ed.), *Soviet Foreign Policy, 1917–1991: A Retrospective* (London, 1994). Esp. chapters by Richard K. Debo, Carole Fink, and Gabriel Gorodetsky.

GRIESER, HELMUT, *Die Soujetpresse über Deutschland in Europa, 1922–1932: Revision von Versailles und Rapallo-Politik in soujetischer Sicht* (Stuttgart, 1970).

HIDEN, JOHN and LOIT, ALEKSANDR (eds.), *Contact or Isolation? Soviet–Western Relations in the Interwar Period. Symposium Organized by the Center of Baltic Studies, October 12–14, 1989*, University of Stockholm (Stockholm, 1991). Esp. the chapters by Daniel F. Calhoun, Suzanne Champonnois, and Patrick Salmon.

HILDEBRAND, KLAUS, *Das deutsche Reich und die Soujetunion im internationalen System, 1918–1933* (Columbia, 1974).

HOGENHUIS-SELIVERSTOFF, ANNE, *Les Relations franco-soviétiques, 1917–1924* (Paris, 1981).

HOLLOWAY, DAVID and NAIMARK, NORMAN (eds.), *Re-examining the Soviet Experience: Essays in Honor of Alexander Dallin* (Boulder, Col., 1995).

HUGHES, MICHAEL, *Inside the Enigma: British Officials in Russia, 1901–1939* (London, 1997).

HULSE, JAMES W., *The Forming of the Communist International* (Stanford, Cal., 1964).

HUMBERT-DROZ, JULES, *L'Origine de l'Internationale Communiste de Zimmerwald à Moscou* (Neuchâtel, 1968).

—— *De Lénine à Staline: dix ans au service de l'internationale communiste, 1921–1931* (Neuchâtel, 1971).

JACOBSON, JON, *When the Soviet Union Entered World Politics* (Berkeley, Cal. and London, 1994).

KENNAN, GEORGE F., *Soviet–American Relations, 1917–1920*, 2 vols. (London, 1956–8).

LINKE, HORST GÜNTHER, *Deutsch-soujetische Beziehungen bis Rapallo*, 2nd edn. (Cologne, 1972).

McDERMOTT, KEVIN and AGNEW, JEREMY, *The Comintern: A History of International Communism from Lenin to Stalin* (Basingstoke, 1996).

MACFADDEN, DAVID, *Alternative Paths: Soviets and Americans, 1917–1920* (New York, 1993).

MAWDSLEY, EVAN, *The Russian Civil War* (Boston and London, 1987).

MELOGRANI, PIERO, *Lenin and the Myth of World Revolution: Ideology and Reasons of State, 1917–1920* (Atlantic Highlands, NJ, 1989).

NARINSKI, MIKHAIL and ROJHAN, JÜRGEN (eds.), *Centre and Periphery: The History of the Comintern; The History of the Comintern in the Light of New Documents* (Amsterdam, 1996).

NATION, R. CRAIG, *Black Earth, Red Star: A History of Soviet Security Policy, 1917–1991* (Ithaca, NY, 1992).

NEKRICH, ALEXANDR, *Pariahs, Partners, Predators: German–Soviet Relations, 1922–1941* (New York, 1997).

O'CONNOR, TIMOTHY EDWARD, *Diplomacy and Revolution: G. V. Chicherin and Soviet Foreign Affairs, 1918–1930* (Ames, Iowa, 1988).

REES, TIM and THORPE, ANDREW, *International Communism and the Communist International, 1919–1943* (Manchester, 1998).

ROSENBAUM, K., *Community of Fate: German–Soviet Diplomatic Relations, 1922–1928* (New York, 1965).

ROSENFELD, GÜNTER, *Sowjetrussland und Deutschland, 1917–1922*, 2nd edn. (Cologne, 1984).

—— *Sowjetunion und Deutschland, 1922–1933* (Berlin, 1984).

SABAHI, HOUSHANG, *British Policy in Persia, 1918–1925* (London and Portland 1990).

SALMON, PATRICK, *Scandinavia and the Great Powers, 1890–1940* (Cambridge, 1997).

SALZMANN, STEPHANIE, *Britain, Germany and the Soviet Union: Rapallo and After, 1922–1934* (London, 2003).

TALWAR, S. N., *Under the Banyan Tree: The Communist Movement in India, 1920–1964* (New Delhi, 1985).

THOMPSON, J. M., *Russia, Bolshevism and the Versailles Peace* (Princeton, 1966).

TROTSKY, LEON, *The First Five Years of the Communist International*, 2 vols. (New York, 1945–53).

TUCKER, ROBERT C., *Stalin as Revolutionary, 1879–1929: A Study in History and Personality* (London, 1974).

—— *Stalinism: Essays in Historical Interpretation*, 2nd edn. (New Brunswick, NJ, 1998).

ULAM, ADAM, *Expansion and Coexistence: The History of Soviet Foreign Relations, 1917–1967* (London, 1968).

ULDRICKS, TEDDY J., *Diplomacy and Ideology: The Origins of Soviet Foreign Relations, 1917–1930* (London and Beverley Hills, 1979).

ULLMAN, RICHARD H., *Anglo-Soviet Relations, 1917–1921*, 3 vols. (Princeton, 1961–73). Vol. 1: *Intervention and the War* (1961); Vol. 2: *Britain and the Russian Civil War* (1968); Vol. 3: *Anglo-Soviet Accord* (1973).

VIGOR, PETER HAST, *The Soviet View of War, Peace, and Neutrality* (London and Boston, 1975).

VOLODARSKI, MIKHAEL, *Soviet Union and its Southern Neighbours: Iran and Afghanistan, 1917–1933* (London, 1994).

WANDYCZ, P. S., *Soviet–Polish relations, 1917–1921* (Cambridge, 1969).

WHITE, STEPHEN, *Britain and the Bolshevik Revolution: A Study in the Politics of Diplomacy, 1920–1924* (London, 1979).

—— *The Origins of Détente: The Genoa Conference and Soviet–Western Relations, 1921–1922* (Cambridge and New York, 1985).

WILLIAMS, ANDREW J., *Trading With the Bolsheviks: The Politics of East–West Trade, 1920–1939* (Manchester, 1992).

ZEIDLER, MANFRED, *Reichswehr und Rote Armee, 1920–1933: Wege und Stationen einer ungewöhnlichen Zusammenarbeit* (Munich, 1993).

Articles

AKHTAMZIAN, A. A., 'Soviet–German Military Cooperation, 1920–1933', *International Affairs*, 7 (1990).

ANDREW, CHRISTOPHER M., 'The British Secret Service and Anglo-Soviet Relations in the 1920s: From the Trade Negotiations to the Zinoviev Letter', *Historical Journal*, 20 (1977).

—— 'More on the Zinoviev Letter', *Historical Journal*, 22 (1979).

AVINERI, SHLOMO, 'Marxism and Nationalism', *Journal of Contemporary History*, 26 (1991).

CARLEY, MICHAEL JABARA, 'From Revolution to Dissolution: The Quai d'Orsay, the Banque Russo-Asiatique, and the Chinese Eastern Railway, 1917–1926', *International History Review*, 12 (1990).

—— 'Prelude to Defeat: Franco-Soviet Relations, 1919–1939', in Joel Blatt (ed.), *The French Defeat of 1940: Reassessments* (Providence, RI, 1998).

—— and DEBO, R. K., 'Always in Need of Credit: The USSR and Franco-German Economic Cooperation, 1926–1929', *French Historical Studies*, 20: 3 (1997).

CHUSSUDOVSKY, EVGENY M., 'Genoa Revisited: Russia and Coexistence', *Foreign Affairs*, 50 (1972).

CLEMENS, WALTER, 'The Burden of Defense: Soviet Russia in the 1920s', *Journal of Slavic Military Studies*, 9: 4 (1996).

COURTOIS, STÉPHANE, 'Le Système communiste international et la lutte pour la paix, 1917–1939', *Relations Internationales*, 53 (1988).

CROWE, SIBYL, 'The Zinoviev Letter: A Reappraisal', *Journal of Contemporary History*, 10: 3 (1975).

DAVIES, NORMAN, 'The Genesis of the Polish–Soviet War, 1919–1920', *European Studies Review*, 5 (1975).

—— 'The Missing Revolutionary War: The Polish Campaigns and the Retreat from Revolution in Soviet Russia, 1919–1921', *Soviet Studies*, 27 (1975).

DOHAN, MICHAEL R., 'Foreign Trade', in R. W. Davies (ed.), *From Tsarism to the New Economic Policy: Continuity and Change in the Economy of the USSR* (London, 1990).

ENGERMAN, DAVID C., 'Economic Reconstruction in Soviet Russia: The Courting of Herbert Hoover in 1922', *International History Review*, 19: 4 (1997).

FINK, CAROLE, 'European Politics and Security at the Genoa Conference of 1922', in C. Fink, I. V. Hull, and M. Knox (eds.), *German Nationalism and the European Response, 1890–1945* (Norman, Okla, 1985).

FISHER, JOHN, ' "On the Glacis of India": Lord Curzon and British Policy in the Caucasus, 1919', *Diplomacy and Statecraft*, 8, 2 (1997).

—— 'The NEP in Foreign Policy: The Genoa Conference and the Treaty of Rapallo', in Gabriel Gorodetsky (ed.), *Soviet Foreign Policy, 1917–1991: A Retrospective* (London, 1994).

GINSBURG, GEORGE, 'The Theme of Rapallo in Postwar Soviet–West German Relations', *Soviet Union/Union Soviétique*, 13 (1986).

GORLOW, SERGEI, 'Die geheime Militärkooperation zwischen Sowjetunion und dem deutschen Reich, 1920–1933', *Vierteljahrshefte für Zeitgeschichte*, 44 (1996).

GORODETSKY, GABRIEL, 'The Formulation of Soviet Foreign Policy-Ideology and *Realpolitik*', in id. (ed.), *Soviet Foreign Policy, 1917–1991: A Retrospective* (London, 1994).

HANSON, STEPHEN and KOPSTEIN, JEFFREY, 'The Weimar/Russian Comparison', *Post-Soviet Affairs*, 3 (1997).

HIMMER, ROBERT, 'Rathenau, Russia and Rapallo', *Central European History*, 9 (1976).

HUGHES, MICHAEL, 'The Virtues of Specialization: British and American Diplomatic Reporting in Russia, 1921–39', *Diplomacy and Statecraft*, 11, 2 (2000).

JACOBSON, JON, 'The Soviet Union and Versailles', in M. F. Boemecke, G. D. Feldman, and E. Glaser (eds.), *The Treaty of Versailles: A Reassessment after 75 Years* (Washington, DC and Cambridge, 1998).

KUBÁLKOVÁ, V., 'The Soviet Concept of Peaceful Coexistence: Some Theoretical and Semantic Problems', *Australian Journal of Politics and History*, 24 (1978).

LERNER, WARREN, 'The Historical Origins of the Soviet Doctrine of Peaceful Coexistence', *Law and Contemporary Society*, 29 (1964).

LINKE, HORST, 'Der Weg nach Rapallo. Strategie und Tatik der deutschen und sowjetischen Aussenpolitik', *Historische Zeitschrift*, 264 (1997).

MADEIRA, VICTOR, 'Moscow's Interwar Infiltration of British Intelligence', *Historical Journal*, 46, 4 (2003).

MISIUNAS, ROMUALD J., 'The Role of the Baltic States in Soviet Relations with the West During the Interwar Period', in John Hiden and Aleksandr Loit (eds.), *The Baltic in International Relations Between the Two World Wars: Symposium Organized by the Center for Baltic Studies, November 11–13, 1986, University of Stockholm* (Stockholm, 1988).

PARTENAUDE, BETRAND M., 'The Strange Death of Soviet Communism: The 1921 Version', in David Holloway and Norman M. Naimark (eds.), *Reexamining the Soviet Experience: Essays in Honour of Alexander Dallin* (Boulder, Col., 1995).

PETRACCHI, GIORGIO, 'La cooperazione italiana, il Centsojuz e la ripresa dei rapporti commerciali tra l'Italia e la Russia sovietica, 1917–1922', *Storia Contemporanea* (1977).

POGGE VON STRANDMANN, HARTMUT, 'Rapallo–Strategy in Preventive Diplomacy: New Sources and New Interpretations', in V. K. Berghahn and Martin Kitchen (eds.), *Germany in the Age of Total War* (London, 1981).

RALEIGH, DONALD J., 'The Soviet Union in the 1920s: A Roundtable', *Soviet Studies in History*, 28 (1989).

SCHRAM, STUART R., 'Christian Rakovskij et le premier rapprochement franco-soviétique', *Cahiers du Monde Russe et Soviétique*, 1 (1960).

STONE, DAVID R., 'The Prospect of War? Lev Trotskü, the Soviet Army, and the German Revolution in 1923', *International History Review*, 35: 4 (Dec. 2003).

THORPE, ANDREW, 'Comintern Control of the Communist Party of Great Britain, 1920–1943', *English Historical Review*, 112: 453 (1998).

TOMASELLI, P., 'C's Moscow's Station–The Anglo-Russian Trade Mission as Cover for SIS in the Early 1920s'. *Intelligence and National Security*, 17, 3 (2002).

TUCKER, ROBERT C., 'The Emergence of Stalin's Foreign Policy', *Slavic Review*, 36 (1977).

—— 'Stalinism as Revolution from Above', in id. (ed.), *Stalinism: Essays in Historical Interpretation* (New York, 1977).

ULDRICKS, TEDDY J., 'Russia and Europe: Diplomacy, Revolution, and Economic Development in the 1920s', *International History Review*, 1 (1979).

WHITE, STEPHEN, 'Communism and the East: The Baku Congress, 1920', *Slavic Review*, 33 (1974).

—— 'Colonial Revolution and the Communist International, 1919–1924', *Science and Society*, 40 (1976).

—— 'Communist Ideology, Belief Systems, and Soviet Foreign Policy', in Erik P. Hoffmann and Frederic J. Fleron (eds.), *The Conduct of Soviet Foreign Policy*, 2nd edn. (New York, 1980).

—— 'Ideology and Soviet Politics', in id. and Alex Pravda (eds.), *Ideology and Soviet Politics* (New York, 1988).

4

The Primacy of Economics: Reconstruction in Western Europe, 1919–1924

I

Once the peace treaty was signed and the European leaders returned to their capitals, the most pressing problems they faced were financial and economic.[1] The war had wrecked international finance and trade, it had distorted or destroyed productive enterprises, and non-European competitors had appeared in world markets who would be difficult to dislodge. The length and costs of the war meant that victors and vanquished alike were left with inflated money supplies, massive budgetary deficits, huge debts, and, in the case of most, collapsed or overstrained tax structures. Almost all the European states had left the gold standard (Britain left officially on 31 March 1919), the supposedly self-regulating mechanism which had controlled exchange rates and had provided the necessary backing for international trade. Only the United States, in its newly established world creditor position, was in a position to return to gold in June 1919. The search for financial stability and balanced budgets in Europe was made more difficult, not only by the political and social consequences of the war, but also by the common desire to restore the traditional financial and trading structures of the past. New realms of competition in finance and trade further complicated matters. Though the war years had created close links between British and American financial experts, London and New York soon became rival financial centres. The British and Americans battled for control over air and cable routes and for access to raw materials and investment opportunities, particularly in areas of the world where the British had previously enjoyed a strong market advantage such as South America, the Middle East, and east Asia. In trade as in finance, there was both compe-

---

[1] See Appendix A-1 for comparative values of currency. The exchange rate was approximately 4 gold marks to the dollar and 20 to the pound. After 1918 the gold mark was no longer circulating in Germany, but continued to be used as a legal denomination as the paper mark fluctuated widely and depreciated quickly.

tition and co-operation as the British responded to the new American presence. Reconstruction would not be easy. The problem was a general European one, but it would be the French, British, German, and, critically, the American positions that were of central importance for the economic future of the continent as well as for the political balance of power. While the peace settlements cast a long shadow over Anglo-French relations, few anticipated that the long drawn-out struggle over German reparations would increasingly dominate European international relations during the early post-war years.

As after most coalition wars, the former allies found more to divide than to unite them. The final American rejection of the Versailles treaty on 19 March 1920 meant the end of the American security guarantee for France. This was greeted with some relief in London, where it was decided that Britain could shed a responsibility that it was reluctant to assume. The Anglo-French guarantee had been ratified but was now left in abeyance. The French search for a security substitute was a recurring theme for the next decade and beyond. There was little enthusiasm in London for a Belgian treaty; the Franco-Belgium agreement was concluded without a British equivalent, to the regret of the Belgians who wanted to avoid subservience to their over-powerful neighbour. There were sharp differences, too, in central Europe, where France looked to strengthen her position in ways which the British opposed, and in south-eastern Europe, where the two powers became bitter rivals. Outside Europe, the British strongly resented sharing the former Turkish territories with France and the division of the spoils drove the powers apart. The future of relations with Bolshevik Russia similarly led to tensions between London and Paris. These matters, political and financial, were discussed at frequent summits between political heads at numerous meetings and conferences, many held in the spas and gambling resorts of Europe. The austere Raymond Poincaré referred to them contemptuously as 'la politique des casinos'. Unofficial consultations, often associated with the peripatetic League (the Geneva buildings were not completed until 1924), and formal conferences were held to complete the work of peacemaking. Fifteen inter-Allied and ten German–Allied conferences struggled with the most intractable problem of all, that of reparations, between 1921 and 1924.

French statesmen believed that their country had a moral entitlement to reparations. It had suffered far more both in human and material terms than the British, the Americans, or the Germans. The destruction of its ten richest departments placed an additional heavy burden on already indebted post-war governments. French governments had relied far more heavily on borrowing (especially in the form of short-term debts to the public) than on taxation in order to finance the war; the servicing of the public debt in 1920 amounted to 65 per cent of the national income.[2] Even after 1919, the government continued to seek support from still-willing citizens and from the Bank of France to cover its massive budgetary deficit. When these sources proved inadequate the government turned to New York and London, only to find the financial environment increasingly hostile. American Treasury plans in 1919 and 1920 to make government loans to the French for reconstruction ran into sharp opposition in Congress. Only modest steps were taken to rationalize the incredibly complex French budgetary procedures. Neither the Clemenceau government nor its successors in the early 1920s were willing to introduce tax programmes that would have reduced the gap between expenditure and revenue. Elections in late 1919 had produced a Chamber weighted towards the right; in the presidential ballot which followed Clemenceau seemed the natural choice, but the left-leaning, anticlerical 'Tiger' who had abandoned the Rhine for stillborn security pacts had many enemies and was rejected by the Assemblée in favour of the insignificant Paul Deschanel. Alexandre Millerand formed the new legislature's first cabinet in January 1920, setting a pattern for his immediate successors by reserving the foreign ministry for himself, but resigned as premier in September to replace the sick Deschanel as a far more activist president. Millerand's *Bloc National*, a conservative-republican alliance, had to deal with France's immediate financial problems. It was essential that money should not lose its value and that the vast rentier class should be protected from devaluation. At the same time, the need to meet the costs of war and to finance reconstruction and pensions to ex-servicemen made cuts in government expenditure politically impossible. The battles over taxes and public spending produced only a succession of budget deficits that were mainly met through the sale of short-term bonds. Between 1919 and 1923 governments were spending twice as much as they were collecting; these deficits were sometimes disguised, but were not eradicated until the books were finally balanced in 1926.

The sharp world depression of 1920–1 following the immediate post-war boom temporarily improved the French position. Such was the appreciation of the franc between December 1920 and April 1922 that J. P. Morgan & Co., who handled French finances in the United States, suggested the franc be stabilized at current values, but the government unwisely preferred to wait until it reached its pre-war parity on gold. No plan of action was adopted to achieve this goal. While incurring large budget deficits, the government practised monetary deflation.

[2] Figures from Barry Eichengreen, *Golden Fetters: The Gold Standard and the Great Depression, 1919–1939* (Oxford, 1992), 81.

The François–Marsel convention of 1920, requiring the Treasury to repay its Bank advances at the rate of at least 2 billion francs each year, represented a partial victory for the Bank of France, which came to focus almost entirely on the curtailment of its advances to the government and a decrease in the amount of money in circulation as the way to control inflation and restore the franc to its pre-war parity. After a first payment in December 1921, the Treasury found it difficult to meet its obligations and questioned the relevance of the Bank's monetary programme to France's financial difficulties.

After May 1922 the franc resumed its downward path, intensifying the financial pressures on the government. Domestic borrowing could continue only because French bondholders were convinced that large German payments would be forthcoming. These would lead to a massive reduction in the national debt, a balanced budget, and a strong franc. Should investors lose confidence and present their short-term loans for redemption, or convert them into high-interest long-term securities, as was to happen in 1924, the domestic loan market would collapse and the franc rapidly depreciate. There were laws against the export of French capital, but no controls over foreign holders of francs, making Paris vulnerable to speculative operations should the latter decide to sell. The French hoped to secure some relief from their budgetary pressures through negotiations for the cancellation or massive reduction of French war debts to the United States. The American Congress, determined to keep control over the debt–refunding negotiations, created the World War Foreign Debt Commission in 1922 and demanded the repayment of debts within twenty-five years at an annual interest rate of not less than 4.25 per cent. All debtors were asked to send delegations to Washington to begin talks. In May the French sent Jean Parmentier, a high official in the Ministry of Finance, to the capital to convince the Americans that any form of repayment would endanger the franc and make the financial position of the government even more precarious than it was. Though American officials were sympathetic, Republican policy-makers were not prepared to challenge the Congressional refunding terms before the November elections.

The assumption in France that reparations would be paid became an essential factor in sustaining government borrowing at home. As the gap between expenditure and revenue widened, a reparations settlement became a financial imperative. The French were optimistic about the role of the all-powerful Reparations Commission, where, after the American withdrawal, they claimed the chair and the casting vote in case of a tie between the national representatives. Yet while French views were in the ascendant, British reluctance, American disinterest, and outright German resistance combined to block all favourable settlements

TABLE 8. Percentage Estimates of French Budget Deficits, 1920–1926 (as a share of public expenditure)

	Dulles	Haig	Ministry of Finance
1920	65.4	82.0	43.2
1921	54.8	58.3	28.2
1922	50.5	45.5	21.6
1923	39.5	43.1	30.8
1924	22.6	21.5	16.8
1925	13.7	12.9	4.2
1926	−0.1	3.8	−2.4

Note: A minus sign preceeding the deficit share for 1926 denotes a surplus.

Source: Barry Eichengreen, *Golden Fetters* (1992), 178.

of the reparations issue. Clemenceau's parting advice on leaving office, that: 'We must show the world the extent of our victory, and we must take up the mentality and habits of a victorious people, which once more takes its place at the head of Europe', proved difficult to translate into action in the face of France's continuing financial weakness.[3]

The British, too, emerged from the war in a weakened financial position. There had been a considerable sale of overseas assets quite apart from domestic war debts, and some $3.2 billion lent to allies, which would be difficult to recoup. The British owed the Americans $4.3 billion and were, for the first time, in debt to their transatlantic cousins, though still in a creditor position worldwide.[4] With a far more effective tax structure than the French, British governments had covered more of their war costs through taxation, but there was still a large budgetary deficit in March 1919. The removal of wartime controls fuelled an inflationary spiral; the pound, off gold and no longer pegged to the dollar, began to fall below its pre-war dollar–exchange rate. Lloyd George's Coalition government was determined to put its financial house in order. The Treasury, the Bank of England, and the City (London's financial district) charted a strict deflationary policy, arguing that by cutting expenditure, restricting government borrowing, and raising interest rates to discourage private investment, the country would be prepared for a return to gold and the restoration of the international financial structure. Even when it became clear by the summer that the post-war boom was over and that further deflation

[3] Quoted in David Robin Warson, *Georges Clemenceau: A Political Biography* (London, 1974), 387.

[4] Figures from Eichengreen, *Golden Fetters*, 85.

would depress trade and create massive unemployment, Austen Chamberlain, the chancellor of the Exchequer, persisted with these policies, and his second budget of 1920 already showed a surplus available for debt redemption. It has been argued in retrospect that a less restrictive policy would have aided British industry and that the concentration on strengthening the pound proved too costly: French inflationary policies allowed a degree of growth, fuelled by industrial expansion, that the British did not share. At the time, however, the Anglo-Saxon financial establishments shared a common reading of the situation and accused the French of reckless accounting. Nonetheless, Britain's deflationary policies did not stop the pound's deterioration in relation to the dollar, nor reverse the flow of gold to the United States. The government insisted that London could meet the competition from New York and resume its place as the centre of the world's financial system. Far more money was available in New York, and ultimately this proved decisive, but the shift of financial power was incomplete. Imperial ties, habit, and geography meant that many continued to look to London. The need to strengthen the pound was seen, above all in the influential City of London, as more important than worries about British trade. There was, in the immediate post-war period, little opposition to the Treasury position or any challenge to its assumption that balanced budgets, stabilized currencies, and the reintroduction of the gold standard were essential for economic recovery.

Like the French, the British hoped to secure, if not the cancellation of the war-debt payments owed to the Americans, then at least better terms than Congress had set. The two countries failed to form a common front and each negotiated separately, fearing that any settlement would prejudice future arrangements. In an attempt to shame the Americans into cancellation, the British used their creditor position in Europe. The 'Balfour note' of 11 August 1922 informed Washington that Germany and the continental allies would have to pay Britain only enough to cover Britain's war debts to the United States. The note not only angered the Americans but alarmed the French who, with the expiry of the British three-year moratorium on their debt, would be pressed for payment. The British, bowing to the inevitable, decided to settle with the Americans. To postpone payment further, argued Montagu Norman, the governor of the Bank of England, would antagonize the Americans and weaken Britain's creditor status. A strong delegation, with Stanley Baldwin, the chancellor of the exchequer, and Norman, arrived in Washington in early January 1923. A bargain was struck, far more favourable to the British than the original Congressional terms. The British were to repay their debt (by 1923, $4,600 million or about £980 million at par) in full over sixty-two years with interest increasing from 3 to 3.5 per cent. Contemporaries thought the arrangements were harsh, though the technical details forgave some debt and implied future reduction. The actual charge on British overseas investment was small, but the continued weakness of the British economy and the costs of maintaining a possibly overvalued pound after 1925 made payments to the Americans a focus of continuing discontent. As the United States was a creditor nation and the possessor of a favourable trade balance, the repayment of war debts posed a difficult problem for its European debtors.

In the face of a sharp recession and mounting unemployment, the London government insisted that financial instability was the cause of the present malaise and that a settlement of the reparation question was the way to restore world trade and British prosperity. France, if necessary, would have to be forced into line. Lloyd George hoped that a fixed reparations sum could be determined within six months and that the Germans themselves would set the figure. He would try to increase the British share of the total by insisting on a 'fair' proportion of whatever the Germans could pay. No British government in the 1920s, despite some dissenting voices in the Treasury, was willing to abandon reparations or cancel Allied war debts without receiving an American quid pro quo.

Whether viewed from London or Paris, the financial role of the United States was seen as imperative for the stabilization of Europe, despite its rejection of the Treaty of Versailles. The unwillingness of the American government to intervene in the reparation question despite the belief that a moderate settlement was essential for European recovery aggravated the conflicts between Britain and France. Any settlement of the 'German problem' appeared to depend on American capital flows to Europe which the new Republican administration was unwilling to underwrite. War debts amounting to some $11.9 billion had to be repaid, and were not considered in Washington as part of the more general European settlement on reparations. 'It is highly improbable that either the Congress or popular opinion in this country will ever permit cancellation of any part of the debt of the British Government to the United States', President Wilson warned Lloyd George in November 1920, either in order to allow the remission of other Allied debts to Britain or 'as an inducement towards a practical settlement of the reparation claims'.[5] Nevertheless, the ways in which the Americans exercised their financial and economic power would critically affect the future of the peace settlement.

---

[5] Wilson to Lloyd George, 2 Nov. 1920, quoted in Arthur Turner, *The Cost of War: British Policy on French War Debts, 1918–1932* (Brighton, 1998), 29–30.

Washington was not blind to the necessity of encouraging European reconstruction. Successive governments were aware that there could be no retreat into economic isolation, but there was no unanimity on what was needed. The Republican administrations of presidents Warren Harding (1920–3) and Calvin Coolidge (1923–8) wanted to see the European nations restored to financial solvency and economic growth, but moved cautiously, taking account of their own fiscal priorities, inflationary fears, and strong protectionist and isolationist sentiment. The importance of the European continental market was clearly demonstrated during the downturn of 1920–1, when both agricultural and raw-material exports fell and farm groups and business interests demanded government action. Fearful of the consequences of the country's creditor position and expecting a flood of European imports which never took place, protectionists found in President Harding a willing champion. His government resisted assuming official obligations in Europe or any form of co-operation with League-sponsored activities. American abstention doomed plans for an 'International Bank of Issue' to underwrite reconstruction loans proposed in Brussels in October 1921. American insistence that war-debt repayment take precedence over reconstruction loans, and disagreements over what should be left to market forces to regulate, buried alternative European suggestions. Nor were the Americans represented at the Genoa conference in 1922, when Lloyd George made his unsuccessful bid for European economic and monetary reconstruction under British direction. Proposals for central bank co-operation and the promotion of exchange and price-level stability were mainly of academic interest without the participation of the United States, the only state able to sponsor such schemes. The official abstention of the American government from such meetings strengthened the role of the largely independent Federal Reserve Bank of New York (FRBNY) and gave new prominence to the New York investment banks. As capital-hungry European governments turned to the United States, a complicated relationship developed between Washington, the FRBNY which influenced interest and exchange rates, and the private bankers. Caught up in the immediate postwar inflation, the American Treasury and the FRBNY favoured an orthodox deflationary approach and a return to balanced budgets and the gold standard. The Republican administration was not adverse to private loans to the Europeans, but wanted safeguards for American investors and for domestic industry. This uneasy compromise between public and private obscured existing dividing lines. Any European government wanting to raise money in the United States had to turn to its investment houses, mainly J. P. Morgan & Co. in New York, who came to play, with some reluctance, a major political role in international diplomacy. Such firms were not free agents but merchant banks with clients to serve.

The reparations battles between London and Paris were further complicated by the actions of Germany, a country which, though defeated, did not fully accept the consequences of its defeat. As the imperial German government had not financed the war by rigorous taxation but by long-term borrowing and increasing its floating debt, the Weimar republic inherited the defeated empire's massive national debt and depreciated currency. It was faced, too, with the demands for 'interim payments' of cash and goods included in the Versailles treaty. Tax and non-tax revenue covered only half of the government spending in 1919–21, though tax reforms introduced in June 1921 by Mathias Erzberger, the German finance minister, who was assassinated two months later, brought a brief improvement. Taxation continued to cover only a small percentage of government expenditure. The budgetary deficits of 1919–23 were met mainly by increases in the floating debt, by loans from banks and other institutions, and by printing paper marks. Contrary to the expectations of Keynes and other like-minded Cassandras, Germany shared in the prosperity of the immediate postwar boom. The German government embarked on an expansionist economic policy, fighting hard to regain lost export markets and unfreezing blocked assets. Domestic demand was buoyant after five years of war, and despite the demobilization of millions of men unemployment remained low. German industry recovered rapidly, making use of government funds to cover losses to the Allies and reconversion to peacetime activity, and having at its disposal war-generated cash balances and a share of the foreign capital attracted by a favourable exchange rate. It has been estimated that there was a net capital influx into Germany of about 13 billion gold marks in the years 1919–23, much of it speculative investment by small private investors, with the greater part coming in 1919, 1921, and the first half of 1922.[6] German industrialists acquired new enterprises and integrated, rationalized, and modernized their firms. When exchange restriction were lifted, they sent capital abroad in anticipation of further depreciations of the mark. The volume of German exports in 1919 and 1920 rose; goods were sold or 'dumped' in increasing quantities at low prices on foreign markets, but the volume

---

[6] Figures from Niall Ferguson, *Paper and Iron: Hamburg Business and German Politics in the Era of Inflation, 1897–1927* (Cambridge, 1995), 243. Carl-Ludwig Holtfrerich has estimated that Americans purchased (and eventually lost) some $300 million-worth of mark denominated bonds during these years. Stephen Schuker estimates American losses at 6 billion gold marks ($1.5 billion). Carl-Ludwig Holtfrerich, *The German Inflation, 1914–1923* (Berlin and New York, 1986), 287; Stephen A. Schuker, *American 'Reparations' to Germany, 1919–1933: Implications for the Third World Debt Crisis* (Princeton, 1988), 118–19.

of imports, mainly food and raw materials needed for the expanding industries, also rose. The trade deficit that resulted was covered by the large number of small-scale foreign purchases of paper marks. The mark continued to depreciate but German industrial output maintained its upward momentum. Given the revolutionary situation of 1918–19, industrialists struck bargains (which they hoped to undo as soon as possible) with their labour forces, recognizing their unions and conceding an eight-hour day and new working and welfare conditions. Inflation allowed the employers to cover the new demands of the workers without harm to themselves. Workers benefited, too, from an expanded social welfare scheme and the government's concern to maintain employment levels. Even when the political truce became strained, sections of the working class continued to profit from the inflation.

It was, and is, argued that inflation created a tacit 'inflationary consensus' linking German industrialists, organized labour, and debtor groups together, and that any real attempt at fiscal and monetary stabilization would have led to its destruction and the collapse of the social peace. Apart from the agricultural sector, which failed to prosper, it was the rentiers, people on fixed incomes or with liquid assets, shopkeepers, professionals, and the self-employed who suffered most from the state's disregard for their fortunes. The more organized, politically influential groups acquired a vested interest in the continuation of inflation. Current research differentiates between the short- and longer-terms costs

TABLE 9. Dollar Exchange Rate of the Paper Mark in Berlin, 1918–1923 (in monthly averages)

Month	1918	1919	1920	1921	1922	1923
Jan.	5.21	8.20	64.80	64.91	191.81	17,972
Feb.	5.27	9.13	99.11	61.31	207.82	27,918
March	5.21	10.39	83.89	62.45	284.19	21,190
April	5.11	12.61	59.64	63.53	291.00	24,475
May	5.14	12.85	46.48	62.30	290.11	47,670
June	5.36	14.01	39.13	69.36	317.14	109,966
July	5.79	15.08	39.48	76.67	493.22	353,412
Aug.	6.10	18.83	47.74	84.31	1,134.56	4,620,455
Sept.	6.59	24.05	57.98	104.91	1,465.87	98,860
Oct.	6.61	26.83	68.17	150.20	3,180.96	25,260
Nov.	7.43	38.31	77.24	262.96	7,183.10	2,193,600
Dec.	8.28	46.77	73.00	191.93	7,589.27	4,200,000
Average	6.01	19.76	63.06	104.57	1,885.78	534,914

Source: Gerald D. Feldman, *The Great Disorder* (1993), p. 5. Note variations and author's important revisionist interpretation of course and consequences of inflation and hyper-inflation.

and between the economic and political effects of the inflation. The longer-term consequences, particularly after inflation reached hyperinflation levels, wiped out the short-term economic benefits. In the early 1920s the Weimar parties (the Social Democrats, Centre, and German Democratic party), faced with large budgetary deficits, found the inflationary fiscal and monetary policies easier and safer to maintain than sorting out the distributional conflicts required for any effective tax programme or cuts in expenditure that would have brought the budget under control. Even in the period of 'relative stabilization', March 1920 to May 1921, when the mark recovered, prices fell, and the rate of inflation was cut to its post-war low, no political consensus was achieved. The stabilization that might have been possible in 1921 never took place. The Weimar governments were too weak and dependent on the producers of wealth to impose policies that they feared would damage the boom economy, create unemployment, and shake the fragile political stability of the state. Both the inflation and hyperinflation fatally damaged the political fabric of the Weimar republic, for the demoralization and alienation of large sections of the electorate in the early 1920s weakened the appeal of democratic politics. German attention was focused on the reduction or abolition of the Versailles treaty reparations obligations. The country's financial and fiscal woes were blamed on the Allied demands rather than on budget deficits and the depreciating currency, both of which resulted, in the first instance, from the lack of political consensus about tax incidence and income distribution. Opposition to paying reparations, even when massively reduced, became one of the few bonds which held the Weimar parties together and kept the right wing in check. Policy-makers debated whether a show of compliance ('fulfilment') or resistance was the best tactic to convince the Allies that their demands were unreasonable and dangerous both to Germany and to themselves. At the same time, no German cabinet—and there was a move to the political right in 1920— adequately addressed the question of financial reform and the unbalanced budget. To cover its budgetary deficits, the government continued to resort to loans and the printing press (i.e. printed money).

German recalcitrance over reparations made agreement ever more impossible and underlined the opposing views of the two main European powers over how their former enemy should be treated. The debates over how much the Germans were to pay and in what form went far beyond purely financial issues. They dramatized Anglo-French differences over the enforcement of the Versailles settlement. As reparations payments became one of the main means for maintaining French superiority over Germany, they were critical to the outcome of the struggle between France and Germany for the future political and economic domination of Europe. The failure of the French attempt at unilateral action in 1923–4, though it brought Weimar to the point of dissolution, opened the way for decisive American financial intervention and highlighted the degree to which the European diplomatic map was changed by the exercise of American financial power. Most significantly, it also produced the first revision of the Versailles status quo in the German direction.

II

The reparations problem brought Anglo-French differences, apparent already at the peace conference, to the forefront of their relations. In a series of private talks between Millerand and Lloyd George, the two men argued over the proper response to the German failure to fulfil either the disarmament or the reparations clauses of Versailles. The French premier insisted that only coercion would bring German compliance: the Allies should agree on their demands and on the sanctions to be imposed if Germany failed to fulfil them before talking to Berlin. Believing that you do not kill the cow if you want her milk, Lloyd George wanted Germany to acknowledge her liability and suggest the best method for liquidating it. The British prime minister was convinced that only when Germany's liability was definitively fixed and accepted would it be able to raise the necessary international loan to cover its unfavourable balance of payments, regain its economic stability, and pay the reparations that he was unwilling to forgo. At a meeting of the Supreme Council in London in February–March 1920, Millerand, playing to the home gallery in Paris but also wanting to convince the British of German bad faith, demanded and was refused an immediate occupation of the Ruhr in retaliation for Germany's deliberate failure to meet her reparation quotas. Though he quickly backed down, his proposal intensified British fears about France's future ambitions. These were reinforced when France unilaterally occupied Frankfurt, Darmstadt, and three other German towns on 6 April 1920. The occupation was meant to ensure that German troops sent into the demilitarized zone to deal with left-wing unrest after the failed right-wing Kapp putsch on 12 March would be withdrawn. Anger in London was directed exclusively against Paris. 'This is a very serious departure by the French Government from united action', Lloyd George thundered. 'We may be landed one day in war with Germany through French action. Or we may have to repudiate our allies.'[7] At San Remo on 18

---

[7] Quoted in Thomas Jones, *Whitehall Diary*, ed. Keith Middlemas (London and New York, 1969–71), i. 108–11. Lloyd George was particularly incensed by the French use of North African troops in the occupation.

April 1920 the Supreme Council, at Lloyd George's urging, agreed to meet with the Germans. In anticipation of a reparation offer from Berlin, the Allies attempted but failed to arrive at any decision about Germany's total liability or about the equally vexed question of the priority of payments, settled at Paris, but repeatedly reopened by the French. With agreement impossible, the question of provisional schedules for payment was referred to a group of financial experts. Meeting again at Boulogne, on 21 June, the Allied heads again dodged the question of total liability and adopted a totally unrealistic schedule of payments that no one expected Germany to accept.

The Germans made settlement difficult. At Spa on 6 July 1920, the first occasion since Paris when a German delegation met directly with the Allies, the German representative, the highly energetic buccaneer industrialist Hugo Stinnes, took such a belligerent stand that even Lloyd George was appalled. The question of coal dominated the discussions, overshadowing even the bitterly disputed disarmament issue. The Germans had fallen seriously behind in their deliveries of reparation coal, so important for France, and Millerand and Foch were prepared to use the threat of a Ruhr occupation to enforce compliance. While the Germans debated among themselves about how much coal they could offer, the British and French clashed over the coal price to be credited to reparations. Millerand, mainly to win the promise of British co-operation if coercion was necessary, agreed to Lloyd George's demand that the coal delivered should be credited to reparations at the high world-market or British export price rather than the German internal price. He consented, also, to the payment of a cash supplement of 5 gold marks a ton, ostensibly to subsidize food for the Ruhr miners. As a result of the Spa arrangements, not only was less reparation coal delivered but the French had to pay a higher price for what they received. The conflict allowed the Germans to exploit the divisions between Britain and France to their advantage. At Spa, too, the powers finally decided how to divide the reparation shares among themselves (France 52 per cent, Britain and Empire 22 per cent, Italy 9.3 per cent, Belgium, 8 per cent, Yugoslavia 5.9 per cent, and 3 per cent for the rest), when and if they could agree on the question of total liability.[8]

The Germans were prepared to gamble on the possibility that the French threats of occupation were bluff, a view strengthened by the Anglo-French disputes. Unwilling to accept the legitimacy of reparations, German policy-makers were encouraged in their opposition by Keynes, whose *Economic Consequences of the Peace* was highly popular in

[8] Sally Marks, *The Illusion of Peace: International Relations in Europe, 1918–1933* (2nd edn. Basingstoke, 2003), 45.

Germany and who was in continuous communication with the highly influential Hamburg financiers Carl Melchior, a close personal friend, and Max Warburg. At best, the moderates argued that some gesture towards compliance should be made. Coal and steel representatives, benefiting from the inflationary situation, argued for temporization. Germans assumed that the currency depreciation would assist them in the battle for revision. It was accepted by many that the depreciation of the mark and the continued trade deficits, generating a flood of cheap exports (as in 1919–20), would force the Allied powers to reduce the reparation bill. In practice, after the success of 1919, only a small trade surplus was produced in 1920 and a deficit resulted in 1921 and 1922. Though the volume of exports grew, the demand for imports grew faster, assisting the recovery of world trade but not generating the pressure on American and Allied markets that would lead to a campaign for reparation reduction. The economic historian Niall Ferguson argues that 'Currency depreciation continued to be regarded as the secret economic weapon of German revisionism because of its stimulating effect on German exports. If the Allies could be persuaded that the peace terms were the root cause of both, then a revision of the treaty might be possible.'[9] As a revisionist tactic, depreciation failed to achieve its purpose. The entrance of the German People's party (DVP), the party of heavy industry, and the departure of the Social Democrats (SPD) from the cabinet in June 1920 made any equitable reform of the tax structure more unlikely. The fast approach of the reparation decision deadline set by the treaty, 1 May 1921, meant that the question dominated German politics.

The French, whose need for relief increased as their own budgetary problems mounted, turned to other alternatives. Proposals for an exchange of German coal for French iron ore and for the creation of a joint steel cartel had existed since the autumn of 1919. Jacques Seydoux, the deputy director of the department of commercial affairs at the Quai d'Orsay, suggested at the time of the Spa talks that, in return for certain reparation advantages, a sum of paper marks should be raised by the German government and placed at the disposal of the reparation creditors who would buy what they wanted in Germany. The plan was enlarged at a meeting of financial and economic experts in Brussels in December 1920 to include French ownership of stock in German industry. As with previous proposals, these stalled in the face of divisions between French producers and opposition from the Ruhr magnates. While the French needed coal from Germany and outlets for their excess ore and raw iron capacity, German industrialists were less

[9] Ferguson, *Paper and Iron*, 311.

dependent on French resources or markets. The German negotiators insisted on separating the reparation and industrial talks, and then proved hostile to the whole scheme. The British, for their part, disliked any direct Franco-German arrangements that left them out.

No progress was made on either the industrial or reparations front at Brussels in December 1920, though proposals and counter-proposals were made. By the time the Supreme Council met in Paris on 24 January 1921 to discuss German disarmament, the trial of German war criminals, and reparations, Aristide Briand had become premier (16 January) of France. The master of Third Republic politics, forming his seventh cabinet, had promised his supporters quick reparation results. Though never comfortable as a nationalist, he was not yet the symbol of international reconciliation he would later become, and was prepared to take a tough line with Berlin. Recognizing that the Chamber's expectations were impossibly high, he fought for the postponement of a final settlement in favour of a provisional arrangement. This was rejected by Lloyd George, who still felt that German recovery depended on the establishment of a fixed liability. The conference arrived at a compromise scheme, suggested by the Belgians, featuring a levy on German exports which would both ease Germany's burden during any economic downturn and provide a politically desirable ambiguity about the actual sums to be received. From Briand's point of view it was of the greatest importance that Lloyd George agreed to the imposition of sanctions should the Germans reject the proposal.

The Germans were at first evasive and then, in March, made a derisory counter-offer of 22 billion gold marks, provoking Lloyd George to suggest that they would soon be asking the Allies for reparations. Sent home under the threat of sanctions if they did not come back with a more serious proposal, the German foreign minister offered to follow the Paris schedule for five years, but only if Upper Silesia remained German. On 9 March 1921 the Allies occupied the Ruhr ports of Düsseldorf, Duisburg, and Ruhrort on grounds of reparation and disarmament defaults. As compensation for a move which he much disliked, Lloyd George demanded and won a 50 per cent levy on German exports. Besides protecting British industry from possible German 'dumping', it appeared to give Britain more than its allotted share of reparations, since only Britain imposed the levy until 1923, when the French, to British and German fury, did as well. Lloyd George's move was an illusionist's trick, opposed by both Treasury and City advisers, but the prime minister, while surreptitiously encouraging German intransigence, had his way.

Facing a major world recession and rising unemployment figures, the British cabinet blamed the downturn in the economy on French intransigence over reparations. Lloyd George, suspicious of Briand's intentions but wanting to get the British share of a reduced reparation bill, pressed for threats rather than action to encourage the Germans to propose an acceptable sum. Briand, under considerable political pressure, needed a firmer policy. In March and April Germany was declared in default on payments on the interim 20 billion gold marks that was due, but no additional sanctions were imposed. With France seemingly moving closer to a Ruhr occupation, the Belgians suggested a compromise total figure of 132 milliard gold marks[10] plus the Belgian war debt and a warning to the Germans that, unless they accepted the Reparation Commission's assessment and a forthcoming decision on ways of payment and guarantees, military sanctions would be imposed. Concerned with the deadlock over the interim payments, Briand and Lloyd George met on 23–5 April. The former, pressed at home, wanted to take action on the basis of the German default on the interim 20 billion gold marks; Lloyd George did not want to act unless Germany refused the Final Schedule.

The Reparation Commission accepted and announced on 27 April the Belgian figure of 132 milliard gold marks plus the Belgian war debt as the total liability of all the Central Powers, a sum that had little relationship either to the creditors' bills or to the still undetermined Germany capacity to pay. The London Schedule of Payment, prepared by the Supreme Council in consultation with a committee of experts, was presented to the Germans in the form of an ultimatum threatening the occupation of the Ruhr. It was paradoxical that, under these conditions, it was the mildest scheme yet devised by the creditors. The final bill to the Germans was far lower than the total sum of 132 milliard gold marks. The bill was divided into three parts. Berlin was required to cover the interest and amortization of an initial series of 'A' bonds amounting to 12 billion gold marks (the unpaid balance of the Versailles interim 20 billion due) and 'B' bonds amounting to 38 billion gold marks, with a fixed annuity of 2 billion gold marks plus a variable amount equal in value to 20 per cent of German exports. Only when the proceeds of German foreign trade were sufficient to pay off the 'A' and 'B' bonds, as well as to pay the interest on the remaining debt, would the 'C' bonds, worth 82 billion gold marks, covering more than half of the theoretical total of German obligations, be issued. The experts did not believe that the 'C' bonds could ever be issued; they were primarily a device for satisfying French wishes in theory if not in practice. Interest on the debt which the Germans were expected to pay covered only 'A' and 'B' bonds. In this manner, the German debt was

---

[10] A British milliard is the equivalent of an American billion.

reduced to 50 milliard gold marks, to be paid over thirty-six years, according to a complex schedule that provided for deliveries of both cash and kind. This was not the scheme that the experts had wanted. Their idea was to set a fixed sum that would provide a baseline for further credit operations. The Supreme Council undid the package by reverting to the variable percentage linked to German exports that made it difficult to judge what sums could actually be obtained. It was expected that the Germans would accept the London Schedule; even Keynes recommended acceptance, though he believed a further downward revision would have to follow. Faced with united Anglo-French action, an Entente ultimatum, and a Polish move into Upper Silesia and clashes between Polish and German forces, the government of Konstantin Fehrenbech in Berlin fell on 4 May. The London Schedule of Payments was presented to Germany on 5 May. It was a minority coalition of the SPD, Centre, and DDP parties under Joseph Wirth, a Centre party politician, that had to deal with the London Schedule.

The historical debate over the feasibility of the London Schedule continues unabated.[11] Professors Gerald Feldman and Barry Eichengreen, among others, have argued that reparations were a destabilizing factor on the German economy. To have covered the annual payments would have required massive government intervention to increase exports and cut imports in order to produce the export surplus needed to transform the necessary percentage of national income into foreign currency. Only a wartime government or a dictatorship, and certainly not the weak Weimar governments, could have taken such actions. Even had Germany managed this trade surplus, would the Allied countries have accepted such a flood of exports, especially after the world economic boom collapsed at the end of 1920? While not large relative to the economies concerned, they would have affected those industries, such as iron, steel, and textiles, already under considerable competitive pressure. These arguments over the transfer problem were extensively

---

[11] Cf. the arguments in G. D. Feldman, *The Great Disorder*; Eichengreen, *Golden Fetters*; Bruce Kent, *The Spoils of War: The Politics, Economics and Diplomacy of Reparations, 1918–1932* (Oxford, 1989); P. Krüger, 'Das Reparationsproblem der Weimarer Republik in fragwürdiger Sicht: kritsche Überlegungen zur neuesten Forschung', Vierteljahrshefte für Zeitgeschicte, 29 (1981); Carl-Ludwig Holtferich, *Die deutsche Inflation, 1914–1923*, with those in Sally Marks, 'The Myth of Reparations', *Central European History*, 11 (1978), and 'Smoke and Mirrors: In Smoke-filled Rooms and the Galerie des Glaces', in Boemeke, Feldman, and Glaser (eds.), *The Treaty of Versailles*; Schuker, *American 'Reparations' to Germany, 1919–1933*. Also see Niall Ferguson, *The Pity of War*, 414, where he suggests that Germany's debt burden, both internal and external, in 1921 would not have been larger in terms of the ratio between national debt and gross national product than that of Britain in 1815.

used by critics of the 'draconian' reparations bill, although the issue proved to be purely academic as no such problem arose. Other historians, including Stephen Schuker and Sally Marks, argue that the actual, as distinguished from the theoretical, demands made on Germany were well within its financial capacity to pay, had the political will been present. The demands made in 1921 were considerably less than the total sum nominally set: 82 billion gold marks of the total were 'notional', because at that late date Germany would never surrender the coupons and therefore the bonds were worthless. Besides, any default on the 'A' and 'B' bonds, however small, would make it impossible for the Allies even to ask for the coupons. The Allies had reverted to the 50 billion gold marks sum discussed in 1919, but, for political reasons, they disguised it in a complicated payment formula. The 50 billion sum was 10 billion gold marks less than Keynes had thought payable at the time of the peace conference. Between 1920 and 1923 German payments to the Allies amounted to between 8 billion and 13 billion gold marks, some 4 to 7 per cent of the total national income. In the hardest year, 1921, the figure rose to some 8.3 per cent, a considerable but not impossible burden and far less than claimed by Chancellor Wirth at the time.

Though the issue was and continues to be obscured by the 'smoke and mirrors' it generates, it does appear that Germany could have paid the actual sum demanded in 1921.[12] The question, as most commentators agree, was a political and not a financial one. If the German government had met its treaty obligation to tax as heavily as the victor powers, it would have had sufficient funds to pay her reparation bill and

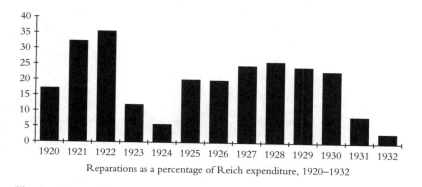

Reparations as a percentage of Reich expenditure, 1920–1932

Fig. 1. German Reparations, 1920–1932

Source: N. Ferguson, *Paper and Iron: Hamburg Business and German Politics in the Era of Inflation 1897–1927* (Cambridge, 1995), 279.

[12] Sally Marks, 'Smoke and Mirrors', 370–7.

been able to secure foreign loans. There would have been no need for an immediate trade or balance-of-payments surplus if a foreign loan had been forthcoming (as happened in 1924), though at some future stage domestic restraint would have been necessary to service the debt without inflation. Even without international loans, the inflow of foreign capital from 1919 until the summer of 1922 covered all the reparations paid by the Germans. Keynes summed up the situation when, in August 1922, he assured his Hamburg audience that the French were only bluffing and that inflation had many advantages. 'The burden of internal debt is wiped off. The whole of Germany's payments to the Allies so far . . . have been entirely discharged by the losses of foreign speculators', he said. 'I do not believe that Germany has paid a penny for these items out of her own resources . . .'[13] In the final reparation balance sheet, the money lent or invested in Germany exceeded its total reparation payments. Between 1919 and 1932 it is estimated that Germany paid 19.1 billion gold marks in reparations; during the same period she received 27 billion gold marks in net capital inflows, mostly from private investors, mainly American, who subsequently lost considerable sums following the German defaults in 1923 and 1932.[14]

The London Schedule was not a good bargain for France. The French would receive, at best, 52 per cent of 50 billion gold marks, a sum far short of Briand's estimate of France's civilian claims. France again tried to argue for a priority for the devastated areas, but had no legal basis for her claim beyond the priority already given to Belgium in the Treaty of Versailles. The coating on the French pill was thin. It was agreed to issue a six-day ultimatum along with the London Schedule. Briand would be allowed to mobilize the French class of 1919 (the mobilization was a disaster, intensifying French insecurity) in order to satisfy his right-wing supporters in the Chamber. Why did Briand accept such a poor bargain? He was under strong political pressure to get something concrete from Berlin; the total overall sum was less

[13] Ferguson, *Pity of War*, 405.
[14] Ibid. 417; Stephen Schuker's innovative study, 'American "Reparations" to Germany, 1919–1933', in Gerald D. Feldman *et al.* (eds.), *Die Nachwirkungen der Inflation auf die deutsche Geschichte, 1924–1933* (Munich, 1985), 364, 371, gives different figures. For November 1918 through June 1931, he estimates that German reparations amounted to 22,891 billion RM, of which 16.831 billion RM (including part of the Young loan that went directly to its creditors) were a charge on the German balance of payments. The gross burden on the German economy of all amounts paid came to 2.72% of national income. Admitting that it is far more difficult to estimate the net capital flow into Germany, Schuker argues that the German gains from the net transfer for 1919–31 were no less than 17.75 billion gold marks (2.1% of national income), and that the Americans carried the burden of loss. For a discussion of these figures, see Eichengreen, *Golden Fetters*, 129, n. 11.

important than an immediate payment. The French financial situation was becoming precarious. The French intended to market the German bonds to get quick cash, leaving Germany to pay the bondholders, but German resistance and non-payment rendered this impossible. Hopes for a war-debt settlement with Washington or London were rapidly fading. The latter became clear in December 1921, when a French offer to reduce the reparations total by concentrating French claims on physical damage, and linking the remaining German obligations to the cost of inter-Allied war debts with the bulk of the German proceeds going to Britain, was rejected by Lloyd George. He insisted that any cancellation of war debts would depend on prior American action that was not forthcoming. Finally, though the British refused to coerce the Germans into compliance with the treaty terms, Briand had no wish to estrange his ex-ally and no stomach for isolated action. The public reaction to the terms, however, led Briand both to reconsider the possibility of direct contacts between Paris and Berlin and to a public declaration of France's independence in the Chamber. France still sought Allied solidarity, 'but if the demands of this solidarity compromise the vital interests of France and of her security, then solidarity would no longer be possible. We have the right and the duty to assure our national existence. All our allies must understand this.'[15]

III

From May 1921 until the collapse of the mark in the summer of 1922, the German governments, with widespread support, insisted that reparations was priming the inflation and currency deprecation. Germany's financial and fiscal woes continued to be blamed on the Allied demands rather than on the budget deficits and the depreciating currency. In the fierce German debates that followed the receipt of the London Schedule, even those recommending acceptance did so in the belief that compliance rather than opposition would lead to revision. *Erfüllungspolitik*, fulfilment within reason, was not designed to pay reparations but intended to bring about their reduction. Acceptance of the London terms brought no reordering of the German finances. Wirth's limited efforts to meet Allied demands for financial reform, modest tax reforms, and cuts in expenditure were intended mainly to keep the reduced payments he was able to win and to qualify for an international loan. Admittedly, Wirth's room for political manoeuvre

[15] Briand, speech in the Chamber, 11 July 1921, quoted in Walter A. McDougall, *France's Rhineland Diplomacy, 1914–1924: The Last Bid for a Balance of Power in Europe* (Princeton, 1978), 164.

was limited, as he tried to get the businessmen's and workers' parties to agree on a common programme. The leaders of the all-important Hamburg group of bankers and industrialists refused to join the cabinet, and the support of the commercial groups on whom Wirth became increasingly dependent was uncertain and capricious. At the same time the Germans were deliberately dumping paper marks on the market, causing the depreciation which they blamed on reparations.

From May until November 1921 the situation deteriorated as the Germans lost confidence in their currency and the government proved incapable or unwilling, or both, of putting through a successful tax programme. In order to pay the first billion gold marks due to the Allies in August 1921, the Wirth government resorted to all forms of financial gymnastics that the chancellor warned could not be repeated. It was difficult to raise money abroad given the extent of Germany's external indebtedness. The exchange rate plummeted during the summer months and was never really to recover. As the politicians could not agree on a tax programme, deficits had to be met by borrowing from German banks and presenting Treasury bills for discount to the Reichsbank, that is, turning bills into paper money. Efforts to limit the inflation were totally inadequate; the government was unwilling to risk introducing deflationary measures, particularly in the highly unpopular context of making payments to foreigners. Germany's industrial leadership, benefiting from the inflationary boom, was prepared to keep it going as long as possible and did little or nothing to assist the government's efforts at 'fulfilment'. The chancellor and other political leaders rejected the Allied view that Germany had only to stop printing notes, tax, and balance her budget to bring inflation under control. They also insisted upon the impossibility of complying with the Reparation Commission's demand for a cut in German domestic purchasing power and the acceptance of a lower standard of living (comparable to that of Britain and France) and level of consumption. Supporters and opponents of fulfilment, particularly the latter, were willing to take massive risks in order to prove that the Allied claims could not be met.

A new German initiative in the summer reopened the old possibility of a direct Franco-German settlement. Meeting in Wiesbaden on 12 June 1921, Walther Rathenau, newly named as Wirth's minister of reconstruction, and Louis Loucheur, France's minister for the liberated regions, concluded a 'businessman's bargain' by which the Germans would pay part of their reparation debt through deliveries in kind. The accord, actually not signed until 7 October, went far beyond the original German offer of men and equipment for the reconstruction of the devastated territories. In Loucheur's hands it became a complex arrangement involving the shipment of up to 7 billion gold marks-worth of German goods to French businessmen by May 1926 in lieu of cash payments. A formula highly favourable to France was devised on the value of German exports to be credited to its reparation account and the prices German exports were to be sold at in France. Agreements would be made between the industrialists of both countries and deliveries would be restricted to the devastated areas. France would clearly benefit from an independent reparation settlement with Germany. Briand's support for the scheme was part of his effort to strike an independent path on the reparation front that would weaken dependence on Britain. In the background were Jacques Seydoux's earlier hopes for a Franco-German partnership that would become the driving force for the reconstruction of Europe. The financial experts warned Briand about the difficulties of extracting cash payments from Germany given the falling value of the mark. The marked preference of the Finance Ministry for reparations in kind was not shared by all French industrialists, many of whom considered the Wiesbaden accords more favourable to the government than to themselves. Some stressed the devastating impact of German imports and labour on French manufacturers and workers, even if restricted to the devastated areas. On the German side, Rathenau viewed the arrangement as a starting point for a rapprochement that could lead to the revision of the London Schedule. A flood of German exports into France would alert the Allies to the dangers and ultimate absurdity of reparation payments. Having earlier consulted various German industrialists about the proposals, Rathenau was shocked to find that the highly influential Stinnes thought the agreement 'extremely bad', and that his industrial supporters were prepared to sabotage Rathenau's efforts. Opposition in both countries, as well as British and Belgian protests, rendered the scheme a dead letter.

IV

By mid-August 1921, when Briand played host to the Supreme Council, no reparation money had reached France and fears began to mount of a German default. Anglo-French differences again resurfaced; the Briand government agreed to lift some of the March sanctions but was insistent on maintaining the occupation of the three towns, so disliked by Lloyd George, who, however, insisted that the export levy should be kept. There were clashes over German disarmament, which the French took more seriously than the British, over the Polish–German dispute in Upper Silesia, and—of great importance for the British—clashes in the Middle East, where the defeat of Mustapha Kemal had become a major strategic question. While the British and French both believed that the

Germans were purposely promoting inflation and courting bankruptcy in order to avoid paying reparations, there was no Allied agreement on how they could be compelled to introduce the necessary reforms.

In the late summer and autumn of 1921 the condition of the mark worsened. The German business community deserted their own currency. The government was under enormous pressure, from the Allies but also from the left-wing parties and, most importantly, from the influential Hamburg merchants and bankers, to reassert its controls over exports, imports, and foreign exchange. Nonetheless, reparations remained the universal scapegoat, and few actually believed that any reform measures would alter the domestic situation unless Germany won a moratorium on its immediate payments. Hopes as well as fears about tax reforms encouraged some groups on the right to take a more conciliatory line with the Wirth government. The Federation of German Industry (RdI) considered an overseas reparation loan to cover the London Schedule instalments due in January and February 1922. However, the opposition of key industrialists, including Stinnes and the heavy industrialist Alfred Hugenberg, who hated the Weimar republic and wanted to undermine Wirth's policies, stalled the credit action. The enlargement of the cabinet in late September to include Gustav Stresemann's DVP, with its important industrial wing, still failed to give the chancellor the greater political manoeuvrability that he sought.

The relatively unfavourable League decision on Upper Silesia of 12 October, giving Germany over half the territory but dividing the industrial area and leaving the principal industrial plants, much of the mineral wealth, and some 350,000 Germans in Polish hands, was a major defeat for Wirth. It came as a blow to German *amour propre* (though the German industrialists had taken steps to safeguard their positions), and an illustration of the hollowness of the claim that fulfilment would help to preserve the territorial integrity of the Reich. The pressure on the chancellor intensified and he resigned office on 22 October. As no one was willing to replace him, Wirth reconstituted his cabinet, recruiting individual members of the former coalition parties rather than the parties themselves, each of which had its own demands. The DDP insisted that Rathenau, already weakened by the attacks on his Wiesbaden policy and the Upper Silesia debacle, be dropped from the cabinet. The DVP had second thoughts about entering the 'cabinet of personalities'. The RdI leadership, sharply divided over any credit offer, demanded rigorous economies and the denationalization of the railways (Stinnes had his eye on private purchases), a political non-starter, as the price of its collaboration. The retreat of the RdI in November and the negative attitude of the right-wing parties in the Reichstag ended the hopes of rescue from the German industrial and commercial sectors. Wirth's attempts at stabilization through indirect tax increases and cuts in subsidies brought higher consumer prices and labour demands for higher wages. While the trade unionists would accept the end of food subsidies and some new arrangements for the nationalized railways, they feared that foreign demands for financial controls would lead to unemployment and demanded that the industrialists provide a safety net. The direct confrontation between labour and industry, each willing to pay reparations if someone else carried the bill, further weakened the government. The tax reforms were a case of too little and too late, as inflation destroyed its benefits before they were put into operation.

As the mark fell, German big business put funds abroad in steady currencies to escape the effects of inflation. While the continuing deterioration of the mark undermined Germany's credit position abroad, Wirth insisted that only a moratorium could save the situation. The German finance minister announced on 4 November a budgetary deficit of 110 billion paper marks, of which 60 billion were attributed to treaty claims. The value of paper marks dropped sharply. The British representative on the Reparations Commission, the sympathetic Sir John Bradbury, warned Berlin that even if Germany was freed from its subsequent 1922 payments, it would still have to meet its interim obligations before a moratorium would be given. When the Commission visited Berlin in mid-November the Germans spoke of industry raising 500 million gold marks abroad, but the RdI, which had already rebuffed the government in early November, knew that the possibility of such a credit action was fading. The commissioners were not deceived. 'I do not want to have to grant a moratorium without making the industrials bleed', Bradbury wrote to Basil Blackett at the Treasury.[16]

Rebuffed at home, the Germans turned to London. The British had objected to the Wiesbaden accords which, like earlier payments in kind, would have given the French a reparations priority. Nor were the Belgians or Italians enthusiastic about the possibility of a new continental economic bloc. Even before the Wiesbaden accords were signed, Rathenau proposed linking expanded exports to Russia with the payment of reparations to Britain. In November a stream of German visitors came to London. The head of the Reichsbank came to appeal for credits, and though the Francophobe Montagu Norman, the long-serving, secretive, and manipulative governor of the Bank of England (1920–44), turned him down, he suggested that the British would be sympathetic both to a moratorium and to revision of the London

[16] Quoted in Charles S. Maier, *Recasting Bourgeois Europe: Stabilization in France, Germany, and Italy in the Decade after World War I* (Princeton, 1975), 266–7.

Schedule. Lloyd George showed no interest in Stinnes's railway schemes, but his Russian ideas resonated with the prime minister's own plans. Rathenau, now an unofficial courier after the reconstruction of the Wirth cabinet, also arrived in London, determined to attack the widespread view that Germany was courting bankruptcy through inflation, and seeking the much-needed British assistance. Rathenau returned empty-handed. The French, of course, were extremely upset at these signs of Anglo-German collaboration behind their backs. In the midst of the swirling mass of conflicting ideas and prescriptions, Lloyd George turned to a new possibility that would diminish the importance of reparations by enlarging the European market through the inclusion of Russia.

V

The British prime minister was in an exposed political position. The deflationary policies supported by the Treasury and Bank of England had worked, but at high cost. Inflation was halted and wholesale prices rapidly declined, yet the pound was still well below its pre-war dollar value. The British would have to bear the full domestic costs of the return to the gold standard that was generally assumed to be the necessary prelude to prosperity. By the end of 1921 unemployment stood at 2 million, 16 per cent of the registered workforce. Few attributed these difficulties to the government's deflationary policies. The visible shrinkage of the export industries was blamed on the unsettled condition of Europe. Government spending was further curtailed during 1922, but though budgetary surpluses were maintained, there was no upswing in the economy. The political pressure for a workable reparation scheme increased, as did criticism of French obstructionism, even among traditional Francophiles in the Conservative party. The chancellor of the Exchequer warned that Germany's financial collapse in the absence of a moratorium would menace the stability of Europe and endanger the London banks, who had £5–6 million outstanding in credits to German importers. Lloyd George faced other difficulties as well. Since the peace conference he had depended on his diplomatic achievements to maintain his hold over the Coalition government. Instead, Britain faced difficulties in Egypt, India, Iraq, and Palestine and the ever-present possibility of a major eruption in Ireland, the latter absorbing much of the prime minister's time until the conclusion of the Anglo-Irish Treaty in November 1921. Success at the Washington naval conference at the end of the year was highly welcome, but Arthur Balfour, the main British negotiator, not Lloyd George, who stayed in London rather than risk failure, reaped the major share of the praise. The news from the Near East was particularly discouraging, since Lloyd George refused to abandon the Greeks, and Kemal's victories, assisted by the defection of the French and Italians to the Nationalist side, made it imperative that the prime minister should refurbish his reputation in Europe.

For a way out of his difficulties, Lloyd George intended to call a world economic conference, which he would dominate, centring around the idea of an international consortium for the economic reconstruction of Russia. His ambitious plans for the reintegration of the Soviet Union into the European economy were as imaginative as they proved fruitless. Prompted by Lenin's efforts to secure foreign relief aid, investment, and trade, Lloyd George hoped that the Bolsheviks might prove amenable to western conditions for recognition and investment. In view of the American relief efforts in Russia, so effectively organized by Hebert Hoover, and the possibility that the Harding government would consider a more positive economic role in Europe, Lloyd George thought that the Americans might participate in his conference. The Foreign Office was generally sceptical of the whole idea, but the cabinet proved somewhat more sympathetic. Though, most unusually, Lloyd George was forced to accept limits on his powers to negotiate, he won cabinet and parliamentary backing for his adventure. Curzon was interested in the Middle East; Lloyd George in 'his' economic conference. Curzon thought Lloyd George an amateur dabbling in foreign affairs; the prime minister dismissed Curzon as a snob, and had no intention of letting the Foreign Office mess up his plans.

Relations with Paris continued to prove difficult. On 14 December Wirth informed the Reparation Commission that Germany could not pay the reparation instalments due in January and February 1922. The German announcement undercut Briand's position. Despite some pressure for coercive measures, there had been considerable backing for his cautious policies. The French premier won an important vote of confidence just before he left for the Washington naval conference in November 1921. There followed a series of disagreements with London. On 21 October the French representative, Franklin-Bouillon, signed an agreement with the Kemalist Turks signalling the end of Anglo-French co-operation in the Near East. At the Washington conference Briand found himself isolated and under pressure from both the British and Americans. His efforts to pave the way for a sympathetic consideration of France's financial difficulties was ruined by a press campaign portraying France as the chief militarist power in Europe. Hopes that the British might break the reparations deadlock by a unilateral renunciation of war debts was blocked by Lloyd George, who was unprepared for any change in policy without an equivalent American action.

The clashes between London and Paris, naturally welcomed in Berlin, were aggravated by the personal antipathies that raised the diplomatic fever chart every time Lloyd George and Briand met. Relations were not improved by Curzon's known dislike and distrust of Briand and his knowledge, through decrypts of the French diplomatic traffic (the French codes were read until 1934), that his feelings were reciprocated. It is, nonetheless, hard to believe, despite official utterances about French bomber capacity and the dire consequences of a French occupation of the Ruhr, that the British really feared French hegemonic designs. Fundamentally neither Lloyd George nor Lord Curzon could contemplate the disruption of the Entente, but each was determined to extract a high price for co-operation. The British hoped to use France's fear of Germany to secure major imperial concessions in return for (but also as preconditions for) a reparations settlement. In refusing both security and reparation guarantees, the British denied the French the quid for which they were being asked to provide the quo.

For the French, the reparations and security questions were always linked. Early in December 1921 the snobbish and already distrusted French ambassador, Count Beaupoil de St-Aulaire, supposedly on his own initiative, raised the possibility of a broad Anglo-French pact with Lord Curzon. It was an idea repeatedly canvassed at the Foreign Office but never welcomed by the cabinet. For France, any such guarantee had to include some recognition of the special situation in the Rhineland. Meeting in London on 20 December to consider the German request for a moratorium, Briand approached Lloyd George with the possibility of a broad defensive alliance. Lloyd George spoke only of a simple guarantee of France's eastern frontiers against German invasion, but no support should France assist her 'unstable and excitable' eastern allies. The possibility of a pact was not dismissed; Lloyd George wanted support for his schemes for European reconstruction and rapprochement with the Soviet Union. The British waited to see what Briand would offer. At the London meeting with Briand, abbreviated because the French premier hurriedly returned to Paris, without his bags or valet, to face a hostile parliamentary *interpellation*, the two leaders agreed that loans to Germany were the only means of achieving rapid German stabilization, but could not agree on a specific scheme. The French thought that German unwillingness to pay, not incapacity, was the problem, but Lloyd George refused to consider any action that would weaken the German government and alienate the Americans. There were autumn meetings between British and French financial experts, attended by Rathenau, to discuss reparations and an international syndicate to rebuild Russia. British, French, and German industrialists considered a division of the Russian markets. Briand was not fundamentally interested in Lloyd George's economic conference scheme, and warned the prime minister that he would want tight assurances on Soviet debt payments before agreeing to negotiations which would be very unpopular at home. Nonetheless, conciliatory by nature and anxious to move in step with the British, he was prepared to go along with Lloyd George's grand design.

The Cannes meeting of the Supreme Council on 4–10 January 1922 started well. Lloyd George's opening speech won general endorsement, and his proposals (the 'Cannes resolutions') establishing the basis for economic and political relations with the Soviet Union were accepted with only a few minor amendments. It was agreed to separate the reparation deliberations from the issue of European reconstruction; the former was put in the hands of a special committee of experts. Securing support from the Italians by picking Genoa as the location for his international conference, Lloyd George pushed through his programme. The Cannes resolutions contained deliberate ambiguities and contradictions, as the prime minister tried both to protect the capitalist powers and foreign investors from Bolshevik practices and assure the Soviets that they could maintain their own system of ownership, internal economy, and government. Contrary to Briand's wishes, Moscow was never asked for and never volunteered an explicit acceptance of the resolutions. Lloyd George overrode the French premier's objections about inviting Rathenau, soon to become Wirth's foreign minister, to appear before the Supreme Council at Cannes. Despite hesitant agreement on some points, an impasse was reached over the Anglo-French security alliance. The British premier proposed a ten-year non-reciprocal defensive pact in case of unprovoked German aggression against the soil of France. There was no military convention; the draft promised only consultation if the Rhineland militarization ban was violated. Briand rejected the offer and demanded a much broader treaty, including the defence of the status quo on Germany's eastern frontiers. The British cabinet found the French proposal unacceptable and preferred to retain its free hand regarding Germany, considered 'the most important country in Europe' for trading purposes. Lloyd George offered too little to Briand. He openly bullied the French premier, who knew that his minority centre-left government was weak and losing parliamentary support. A press photograph of Briand being given a golf lesson by Lloyd George, who was shown leaning over the French premier, was seized upon as symbolic of the relationship between the two men. Parliamentary resolutions and telegrams leaked to the press from President Millerand (well informed of the British position through reading the prime minister's communications to London) forced Briand to beat a hasty retreat from Cannes on the very day that Rathenau arrived. On 12 January Briand resigned as premier, bringing the Cannes conference to an end. He kept his political independence from the Anglophobe right by refusing to compromise the policy of the Entente, but knew that he lacked anything like a stable majority.

Briand's successor was the former wartime president Raymond Poincaré, who would rely on a centre-right following. A lawyer from Lorraine, he was famed for demanding clarity and precision in any contract to which he was a party. Cold, unemotional, and honest beyond reproach, yet sometimes indecisive and even timid, it is hard to imagine a politician more different from Lloyd George. Not unexpectedly, personal relations between the two men were even worse than between Lloyd George and Briand. The French master of deductive logic was far more flexible than his critics assumed. He knew that the strict enforcement of the peace treaties was impossible and that little would be achieved by insisting on the letter of the law. Without Briand's oratorical powers or breadth of vision, Poincaré shared the same realistic appraisal of the limits of French power. Informed observers correctly predicted that Poincaré would continue Briand's cautious policies and try to keep the lines to London open. There was more continuity than change in French policy, with Poincaré remaining as premier until the parliamentary elections in June 1924.

Poincaré was not a great believer in summit diplomacy, nor did he like the idea of the Genoa conference. When Lloyd George stopped in Paris on 14 January 1922 on his way home from Cannes, the premier-designate made clear his doubts. He also told Lloyd George that any security pact would have to involve reciprocal guarantees and a military convention. In response, Lloyd George pointed to all the other questions left unsettled at Cannes—Turkey, reparations, Tangiers—while refusing any joint planning or specific military agreement. The real importance of any pact, he claimed, was the moral value of Britain's general commitment to aid France. 'If the word of the British people was not sufficient for France,' Lloyd George insisted, 'he feared the draft treaty must be withdrawn. The British people would honour their pledge, if France were attacked, with the whole of their strength, but they would never bind themselves by military conventions as to the forces which they would maintain in present conditions during a time of peace.'[17] At this Poincaré retreated slightly, and Lloyd George agreed to wait for a further French proposal. In the draft treaty sent to London, Poincaré dropped the military convention but called for a reciprocal guarantee in case of unprovoked aggression, which would include any

---

[17] Lloyd George, meeting with Poincaré in Paris, 14 Jan. 1922, quoted in Anne Orde, *Great Britain and International Security, 1920–1926* (London, 1978), 24.

violation of the demilitarized Rhineland. Lord Curzon was cool; he wanted France to settle all outstanding questions before proceeding to any treaty. He insisted that the cabinet would never accept an obligation to defend the Rhineland against German reoccupation or for the defence of the status quo in eastern Europe, for this would tip the European balance too far in the French direction. When the British decided to suspend the negotiations, Poincaré warned that France would attend Genoa only if there was no discussion of either disarmament or reparations, as agreed at Cannes. At a glacial meeting in Boulogne on 25 February, Lloyd George agreed to accept some of the French conditions and promised to reconsider the security pact yet again. He was determined to go ahead, despite Poincaré's disdain for the prime minister's European reconstruction plans. Lloyd George had already suffered a domestic political setback; he badly needed a success in Genoa that would allow him to play the part of European peacemaker.

Delegates from thirty-four nations assembled at Genoa; the conference lasted from 10 April to 19 May 1922. Lloyd George aimed at a fundamental reshaping of the European order. He hoped to bring Russia back into Europe, using Germany as an accomplice. He sought treaty revision in favour of the defeated powers, Germany, Austria, and Hungary. All the powers of Europe, and not just the victors, would join in a toothless ten-year pact renouncing aggression and agree to collaborate on peaceful means to prevent it. He wanted American underwriting and participation in the restoration of Europe's financial and economic stability. Lloyd George's brainchild was to bypass the Versailles settlement which, due to Britain and Germany, had become almost impossible to enforce. Whether a 'quixotic diversion' or an 'imaginative gesture', Genoa proved to be a total failure. No proper preparations were made and no pre-conference consensus established. The agenda was overcrowded with issues and participants. There was too much publicity, as press photographers and journalists crowded the Italian city, and too much secret diplomacy, the inevitable result of conference conditions. The Soviets would not accept what offers Lloyd George could make. The cabinet had insisted that the prime minister was not to act without Britain's allies; he was prohibited from offering direct assistance or *de jure* recognition. Nor would the French, with their very different diplomatic agenda and over 1 million tsarist bondholders, swallow their objections to a deal that did not provide debt repayment to France (except as part of a comprehensive general settlement) and its bondholders. Lenin would not accept one-sided bargains. There could be no debt repayment or restoration of property without the promise of substantial loans and full recognition. Since 1919

Lloyd George had accepted the necessity of dealing with the Bolsheviks; this first 'detente' brought few rewards.

Lloyd George's hopes to secure a moratorium on German reparations and prepare the way for Germany's reintegration into a European system on a basis of equality were torpedoed by France and Germany. The former had insisted that neither reparations nor disarmament should be discussed at Genoa. Backed by Edvard Beneš and his 'Little Entente' partners, Romania and Yugoslavia—an unusual example of Little Entente unanimity—the French vetoed the draft plan for a non-aggression pact, framed in imitation of the 1921 Four Power Pacific agreement. The eloquent 'moral statement' ('pure verbiage', according to Eyre Crowe, the sceptical Foreign Office permanent under-secretary) would have weakened, as was Lloyd George's intention, hopes of British participation in the League's system of collective security. Nations would be under no obligation to take up arms to assist allies, fulfil League obligations, or enforce existing treaties. It was adopted in a very truncated form.

The Germans had already angered the French by rejecting the conditions set down by the Reparation Commission for a moratorium before the Genoa conference assembled. News of the Rapallo agreement infuriated Poincaré, who had stayed in Paris, unwilling to confront Lloyd George directly. Louis Barthou, the deputy premier who headed the French delegation, was instructed to pull out of the conference if Russia and Germany did not immediately renounce the treaty. Because Lloyd George wanted the talks with the Russians to continue, he swallowed his own dismay and sought to contain the diplomatic damage. Assisted by the Italian foreign minister, Carlo Schanzer, he tried to moderate the anger of the French, Belgian, and Japanese delegates and managed to secure their agreement to a reworked note of censure sent to the Germans. He owed much to Barthou, who ignored Poincaré's instructions and accepted the differential treatment given to Germany and Russia and refused to bring up the German violations of the Versailles arms provisions. Poincaré tightened his control over the French negotiators and upbraided his deputy for being too conciliatory, but did not oppose Barthou's conciliatory tactics. With his eye firmly on the looming battle over reparations, Poincaré was unwilling to torpedo the conference altogether. Mainly due to Lloyd George's 'diplomatic acrobatics', the Germans grudgingly accepted the letter of censure and the ban on participation in the Allied–Soviet talks. Rapallo did not lead to a German or French walkout or to the disruption of the negotiations with Chicherin.

The Americans had refused to come to Genoa. The usually feuding departments in Washington (State, Treasury, and Commerce) agreed that the conference was premature, and little more than a British political move designed to deal with their own problems rather than to address the fundamental prerequisites for European reconstruction. The highly influential secretary of commerce, Herbert Hoover, insisted that the Europeans would have to put their own financial houses in order before anything further could be done. The Americans did not regret their absence; their unofficial observer at Genoa reported on the confusions and divisions among the allies, and warned against being 'dragged in as an easily hoodwinked creditor who innocently goes afield to meetings of his debtors'.[18] Without American participation, the recommendations of the experts on the financial and economic commissions at Genoa were of little substantive value. The Americans took a more active interest in the forthcoming meeting of an international bankers committee in Paris in May, created by the Reparation Commission to consider an international loan for Germany. Anxious to avoid any appearance of official involvement, Secretary of State Hughes vetoed the appointment of Benjamin Strong, the governor of the FRBNY, in favour of J. P. Morgan, who would go to Paris as a private banker. This businessmen's approach to the reparations problem suited the Americans; it would neither involve the government nor link reparations with war debts and jeopardize war-debt payments.

The Genoa conference broke up in some acrimony. Nothing was accomplished and considerable damage had been inflicted on Anglo-French relations. Lloyd George had overreached himself. His grand design was far too ambitious and ended in failure. The Welsh Wizard's bag of tricks was almost empty.

VI

On 24 April Poincaré delivered a blustering speech at Bar-le-Duc, his birthplace, located close to Verdun, the very symbol of French sacrifices in the recent war. It was intended to return the British to fundamentals, above all to the possibility of a German default on the reparation payment due on 31 May and the prospect of a French punitive response. Germany's relations with the Reparations Commission had become increasingly difficult since January, when in response to German requests for a moratorium the Commission had agreed to a schedule of reduced payments but demanded certain fiscal and budgetary reforms in return. While the inflationary boom continued, the Wirth government

---

[18] Stephen A. Schuker, 'American Policy Towards Debts and Reconstruction at Genoa, 1922', in Carol Fink, Axel Frohn, and Jürgen Heideking (eds.), *Genoa, Rapallo and European Reconstruction in 1922* (Cambridge, 1991), 116.

was not prepared to take the risks of a policy of deflation which such demands as a limitation on note issues, tax increases, voluntary and involuntary loans, and the abolition of subsidies implied. As Rathenau revealed in remarks to the cabinet in March, the policy of fulfilment was 'no end in itself'; the problem of the government was to see how far it could go towards revision without unduly provoking the Allies—to see 'how far the ice is capable of bearing the load'.[19] The conflict came to crisis point on 21 March, when the Commission set as one of its conditions for a further reduced schedule of payments that 60 billion paper marks in additional taxes be voted by 31 May and that the Germans accept the supervision of the Committee of Guarantees to monitor their financial and budgetary reforms. The Germans were furious. Wirth defended the fulfilment policy, but he, Rathenau, and even Stresemann, who had his eye on forming his own cabinet, denounced the Allied demands. Stresemann blamed reparations for ruining the currency and the morale and lives of the middle class. Rightly believing that Lloyd George would not permit the reparation question to cloud the meeting at Genoa, the Germans rejected the Reparation Commission's demands on 7 April.

While Wirth and Rathenau were prepared to take their chances at Genoa, the German finance minister, Andreas Hermes, who had opposed the Rapallo policy from the start and was fixated on the 31 May ultimatum, went off to Paris for talks with the Reparations Commission and reached an agreement. The 31 May ultimatum remained but Germany effectively received a partial moratorium on condition of debt restriction and new taxes. German acceptance was made contingent on the approval of a loan. The Germans also accepted the supervisory authority of the Committee of Guarantees, after being given assurances that there would be no breach of German sovereignty. The bargain was accepted by the Germans mainly to avoid the 31 May deadline, but also because of news that Bradbury would resign and leave the Germans to the tender mercies of the French unless the 'Bradbury plan' was accepted. On 9 June the Bankers' Committee, consisting of Belgian, British, French, German, Italian, and Dutch representatives as well as the American bankers led by Morgan, reported that it was not possible to grant a loan to the Germans under present conditions. The Germans, though denied their loan request, were actually relieved. It was now up to the French, whose representative did not sign the report, to agree to revision before any loan would be given and reparations paid. The committee's decision that there could be no loan while the London schedule remained unchanged was a real

[19] Quoted in Trachtenberg, *Reparation in World Politics*, 214.

blow to Paris. The committee insisted that Germany put its finances on a stable basis. The little that the Wirth government accomplished in the way of reform was soon threatened by a new wave of depreciation set off by the Bankers' Committee report.

While the German leaders considered they had won a 'victory' and that their tough stand on reparations would bear fruit, ordinary Germans lost confidence in the mark. As the value of the mark fell, prices and wages spiralled upwards. The economic crisis deepened; the government marked time and waited for the forthcoming visit of the Committee of Guarantees in December. A Jewish outsider (only one of two Jews who held ministerial office in the Weimar republic) under assault from the anti-Semitic German right wing, the highly strung Rathenau was badly shaken by the demoralization caused by the inflation and by the many threats that he received. On 24 June 1922 he was murdered by two right-wing thugs. The killing created great indignation in Germany and provoked a strong reaction against the political right. A law was introduced imposing severe penalties for conspiracy to murder and providing a means for prohibiting extreme parties, but its effect was weakened by the predilection of judges to enforce it more strictly against the communists than against the right. The assassination resulted in a sharp fall in the value of the mark; inflation turned into hyperinflation, with disastrous effects on the economy and on the lives of many individuals. Confusion and fear undermined traditional values; profiteering became common among people who traditionally prided themselves on their rectitude. Poverty-induced crime created its own excuses. Wirth's efforts to stem the tide through domestic action were blocked by the newly independent Reichsbank and by the obstruction of the industrial and commercial communities. On 4 July the Reichstag ratified the Treaty of Rapallo. The mark continued its downward plunge. On 12 July Wirth asked for a complete moratorium on cash reparations until 1925.

The German national income remained high throughout 1922 even as the mark lost value. Despite the financial chaos, Germany was still enjoying boom conditions, with home demand buoyant and high employment. The major economic interest groups were unwilling to accept the deflationary consequences of stabilization, particularly when their sacrifices would enrich ex-enemies. It proved impossible to raise a hard-currency loan or to impose a tax on capital. Wirth's renewed efforts to enlarge his political support were doomed to failure; the DVP insisted on the end of the eight-hour day as the price of co-operation, a demand which was anathema to the Social Democrats. The most influential economic groups in Germany believed that the domestic stalemate would convince the Allies to accept both a moratorium and the reduction of the reparation bill. The accelerating depreciation and the warnings from the Reparation Commissioners finally forced the Germans to address their domestic situation. During the autumn of 1922 a fierce and complex debate over the question of currency reform took centre stage, but no real effort was made to deal with the financial crisis. It was only on 14 November, after calling in foreign experts for advice, that in a reparation note to the Allies the Wirth government conceded that a temporary action supporting the mark was possible and finally provided the concrete proposals for reform demanded by the Reparation Commission. On the same day Wirth's attempt to establish the Great Coalition collapsed when the SPD refused to remain in a government that included the DVP. The former civil servant and head of the Hamburg–America line, Dr Wilhelm Cuno, took over when Wirth resigned. Hardly a high-flier, his cabinet of 'experts' proved as incapable of dealing with the country's problems as its predecessor.

The French attitude stiffened. French obduracy was linked with the American demands for debt payment and the continuing signs of German intransigence. Poincaré was blamed by the left for his failure to achieve an understanding with London, and by the right for his timidity towards Britain and Germany. The parties of the moderate left began to desert the government and Poincaré was caught by his dependency on a right-nationalist majority. The failure of the Bankers' Committee to back a loan ended hopes for rapid reparation payments. Attacked by speculators, the franc began to weaken. Poincaré tried, as Briand had before him, for a reparations-in-kind solution. Proposals for an industrial entente lacked the backing of the Ruhr industrialists, who refused to bargain until the French evacuated the Saar. There was one breakthrough at the private level. The Gillet–Ruppel accord, signed on 6 June, provided considerable freedom for contracts between individuals in the devastated territories and German suppliers. Stinnes, a man of extraordinary daring, seized the opportunity to conclude a bargain with Guy de Lubersac, a French industrialist, for deliveries of wood and other construction materials to the devastated territories, to be credited to reparations at a price not exceeding the domestic price in France. The French agreed to have part of their reparation coal distributed to the German firms involved. The firms of both men would act as intermediaries in the distribution of orders and contracts and receive a commission for their efforts. Stinnes's activities raised a storm of criticism in Germany, where he was accused of making profits out of his country's miseries, but he was in such a strong position that that he could make his own terms. Stinnes's influence both on the international and domestic stages undercut Wirth's authority and helped to ruin his effort to create a

'Great Coalition' that would include Stresemann's DVP and the Social Democrats. De Lubersac, with less influence in France, was permitted to go ahead, but the distribution of reparation coal was made dependent on Germany fulfilling the entire programme of the Reparations Commission and satisfying French demands.

Poincaré continued to drag his feet during the autumn. There was increasing concern about the state of the French finances, for though France practised strict monetary deflation, the large budgetary deficits were being covered by borrowing, mainly through the sale of short- and long-terms bonds to the French public. In 1922, as doubts grew about the German payments intended to cover reconstruction costs, both French and foreign holders of francs began to take alarm. In May the franc began a very slow depreciation. At the same time the upturn of the economy made it difficult for the Treasury to raise funds. When interest rates on long-term bonds to finance reconstruction in the devastated areas were raised to attract buyers, French investors sold off some short-term bonds to take advantage of the offer. For the first time the Treasury failed to raise the money it needed. Alarm bells began to ring. Ministers began to ask how long French investors would continue to take up the bonds used to finance reconstruction, bonds which were already imposing an 'intolerable burden' on the state. The Ministry of Finance warned of the necessity of achieving real financial gains instead of perpetuating illusions. Far-sighted officials at the ministry, discounting the possibility of a foreseeable reparation settlement, wanted a radical reduction in government expenditure and a positive move towards a balanced budget. In the prevailing political mood, cuts in expenditure were impossible. They would, in any case, signal the failure of the government's German policy. The more Poincaré needed a reparation settlement, the less likely it appeared. American bankers would not consider an international loan for Germany unless France first agreed to a downward revision of reparations. Poincaré would not act unless the Americans and British annulled or reduced the French war debt (though this would hardly cover French financial needs), or until he had concrete ('productive') guarantees of future German payment.

There was no help from London in the summer of 1922. The dispatch of the 'Balfour note' on 1 August was seen as a slap in the face to France. Faced with stalemate on every side, Poincaré grew increasingly angry. Believing that the Germans were deliberately courting financial disaster in order to avoid paying reparations, he argued that only direct intervention would force them to mobilize the country's wealth. When the Germans asked for a new moratorium on 12 July, Poincaré demanded 'physical pledges' (*gages*) in return. He explained in August that these should include the Allied exploitation of state mines and forests, collection of German customs duties, the transfer of a majority of the shares of the chemical and dye companies on the left bank of the Rhine to the Allies, and the re-establishment of the customs line east of the occupied Rhineland which might include the Ruhr.

Lloyd George, after the Genoa fiasco, had again to face the reparation impasse. It was thought in London that Germany needed a long and complete moratorium and an international loan. Bradbury, the British representative on the Reparations Commission, among others, was outraged by the flagrant examples of German financial irresponsibility. The prime minister, nevertheless, held to his view that the logjam preventing the rationalization of German finances could only be broken by a change in French policy. His aim was a settlement productive of hard cash for Britain but a much-reduced reparations bill for Germany. It did not help that Lloyd George and Curzon found Poincaré, 'that horrid little man', intolerable. His acerbic tongue and abrasive person-ality grated on their nerves; they thought him 'shifty', and would not have been averse to his fall from office. When the Supreme Council met in London on 22 August both prime ministers blamed German mis-management for the financial chaos and raging inflation, but Lloyd George refused to consider the *gages* that Poincaré demanded as security for any moratorium. He similarly rejected more modest proposals due to suspicions about Poincaré's ultimate objectives in the Rhineland and Ruhr. Though Lloyd George, already in deep political difficulties, may have seen the need to move in the French direction, he could not rise above his dislike of the French premier.

The British leader's days in office were numbered. The crisis at Chanak, the armistice with the Kemalists on 11 October, and a Con-servative revolt at home led to his replacement on 23 October by Andrew Bonar Law. Lord Curzon remained as foreign secretary. By this time there was little room for manoeuvre left on the reparation front, as the spectre of a Ruhr occupation loomed ever larger. After the failure of the August Supreme Council meeting, the Reparation Com-mission refused a definite moratorium without radical reforms but permitted the Germans to cover the December payments with six-month Treasury notes. Coercive action was avoided only because the Belgians, fearing an Anglo-French rupture, agreed to postpone for six months the remainder of the 1922 reparations due to them. The Cuno government failed to secure backing for a reform programme despite frantic efforts to win domestic support. The German proposals, request-ing a four-year moratorium without providing guarantees for future payment, were dismissed even by the usually sympathetic British Foreign Office as inadmissible. The Germans appealed to the Americans but J. P. Morgan refused to head an international bank consortium that would raise a large loan. When, at the end of the year, the Germans came up with yet another offer, it was so demonstratively inadequate that Carl Bergmann, the German reparations adviser, was relieved not to have to present it to the Allies at their January meeting.

Poincaré came under a barrage of domestic criticism. He was sharply attacked when the 1923 budget was discussed in the Chamber, and was isolated within his own cabinet. André Maginot, the minister for war, backed by Foch, urged immediate military action in the Ruhr. Even the Quai d'Orsay had given up hopes of a negotiated reparations agreement. On 27 November contingency plans were approved for a progressive occupation of the Ruhr (the Foch plan), which it was hoped might prove more acceptable to the British than more radical occupation proposals. Only de Lasteyrie, the minister of finance, spoke for negoti- ations. A press communiqué warning of French coercive action unless the reparation and war-debts problems were settled provoked adverse comments abroad. Poincaré still thought that Bonar Law might prove more sympathetic to France's financial difficulties than his predecessor, and that a compromise solution could be found. If the British refused to co-operate, he was prepared to proceed without them and take action in the Ruhr and on the left bank of the Rhine. In London on 9 December Bonar Law, indeed more agreeable than Lloyd George, suggested that Britain might be willing to go back to the Balfour declaration of August 1922 if France would reduce the reparations owed by Germany. Poincaré did not rule out a bargain, but his response was generally negative. Bonar Law reported to Curzon that the French premier was intent on the occupation of Essen and would only reduce French claims to the extent that Britain would reduce the French debt. There was 'really therefore nothing to do but play for time for the sake of Lausanne'.[20] Anxious to avoid an open quarrel while Curzon was negotiating with the Turks at Lausanne, Bonar Law resorted to delaying tactics and prevailed on Poincaré to adjourn their discussions until 2 January 1923.

While Bradbury and the British Treasury prepared proposals for the Paris conference, the British tried out other possibilities: a new offer from the Germans to be presented in Paris and, more hopefully, an appeal to the American secretary of state, Charles Evans Hughes. The Cuno government, in a desperate attempt to enlist the Americans, had approached Hughes on 12 December, warning that Poincaré was seek- ing indirect annexation of the Rhineland and, if successful, would prolong the European political crisis. In Washington, the visiting Ger- man foreign minister proposed an international committee of experts, with American participation, to regulate reparations and a thirty-year

---

[20] Quoted in O'Riordan, *Britain and the Ruhr Crisis*, 24.

non-agression pact. Hughes listened sympathetically but Poincaré ignored the German proposals. As neither the Americans nor British would join a non-aggression pact, that idea was dropped, but the German démarche was not without effect. French action in the Ruhr and Rhineland would adversely affect American economic interests and delay the process of European pacification in which the United States had a stake. On 29 December, four days after the Reparation Committee had declared Germany in default, in a speech at Yale University Hughes offered to set up a committee of experts to consider the German capacity to pay and to propose a new reparations settlement if the Europeans agreed in advance to accept its recommendations. Hughes promised his government's support and private American capital to underwrite any acceptable scheme. Ten months later, his offer would bear fruit.

In Paris there was no breakthrough at the 2 January meeting. Poincaré refused to hear any further German proposals. He outlined the sanctions that France wanted taken in order to secure reparations. Bonar Law presented the British proposals. Britain would annul the Allied debts owed to her and German reparations would be reduced accordingly, a trade-off that would have involved a reduction of French reparations receipts from 52 to 42 per cent of the total. The Belgians would renounce their priority to reparation payments to compensate the French. The Germans would enjoy a complete moratorium for four years, with payments in kind excluded. A new schedule of low graduated payments for the next ten years was to be followed by annual payments of 3.5 billion marks thereafter. If Germany failed to satisfy its obligations, sanctions would be imposed. There was no reference to any specific productive pledges. Poincaré had no interest in such a plan, and discouraged Bonar Law's less than genuine gestures of friendship. The British proposal, drawn up by Bradbury and the Treasury, reflected their distrust and dislike of the French and appeared deliberately provocative. The technical details were so complicated that the German representative sent to Paris, Carl Bergmann, quipped, 'I would rather pay reparations than try to understand the Bonar Law Plan'.[21] George Theunis, the Belgian premier and finance minister, was shocked by the extreme leniency shown towards Germany and horrified by the challenge to the Belgian reparation priority. More to the point, he knew that Belgium was suffering from the same monetary and financial problems as France and was in desperate need of German payments. The Belgian decision to support the threatened French action in the Ruhr was not

[21] Quoted in Stephen A. Schuker, *The End of French Predominance in Europe: The Financial Crisis of 1924 and the Adoption of the Dawes Plan* (Chapel Hill, NC, 1976), 23.

unconditional; Theunis had no wish to be dragged into a French adventure that might alienate the British, and tried to safeguard Belgian independence. Mussolini, recently installed in the driver's seat in Rome (on 29 October), also rejected the British plan and agreed to follow the French into the Ruhr. Two engineers would be sent to show Italian solidarity with France. Goaded by British unwillingness to compromise on Italy's war debts, and with wild dreams of creating an anti-British coalition, Mussolini demanded a share of German coal as the price of co-operation. Poincaré had no love for the new Italian leader, but agreed to Mussolini's terms.

There was no possible agreement between the French and the British at Paris. The French had laid their plans for a full military occupation of the Ruhr. Early on the morning of 4 January the order went out for the occupation to begin on 11 January. Faced with the reality of the occupation, the British were left straddling the fence, unwilling to commit themselves to join in what the Foreign Office believed was a futile and dangerous intervention, but equally unwilling to break with France and side with Germany. The weakness of the newly created Bonar Law cabinet and the divisions of opinion reflected in the press encouraged equivocation. Once the French actually occupied the Ruhr, Britain adopted a policy of 'benevolent neutrality', a confusing and confused course of action which proved untenable in practice.

Why did the French enter the Ruhr? The answer is far from simple; in part because the chief policy-makers in Paris and in the Rhineland had different objectives, but also because Poincaré, who made the key decisions, was prone to procrastination and vacillation. There were those who hoped to return to the Rhenish policies that Clemenceau had been forced to abandon in 1919, but also those who started out with far narrower economic and security objectives in mind and viewed the occupation as a means of permanently solving France's critical shortage of coke. The Ruhr itself was 'la gage par excellence' that could be used to restrict German industrial production and force Berlin to abide by the terms of the Versailles treaty. Some, like Charles de Lasteyrie, the minister of finance, objected to the plans and repeatedly warned Poincaré of the worsening financial position at home and the unacceptable costs of occupation. The minister dismissed the Quai d'Orsay's Jacques Seydoux's highly favourable financial projection, insisting that everything depended upon the attitude of the German authorities. Poincaré, in fact, did not expect a major financial return from the Ruhr, but thought that de Lasteyrie was unduly pessimistic.

Poincaré's intentions are still the subject of debate. He was neither the tool nor the spokesman of the French metallurgists, whom he very much distrusted. Nor was he decisively swayed by the advice of any single adviser, civilian or military. He was, above all, a politician, acutely aware of the mood in the Chamber and the pressures in the country at large for positive action. The premier dragged his feet over the occupation, exploring without success a host of other possibilities in the summer of 1922. As late as 13 November of that year, Millerand claimed that at the Council of Ministers Poincaré, 'to the general surprise, violently denounced "the dangers which he foresaw from the enterprise". I interrupted him: "The military operation will not be a disaster or a bankruptcy." To which Poincaré exclaimed, "I resign!" '[22] Such histrionics notwithstanding, it remains unclear whether Poincaré was mainly concerned with reparations or had broader security objectives in mind. He knew that action in the Ruhr could affect the Rhineland both economically and politically, and that a 'neutral' Rhineland, particularly one without Prussians, would help to solve the French security problem. Above all, the French premier did not want to break with the British. As far as he was chiefly concerned with achieving a solution of the reparations question, he knew this depended on British and American co-operation. It was clear that Britain would not join the occupation, but Poincaré believed, rightly, that they would do nothing to stop French action. He harboured some hopes that London might come to accept a radical adjustment in Franco-German relations. Even the experienced René Massigli at the Quai d'Orsay harboured such illusions (for which Lord Curzon was partly to blame), and argued that the British public could be convinced that the struggle in the Ruhr was not solely about reparations but about a new 'formula of political civilisation'.[23] As the struggle lengthened, and the tide moved in the French direction, Poincaré, after considerable hesitation, was tempted to turn the situation to France's permanent advantage while Germany lay prostrate.

The French occuption was launched on 11 January for a multitude of reasons, but no unity of purpose or clarity about objectives emerged. A number of possibilities were pursued simultaneously, creating considerable confusion both in Paris and in the Ruhr and Rhineland. Few of the French leaders (Foch was one of the exceptions) considered what might happen should the Germans resist the occupation. Consequently, in May 1923, faced with the fact of German opposition, Foch, Millerand, and Seydoux, among others, complained about the lack of organization and the absence of any programme of future action. The ultimate purpose of the occupation remained undefined.

[22] From Millerand's unpublished memoir, 'Mes Souvenirs (1859–1941), Contribution a l'Histoire de la Troisiéme République', 114. I owe this reference to Dr Andrew Barros of the Université Québec à Montréal.
[23] Millerand Papers, Massigli to Laroche, 13 July 1923.

VII

The occupation of the Ruhr, long anticipated by some and feared by others, was finally at hand. On 9 January 1923, after listening to the German representatives, the Reparation Commission (with Bradbury abstaining) ruled that Germany had 'voluntarily defaulted' on her coal deliveries, which were below quota as usual. Two days later French and Belgian engineers, the Mission Interalliée de Control des Usines et des Mines (MICUM), marched into Essen accompanied by a military force, intending to establish their supervision over the coal-mines. By 15 January the entire Ruhr valley was in French and Belgian hands. Some 19,000 French soldiers (later augmented) and 2,500 Belgians were involved in the initial occupation. Poincaré had expected that the French and Belgian authorities would extract sufficient timber, coke, and coal to force the Germans to 'surrender'. It was decided at a conference in Paris at the end of January, with Poincaré present, that recalcitrant senior German officials on the railway and in the post offices should be expelled, that customs barriers should be created along the eastern frontiers of the occupied regions and along the bridges and ports of the Rhine, and that imports and exports from the Ruhr should be subjected to licence and tax. In early February Tirard was instructed to proceed to the economic separation of the Ruhr and Rhineland from the rest of unoccupied Germany.

Contrary to what the French expected, along with formal protests from Berlin, the occupation triggered off a German reaction, initially largely spontaneous but soon organized and financed by the German government. 'Passive resistance' ranged from non-cooperation on the part of factory- and mine-owners and workers, and strikes by railway workers, to actual acts of sabotage. Ruhr managers, miners, and railway workers refused to work. The Stinnes and Thyssen empires shut down. The action had wide support and spread to the Rhineland. By the spring of 1923 there was little movement in or out of the Ruhr, and the French iron and steel industries began to suffer. The customs barrier became a blockade of the occupied territories. The occupiers established their control over the entire railway network in the occupied territory: a railway *Régie* (administration) was created, and French and Belgian personnel took over its management and operations. They could now move the stockpiled coal and coke so that at least some French furnaces could work, but the miners refused to replenish these stores. The French were convinced, rightly, that they could stand the strain of the occupation longer than Germany, but also, wrongly, that even a costly victory might be worth the price. The occupiers seized control of

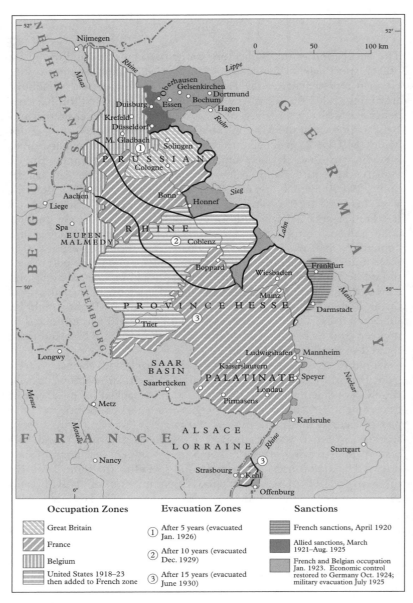

Map 10. The Rhineland

the Rhineland Commission in Coblenz, which the Americans, in accordance with Congressional demands, had just evacuated, and used its powers to impose their control over the occupied territories. In response to German resistance, Paul Tirard, the French high commissioner in the Rhineland, proceeded to implement, through the Rhineland Commission, many of those measures of legislative, executive, and judicial control for which he had lobbied since 1920. The first wave of expulsions of senior functionaries (most of them Prussians) began in February; a second, far more extensive and systematic expulsion of those opposing the occupation took place in April. By 1 October some 8,400 people (expellees and their families) in the Ruhr and 130,000 on the right bank of the Rhine left the occupied territories for Germany. The extension of French power (including the closing of the Rhine bridgeheads and the occupation of the strips of territory on the Right Bank between the Cologne, Coblenz, and Mainz bridgeheads) provoked further German resistance. Both the French and the Germans resorted to tough tactics to achieve their goals.

As the French became more deeply committed to the occupation, officials in Paris became increasingly optimistic. It was not only the Quai d'Orsay's powerful under-secretary, Jacques Seydoux, who spoke of a graduated evacuation of the Ruhr as reparations were paid and of a continued and lengthly occupation of the Rhineland. There were numerous calls for an autonomous Rhineland or a permanent French presence in the region, and detailed consideration of such scenarios by the CSDN in Paris. Admittedly, Poincaré's top aide at the Quai d'Orsay, the director of political affairs and a leading proponent of an aggressive policy, Peretti de la Rocca, scribbled on one of the more ambitious of these proposals: 'Admirable project, if Britain did not exist.'[24] Poincaré himself remained hesitant and uncertain about the possibilities of Rhineland separatism. A visit to London in April 1923 by Louis Loucheur, which Loucheur mistakenly assumed would lead to Anglo-French negotiations, revealed the extent of French ambitions to the startled Conservative prime minister, Bonar Law, and Stanley Baldwin, his chancellor of the Exchequer. The Opposition leader, Ramsay MacDonald, objected strongly to Loucheur's suggestions for the creation of an autonomous, neutralized Rhenish state. Nor were the Belgians happy, as French intentions shifted from a temporary occupation to ensure German payments to more ambitious possibilities. Theunis had hoped for a quick German capitulation and a moderate settlement in which Belgium would play the mediating role. Admittedly, the Belgians raised no objections to the establishment of the rail

[24] MAE, Rive Gauche, vol. 29, memo by Peretti, 30 Mar. 1923.

Régie, and participated fully in taking the productive pledges, but Theunis wanted to get out of the Ruhr as quickly as possible and, above all, to avoid a permanent French presence in the region. By midsummer, having tried unsuccessfully to get the British involved, Brussels began to lose confidence in the occupation. Unable to grasp what Poincaré intended, and facing opposition at home from Flemings and socialists, the Belgians pressed for a resolution of the conflict.

British troops had remained in their Rhineland occupation zone, which separated the French and Belgian zones; their presence was welcomed by both the French and the Germans. The so-called British policy of 'benevolent neutrality' meant, as far as possible, one of non-intervention. Total inaction was impossible. The British allowed the French the use of a railway line that crossed a small corner of their zone and sanctioned the daily running of ten military and two food trains. There were difficulties, too, with the French and German retaliatory customs duties, and London had to negotiate to win some degree of protection for British traders. While some British industries, coal, steel, and chemicals, benefited from the crisis and the temporary elimination of Ruhr competition, in the longer term the German hyperinflation and the dislocations of European trade were damaging to British commerce. Lord Curzon returned to London from Lausanne in February and resumed control of the Foreign Office; until April British policy was characterized by its passivity. Public sentiment, at first divided, shifted away from France and towards Germany, but Bonar Law's Conservative backbenchers remained staunchly Francophile. At the Treasury and at the Foreign Office, where senior officials were highly suspicious of French intentions, many hoped that the occupation would fail and that Paris would see the folly of its ways. Even Eyre Crowe, the traditionally Francophile permanent under-secretary at the Foreign Office, insisted that the occupation of the Ruhr was illegal and believed that a more active anti-French line was necessary. Britain would be 'squeezed out' by the French and Belgians, Crowe warned, and the 'whole situation in Europe brought to ruin through French obstinacy'.[25] Curzon remained cautious, anxious to avoid any direct action that could be interpreted as anti-French. He tried to pressure Poincaré to define his objectives in the Ruhr in order to provide a basis for opening negotiations, but the French leader claimed that these were already clear and that France would only withdraw from the Ruhr when Germany had paid its reparations. On 20 April, in a speech to the Lords, Curzon invited the Germans to break the deadlock with some sort of offer, dangling the possibility of future assistance if talks should begin.

[25] Minute by Crowe, 14 May 1923, PRO, FO 371/8636.

Though this tentative move marked the beginning of a change in British diplomacy, Curzon soon became engrossed in domestic affairs which preoccupied him for some weeks. Bonar Law, whose health had collapsed, resigned on 20 May. Lord Curzon had previously acted as deputy prime minister for Bonar Law and expected to succeed him, but the less experienced and relatively unqualified Baldwin was appointed instead.

The German government took steps to support the population of the occupied areas while doing everything possible to strengthen the resistance movement. In the early months of 1923 the government worked out a system of Rhine–Ruhr aid by which the government and employers agreed to pay the full salary of workers on strike against the occupation. The Reichsbank extended short-term paper-mark credit to the industrialists, while special agencies and private associations distributed unemployment relief to workers. These payments fuelled the already rampant inflation fed by the continuous use of the printing press. An effort to launch a gold note loan in the winter and spring of 1923 failed utterly. There was a massive increase in the number of banknotes in circulation; local government authorities and the larger industrial and commercial firms began to print their own, adding to the financial chaos. The government searched for ways to regain control, but Chancellor Cuno's efforts were continually blocked by the unwillingness of the industrialists to commit their assets without compensation at the expense of the workers. As real wages began to lag behind price increases and unemployment rose, the mood of the working classes changed. Passive resistance became an end in itself. Rather than uniting Germany, resistance to the occupation increased its domestic divisions, as each interest group accused the other of making the lesser sacrifice. The hyperinflation began to hit all levels of society and not just those that had suffered earlier. The resulting demoralization proved a lasting blow to the young republic.

During the last week of July a rash of strikes and rioting swept the Ruhr and unoccupied Germany. Local authority began to collapse in the Rhineland, where Poincaré, who needed right-wing support, refused to end France's long-standing subsidy, though he gave the separatist leaders, whom he distrusted and even despised, no personal encouragement. In Saxony and Thuringia the Communists and Socialists created coalition governments and joined in common defence organizations against possible action by the Reichswehr. In Bavaria, the ultra right-wing nationalist movements showed their strength; Adolf Hitler's National Socialist German Workers Party (NSDAP) gained new recruits and importance. The political unity of the Reich was coming under strain. When the Reichstag convened in the first week of August, the bankruptcy of the Cuno government was obvious.

Ironically, just before Cuno's fall the Reichstag accepted new gold-based taxes, which comprised the 'first solid step toward stabilisation'.[26] By 11 August, when Cuno resigned, Germany was in a state of acute crisis. Gustav Stresemann, head of the conservative DVP, formed the first great coalition government with four Social Democratic members in the cabinet, including Rudolf Hilferding as finance minister. The autumn of 1923 was one of the nadir points in Weimar's history.

In response to Curzon's April speech in the Lords, the Germans made an offer (largely drafted by Keynes) involving a four-year unsecured moratorium but with no guarantees of future payment. It was totally unacceptable, and Curzon demanded a better proposal. Berlin offered, on 7 June, to accept an impartial committee of experts to determine German liability and offered certain guarantees to ensure reparation payments. There was no proposal to end passive resistance, without which Poincaré refused to negotiate. He already had doubts about a new committee that would derogate from the authority given to the Reparation Commission. The French and Belgians demanded concerted pressure on Germany to abandon passive resistance; Curzon stalled and countered by asking for a clearer definition of French policy in the Ruhr in the event of German capitulation. By this time the French were growing more confident of success and showed no inclination to rush into talks. On the contrary, the far-reaching goals discussed earlier at the Quai d'Orsay seemed well within their grasp. Alarmed by their intransigence, and by fears that Germany might collapse into chaos, officials in London began to press for intervention to restrain the French. Curzon finally lost patience and authorized the drafting of a strongly worded rebuff to Paris. The note, drafted by Crowe and sent on 11 August, asserted that the occupation was illegal (a disputed judgement) and would not bring the payment of reparations any closer. Instead, it was proposed that a committee of experts, including German and American representatives, should conduct an inquiry into Germany's capacity to pay reparations. The note ended with a threat to 'contemplate' the possibility of separate action to hasten a solution. This closing flourish, which had no actual cabinet sanction, was a bluff that failed. France's detailed reply was a point-by-point dismissal of the British case, and the Belgian answer, if less hostile, was equally negative. There was no follow-up from London. It was vacation time and the cabinet dispersed; even the industrious Crowe went on holiday.

Some senior Conservatives thought that Curzon's note had been too peremptory, and demanded that Baldwin should meet with Poincaré

---

[26] Charles S. Maier, *Recasting Bourgeois Europe*, 373.

and repair the damage. Baldwin, contemplating an election on the issue of protection, moved to conciliate the restive Francophiles in his party. Returning from holiday at Aix-les-Bains, he met with Poincaré in Paris on 19 September. Exuding goodwill and anxious to appease the French leader in the hope of ending the 'mésentente cordiale', Baldwin accepted Poincaré's assurances that he was ready to negotiate with Germany and had no intention of breaking up the country. He hardly noticed that nothing was said about evacuating the Ruhr. To make matters worse, in Curzon's view, the press communiqué issued after the meeting underlined the 'common agreement of views' between the two prime ministers. Curzon was aghast at what he regarded as Baldwin's inept forfeiture of all British pressure on France. Poincaré appeared to hold all the trump cards. As Austen Chamberlain complained to his sister: 'It seems to me that we are becoming the scold of Europe. We run about shaking our fists in people's faces, ascertaining that this must be altered and that must stop. We get ourselves disliked and distrusted and misunderstood, and in the end we achieve nothing and relapse into humiliated silence or laboriously explain how pleased we are.'[27]

There seemed no solution to the impasse but a German surrender. The British proved unresponsive to Stresemann's appeals for assistance. Continuation of the struggle would lead to the disintegration of the economy and possibly the state. Stresemann's efforts to open talks with the French without abandoning passive resistance were met with silence, Poincaré demanded that the Belgians, who had welcomed Stresemann's overtures on 1 September, reject them out of hand. On 26 September the German chancellor, showing that pragmatic sense and tactical flexibility that marked his subsequent career, gave way, stopping the subsidies to the Ruhr while maintaining most of the other measures of resistance. He expected that Poincaré would now negotiate. Instead, the latter refused to talk until all the resistance ordinances had been repealed and the Ruhr magnates and workers had restored production and resumed deliveries to France. Poincaré's silence perplexed and angered many of his own countrymen, as well as the British and Americans.

There are various possible explanations for Poincaré's behaviour. He might have wanted to take further advantage of German weakness to enhance the French position before entering into new discussions over reparations. It might have been some indecisiveness or even timidity that prevented his taking further action, or a fundamental respect for legality and order which served as a restraint at this time of crisis. Or, as

[27] Austen to Ida Chamberlain, 22 Sept. 1923, Austen Chamberlain Mss., AC 5/1/290.

he told French critics of his action, he could well have thought that French financial recovery and European stabilization depended on the Entente with Britain, which would never countenance an exclusive French deal with Germany. He knew that Washington would oppose any such settlement. If his primary aim was to bring about a favourable solution to the reparations problem, however, his subsequent moves in the Ruhr and Rhineland only confirmed Anglo-American suspicions that he was aiming at the dismemberment of Germany and intended a radical readjustment of the Versailles peace settlement. Poincaré missed a chance to act at the most opportune moment, if not in October, then after the November MICUM agreements. Thanks to Baldwin's intervention, France's diplomatic situation had briefly improved. In October the Ruhr authorities began direct negotiations with the industrialists, workers, and local authorities in the occupied territories. On 7 October the MICUM agreement was concluded with Otto Wolff of the Rheinstahl and Phönix works, with excellent terms for France. Conversations had been started two days earlier with a delegation of six industrialists led by Hugo Stinnes, despite Stresemann's unwillingness to recognize their right to negotiate in the name of Germany. While these talks were continuing, Poincaré refused to allow the French industrialists to enter the negotiations or to consider any broader agreements to be purchased by concessions over reparations. He made no proposal to the Reparation Commission at a time when France, with Belgium still in tow, was clearly in the ascendant.

It is highly doubtful that Poincaré, with his eye on a reparations settlement, would have set an independent Rhineland as a condition for evacuation, although some of his officials believed, particularly after the ending of passive resistance, that it was now possible to restructure the European balance of power in France's favour. Poincaré may have intended to treat the two issues, the Ruhr and the Rhineland, separately, despite their obvious interconnection. The economic debacle in the Rhineland and local French patronage stimulated separatist feeling, but the whole previous history of the separatist movements suggested that genuine separatism appealed only to a minority and that the activists, a motley crew at best, were not necessarily pro-French. Yet incompetent, irresponsible, and quarrelsome leaders set the stage in the summer of 1923 for a series of demonstrations in favour of Rhenish independence. Poincaré had avoided personal contacts, and expressed his doubts about the limited backing offered by Paul Tirard and General Degoutte to the leaders of the Rhenish movement. During the summer months he nevertheless sanctioned support for their summer rallies, despite fierce quarrels between the separatist leaders and the frustration of French hopes that unity could be imposed on their competing organizations.

An open and bloody clash at Düsseldorf on 30 September 1923 between the forewarned German police and the separatists, resulting in a rout of the latter, might have caused second thoughts in Paris, but Peretti, for one, thought that this example of Prussian brutality might be exploited to strengthen separatist feeling.[28] Poincaré's reaction was ambiguous. Though he was warned that majority opinion on the Left Bank was anti-separatist, and was concerned about the unpredictability of the separatists' behaviour, he took no steps to check the continuing collaboration between the occupation authorities and the separatists.

To the surprise of the French, though not of the Belgians, there was a putsch in Aachen in the Belgian zone in the early hours of 21 October and a separate Rhenish republic was declared at Coblenz. The movement spread to the French zone. The separatists seized Bonn and Duisburg; Hans Dorten and Joseph Dorten, their less-than-respectable leaders, proclaimed themselves co-directors of a provisional regime in the Rhineland on 22 October. To the general surprise of the French officials, including Tirard, Poincaré decided to back the insurgents. The premier had never declared himself before in favour of an independent state, separated from the rest of Germany, and his representatives in the Rhineland were about to open conversations with the 'legalists', the more respectable Rhinelanders, which he had welcomed. Admittedly, there was considerable confusion both in Paris and in the Rhineland. The telegraphic instructions sent by the Quai d'Orsay to its representatives showed signs of haste and improvisation. If Tirard, who had previously been instructed to follow a policy of 'benevolent neutrality', was surprised by Poincaré's decision, he quickly changed tactics and gave his open backing to the separatists. With rising doubts about the competence of the separatist leaders, he warned the Quai d'Orsay that, without any administrative capabilities of their own, they would depend on the French authorities to keep the public services going. On 23 October, in a separate and independent action, an autonomous Palatine republic was proclaimed at Speyer, with considerable backing from the population who, for both economic and political reasons, were anti-Bavarian and who had no sympathy with the rightist-authoritarian separatists in Munich. Tirard asked for instructions. Poincaré wanted to withhold financial backing until he knew whether the Speyer government would support France. 'Your telegraphic intelligence has proven contradictory and unintelligble', he complained to Tirard.[29] The French subsidized the insurgents, though General de Metz, the French delegate-general in Speyer, pursued an independent course in

---

[28] McDougall, *France's Rhineland Diplomacy, 1914–1924*, 302.
[29] Quoted in ibid. 309.

the Palatinate, often without Quai d'Orsay backing. Tirard came to Paris on 29 October to express his doubts about the 'provisional governments' in the Rhineland, warning that if the Germans cut off all unemployment relief for the occupied territories, the full financial burden would full on France. There was far more to be gained from negotiations with the respectable representatives from the Rhineland, he argued, who were already in contact with him. Poincaré authorized the talks. His maximum programme might have been the total independence of the Rhineland under the auspices of the League of Nations, but he was prepared to accept some form of autonomous Rhineland within the Reich. Time was of the essence. Support for the dubious separatists could be used to hasten agreements with the notables. The former could be abandoned at any time, but their movements had a limited due date.

The international background to these events was rapidly changing. During the autumn of 1923 the British began to feel that a far more interventionist policy was necessary. Even in the Cologne zone of occupation they had tended to follow a policy of delay and obstruction rather than confrontation. Curzon's Francophobia was mounting. In October he learnt, through wiretaps and decrypted messages exchanged between Poincaré and the French ambassador in London, of a plot to persuade Baldwin to replace him with a more Francophile foreign secretary. His distrust of Poincaré had already reached epic proportions over the latter's actions in the Near East; he now refused even to meet Ambassador St Aulaire. Convinced that Poincaré would be defeated by the problems of the occupation, the Treasury, if not the Foreign Office, was willing to let Germany go to the wall to expose the weakness of the French position. Curzon's speech to the Imperial Conference on 5 October accused the French of aspiring to attain the domination of the European continent. He again asked Poincaré for an expression of his views, but elicited no response. While waiting for Poincaré, the British looked across the ocean.

There were some favourable signs. The phlegmatic and notoriously silent Calvin Coolidge, who became president in early August after Harding's sudden death, delivered a speech on 9 October referring favourably to the December 1922 proposal by Charles Hughes for convening a committee of experts. On 15 October, in response to a British request, Hughes, still secretary of state in the new administration, indicated that any unanimous communication from the European states would be given careful consideration. At first Hughes explored the British suggestions of an economic conference on reparations to investigate Germany's capacity to pay reparations and present a plan for their payment, but he much preferred the more informal approach suggested in his earlier speech at New Haven. The creation of an expert committee on reparations, in which the Americans would participate, would avoid any discussion of war debts and encourage a non-political approach to the reparation question. Though preoccupied with the forthcoming general election, Curzon, undoubtedly encouraged by Hughes, informed the French, Belgian, and Italian governments of the possibility of either an international economic conference idea or the creation of a committee of experts charged by the Reparation Commission to make recommendations. Poincaré responded that he would not countenance a conference, but on 25 October, after soundings in Brussels and Washington, he agreed in principle to the setting up of an advisory committee, with American participation, by the Reparation Commission, though with specific conditions which he made clear in the days that followed. Poincaré had accepted a proposal that he had refused in the summer, clearly hoping to use the Ruhr card to set the terms and conditions of the inquiry. He demanded that the Reparation Commission appoint the experts, that no reduction be made in the total amount of the German debt as fixed on 21 May 1921, that passive resistance cease, and that the occupation should continue. He insisted, too, that any European invitation to the Americans should make clear that the commission's inquiry could only consider Germany's present capacity to pay. Poincaré somewhat weakened his hand when he agreed that the French representative and chairman of the Reparation Commission, Louis Barthou, should put this last proposal to his fellow commissioners. Poincaré was now committed to an inquiry.

In the hope that the Americans were prepared to participate in a general war-debt (hopes that were quickly dispelled) and reparations settlement that would relieve the financial pressures on France, Poincaré finally cashed in on his Ruhr gamble. It has been suggested that there was a connection between Poincaré's decision on 24 October to support the separatists and his willingness to accept the creation of a committee of experts.[30] His political situation was beginning to deteriorate, the Belgians were opposed to the current policy of underwriting the separatists, and the Americans refused to negotiate over war debts. It was a gamble, but he had some cards to play. It might be that the separatists' movements might herald Germany's decomposition, or at the least force the notables to negotiate terms that would lead to the detachment of the Rhineland from the Reich. France would be, in any case, in a far better position to impose its terms on the committee of experts.

A public warning from Baldwin on 25 October that Britain would not tolerate the disintegration of Germany or the breaking off of any

---

[30] Jeannesson, *Poincaré, la France et la Ruhr*, 338.

part into a separate state was decisive for the Belgians. Henri Jasper, the Belgian foreign minister, was determined to clear its Rhineland zone of separatists, who were already warring against each other. Their expulsion left them isolated in the French zone and deprived France of its only ally. On 10 November Lord Curzon warned the French that the establishment of a Rhenish republic would mean the sacrifice of French reparations. Poincaré made desperate but unsuccessful efforts to win back the Belgians, who would only negotiate if the British joined the talks. By the end of November the movements in the French zone were faltering. General Degoutte refused to permit any separatist agitation in the Ruhr for fear of disrupting talks with the German industrialists. In the (Speyer) Palatinate, where there was a genuine movement of protest, the new government flourished during the winter months. Its financial decrees had to be approved by the Rhineland Commission, however, where the British could block registration. Poincaré's personal prestige was engaged, but with the French franc under pressure and the Belgians unwilling to act while Britain and France were quarrelling, the French opted for retreat after a British investigation and threats in January 1924 to disclose its findings about France's actions. The Rhineland Commission arranged for the financial stabilization of the Palatinate and its return to Bavarian sovereignty. It was a 'costly adventure' for Poincaré and France. The story had a tragic ending when, without German relief and cut off from French subsidies, a band of unemployed workers, incited by nationalist provocateurs, set fire to a separatist garrison on the night of 13 February and shot or hacked to death those who fled. It was a bloody ending to the separatist cause.

The main French efforts shifted at the end of October to the negotiations with the Rhenish notables, including Konrad Adenauer, the mayor of Cologne, and Louis Hagen, a Rhenish banker and close associate. The French followed the same course of action in the Rhineland as in the Ruhr, hoping to achieve their ends through talks with the men of influence. Faced with the impoverishment and demoralization of the local population, the Adenauer group demanded from Berlin either the continuation of the Reich subsidies or the right to negotiate directly with the French. Stresemann, dealing concurrently with a leftwing revolt in Saxony and Thuringia and a National Socialist putsch involving General Ludendorff in Munich, had little choice. Subsidies were at first continued but were dropped in late November, lest they destroy the credibility of a new currency scheme initiated earlier that month. At the long-delayed meeting (the delays due first to the French and then to the Germans) of Tirard and Adenauer in mid-November, the Rhenish leader spoke of an economic entente between French and German industry and held out the possibility of an autonomous Rhenish republic achieved through constitutional means. The notables did not offer enough to interest Tirard; the rejection of their proposals led to the break-up of the Committee of Fifteen and the constitution of a broader Committee of Sixty, but Adenauer remained its chief spokesman. At the end of November he rejected Tirard's principles for the foundation of a Rehnish state, and argued that any political settlement in the Rhineland would have to be accompanied by a general reparations and economic agreement. Poincaré was furious at this apparent retreat, for time was running out with the collapse of the Matthes/Dorten government in the Rhineland. A change in the German government in late November and a new cabinet with a Centrist and native Rhinelander, Wilhelm Marx, as Chancellor and Stresemann as foreign minister, ruling under emergency law, increased the pressure on Adenauer. Though Marx allowed Adenauer to continue the talks, the new cabinet would not accept any change in the status of the Rhineland. Adenauer's own position was complicated, but he responded to the changed situation in Berlin. Whereas he had previously aimed at an administratively independent province joined confederally with the Reich, in the later talks with the French, after the collapse of the Rhenish currency scheme in December, he shifted their focus from the political to the economic plane. By early January, with the franc under serious pressure and the mark recovering, the talks were abandoned. The German delaying tactics proved successful.

French hopes to establish a Rhenish bank also collapsed in December 1923–January 1924. The French had long planned to create a Rhenish gold note bank whose notes would run throughout the occupied provinces. If they were the major underwriters, they would gain financial control over the Rhenish territories and could hasten the separation of the Rhineland from the Reich. Early attempts to establish a Rhenish bank had met with opposition from de Lasteyrie, who feared the effects on France's own weakened financial state. In late October, when the German government finally decided to create a new gold-backed currency, the French made a final attempt to fulfil their ambitions. With the imminent ending of Reich relief, Louis Hagen, the Rhenish banker, backed the idea of a gold-based Rhenish currency as a way to restore the province's prosperity. The bank was to be financed mainly by the Rhinelanders with Belgian and French assistance, but it would depend on British and German acquiescence. The scheme had to be put into operation before the Rhineland Commission gave its approval to the German Rentenbank and the entry of the new German currency into the occupied territories. The weakness of the French franc and British opposition and support for the Rentenmark made it impossible for the French to raise the necessary capital. The Belgians refused their support unless the Rhinelanders had the major interest in the bank and it had the approval of the Germans. In early December the Marx cabinet vetoed the separate currency plan and denounced Rhenish autonomism. The combined opposition of the Weimar government and the Reichsbank more than outweighed the limited support from some German industrialists, like Hugo Stinnes, who had vastly expanded his empire by buying up failing firms and was now in need of liquid assets.

The ongoing MICUM negotiations with the Ruhr industrialists were more successful. Agreements were concluded in October and November 1923 providing for the resumption of deliveries of coal to France and the payment of further reparation in cash and kind. The final MICUM agreements were concluded on 23 November, with France assured of anything up to a quarter of German production until April 1924, when the agreements would come up for renewal. Once again Stresemann was forced to allow the talks to take place. He reluctantly agreed that the coal taxes should be treated as taxes to the state. All other payments would be counted as reparations, to be used to defray occupation costs but ultimately credited towards the reparation account. It was a relatively heavy burden on German industry, for Berlin did not reimburse them. Ruhr firms with strong organizations and limited debts weathered the storm, but others, even the Stinnes organization, built mainly on the benefits of the inflation, were soon in serious difficulties. The French had won the deliveries of coal and coke that had been the aim of every successive French government. The agreements, which were extended to other Ruhr industries, might have been used to extract further concessions from the Germans, but the French steel industry, coal producers, and government could not agree on a common front. Poincaré, like Stresemann, was suspicious about private arrangements between industrialists that might benefit the steelmen but not France. In need of capital (the Rentenmark did not circulate in the occupied territories, as the Germans feared its seizure by the French) the Ruhr metallurgists, led by Stinnes, in the winter of 1923–4 offered blocks of stock in their mines and industries for sale. Again, fears of being dominated by the more powerful Germans, divisions in the ranks of the Comité des Forges and differences between the government and the metallurgists blocked these efforts to promote Franco-German integration. Similarly, a grand solution to the reparations and metallurgical problems, proposed by Arnold Rechberg, long a German advocate of Franco-German economic co-operation, failed to elicit support from either the German or French governments. By January Stresemann was in a position to intervene in order to safeguard the Reich's future economic interests, but had to yield to his industrialists' demand for sharing the payments burden. Poincaré, it is true, won an extension of the MICUM accords after the mid-April terminal date. Tolerated in Berlin mainly to avoid conflict during the discussions of the Dawes plan, they had to be abandoned, along with French hopes to maintain their interests in the Ruhr mines and steel plants, with the implementation of the new reparation agreement.

VIII

The newly constituted committee of experts met on 30 November. Following proposals by Bradbury, the British representative, designed to appeal to French *amour propre* while still leaving the way open for the broader inquiry demanded by the Americans, the Reparation Commission agreed to set up two expert committees. The first would consider different means of balancing the German budget and stabilizing the currency; the second, designed to placate the French, would estimate the amount of capital exported by Germany and see to its return. France's representative, Barthou, who had developed doubts about the utility of the Ruhr occupation, convinced Poincaré that he had to negotiate. The premier was far less well placed than he had been in September when passive resistance had ceased. He had refused to consider a bilateral treaty with the Germans, allegedly supported by President Millerand, drawing together Ruhr coal, Lorraine iron ore, and French security on the Rhine. 'Discussions with Germany would upset England', he told Charles Reibel, the minister for the liberated regions. 'If they wanted to force me into that policy, I would hand in the resignation of the cabinet.'[31] The franc continued its uneven decline on the exchanges and the cost of living began to rise, affecting basic food items, and Poincaré's political position weakened. Voters began to weary of the occupation that was not bringing any visible economic benefits at a time when small investors were losing from the weakening of the franc. The hard-pressed premier realized that he had to accept the expert committee if France was not to be isolated from the Anglo-American powers whose financial support was becoming imperative. Though repeatedly trying to restrict the scope of the Dawes committees' work and seeking fresh Anglo-American guarantees, he was forced to retreat.

Just as the experts on the two committees began work, on 14 January 1924, there was a panic on the Bourse, and for two weeks the franc plunged downward. The government responded by introducing the

---

[31] Quoted in John F. V. Keiger, 'Raymond Poincaré and the Ruhr Crisis', in Robert Boyce (ed.), *French Foreign and Defence Policy, 1918–1940: The Decline and Fall of a Great Power* (London, 1998), 64.

new tax programme, which was pushed through a reluctant Chamber and an even more hostile Senate in March. In the heated pre-election atmosphere, domestic issues rather than the occupation of the Ruhr became the bread and butter of daily debate. Poincaré, worn out by the weeks of parliamentary obstruction, started to lose his famous resilience. Despite the Chamber's approval of the new tax package, the franc again plummeted. There was panic on the exchanges, fuelled by foreign speculators operating out of Amsterdam and involving some of the most respected banks in central Europe. Neither the German nor the British governments directly intervened, but both welcomed the franc's distress. New York and London responded to a French appeal; a dollar credit granted by J. P. Morgan to the Bank of France helped to save the franc. Neither the bankers nor the American government tied the loan to France's acceptance of the experts committees' recommendations, but the French were already prepared to abandon the measures hampering economic activity in the Ruhr once Germany put the new reparation settlement into effect.

As France focused on the elections scheduled for 11 May, there was no enthusiasm for higher taxes and the maintenance of the occupation forces in the Ruhr, though the latter's costs were covered by the German payments. The Germans, on the contrary, were well on the way to recovery and to a revival of public confidence. Marx's centre-liberal coalition was conducting business under an emergency law of limited duration. Executive power had been ceded to General von Seeckt, the head of the army command, whom Marx and Stresemann as well as right-wing groups had courted in the hope of maintaining order. The emergency law, which lasted until the spring of 1924 because of left- and right-wing unrest, including the Hitler–Ludendorff attempted putsch in Munich on 9 November, contained the disintegrative forces in the republic but at a considerable price. The KPD, it is true, because of its failed actions in Saxony and Thuringia, lost much of its offensive power and was soon immobilized by internal divisions. Until 1930 it posed no threat to the stability of the state. More worrying was the ambiguous attitude of the Reichswehr leaders at the moment of crisis in Bavaria, and the persistence of anti-Weimar feeling even after Reich authority was restored. Even more dangerous to the future of the republic were the effects of the hyperinflation on its most respectable and law-abiding citizens, who had seen the collapse of their society and who blamed, not wholly without reason, the erosion of their savings, salaries, wages, and profits on elected politicians.

Fear of economic collapse and political disintegration forced the different interest groups to support a programme of financial stabilization. It was a long, piecemeal, and arduous battle for the Marx–

Stresemann cabinet. The new Rentenmark, promised in mid-October, was not made available until a month later, and then in restricted quantities. At the start of November the price of bread had risen to 165 billion marks, 10,000 times its price three weeks earlier. It was only when Hjalmar Schacht was appointed 'currency commissioner' on 12 November and subsequently made president of the Reichsbank that the way was paved for a conversion of the old mark into the new currency and that the Reichsbank ceased to print paper money. Schacht's Gold Discount Bank was backed by British and American credits. On 7 April 1924, in the face of new inflationary pressures, Schacht imposed an effective credit freeze that assured the success of the currency stabilization programme. Steps were also taken to balance the budget through the ending of subsidies to the Rhine and Ruhr and by major cutbacks in the civil-service sector. The introduction of a basic and hard-won reform of the tax system forced the states and communes to try to put their own financial houses in order. The new reforms were carried through, not by the Reichstag but by a series of emergency decrees using the presidential powers under Article 48 of the constitution. A budgetary surplus was produced by the end of 1924.

Financial stabilization was a brilliant coup, but it was not without its costs. The impact of the credit restrictions on the small and medium business sectors of the economy was severe and had future political implications. Much of the Nazi vote in 1930 represented these hard-hit small farmers and small businessmen. Further, as a result of the November action money become extremely scarce. The prospect of very high interest rates and a new stable currency, in addition to the possibility of an international reparations settlement, abruptly made Germany an attractive investment prospect. New York banks began to lend short-term on a large scale. The Reich was suddenly awash with short-term credit, which it used for structural investment. Borrowing short and lending long made it vulnerable to any future financial crisis. Stabilization was achieved in dire circumstances without international action, raising the possibility that similar action might have been taken in 1921. Admittedly, Stresemann's 'Grand Coalition' had to be sacrificed in the process. The SPD, the largest party in the Reichstag, intent on preserving the eight-hour day, refused to join Marx's minority government in late November. Employers were able to turn back the clock on some of the benefits won by labour in 1919. The stage was set for confrontation. The stabilization failed to promote the political consensus required for the effective functioning of the republic. Most politicians agreed that if the stabilization programme was to endure, a further revision of the reparation settlement was required.

IX

The expert committees set up by the Reparation Commission began their work in January 1924. Washington appointed a powerful delegation headed by Charles Dawes, a Chicago banker and former director of the budget, a known Francophile and a first-rate publicist; Owen Young, chairman of General Electric and the Radio Corporation of America; and the Californian banker Henry M. Robinson. The Coolidge administration protected its position by insisting that members act as private individuals, yet its unofficial support as well as American financial power assured the American delegates a dominating role. The first committee, under the chairmanship of Dawes, not only dealt with the German budget and monetary system but also with the preparation of a new reparations plan. The very precise technical details were mainly worked out by Sir Joshua Stamp of Britain and Émile Francqui of Belgium. The second committee soon concluded that only the restoration of confidence in the Germany currency would stop the flight of additional capital abroad and allow for the repatriation of funds. Members could not agree on their estimates of German capital exports, and so the committee proposed what they thought was a plausible compromise figure.

The 'Dawes plan', produced on 9 April 1924, called for the reorganization of the German monetary system with some foreign supervision, tax reforms, an international loan, and the appointment of an agent-general who would administer the new system bypassing the Reparation Commission. Germany would pay little the first two years (the payment of 1 milliard gold marks in 1924–5 was covered by the international loan), increasing amounts for two years, and then 2.5 milliard gold marks for one year. From 1929 it would pay annual annuities of 2.5 milliard gold marks supplemented by a sum linked to an index of German prosperity. These annuities were relatively modest (Germany met each payment almost in full, thanks to the flood of American investment) and covered all of Germany's financial obligations under the Versailles treaty. The Dawes plan marked a sharp de facto reduction of the German debt. Under the London Schedule of Payments, the Germans assumed an immediate liability of 50 billion gold marks. The 1924 value of the Dawes plan was the equivalent to a capital sum of 39–40 billion gold marks if the maximum sixty-four-year timetable was maintained without change. As no one realistically anticipated such a period of payments, the sums demanded were actually far less.[32] To

---

[32] Figures from Schuker, *The End of French Predominance in Europe*, 183.

assist Germany, there would be an international loan of 800 million marks; another 200 million marks would come from the Reichsbank. Only half the annual standard payment would be charged to the German budget. The rest would come from bonds issued on the assets of German industry and the railway system, which became a public corporation issuing bonds of its own. The bonds were on deposit at the Reparation Commission.

Since the great inflation had virtually cancelled the national and corporate debt of Germany, it was obvious that with these payments the tax burden on Germany would be well below the stipulation in the Versailles treaty that it should be commensurate with that borne by the Allied peoples. Though it was thought that the Reich could raise 4.5 billion gold marks annually if it taxed as heavily as the British, the sum set was only slightly more than half this figure, because the British objected to high reparation payments. The low tax figure was blamed on the unreliability of existing statistics and on the belief that Germany could transfer only a part of what she raised through taxation to her creditors abroad. As this amount could only be determined at some later date, the sums collected were to be deposited to the account of a new agent-general for reparations in Berlin. To facilitate their handover, a Transfer Committee of five international experts was created who, with the agent-general, would determine the amounts paid to the Allies. The committee could recommend suspension of payments if the stability of the mark was in danger. It would be an American, S. Parker Gilbert, a former under-secretary of the Treasury, who would serve as agent-general for reparations throughout the life of the Dawes plan. It was believed, at least by the Americans, that the Germans would meet their reparation bills through taxation and that the agent-general would decide if sufficient foreign exchange was available to transfer sums to Germany's creditors. The transfer procedures, a problem which pre-occupied many contemporaries, were thought essential to the success of the new system. The creditors could take their payments in kind instead of cash. Owen Young expected, too, that in the early years a good part of the reparation balance would be used in Germany to be lent to credit-short German industry. The whole idea was to provide for a variety of options for the creditors while stimulating German recovery. It was not anticipated that the success of the Dawes plan would depend on a continuing flow of American money.

All the powers reluctantly approved the plan; the French and Germans only after considerable Anglo–American pressure. Poincaré, in particular, thought it a poor bargain for France. He had intended that France would keep its financial and economic pledges as well as its troops in the Ruhr until the Germans began to pay reparations. For the moment the occupation continued, but all his schemes to retain control over trade and industry in the occupied territories had to be abandoned. The Americans and British insisted on the restoration of the fiscal and economic unity of the Reich. All restrictions on Germany's economic activities were to be withdrawn and were not to be reimposed except in the case of a 'flagrant failure' to fulfil the Dawes conditions. Nothing was said about sanctions against default; the decision was left to the creditor nations. In Paris, Poincaré was isolated in his reluctance to accept such poor terms for France. The swing against the premier, despite Millerand's efforts to save him, to the point of compromising the presidential office, was irreversible. On 11 May the 'Cartel des Gauches' won a massive electoral victory and Poincaré resigned. The Radical Socialist, Édouard Herriot, who was neither radical nor socialist, became premier, with the support of those weary of foreign adventures and anxious to concentrate on France's domestic difficulties. 'Herriot is the exact opposite of Poincaré', reported the British minister in Paris, Eric Phipps. 'Not only, as he himself said, has he nothing up his sleeve, but he has no sleeve.'[33] Herriot took office with the declared intention of ending the Ruhr escapade and terminating France's revisionist policies in the Rhineland. The premier's cultural interests were as broad as his girth, but he knew nothing about finance. He was not served well by his quarrelling bureaucrats nor by the French metallurgists, who failed to develop clear-cut policies. Having already accepted an 'international solution' to the reparation question, French bargaining room was limited, but Herriot's soft approach and anxiety to appease the British resulted in unnecessary retreats. How little France achieved from the Ruhr occupation became clear only at the summer's London conference on the Dawes plan.

The new British Labour prime minister and foreign secretary, James Ramsay MacDonald, proved an adroit negotiator. Determined to make a success of his first incursions into the world of diplomacy and to demonstrate the Labour party's capacity to rule, he rose to the challenge. The British momentarily recaptured the initiative in European affairs that they had lost when France marched into the Ruhr fifteen months earlier. His success owed much to the nature of the Anglo-American partnership. Though secretary of state Hughes took a far more active political role in creating the conditions for the acceptance of the Dawes plan than he, at first, anticipated, his intention throughout these months was to leave the political manoeuvring needed to bring France and Germany together in MacDonald's hands, and to distance the United States from the bargaining. The United States 'returned' to Europe in

---

[33] Quoted in Schuker, *The End of French Predominance in Europe*, 233.

November 1923 under the very special conditions imposed by Washington. American experts participated in the independent expert inquiry, but once the deliberations began, Secretary of State Hughes returned to his policy of 'neutrality' underscoring that Washington would not become a 'dictator in the reparations policy'.[34] MacDonald, committed to proposals that would bring American financial assistance to Europe, seized his opportunity, with Hughes's backing, to take the political initiative in securing French and German agreement to the Anglo-American terms. There were many doubts about the Dawes plan in London, but the British prime minister had Montagu Norman's backing and was determined on success. Admittedly, he played a double game with the French, holding out to his socialist counterparts in Paris the prospect of co-operation on security and war debts while knowing that Britain would not compromise on either. During Herriot's visit on 21–2 June to Chequers, the prime minister's official country residence, the French premier agreed to an economic evacuation of the Ruhr two weeks after the German government complied with the measures outlined by the Dawes committee. The adverse reaction in Paris to his surrender was so powerful that MacDonald made a high-profile visit to the French capital to arrange for an ostensible restoration and strengthening of the authority of the Reparation Commission. This merely coated the pill that Herriot would swallow when he attended the London conference in July.

The Dawes plan proved acceptable to the Germans because it got the French out of the Ruhr and provided relief from higher reparation payments. Marx and Stresemann had won the restitution of German economic sovereignty in the Ruhr and Rhineland and the much-needed foreign credits. Though the experts avoided any discussion of Germany's total liability, the Dawes plan annuities marked a sharp reduction in the German debt and left the door open, as Stresemann calculated, to further downward revision when the higher reparations schedule came into force. Though there were protests in Germany that the annuities were too high, Stresemann knew that they could be covered. Most important of all, the Americans had returned to Europe, which Stresemann believed essential for German recovery, its reintegration into Europe, and its future return to great-power status. The Americans were delighted by the reparation breakthrough that had always been, along with disarmament, their major aim. A settlement had been reached, for which the Coolidge administration could take the

---

[34] Patrick O. Cohrs, 'The First "Real" Peace Settlement After the First World War: Britain, the United States and the Accords of London and Locarno, 1923–24', *Contemporary European History*, 12: 1 (2003).

full credit, without any reference to the war-debt question and without involving the United States in Europe's political conflicts. The Americans acting as 'honest brokers' had produced a workable scheme in which they would play a continuing part, but within the limits of what was politically practical at home. Private American investors would carry the responsibility of underwriting European prosperity.

Among the other powers with an interest in the reparations settlement, the Belgians, who worked closely with the British, had hopes of recreating the Brussels–London–Paris links so essential for their security. They could disentangle themselves from the Ruhr and secure their share of the reparations payments. The Italians, who had panicked as the occupation lengthened, needed both French and German friendship for economic reasons. Mussolini could not afford to alienate either the British, if his imperial aspirations were to be satisfied, or the Americans, from whom he wanted loans and war-debt relief. As he had tried to sell his support to each power in turn, he managed to increase distrust of Italy in every foreign capital. A domestic political crisis in Rome precluded an active part in the work of the Dawes committee, and the Italians emerged from the proceedings with almost nothing.

As the terms and implementation of the Dawes plan involved changes to the Versailles treaty, an international conference was necessary. The London conference opened on 16 July 1924. It was here that the continuing power struggle between France and Germany was resolved in the German favour. For all the participants, the most hopeful aspect of the settlement was the participation of the Americans and the promised influx of American capital. For the first time since the peace conference, an authorized American delegation took its place alongside the continentals. The American secretary of state, the secretary of the Treasury, and Thomas Lamont, a partner of J. P. Morgan's, were unofficially present to make their weight felt. In July and August Hughes himself would take an active part in promoting a settlement, even travelling to Berlin to encourage the Germans to compromise. American diplomats in Europe played their part in smoothing the path to agreement. The success of the conference, however, owed a great deal to Ramsay MacDonald, who put the necessary political framework into place. Without this the financiers, with whom the prime minister kept in the closest contact, could not have used their powers to shape the final terms of the settlement.

The relative speed of the settlement disguised the intensity of the battle waged behind the scenes. At the conference the financial power of the Anglo-American financiers, above all that of J. P. Morgan & Co., was translated into political terms. Though reluctant to be drawn into European quarrels, neither the American government nor

Morgan's could avoid involvement if American money was to be mobilized for European purposes. In the later stages of the negotiations the Morgan partners were doubtful whether the terms being discussed were good enough to safeguard the interests of their bondholders. They remained hesitant about selling the Dawes bonds on the American market without further safeguards against a possible French resort to sanctions. MacDonald found it expedient to encourage the bankers, known for their Francophile sympathies, to press for French concessions. In a memorandum presented by Lamont on 15 July, the financiers demanded the immediate military evacuation of the Ruhr, the reduction of the powers of the Rhineland Commission, a timetable for the Rhineland withdrawal, and an assurance that the Transfer Committee would become the sole body competent to declare default. The Anglo-American aim was to deprive France of any legal sanction to march should the Germans default, and to make certain that the power over reparation transfers and judgements of default would rest with the Dawes plan machinery rather than with the French-favoured Reparation Commission. These terms narrowed the French ability to determine or respond to any German evasion of the Dawes provisions. The intervention by the Morgan partners, backed by indirect pressure from Hughes on Herriot and Theunis, was the crucial factor in the subsequent proceedings. It was agreed that the Americans would participate in the deliberations of the Reparation Commission when a declaration of default was considered. If the decision was not unanimous, the minority could appeal to an arbitration panel of three members headed by an American. The power to consider sanctions was reserved to the Reparation Commission, which now included a new American 'citizen member'. Possible action by individual states was not discussed.

Herriot battled to salvage something tangible in return for accepting the Anglo-American terms, yet in almost every instance he lost the struggle. The French premier, his country still under severe financial strain, wanted to remove troops from the Ruhr but needed compensation. He wavered among various possibilities; his less-than-helpful advisers repeatedly shifted their grounds and had no proposal ready when the Germans arrived in London (the British and Americans had insisted on their participation in the proceedings) demanding an immediate withdrawal from the Ruhr as the price of acceptance. Direct negotiations with the Germans, treated as full equals, began on 5 August. Pressed by MacDonald, who was highly revisionist in his views about the origins of the Great War and considered the Ruhr occupation immoral as well as illegal, and by his Francophobe chancellor of the Exchequer, Philip Snowden, Herriot proved no match for his 'friends' or foes. The real turning point came when the French premier was faced by what was, in effect if not in form, an ultimatum from the Morgan partners, who were at the same time discussing the French financial position in Paris, that France should abandon its rights to impose physical sanctions on Germany in case of a German default. Once the French were forced to give way on this issue, J. P. Morgan and Lamont travelled to the continent to convince bankers to take up their projected share of the Dawes loan. In order to get the French government to coerce their reluctant bankers, Morgan warned the minister of finance that Morgan's would not float the promised $100 million loan in New York unless the Paris bankers co-operated. The partnership between Morgan's, the Bank of England, and the British government left the French with few alternatives. Herriot agreed to evacuate the Ruhr within a year after the Dawes plan went into operation, without securing any quid pro quo. There was a crisis in the final days of the conference when Stresemann, aided by MacDonald, tried to push Herriot into further shortening the evacuation. Primed by Norman, Snowden suddenly intervened and threatened to force Herriot's hand by revealing the Morgan terms for the Dawes loan. Lamont successfully blocked this blackmail attempt, which would have placed the onus of failure on the bankers.

The French found it difficult to secure any financial or economic benefits from the Ruhr evacuation. The British insisted on the Spa percentages of 1920 and the settlement of French war debts. In London, Seydoux and Clémentel proposed to Stresemann a trade agreement that would be linked to a more rapid evacuation timetable for the Ruhr. Their proposals had been foreshadowed in the earlier attempts of the Comité des Forges to capitalize on the Ruhr occupation. The German metallurgists had rejected these overtures in the spring of 1924; they proved equally averse to the more modest suggestions that they join a rail or steel cartel organized by France. The Germans had everything to gain by waiting, as they began to recover from the Ruhr debacle and turned their attention to the rationalization of their industries. The French were under time pressure; the five-year Versailles treaty protections would run out in 1925 and the lack of coke and markets would put the Lorraine producers at a disadvantage. The Clémentel–Seydoux proposals were a last-minute affair; the French industrialists proved unable and unwilling to suggest a concrete programme and, as usual, the French bureaucrats quarrelled among themselves. Stresemann, despite warnings from the German industrialists, was willing to bargain for a shortening of the evacuation timetable. It was the French who abandoned their efforts in the face of domestic doubts and strong criticism from the British and Belgians. Stresemann was content to let the matter rest. The French would resume the talks only after the Germans had recovered their full sovereignty and economic strength.

On the related problem of the Rhineland, Herriot started out with more pieces on the board than he played. MacDonald wanted to withdraw the token British force as soon as possible, but preferred to wait until the French and Belgians agreed to total evacuation. Nor did the Germans want the British to leave until the other occupying forces followed suit. Herriot could have demanded concessions, but he was so fearful of losing Britain's support that he accepted that the Rhineland withdrawal clock had already started to run, despite Germany's failure to fulfil the terms of the Versailles treaty. To save something for France, he insisted that the British evacuation of the Cologne sector be linked to German compliance with the disarmament terms following a report from the Inter-Allied Military Control Commission (IMCC). Even here, he gained little. The IMCC, which had been withdrawn from Germany during the Ruhr crisis, was to be disbanded after its final investigation was concluded. A League of Nations committee had established general principles for the military surveillance of the ex-enemy countries, and this seemed a possible way for the former Allies to keep an eye on German action without the moral opprobrium attached to the IMCC. There was, in truth, little France could do about German rearmament once it lost the ability to impose treaty sanctions. The German military had already trained, in one fashion or another, about half-a-million men since the Versailles treaty was signed. Quite apart from clandestine rearmament, assisted by the Soviets, the building up of heavy industry for export purposes provided the industrial potential needed for modern warfare. France's military leaders acquiesced in Herriot's decision to wind up the control commission, knowing that no League committee, without the intelligence network of the IMCC, could create an effective inspection system. Even the IMCC could do little more than record and report German evasions. It issued a critical interim report in December 1924 and the Allies agreed to postpone the Cologne evacuation. By the time its next report of 15 February 1925 giving details of German evasions was received, the Locarno negotiations were under way and the whole question seen in a new framework. Led by Britain, the Allies agreed to Stresemann's demands that the Cologne zone evacuation begin in January 1926, though Germany had not fulfilled the treaty's disarmament clauses.

During the London conference Herriot raised the possibility of a defensive pact; his vague security proposals were hardly taken seriously by a Labour government set against any form of further continental involvement. An attempt to use the League for the same purpose was blocked by a similar, if more disguised, British veto. The London agreements left France more exposed than she had been before the Ruhr invasion. She could no longer, in practical terms, look to an extended occupation of the Rhineland or a reoccupation of the Ruhr as a means of coercing Germany. The Reparation Commission was effectively bypassed by the new Dawes structure, further reducing French influence. Having proved unable to revise the 1919 settlement in its favour, France possessed fewer pawns to maintain her existing European position. MacDonald set the tone at the final plenary session of the conference. 'We are now offering the first really negotiated agreement since the war', he observed. 'This agreement may be regarded as the first Peace Treaty, because we sign it with a feeling that we have turned our backs on the terrible years of war and war mentality.'[35] While the German delegates might have rejoiced at such words, the implicit repudiation of Versailles could not sit well with the French. The 1919 pattern of European relations had been broken, and remained to be rearranged.

X

The London agreements revealed that France could not enforce or revise the terms of the Treaty of Versailles without British support. It may be that the French lacked the drive and the emotional reserves to pursue an independent policy in Europe. Drained by the experience and costs of the war, its electorate was unwilling to make the financial sacrifices that such a policy entailed. No one was prepared to carry the tax bill that would have made American loans unnecessary. The ambitious plans of France's wartime leaders had little appeal for a tired generation. Insofar as the reparation battle was a political struggle for power, the outcome was determined by the Anglo–American intervention. The French inability to capitalize on the Ruhr evacuation meant that it lost the chance to build on the position that Clemenceau had won in 1919.

The British had thrown their weight against Poincaré's policies. No British statesman would allow France to increase its power at the expense of Germany and alter the Versailles balance in its favour. However distrustful of Germany, most British politicians (the military leaders thought differently) argued that the security and prosperity of Europe depended on the recovery of Germany. The policy of appeasement had limits; the British would not sever the Anglo–French connection, but they exaggerated French power and underestimated the German capacity for recovery. This British misreading of the power equation contributed to Germany's continental dominance, which was not what London intended. In the background was the fear, particularly in the Curzon Foreign Office, that if thwarted the Germans would make common cause with the Russians, threatening both the European

---

[35] Quoted in Schuker, *The End of French Predominance*, 383.

equilibrium and Britain's all-important imperial interests. After Genoa the British concentrated on bringing Germany into the western fold as the foil to the Rapallo connection. Between 1919 and 1925 Britain's statesmen used their considerable diplomatic skills to try to create a balance that would not require their constant intervention. Their influence depended as much on French and German weakness as on Britain's global strength. Insofar as Britain's power in Europe depended on its financial role (it was still a major world exporter of capital) and its naval and imperial supremacy, the first two were sustained through arrangements with the United States, a country unwilling to fully exploit its potential power or to take responsibility for maintaining the peace of Europe. The temporary partnership with the Americans in mid-decade allowed the British to enhance their position beyond their actual power.

Gustav Stresemann had taken the first successful step in subverting the Versailles treaty. The country owed much to his realism, skill, and ruthlessness. Germany had survived the Ruhr occupation and the follies of passive resistance. It had succeeded in restoring its threatened unity and sovereignty. It won, in the Dawes plan, the much-desired revision of the peace treaty's reparation clauses and was free to benefit from the ending of its temporary restraints on trade and commerce. German aspirations remained unsatisfied; even the moderates argued that the Dawes proposals were an onerous burden that had to be accepted to free the Ruhr and Rhineland. Stresemann looked forward. He saw how Germany's economic assets could be used to enlist Anglo-American support for future treaty revision. Stresemann's main aim was, in the first instance, to free German soil from all foreign occupiers. Only then could he plan for the achievement of more far-reaching revisionist aims. The former believer in the stab-in-the-back myth would focus not on Germany's former military prowess but on its ability to exploit the more open-ended diplomatic situation.

The massive infusion of American capital into Europe was to highlight the differentials in financial and economic power between the United States and the states of Europe. The Dawes loan bonds were over-subscribed within fifteen minutes of the market openings. The subsequent demand for German bonds went far beyond the Dawes stabilization loan. American lending to Germany soared during the summer of 1925. American bankers waxed enthusiastic about conditions for investment; foreigners were encouraged to borrow money in the United States by low interest rates. A multitude of small competing firms broke the Morgan monopoly, and the restraints and controls once imposed by that powerful firm disappeared in the resulting scramble. Lending peaked in the middle of 1927, after which the deceleration in long-term borrowing was followed by a sharp upturn in short-term loans. The more responsible bankers warned of the danger of over-lending, but neither they nor the American government could control the avalanche. The Commerce Department under Herbert Hoover moved to have the administration restrict the volume of German loans; their efforts were vetoed by the State and Treasury departments, unwilling to pass official judgement on private investments. To protect existing bondholders, the Americans became committed to a continuing and virtually uncontrolled flow of capital into Germany as long as the market appeared attractive to would-be lenders. The burden of restriction was shifted to the German government, which proved unwilling to take the inevitable economic and political risks of direction. Bondholder interest in the viability of the German economy was only one aspect of the continuing American involvement in European matters; the war–debt issue remained on the agenda, as well as the question of disarmament. The post–Dawes flood of capital and goods across the Atlantic and the rise of direct investment meant that the reconstructed financial system would rely heavily on American participation. American capital became 'one of the motors of European prosperity'.[36] The 'golden age' which Montagu Norman predicted for his own country never arrived. Symbolically, the new mark was based on the dollar and not on the pound.

It was the American financial intervention in 1924 that allowed Britain, at no expense to itself, to change the Versailles balance and adjust the European scales in the German direction. Washington felt that it had done all that was necessary to safeguard American interests and to promote the European peace. It had 'depoliticized' the reparations question. The influx of private American capital would promote the economic stabilization of Europe that would lead, in turn, to a new and more satisfactory political equilibrium. The Republication administration was proud of its success; it saw no reason to depart from the policies that had served the country so well. Europe's political problems, in fact, had not been solved. It would be left to the Europeans to construct the political edifice that American money had made possible

Books

ALDCROFT, DEREK HOWARD, *From Versailles to Wall Street, 1919–1929* (London, 1977).

ARTAUD, DENISE, *La Question des dettes interalliés et la reconstruction de l'Europe, 1917–1929*, 2 vols. (Lille and Paris, 1978).

BARIÉTY, JACQUES, *Les Relations franco-allemandes après la première guerre mondiale, 10 novembre 1918–10 janvier 1923: de l'exécution à la négociation* (Paris, 1977).

[36] Denise Artaud, 'Reparations and War Debts: The Restoration of French Financial Power, 1919–1929', in Boyce (ed.), *French Foreign and Defence Policy*, 104.

BECKER, JEAN-JACQUES and BRENSTEIN, SERGE, *Victoire et frustrations, 1914–1929* (Paris, 1990).

BELL, P. M. H., *France and Britain: 1900–1940. Entente and Estrangement* (New York, 1996).

BENNETT, G. H., *British Foreign Policy During the Curzon Period, 1919–1924* (London, 1995).

BOURNAZEL, RENATA, *Rapallo: naissance d'un mythe. La politique de la peur dans la France du Bloc National* (Paris, 1974).

BOYCE, ROBERT W. D., *British Capitalism at the Crossroads 1919–1932: A Study in Politics, Economics and International Relations* (Cambridge, 1987).

BRACHER, KARL DIETRICH, FUNKE, MANFRED, and JACOBSON, HANS-ADOLF (eds.), *Die Weimarer Republik, 1918–1933: Politik, Wirtschaft, Gesellschaft* (Düsseldorf, 1987).

BUNSELMEYER, ROBERT E., *The Cost of the War: British Economic War Aims and the Origin of Reparation* (Hamden, Conn., 1975).

BUSSIÈRE, ÉRIC, *La France, la Belgique et l'organisation économique de l'Europe, 1918–1935* (Paris, 1992).

CAIN, P. J. and HOPKINS, A. G., *British Imperialism: Crisis and Deconstruction, 1914–1990* (London, 1993).

CARSTEN, F. L., *The Reichswehr and Politics 1918 to 1983* (Oxford, 1966).

COSTIGLIOLA, FRANK, *Awkward Dominion: American Political, Economic and Cultural Relations with Europe, 1919–1933* (Ithaca, NY, 1984).

DEPOORTERE, ROLANDE, *La Question des réparations allemandes dans la politique étrangère de la Belgique après la première guerre mondiale, 1919–1925* (Brussels, 1997).

DRUMMOND, IAN M., *The Gold Standard and the International Monetary System 1900–1939* (Basingstoke, 1987).

EICHENGREEN, BARRY, *Golden Fetters: The Gold Standard and the Great Depression, 1919–1939* (New York and Oxford, 1992).

ERDMANN, KARL DIETRICH, *Adenauer in der Rheinland politik nach dem Ersten Weltkrieg* (Stuttgart, 1966).

FAVEZ, JEAN-CLAUDE, *Le Reich devant l'occupation franco-belge de la Ruhr en 1923* (Geneva, 1969).

FEINSTEIN, CHARLES H., *Banking, Currency and Finance in Europe Between the Wars* (Oxford, 1995).

—— TEMIN, PETER, and TONIOLO, GIANNI, *The European Economy Between the Wars* (Oxford, 1997).

FELDMAN, G. D., *The Great Disorder: Politics, Economics and Society in the German Inflation, 1914–1924* (New York and Oxford, 1993).

—— HOLTFRERICH, CARL-LUDWIG, PITT, PETER-CHRISTIAN, and RITTER, GERHARD A. (eds.), *The German Inflation Reconsidered: A Preliminary Balance* (Berlin and New York, 1982).

FERGUSON, NIALL, *Paper and Iron: Hamburg Business and German Politics in the Era of Inflation, 1897–1927* (Cambridge, 1995).

FERRIS, J. R. *Men, Money, and Diplomacy: The Evolution of British Strategic Policy, 1919–1926* (Ithaca, NY, 1989).

FINK, CAROLE, *The Genoa Conference: European Diplomacy, 1921–1922* (Chapel Hill, NC, 1984).

—— HULL, ISABEL V., and KNOX, MACGREGOR (eds.), *German Nationalism and the European Response, 1890–1945* (Norman, Okla., 1985). Esp. chapters by Magda Ádám, Peter Krüger, Giorgio Petracchi, Stephen A. Schuker, and Andrew Williams.

—— FROHN, AXEL, and HEIDEKING, JÜRGEN (eds.), *Genoa, Rapallo and European Reconstruction in 1922* (Cambridge, 1991). Esp. the chapter by Stephen A. Schuker.

FISCHER, CONAN, *The Ruhr Crisis 1923–1924* (Oxford, 2003).

FRANK, ROBERT, *La Hantise du déclin: la France 1920–1960: finances, défense et identité nationale* (Paris and Berlin, 1994).

GRAYSON, RICHARD S., *Austen Chamberlain and the Commitment to Europe: British Foreign Policy, 1924–29* (London, 1997).

HEIDEKING, JÜRGEN, *Aropag der Diplomaten: Die Pariser Botschafterkonferencz der europäischen Hauptmächte und die Probleme der europäischen Politik, 1920–1931* (Husum, 1979).

HOGAN, MICHAEL J., *Informal Entente: The Private Structure of Co-operation in Anglo-American Economic Diplomacy, 1918–1928* (Columbia, Mo., 1977).

HOLTFRERICH, CARL-LUDWIG, *The German Inflation, 1914–1923: Causes and Effects in International Perspective*, trans. Theo Balderston (New York, 1986).

JEANNESSON, STANISLAS, *Poincaré, la France, et la Ruhr, 1922–1924* (Strasburg, 1998).

KAHN, ALFRED E., *Great Britain in the World Economy* (London, 1946).

KENT, BRUCE, *The Spoils of War: The Politics, Economics and Diplomacy of Reparations, 1918–1932* (Oxford, 1989).

KÖHLER, HENNING, *Adenauer and die Rheinische Republik* (Opladen, 1986).

LANDES, DAVID S., *The Unbound Prometheus: Technological Change and Industrial Development in Western Europe from 1750 to the Present*, revised edn. (New York, 2003).

LAUBACH, ERNST, *Die Politik der Kabinette Wirth, 1921–1922* (Lübeck and Hamburg, 1968).

LEFFLER, MELVYN P., *The Elusive Quest: America's Pursuit of European Stability and French Security, 1919–1933* (Chapel Hill, NC, 1979).

LINK, WERNER, *Die amerikanische Stabilisierungspolitik in Deutschland, 1921–1932* (Düsseldorf, 1970).

LOURIA, MARGOT, *Triumph and Downfall: America's Pursuit of Peace and Prosperity, 1921–1933* (Westport, Conn. and London, 2000).

MCDOUGALL, WALTER A., *France's Rhineland Diplomacy, 1914–1924: The Last Bid for a Balance of Power in Europe* (Princeton, 1978).

MCKERCHER, B. J. C. (ed.), *Anglo-American Relations in the 1920s: The Struggle for Supremacy* (Basingstoke, 1991). Esp. chapters by Burk, Dayer, and McKercher.

MAIER, CHARLES S., *Recasting Bourgeois Europe: Stabilization in France, Germany and Italy in the Decade after World War One* (Princeton, 1975).

MAISEL, EPHRAIM, *The Foreign Office and Foreign Policy, 1919–1926* (Brighton, 1994).

Mantoux, Étienne, *The Carthaginian Peace, or the Economic Consequences of Mr. Keynes* (Oxford, 1946).

Maxelon, Michael-Olaf, *Stresemann und Frankreich 1914–1929* (Düsseldorf, 1972).

Milward, Alan R. and Murray, Williamson (eds.), *Military Effectiveness.* Vol. 2.: *The Interwar Period* (Boston, 1988). Esp. the article by Manfred Messerschmidt.

Mouré, Kenneth, *The Gold Standard Illusion: France, the Bank of France, and the International Gold Standard, 1914–1939* (Oxford, 2002).

Munting, Roger and Holderness, B. A., *Crisis, Recovery and War: An Economic History of Continental Europe, 1918–1945* (New York and London, 1991).

Orde, Anne, *Great Britain and International Security, 1920–1926* (London, 1978).

—— *British Policy and European Reconstruction After the First World War* (Cambridge, 1990).

Parrini, Carl, *Heir to Empire: United States Economic Diplomacy, 1916–1923* (Pittsburgh, 1969).

Poidevin, Raymond and Bariéty, Jacques, *Les Relations franco-allemandes, 1815–1975* (Paris, 1977).

Rosenberg, Emily S., *Spreading the American Dream: American Economic and Cultural Expansion, 1890–1945* (New York, 1982).

Rowland, Benjamin M. (ed.), *Balance of Power or Hegemony: The Interwar Monetary System* (New York, 1976).

Rupieper, Hermann-Josef, *The Cuno Government and Reparations, 1922–1923: Politics and Economics* (The Hague and London, 1979).

Schröder, Hans-Jürgen (ed.), *Confrontation and Cooperation: Germany and the United States in the Era of World War I, 1900–1924* (Providence, RI, 1993). Esp. chapters by Glaser-Schmidt, Schuker, Berg, and Behnen.

Schuker, Stephen A., *The End of French Predominance in Europe: The Financial Crisis of 1924 and the Adoption of the Dawes Plan* (Chapel Hill, NC, 1976).

—— *American 'Reparations' to Germany, 1919–1933: Implications for the Third World Debt Crisis* (Princeton, 1988).

Schwabe, K. (ed.), *Die Ruhrkrise 1923: Wendepunkt der internationalen Beziehungen nach dem Ersten Weltkrieg* (Paderborn, 1985). Esp. chapters by Bariéty and Schwabe.

Silverman, Dan P., *Reconstructing Europe After the Great War* (Cambridge, Mass., and London, 1982).

Trachtenburg, Marc, *Reparation in World Politics: France and European Economic Diplomacy, 1916–1923* (New York, 1980).

Turner, Arthur, *The Cost of War: British Policy on French War Debts, 1918–1932* (Brighton, 1998).

Watt, Donald Cameron, *Succeeding John Bull: America in Britain's Place, 1900–1975. A Study of the Anglo-American Relationship and World Politics in the Context of British and American Foreign-policy Making in the Twentieth Century* (Cambridge, 1984).

WEILL-RAYNAL, ÉTIENNE, *Les Réparations allemandes et la France*, 3 vols. (Paris, 1938, 1947).

WILSON, KEITH M., *A Study in the History and Politics of* The Morning Post, *1905–1926* (Lewiston, NY, 1990).

Articles

BURK, KATHLEEN, 'The House of Morgan in Financial Diplomacy, 1920–1930' in B. J. C. McKercher (ed.), *The Struggle for Supremacy: Aspects of Anglo-American Relations in the 1920s*, (Edmonton, 1990).

—— 'The Lineaments of Foreign Policy: The United States and a "New World Order" 1919–39', *Journal of American Studies*, 26 (1992).

CAIRNS, JOHN C., 'A Nation of Shopkeepers in Search of a Suitable France: 1918–1940', *American Historical Review*, 79 (1974).

COHRS, PATRICK O., 'The First "Real" Peace Settlement After the First World War: Britain, the United States and the Awards of London and Locano, 1923–1925', *Contemporary European History*, 12: 1 (2003).

FERGUSSON, NIALL, 'The Balance of Payments Question; Versailles and After', in M. F. Boemeke *et al.* (eds.), *The Treaty of Versailles: A Reassessment After 75 Years* (Cambridge, 1998).

FERRIS, J. R., 'The Greatest Power on Earth: Great Britain in the 1920's', *International History Review*, 13, (1991).

GLASER-SCHMIDT, ELISABETH, 'Von Versailles nach Berlin: Überlegungen zur Neugestaltung der deutsch-amerikanischen Beziehungen in der Ära Harding', in Norbert Finzsch and Hermann Wellenreuther (eds.), *Liberalitas: Festschrift für Erich Angermann zum 65. Geburtstag* (Stuttgart, 1992).

—— 'The Making of the Economic Peace', in M. F. Boemeke *et al.* (eds.), *The Treaty of Versailles: A Reassessment After 75 Years* (Cambridge, 1998).

GUINN, PAUL, 'On Throwing Ballast in Foreign Policy: Poincaré, the Entente and the Ruhr Occupation', *European History Quarterly*, 18 (1988).

JEANNESSON, STANISLAS, 'Pourquoi la France a-t-elle occupé la Ruhr?' *Vingtième Siècle. Revue d'Histoire.* 51 (1996).

JORDAN, NICOLE, 'The Reorientation of French Diplomacy in the Mid-1920s: The Role of Jacques Sydoux', *English Historical Review*, 117: 473 (2002).

KEIGER, J. F. V., 'Raymond Poincaré and the Ruhr Crisis', in Boyce (ed.), *French Foreign and Defence Policy, 1918–1940: The Decline and Fall of a Great Power* (London, 1998).

LEFFLER, MELVYN P., 'Political Isolationism, Economic Expansionism, or Diplomatic Realism? American Policy Toward Western Europe, 1921–1933', *Perspectives in American History*, 8 (1974).

—— '1921–1932: Expansionist Impulses and Domestic Constraints', in William H. Becker and Samuel F. Wells, Jr. (eds.) *Economics and World Power: An Assessment of European Diplomacy Since 1789* (New York, 1984).

McKERCHER, B. J. C., 'Wealth, Power, and the New International Order: Britain and the American Challenge in the 1920s', *Diplomatic History*, 12 (1998).

MAIER, CHARLES S., 'The Two Postwar Eras and the Conditions for Stability in Twentieth-Century Western Europe', *American Historical Review*, 86 (1981).

MARKS, SALLY, 'Poincaré-la-peur: France and the Ruhr Crisis of 1923', in Kenneth Moure, and Martin S. Alexander (eds.), *Crisis and Renewal in France (1918–1962)* (London, 2002).

—— 'The Myth of Reparations', *Central European History*, 11 (1978).

—— 'Ménage à trois: The Negotiations for an Anglo-French-Belgian Alliance in 1922', *International History Review*, 4 (1982).

—— 'The Misery of Victory: France's Struggle for the Versailles Treaty', *Historical Papers* (1986).

—— 'Smoke and Mirrors: In Smoke-Filled Rooms and the Galerie des Glaces', in M. F. Boemeke *et al.*, (eds.), *The Treaty of Versailles: A Reassessment After 75 Years* (Cambridge, 1998).

POGGE VON STRANDMANN, H., 'Rapallo: Strategy in Preventive Diplomacy. New Sources and New Interpretations', in Volker R. Berghahn and Martin Kitchen (eds.), *Germany in the Age of Total War* (London, 1981).

SOUTOU, GEORGES-HENRI, 'Problèmes concernant le rétablissement des relations économiques franco-allemandes après la premiere guerre mondiale', *Francia*, 2 (1974).

—— 'Die deutschen Reparationen und das Seydoux Projekt, 1920–1921', *Vierteljahreshefte für Zeitgeschichte*, 23 (1975).

—— 'Une autre politique? Les tentatives françaises d'entente économique avec l'Allemagne, 1919–1921', *Revue d'Allemagne*, 8: 1 (1976).

—— 'Le Coke dans les relations internationales en Europe de 1914 au plan Dawes (1924)', *Relations Internationales*, 43 (1985).

Theses and Manuscripts

BARROS, ANDREW, 'France and the German Menace, 1919–1928', Ph.D. thesis, Cambridge University (2001).

KRÜGER, PETER, ' "Schubert, Maltzan und die Neugestaltung der auswärtigen Politik in den 20er Jahren", Vortrag anläßlich einer Gedenkfeier des Auswärtigen Amtes für die Staatssekretäre Ago Freiherr von Maltzan und Dr. Carl von Schubert', unpublished mss. (1987).

5

The Primacy of Nationalism: Reconstruction in Eastern and Central Europe

I

The map of western Europe was dramatically changed in 1919; that of eastern Europe was unrecognizable. The peace treaties resulted in the greatest expansion of sovereign states witnessed since the Peace of Westphalia. Instead of the three great empires of Germany, Austria–Hungary, and Russia, there were now eight new or restored countries: Finland, Estonia, Latvia, Lithuania, Poland, Czechoslovakia, Hungary, and Austria. In the Balkans there was one new state, Yugoslavia, but all the other countries, Albania, Bulgaria, Greece, and Romania, won or lost territories and emerged with new shapes and populations. This radical redrawing of traditional boundaries left the successor states divided and vulnerable. They had very different national characteristics, ethnic compositions, interests, and enemies. Each was defined by its dominant nationality, yet most were multinational without including all their co-nationals. Their leaders were faced not only with ethnically disparate populations but with deep social and economic differences that made integration, both internal and regional, difficult if not impossible.

Regional terminology can be a useful form of historical generalization, but the commonality of 'eastern Europe' was purely geographic. The term, regularly used between the wars, referred to a vast territory with an infinite variety of peoples, nationalities, religions, languages, histories, geographies, and climate. Even the sub-terms used to describe the lands between Germany and Russia—the Baltic, central Europe, east-central Europe, south-east Europe, the Balkans—suggest shared characteristics or a degree of unity rarely, if ever, found in practice. The largest and most powerful country, Poland, had a population of 30 million people; the smallest and weakest, Albania, had barely a million inhabitants. There were striking economic contrasts between the highly industrialized Czechoslovakia and Austria, the semi-industrialized states of Poland and Hungary, and the almost wholly agricultural states of the

Balkans. The statesmen of the countries along the Danube hardly thought of themselves as constituting a Danubian 'bloc'; if they entertained any such thoughts, each conceived of different plans for its constitution. The German term *Mitteleuropa*, codified in its modern usage by Friedrich Naumann in 1915 and initially including Germany, came to refer as well to Poland, Czechoslovakia, Austria, and Hungary, countries that shared little beyond their historical past and the fact that they could, in the event of a German wartime victory, as Naumann argued, become Germany's economic and political satellites. As a result of the war, the reduction of old states and the creation of new ones provided a less precise definition of 'central Europe'. Ödön von Horváth, author of the well-known *Tales from the Vienna Woods* (1930), gave himself as an example of the central European mix. 'If you ask me what is my native country, I answer: I was born in Fiume, I grew up in Belgrade, Budapest, Pressburg, Vienna and Munich, and I have a Hungarian passport; but I have no fatherland. I am a very typical mix of old Austria-Hungary; at once Magyar, Croatian, German and Czech; my country is Hungary, my mother tongue is German.'[1] The arguments over nomenclature, then as now, were not purely semantic; alternative 'mental maps' embodied illusions and realities that deeply affected internal and external behaviour.

Peace returned slowly to eastern Europe, and it was only in 1922 that the post-war period of small wars came to an end. The impact of the war on these nations had varied with their distance from the battlefield and whether they were on the side of the winners or losers. Poland and Serbia (Yugoslavia) suffered heavy war damage, major military operations took place in Romania, while Czechoslovakia and Austria escaped completely. The difference between their conditions, quite apart from the disparity in size and economic inheritance, also depended on their treatment by the peacemakers. Hungary incurred more disturbances as a consequence of the peace than of the war. Bolshevik Russia recognized the independence of Finland in 1918 and signed peace treaties with Estonia, Latvia, and Lithuania in 1920. The 'nursery brawls' in which Poland engaged between 1919 and 1921 destabilized the region as it worked out its new frontiers. The Polish border with Russia was determined by the terms of the Treaty of Riga in 1921 but lacked international recognition until 1923. The Upper Silesian plebiscite took place on 20 March 1921, with the subsequent League division of the territory displeasing both Poles and Germans. In east-central Europe and in the Balkans, even after the peace treaties were finally

[1] Jacques Rupnik, 'Central Europe or *Mitteleuropa*', *Daedalus*, 119: 1 (Winter, 1990), 251.

signed, settled conditions were hard to re-establish. Romanian and Czechoslovak troops occupying parts of Hungary only withdrew beyond their new frontiers in 1920 and the Yugoslavs only in 1921. The territorial disputes between Austria and Hungary, Hungary and Romania, Bulgaria with Romania, Romania with Russia over Bessarabia, and Yugoslavia with Italy continued well into the middle of the decade and beyond. Greek claims to northern Epirus in Albania were rejected and its dreams of a 'Greater Greece' (controlling both sides of the Aegean Sea) ended with the armistice concluded with the Turks on 11 October 1922, the verdict in both cases confirmed in the Treaty of Lausanne (24 July 1923). New disputes were created when Allenstein and Marienwerder voted in a plebiscite on 11 July 1920 to form part of German East Prussia, severed from the main bulk of Germany by the Poznán (Poznania) 'corridor' which secured Poland's access to the sea. Still others came from the creation of Danzig as a Free City on 15 November 1920 and from the Polish seizure of Vilna (Vilnius) in October 1920, as well as by the Lithuanian occupation of the Memel district in January 1923. Happily, after the Soviet–Polish conflict there were no wars in the region, either between status quo and revisionist powers or with any outside power.

The Habsburg empire, said a wit, 'was like a beautiful old vase, whose value no one appreciated until it fell and broke into a thousand pieces'.[2] The broken shards of the old empire were sharp. There may not have been war in eastern Europe during the 1920s, but the toxic mix of internal and external disputes, whether political, ethnic, or economic, meant that there was no peace either. With few exceptions, survival of the states depended on the governing capacities of narrow political elites and their ability to begin the process of economic rehabilitation that could bring some measure of internal stability. If the states in the region maintained their independence and outward unity, they did so at the expense of democratic politics and the toleration of ethnic and religious diversity. All the elected post-war governments, many following French models of government, with weak executives and strong legislatures, found it difficult to deal with multinational populations and conflicting economic demands without resorting to authoritarian rule and central-izing policies. Political fragmentation, often the result of ethnic divi-sions, resulted in rapid turnovers in governments and the discrediting of parliamentary institutions. What progress was made towards stabil-ization was often the result of the impositions of authoritarian regimes. It was primarily in Czechoslovakia, the country whose degree of

---

[2] Thomas Montgomery-Cunningham, *Dusty Measure: A Record of Troubled Times* (London, 1939), 303–4.

industrialization, social structure, and high literacy rates most closely approximated those of the west, that democracy took root and even here much was owed to the ability of the president, Tomáš Masaryk, to keep the multitude of parties working together. By 1934 it alone among the nations south of Denmark and east of Switzerland was still a functioning democracy.

Pressures from ethnic minorities and peasant parties in a region where 65 per cent of the active population was engaged in agriculture, many under semi-feudal conditions, provided an immediate political agenda both for the established and new successor states. While it was true that more people than ever before were living under governments of their own nationality, the peace treaties created new problems. The Paris treaties gave 60 million people a state of their own but turned another 25 million into minorities.[3] The actions of the majority, at a time when the rhetoric of politics was both democratic and nationalistic, preserved unity only at the cost of fanning ethnic discontent. With the exception of Albania (where nine out of ten inhabitants were Albanian and 60 to 70 per cent Muslims), most of the states of central and eastern Europe were, to some degree, multinational. Even in truncated Hungary and Bulgaria, there remained pockets of ethnic minorities. Where internal minority pressure was negligible, outside irredentist movements kept nationalist protest alive. The peacemakers' hopes for the assimilation and toleration of minorities proved illusory. Assimilation was rare and restricted mainly to the old-established minorities for whom the new frontiers brought few changes. The peace settlements, even where most responsive to the claims of self-determination, exacerbated traditional rivalries, both because of the new emphasis on Wilsonian principles and because the new governments, controlled by dominant ethnic groups, introduced policies sometimes more intolerant of minority rights than their Habsburg and Romanov predecessors. When criticized in this respect, politicians of the dominant ethnic groups claimed that such practices were necessary to reverse decades, even centuries, of discrimination against their co-nationals. Western diplomats, especially in the early 1920s, tended to accept their arguments. Centralizing policies intensified the self-consciousness and discontent of those condemned to the position of second-class citizens. The safeguards offered by the League of Nations under the highly innovative 'minorities treaties' proved far too weak to correct the inequalities that geography and the conditions of state-building made inevitable. In Yugoslavia minorities were treated as 'foreigners' in their own homelands. The specially crafted protection clauses for the Jewish minority did little to prevent

---

[3] Mark Mazower, *Dark Continent: Europe's Twentieth Century* (London, 1998), 41.

the imposition of restrictive and discriminatory legislation. Czechoslovakia proved to be the singular exception to this generally dismal picture. As the Jews were not a nationality and lacked even 'surrogate' spokesmen, many abandoned hope of relief through the League's protective system. It was often the multiplicity of minority groups and their divisive economic, religious, and cultural identifications that prevented united action against the dominant nationality. Continuing ethnic tensions acted as a destabilizing force in domestic politics, contributing to the proliferation of political parties, obstructing or paralysing existing governments, and sometimes hastening the abandonment of democratic forms. More often than not, relations with bordering states were adversely affected, deepening the gulf between the winners and losers from the peace settlements and multiplying the differences between the status quo and revisionist states. There was no 'melting pot' in the countries of eastern Europe.

II

Reborn Poland created itself from the three former partitioning states, Russia, Austria, and Prussia, each of which left its own legacy. The 'Austrian' Poles were the most experienced politically, the 'Russian' Poles the least. The 'Prussian' Poles had roads and houses and enjoyed some measure of prosperity. With the country so divided, ethnic Poles (just under 70 per cent of the population) rarely agreed on official policy towards the minorities. The highly nationalistic and anti-Semitic right and right-centre parties in the unstable coalition governments of the 1920s introduced legislation that fuelled grievances among the politically self-conscious and economically progressive Germans in the western regions (Pomerelia, Pozonia, and Silesia) of the state, as well as in the eastern lands populated by the far less advanced and mainly peasant Ukrainian, Belorussian, and Russian ethnic groups. The Socialist, Peasant, and other left-of-centre parties preferred to concentrate on economic and social questions rather than on minority issues. The small but active Communist party wanted the eastern territories joined to the Soviet Ukrainian and Belorussian republics. Dmowski's National Democrats wanted to assimilate the Slavic minorities but not the Jews, viewing the ancient Jewish presence in Poland as a 'permanent outrage'.[4] Jews constituted nearly 8 per cent of the population; most lived in poverty and were politically inert, but there was also an entirely separate, important, and influential urban representation, making up some 31 per cent of Poland's total urban population. Anti-Semitic

---

[4] David Vital, *A People Apart: The Jews in Europe, 1789–1939* (Oxford, 1999), 767.

TABLE 10. Estimates of Religious Affiliation in South–East Europe, 1930 (★ = year of census)

	Albania 1930★		Bulgaria 1934★		Czechoslovakia 1930★		Hungary 1931★		Poland 1931★		Romania 1930★		Yugoslavia 1930★	
	(000)	(%)	(000)	(%)	(000)	(%)	(000)	(%)	(000)	(%)	(000)	(%)	(000)	(%)
Roman Catholic		10.1	46	0.8	10,831	73.5	5,634	64.9	20,670	64.8	1,200		5,218	37.4
Uniate/Greek/Armenian					584	4	201	2.3	3,336	10.4	1,426		45	0.3
Orthodox		19.7	5,130	84.4			40	0.5	3,762	11.8	13,200		6,785	48.7
Protestant			8	0.1	1,130	3.7	2,347	27	835	2.6	1,295		231	1.6
Jewish			48	0.8	357	2.4	445	5.1	3,114	9.8	1,500		68	0.4
Muslim		70.2	821	13.5							260		1,516	11.2
Others			25	0.4	800		21	0.2	198	0.6	140		18	0.1

Sources: Milan Hauner, 'Demographic Structure of Eastern Europe Between the Two Wars', *Papers in East European Economics*, 40 (Oxford, 1974); Hugh Seton-Watson, *Eastern Europe between the Wars, 1918–1941*, 3rd edn. (New York, 1962).

Map 11. Independent Poland, 1918–22

legislation both encouraged the spread of Marxist and Zionist ideas and alienated those Jews who had left the *shtetl* to move into the mainstream of Polish life. Unfortunately for all concerned, Poland was the country with the largest free Jewish population in Europe, and their visible presence in the cities and towns of Poland repeatedly acted as an anti-Semitic lightning rod.

Poland's territorial gains during and after the peace conference increased its vulnerability to nationalist discontents. There were continuing tensions in Upper Silesia as well as in the 'Polish corridor' (where the Poles constituted two-thirds of the population), in Posen and West Prussia, and in the free city of Danzig. In the east, where the Poles pushed their borders into Russian territories, centralizing legislation and the unwillingness to concede any form of autonomy aggravated age-old hatreds between the different Slav groups inhabiting the vast areas which had once belonged to the medieval Polish-Lithuanian Commonwealth. The seizure of Vilna, with its Jewish majority and Polish, Lithuanian, and Belorussian inhabitants, poisoned relations with Lithuania, which refused to give up its claims to the former capital.

The main consequence of the ethnic question was to add to the fractiousness of Polish politics in the all-powerful Sejm. Parties and political clubs increased in number; new factions based on ideological, nationalist, or economic lines made compromise difficult if not impossible. The coalition governments of the period were highly unstable, and in the background the pro and anti-Piłsudski forces were in constant contention. Between 1921, when the new Polish constitution was adopted, and the Piłsudski coup of May 1926 that marked its abandonment, the country again and again seemed to be on the verge of political disintegration.

Czechoslovakia's multinational, factional party-political climate was not naturally conducive to parliamentary democracy. After a brief period of Socialist rule, a five-party de facto coalition (Agrarians, National Democrats, Social Democrats, Socialists, and Catholics) was created which continued in power throughout the inter-war period. Without the coalition, the multitude of diverse political forces would have made parliamentary government impossible. Headed by the Agrarians, who represented the prosperous Czech peasantry, it was kept together not only by self-interest but by the strong counter-pressures exerted by 'the Castle', the highly influential, small, pro-western, and mildly socialist group around the president, Tomáš Masaryk, and by the president's own personal exertions. If the Prague government functioned more successfully than most, much of the credit must be given to Masaryk, the son of a Moravian estate worker who became a scholar and then a nationalist politician. His unique position and prestige as Czechoslovakia's founder secured a key unifying role for him in the country's political life. Elected four times as head of state, each time opposed by the right, the communists, and the German, Slovak, and Hungarian dissidents, Masaryk's conception of the Czech nation was not all-embracing. It ignored the Catholicism of much of the population and distinguished Czechs from Germans and Slovaks. Masaryk's vision encompassed a country linked to the west rather than to the Bolshevik east, and committed to a form of democratic rule that was totally unfamiliar to the eastern half of Czechoslovakia and from which it derived few advantages. While exceptional among the successor states in its political stability, Czechoslovakia followed the general pattern in its treatment of the ethnic minorities who constituted slightly more than one-third of the entire population.

The Czechs ruled over the prosperous Sudeten Germans of Bohemia, Moravia, and Silesia, the overwhelmingly rural Slovak population, and the even more backward Ruthenes of Sub-Carpathia, whose condition in their new country was not much better than under the Hungarians. Slovakia inherited, on economic and strategic grounds, a 750,000-strong disgruntled Hungarian minority, most of them living on the large Danube island of Grosse Schütte. The Jews, who lived in all parts of the republic, mainly in the cities, after a period of initial difficulty flourished under a regime without anti-Semitic legislation and became strong supporters of the Masaryk state.

Apprehensive about the centrifugal forces in the newly created country, the Czechs rejected calls by the regional minorities for local political autonomy and implemented social, cultural, and economic legislation that reinforced political unity. Foremost among the minorities were the Sudeten Germans, a quarter of the new state's population, who had acquired a common identity and political representation during 1918–19. At first, relations with the Czechs were hostile, and even violent, but once the constitution was adopted in February 1920 most Sudeten Germans entered the body politic. They formed their own parties, took part in elections, and won seats in both houses of the Assembly. Inevitably, the views of the Czech founders shaped the nature of the multinational state. All the Czech leaders, including Masaryk, wanted a unitary and bureaucratically centralized nation-state in which the Sudeten Germans would be included as a minority. The latter, by contrast, wanted a 'state of nationalities' based on a confederation of autonomous areas where the local authorities would have paramount influence. The Sudeten Germans were divided between those willing to participate in government and a steadily decreasing minority who preferred non-cooperation and obstruction. Though the former prevailed and took an active part in parliamentary politics, no links were forged

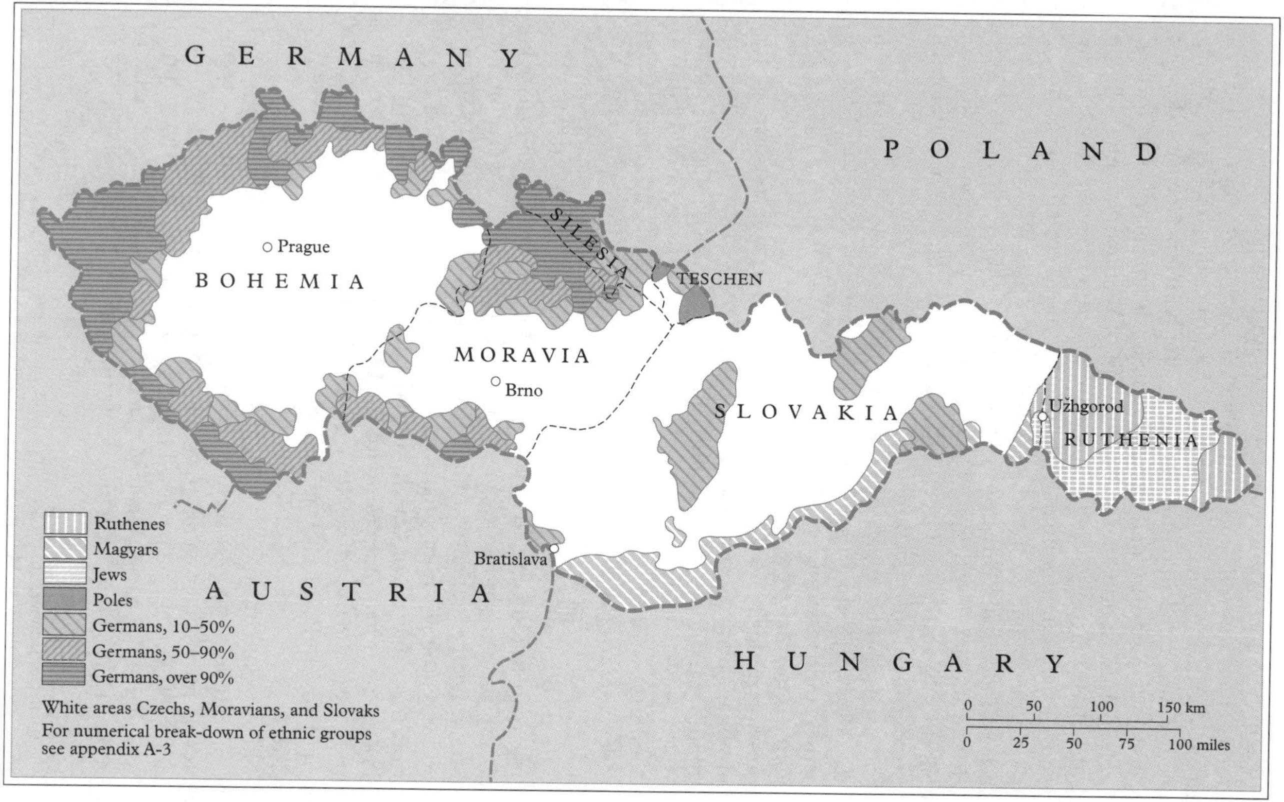
GERMANY
POLAND
Prague
BOHEMIA
SILESIA
TESCHEN
MORAVIA
Brno
SLOVAKIA
Užhgorod
RUTHENIA
Bratislava
AUSTRIA
HUNGARY
Ruthenes
Magyars
Jews
Poles
Germans, 10–50%
Germans, 50–90%
Germans, over 90%
White areas Czechs, Moravians, and Slovaks
For numerical break-down of ethnic groups see appendix A-3
0 50 100 150 km
0 25 50 75 100 miles

Map 12. Inter-War Czechoslovakia: Ethnic-Linguistic Composition

between the Sudeten and Czech parties and even common economic interests failed to erode the nationalities barrier. It was not until 1926 that the German parties were admitted into the ruling coalition. While not fully integrated into the new state, the Sudeten Germans did not challenge its authority and there was little, if any, irredentist feeling. Czech affairs were low on the overlong list of Weimar priorities. On the whole, Berlin favoured Sudeten participation in Czech politics in the hope that they might influence Prague in a pro-German direction.

The Slovaks and Ruthenes of Sub-Carpathia populated the poorest and least industrialized regions of the country, where birth rates were high and literacy levels low. They had little in common socially and economically with their Czech rulers and suffered from the differential treatment that favoured Bohemia over all other regions. The Slovaks, whose lands had been part of Hungary, had never possessed their own state. After 1918 they had their own representatives in the National Assembly and a minister who represented Slovakia in Prague. No significant powers were devolved to Bratislava, the Slovak capital. The Protestant minority of Slovakia was favoured at the expense of the Catholic majority. Nationalist discontent, fed by the fiercely reactionary Catholic priesthood, was channelled into the increasingly popular Slovak People's party under the leadership of Father Andrej Hlinka, the leading advocate of Slovak political and cultural autonomy. Until the depression radicalized politics, the Slovaks did not challenge the unitary state. Local agitation centred on demands for a greater share of the funds dispensed by Prague and some measure of autonomy. The Hungarians in Slovakia, many of whom were former landowners who had lost their political power along with their lands, were, on the contrary, strong irredentists who looked to Budapest. Ruthenia, populated by Ruthenes, Hungarians, and Jews, was a desperately poor area, cut off from the rest of Czechoslovakia and lying on the eastern tip of the republic. It had more ties with the Ukraine and with Hungary than with Prague, and might well have gone to Russia had the Bolsheviks not been in power. Political awareness remained minimal and the few active politicians concentrated on economic grievances.

No government in Belgrade could have created a unitary state from the multitude of peoples included within Yugoslavia's borders, a country even more heterogeneous in its ethnic and religious composition than Czechoslovakia. The new kingdom 'resembled a miniature edition of the old multi-racial Dual Monarchy', with its numerous national groups and religions.[5] Yet the constitutional monarchy established in

---

[5] Gerhard Schrieber, 'Germany, Italy and South-east Europe: From Political and Economic Hegemony to Military Aggression', in Gerhard Schreiber, Bernd Stegemann,

1921 was a centralized rather than a federal state, which would have been far more appropriate to its origins and character. The leaders of pre-war Serbia continued to rule a much enlarged state unsuited to their existing administrative machinery. The Serbs, Orthodox in religion, constituted only 43 per cent of the total population of the post-war kingdom. The Serb monopoly of power was bitterly contested by the Catholic Croats who, while less than a quarter of the Yugoslav population, had enjoyed considerable autonomy under the Habsburgs and deeply resented the control exercised from Belgrade by Nikola Pašić's Serb Radical party. The Serbs prevailed mainly by force, but also by offering administrative rights and cultural and economic concessions to the self-conscious Slovenes in the territories once part of Austria, and to the Bosnian Muslims. There were also Montenegrins, Bulgar-Macedonians and Albanians, Greeks, and Turks living in the country. The first two groups were treated as Serbs but the Albanians were deprived of any form of autonomy. Those living in the Kosovo region demanded union with neighbouring Albania, a state that won recognition of its independence and 1913 borders in 1920. Albanian demonstrations were put down by military force and Serb army veterans were brought in and settled in their midst. There was also a significant number of disaffected Germans in the north-west, and Hungarians, mainly in the Vojvodina region in the north, who had previously enjoyed significant influence but were now politically impotent. The struggle between Serbs and Croats cast its heavy shadow over the country's political life, even when King Alexander I imposed his royal dictatorship in 1929 and transformed the Kingdom of Serbs, Croats, and Slovenes into the Kingdom of Yugoslavia. The country's divisions, regional, ethnic, and religious discontents provided abundant opportunities for Italian meddling when Mussolini turned his attention to the revision of the Adriatic peace settlement. Apart from Italy, Hungary was perceived as posing the next most dangerous challenge to Yugoslavia's security, resulting in alliances with Czechoslovakia and Romania.

Romania struggled with democracy. Despite the introduction of universal male suffrage and the creation of a democratic government, King Ferdinand retained considerable power under the new constitution of 1923. With his backing and the use of traditionally corrupt electioneering methods, the Liberals under Ion Brătianu, whose family had dominated Romanian politics since the nineteenth century, won control of the government in 1922 and stayed almost continually in

and Detlef Vogel (eds.), *Germany and the Second World War*, Vol. 3: *The Mediterranean, South-east Europe, and North Africa 1939–1941*, trans. Dean S. McMurry, Ewald Osers, and Louise Willmot (Oxford, 1995), 318.

office until 1928. Brătianu was a rigid centralist, whose administrative policies alienated the Hungarians in Transylvania and Bessarabia as well as the other ethnic minorities. His autocratic government survived until his autarkic economic policies at the expense of the peasantry drove the opposition parties together. The Liberals also had difficulties with the ailing king's heir, Prince Carol, who refused to give up his mistress, Elena Lupescu, and return home from Paris. He was finally forced in 1925 to renounce the succession in favour of his own infant son Michel and a regency. The death of Ferdinand in the summer of 1926 and of Brătianu, who had held the Liberals together and given the party a sense of direction, in 1927 heralded the end of the period of Liberal rule. Iuliu Maniu's National Peasant party, appointed by Romania's regents, acceded to power. The new government, a coalition elected in Romania's most democratic election of the whole inter-war period, held office from November 1928 until October 1930. In this brief time of constitutional rule, the National Peasants focused on the need to decentralize the government and assure civil and political rights. Maniu came to grief when the exiled ex-king returned to the capital in June 1930 and, as King Carol II, made clear his intention to establish his personal rule.

Though the peace treaties doubled the size of Romania's territory and population, Romanians still represented over 70 per cent of the enlarged state. They had a clear majority in the Old Kingdom and at least a near or bare majority in the new provinces, Transylvania, Bessarabia, the Banat, Bukovina, and Dobruja. The 2.1 million Hungarians, living mainly in Transylvania, the Banat, and Bukovina, were the most openly dissatisfied minority, as the once dominant Magyars lost their extensive lands and had to accept Romanian political rule. The Hungarian landlords appealed to the League of Nations under the minority treaties, but could not mount a real challenge either to the agrarian reform programme or to Romanian domination of their new provinces. The other minority groups caused fewer problems. The Germans of southern and south-eastern Transylvania, living in long-established and self-supporting Lutheran communities, were politically active but not irredentist. The Bulgarian peasants in Dobruja, who felt disadvantaged when Romanian settlers were given preference, were not a significant political force. The Ukrainian and Russian peasants, who benefited from the land reforms at the Hungarians' expense, were excluded from political life. The sizeable Jewish minority (4.2 per cent of the population and 14 per cent of the urban population), who had already been the object of European concern at the Congress of Berlin in 1878, were finally given citizenship under the treaties signed by Romania. They were important in the economic and professional life of the country, but remained an unassimilated group and were the object of considerable ill feeling. The Gypsies, the largest group in any country, were powerless and easier to ignore than the Jews.

Though the minorities problem, particularly Hungarian discontent, plagued the Romanian leaders, their main concern focused on Russia's unwillingness to recognize the Romanian wartime acquisition of Bessarabia. Since neither Czechoslovakia, Yugoslavia, or France, Romania's allies and friends, shared its extreme hostility towards Moscow, the Romanians concluded a treaty with Poland in 1921, which became a mutual defence treaty in 1926. For most of the 1920s the Russians did not actually challenge the Romanian possession of the province, though they continued to contest Bucharest's action.

Among the defeated nations in Eastern Europe, Hungary was the most revisionist. After the fall of Béla Kun, it developed close relations with Britain. In November 1919 Sir George Clerk, the British minister-designate to Czechoslovakia, who was much influenced by the strong supporter of the successor states R. W. Seton-Watson and his journal *The New Europe*, was sent to Budapest to oversee the Romanian evacuation of the Hungarian capital and to replace the existing administration with one that was capable of signing the peace treaty. It was due to Clerk's mediation that the Conservatives were confirmed in power in Hungary and that Admiral Miklós Horthy, formerly in command of the Austro-Hungarian navy and one of the leaders of the counter-revolutionary movement during the Béla Kun regime, became governor-regent of Hungary. Clerk, who regarded Horthy as a 'gentleman' who could be trusted, accepted the latter's quickly violated pledge that there would be no 'White terror' in Hungary. While there was no way of disregarding the general clamour for territorial revision, Horthy concentrated on building stable institutions and fostering economic development. He found two remarkable men, both of aristocratic gentry descent, Count István Bethlen (1920–31) and Count Pál Teleki (1920–1 and 1939–41), to serve as prime minister. Teleki, who briefly preceded Bethlen in 1920, started the politics of limited consensus which Bethlen developed into a political art. By limiting the franchise, playing off the many small parliamentary groups, and controlling the press, he established his domination over parliament. Through a series of measures combining cajolery and coercion, Bethlen weakened the socialists and pacified the far right. His centrist coalition, the Party of Unity (known as the Government party), founded in 1922 and completely controlled by Bethlen, rested on the landed magnates and their huge estates. During the early 1920s Bethlen secured British support for his domestic and foreign policy, but by the mid-decade, as he moved towards a highly authoritarian government and set his eye on the revision of the peace treaty, the British lost interest. It was a course that Bethlen had always kept in mind but whose practical prerequisites, a stable economy and a reliable ally, were absent until the latter half of the decade.

The Budapest government harboured deep and continuing irredentist ambitions for their co-nationals in Transylvania and Slovakia. Its scarcely disguised intentions and the two abortive efforts of ex-Kaiser Karl to regain the Hungarian throne in 1921 (opposed by Bethlen) set the seal on the creation of the 'Little Entente', so named by the contemptuous Budapest press, that brought together Czechoslovakia, Romania, and Yugoslavia as allies against Hungary. Within the much-reduced Hungarian state, the ethnic minorities caused few difficulties. Eighty-seven per cent of the country's population, including Jews and Gypsies, was Hungarian-speaking, and the largest minority, the bilingual Germans, as well as the Croats, were well integrated into Hungarian life. The few remaining Slovaks in the country continued to voice their grievances; the even fewer Romanians in south-east Hungary accepted the status quo.

Bulgaria's population was over 83 per cent Bulgarian-speaking and Orthodox in religion. There were few difficulties with the Turks, the largest minority (just over 11 per cent of the population), who were given their own schools, nor with the equally mistrusted and powerless Muslim Bulgarians or 'Pomaks'. The exodus of Turks, Greeks, and Romanians that had begun after the Second Balkan War (1913) continued during the 1920s. Some 250,000 Bulgars came in from surrounding areas, many in need of public support, putting considerable pressure on the central authorities. It was mainly the Bulgarian Macedonians, far smaller in number than the Turkish minority, who, as sympathizers or members of highly organized, irredentist organizations created the greatest turmoil in the country. The terrorist group IMRO (Internal Macedonian Revolutionary Organization, founded in 1893) was the most powerful terrorist movement in the Balkans, and proved to be a highly disruptive political force. Assisted and funded by backers in Sofia, IMRO was divided between those wanting the whole of Macedonia annexed to Bulgaria and those who favoured a separate Macedonia in a Balkan federation. Repeated incursions across the frontiers threatened Bulgaria's relations with both Yugoslavia and Greece. In a country where the parties of the left were particularly strong, the ruling radical Bulgarian Agrarian National Union party (1919–23), which came to power after the elections of August 1919 led by Alexander Stamboliiski, wanted to concentrate on domestic reform and avoid foreign complications. Stamboliiski sought agreements with both Belgrade and Athens and participation in the League of Nations (Bulgaria was the first of the defeated nations to be admitted in 1920). The Macedonian extremists, however, were vociferous and the raids of IMRO into Yugoslav territories particularly damaging to Stamboliiski's plans. The Convention of Niš concluded with Belgrade in March 1923 was intended to settle the border with Yugoslavia and rein in the terrorists. In the event, it served only to infuriate them further and added volume to the growing chorus of internal opposition to Stamboliiski's radical agrarian and *dirigiste* economic programmes. The terrorists, who hated Stamboliiski for signing the notorious Treaty of Neuilly that gave most of Macedonia to Yugoslavia, joined the successful coup mounted by a variety of opponents in 1923; Stamboliiski was captured, tortured, and decapitated. The new regime, which moved massively against the left after a belated Moscow-inspired insurrection, ruled mainly by violence but proved as incapable as Stamboliiski at controlling the terrorists. With secret Italian assistance, as well as help from the Bulgarian ministry of war, IMRO created its own state within a state in Petrich, a 'no-go' area where the Bulgarian, Greek, and Yugoslav borders met, and continued its destructive incursions into Yugoslavia. By the time IMRO was finally disbanded in 1934, it had accentuated the trend towards violence in Belgrade and had caused irreparable damage to inter-state relations.

Like the Bulgarians, but on a much larger scale, the Greeks faced the problems of settling incoming refugees. In addition to the flood of people from Asia Minor, displaced after the Treaty of Lausanne on the old Ottoman basis of religion, there were Greeks coming from Bulgaria under a voluntary exchange agreement and refugees from southern Russia fleeing the revolution. Most refugees were settled in rural areas, particularly in Macedonia and Thrace, areas which Greece had only recently acquired. Others were left on the fringes of large towns or in shanties around Athens–Piraeus and became radicals in politics, The huge intake of refugees had its effect on national politics, but, except during the brief dictatorship of General Theodoros Panaglos (1925–6), who threatened to renew the war against Turkey and very briefly occupied a part of Bulgaria after a border incident with the Macedonian terrorists, Greek attention was focused on its internal politics and public finance. Internal conditions remained chaotic and governments highly unstable, even after the debacle in the Middle East. Between 1924 and 1928, when Venizelos again became prime minister, Greece experienced eleven governments, eleven military coups, three elections, and two military dictatorships.[6]

For the most part, in almost every country the centralizing policies of the dominant ethnic group prevailed. No multinational state was torn apart by ethnic divisions. While old hatreds between neighbouring people were intensified by the peace settlements and the new ethnic

---

[6] Schrieber, 'Germany, Italy, and South-East Europe', 334.

conflicts sometimes aggravated border disputes, the status quo was maintained. The revisionist powers were too weak to challenge the peace settlements and no outside country, not even Italy, the most restless of the major victor countries, was ready to take up the revisionist cause. The main external consequence of these tensions was to make regional co-operation, political or economic, more difficult. There was no movement towards the economic confederation of the former Austro-Hungarian lands nor any association of the Balkan states. It was inevitable, given the fragmented character of the region and the multitude of border and ethnic disputes, that local leaders should search for outside support and that the great powers should fish in the troubled waters. While wanting great-power support for some purposes, countries like Poland and Czechoslovakia on the one hand, and Hungary and Bulgaria on the other, had specific regional aims which their patrons did not share and which would weaken or undermine their support. The main interested countries, France, Britain, Italy, and Germany, each had its own agenda, almost invariably pursued in rivalry with the others, exacerbating local tensions. The majority of the multinational states felt under no compulsion to compromise with their ethnic minorities, while enjoying the breathing space provided by the withdrawal of Germany and the Soviet Union and the weaknesses of the defeated states.

III

Apart from nationality questions and divisive domestic politics, it was the comparative poverty of the countries in eastern Europe that most threatened their future development. Even before 1914, most of the region lagged behind the west in terms of agricultural output and industrial development. Economic progress within the area was highly uneven. The Habsburg monarchy included the rich and industrialized regions of Lower Austria and Bohemia as well as the poverty-stricken lands of Galicia, Bukovina, and Dalmatia. Trade was largely internalized and foreign trade actually declined in the years before the war. Most of the rest of east-central Europe was mainly agricultural and dependent on peasant labour. Though the war and peace caused economic upheavals, the region, with one or two exceptions, remained mainly agricultural and without the capital to finance stabilization or industrialization. The effects of the war and the drawing of new boundaries led to the interruption of normal trade and the collapse of traditional markets. The disappearance of the pre-war empires inevitably led to the reordering of the economic map of eastern Europe. The number of independent economic units rose from twenty-six to thirty-eight, the length of customs frontiers increased, and the number of separate currencies in

TABLE 11. Population Dependent on Agriculture
in Eastern Europe, 1921–1931 (%)

	1921	1930/1
Czechoslovakia	40	28
Hungary	56	54
Poland	64	65
Romania	75–80	78
Yugoslavia	75–80	79
Bulgaria	75–80	80

Sources: League of Nations, *Industrialisation and Foreign Trade*
(Geneva, 1945), 26–7; N. Spulber, *The Economics of Communist
Eastern Europe* (New York, 1957), 8; W. E. Moore, *Economic
Demography of Eastern and Southern Europe* (Geneva, 1945), *passim*.

circulation increased from thirteen to twenty-seven.[7] The creation of
the Baltic states and the practical ending of trade with Russia added to
the fragmentation and to the disruption of trade lines. Heightened
nationalism led to the deliberate severing of former economic ties and
intensified the search for markets outside of the region. The shift of
trade away from neighbours and towards western Europe left the
majority of the eastern European states vulnerable to changes in the
world economy and without any means of mutual defence.

The immediate impact of the war was to create economic chaos, high
inflation, and debased currencies. Austria, Poland, and Hungary were
the hardest hit. Austria was kept alive through relief supplies, mainly
American. Agricultural production reached only half its pre-war level in
1920 and Hungary had no substantial surplus food to export to Austria as
had been customary before 1914. Austrian industrial output barely
exceeded one-third of 1913 levels and unemployment reached unprecedented proportions. The need to provide cheap food for the population to avoid revolution fuelled the wartime inflation. In desperation,
the Vienna government appealed to the victors for credits to keep the
government afloat. An Austrian subcommittee of the Reparation Commission argued for a postponement of reparation claims in November
1920 but did not conclude its deliberations until the following year.
Instead of looking at ways to extract wealth from Austria, it began to
assess the methods by which foreign aid could be channelled into the

---

[7] Ivan T. Berend and György Ranki, *Economic Development in East-Central Europe in the
19th and 20th Centuries* (New York, 1974), 201. The totals would be higher if the Baltic
states were included.

country. The Béla Kun government in Hungary also failed to halt the drastic drop in agricultural and industrial production, nor could it control the galloping inflation during the life of the 133-day republic. The economic chaos, aggravated by the campaigns of the invading Romanian army, grew worse after the counter-revolution. The massive drop in agricultural exports made it difficult to secure the capital and raw materials needed to stimulate industrial production. Poland had been the scene of terrible fighting that left behind a trail of physical destruction. The weak infant economy bore the costs of hostilities with the Ukrainians, Germans, Lithuanians, and Russians, often fought simultaneously, between 1918 and 1921. The government had the seemingly impossible task of bringing together regions that had belonged to three different empires and that were of very uneven economic development. Financial confusion and rampant inflation undercut any efforts to stabilize the currency. Poland's unusually protracted and severe currency depreciation paralysed parts of its economy, though it also speeded up economic unification by creating a level playing field and forcing the previously unconnected economic actors to trade with each other.

Elsewhere, governments grappled with war-induced shortages of food and raw materials and high inflation. Yugoslavia and Romania, each of which suffered considerable physical damage in the war, lost livestock (the main portion of Serbia's rural production) and agricultural equipment and suffered drastic reductions in agricultural output. Romanian oil production plummeted, though its inflation was less severe than in Austria or Hungary as its continuing, if diminished, oil and grain exports somewhat improved the foreign trade balance. The Brătianu government in Bucharest was insistent that the country should put its house in order without foreign loans and placed strict limitations on foreign investment and imports of foreign manufactured goods. Native capital still dominated the oil firms and the import of foreign manufactured goods fell steadily. In Bulgaria, too, though agricultural production figures fell sharply and foreign trade was curtailed, inflation was relatively mild and the budget balanced in 1921–2.

Czechoslovakia was the first country to recover and return to pre-war levels of production. The country had the important advantage, economic-financial as well as psychological, of being treated as a victor nation. It inherited some of the most advanced industrial and banking facilities of the pre-war Habsburg monarchy and benefited, too, from a series of able finance ministers, who cut the old ties with Vienna and rapidly created an independent currency. While the Austrian inflation became a hyperinflation threatening the existence of the government, in Czechoslovakia the Austro-Hungarian krone was quickly withdrawn from circulation; the notes were over-stamped by the Ministry of

Finance and released for domestic purposes. The new crown (*koruna*) was stabilized in 1921–2. The state survived the ending of the inflationary boom and the introduction of deflationary measures during 1922–3. Though the subsequent overvaluation of the currency (in part the result of an artificial demand for Czechoslovak goods during the Ruhr occupation) checked the growth of the export market, both industrial production and exports resumed their upward trend in the latter half of the 1920s, when Czechoslovakia benefited from the general improvement in the world economy. Alone among the states of eastern Europe, Czechoslovakia was able to generate sufficient capital from her industrial exports to finance her own economic development, invest abroad, and buy back foreign-owned securities to ensure her economic independence.

The immediate post-war inflation had positive as well as negative effects on the process of recovery. In Austria, Hungary, Czechoslovakia, and especially Poland, for a short period at least, inflation stimulated investment, and encouraged the creation of new firms and the restocking of inventories. Foreign investment, cancelled debts, cheap loans, and the flight of capital into goods and buildings led to industrial growth. In the case of Austria, the temporary boom increased the gap between production and consumption and between imports and exports, thereby weakening the whole economic structure. Bulgaria, Romania, and Yugoslavia enjoyed their first spurt of industrial development between 1919 and 1924; in Yugoslavia industrial investment reached its inter-war peak during the inflation period. By the time the inflation ran its course, industrial output was approaching approximately 75 per cent of pre-war levels. But these early stirrings in the agrarian states were not enough to

TABLE 12. Index of Eastern European Manufacturing Output, 1920–1929 (1913 = 100)

	1920/1	1925	1929
Czechslovakia	69.8	136.4	171.8
Hungary	64.0	76.7	113.9
Poland	35.1	63.1	85.9
Romania	47.2	92.2	136.9
Yugoslavia	–	–	140.0
Europe (18 countries)	66.9	89.6	110.7
World Total	93.2	120.7	137.5

Sources: League of Nations, *Industrialisation and Foreign Trade* (Geneva, 1945), 136–7; I. T. Berend, and G. Ranki, *Economic Development in East Central Europe in the 19th and 20th Centuries* (New York, 1974), 298–300.

change the balance of economies still almost totally dependent on agriculture for economic growth, even when, by the mid-1920s, most were reaching or surpassing their pre-war levels of industrial production. Hungary, for instance, doubled its industrial production and expanded its textile and chemical industries, but still depended on agricultural exports, primarily wheat, for the raw materials and machinery essential for industrial growth.

Agricultural weakness continued despite major land reforms in most of the eastern European countries. The example of the 1917 Russian revolution, the mass migrations of 1917–19, and the emergence of strong peasant parties made a response to the widespread demand for land redistribution expedient. The most radical changes took place in the Baltic, especially in Estonia and Latvia where the Baltic German landowners were expropriated, in parts of Yugoslavia, and in Romania, particularly in Bessarabia and Transylvania. There was a radical agrarian programme, too, in Bulgaria, though expropriation was unnecessary for the country was and remained a nation of small peasant holdings. In Greece, after a slow start, the influx of refugees forced the government to institute a radical redistribution programme. Some 40 per cent of the country's land was redistributed, the highest proportion in the Balkans, with almost all of it going to refugees. In Czechoslovakia, where the land problem was most acute in predominantly rural Slovakia, the implementation of reforms was slow and compensation high. In general, it was the capable and well-organized Czech peasantry rather than the Slovaks and Ruthenes who benefited most. In Poland, the power of the landowners was such that only one quarter of the land belonging to the large estates was expropriated and about 20 per cent of the arable land remained in the hands of the big landowners. Hungary was a special case. The country had historically been bedevilled by the persistence of huge *latifundia* owned by aristocrats and the Catholic Church. The landowners managed to sabotage early attempts at land reform and the Bolshevik Béla Kun regime did not have the time to implement its intended reforms. After its fall, the traditional landowning class returned to power and regained or held on to its vast holdings. As late as 1935, 43.1 per cent of the land was held by less than 1 per cent of the population. Albania, too, was an exception. It alone in south-eastern Europe had no peasant or Communist party and there was no change in the landowning system. The country, torn by civil war and the conflicting interests of its neighbours, remained the least economically developed state in Europe.

Land reform did not solve the problem of agricultural backwardness. Even where radical land distribution took place, the new farms were too small to be profitable and rising population figures, due to a lower death rate and reduced emigration overseas, put new and heavy pressure on peasant families. In Poland and Hungary, where the persistence of the large estates created social and economic problems among the mass of landless labourers and productivity remained low, there was little incentive for improvement. The most notable recovery in the mid-1920s occurred in Romania and Yugoslavia, where increased yield resulted from new land brought under cultivation and the use of additional labour rather than from improved methods of farming. Agricultural recovery was helped, too, by the high post-war demand for food and rising agricultural prices on the world market. Neither of these conditions lasted beyond 1927–8. If real progress was to be made, these agriculturally dependent countries needed to diversify their exports, still heavily centred on grain, and radically modernize their farming techniques. Even in the best years between 1924 and 1928, the food-exporting states of south-east Europe could not challenge the far more efficient American and Canadian agricultural producers. For countries dependent on grain exports to finance loans and industrial expansion, any major fall in world prices would pose catastrophic problems.

The weaknesses in agriculture and in the foreign trade sector were compounded by the actions of the new post-war governments. The Allied powers recognized the economic costs of the political disintegration of the Habsburg monarchy and, in competition with each other, pressed for the creation of regional economic federations. Instead, seven separate and independent customs systems were created within the former territories of the Dual Monarchy. Each of the successor states was determined to establish and maintain its full economic independence. Despite the peace-treaty provisions for preferential customs treaties and the agreements proposed at the Porto Rosa meeting called by the Italians in October–November 1921 to ease barriers and restrictions, governments resorted to prohibitions of imports and exports when the latter did not serve the state's interests. When currencies were finally stabilized, the governments applied high customs duties in the interests of self-sufficiency and freedom of action. Czechoslovakia and Austria encouraged agricultural production at home by setting high tariffs on imports of cereals and livestock. The agrarian countries of the Danube valley, in turn, raised tariffs against industrial imports from Czechoslovakia and Austria. These protective measures reduced intra-regional trade and encouraged a shift away from the Danubian basin to the markets of western Europe and the American continent. Immediately after the war, 52 per cent of all Czechoslovak exports went to the Danubian states; by 1924 this total was reduced to 37 per cent and by 1929 to 31 per cent. The protectionist policy introduced by the Czech agrarians made it impossible for Romania and Yugoslavia,

Czechoslovakia's partners, to buy Czech industrial goods, including armaments. Agricultural products and raw materials were their only exchange commodities. Czechoslovakia and even impoverished Austria looked to the United States and Canada where, despite transport costs, agricultural prices were competitive and Czech exports buoyant. Yugoslavia's regional trade dropped significantly compared to Serbia's pre-war figures; Italy rapidly became its best market. The Hungarians, determined on a course of forced industrialization paid for by the peasantry, maintained high protective walls and deliberately restricted their trading with neighbours. Outside efforts to open up new markets within the region or to introduce more liberal trading practices repeatedly failed. Soviet initiatives at the conferences of Riga in March 1922 and Moscow in December 1922 produced minimal results. No progress was made at the 1922 Genoa conference when the Little Entente powers, backed by France, buried the Porta Rosa recommendations. Proposals for preferential tariff arrangements were also stultified by Britain's insistence on most-favoured-nation status despite London's pressure for tariff reductions. By the time the World Economic Conference assembled in 1927, the tariff level throughout eastern Europe was considerably higher than in 1914. Poland was the sole exception, only because of the very high pre-1914 Russian tariff. The policy of 'beggar one's neighbour' not only increased the vulnerability of these states to the conditions of the world markets but failed to bring sufficient benefits to either agriculture or industry to cushion their economies when the world markets contracted.

IV

With the notable exception of Czechoslovakia, governments in east-central Europe, while determined to establish their economic independence, found they did not have the capital resources needed for stabilization and recovery. In the immediate post-settlement period, reparations and war debts (the defeated nations had to assume their predecessors' obligations) represented a considerable burden on the weak economies of the states concerned, but also proved major obstacles to securing immediate credits and loans. Though reparation payments for the ex-enemy countries came to be postponed, reduced, and abandoned in the case of Austria, and more generous terms negotiated for war debts, they were not cancelled and continued to complicate the process of financial rehabilitation. Relief supplies, mainly financed by the United States, and to a lesser extent by Britain and Canada, flowed into Austria, Poland, Czechoslovakia, Romania, and Yugoslavia and were even sent to Hungary and Bulgaria, though on far less favourable terms. Relief loans and other forms of inter-governmental lending failed to cover short-term needs, and attempts to secure private credit and investment were more often than not unsuccessful. In London, private bankers proved unenthusiastic even before the Bank of England imposed its not entirely effective embargo on private foreign lending in 1921. Where credits were secured, their costs increased the burden on already indebted governments. Representatives from firms in the United States, Britain, France, and Italy appeared in the capital cities looking for speculative or more long-range bargains. Syndicates were formed to obtain concessions either through official channels or on a more ad hoc basis. Anglo–American relief workers often took advantage of the local situation to become concession hunters themselves or to prepare the way for fellow nationals ready to combine philanthropy with profit. Meanwhile, there were appeals for help to the Supreme Council in Paris from the Austrian chancellor and requests for loans and credits from Czechoslovakia, Hungary, Yugoslavia, and the hard-pressed Poles.

Though most of the Anglo–American experts at the peace conference thought that the economies of the states in central and eastern Europe could be reconstructed through private enterprise, officials began to discuss how loans and credits could be funnelled into east-central Europe. Bankers and financial experts agreed that European economic recovery would occur only if governments stabilized their currencies, cut their expenditures, balanced their budgets, and established independent and politically 'neutral' central banks. Such programmes of reform seemed beyond the range of possibility for the states of east-central Europe, given their political and economic situations. International intervention began in a significant form with two major stabilization loans, to Austria in 1922 and to Hungary in 1924. In both, the Financial Committee of the League of Nations, encouraged and supported by Montagu Norman, the governor of the Bank of England, played the central role. It was the increasingly precarious situation in Austria that resulted in the international effort to provide the Austrians with a long-term loan—650 million gold crowns—guaranteed by Britain, France, Italy, and Czechoslovakia, in return for acceptance of a closely monitored plan of radical reform devised by the League's Financial Committee. The mechanism adopted was derived from a Czech application for an international loan issued in London, Amsterdam, and New York in 1922, and the decision to use the League of Nations as an arbiter in case of any clash between the Czech government and the lenders about security. Because of the American participation in the issuing of the stabilization loan, the new Austrian currency was stabilized against the dollar. The rigorous regime imposed on Vienna included strict control over Austria's internal economy and the appointment of a commissioner-general (or 'financial director') who forced through deflationary policies that successfully revalued the currency and eliminated social-welfare schemes, in the process alienating the Social Democrats and much of the working class. Recovery was quick but, after paying off previous debts, supporting the currency, and balancing the budget, there was little capital left for restructuring Austrian industry. The League's direct control of the Austrian budget was only lifted in 1926. Recovery and stabilization were accomplished in ways advantageous to Austria's new creditors. Her banks and associated industries were internationalized and the British, French, Americans, Belgians, Dutch, and Swiss became major shareholders. The financial and commercial fate of Austria was now tied to developments outside Vienna.

The Austrian stabilization loan became the model for subsequent League action. The loan to Hungary in 1924 followed the Austrian pattern in securing the loan on designated revenues, providing for a new bank of issue, introducing a programme of financial reform, and appointing a neutral controller-general. It was mainly due to the persuasion of the British Treasury and the participation of the Bank of England that the Hungarian loan was successfully issued in July 1924 with nearly £8 million out of a total of £14,200,000 subscribed in London.[8] France did not participate because of its own financial difficulties and the lack of interest among French banks. Ironically, the loan had raised, in a miniature but striking fashion, the fundamental problem with Montagu Norman's claim that central bankers were neutral actors on the international stage. He had revoked his support for the Hungarian loan in December 1923, claiming that the loan conditions made it a poorer risk than its Austrian counterpart, but the following April performed a dramatic *volte-face* when the chancellor of the Exchequer in the Labour government, Philip Snowden, intervened. 'The British government now deem it politically expedient to proceed with the Scheme,' Norman wrote, 'and, although on the question of principle my views regarding the proposed foreign Loan, looked at solely from the economic aspect, remain unchanged, I shall nevertheless, in view of this decision, now give it <u>every support</u> in my power.'[9]

Behind Norman's interventionism and his advocacy of the League solution to the problems of central Europe was his belief that it was essential to separate the political from the financial and economic realms

---

[8] Anne Orde, *British Policy and European Reconstruction After the First World War* (Cambridge, 1990), 273.

[9] Norman to Gerard Vissering (president of the Nederlandsche Bank), 12 May 1924, Bank of England G3/180. (The underlining is Norman's.)

of international policy. He wanted to remove the management of the latter from the inept hands of the politicians and allow the central bankers to address the problems of economic reconstruction. Norman came to believe that central bank co-operation could provide the solution to Europe's post-war economic difficulties. In reality, such co-operation represented only some future goal. Though Norman succeeded in establishing personal and institutional links with Benjamin Strong and the Federal Reserve Bank of New York, and with prominent central bankers of some neutral states in Europe, he had yet to create the base for successful central bank co-operation. In its absence, arranging support for League stabilization schemes was the next best solution, and the League's Financial Committee the closest equivalent to a neutral and impartial body of banking and financial experts. Norman had personal and professional ties with the members of the Financial Committee, which was dominated by its three British representatives (other countries had only one), including its chairman, the British senior civil servant Sir Arthur Salter. It was hardly surprising that it was widely believed, particularly in Paris, that the 'Norman conquest' of central Europe took place on the back of the Financial Committee and that Britain was using the League to further its own brand of financial imperialism on the continent.

Norman claimed otherwise. 'The quarrels in Austria between the protagonists of the French on the one side and of the British on the other have been very unfortunate,' he wrote to Strong in 1921, 'and of course all spring from the fundamentally different standpoints of the two countries. Our basis is economic, the French basis is political, and nowhere is the distinction more clearly seen than in Austria.'[10] Norman's policies were hardly as politically neutral as he professed, and the lines drawn between politics and finance proved less clear in practice than in theory. Rebuilding the economies of central and eastern Europe was a way of restoring British monetary and financial stability. Predicated on the concept that the pound must rejoin the gold standard at the earliest opportunity, Norman and his circle hoped to return sterling and the City of London to their pre-war eminence. Norman missed no opportunity to attempt to link the new central banks to the Bank of England and to tie their stabilized currencies to the pound sterling, at least for the terms of the loan projects. Despite Norman's efforts, the Austrian crown was stabilized against the dollar, but the newly created National Bank of Hungary was required to deal exclusively with the Bank of England and the korona was stabilized against the pound. Norman could be ruthless in mobilizing Britain's financial

---

[10] Henry Clay, *Lord Norman* (London, 1957), 184–5.

power and political influence to achieve his ends. In December 1921, seeking to reconcile Austria with its neighbours, the British warned the Czechs that unless they were more forthcoming in their attitude towards Vienna, there would be no British loans to Prague. Similar tactics were used in 1923, when Norman took up the cause of a League loan for the Hungarians and sought Foreign Office help to bring Romania and Czechoslovakia into line. The two powers were forced to give way and agree to abandon their liens on Hungary's assets for reparation payments.

Between 1924 and 1927 the League's Financial Committee sponsored a number of further loans to small states, including refugee loans to Greece and Bulgaria, to the Free City of Danzig, and to Estonia. Most loans were given to balance budgets and to stabilize depreciated currencies. The City of London provided almost half of the League loans (49.1 per cent of £81.2 million subscribed) to eastern Europe; the American contribution was less than half that (19.1 per cent) and no other European country was able to take more than a small tranche of the loan issues.[11] It was only during and after 1927, with the increased availability of American capital, that the Americans began to assert their autonomous financial power and that the role of the Financial Committee and British influence was radically reduced. The Bank of France, too, after the stabilization of the franc in 1926, appeared on the scene as a rival to the Bank of England. In Poland, after an exchange-rate crisis in 1926 following the introduction of a new currency, an American stabilization plan was adopted, setting less strict conditions than would have been demanded by the League. A loan was arranged by the FRBNY with French support. Half the loan, used mainly for currency stabilization, came from the United States and the rest from Britain, France, Switzerland, and Holland. In the case of Romania, the Liberal government of Iuliu Maniu, which was more willing than its predecessors to seek outside assistance, appealed to the French and the Bank of France to cover the final stages of its currency stabilization. This loan in 1929, the last to be linked to the gold exchange system, took the form of a joint central bank credit with each of the four major central banks in France, Britain, the United States, and Germany taking equal shares. Though France played an important part in the financial reconstruction of Poland, Romania, and Bulgaria (the stabilization loan of 1928), its role was limited by the need for outside (mainly American) participation and its 'financial weapon' was not very powerful.

[11] Orde, *British Policy and European Reconstruction*, 328. In terms of non-League lending during the 1920s, the USA was by far the largest source of all loans, both long- and short-term (55.2% and 26.2% respectively of loans extant in 1931). Ibid. 329.

The League loans, though they undoubtedly assisted financial stabilization, failed to bring about any major improvement in the borrowers' capacity to meet their long-range obligations. The Austrians were unable to solve their basic problem, which stemmed from their weak trading position. Political obstacles were raised against every proposal for enlarging the Austrian market and expanding its regional trade. The future of the country remained highly problematic, and some both in Vienna and London spoke approvingly of *Anschluss*. The Hungarian situation initially looked more propitious. Its economic reserves were sufficient to secure the interest service and the amortization of the League of Nations loan. Much of the budget deficit was financed from internal resources; a policy of strict financial austerity was introduced, and enforced mainly at the expense of the urban middle classes. By the middle of 1925 the League's financial controller-general in Budapest, who ultimately proved to be little more than a statistical observer, could report that Hungary had not only balanced its budget but had produced a substantial surplus. Once financial stability and liquidity were established, foreign banking houses were willing and even eager to extend long-term loans to Hungarian enterprises and projects. Yet stabilization and the 'loan culture' that it spawned did not yield a permanent solution to the country's economic disabilities. The bulk of western loans to Hungary did not go to productive enterprises; 40 per cent of the long-term loans were used to service and amortize other loans, including pre-war debts. Renewed indebtedness and dependence on foreign capital left Hungary unprotected from the ravages of the depression. The inexpedient utilization of loan capital was not peculiar to Hungary. Most loans were short term and were used to cover budget deficits and interest charges, to repay previous borrowings, or to convert old debts into new ones. Some were spent on military equipment or channelled into public welfare schemes for political purposes. Relatively few encouraged industrial output. While loan credit assisted the consolidation of the existing regimes, it did nothing to discourage their economic particularism.

There is no doubt about the importance of international investment in eastern Europe during the 1920s and beyond, but there is some debate about its effects on the recipient states. Foreign investment was highly concentrated in the extractive and capital goods industries in Poland and Czechoslovakia, and in the oil industries of Romania (Britain was the dominant investor). Capital tended to go, moreover, to the largest companies in the most highly concentrated industries, that is, into mining and metallurgic companies in Czechoslovakia, Poland, and Yugoslavia, oil companies in Romania, and tobacco and sugar refining industries in Bulgaria, increasing their size and encouraging mergers and cartelization. As foreign investors favoured industries where they had similar or related enterprises elsewhere, investment, while encouraging industrialization, came to serve the interests of the capital-exporting countries rather than those of the recipient nations. Imbalances were created that were not to the latter's long-term advantage. Neither loans nor foreign participation in industry was sufficient to stimulate long-term economic growth and industrial development, nor did they create the domestic and foreign export markets necessary for sustained expansion. In financial terms, it was mainly British and French investment capital that replaced ex-enemy funds, though capital also came from the United States, Italy, Belgium, Holland, and Switzerland. The peace treaties offered special privileges to the victors that allowed them the opportunity to replace the Germans and Austrians who had dominated the financial life of the Danubian basin. The Entente powers were given most-favoured-nation treatment for the first five years after 1919 and special regulations strengthened the position of their investors. The 'nostrification' clause (Article 297 of the Versailles treaty) allowed the victors to acquire capital shares of Central Power nationals in enterprises within their borders, either as reparations or with just compensation. Czechoslovakia and Romania became the chief regional beneficiaries. The Czechs took over the branches of the pre-war Vienna banks in their country and, subsequently with capital to export, acquired shares in enterprises in Romania and Yugoslavia. The Romanians took over a considerable part of the substantial German and Hungarian holdings in their banks, mines, and industrial plants. In Yugoslavia, only modest acquisitions were made and the old concerns continued their activities under new names. In Poland, where the pool of private investors was small and lacking in initiative, the French, as well as others, capitalized on the situation.

In the troubled conditions of 1918–20 concession hunters acquired assets in return for exports or took advantage of strong currencies to purchase devalued shares. The French and British governments lent their active support to private concerns seeking east-central European securities, the former more interventionist than the latter, who used more indirect methods of persuasion. Both governments encouraged the purchase of equity capital in the Vienna and Prague banks, the former with their important pre-war links with the leading industrial firms of the old Habsburg monarchy and their contacts in the Balkans and Turkey. Approaches were sometimes made directly by Viennese and Czech bankers anxious to secure capital for new share options. Unusually, two banks, the Austrian Länderbank (which already had a sizeable French participation) and the Anglo-Austrian bank (where the Bank of England was among the bank's British creditors) were totally transformed into French and English banking institutions. The head-quarters of the Länderbank was moved to Paris and, under strong pressure from the Quai d'Orsay, was taken over by Paribas and renamed Banque des Pays de l'Europe Centrale, with Jules Cambon, a former French ambassador, as president. The bank, the fifth largest in Austria, was a savings rather than an investment bank and proved a disappointment both to the Quai d'Orsay and to its French investors. The Czech branches of the bank were turned into an autonomous concern with a continuing French presence. The Anglo–Austrian bank stayed in Vienna but came under the patronage of the Bank of England. After lengthy and difficult negotiations, a separate Anglo–Czech bank was established under almost complete British control. In time the British disposed of the Austrian branches of the Anglo–Austrian bank, but the Bank of England, with Treasury approval, indirectly became a shareholder in Rothschild's Credit-Anstalt, the only remaining important Viennese bank in the early 1930s. By that time, more than half of the shares of this giant holding company were held by foreigners and 40 per cent of its business was conducted outside Vienna. Such direct absorptions were exceptional. More gen-erally, foreign investors were encouraged to acquire participating shares in the joint-stock capital of the largest commercial banks and industrial companies of the successor states. It was common practice for the large commercial banks to borrow abroad and to channel the funds to industries in their own countries and elsewhere in south-east Europe. Some of the larger industrial firms sought credits directly from foreign banks or from issues floated on the New York or London markets on their behalf. Trusts were created in London and New York to hold portfolios of central European industrial shares. Western stock ownership in the commercial banks did not necessarily mean control or direction. As the Vienna banks grew less important, the other national banks gained in strength and expanded their hold over subsidiaries in their own countries. Many of the Prague banks remained in Czech hands. The highly prestigious Zivnostenska Banka in Prague, which had holdings outside Czechoslovakia, was exceptional in that it had no foreign capital at all. Hungarian banks continued to pursue their own national strategies despite international boards of directors.

The British established and maintained the leading investment pos-ition in the region; they were either the ranking or second ranking investor in almost every country with the exception of Poland. This investment, of course, represented only a small part of the British total. By 1930, 58 per cent of British investment was in the empire, 20.8 per cent in South America, 7.9 per cent in Europe, and 5.4 per cent in the

United States.[12] The percentage of total investment in Europe was much lower than either that of the French (60 per cent) or the Americans (30 per cent) who, in any case, were far more interested in Germany than in east-central Europe.[13] In terms of total value, French investment may have been slightly higher in the region than that of Britain. A good deal of French capital went into short-term ventures in London and New York, but France enjoyed the dominant investment position in Poland, maintained a strong presence in Czechoslovakia, and was a major player in Yugoslavia, Romania, and Bulgaria. As in the case of Britain, French trade did not follow investment despite hard bargaining with the Poles and the Czechs and demands for most-favoured-nation status. Even Italy, with a smaller investment of capital, was often more successful than France, as in Yugoslavia.

While both Entente powers were equally anxious to prevent the 'bolshevization' of the region or the revival of German economic predominance, each sought to create its own sphere of influence in the Danubian area. As early as 1922 the region was divided into two rival camps. The French plans for central and south-eastern Europe were highly ambitious. Officials in the Quai d'Orsay believed that, by building up French economic power in the region, France could extend its political influence and strengthen its barrier against both German and Russian expansion. The British goals were far less political, but the Foreign Office hoped that by creating a Danubian bloc consisting of Austria, Hungary, and Czechoslovakia, Britain might play a leading role in the stabilization of the region and secure a base for the expansion of investment and trade. More inclined than the French to let British traders and investors find their own way without government assistance, the Foreign Office concentrated its efforts on encouraging the recovery of Austria and Hungary and their integration with Czechoslovakia into a Danubian bloc.

Though the French had to abandon their far-reaching wartime plans for a vast economic, industrial, and commercial union in Europe under their direction, many politicians, officials, and some industrialists still looked to eastern Europe to secure the scarce raw materials, particularly coal and oil, that would enable the country to balance Germany's greater economic potential. This explains the particular interest that French officials took in the Saar coalfields, the mines of Upper Silesia, the mines and steel plants of Teschen, and the Galician and Romanian oilfields.

[12] Orde, *British Policy and European Reconstruction*, 327–8.
[13] Alice Teichova, *An Economic Background to Munich: International Business and Czecho-slovakia, 1918–1938* (Cambridge, 1974), 3. The Orde and Teichova figures differ somewhat; both are based on Royal Institute of International Affairs, *The Problem of International Investment* (London, New York, and Toronto, 1937).

The Quai d'Orsay took the initiative in persuading often reluctant French industrialists to invest in Polish metallurgy and mining projects and in Romanian oil. Politicians and officials in the Quai d'Orsay and Ministry of Finance thought that through loans and the acquisition of shares in the leading banks of Austria and Czechoslovakia, France could acquire a dominant influence in the economic life of the region where banks and industry were intimately linked. 'The *tentative* was not a normal and inevitable development of French capitalism,' Georges Soutou suggests, 'but a governmental and administrative attempt to modify the structure of the latter.'[14] The difficulty was that France lacked the financial resources to carry out its grand designs (the 'imperialism of the poor') and that, despite official encouragement, French bankers and industrialists pursued their own interests, often thwarting the Quai's broader and more long-range objectives. The French faced competition with the richer British and American investors and the resistance of the recipient states, which preferred multinational investment to exclusive French control. Extensive but dispersed investments did not lead to French domination of any single government or produce the blocs it wanted. Such investment could not be turned into political power.

The French started out with high hopes. Their troops were in occupation of Austria in 1919 and controlled all the railway lines to Vienna, the natural focus of early foreign competition. By gaining control of the great pre-war Vienna banks, the French hoped to move into the rest of central and south-east Europe, including the Balkans. In 1920, when Alexandre Millerand became premier and the extremely active Maurice Paléologue, the ex-ambassador to Russia, returned to the Quai d'Orsay as secretary-general, they seized on the idea of making Hungary rather than Austria the 'axis' of a politically reliable and economically integrated Danubian bloc under French control, despite an already established British position in Budapest. Political and economic talks were opened in Paris in March 1920 between the French, the Hungarians, and the managers of the important Schneider–Creusot company. In return for promises to back Hungary's demands for significant boundary changes in the still unsigned Treaty of Trianon, Paléologue won extensive concessions for the concern. The scheme aroused intense anger in London and Rome and produced high alarm in Prague and Belgrade. It faltered, in the first place, on political grounds, because of Hungarian demands for treaty revision which

---

[14] Georges Soutou, 'L'Impérialisme du pauvre: la politique économique du gouvernement français en Europe Centrale et Orientale de 1918 à 1929', *Relations Internationales*, 7 (1976), 220.

France could not really back, but also because of strong British objections at a time of considerable Anglo-French tension. By the summer of 1920 the French were in retreat, though conversations continued even after the Hungarians signed the Trianon treaty on 4 June 1920. These abortive commercial negotiations had important, if unintended, political consequences. They served to push Czechoslovakia, Yugoslavia, and Romania together in opposition to what was seen as a French attempt to establish its hegemony over the Danubian region through Hungary. The Czechoslovak–Yugoslav agreement was signed in Belgrade on 14 August 1920; Marshal Joffre was dispatched to Bucharest to block Beneš's effort to conclude a similar agreement with Romania. Both the British and the Italians welcomed the Prague counter-move as a means of checking the spread of French influence. It was only in the autumn of 1920, after Millerand became president and Paléologue was dropped and replaced as secretary-general by the experienced, influential, and imperturbable Philippe Berthelot, that the French shifted the centre of their activities from Budapest to Prague. Berthelot emerged as one of the foreign ministry's strongest supporters of the 'Little Entente'.

France's early ambitions were not sustained. Too often, quick profits were favoured over the kinds of development that would have created allies. It was mainly in Czechoslovakia that France's political and economic interests converged. Eugène Schneider, France's leading iron and steel producer and the president of the Comité des Forges, was in every way the exception to the rule in his involvement in eastern Europe, in the range and importance of his acquisitions, and in his close partnership with the Quai d'Orsay. Even while the peace negotiations were being conducted, discussions took place between Beneš, officials from the ministries of foreign affairs and finance, and the representatives of the Schneider company which led to the latter's acquisition of a majority stake in the Skoda armaments works. The latter became a huge combine, with mining, metallurgic, and engineering interests in Czechoslovakia and elsewhere in south-east Europe. Through its many subsidiaries and cartel arrangements, the Schneider–Creusot concern acquired an often controlling interest in Czechoslovakia's basic industries and an important voice in the banking and industrial enterprises of other states, such as Poland and Hungary. Through the Union Européenne Industrielle et Financière (UEIF), an investment company created by Schneider & Cie. and two other concerns, the Schneider group came to control a vast empire with a minimal outlay of capital. Schneider's activities constituted one of the few really successful moves in extending French power in central Europe. Partly because of the Czech base of so many of his concerns, however, even he found it difficult to integrate industries across national lines.

British goals in east-central Europe were less clearly defined; they had no security interests of the kind that shaped French policy. Official concerns were more narrowly economic than those of France, but this did not preclude interference in the political life of the Danubian states. The government wanted to prevent the spread of Bolshevism, and this was an important factor in the British commitment to the reconstruction of Austria and Hungary. The first British efforts to create a Danubian bloc began in Vienna, where everything possible was done to check the spread of French influence and to encourage the financial rehabilitation of the state. It soon became obvious that Austria would have great difficulty in recovering, and by 1922 hopes had faded that it could resume its pre-1914 banking and industrial role. There was a brief interval, between 1920 and 1921 when the Foreign Office looked to Prague to take the lead in creating the desired Danubian federation. There was considerable competition between the British ministers in Vienna, Prague, and Budapest, each anxious to make his respective capital the centre of British activity in the region. Increasingly, the Foreign Office and the Bank of England took the view that the Czechs were too anti-Hungarian and too favourable to the French to provide a reliable base for the extension of British influence. The pro-Hungarian faction in the Foreign Office prevailed, and, due in large measure to the efforts of the extraordinarily sympathetic and totally uncritical minister in Budapest, Sir Thomas Hohler (January 1920–May 1924), British influence there was maintained. Admittedly official support did not extend to Hungarian territorial revisionism. Austen Chamberlain, who became foreign secretary in November 1924, tried to dampen Hungarian hopes for territorial changes without openly admonishing the Bethlen government. British interest in Budapest soon faded, as it did in most of east-central Europe. It was clear before the middle of the decade that there was no way of achieving the 'ultimate solution for Eastern Europe', an economic federation, including the half-dozen countries in or near the Danube, freed of customs barriers. Whatever their support for Danubian economic co-operation, the British would not abandon their own most-favoured-nation status in any of the east-central European states. The establishment of the Little Entente and the French alliances with Poland (1921) and Czechoslovakia (1924) made it impossible for London to bridge the gap between former friends and foes or to counter the French political advantage. The Foreign Office grew tired of dealing with 'squabbling states' and their 'impossible leaders', and saw little reason to become involved in their tangled affairs and distasteful politics.

The German economic stake in eastern Europe remained of considerable importance at a time when its political position was weak. Once the key foreign investor in the Habsburg empire, Germany lost about 60 per cent of its pre-1914 investment in eastern Europe. Early German attempts to create new networks in Austria, Czechoslovakia, and Hungary failed mainly because of French opposition. It was only gradually that German industry began to re-establish itself in what had once been major markets; the ending of the Versailles restraints in 1925 provided a major boost that was quickly exploited. Co-operation between government, banks, and business was a major feature of post-war German policy well before the country regained its full economic sovereignty. Reforms introduced into the German foreign ministry after the war strengthened its commercial section, and important diplomatic posts, for the first time, were given to outsiders. The German economic initiatives were most successful in the Baltic, where the German government worked in the closest co-operation with financial and industrial circles as well as with the Baltic Germans. Provisional trade agreements with Latvia in 1920 and with Estonia and Lithuania in 1923 opened the way for German business. Conscious of the needs of East Prussia and the importance of exports for any resolution of the reparations question, the Germans were willing to compromise any outstanding differences in order to gain entry into the Baltic markets. German behaviour contrasted sharply with that of the British, who had played the key role in securing the independence of the Baltic states and were much favoured by their new governments. British importers and exporters, in a privileged position immediately after the war, began to lose interest when it became apparent that the republics would not become the 'springboard' to the supposedly rich markets of Russia.

The Germans made use of the German minority living in the cities of the Baltic states, above all in Riga, as the foreign ministry began its active campaign for settling disputes, mainly about reparations and questions relating to the Baltic Germans. By the end of 1921 German finance began to enter the area and trade soon followed. Germany soon surpassed Britain in exports to the Baltic and took the lead in the admittedly disappointing transit trade to Russia. The Ruhr crisis led to a redoubling of official efforts to conclude separate economic agreements with each of the Baltic countries and with Moscow. The Germans wanted an economic arrangement that would bring together Lithuania, Estonia, Latvia, and Russia and would leave Poland isolated. Their sustained efforts, assisted by Baltic worries about the growth of Polish–French influence in the region, began to pay important dividends. The British continued to be the principal importer of Baltic goods, mainly timber and agricultural products, but the money earned from Britain was spent in Germany. The Wilhelmstrasse (German foreign ministry) had to face considerable suspicion and Baltic governments continued to look to

London for the protection of their interests, but persistence brought success. The Rapallo treaty with Russia, it is true, proved a double-edged sword, useful in keeping Poland off balance but often an impediment to good relations with the Baltic republics. The German foreign ministry had to convince the Baltic states that Germany could provide a bridge to Moscow and would try to secure a Soviet commitment to their independence. An attempted communist coup in Estonia in 1924 made the German task no easier. There were also problems with Finland, Germanophile because of the military assistance given against the Bolsheviks in 1918 but strongly anti-communist. The Germans used their influence to help turn the Finns away from anti-Soviet Baltic alliance projects towards the more neutral Scandinavian countries.

TABLE 13. Baltic Trade with UK and Germany (% of total value)
(a) Exports

	Estonia		Latvia		Lithuania	
	UK	Germany	UK	Germany	UK	Germany
1920	45.2	3.9	67.5	1.2		
1921	39.6	3.9	35.6	17.9	27.1	51.0
1922	22.2	12.7	40.3	13.0	39.0	36.2
1923	34.1	10.8	46.3	7.6	26.9	43.3
1924	33.5	22.6	41.5	16.4	27.9	43.0
1925	25.0	31.2	34.6	22.6	24.2	50.7
1926	28.8	23.1	34.0	24.3	24.9	46.8
1927	31.4	29.8	34.0	26.4	24.8	51.5

(b) Imports

	Estonia		Latvia		Lithuania	
	UK	Germany	UK	Germany	UK	Germany
1920	26.2	29.9	20.7	18.6		72.0
1921	27.9	40.2	14.3	48.1	0.9	70.7
1922	14.9	54.7	18.7	42.6	1.8	78.0
1923	19.7	51.0	17.0	45.2	5.3	80.9
1924	14.0	36.6	16.2	39.0	8.1	62.6
1925	12.3	29.4	13.8	41.5	8.3	56.6
1926	12.1	29.1	9.9	39.9	7.9	53.8
1927	14.3	26.4	10.6	40.6	6.8	53.2

Source: M. Hinkkanen-Lievonen, British Trade and Enterprise in the Baltic States, 1919–1925 (Helsinki, 1984), 282–3.

The German economic success in the Baltic was paralleled by an expansion of trade in central Europe and the Balkans. Export totals throughout the 1920s were still well below 1913 levels, but the Germans staged an impressive comeback. The complementary structure of the economies of Germany and the eastern European states, as well as traditional networks of business contacts, opened possibilities not available to France. I. G. Farben, for example, began by using indigenous agent firms, which were gradually replaced by companies established under the laws of the host country. Its well-organized sales force and subsequent cartel arrangements meant that the company could market its chemical products in Austria and move from there into south-eastern Europe. The successor states became the third largest world market for the German chemical industry. The Germans needed raw materials and markets for their industrial goods; the eastern European states could supply the former and required the latter. In Poland and Czechoslovakia, but also in Romania and Yugoslavia, Germany was an important customer, in the first two cases the single most important customer outside eastern Europe. Many eastern European states (Yugoslavia, because of its trade with Italy, and Poland were exceptions) ran negative trade balances with the Weimar republic. The latter's positive balance, with fluctuations after 1925, stood in marked contrast to France's negative trade balance throughout the decade. In 1924 Germany took 43.2 per cent of Poland's exports and supplied 33.8 per cent of its imports. Apart from being Poland's most important trading partner, Germany was an important source of short-term credit. It was only during the tariff war that the overall volume of trade fell as Poland turned to the Scandinavian countries for substitute markets. Poland was in a special category; the lost lands of the east never vanished from the German political agenda. It was, after all, the question that had raised the deepest sense of betrayal when the peace terms became publicly known. The German government tried, without success, to use its economic power to win territorial concessions from the Poles when the Versailles treaty duty-free provisions and the Polish–German Upper Silesian free-trade agreements lapsed. In 1924 the introduction of temporary German quotas on imports from eastern Silesia seriously hurt the Polish coal miners, but the Poles rejected the new and unsatisfactory German terms of 1925 and a 'tariff war' between the two countries began. Under Foreign Minister Stresemann's aegis, Germany would change its tactics but not the pursuit of territorial revision.

The Germans were well aware of the value of trade in strengthening their political standing. Stresemann, in particular, argued that, in the absence of military forces, Germany's economic power was one of her most important assets in the return to great-power status. With the exception of Poland, the Germans were very cautious about using trade as a means of increasing their political influence in the capitals of the states concerned. While willing to support nationals in their commercial endeavours, Weimar governments generally refused to become involved in regional disputes and preferred a course of political neutrality. In the Baltic and in Czechoslovakia the Germans had every interest in the preservation of the independence of the new states and, though supporting links with German-speaking groups, used them mainly to encourage good relations and trade with Germany. For most, the primary interest was to re-establish former export positions; both the government and business considered south-east Europe to be their natural market. In the mid-1920s, there were some expressions of concern, and not just in Poland, that Germany's economic expansion in eastern Europe might lead to a revival of its *Mitteleuropa* ambitions and prove less desirable than was thought.

V

Given their size, domestic difficulties, jealousies, and conflicts, it was inevitable that the states of eastern Europe would remain vulnerable to the ambitions of the larger powers. Most governments, overwhelmed with the problems of state-building, could do little more than seek bilateral arrangements to settle commercial and territorial disputes with neighbours where they did not engage in acrimonious dispute. Two states—Poland, the largest of the successor states, and Czechoslovakia, the strongest economically—sought to protect themselves from future dangers through regional associations and alliances with France. The two countries became the most active diplomatic players in the region. But despite their common links to France, there was no real agreement between them. There were imponderables, such as background, temperament, and culture, that kept the two nations at loggerheads, quite apart from the geographically insignificant but fiercely contested territorial disputes and their differing attitudes towards the Soviet Union. As competitors for the leadership of the small states in eastern Europe, the Poles and Czechs surveyed the European scene from very different vantage points. Marshal Piłsudski thought that an enlarged Poland, supported by the French army, could defend itself against Germany and Russia, both of whom he regarded as equal and permanent threats to Polish independence. He dismissed the League of Nations as irrelevant, and after Germany's admission judged it inimical to Poland's interests. Edvard Beneš, who shaped Czech foreign policy almost single-handedly throughout the inter-war period, insisted that his country's security lay in the creation of a stable international environment and that Czechoslovakia should have no permanent enemies. He showed considerable confidence in the Geneva system and became one of its most recognizable figures.

Poland, because of its size, geography, and army, assumed that it could take a major role in organizing the states lying between Germany and Russia in order to defend its western and eastern frontiers. Its concerns extended into the Baltic and into the Balkans as well. Although from the time of the peace conference, Marshal Piłsudski believed that Poland would have to act on its own behalf to change the balance of power in eastern Europe, both his followers and opponents soon realized that the maintenance of the Polish frontiers would depend on French assistance. Successive Polish foreign ministers, whether on the left or right, had few alternative options. The Polish room for manoeuvre, despite the propensity of its ruling aristocratic elite to think in grandiose terms, was more limited than that of its strategically less vulnerable southern neighbour. Situated between two giants, Germany and Russia, it had to fear not only the expansionist policies of either but the possibility that the two pariahs of Europe would link arms, confronting Poland with the prospect of a new partition. Unfortunately, some Poles continued to harbour ambitions that far outstripped the country's means. Piłsudski's vision of a great central European federation consisting of a free Poland, Lithuania, Belorussia, and the Ukraine, strong enough to withstand enemies on both frontiers, had to be modified after the Polish–Soviet War of 1920–1. Nonetheless, the ideas of this charismatic soldier-statesmen provided a dangerous legacy for his successors, even after his temporary retirement from politics in 1922. The Treaty of Riga (1922) following the Polish–Soviet War left both sides dissatisfied. On the eastern frontier, clashes continued as the Russians took up the claims of the Soviet Ukrainian government to East Galicia. Ukrainian nationalists in the disputed territories fled to Czechoslovakia, where they found Prague sympathetic to their cause. Piłsudski's belief that neither the Soviet Union nor Czechoslovakia would survive in their existing forms encouraged false hopes. His coup in Vilna, intended to force the Lithuanians to accept either union or federation, made it difficult if not impossible to create the highly desirable Baltic combination that he sought. Neither Latvia nor Estonia would move without its neighbour. Instead of following a circumspect policy during the early years of the reborn Polish state, the Poles started out on a high and expensive road of expansion. During the 1920s Poland's military expenditure took almost 30 per cent of its national income.

Poland's geographic situation was the decisive factor in its foreign policy. No one in Warsaw needed instruction in the lessons of the past.

Its rebirth, however, after 123 years of division, engendered exaggerated views of future influence. Even when Piłsudski's federation ideas were abandoned, Polish statesmen still believed that their country could create and lead a central European grouping that would stand as a barrier to German and Soviet expansion. Poland was Europe's fifth largest country and sixth most populous state, but neither its political nor economic situation encouraged optimism about its future leadership role. The Polish–Soviet war deepened the quarrels between Piłsudski's followers and Dmowski's National Democrats and accentuated the differences between the parties of the left and right. The Polish constitution, adopted in March 1921 and framed by the National Democratic majority, was specifically aimed at curbing Piłsudski's power and was never accepted by his supporters. Poland's foreign secretaries, who followed each other in quick succession (ten between 1919 and 1925), found it difficult to carry through any consistent policy. Suffering from a protracted and paralysing process of depreciation until the American intervention of 1926–7, its governments were unable to deal with the rampant inflation. Its crippling lack of domestic capital made it particularly dependent on foreign investment for rational and sustained industrial growth; the French proved unable or unwilling to meet its needs.

The gap between Polish aspirations and resources was magnified by France's own security interests. The French viewed an enlarged Poland, a Polish–Czechoslovak alliance, and Polish adhesion to the Little Entente as the substitute for their lost Russian partnership. Few at the Quai d'Orsay questioned the importance of Polish assistance in containing Germany, but it was the defeat of General Wrangel and the collapse of French hopes for a White victory in Russia that opened the way for a Franco-Polish alliance. There were some doubts in Paris about the wisdom of an alliance that committed France to the defence of Poland's eastern as well as western borders. Marshal Foch argued that the continuing enmity between Poland and Russia would involve an unwilling France in their quarrels. Due to the efforts of Millerand and Piłsudski, the text of the Franco-Polish political and secret military convention was signed on 21 February 1921. It was an unequal partnership, and the Poles took umbrage at their client status. They had won the substance of their demands but at a high commercial price, including concessions in East Galicia and Upper Silesia and most-favoured-nation status for French exports. Briand, trying to win time in order to secure the revival of the 1919 British guarantee, and knowing of Lloyd George's anti-Polish sentiments, insisted that agreement had to be reached on the remaining troublesome economic issues before the political and military accords could come into operation. It was not until Poincaré took office that the economic agreements were signed and the alliance activated.

The political agreement was accompanied by a secret military convention providing for joint action in case of German aggression and French material and technical assistance in case of a Polish–Russian war. The French hoped that Poland would provide a defence against German revisionism and a barrier to the spread of Bolshevism; the Poles saw France as the protector of its independence and territorial integrity on both frontiers. Predictably, the new alliance was ill-received in London. The British did not look kindly on French attempts to spread their influence in central Europe and, particularly in moments of crisis, accused them of harbouring hegemonic designs. No French leader succeeded in modifying the veto on any British eastern guarantee; London's negative attitude complicated and made more difficult France's search for British support in the west.

Most French leaders considered Poland a valuable asset and ignored the possible liabilities of their new alliance. Whatever their doubts about the specific policies of their ally, they loyally supported the Poles even at the risk of quarrelling with Britain. It was due to French pressure on Lord Balfour, the former British foreign secretary, that the final division of Upper Silesia went in the Polish favour. Though French support for Warsaw during the Polish–Soviet war was far less vigorous than was publicly claimed, the Quai d'Orsay was undoubtedly relieved when the Poles checked the Russian advance and strongly backed Poland's subsequent diplomatic efforts to strengthen its position in the east. The French supported Polish efforts to create a northern pact in 1921 and again in March 1922, just before the Genoa conference, when the foreign ministers of Estonia, Latvia, Finland, and Poland, meeting in Warsaw, concluded a pact (never ratified by Finland) providing for political and economic co-operation as well as concerted action in case of an attack on any member. The Russians reacted by inviting the four participants to Riga (the Finns refused and sent an unofficial observer), and secured an accord calling for the recognition of the Soviet Union. The Riga meeting at the end of March was seen in Moscow as a successful check both to the overambitious Polish government and to its French patron. It was mainly the quarrels with Lithuania over Vilna that continued to frustrate Polish ambitions to create an anti-Soviet northern bloc.

The continuing disputes between Poland and Czechoslovakia made it particularly difficult to fulfil any dreams of building barriers against German and Russian expansion from the Baltic to the Black Sea. The French efforts to promote military co-operation between the two states were repeatedly checked by the two countries' territorial disputes and their very different attitudes towards Moscow. It may be that the French leadership, despite the earlier alliance with Poland, felt closer in spirit to the stolid Czechs than to the politically unstable and often rash and intransigent Poles, but they brought pressure on both governments in their vain attempt to secure agreement. It was in part French prodding that led Konstanty Skirmunt, one of Dmowski's collaborators, who became foreign minister in June 1921, to seek a rapprochement with Prague. The commercial and political treaties concluded in October and November 1921 were the closest the two countries came to an alliance. The Skirmunt–Beneš pact provided for mutual territorial guarantees and benevolent neutrality in case of war, including the transit of war materials. In a secret protocol Beneš offered limited diplomatic backing in East Galicia and support for international recognition of the Riga settlements in return for Polish backing against any attempt of the Habsburgs to reclaim the thrones of Austria or Hungary. The Polish claims on the border commune of Javorina, a tiny Tatra village of 400 inhabitants, and the old disputes over Teschen, Spiš, and Orava were left over for future discussion. The Sejm proved reluctant to ratify the agreement without these territorial concessions and, with the fall of Skirmunt after the Genoa conference and the beginning of a period of intense political strife in Warsaw, hopes for ratification faded. Beneš lost interest and turned his attention to the Little Entente.

The Poles took other steps to guard their position against Soviet Russia. They sought agreements with Hungary and Romania. These moves, much favoured by Piłsudski in 1920, had been checked when France abandoned its Hungarian plans and Beneš succeeded in winning Romanian support for his proposals for anti-Hungarian ententes. The Poles maintained their contacts with Budapest and refused to recognize the validity of the Treaty of Trianon, which had ceded Transylvania to Romania. There was more success with the Romanians. The shrewd and resourceful Romanian foreign minister, Take Ionescu, was determined to exploit his common borders with Poland and Czechoslovakia to win protection against both the Soviet Union and Hungary. He initially favoured an enlarged five-power alliance which would include France, Poland, Czechoslovakia, and Yugoslavia, but this met with opposition from both the Czechs and Poles, the latter preferring a separate regional bloc. Ionescu solved the Romanian security dilemma by concluding an alliance with Poland on 3 March 1921 and signing bilateral agreements with Czechoslovakia and Yugoslavia on 23 April and 7 June 1921 respectively. The Polish–Romanian pact, encouraged by France, provided for mutual assistance against an attack from the Soviet Union, and contained a secret protocol keeping open the possibility of enlargement, though this remained an unfulfilled gesture.

The success of Czechoslovak diplomacy depended largely on the adept stewardship of Dr Edvard Beneš, who never lost his grip on the direction of foreign policy throughout the entire period from 1919 to 1938, even when he was in political difficulties. Apart from consultations with President Masaryk, he took no counsel, revealed little about his intentions, and was probably happier in Geneva than in Prague. A calculating realist in foreign affairs, Beneš favoured a middle-of-the-road approach to diplomacy, relying on his negotiating abilities to find the way out of difficult, if not dangerous, situations. Beneš's advocacy of the *solution moyenne* was intended to underpin Czechoslovakia's role as an intermediary between France and Britain, bringing them together in the interest of preserving the peace settlements so advantageous to Czechoslovakia. The 'Grand Master of Compromise' put excessive reliance on what could be accomplished through personal diplomacy and cautious piloting. There were successes—the negotiation of the treaties with Yugoslavia and Romania and the alliance with France—but also failures which must be attributed, in part, to the foreign minister's ceaseless activities. One of the most striking was Beneš's inability to establish a good relationship with the British, who came to dislike and distrust him. Foreign Office officials shared Lord Curzon's belief that Beneš 'travels too much and talks too hard'.[15] His interminable journeying and sojourns in Geneva earned him the reputation in London of being the 'Jack Horner' of European diplomacy. Beneš was also partly responsible for the failure to conclude an agreement with Poland; the foreign minister rejected Polish advances on more than one occasion and blocked its admission into the Little Entente circle. Beneš viewed his Polish neighbour as the great troublemaker of the north and insisted that Polish policies were antagonizing Britain as well as Germany and Russia. He made little secret of his doubts about the permanence of Poland's German acquisitions. He thought that the Polish war with Russia and the occupation of East Galicia would permanently alienate the Soviet Union, which he viewed as a future market for the Czechs and a possible ally against German revisionism. Above all, Beneš feared that Anglo-French differences over Poland would weaken their joint defence of the status quo upon which the safety of Czechoslovakia rested.

Beneš rapidly emerged as the man of Geneva, six-times chairman of the League Council, president of the Assembly, and chairman and *rapporteur* of innumerable League committees. With French support, he took a directing role in the discussions of the 1923 Treaty of Mutual Assistance and, with the Greek representative, Nicolas Politis, in the drafting and mobilization of support for the Geneva Protocol in 1924.

[15] Quoted in Gábor Bátonyi, *Britain and Central Europe, 1918–1933* (Oxford, 1999), 183.

This again put him into opposition to the British, who objected to his 'pactomania' and his search for an enhanced League security role. Austen Chamberlain was particularly contemptuous of what he took to be Beneš's self-aggrandizement and strongly opposed his candidature for the post of secretary-general of the League in 1925. Even when Beneš's international reputation was at its height, his influence on European affairs was more illusory than real. League diplomacy was often little more than great-power diplomacy dressed in Wilsonian clothes, and the importance of the representatives from the small states, however active, was necessarily limited. Beneš, however, was not a naive optimist. Collective security was an insurance policy for the maintenance of the status quo and a means of protecting the interests of the states most at risk from revisionism. It was a commentary on the limits of small-power diplomacy that Beneš's supposedly highly rational and scientific policies were no more successful than those of the 'romantic' Poles, and that neither had any choice but to look to France for protection.

Czechoslovakia enjoyed greater political stability, more defensible borders, and far more impressive economic resources than its neighbour. The clashes between the Agrarian party coalition and the 'castle group' around Masaryk in Prague did not spill over into the international arena and made relatively little difference to Beneš as he held court in Geneva. Unlike Poland, Czechoslovakia enjoyed a speedy financial and economic recovery that enabled it to take an active part in the economic rehabilitation of the Danube basin. Despite Beneš's strong support for disarmament, his country became the leading small-arms manufacturer in Europe and a major competitor with the French and British in the export of heavy armour. Czechoslovakia's greatest advantage over Poland was geographic; the much smaller country was not squeezed between two great dissatisfied powers. In the 1920s, though Germany remained a future threat, Berlin showed only limited interest in the Sudeten Germans and had no territorial disputes with Czechoslovakia. Strongly anti-Bolshevik at home, Beneš was far less Russophobic than the Polish or Romanian leaders and thought that economic co-operation with Moscow was both possible and profitable. It was for these reasons that the Czechs believed they could afford a certain measure of detachment from the great-power rivalries in Europe.

The Czech leaders intended that Czechoslovakia should be the major player in the Danube basin. Beneš used the Hungarian danger and Millerand's abortive efforts in Budapest to approach Belgrade in the summer of 1920 and to conclude an alliance (14 August 1920) with Yugoslavia. The abortive attempts made by ex-King Charles in April and October 1921 to regain the Hungarian throne helped to strengthen the ties not only with the Yugoslavs but with Romania. Beneš made a great deal of the ex-king's second return in October, to the point of threatening a Czech–Yugoslav invasion of Hungary and resorting to partial mobilization. Even in the face of British and Italian anger, he managed to secure Allied support for the permanent banning of the entire Habsburg dynasty from the Hungarian throne. While the Romanians refused to mobilize their army and entertained some doubts about Beneš's extreme bellicosity, they gave their approval to the joint Czech–Yugoslav action. The bilateral agreements between Czechoslovakia and Yugoslavia (14 August 1920), Romania and Czechoslovakia (23 April 1921), and Romania and Yugoslavia (7 June 1921) constituted the basis of the Little Entente. The treaties were narrowly focused and specifically directed against Hungary. In their origins, they were not only anti-Hungarian but also anti-French. It was the change in France's position and her abandonment of Hungary in 1920 that proved critical for the Little Entente's future history. The Czechs were correspondingly cool towards the first French attempts to conclude an agreement with Prague. General Foch visited the Czech capital in 1921 to discuss the details of a political and military agreement, but neither Masaryk nor Beneš thought the time ripe. Even when Poincaré replaced Briand (who secretly favoured a Habsburg restoration in the interests of Danubian unity), Beneš, in the face of British hostility to the alliance, was still reluctant to conclude an agreement that was aimed solely at Germany or to turn the Little Entente into an anti-German military pact. He saw the grouping as a self-defence structure intended to keep the great powers out and to allow the three countries, individually small and isolated, the opportunity, in theory if not in practice, to speak with a single voice.

Nothing more than their common dislike of Hungary kept the three states together. Romania and Yugoslavia had more to fear from their respective enemies, Russia and Italy, than from Germany, which represented the greatest future danger to Czechoslovakia. Their treaty was also directed against Bulgaria with whom Czechoslovakia had no quarrel. The bilateral agreements had no economic basis; each country insisted on functioning as a separate economic unit and economic borders followed national lines. Nationalism triumphed over economic good sense. Each country looked for supporters outside of the Little Entente and concluded separate treaties. The Czechs, despite continuing suspicion of Vienna, did not rule out some form of understanding with Austria, whose continuing independence was of considerable importance to Prague. In January 1920 the Austrian chancellor visited the Czech capital; his country needed food and coal which he hoped the Czechs would provide. Three secret protocols for a political

and military alliance against Hungary were signed, though little economic relief for the Austrians followed. The Austrian quarrel with the
Hungarians over the small Burgenland strip and the return of the
Habsburg king to Hungary again brought the two states together. In
the Treaty of Lány, concluded in December 1921, the Austrians secured
financial assistance in return for assurances against the return of the
Habsburgs or an *Anschluss* with Germany. The agreement was welcomed by Romania and Yugoslavia, the latter anxious to re-establish
Serbia's pre-war commercial relations with Austria. The Czechs were
not overly anxious to move too close to their ex-rulers, while for their
part the Austrians had little interest in aligning themselves with the Little
Entente, which would compromise their neutrality and offend the
Germans. British pressure played its part in the Czech offer of financial
support to Austria in 1922. The German representative in Vienna,
noting the action, reported: 'the well-behaved Austrian child has received a *Zuckertüte* from its godfather...because it has obediently
shaken hands with its sister, Czechoslovakia, instead of reaching for
mother Germania's apron.'[16] At the 1922 Genoa conference neither
Romania nor Yugoslavia was willing to forego its liens on Austria's
assets so as to facilitate an international loan. Despite the Austrian prime
minister Johann Schober's hopes for Beneš's support, the latter defended
his allies. At the same meeting the Little Entente vetoed proposals,
supported by Italy and Hungary, that would have given substance to
the Porto Rosa recommendations and improved Austria's trading positions. Beneš preferred bilateral to multilateral trade agreements; the one
signed with Austria actually lowered tariffs on almost a third of the
products exchanged between the two countries. The Czechs feared that
any kind of economic integration in the region might lead to the
political federation they so strongly opposed.

Opportunities for joint action between Poland and Czechoslovakia
were repeatedly lost. The two countries failed to work together at
Genoa in 1922. The Poles wanted international recognition of their
Russian and Lithuanian borders and acceptance of their occupation of
eastern Galicia. Czechoslovakia and Yugoslavia, lacking contiguous
borders with the Soviet Union, were not disposed to sanction the
political recognition that such action might imply. The Romanians
were adamant that there should be no change in Russia's status without
recognition of their possession of Bessarabia. While the main Polish
interest in the Genoa conference was the recognition of its eastern

[16] Frank Hadler, 'The European Policy of Czechoslovakia on the Eve of the Genoa
Conference of 1922', in Fink, Frohn, and Heideking (eds.), *Genoa, Rapallo and European
Reconstruction in 1922*, 177.

frontier with Russia, Beneš was unwilling to go beyond some form of economic co-operation with Russia. At the March 1922 Little Entente meeting in Belgrade, while Beneš was shuttling between London and Paris promoting co-operation, the Poles, under Skirmunt's leadership, tried to promote an agreement with the Little Entente powers. On his return Beneš succeeded in burying the idea. Beneš, however, lost ground at the Genoa conference. Lloyd George blamed him for the failure of his rescue plans for the Austrian republic, and was annoyed at the Little Entente's continuing hostility to Hungary. Lloyd George's strong personal antipathy towards Beneš deeply upset Masaryk, who sought British backing to offset Prague's dependence on France. Beneš's chief success at Genoa was the commercial treaty concluded with Chicherin and signed in Prague on 5 June. It hardly compensated for the failure to keep 'one foot on each of two horses', as Beneš's policy towards France and Britain was described.[17]

The Poles, too, gained little at Genoa, and the Rapallo treaty was a real blow to their interests, bringing together their two most dangerous neighbours. They had failed to create a Baltic bloc or to negotiate an alliance with the Little Entente states and had upset the French by pursuing an independent line. Lloyd George, who welcomed Skirmunt's more conciliatory attitude towards Moscow, refused his request for a territorial guarantee of Poland. In the face of the German–Russian agreement, Skirmunt abandoned his efforts to get the eastern boundaries acknowledged. The failure to bring back anything concrete from the conference weakened his standing at home. Piłsudski deplored Skirmunt's policies and his followers demanded that Poland take a more isolationist stand, equally detached from France and Britain. The Ponikowski–Skirmunt cabinet fell. The Sejm elections in November 1922, following fierce and bitter political conflicts, resulted in a stalemate between the parties of the left and right. Piłsudski refused to stand as a candidate for the presidency under the new constitution; the elected president was assassinated by a nationalist fanatic a week after his inauguration. It was only then that some degree of sanity returned to the Warsaw scene. The new left-wing cabinet, headed by General Władysław Sikorski, had a firmer grasp over the political situation than its predecessor and was further helped by Piłsudski's temporary retirement from politics. The new foreign minister, Count Aleksander Skrzyński, a highly experienced diplomat, was left to pilot Poland through the delicate waters of the next highly difficult year.

The French–Belgian–Italian occupation of the Ruhr was an anxious time for both Poland and Czechoslovakia. The Poles feared that the

---

[17] Quoted in Bátonyi, *Britain and Central Europe*, 190.

French action would drive Germany closer to Russia and that the Germans would seek compensation in the east for their losses in the Ruhr. At the same time, the Russians intervened to warn against Polish action should the communist revolution in Germany succeed. In line with Moscow's own ambiguous policies in Germany, Warsaw was cautioned against any aggressive moves in East Prussia or Upper Silesia. The Poles used the crisis to secure the international recognition of their borders that they failed to gain at Genoa. One day before the occupation of the Ruhr, the Lithuanians, courted by both the Germans and Russians, seized Memel, an autonomous, formerly German port. In these circumstances it was rightly believed in Warsaw that Britain would no longer oppose the Polish occupation of Riga. The Polish case for border recognition was further strengthened by Mussolini's favourable attitude, the consequence of an advantageous oil agreement with Warsaw. Enmeshed in the Ruhr difficulties and faced with both French and Italian demands for recognition, the British gave way. On 14 March 1923 the Conference of Ambassadors, acting in the name of the great powers, recognized the Polish–Lithuanian and Polish–Soviet frontiers. Warsaw refused to concede any form of autonomy to the East Galicians (Poles constituted only 35 per cent of the population) or offer any protection to the Ruthene minority.

Czechoslovakia, too, was placed in an awkward situation by the French Ruhr action. Its important economic ties with Germany made it vulnerable whatever the short-term economic advantages derived from the occupation. Both Masaryk and Beneš were privately critical of Poincaré's action, but their efforts at mediation were entirely futile. Faced with the breakdown of relations between Britain and France, which he considered the sine qua non of European stability, Beneš, with a seat on the Council following Czechoslovakia's election in 1923, turned his attention to the League. While the Ruhr crisis was at its height, he took the initiative in soliciting support for the Treaty of Mutual Assistance, only to be faced with a British veto. The movement towards an alliance with France gathered momentum. The French, through General Mittelhauser, the French chief of staff of the Czecho-slovak army, brought increasing pressure on the Prague government for an open military alliance. This time Beneš's reply was positive enough to encourage the French to work out the terms of an alliance which were dispatched to Prague in June 1923. There were differences between Masaryk and Beneš; the former was more reluctant to abandon the possibility of British friendship. All through the summer and autumn of 1923 he insisted in London that Czechoslovakia would maintain its independence from France and resist its pressure for a military conven-tion. Responding to Masaryk's objections to the alliance Beneš tried to delay matters, but the French were increasingly impatient. In mid-October Masaryk and Beneš made their much-discussed visits to Paris, Brussels, and London. The talks with the French were highly product-ive and pointed to the forthcoming alliance; those with the British were more satisfactory than usual, possibly because Masaryk was critical of Poincaré's Ruhr policy and Lord Curzon was assured that there would be no Czech military alliance with France. The Czech leaders might have preferred the existing informal arrangements, but the French were insistent.

Beneš's options were few. The Anglo-French entente had become a *mésentente*. The domestic difficulties in Germany, particularly in Bavaria, could easily have spilled over into Czechoslovakia. In early November 1923, to Beneš's considerable alarm, Crown Prince Wilhelm crossed the border into Germany. The British dismissed Beneš's exaggerated appre-hensions about a possible Hohenzollern restoration but the French and Belgians backed his futile demands that the German government expel the prince. The way was clear for the Masaryk–Beneš visit to Paris in December, when the Franco-Czech bargain was concluded, and on 25 January 1924 the treaty of alliance was signed. The agreement provided for consultations and concerted action in case of threats to the security of either country or to the existing peace settlement. Its terms, which included provisions against the restoration of the Habsburgs and Hohenzollerns, as well as against *Anschluss*, were intentionally loose. As Beneš insisted, no military convention was concluded but he agreed to an exchange of military letters, signed six days after the treaty of alliance, outlining the conditions for general-staff collaboration against aggression by any common enemy against either state and for plans to provide mutual assistance in case of need. It was a military alliance in everything but name. Unable to push the Czechs in the direction of Warsaw or to convince Beneš to enlarge the Little Entente to include Poland, France's eastern alliance system still lacked strategic credibility.

Beneš had returned to the oldest form of national self-defence, an alliance with a stronger military power. The British Foreign Office washed its hands of Prague; it was widely believed in London that a military alliance had been concluded. The partnership between the French and Czechs over security and disarmament questions in Geneva further alienated the British, despite the change in government in London and Ramsay MacDonald's debut as Labour prime minister and foreign secretary. The Italians, too, took umbrage at the new alliance, which they saw as a further extension of French influence in the Balkans. Nor were the Poles particularly pleased; they felt that the new alliance weakened their influence in Paris and would pull the French in the direction of Moscow. While repeatedly assured that no military convention had been concluded, the Polish leaders remained unconvinced.

The British and Italians insisted that there should be no parallel French treaties with Yugoslavia and Romania. There had been, in fact, a cautious response to Poincaré's advances in this direction. Alliances with France could bring more risks than benefits. The Yugoslavs preferred a bilateral settlement with Rome. On 27 January 1924 Mussolini concluded a friendship treaty with Belgrade. Despite their considerable shock, the French continued their talks in Belgrade. Though they wanted close and regular co-operation between the two general staffs, they were not prepared to back a Yugoslav attack on Bulgaria, with whom the French had no quarrels. The French negotiations with the Romanians also stalled; Bucharest wanted an agreement that would specifically guarantee the Romanian–Soviet frontier and Romania's right to Bessarabia. The Romanians wanted a pact along the lines of the Franco–Polish and Romanian–Polish agreements. The French were only interested in a military agreement aimed at Germany and were not prepared to sacrifice their freedom of manoeuvre in the east. The Romanians knew, too, that the British looked on French pact-making with extreme disfavour and were reluctant to antagonize London. The Czechs lost what little enthusiasm they had for such additional agreements. Still engaged in the Ruhr, the French were unwilling to take on new obligations in the Balkans and preferred to wait for a more auspicious moment. French weakness provided Mussolini with opportunities for action. A friendship treaty with Romania along the lines of the Italian–Yugoslav agreement was ruled out because of the Italian recognition of the Soviet Union in January 1924, but a move towards Prague might prove useful. Ignoring French warnings, Beneš arrived in Rome in April and concluded a commercial and a friendship treaty that committed the signatories to the defence of the status quo and the prevention of a Habsburg restoration. It was a very limited agreement and, on Beneš's side, probably little more than a warning to Paris that Czechoslovakia would continue to pursue an independent policy. There was no love lost between Beneš and Mussolini and neither trusted the other. In the spring of 1924 French diplomacy had suffered a double check, in the Ruhr and in the Danubian basin.

Contrary to every French hope, there was still no movement on the Czech–Polish front. Beneš's growing international reputation and his triumph in Paris grated on Polish nerves; the *commis voyageur* had a poor press in Warsaw. While the rightist parties were conciliatory, the Polish left, especially those circles close to Marshal Piłsudski, questioned the usefulness of any rapprochement with Prague. The Czechs, for their part, saw no advantage from taking on Poland's problems when France was moving towards the de facto recognition of the Soviet Union and the resolution of the Ruhr crisis on Anglo-American financial terms was opening dangerous questions of treaty revision. There were differences, too, in the Czech and Polish reactions to the electoral changes in France. Beneš had enthusiastically welcomed the changes of government both in London and Paris. He still hoped that the security issue might be solved through the League and threw his full weight behind the 1924 Geneva Protocol. The return of two left-wing governments held out the prospect of a reconstitution of the Anglo-French entente and would improve the chances of a Geneva success. In Warsaw, the victory of the Cartel des Gauches under Herriot set off warning bells of future difficulties. An adverse change in French priorities was widely anticipated. A powerful attack on the Polish National Democratic foreign secretary, Count Maurycy Zamoyski, for being too subservient to the French led to his resignation in July and his replacement by Count Skrzyński. Returning to the foreign ministry for a second time, Skrzyński tried to improve relations with Herriot's government and offered to start a dialogue with the Czechs. Neither initiative met with success. Franco-Polish co-operation was closely associated with the parties of the right, and Herriot's determination to re-establish the Anglo-French entente in the summer of 1924 boded ill for Warsaw. There were fears that Poland might have to pay the price for improved French relations with Germany. Conscious of the uneasiness in Warsaw, the Herriot government backed the new Franco-Polish consortium formed to extend the port at Gydnia and concluded a more equal trade agreement with Warsaw in December. The Czechs saw Skrzyński as Piłsudski's man and treated the new minister's attempt to re-open talks with considerable suspicion.

The early rumours of a western security pact unsettled both Poles and Czechs. It could be said the Skrzyński was panicked while Beneš remained philosophical. The Polish leaders distrusted Stresemann though they retained their faith in France. Many, and not just the Poles, regarded the German security plans as nothing more than the prelude to an attack on Poland and viewed Berlin's offer of an arbitration agreement as a device for airing Germany's frontier grievances. Efforts by Herriot and Chamberlain to calm the rising panic in Warsaw were only partly successful, though Skrzyński, recognizing the limited possibilities for Polish action, did his best to calm the Polish public. It was not just the Polish–German border that was at risk. The Poles had long been concerned with the possibility of a change in the French attitude towards Russia. After the conclusion of the Rapallo treaty during the Genoa conference, Marshal Foch had visited Warsaw hoping to win modifications of the 1921 alliance by excluding the Soviet Union from its provisions. The Poles refused to discuss what they considered a dangerous change. In 1924 the Herriot government, following the British example, and hoping to separate Russia from Germany, began its own negotiations with Moscow. On 24 October the Soviets won full diplomatic recognition and the restoration of normal diplomatic relations with France. Would this mean a French reassessment of the Franco–Polish pact? There were also problems in the east: the Poles were caught up in the manoeuvring between Moscow and Berlin as the Soviets tried to use the 'Polish card' to draw Stresemann away from the western powers. In December 1924, and again in October 1925, Chicherin visited both Warsaw and Berlin, offering the Poles a non-aggression pact and using the unlikely threat of a Franco–Polish–Soviet accord to bring the Germans closer to Russia. The Soviet non-aggression treaty, following the same form as used in the bilateral treaties with Turkey, Iran, and Afghanistan, bound the signatories not to intervene in any conflict with a third party as well as to agree not to attack each other. The Poles would not be wooed; they insisted that any treaty with Moscow would have to include the Baltic states and Finland. Chicherin had little satisfaction from Stresemann. The latter wanted to keep his eastern line open, not least for its salutary effects on London and Paris, but the western security accords were his first priority.

Beneš showed less open concern with the new stirrings in western Europe. When it became clear that the new British Conservative government that took office in November 1924 would reject the Protocol, Beneš sought further reassurance from France. He needed to know that Germany would not be given a free hand in the east nor be allowed to unite with Austria as continuing economic difficulties again raised the spectre of *Anschluss*. Not for the first or the last time, Beneš distinguished between the interests of Czechoslovakia and Poland, suggesting, privately at least, that some measure of Polish border revision was desirable and the inevitable consequence of the new security negotiations. As the talks proceeded the Czechs showed considerable interest in the German proposed arbitration pact, and made their own *démarche* without consulting Warsaw. Even during this period of high anxiety the two central European governments failed to work together. Despite all of Beneš's efforts to distinguish Czechoslovakia from Poland, both countries were treated identically by Stresemann, who refused to allow France to guarantee the German arbitration pacts. He was determined to restrict the participation of the central European powers to the very last stages of the Locarno talks when these pacts would be discussed. Poland and Czechoslovakia only entered the negotiations on 15 October 1925, the day before the initialling of the final Locarno agreements. In his intentionally overstated speech to the nationalists, Stresemann recalled the scene:

The psychology of the gentlemen was different. Mr. Beneš, that skilful politician, acted after he had not accomplished anything as if he had. He put on a big
smile and appeared to be happy. Mr. Skrzyński could not conceal his agitation. . . . Mr. Beneš and Mr. Skrzyński had to sit there waiting in the anteroom
until we let them in. That was the situation of the states that were previously
coddled because they were the servants of others and that were dropped in the
moment when it was believed that there could be an understanding with
Germany.[18]

VI

Small states live in the shadows of large ones. It was always clear that
German recovery would leave Poland and Czechoslovakia at risk and
that any agreement between Moscow and Berlin would pose a double
threat to the former. The only real alternative to seeking outside
assistance would have been the fulfilment of Piłsudki's plans for a central
European federation, but his dream had no reality once the Soviet
Union survived foreign intervention and the Polish attack. Each of
the two central European powers tried to create regional pacts; either
these failed to materialize or provided, as in the case of the Little
Entente, only minimal protection from a non-existent regional danger.
If Warsaw and Prague had buried their differences and concluded an
alliance they would have been in a stronger position, not only towards
their enemies but with regard to France. Together they could have
exerted far more pressure on Paris than they could do individually.
Only France could provide the protection they needed. Both Poland
and Czechoslovakia would have welcomed British underwriting, but
London was uninterested, if not hostile. The Italians had their own
revisionist scenario: Mussolini's ambitions centred on Albania and
Yugoslavia, but his flirtations with the Hungarians and interests in the
Danube basin and the Balkans made him an unsuitable friend. The Poles
and the Czechs faced the daunting possibility that in safeguarding its
western borders France might compromise the security interests of its
two eastern allies. Their fears were for the future. France still had the
margin of military power that provided safety, but the future evacuation
of the Rhineland and the failure to create an eastern Locarno would
leave them at risk. Their statesmen were forced to play a careful game; it
hardly helped that they could not settle the differences between themselves. Concentrating on the inter-relationships between the two major

[18] Gustav Stresemann, *Vermächtnis. Der Nachlass in drei Bänden*, ed. Henry Bernhard, 3
vols. (Berlin, 1933), ii. 233–4. For the whole speech, see Austwärtiges Amt, *Akten zur
deutschen auswärtigen Politik, 1918–1945, series B (1925–1933)*, vol. I, *Dezember 1925–Juli
1926* (Göttingen, 1966), App. II, 727–53.

peripheral players and the great powers does scant justice to the complexities of eastern European relations during the 1920s. Yet Poland and Czechoslovakia, more than any of the other regional states, held the key to any diplomatic refiguration of east-central Europe. From the perspective of western Europe, all these states, whether old or new, were only secondary actors in the process of European stabilization.

Books

General

BEREND, I. T., *The Crisis Zone of Europe: An Interpretation of East-Central European History in the First Half of the Twentieth Century* (Cambridge, 1986).

CRAMPTON, R. J., *Eastern Europe in the Twentieth Century* (London, 1994).

GLATZ, FERENC (ed.), *Modern Age—Modern Historian: In Memoriam, György Ránki (1930–1988)* (Budapest, 1990).

GLENNY, MISHA, *The Balkans, 1804–1999: Nationalism, War and the Great Powers* (London, 1999).

JOHNSON, LONNIE R., *Central Europe: Enemies, Neighbours, Friends* (Oxford, 1996).

MACARTNEY, C. A. and PALMER, A. W., *Independent Eastern Europe: A History* (London, 1962).

PALMER, ALAN, *The Lands Between: A History of East-Central Europe Since the Congress of Vienna* (London, 1970).

PAVLOWITCH, STEVAN K., *A History of the Balkans, 1804–1945* (London, 1999).

POLONSKY, ANTONY, *The Little Dictators: The History of Eastern Europe Since 1918* (London, 1975).

ROTHSCHILD, JOSEPH, *East Central Europe Between the Two World Wars* (Seattle, 1974).

SCHMIDT-HARTMANN, E. and WINTERS, S. B. (eds.), *Grossbritannien, die USA und die böhmischen Länder, 1848–1938. Vorträge der Tagung des Collegium Carolinum in Bad Wiessee vom 2. bis 6. November, 1988* (Munich, 1991).

Politics

ÁDÁM, MAGDA, *The Little Entente and Europe, 1920–1929* (Budapest, 1993).

AYÇOBERRY, PIERRE, BLED, JEAN-PAUL, and HUNYADI, ISTVAN, *Les Conséquences des traités de paix de 1919–1920 en Europe centrale et sud-orientale* (Strasburg, 1987).

BÁTONYI, GÁBOR, *Britain and Central Europe, 1918–1933* (Oxford, 1999).

BERGHAHN, V. R. and KITCHEN, M. (eds.), *Germany in the Age of Total War* (London, 1981).

BOIA, EUGENE, *Romania's Diplomatic Relations With Yugoslavia in the Interwar Period, 1919–1941* (Boulder, Col., 1993).

CAMPBELL, FENTON GREGORY, *Confrontation in Central Europe: Weimar Germany and Czechoslovakia* (Chicago and London, 1975).

CAMPUS, ELIZA, *The Little Entente and the Balkan Alliance* (Bucharest, 1978).

CIENCIALA, ANNA M. and KOMARNICKI, TITUS, *From Versailles to Locarno: Keys to Polish Foreign Policy, 1919–1925* (Lawrence, Ka., 1984).

DAVIES, NORMAN, *God's Playground: A History of Poland*. Vol. 2: *1795 to the Present* (Oxford, 1981).

DEBICKI, R., *Foreign Policy of Poland, 1919–39* (London, 1963).

DRAGNICH, ALEX N., *The First Yugoslavia: Search For a Viable Political System* (Stanford, Cal., 1983).

FRANKE, REINER, *London und Prag: Materialien zum Problem eines multinationalen Nationalstaates, 1919–1938* (Munich, 1981).

GROMADA, THADDEUS V. (ed.), *Essays on Poland's Foreign Policy, 1918–1939* (New York, 1970). Esp. the chapter by Piotr Wandycz.

HIDEN, JOHN, *The Baltic States and Weimar Ostpolitik* (Cambridge, 1987).

—— *Germany and Europe, 1919–1939*, 2nd edn. (Harlow and New York, 1993).

—— and LOIT, ALEKSANDER (eds.), *The Baltic in International Relations Between the Two World Wars: Symposium Organised by the Centre for Baltic Studies, November 11–13, 1986, University of Stockholm* (Stockholm, 1988).

—— and SALMON, PATRICK, *The Baltic Nations and Europe: Estonia, Latvia and Lithuania in the Twentieth Century*, rev. edn. (London, 1994).

HOVI, K., *Interessensphären im Baltikum: Finnland im Rahmen der Ostpolitik Polens, 1919–1922* (Helsinki, 1984).

KARSKI, JAN, *The Great Powers and Poland, 1919–1945: From Versailles to Yalta* (Lanham, Md., 1985).

KLIMEK, ANTONÍN, *Diplomacy at the Crossroads of Europe: Czechoslovak Foreign Policy, 1918–1938*, trans. Libor Trejdl (Prague, 1989).

KORBEL, JOSEF, *Poland Between East and West: Soviet and German Diplomacy Toward Poland, 1919–1933* (Princeton, 1963).

LATAWSKI, PAUL (ed.), *The Reconstruction of Poland, 1914–1923* (London, 1992).

LOW, ALFRED, *The Anschluss Movement 1918–1919 and the Paris Peace Conference* (Philadelphia, 1974).

—— *The Anschluss Movement, 1931–1938 and the Great Powers* (New York, 1985). See chapters 1 and 2.

LUZA, RADOMIR and MAMATEY, VICTOR S. (eds.), *A History of the Czechoslovak Republic, 1918–1948* (Princeton, 1973). Esp. chapters by J. W. Bruegel, Zora P. Pryor, and Piotr Wandycz.

MORISON, JOHN (ed.), *Eastern Europe and the West: Selected Papers from the Fourth World Congress for Soviet and East European Studies, Harrogate, 1990* (Basingstoke, 1992). Esp. chapter by Thomas C. Sakmyster.

NAGY, ZSUZSA L., *The United States and the Danubian Basin, 1919–1939* (Budapest, 1975).

OLIVOVÁ, VERA, *The Doomed Democracy: Czechoslovakia in a Disrupted Europe, 1914–38*, trans. George Theiner (London, 1972).

Recherches sur la France et le problème des nationalités pendant la Première Guerre Mondiale: Pologne, Ukraine, Lithuanie, Travaux du Centre Histoire des relations internationales et de l'Europe au XXe siècle de l'Université de Paris IV (Paris, 1995).

RECKER, MARIE-LUISE (ed.), *Von der Konkurrenz zur Rivalität: das britisch-deutsche Verhältnis in den Ländern der europaischen Peripherie, 1919–1939* (Stuttgart, 1986).

RIEKHOFF, HARRALD VAN, *German–Polish Relations, 1918–1933* (Baltimore, 1971).

SANDU, TRAIAN, *Le Système de sécurité français en Europe centre-orientale: L'exemple roumain, 1919–1933* (Paris, 1999).

SCHOTT, BASTIAN, *Nation oder Staat?: Deutschland und der Minderheitenschutz: zur Völkerbundspolitik der Stresemann-Ära* (Marburg and Lahn, 1988).

STONE, NORMAN and STROUHAL, EDUARD (eds.), *Czechoslovakia: Crossroads and Crises, 1918–88* (Basingstoke, 1989).

SUPPAN, ARNOLD, *Jugoslawien und Österreich 1918–1939: bilaterale Aussenpolitik im europäischen Umfeld* (Vienna and Munich, 1996).

TEICHOVA, ALICE, *Kleinstaaten im Spannungsfeld der Grossmächte: Wirtschaft und Politik in Mittel-vund Südosteuropa in der Zwischenkriegszeit* (Munich, 1988).

Economics

ALDCROFT, DEREK H. and MOREWOOD, STEVEN, *Economic Change in Eastern Europe Since 1918* (Aldershot, 1995).

BEREND, IVAN T. and RANKI, GYÖRGI, *Economic Development in East-Central Europe in the 19th and 20th Centuries* (New York and London, 1974).

COTTRELL, PHILIP L. and TEICHOVA, ALICE (eds.), *International Business and Central Europe, 1918–1939* (Leicester, 1983).

HINKKANEN-LIEVONEN, MERJA-LIISA, *British Trade and Enterprise With the Baltic States, 1919–1925* (Helsinki, 1984).

HOLTFRERICH, CARL-LUDWIG, REIS, JAIME, and TONIOLO, GIANNI, *The Emergence of Modern Central Banking from 1918 to the Present* (Aldershot, 1999).

JAMES, HAROLD, KINDGREN, HAKAN, and TEICHOVA, ALICE, (eds.), *The Role of Banks in the Interwar Economy* (Cambridge, 1991).

KASER, M. C. and RADICE, E. A. (eds.), *The Economic History of Eastern Europe, 1919–1975*, 3 vols. (Oxford, 1985). Esp. chapter by Teichova in vol. 1.

MATIS, HERBERT and TEICHOVA, ALICE (eds.), *Österreich und die Tschechoslowakei, 1918–1938: die wirtschaftliche Neuordnung in Zentraleuropa der Zwischenkriegs-zeit* (Vienna, Cologne, and Weimar, 1996).

RÁNKI, GYÖRGY, *Economy and Foreign Policy: The Struggle of the Great Powers for Hegemony in the Danube Valley, 1919–1939* (Boulder, Col. and New York, 1983).

RECKER, M. L., *England und der Donauraum, 1919–1929: Probleme einer europäischen Nachkriegsordnung* (Stuttgart, 1976).

SPAULDING, ROBERT MARK, *Osthandel und Ostpolitik: German Foreign Trade Policies in Eastern Europe from Bismarck to Adenauer* (Providence, RI, 1997).

TEICHOVA, ALICE, *An Economic Background to Munich, International Business and Czechoslovakia, 1918–1939* (London, 1975).

—— (ed.), *Österreich und die Tschechoslowakei 1918–1938: die wirtschaftliche Neuordnung in Zentraleuropa in der Zwischenkriegszeit* (Vienna and Cologne, 1996).

Articles

Politics

ÁDÁM, MAGDA, 'France and Hungary at the Beginning of the 1920s', in Béla Király, Peter Pastor, and Ivan Sanders (eds.), *War and Society in East Central Europe*. Vol. 6.: *Essays on World War I: Total War and Peacemaking, a Case Study on Trianon* (New York, 1982).

BARIÉTY, JACQUES, ' "L'Accord révisionniste" franco-hongrois de 1920. Histoire d'un mythe', in *Les Conséquences des traités de paix de 1919–1920 en Europe centrale et sud orientale. Colloque de Strasbourg 24–26 mai 1984* (Strasburg, 1987).

CORNWALL, MARK, 'A Fluctuating Barometer: British Diplomatic Views of the Czech–German Relationship in Czechoslovakia', in Bad Wiesseer Tagungen des Collegium Carolinum, *Great Britain, the United States and the Bohemian Lands, 1848–1938* (Munich, 1991).

GASIOROWSKI, ZYGMUNT J., 'Polish–Czechoslovak Relations, 1918–1922', *Slavonic and East European Review*, 35 (1956–7).

—— 'Polish–Czechoslovak Relations, 1922–1926', *Slavonic and East European Review*, 35 (1956–7).

—— 'Stresemann and Poland Before Locarno', *Journal of Central European Affairs*, 18 (1958).

HANAK, HARRY, 'British Attitudes to Masaryk', in id. (ed.), *T. G. Masaryk, 1850–1937*. Vol. 3: *Statesman and Cultural Force* (London, 1990).

HIDEN, JOHN, 'The Weimar Republic and the Problem of the Auslandsdeutsche', *Journal of Contemporary History*, 12 (1977).

—— 'Weimar Revisionism and Baltic Security', in id. and A. Loit (eds.), *The Baltic in International Relations Between the Two World Wars* (Uppsala, 1988).

HOVI, KARLEVO, 'The French Alliance Policy, 1917–1927: A Change of Mentality', in J. Hiden and A. Loit (eds.), *Contact or Isolation? Soviet–Western Relations in the Interwar Period. Symposium Organised by the Center of Baltic Studies, October 12–14, 1989, University of Stockholm* (Stockholm, 1991).

MICHEL, BERNARD, 'Edouard Beneš et la France, 1918–1938', in L. Schelbert and Nick Ceh (eds.), *Essays in Russian and East European History: Festschrift in Honour of Edward C. Thaden* (Boulder, Col., 1995).

ORDE, ANNE, 'France and Hungary in 1920: Revisionism and Railways', *Journal of Contemporary History*, 15 (1980).

SAKMYSTER, THOMAS, 'István Bethlen and Hungarian Foreign Policy, 1921–1931', *Canadian–American Review of Hungarian Studies*, 5: 2 (1978).

ZINNER, P. E., 'Czechoslovakia: The Diplomacy of Eduard Beneš', in G. A. Craig and F. Gilbert (eds.), *Diplomats, 1919–39* (Princeton, 1953).

Economics

NÖTEL, RUDOLF, 'Money, Banking and Industry in Interwar Austria and Hungary', *Journal of European Economic History*, 13: 2 (1984).

ORDE, ANNE, 'Baring Brothers, the Bank of England, the British Government and the Czechoslovak State Loan of 1922', *English Historical Review*, 106 (1991).

PÉTERI, GYÖRGY, 'Tying Up a Loose End: British Foreign Economic Strategy in 1924: The Hungarian Stabilisation', *Acta Historica Academiae Scientiarum Hungaricae*, 30: 3/4 (1984).

—— 'Central Bank Diplomacy: Montagu Norman and Central Europe's Monetary Reconstruction after World War I', *Contemporary European History*, 1: 3 (1992).

SHISHKIN, VALERI A., 'The External Factor in the Country's Socio-economic Development', *Soviet Studies in History*, 28 (1989).

TEICHOVA, ALICE, 'Versailles and the Expansion of the Bank of England into Central Europe', in Norbert Horn and Jürgen Kocka (eds.), *Recht und Entwicklung der Großunternehmen im 19. und frühen 20. Jahrhundert: Wirtschafts-, sozial-und rechtshistorische Untersuchungen zur Industrialisierung in Deutschland, Frankreich, England und den USA* (Göttingen, 1979).

—— 'Structural Change and Industrialisation in Interwar Central-east Europe', in P. Bairoch and M. Lévy-Leboyer (eds.), *Disparities in Economic Development Since the Industrial Revolution* (London, 1981).

—— 'Industry', in M. C. Kaser and E. A. Radice (eds.), *The Economic History of Eastern Europe 1919–1975*. Vol. 1: *Economic Structure and Performance Between the Two Wars* (Oxford, 1985).

—— 'East-central and South-east Europe, 1919–39', in P. Mathias and S. Pollard (eds.), *The Cambridge Economic History of Europe*. Vol. 8: *The Industrial Economies: The Development of Economic and Social Policies* (Cambridge, 1989).

—— 'Eastern Europe in Transition: Economic Development During the Interwar and Postwar Period', in id. (ed.), *Central Europe in the Twentieth Century: An Economic History Perspective* (Aldershot, 1997).

Theses

LOJKO, MIKLOS, 'Britain and Central Europe, 1919–1925', Ph.D. thesis, Cambridge University (2001).

PROTHEROE, GERALD JAMES, 'Watching and Observing: Sir George Clerk in Central Europe, 1919–1926', Ph.D. thesis, University of London (1999).

6

Revolution from the Right: Italy, 1919–1925

I

Italy's pre-war leaders had indulged in expansionist dreams in Africa, in the 'unredeemed lands' along the north-east frontier of the Habsburg empire, and in Albania. Having entered the war to give reality to these ambitions, and failing to secure the promised fruits of victory, they not only harboured these previous designs but added additional items to the old imperial menu. There were elements of continuity between the irredentist and expansionist goals of liberal Italy and Mussolini's fascist state, but the Duce added a new ideological framework to the quest for greatness that shaped the state's future development. Powerful domestic constraints, political and economic turmoil before 1922, and political uncertainties, internal opposition, and lack of resources after Mussolini's 'march on Rome' blocked further improvements in Italy's international position. It was not until the mid-1920s that Mussolini started to exploit the unsettled European situation in order to create the 'new Italy' and the 'new Italian' which would confirm his power and assure the triumph of fascism. Success proved elusive and rhetoric proved louder than action. As long as Italy remained 'the least of the great powers', Mussolini's militarist posturings and diplomatic manoeuvrings roused few apprehensions in European ruling circles. Western statesmen treated him with condescension, sometimes mixed with a degree of admiration, which acted as a spur to his aggressive intentions. In sharp contrast with their attitude towards the Soviet Union, they sought Mussolini's participation in the European reconstruction process and minimized the danger of his radical nationalist revolution.

Italy's leaders found themselves in an ambiguous situation after the conclusion of the peace treaties. They had everything to gain from the maintenance of the Versailles settlement; they had won the Brenner frontier, the South Tyrol, and a promised share of reparations. The independence of Austria was regarded as a guarantee of Italian security against future German revisionism. Yet nationalists and liberals alike had

Map 13. Fascist Italy in the 1920s

wider ambitions in the Adriatic and Mediterranean, in the Middle East and Asia Minor, in the Caucasus and in East Africa. Such irredentist and expansionist goals meant that Italy was a revisionist power, hoping for changes in the peace treaties and for the fulfilment of promises made during the war. The combination of support for Versailles and hopes for revision set the parameters of Italy's immediate post-war agenda. Future gains were somewhat problematic. The inept and damaging diplomacy of the Italian peacemakers at Paris confirmed the Allied view that the 'sturdy beggar' of the conference had demanded far more than she deserved. Yet while continuing to treat Italy as a second-class member of the great-power circle, the victors needed Italian co-operation for the restoration of order and stability in Europe and for the settlement of their extra-European problems. France, sharing a frontier with Italy, was more directly engaged than Britain in the search for a viable diplomatic relationship with Rome. At the peace conference Clemenceau, Poincaré, and Camille Barrère, the long-serving French ambassador in Rome, failed to agree on a common approach to the Italian problem. The fears that a dissatisfied Italy would be driven into the arms of Germany and that the left would take power if Orlando and Sonnino returned empty-handed had to be balanced against the need to conciliate Woodrow Wilson, Italy's chief adversary. Clemenceau's pro-Wilson and anti-Italian attitudes prevailed, but the value of co-operation with Rome against German revisionism had to be weighed against the distaste for Italian expansion into areas marked out for the expansion of French influence. The Italians came to blame the French for the frustration of their territorial ambitions both in Europe and in Africa.

The Franco-Italian contest for political influence and economic expansion was at its most intense in south-east and central Europe as Italy attempted to extend its gains and influence in Belgrade, Vienna, and Budapest. Sonnino's proposal in 1919, as a counterweight to France, for a rapprochement between Romania and Hungary under Italian auspices to check Yugoslavia, failed when the Romanians took matters into their own hands and occupied Budapest. In 1920 he suggested to foreign minister Count Sforza that the Italians conclude an alliance with the ex-enemy nations to secure what had been lost at the peace conference. It was an idea that appealed to the nationalists and to Benito Mussolini on the eve of his elevation to power. As before 1914, Italian industrialists were far more interested in eastern Europe, the Balkans, and Anatolia than in the 'oases of North Africa or the far-off hills of Ethiopia'. They sought secure and reliable sources of raw materials for the war-expanded industrial sector: imports of wheat from Romania and the Ukraine, oil from Romania and the Caucasus, and charcoal from Asia Minor, which were to be paid for by exports of port equipment, railways, and modern machinery. Above all, Italy required oil if the country was to make the transition from a coal-based economy almost entirely dependent upon imports from Britain. The peace negotiators and the industrialists were equally enthusiastic about Lloyd George's offer of a protectorate over the Caucasus, with its promise of access to the Baku oilfields. When these illusions had to be abandoned, the focus shifted to the Romanian oilfields, already pre-empted by the unsympathetic Allies and Americans. Though their wider ambitions were unfulfilled, the Italians were able to establish an important investment and trading presence in the former lands of the Dual Monarchy and in the Balkans, including major stakes in several Hungarian banks, a presence in the Romanian, Yugoslav, and Hungarian timber industries, and shares in the Polish textile industry. Italian trade with Bulgaria, Hungary, Romania, and Yugoslavia rapidly increased and its dominant trading position in Yugoslavia, notwithstanding political conflicts, was maintained until 1935. Italian investors exploited the Anglo-French rivalry in eastern Europe, often aligning with the British against the French with some degree of success.

Chaotic domestic conditions in Italy dominated the short-lived post-war ministries (six between 1919 and 1922) and left little time or inclination for foreign adventures. Operating in an atmosphere of political turmoil and social confrontation in the cities and countryside, foreign ministers followed the path of strategic retreat without abandoning their irredentist goals. Even Camille Barrère, the long-serving French ambassador to Rome (1898–1924), who took a highly alarmist view of Italian Francophobia in 1919–20, was more concerned by the inability of the Rome governments to deal with the agitation of the socialists, communists, and anarchists than with the dangers of Italian expansionism. For among all the victor nations, Italy proved the least able to deal with the political and societal disruptions of the war. Apart from the Soviet Union, it was the first nation to face the kinds of civil

TABLE 14. Balance of Italian Trade with South-East Europe 1920–1924 ($m.)

	Albania	Bulgaria	Czechoslovakia	Hungary	Poland	Romania	Yugoslavia
1920	−3.2	−9.5	4.2	−12.4		−34.5	−44.5
1921	−3.8	−5.3	2.3	−5.7		−25.5	−11.2
1922	−2.1	0.3	14.0	−0.3	−4.2	4.7	1.1
1923	−3.6	−4.8		1.4	−4.9	−3.2	15.2
1924	−3.0	−3.7	−7.8	−3.0	−22.2	−10.4	23.2

Source: Adapted from M. Kaser and E. A. Radice (eds.), *The Economic History of Eastern Europe 1919–1975* (Oxford, 1985), i. 523–9.

discord that would destroy the liberal state and ultimately help to undermine the European international order. Nationalist rhetoric would have been less damaging to the political fabric of the country had the transition from war to peace been less tumultuous. It was a combination of the political and economic dislocations of the war and the incompetence and cowardice of the Italian ruling elite that brought about the collapse of liberal Italy.

The war had inflicted a terrible cost on the country. Instead of the short war that Italian politicians hoped would unify the nation and give Italy the world status that they sought, the country became mired in a lengthy and murderous struggle that brought inadequate rewards. The Italians lost 680,000 men, and another 30,000 died from wounds or war injuries. The financial costs of the years 1914–19 came to about 26.5 billion lire, with another 10.8 billion lire in war-related expenses that would become due between 1919 and 1924.[1] The Italian government was saddled with a foreign debt of $2.96 billion, owed to the United States, Britain, and France, a heavy burden for a country with a low pre-war national income. Like other European countries, Italy suffered a severe post-war inflation. The value of the lira plummeted, prices rose, and wages fell. Industrial production was cut, export industries contracted, and, with demobilization, unemployment swelled. Italian emigration figures rose from 253,200 in 1919 to 641,600 in 1920, but the traditional escape valve was closed when the Americans imposed an annual quota of 40,000 emigrants in 1921 and instituted a restrictive immigration policy. In the cities, workers organized themselves to secure higher wages; unprecedented large-scale strikes took place, marked by violence and workers' deaths. Where the workers secured wage increases, their victories fanned the resentment of those dependent on fixed incomes whose salaries lagged far behind the rising cost of living. The strikes frightened not only factory-owners but other sections of the middle class, who were convinced that the government was incapable of controlling the situation and anticipated with horror the spread of 'Bolshevism'. The Socialist party added fuel to the flames by issuing highly inflammatory class-war propaganda suggesting that revolution was imminent. The countryside, too, was in turmoil, convulsed by land seizures and by struggles between those who benefited from the war and those left out, including landless labourers returning from the army. During 1919–20, the landless seized properties from the great proprietors and, to the fury of the latter, the government recognized

[1] Brian R. Sullivan, 'The Strategy of the Decisive Weight: Italy, 1882–1922', in Williamson Murray, MacGregor Knox, and Alvin Bernstein (eds.), *The Making of Strategy: Rulers, States and War* (Cambridge, 1994), 343.

these illegal occupations. Overpopulation in such rich agricultural areas as Emilio and the Po valley had left agricultural workers at the mercy of their hirers. The war had taken the surplus labour to the front, and suddenly existing agricultural unions could dictate terms to the capitalist farmers of the Po valley. Wages doubled and local socialists achieved political power, to the double discomfiture of the small proprietors and tenant farmers whose social status as well as economic well-being was threatened from below.

The government's efforts to control this situation proved totally inadequate and the means used to relieve the underlying economic distress served only to fuel the inflation and increase the budget deficit without bringing relief or pacifying the rebellious. The old laissez-faire and non-interventionist methods of the past were hardly appropriate for dealing with the social ferment of post-war Italy. The inadequacies of the Rome authorities further undermined confidence in parliamentary government even among its traditional supporters. Narrow coalition governments and the manipulative parliamentary and electoral practices of the past could not deal with the mass parties and radicalized politics of the post-1918 years. The pre-war elites, still in control of the reins of power, found themselves in a highly uncongenial and almost unrecognizable world. They faced the backlash of the emotions generated by the war and the peace. Gabriele d'Annunzio's Fiume adventure in September 1919, riding the crest of the nationalist wave, cast an all too revealing light on the highly charged state of feeling in the country and the pusillanimity of its political leaders. The irredentist Nationalist party, playing on the theme of *la vittoria mutilate* ('the mutilated peace') found an expanded audience. The Socialists and newly founded *Partito Popolari*, or Christian Democratic party, won more than half the seats in the Chamber of Deputies in the unusually open election of November 1919. Under the system of proportional representation introduced for the elections the Socialists became the majority party, but as they did not have enough seats to rule alone and would not join the Popolari in a coalition government, they formed a permanent opposition to any governing party or parties. None of the pre-Mussolini cabinets could adapt the traditional oligarchic political structure to the fractious opposition in the chamber. The extremist parties took to the streets, and ex-servicemen, unable to find jobs, sold their wartime skills both to Benito Mussolini's supporters and to the Socialists battling against them. Such veteran movements were hardly restricted to Italy, but the Italian political structure was too weak and the ruling elite far too narrow to withstand the assault on the state's institutions and their crumbling foundations.

Under such conditions it is hardly surprising that both Francisco Nitti (June 1919 to June 1920) and the veteran politician Giovanni Giolitti

(June 1920 to July 1921) favoured retrenchment and conciliation. Nitti, an ex-professor of political economy from Naples, led a split Radical party without the support of Giolitti, his former patron, or the latter's followers. Nitti cancelled the Italian expedition to the Caucasus and was prepared to negotiate with both Yugoslavia and Greece. He opened talks with Kemal after the latter's Turkish troops defeated the Italians at Konia in Anatolia in May 1920. The Nitti government sought to resolve the Adriatic dispute with Yugoslavia. Once Woodrow Wilson's political impotence was confirmed, direct talks were opened between the prime minister and Ante Trumbić, the Yugoslav leader. Progress was slow, in part because the Yugoslavs insisted on a partition of Albania that Nitti would not accept. Tomaso Tittoni, Nitti's foreign minister, had more success with the Greeks. He concluded a convention with the Greek prime minister, Venizelos, in July 1919, followed by a treaty on 10 August 1920, intended to come into force at the same time as the Treaty of Sèvres, on 20 July 1919. The Italians were given the already Italian-occupied Dodecanese islands, with the exception of Rhodes, while Smyrna was recognized as Greek and Italian influence in Asia Minor confined to a coastal strip from Scalanuova to Mersina. The two powers divided Albania, with the Greeks in northern Epirus and the Italians given a mandate for central Albania. The Italians were, in addition, a signatory to the tripartite agreement, also signed in 1920, dividing Anatolia into spheres of Italian and French economic influence. Both agreements were only on paper and were abandoned in the face of Kemal's successful military campaign.

The Italians were still overextended when Nitti, after three unsuccessful attempts to create a viable government, resigned on 9 June 1920. His successor, the vastly experienced Giovanii Giolitti, whose first ministry dated back to 1892, and his resourceful foreign minister, Count Sforza, the ablest of the post-war heads of the Consulta (foreign ministry), had greater success in shaping a more realistic foreign policy. Sforza turned his attention to the situations in Albania and Yugoslavia. Besieged by the Albanians, his troops decimated by malaria, and faced with the mutiny of an Italian regiment embarking for Albania, Giolitti agreed in August 1920 to evacuate the country entirely, ending a futile and expensive campaign. The Italians dropped their claims to a mandate, renounced the Tittoni–Venizelos treaty, and concluded an agreement with the provisional government in Tirana recognizing Albanian independence within its 1913 boundaries but still leaving Italy with a predominant place in the Adriatic state. Progress towards a settlement with Yugoslavia was slow. It was only after the Senate rejection of the Versailles treaty in March that the Allies were free to act. Count Sforza drew closer to Paris, and the French, troubled by the growing chaos in

Italy and anxious to assist the Giolitti government, pressed the Yugoslavs to accept Sforza's peace terms. The Italians agreed to abandon their claims in Dalmatia in exchange for Belgrade's recognition of their demands in Istria. On 12 November 1920 the Treaty of Rapallo was signed. Italy won almost all of Istria, but Fiume was made a free city under bilateral control. The Italians also took possession of four islands off the coast of northern Dalmatia wanted by the navy and were given sovereignty over Zara. The rest of Dalmatia was left to Yugoslavia. These were the same proposals that Tittoni had made in August 1919, which Lloyd George and Clemenceau had accepted but Wilson rejected. At the last minute, to sweeten the Fiume pill for the Yugoslavs, Sforza promised Yugoslavia, in a secret letter, that the secondary harbour of Port Baros, adjacent to Fiume, and the all-Slav suburb of Susak would go to Belgrade. Once the new status of Fiume was recognized there was no reason for D'Annunzio to remain. At the end of December 1920 Italian forces bombarded the city and forced the poet-dictator to finally leave the scene, though not before berating the Italian populace for its failure to overthrow the Giolitti government in Rome.

Sforza's diplomacy, particularly the Treaty of Rapallo, was not universally popular. The right was highly critical, though Mussolini, in an action he later 'forgot', approved of the Yugoslav settlement. The 'free city' survived until 1923, when Mussolini ordered its re-occupation. Sforza also tried to improve Italy's image in the Balkans. Never sympathetic to Hungarian revisionism but hardly enthusiastic about the prospects of a Slav-dominated alliance in the Balkans, he went out of his way nevertheless to welcome the creation of the Little Entente. When former emperor Charles landed in Hungary in his first attempt to regain the Habsburg throne in March 1921, the Italians joined the French and British in the successful diplomatic action to eject him. Sforza also turned his attention to Ankara, where in return for promises of economic concessions in Anatolia, he backed Mustapha Kemal's claims against the Greeks.

Giolitti's attempts at conciliation at home proved far less successful than Sforza's diplomacy. The premier's assumption that all the discordant elements in Italian life could be reconciled under an enlightened parliamentary regime, and that liberals, fascists, and socialists could work under the 'common rule of the liberal state, which tolerates everything and survives everything', soon proved wanting.[2] Even Giolitti's successful handling of the so-called occupation of the factories, when he refused to intervene against the workers who had seized control of some of the larger industries in the north, failed to pay the anticipated

[2] Renzo De Felice, *Mussolini il rivoluzionario* (Turin, 1965), 607.

political dividends. The petering-out of the occupation exposed the ineptness of the socialists, but this demonstration of their weakness failed to reassure the property-holders. Real and illusory fears led moderates and conservatives to turn to the fascists for deliverance from 'democratic excesses' and 'proletarian attacks'. Alarmed by the electoral appeal of the mass parties and blind to the dangers of a revolutionary party of the right, Giolitti and his liberal followers assumed that Mussolini and the fascists could be used to restore order in the state. Uncertain of his support in the country, Giolitti, having decided on an election in the spring of 1921, organized a national bloc that included both nationalists and fascists. It was a fatal move; in effect, Giolitti had offered Mussolini the gift of political respectability. His initiative was welcomed by both liberals and radicals and by the foreign diplomats in Rome, including Barrère, who saw Mussolini as the only alternative to the triumph of the left and assumed, like so many Italians, that he could be absorbed into the existing political structure once he had served his political purpose. Despite the political manoeuvring, Giolitti failed to obtain a working majority. The fascists won only thirty-five of the 535 seats in the Chamber of Deputies. Mussolini aligned himself with the opposition and sat, on the rare occasions when he came to parliament, on the extreme right. Without sufficient support for his reform policies, Giolitti resigned in June.

Ivanoe Bonomi, the next prime minister (June 1921 to April 1922), a colourless and irresolute figure who had been expelled from the Socialist party for supporting the Libyan war, depended on a highly unstable coalition of Populari and Socialists to buttress his ministry. He tried to maintain a neutral position between the socialists and fascists, whom he sought to reconcile. Given Mussolini's opportunism and the eclectic nature of the provincial fascist groups, such an outcome seemed possible. Mussolini opted for respectability, discarding his uniform for stiff butterfly collar and spats, shaving each day, and even cleaning up his 'excessively sordid language'. The *ras*—local fascist bosses such as Dino Grandi at Bologna, Italo Balbo at Ferrara, and Roberto Farinacci at Cremona, who took their name from the tribal chieftains in Ethiopia, and whose armed bands extracted the protection money that sustained their activities—rejected respectability and opposed the centralization of power in Mussolini's hands. They rebelled against Mussolini's sudden adoption of Bonomi's idea of a pact with the socialists in August 1921, refusing to embrace the men whom they previously had been hired to kill. When Mussolini resigned, the *ras* realized that they needed him as much as he needed them. The resulting pact between the leader and the local bosses gave fascism its special character right until the end. Mussolini was no Hitler. Though fascism was a minority movement composed of diverse groupings, the Bonomi government tolerated its spreading influence and violent tactics, firmly convinced that once the crisis was ended the fascists could be tamed.

The election of 1921 revived the demands for an active foreign policy; Mussolini joined the nationalist clamour. Bonomi's only aggressive action was in Tripolitania, where troops were used to regain control over the native people lost during the wartime Arab revolt. In order to buttress the unstable Bonomi coalition, the foreign minister, Pietro Thomasi della Torretta, an Italian aristocrat and career diplomat, sought commercial concessions from the Turks and opened talks with the Soviet government, a move popular with the socialists on ideological grounds and with both the Milanese financiers and industrialists and the fruit growers in the south. The diplomats of the Consulta preferred to orient Italian policy towards London, for they wanted a war–debt settlement and loans which only the Anglo-Americans could offer. At the Washington naval conference (November 1921–February 1922) the Italians ingratiated themselves with both. With British backing they won parity in battleships with France, saving themselves from a naval race that they certainly would have lost. The naval victory fed hopes of establishing Italian supremacy in the Mediterranean. By the summer of 1922 the naval chiefs were discussing plans to ward off any British interference in their Mediterranean ambitions. Italy's 'imprisonment in the Mediterranean', a popular theme in naval circles, became one of Mussolini's most enduring preoccupations. Bonomi's goals at Washington were more centrally focused on winning a favourable war–debt settlement, but it would be Mussolini who would reap the financial benefits from the Italian success at the conference.

In Washington, and over reparations, the Italians sought out the British. With his proposed world economic conference in view, Lloyd George began to court the Bonomi government, and his wooing reached its height just before the Genoa conference opened. The site itself, a totally inappropriate setting for the gathering, was picked in the vain hope of bolstering Bonomi's weak position. By the time the conference opened, his government had fallen and Italy was without political leadership for nearly four weeks. As the deputies of the dead-locked Chamber argued, sporadic battles took place all over northern Italy, with the fascist outrages tolerated, if not condoned, by the local authorities. Another weak caretaker coalition, led by the timid, inexperienced Giolitti loyalist Luigi Facta, took office when all of Italy's leading liberal politicians refused. The government lasted only from February to October 1922, and was always under pressure from the right, which complained about Italian subservience to France in Europe and to Britain in the Mediterranean. Nationalists and socialists demanded the revision of the peace treaties. The Italians wanted the Genoa conference postponed, but the opening date was set for the beginning of Holy Week, an embarrassing decision for a government anxious to promote closer relations with the new pope, Pius XI.

The Genoa conference proved to be the international swansong of Italy's liberal system of government. Carlo Schanzer, who had represented Italy so successfully at the Washington conference, became Facta's foreign minister. He loyally supported Lloyd George's policies, seconding his efforts to avoid the rupture of the talks after the Soviet– German agreement at Rapallo and backing the prime minister over Turkey in the hope of concluding an Anglo-Italian pact that would lead to gains in the Near East and Africa. The Italian–Yugoslav dispute cast its shadow over the proceedings. Contrary to Sforza's earlier promises, Italian troops remained in Fiume and occupied parts of Dalmatia, while the Facta government refused to recognize Belgrade's claim to Port Baros. Under extreme pressure from the nationalists, Schanzer sought to open conversations with the Yugoslavs for a revision of the Treaty of Rapallo, but Lloyd George had little time for Adriatic questions and Nikola Pašić, the Serb leader, supported by the French and Czechs, rejected the Italian overtures. Schanzer also tried to persuade the successor states to lower their economic barriers as had been recommended at the Porto Rosa conference (October–November 1921), but was again rebuffed. There were some successes. Commercial treaties were concluded with Poland, Romania, Finland, and Estonia, though attempts to negotiate a more advantageous treaty with Moscow failed when the Russians insisted on maintaining the status quo. When Schanzer came to London in July expecting a reward for his loyalty, Lloyd George did not even offer a conciliatory pat on the back. Schanzer's list of demands would be inherited by Mussolini: full participation in future discussions over Tangier, acquisition of the Jubaland in Kenya on the border of Italian Somaliland, economic concessions in the British mandates of Iraq and Palestine, the adjustment of the Libyan– Egyptian frontier, co-operation in Abyssinia and Senussia (part of Libya), and support for the retention of the Dodecanese islands. Lloyd George refused to discuss Fiume, Austria, war debts, or reparation shares, and Schanzer returned to Rome much depressed. Not surprisingly, having dutifully supported Lloyd George's anti-Turk policies in the spring and summer of 1922, Schanzer refused to back him at Chanak.

Disappointment over Genoa compounded the Facta government's difficulties with the Chamber, and Facta resigned on 19 July only to form a second hopelessly divided ministry that staggered on until the autumn. The government looked on passively when Mussolini seized on the excuse of a senseless general strike to send his thugs to beat up the socialists and raze their buildings in Ancona, Leghorn, Genoa, and other cities. After a three-hour battle the fascists won control of Milan, the 'brain centre of Italian socialism', which provided most of the socialist funding. It was a dress rehearsal for the October takeover of the non-fascist councils in most of the other major cities. While the fascists continued their campaigns of bullying, burning, beating, and murdering, Mussolini, posing as the defender of law and order, proceeded to negotiate with the leaders of all parties, right, centre, and left, and with the Church and Freemasons as well. As the government did nothing to stop the street-fighting, large sections of the middle class looked to Mussolini to save Italy from ruin and the triumph of Bolshevism. Each of the liberal leaders, Giolitti, Salandra, Orlando, and Facto, tried to enlist fascist participation in their future ministries. It was with some reason that Mussolini boasted that only he and the king were in charge of events.

II

Early on the morning of 29 October 1922 Vittorio Emanuele invited Mussolini to form his own cabinet. The king had yielded to an ultimatum, but his action was highly popular and had the support of his senior military and naval advisers. The troops in Rome could have defeated the fascist forces but were never asked to take action. The new premier arrived in Rome by sleeping-car on the morning of 30 October and was welcomed by cheering crowds. His followers, in an extraordinary array of picturesque uniforms, arrived by train over the next two days and were hailed as liberators. Parliamentarians rushed to ingratiate themselves with the new premier. Only the socialists refused to join Mussolini's cabinet, but there was no general strike or any public demonstration of disapproval. The generals and admirals welcomed the advent of a leader, a decorated war veteran, known to be a nationalist with extensive expansionist ambitions. In the past the military had been in the forefront of the moves to acquire territories that Italy could not possibly defend. They could hardly guess that they would soon try to restrain their new master from such ill-considered adventures. The 'march on Rome' was the first of the myths spun by a master myth-maker.

Posterity has been kind to Mussolini. Compared to Hitler or to Stalin, the Duce emerges as a minor villain, a bully-dictator who wooed and won the Italian people by posturing and propaganda and who might have died in bed had he shown greater judgement. Mussolini has been fortunate, too, in his biographer, Renzo De Felice, whose awe-inspiring, multi-volume, archive-based biography pictured a gentler and more humane Mussolini than most historians now accept. De Felice stresses Mussolini's 'hyper-realism' throughout the 1920s and early 1930s and, where he deals with Mussolini's foreign policy, emphasizes the lines of continuity with those of his liberal predecessors. Even after the Ethiopian campaign, when De Felice argues that the Duce abandoned the pragmatic policies of the *peso determinante*, he insists that the Italian leader still sought an accommodation with Britain and 'inwardly would not have wanted the "inevitable war" of which he spoke ever more frequently'.[3] The overall impact of De Felice's seven volumes was not only to distance, quite correctly, both the man and his imperial aspirations from the incomparably more barbarous German dictator and Hitler's racially driven vision of European dominion, but to emphasize the Duce's essentially opportunistic approach to foreign affairs. De Felice's growing circle of critics convincingly argue that he has underplayed Mussolini's 'will to war' and obscured the extent of his culpability for the chain of events that led to his own and his country's downfall. Some historians have questioned De Felice's pragmatic, opportunistic, and conditional interpretation of the Duce's foreign and imperial policies and have called for a radical revision.

It is easy to underestimate Mussolini, as so many contemporaries did. He was no fool, no *César de carnaval* (the French diplomat Paul-Boncour's description), nor even a 'Napoleon turned pugilist'. He was intelligent and quick of mind. Though uncouth and deliberately ill-mannered, he was from childhood encouraged to read and exposed to political ideas. His mother, a good Catholic, was the local schoolmistress and his father, a tough, heavy-drinking, and intermittently employed blacksmith, was one of the earliest self-proclaimed socialists in Italy and active in local co-operative and socialist movements. Widely read during his years as journalist and agitator, it was probably Marx who had the greatest influence on Mussolini. Later, as dictator, he became fascinated by statistics, boasting to his minister of national education, Giuseppe Bottai, that 'I am the unique reader of the *Annual of Statistics*', and finding in the demographic tables proof of the linkages between birth rates, decadence, and power that became such an integral part of his thinking.[4] Mussolini had charisma, charm, and, according to some, an ironic sense of humour that could be used to devastating effect. In time he came to exude a sense of authority, enhanced no doubt by

[3] Renzo De Felice, *Mussolini l'alleato*. I, i, *L'Italia in guerra, 1940–43* (Turin, 1990), 61. Trans. in MacGregor Knox, 'The Fascist Regime, its Foreign Policy and its Wars: An "Anti-anti-Fascist" Orthodoxy?', *Contemporary European History*, 4: 3 (1995), 354–5.

[4] Brian Sullivan, 'Fascist Italian Perceptions of the Nazis', in Martin S. Alexander (ed.), *Knowing Your Friends: Intelligence Inside Alliances and Coalitions from 1914 to the Cold War* (London, 1998), 89.

sitting in 'what seemed to be the largest room in the world, at the far end of which was an equally colossal table. It seemed as if I were walking in treacle, yet the marble floor was also very slippery. I felt sure that I should either never arrive at all at the other end or should skid there in a sitting posture.'[5]

There was a more ominous side to Mussolini's multi-faceted personality. From an early age he exhibited a streak of brutality and cruelty that would later characterize the treatment of his mistresses, political opponents, and those who were the victims of his bloody colonial campaigns. As a youth and young man he loved to fight. He was a 'notorious dueller', who took pleasure 'at the thought that his schoolfellows would still carry the scars of wounds he had inflicted'.[6] He delighted in physical action and was addicted to bouts of exercise, occasionally inviting foreign journalists to see him fence, play tennis, or ride (a recent accomplishment of which he was exceedingly proud) in order to impress them with his vigour. He enjoyed dangerous sports, fast cars, and aeroplanes, which he piloted himself. This pleasure in action and violence was genuine but also an essential part of his cultivated manly image. Virility, physical prowess, and courage were to become the coveted features of the refashioned Italian male destined to realize Mussolini's vision of the new Imperial Rome. The leader believed that his followers had to be toughened and the image of the fat, easygoing, opera-singing Italian replaced by that of the fierce, action-seeking, war-worthy male. Italy had to be feared before it could be respected. According to Mussolini, it was 'only blood that makes the wheels of history turn'.[7] He believed in the therapeutic value of the 'bath of blood' and, like so many of the pre-1914 generation who had imbibed the Social Darwinian waters, saw war as an ennobling experience for men and nations. Well before Mussolini openly proclaimed that Italy's destiny could be fulfilled only through war, he was extolling the virtues of militarism and the role of force in unifying the nation and in the conduct of its affairs.

It is admittedly difficult to locate the 'real' Mussolini. As a great impresario and propagandist, he created his own parts and played a number of public roles with appropriate costumes. There was civilian dress in the 1920s, with a partiality for winged collars and spats, and a vast variety of military uniforms during the 1930s. One of his favourite public poses was to stand with chest thrust forward and large head thrown back or, at a later date, to appear as the stern, scowling, helmeted

---

[5] Sir John Wheeler Bennett, *Knaves, Fools and Heroes: Europe Between the Wars* (London, 1974), 82.
[6] Denis Mack Smith, *Mussolini* (paperback edn., London, 1993), 3.
[7] Ibid. 24.

military leader. Roles, moods, and opinions, in private as in public, changed in accordance with the audience. Mussolini came most alive when haranguing the crowds from the balcony—in his own words, his 'stage'. Like Hitler, who greatly admired Mussolini's ability to enlist mass support, he seemed to draw lifeblood from the assemblages of people gathered below him. At an early age he acquired a reputation for being solitary and misanthropic. In power he cultivated his isolation, permitting no intimates and adopting an abstemious lifestyle except when it came to women. The desire to make his mark was always strong. His mistress and early official biographer, Margherita Sarfatti, describes Mussolini soon after taking office as saying, with appropriate gestures, 'I am possessed by a frenzied ambition which torments and devours me from within like a physical illness. It is, through my own will power, to carve a mark on the age—like a lion with his claws, like this.'[8] Unfortunately both for himself and for his country, his ambition was fulfilled.

Mussolini was hardly a systematic thinker. He wrote no equivalent to *Mein Kampf*. He never developed the singular and all-embracing ideology that allowed Hitler to turn his fearsome doctrine of racial expansionism into political reality, nor did his programme of 'domestic regeneration and radical revisionism' make the same impact on Italians that Hitler's doctrines made on the German people. There always remained competing claims and loyalties in Italy that Mussolini could not ignore, abolish, or totally destroy. It was probably not until after he assumed full control of the state in 1925 that his ideas about creating a new Italy regenerated through conquest and expansion, and capable of inspiring others as had Ancient Rome, began to coalesce into a programme of action that would confirm his dictatorship and the new fascist state. Professor MacGregor Knox, the main exponent of an ideological interpretation of Mussolini's policies, traces their roots to such influential post-Risorgimento writers as Alfredo Oriani, who believed that war and bloodshed were necessary for the unification of Italy, as well as to the doctrines of revolutionary Marxism which Mussolini espoused as a student, journalist, and propagandist. The war of 1914–18 acted as the catalyst in transferring Mussolini's revolutionary focus from class to nation. Italy's participation in the conflict was a golden opportunity to shake the country out of its former stupor, and its decision to fight confirmed Italy's right to achieve its 'higher destinies'. No longer would foreigners see Italy as a land 'of travelling storytellers, of peddlers of statuettes, of Calabrian *banditi*'.[9] Ousted

---

[8] M. G. Sarfatti, *Dux* (Verona, 1932), 314.
[9] MacGregor Knox, *Common Destiny: Dictatorship, Foreign Policy and War in Fascist Italy and Nazi Germany* (Cambridge, 2000), 61–2.

from the Socialist party because of his support for intervention, Mussolini embraced the nationalist cause, fusing together the myths of revolution and nation.

In later years Mussolini would affirm that the Fascist party, Italy's revolutionary elite, was created from the war and victory, though he acknowledged that the 'march on Rome' was 'a revolutionary deed and a victorious insurrection, [but] not a revolution. The revolution comes later.'[10] Mussolini had appropriated the full panoply of liberal and nationalist irredentist and expansionist goals, but it was the domination of the Mediterranean that was central to his vision of Italy as the 'worthy heir of Rome'. Italy was imprisoned within the Mediterranean, and France and particularly Britain, with its control of Gibraltar and Suez, were the jailers, able to cut off its access to the oceans through which imported food and essential raw materials came. Four weeks before becoming prime minister Mussolini insisted that the Italians must concentrate on 'making the Mediterranean our lake . . . and expelling those in the Mediterranean who are parasites'.[11] Britain was the chief 'parasite'. The Corfu adventure, Mussolini's first foreign-policy initiative, though portrayed as a fascist success, exposed Italy's extreme vulnerability to British attack. The highly unwelcome naval warnings that Italy's coastal cities and shipping lanes were defenceless explain Mussolini's fixation. On 6 March 1925, 'with a fixed stare' resembling that of a 'fanatic', Mussolini told Salvatore Contarini, his shocked secretary-general at the foreign ministry, that 'Gibraltar, Malta, Suez, Cyprus represent a chain that allows England to encircle and imprison Italy in the Mediterranean. If this chain had another link added to it, Albania, we would have had to break it with a war. A short war which would only have lasted a few weeks because today Italy is no longer the Italy of the days of Giolitti, or, worse, of Count Sforza!'[12] The Duce returned to the same theme in the autumn of 1926, when he told his senior officers that 'a nation which does not have free access to the oceans cannot be considered a great power; Italy must become a great power.'[13] The same note was struck again in 1929, in 1935, and in 1940.

---

[10] Knox, *Common Destiny*, 69.

[11] Brian R. Sullivan, 'A Thirst For Glory: Mussolini, the Italian Military, and the Fascist Regime, 1922–1940', unpubl. Ph.D. thesis, Columbia University (1981), 99.

[12] MacGregor Knox, 'Il fascismo e la politica esteri italiana', in Richard J. B. Bosworth and Sergio Romano (eds.), *La politica estera italiana (1860–1985)* (Bologna, 1991), 298.

[13] Brian R. Sullivan, 'The Italian Armed Forces, 1918–1940', in Alan R. Millett and Williamson Murray (eds.), *Military Effectiveness*. Vol. II: *The Inter-War Period* (London, 1988), 180; also in Knox, 'Il fascismo e la politica esteri italiana', 298.

In December 1924 the German ambassador to Italy (1921–30) and future foreign minister to Hitler (1932–8), Constantin von Neurath, sent a dispatch to Berlin warning that Mussolini was attempting to make the Mediterranean a *mare italiano* and that he had begun to prepare for battle against France, his main adversary. In the inevitable future war between France and Germany, Neurath reported, 'Italy, led by Mussolini, would place itself at Germany's side in order to crush France jointly. If the endeavour succeeded, Mussolini would claim as his booty the entire French North African coast and create a great "imperium latinum" in the Mediterranean. Then he might also judge the moment had come to have himself acclaimed emperor, and to push aside easily the unwarlike king.'[14] Mussolini was courting Stresemann at the time and may have been saying what he thought the Germans would like to hear, but Neurath's account proved all too prescient. After 1925, when Mussolini's goals became more clearly defined, he turned the usual demographic argument on its head, arguing that it was essential, if Italy was not to follow the French and British examples of steady decline because of falling birth rates, that its population should increase from 40 million to 60 million people by mid-century. This was the only way for Italy to fulfil its imperial destiny. The campaigns to 'ruralize' Italy and the 'battle for grain' were more than domestic rallying cries; they were part of Mussolini's efforts to prepare the country, both demographically and economically, for the achievement of its future imperial role. According to the Italian leader: 'In an Italy entirely reclaimed, cultivated, irrigated and disciplined, in other words a Fascist Italy, there is space and bread for another ten million men. Sixty million Italians will make the weight of the numbers and their power felt in the history of the world.'[15]

As Duce, he impressed a wide array of foreign visitors, politicians, diplomats, and journalists who, however condescending in their attitudes towards the Italians, admired the dynamism of their new leader. There was an element of unconscious smugness and contempt that led many British politicians and diplomats to condone Italian fascism and make allowances for Mussolini's sensitivity about his own and his country's ranking in the international order. Angrily rejecting the suggested analogy between the fascist and Soviet regimes, Austen Chamberlain wrote, ' . . . are these generalities very helpful? Was life safer in Italy before the March on Rome? Was law better observed? Was the average Italian as free even as he is today? There is no greater mistake

---

[14] Jens Petersen, *Hitler, Mussolini: Die Entstehung der Achse Berlin–Rom, 1933–1936* (Tübingen, 1973), 495.

[15] Knox, *Common Destiny*, 71.

TABLE 15. Italian Migration, 1920–1940

	Emigration	Immigration	Emigration to USA
1920	614,000		95,145
1921	201,300	124,000	222,260
1922	281,300	110,800	40,319
1923	390,000	119,700	46,674
1924	364,600	172,800	56,246
1925	280,100	189,100	6,203
1926	262,400	177,600	8,253
1927	218,900	140,400	17,297
1928	150,000	98,900	17,728
1929	149,800	115,900	18,008
1930	280,100	129,000	22,327
1931	165,900	107,700	13,399
1932	83,300	73,200	6,662
1933	83,100	65,800	3,477
1934	68,500	49,800	4,374
1935	57,400	39,500	6,566
1936	41,700	32,800	6,774
1937	59,900	35,700	7,192
1938	61,500	36,900	7,712
1939	29,500	87,300	6,570
1940	51,800	61,100	5,302

Sources: B. R. Mitchell, *International Historical Statistics, Europe 1750–1993*, 4th edn. (Basingstoke, 1998), Sec. A9; US immigration: *US Historical Statistics, Colonial Times to 1970* (Washington, DC, 1989). American Immigration Acts 19 May 1921, 26 May 1924.

than to apply British standards to un-British conditions. Mussolini would not be a fascist if he were an Englishman in England.'[16] Chamberlain admired Mussolini and sought his friendship, explaining the contrast between his greatness and his 'childish sensitivity' by comparing him to Bismarck. Chamberlain's wife Ivy, much taken with the Italian leader, provided him with one of his great propaganda triumphs in London when she convinced him to stage a massive Italian art exhibition at the Royal Academy in 1930. All objections from Italian museums and collectors were swept aside, and the exhibition, that included such masterpieces as Botticelli's *The Birth of Venus* and Donatello's *David*, enormously enhanced the reputation both of Mussolini and his fascist state in certain circles. Winston Churchill, who applauded the fascist struggle against the 'bestial appetite and passions of Leninism', was quick

[16] Minute by Sir A. Chamberlain, 5 Nov. 1926, quoted in P. G. Edwards, 'The Foreign Office and Fascism, 1924–1929', *Journal of Contemporary History*, 5: 2 (1970), 157.

to recognize the importance of the Duce's accomplishments. Just weeks before the Italian attack on Abyssinia, he was still praising Mussolini, 'so great a man, so wise a ruler', who was presiding over a 'revivified Italian nation'.[17]

III

Mussolini owed his ascent not to a revolution, but to the assistance of the king, the heads of the armed forces, and most of the existing political establishment. He was not even in full control of the many semi-independent local fascist groups, losing popularity as the need for their services diminished. The army and navy, whose obedience and first loyalty was to the king, expected to be rewarded for standing aside during the 'March on Rome'. Army appropriations had been cut by the Facta government, and the army leaders looked to more than restitution; the navy sought funds for a Mediterranean fleet that could challenge France. The independent air force, a 'fascist creation' established in 1923, also required substantial funding. Mussolini was as generous as possible (already in 1922–3 the military consumed 22.4 per cent of the state's expenditure), but it was not until 1926, when the Italian war-debt agreement with Britain expanded the state's access to foreign capital markets, that the funds needed for rearmament began to be released. The army's attention remained focused on Yugoslavia and the defence of Italy's Alpine frontiers. Conscious of its weakness, these concerns

TABLE 16. Italian Army Size and Military Expenditure, 1922–1930

	Army size	Expenditure (Lire bn.)	State budget (Lire bn.)
1922/3	175,000		
1923/4	250,000		
1924/5	250,000		
1925/6	250,000	2.795	23,000
1926/7	251,155	3.112	24,600
1927/8	251,300	2.705	29,650
1928/9	257,962	2.856	20,840
1929/30	253,150	2.943	20,860

Sources: Lucio Ceva, Le forze armate (Turin, 1981), 223; id., L'Esercito Italiano, tra la 1 e la 2 Guerra Mondial (Rome, 1954), 209.

[17] Quoted in R. A. C. Parker, Churchill and Appeasement (London, 2000), 76.

took precedence over the needs of the navy and Mussolini's Mediterranean dreams.

Mussolini added the foreign ministry to an already long list of his offices, and moved the ministry from the Consulta to the more centrally located Palazzo Chigi, where he could more easily address the assembled crowds below. Many career diplomats welcomed the return of discipline and order. Few resigned—Count Sforza, the ambassador to France, was one of the exceptions. The highly experienced secretary-general, Salvatore Contarini, a conservative nationalist, hoped that the restitution of strong government would end the period of diplomatic impotence and enable the Italians to win the concessions that had so far eluded them. The professionals feared Mussolini's bluster and rashness far more than his ambitions, and counted on their ability to control their bombastic and ill-mannered master. Contarini appeared confident about the Consulta's future relationship with its chief: 'We must use Mussolini like the blood of San Gennaro', the secretary-general recommended, 'exhibit him once a year and then only from afar.'[18] Contarini, like many of his subordinates, was a cautious revisionist, hoping to establish spheres of influence in the Balkans and Danubian basin and to promote a policy of careful imperial expansion. Much could be accomplished in regaining Italian prestige if Mussolini was kept under official control. Mussolini may have exchanged his black shirt for morning coat, but he was not constrained by his officials. In his first address to the Chamber, on 16 November 1922, he denounced the 'inferior way' that Italy had been treated in the past and warned that the peace treaties were neither eternal nor immutable. Italy would give 'nothing for nothing'. In this speech, too, he showed his interest in opening relations with Moscow, a move not favoured by the diplomats. Yet they welcomed the signs that Mussolini recognized that he was a novice in international affairs and would accept their advice and instruction in diplomatic manners.

At first, Mussolini adopted a conciliatory policy towards Belgrade and a positive attitude towards the Little Entente. This did not prevent personal approaches to the Bulgarians, where a comparatively stable government, dependent on repressive measures to maintain its power, included supporters who were ideologically close to the Italian fascists. There were covetous glances at Albania, soon again convulsed by a civil war between two major factions, one headed by Ahmed Zogu, prime minister from December 1922 to February 1924, and the other by Fan Noli, an Orthodox priest with Italian patronage, who seized power and forced Zogu into exile in Yugoslavia. The Italian interest in Albania was

---

[18] Mario Luciolli, *Palazzo Chigi: anni ruventi* (Milan, 1976), 53.

more than a matter of raw materials, though its oil deposits were of some importance. Italian tutelage over the tiny state would be a blow to Yugoslavia and provide access to the Adriatic and a foothold in the lower Balkans. In the face of Kemal's successes, which effectively excluded Italy from Anatolia, Mussolini looked for alternative pickings in the Middle East and continued the search for the African colonies that had begun under his liberal predecessors. Curzon and Poincaré, at Mussolini's insistence, journeyed to Territet in Switzerland in November 1922 to endure their first experience of fascist diplomacy. Mussolini claimed that he won an agreement to acknowledge Italian sovereignty over the ethnically Greek but Italian-occupied Dodecanese islands and the promise of a mandate in Iraq. At Lausanne, Curzon haughtily dismissed his claims and warned that the discussions would go on without the Italians if they should withdraw. The British foreign secretary also proved difficult over Jubaland, which he wanted to use as a carrot to persuade the Italians to cede the Dodecanese islands to Greece. Despite all the efforts of the Italophile French ambassador in Rome, the French proved equally uncooperative about meeting Italian demands for a share of the Anglo-French economic privileges in the Middle East and were not forthcoming about colonies in Africa. In 1924 Mussolini considered taking action against Turkey, hoping to take advantage of its quarrels with Britain over Mosul to make his own demands at Ankara.

There were other continuities with the liberal regime. The Colonial Office looked to the pacification of Libya and Italian Somaliland as the prelude to the conquest of Ethiopia (Abyssinia). The war for the reconquest of Libya, lying between French Tunisia (populated by twice as many Italians as French) and Egypt (nominally independent since 1923 but still British-controlled) continued under Giuseppi Volpi, the governor of Libya, who by 1925 had brought most of the tribes of Tripolitania back under Italian control. The struggle against the Senussi nomads of Cyrenaica proved far more difficult and a fierce war against the rebels lasted until 1932, when General Pietro Badoglio, the governor of the two North African provinces Tripoli and Cyrenaica, and General Rodolfo Graziani moved the whole local population of Cyrenaica, with all their goods, into concentration camps to cut the rebels off from the sources of their supplies. In 1925 a series of campaigns was launched from southern Somalia to destroy the independent sultanates in the north of the country. The governor of Somalia, the ex-*squadrista* Cesare De Vecchi, whom Mussolini wanted out of Rome, waged a terrible war, using Askari battalions recruited in Eritrea and Ethiopia to do the fighting. Though the Ethiopians had to be conciliated while recruiting continued, during 1925 Mussolini began to think of a full-scale invasion of the country. In March 1926 long-range planning for the conquest of Ethiopia began. The North African campaigns were unexpectedly lengthy, bloody, and costly. The colonies were unsuited for Italian settlement and the costs of maintenance far higher than the dividends, but Mussolini, with his dreams of an Italian empire stretching from the Mediterranean south-west to the Atlantic, was determined to extend his dominions in the horn of Africa.

Mussolini's first personal forays into international waters, the meeting with Poincaré and Lloyd George at Territet before the Lausanne conference and his one-day appearance at the conference, were less than successful. At best, the new leader demonstrated his independence and may have allayed suspicions arising from his belligerent Chamber speech, but he achieved nothing concrete. Both in Lausanne and in London in December 1922, where he went to discuss reparations, he was ill at ease, and the London trip in particular convinced him that it was better to stay at home. A few months later, restless and impatient with the constraints of old-fashioned diplomacy, Mussolini was ready to slip the foreign ministry leash. He was prepared to seize Corsica and to annex Corfu even if it meant a Mediterranean war. He decided to take Fiume, increase the pressure on Yugoslavia, and weaken the Little Entente by isolating Czechoslovakia, a policy strongly opposed by Contarini. Shortly before the Corfu incident, after Belgrade declined to allow the Italians to take Fiume in return for Yugoslav control over Port Baros and its delta, Mussolini appointed an Italian general as military governor of the contested city. Overlapping with the Corfu crisis, it looked as if Mussolini was preparing another coup in the northern Adriatic.

The Corfu crisis, in September 1923, arose out of the Italian–Greek quarrel over Albania. Relations between Rome and Athens were already tense when General Enrico Tellini, the Italian chairman of the Anglo–French–Italian commission determining the frontiers of Albania, was shot about 15 miles from the Greek town of Janina. Mussolini reacted rapidly, ordering the occupation of the Greek island of Corfu on the following day and dispatching an ultimatum to Athens designed to be rejected. Greece accepted all but two of the Italian terms: the demand for 50 million lire indemnity and the participation of the Italian military attaché in an investigation at the site of the murder. In response, the Italians occupied Corfu on 31 August, just as Germany was edging towards capitulation in the Ruhr. The Greeks appealed to the League of Nations; Mussolini insisted that the matter be settled in the Conference of Ambassadors, correctly believing that Poincaré would support his cause. In accordance with French wishes, and with reluctant British concurrence, the League was circumvented. The Conference of Ambassadors decided that the Italians should evacuate the island but collect their indemnity. The Greeks were furious and their supporters in the Assembly outraged. British insistence and naval threats, as well as the need to calm the powers before his leap at Fuime, led Mussolini to evacuate the island. What had appeared as a brilliant coup to dominate the Adriatic (the island guarded the south entrance to the Adriatic) and isolate Yugoslavia turned into a confrontation with Britain which horrified both the diplomats and the naval chiefs. Mussolini came to regard the Corfu occupation as the 'finest page' in the early history of fascist diplomacy. He had won, after all, an important psychological victory at Athens and had bested the League of Nations, an institution for which he had little regard. Poincaré, knowing nothing of Mussolini's plans for raising a separatist revolt in Corsica, might have paid the price in return for support in the Ruhr, but the British would not allow the Italians to stay in Corfu.

Forebodings at the Consulta were almost immediately confirmed by Mussolini's second Adriatic coup. On 16 September the Italian military governor was dispatched to Fiume. Within a few hours, and without any bloodshed, Italy took over the administration of the still-disputed city. Yugoslavia had to accept the fait accompli, as France urged moderation and conciliation in Belgrade. The decision had already been made to abandon Fiume, but Pašić, the Serb foreign minister, wanted a price that would make the Italian occupation acceptable to the anti-Italian Croats and compensate for the anger in Prague should the settlement lead to a more general reconciliation with Rome. The January 1924 Italo-Yugoslav accord was seen as a diplomatic victory for Mussolini. The Yugoslavs accepted the Italian annexation of Fiume in return for commercial privileges in the city, the acquisition of Porto Baros, and a further reduction in Italy's narrow strip of land on the Adriatic coast connecting Fiume with Italian Istria. The agreement was followed by an Italo-Yugoslav 'friendship pact' providing for benevolent neutrality in the case of attack by any third party and a vague formula for aid against outside incursions (that is, the Macedonian bands threatening Yugoslavia's southern border) into either country. Welcomed by the Italian diplomats, Mussolini never accepted their view that the pact should mark the beginning of a new chapter in Italian–Yugoslav relations and open the way for good relations with Czechoslovakia and Romania. He already had his eye on plans for checking French hegemony in the Balkans. The Pact of Rome did not touch on the Albanian problem which for the moment, whatever Mussolini's future plans for the disturbed province, was put on ice.

After Corfu and Fiume, Mussolini returned to the more conventional paths favoured by the foreign ministry. There was no attempt to encourage either Hungarian or Bulgarian revisionism, though Mussolini looked for a way to undermine French influence by weakening the ties between the Little Entente powers. From the Italian point of view an arrangement with the Romanians seemed the most promising solution. Bucharest wanted Italian support for international recognition of their acquisition of Bessarabia; Mussolini characteristically demanded oil concessions and commercial advantages in return for intervention in Moscow. The talks did not prosper, and were further stalled when Mussolini began to push for an agreement with the Russians. Unlike Contarini, Mussolini had no confidence in Beneš and believed Czechoslovakia to be already under the influence of France. The seemingly conciliatory Italian approach to Yugoslavia led Beneš to Rome, though he continued to harbour the deepest suspicions of fascist Italy and expected Mussolini to fall. The Czech foreign minister first visited the capital in 1923 but failed to convince his suspicious host that Czech relations with France were still unsettled. By the time of his second visit he had already concluded the treaty with France (January 1924), but still hoped to play his own hand in the Balkans by using Italy as a counterweight to the French. Convinced that France and Czechoslovakia were intent on blocking Italian expansion in the Danubian basin, Mussolini saw no advantage in any settlement with Prague. Whereas Contarini wanted to exploit France's isolated position after the Ruhr occupation and to work with the Little Entente powers to reduce French influence in south-east Europe, Mussolini had more ambitious ideas. He and Beneš initialled a 'Pact of Sincere Collaboration' from which the original phrase 'of Friendship' had been omitted. The French had some doubts about the Italo-Yugoslav accord of 1924, which they feared would encourage both Italian and Yugoslav expansionism, the former in Albania and the latter at Salonika in Greece. With reason, they viewed the new arrangements as a Yugoslav step away from the Little Entente and an attempt to reduce Belgrade's dependence on France. Nonetheless, they welcomed an agreement that might ease their relations with Rome without alienating the small nations of eastern Europe. While the treaty was being negotiated, the Quai d'Orsay took up Contarini's hints of a possible pact *à trois* or even a pact *à quatre* with France and Czechoslovakia. Once the bilateral agreement was concluded, however, Mussolini could afford to bypass Paris and insisted on the settlement of the Tunisia question as the price for any bilateral treaty with France. Rebuffed in their efforts to court Rome, the French responded by turning back to Belgrade. The offer of an alliance to the Yugoslavs, intended to coax her back into the French camp, was delayed when negotiations for a western security pact culminating at Locarno made it advisable to keep on good terms with the Italians.

Like some of his liberal predecessors and, at first, against the inclinations of his officials, Mussolini favoured an agreement with the Soviet Union. His anti-Bolshevik posturing, a combination of anti-communism, anti-socialism, and a visceral anti-Slavism, was intended primarily for domestic purposes and did not blind him to the political and economic usefulness of a treaty with Moscow which would appeal to left-wing workers and to sections of the industrial and commercial middle class. The industrial giants Fiat, Pirelli, and Rossi, and the wine exporters had made the Italian pavilion at the Russian trade fair in August 1923 the largest and most ambitious of all the foreign exhibition halls. There was considerable Italian newspaper comment about the similarities and differences between fascism and Bolshevism and their common opposition to liberal democracy. The aftermath of the Corfu crisis alerted Mussolini to the advantages of bringing the 'Soviet card' into the European game. It would strengthen Italy's bargaining position with regard to the western powers and might assist in the creation of an anti-French bloc in the Balkans and in the fulfilment of Italian ambitions at Turkish expense. To Mussolini's great annoyance, because questions of prestige were also involved, it was Britain and not Italy which became the first Allied power to recognize the Soviet Union. The British treaty, moreover, allowed the Russians to revise the terms of a Russo–Italian trade treaty to their own advantage. The great Soviet market never materialized. There was a brief, if impressive, growth in Italian exports to Russia in 1925–6 but thereafter a sharp drop until 1928–9. The Soviets bought their machinery and industrial goods from Germany, Britain, and the United States, countries where they could obtain substantial long-term credits. Russian exports to Italy, by contrast, increased significantly and remained at a high level, with oil constituting one of the major items. Between 1925 and 1927 the Soviet Union provided the expanding Italian navy with most of the fuel it needed to put to sea. As the Italians suffered from a long-term shortage of fuels (hence the importance of the German coal reparations to Italy), this useful source lessened its dependence on the highly priced oil of the international oil trusts.

Much of Mussolini's early diplomacy was carried on behind the backs of his professional advisers. Never happy with the Palazzo Chigi and highly suspicious of the conventions of European diplomacy, he developed his own network of trusted agents, political mediators, industrialists, and businessmen who acted as go-betweens with the foreigners Mussolini wished to cultivate. Contact was made with Macedonian terrorist groups and with Croat dissidents (despite Italian claims on Croat-inhabited Macedonia), with right-wing German groups, including the National Socialists, and with members of the Austrian *Heimwehr*.

Money was sent to anti-British groups in Egypt and to anti-French groups in Syria and Lebanon. Arms were dispatched to Yemen and communists were encouraged to move into the Arabian peninsula. Mussolini even had the idea of using Afghanistan as the point of Italian entry into Central Asia. His meddling constituted little more than a wish to stir up trouble. The foreign ministry was often bypassed, as were official agents abroad. The Italian trade mission in Moscow, for instance, was kept in the dark about Mussolini's contacts with the Soviet leadership. Much of this secret diplomacy ran counter to the policies of Italy's accredited representatives. In Austria and Germany Mussolini funded groups who were in opposition to each other as well as to the governments in power. He never considered that the funding of nationalist unrest in neighbouring countries, as in Yugoslavia, might adversely affect the policy of ruthless Italianization in the Alto Adige (South Tyrol) and in the mainly Slav and Croatian provinces in the Julian Alps. The use of private channels, the secret dispatch of money and arms, the recruitment of expatriate Italians for the fascist cause, and the extensive use of propaganda in all forms became the hallmarks of the new fascist diplomacy.

Mussolini's early foreign adventures were much applauded in Italy and his name and picture frequently appeared in the world's newspapers. He gloried in his reputation as a troublemaker and was not deterred by foreign critics, mainly on the left in France and Britain, who thought him a dangerous megalomaniac who might, if cornered, commit some 'mad dog act' and destroy the fragile peace. In fact Mussolini was not yet in a position to do more than stir the troubled waters. He could not engage against any state, however weak, that could call on the protection of a major power. When it came to the latter, he sought to exploit the opportunities for enhancing Italian influence by placing a price on Italian support. The Italians benefited from the French need for backing against Germany and from the Anglo-French tensions over reparations and sanctions. Mussolini's attempts to act as 'arbitor mundi', however, tended to annoy the British without bringing rewards from France. The decision to send some engineers into the Ruhr alongside the French and Belgians in January 1923 was taken only after considerable wavering and the testing of more attractive options. By taking part in the occupation Mussolini hoped at least to prevent the French from forcing the Germans into a new reparations agreement that would exclude Italy or threaten German coal deliveries to Italy. On the eve of the occupation he even proposed a continental bloc against Britain, subsequently dismissing the idea as 'absurd' when reports of his proposals appeared in the Italian newspapers. Panicked by the prospect of an extensive military excursion into the Ruhr and a conflict between Britain and France,

Mussolini sought American intervention and returned to the more traditional Anglophile policies of the diplomats. In the end, two years of active Italian diplomacy resulted in increased coal deliveries from Germany but not the larger share of reparations nor any of the other financial advantages, such as a generous debt settlement by the British, that Mussolini anticipated. The attempts to keep a toe in each camp resulted only in minimal rewards, while the courting of all the governments involved only intensified their suspicions and further marginalized the Italians in the spring and summer of 1924.

In the aftermath of the Ruhr crisis Italy's relations with France again deteriorated and the victory of the Cartel des Gauches in May 1924 added an ideological dimension to the prevailing tension. The Italians took extreme umbrage at an anti-Italian press campaign in Paris and at French protection of the *fuorusciti*, the anti-fascist exiles who fled to France. Philippe Berthelot's return to the secretary-generalship at the Quai d'Orsay after his exile under Poincaré reinforced the anti-Italian currents there. French officials coolly appraised Mussolini's list of unfulfilled demands in return for support against Germany. The old conflicts over French-controlled Tunisia with its Italian majority, the Libyan frontiers with Tunisia and Algeria, and Tangier, where Mussolini bitterly resented Italy's exclusion from the international settlement of the city's status, were still on the agenda. The French proved stiff in their transactions, condescending in their attitudes, and generally unwilling to pave the way towards friendship with concessions to Mussolini's *amour propre*.

Mussolini had more success in London once Lord Curzon, who saw no reason to satisfy Italian appetites, left the Foreign Office. Just before the change of government in London, Curzon again insisted that Italian demands for an enlarged Jubaland should be linked to a division of the Dodecanese islands with Greece. The new Labour prime minister and foreign secretary Ramsay MacDonald, despite Labour's disapproval of fascism, proved more obliging than Curzon and ceded Jubaland without any Aegean quid pro quo. The Greeks, too, were more receptive to an arrangement. The recently elected (December 1923) Greek constitutional assembly opted for a republic, a decision overwhelmingly endorsed by a plebiscite in April 1924, and with Venizelos again in exile, the new government in Athens was willing to recognize the annexation of the Dodecanese islands if their Greek inhabitants were granted local autonomy. While protracted and unsuccessful efforts were made to meet this condition, there was a rapprochement between the two governments, who joined diplomatic forces to see what could be won from Kemal in Asia Minor. In the spring of 1924 and again in 1925–6 there were conversations about an assault on Turkey. In June 1924

Mussolini instructed his minister of war, General Antonino Di Gorgio, to prepare plans for a campaign against Turkey, though the latter warned his master that the Italians could not mount such an invasion. In the winter of 1925–6 Mussolini and the bombastic Greek dictator Theodoras Pagalos (1925–6) again planned for an assault on the Turkish mainland; Italian troops were actually assembled for the attack. Cooler military heads in Rome thwarted Mussolini's thirst for action.

The murder of Giacomo Matteotti on 10 June 1924 forced Mussolini onto the defensive. Matteotti, the socialist leader, had tried to have the corrupt and violent March election declared invalid, and a furious Mussolini publicly called on his 'bully-boys' to 'teach him a lesson'. Leading figures in the fascist hierarchy were involved and the murderer came to the Duce's office a few hours after the assassination. It rapidly became clear that Mussolini was implicated; public opinion was outraged, and if the opposition groups had united Mussolini would not have survived. As the very continuation of the fascist regime came under threat, Mussolini had to fight for his political life. It says much about the nature of the fascist movement that he recovered his position mainly with the assistance of the king, the Church, and the conservative and liberal leaders while many of the fascists deserted him in the winter of 1924–5. It was only in January 1925 that Mussolini emerged triumphant, with a speech to the reassembled parliament taking full responsibility for all that had happened and promising to put the country to rights, something which could only be done through a personal dictatorship. Within months the party and the state came under his complete control. The murder led to a sharp but short outburst of indignation in the foreign press. Moscow temporarily renewed the ideological war of words. There were expressions of indignation and horror in both Paris and London, though even at this difficult moment Mussolini was able to censor foreign reporting of these events. Possibly exaggerating the ill-effects of the murder on foreign opinion, Mussolini was prepared to take a prudent line abroad and maintained a very low profile at the 1924 London reparations conference.

Italian diplomats thought that the time was ripe for an understanding with France over Tangier and Tunisia, and talks were resumed. In November 1924, too, a new overture was made to the Soviets and the Narkomindel, after some hesitation, agreed to open discussions about a possible political agreement. In line with Mussolini's more cautious policy, the unofficial contacts with the leaders of the Reichswehr and of the *Stahlhelm* veterans groups were interrupted. Though some of Hitler's supporters found refuge in Italy after the abortive Munich putsch of November 1923 and Mussolini began sending funds to the Nazis after Hitler was released from prison in late 1924, requests that

Hitler should be received in Rome were repeatedly rebuffed. It was, above all, Mussolini's extremely careful handling of the Albanian civil war which showed the extent of his temporary loss of nerve. Both Zogu and Noli appealed to Mussolini for help during the summer of 1924, but he avoided taking sides. When open warfare broke out he preferred to conclude a non-intervention pact with the Yugoslav government, hoping to neutralize Belgrade while Italy was too weak to act. Even when the defeated Zogu, who fled to Belgrade and raised a military force with Yugoslav help, unseated Noli in December 1924, Mussolini refused the latter's appeals for assistance. Once in power, Zogu changed his tune and sought Italian backing against his former patrons who stood in the way of his irredentist ambitions in Yugoslavia. Still Mussolini waited to see what economic concessions Zogu would offer and how the situation would develop before concluding any political agreements with the Albanian leader. It was only in March 1925 that a trade treaty was ratified and Italy given the right to prospect for oil, a valuable concession in the rivalry with Britain. Along with a loan agreement and full control over the National Bank of Albania, the Italians could dominate the small country's economy and finances, and through a 'systematic policy of pauperization' maintain and increase Zogu's dependence on Italy. A secret exchange of letters in August 1925 created a military alliance. In return for an Italian commitment to support Albania should its territorial integrity and sovereignty be threatened, the very reluctant Zogu agreed to declare war on any state that attacked Italy if assistance was requested and promised not to enter into any alliance or military agreements with third parties without the simultaneous participation of Italy. Having regained control in Rome, Mussolini could contemplate turning Albania into an Italian satellite and using it as a springboard for a campaign against Yugoslavia.

It was in December 1924, at a Council meeting of the League of Nations in Rome (the invitation itself a sign of Mussolini's hope to minimize the effects of the Matteoti murder), that Mussolini and Austen Chamberlain, the foreign secretary in the new Conservative government, first came together. It was an important diplomatic breakthrough for Mussolini. The new friends (Lady Chamberlain prominently displayed the gift of a fascist pin) found a common cause in their opposition to the Paris-backed Geneva Protocol which Mussolini had initially supported. Chamberlain's friendship significantly improved Italy's international position as Mussolini set out to consolidate his rule at home and sought to regain his voice in European matters. Chamberlain's repeated visits to Rome (five in all, four in two years) convinced the Italian leader that he could count on British backing in the Balkans and in Africa. The friendship with Chamberlain was particularly important when the Germans made their offer to guarantee the western frontiers.

The move to establish a dictatorial regime was bound to have its effects on the foreign ministry, but change came slowly. In May 1925 Dino Grandi, one of the early fascists who had led the *squadristi* in Bologna, was made under-secretary at the Palazzo Chigi, signalling Mussolini's intention to 'fascisticize' the ministry. In truth, his name was suggested to Mussolini by Contarini, who judged that Grandi would prove an 'acceptable' fascist who would prove no threat to the professionals. Mussolini also appointed Pietro Badoglio as chief of the Supreme General Staff, a new position that gave Badoglio the powers of an army chief of staff with the added authority to issue strategic directives to the navy and air force. Mussolini made himself the minister for each of the services in 1925, a highly unsatisfactory administrative situation that was to continue until 1929 and only hindered the badly needed process of modernization and co-ordination of strategy. In line with Mussolini's plans for the domination of the Mediterranean, funds should have been diverted from the army to the navy and air force. Instead, the army continued to get the major share of the estimates and kept Yugoslavia and France within its sights.

The German offer of a Rhine guarantee in January 1925 turned attention back to western Europe and to the Brenner and Alto Adige, where since 1923 the programme of fierce Italianization had aroused considerable unrest among its formerly Austrian population. Though the Palazzo Chigi saw in the new European security talks a chance to strengthen the links with London and an opportunity to demonstrate Italy's European credentials, Mussolini's attitude was more ambiguous. A Franco-German settlement might focus German attention on the Brenner and divert the French from the Rhineland to the Balkans. It would only be acceptable if there were a Brenner guarantee and if the Italians could win colonial concessions from France as the price of co-operation. It soon became clear that neither the Germans nor the British would consider a guarantee of all the German borders. The French sought Italian co-operation. In March 1925 they proposed a guarantee of a single frontier running from the Rhine to the Adriatic and sought Mussolini's assistance in propping up Austria's tottering economy. Mussolini was not prepared for concerted action with the French; he did not want either France or the Little Entente powers to meddle in Austria. There were no French colonial inducements to co-operation, though Briand spoke of future talks on Tunis, Tangier, and the African colonial mandates. The earlier Franco-Italian colonial talks were stalemated. Mussolini was correspondingly evasive and claimed that *Anschluss* was a greater threat to France than to Italy. He was alarmed, however, when in a conversation with the Italian ambassador in Berlin, Stresemann referred to the growing public interest in a union with Austria and remarked that other countries took a less intransigent stand than Italy. Before the Senate on 20 May, Mussolini announced that the Brenner as well as the Rhine must be guaranteed. Tempers rose, but quickly cooled as neither Stresemann nor Mussolini was ready to press the issue.

The Italian leader had no particular wish to see the Rhineland talks succeed, though he was courted both by Chamberlain and Briand. Chamberlain offered to recognize Italy's 'special authority' in Balkan affairs. Briand backed Chamberlain's initiative, to the horror of the Quai officials, and suggested a guarantee of the 'reciprocal security of respective frontiers'. He promised to regard any *Anschluss* attempt as a *casus belli*.[19] Mussolini was not tempted. He regarded a unilateral guarantee as a 'dubious antidote' to the 'two different categories of treaties', that is, for the western and eastern frontiers, and denied that he had ever received Chamberlain's Balkan offer. Worried by information that Mussolini might seek a bilateral agreement with the Germans or conclude an exclusive deal with the Austrians, Briand tried again in September to secure Italian co-operation in supplementing the Rhineland accords. Mussolini showed no interest, as nothing was said about either Tunisia or Tangier. He pointed out that France was destroying the indivisibility of the peace by separating its own security problems from those of eastern Europe. He claimed that Italy was not vitally interested in the fate of the Rhine and that it was easier for Italy to defend the Brenner than for France to stand on the Rhine. Pressed hard by the Palazzo Chigi officials to join the Allied discussions, Mussolini stood apart, reluctant to take on any commitment north of the Alps. There matters stood, as Chamberlain, Briand, and Stresemann agreed that their experts should consult together on the terms of the agreement.

It was neither the urgings of his officials nor the pressure from Chamberlain and Briand that convinced Mussolini to join the negotiators. It was mainly that he realized that Italy could not absent itself from a major revision of the peace treaties, particularly when it was to be recognized, along with Britain, as one of the guaranteeing nations. Mussolini's last-minute dash by special train, racing car, and speedboat to Locarno fooled no one. He was hissed by anti-fascist demonstrators and snubbed at diplomatic parties. Despite his brief appearance and signature on the agreement, Mussolini was preparing to embark on a more active foreign policy.

[19] H. James Burgwyn, *Italian Foreign Policy in the Interwar Period, 1918–1940* (Westport, Conn., 1997), 30.

IV

At the start of 1926 Mussolini announced that 'the fascist revolution will have in 1926 its Napoleonic year'. In April, in a bellicose speech at Tripoli, he proclaimed Italian supremacy in the Mediterranean, leading the French to take a number of defensive naval and military steps. In the same year he told the leaders of the armed forces of 'his intentions to conquer the Mediterranean basin, necessitating some form of conflict with Britain and France'.[20] It was not hard to foresee that with Mussolini's emergence as the unchallenged master of Italy, he might make some move in south-east Europe in order to challenge the dominant position of France. The potential Italian threat to Yugoslavia and the status quo in the Balkans was not enough to force France to make the necessary concessions in the Mediterranean that Mussolini demanded as the price for a general entente. The long-term dangers of Mussolini's restlessness were partly masked as long as Italy and France were joined in their opposition to German revisionism. The Brenner frontier and the Alto Adige problem, quite apart from the personal antipathy between Mussolini and Stresemann, provided a reinsurance treaty for France. The Locarno treaties made it less necessary for the French to enrol the Italians in an anti-German bloc. The political atmosphere was hardly conducive to negotiations while the Cartel des Gauches (May 1924–July 1926) remained in power in Paris. The distaste of the centre-left parties for the fascist regime and the public support given to the Italian political refugees infuriated Mussolini, who accused the French government of complicity in the anti-fascist press campaigns run by some of the Paris journals. There was no love lost between the 'two Latin sisters', whatever might have been the practical reasons for agreement.

The Duce's reluctance to join the Locarno proceedings did not unduly trouble the British. Austen Chamberlain believed that 'we might easily go far before finding an Italian with whom it would be as easy to work', and was willing to give due regard to Italian sensibilities about being treated as a second-rate power.[21] Though the British were as unwilling to engage themselves over the Brenner as over the Vistula, they regarded French activities in the Balkans and Danube region with some suspicion and anxiety. Chamberlain felt, moreover, that the Quai d'Orsay could be more magnanimous in its treatment of Mussolini's colonial claims. He was fully prepared to believe in Mussolini's pacific

---

[20] Sullivan, 'A Thirst For Glory', 7.
[21] M. H. H. Macartney and P. Cremona, *Italy's Foreign and Colonial Policy, 1914–1937* (1938), 123.

sentiments and support for European stability. It was only in 1928 that the British foreign secretary began to question Mussolini's intentions. In fact the Duce had been reluctant to sign the Locarno treaties because he had little interest in the consolidation of the status quo. The drawing together of France and Germany would frustrate rather than advance his hopes to exploit the weaknesses in the European balance. Though Italy had already been revisionist in its foreign policy before Mussolini's accession to power, it could not then or after his appointment afford to forgo the benefits of the Treaty of Versailles. Nor could it challenge the territorial arrangements resulting from the other peace settlements without some form of outside assistance. Given the fragmented character of south-eastern Europe and the divisions between the beneficiaries and losers of the war, however, there was ample opportunity for a destabilizing foreign policy without resorting to the military action that Mussolini might have favoured, but lacked the means to launch.

Books

BARROS, JAMES, *The Corfu Incident of 1923: Mussolini and the League of Nations* (Princeton, 1965).

BOSWORTH, RICHARD J. B., *The Italian Dictatorship: Problems and Perspectives in the Interpretation of Mussolini and Fascism* (London, 1998).

—— *Mussolini* (London, 2002).

—— and ROMANO, SERGIO (eds.), *La politica estera italiana, 1860–1985* (Bologna, 1991). Esp. chapters by Marcello De Cecco and Gian Giacomo Migone, Claudio G. Segré, and Brunello Vigezzi.

BURGWYN, H. JAMES, *The Legend of the Mutilated Victory: Italy, the Great War, and the Paris Peace Conference, 1915–1919* (London and Westport, Conn. 1993).

—— *Italian Foreign Policy in the Inter-war Period, 1918–1940* (Westpoint, Conn., 1997).

CAROCCI, GIAMPERO, *La politica estera dell'Italia fascista* (Bari, 1969).

CASSELS, ALAN, *Mussolini's Early Diplomacy* (Princeton, 1970).

CEVA, LUCIO, *Storia delle forze armate in Italia* (Turin, 1981).

D'AMOJA, FULVIO, *La politica estera dell'Impero* (Milan, 1967).

DI NOLFO, ENNIO, *Mussolini e la politica estera italiana, 1919–1933* (Padua, 1960).

MACK SMITH, DENIS, *Mussolini's Roman Empire* (Harmondsworth, 1979).

PETERSEN, JENS, *Hitler–Mussolini. Die Entstehung der Achse Berlin–Rom, 1933–1936* (Tübingen, 1973).

PETRACCHI, GIORGIO, *La Russia rivoluzionaria nella politica italiana: le relazioni italo-sovietiche, 1917–1925* (Rome, 1982).

ROCHAT, GIORGIO, *Guerre italiane in Libia e in Etiopia: studi militari, 1921–1939* (Paese, 1991).

—— *L'esercito italiano in pace e in guerra: studi di storia militare* (Milan, 1991).

RUMI, GIORGIO, *Alle origini della politica estera fascista, 1918–1923* (Bari, 1968).

RUSINOW, DENNISON I., *Italy's Austrian Heritage, 1919–1946* (Oxford, 1969).

SHORROCK, WILLIAM I., *From Ally to Enemy: The Enigma of Fascist Italy in French Diplomacy, 1920–1940* (Kent, Ohio, 1988).

TORUNSKY, Vera, *Entente der Revisionisten? Mussolini und Stresemann, 1922–1929* (Cologne and Vienna, 1988).

ZAMAGNI, VERA, *The Economic History of Italy, 1860–1990* (Oxford, 1997).

Articles

BRECCIA, ALFREDO, 'La politica estera italiana e l'Ungheria, 1922–1933', *Rivista di studi politici internazionali*, 47: 1 (1980).

CASSELS, ALAN, 'Mussolini and German Nationalism, 1922–25', *Journal of Modern History*, 35: 2 (1963).

—— 'Locarno: Early Test of Fascist Intention' in Jonson Gayner (ed.), 'Locarno Revisited: European Diplomacy', conference paper (to be published).

ERLICH, HAGGAI, 'Mussolini and the Middle East in the 1920s: The Restrained Imperialist', in Uriel Dann (ed.), *The Great Powers in the Middle East, 1919–1939* (New York, 1988).

GUILLEN, PIERRE, 'Les Vicissitudes des rapports économiques franco-italiens dans les années vingt', in Enrico Decleva and Pierre Milza (eds.), *La Francia e l'Italia negli anni venti: tra politica e cultura* (Milan, 1996).

—— 'Franco-Italian Relations in Flux, 1918–1940', in Robert Boyce (ed.), *French Foreign and Defence Policy, 1918–1940: The Decline and Fall of a Great Power* (London, 1998).

KENT, MARIAN, 'Guarding the Bandwagon: Great Britain, Italy and Middle Eastern Oil, 1920–1923' in Edward Ingram (ed.), *National and International Politics in the Middle East: Essays in Honour of Elie Kedourie* (London, 1986).

KNOX, MACGREGOR, 'Conquest, Foreign and Domestic, in Fascist Italy and Nazi Germany', *Journal of Modern History*, 56: 1 (1984).

—— 'Il Fascismo e la politica estera italiana', in Richard J. B. Bosworth and Sergio Romano (eds.), *La politica estera italiana, 1860–1985* (Bologna, 1991).

—— 'The Fascist Regime, its Foreign Policy and its Wars: An "Anti-Anti-Fascist" Orthodoxy?', *Contemporary European History*, 4: 3 (1995).

MARKS, SALLY, 'Mussolini and Locarno: Fascist Foreign Policy in Microcosm', *Journal of Contemporary History*, 14 (1979).

MOUTON, MARIE-RENÉE, 'L'Italie et le mandat français en Syrie, 1922–1923', in Enrico Decleva and Pierre Milza (eds.), *La Francia e l'Italia negli anni venti: tra politica e cultura* (Milan, 1996).

PETERSEN, JENS, 'Die Außenpolitik des faschistischen Italien als historiographisches Problem', *Vierteljahrshefte für Zeitgeschichte*, 22 (1974).

—— 'Il Mussolini di Renzo de Felice', *Passato e presente*, 1 (1982).

PETRACCHI, GIORGIO, 'Ideology and Realpolitik: Italo-Soviet Relations, 1917–1933', *Journal of Modern History*, 2: 3 (1979).

POULAIN, MARC, 'L'Italie, la Yougoslavie, la France et le pacte de Rome de janvier 1924: la comédie de l'accord à trois', *Balkan Studies*, 16 (1975).

SHORROCK, W. I., 'France, Italy and the Eastern Mediterranean in the 1920s', *International History Review*, 8 (1986).

SULLIVAN, B. R., 'The Italian Armed Forces, 1918–1940', in Allan R. Millett and Murray Williamson (eds.), *Military Effectiveness*. Vol. 2: *The Interwar Period* (London, 1988).

VIGEZZI, BRUNELLO, 'Politica estera e opinione pubblica in Italia dal 1870 al 1945', *Nuova Rivista Storica*, 63: 5/6 (1979).

WEBSTER, RICHARD A., 'Una speranza rinviata: l'espansione industriale italiana e il problema del petrolio dopo la prima guerra mondiale', *Storia Contemporanea*, 11: 2 (1980).

Theses

SULLIVAN, B. R., 'A Thirst for Glory: Mussolini, the Italian Military and the Fascist Regime, 1922–1936', Ph.D. thesis, Columbia University (1984).

7

The Geneva Dream: The League of Nations and Post-War Internationalism

I

The League of Nations was, in the words of its most tireless champion, Lord Robert Cecil, 'a great experiment'.[1] President Wilson's creation injected a new multinational dimension into the traditional modes of diplomatic negotiation. Apart from those who embraced the Marxist-Leninist approach to diplomacy, the system of international relations embodied by the League appeared to many to offer the most viable alternative to the balance-of-power mechanism that had failed so disastrously in 1914. It was not, of course, the League that Wilson had envisaged, quite apart from the absence of the United States itself. The 'Geneva system' was not a substitute for great-power politics, as he had intended, but rather an adjunct to it. It was only a mechanism for conducting multinational diplomacy whose success or failure depended on the willingness of the states, and particularly the most powerful states, to use it. The growth of the new institution was fostered by the increasing internationalization of so many questions previously considered solely of national concern, but it always operated within prescribed limits. The sovereign state was the only source of the League's power. There could be no authority above that of the state, and no state could be legally bound without its own consent. The League of Nations was never intended to be a superstate. It was an experiment in internationalism at a time when the counterclaims of nationalism were running powerfully in the opposite direction.

The League of Nations was inextricably intertwined with the peace settlement. Its 'Covenant' was enshrined within the Treaty of Versailles as its first twenty-six articles. This posed special difficulties from the start. There was a basic contradiction between the treaty that ended the war and a Covenant that proposed a new form of international security.

---

[1] Viscount Cecil, *A Great Experiment* (London, 1941).

The Versailles treaty served the interests of the triumphant Allies and confirmed the new European equilibrium; the League was to serve the interests of all, with the security of each dependent on the security of all. The League had been created by the victor powers and the defeated were excluded from immediate membership. The new body was given specific duties associated with the peace treaty with regard to the Saar, Danzig, and Upper Silesia. Yet to work properly the new system of security needed to be universal and the League's orientation global. From the start, despite the American input to its creation and its many non-European members, the League was a Eurocentric institution, and this European bias was intensified when the American Senate rejected the Versailles treaty in March 1920. Yet neither the British nor the French, who had little confidence in the structure, saw the League as providing the answer either to the stabilization of Europe or to the future security of France. The League was marginal to Lloyd George's way of thinking. He much preferred the meetings of political heads of state, where he and his French counterpart could settle their differences in private. Popular opinion and political considerations rather than enthusiasm or confidence dictated a public policy of qualified support. Privately, Lloyd George believed that a League without the United States was a worthless if not a dangerous institution. While Britain remained an active member and the League's chief financial supporter, Lloyd George made certain that it dealt with questions of relatively little importance. The French leadership, too—and there was little difference between the openly sceptical Clemenceau and his successors—nurtured the League only insofar as it could be turned into the instrument that had been rejected at the peace conference. With great speed, after the Anglo-American guarantee lapsed, the French negotiated bilateral arrangements with Poland and Czechoslovakia to buttress their security position. They also began the search for an alliance with Britain that became a recurring theme in Anglo-French relations. In parallel actions, the French took the initiative at Geneva to strengthen the League's collective enforcement role which the Covenant only imperfectly institutionalized. It was one way to secure British underwriting of France's security needs.

The League was created, first and foremost, to be a security organization. The core of the Covenant lay in those clauses outlining the new security system: the obligations of members, the rules for the settlement of disputes, and the sanctions to be applied to transgressors. It was here that the clash between the hopes of the drafters and the realities of the international system were most apparent and that the weaknesses of the new system most clearly revealed. Article 10, so important to Wilson, guaranteed the territorial integrity and political independence of member states, yet it stopped short of its logical conclusions. Members were not bound to take any specific actions and the Council could only 'advise upon the means by which this obligation shall be fulfilled'. This article appeared dangerous because it added an unnecessary element of inflexibility to the system. Given the way the new territorial lines were drawn and the still undetermined future of so many national boundaries, any guarantee of the status quo was more likely to provoke conflict than to assure peace. It highlighted the division between the states (France, Poland, and the Little Entente powers) which had everything to gain from the existing situation and those (Britain, Italy, and Japan) which were anxious or at least prepared to consider future revision. It was one of the reasons for the US Senate's rejection of the entire treaty and was much disliked by the British. Article 19, framed by Cecil to provide greater flexibility for revision, was invoked only once, in 1920. It proved a cumbersome and inappropriate method for dealing with change in the inter-war years, a period of unusual fluidity in the international system. It was Article 11, which declared any war or threat of war to be a matter of concern for the entire League and reflected the more limited British view of what an international body could achieve, that turned out to be the most commonly used method of bringing disputes to the League's attention. In this respect the new body acted as a commission of conciliation. For war was neither outlawed nor excluded by the Covenant. While states had to accept arbitration or ask for Council intervention in disputes, through Articles 12 to 15, if this failed they were free to 'resort to war' after a three-month delay. Little use was made in the 1920s of the articles that set in motion the automatic and immediate application of non-military sanctions under Article 16, the most innovative part of the Covenant. If these deterrents, economic, financial, and diplomatic, failed, the Council could recommend to the states what military measures might be applied against the transgressor. Intended to prevent states from going to war, the final sanction in the Covenant was the resort to arms. If moral force failed, Wilson told the peace conference on 31 May 1919, 'we must not close our eyes to the fact that in the last analysis the military and naval strength of the great Powers will be the final guarantee of the peace of the world'.[2] Though theoretically the obligations imposed on all states were equal, in the absence of the United States the burden of enforcement would rest upon France and Britain. This made it more difficult to translate an imperfect collective security system into a working mechanism. The problem ran much deeper than the issue of American participation.

[2] Wilson, speech to the Paris peace conference, 31 May 1919, quoted in Salvador de Madariaga, *Disarmament* (London, 1929), 28.

There was no way to guarantee that members would fulfil their responsibilities and enforce the sanctions outlined in Article 16, yet the system depended on the assumption that states would be deterred from 'illegal' war because they knew that sanctions would be imposed. The circularity of the argument exposed one of the League's fundamental weaknesses, for which there could be no cure.

There was a considerable debate, at the time and later, over whether the system of mutual security rested on world opinion or the application of force. The gap between the normative rules in the Covenant and the realities of international behaviour was recognized from the start. In the very first years of the League's existence efforts were made to modify Articles 10 and 16. The British warmly supported the Canadian attempt to weaken the security provisions in the two articles and would have happily abandoned the former if that would have satisfied the Americans. Though not actually amended, the articles were so modified by interpretation that Article 10 lost all significance and Article 16 was seriously qualified. Rules of guidance adopted in 1921 allowed the states to decide whether a breach of the peace requiring economic sanctions had occurred. The Assembly also redefined the concept of 'immediate and absolute' action to include a 'gradual and partial' boycott. As a result of a French veto these rules never acquired legal force, but on the one occasion when sanctions were imposed, against Italy in 1935, it was the French who insisted on their relevance. The debates over Articles 10 and 16 in 1921 and 1923 divided the League membership into contending blocs under British and French leadership. Their battles over the security provisions of the Covenant continued into the 1930s.

The so-called 'gaps' in the Covenant stemmed from the realities of international life. So did the implementation of other provisions; internationalism and equality between member states were limited in practice. State sovereignty was absolute. From the start, states were free to join the League on the basis of minimum qualifications or to leave after satisfying purely formal conditions. The unanimity rule in the Covenant preserved state independence, for it meant that no state could be bound to a decision against its own will, while various provisions safeguarded 'regional understandings' and the domestic jurisdiction of the state from outside interference. Though the League was to be more than an enlarged version of the nineteenth-century Concert of Europe, the founders recognized the superior position and responsibilities of the great powers. The Council and Assembly had concurrent jurisdiction over breaches of the peace and were given parallel authority to deal with any matter coming under the League's auspices, but Articles 11 through 17 provided the Council with a special role in the actual settlement of disputes and the application of sanctions. Article 4 permitted the

Council to deal with 'any matter within the sphere of action of the League or affecting the peace of the world'. According to the Covenant, the Council was to meet at least once a year, the Assembly at 'stated intervals'; in practice, the Council met quarterly and the Assembly annually in September. The Council became the League's administrative body, the permanent status of its great-power members confirming the traditional distinctions between categories of states. Though the small powers increasingly referred threats to the peace to the Assembly, the latter was seen as a public forum in which world opinion could be mobilized rather than as the initiator of positive action. While it was the smaller states that felt they had the most to gain from the new organization, even here their statesmen were driven to look elsewhere for protection. In view of growing British political disinterest, the more vulnerable states gravitated towards France. The small states were divided on whether the security provisions should be strengthened or weakened, depending on the views of their would-be protectors. The unattached states, mainly the neutrals (non-belligerents during the war) and the Baltic nations, tended to support the existing League guarantees. Whatever their positions, the representatives of the smaller nations found in Geneva an important public platform and a unique opportunity to be heard in the corridors of power. Giuseppi Motta of Switzerland, Edvard Beneš of Czechoslovakia, Joseph Bech of Luxembourg, and Paul Hymans of Belgium became familiar figures on the international stage when the League ended its itinerant existence in 1922 and took up residence in Geneva. Those outside the organization showed, at first, little inclination to co-operate with the new body. The Harding administration would have nothing to do with the League: the State Department did not even reply to League enquiries. In 1923, when Secretary of State Hughes agreed to send an 'unofficial observer' to the League's Opium Committee and to appoint a consular official in Geneva to report on League matters, care was taken not to ask Congress for representational costs. Russian contact was restricted to humanitarian and technical matters, co-operation with the League's high commissioner Fridtjof Nansen for the repatriation of prisoners of war and Russian refugees wishing to return to their homeland, and seeking advice on epidemics from the League's Health Organization. Lenin viewed the League as a 'band of robber nations'; it was, according to Chicherin in 1924, 'a poorly screened coalition of victor-Powers created in order to secure their acquisitions and conquests'.[3] Even when

---

[3] Ingeborg Plettenberg, 'The Soviet Union and the League of Nations', in *The League of Nations in Retrospect: Proceedings of the Symposium. Organised by the United Nations Library and the Graduate Institute of International Studies, Geneva, 6–9 November, 1980* (Berlin and New York, 1983), 148.

the Bolshevik government sought to end its diplomatic isolation, the League was still considered an instrument for the maintenance of an unjust and capitalist post-war order. Not everyone agreed that the 'great experiment' was one worth making.

II

If the League was accepted as part of the international landscape, it was because it did not attempt too much. The very choice of Sir Eric Drummond, a British Foreign Office official, to be the League's first secretary-general rather than a political figure like Venizelos of Greece or Masaryk of Czechoslovakia underlined the limited conception of the organization's future role. Drummond, a cautious Scot, possessed a sharp awareness of the realities of power. He cultivated his connections to London while trying to remain on good terms with Paris; he was always more concerned with conciliating the great powers than with the sensibilities of the small. In these early years he kept a close watch on Washington, hoping to bring the United States into the League's orbit but above all avoiding action which might increase its hostility. Drummond preferred working quietly behind the scenes and intentionally minimized his public role. His restricted view both of his own position and the possibilities for League action, though not accepted by the members of the Secretariat, was understandable if not always defensible, given the generally sceptical and sometimes openly hostile environment in which the League operated and the reluctance of the member states to finance the new institution. The average annual cost of the League, the International Labour Organization, and the Permanent Court of International Justice at the Hague during the years 1920 to 1946 was just $5.5 million. Despite this shoestring budget, League officials were constantly badgered, particularly by the British, about costs, waste, and unnecessary expenditure.

To establish its position, the Council of the League moved rapidly to carry out the tasks assigned to it by the 1919 peace treaties. A plebiscite was carried out in the districts of Eupen and Malmédy in 1920 and the two districts were consequently transferred to Belgium. In the Saar, the Council created a five-member Governing Commission under a French chairman; almost immediately it found itself in open dispute with the Saarlanders. Tensions came to a head during the Ruhr crisis when the Saar coal-miners went on strike against their French owners. The League Council approved the doubling of the French military force and backed strict limitations on civil liberties, despite strong protests from the British and an outcry from the Germans. Once the Ruhr was evacuated and calm restored, the Council moved to replace the somewhat authoritarian French chairman with a Canadian and then an American appointee. Peace was maintained. In Danzig, too, the Council found ways to contain the potentially explosive situation in which the rights of the resident majority German population clashed with the political and economic interests of the Polish government. The Council appointed a high commissioner (the first three were British) who, along with representatives of the Free City, created a constitution guaranteed by the League. The high commissioner, who resided in Danzig, was responsible for enforcing the settlement but the League Council was frequently asked to intervene in the numerous disputes between the free city and the Poles. The successful running of the city depended on a degree of economic prosperity as well as the general state of Polish–German relations. Much was owed to Drummond, who used his influence to keep Germans and Poles apart, defusing situations that might heighten the tension between Warsaw and Berlin.

The drafters of the Covenant believed that the main purpose of the League was to promote the peaceful resolution of conflicts between member states through arbitration, mediation, and conciliation. Given the circumstances of its birth, the League confined itself during its early history to the 'small change' of world affairs. It dealt with minor disputes and limited issues and not with the fundamental problems of reconstruction. During the first decade of its existence the Council, with the assistance of the secretary-general, intervened in seventeen disputes likely to lead to confrontation and on seven or eight occasions actually brought open hostilities to an end. There was no progression in the League's success rate. Much depended on the attitude of the great powers on the Council, the local circumstances of the dispute, and the willingness of the disputants to accept proffered solutions. None of these cases involved the use of sanctions, so the League's security system was not tested. On the contrary, the discussions on sanctions during the Corfu and Greek–Bulgarian disputes revealed the legal and practical complications of applying Article 16 and confirmed British hostility towards its implementation. At first the Council was only asked to take on cases where for one reason or another the Allied governments preferred not to act, such as the many clashes between states on the periphery of the former Russian empire where unsettled border conditions and nationalist aspirations were resolved by force. By 1926 Britain herself appealed to the League for a decision in its clash with Turkey over Mosul. However, the fundamental point had not changed: it took great-power agreement to reach any solution, which was in effect what the original drafters of the Covenant had intended.

The first dispute successfully resolved in 1920, despite Soviet objections, was between Finland and Sweden over the Åaland Islands. It proved far more difficult to settle the question of Vilna, which was occupied by the Poles in 1920 in open breach of the truce imposed on Poland and Lithuania pending a Council decision on the boundary line between the two states. Fighting broke out and League efforts to organise a plebiscite failed. The Poles remained in possession of the city and the Lithuanians continued to protest. In 1923 the Conference of Ambassadors and not the League awarded the city to the Poles. It was not until four years later that the Council forced the two countries to negotiate. Both Germany and the Soviet Union had a specific interest in the outcome; both tried to worsen Polish–Lithuanian relations. Stresemann, as Germany was now a League member, and Maxim Litvinov, the deputy commissar for foreign affairs, in Geneva as an observer for the first time, supported the Council's action. The public handshake between the two hostile dictators, Piłsudski and Voldemaras, ended the threat of war but not the bitter feelings on both sides. A series of minor quarrels kept Polish–Lithuanian relations on the Council agenda until March 1938, when a more aggressive Polish prime minister, taking advantage of the turbulence of the time, forced Lithuania to resume normal diplomatic relations under the threat of immediate invasion. The Poles and Lithuanians were also involved in the dispute over Memel, the former German port on the Baltic Sea given to the Lithuanians in 1919. Fighting between the two powers delayed its transfer and the Poles, backed by the French, argued that Memel, like Danzig, should be made a Free City. The prickly question was handed over to the Council under Article 11 in September 1923. The Council followed what would become normal procedure in subsequent years. The secretary-general conferred with the British representative on the Council, in this case Robert Cecil, who in turn consulted with the French and Italians. Assured of great-power co-operation, the Council created a commission of inquiry composed of individuals from states not involved in the conflict. An American chairman, Norman Davis, and his associates recommended that Memel be recognized as Lithuania's main port but that the Poles be granted equal rights with others to use its facilities. Neither of the rivals were satisfied yet both agreed to accept the ruling. The commission's proposals to protect the rights of the local German population proved inadequate and the German government took up the cause of the German Memellanders, who never accepted their Lithuanian masters and found it intolerable to be governed by their 'inferiors'. Again, these national disputes required repeated Council intervention to keep the peace until Hitler took the matter into German hands in March 1939.

There was no agreement between the powers on the division of Upper Silesia, the peace-treaty flashpoint in Polish–German relations.

Poland's claims were pressed by France while Britain and Italy supported Germany. The question was left to the Council to settle, and a complex arrangement (the final award of May 1922 consisted of 606 clauses) was devised by which Germany was awarded two-thirds of the territory and Poland given the lion's share of the area's mineral wealth and industrial plants as well as 350,000 Germans. The issue was bitterly fought between Paris and London, and the League decision was strongly criticized by the Foreign Office. There was uproar in Germany, where it added to the unpopularity of the weak Wirth government. Again, the Silesian judgement was maintained until the advent of Hitler. The territories prospered, but national tensions persisted. The Germans in Polish Silesia, though a minority, were landowners, industrial leaders, and professional men who organized a special pressure group, the *Volksbund*, to bring their grievances to the notice of the Minorities Commission with German support. The Poles in German Silesia, on the other hand, were peasants and workers who were far less politically literate and were poorly organized. This was the background to a sharp clash in 1928 between Stresemann and Zaleski, the Polish foreign minister, over minority rights.

The Italian seizure of Corfu in September 1923, arising out of disputes with Greece over Albania, illustrated how the 'least of the great powers' could get its way when France and Britain agreed to sacrifice justice for co-operation. Feelings ran high in Geneva. The Assembly, which met in September, took up the Greek cause when it appealed to the Council under Articles 12 and 15 of the Covenant. The Italians, however, insisted that the issue be settled by the Conference of Ambassadors, denying that the Council had any competence in a matter that was neither an act nor a threat of war. The real difficulty was that the League could not act initially because the British and French were in disagreement. The British favoured Council intervention but the French, involved in the Ruhr, supported Mussolini. On consideration the British drew back, unwilling to consider a naval demonstration, one possible League sanction, on their own. It was believed that the application of Article 16 was an inappropriate and inflexible way to cope with threats to the peace except in the context of an all-out war. The Italians got their way; it was the Conference of Ambassadors rather than the Council that took the operative decisions, though the British, conscious of domestic opinion, somewhat disguised the extent of their retreat. An investigating commission consisting of British, French, Japanese, and Italian representatives was constituted. When their report was received, only the Italian member considered that the Greek government was to blame, yet the conference judged that the Greeks should pay compensation. The Italian troops left Corfu but there was widespread anger in Geneva. Mussolini had succeeded in having the conflict settled in a forum where Italian interests would be safeguarded and the Covenant ignored. The Council submitted the interpretative questions rising out of the Italian action to a special commission of jurists; in all cases but one the jurists unanimously found against the Italian interpretation of the League's competencies. Because it was in everyone's interest to avoid further wrangles, the legal question was removed from the Council agenda and the ambiguities in interpretation ignored. The Corfu case was a victory for *realpolitik*, the outcome hardly surprising given the attitudes of the key Council members. Though the French were perfectly content with the outcome of the Corfu incident, they argued that the system needed to be improved and tightened. Without concerted arrangements made beforehand and without designating against whom and in what circumstances sanctions would be applied, the advantage was with the aggressor. No British government publicly revealed its deep reservations about the whole feasibility of sanctions; the odium at home and in Geneva would have been too great. Sanctions remained the 'big stick' in the cupboard, though the British were convinced that the stick was made of paper.

The bitter taste left by this League 'failure' was forgotten two years later with the speedy resolution of the conflict between Bulgaria and Greece. In this case sanctions were threatened and the deterrent proved successful. In October 1925 Greek troops crossed over into Bulgaria and the Bulgarians, who were in no position to riposte, appealed to the Council. The secretary-general acted quickly and summoned the Council to meet in Paris. Briand, the acting president of the Council, took the initiative in demanding that both parties cease their military action and withdraw their forces within sixty hours. This appeal was backed by the Council; Briand had the support of Britain, unexpectedly represented by Austen Chamberlain who had just returned from Locarno and Italy. The combined pressure on the Greeks proved sufficient without invoking Article 16. An observer party was sent, a ceasefire arranged, and a commission of inquiry constituted. The verdict went against the Greeks, who were forced to pay £45,000 in reparation. Chamberlain, who chaired the subcommittee reporting to the Council, left the Greeks no option but to accept the Council's decision. Great-power solidarity rather than the sanctions weapon determined the outcome. The successful resolution of the conflict was hailed as a victory for the League and contributed to an unwarranted optimism about the effectiveness of its coercive machinery.

If most of the League's successes during the 1920s involved small states, the clash between Britain and Turkey over oil-rich Mosul in October 1924 suggested that the Council's procedures could be used to keep the peace in matters involving a great power, if that power was co-operative. The British appealed for a decision over Mosul in accordance with the agreement reached with the Turks at Lausanne in 1923. The Kurds, who were the majority in the disputed provinces, wanted independence; if not, they preferred incorporation into Britain's mandate of Iraq, if the mandate was continued for twenty-five years, rather than return to Turkey. Despite delays, an inadmissible British claim for further territory for Iraq, and a Turkish rejection of the League procedure that was settled by a much-debated Permanent Court of International Justice ruling, the Council decision that Mosul should go to Iraq was implemented. The treaty between Turkey, Britain, and Iraq acknowledging the new boundary, almost identical with Lord Curzon's suggested frontier at Lausanne, was signed at Ankara in June 1926. Turkish anger at the decision was mollified by a League-arranged loan, and in 1931 Mustapha Kemal suggested that Turkey would welcome an invitation to join the League.

Though most of these disputes might have been settled by the great powers without the League, Geneva provided a new means of settlement and the Council's participation made it easier for the loser to accept unwelcome judgements. The flexible modes of procedure followed by the Council, the role of the Council president and the secretary-general, the use of the special commission, and the judicious employment of both private persuasion and public admonition added a new dimension to the older forms of diplomacy. A peacekeeping role that did not involve sanctions suited the British, who viewed the Geneva system primarily as a way to promote friendly co-operation, if not the French, who wanted something more. As the decade came to a close, this aspect of the League's peacekeeping function had become part of the international landscape. Whatever the reservations in the chancelleries in Europe, they were not shared by the general public, particularly in Britain, where considerable press attention was given to the League's successes and where the League of Nations Union, one of the most influential and largest pressure groups of the 1920s, kept up a considerable campaign in favour of the League's role as peacekeeper.

III

The League also went to work implementing other aspects of the peace settlements. The Council and the Secretariat, though always in modest ways which would not challenge the authority of the member states, developed techniques for implementing the treaty clauses covering mandated territories and minority rights and for handling the new refugee problem which became a permanent feature of the post-war scene. The Covenant provided for a Permanent Mandates Commission (PMC) of experts to advise the Council and receive annual reports from each of the mandatory powers for the fifteen mandated territories. Neither the Council nor the PMC could coerce the mandatory power; the commission could not even visit the territories or question the inhabitants. Instead, by relying on consultation and co-operation rather than on close surveillance or sharp criticism, the mandatories were led to consider the interests of the local population. The detailed examination of annual reports and local petitions by experts who, like the commission's chairman Marquis Alberto Theodoli, were sympathetic but critical, had a positive effect on the mandatory representatives. The French were particularly sensitive to criticism about their policies in Syria and Lebanon; the British were forced to change tactics, more often with regard to Tanganyika than to Palestine; the Iraqis, who with British support emerged from mandate status to full sovereignty, were persuaded to make concessions to their own minorities. The PMC was assisted by a small secretariat headed by William Rappard, a forceful and dedicated Swiss jurist, who was determined to make the mandate system an effective demonstration of the League's protection role. Neither he nor the commission as a whole questioned the moral basis of colonialism. The mandate system was based on the assumption that the world order was a hierarchical one but that the self-proclaimed civilized nations had a duty to improve the lot of the more backward people under their control. The mandatory powers were reminded that they had duties as well as rights, and for the 'A' mandates this included preparation for self-government. This was a highly legalistic and limited system of control, but it was the first international attempt to tackle the problems of dependent territories and to give a practical meaning to 'reciprocal interest' and 'collective responsibility'. The often-protracted discussions between the commission and the mandate representatives encouraged unrest in the mandates and even in neighbouring colonial territories under direct rule, but this side-effect of the protection system did not detract from the influence of the commission. While it has been cogently argued that the mandate system was little more than a form of neo-colonialism, the work of the Mandates Commission undoubtedly contributed to the moderation of the existing structure of colonial rule in favour of the indigenous people.

The Great War had been 'a watershed in the history of nationalism'. Stalemated on the battlefield, the belligerents had encouraged uprisings of every kind against the existing authorities. The Turkish attempt to wipe out the Armenians in 1915, resulting in the murder of between 800,000 and 1.3 million people, and the ethnic struggles in Poland between 1918 and 1920, which involved the decimation of the Jewish population of the Ukraine on a scale and in a manner not seen before, gave substance to liberal fears that nationalism and self-determination might unleash uncontrollable and murderous instincts. The idea of protecting minorities by law was taken up by women's groups, socialists, and pacifists at the end of the war. At the Paris peace conference the *Comité des Délégations Juives auprès la Conférence de la Paix*, an organization created by eastern European Jews and joined by some American Jews, agitated for the recognition of a collective Jewish identity and for the provision of the largest measure of Jewish autonomy possible. The Germans, too, even before the Versailles treaty was completed, were preparing to argue the case for minority rights to protect Germans living outside of Germany's borders. The representatives of the great powers, aware of the problem, were not particularly anxious to tackle questions of political or cultural autonomy, while the successor states had every interest in burying the issue altogether. Nevertheless, as the creations of 1919 had left many minority groups, long at odds with their new political masters, exposed to dangers that were magnified by the granting of self-determination to some but not to all national groups, the peacemakers felt they had to offer some measure of protection. In so doing, albeit in a much-qualified manner, they extended the rules of international law. After the rejection of proposals to include the protection of minorities within the Covenant itself, the minority issue was finally directly and separately addressed at the peace conference with the creation of the Committee of New States in May 1919. It was no easy task: the committee was pressed for time (the German delegation was already in Paris), subject to all kinds of political constraints, and had in the background reports of fresh violence in eastern Europe. Dominated by its British and American members, the committee drafted model minority treaties, first for Poland and then for Czechoslovakia and Yugoslavia, Greece, and Romania. Despite bitter protests from their representatives, the Polish government, as a condition for recognition, had to grant in Articles 1–8 complete 'protection of life and liberty to all inhabitants' regardless of 'birth, nationality, language, race or religion' and to guarantee the free exercise of any 'creed, religion or belief' not inconsistent with public order or public morals.[4] Article 9 gave special protection to the rights of non-Polish-speaking citizens. The Jews were dealt with specifically in two further articles. Article 10 laid down that the 'Jewish communities of Poland' could establish educational committees of their own choosing and would receive a share of public funds,

---

[4] Quoted in Carole Fink, 'The Minorities Question at the Paris Peace Conference: The Polish Minority Treaty, June 28, 1919', in Boemeke, Feldman, and Glaser (eds.), *The Treaty of Versailles*, 269–70.

while Article 11 guaranteed that the Jewish Sabbath was to be respected and not used as a weapon against the Jews. This was not the recognition of 'national autonomy' that many of the Jewish representatives in Paris wanted, but it was at least an implicit recognition of the separate character of Jewry as being legitimate and inviolable. This measure of legitimacy applied only to the Jews in Poland; the special clauses relating to the Jews were not included in the other minority treaties. Still, it held out the hope of future amelioration at a time when the Jews were facing new and highly dangerous challenges to their very existence.

Poland provided the model for the whole series of subsequent minority treaties protecting the interests of racial, religious, and linguistic minorities. By 1924 thirteen states (Albania, Austria, Bulgaria, Czechoslovakia, Estonia, Greece, Hungary, Latvia, Lithuania, Poland, Romania, Turkey, and Yugoslavia) had recognized minorities as collective entities and had agreed to respect their 'national' rights. Upper Silesia and, in 1932, Iraq were added to the list. The treaties were only applied to new or immature nations that had to be taught the rules of civilized behaviour; it was assumed that the great powers were in no need of such instruction. The successor states bitterly resented being singled out in this fashion; they struggled continuously either to extend the system to all or to dissolve it entirely. A universal regime was opposed by committee members on the grounds that it would involve an unacceptable right to interfere in the internal constitution of every country and would mean the negation of state sovereignty. It was hoped that the minorities, properly protected by international law, would eventually feel secure enough to assimilate into the life of a unitary nation-state. It was a final irony that the 'assimilationist' thesis should have been stood on its head by the National Socialists in Germany, who by giving a racial definition to nationality prepared the way for discrimination and exclusion before the Second World War. The exchanges of population, as in the Greco-Turkish case of 1923, were seen as exceptional and made necessary only because of the seeming impossibility of any other solution. While they did little to diminish the animosity that the Greek–Turkish war engendered, these population exchanges removed a source of considerable danger to relations between the two states.

In a modest way the peacemakers extended the rules of international law. The treaties did not guarantee 'human' but minority rights. The latter went far beyond the protection of religious freedom, as had been done with regard to Belgium in 1830 and Romania in 1878. The treaty states were required to assure equal civil and political rights; minorities were free to maintain their own religious, social, and educational institutions. In some instances specified minorities—the Ruthene province in Czechoslovakia, the non-Greek communities of Mount Athos, and the non-Muslim minorities in Turkey—were given additional protection. Besides the treaties' limited application to certain states only, rights of appeal and the procedures for the redress of grievances were very restricted. The minorities or their defenders could not appeal directly to the League Council, which alone had the right to call attention to infractions or the danger of infractions, and only the Council could take action. Complicated procedures for receiving and considering petitions were established in October 1920 which continued to be followed until the reforms of 1930. Approximately 55 per cent of all petitions were found receivable; complaints, along with the offending government's defence, could be put on the Council's agenda by its Minorities Committee, by a Council member, or by any League member under Article 11 (Lithuania used this procedure against Poland and Albania against Greece). After 1928, as a result of a Council ruling, this last practice ceased. Although the League could refer cases to the Permanent Court of International Justice, this was rarely done and minorities were not allowed to appeal to the court directly. In theory, the Council's powers of redress were extensive. In practice, the state charged with violation had the right to sit as a voting member of the Council, so no actual coercive action could be taken. The emphasis was placed on negotiations between the Minorities Committee and the offending government. The real work was done by the minorities section of the Secretariat, a small group with never more than nine members, which was also responsible for the affairs of Danzig and the Saar. Its dedicated staff consulted with the government concerned either in Geneva or, in contrast to the Mandates Commission, in the country itself. Members could collect information locally and consult with petitioners, who had no further formal role in the investigative process. By operating in an informal and unpublicized fashion, it sought to find solutions acceptable to 'offenders' who generally preferred to avoid public censure. Minority groups protested against their official exclusion from the investigatory process and the behind-the-scenes approach which protected the accused government from unwelcome publicity. Pressure in 1930 by the Canadian Council representative, Raoul Dandurand, backed by Stresemann following a dispute with Poland over German minority rights in Upper Silesia, produced moderate procedural changes that regularized the report system and provided for greater publicity with regard to both complaints and recommended action.

The record of the League during the 1920s was uneven. As the minorities section tried to avoid reference to the Council, less is known about its successes than its failures. The quiet and continuing efforts of the minorities section did produce positive results: compensation for expropriated property, the withdrawal of some restrictions on the educational, cultural, and religious activities of the minorities, and the punishment of individual civil servants found guilty of acts of violence and brutality. Minority groups continued to complain that it was difficult to mobilize public sympathy unless the minorities section would make their grievances more widely known. Unwilling, perhaps, to recognize that nothing that the League could do would change attitudes which made discriminatory legislation politically popular, spokesmen for the minorities had to rely on publicity. The success of the system depended on the co-operation of the states. It appears that Lithuania and Turkey were extremely hostile towards the League's efforts, which proved useless there. Poland, Greece, and Romania, on the other hand, whose actions produced a continuous flow of complaints, did modify offensive behaviour when subjected to strong pressure. The Polish case had important political overtones, particularly after Germany joined the League. For domestic purposes, Stresemann used the protection of the German minorities to gain nationalist support for the League. The German representatives at Geneva encouraged petitions, mainly as an anti-Polish move, but avoided escalating quarrels that might put in question Germany's League standing. It was in the 1930s that the minority question became an explosive issue and the weaknesses of the system fully exposed. The number of petitions fell dramatically from its peak of 204 in 1930–1 to fifteen in 1936. The qualified optimism of the 1920s evaporated in the colder political climate. Germany was found to be at fault in the 'Bernheim case' of 1933, concerning a German citizen of Jewish origin who had lived in Upper Silesia, a case specifically brought to test the minorities protection system. The Germans responded to the Council's request for reform, and conditions in Upper Silesia were somewhat improved. A few months later the Germans asked that the Assembly consider the League's annual minority report. Two French proposals, made with the Bernheim case in mind, to extend minority protection gained general support but were blocked by the German delegates three days before Germany withdrew from the League. In 1934 the Poles withdrew from the minorities protection system entirely. In the larger context, the minorities protection system could operate only because the treaty-bound states were weak; the stronger nations could act with impunity.

Did the League-sponsored system magnify antagonisms by allowing complaints to go forward? It seems highly unlikely. The national, ethnic, and religious divisions that produced discrimination were so deeply embedded in the societies concerned that neither the presence nor the absence of the League regime made any difference in this respect. At the very least, those at risk had some hope of being heard and the international community took note of the need to protect the rights of persons belonging to national or ethnic, religious, and linguistic minorities. Given the present muddled and generally unsuccessful attempts to deal with the dilemmas of nationalism and national rights, one can only envy the confidence and the ambition of a relatively small group of men and women who not only believed that the protection of minorities was an international responsibility, but who assumed that the League's 'powers of persuasion' would convince governments, however reluctant, to accept externally established standards of behaviour.

Parallel steps were taken to tackle the 'refugee problem' on an international basis. Much of the credit for what was done must be given to Fridtjof Nansen, the famed explorer, who had been appointed by a reluctant Council to work on behalf of the repatriation of prisoners of war. As well as his position as high commissioner for Russian refugees, Nansen was also involved in famine-relief work in the Soviet Union, and through arrangements with Chicherin, the Soviet commissar for foreign affairs, provided an administrative framework for the League's modest efforts in this direction. Nansen remained as high commissioner from 1921 until his death in 1930; by 1923 the adjective 'Russian' was dropped from his title and the commissioner took on other tasks, above all the settlement of Greek refugees in western Thrace, an exchange involving considerable numbers of people. Eventually this work, as well as the Bulgarian refugee problem, was handled by specially appointed League bodies. After 1924 the technical work was done by the International Labour Organization (ILO), and Nansen's staff was transferred from the League Secretariat to the ILO. The newly named Refugee Service was responsible to both the high commissioner and the ILO, an unsatisfactory arrangement changed at the end of 1929 when staff and responsibilities returned to the high commissioner.

It was due to Nansen, an extraordinarily creative and personally spartan and selfless figure, and the ILO Refugee Service that the first modest but practical steps were taken to deal with what appeared to be overwhelming numbers of displaced people. Various innovative ways were found to deal with what unexpectedly became a continuing problem whose dimensions, contrary to what was thought at the time, grew rather than diminished. The 'Nansen passport', introduced in 1922 for Russian refugees, was extended to cover other specified refugee groups. Arrangements made with regard to the legal status of Russian refugees in 1928 were similarly extended in 1933 and 1938. The ILO Refugee Service between 1925 and 1929 was able to match refugees looking for jobs with potential employers in other countries; help was given with emigration formalities and transport arrangements.

TABLE 17. Eastern European International Refugees Report, 1927–1930

	1927		1930			
	Russian	Armenian	Russian	Armenian	Syrian	Turkish
Austria	2,465	270	2,401	263		
Cyprus ⎱ British	40	2,500	40	2,500		14
Palestine ⎰ Empire	30	1,500	28	2,000		
Iraq	222	6,784	30		3,600	5
Bulgaria	26,494	22,000	23,848	22,000		3
China	76,000	450	119,294	500		
Czechoslovakia	30,000	200	23,800			
Danzig	300	200	269			
Denmark	300		300			
Estonia	18,000		16,822			
Finland	14,313		14,314			
France	400,000		400,000			5
Germany			100,000			
Greece	2,075	42,002	2,026	38,834	600	37
Hungary	5,294	15	4,751	15		
Italy	1,154	603	1,154	603		
Japan	2,356	24	2,356	24		
Latvia	40,000					
Lithuania	10,000					
Norway						
Poland	90,000		99,815	1,000		
Romania			70,000			
Spain	500		500			
Sweden	1,000		1,000			
Switzerland	2,268	250	2,266	250		
Syria		86,500		85,842	1,500	30
Turkey	3,000	4,963	866			
Yugoslavia	25,350	543	26,521			
Southern Russia					15,000	
Albania						2
Egypt						14
Other countries						51
Total	751,161	168,804	912,401	153,831	20,700	161

Sources: League of Nations A.48. VII, p. 25, Report to the Eighth Ordinary Session of the Assembly (Geneva 1927): id., Report to the Secretary General on the future Organization of Refugee Work, Annex 1, p. 12 (Geneva, 1930).

Nansen's main concern towards the end of his life was with the resettlement of the Armenian refugees in Soviet Armenia. League support was extremely limited; only the barest administrative expenses were paid (Nansen had no salary) and funds had to be raised from outside sources. Some money was raised from the refugees, who were required to pay for the annual stamp on their Nansen passports. Other contributions came from private and public sources. In 1927 the fund reached 66,000 Swiss francs; by 1935 it amounted to 338,000 Swiss francs. Nansen's hopes were repeatedly frustrated by the lack of even small sums of money. The prospects were hardly encouraging when the new and autonomous Nansen International Office for Refugees was created in 1931 with a minute administrative budget. The Assembly decided at the same time that it was to be closed down at the end of 1938, a reflection of the still common assumption that the refugee problem was a temporary one for which solutions would be found. Further innovative approaches to solving the refugee problem during the early 1930s were stifled by the unwillingness of the League statesmen to face questions that were becoming politically embarrassing at home as well as highly contentious abroad. As the number of 'political' refugees swelled, the member states became increasingly reluctant to extend the scope of the League's responsibilities. The first steps taken to force nations to recognize that there were responsibilities that did not cease with their national borders were hardly sufficient to cope with the refugees from Russia, Mussolini's Italy and Franco's Spain, quite apart from Hitler's later massive assault on what was left of the international regime.

IV

Pre-war trends toward international humanitarian co-operation both on the part of governmental and private organizations meant that it was expected that the League Covenant should include some provision for promoting prosperity, welfare, and social justice. The non-political dimensions of inter-state relations had to be recognized despite the reluctance of some of the peacemakers. Many of the League's new institutions had their origins in the public international unions and bureaux of the late nineteenth century. Their representatives and supporters as well as propagandists for other causes came to Paris in 1919 to press the case for international recognition. The newly created International Labour Organization (Part XIII of the Versailles treaty) and Articles 23 to 25 of the Covenant were based on the contested and unsubstantiated claim, in the words of the ILO constitution, that 'Universal and lasting peace can be established only if it is based on social justice'. Few statesmen accepted the premise that war was the product of human injustice and that the improvement of the conditions of life would promote peace. Yet it was under this banner that the fifteen members of the Commission on International Labour Legislation, representing the voice of labour, achieved recognition and independent status for the ILO. British influence and the eloquent pleas of General

Smuts overcame President Wilson's objections to the vague mandate given the League for action in non-political matters. Though the League was intended to be little more than an umbrella organization for pre-war humanitarian bodies, the unwillingness of the Americans to associate themselves with the new international organization left many of these outside the League circle. As a result of the efforts of a few individuals and the members of the League Secretariat, a massive proliferation of new specialized bodies took place under Article 23, ranging in their concerns and membership from the Committee on Communications and Transit to the highly informal International Committee on Intellectual Co-operation, whose members paid their own fares to annual meetings. As in so many other respects, the expansion of the League's activities was both a response to existing conditions and a catalyst for further growth. Despite the League's Eurocentric political bias, the work of these agencies was truly international and non-League members were gradually drawn in. The Secretariat assumed a back-up function that became integral to the internationalization of problems dealt with by private individuals and associations who benefited from the exchange of views and documentation that it could provide. Debates in the Assembly publicized its activities and made the mobilization of public and official support more effective and efficient.

The work of the League in these non-political spheres had two different aims: to establish its competence and expertise in order to gain the confidence of member states, and to make the League itself meaningful to the states by involving them continuously in its efforts. While it could count on the applause of some, there were always those League members who felt that their activities violated the principles of state sovereignty. And even where no objections on principle were raised, representatives were not inclined to dig into their national pockets to foster the League's humanitarian work. Only the small Secretariat provided the continuity and 'institutional memory' so essential to success. The early appointees to the Secretariat were men of considerable independence, with broader horizons and greater ambitions than the secretary-general. Whatever the length of their tenure, men like Jean Monnet, William Rappard, Sir Arthur Salter, and Thanassis Aghnides left permanent marks on the infant organization and contributed to the development of an international civil service. The Secretariat, moreover, encouraged co-operation with whatever groups, official or private, that would further the League's work. It was not only in the financial and economic fields that the appetite for expert advice created a demand for the League's services. Many of the committees and commissions that developed in the 1920s were small, underfunded, and dependent on the work of a few activists, but their existence increased the reputation and responsibilities of the League. Whether with regard to the protection of women and children or to technical assistance and health programmes, the League's humanitarian work involved political decisions, often of a contentious nature. In 1929 China asked for assistance in the field of public health and in 1931 requested financial and economic advice. Salter went out for a six-week visit and, along with two other League officials, devised and introduced a plan of reconstruction that so angered the Japanese that it had to be withdrawn. The Secretariat was always cautious and highly conscious of its limited mandate.

In the 1920s the League contributed to the multilateral economic and fiscal discussions that so dominated international diplomacy; one of its key functions was to create data banks and to foster the exchange of information and views. Already in October 1920 the League Council, following the recommendations of Léon Bourgeois, created a committee that was divided into two sections, an economic section staffed by 'experts' acting in their personal capacities and recruited from government departments of trade and commerce, and a financial section made up of officials from finance ministries and distinguished bankers. Close links with ruling elites at home proved necessary and exceedingly useful. Experts worked closely with the Council, reinforcing the dominant role of the wealthier and larger states, with Britain, in the absence of the Americans, setting the pace. Participants in both committees favoured the more orthodox multilateralist and free-trade approaches of the absent official American representatives whose support was so essential for continental reconstruction. The Economic Committee worked slowly, unwilling or unable to act until questions were 'ripe' for consideration. Much effort was expended on such technical questions as the unification and simplification of customs duties and bills of international credit, while the more critical questions of tariffs and other forms of import-and-export prohibitions were postponed until an international consensus had emerged. The failure to tackle such key questions was sharply criticized at the World Economic Conference of 1927 and the role of the experts queried. Appointed in their personal capacity, rather than as state representatives, they were accused either of being spokesmen for their countries or, on the contrary, of being too theoretical and apolitical in their approach to contemporary questions. The Financial Committee was more active and successful. The committee, mainly consisting of bankers and finance ministry officials, opened the way for new forms of assistance to states in financial difficulties even while it looked backwards to the restoration of the pre-war financial system and the return to the so-called automatic gold standard.

The League sponsored or serviced most of the more important financial and economic conferences of the period. The Brussels conference of 1921, the first international conference devoted only to financial and monetary problems, drew on the expertise of civil servants, parliamentarians, businessmen, and financiers. A mass of statistical information was collected. The experts' recommendations for dealing with the current financial difficulties were highly orthodox, but few of the concrete proposals for dealing with inflation, exchange-rate instability, and the lack of capital for reconstruction and monetary stabilization could be implemented. The most innovative proposal, the establishment of an international commission of the League of Nations to sponsor reconstruction loans and international credits, was opposed by the United States which alone could finance loans on the necessary scale. Other less utopian schemes were similarly stillborn, given American 'ambivalence toward international entanglements, the struggle over war debts and reparations, and disagreements among policymakers over whether financial problems could simply be delegated to the market'.[5] A second international financial conference, initiated by Britain and France in the hope that the Americans would attend but serviced by the League, took place in 1922 as part of the Genoa conference. Far less ambitious in their aims, the delegates focused primarily on the restoration of the gold standard and the promotion of exchange-rate stability. Once again the questions of war debts and reparations, as well as official American abstention from the proceedings and their opposition to the extension of the gold-exchange system, made progress difficult. The French, Belgians, and Italians had no wish to stabilize their currencies, which had depreciated more rapidly than sterling, at pre-war parities. They believed that devaluation would lead to a loss of confidence in their currencies, hurt the politically important middle classes, raise prices, and result in unemployment and social unrest. They preferred to wait until their currencies naturally regained their pre-war value before acting. The gold-exchange system, supported by the British but only partially endorsed at Genoa, enabled London to continue as a major financial centre while disguising the full impact of Britain's growing trade deficit. The system was viewed by the Americans as an unwarranted and dangerous official intrusion in the international monetary system and as a British device intended to divert business from New York to London. The French also opposed formalizing the gold-exchange system. Citing their own experiences with the Bank of France, they disliked giving additional discretionary powers to the central banks and opposed changes that would reinforce the financial

---

[5] Eichengreen, *Golden Fetters*, 157.

predominance of London and New York. While governments were still arguing about war debts and reparations, it was unlikely that central bankers, however independent, could successfully collaborate in restoring the stability of the international financial system. The League's most ambitious effort was the Economic Conference of 1927 with its broad mandate and large membership—194 delegates and 226 experts, all chosen as private individuals, from fifty member and non-member states including the United States, Soviet Union, and Turkey. The French were the prime movers; the British had dragged their feet, fearing its possible anti-American bias and attacks on their own economic practices. There was extensive preparation for this four-day meeting, with some seventy separate studies issued by the economic and financial section of the Secretariat. The emphasis was shifted from the financial sphere to questions of international trade since, with the stabilization of most national currencies, it was believed that the period of disordered public finances and depreciated currencies was reaching an end. There were many recommendations for removing the hindrances to the 'free flow of labour, capital and goods', but few were implemented. The prophetic warnings and the wise words of 1927 were soon forgotten when governments were faced with the problems of shrinking trade, depressed prices, and rising unemployment. The push towards international co-operation provided by the League, through its technical and auxiliary functions, was already losing ground in the colder economic climate of the early 1930s.

In its economic, social, and humanitarian work the League made painstaking progress. The Secretariat and the technical organizations were able to collect and collate information on a world scale and to create international standards of behaviour. In many instances they successfully convinced the governments of both member and non-member states to adjust their national legislation to meet such standards. Constructive precedents were set for combining the work of the League with private and public organizations and for working out common modes of procedure in the pursuit of economic, social, and cultural goals. A few visionaries hoped that, in dealing with problems that lay outside the realm of traditional diplomacy, the League would provide examples of international co-operation that could be transferred to the political arena. It was only in the late 1930s, when the League had lost all its political credibility, that its functional work came to be regarded as its most important and main redeeming feature. In the 1920s European statesmen paid little attention to the League's expanding humanitarian role and focused instead on its peacekeeping activities, where progress was modest, and on the search for a disarmament formula, which never came within its grasp.

V

Given the enormity and costs of the Great War and the heavy burden placed on all European populations, it was inevitable that post-war governments should be urged to cut their armed forces and their expenditure on arms. Geneva became the natural focal point for much of this agitation. The pursuit of disarmament absorbed more of the League's attention, time, and energy than any other problem. It turned out not only to be a futile quest but one that helped to destroy the League's credibility in the political arena. Owing to President Wilson's insistence, Article 8 of the Covenant asserted that 'the maintenance of peace requires the reduction of national armaments to the lowest point consistent with national safety and the enforcement by common action of international obligations', and required the Council, aided by a permanent commission (Article 9), to formulate plans for such a reduction. Both the preamble to Part V of the Versailles treaty and the official Allied reply to German objections to the peace treaty presented the German disarmament requirements as being 'first steps towards that general reduction and limitation of armaments which they seek to bring about as one of the most fruitful preventatives of war, and which it will be one of the first duties of the League of Nations to promote'.[6] Behind these promises, which had a powerful moral force regardless of whether they were legally binding, was the widespread belief on both sides of the Atlantic that great armaments led inevitably to war and that the arms race had led directly to the catastrophe of 1914. Apart from the Bolshevik view that war was implicit in the final stage of capitalist development and the 1914–18 conflict only the first of a series of imperialist wars, there were many variants on this theme. They extended from conspiracy theories about the influence of the makers of armaments (the so-called 'merchants of death') and international bankers, to the more sophisticated claims that war expenditure stimulated nationalism, encouraged national enmities, and diverted resources from more productive and socially useful purposes that would reduce the risk of conflict. It was owing to the efforts of a few individuals that the question of international disarmament was seriously pursued after the first flush of enthusiasm had died. Once it was started, however, the growing strength of public feeling on the subject meant the process acquired a momentum of its own. No government wished to be blamed for failure. Whatever the difficulties, the disarmers argued that the

---

[6] 'Reply of the Allied and Associated Powers to the Observations of the German Delegation on the Conditions of Peace', 16 June 1919.

post-war period was an ideal time to implement the Covenant's promise. Despite evasion of their armament restrictions, of far more concern to the French than the British, the Germans were effectively disarmed and posed no immediate threat to peace. The images of the recent war were fresh and the case for disarmament had strong support at the popular level in Britain and France. There were powerful financial reasons for all states to seek an arms-limitation agreement.

The difficulties of international disarmament were real and apparent from the start. Without resolute political leadership it proved difficult to advance the case for arms limitation. When it came to discussing troops, ships, or planes, the military men came into their own and the prospects of an arms agreement receded. Many technical difficulties were political arguments 'dressed up in uniform', but there were also formidable problems to be overcome when the different services of more than forty nations had to be considered. Weapon systems were different, equivalents hard to find, and ratios difficult to establish. Methods of control and inspection raised fundamental questions about sovereignty and independence. The problems of general disarmament were and are always daunting. While the smaller nations were the most insistent that action was required, neither of the two key League members, Britain and France, thought that disarmament would promote peace. None of the service chiefs in either country believed in arms reduction. On both sides of the Channel they shared the assumption that there was no substitute for military power in underwriting the safety of the state. Before 1925 there was no British disarmament policy. Soon after the war ended the army reverted to voluntary service and drastic cuts were made in Britain's military establishment. The decision reached in 1919 that there would be no European war for the next ten years, the so-called 'Ten Year Rule', became the basis for Treasury demands for reductions in all three service estimates. It imposed its control only over the army. In 1922 and 1924 the air force and navy successfully sustained their claims for increased expenditure. Throughout the 1920s the British were spending as much, if not more, than any other power on their armed services, and the figures never fell below their pre-1914 levels. The services never got all they wished, and in absolute terms the money spent on the three services fell from 1925 until 1934. The British consequently argued in Geneva that they were already disarmed and barely had the necessary troops to carry out their existing imperial responsibilities. The burden on the navy was exceptionally heavy; it had no option but to underwrite Britain's global position, but even the 'senior service' suffered from drives for economy. Herein lay another reason for successive cabinets to seek reductions in Britain's European commitments.

The French position was entirely consistent and perfectly logical. The Versailles treaty had not provided the measure of safety considered necessary before Germany returned to her great-power status. There was no Anglo-American guarantee or British alliance. There were even difficulties in underwriting the treaty position and enforcing German disarmament. The only way the continental status quo could be preserved was to maintain France's military strength. Ultimately, the French army was the guarantor of the peace of Europe. Such was the dread of German revival that numerical superiority in soldiers and in armaments did not calm French fears. Germany's superiority in population and industrial potential required constant vigilance. Those in control of French defence policy knew that, despite its quantitative superiority, the French army was poorly equipped, inadequately trained, badly led, and suffering from poor morale. Its large air force, despite British talk of the French bombing threat, consisted mainly of obsolete planes. Only the French navy, after the Washington Naval Conference, was set on a programme of expansion and improvement. No French prime minister would consider a reduction in French forces without a strengthened security system backed by effective sanctions. The French never fully spelled out what they meant by such a system, but its effectiveness, in the absence of a British guarantee which was France's first priority, depended on the British assumption of expanded League responsibilities that London was clearly reluctant to assume. In the French view, security had to precede disarmament.

The League's initial efforts to promote disarmament brought little progress or credit. All governments theoretically favoured disarmament; in practice, each was mainly anxious to see the others disarm. On 17 May 1920 the League Council created its Permanent Advisory Committee (PAC) on military, naval, and air matters, composed of representatives drawn from the armed services of the member states. Any hopes that they might agree on how force levels might be set were rapidly dispelled. The discussion led only to the unsurprising conclusion that disarmament was impracticable. The first League Assembly, meeting in September 1920, would not let the matter rest, and when the three Scandinavian members put disarmament on the agenda there was a general demand that a broader group of experts should be assembled who did not have their hands tied by governments. As a consequence, the Council created, in addition to the PAC, a Temporary Mixed Commission (TMC) composed of experts competent in 'political, economic and social matters', along with representatives from the PAC, the League Financial Commission, and the ILO. For its first two years of work, however, the TMC confined itself to examining how to control the traffic in and private manufacture of armaments, and to conducting a statistical inquiry into the present state of armaments possessed by League members. It was the success of the Washington Naval Conference (12 November 1921–6 February 1922) that encouraged Assembly optimism on the possibilities of more ambitious measures. Though the internationalists disliked talks that were held outside the League, at Washington agreement was reached and battleships were actually scrapped.

The Washington treaties were the product of specific domestic requirements in each of the three chief negotiating states, and were linked with political agreements affecting China and the Pacific area. The United States, the strongest potential naval power, was willing to make concessions to avoid the expenditure of a naval race. The American shipbuilding programme of 1916 was already stalled, with no ship more than 45 per cent completed. Warren Harding, the new Republican president, was faced with a major Congressional attack on the completion of the programme just when the Navy Department had submitted yet another construction bill. Though the 'big navy' group won powerful support in the Senate, conventional wisdom in a country recovering from a post-war recession suggested that money spent on defence was money wasted. The shaggy-haired Republican senator from Idaho, Senator William Borah, brought together a formidable collection of women, labour, churchmen, pacifists, and teetotallers to oppose the president's bill. Borah's resolution of December 1920 calling on the president to work towards a naval limitation treaty with Britain and Japan won adherents in the Senate. Charles Evans Hughes, the secretary of state, while neither for nor against naval building, was extremely hostile towards the Anglo-Japanese alliance and prepared to co-operate with the British only if the alliance was terminated. Japan, seen as the most probable future threat to the Pacific equilibrium, had progressed furthest with its naval plans, but financial resources were undoubtedly strained. Completion of its naval building programme would account for half the Japanese budget at a time when exports were down and tax revenues reduced. The Japanese premier, Hara Kai, a former diplomat who would be assassinated on the day the Washington conference opened, was engaged in a major political battle in Tokyo. He needed, for political and economic reasons, an agreement with the United States even if this meant withdrawing from activist policies in China and possibly abandoning the Anglo-Japanese treaty. It was important that Japan's new place in north-east Asia be recognized, but a conservative position might bring useful recompense. The British, too, who were about to take their own conference initiative when the American invitation arrived, found it more advantageous to negotiate with the United States than to engage in a costly capital-ship naval race that they might lose. If America chose 'to put up the money and persevere, [it would] have a good chance of becoming the strongest Naval Power in the world', Winston Churchill warned on 23 July 1921, 'and thus obtaining the complete mastery of the Pacific'.[7] In early 1921 the British government gave the go-ahead for the construction of eight super-dreadnoughts, but preferred to compromise. The Admiralty talked almost exclusively of a 'one power standard' or 'equality with any other power'. Building ships in response to the American threat at a time when an 'anti-waste' campaign had been launched fuelled a bitter Treasury–Admiralty battle. Lloyd George desperately wanted a foreign-policy success to restore his political credit; the Irish problem was barely settled and there were difficulties in both Europe and in the Middle East. Slowly and reluctantly, the Foreign Office decided that in the interests of American co-operation, the Anglo-Japanese alliance would have to go. As the Dominions were divided over the wisdom of such a move, a tripartite solution was the best possible compromise.

Once Harding issued his invitation to Washington, the British fused their naval and Pacific policies. They expected little from the conference or from Hughes. The delegation led by Arthur Balfour, after a very stormy crossing, found it was in no position to refuse the Hughes proposal for a ten-year building holiday for capital ships. Britain, the United States, and Japan accepted the proffered 5–5–3 ratio in tonnage for capital ships. France, after raising major objections, accepted a capital-ship ratio of 1.75 and parity with Italy on the condition that these limits did not apply to smaller ships, namely cruisers and submarines (which the British wished to abolish entirely). The 'Washington system' was a limited one; the parity arrangements applied only to capital ships and for a ten-year period. The British would not extend the ratios to other classes of auxiliary vessels. As the British had a substantial advantage in cruisers, essential for the protection of their worldwide trade, they agreed only that cruisers should not exceed 10,000 tons or mount anything larger than eight-inch guns. The British still led the Americans in tonnage and number in every category of ship. The Admiralty was prepared to accept the new ratios; its chief concern was with the ten-year holiday, that would damage Britain's shipbuilding capacity. The Japanese had to accept a lower ratio than they wished but won a non-fortification clause preventing either the British or the Americans from developing or operating bases within 3,000 miles of Japan. Pearl Harbor and Singapore, exempted from the agreement, were their nearest bases;

[7] Erik Goldstein, 'The Evolution of British Diplomatic Strategy for the Washington Conference, 1921–22', in Erik Goldstein and John Maurer (eds.), *The Washington Conference, 1921–22: Naval Rivalry, East Asian Stability and the Road to Pearl Harbor* (London, 1994), 15.

neither could challenge the Japanese domination of east Asian waters. On the political side, neither the Four Power treaty, in which the four signatories (the United States, Britain, Japan, and France) guaranteed each others' rights in insular possessions in the Pacific and agreed to concert together if their rights were threatened, nor the Nine Power treaties, which guaranteed the territorial integrity and administrative independence of China and reaffirmed the 'Open Door' principle, committed any of the participants to action. The Americans were freed from the threat of the Anglo-Japanese alliance which had previously been central to their naval planning. The British, having won a face-saving way of withdrawing from the Japanese alliance through the Four Power pact, thought they could placate the Japanese and get the Americans to share their policing responsibilities in the Far East. The Nine Power treaty was without real substance. It contained no means of enforcement and the Japanese believed that it did not apply to Manchuria, the part of China they were intent on controlling. The changed status quo in the Pacific was recognized and momentarily stabilized. It was enough to make possible the negotiation of an arms-reduction treaty. The Treaty of Locarno did not provide a similar basis for general disarmament in Europe.

Though the Washington treaties have evoked a great deal of historical criticism, in recent years a more positive verdict has emerged. The British had retained their naval supremacy without engaging in a costly race with the Americans, who did not build up to the treaty limits. The Royal Navy scrapped mainly old and obsolete vessels and abandoned only a paper programme of new construction. Having decided that the Royal Navy needed a 50 per cent margin of capital-ship superiority over the Japanese, the Washington conference gave the British 60 per cent. In European waters the Royal Navy was assured total dominance. The British were defeated solely on their demand that submarines should be outlawed. More contentious is the issue of the abandonment of the Japanese alliance, though it seems doubtful whether its retention would have kept the Japanese navalists in check or prevented Japanese expansion in China. The Americans did well out of the treaty, given the fact that Congress was reluctant to appropriate money for building a fleet, especially expensive capital ships. It might well have baulked at appropriating the large sums needed to develop bases in the western Pacific for an offensive war. The Japanese home islands were safer than before and Tokyo saved from a costly naval building programme that might have triggered an American response. Each of the three main naval powers emerged in a better position than would have been the case had there been no naval limitation treaty at all. France suffered a diplomatic check, but the French navy achieved its minimum demands and was left free to build the number of light ships and submarines needed to secure its naval objectives. The French lost the propaganda battle and were portrayed in the American press as bellicose militarists. The French delegation had no opportunity to act as mediators between Britain and the United States, as Briand had hoped. Worse still, Briand, who resented Britain's failure to consider France's entitlement to special treatment, handled the situation badly and left the conference having alienated both the Anglo-Saxon powers. His attempts to link naval and land disarmament angered the Americans, and his efforts to smooth the way for a sympathetic consideration of France's financial difficulties were ruined by the American press campaign. The Italians felt that they had won a victory in securing parity with France, and in principle this was a check on French ambitions. Given that French finances precluded building capital ships (France already led Italy in this category) and it was assumed that the Italians would be financially unable to build up to the tonnage limited in other categories, the French navalists should have been content with what had been achieved at Washington. The relegation of France to the second rank of naval powers, however, and the forced acceptance of parity with Italy was a severe blow to the *amour propre* of the naval establishment.

The treaties won considerable popular acclaim (except in some naval circles, above all in Japan) and raised considerable hope that they would mark, in President Harding's words, 'the beginning of a new and better epoch in human affairs'.[8] There were high expectations not only that other naval agreements would follow but that the Washington example would serve as the first step towards a general disarmament programme. There were obvious reasons for the optimism about naval disarmament in the 1920s. Technically, naval limitation was a less complex problem than land or air disarmament. Fewer states were involved and the major naval powers could arrange matters to their satisfaction without the interference of small and often landlocked nations. There was not the same variety of weaponry, concealment was difficult, the construction of ships was slow, and the possibilities of conversion limited. Shipbuilding was a highly expensive proposition and the 'High Seas' governments wanted to avoid naval races where it was possible. Naval-limitation systems could be self-contained, as the French discovered when they unsuccessfully tried to extend the Washington discussions to include land forces. The naval treaty, however, could not be applied to other naval sub-systems, nor could naval disarmament be linked with other forms of arms reductions. A League-sponsored meeting at Rome in

[8] T. Buckley, *The United States and the Washington Conference, 1921–1922* (Knoxville, Tenn., 1970), 172.

February 1924 broke up without any results at all. France and Italy would find their Mediterranean concerns of far greater concern than the global naval balance, and the British failed to bring either naval power into the extended Washington system after 1930.

The French failure at Washington was compounded by the collapse of the Cannes negotiations in January 1922, when once again the British refused to provide the extensive treaty guarantees that Briand and Poincaré so anxiously sought. France was also faced with further unwelcome disarmament proposals on the League's Temporary Mixed Commission during early 1922. The British delegate, Lord Esher, put forward the formula of applying ratios, like the Washington treaty's naval ratios, to the size of European armies (colonial forces were excluded from the calculations). The French hated this 'simplistic' and 'entirely arbitrary' scheme, and since it lacked any official British support it was soon abandoned. It was with French backing that the representatives of the smaller states, including Edvard Beneš of Czechoslovakia and Paul Hymans of Belgium, took the initiative in raising the security question as the necessary preliminary to any disarmament agreement. On 27 September 1922 the Third League Assembly adopted 'Resolution XIV' underlining the indissoluble connection between security and disarmament and making a disarmament agreement conditional upon the conclusion of a general defensive pact. The result of this was new action in the Temporary Mixed Commission during 1923. The Anglo-French experts produced separate treaties which were eventually combined to form a single Draft Treaty of Mutual Assistance. Presented to the General Assembly in September 1923—hardly an auspicious time in Franco-German or Anglo-French relations—the Draft Treaty required all signatories to come to the aid of any signatory on the same continent who was the victim of aggression. The powers of the Council were expanded and strengthened; it could designate the aggressor and decide on the application of sanctions, including the organization of military forces. This mutual guarantee was tied to the acceptance of a general disarmament plan and provision was made for a detailed disarmament scheme to follow. Most of the European states, including France, accepted the Draft Treaty, though many with reservations. Despite its British origins, Ramsay MacDonald's Labour government buried the proposal when it rejected the plan on 5 July 1924. The most important objection was the increased burden placed on Britain's overstretched armed forces. The expanded role of the Council would turn the League into that 'super-state' rejected by all British governments. The Dominions, particularly Canada, and the Scandinavian countries were equally hostile, nor did the scheme find any favour with the American, Soviet, or German governments. Even the French were doubtful whether the provisions for assistance were sufficient to warrant reductions in their military forces.

Such was the momentum, however, behind the French effort to find some way out of their security dilemma and the desire of the Assembly for a disarmament conference that the discussions had to continue. No Labour government in London, kept in power by the Liberals, among the most active political supporters of the League, could turn its face against disarmament. Already in his letter rejecting the Draft Treaty, MacDonald had declared his intention of calling a worldwide disarmament conference at an appropriate moment. Having checked the French during the London reparation talks of August 1924 and rejected Herriot's attempt to secure some kind of Anglo-French pact, the Labour prime minister felt it politic to take some step in France's direction. The Foreign Office, conscious of the French malaise, discussed the possibilities of a mutual guarantee against aggression which Germany could join. Such a pact would get the French out of the Rhineland, remove one of the main sources of German discontent, and encourage a new spirit of co-operation among the nations of Europe. This was the background to the 'Geneva Protocol for the Pacific Settlement of International Disputes', the word 'protocol' used to indicate that the proposal was a gloss on the Covenant and not a departure from it. Both the socialist leaders, MacDonald and Herriot, attended the League Assembly in September 1924, the first time that either country was represented by its prime minister. MacDonald spoke of the need to admit Germany to the League and argued the case for compulsory arbitration. Herriot raised the question of sanctions: arbitration alone would not provide the compulsion needed to assure compliance and security. Further impetus for action came from an unconfirmed rumour that the Americans were about to call another disarmament conference outside the League. The 'Geneva Protocol' embodied a triple formula: arbitration, security, and disarmament. Its terms were hammered out in two committees: one on security, brilliantly chaired by Beneš of Czechoslovakia, and the other on the system of compulsory arbitration, headed by the Greek delegate, Politis. An automatic system for the settlement of all disputes was created, with the failure to accept arbitration regarded as the test of aggression. The Geneva Protocol was intended to fill the 'gap' in the Covenant created by Articles 12 and 15; under the new terms, no state could resort to war except with the consent or at the behest of the Council. Any state going to war after a judgement of the Permanent Court of International Justice, an arbitration body, or the Council was automatically judged the aggressor and would be subject to sanctions. All signatories would refer their judicial disputes to the Permanent Court and accept its judgement as final. In the case of non-judicial disputes, where no unanimous decision could be reached in the Council the case would automatically be referred to arbitration and the award made binding. The Protocol would come into operation when a disarmament conference, called for June 1925, agreed on a general disarmament plan.

This tightening of the League's general security system (matters falling within the state's domestic jurisdiction, of course, were excluded) still left the final power of enforcing sanctions to the individual states. At most, it provided a correction to the juridical weakness of the Covenant. In the British view, the Protocol, even more than the Draft Treaty, would have placed an intolerable burden on their fleet and add unnecessary and dangerous commitments in areas where Britain had only limited interests. It was not an obligation that the government, or any of the Dominions, which strongly opposed the Protocol, was willing to accept. Acceptance would freeze the European status quo at a time when the Labour government was intent on some form of continental revision. The British representatives in Geneva had played a major role in the Protocol's drafting during the autumn of 1924. In its final form, however, it would have extended the powers of the League in just those directions that no cabinet could sanction. This 'harmless drug to soothe nerves'— MacDonald's words—had little chance of success in London. It is doubtful that the Protocol would have been approved even if MacDonald had stayed in office. The victory of the Conservatives in the October 1924 election assured its rejection. The new cabinet was overwhelmingly opposed to its terms, the Foreign Office vehemently hostile, and the service chiefs alarmist about its interventionist implications. The new proposal evoked a similarly hostile reaction in Washington, where it was feared that the provisions regarding non-members might involve European action against the United States. The risk was negligible, but American hostility reinforced British and Canadian opposition. Foreign Secretary Austen Chamberlain's rejection in March 1925, which he explained earlier to Lord Crewe, reflected the majority view:

A form of guarantee which is so general that we undertake exactly the same obligations in defence, shall I say of the Polish corridor (for which no British Government ever will or ever can risk the bones of a British grenadier) as we extend to those international arrangements or conditions on which, as our history shows, our national existence depends, is a guarantee so wide and so general that it carries no conviction whatever and gives no sense of security to those who are concerned in our action.[9]

---

[9] Chamberlain to Lord Crewe, ambassador to France, 16 Feb. 1925, *Documents on British Foreign Policy, 1919–1939*, ser. I, vol. 27, no. 200, 303–4. Henceforth cited as *DBFP*.

The British rejection sealed the fate of the Geneva Protocol. It remains an open question whether the Geneva Protocol's acceptance would have sufficiently reassured the security-seeking states, above all France, to allow progress towards disarmament. It is questionable whether the Protocol alone would have provided the certainty needed to make a collective security system viable. Even in a more limited system, created to meet an outside threat, there always remains an element of doubt as to whether member states will fulfil their obligations. In an inclusive system, where every state could be the aggressor or the victim of aggression and all are pledged to act, there was no way of assuring compliance. Much of the subsequent history of the disarmament talks was concerned with the differences between Britain and France and the question of priority, whether disarmament would lead to security or security precede disarmament. Britain was concerned, as at the peace conference, with European stability, still hoping to reduce European commitments in favour of its worldwide interests. As long as the 'German problem' remained on the agenda it had to play a major continental role. The continuing involvement in Europe did not mean, however, accepting an alliance on French terms or taking on added responsibilities through an extension of the League's security functions. On the contrary, London sought to weaken the French links with its east European allies and would try to modify the Covenant's security provisions. The French and their allies had everything to gain from a strengthened League committed to the support of the status quo. As constituted, the League did not provide the security that France required to reduce its military forces further than financial exigencies made necessary. As France remained, for the moment, the strongest military power in Europe, there could be no viable disarmament agreement without her. Using this powerful card, the French sought to gain through the League the backing from Britain that she had not yet won from London. More was at stake than the differing interests of land and maritime powers, though these, too, added to the difficulties of bridging the gap between the two most powerful European states. In the absence of any other comprehensive alternative, whatever its weaknesses, the Geneva Protocol would later be seen in Paris as the best means to enhance her security.

The security problem that had led MacDonald and Herriot to the Protocol would be settled in a different way at much less potential cost from the British point of view. Chamberlain, while globalist in his outlook, gave precedence to European affairs, and sought 'special arrangements to meet special needs'.[10] His March 1925 speech to

[10] Richard S. Grayson, *Austen Chamberlain and the Commitment to Europe: British Foreign Policy, 1924–29* (London, 1997), 55.

the League Council pointed to a regional arrangement guaranteeing the Franco-German borders. The somewhat cold and reserved British foreign secretary, unfairly judged as a political washout, helped to create the conditions for what was seen as a new chapter in European diplomacy. Some hoped that this and similar regional security guarantees might be the key that would open the way for general disarmament.

Books

AHMANN, ROLF, *Nichtangriffspakte: Entwicklung und operative Nutzung in Europa, 1922–1939. Mit einem Ausblick auf die Renaissance des Nichtangriffsvertrages nach dem Zweiten Weltkrieg* (Baden-Baden, 1988).

—— BIRKE, A. M. and HOWARD, M. (eds.), *The Quest for Stability: Problems of West European Security, 1918–1957* (Oxford, 1993). Esp. chapters by Erwin Oberländer, Keith Robbins, Zara Steiner, and Philip Towle.

ARMSTRONG, DAVID, *The Rise of the International Organisation: A Short History* (London, 1982).

BOEMEKE, MANFRED F., FELDMAN, GERALD D., and GLASER, ELISABETH (eds.), *The Treaty of Versailles: A Reassessment After 75 years* (Washington, DC and Cambridge, 1998). Esp. chapters by Carole Fink and Antoine Fleury.

CLARK, IAN, *The Hierarchy of States: Reform and Resistance in the International Order* (Cambridge, 1989).

CLAUDE, INIS L., *Power and International Relations* (New York, 1962).

—— *Swords into Ploughshares: The Problems and Progress of International Organisation* (London, 1964).

DINGMAN, ROGER, *Power in the Pacific: The Origins of Naval Arms Limitation, 1914–1922* (Chicago, 1976).

DINSTEIN, YORAM (ed.), *The Protection of Minorities and Human Rights* (London, 1992).

GOLDSTEIN, ERIK and MAURER, JOHN (eds.), *The Washington Conference, 1921–1922: Naval Rivalry, East Asian Stability and the Road to Pearl Harbor* (London, 1994).

HALL, CHRISTOPHER, *Britain, America and Arms Control, 1921–37* (Basingstoke, 1987).

HINSLEY, F. H., *Power and the Pursuit of Peace* (Cambridge, 1963).

JOYCE, JAMES AVERY, *Broken Star: The Story of the League of Nations, 1919–1939* (Swansea, 1978).

McKERCHER, B. J. C., *Anglo-American Relations in the 1920s: The Struggle for Supremacy* (Basingstoke, 1991).

—— (ed.), *Arms Limitation and Disarmament: Restraints on War, 1899–1939* (Westport, Conn., 1992).

MAZOWER, MARK, *Dark Continent: Europe's Twentieth Century* (London, 1998). Esp. chapter 2: 'Empires, Nations, Minorities'.

NORTHEDGE, F. S., *The League of Nations: Its Life and Times, 1920–1946* (Leicester, 1986).

OSTROWER, GARY B., *The League of Nations from 1919 to 1929* (Garden City Park, NY, 1995).

PEGG, CARL H., *Evolution of the European Idea, 1914–1932* (Chapel Hill, NC, 1983).

SCHOT, BASTIAN, *Nation oder Staat?: Deutschland und der Minderheitenschutz: zur Völkerbundspolitik der Stresemann-Ära* (Marburg an Lahn, 1988).

SCOTT, GEORGE, *The Rise and Fall of the League of Nations* (London, 1973).

SKRAN, CLAUDENA M., *Refugees in Inter-war Europe: The Emergence of a Regime* (Oxford, 1995).

United Nations Library and the Graduate Institute of International Studies, *The League of Nations in Retrospect: Proceedings of the Symposium. Organised by the United Nations Library and the Graduate Institute of International Studies, Geneva, 6–9 November, 1980* (Berlin and New York, 1983).

WALTERS, F. P., *History of the League of Nations*, 2 vols. (London, 1952).

WEINDLING, PAUL (ed.), *International Health Organisations and Movements, 1918–1939* (Cambridge, 1995).

Other Specialized Books

BARROS, JAMES, *The Aaland Islands Question: Its Settlement by the League of Nations* (New Haven, Conn. and London, 1968). See Sierpowski article for present view.

—— *The League of Nations and the Great Powers: The Greek–Bulgarian Incident, 1925* (Oxford, 1970).

—— *Office Without Power: Secretary-General Sir Eric Drummond, 1919–1933* (Oxford, 1979).

DAVIS, KATHRYN WASSERMAN, *The Soviets at Geneva: The USSR and the League of Nations, 1919–1933* (Westport, Conn., 1977).

EGERTON, GEORGE W., *Great Britain and the Creation of the League of Nations: Strategy, Politics, and International Organisation, 1914–1919* (Chapel Hill, NC, 1978).

FERRIS, JOHN ROBERT, *Men, Money, and Diplomacy: The Evolution of British Strategic Policy, 1919–26* (Ithaca, NY, 1989).

FRENTZ, CHRISTIAN RAITZ VON, *A Lesson Forgotten: Minority Protection Under the League of Nations. The Case of the German Minority in Poland, 1920–1934* (New York, 1999).

KIMMICH, CHRISTOPH M., *Germany and the League of Nations* (Chicago and London, 1976).

KITCHING, CAROLYN, *Britain and the Problem of International Disarmament, 1919–1934* (London, 1999).

LAMBERT, ROBERT W., *Soviet Disarmament Policy, 1922–1931* (Washington, DC, 1964).

MOUTON, MARIE-RENÉE, *La Société des Nations et les intérêts de la France, 1920–1924* (Bern, 1995).

OSTROWER, GARY B., *Collective Insecurity: The United States and the League of Nations During the Early Thirties* (Lewisburg and London, 1979)

PENTZOPOULOS, DIMITRI, *The Balkan Exchange of Minorities and its Impact upon Greece* (Paris, 1962).

Articles

BLANKE, R., 'The German Minority in Inter-War Poland and German Foreign Policy—Some Reconsiderations', *Journal of Contemporary History*, 25 (1990).

BLATT, JOEL, 'The Parity That Meant Superiority: French Naval Policy Towards Italy at the Washington Conference, 1921–22, and Interwar French Foreign Policy', *French Historical Studies*, 12 (1981).

—— 'France and the Corfu–Fiume Crisis of 1923', *The Historian* (1988).

BURNS, MICHAEL, 'Disturbed Spirits: Minority Rights and New World Orders, 1919 and the 1990s', in S. F. Wells, Jr. and P. B. Smith (eds.), *New European Orders, 1919 and 1991* (Washington, DC, 1996).

BUSSIÈRE, E., 'L'Organisation économique de la SDN et la naissance du régionalisme économique en Europe', *Relations Internationales*, 75: 3 (1993).

CARLTON, D., 'Disarmament With Guarantees: Lord Cecil 1922–1927', *Disarmament and Arms Control*, 3 (1965).

CROZIER, ANDREW J., 'The Establishment of the Mandates System, 1919–1925: Some Problems Created by the Paris Peace Conference', *Journal of Contemporary History*, 14 (1979).

DUNBABIN, J. P., 'The League of Nations' Place in the International System', *History*, 78 (1993).

FERRIS, JOHN R., 'The Symbol and Substance of Seapower: Great Britain, the United States, and the One-Power Standard', in B. J. C. McKercher (ed.), *Anglo-American Relations in the 1920s: The Struggle for Supremacy* (Basingstoke, 1991).

FINK, CAROLE, 'Defender of Minorities: Germany in the League of Nations, 1926–1933', *Central European History*, 5 (1972)

—— 'Stresemann's Minority Policies, 1924–1929' *Journal of Contemporary History*, 14 (1979).

—— 'The League of Nations and the Minorities Question', *World Affairs*, 157 (1995).

HENIG, RUTH, 'New Diplomacy and Old: A Reassessment of British Conceptions of a League of Nations, 1918–20' in M. Dockrill and J. Fisher (eds.), *The Paris Peace Conference, 1919: Peace without Victory?* (Basingstoke, 2001).

LEE, MARSHALL, 'The German Attempt to Reform the League: The Failure of German League of Nations Policy, 1930–1932', *Francia*, 5 (1977).

MAIER, C. S., 'The Two Post-War Eras and the Conditions for Stability in 20th Century Western Europe', *American Historical Review*, 86 (1981).

MAZOWER, MARK, 'Minorities and the League of Nations in Interwar Europe', *Daedalus*, 126 (1997).

MOUTON, M. R, 'La SDN et la protection des minorités nationales en Europe', *Relations Internationales*, 75: 3 (1993).

NIEMEYER, GERHART, 'The Balance-Sheet of the League Experiment', *International Organization*, 6 (1952).

SCHROEDER, PAUL, 'Historical Reality vs. Neo-realist Theory', *International Security*, 19 (1994).

SHARP, ALAN, 'Britain and the Protection of Minorities at the Paris Peace Conference', in A. C. Hepburn (ed.), *Minorities in History* (London, 1978).

SIERPOWSKI, STANISLAW, 'La Société des Nations et le règlement des conflits frontaliers de 1920 à 1924', in Christian Baechler and Carole Fink (eds.), *The Establishment of European Frontiers After the Two World Wars* (Berne and New York, 1996).

YEARWOOD, PETER J., ' "Consistency with Honor": Great Britain, the League of Nations, and the Corfu Crisis of 1923', *Journal of Contemporary History*, 21 (1986).

Theses

METZGER, BARBARA, 'The League of Nations and Human Rights: From Practice to Theory', Ph.D. thesis, Cambridge University (2001).

8

New Dawn? Stabilization in Western Europe After Locarno

Treaty Revision and the Construction of the New Political Equilibrium

I

'The old Europe was consumed in the fires of the Great War,' pronounced the new British foreign secretary, Austen Chamberlain, in January 1925, 'and the new Europe has yet to be built on foundations that may give peace and security to the nations of the old world.'[1] As the second half of the decade began, the post-war reconstruction was far from complete and such goals were for the future. It was with the adoption of the Dawes plan that the statesmen and publics alike began to hope that they might become reality. International relations in the early 1920s had been characterized by multiple and often independent and unrelated strands of diplomacy, leading in many directions. From 1925 these diverse threads started to pull together and lines of common development began to emerge.

With the acceptance of the Dawes plan, a revision to the Versailles treaty to which the Germans had freely assented, it seemed that the reparations conundrum had been resolved for the immediate future. Western European attention again focused on security issues. As a consequence, for the next five years the direction of foreign affairs returned to the foreign secretaries of the three major western powers. Aristide Briand, Austen Chamberlain, and Gustav Stresemann dominated the European stage. Assisted by their professional diplomatic advisers, also restored to their earlier prominence, the statesmen looked for ways to balance French claims for security with German demands for treaty revision. In doing so they imparted a more positive sense of direction to the process of stabilizing Europe, guided by at least some measure of common purpose. They began to harness the powers and

[1] Speech by Sir Austen Chamberlain, Birmingham, 31 Jan. 1925, quoted in *The Times*, 2 Feb. 1925.

potential of the League of Nations, bringing it to the centre of the process of international negotiation. This applied not only to the general issues of implementing the peace settlement, but also to renewed efforts at international economic and financial co-operation and a relaunched disarmament effort. The problems which confronted Europe were the same as before, but progress now seemed possible. A new dawn for post-war Europe, it seemed, might be breaking.

The problem of French security would not go away. In anticipation of the rejection of the Geneva Protocol, Chamberlain initiated a Foreign Office search for some kind of substitute formula. He came to office after a series of political defeats but still in a position to make his weight felt in the Baldwin cabinet. Stiff and cold in manner, he was determined to mark his reunion with the Conservatives (he had loyally supported Lloyd George in 1922 against Bonar Law) with a successful foreign policy. He studied and mastered the main features of the diplomatic scene and came to share the views of those officials who believed that Britain's resources were overextended but who rejected the possibility of continental isolation. Though global in his outlook, Europe was the centre of his immediate concerns and he saw Franco-German tensions as the crux of the continent's problems. He believed that the only way to promote conciliation was to reduce French fears of a resurgent Germany. In considering the alternatives suggested by ministerial colleagues and Foreign Office advisers, Chamberlain, the most Francophile member of the cabinet, opted for a tripartite alliance in which Britain would guarantee the security of France and Belgium. Only the promise of British support in case of German aggression would make a Franco-German rapprochement possible. The cabinet proved totally opposed to the idea of a defensive alliance, though Chamberlain continued to argue his case until the very eve of his departure for Geneva. While these discussions continued he would not take up a new German initiative of 20 January 1925 for a Rhineland pact between Germany, France, and Britain. On the contrary, he viewed Stresemann's proposal with suspicion and had serious reservations, never entirely abandoned, about the German foreign minister's purpose in offering a guarantee of the Franco-German border.

On the German side the proposal had a long history. The Cuno government had made a similar offer in 1922 and the possibility was again discussed in the Wilhelmstrasse before the Ruhr invasion. Lord D'Abernon, the highly influential and fiercely pro-German British ambassador in Berlin, consistently argued that Germany required protection against an aggressive France. In writing to MacDonald in 1923, he raised the prospect of an 'iron curtain' (one of the first uses of the term) between France and Germany, with the Rhineland as a barrier against aggression from either country. The occupation of the Ruhr postponed any serious consideration of D'Abernon's ideas. On 29 December 1924, however, after a visit to London where rumours were already circulating of a possible Anglo-French alliance, D'Abernon suggested to his close friend, Friedrich von Schubert, the shrewd, recently appointed state secretary at the Wilhelmstrasse, that the Germans offer the British a multilateral non-aggression pact of the Cuno variety. There were good reasons why the Germans began their own discussions about a possible initiative. The dispute with the Allies over the timing of the Cologne evacuation proved a sharp setback to Stresemann's hopes that the London agreements would mark the beginning of a new era of co-operation. In December 1924 the Allied Conference of Ambassadors, reacting to the Military Control Commission's report of German violations of the Versailles treaty's disarmament clauses, followed the French lead and delayed the evacuation of the Cologne zone scheduled for January 1925. While the Germans fumed over this indefinite postponement, the possibility of an Anglo-French mutual-defence pact raised the even more threatening possibility of German isolation.

Stresemann viewed collaboration with the western powers as the most suitable vehicle for German recovery and the country's return to full equality of status. This latter goal was already foreshadowed in his handling of the League question, when in early 1924 the British had raised the prospect of German entry. Even at that time Stresemann made it clear that Germany would demand a permanent seat on the Council. He underlined, too, his fears about the absence of the Soviet Union from Geneva. When the subject was again raised in the autumn of the same year, the Wilhelmstrasse responded cautiously, repeating Stresemann's demands for a permanent seat and special exemptions from Article 16, the sanctions clause. German worries were mainly about Russian opposition to German entry into an organization of anti-Soviet capitalist powers. Stresemann was strongly anti-Bolshevik and never accepted the views of those who believed a rearmed Germany, allied with the Soviet Union, could embark on a war of revenge against France. 'Soviet Russia is very greatly overestimated here; it cannot bring us much economically, nor can it offer us much militarily,' he told the DVP national executive on 19 March 1927, 'and those who believe that we would get out of everything, if we joined the Soviet Union are, I believe, the maddest foreign policy makers.'[2] If he lacked ambassador Brockdorff-Rantzau's enthusiasm for the Rapallo connection, he did not intend to abandon it. It increased Germany's

[2] Jonathan Wright, 'Stresemann and Locarno', *Contemporary European History*, 4: 2 (1995).

options in the east, particularly with regard to Poland, and might one day, should there be a clash between the western powers and the Soviet Union, allow Germany to play a mediating role between east and west. The ever-practical statesman fully understood that the Moscow link could be useful in managing relations with the western powers. At home it continued to enjoy considerable support in the German military and industrial elites whose backing Stresemann needed. The Wilhelmstrasse was content that the League issue should be held in abeyance until the next meeting of the Assembly in September 1925. The door to Moscow was left open. In December 1924 the Soviets followed up Brockdorff-Rantzau's earlier reply to their previous approaches which stressed their common interest in revising the Polish frontiers according to ethnographic principles. Chicherin's 'December Initiative' proposed a comprehensive political agreement that would be embodied in a formal treaty. Both countries would promise not to join any kind of political or economic coalition directed at the other. Neither power would guarantee or recognize the existing borders of Poland. It was a defensive move on the Soviet part that failed to elicit a response from the Germans for some five months. In early January 1925, while preparing the terms of the Rhineland pact, the Wilhelmstrasse announced that a delegation would return to Moscow to conclude work on a new commercial treaty. The decision, however, had been taken that the talks with Britain and France should take priority over any neutrality agreement with the Soviet Union. In this Stresemann had the full support of the senior officials at the Wilhelmstrasse. Even Ago von Maltzan, the main architect of the Rapallo agreement, who left Berlin to go as ambassador to Washington in 1925, had joined the 'westerners' at the Wilhelmstrasse.

Chamberlain's main concern with Stresemann's offer of a comprehensive arbitration treaty or guarantee of the status quo on the western frontier was to avoid any affront to the French. There was always the fear that the Germans were attempting to split the Allies. The French ambassador in London was immediately informed of the unilateral German approach, and after Chamberlain's sharp retort to the German ambassador, the same proposal was presented in Paris on 9 February. The crucial questions for the French were still the British decision about the Geneva Protocol and the possible offer of the much-coveted defensive alliance. These were under discussion when the 'premature' German overture was made. Premier Édouard Herriot, who had weakened his bargaining hand during the previous summer's negotiations in London, hoped that Austen Chamberlain might prove a better friend to France than MacDonald. On his way to Geneva to announce the British rejection of the Protocol, the British foreign secretary stopped in Paris. It was a natural stopping-point on what would soon become his regular expeditions to Geneva. It was only on the very eve of his departure from London that Chamberlain had abandoned the proposed Anglo-French pact in the face of the overwhelming objections of his cabinet colleagues. At two cabinet meetings the foreign secretary, who had moved slowly towards a more favourable consideration of the German offer, picked up Winston Churchill's rather vague suggestion that the possibility of a four-power security pact might be discussed with Herriot. It would take Chamberlain's threat of resignation and further arguments in the cabinet in his absence (with Eyre Crowe, the Foreign Office permanent under-secretary, playing a vital part) before Baldwin authorized the specific offer of British participation in future talks for a quadrilateral pact. Although Chamberlain had triumphed over his cabinet opponents, a group which included many of the party's 'heavyweights'—Balfour, Curzon, Churchill (who preferred isolation to a pact with France), Leo Amery, and Lord Birkenhead, none of whom wanted any specific offer made to Herriot—the foreign secretary failed to win the form of support for France that he really wanted. Though he took full command of the talks which followed and was backed by Balfour, he could only make carefully circumscribed offers to the French. Chamberlain saw himself during the next months as the mediator between France and Germany, working to open negotiations that would bring about the reconciliation that was essential to the peace of Europe. It was the position that Lloyd George had vainly sought but which Chamberlain's cabinet colleagues would accept only as long as the costs to Britain were minimal.

The announcement that Britain would neither accept the Protocol nor pursue a bilateral Anglo-French pact left Herriot in a state of shock; he had anticipated the former, if not the latter. There was little choice for the French at a moment when the Herriot cabinet was struggling with its financial difficulties and a rapidly depreciating franc. There were a number of immediate French worries about the German offer, above all the omission of any reference to the Belgian frontier or to Germany's southern boundaries. They were alarmed, too, by the distinction made between Germany's western and eastern frontiers which would leave France's eastern allies unprotected. Chamberlain's offer at Geneva to consider 'special arrangements in order to meet special needs' provided the only opening for further security talks, and the German pact the most practical way of approaching London.[3] From March until the middle of May, while the British and French sought elucidation from Berlin, Chamberlain and Herriot sought to define the terms of an agreement that would meet their different objectives. The task was

[3] Chamberlain to Lord Crewe, 16 Feb. 1925, Chamberlain Mss. AC 52/189.

complicated by Lord D'Abernon's 'creative' role in defining the German position. There were cabinet crises in France, where Painlevé replaced Herriot on 17 April, with Briand as his foreign secretary, and in Belgium, where after general elections held on 5 April a new cabinet was formed with the leading Socialist, Émile Vandervelde, taking the Foreign Ministry portfolio. After making no reference at all to Belgium in their original draft, the Germans agreed to include the Belgian frontier in their guarantee and to invite the Belgians to participate in later meetings.

The election on 26 April of General Paul von Hindenburg, the ex-commander-in-chief of the German army, as president of Germany (due in part to Stresemann's mishandling of the election) raised the fever chart all over Europe but especially in Paris, despite Stresemann's assurances that the victory of the nationalists' candidate would have no influence on German foreign policy. The sticking point in the interchanges with Germany, as between Britain and France, was the position of the eastern frontiers. The Germans were not prepared to guarantee the Polish frontier in any way nor to accept any reference to the inviolability of Polish territory. The most they would offer were bilateral arbitration treaties with Poland and Czechoslovakia. Mention has been made of the extreme apprehension of the Poles and Edvard Beneš's unease despite his efforts to distinguish between the dangers to Warsaw and Prague. Chamberlain, at Geneva, tried to calm the nervous Count Skrzyński, the Polish foreign minister. Skrzyński was advised that since Poland was faced with two dangerous neighbours, it would be better to cultivate good relations with Germany than with the Soviet Union. Such words of wisdom hardly reassured Poland's young, handsome, and astute foreign minister. Once the new Painlevé government took office in April, Briand and Chamberlain worked out a joint position on the eastern treaties. Briand wanted a guarantee of the German arbitration treaties with Poland and Czechoslovakia; Chamberlain made clear his government's unwillingness to undertake any new obligations beyond the western borders.

Nor would Britain consider a guarantee of the Brenner frontier. Mussolini had raised the Brenner issue when first approached about participating in the talks. In May 1925 Stresemann, in less than friendly exchanges with Mussolini, had rejected the Italian approach for a mutual guarantee. Both sides agreed to accept the stalemated situation. The Italian leader, having recovered his diplomatic nerve after the Matteotti crisis, was not interested in Briand's offer in the summer of 1925 of a separate pact with Italy guaranteeing all their respective frontiers. Thinking in terms of a more assertive foreign policy, he saw France as Italy's chief adversary and the obstacle to the fulfilment of his ambitions.

Mussolini stood apart, neither wanting to join nor to be excluded from the great-power deliberations. Briand put the case well when he told Chamberlain at Locarno on 7 October that 'Italy seemed to him to resemble a submarine that was floating just below the surface of the water undecided into which ship to fire its torpedo'.[4]

The remaining Anglo-French differences were rapidly overcome when Briand and Chamberlain met at Geneva in early June; the difficulties were now in Berlin. Chamberlain and Briand agreed that France should guarantee the German eastern arbitration treaties and that Germany should enter the League without reservations. The Germans would accept neither condition, for both involved issues not open to compromise. The Luther cabinet was divided; the chancellor wavered in his backing for the French (actually Anglo-French) version of the pact that reached Berlin on 16 June. Even the usually optimistic D'Abernon was doubtful about its acceptance. Soviet apprehensions and pressure on the Germans mounted during the spring and summer, as it became obvious that Stresemann was negotiating with the western powers while postponing any serious talks with the Russians. The Germans continued to procrastinate, offering only verbal assurances and vaguely worded formulas. In June and again on 1 October, the eve of Stresemann's journey to Locarno, the Soviets threatened to reveal the extent of the Russo-German military conversations and the German offer, referring to conversations held in Berlin in December 1924, to co-operate in 'forcing back Poland to its ethnographic borders'.[5] Stresemann, seconded by von Schubert, gave priority to the western negotiations but needed to disguise any difficulties with Moscow. He warned D'Abernon on 10 June, when the western talks were reaching their critical stage: 'We cannot forgo the Russian connection, such as it is, without having something positive on the other side. I have a stiff fight in front of me.'[6]

Chamberlain, who was following a policy of 'passive inactivity' towards Russia and had no intention of building an anti-Soviet European bloc, as was suspected in Moscow, grew anxious at the German delay to the point of suspecting the ultimate intentions of the Luther cabinet. The foreign secretary's support for the quadrilateral pact undoubtedly had as one of its objects the attachment of Germany to the western camp. As he told the Polish ambassador in the summer of 1925 and repeated to Briand on the eve of Locarno, 'at the present time the

---

[4] *DBFP*, ser. I, vol. 28, no. 522.
[5] Jon Jacobson, *When the Soviet Union Entered World Politics* (Berkeley and London, 1994), 160.
[6] E. Vincent D'Abernon, *An Ambassador of Peace* (London, 1930), iii. 169.

European powers on the one hand and the Soviet Government on the other were fighting for the soul of the German people'.[7] Accounts of discussions between Berlin and Moscow were bound to make him uneasy, despite D'Abernon's over-sanguine reports from Berlin minimizing the dangers of Russo-German co-operation. While they waited, Chamberlain and Briand discussed possible final drafts and the form future negotiations should take. In the interests of securing what seemed to be almost in his grasp, the now enthusiastic British foreign secretary agreed that the proposed guarantee should not apply to the Dominions or India lest their opposition, a contributing factor to the defeat of the Geneva Protocol, raise last-minute difficulties.

Small crises indicated a certain reluctance on both the French and German sides to advance matters. The French at first baulked at fulfilling their 1924 London conference promises to evacuate the three German cities occupied in March 1921 as well as the Ruhr. Briand demanded a quid pro quo in the form of concessions in the continuing Franco-German commercial negotiations. He absolutely refused to discuss the evacuation of Cologne or the withdrawal of troops from the rest of the Rhineland. Briand's permanent officials, including the influential Phillipe Berthelot, the secretary-general again in charge of the Quai d'Orsay, dragged their feet. They were far more inclined than their chief to consider the details of the new arrangements, particularly their effect on France's eastern alliances. The Germans, too, were uneasy. At best, the tone of the German answer to the French note was discouraging, reflecting Stresemann's need to court the centre and right-wing parties, including his own German People's Party, and to keep a wary eye on Moscow. There were severe strains between the coalition parties; the DNVP strongly opposed the foreign minister's policies and Luther, trying to keep his cabinet together, contemplated sending Stresemann as ambassador to Britain. Even though Stresemann won his political battles and dispatched the German reply on 20 July, he knew his situation was highly unstable. The Germans were adamant in their opposition to a French guarantee of the eastern treaties and to the Allied demand for their unconditional entry into the League. Sharply pressed by both London and Paris to advance matters, Stresemann reluctantly agreed to send the *Auswärtiges Amt*'s (foreign ministry's) legal adviser, Friedrich Gaus, to a meeting of jurists in London during the first days of September to prepare drafts for the foreign ministers' consideration. After blowing cold and hot, Mussolini was finally convinced that Italy could not afford to be absent and sent his representatives to London and then to Locarno. Much of the success of the jurists' meetings was due to

---

[7] Austen Chamberlain Papers, AC 50/104; *DBFP*, ser. Ia, vol. 3, doc. 201.

Chamberlain's warnings to the French not to raise the eastern question until the foreign secretaries assembled. Enough progress was made by the jurists in September, especially after Washington urged completion of the pact, for invitations to be issued for the foreign ministers' conference to start at Locarno on 5 October.

German acceptance of the invitation was made subject to an Allied repudiation of the war-guilt clause and prior evacuation of the Cologne zone. Chamberlain was furious at this last-minute effort to extract further concessions. 'Your Germans—I use the possessive prounoun as one says to one's wife: your housemaid—are very nearly intolerable', the foreign secretary complained to D'Abernon. 'From first to last very nearly every obstacle to the Pact negotiations has come from them. Briand has almost taken my breath away by his liberality, his conciliatoriness, his strong and manifest desire to promote peace. The German attitude has been just the contrary—niggling, provocative, crooked.'[8] The British foreign secretary's distrust of the Germans reached its height on the eve of Locarno. His relations with Stresemann were never as close or warm as those with Briand even after he became convinced that Stresemann really believed in the new course that the latter had initiated. In the event, Stresemann attended the conference without the acceptance of his conditions. The final and most important compromises at Locarno were worked out between the British, French, and German foreign ministers aboard the *Orange Blossom* during a difficult five-hour cruise on Lake Maggiore. While the pact would make no mention of France's guarantees to Poland and Czechoslovakia, the French would be free to act in their defence against a German threat under the Covenant's Articles 15 (an attack after the failure of conciliation) and 16 (an attack without first resorting to conciliation). There would be no specific reference to the German eastern arbitration treaties to be concluded simultaneously with the mutual-security pact. The 'texte du bateau' limited League members' resistance to aggression to ways 'compatible with its military situation and geographic position'. Only the Belgian foreign minister objected to the possible German exclusion from participation in economic as well as military sanctions. In this respect Chamberlain's support for Stresemann proved decisive, and the German terms for entry into the League were accepted. Stresemann reassured Moscow that Berlin would not join in any League sanctions directed at the USSR nor guarantee the borders of Poland in any way. The Germans fulfilled both of Chicherin's key demands. The Germans had to admit during the Chicherin–Stresemann meeting that Brockdorff-Rantzau had taken the initiative in speaking of military

---

[8] Austen Chamberlain Papers, PRO, FO 800/258, pp. 556–7.

co-operation to 'smash the present-day Poland', but the commissar dropped the threat of a 'calculated indiscretion'.[9]

Though the German foreign minister had achieved his most important requirements, with an eye to the nationalists he sought more immediate advantages. In further conversations with Briand and Chamberlain, Stresemann presented a list of additional demands, including an amnesty for Germans imprisoned by the French during the Ruhr occupation, the lifting of restrictions on German civilian aviation, and, most importantly, a lenient interpretation of the Allied disarmament demands. More objectionable from the Allied point of view, he again asked for the rapid evacuation of the Cologne zone, earlier dates for the evacuation of the rest of the Rhineland and the Saar plebiscite, and the easing of the conditions of the present occupation. Both Briand and Chamberlain bristled at such last-minute conditions. Chamberlain secured agreement on the beginning of the Cologne evacuation, now set for 1 December 1926. As for the rest of Stresemann's *Rückwirkungen*, the German foreign secretary had to accept the promise that his demands would be favourably considered once the agreements were concluded and détente established. The Germans made one last effort to avoid Allied control over German disarmament by threatening not to join the League unless its powers for surveillance were modified. Chamberlain and Vandervelde, the Belgian foreign minister, exploded at this final 'pistol at our heads' and the Germans retreated.

The Locarno settlements were initialled on 16 October and signed in a quiet ceremony, due to Queen Alexandra's death, in London on 1 December. They consisted of a mutual guarantee of the western frontiers of Germany and the demilitarized Rhineland by the five European powers. France and Germany, and Belgium and Germany agreed not to attack or invade or make war against each other except as a result of a decision of the League or as the consequence of a violation of the Rhineland guarantee. The countries pledged themselves to accept arbitration in case of unresolved disputes. Alleged breaches of the treaty would be brought before the League, 'flagrant violations' would result in immediate action by the guarantors, Britain and Italy, without recourse to the League. The distinction represented an earlier Anglo-French compromise. The pact provided no definition of the term 'flagrant'. Chamberlain told the House of Commons that Britain was not prepared 'to sit still while the demilitarisation of the Rhineland zone is rendered ineffective'.[10] Nonetheless, he assured the Committee for

---

[9] Quoted in Jonathan Wright, *Gustav Stresemann: Weimar's Greatest Statesman* (Oxford, 2002), 323 and 324.

[10] Quoted in Jon Jacobson, *Locarno Diplomacy: Germany and the West, 1925–1929* (Princeton, 1972), 34.

Imperial Defence that he regarded British liabilities as reduced and not extended by Locarno, and that the guarantors and not the aggrieved party would decide whether any so-called violation implied an intention to go to war except in case of a direct attack across the frontier. The French did not get the automatic guarantees that Briand sought. The borders in the east were neither recognized nor guaranteed. The right of France to act against a German threat to her eastern allies meant that if Germany attacked Poland or Czechoslovakia in breach of her League obligations, the French could come to their assistance and Germany could not evoke the Rhine pact against France. To partly compensate for the failure to win guarantees in the east, France concluded at Locarno separate non-aggression treaties with both her allies that were referred to but not included in the general protocol. The German arbitration treaties with Poland and Czechoslovakia were negotiated simultaneously but independently of the Locarno pact. There were no guarantors.

II

Who were the winners and losers at Locarno? The Germans had won a great deal, though achievement depended on future Allied actions. They had taken a major step towards international respectability and would enter the League with a permanent seat on the Council. In return, they had freely accepted the Versailles verdict on the western frontiers and the demilitarized Rhineland. The loss of Alsace-Lorraine, as Stresemann assured his domestic critics, was little more than an acknowledgement of what could not be changed until Germany had an army. He denied the Anglo-French contention that the French could intervene immediately and unilaterally in cases of serious demilitarization violations by Germany. The German foreign minister was on stronger ground when he argued in Berlin that he had yielded nothing on Germany's eastern frontiers and had kept the door open to a compromise with the Russians by the qualified interpretation of Article 16. Stresemann believed that insofar as France's eastern guarantees were now linked to the League, he had weakened the Franco–Polish alliance of 1921. Stresemann had prevented the conclusion of an Anglo–French alliance; this was a major relief. Though he undoubtedly exaggerated what would be won in the immediate future for domestic political purposes, he could claim rightly that the Allies had agreed to reconsider the Versailles provisions for German disarmament and to review the terms and length of the Rhineland occupation, his most important immediate objective. The fulfilment of these demands was a question of time and persistence. These concessions (rights in the German view), the anticipated first fruits of the *Locarnogeist*, would hasten Germany's return to full sovereignty and great-power status. By accepting the status quo in the west and leaving his hands free in the east, Stresemann had opened the possibility of peaceful territorial revision in the future. With Germany in no position to exert any military power, there was far more to be achieved within the framework of European co-operation than through unilateral action. The tariff war against Poland launched in June 1925 indicated that the Berlin government would try to use her commercial power to weaken and isolate the Polish state though Stresemann, prompted by Schubert, developed doubts about its utility. Stresemann's confidential assurances to Chamberlain that the German government would renounce the use of warlike measures to alter the present German–Polish frontier but hoped that the frontier would be altered in some other way, was politically shrewd and pragmatically sound. In fact, none of the proposals discussed for the future peaceful revision of the Polish borders had any substance, and while this remained one of Germany's most important tasks, she lacked the means to achieve it.[11] Nevertheless, Stresemann did not have an easy time when he returned to Berlin. The DNVP, the largest nationalist party, left the government on 26 October; the government lost its majority and was dependent on the SPD and DDP to provide the votes to ratify the Locarno treaties. Stresemann held out the goal of 'a peaceful Germany at the centre of a peaceful Europe', and stressed the common Franco-German interest in loans from America for which a peaceful Europe was an essential prerequisite.[12] The agreements were accepted on 27 November by a vote of 292 to 174. The lukewarm reaction of some of the supporting parties was a warning to Stresemann and an irritation to Chamberlain. At the signing ceremony in London, Stresemann again demanded concessions only to be warned off until a later and more appropriate time.

The Locarno agreements were warmly received in Paris. The pact ended the fear of French isolation, associated Britain with the defence of France, improved relations with the United States, who supported the agreements without taking part in their negotiation, reduced the danger of a German–Soviet alliance, and created a new atmosphere in which to promote Franco-German co-operation. From the first, Briand's main priority was to secure the formal British guarantee that had eluded France since 1919. In contrast to the ambiguous situation in 1914, France could now count on British military assistance should Germany

---

[11] Peter Krüger, *Der Aussenpolitik der Republik von Weimar* (Darmstadt, 1985), 298–314.
[12] Quoted in Wright, *Gustav Stresemann*, 342.

attack its borders. The form and price to be paid for her new security on the Rhine had still to be negotiated. Briand agreed to work for the alleviation of the Rhineland regime and to arrange for the rapid evacuation of Cologne. He promised further disarmament concessions to speed the withdrawal of the IMCC. As was explained to Stresemann, once the IMCC was disbanded, League supervision of German disarmament would not entail a permanent, on-site organization. While refusing any public statement on the continuing occupation of the Rhineland, he suggested to Stresemann that the Locarno détente would open the way for the settlement of all outstanding Franco-German problems. Briand told the Chamber foreign affairs committee after the meetings at Locarno that the Rhineland occupation was a 'bargaining tool' and not a permanent strategic advantage, a view that he continued to hold at the time of the Hague conference in August 1929. He expected to use the fulfilment of Stresemann's demands as a way to improve France's financial and economic position as it faced its economically more powerful neighbour.

The French willingness to bargain over the Rhineland was due, in part, to the occupation's diminishing value as the treaty date for evacuation drew nearer. A fundamental change in French military strategic thinking reduced the importance of the occupation. Throughout these months Foch and Pétain continued to argue over whether French strategy should include preparations for an offensive in the Rhineland as the former wanted or the adoption of a defensive strategy as proposed by Pétain and his followers. At a key meeting in December 1925 Pétain and his followers, in opposition to Foch, emphasized the need to secure French soil against attack and advocated a continuous front strengthened by fortifications. Financial pressures, public sentiment, and the projected changes in the organization of the army favoured Pétain's defensive strategy which both Briand and Poincaré supported. Plan 'B' of June 1926, while still referring to offensive action, made its implementation highly improbable. The new French defensive line was to be established well behind the Rhine and, in case of attack, French reserves would be rushed to Belgium and would not be available to support an offensive action. Furthermore, due to popular demand and electoral promises, the army, having accepted an eighteen-month military service in 1923, now anticipated a further reduction in service to one year. Combined with the diminishing pool of conscripts resulting from its shrinking population figures, France would have only a small army to defend her borders until her reserves were mobilized and her scattered colonial forces, half the active army, returned to France. Such considerations gave further weight to the those favouring the defensive strategy.

Financial and commercial reasons favoured accommodation with Germany and explain the popularity of Briand's policies in the Chamber. Briand saw in future Franco-German co-operation a way to reduce both countries' dependence on American financial liberality. At the same time, as the Versailles restrictions on German economic freedom lapsed in 1925, the French were anxious to conclude tariff and cartel arrangements with their German counterparts. The industrial supporters of the right-centre parties and the wine-growers of southern France, who constituted the backbone of the Radical party, needed major concessions from the Germans. In September 1925 Louis Loucheur, finance minister under Painlevé and Briand, suggested the idea of an international economic conference sponsored by the League of Nations in order to promote the rationalization of European production and consumption and to combat the European 'race for high tariffs that is comparable to the pre-war armaments race'.[13] At the end of September 1926, even before the World Economic Conference met, steel producers in France, Germany, Belgium, Luxembourg, and the Saar formed a steel cartel designed to establish a system of quotas for crude steel. Due to Briand's intervention, the German government brought pressure on its producers to compromise when they proved unduly stiff over marketing arrangements. It seemed possible that Loucheur's vision of a 'Europe of producers' could be extended to coal and even to producers of semi-finished iron products. In August 1927, after three years of negotiation, France and Germany signed a comprehensive commercial accord that extended general and unconditional most-favoured-nation status to both signatories. The treaty involved an adjustment of French duties in favour of German trade, partly at the expense of other countries including Britain. It was welcomed by both governments. French politicians of the right, many with industrial connections, strongly favoured an 'economic Locarno', with only the small minority of right-wing nationalists opposing these closer ties to Germany. Even French producers and bankers who had relatively large investments in Poland, Czechoslovakia, and Romania were favourably disposed to the new arrangements. Major metallurgical figures, the Laurents, de Wendels, and Schneider, believed the new cartel arrangements could be concluded without sacrificing France's privileged position in eastern Europe. They hoped to benefit from cartel market quotas that would restrict sales but provide higher profits. Briand was moving with, and not against, the economic tide and strengthening his political base.

[13] Stephen B. Carls, *Louis Loucheur and the Shaping of Modern France, 1916–1931* (Baton Rouge, La. and London, 1993), 264.

The critical point about the Locarno pact for Briand was the British participation in the new security arrangements. In the last resort, the new guarantee was of more lasting value to France than the eastern alliances. Briand believed that, for the moment, Poland was strong enough with French backing to defend itself against an unarmed Germany. It was essential that Warsaw should not, by provoking either Germany or Russia, precipitate a Russo–German alliance, an alignment feared by both Briand and Chamberlain. The French had long wished to minimize their responsibilities in any Polish–Soviet conflict. Once the Locarno agreements were concluded, Briand was prepared to try for a détente with the Soviet Union hoping to separate Moscow from Berlin. The alternative tactic was to attach Germany to the western powers. Having won as much protection for his eastern allies as the British and Germans would allow, Briand sought a way to reduce German–Polish antagonisms. Both he and Poincaré favoured changes on the German–Polish frontier. Briand was thinking of a 'Corridor–Memel' exchange, despite the diplomatic complications and Polish objections to abandoning the Corridor. Briand and Stresemann reached a somewhat ambiguous understanding. The Frenchman recognized Germany's hopes for future revision but postponed discussions until some future time.

The British were well satisfied with the new agreements. Chamberlain later declared that Locarno marked 'the real dividing line between the years of war and the years of peace'.[14] The British foreign secretary won, at very little cost to his country, a détente in the five-year struggle between victors and vanquished. Britain's new European responsibilities were confined to the Rhine frontier. The stage was now set for France and Germany to settle their differences in a conciliatory frame of mind with Britain acting in its favourite role of moderator. With the road open for peaceful change on the continent, the London government could turn its attention to domestic and imperial concerns as in the golden period of the 'Pax Britannica'. The new pact was seen as a way of minimizing the danger of war and restricting Britain's military obligations should the peace collapse. Britain was pledged only to immediate military action in case of 'flagrant aggression' in the west; all other forms of attack would be considered by the League Council where Britain could accept or reject sanctions. No steps were taken to follow up the guarantee with any form of military planning. In their annual review of imperial defence for 1926, the chiefs of staff warned that, with regard to continental commitments, the services could only 'take note of them' and that no provision to meet them was 'practicable'. There was a small expeditionary force and a limited number of

---

[14] N. H. Gibbs, *Grand Strategy* (London, 1976), 43.

RAF squadrons available for use in Europe, but these were little more than a 'pledge' that Britain would fulfil its guarantees. Given the assumption that war was not to be expected during the next ten years, the chiefs of staff felt free to concentrate their attention on imperial defence in the face of insistent Treasury demands for further economies

Austen Chamberlain had succeeded in distancing Britain from any involvement in eastern Europe, though he conceded the French right to go to the assistance of her eastern allies should they be attacked by Germany. The foreign secretary shared the view of his officials that the Polish–German border was basically unstable and that the mistakes of Versailles would have to be corrected. He dismissed the warnings of his historical adviser, James Headlam-Morley, that 'if there were to be a new partition of Poland, or if the Czechoslovak state were to be so curtailed and dismembered that in fact it disappeared from the map of Europe . . . the whole of Europe would at once be in chaos. There would no longer be any principle, meaning or sense in the territorial arrangements of the continent.'[15] Headlam-Morley's 'improbable' scenario of an Austria joined to Germany, the discontented minority in Bohemia demanding a new frontier, and the Hungarians, in alliance with the Germans, recovering the southern slope of the Carpathians, seemed far-fetched in 1925. 'This would be catastrophic,' he predicted, 'and even if we neglected to interfere to prevent it happening, we should be driven to interfere, probably too late.' Chamberlain was 'not at one' with his historical adviser and drew a far sharper line between British interests in western and eastern Europe: 'in Western Europe we are a partner', but 'in Eastern Europe our role should be rather that of a disinterested *amicus curiae*'.[16] Chamberlain's security concerns did not extend to Poland and Czechoslovakia or to the Balkan states. The Poles were particularly troublesome, though Beneš, whatever his own disappointments, used his influence to bring them into line. Writing to his sister, Chamberlain quoted, with approval, Briand's remark that Poland was 'the rheumatism of Europe . . . catching you in the back when you try to move'.[17] Whatever the foreign secretary's doubts about the durability of the eastern frontier settlements, he thought it much too early to discuss territorial revision and cautioned the Germans as well as the Poles to allow the question to sleep for a generation. Chamberlain believed that Germany's adhesion to the Locarno pact and its forthcoming entrance into the League would anchor her in the west and reduce the threat of a German–Soviet alliance. He

[15] Memorandum by Headlam-Morley, 12 Feb. 1925, PRO, FO 371/11064.
[16] Ibid., minute by Chamberlain.
[17] Chamberlain to Hilda Chamberlain, 22 Sept. 1925, AC 5/1/365.

did not consider the Soviet Union to be a major threat in Europe and would have preferred to have left the Russians ignored and isolated. Knowing that Stresemann would nurse his links with Moscow, Chamberlain was convinced that the Locarno grouping offered Stresemann far more than he could gain from the USSR. Though troubled by the exchanges between Berlin and Moscow, he was less alarmed than Briand by the German chancellor's insistence on conditions that would reduce Soviet anxiety about Germany's entrance into the League.

Even the usually cool-headed Foreign Office officials were caught up in the wave of optimism that the Locarno settlements unleashed. Much praise was lavished on Chamberlain, who was seen as the true begetter of the peace. Engaging in a moment of self-congratulation (Chamberlain had recently read Charles K. Webster's study of Castlereagh, and was much impressed by the parallels in their policies), the foreign secretary declared: 'British friendship is cultivated, British counsel asked, British aid sought, and as in the days of Castlereagh, Great Britain stands forth again as the moderator and peace maker of the new Europe created by the Great War.'[18] Chamberlain went on to create a unique place for himself at Geneva and, in contrast to Lloyd George after the peace conference, enhanced his reputation by careful statesmanship and an attention to detail that won trust and professional acclaim.

Belgium's gains were limited for neither the British nor the French paid much attention to its requirements. Mainly due to the efforts of its statesmen, it was a signatory of the treaty and won a guarantee of its border with Germany. At long last Belgium secured the much-sought guarantee from Britain, but without the military back-up which would reduce its dependence on France. The Germans continued to press for the retrocession of Eupen and Malmédy in return for a settlement of Belgium's marks claims (the redemption of marks that had flooded Belgium during the war and armistice), but no such revision took place. The treaty, quite incidentally and for other reasons, included in its preamble a reference to the abrogation of Belgian neutrality, cancelling the 1839 treaties which had imposed humiliating limitations on Belgian sovereignty. The Italians, like the Belgians, participated in all the conference meetings without making any impact on the greatpower talks. Mussolini gained nothing in return for the unwanted guarantee of the western borders.

The real losers at Locarno were Poland and, to a lesser extent, Czechoslovakia. The terms of the treaties provided no safeguards for the eastern frontiers. The Poles always assumed that their future security rested on the promise of unqualified French military support. Beneš

[18] DBFP, ser. Ia, vol. 1, no. 1.

sought the protection of France in 1924 despite his hopes for the League and belief that Czechoslovakia could play a more independent role in Europe than its neighbour. French assistance was now qualified and could be delayed. Under the former treaties of alliance France could give immediate assistance to her allies in any situation; after Locarno she could invade Germany from the west only if attacked or if the demilitarized zone was violated. The French guarantees were linked to the decisions of the Council of the League. The terms of the Polish guarantee were less favourable to Poland than the 1921 treaty. The Franco-Czechoslovak treaty of mutual guarantee was, in some ways, more precise than the 1924 agreement but hardly compensated for the French move towards Germany. Stresemann never disguised his belief that Locarno would provide the basis for future territorial revision, but he accepted that Germany was not yet in a position to make such claims and believed that it could afford to wait. The Polish attempts to buttress their position met with little sympathy in Paris or in London. Skrzyński's repeated pleas for a tripartite treaty or an anti-Soviet pact were hardly taken seriously. He failed, too, in a last-minute attempt to include a ban on war in all circumstances in the German–Polish arbitration treaty. Skrzyński's conciliatory tactics resulted more from his fears of Polish isolation than from any misapprehension of the real situation. He knew that Poland faced the possibility of an early French withdrawal from the Rhineland and that she could find herself the victim of further Franco-German arrangements. Skrzyński accepted the existing situation because he had no alternative; there was no purpose in advertising Poland's weakness and dependence on France's goodwill. The Poles could not count on backing from Beneš. Even at Locarno, the Czech foreign minister openly discussed the inevitable return of the 'Corridor'. While the new agreements were not a direct threat to Czech security, Beneš, like Skrzyński, was treated as a second-class citizen by the Germans. The new arrangements in the west restricted Beneš's freedom of diplomatic manoeuvre, but his earlier efforts to mediate between Britain and France had never been crowned by much success. In December 1925 there was talk of a central European Locarno involving the Poles, Yugoslavs, Romanians, and Hungarians, but Little Entente enmity towards Hungary and Mussolini's own ideas for the future of the Danubian and Balkan nations defeated the idea.

Both Skrzyński and Beneš had to defend the Locarno treaties against hostile criticism in their respective parliaments. The already difficult Polish political situation, the product of divisions in the powerful Sejm and the dissatisfactions of the non-Polish national minorities, was compounded in 1925–6 by the rampant inflation and trade war with Germany. In November a new ministry was formed under Skrzyński, who remained foreign minister as well as premier. In the background, Marshal Piłsudski thundered against the abuses of the parliamentary regime and called for the 'moral regeneration' of Poland. The marshal was highly critical of the Locarno settlement, as were the army leaders and the parties of the right. Skrzyński, on the defensive, pleaded for the inevitability of the settlements and the breathing space they could provide for the struggling Polish republic. He refused to admit publicly that French obligations to Poland had been diminished or limited in any way. In February the Poles agreed to suspend the expulsion of German 'optants' (those who chose German citizenship), one of the political conditions demanded by Berlin when new tariff arrangements were debated in 1925. Chamberlain lectured the German ambassador about his unnecessary and undeserved complaints against the Poles. The latter took hope where they could. They were pleased by France's support for their ultimately unsuccessful bid for a permanent seat on the council. They welcomed the renewal of the alliance with Romania, guaranteeing the existing frontiers in March 1926. What little optimism existed in Warsaw was soon dispelled by the signing of the Russo-German treaty of Berlin in April and the unexpectedly mild Anglo-French reaction to its announcement.

Beneš, too, encountered political difficulties, and his hopes for a central European Locarno made little progress. The French delayed the conclusion of their own treaty with the Yugoslavs, preferring a tripartite French–Italian–Yugoslav pact which would lead Mussolini to support the regional status quo. The Little Entente powers, meeting on 10 February 1926, were concerned mainly with signs of Hungarian revisionism and supported the ongoing talks with France and Italy out of weakness rather than conviction. Mussolini, less than enthusiastic about Locarno, rejected the tripartite pact and decided to take the initiative in Belgrade. With his veto, the possibility of a more stable alignment in south-east Europe began to fade. Little united Rome, Paris, and Prague except their mutual dislike of *Anschluss* which Germany now might urge. There was also the problem of the Soviet Union, one of the main points of division between Czechoslovakia and Poland. As there could be no common Little Entente policy towards the Russians because of the Romanian–Soviet quarrel over Bessarabia, Beneš acted alone. Counting on Russian fears of isolation, the Czech foreign minister offered Moscow *de jure* recognition in return for major economic concessions, the minimum price demanded by the anti-Bolshevik right-wing parties in Czechoslovakia. The Russians rejected Beneš's terms and the talks were consequently abandoned. The Russo-German treaty of Berlin (26 April 1926) alarmed the Czechs almost as much as the Poles, for Beneš saw the treaty as a destabilizing

force in central Europe and a blow to the future effectiveness of the
League. The one positive consequence of Beneš's endless diplomatic
activity was the renewed conversations with the Poles. Skrzyński travelled to Prague in mid-April; an arbitration treaty was ratified, progress
made towards the conclusion of a commercial treaty, and the questions
of Council representation and the Geneva disarmament talks amicably
debated. A liquidation agreement was concluded defining the position
of mutual minorities. If the Polish minister raised the possibility of an
alliance, as was widely reported in the press, Beneš showed no signs of
responding. Quite apart from doubts about Skryzński's political future,
he was not going to invite German and Russian reproaches for an
alliance of doubtful value. The spirit of Locarno had not reached either
the Vistula or the Danube.

For Stalin and most of the Soviet leadership Locarno was 'an example
of the matchless hypocrisy of bourgeois diplomacy, when by shouting
and singing about peace they try to cover up preparations for a new
war'.[19] Though there was undoubtedly an element of exaggeration in
Stalin's alarm, both because of the intra-party disputes and the hope to
rally national communist parties to the defence of the Soviet Union,
many shared his assumption that the 'guarantee pacts' were aimed at
Russia. Chicherin, who was much less concerned than Stalin and
Bukharin, took immediate steps to contain the supposed threat to the
USSR. Soon after the conclusion of the Locarno treaties negotiations
were opened with the Germans. The Neutrality and Non-Aggression
pact was not concluded until 24 April 1926, the delay mainly due to
Stresemann's unwillingness to sign the treaty until the issue of Germany's League Council seat was settled. The new pact guaranteed that
Germany would not be recruited into an anti-Soviet bloc. Each side was
pledged to neutrality in case of war involving a third power and
promised to refrain from concluding any treaty directed against the
other party. Chicherin was again hopeful, as after Rapallo, that the
new bilateral arrangement would prove the model for treaties with
other states, providing a security structure for Russia outside of the
League of Nations and multilateral regional pacts. From Stresemann's
point of view the Treaty of Berlin increased Germany's range of diplomatic options in both west and east. The new treaty pleased both pro-
Rapallo diplomats at the Wilhelmstrasse and the Reichswehr officers,
who welcomed Soviet feelers for closer co-operation. The new treaty
did not restore the earlier relationship between the two states and Soviet
anxieties were not assuaged. Germany and the Soviet Union were less
dependent on each other than in 1922. The Germans had attractive

[19] Stalin, *Works* (London, 1954), vii. 282.

TABLE 18. German Government Revenue, Expenditure and Debt 1926/7–1932/3 (m. RM)

	1926/7	1927/8	1928/9	1929/30	1930/1	1931/2	1932/3
Expenditure							
Public Administration							
Reich[a]	17 201	18 801	20 801	20 872	20 406	16 977	14 535
Länder[a]	6 562	7 155	8 376	8 043	8 163	6 625	5 735
Communes[a]	4 123	4 357	4 585	4 564	4 487	3 907	3 349
Hansa Cities[a]	6 734	7 422	8 029	8 461	8 021	6 998	6 289
Social Insurance[b]	528	595	640	675	647	524	491
	2 843	4 108	4 862	5 314	5 718	5 626	4 168
Total expenditure	20 397	22 460	25 043	25 736	25 400	21 971	18 168
(as % of GNP)	26.9	26.8	28.4	29.6	32.1	33.3	31.8
Revenue							
Public Administration	17 286	18 762	19 613	20 082	19 890	16 458	13 780
Reich	6 819	7 113	7 300	7 730	8 041	6 440	5 589
Länder	3 577	3 942	4 144	3 994	3 928	3 432	2 845
Communes	6 387	7 124	7 541	7 713	7 325	6 093	4 952
Hansa Cities	503	583	628	645	596	493	394
Social Insurance[b]	3 371	3 990	5 551	6 029	5 912	5 470	4 390
Total Public Revenue	18 412	21 307	22 816	23 205	23 104	20 694	16 684
Increase in Public Debt	1 742	1075	3 561	3 159	2 704	155	170
Increase in Debt as % of GNP	2.3	1.3	4.0	3.6	3.4	0.2	0.3

Source: Harold James, *The German Slump: Politics and Economics* (1986), 52. See Appendix A-4 for a different breakdown of German Expenditure.
[a]Expenditure figures for Reich, Länder, Communes, and Hansa Cities include payments to other public authorities. These have been removed in the total.
[b]Calendar year, *not* budget year (1 April–31 March).

alternatives to the Moscow line and the Soviets, preparing to embark on a massive industrialization programme, looked beyond Germany to the United States, Britain, and France for the capital and technology needed. The Germans were prepared to broker agreements between the USSR and the western states but the Russians were intent on concluding their own bilateral treaties with the industrialized powers. No invocation of the strength of the Rapallo relationship could obscure, moreover, differences of interest over Poland. Chicherin had made extensive use of the Polish card both to get the new German treaty and, less successfully, to make Poland the subject of common agreement. Before beginning the negotiations with Berlin he had proposed offering the Poles a non-aggression pact guaranteeing Poland's eastern but not its western frontiers. Stresemann, with no interest in such a possibility, warned that any separate treaty with Poland was incompatible with the projected German–Soviet pact. In August 1926, despite the German warning, the Russians publicly offered the Poles a bilateral treaty of non-aggression and neutrality, an offer that was rejected as it could not be extended to include the Baltic states. In response, the Soviet Union concluded a non-aggression pact with Lithuania in September. The Russians could not afford to abandon their efforts to neutralize Poland, the 'door' to the Soviet Union. Germany and Russia each had its own scenario with regard to their shared neighbour. The Treaty of Berlin was neither the highpoint of the Soviet–German relationship nor a major step in its decline.

If in the east the Locarno treaties raised apprehensions, in the west they produced a sense of hope and euphoria. Insofar as the real divisions between the states during the 1920s were those between those states which wanted to maintain the status quo and those hoping to change it, Locarno was a victory for the latter. The French had opted for the British scenario of peaceful change. The *esprit de Locarno* pointed to a period of future negotiation. Austen Chamberlain believed that Briand was accepting most of the risks of the new agreements, even if most of the concessions made to Germany would be the subject of future negotiation. In one sense Locarno was the continuation of the French retreat from the defence of the Versailles settlement that began with the acceptance of the Dawes plan and the conclusion of the London agreements. In another, it represented a French effort to find an alternative policy to those that had failed. The treaties were something new in form and direction. They were a regional mutual security pact, falling somewhere between the alliances of the past and the collective security arrangements discussed at Geneva. They opened the way to a peaceful European settlement but did not secure it and left the situation on the eastern borders of Germany more precarious than they had been previ-

ously. The terms were negotiated in the old way by the foreign secretaries of the three major European players. They represented a triumph
for the 'old diplomacy' and were seen by non-participants as a possible
check to the embryonic security system embodied in the Covenant. For
them, the Treaty of Locarno, whatever its virtues, implied a retreat from
the concept of the 'indivisibility of peace' (Litvinov's phrase). It was an
arrangement which involved neither the United States nor the Soviet
Union, and was welcomed as such by both Chamberlain and Briand.
Behind the treaty, nevertheless, was the continuing flow of American
capital to Germany and Washington's backing for the new diplomatic
configuration. Without the adoption of the Dawes plan and the London
agreements, there could have been no political breakthrough, though
the Americans maintained their attitude of aloof detachment from the
Locarno-initiated stabilization process. The Russians, for their part,
could not check the German rapprochement with France and Britain,
but were able to keep the line open to Berlin.

The difficulties of readjusting the Versailles balance between France
and Germany in the latter's direction were compounded by the absence
of an agreed outside threat that would force them together. Much
depended on Britain's ability to influence the pace of change. In the
long run, the British and French were gambling on German acceptance
of a less than equal position until some future undetermined date. As
Chamberlain had written earlier to Lord Stamfordham, the king's private secretary:

I regard it as the first task of statesmanship to set to work to make the new
position of Germany tolerable to the German people in the hope that as they
regain prosperity under it they may in time become reconciled to it and be
unwilling to put their fortunes again to the desperate hazard of war. I am
working not for today or tomorrow but for some date like 1960 or 1970
when German strength will have returned and when the prospect of war will
again cloud the horizon unless the risks are still too great to be rashly incurred
and the actual conditions too tolerable to be jeopardised on a gambler's throw.[20]

Yet the equivocal nature of Britain's commitment in Europe was an
important weakness in the mid-decade stabilization which followed.
Britain's real influence stemmed from its willingness to guarantee
France's future security, yet the Locarno guarantees were partial and
carefully circumscribed. No British government could or would engage
itself in eastern Europe. British obligations were also restricted in the
west and purposely linked to the League's weak and non-binding

---

[20] Chamberlain to Lord Stamfordham, 9 Feb. 1925, Austen Chamberlain Mss., PRO,
FO 800/257.

security system. It was hoped in London that the western guarantees would never have to be honoured. There was no military follow-up to the political arrangements. The memories of the Somme and Passchendaele closed the door to any broader interpretation of Britain's responsibilities in Europe beyond Locarno.

III

Stresemann, Briand, and Chamberlain dominated the diplomacy of the later twenties. The challenge to their statesmanship was almost as great as that faced by the 1919 peacemakers. Whatever may have been the private and public rejoicing after Locarno, the men who went boating on Lake Maggiore knew that they were at the start of a difficult road. The initiative lay with Stresemann; he set the menu for revision but its length and timing depended on France. In recent years the German foreign secretary has been identified as Weimar's greatest statesman. His full-length portrait hung in the room of Hans-Dietrich Genscher (Chancellor Kohl's foreign minister) at the Foreign Ministry in Bonn, a reminder of Stresemann's *Westorientierung und Ostpolitik* legacies and a pointer to the reconstruction of a usable historical past. The man who started his political career as a nationalist member of the National Liberals and the wartime spokesman for a 'greater Germany' is now remembered for his loyalty to the Weimar republic and his vision of a Germany operating within the constraints of a European concert of powers. It was only gradually and with some reluctance that the head of his new right-centre party, the German People's Party (DVP), created in 1919, came to terms with the republic, though he had long favoured a parliamentary regime. The highly intelligent and charismatic leader was an outsider in German politics, a parvenu who rose by his own efforts from the Protestant lower middle class (his father produced and sold bottled beer, hence the jibe, 'bottled beer Gustav') to social acceptability and political eminence. Never quite trusted because of his political agility and adaptability to circumstances, he was more pragmatic than many of his political colleagues. He had learned much from the German defeat in 1918 and from the republic's near collapse during the Ruhr crisis. Unlike so many others, he accepted the reality of military defeat and argued that Germany's economic strength and not 'old, buried guns' was its best card for its return to great-power status. The former economic imperialist became convinced that German recovery was dependent on rejoining the international economy, but also that the future of the world economy required the recovery of Germany. The Ruhr occupation hammered the lesson home. Stresemann recognized the vital role the United States could play in Germany's rehabilitation.

The fact that Germany could enlist American as well as British capital against 'French imperialism' in 1924 made American participation in the reparation talks a defining political event for Stresemann. Stresemann placed considerable reliance on Franco-German economic co-operation as a way to calm French fears about future German hegemony. The brutal demonstration of Germany's internal and external weakness during his hundred-day chancellorship in 1923 convinced him that the future security of Germany, in the largest sense, depended on finding a peaceful and acceptable solution to the Franco-German problem. For Stresemann, Locarno was only the first milestone on a long road. The German motive was defensive, to avoid the possibility of a renewed pact between France, Britain, and Belgium and to secure a Cologne evacuation without disarmament. In the future Germany had to become *bundisfahrung* (alliance-worthy) in order to protect its interests. This could only be accomplished by recognizing the western frontiers and joining the League of Nations, which in its very early years Stresemann had treated as an irrelevancy. Like almost every other German politician, Stresemann was a nationalist and revisionist. The goals outlined in the famous and much-quoted letter to the German crown prince in September 1925 provide some insight into his long-term thinking, though the letter was composed with an eye to its recipient's nationalist sympathies. There was to be an end to the foreign occupation of Germany and reparations were to be made tolerable. Germany must protect 'those ten or twelve millions of our kindred who now live under a foreign yoke in foreign lands'. The German–Polish frontier had to be changed, with Danzig, the Polish Corridor to the sea, and the portion of Upper Silesia awarded to Poland in 1921 returned to Germany. In the background was the *Anschluss* with German Austria. With an eye to the crown prince's advisers, Stresemann added a warning against the utopia of flirting with Bolshevism.[21] He made no secret of his immediate goals, telling Briand and Chamberlain that Germany looked to the early evacuation of the Rhineland, a favourable settlement of the Polish Corridor and Danzig, and the return of some former German colonies as mandates. In return, he intended that Germany should abandon the possibility of future military action and accept and promote the rules of peaceful intercourse. Yet even with regard to the first, non-territorial goal of liberating German territory from foreign occupation, he had to refrain from pushing too hard or too early for fear of compromising Briand's position. The Rhineland issue, with its linkage to reparations,

---

[21] Arnold Harttung (ed.), *Gustav Stresemann, Schriften*, Nachlass Bd. 29 (Berlin, 1976), 336–40.

not only highlighted the difficulties in achieving détente but weakened
the impulse towards accommodation.

Stresemann, a complex and highly flexible individual, developed a
wider vision of European relations in which a peaceful Germany could
play a major part. His pursuit of peaceful accommodation was intended
both to restore Germany as a great power and to create a domestic
consensus that would strengthen the republic. At the coalface of
Locarno politics, whether in the west or east, Stresemann was a pragmatic realist, exploiting or creating the opportunities for the full recovery of German power. While Stresemann wanted Germany to rejoin the
concert, it had to be as a full partner with 'equal rights'. Whatever his
sympathies with Briand's need to safeguard France's future safety, the
German foreign minister intended to use Locarno as the springboard for
revision; he came to hope that this revision could be realized with the
consent and support of his Locarno partners. He never believed that war
was a feasible or desirable option for Germany. Like Briand, Stresemann
believed in the 'management of peace'. He told his party conference
in October 1926: 'I firmly believe that the new Germany and its
re-ascendancy can only be founded on peace. But how should this
peace be established if it is not based on a reconciliation between
Germany and France?'[22] British and American support (if forthcoming)
might reassure the French, but only co-operation with France would
permit genuine revision. Stresemann respected Briand and appreciated
his difficulties; he responded well to the Frenchman's charm and wit.
Though he never particularly warmed to Chamberlain, whom he found
'condescending' in manner and unnecessarily rigid over colonies, he was
too astute to ignore the advantages of working with the 'honest broker'
who could swing the European balance in the German direction. It may
be true that Stresemann's search for a peaceful accommodation with
France developed into a more far-reaching attachment to European co-
operation. The foreign minister and his supportive secretary of state,
Carl von Schubert, understood the need to address the problems
of a changing international system at a time of unusual instability.
Stresemann welcomed the League meetings both as providing opportunities for regular contacts with Briand and Chamberlain and for their
domestic political value. Like the other two statesmen, he never saw the
League as a substitute for great-power diplomacy but as a useful means
of promoting co-operation and, for home purposes, advancing the cause
of minority rights.

---

[22] Jonathan Wright, 'Stresemann's Concept of International Relations', in A. M.
Birke, M. Brechtken, and A. Searle (eds.), *An Anglo-German Dialogue: The Munich
Lectures on the History of International Relations* (Munich, 2000).

Neither Stresemann nor Briand was able to bridge the gap between German aspirations and French fears. German gains were seen in Paris as France's losses, while insofar as Stresemann was unwilling to abandon the hope of territorial change in the east (though prepared to postpone it), he stoked those very insecurities that Locarno was intended to diminish. If Stresemann's freedom of manoeuvre was circumscribed by this basic clash of national interests, it was further narrowed by the persistence of powerful nationalist sentiments in Germany. It was an uphill battle, both to build viable governments of the centre and to educate the electorate in the virtues of restraint. The task became more difficult after 1928. Given Stresemann's difficulties with his own Reichstag party, a section of which always looked to the nationalist right, and the fundamental fragility of the Weimar political structure, he had to exaggerate what could be achieved and the speed with which change would take place. No foreign minister was more acutely conscious of the importance of securing political backing. Stresemann's mornings were spent at the ministry; the rest of his day was devoted to politicking in the Reichstag and chancellery. His attention to the politicians of the main parties paid dividends, but no achievable diplomatic success could compensate for the instabilities of the Weimar state. It was not easy to preach patience in a country whose chief *raison d'être* rested on its opposition to an imposed peace and foreign exploitation. When the economic scene darkened, nothing Stresemann had accomplished prevented the upsurge of xenophobic feelings. Already before his death in October 1929, at the early age of 51, he had become highly apprehensive about the future. He could deal with nationalists like Hugenberg but already foresaw that the National Socialists posed a far more destructive threat to the existence of the republic to which he was deeply committed, as well as to the peaceful path to revision that he championed.

If Stresemann still remains an elusive figure, Briand's reputation, even in his own lifetime, was the subject both of extravagant praise and harsh denunciation. Along with General de Gaulle, he is the French statesman 'most cited on the plaques of the streets of France', but he has been, until recently, mainly forgotten by his countrymen and women.[23] He has been portrayed successively as the 'pilgrim of peace' (see the bronze sculpture on the gate of the Quai d'Orsay, put up in the 1930s), condemned as the appeaser of Germany and the propagator of dangerous illusions, and currently praised as the prophet of European

---

[23] Jacques Bariéty, 'Aristide Briand, les raisons d'un oubli', in Antoine Fleury, in collaboration with Lubor Jilek (eds.), *Le Plan Briand d'Union federale européene* (Berne, 1998), 1.

integration. Briand's great gifts of oratory and persuasion and his lack of order and precision have made a balanced assessment difficult. He read little and wrote less. He was a silver-tongued statesman who delighted in the spoken word, the conciliatory phrase, and the oratorical gesture. Stresemann spoke bluntly when confrontation loomed; Briand retreated into generalities. Where Stresemann's demands were clearly formulated, Briand's were deliberately vague. Policy details could be left to officials, above all to his expert secretary-general, Philippe Berthelot, who would act as a brake on Briand's more fanciful ideas; but the French foreign minister was an adroit and subtle negotiator in his own right. The great advantage of retreating into generalities was to leave the door open for future bargaining.

Briandisme came to mean a policy of conciliation and appeasement and eventually also advocacy of the creation of a European federal union independent of American financial and economic power. This was, in part, the image of French diplomacy which Briand cultivated, with all the personal warmth and natural charm that so attracted Austen Chamberlain and so many others. But behind the cigarette smoke, the sleepy and heavy-lidded eyes, the walrus moustache, and the persuasive voice, there was the shrewd and highly experienced statesman with a sharp sense of his country's capabilities and limitations. There was more substance and calculation to *Briandisme* than the minister's speeches to the Chamber of Deputies or to the League Assembly conveyed. Briand's policies did not rest on an illusory view of the world. On the contrary, despite the high rhetoric, his reading of the European situation was often as realistic as that of Stresemann. Having long recognized that victorious France was *épuisée et exsangue* (exhausted and bloodless), and that it could not impose its will on Germany, he was prepared to work for détente. The Franco-German situation had to be resolved if France was to regain its balance and live with some degree of confidence in the future. Briand hoped that this rapprochement could be built on their common interests in peace and economic prosperity. Yet, however necessary rapprochement was, Briand was well aware of the risks involved and had no intention of sacrificing the existing safeguards of French security. He relied on the promise of British protection in case of war, on the hope of Anglo-American financial assistance, and on the maintenance of the eastern alliances to buttress French security. He hoped, too, that Germany and Russia would be kept apart and contemplated a closer relationship with the Soviet Union. He was cautious about moving too fast in dealing with Germany, believing that a nation of 40 million people was always at risk from a neighbour of 70 million which was growing at a faster rate and equipped with a superior industrial base. The exaggerated estimates of current German power produced by the French intelligence services were widely accepted. The balance of the *forces profondes* spoke for themselves. Briand's vision, as he told the Chamber's foreign affairs commission in April 1926, of a time when Europe 'will do like America and make a federal state', included the hope that Germany's absorption into Europe would dilute its threat to France and make possible the next step forward towards an endurable peace.[24] By temperament and choice Briand sought compromise and consensus, but he genuinely believed that the conciliation of Germany was unavoidable. No alternative policy was practical.

Briand was under considerable pressure to deliver the rewards of his diplomacy; much, too much, depended on movements in Germany and Britain over which he had no control. There were influential political forces in France favouring co-operation with Germany; conciliation appealed to a wide range of disparate political and economic groups. If Raymond Poincaré was ultimately more suspicious of German intentions than Briand, the differences between the two men were more marginal than substantive. There were dangers in Briand's preference for deliberate evasion. He never made clear the required safeguards for French 'security'. He failed to state what France would accept in the way of treaty revision and misled Stresemann as a result. Briand never examined the true worth of the British guarantee and relied too heavily on Chamberlain's support. The ambiguities in his eastern policies confused allies and friends. Above all, he was unable and perhaps unwilling to deliver what Stresemann needed to keep the process of accommodation on track. Locarno left room for concessions to encourage Germany along the path of peaceful revision but Briand was too cautious to abandon the fundamental Versailles restraints on German power. An ambiguity of purpose lay at the heart of the problems of the 'Locarno system'. Never doubting that France needed protection against its more powerful neighbour, Briand simultaneously sought a Franco-German partnership that would reduce French dependence on Britain and the United States. He therefore encouraged Stresemann's policy of peaceful revision while trying to limit Germany's powers of recovery through a series of bilateral and multilateral agreements. As the ambiguities and contradictions in Briand's position were revealed his nationalist critics found much ammunition, yet they could offer no real alternative answer to France's security dilemma.

At Locarno Briand had put the French security eggs in the British basket. It was this which made Austen Chamberlain the key player in

[24] AAN, Proces-verbal, Commission des Affaires Étrangeres, Assemblée Nationale, 23 April 1926: see Andrew Barros, 'France and the German Menace, 1919–1928' unpubl. Ph.D. thesis, Cambridge University (2001), 310.

the Locarno combination. The much-quoted Churchill quip, 'Austen always played the game and always lost it', may be relevant to Chamberlain's failure to become prime minister but cannot be applied to his actions at Locarno. After initial hesitations before the Locarno agreements were concluded he became their enthusiastic supporter, seeing in them the solution to Britain's overextended world responsibilities. Britain's function was to foster a feeling of security on the continent which would dampen war spirits. In reassuring France through limited commitments in Europe while encouraging German hopes for peaceful revision, Chamberlain believed he could open the way for Franco-German reconciliation. In the knowledge of British support, he hoped that Briand would be generous, while the Germans, fearful of British opposition, would not move too quickly or demand too much. The stabilization of German political life and Germany's development into a pacific member of the European community would encourage the French to follow the policy of accommodation in which Chamberlain genuinely believed. How far he could actually bridge the gap between France and Germany was circumscribed by the unwillingness of the cabinet and the military to consider any responsibilities beyond the limited commitment offered in 1925. From the start of the negotiations, Chamberlain depended on his diplomatic acuity and Britain's considerable prestige for success. Much was made of the intangible benefits of Locarno. The foreign secretary clearly hoped that Britain would never be called upon to honour her commitments.

Chamberlain did not look for quick or spectacular results but for a gradual change in the international environment. There were positive advantages in the usual pragmatic approach that characterized traditional British diplomacy, and it was one that served Chamberlain well in his dealings with Briand and Stresemann. Yet while Chamberlain could encourage and reassure, both of which he did exceedingly well, there were limits to what he could accomplish. It can be argued that Chamberlain was not a genuine neutral. Though sometimes irritated by France's exaggerated preoccupation with 'security', he would neither force Briand's hand nor desert him.

Though he never truly warmed to him, Chamberlain did come to trust Stresemann. Writing to D'Abernon in October 1930, Chamberlain reminisced that:

it was by degrees and, as it were, reluctantly, that Stresemann became a convert to his own policy and accepted its consequences. I am not at all sure that his first idea was not to divide France and England, or at least to make it certain that we should not revive the Treaty of Alliance ... [I]t does not detract from the courage and loyalty with which he pursued the policy as it developed in our hands and the skill with which he drew from it all the advantages it offered.[25]

Chamberlain recognized the strength of nationalist feeling in Germany and the need to provide Stresemann with rewards for co-operation. He urged Briand to be more conciliatory over the evacuation of French troops from Germany and the dismantling of the Military Control Commission. He did his best to maintain an 'even hand', taking pains to avoid offending either leader. His sincerity and honesty were powerful assets in Geneva, compensating for the pomposity and formality of dress—the morning coat, well-pressed trousers, boutonniere, top hat, and monocle—that made him such an excellent subject for the cartoonist. Though he genuinely tried to play the 'honest broker', Chamberlain always believed that Briand had taken the greater risks in concluding the Locarno agreements. It was with some justice that Stresemann, who found Chamberlain distant and reserved, never fully trusted his neutrality.

The fundamental questions raised by the Locarno treaties were neither asked nor answered in London. As British power was imperial, naval, financial, and economic, there was little to fear from a modest adjustment of the European balance in Germany's favour, but it was not in Britain's interest to help Europe's greatest power to continental predominance. No member of the Conservative cabinet, Churchill excepted, spoke of Britain's ultimate dependence on France's military superiority over a disarmed Germany. It was only if conciliation failed that the military balance would become important, and Locarno was intended to avoid just such a possibility. As long as Britain's specific economic interests were protected, Chamberlain was prepared to leave the settlement of such issues to the Germans and French. Unlike his Locarno partners, Chamberlain was a globalist with interests to defend in many other parts of the world beyond Europe. In the summer of 1928, when Stresemann made his bid for the early evacuation of the Rhineland, the British were engaged in a difficult clash with the Americans. While these global preoccupations explain why Britain was so anxious to establish an equilibrium in Europe, they also restricted what the British were willing to do to sustain it. It was highly unlikely that Chamberlain shared Briand's European vision; he had to think in more global terms. His aim was to re-establish the concert system based on the reconciliation of France and Germany and operating through the League of Nations, whose utility he clearly recognized. When his hopes in this direction began to fade, he was prepared to throw his

[25] Chamberlain to D'Abernon, 1 Oct. 1930, British Library Add. Mss. 48926B, fos. 245–8.

diplomatic weight on the side of France, for, like Briand, he recognized the potential danger of a revived and unreconciled Germany and the need to keep the existing safeguards while its future remained uncertain. Austen Chamberlain stood squarely in the long tradition of British appeasement, the adjustment of continental relations through the application of reason and compromise. An island kingdom that stood at the heart of a great empire could afford to take a more detached view of the continental conflicts than those who were neighbours. What Britain could not do, as Chamberlain fully understood, was to stand apart from the readjustments that had to be made if these conflicts were not to simmer and burst into flames.

IV

The Locarno treaties could not take effect until Germany entered the League, and careful preparations were made for her rapid admission. The German application was dispatched on 8 February 1926; four days later the Council called for an extraordinary session of the Assembly to meet on 8 March to consider the request. Complications immediately ensued. The German submission provided the middle-ranking powers with an opportunity to press once again for permanent representation on the Council. The whole question of the size of the Council, the differences between permanent and non-permanent members, and the geographic distribution of seats (the non-European states felt particularly aggrieved) had long been a point of bitter contention between the League representatives. With the subject reopened, Brazil and Spain, both non-permanent members on the Council, and Poland, seeking representation for the first time, demanded permanent seats. Poland's demand set off warning bells in Berlin. The situation was further complicated by an Anglo-French compromise, reached without consulting Stresemann, to back Poland and Spain, their respective protégés. Stresemann demanded that Germany alone should be given a permanent seat upon entry. Others supported the German objections to an enlarged membership. Sweden, a non-permanent member of the Council, became the spokesman for a group of states (Norway, Denmark, the Netherlands, Finland, Switzerland, and Belgium) who objected to any distinctions being made between middle and small powers. Sweden and Denmark, who had opposed Poland's earlier efforts at an alliance with Finland and hoped that German participation in the League would weaken its links with the Soviet Union, took up a principled defence of maintaining the distinction between great and small powers. Misled by Chamberlain's willingness to let Sweden carry the odium of blocking Polish entry on a question of principle, Östen Undén, the Swedish foreign minister and representa-tive, took a strong line in Geneva until he found himself in danger of isolation when Chamberlain altered his stand and sought an acceptable compromise.

By the time the Assembly met in March 1926 passions were running high. The Germans refused to enter the League until the dispute over the Council seats was settled. Chamberlain pushed the Spanish claims; France was committed to Poland. Both demanded German support for their respective candidates. Briand threatened resignation if Poland was refused a Council seat. The sustained deadlock turned opinion against the Germans, and the British brought heavy pressure on the Swedes to abandon their veto on expansion. Identified too closely with Germany and concerned that the League would suffer if the conflict continued, Sweden offered to vacate its Council seat in favour of Poland. The Germans accepted this solution only if Czechoslovakia made way for the Netherlands. Undén and Beneš, with little enthusiasm, agreed to the German demand but the Brazilians threatened to use their veto against German admission into the Council. A specially constituted League committee including both present and would-be Council members (so that Germany could participate) was created, and German entry postponed until September. At the final March Assembly session the smaller states denounced the manner in which the Council issue had been handled by the Locarno powers behind closed doors and insisted on continuing the struggle.

The whole affair was a blow to the prestige of the League and to the morale of its strongest defenders. In Germany, criticism, except on the far right, was directed less against Stresemann than against an institution that allowed second-rate countries to thwart the will of the mighty. Stresemann argued that the Allied effort to pack the Council had been blocked and that Germany had entered the 'inner circle' of great powers even before her formal admission to the League. He used the debacle to demand further concessions from the French and British in the ongoing negotiations over the Rhineland occupation forces and the ending of IMCC control. In the late summer, after further conflicts between the Locarnites and a new revolt by the smaller powers, the committee reached a compromise solution. Germany alone would be given a permanent seat and the number of non-permanent seats would be increased from six to nine, one-third to be filled every year for three-year terms, with a maximum of three states eligible for re-election. A new category of semi-permanent members was created. Poland accepted the arrangements but Brazil and Spain left the League in indignation. Spain returned in 1928; Brazil remained outside. Against the will of the smaller European states, the Council was enlarged and, through informal arrangements, the non-European powers gained greater representation in the distribution of the temporary seats. The Germans entered the League on Stresemann's terms. As a permanent member of the Council, Germany won formal parity with the great powers and could bargain as an equal. In Berlin the solution was hailed as a German victory.

The conclusion in April of the Russo-German non-aggression treaty was another bump in the road. The permanent officials at the Quai d'Orsay found the treaty terms 'execrable'. Briand's attitude hardened over such issues as German civilian aircraft (considered easily convertible into military aircraft), disarmament violations, nationalist activities in the Rhineland, and further troop reductions in the Rhineland and Saar as had been promised in January. The British, repeatedly reassured by D'Abernon, were less alarmed. Due to Chamberlain's insistence, Briand overruled his officials and agreed to abandon the idea of a formal protest. Chamberlain convinced him that a sharp reaction would drive Germany towards closer co-operation with Russia. Briand had a difficult time in the Senate when defending the Locarno accords, which were confirmed nevertheless by an overwhelming majority. The military men showed their displeasure by refusing to consider any disarmament proposals at Geneva until the question of French security was settled. Briand's fears were compounded by worries, after Piłsudski's May 1926 coup in Poland, of a possible Polish–Soviet conflict, but his efforts to negotiate an eastern settlement with the Germans failed.

On 10 September 1926, the twelfth anniversary of the Battle of the Marne, the German delegation was received into the League. Stresemann spoke simply and modestly. Briand rose majestically to the occasion as the League's chief spokesman with a stirring appeal: 'Away with rifles, machine guns, cannon. Clear the way for conciliation, arbitration and peace.'[26] He smoothed the ruffled feathers of the smaller states by promising that future negotiations would take place 'in the spirit of the League'. Chamberlain was thrilled at what he saw as a British triumph that would 'close the war chapter and start Europe afresh'. Germany's admission to the League altered its status and made Geneva the focal point of European diplomacy. Whether the League itself benefited from this new addition to its membership structure is more debatable. The three foreign secretaries met regularly at Geneva, representing their countries at the quarterly Council meetings. Stresemann was absent only once, because of illness in the summer of 1928. The real centre of decision-making rested with Briand, Chamberlain,

---

[26] *League of Nations Official Journal*, Special Supplement, no. 44. *Records of the Seventh Ordinary Session of the Assembly* (Geneva, 1926), 53.

and Stresemann who settled the questions of the day in the hotel rooms of Geneva. It was at these 'Locarno tea parties' that the three, sometimes with others in attendance, discussed their problems, set the agenda for Council meetings, and drafted the texts of the resolutions to be proposed and accepted. The smaller powers chafed at this revival of the old Concert of Europe, now a concert of three. Even Belgium, which before 1924 had played at least a lubricating role in Anglo-French relations, was not a regular participant, though it was still included when German questions were discussed. Its influence was further reduced when the rule of small-power rotation was introduced and it lost its Council seat. While Geneva became a permanent fixture on the diplomatic map and the men who sat around the horseshoe table commanded a world audience, the Council itself was increasingly engaged in matters of secondary importance. The entry of Germany into the League underlined the distinction between the great and small states already acknowledged at the time of its founding. The three summiteers, well versed in the cut and thrust of parliamentary debates, believed in the efficacy of face-to-face negotiations. Stresemann and Briand could calculate how far domestic interests could be compromised in the interests of harmony without losing political backing. Council and Assembly meetings provided public platforms for the expression of their views.

Each of the three leaders saw how the League could be used for the promotion of their respective national interests. Stresemann basked in the opportunities for press exposure and publicity. The attention of the fourth estate was particularly important for the German leader in his task of winning home support for his policy of 'national realism'. He brought with him to Geneva an impressive delegation of officials and parliamentary representatives from different parties to underline the significance of Germany's re-entry into world politics. Somewhat to the surprise of the Allied delegates, the Germans proved to be good League citizens, taking their duties seriously and contributing to the work of the Secretariat and the League committees. The German representatives cultivated delegates from the smaller nations, ex-allies and neutrals, in order to re-establish ties of common interest. Germany's active presence in Geneva was intended to show how the advantages of great-power status could be achieved without military strength or threats of confrontation. Briand, apart from the unique opportunities the League presented for his extraordinary powers of public persuasion, believed that the Geneva system could be used to assist the process of diplomatic adjustment. The League's commissions and committees blunted the edge of direct confrontation and encouraged the participants to work together. They also provided opportunities for delay. Briand's high reputation in Geneva brought him kudos at home, above all from his old supporters in the radical and socialist camps. His speeches conveyed a sense of hope and conviction that left only the most cynical listener unmoved. Even Austen Chamberlain, who disliked the 'jamboree' atmosphere of Geneva and whose somewhat patronizing tone reinforced the 'nanny' view of British diplomacy, used the League to extend British influence. He dispensed advice to the representatives of the powers, large and small, and was able to smooth ruffled feathers. It was for excellent reasons and with beneficial results that Chamberlain kept British League policy under his personal direction after a period of divided control in London.

The real bargaining between the Locarnites took place in private. This form of personal and highly informal diplomacy had advantages but also drawbacks. Compromises reached to avoid disagreements subsequently proved to be impractical or politically unacceptable. Some differences could not be resolved, and there were outbursts of temper. The outward appearance of harmonious relations naturally encouraged expectations of success. The public was consequently left unprepared for the inevitable disputes between men who represented countries with divergent interests. A lunchtime meeting in September 1926 between Briand and Stresemann at Thoiry, the small French village near Geneva, proved how dangerous and damaging private conversations could be. The four-and-a-half-hour meal was the culmination of a long chain of diplomatic manoeuvring and was widely reported to herald a vital breakthrough in Franco-German relations. Much was expected. Instead, this attempt at an overall solution led to recriminations on both sides.

Quite apart from Chamberlain's urgings and his own willingness to further the conciliation process, Briand was prepared to go beyond the immediate issues dividing France and Germany in order to seek a comprehensive agreement with Stresemann. France's financial difficulties and the plummeting franc were the keys to the Thoiry lunch. The Cartel des Gauches, unable to find a solution for the country's financial woes, was beginning to disintegrate; German reparations again appeared as a possible source of relief. Shortly after signing the Locarno accords, the French authorities considered the possibility of commercializing the Dawes plan obligations, that is, the German railroad bonds and industrial debentures earmarked as security for the Dawes annuities and held by the Transfer Committee. These bonds could be floated on the world's stock exchanges, mainly New York, and the French, who under the terms of the Spa Protocol of 1920 were entitled to 52 per cent of the proceeds, could claim their cash. Nothing could be done without the consent of the Reparation Commission and the co-operation of the American banks. The French also needed German assistance: the latter would have to guarantee future payment of interest on the commercial bonds if they were to attract buyers. In the late autumn of 1925 French officials at the Ministry of Finance and Quai d'Orsay considered linking German co-operation over financial and commercial questions with the early evacuation of the Rhineland. Apart from France's financial requirements, this was also the time when French and German industrialists were negotiating cartel and tariff arrangements and when the all-important new Franco-German commercial treaty, signed in July 1926, was still under consideration. The French sounded out Parker Gilbert, the reparation agent-general, and the representatives from American financial houses. The Germans, appreciating the opportunities presented by the collapse of the French franc, along with the difficulties of the Belgian franc and Polish zloty, took their own soundings. The price for German co-operation, as discussed by Stresemann, included the fixing of Germany's total reparations obligations, an end to the Rhineland occupation, the return of the Saar, and the settlement of the Polish border. In conversations with the Belgians and Poles in the spring of 1926, Hjalmar Schacht, the president of the Reichsbank, offered to trade German financial assistance for Eupen-Malmédy and the Polish Corridor. Schacht's proposals were unacceptable to the Poles or to the British; the Belgian talks continued but raised a storm in Paris. The financial débâcle in Paris in early July 1926 and the news of the German–Belgian talks produced a new flurry of activity in Paris and Berlin. Each side knew that the other was prepared to talk.

Stresemann, cautiously optimistic, waited for an approach from Briand; while he waited, the French financial crisis brought down the Briand cabinet. Raymond Poincaré took office on 23 July 1926 as premier and finance minister in the new 'Union Nationale' cabinet. Briand returned to the foreign ministry to serve under his old rival, who needed to draw on the ex-premier's popularity in left and right-centre circles to assure the success of his anti-inflation programme. Like Briand, Poincaré wanted to commercialize part of the Dawes bonds but hoped this could be done without American or German assistance. He nevertheless agreed that Briand should consult with Stresemann. The latter, in anticipation of the next League meeting in September, indicated that he would welcome a private exchange of views and if the new French cabinet was still interested to discuss the question of German financial assistance through the mobilization of the Dawes obligations. Briand, though welcoming the meeting, gave no hint of offering further concessions to the Germans. On the contrary, he successfully appealed to Chamberlain for support on the German disarmament violations and again warned the Belgians against the cession of Eupen-Malmédy to Germany. Reacting negatively to the reports of Schacht's multifarious activities and conscious of Poincaré's strong objections to the restoration of the provinces, Briand warned Stresemann against 'imprudent initiatives'. The Belgians retreated; on 23 August the Belgian premier publicly insisted that 'there have never been any official dealings and I assure you that there will not be any on the subject of Eupen-Malmédy'.[27] Following Poincaré's appointment, the French franc began its recovery. Though commercialization was still a desirable strategy, Briand, who may not have understood what was actually involved, had more freedom to negotiate.

The question came to a head shortly after Germany's reception into the League on 10 September. No one knows exactly what transpired at Geneva or what was said or promised at Thoiry during a long and rich lunch. These dealings were private and unofficial, and only a few people knew of the exchanges. No official record was kept of the Thoiry meeting and Stresemann's first-hand account differs markedly from the notes kept by Professor Hensard, Briand's translator, and used by the Quai d'Orsay.[28] Both accounts make it clear that, as the world press informed their readers, the two statesmen were intent on a 'complete solution'. Stresemann asked for the evacuation of the Rhineland within a year, the immediate return of the Saar to Germany, the purchase of Eupen-Malmédy, and for the IMCC to be withdrawn and replaced by a League organization to monitor the demilitarized zone. In return, the Germans offered support for the marketing of about 1,500 million gold marks-worth of the railway bonds deposited with the Reparation Commission. Half the proceeds would go to Germany's creditors and be deducted from her final reparations bill; the other half, amounting to 780 million gold marks, would go to France. The Germans would also pay between 370 and 400 million gold marks for the Saar mines. Stresemann's account suggests that a bargain was struck and that the experts only had to work out the details. The French were to claim that this was a far-reaching but general discussion, 'a preface' (Briand's words) to the more thorough examination of the problems raised. Both men intended that their conversations should be followed by detailed technical studies and that their governments should be asked to sanction further negotiations. When the discussions were abandoned less than two months later, each foreign minister blamed the other for initiating the talks and for their failure.

[27] Sally Marks, *Innocent Abroad: Belgium at the Paris Peace Conference of 1919* (Chapel Hill, NC, 1981), 353.

[28] These notes were apparently altered on Briand's orders at the beginning of November and therefore are less reliable than was once thought. Jacques Bariéty, 'Finances et relations internationales a propos du "plan de Thoiry" (Septembre 1926)', *Relations Internationales*, 21 (Spring, 1970), 69.

The Thoiry scheme would have given Stresemann much of what he had sought at Locarno. In return for a limited debt commercialization, he would secure the liberation of German territory from foreign occupation. Though commercialization might prejudice German hopes for future reductions in the reparation burden, the political rewards were well worth the possible financial sacrifice. There was not much enthusiasm in Paris for Briand's *solution d'ensemble*. Neither Poincaré nor the Quai d'Orsay officials were prepared to make the 'grand gesture' without getting far more substantial rewards in return. It seems highly probable that Briand promised more than he could deliver and later covered his retreat by changing the details of the story. There were denials of the German version of the promises made at Thoiry, and Stresemann had to accept the collapse of the bargain. Briand had gone to Thoiry without any mandate from the cabinet and knowing that Poincaré opposed the linkage between transfer guarantees and the shortening of the occupation. When he returned to Paris he found that Poincaré still hoped to mobilize a first tranche of the Dawes obligations on the American market without German concurrence. The premier wanted simultaneous and complete mobilization of the Dawes obligations in return for the evacuation of the Rhineland. Briand's advisers demanded a more generous financial settlement, new guarantees of the status quo in the east, and specific pledges against *Anschluss* before concluding a general settlement. Nothing offered at Thoiry gave the French any security from a change in German policy and a future assault on France. Briand had to retreat. As the franc began its rapid recovery on the exchanges and was formally stabilized in December 1926, the Thoiry scheme lost its immediate *raison d'être* in Paris. Poincaré had succeeded without either American or German assistance. The Belgians, whose financial position had markedly improved by September, and the Italians both opposed commercialization, preferring to take their scheduled annuities under the Dawes plan. The French, intending to use the Rhineland evacuation as a bargaining card, could afford to wait. Marshal Foch publicly opposed a premature withdrawal from the Rhineland while the French army was in the process of reorganization and the eastern fortifications not yet constructed. Poincaré had assured the Conseil Superieur de la Guerre that these conditions would be met. Giving up the most important physical guarantee of French security was worth a high return.

The final blow to the bond sales idea came from the Americans and British. The Thoiry scheme, in the American view, was little more than a loan to France with the German railways as security. The American Treasury wanted to keep its financial pressure on France (a ban on loans was still in place) until the Mellon–Bérenger agreement was ratified.

The American bankers were equally hostile; their opposition was critical, for the German railway bonds would have to be floated on the New York market, the only possible financial venue. In London, Austen Chamberlain was more sympathetic towards the idea when first approached by Briand in early June. The Treasury and the Bank of England, however, were resolutely opposed to the idea of mobilization. By October, Chamberlain, who generally disliked Franco–German bargains negotiated outside the Locarno framework, had joined the opponents to the scheme. On both sides of the Atlantic officials wanted to keep the Dawes regime intact until a final resolution of the whole reparations question could be negotiated. With an American election due in November 1928 and the Germans facing the introduction of a higher Dawes payments schedule, it might be possible to negotiate a final settlement that would clear the international financial slate.

Stresemann was genuinely confused about Briand's failure to pursue the Thoiry initiatives. He had doubts about the financial proposals, especially as he counted their costs, but was anxious to explore every means of achieving the early evacuation of the Rhineland. Briand was not forthcoming; he would not even discuss the Saar. On 11 November Briand ended the talks in Paris with the sympathetic German ambassador, Hoesch, stating only that 'the prompt fulfilment of the Thoiry idea had been crushed by technical obstacles'.[29] In the vain hope of keeping alive the possibility of further dialogue with Briand, Hoesch blamed Poincaré and the French cabinet for blocking Briand's efforts and accused Berthelot and Seydoux at the Quai d'Orsay of disloyalty towards their chief. It suited Briand that the premier should take the blame for the failure of Thoiry, for it allowed him to temporize without compromising his image as the spokesman for conciliation. Stresemann was still hopeful of a breakthrough on the Rhineland evacuation and was willing to smooth Briand's path to achieve an agreement. On 7 October 1926 the steel cartel arrangements were concluded between the German, French, Belgian, Luxembourg, and Saar industrialists. The British were invited to join but appeared uninterested. Franco–German co-operation was taking a concrete form. To keep some momentum in the peace process, Stresemann concentrated on the issue of the IMCC, the part of the Thoiry scheme most likely to produce an agreement. The three foreign ministers, after protracted and difficult negotiations, agreed that the IMCC should be withdrawn by 31 January 1927 and that the remaining disarmament problems should be negotiated between the Germans and the Conference of Ambassadors, with reference to the League Council if no agreement was reached. Briand, pressed by Foch

[29] Quoted in Jacobson, *Locarno Diplomacy*, 90.

and the military, argued for the permanent on-site inspection of German disarmament and a standing League agency to monitor the demilitarization of the Rhineland. The idea, suggested by Joseph Paul-Boncour, a prominent Socialist deputy and delegate to the League of Nations, met with no sympathy in Berlin, but Stresemann agreed to postpone further talks until the League meeting in March 1927. For all practical purposes the Germans had won their point. The withdrawal of the IMCC meant the end of Allied control over German disarmament. The bickering continued. The Germans were slow in fulfilling their part of the bargain, which involved dismantling the fortifications at Königsberg, Kusten, and Glogau that threatened the Poles. For prestige reasons they were reluctant to allow the technical experts to inspect the demolished eastern fortifications. The matter dragged on until July, when the IMCC finally left Berlin without all the disarmament conditions fulfilled.

V

In December 1926 the Nobel Peace Prize, awarded to Chamberlain (and Charles Dawes) in the previous year, was shared between Stresemann and Briand. Stresemann was hopeful; he promised supporters that 1927 would be the year of evacuations. On his return from the December meeting at Geneva he announced to the press his intention to demand the withdrawal of all Allied troops from the Rhineland at the next Council session. He thought that, with American assistance, some form of overall financial settlement would be possible. It was, on the contrary, during 1927 that the French attitude hardened. Briand sought to postpone any further major concessions and Chamberlain, preoccupied with Far Eastern and Russian affairs, was less inclined than earlier to push him along the path of conciliation. Briand faced a revolt led by the nationalist and anti-German minister of pensions, Louis Marin, for agreeing to withdraw the IMCC before the disarmament question was completely settled. There were rumours even before Briand went to Geneva of growing cabinet opposition to his policies, and during his absence an attempt was made to curtail his negotiating freedom. The press, inspired by the nationalists, carried reports of cabinet rifts and rumours of disaffection at the Quai d'Orsay. Secretary-General Berthelot felt it necessary to publicly declare his support for Briand's policies. With an election to be fought in May 1928 and party divisions over the level of de facto official franc stabilization, Briand's political position seemed safe. Poincaré could ill afford to lose his most influential colleague. It seems probable that Briand had already decided to take a stiffer line with the Germans before the right-wing campaign reached its peak, but he was clearly conscious of

Poincaré's opposition and the political backwash to the Thoiry conversations.

In a withering attack on his opponents on 20 January 1927 before the Chamber's foreign affairs committee, Briand defended the IMCC withdrawal and rounded on his critics, rebutting their charges of sentimentalism. He insisted that Thoiry was nothing more than a general discussion with Stresemann agreeing to make proposals for reciprocal security controls. Though he concentrated on defending the general lines of his policy, he reminded his listeners that he was not averse to force when necessary and had ordered the 1921 occupation of the three German towns. Much of this was repeated to the waiting journalists, who were assured there would be no early evacuation of the Rhineland without guarantees of French security and reparation payments. French apprehensions about the future direction of German policy remained strong. Demonstrations for *Anschluss* both in Germany and in Austria, and difficulties with Italy in south-eastern Europe, gave added weight to Quai d'Orsay advice to 'make haste slowly'. The preoccupation with Germany's power and the fears of its military revival continued to colour French perceptions of their neighbour. Discussions of the new army laws in the Chamber of Deputies focused political attention on the strength of the German army and the need to retain the *couverture* provided by the Rhineland occupation for as long as possible. Stresemann was warned not to raise the questions of evacuation or further troop reductions at the March 1927 Council meeting, when he would act as chairman for the first time.

Though ostensibly the March meeting was a successful one, in fact the private gatherings of the Locarnites were marked by considerable acrimony and ill-will. Briand would not discuss the early evacuation of the Rhineland and Stresemann agreed that when the subject was formally raised, Germany would base its legal claim on Article 431 of the Versailles treaty rather than on its Locarno rights. Chamberlain cautioned the German foreign minister against pressing Briand too hard, given the weakness of the latter's political position. The two men commented on Briand's unusual listlessness and signs of fatigue, but Stresemann took umbrage at the Frenchman's 'unnecessarily unfriendly and malicious tone'.[30] Rather than launching a counter-attack, Stresemann, misled by Hoesch's reading of the forthcoming French election, thought it more prudent to wait on the evacuation issue until after the elections, when Poincaré might be checked and Briand's position strengthened. It was now Stresemann who found himself under attack in Germany. His Reichstag critics made much of the lack of progress

³⁰ Jacobson, *Locarno Diplomacy*, 115.

since Locarno. The government was badly in need of a foreign-policy success and the German public expected that the Rhineland occupation would shortly be ended. Stresemann threatened to resign unless there was some progress on troop reduction. Briand promised to approach the cabinet and general staff on the question of troop reductions but only if the military experts attached to the Allied embassies in Berlin could inspect the fortifications around Königsberg to check they had been destroyed. This was not much to bring back to Berlin. Chamberlain was not in a position to act in Paris. He was preoccupied with the difficulties in China and the May breach with the Soviet Union. The forthcoming summer naval disarmament discussions in Geneva were bound to be difficult in view of the opposing positions of the British and American admirals. The foreign secretary had to view the Briand–Stresemann sparring match in a broader context.

When Briand accompanied the French president to London on 16 May, a visit intended to strengthen the entente, he discussed the Soviet question with Chamberlain. The latter again stressed that the western battle was for the 'soul of Germany'. The Germans, who knew little about the details of the meeting, took alarm at the apparent demonstration of the 'solidarity of the Entente Cordiale', the term used in an uninformative and short press communiqué. The German ambassador in London suspected an Anglo-French bargain, that is, support on the Rhineland in return for French concessions elsewhere. Chamberlain denied that any new engagements were undertaken and insisted that the Russian question had hardly been mentioned. While somewhat exaggerating the innocence of the meeting, Chamberlain had not entered into any bargain and in fact had urged Briand to take action on the troop-reduction issue, for 'the more difficult our relations with Russia became, the more important was it that we should attach Germany solidly to the Western Powers'.[31] Chamberlain neither threatened nor cajoled the Germans with regard to Russia, and only once, in early June, when it was feared that the Soviets might respond to the murder of their representative in Warsaw with an ultimatum to the Poles, asked Stresemann to intervene with Chicherin.

General alarm at the deterioration of relations between Paris and Berlin led to greater cordiality in Geneva in June. Stresemann and Briand sought to find some common ground, though again the Germans failed to pin Briand down on the question of troop reductions. On this issue Stresemann secured Chamberlain's backing, and the British foreign secretary agreed to make a positive statement in the Commons. The inspection question was finally settled when military experts,

[31] Memorandum by Chamberlain, 21 May 1927, Chamberlain Papers, AC 50/536.

guided by German generals, were allowed to complete their tour of the Königsberg fortifications. On 22 July the Conference of Ambassadors formally announced that the IMCC had been dissolved on 31 January 1927. Whatever was gained in the way of improved relations at Geneva was spoiled by a stiff speech by Poincaré at Luneville in June and Stresemann's equally tough statements in the Reichstag and at the Nobel Peace Prize ceremony later in the month. Foreign bayonets in the Rhineland, he informed his audience, were incompatible with Locarno, for Germany had renounced all thought of *revanche* and was working only for peace. Chamberlain wrote to his ambassadors in Paris and Brussels of his fears about the decline in the 'spirit of Locarno'. Briand was playing for time, looking for a reparations–withdrawal bargain after the American elections in November 1928. He was beginning to run out of plausible delaying tactics. There was some modest progress in the summer of 1927 when, faced with French obstruction, Chamberlain forcefully intervened in the troop-reduction dispute. Poincaré and Briand together compelled the French cabinet to agree to the withdrawal of 8,000 men from the Rhineland, less than Chamberlain wanted but more than previously offered. With British and Belgian cuts of 1,000 men each, the total occupation force was now reduced to 60,000 men, mainly French. In August the all-important Franco–German tariff agreement was concluded and Stresemann offered his support in the chemical cartel negotiations in an effort to improve the atmosphere. Stresemann was impatient. There was increasing rest-iveness among his Reichstag critics as Briand dragged his feet over evacuation. Though Stresemann had been persuaded not to publicly press for the evacuation of the Rhineland until after the French elections in May 1928, the negotiating timetable was put in question when Parker Gilbert published his December 1927 annual report recommending a new and final reparation settlement. The old question was back on the international agenda.

Politically, the 'new dawn' of Locarno seemed to be faltering. Pro-gress had been made, mainly at French expense, but after two years of almost continuous negotiation there was little sign of the mutual trust, the 'ethereal bonhomie', which Chamberlain had hoped would tran-scend the written pacts and permeate the conduct of diplomacy gener-ally.[32] Stresemann needed faster progress on the Rhineland withdrawal, while in Paris there were increasing doubts about the evacuation or on any further move on disarmament at Geneva. The Locarno rap-prochement was reaching its limits.

---

[32] David Dutton, *Austen Chamberlain: Gentleman in Politics* (Bolton, 1985), 259.

Re-creating Europe's Financial and Trading Systems, 1924–1928

I

The process of re-creating Europe's financial and trading systems had gone ahead in parallel with the new political approaches surrounding the Locarno agreements. The adoption of the Dawes plan had opened the way for a new chapter in the post-war financial reconstruction of Europe as the American intervention broke the logjam created by reparations. Neither the British nor the Germans believed that the long-range reparation schedule would be fulfilled, and the latter spoke openly of revision within three years. The French were already planning to link the war-debts question to some future final German payment. For the moment, however, the German mark was stabilized with the assistance of an American-backed international loan and the gold mark linked to the dollar. The £800 million Dawes loan issued on 10 October 1924 was a resounding success, oversubscribed thirteen times in London and nearly ten times in New York. Capital-hungry *Länder* and municipal governments in Germany as well as industrialists looked to the New York market for future investment funds.

Contrary to expectations in both Germany and the United States, the successful Dawes issue was not immediately followed by a flood of American loans to Germany. The flow of funds began only in the late summer and autumn of 1925 and went mainly to the *Länder* governments and municipalities. Municipal bonds seemed safe and secure investments, particularly as American investors had few incentives to put their money in German industries that might compete with their own. Though J. P. Morgan & Co. shunned the German market, there were many other firms in the United States eager to make the most of this new bonanza. Between 1925 and 1928 as much as one-third of Germany's total investment was financed by capital imports, of which the largest share by far came from Wall Street. In Germany control over public investment and the decisions over where the foreign capital should go became a divisive political issue. Hjalmar Schacht, the president of the almost totally independent Reichsbank, feared that any large, unregulated capital inflow would undermine the Reichsbank's control of the currency and defeat its tight money policies. He tried, at first with only limited success, to strengthen the bank's supervision of foreign loans. In his campaign for the regulation of public borrowing and restraints on excessive government spending, he won the backing of some German industrialists, who shared his dislike of the *Kalte*

Sozialisierung (cold socialism) of the municipalities and their high spending programmes financed through borrowing. This temporary combination—for most industrialists disliked the Reichsbank's restrictive credit policies—resulted in a victory for Schacht in 1925 when the newly created Advisory Office for Foreign Credit was empowered to establish and enforce criteria for *Länder* and communal borrowing. Schacht hoped that American funds could be channelled directly into 'productive' investment, but despite the new controls and a complete stop on public loans in 1927, a sizeable part of the long-term American loans continued to go to the municipalities. The latter also resorted to the domestic market or to short-term foreign loans over which Schacht had no control.

At first the Berlin government's deflationary policies during 1924 and 1925 created large budgetary surpluses which, with the new loans, easily covered the modest Dawes payments. But the drastic restrictions on government expenditure and domestic credit, combined with a fall in the consumption and production of basic industrial products, intensified the downward movement of the economy. Towards the end of 1925 national income and imports began to fall, though exports continued to rise, and after a few months the unemployment figures started to climb. The parties of the industrialists and labour looked to the government for relief: the former wanted tax cuts and lower interest rates, the latter, work-creation schemes and expanded unemployment benefits. It was clear to some German analysts that under the existing deflationary conditions Germany could produce the surplus needed to cover its reparation obligations without an increase in world trade or the flood of German exports that neither the British nor French wanted. The domestic costs of fulfilment, however, were judged excessive and politically unacceptable. During this short but intense economic crisis, the government capitulated to those intent on securing relief through government action. These included agriculturalists, who were among the heaviest and most favoured borrowers, industrialists alienated by the tight money policies of Reichsbank, and labour groups seeking relief for unemployed workers.

The Luther government (January 1925–May 1926) used tax cuts and its own surpluses to make capital available at reduced interest rates. The budget surpluses disappeared and gave way to heavy deficits in the summer of 1926. The cabinet again cut taxes and was forced to increase its spending, moves which inevitably initiated fierce political controversies. The deepening of the crisis carried its own corrective, and during the second half of 1926 there was an upward turn and a temporary truce in the distributive battles, albeit one purchased through government deficit financing and foreign loans. The industrialists were

appeased with subsidies and tax cuts, the farmers with tariff protection
and easy credit policies, the civil servants with wage increases of up to
32 per cent in 1927. Workers, too, demanded and won wage increases
that were well ahead of any gains in productivity, which actually began
to fall in 1928. The economic prosperity of the so-called 'golden years'
and the social stability purchased through government largesse provided
the background for Stresemann's efforts to return Germany to full
membership in the great-power councils of Europe. The German
respite was short. The deep structural flaws in what the economic
historian Klaus Borchardt has called the 'sick Weimar economy' man-
ifested themselves in an economic crisis that began in 1927–8, preceding
both the world depression and the collapse of parliamentary rule in
Germany. The basic instability of the German economy, while connected with the less favourable international environment, was due
mainly to endogenous factors (Borchardt stresses the upward pressure
on wages) that left Germany particularly vulnerable to the global depression.

The Dawes settlement did not solve the financial problems of the
French. The real problem was that there was no agreement as to who
was to carry the burden of taxation needed to restore the fiscal equilibrium, so that the budget remained in deficit. The Bank of France saved
the situation in March 1924 by offering a credit guaranteed by its gold
reserves, but demanded in return that the government balance the
budget and suppress new expenditure not covered by tax receipts.
With the new tax reforms and the loans from New York and London,
the fiscal position began to improve and the budget deficit was cut.

Unfortunately this was only a temporary improvement. The Cartel
des Gauches which came to power in May 1924 had only a tenuous
majority in the Chamber, and suffered from deep divisions over the
financial issues that dominated its period in office. Premier Édouard
Herriot, the ex-professor of literature, was an innocent when it came to
financial affairs and was anxious to link his left-wing party with the Bank
of France. On taking office, he and his finance minister, Étienne
Clémentel, were given contradictory advice by the Bank and by the
Finance Ministry, and opted to follow the orthodox deflationary programme recommended by the former. The Bank argued that expenditure had to be cut and that the legal limitations on Bank advances to the
state and on the currency in circulation had to be maintained to avoid
inflation. The Finance Ministry would have welcomed the ending of
these constraints, and favoured a modest inflation that would have
allowed it to consolidate the floating debt and to meet the payments
on all its outstanding obligations without resorting to indirect advances
from the Bank as had become customary. The director of the Finance

Ministry explained the case against deflation and the repayment of the Bank advances, but such was the fear of inflation and the anxiety to work closely with the Bank of France that Herriot and Clémentel ignored his advice. They committed themselves to a policy from which they could not retreat without a serious loss of face and credibility. Their position was made worse when they learned, in October 1924, that the Bank of France had been manipulating its weekly balances in order to conceal the true number of notes in circulation, a practice that had already begun under Poincaré in March 1924. The Cartel leaders, hoping that the Bank could return to proper account-keeping, kept quiet, but by mid-December the knowledge of the *faux bilans* (false balances) had spread. Herriot and Clémentel were in the invidious position of assuring the Chamber that they would maintain the strict limits on note circulation to avoid inflation while that limitation had already been breached. The Bank of France, unable to keep the note issue under control, in effect denied its responsibility and insisted that the government should rectify the situation. Nothing that Herriot tried could restore confidence in the government's handling of its monetary and financial policy. The exchange-rate crisis reappeared and the value of the franc began an almost continuous decline, with the exception of two periods in the summer of 1925 and again in late May 1926 when there were major interventions in the exchange markets. On 30 March 1925 Clémentel admitted defeat and agreed to introduce legislation to raise the note ceiling. Knowing that his cabinet could not survive the revelations of the Bank's illegalities, Herriot attempted to preserve his reputation by announcing the capital tax, proposed by the Socialists to remedy the budget deficit, that he knew would be rejected by the Senate. The adverse vote led to his resignation in April and a new Cartel des Gauches cabinet under the leadership of Paul Painlevé.

It was all something of a political charade, for there was no agreement among the members of the new cabinet on a tax-reform programme. Joseph Caillaux, the new finance minister, proved as incapable of solving France's financial problems as his predecessor. He dropped the threat of a capital tax which had already triggered a capital outflow and vainly appealed for opposition support for higher indirect taxes and other measures to encourage the repatriation of capital. The seemingly helpless Painlevé government looked to London and New York for stabilization loans, but the unresolved war-debts issue stood in the way. The British had already closed their market to French securities and, from April 1925, no loan could be raised in the United States without government approval, which meant no loans at all until France settled its war debts. Caillaux was forced to begin negotiations with Winston Churchill, the Conservative chancellor of the Exchequer, in August

1925 and with the Americans in September. Caillaux's whole reform programme depended on his ability to secure the funds needed to balance the budget and stabilize the franc. The London talks went well and were successfully concluded in July 1926. The agreement provided for the sum of £653 million in sixty-two annual payments, with annuities rising progressively from £4 million in 1926–7 to £14 million for the last thirty-one years. The British agreed that French payments would at first be small to facilitate the task of rehabilitating French finances, but there was to be no safeguarding clause linking French payments to the receipt of German reparations. An exchange of letters recorded the two country's different views. The French demanded that their total debt payments to Britain should not exceed the Dawes receipts from Germany; the British insisted there could be no deductions in French payments because of German defaults. Though the Caillaux–Churchill agreement was not ratified until 1929, the first payments were arranged by annual agreement between the two Treasuries. The talks in Washington were far more difficult, despite the hopes of the American Treasury that a war-debt settlement would lead to the much-desired stabilization of European currencies and the restoration of European markets. There was a dispute over the total sum France should pay and over the French demand for a safeguarding clause and transfer protection. Bureaucratic divisions and the opposition of Senators Borah and Smoot to a lenient policy damaged the prospects of success. The War Debt Committee turned down Caillaux's proposed solution on political and fiscal grounds. Caillaux, in turn, rejected a last-minute proposal from Andrew Mellon, the secretary of the Treasury, as too unfavourable to French interests.

The franc continued to fall and the first half of 1926 brought no improvement. The French internal debt soared and, to cover its obligations, the government had to borrow heavily from the Bank of France, further weakening financial confidence. Conflicts over fiscal policy brought the Painlevé government down. A new ministry, with Briand as premier and foreign minister and Louis Loucheur, the most politically influential industrialist in the Gauche Radical party, as finance minister, was equally unsuccessful in its attempts to impose new taxes and balance the budget. Briand and Loucheur agreed that only a resolution of the war-debt issue and American loans would permit the much-needed stabilization of the franc. In January 1926 Henri Bérenger, a man of 'inexhaustible energy' who had been *rapporteur* of the Senate finance commission, was sent as a special envoy to the United States to negotiate an agreement. Matters moved slowly and an accord was not signed until the end of April, just after the Senate ratified an Italian debt settlement with extremely generous terms for Mussolini.

The Mellon–Bérenger agreement provided for the payment of a total debt of $4,025,000,000 over sixty-two years at an annual average interest rate of 1.64 per cent. The French had to accept a total payment of $6,847,674,104 (far more than Caillaux had offered) and failed to win a safeguard clause, but the War Debt Commission agreed to set the first five annuities below $40 million and France won special postponement privileges during the early years of the settlement. The favourable interest terms cancelled 52.8 per cent of the debt. In a fatal move adopted to avoid an acrimonious debate in the American Senate, Mellon suggested that the Senate finance committee defer action until after ratification by the French. The new accord proved highly unpopular in Paris. Instead of cancellation, which most Frenchmen believed justified by their war sufferings, France would ultimately have to pay far more than it originally borrowed. The agreement could not be submitted to the Chamber of Deputies for ratification until the American loans improved the political climate.

As soon as the agreement was signed in Washington the French appealed for loans and credits, but the New York bankers, backed by Benjamin Strong, head of the FRBNY, refused to co-operate. They insisted that the French first put their political and financial house in order and agree on a coherent and comprehensive financial reform programme. The result was political chaos in Paris. The Briand cabinet was overthrown; a new Briand cabinet was formed on 23 June, again with Caillaux as finance minister and the able Émile Moreau appointed as governor (1926–30) of the Bank of France. In an effort to deal with the country's financial problems, Caillaux demanded decree powers to implement a major reform package that included new taxes, a balanced budget, and a special fund to amortize the floating debt. His attempt met with total failure in the Chamber, where old suspicions regarding his pre-war pro-German policies rose to the surface and united the opposition parties. As the franc continued to fall and wholesale prices soared in the summer of 1926, the United States became the scapegoat for French discontent. Twenty thousand French veterans and mutilated ex-soldiers paraded down the streets of Paris protesting against the Mellon–Bérenger accord. American tourists were jostled and the mood became increasingly ugly. The extreme right, financed largely by the perfume manufacturer Pierre Coty, denounced the Briand administration and held up Italian fascism as a model. The Americans responded in kind. Taking their lead from William Borah, and infuriated by the 'Uncle Shylock' accusations of the continentals, senators refused to consider further concessions to the French. Promising talks between Strong and Émile Moreau about FRBNY aid to the Bank of France were buried in the wave of Washington indignation over European ingratitude and envy. There was panic in Paris, talk of street-fighting and even a possible coup. French bankers sent their families out of the city. On 17 July the Briand–Caillaux cabinet fell. Four days later the new Herriot ministry was overthrown. The Cartel des Gauches had used up its political capital.

The situation seemed desperate in July 1926, when Raymond Poincaré formed his coalition cabinet. The combination of conservative radicals, centre, and centre-right forces had been discussed since early June, but it was Poincaré and not Briand who reaped the harvest. The costs of financial instability convinced the left that financial reform had to precede social action. The moderate-left deputies abandoned their opposition to Poincaré, a staunch opponent of the capital levy, and gave him their support. Backed by a majority that excluded the mainly working-class parties of the left and the anti-German nationalists of the right, Poincaré's new platform brought about an immediate return of confidence. Even before the premier introduced his economic measures the franc began to recover. Expatriated French capital and foreign funds returned to Paris. Budget cuts, a new and more realistic tax programme, and a special commission charged with the redemption of the public debt with income derived from specified taxes opened the way to stabilization. 'Poincaré-la-confiance' was the hero of France. The return of confidence was critical. The budget was already close to balance because of the fall in reconstruction costs, while significant progress had been made on war-debt settlements. Anglo-Saxon bankers agreed that the French needed a comprehensive plan to stabilize their short-term finances and the franc, but this could be done only by a new coalition of parties. The grant of full powers to Poincaré signalled parliamentary support for the programme of reform. The change in the political balance reassured both French and foreign investors. The franc was soon gaining more than it lost, and the political arguments in Paris now centred on alternative stabilization rates.

Poincaré still hoped to cover the domestic costs of stabilization through foreign credits, but Washington decreed that no financial aid could be given until the Mellon–Bérenger agreement was ratified. In the end, Poincaré succeeded without any foreign assistance. De facto stabilization took place in December 1926 when the Bank of France initiated operations to maintain the value of the franc at about 4 cents. At the same time Poincaré arranged that France would begin paying its debt to the United States even though the Mellon–Bérenger agreement remained unratified. Poincaré was all in favour of allowing the franc to appreciate and delayed stabilization for as long as possible, using the fear of a future financial crisis as a way to keep his uneasy coalition together. It was Moreau and his senior colleagues at the Bank of France who campaigned for prompt *de jure* stabilization. On 25 June 1928 France would return to the gold standard at the existing exchange rate, set at one-fifth of pre-war parity, effectively undervaluing the franc. Though Poincaré, after the May 1928 elections, created the political conditions needed for *de jure* stabilization, the timing, rate and method were determined by Émile Moreau and the Bank of France. The value of the franc was set to maintain French prices below the level of world prices in order to avoid economic instability and dislocation. France returned to gold without the deflationary problems suffered by the British. The French focussed on their domestic situation and were determined to avoid inflation; it was assumed that the gold standard would restore and maintain the international equilibrium. Once the franc was re-pegged there was a massive demand for domestic currency. This could be met only by the Bank of France offering high interest rates to attract gold, as fears of inflation had led to limits on alternative methods of expanding the currency. Such was the strength of the franc that the Bank of France acquired large holdings of foreign exchange which were converted into gold. In 1927 this conversion put considerable pressure on the Bank of England, already facing a movement of funds back to Germany and France and anxious to defend the limited gold stocks it held. Impressed by the precariousness of the British

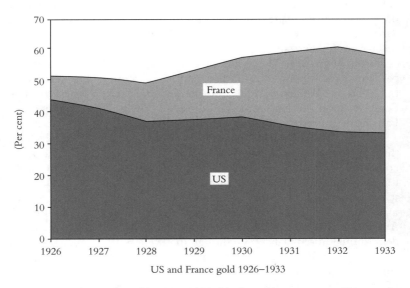

US and France gold 1926–1933

Fig 2. US and French Gold, 1926–1933 (% of world monetary gold reserve)

Source: K. Mouré, *The Gold Standard Illusion* (2002), 190.

position, the French, whose sterling balances exceeded the Bank of England's gold reserves, stepped back. It was due mainly to the intervention of Strong and the co-ordinated action of the central bankers of the countries concerned that the British were rescued, albeit temporarily. Gold continued to flow into the Bank of France during 1928 and 1929 making the country the world's largest importer of gold. Together with the Americans, their policies began to drain off the gold reserves of other countries, significantly reducing the monetary gold reserves available in the international system and reinforcing the contractionary pressures exerted by the gold standard. Britain, the most vulnerable link in the system, was most at risk.

In London, during the spring of 1925, the British had to consider the return to gold. In an effort to prevent American financial hegemony, on the day the Dawes loan was floated Montagu Norman imposed an informal ban on foreign lending, save for League-sponsored reconstruction loans, as a means of strengthening the pound. The central banker had the backing of Strong, who reduced the American discount rate in order to build up sterling. The FRBNY provided the Bank of England with a credit of $200 million and Morgan's opened a line of credit for the government worth $100 million, both for two years. There were objections to the return to gold from many sources. John Maynard Keynes preferred a managed currency that would ensure the stability of domestic prices; Lord Beaverbrook, the highly influential newspaper baron, shared Keynes's concern that Britain would be shackled to the United States; and politician-banker Reginald McKenna feared that stabilization would result in a stiff deflation. Nonetheless, the pressure for immediate action from the Treasury and the Bank of England, prodded by Strong, intensified. Norman viewed the return to gold at pre-war parity as a means of re-establishing London's central place in the world's financial system. Churchill, worried by the effects of deflation on industry and employment at a time when there were already a million and a quarter unemployed, temporized and suggested delay, but he was forced to bow to prevailing expert opinion. While later admitting that the decision was the biggest blunder of his life, he was hardly in a position to withstand the overwhelming official backing for a return to gold at pre-war parity. On 28 April 1925 Britain returned to the gold standard at $4.86.

The decision is often cited as a striking example of the tendency of British government to favour finance over industry. Some historians (economic historians are as prone to changes of interpretation as their non-quantitative colleagues, who find themselves at their mercy) favour the theory that the pound was undervalued and that the real error in 1925 was not the return to pre-war parity but the adoption of fixed rates of exchange. Such a view was nowhere in evidence at the time. There are, moreover, still many historians who argue that a lower parity 'would have stimulated greater economic activity and lowered unemployment'.[33] The weaknesses of the staple export industries and unemployment in the regions where they were situated were old problems that dated back to the pre-war period. They were further aggravated by wartime import substitution in countries that had formerly depended on British imports. In the long and much-debated list of explanations for Britain's export difficulties, economic historians have blamed the adverse patterns of world trade, changes in empire production, high internal costs of production, and the fragmentation and institutional rigidities of the staple industries which continued to dominate Britain's export trade. Little was done either by the banks or the government to promote industrial reform and few of the industry's leaders were prepared for shake-ups of a more radical kind. The return to gold was linked to the high unemployment figures and to the severe struggles over wages among those employed. Government critics insisted that Norman's dear-money policies were responsible for the difficulties in the coalfields which culminated in the traumatic nine-day General Strike of 1926, the blackest time of a very black year. The Baldwin government tried various ways to stimulate the economy without lowering interest rates and to assist industry without resorting to protection, which had considerable support. There was a budget deficit in 1926–7 but a surplus in 1927–8, due mainly to the adoption of unrepeatable financial expedients. Churchill, a staunch free-trader, reimposed the McKenna duties, removed by his Labour predecessor, on motor cars, cycles, watches, and other assorted items and added new duties on silk and rayon. Having paid the political costs of backing protection in 1923, the Conservative cabinet was not prepared to go down the protectionist road. The government's deflationary regime provoked angry debates that pitted industrialists against financiers, spokesmen for the 'new industries' against those for the 'old', and protectionists against free-traders. While few if any actually called for the rejection of the gold standard, dissatisfaction with its 'automatic application' swelled the minority of critical voices. Each of the political parties looked in vain for alternative ways of addressing the electorally important unemployment problem.

Returning to the gold standard did not fulfil Norman's hopes of re-establishing London as the world financial centre. By 1929 the Americans had replaced the British as the chief source of foreign borrowing. New American issues in 1927 and 1928 were twice those of Britain. Between 1924 and 1928, 58.5 per cent of new British capital

---

[33] G. C. Peden, *The Treasury and British Public Policy, 1906–1959* (Oxford, 2000), 202.

TABLE 19. Trends in British and American Lending 1924–1929 (current prices)

UK Lending, Annually by Region 1924–1929 (US $ mil.)					
	Europe	Asia	Africa	Canada	Latin America	Total
1924	159	314	66	20	31	590
1925	53	216	72	10	68	419
1926	120	226	32	29	129	536
1927	105	238	136	34	126	639
1928	164	232	80	98	96	670
1929	105	139	51	74	78	447
Total	706	1365	437	265	528	3301

US Lending, Annually by Region 1924–1929 (US $ mil.)					
	Europe	Asia	Africa	Canada	Latin America	Total
1924	527	100	0	151	191	969
1925	629	147	0	151	191	1076
1926	484	38	0	226	377	1125
1927	577	164	0	237	359	1337
1928	598	137	0	185	331	1251
1929	142	58	0	295	176	671
Total	2957	644	0	1245	1625	6429

Source: League of Nations, *Balances of Payments 1930* (1932), 30

Average Annual Long-Term Capital Exports,
United States and Britain 1919–1938 (US $)

Country	1919–23	1924–28	1929–31	1932–38
USA	531	1412	595	28
UK	416	587	399	143

Source: United Nations, Department of Economic Affairs, *International Capital Movements during the Inter-War Period* (1949), 25.

went to the empire and most of the new money available to Europe, Latin America, and the Far East came from the United States.[34] There are problems in drawing comparisons; the distinction between short-term and long-term lending is far less clear in practice than in theory. The United States, moreover, did not develop an acceptance market

---

[34] See table on new capital issues, empire and foreign, 1900–1938, in P. J. Cain and A. G. Hopkins, *British Imperialism: Crisis and Deconstruction, 1914–1990* (Harlow, 1993), 45. Stephen Schuker, *American 'Reparations' to Germany, 1919–1933: Implications for the Third-World Debt Crisis* (Princeton, 1988), 92–5.

comparable to that of Britain, so that the City of London continued to take the lion's share of financing international trade both within and outside the empire. Whatever the qualifications, however, global financial power was clearly shifting to the United States. Faced with the competitive pulls of New York and later Paris, London, with its high liabilities and small gold reserves, was at risk. Though an earner of current-account surpluses and a major lender of capital, Britain's short-term obligations to those countries who kept their balances in the form of claims far exceeded the amount of gold held by the Bank of England. Sterling liabilities were about four times greater than British gold reserves. In contrast to the situation before 1914, in the more competitive atmosphere of the late 1920s this small metallic base became a source of danger. Norman's domestic freedom of action became increasingly circumscribed: he could not ignore the political consequences of the Bank's actions. Though he had the right to set the Bank rate without consultation with the Treasury, there were repeated complaints from Churchill and his officials that the Bank's high interest rates were discouraging trade and increasing unemployment, and that the Bank should be prepared to lose some of its gold reserves in the national interest. The Bank rate of 5 per cent, introduced in December 1925 and thought far too high by the Treasury, was reduced to 4.5 per cent in April 1927 and kept at that level until February 1929, when Norman, fearing for the Bank's gold reserves, raised it to 5.5 per cent despite strong protests from Churchill, and then to 6.5 per cent in September. The Bank rate had become a political issue.

Other countries quickly followed the British example over the return to gold: by the end of 1925 thirty-five currencies were officially convertible into gold or had been stabilized *de facto* for at least a year.[35] In France, Belgium, Italy, Greece, and Poland currencies continued to depreciate. The first two returned to gold in 1926, and the latter three in 1927. A new Belgian cabinet in the summer of 1926 with a reforming financier-statesman, Émile Francqui, appealed for international support. It was Norman, backed by Strong, who invited the other central bankers to take part in a credit to the Belgians, opening the way for a stabilization loan from private international bankers. On 25 October 1926, helped by the firmness of the French franc and the Francqui financial reforms at home, Belgium returned to a gold-exchange standard, though at an undervalued exchange rate which helped the Belgian export trade partly at British expense. The Belgians subsequently enjoyed a period of reasonable growth and low unemployment. It was

---

[35] Barry Eichengreen, *Gold Fetters: The Gold Standard and the Great Depression, 1919–1939* (Oxford, 1992), 192.

again Norman and Strong who worked together to arrange the central bank credit for the Italian stabilization operation which took place on 22 December 1927. Relations between France and Italy were too strained politically for the former's participation. The private loan of $50 million, made to the Bank of Italy, was divided between Morgans of New York and a London group of bankers including Morgan Grenfell. The fascist government also negotiated a credit arrangement with the Bank of England and the Federal Reserve for $75 million (sixteen institutions took part) in case it required emergency funds to support the lira. Norman and Strong accepted less strict standards for Italy than were demanded elsewhere. Behind their acquiescence lay Italy's successful negotiation of the American war-debt agreement and the generally sympathetic attitude of Wall Street towards the restoration of Italian order and stability. The Italian lira was overvalued at 92 to the pound (as against nearly 145 in 1925); both its setting and its maintenance became matters of fascist prestige.

Mussolini was determined to return to the rate he had inherited in 1922. He warned his followers that 'the fate of the regime is bound to the fate of the lira'.[36] There was to be no compromise, despite the opposition of most of Italy's major industrialists and financiers who were worried by the threat to exports, the squeeze on liquidity, and the cost to the economy of the severe deflation which would result from the overvalued lira. In preparation for the return to the gold standard a series of deflationary measures were introduced in Italy involving large cuts in wages and prices. To the astonishment of many foreign observers, the Italian government could not only impose the high rate of exchange but maintain it. In addition to the traditional monetary and financial means at the disposal of the government, Mussolini mobilized the political apparatus of the fascist state to win 'the battle of the lira'. The leading Italian industrialists, who strongly objected to the sharp upward revaluation of the lira, had to accept the *quota novanta*. In return for capitulation, they were offered tax cuts, new government orders, increased tariffs, and, most important of all, wage reductions, ranging from 10 per cent to 20 per cent, which were greater than the imposed price cuts. Mussolini was also prepared to accept their demands for mergers. Eighteen separate loans to Italy were floated in the United States from 1925 to 1927 for a total of $271,400,000, most going to the government, municipalities, and public utilities.[37] About 70 per cent of this

[36] Charles Maier, *Recasting Bourgeois Europe: Stabilization in France, Germany, and Italy in the Decade after World War I* (Princeton, 1975), 574.
[37] Roland Sarti, 'Mussolini and the Italian Industrial Leadership in the Battle of the Lira, 1925–1927', *Past and Present*, 47 (May 1970), 105.

capital eventually found its way into industrial enterprises, mainly into the electrical sector and to the larger and older firms, compensating for the tightness of domestic credit. Mussolini's victory over the industrialists heralded a shift from the anti-interventionist rhetoric used to attract their backing in the early days of his power to the introduction of a more centralized system of state control under the greatly strengthened dictatorship. Deflation allowed the government to acquire far greater control over the general direction of the economy. In return, the larger firms were given ample opportunity to restructure their industries and, under the banner of modernization and scientific management, to demand far more from their workers. In the difficult post-stabilization climate, the industrialists were forced to turn to the state for protection against foreign competition. Tariffs, subsidies, and labour regulations opened the way for still further government intervention in the economy. The economic cost of the *quota novanta* was high: unemployment nearly tripled between 1926 and 1929, exports fell, and growth in the manufacturing sector slowed. In the new partnership between government and industry, it was the workers who lost the most and paid the heaviest price for Mussolini's victory.

Already during 1927, there were fears of some future financial crisis unless the central bankers took decisive action. In the first week of July an informal gathering of European central bankers took place at the Long Island home of the secretary of the United States Treasury. Initially called to discuss the effects of the French decision in May 1927 to convert their sterling balances into gold, the bankers turned their attention to the difficult problem of the world deflationary price trends, which was attributed to the defensive actions taken in response to the drain of gold into the United States (cf. discussion on p. 438–9). Subsequent to the meeting, mainly because of Strong's intervention, the FRBNY reduced its discount rate and conducted $80 million of open market purchases. The lower interest rate in New York and the relatively higher rates in Europe encouraged the outpouring of American dollar loans and gold began to flow out of New York. Strong's move was intended to help the Europeans but also to stimulate the American economy. However, he came under heavy political attack and was accused of allowing European interests to take precedence over American needs and of diverting capital to Europe that was needed by the farmers at home. The summer franc–pound crisis alerted Strong and his colleagues to the dangers of the gold-exchange system. The perfectly proper French move to convert its sterling holdings into gold had threatened the whole gold standard. Only difficult and complicated negotiations had averted a crisis. The United States, France, and Germany took steps to reduce their foreign-exchange balances but other

European countries increased their reserves, so no overall reduction occurred. The pattern of international settlements and the stability of the gold standard depended on the American willingness to recycle its balance-of-payments surpluses. As long as American lending continued, the gold standard remained viable. Low American interest rates and expansionary monetary policies had encouraged capital to flow outwards and eased the process of European recovery and stabilization. In the two instances, 1924 and 1927, when the United States moved to release gold in order to help countries stabilize their currencies and rebuild their reserves, there was no conflict between its domestic and international objectives. During Strong's usual summer visit to Europe in 1928, the Federal Reserve Board cautiously reversed policy, raised the discount rate, and tightened the money supply in order to cut excessive speculation on Wall Street. American foreign lending fell and short-term capital began to flow into the United States instead of moving abroad. Together, France and the United States increased their official gold holdings by over £140 million, or twice the annual world production of gold between 1928 and 1930. The flow of gold back to the United States, coupled with France's increase in its gold reserves, increased the pressure on countries with already weak balances of payments. Debtor nations, reliant on capital imports, began to feel the effects during the latter half of 1928 and turned to stringent monetary and fiscal policies to defend their gold parities and to maintain their debt payments. As the American contraction continued in a futile effort to contain the Wall Street boom, other governments responded by cutting their domestic spending, even if this threatened to result in recession and higher unemployment. It was this general restrictive shift in 1928, and not just the American action alone, economic historian Barry Eichengreen argues, that explains the seriousness of the global contraction in 1929. The gold standard was the mechanism by which the destabilizing action taken in the United States in 1928 was transmitted to the rest of the world, greatly magnifying the effects of the initial shock in the process. Only co-ordinated action by the states might have helped to resolve the crisis, and this was not forthcoming. This failure of co-operation was central to the story of the collapse of internationalism between 1928 and 1933, which in turn led to the adoption of nationalistic, autarchic, and 'beggar-thy-neighbour' policies in the years that followed.

II

With the general return to the gold standard, the European governments believed that they had completed the first stage of economic reconstruction. The recommendations made by the experts at Brussels in 1920 and at Genoa in 1922 had been partially, if imperfectly, implemented. Nearly all the European countries had brought inflation under control, stabilized their currencies, adopted some form of gold or gold-exchange standard, and created central banks. The League's financial committee had helped both Austria and Hungary to stabilize their currencies with the assistance of international loans. The Norman–Strong relationship, which was the main instrument of central bank co-operation, had played a major part in the restoration of the gold standard in much of the rest of Europe. France was the major exception. With the European political atmosphere conducive to co-operation, it was time to turn attention to the question of international trade.

It was already obvious to Europe's leaders that, though their countries were reaching pre-war production levels both in agriculture and in capital-goods industries, Europe's share of world trade had not kept up with its expansion. The massive documentation collected for the World Economic Conference held in Geneva on 4 May 1927 and later League surveys confirmed these impressions. The former provided a detailed picture of the world economy and showed the degree to which the damages inflicted by the war had been absorbed. World population had grown markedly since 1913; the European states, with the exception of Russia, were making good the population losses of the war (a 6.5 per cent increase on the 1913 figure). World raw-material production was everywhere higher in 1925 than in 1913, with the greatest increases in the Caribbean, and South and North America, and the smallest in east and central Europe.[38] Later published League figures (1929 and 1931) showed that production of foodstuffs and raw materials for the whole of Europe, including Russia, had returned to 1913 levels by 1925; for east and central Europe, without Russia, by 1927. Europe's share of world production returned to the 1913 level in 1927. The figures for industrial production were less complete; the most marked growth occurred during the second half of the decade. Belgium, France, Germany, Luxembourg, and Sweden witnessed the most impressive increases in western Europe; Czechoslovakia, Hungary, and Romania in the east. The advances were strongest in the capital-goods industries (iron and steel, engineering, electricity, motors, and chemicals) and lower in consumer-oriented industries. The total European share of world trade had fallen from 58.5 per cent in 1913 to 47.9 per cent in 1926.[39]

---

[38] Figures from League of Nations sources printed in Ann Orde, *British Policy and European Reconstruction after the First World War* (Cambridge, 1990), 318.

[39] Ibid.

Speakers at the plenary sessions of the World Economic Conference compared Europe's difficulties with the prosperity of the United States. Their concerns mirrored a far more general apprehension of America's global economic role and the flooding of European markets with American goods. Some viewed the popularity of American films and jazz as a challenge to assumptions about European cultural superiority. The American example elicitied admiration, envy, and hostility. In private, if not in public, German, French, and British businessmen blamed America's high tariff policies for their failure to penetrate the American market. While few were openly critical of American investment, there was considerable anxiety about the growth of American direct investment, particularly in France and Germany, though it was Britain that was the main American target. There were worries, too, about the increase in American exports to Europe, no longer confined to agricultural goods but including impressive quantities of finished manufactured products. The gap between American exports and imports, European spokesmen insisted, was substantial and American tariff policy inimical to the expansion of the European trade. Many explanations of the 'American miracle' were offered at the time. British and continental industrialists went off to the United States to view its industrial practices at first hand in the hope of applying the new managerial techniques to their own. There was much discussion of 'Fordism' (assembly-line production) and 'Taylorism' (scientific management, including time controls), but attempts at rationalization along American lines were either half-hearted or impossible to implement under European conditions. In most countries rationalization involved little more than expansion and mergers rather than technological innovation or changes in management techniques. Some labour leaders, particularly in Britain, noted that the growth of American industry meant increased employment, higher wages, and rising standards of living for the workforce. There was a varied response to the American presence in both the European and global markets, but many believed that positive steps would have to be taken in Europe if the economic balance of power was not to shift permanently across the Atlantic.

Delegates at the World Economic Conference concentrated on Europe's difficulties, which were blamed on the dislocations of the war and the subsequent fragmentation of the European market. The most obvious target was the increase in national tariffs resulting from the creation of new statutes and currencies and the addition of some 20,000 kilometres of new tariff barriers. Such unanimity disappeared, however, when delegates came to propose remedies for the general trend towards protection, particularly in states with large agricultural sectors or politically important agricultural interest groups. British delegates, supported

TABLE 20. Tariff Levels in Europe as % of
1913 Levels

	1927	1931
Germany	122.0	244.0
France	97.5	160.0
Austria*	77.0	158.0
Czechoslovakia*	137.0	220.0
Poland†	74.0	93.0
Romania	140.0	207.0
Hungary*	144.0	207.0
Yugoslavia‡	144.0	207.0
Bulgaria	296.0	420.0
Italy	112.0	195.0
Belgium	77.5	122.0
Switzerland	160.0	252.0
Sweden	72.5	97.0
Finland	91.0	134.0
Spain	132.0	93.0

Notes: *1913 = Territories of former Austria-Hungarian
empire; † 1913 = Russian empire; ‡ 1913 = Serbia

Source: H. Liepmann, *Tariff Levels and Economic Unity in
Europe* (1938), 415; an examination of tariff policy, export
movements and the economic integration of Europe,
1913–193.

by the Americans, favoured tariff reductions, the complete removal of
all 'artifical' restrictions on trade, and the unconditional application of
the most-favoured-nation treatment regardless of the nature of the
agreement. Daniel Serruys, France's ablest commercial negotiator and
director of the treaty department of the Ministry of Commerce, proposed that tariffs should be set according to the principle of reciprocity
or conditional most-favoured-nation treatment. The French favoured
regional pacts with the discriminatory use of most-favoured-nation
privileges which would be extended to third parties only if they offered
reciprocal reductions. He nonetheless accepted British draft proposals
that included the endorsement of the most-favoured-nation clause in its
most unconditional form. With only Russia and Turkey abstaining, the
conference adopted a series of resolutions intended to liberalize trade
and promote tariff reduction. Trade barriers such as import-and-export
restrictions were to be condemned and a conference called in the
autumn to abolish them. The fundamental Anglo-French clash was
left unresolved. In its final report the conference recommended that
tariff levels should be reduced through the use of bilateral and plurilat-

eral (the League term for multilateral) conventions and global agreements, and endorsed the most-favoured-nation principle. The latter was referred to the League's Economic Committee and debated in March 1928, when the differences between Britain and the continental states, led by France, dominated the discussion.

The final recommendations of the conference were hailed as a victory for liberalization. At the time the meeting was seen as an important landmark along the path of international economic co-operation. The very size and composition of the conference encouraged modest hopes for future progress. The participants, though sounding a cautionary note, were not without hope that Europe would get its act together and improve the conditions of world trade. Insofar as concrete proposals were adopted, there was, of course, no assurance that governments would accept them. The Americans gave notice that Washington would not be bound in any way by the conference resolutions. Where the conference recommendations were adopted by the League Assembly, it was a laborious process to translate them into action. It was only after three Prohibitions (quantitative trade controls) Conferences in 1927, 1928, and 1929 that one of the most widely anticipated benefits of the World Economic Conference, a convention banning quantitative restrictions on trade, was adopted in December 1929 by seventeen countries, including the United States and the most important European trading countries. The question of ratification was dropped and the draft protocol, which went into effect on 1 January 1930 for five years, contained qualifications which permitted states to keep their freedom of action. There were even greater problems over the question of tariff reduction. Subsequent conferences on the tariff issue highlighted the disagreements between Britain and France and added to their mutual belief that each country was the cause of the other's difficulties. In particular, the British government's insistence on maintaining a free-trade regime, already under serious attack at home, and most-favoured-nation rights in their most unconditional form, proved unacceptable to France and many of the other continental states. The disputes continued in the League's Economic Committee, where, by an overwhelming majority in March 1928, it was agreed that plurilateral conventions should be exempt from most-favoured-nation agreements as long as they were open to other countries prepared to make comparable concessions. In opposition to the British, representatives were not prepared, in Serruys's words, to exchange 'an open door for a closed door'.[40]

---

[40] Robert W. D. Boyce, *British Capitalism at the Crossroads, 1919–1932: A Study in Politics, Economics and International Relations* (Cambridge, 1987), 132.

In May 1928 the League's Economic Consultative Committee, set up to monitor the progress in applying the resolutions of the World Economic Conference, was cautiously optimistic. The all-important Franco-German trade agreement of 1927, based on the most-favoured-nation principle (the French withheld its application to the United States), and the Prohibitions Convention were cited as signs of progress. One year later the same committee warned that progress had been halted, and that unless immediate action was taken a new era of protectionism would begin. The beginning of the Congressional debates leading to the adoption of the Hawley–Smoot tariff of 1930, raising American import duties to their highest levels in American history, was symbolic of the movement towards intensified economic nationalism all over the world.

At the same time, debates about European recovery were about to take a tack back to an old issue. When Parker Gilbert published his December 1927 annual report recommending a new and final reparation settlement, the question of recovery once again became tied to the issue of reparations. Whereas until this point the security issue had dominated the political discussions, the reparations issue again became the driving force behind the negotiations. The unfortunate linkage between the two questions would last until 1932. What lay behind Gilbert's intervention? In the first half of 1927 the German economy seemed exceptionally strong and the unemployment figures demonstrably lower. German recovery was being financed by German banks, for the country had been living without foreign loans since December 1926, when their tax benefits had been removed in an effort to control the flood of foreign capital. Faced with a stock-market boom in the spring of 1927 that endangered the Reichsbank reserves, Schacht threatened to withdraw discounting privileges at the Reichsbank if the private bankers continued to lend to stock-market speculators. The private bankers, heavily in debt to the Reichsbank, surrendered at once and cut their stock-market credits. On 12 May 1927, 'Black Friday', there was a rapid withdrawal of foreign funds and a loss of Reichsmarks from the Reichsbank reserve. The government reacted by restoring the tax benefits to foreign lenders and the Reichsbank raised its discount rate from 5 per cent to 6 per cent. Schacht's earlier refusal to raise the discount rate to control the stock-market speculation has occasioned considerable controversy. Neither contemporaries nor historians have been able to unravel the motives of the highly unpredictable Reichsbank president, an enigmatic figure as dedicated to orthodox fiscal policies as he was to his own self-advancement. Schacht's action may have been a move to protect the Reichsbank reserves and the consequences unexpected, but he had never disguised his opposition to reparation payments and he may have created the crisis to expose the full extent of Germany's financial weakness. In the months that followed the return of foreign lending, Schacht insisted, to all who would listen, that the government borrowing policies must cease, foreign loans must be controlled, and the reparation settlement renegotiated. Instead, the Reich increased its subsidies to the states and allowed the municipalities to use their spending and borrowing authority to finance civic improvements. In July 1927 the Reichstag passed a grossly underfunded unemployment insurance scheme which became an enormous drain on both the Reich and *Länder*. There followed a period of pork-barrel handouts by which the government bought off its many claimants.

Schacht was not alone in his worries about the government's actions and its future reparation policy. The German finance minister warned the Reichstag in February 1927 that the country would be faced with the higher Dawes schedule to start in September 1928 and that it could not pay the sums involved. Stresemann preferred not to raise the reparations question, but the public warnings and Schacht's campaign made delay difficult. Schacht, moreover, found an important ally in S. Parker Gilbert. The establishment of an Office of the Agent-General for Reparation Questions as part of the Dawes settlement had created a new post of great individual influence. S. Parker Gilbert, the 32-year-old former US Treasury official acceptable to the Morgan partners, was appointed agent-general. The young, taciturn workaholic was to see that the Germans paid the maximum amount possible to the Allies, without threatening the stability of the currency or creating the inflationary conditions that would kill the goose that laid the reparation-payment egg. Determined that the Dawes plan should be a success, he felt free to offer advice to the Berlin authorities to this end. He cultivated no one in Berlin, neither politicians nor bureaucrats, and his one alliance—a temporary one at that—was with the all-powerful Schacht. The American, while not sharing Schacht's belief that foreign loans were providing the funds for reparations payments, strongly disapproved of the Reich government's spending policies. He argued that German deficit spending would lead to inflation, encourage imports, and create an adverse balance of payments negatively affecting the annuity payments. In December 1927 Gilbert proposed the adoption of a new definitive schedule of payments, the cancellation of transfer protection, and the end of foreign supervision over German finances. His intervention was, for the most part, the consequence of the high borrowing policies of the German government and concern for the position of Germany's creditors. He feared that the higher standard Dawes annuity might draw so heavily on Germany's foreign reserves, already under strain because of interest payment on Germany's large loans, that transfer would have to be suspended to the detriment of its reparation creditors. The Americans were beginning to worry about the implications of a German financial crisis. There were predictions that reparation payments would take precedence over interest on private loans, a view on which Gilbert refused to comment. American nervousness was such that, in September 1927, the State Department intervened and banned a loan to the state of Prussia. It was a solitary effort and the question of regulating the flow of funds was again returned to the Germans. The combined efforts of Schacht and Gilbert to restrict German borrowing made little impact on the Reich government, which was convinced that cuts would bring about a major political crisis. It was against this background, and in response to American apprehensions about the safety of its citizens' investments, that Gilbert, acting on his own initiative and without consulting the indignant members of the Reparation Commission, advocated his new proposals for the settlement of the reparation question.

One month after the Gilbert report was published, Joseph Paul-Boncour, the French delegate to the League of Nations, in a press interview again called for a permanent civilian body to monitor the demilitarized Rhineland. In two speeches delivered to the Reichstag on 30 January and 1 February 1928, using the Paul-Boncour interview as a pretext, Stresemann opened the campaign for the full evacuation of the Rhineland. Abandoning the agreement not to raise the issue publicly until after the French elections, he asserted, in no uncertain terms, Germany's legal right to immediate evacuation. The next months were marked by an intensification of the Franco-German conflict, made worse by the weakening of Britain's role as mediator between the two countries. The last chapter in the Locarno story opened in the summer of 1928.

A. Treaty Revision and the Construction of the New Political Equilibrium

Books

BAECHLER, CHRISTINE, Gustave Stresemann: de l'impérialisme à la sécurité collective (Strasbourg, 1996).

—— and FINK, CAROLE, *The Establishment of European Frontiers After the Two World Wars* (Bern and New York, 1996).

BARIÉTY, J. and POIDEVIN R., *Les Relations Franco–Allemandes, 1815–1975* (Paris, 1977).

BERG, MANFRED, *Gustav Stresemann und die Vereinigten Staaten von Amerika: weltwirtschaftliche Verflechtung und Revisionspolitik, 1907–1929* (Baden-Baden, 1990).

BOYCE, ROBERT W. D. (ed.), *French Foreign and Defence Policy, 1918–1940: The Decline and Fall of a Great Power* (London, 1998). Esp. chapters by Denise Artaud and Robert W. D. Boyce.

CARLIER, CLAUDE and SOUTOU, GEORGES-HENRI, *1918–1925. Comment faire la paix?* (Paris, 2001)

FERRIS, J., *The Evolution of British Strategic Foreign Policy, 1919–1926* (London, 1989).

GATZKE, H. W., *Stresemann and the Rearmament of Germany* (Baltimore, 1954).

GEYER, M., *Aufrüstung oder Sicherheit: Die Reichswehr in der Krise der Machtpolitik, 1924–1936* (Wiesbaden, 1980).

GRAYSON, RICHARD S., *Austen Chamberlain and the Commitment to Europe: British Foreign Policy, 1924–1929* (London, 1997).

JONES, LARRY, *German Liberalism and the Dissolution of the Weimar Party System, 1918–1933* (Chapel Hill, NC and London, 1988).

KAISER, ANGELA, *Lord D'Abernon und die englische Deutschlandpolitik, 1920–1926* (Frankfurt a.M., 1989).

KRÜGER, P., *Die Außenpolitik der Republik von Weimar* (Darmstadt, 1985).

LEE, MARSHALL M. and MICHALKA, WOLFGANG (eds.), *Gustav Stresemann* (Darmstadt, 1982).

LEFFLER, MELVYN P., *The Elusive Quest: America's Pursuit of European Stability and French Security, 1919–1933* (Chapel Hill, NC, 1979).

MAIER, CHARLES S., *Recasting Bourgeois Europe: Stabilisation in France, Germany and Italy in the Decade after World War I* (Princeton, 1975).

MAXELON, MICHAEL-OLAF, *Stresemann und Frankreich 1914–1929* (Düsseldorf, 1972).

MICHALKA, WOLFGANG and LEE, MARSHALL M., *German Foreign Policy, 1917–1933: Continuity or Break?* (Leamington Spa, 1987).

NIEDHART, G., JUNKER, D., and RICHTER, W. M. (eds.), *Deutschland in Europa: nationale Interessen und internationale Ordnung im 20. Jahrhundert* (Mannheim, 1997). Esp. chapters by Manfred Berg, Gottfried Niedhart, Adam Daniel Rotfeld, Stephanie Salzmann, Ralph Schattowsky, and Clemens Wurm.

ORDE, ANNE, *Great Britain and International Security, 1920–1926* (London, 1978).

PEDEN, G. C., *The Treasury and British Public Policy, 1906–1959* (Oxford, 2000).

PITTS, VINCENT J., *France and the German Problem: Politics and Economics in the Locarno Period, 1924–1929* (New York, 1987).

POST, GAINES, *The Civil-Military Fabric of Weimar Foreign Policy* (Princeton, 1973).

RÖDDER, ANDREAS, *Stresemanns Erbe: Julius Curtius und die deutsche Außenpolitik, 1929–1931* (Paderborn, 1996)

ROSENBERG, EMILY S., *Spreading the American Dream: American Economic and Cultural Expansion, 1890–1945* (New York, 1982).

SALZMANN, STEPHANIE, *Great Britain, Germany and the Soviet Union* (Woodbridge, Suffolk, and Rochester, NY, 2003).

WRIGHT, JONATHAN, *Gustav Stresemann: Weimar's Greatest Statesman* (Oxford, 2002).

ZEIDLER, MANFRED, *Reichswehr und Rote Armee, 1920–1933: Wege und Stationen einer ungewöhnlichen Zusammenarbeit* (Munich, 1993).

Articles

BARIÉTY, JACQUES, 'Les Relations franco-allemandes de 1924 à 1933', *Annales de la Société d'Histoire de la IIIème République* (1962–3).

BARIÉTY, JACQUES, 'La Tentative de construction de la paix, 1924–1930', in Raymond Poidevin and Jacques Bariéty (eds.), *Les Relations franco-allemandes, 1815–1975* (Paris, 1977).

—— 'Finances et relations internationales: A propos du "plan de Thoiry" (septembre 1926)', *Relations Internationales*, 21 (1980).

COHRS, PATRICK O., 'The First "Real" Peace Settlement After the First World War: Britain, the United States, and the Accord of London and Locarno, 1923–1925', *Contemporary European History*, 12: 1 (2003).

EDWARDS, P. G., 'Britain, Mussolini and the "Locarno–Geneva System" ', *European Studies Review*, 10 (1980).

GOLDSTEIN, ERIK, 'The Evolution of British Diplomatic Strategy for the Locarno Pact, 1924–1925', in M. Dockrill and B. McKercher, *Diplomacy and World Power: Studies in British Foreign Policy 1890–1950* (Cambridge, 1996).

JACOBSON, JON, 'Is There a New International History of the 1920s?', *American Historical Review* 88 (1983).

—— 'Strategies of French Foreign Policy after World War 1', *Journal of Modern History*, 55, 2 (1983).

McKERCHER, B. J. C., 'Austen Chamberlain's Control of British Foreign Policy, 1924–1929', *IHR* 6 (1984).

SCHULIN, E., 'Zur Enstehung des Rapallo–Vertrages' in H. Von Hentig and A. Nitschke (eds.), *Was die Wirklichkeit Lehrt. Golo Mann zum 70. Geburtstag* (Frankfurt, 1979).

TURNER, HENRY ASHBY, Jr., 'Eine Rede Stresemanns über seine Locarnopolitik', *Vierteljahrshefte für Zeitgeschichte*, 15 (1967).

WRIGHT, JONATHAN, 'Stresemann and Locarno', *Contemporary European History*, 4 (1995).

B. Re-creating Europe's Financial and Trading Systems, 1924–1928

ARTAUD, DENISE, *La Question des dettes interalliés et la reconstruction de l'Europe, 1917–1929*, 2 vols. (Lille and Paris, 1978).

BALDESTON, THEO, *The Origins and Course of the German Economic Crisis: November 1923 to May 1932* (Berlin, 1993).

BOYCE, ROBERT W. D., *British Capitalism At the Crossroads, 1919–1932: A Study in Politics, Economics and International Relations* (Cambridge, 1987).

CLARKE, STEPHEN V. O., *Central Bank Cooperation, 1924–1931* (New York, 1967).

EICHENGREEN, BARRY, *Elusive Stability: Essays in the History of International Finance, 1919–1939* (Cambridge, 1990).

—— *Golden Fetters: The Gold Standard and the Great Depression, 1919–1939* (New York, 1992).

—— and WYPLOSZ, CHARLES, *The Economic Consequences of the Franc Poincaré* (London, 1986).

FEINSTEIN, CHARLES H. (ed.), *Banking, Currency, and Finance in Europe between the Wars* (Oxford, 1995). See Feinstein, Temin, Balderston, Hardach, Toniolo, and articles with regard to countries not covered in this chapter.

—— PETER, and TONIOLO, GIANNI, *The European Economy Between the Wars* (Oxford, 1997).

JAMES, HAROLD, *The Reichsbank and Public Finance in Germany, 1924–1933: A Study of the Politics of Economics During the Great Depression* (Frankfurt, a.M., 1985).

—— *The German Slump: Politics and Economics, 1924–1936* (Oxford, 1986).

—— *The End of Globalization: Lessons from the Great Depression* (Cambridge, MA., 2001).

—— LUNDGREN, HAKAN, and TEICHOVA, ALICE (eds.), *The Role of Banks in the Interwar Economy* (Cambridge and Paris, 1991).

KEETON, EDWARD DAVID, *Briand's Locarno Policy: French Economics, Politics and Diplomacy, 1925–1929* (New York and London, 1987).

KENT, BRUCE, *The Spoils of War: The Politics, Economics and Diplomacy of Reparations, 1918–1932* (Oxford, 1989).

LEWIS, W. A., *Economic Survey, 1919–39* (London, 1949).

LINK, WERNER, *Die amerikanische Stabilisierungspolitik in Deutschland, 1921–1932* (Düsseldorf, 1970).

MOURÉ, KENNETH, *The Gold Standard Illusion: France, the Bank of France, and the International Gold Standard* (Oxford, 2002).

Other Specialized Books

BORCHARDT, KNUT, *Perspectives on Modern German Economic History and Policy*, trans. Peter Lambert (Cambridge, 1991).

CAIN, P. J. and HOPKINS, A. G., *British Imperialism: Crisis and Deconstruction, 1914–1990* (London, 1993).

ELBAUM, BERNARD and LAZONICK, WILLIAM (eds.), *The Decline of the British Economy* (Oxford, 1986).

FEINSTEIN, CHARLES H. (ed.), *Banking, Currency and Finance in Europe Between the Wars* (Oxford, 1995).

HOWSON, S., *Domestic Monetary Management in Britain, 1919–1938* (Cambridge, 1975).

KAHN, ALFRED E., *Great Britain in the World Economy* (New York, 1946).

MCNEIL, WILLIAM C., *American Money and the Weimar Republic: Economics and Politics on the Eve of the Great Depression* (New York, 1986).

MOGGRIDGE, D. E., *British Monetary Policy, 1924–1931* (Cambridge, 1972).

NEWTON, SCOTT and PORTER, DILWYN, *Modernization Frustrated: The Politics of Industrial Decline in Britain Since 1900* (London, 1988).

ORDE, ANNE, *British Policy and European Reconstruction After the First World War* (Cambridge, 1990).

POHL, KARL-DIETRICH, *Weimars Wirtschaft und die Außenpolitik der Republik, 1924–1926: vom Dawes-Plan zum internationalen Eisenpakt* (Düsseldorf, 1979).

TEMIN, PETER, *Lessons From the Great Depression* (Cambridge, Mass., 1989).

TONIOLO, GIANNI, *L'economia dell'Italia fascista* (Rome, 1980).

TURNER, ARTHUR, *The Cost of War: British Policy on French War Debts, 1918–1932* (Brighton, 1998).

Articles

BARIÉTY, JACQUES. 'Problèmes concernant le rétablissement des relations économiques franco-allemandes après la Première Guerre Mondiale', *Francia*, 2 (1974).

BERNAKE, BEN and JAMES, HAROLD, 'The Gold Standard, Deflation, and Financial Crises in the Great Depression', in Glenn, Hubbard R. (ed.), *Financial Markets and Financial Crises* (Chicago, 1991).

BOUVIER, JEAN, 'The French Banks: Inflation and the Economic Crisis, 1919–1939', *Journal of European Economic History*, 13: 2 (1984).

BOYCE, ROBERT W. D., 'Creating the Myth of Consensus: Public Opinion and Britain's Return to the Gold Standard in 1925', in P. L. Cottrell, and D. E. Moggridge (eds.), *Money and Power: Essays in Honour of L. S. Pressnell* (Basingstoke, 1988).

CIOCCO, PIERLUIGI and TONIOLO, GIANNI, 'Industry and Finance in Italy, 1918–1940', *Journal of European Economic History*, 13: 2 (1984).

COHRS, PATRICK, 'The First "Real" Peace Settlements After the First World War: Britain, the United States and the Accords of London and Locarno, 1923–1925', *Contemporary European History* (2003).

EICHENGREEN, BARRY, 'The Origins and the Nature of the Great Slump Revisited', *Economic History Review*, 45: 2 (1992).

JORDAN, NICOLE, 'The Reorientation of French Diplomacy in the Mid-1920s: The Role of Jacques Seydoux', *English Historical Review*, 117: 473 (2002).

MAIER, CHARLES S., 'The Economies of Fascism and Nazism', in id. (ed.), *In Search of Political Stability: Explorations in Historical Political Economy* (Cambridge and New York, 1987).

PIESCHE, M., 'Die Rolle des Reparationsagenten Seymour Parker Gilbert während der Weimarer Republik, 1924–1930', *Jahrbuch für Geschichte*, 18 (1978).

ROWLAND, BENJAMIN M., 'Preparing the American Ascending: The Transfer of Economic Power from Britain to the United States', in id. (ed.), *Balance of Power or Hegemony: The Interwar Monetary System* (New York, 1975).

TEMIN, PETER, 'The Beginning of the Depression in Germany', *Economic History Review*, 24 (1971).

—— 'Transmission of the Great Depression', *Journal of Economic Perspectives*, 7: 2 (1993).

WENDT, BERND-JÜRGEN, 'Aspects économiques d'une politique de sécurité nationale entre le révisionnisme et l'expansionnisme', *Guerres mondiales*, 154 (1989).

9

Faltering Reconstruction:
Cracks in the Locarno Façade

I

The Locarno powers were reaching a highly dangerous stage in their relationship. Various roads led from the decisions taken in 1928 to the Hague conference of August 1929 that was intended to mark the 'final liquidation of the war'. The two most important were Parker Gilbert's call for a new reparation settlement and the German decision in the summer of 1928 to formally demand the early evacuation of the Rhineland even at the risk of an open quarrel with its Locarno partners. The reparation agent followed up his report of December 1927 with approaches to France's political and financial leaders. Poincaré had pursued the idea of a Dawes bond sale long after Thiory and was not hostile to Gilbert's ideas for the commercialization of the German reparation bonds. At the start of 1928 the reparations agent proposed that Germany should raise, in return for the evacuation of the Rhineland, $4 billion by selling railway and industrial securities that could be used by its creditors to repay the American war debts. Unfortunately for his scheme, the American Treasury refused to consider a reduction in war-debt payments during an election year. Nor were the British or Germans interested in the idea. The former preferred to give the Dawes plan a more extended trial while the Germans wanted to postpone any action until foreign troops left the Rhineland. The French, on the contrary, were anxious to proceed. The Washington administration, in anticipation of the November election, had intensified its pressure on Poincaré to ratify the Mellon–Bérenger agreement. The Americans warned that they would demand repayment of an American war stocks credit, some $406 million, if French ratification did not take place before 1 August 1929. Though Poincaré hoped to shift the burden of paying the Americans onto the Germans, he was unwilling to initiate discussions. It was left to Parker Gilbert to campaign for a staggered commercialization of the Dawes bonds and for a reduced reparation and war-debt settlement.

Exchanges between Stresemann and Briand in early 1928 highlighted their differences. It was Stresemann who invoked the *Locarnogeist* and

Briand who demanded concrete guarantees, the latter still not clearly defined. Stresemann believed that it was time for France, in the interests of peace, to abandon the guarantees of 1919 and to make a meaningful gesture in the German direction. Referring to Briand's famous speech to the Assembly in September 1926, he noted: 'Much has been said about discarding machine guns and cannons, but machine guns and cannons are still staring [Germany] in the face in the Rhineland.'[1] He claimed that it was Germany and not France that was disarmed and defenceless, and that the maintenance of the occupation was producing 'a psychological obstacle' to any German understanding with France. Briand's answering Senate speech, unusually direct and to the point, promised that evacuation would take place in the near future but denied that Locarno and the goodwill it generated were sufficient to allow the withdrawal of troops. Germany would have to fulfil its obligations under the Treaty of Versailles before the occupation could end. The 'spirit of Locarno' provided no guarantee against German rearmament, the remilitarization of the Rhineland, or the non-payment of reparations. The French wanted solid assurances of reparations and security, assurances that were permanent and institutional and not dependent on individuals and goodwill. René Massigli, the Quai official, insisted that 'it is important to maintain very firmly the principle of our Treaty right not to proceed' with evacuation without compensation'.[2] For his part, Chamberlain was known to favour early withdrawal with some form of quid pro quo but preferred to postpone the reparation question until after the American elections. The British foreign secretary was overstretched; in the spring of 1928 he had to deal with Egyptian, American, and Chinese affairs as well as his European problems. These multifarious duties may explain his willingness to generally support Briand without taking any positive role in Geneva. In subsequent discussions Briand took the lead.

As all but the Germans anticipated, the spring elections in France (22–9 April) returned Poincaré and the Union Nationale to office. The Socialists and Radical Socialists lost seats in the National Assembly, though it was not yet clear whether Briand had suffered any real diminution in influence. Once the elections were over, Stresemann felt free to officially raise the evacuation question. There were pressing political reasons for his action. In the German elections on 20 May the SPD had increased its share of the votes, and the head of the parliamentary party, Hermann Müller, was asked to form the broadest possible

---

[1] Jacobson, *Locarno Diplomacy*, 147.
[2] Memorandum on negotiations leading to the evacuation of the Rhineland, MAE, Massigli Papers, PA-AP 217, 7/120.

government as the Social Democrats, even with the Democratic and Centre parties, were still short of a working majority. It was due to Stresemann's intervention that the new government was formed at the end of June. Müller's 'cabinet of personalities' only became the 'Great Coalition' at the beginning of 1929. Little in the way of domestic policy united its members; it was mainly Stresemann's influence and the hope of foreign-policy success that gave the government some semblance of unity. On 3 July 1928 the Müller government presented its foreign-policy platform to the Reichstag. Its programme included the promotion of general disarmament, the immediate and unconditional evacuation of the Rhineland, the return of the Saar to Germany, and a reparation settlement within what Germany deemed its capacity to pay. The cabinet would try to maintain its position and stabilize the republic through a successful foreign policy. Yet it was clear from soundings in London and Paris that there was no sympathy for the unconditional evacuation of the Rhineland. The German ambassador in London reported that Britain was moving closer to France and Germany could not count on its support in its dealings with the Quai d'Orsay. The summer's Anglo–French agreement on armaments, even though ultimately abandoned, was seen in Berlin as a signal that Britain was prepared to abandon the Locarno 'troika' for a partnership with France.

At the end of July Chamberlain collapsed and a chill developed into pneumonia. To recover his nerves and health he left on a long cruise followed by an extended holiday in California, and did not return to London until November 1928. Stresemann, who had been seriously ill for some time, and was recovering from a stroke, made the rounds of the European spas in a vain attempt to regain his health. The Wilhelmstrasse, nevertheless, felt confident enough to take up the issue of evacuation even if it meant a major battle of wills with France and Britain. Carl von Schubert, the state secretary who took over Stresemann's duties during the latter's convalescence, outlined the programme for German action. His proposals were discussed in the cabinet and approved by the absent foreign minister. By making public the demand for total evacuation, Schubert argued that Germany would be able to define and dramatize the conflict with the Allies and reveal the breakdown in the Locarno collaboration. This would embarrass France and Britain, who would have to re-examine their policies to Germany's advantage. The cabinet gave its approval to Schubert's tactics. The timing of the démarche, with an eye to the next meeting of the Council in September, was dictated by the growing feeling in Berlin that it was urgent to act for domestic political reasons. The Rhineland question would be publicly aired in Geneva and the powers asked whether they intended to pursue the Locarno understanding and agree to evacuation, not as the end result of Locarno but as a stage in its development. If this approach failed, the government might make a legal claim under Article 431 or appeal for the application of the Locarno arbitration procedures. If revision of the Dawes plan was raised, the Germans should consent to exploratory but independent negotiations. On 28 July instructions were sent to the German ambassadors in Paris, London, Brussels, and Rome to ask their host governments whether they were prepared to discuss the Rhineland question in a friendly manner. It was the beginning of the German diplomatic offensive to end the military occupation of the Rhineland.

At the end of August Stresemann, despite his doctor's orders to the contrary, came to Paris at the end of August for the signing of the Kellogg–Briand pact, that 'pious gesture' meant to outlaw aggressive war forever. The positive public feeling generated by the pact made some think that a new phase in European diplomacy had begun; by the end of the year the renewed optimism about the future had begun to fade. The first German foreign secretary to visit the capital since Bismarck in 1871, Stresemann intended to use the occasion to sound out Briand and Poincaré about the Rhineland evacuation. Briand was encouraging but purposely vague when speaking of financial compensation. The conversation with Poincaré was far more important. After preliminary and heated exchanges over *Anschluss*, being publicly discussed in Vienna and Berlin, the two men found common ground in complaining about the overmighty American financial position and in exploring a possible war-debt and reparation arrangement. Poincaré argued that nothing could be done until after the American elections in November. It was only at the end of the talks that Stresemann turned to the forthcoming meeting at Geneva. Poincaré insisted that the evacuation had nothing to do with Locarno or the Kellogg pact and would have to be solved in conjunction with the pending financial arrangement. Stresemann, in turn, warned the premier that the Thiory terms no longer applied and that the Americans would not buy the bonds in light of the American stock-market boom, a view he claimed was shared by Parker Gilbert. The conversation was broken off when Stresemann's doctor intervened.

None of the Locarno powers were happy about the forthcoming German appeal. The timing was wrong and no one would consider the demand for unconditional evacuation. Poincaré still hoped, despite warnings about American intransigence over war debts, that the Germans would assist him in securing Washington's consent to an all-around settlement and preferred to wait for a more opportune time. The German initiative, however, focused French attention on the question of what compensation could be demanded from Berlin. When the cabinet considered the evacuation question just before Poincaré's meeting with Stresemann, it was clear that its members were deeply distrustful of Germany's long-term intentions and feared that some future German government might not honour its reparation obligations once the troops were withdrawn from the Rhineland. In London the Treasury was unenthusiastic about the commercialization of the Dawes tranche or, indeed, about any reparation settlement before the Americans considered the revision of war debts. No detailed preparations were made for the forthcoming Council and Assembly meetings. The Conservatives, with an election in the offing and under strong pressure from the opposition for a quick evacuation of the Rhineland, were anxious that progress should be made, but wanted to keep in step with the French.

The Geneva conversations in September were difficult and contentious. Chancellor Müller, substituting for Stresemann, found Briand and Lord Cushenden, replacing the absent Chamberlain, evasive when it came to stating their price for evacuation. At the Assembly the exchanges between Müller and Briand were unusually sharp. Müller made a thinly disguised attack on the Anglo-French disarmament policies and took up the minorities case as it affected Austria. Uncharacteristically blunt and outspoken in his angry reply, Briand defended his cautious policy on disarmament by pointing to the German capacity to launch an 'attaque brusque'. He also dealt with the nationalities issue, warning that self-determination should not be used to undermine governments or to disturb the peace, a reference to Poland as well as to Austria. The mood was not improved by pro-*Anschluss* speeches in Berlin by the Social Democratic president of the Reichstag and, in Geneva, by the Austrian chancellor, Ignaz Seipel, who was cautioned against further pro-German demonstrations in his country. At a private meeting of the Locarno power representatives (with the Japanese present) on 11 September, Müller presented the legal case for a Rhineland evacuation. In light of the prevailing views in American financial circles, any reparation–evacuation linkage would mean an almost indefinite and unacceptable postponement of the Rhineland settlement. Müller was willing to join discussions on reparations but could not return to Berlin empty-handed. Briand agreed that the Germans had the right to raise the question under Article 431 but protested that they had received all the concessions discussed at Locarno which did not include the evacuation of the Rhineland. To the surprise of the Germans, he raised again the question of a body for monitoring the demilitarized zone. He indicated that he was prepared for simultaneous negotiations over the Rhineland and reparations, and hoped that the Germans would suggest a feasible solution to the inspection problem. The British, seconded by the Belgians and Italians, also insisted that Germany should make an offer to the other occupiers if the Rhineland occupation was to be terminated. At a second meeting of the six powers Müller and Briand agreed that a committee of experts should be constituted from the interested governments and the United States in order to produce a definitive settlement of Germany's reparation obligations. The French, who wanted a financial settlement that would cover all inter-Allied war debts, suggested, after some prodding from Lord Cushenden, that once the formula for the commission of verification was accepted, France might offer to evacuate the second zone of the Rhineland as a gesture of goodwill. At Cushenden's suggestion, too, there was a break for a few days while Briand and Müller consulted their respective governments.

In Paris Briand found Poincaré and the cabinet far stiffer than he had expected. The best he could obtain was a cabinet agreement that a settlement was desirable and a financial–evacuation bargain acceptable. Briand raised but did not press the question of the second zone, possibly because he feared a negative reaction. Müller also consulted his cabinet and contacted Stresemann. In general, the German ministers were satisfied with the Geneva proceedings. Concerned mainly with the country's financial difficulties and the rising budgetary deficit, the German delegation was instructed to give priority to the reparation settlement and to accept some form of verification system until 1935 with equal guarantees on both sides. It was the latter question that was debated at the final meeting at Geneva, with Briand at last producing a vague formula but leaving the details of the new system to be concluded later. As the discussions came to an end, Müller noted that nothing had been decided about evacuation. Briand claimed that since everyone was anxious to solve the reparations question, Germany was bound to be given satisfaction. Cushenden's statement of the British position was suitably equivocal. Britain would stand by the principles of the Balfour memorandum of 1922 linking payments of war debts to Britain with the latter's payments to the United States, and would act on the evacuation question without necessarily connecting it with any other issue. Cushenden knew that the Treasury would reject any arrangement that did not meet British financial requirements. The British still preferred delay to decision.

The Geneva communiqué of 16 September was suitably phrased to conceal the unsettled issues. The representatives agreed to open nego-tiations on the Rhineland, to appoint a committee of financial experts to discuss a definitive reparations settlement, and to accept, in principle, a 'commission of verification and conciliation', the details to be settled by negotiation. Nothing was said about timing or partial solutions. No reference was made to *Anschluss* or to an 'eastern Locarno' as the Poles had wanted. The communiqué was nonetheless welcomed as a step forward. The Germans had won an assurance that the occupation would be negotiated. The French were promised a new reparation settlement as compensation. Both sides felt that they had secured their primary aims and that the general settlement that had escaped them at Thiory could now be realized. Unfortunately, the grounds for future disputes were already present. The Germans believed they had succeeded in separating the reparations and evacuation discussions, and that even if the former failed the latter would go ahead. The French assumed, because it was what they wanted, that the Germans had tacitly accepted the linkage between the two issues. Briand was quoted in the *Frankfurter Zeitung* on 19 September as saying that complete evacuation could only begin when the reparation question was settled, but he immediately softened the blow by indicating that he expected the financial settlements to be completed in a few weeks and that evacuation would then follow.

II

The Franco–German honeymoon was brief. The 'Geneva communiqué' was the starting point for two years of quarrelling which left the Locarnites with few common interests to compensate for their differences. Neither Briand nor the more suspicious Poincaré was willing to make the *beau geste* that Stresemann wanted unless France was amply rewarded. The hostile public mood in Germany hardly reassured Poincaré's right-wing cabinet. The British response was necessarily muted. The Conservative government was running out of steam, with elections expected in the spring of 1929, the economy had failed to revive, and unemployment was a major problem. With no alternative economic programme to offer, the Labour leaders concentrated on Chamberlain's recent diplomatic failures and the slowness with which the Geneva disarmament talks were progressing. While Cushenden was at the helm he worked closely with Briand, and a much stronger relationship developed between the two countries between the autumn of 1928 and the spring of 1929 when Labour returned to power. Stresemann, aware of the Francophile shift in British sympathies, waited to see whether the British elections would bring in a more sympathetic government. He had to accept, however, that reparations would take precedence over the questions of withdrawal and any change in the status of the Saar.

During the next months Parker Gilbert moved from capital to capital marshalling support for the revision of the Dawes plan. At first he pressed for commercialization to be followed by a scaling down of both reparations and war debts. Faced with an American veto on any kind of Dawes bonds mobilization on the American market until the Mellon–Bérenger agreement was ratified, and a blanket refusal to consider war-debt revision, Gilbert abandoned these proposals in favour of a new general settlement in which German reparation payments would cover the costs of the Allied war-debt settlements. This suited both Washington and Paris. Gradually the hopes of Benjamin Strong and the Wall Street bankers for a final and commercially viable reparations agreement were abandoned in favour of a narrower and more provisional agreement between Germany and her creditors that would satisfy the Republican administration. Gilbert had difficulties with both the British and the Belgians. Though Chamberlain, on his return, was not averse to Poincaré's linkage of a staged evacuation with commercialization, the Treasury opposed negotiations until the Americans revised the war-debt agreements. The Belgians, worried by the prospect of troop withdrawals from the Rhineland, were afraid that any reduction of the German annuities would be at their expense and might endanger the large public-works programme just instituted by the Brussels government. The Belgians had their own preliminary condition for any financial deal, the marks question that remained unsettled after almost ten years. Gilbert had more success in Berlin, particularly after he convinced Stresemann to follow up his demand for troop withdrawals with an offer to have parallel talks on reparation revision. Somewhat surprisingly, Gilbert converted Schacht to the idea of a final settlement, presumably because the Reichsbank president thought that if American bankers were involved, the experts would come up with a realistic assessment of Germany's capacity to pay. There was the added advantage, if Gilbert's suggestions were accepted, of ending the Dawes regime and restoring to Germany her full financial autonomy.

The British Treasury pressed its objections. Churchill was highly dubious about the 'Geneva communiqué' and sought to delay the meeting of the experts. He argued that it was up to the Americans to take the initiative over war debts before the British and French could consider any reduction in German reparations. Nor did he favour an earlier evacuation of the Rhineland unless Germany waived its claims under the Versailles treaty to a reduction of the French army. He again pointed out that 'the Locarno Treaties depend for their efficiency upon the French army', and that the strength of the French army 'protects us against the most probable danger of our being forced to intervene in Europe'.[3] Cushenden was instructed to inform the Locarnites that

---

[3] Martin Gilbert, *Winston S. Churchill*, Vol. 5: *Companion Part I* (London, 1976), 1338.

British war debts would have to be completely covered in any new settlement and that the government would not take part in any effort to arrange for a remission of war debts. It was due to the indefatigable Gilbert that Churchill's opposition was overcome. After a private week-end spent at Chartwell on 12–13 October, he convinced Churchill to accept the new scheme. The latter's conversion was due to Gilbert's assurance that Germany was both able and willing to pay an annuity of 2 billion marks without transfer protection and for a sufficient period of time to allow the Allies to cover all their war debts to the United States. Churchill was so taken with the prospect of shifting the war-debt burden onto the Germans that he accompanied Gilbert to Paris and concluded a bargain with Poincaré on the basis of German annuities of 2 billion a year. The chancellor of the Exchequer insisted that the Rhineland would have to be evacuated and the Churchill–Caillaux agreement on Anglo-French war debts ratified. Poincaré had no difficulty with either condition. The Anglo-French financial entente was now in place.

The sums discussed were close to the figures demanded under the new Dawes schedule which the Müller government had already dismissed as intolerable, particularly as the new payments would be made without transfer protection. Why should the Germans accept such unattractive terms? On 25 October Gilbert was in Berlin reporting on his conversations with Churchill and Poincaré. He told Müller, Hilferding, the minister of finance, and Schacht that Britain and France expected to collect sufficient reparations to cover war-debt payments to each other and to the United States, but gave no figures and apparently denied that they were discussed in Paris. He warned the Germans that they could not expect concessions from their creditors. No one in the cabinet opposed the Müller–Hilferding recommendation that the expert committee be summoned as soon as possible and there was no debate about the sums involved. The politicians apparently shared Schacht's assumption that the experts would link reparations to Germany's capacity to pay and produce a much-reduced reparation bill. These false hopes, the product of wishful thinking but also of the way Parker Gilbert conducted the pre-conference talks, were only gradually dissipated in late October when the reparation agent began to speak of a settlement based on creditor claims rather than on the German capacity to pay.

The German belief that their case would prevail if independent financial experts judged their situation led to a major clash with other powers over whether commercial bankers or government appointees should conduct the forthcoming negotiations. Poincaré and Churchill insisted on the right to instruct their experts and demanded that the expert committee be appointed by the Reparation Commission. The

German case was further weakened when the Americans made it clear that they were not interested in any discussion of Germany's capacity to pay but just wanted a rapid settlement so that the Mellon–Bérenger agreement would be ratified. This did not bode well for the commercial solution that the Germans sought. The French and British clarified their views over their individual requirements. The French wanted an indemnity plus sufficient sums to cover war-debt payments to the United States and Britain. They would not consent to any reduction in France's share of total payments from German assets as set in the Spa agreement. The British asked that the principles in the Balfour note linking reductions in reparations to payments of war debts to Britain should be maintained. They reserved the right to claims from past years when reparation payments were higher than receipts from war-debt payments, as well as the right to veto any mobilization of the German debt considered inexpedient. Dominion claims were to be treated separately and not made part of the British share. In a separate exchange, the French were reminded of the need to ratify the Churchill–Caillaux agreements. The two governments wanted Gilbert to present their aides-memoires to Berlin, but he wisely refused to act as go-between in an action which could only irritate the Germans, who wanted to preserve the full discretion of the committee of experts.

All during October, the Germans took no official action while continuing to argue that there was no legal connection between the reparation and evacuation settlements. At the end of the month they prepared a memorandum insisting that the experts should not be tied by instructions from their respective governments, and that the Reparation Commission should be invited to implement the final settlement only after acceptance by the participating countries. The evacuation question was not raised, but the Germans refused to consider any verification commission for the Rhineland beyond 1935. The quarrelling continued well into December. The Germans clung to the hope that the experts would examine their 'capacity to pay', a brief which Poincaré totally rejected. Both in public and private Briand and Poincaré paraded their unanimity and defended their Locarno policies in anticipation of the new negotiations.

When the very sick Stresemann returned to Berlin in early November, he was faced with a barrage of criticism arising from these declarations of Allied policy. No reference had been made to the evacuation question, and the French and British appeared to be dictating the outcome of the forthcoming conference. Like Schacht, Stresemann hoped that the American interest in safeguarding their German investments could be used to win a major downward revision in the reparation bill, but it seemed that the Americans were interested mainly in securing war-debt payments. Stresemann thought that Germany's growing financial difficulties and its dependence on foreign credit left it little freedom of choice. 'We are not only militarily disarmed, we are financially disarmed,' he told journalists, 'we have no kind of resources left.'[4] Participation in the expert discussions was the least disagreeable of the 'ugly' alternatives faced by the Germans. In his Reichstag speech of 19 November he again tried to separate the evacuation and reparation questions. He told the deputies that Germany would not purchase evacuation through financial compensation or the acceptance of a verification commission lasting beyond 1935. Playing to the public gallery, he accused the British and French of acting in bad faith. The Germans had been pushed into an untenable position. They continued to demand unconditional evacuation, but had agreed to participate in reparation discussions without any guarantee that the evacuation would take place before financial compensation was made. In the Chamber on 4 December, Briand dismissed Stresemann's speech as a tactical move intended to placate German public opinion. He assured the deputies that France would continue to insist on a reparation settlement and the commission of verification as the price of evacuation. In his usual way he extended an olive branch to Stresemann, promising to pursue an understanding with Germany until there was 'a general liquidation of the war'. The British found it more difficult to answer Stresemann's charges. Under mounting criticism, Chamberlain was forced to equivocate about the Rhineland and to avoid choosing between the French and German positions. While claiming that Germany had no legal right to complete withdrawal, Chamberlain let it be known that he favoured early evacuation but took no stand on compensation. Stresemann, assuming that the *entente cordiale* had survived the summer arms-agreement débâcle, looked forward to a Labour victory.

The Germans learned from Gilbert in November that the Allies would demand annuities of between 2 and 2.5 billion marks. Gilbert, whom Stresemann now accused of becoming the French 'pace-maker', warned the foreign minister that refusal would undermine German credit abroad and cut off the flow of short-term credits that continued even after the tightening of the American market for German bonds. The pressure for foreign loans was somewhat eased in 1928–9 as the German economy began to slip into recession. As in the depression of 1926, opposing interest groups looked to the government to take corrective action, and arguments over taxation and spending programmes began to tear apart Müller's fragile coalition. Without any foreign-policy success in sight, ministers turned on Stresemann, com-

---

[4] Gustav Stresemann, *Vermächtnis: der Nachlass* (Berlin, 1932), iii. 231.

peting with the anti-government parties in voicing their sense of disappointment. The republic was on the eve of one of the most difficult
political periods in its short history. It was not just that the Müller
government was badly shaken. The electoral setbacks suffered by the
parties of the middle and right in the May 1928 election (the Nazi vote
was considerably reduced) resulted in their shift to more extreme
positions and ever louder denunciations of Germany's weak and incompetent government. In October, the radical wing of the Nationalists, led
by the anti-republic and racist Alfred Hugenberg, triumphed over the
moderates, and the DNVP joined the ranks of the 'bitter and disaffected
opposition'. There was also a change in the position of the Centre party.
Marx, who had co-operated with Stresemann, was replaced as party
chairman by Ludwig Kass, who had criticized the Locarno agreements
and privately advocated Stresemann's removal from the cabinet.
Briand's 'speech' of 4 December produced a mass of critical German
press comment, much of it aimed at Stresemann.

It was an ill, fatigued, and despondent German foreign minister who
met with his two colleagues at Lugano (the change of venue due to
Stresemann's ill-health) between 9 and 14 December 1928. He re-
proached Briand and Chamberlain for the collapse of the Locarno
collaboration and called their attention to the domestic opposition
to his policies. With 60,000 Allied troops garrisoned in the Rhineland,
he questioned whether he could persuade anyone to support his
programme. Backtracking from the decisions reached at Geneva in
September, he tried to restore the primacy of the evacuation issue, but
Chamberlain backed Briand's demand for simultaneous reparation
and evacuation discussions and both men were adamant that complete
evacuation could take place only after the experts had arrived at a
settlement and agreement was reached on the commission of verification. Briand tried to soothe Stresemann, assuring him that the negotiations over the Rhineland would continue regardless of what happened
in the committee of experts. He drew a highly optimistic picture of their
future deliberations and the speed with which they would achieve a
settlement. Thanks to Chamberlain's prompting, Briand agreed that the
settlement of outstanding issues would be followed by the rapid evacuation of the troops from the Rhineland, though he refused to have his
pledges incorporated into the final press communiqué.

Each foreign minister met with a hostile reaction when he returned
home. Stresemann's failures were noted by his own party as well as by
the right-wing opposition. Plagued by the prolonged difficulties over
settling the terms for the conference of experts, and generally disillusioned about French co-operation, Stresemann turned his attention
to domestic affairs. A cabinet crisis between the ministers and their

respective parliamentary parties was only temporarily resolved in April 1929. The right wing of Stresemann's own party wanted to join the growing 'National Opposition' group that was espousing the most extreme forms of nationalism. Stresemann threatened to leave the party rather than abandon the foreign ministry, but he continued to blame the recalcitrant Allies for frustrating the hopes of Locarno. By this time almost all of Stresemann's reserves of energy and optimism had been depleted. At the March session of the League Council it had been agreed to postpone discussion of the Rhineland until after the financial experts had reported. Stresemann refused to consider the French draft proposal for the verification committee until further discussion in Berlin. The Germans were marking time. Despite appeals from Chamberlain for a more conciliatory approach to Germany in view of his domestic political difficulties, Briand could do little to assist his partner in London, though French success depended heavily on British backing. It soon became obvious that the ebullient Frenchman had spoken too freely about immediate evacuation. Poincaré was insistent that the occupation, the key weapon in any future reparation talks, should continue until France had secured its financial benefits from the commercialization and sale of the German reparation bonds. It was probably due to Poincaré that the idea of parallel negotiations, discussed at Geneva and Lugano, was dropped at the end of January. The Paris press publicized the German failure to renounce its claims in Poland and Austria. The French chiefs of staff, faced with a meeting of the League's preparatory commission on disarmament in the spring, demanded a large budgetary increase to prepare for a possible two-front war against Italy and Germany. Their arguments further fed the anti-German mood. In Britain the Labour and Liberal parties demanded immediate, unilateral, and unconditional evacuation, with the Labour attack gathering force during the run-up to the spring election. There were rumours that Baldwin would replace his 65-year-old foreign secretary in the next cabinet. Unable to get Briand to speed up the Rhineland talks and unwilling to consider unilateral withdrawal as demanded by the opposition, Chamberlain, during January, decided to drop the whole evacuation problem and allow the French to set the terms for the verification commission. He tried to convince the Germans that any British unilateral action would make little difference and would only weaken his ability to influence Briand once the reparation talks were concluded. Chamberlain's relative passivity, arising in part from the same lassitude that had led to his breakdown in the summer of 1928, owed much to his preoccupation with American affairs. The election campaign put the spotlight on the League and on unilateral evacuation. Chamberlain's sympathies were clear. 'Only the future would show whether Germany would really accept her present position, or whether she would once again resort to arms and stake everything on the hazards of a new war', he wrote to Sir Ronald Graham, the ambassador in Rome on 8 April 1929. 'Germany was still restless, still prone to suggest that her good behaviour must constantly be bought by fresh concessions.'[5] Following its election defeat on 30 May, Stanley Baldwin's Conservative government resigned and a minority Labour government with Ramsay MacDonald as prime minister and Arthur Henderson as foreign secretary took office.

III

The real action was taking place in Paris, where the committee of financial experts, an assorted body including the heads of the central banks chaired by the American Owen Young, began its work on 11 February. It would not conclude its labours until 7 June. This was a very experienced group of men, most of whom were already familiar with the complexities of reparations.[6] Supposedly independent and without official instructions, their number included several governors of the various national banks. It was understood from the start that the American government, though not officially represented, was immovable on the war-debt question. The terms of reference were broad but the room for compromise was narrow. No 'complete and final settlement' appeared possible. Hjalmar Schacht of the Reischsbank and Albert Vogler, an industrialist selected to induce his colleagues to accept the committee's recommendations, tried to focus attention on the German capacity to pay. Discussion stopped, however, when Schacht's tentative offer of a non-postponable annuity of 800 million gold marks revealed the startling contrast between what the Germans thought was a reasonable payment and what Gilbert had led the creditors to believe possible. At most, the Germans thought in terms of paying not more than 1 billion gold marks for thirty years, while the French anticipated

[5] Quoted in Jacobson, *Locarno Diplomacy*, 245–6.
[6] The committee's members included—*Belgium*: Émile Francqui, banker; Camille Gutt, banker and former minister of finance; *France*: Émile Moreau, governor of Bank of France; Jean Parmentier, director of Credit Foncier de France; *Germany*: Hjalmar Schacht, president of Reichsbank; Dr Albert Vogler, chairman of directors of Vereinigten Stahlwerke; *Italy*: Dr Alberto Pirelli, president of Pirelli Cable and Rubber Co.; Fulvio Suvich, former under-secretary in Ministry of Finance, vice-president of Italian Petroleum Co.; *Great Britain*: Sir Josiah Stamp, president of LMS Railway Co. and director of Bank of England; Lord Revelstoke, partner at Baring Bros. and director of Bank of England; *Japan*: Kengo Mori, president of Japan Gas Co.; Takashi Akoki, director of Imperial Bank of Japan; *United States*: Owen D. Young (chairman), chairman of General Electric Co. and board of directors of Federal Reserve Bank; J. P. Morgan, Jr., head of J. P. Morgan & Co., New York.

annuities ranging between 2 and 2.5 billion gold marks covering the full fifty-eight-year war-debt payment period. It was left to the American experts to try to bridge the gap between the participants. Young and J. P. Morgan, Jr., both highly experienced negotiators, were optimistic about Germany's capacity to pay and shared the Gilbert–Poincaré argument that the German payments should facilitate the war-debt repayments to the United States. This checked Schacht's hopes for annuities set well below the Dawes levels and of limited duration. Inevitably the Germans, their creditors, and the Americans battled over the proposed annuity figures. Young sent Morgan and Thomas Lamont to convince Schacht that the German figures were unreasonable. Morgan, used to giving orders and unaccustomed to dealing with men like Schacht, returned in a state of virtual breakdown. Almost in desperation, after each of Germany's creditors had separate talks with Schacht, it was agreed to let Young propose a solution. After much argument that lasted over three days, a new schedule representing the 'minimal requirements' of the creditors was presented to the Germans on 13 April. Annuities were set at an average of 2.198 billion gold marks for the first thirty-seven years covering both indemnities and outpayments. They would decline during the next twenty-one years when Germany would pay reparations only to cover outpayments to the United States.

The German counter-proposal, framed without any consultation with Berlin, intentionally raised the political temperature. The German delegates argued that it was impossible to transfer annuities worth more than 1.65 billion gold marks or lasting longer than thirty-seven years without endangering the current German standard of living. After outlining two alternative methods of payment, Schacht went on to link the difficulties of German payments and its adverse balance of payments to the loss of the former German colonies and the eastern agricultural lands. The idea that reparations payments would depend on rewriting the territorial clauses of the Treaty of Versailles was greeted first with astonished silence and then with cries of indignation from the British, Italian, and Belgian experts. Moreau, from the Bank of France, pounded the table, refused to discuss Schacht's proposals. Young moved quickly to salvage the conference; a subcommittee was created to consider an interim solution. Schacht refused to improve on his offer of 1.65 billion gold marks. The negotiations were broken off. The subcommittee was prepared to report its failure and recommend adjournment. There was high alarm in Berlin; Schacht had acted on his own and in defiance of Stresemann's warning not to raise territorial issues. He was instructed to ask for a temporary adjournment of the conference for a few days. As it happened, the British delegate Lord

Revelstoke, who had been trying to reconcile the Germans and their creditors, suffered a stroke and died suddenly. The final session was postponed from Friday, 19 April, until the following Monday. Schacht and Vogler returned to Berlin for consultations; the former had already made it clear that he wanted the negotiations to go on and had agreed that Young should draw up a new schedule of payments. In Berlin the cabinet, who knew little of what was transpiring in Paris, insisted that Schacht had overstepped his authority and should abandon his quasi-political conditions. The discussions on the proposed schedule were to proceed.

In late April there was a massive withdrawal of gold and foreign exchange from Germany. Because of the effects of the increasingly restrictive American monetary policy, borrowing from New York had been curtailed and short-term capital was coming from Paris. French anxieties about the reparation negotiations interrupted this inflow. The Reichsbank lost nearly RM 1 billion of reserves in April alone and was reaching the limits of the 40 per cent statutory gold backing minimum. On 25 April the Reichsbank raised its discount rate from 6.5 per cent to 7.5 per cent to staunch the flow. False press reports, which Schacht claimed were inspired by Moreau, stating that the Transfer Committee had attributed the loss of funds to the Reichsbank's irresponsible discount policy led to increased speculation against the mark. Prodded by Young, Parker Gilbert, who had not suspended the transfer of reparation payments in order to protect the mark, denied the rumours and British and American bankers hastened to support the Reichsbank. The latter's action checked its gold losses, but the Reich government was in a weak bargaining position. The economy was contracting and the government had to subsidize employment insurance schemes and other programmes that increased the budget deficit. Germany could not face the consequences of rejecting the newly proposed Young schedule, though, like Schacht, the government would have liked to avoid direct responsibility for acceptance. Indeed, the question in Berlin was who would take responsibility for a decision that was disliked by all the cabinet members. After a second trip back to the capital, Schacht demanded written authorization before he would agree to accept the Young figures. On 5 May, with many conditions attached, Schacht announced Germany's acceptance of the creditors' terms. His government did not believe the terms either fair or reasonable and did not regard the 'Young plan' as a final settlement. As in 1919 and 1921, the Social Democrats, and in this case Müller and Wirth personally, assumed the responsibility for an unpopular settlement. In his book *The End of Reparations*, published the following year, Schacht disclaimed, with little justification, all responsibility for the settlement and protested that he had been deceived by both the foreign experts and his own government. Despite these later complaints, he remained in Paris after 5 May where negotiations and horse-trading between the creditors continued. Unlike the other German delegate, Vogler, he did not offer his resignation. With Young close to physical collapse, agreement was finally reached between all the parties and the Young committee's report signed on 7 June.

The Germans entered into the reparation negotiations because they had wanted to expedite the withdrawal of foreign troops from the Rhineland. The evacuation issue was not raised in Paris and had no bearing on the Young plan. They accepted the plan because paying the much higher Dawes annuities would have meant tax increases and credit restriction that might have caused a major economic crisis and the danger of political and social upheaval. The Germans expected further negotiations under better conditions. They would continue to stress the country's financial weaknesses, not only to win revision of the Young plan but to achieve territorial revision as well. The German hope that independent experts would examine Germany's capacity to pay, reduce its obligations, and create a schedule based on what Germany could transfer without borrowing was without foundation from the start. No agreement had been reached on the gap between what the creditors hoped to receive and what Germany believed to be her capacity to pay. The terms of the plan were shaped by the creditors' wishes to cover their war debts to the Americans and to each other. Even where the delegates acted in their capacity as 'experts', they were intensely aware of their national interests. Their discussions were not of a purely financial nature; they necessarily involved political decisions. The reparation problem was not, as the Republican administration and Wall Street bankers had hoped, depoliticized. As throughout the decade, and with fatal consequences in 1931–2, political and financial issues were inseparable.

There was one welcome attempt to go beyond the national confines of the reparation question. A new Bank of International Settlement (BIS) was created to replace the Reparation Commission and its attendant appendages as well as the Dawes structure. The proposal was supported by Schacht, who was worried about the impact of reparation payments on Germany's foreign-exchange position, and by Francqui, the Belgian finance minister. It was taken up by Young, who wanted to move reparations from the political to the commercial domain. He called on the American bankers to create a new institution capable of managing the reception and distribution of reparation payments and to assess German requests for their temporary suspension. Sir Josiah Stamp, the British delegate responsible for many of the technical details of the

Young plan, had wider aims in mind. He thought that the new bank should be a clearing-house for transfers of intergovernmental debts and act as a lender of last resort to member central banks. In this capacity it could provide credit facilities to ease the pressure on governments forced to take politically unpopular measures to maintain exchange stability abroad. The French were less than enthusiastic about the bank's discretionary functions and reluctant to consider Stamp's imaginative scheme of an international institution with credit-creating powers. The main blow to the expanded role of the BIS came from Washington. Due to Congressional opposition to any initiative involving reparations, the government refused to allow the Federal Reserve Bank of New York to have anything to do with the BIS. It had to be content with the participation of a syndicate of American commercial banks. If they wished, the participating central banks could treat the BIS funds as reserve assets and call on them to smooth out exchange disturbances. Without the participation of the FRBNY, the resources of the bank would be small and central-bank co-operation would still have to be arranged on an ad hoc basis. The BIS had twenty-one members and two commercial banking groups from the United States. Its capital totalled $100 million, of which only $21 million was paid up before the end of 1931. Assets at their peak in May 1931 were valued at $412 million, about the same as Germany's reparation payments for that year. Most were in dollar investments, with a good portion of the rest in sterling. The BIS represented the first attempt to promote the maintenance of international monetary stability through institutionalized central-bank co-operation. Its weaknesses proved far greater than its strength, as became clear in 1931. It still survives in its original location, Basle, the sole remaining relic of the long reparation struggle that so poisoned international relations during the 1920s.

The Young plan divided German payments into two schedules, the first lasting thirty-seven years (1929–66) and the second twenty-two years (1966–88). During the first period annuities were divided into unconditional and conditional payments. The former, as subsequently modified at the first Hague conference, came to approximately RM 674 million and were subject to commercialization. The figure covered indemnities, outpayments (war debts), and a sum to service the original Dawes loan. The French benefited most from the unconditional payments, receiving 75–80 per cent of the proceeds from the sale of the new annuities. The second portion, the conditional payments, were set on an ascending scale, from RM 1,567 billion in 1930–1 to RM 2,353 billion in the highest year, 1965–6. During the second period the distinction between conditional and unconditional payments was dropped, and the total marginally increased from RM 1,567 billion in 1967–8 to RM

1,684 billion in 1984–5. The figure was dramatically reduced during the last three payment years. Could anyone have seriously believed in 1929 that reparation payments would continue to be paid into the 1980s? Unfortunately, not even hard-headed bankers could escape the French and American demands that reparation payments should last as long as inter-Allied debt-funding arrangements. The need to project entirely illusory figures that involved payments over an extended period of time only served to fuel the nationalist revolt in Germany against the Young plan, where the prospect of this interminable burden of future payments provided excellent political ammunition.

The Müller cabinet won the immediate financial advantages it sought when agreeing to participate in the Paris negotiations. The first thirty-seven-year Young plan annuity averaged 2.05 billion marks, 20 per cent lower than what Germany would have paid if the Dawes plan had remained in operation, particularly as the latter would have been augmented in normal times by the prosperity index. Special concessions in the Young plan reduced the burden even further for the period between September 1929 and March 1930. Only about one-third of each annuity, RM 660 million, was unconditionally payable and only this portion of the debt could be commercialized. The Germans could request a two-year moratorium for conditional payments if they were unable to

TABLE 21. German Reparations, 1919–1932

	Reparations (gold marks)	Reparations as % NNP*	Reich Deficit as % NNP	Reparations as % of Reich Deficit	Reich Deficit without Reparations as % of NNP
1919			17.7		17.7
1920	1,236	3.3	16.2	20.3	12.9
1921	3,659	8.3	12.2	68.2	3.9
1922	2,226	5.3	9.4	56.3	4.1
1923	801	2.1	22.2	9.5	20.1
1924	281	0.6	0.1	112.4	−0.6
1925	1,080	1.6	0.5	297.5	−1.1
1926	1,310	2.0	1.4	141.2	−0.6
1927	1,779	2.2	0.6	389.3	−1.6
1928	2,187	2.6	1.6	157.5	−0.9
1929	1,965	2.5	1.0	237.6	−1.4
1930	1,879	2.6	1.5	176.4	−1.1
1931	561	1.0	0.8	114.7	−0.1
1932	183	0.4	0.7	49.3	0.4

* Net National Product.

Source: Niall Ferguson, *Paper and Iron: Hamburg Business and German Politics in the Era of Inflation, 1897–1927* (Cambridge, 1995).

meet a full payment, and under special circumstances could postpone the internal payment of one-half of the conditional annuity. Conditional annuities were subject to reduction if the United States reduced or cancelled its war-debt demands. Though the Germans protested against the ostensible total amount, they would pay annuities well under 2 billion marks during the first ten years. Before that time elapsed it was assumed that reparations would either be dropped or the Germans would win another reduction. Even in the interim, deliveries in kind would be sharply reduced and all supervision over German finances would cease. The Germans had lost the transfer protection provided under the Dawes plan, and there were debates, as earlier, about Germany's capacity to export sufficient amounts to make the transfer of marks into foreign credits without a major expansion of world trade. Historians still disagree whether even the reduced Young annuities imposed too great a burden on the German budget and balance of payments given the conditions of 1929–30. There was a brief moment at the end of the 1920s when reparations accounted for 3 per cent of the GNP or 7 per cent of the German tax bill, which the Germans thought far too high. It must be remembered, however, that an integral component of the Young plan was a stabilization loan. Germany was lent RM 1.2 billion in 1930, nearly financing its entire reparations payments for the year. Foreign exchange was needed to service the commercial debt and this was done by restricting domestic spending. Due to this contraction, the trade balance in 1929 became a trade surplus in 1930. In the long run the burden of payment was more than compensated for by the inflow of foreign loans and the proceeds from German investment abroad, above all in the United States.[7] The Young payments, which had a very short life, were hardly the main cause of the Reich's financial difficulties or the reason for the limited growth of the German economy. They provided, nevertheless, a convenient target for the nationalists and a rallying cry for those who blamed Germany's troubles on the coalition government and the foreigners.

Among Germany's creditors, the French appeared to have gained the most. They would be able to cover their war debts from the German payment and had won an indemnity as well. Once the French began paying off their debts to the Americans under the Mellon–Bérenger agreement, the sums amounted to about $32 million annually and hardly dented the French balance of payments. American tourists in 1929 spent $137 million in France on holiday. The emotions aroused by the war-debt issue overshadowed all commercial considerations. If the Americans and British were to demand their pound of flesh after

7 Schuker, American 'Reparations' to Germany, 1919–1933, 44–5.

TABLE 22. German Reparations Payments Leading to the Dawes and Young Plans, 1919–1932

1919–1924	German estimate	51.6 bn Gold Marks	
	Allied valuation	8.0 bn Gold Marks	
	Schuker Estimate	10.1 bn Gold Marks	

1925–1932 bn RM			
	Allied demand	Actual	% Nat income
1925	1.0 Dawes	1.1	1.8
1926	1.22 Dawes	1.2	2.0
1927	1.50 Dawes	1.6	2.3
1928	2.50 Dawes	2.0	2.8
1929	1.94 Dawes	2.3	3.2
1930	1.70 Young	1.7	2.4
1931	1.69 Young	1.0	1.8
1932	1.73 Young	0.2	0.4
	Total	11.1	16.7

Source: Steven Schuker, American 'Reparations' to Germany, 1919–1933, p. 33

all that France had suffered in the Great War, the Germans would have to provide it. Hopefully, the French government would be in a position to commercialize part of their unconditional annuity (£25 million of the £33 million) allowing for the prepayment of war debts and tying German reparation obligations more closely to her commercial credit standing. There was some disquiet about how little of the total German obligation was to be commercialized, but these fears did not immediately surface. The Belgians, after considerable difficulty, refused to link their settlement with the return of Eupen-Malmédy to Germany and won separate negotiations with the Germans. The Belgians and the Italians won annuities that covered both war debts and an indemnity. Only the British received no indemnity and had their annuities reduced.

Apart from the United States, where the new administration of Herbert Hoover, elected on 5 November 1928, thought the Young plan would expedite the payment of war debts, the new arrangements generated little positive enthusiasm. In London angry Treasury officials felt that the new settlement was no substitute for the general liquidation of reparations and war debts that they believed was the only solution to the problem of world indebtedness. Young had reduced the Allied claims mainly at the expense of Britain and the Dominions, whose overall share of the spoils was reduced from the Spa total of 22.8 per cent to 19.4 per cent. On the eve of the British elections, goaded by Philip Snowden, the Labour shadow chancellor of the Exchequer, and faced with a deepening financial crisis, Winston Churchill practically repudiated the forthcoming experts' report and promised the renegotiation of the division of the annuities. Snowden also took up the issue of the retention of the German payments in kind for another ten-year period. It was believed that German exports in kind to Italy and France were damaging the already weak British export industries. By 1929 the Italians were taking 97 per cent of their payments in kind from Germany in the form of coal, massively reducing their customary imports from Britain. During the fourth Dawes year German machinery exports to France constituted some 72 per cent of its payments in kind to France. Stamp managed to secure a new arrangement by which payments in kind would immediately be reduced by half but would continue until 1940. Many wanted to see their abolition at once. The actual losses to the British would have been relatively small. Under the Young scheme, receipts would have increased during the next decade and the reductions in the British annuities be postponed until the 1940s. As no one expected the system to last more than a decade, the cost to Britain was nominal. Snowden, nevertheless, sensed an excellent election issue and was prepared to do battle on behalf of his country and people, who had been 'bled white for the benefit of other countries who are far more prosperous than ourselves'.[8]

The Quai d'Orsay and French finance ministry were generally satisfied with the Young plan, but the French deputies were less impressed and disliked the way reparations had been subordinated to war debts. An attempt was made to get the Americans to postpone the 1 August ultimatum on war debts, but Secretary of State Henry Stimson, though sentimental about his shared war experiences with the French, would not be moved. Consequently, Poincaré and Briand were anxious that the Germans should ratify the Young plan as rapidly as possible, for they had to convince the French parliament to ratify the war–debt agreement before the 1 August deadline. The British were also demanding an equal payment as provided for in the *pari passu* clause of the Churchill–Caillaux agreement over war debts. Pressure was brought to bear on Stresemann, but the foreign minister refused to speed up the ratification process unless assured that the political price for the Young plan, that is, the evacuation of the Rhineland and the return of the Saar, would be paid in full. It may have been Briand's concern with the attitudes of the new Labour government in London and the realization that the Rhineland would soon become the main issue for negotiation that explained his more conciliatory approach to Stresemann at the June Council

---

[8] Bruce Kent, *The Spoils of War: The Politics, Economics and Diplomacy of Reparations 1918–1932* (Oxford, 1989), 307.

meeting in Madrid. Briand proposed a political conference to discuss the 'final liquidation of the war', and suggested that as soon as outstanding problems were resolved, the continental countries, possibly with Britain, should consider some form of political and economic consolidation to check an overpowerful United States. This was the theme to which he was to return in the autumn of 1929. Briand also cautioned Stresemann not to raise the Saar question; in turn, he made no demand for a verification commission to monitor the demilitarized Rhineland.

It was only on 21 July that the French Chamber gave its approval to the two war-debt agreements by a narrow vote of 300 to 292. The Senate followed later in the week with a non-binding resolution that made payment contingent on the fulfilment of Germany's reparation obligations. The strenuous efforts made to secure ratification cost Poincaré his health, and he resigned office on 25 July. Briand, in a far more politically exposed position, replaced him at the end of the month and asked the Chamber of Deputies for a three-months 'truce' while the international negotiations lasted. The close Chamber vote reflected its uncertainty about the implementation of the Young plan and the trustworthiness of the Germans. The debates also highlighted the tortuous policies of the cabinet. On the one hand, Poincaré and Briand were assuring the deputies that the Germans would loyally carry out the Young plan; on the other, they were arguing for such safeguards as the mobilization of the unconditional annuities and the creation of a verification and conciliation commission that reflected their own doubts about German probity. What did Poincaré's retirement mean in terms of Franco-German relations? The premier had acted as a convenient foil for Briand's own unwillingness to move too quickly along the path of reconciliation. Because of his public reputation as an anti-accommodationist, Poincaré provided a check on the nationalist opposition to Briand's diplomacy. Undoubtedly the premier was more suspicious about the German capacity for change, but his policy differences with Briand remained minimal. Both men accepted the need to implement the Locarno accords, but both were determined not to sacrifice French security in the process. It was a classic case of squaring the circle. With Poincaré's departure, Briand had a freer hand in the cabinet but not in the Chamber. When Briand presented his 'caretaker government' to the Chamber of Deputies and asked for a political truce, most of the Radicals abstained from voting. They found it difficult to vote for a government whose domestic policies they had long opposed but which was now led by a man whose foreign policy they strongly supported.

Stresemann also faced serious problems. Though the initial reaction of the government to the Young plan was to make the best of a bargain about which they had many doubts, the Müller cabinet had to respond to the opening shots of Alfred Hugenberg's assault on the Young *Diktat*. The 'Campaign against the Enslavement of the German People' mounted by the Nationalists, Stahlhelm, and Nazis, and their successful demand for a plebiscite on the Young plan forced the government to mount a qualified defence. The SPD finance minister, Rudolf Hilferding, argued the financial case for accepting the Young plan. He explained that the reduced Young annuities would help to offset the 150 million mark deficit in the 1928–9 budget resulting from declining government revenues and the increased outlays associated with the winter depression. When Stresemann spoke in the Reichstag he had to counter the Hugenberg assault without in any way imperilling Germany's foreign credit or compromising his negotiations with France. He told the deputies that the Young plan was the only alternative to a damaging financial crisis and emphasized its short-term advantages. With an eye on the opposition, he insisted on the purely German character of the Saar and promised that he would not accept a verification commission after 1935. To placate the French, there was no mention of the Rhineland evacuation or territorial revision, but his speech nevertheless provoked a negative reaction in Paris.

The defeat of the Conservative government in Britain and the replacement of Chamberlain by Henderson, a strong League advocate, was not to France's advantage. Labour had made foreign policy the centre of its election campaign, stressing international arbitration, the limitation of armaments through the League of Nations, the restoration of relations with the Soviet Union, and the pacification and reconciliation of Germany. Copies of its manifesto were circulated in the Foreign Office to remind officials of the impending change in policy direction. Henderson's conception of the role of the League was very different from that of Chamberlain, and the inclusion of Lord Robert Cecil among his foreign-policy advisers suggested a much higher British profile in the disarmament debates. Once in power, the new foreign secretary was to follow a more nuanced course than has been appreciated by later critics, who have accused Labour of being almost pathologically Francophobe. It was clear, however, that the Labour leadership was going to turn its back on ententes and alliances and that relations with France were going to be more difficult than in the past. Henderson's determination to end the occupation of the Rhineland as rapidly as possible altered the relationship with Briand, who clung to the idea of the entente, and changed the diplomatic balance between France and Germany. The new chancellor of the Exchequer, Snowden, continued his anti-Young-plan campaign, ably assisted by Frederick Leith Ross, the only senior Treasury official left with extensive experience in international finance. Leith Ross had already denounced Josiah Stamp's 'craven surrender' to the Latins. He prepared the ammunition Snowden required for an all-out attack on the experts' recommendations. The French were forewarned of Snowden's intentions but hoped they could use their financial muscle to protect their interests. Henderson was willing to leave economic and financial matters to Snowden. While MacDonald took charge of American relations, Henderson focused on European problems and was determined to take up the evacuation question. He argued that Germany had fulfilled the conditions set by the Versailles treaty and that evacuation should take place as soon as the Young plan was accepted. On 17 July 1929 the cabinet decided— though parliament was not informed—that under certain circumstances Britain would resort to unilateral withdrawal. One week later the cabinet accepted Henderson's recommendation that if France and Belgium refused to move their troops by Christmas, Britain would act alone. The French had to face the possibility that the Young plan might be scrapped and the Rhineland occupation ended without any compensation for France. Stresemann's negotiating hand was strengthened and the way prepared for his most important, and last, foreign-policy success.

IV

The first Hague conference began on 8 August 1929 and lasted until the end of the month. It was optimistically titled 'The Conference on the Liquidation of the War'. Delegates came from Britain, France, Germany, Belgium, Italy, and Japan. Two committees were created: a financial committee under Belgian chairmanship to consider the Young plan, and a political committee under Henderson to deal with the Rhineland evacuation. The three major powers had clear but very different goals in mind. Stresemann was willing to accept the Young plan but determined to secure the full and rapid evacuation of the Rhineland. He had decided, moreover, to make use of the French interest in the ratification of the Young plan to get the Saar issue on the Hague agenda, though he agreed to bilateral and informal talks by German and French experts. He would not accept a commission of verification beyond 1935. The French wanted prompt acceptance of the Young plan but wished to delay evacuation until German payments were actually received, and demanded some form of commission to monitor the continuing demilitarization of the Rhineland. Briand would have liked to restrict German military and paramilitary activities on the left bank on the Rhine and wanted other assurances about the Rhineland's disarmament. The British refused to ratify the Young plan without modification and were prepared to use the threat of unilateral evacuation to force through the prompt and complete withdrawal of all Allied troops. Little effort was made to compromise these differences before the meetings began.

The month-long conference was dominated by Snowden's battles with Germany's creditors for a revision of the Young plan to Britain's advantage. The tough and acerbic chancellor of the Exchequer demanded that the Spa percentages be restored, thereby increasing Britain's share of the annuity by an average of £2.4 million. He insisted, too, that Britain should have a larger share of the unconditional annuity, most of which had been promised to France, and that all payments in kind should be dropped immediately. The disputes in the reparation committee became a duel between Snowden and Henri Cheron, Briand's finance minister. Snowden used all his well-known powers of verbal invective on the sensitive Cheron. There was a minor crisis when the chancellor's remark that the French argument was 'grotesque and ridiculous' was taken as a veiled reference to Cheron's ample girth. Though the diplomatic peace was restored, Snowden's adamant stand and refusal to engage in diplomatic pleasantries stalemated the discussions and almost led to the collapse of the conference. The British were accused of behaving like Shylock; one French delegate said that Snowden's behaviour had helped French–German co-operation more than ten years of propaganda.[9] A strong nationalist with little experience of, and even less interest in, the give and take of international meetings, Snowden fervently believed that Britain should not be the 'milch cow of Europe', compelled to make financial sacrifices at the British taxpayers' expense for the benefit of others. He successfully withstood threats from Moreau to remove Bank of France assets from London, as well as an intervention by Ramsay MacDonald to force him to compromise. Though Snowden's credibility was somewhat damaged by MacDonald's actions, he stood his ground. The French, anxious about delaying the implementation of the Young plan, and the Belgians finally capitulated and agreed to satisfy approximately half of the British demand by giving up their share of the surplus from the payments of the last five months of the Dawes scheme. Mussolini had forbidden Pirelli, the Italian delegate, to make any concessions, but combined pressure from the others resulted in an Italian decision to contribute part of the liberation debt from the successor states as a further contribution to the British portion.

It was only at the very last moment, with time running out before the foreign ministers had to go to Geneva, that Snowden agreed to take slightly less than he demanded. He held out until he had won back 83

---

[9] Franz Knipping, *Deutschland, Frankreich und das Ende der Locarno-Ära, 1928–1931* (Munich, 1987), 62.

per cent, or a nominal £2 million per annum, of what had been sacrificed by Stamp under the Young plan. By sheer stonewalling, the chancellor of the Exchanger won an increase from the original French–Belgian–Italian offer of 26.8 million marks to 36 million marks. Britain's share of the unconditional annuity was increased from less than £900,000 to £2,750,000. In addition, the Italians promised that their national railway would purchase 1 million tons of coal for three years at the best British prices to offset the German deliveries of reparation coal. After bringing the Germans in and trying, unsuccessfully, to get Stresemann to accept higher annuities, the four creditor nations finally reached an arrangement with Snowden at midnight on 27–8 August. Given the last-minute rush to reach a settlement, there was no time for negotiations over the questions, highly important for France, of commercialization or guarantees of payment. Reports from the newly appointed expert committees would be considered at a later conference of governments to be held at the Hague early in the new year. Snowden's success in bullying the other creditors was due, apart from his sheer cussedness, to the fear that the British might break up the conference, scotch the Young plan, and revert to the Dawes scheme in the hope of a major crisis and a genuine war-debt–reparation settlement.

Snowden's manoeuvrings almost wrecked the Foreign Office hopes for a Rhineland settlement, for they meant that the political negotiations moved ahead at a faster pace than the financial ones. Briand was at a disadvantage and forced to resort to delaying tactics. He was repeatedly pushed by Henderson and Stresemann to accept complete evacuation and to set a date for the French withdrawal. Henderson was intent on his goal even at the cost of disrupting the Anglo-French entente, and in this sense achieved a major success. The main and most important result of the political negotiations was an agreement that all foreign troops would leave the Rhineland by 30 June 1930. At the start of the talks Briand took a stiff line, stipulating that the evacuation should be subject to a financial settlement that could be 'practically applied' and refusing to set a terminal date for withdrawal. After consulting with the military in Paris, Briand privately informed Stresemann that the French evacuation could not be completed before October 1930. This date would mollify the army chiefs; the 'Maginot line' project for fortifying France's north-eastern frontier was only brought before the Chamber and the first credits for construction authorized in December 1929. Delay, more-over, would have given time for the capitalization of the German reparation debt. Stresemann was unwilling to return to Berlin with the prospect of a one-year delay in freeing German soil from foreign occupation. In a strong personal letter to Briand, he pointed to the dangers of a public uproar. He threatened not to sign the Young plan or to continue the policy of German–French co-operation unless Briand shortened the evacuation period to 1 April. When Briand refused, the British took the initiative. Henderson sought out Stresemann and Wirth and concluded a separate agreement by which the British would complete their evacuation before 31 December 1929 and the Germans would waive claims and occupation costs after 1 September. Briand strongly protested against this unilateral approach. There was an acrimonious conversation between Briand and Stresemann, during which the Frenchman's bitterness at the British desertion was barely disguised and the parallels with British behaviour over the Geneva Protocol recalled for Stresemann's benefit. An abortive meeting of the political committee on the same day to debate the commission of verification revealed the extent of French isolation. Just before its early adjournment Stresemann announced his intention to abandon all indemnity claims against the armies of Britain and Belgium if their troops left the Rhineland by the end of the year. He would do the same for the French only if their troops, too, were evacuated by 1 April 1930. Pressed hard by Stresemann and Henderson, Briand retreated but would not surrender. French troops would leave the Rhineland within six months of the end of winter. Henderson made light of the so-called operational difficulties which precluded a winter evacuation. If British troops could be withdrawn and transported across the Channel in winter, the French could certainly do the same on land. With the British and Belgians behind him, and in the knowledge that German support was being solicited on the parallel reparation negotiations, Stresemann had the upper hand. Briand dropped the Paul-Boncour verification commission and agreed that the Locarno arbitration commissions could be used to handle any disputes over demilitarization. The words 'verification' and 'conciliation' were not even mentioned in the final protocol. There was a further retreat on the evacuation date. If the Young plan was ratified by late October, the French evacuation would be completed before 30 June. The final agreement confirmed the 30 June evacuation. The arguments over dates were a face-saving operation.

It was only when the financial talks were successfully concluded that Stresemann, Briand, Henderson, and Hymans exchanged notes for the evacuation of the Rhineland. At the very last moment Stresemann refused a financial settlement that required German agreement to relatively minor financial concessions, mainly an altered schedule of unconditional payments, unless Briand accepted the 1 April deadline. By this time everyone was too tired to continue fighting and anxious to depart for Geneva. Briand gave in to Stresemann at 2 a.m. on 29 August. The German delegation, despite Schacht's last-minute protests and threats of resignation, agreed to the changes demanded by the creditors.

The Rhineland notes were exchanged and, on 31 August, the Hague Protocol was signed.

This was Stresemann's victory. All the demands made at the Locarno conference in October 1925, with the exception of the return of the Saar, had been achieved. The Germans had originally entered the reparation negotiations for political reasons. Once they had agreed to the terms of the Young plan, despite reservations, they concentrated their efforts on winning the political prize. Stresemann had secured his four-and-a-half-year shortening of the period of occupation in return for minimal concessions. The verification commission was dropped. The Saar question was left pending after discussions between the French and German experts. Stresemann was anxious to proceed, while the French dragged their feet; it was agreed to open formal negotiations in December. Two questions, sanctions in the event of wilful German default and arrangements for a partial mobilization of the unconditional annuities, were to be discussed at the second Hague conference. In Berlin the political agreements were hailed as a major success for Stresemann's diplomacy. The German Foreign Office warned against any provocations or demonstrations during the evacuation; it would be safer not to celebrate too openly. The German delegates were warmly congratulated by President Hindenburg. Respectable nationalists rejected the extremists' demands for the rejection of the Young plan and the impeachment of the ministers responsible. The Nazi–Nationalist campaign against the Young plan, though noisy, lacked cohesion. Only slightly less than 14 per cent of the electorate actually voted for the 'Freedom Law' ('The Law against the Enslavement of the German People') in the 22 December referendum. The campaigners drew a good deal of attention to themselves and their activities did not go unnoticed in Paris. The real importance of the campaign lay in the combined efforts of the disparate right–wing groups who had found a common cause. Within the National Opposition coalition, the Nazis gained in importance at the expense of the Nationalists. Hitler had gained entry into the circles of the 'respectable' right and was fêted in the Hugenburg press by those who thought they could harness his remarkable political skills to strengthen the nationalist movement. It was an illusion for which they were to pay a high price.

The Müller government hoped that the Young plan would ease its financial situation and encourage further foreign lending. The cabinet felt it had to tackle the mounting budget-deficit problems before the plan was implemented. Reich expenditure was still rising in 1929. The number of unemployed reached the 3 million mark by the beginning of 1930 and the central government had to cover the deficits incurred by the underfunded insurance scheme. The projected Young plan savings encouraged the parties of the centre and right to press for tax reductions to encourage industrial investment. An attempt to fund the government debt through a new domestic loan proved a failure, despite generous tax concessions to the wealthy. The resort to short-term borrowing fuelled criticism in industrial and banking circles and made foreigners increasingly pessimistic about Germany's financial future. Matters were not helped by Schacht's bizarre behaviour during the summer of 1929, which deeply annoyed both the French and British. Schacht publicly denounced the Young plan at the end of the year and, having failed to convince Hindenburg to veto its ratification, resigned on 6 March 1930. While Stresemann was at the Hague, the conflict between the SPD and the DVP over the deficit in the unemployment insurance fund threatened the life of the coalition. Against the advice of his doctors, the gravely ill Stresemann returned to Berlin in order to ward off the crisis. In his speech to the DVP Reich committee on 30 September he made an all-out attack on Hugenberg and his allies, warning of a future civil war if the right combined at the next election. His appeal for DVP concessions and continuing support for the left, while helping to save the immediate situation, did not unite his deeply divided party. It was his last rhetorical effort. On the morning of 3 October Stresemann died. He was in sight of the withdrawal of foreign troops from the Rhineland, but his final days were shadowed by fears for the troubled future of the Grand Coalition and the republic that he had so loyally served.

The Hague conference was a diplomatic setback for the French. In both sets of negotiations the British forced Briand to retreat. Snowden's treatment of Cheron left the French seething and the Young plan had been modified in ways contrary to their interests. Briand was forced to give way over the evacuation and had abandoned, for all intents and purposes, the Rhineland verification commission. He had agreed to talks on the Saar, though only an informal exchange of notifications took place at the Hague and the French hoped that the economic problems of the Saar would be settled prior to any political agreement. The British had fought many of Stresemann's battles for him and France was repeatedly isolated. Briand, nevertheless, refused to admit that he had given up much of real substance, and argued that the Young plan provided France with sufficient advantages to warrant acceptance of the earlier date for the Rhineland withdrawal. Unlike Poincaré, he had never believed that the occupation would assure the payment of reparations and considered it as nothing more than a useful threat. With the construction of the Maginot Line, the five-year prolongation was no longer considered a military necessity. Briand even hoped that a compromise over the Saar would bring about the closer Franco–German relationship implicit in Locarno. The balance sheet depended on what France would secure from the Young plan annuities and whether the Anglo-French line could be restored. There was a mixed response to the Hague agreements in Paris. The concessions made to the British and the subsequent Hugenberg–Hitler campaign in Germany raised doubts about the extent of Briand's reparation victory. Could the French capitalize on the portion of the reparation bonds placed on the American market before the troops left the Rhineland? Faced with criticism from moderates as well as extremists, Briand defended his retreat on the evacuation date and inspection issue. It was better to give in than to be publicly defeated, he told the Chamber Foreign Affairs Committee, and pointless to destroy what remained of the ententes with Britain and Belgium. Briand lost political ground, and his right-wing coalition, bequeathed to him by Poincaré, was severely shaken as the nationalists faced the reality of the Rhineland evacuation. His premiership came to an end on 22 October 1929, and President Doumergue asked the intellectually brilliant, dynamic, and witty André Tardieu to head the new ministry.

The second Hague conference took place between 3 and 20 January 1930. So much time had been consumed in settling Snowden's demands that many of the details of the earlier Hague agreement had to be decided at this second meeting. There were difficulties and disputes between the French and Germans over the commercialization of the reparation bonds, the character of the new Bank of International Settlements, the all-important (to the French) question of sanctions, and other measures to assure the demilitarization of the unoccupied Rhineland. For the most part, the French continued to retreat. The Germans refused to clarify details about commercialization and payment. The BIS was located in Basle and not in Brussels, and its role was more restricted than the French and Belgians had wished. The French abandoned the Treaty of Versailles sanctions (the possibility of reoccupying the Rhineland in the event of wilful default), though they received some support from Snowden, who was as anxious as they that Germany should pay its reparation bill. Tardieu secured a weak and vague formula that if the Permanent Court of International Justice (PCIJ), which would hear complaints, found against the debtor, the aggrieved parties were entitled to 'resume their full liberty of action'. The phrase meant anything or nothing, and consequently was acceptable to both the French and Germans. The bilateral conversations about the Saar failed to prosper; the Germans were anxious to buy back the mines and regain control as rapidly as possible, while the French experts fought to retain a share in the mine ownership and to get the best possible customs and trade deals for those French provinces dependent on the Saar markets. Whatever the difficulties, the Young plan was accepted and agreement reached on the withdrawal of troops from the Rhineland. The Hague conference appeared to live up to its promised goal of closing the books on the war.

There was even an attempt to settle the question of east European indebtedness. The Young Committee's recommendation that Germany should not be held responsible for the debts of her former allies Austria and Hungary opened the way for a settlement of the Hungarian reparations. Nothing could be expected in the way of payment from Austria, but Czechoslovakia, Yugoslavia, and Romania sought their due from Hungary despite counter-claims for compensation for losses of Hungarian citizens resident in the successor states. Thanks to French support and a Snowden-like campaign on the part of Beneš, the Little Entente powers won their reparations battle and the British were convinced by Louis Loucheur, the chairman of the Committee on Eastern Reparations, to create a number of financial 'pools' out of which the Hungarian counter-claims would be paid. Beneš managed to cajole the British and French, on the very last day of the conference, to pay part of the Czech liberation debt to Italy from funds that had been earmarked for Britain in order to satisfy Snowden's demands at the first Hague conference. The complex situation, created by the peace settlements, by which all seven of the successor states to the old Habsburg monarchy had inherited its debts but five of them were entitled to reparations was considerably simplified by the combined action of both the great and the small nations.

Much was hoped from the Hague agreements, yet during the next months the European clouds visibly darkened. This was due mainly to the worsening economic situation, but other sources of dissatisfaction and suspicion helped to poison the atmosphere. The Hague agreements were ratified in March 1930 by clear majorities in both the Reichstag and French Chamber of Deputies; in both instances, the debates revealed underlying anxieties about fulfilment. Despite hopes in London that the Hague accords would mark the end of the most troubling legacies of the Paris peace conference, the next months saw repeated disputes between the three governments. The British and Germans feared that the French might not leave the Rhineland because of the delays in the implementation of the Young plan. When the last French troops were withdrawn, along with the Inter-Allied Rhineland High Commission, on 30 June, nationalist celebrations in Germany and the absence of any expression of gratitude for France's prompt withdrawal created great offence. The speech by Julius Curtius, the new foreign minister, to the Reichstag on 25 June calling for the attainment of 'full political freedom and equality of rights' suggested that the German quest for revision had not ended but was about to restart. President Hindenburg's declaration of 1 July deploring the sufferings of the German people at the hands of the foreign occupiers rubbed further salt into the French wounds. The contrast between the French and German conceptions of what had been achieved could not have been more dramatically exposed. Suddenly and unexpectedly, French journalists and writers began to ask whether Europe was entering into a new pre-war period.

V

What had gone wrong? Why had the 'Conference for the Final Liquidation of the War' failed to set the European stage for a new and more harmonious chapter in Franco-German relations? Stresemann, Briand, and Chamberlain were practical men who genuinely sought to promote conciliation between their nations, yet their efforts had ended more in deadlock than in agreement. German revisionism accelerated despite having in Stresemann a foreign minister willing to work within the international system. France still found itself unwilling to make sufficient accommodation to German demands, despite having in Briand the most determined champion of reconciliation with Germany. Britain remained complacent that Locarno was sufficient involvement in continental affairs to achieve a Franco-German settlement, despite having in Chamberlain one of the most interventionist foreign secretaries of the inter-war period. The basic problem was structural: the Treaty of Versailles could not adequately address the fundamental gap between the French and German power positions. There was a basic conflict between French security and German recovery which the treaty did not solve. Any substantive revision of the treaty's terms in the German direction meant a loss of security for France. Though Stresemann and Briand had the imagination and courage to seek some way 'to bridge the apparently unbridgeable', their room for manoeuvre was small. The situation was made worse by the continuing French fears of the future German menace, which not only shadowed relations with Germany but increased France's dependency on Britain. Nor was the latter power willing to shoulder the burden of great-power adjustment. No outside pressures forced the Germans and French to agree. Quite apart from the absence of any clear and present danger to the peace, which lowered the price of failure, there was no common enemy that might have speeded up the process of negotiation. The American contribution to Europe's financial stability and economic prosperity was far too great to be compromised in such a manner, whatever the exasperation with its war-debt claims and trading practices. The Soviet Union was not viewed as the common enemy: all three of the Locarnites were amenable to engagement with Moscow on some level. The fluidity of the European system still left open possibilities for further adjustment; this made it easier to accept the risks of failure.

It was not just the failure of Germany and France to find a modus vivendi, but also the limitations of the American contribution to the final settlement which stalled further progress. Fundamental to the weaknesses of the Young plan was the determination of both the Coolidge and Hoover administrations to follow the same path that had led to the adoption of the Dawes plan and London agreements. Once again, American involvement in the formulation of a new reparation agreement and the subsequent mobilization of the reparations bonds would be left primarily to the banks. Because the circumstances in 1929 were so different from those in 1923–4, the influence of the experts was far more circumscribed than five years earlier. In the American case, there were clashes between Owen Young, the American head of the committee of experts, and the American president and secretary of the Treasury. Republican fears that the Bank of International Settlement would encourage a linkage between war debts and reparations precluded official American participation in its funding. The American government did intervene, but in a negative way, checking Young's efforts to reach a solution that might have compromised American independence. Indeed, they restricted Young in his willingness to further the European negotiations. The failure to achieve a successful breakthrough at the Hague was therefore due in part to the unwillingness of the administration to make the grand gesture and depart from the narrow confines of its version of liberal internationalism.

Democratic politics, party strife, and domestic distributive quarrels acted as major barriers to progress. It was Woodrow Wilson's belief that only democratic states could sustain a collective security system, but democratic forces do not always promote international conciliation. In the case of Germany and France, nationalist sentiment as reflected in the political parties and representative assemblies set limits on what even the most imaginative statesmen could do. Though in some measure both Stresemann and Briand shared the hopes and fears of their respective electorates, they tried to overcome exaggerated suspicions on either side. Neither man could move too quickly ahead of what was politically acceptable. Too short a time had elapsed since the war years, when governments beat the nationalist drums to demonize their opponents, to allow for real conciliation. There could be little more than a beginning to the bridge-building needed to create trust. Stresemann's attempts to sell his new conception of Germany's foreign-policy role proved increasingly unpopular after 1928, as the left and right grew impatient with the slow pace of change. Briand's efforts, too, were checked by rising political resistance to compromises that failed to pay any concrete dividends. Even in Britain, Chamberlain's ability to broker agreements was always restricted by the unwillingness of his own party to engage Britain too deeply in continental affairs. His unwillingness to grasp the nettle of disarmament fuelled Labour and Liberal criticism of his policies. In a very real sense, the failure to advance the stabilization process was more damaging to the Weimar republic than to Britain and France. The very existence of the Weimar republic was bound up with a successful foreign policy. What Stresemann had won was not sufficient to steady the Weimar coalition, as the onset of the depression exposed the fragility of its political base.

None of the Locarnites felt they had achieved their goals. They were soon replaced by men with narrower visions or, some would claim, with a stronger sense of realism. Chamberlain, now in opposition, became one of the sharpest critics of German revisionism in the Commons. Arthur Henderson, his successor, was not without imagination, but his League policy was no more successful than Locarno in strengthening European security. Two weeks after the ratification of the Young plan, on 27 March 1930, following a fierce attack on its economic programme that split the coalition, Müller's cabinet resigned. A minority coalition, including the SPD, the largest party in the Reichstag, took office under the Catholic Centrist Heinrich Brüning. The latter's position depended on President Hindenburg's support and the use of the presidential power of emergency decree under Article 48 of the Weimar constitution and the right to dissolve the parliament. The appointment might have revived the ailing structure of government; instead it proved to be the beginning of the end of the parliamentary system in Germany. Stresemann was replaced by Julius Curtius, who, while preaching continuity in foreign policy, was determined on a more assertive line of diplomacy. The new state secretary, Bernhard von Bülow, who became a member of Brüning's small circle of intimates, sought to strike a more independent note in German affairs, regardless of the French reaction.

Briand was the last of the Lorcarnites to survive politically: his ministry fell in October 1929, but he continued to serve as foreign minister under André Tardieu. Assisted by Berthelot and the almost equally important Alexis Léger, who was personally closer to his ageing chief than the secretary-general, Briand's political influence was visibly ebbing in 1929 and 1930 and his policies lost their *raison d'être* in the absence of positive results. A new generation of more hard-headed politicians came into prominence as Tardieu, who took over the direction of foreign affairs, tried to launch France on a different diplomatic course. The window of opportunity created in 1925 had almost closed.

Books: See bibliography for Chapters 8 and 12.

BECKER, JOSEF and HILDEBRAND, KLAUS (eds.), *Internationale Beziehungen in der Weltwirtschaftskrise, 1929–1933: Referate und Diskussionsbeiträge eines Augsburger Symposiums, 28. März bis 1. April 1979* (Munich, 1980).
BERSTEIN, SERGE, *Histoire du Parti Radical*, vol II; *Crise du Radicalisme, 1926–1939* (Paris, 1982).

BRACHER, KARL DIETRICH, *Die Auflösung der Weimarer Republik: eine Studie zum Machtverfall in der Demokratie* (Düsseldorf, 1978).

CARLTON, DAVID, *MacDonald versus Henderson: The Foreign Policy of the Second Labour Government* (London, 1970).

CARSTEN, FRANCIS L., *Reichswehr und Politik, 1918–1933* (Cologne, 1964).

HOWARD, MICHAEL E., *The Continental Commitment: The Dilemma of British Defence Policy in the Era of the Two World Wars* (London, 1972).

HUGHES, JUDITH, *To the Maginot Line: The Politics of French Military Preparations in the 1920s* (Cambridge, Mass., 1971).

KNIPPING, FRANZ, *Deutschland, Frankreich und das Ende der Locarno-Ära, 1928–1931: Studien zur internationalen Politik in der Anfangsphase der Weltwirtschaftskrise* (Munich, 1987).

KRUEDENER, J. VON, *Economic Crisis and Political Collapse: The Weimar Republic 1924–1933* (New York, Oxford, and Munich, 1990).

LEFFLER, MELVYN P., *The Elusive Quest: America's Pursuit of European Stability and French Security, 1919–1933* (Chapel Hill, NC, 1979).

MAXELON, MICHAEL-OLAF, *Stresemann und Frankreich, 1914–1929: Deutsche Politik der Ost-West Balance* (Düsseldorf, 1972).

MURRAY, WILLIAMSON, KNOX, MACGREGOR, and BERNSTEIN, ALVIN (eds.), *The Making of Strategy: Rulers, States and War* (Cambridge and New York, 1994).

NIEDHART, G., *Die Aussenpolitik der Weimarer Republik* (Munich, 1999).

PEGG, CARL H., *Evolution of the European Idea, 1914–1932* (Chapel Hill, NC, 1983).

PEREBOOM, M., *Democracies at the Turning Point: Britain, France and the End of the Post-War Order, 1928–1933* (New York 1995).

PITTS, VINCENT J., *France and the German Problem: Politics and Economics in the Locarno Period, 1924–1929* (New York, 1987).

ROOTH, TIM, *British Protectionism and the International Economy: Overseas Commercial Policy in the 1930s* (Cambridge, 1993).

SCHMIDT, GUSTAV (ed.), *Konstellationen Internationaler Politk, 1924–1932: Politische und Wirtschaftliche Faktoren in den Beziehungen zwischen Westeuropa un den Vereinigten Staaten* (Bochum, 1983).

STIRK, PETER M. R. (ed.), *European Unity in Context: The Interwar Period* (London, 1989).

WANDYCZ, PIOTR, *The Twilight of French Eastern Alliances, 1926–1936: French–Czechoslovak–Polish Relations from Locarno to the Remilitarization of the Rhineland* (Princeton, 1988).

WINKLER, HENRY, *Path Not Taken: British Labour and International Policy in the 1920s* (Chapel Hill, N.C. and London, 1999).

Articles

ALEXANDER, MARTIN, 'In Defence of the Maginot Line: Security Policy, Domestic Policies and the Economic Depression in France', in Robert W. D. Boyce (ed.), *French Foreign and Defence Policy, 1918–1940: The Decline and Fall of a Great Power* (London, 1998).

BADEL, LAURENCE, 'Trêve douanière, libéralisme et conjoncture, septembre 1929–mars 1930', *Relations internationales*, 82 (1995).

BAECHLER, CHRISTIAN, 'Une difficile négociation franco-allemande aux conférences de la Hague: le règlement de la question des sanctions, 1929–1930', *Revue d'Allemagne*, 12 (1980).

BARIÉTY, JACQUES, 'Les Relations franco-allemandes de 1924 à 1933', *Annales de la Société d'Histoire de la IIIème République* (1962–3).

—— 'Idée européenne et relations franco-allemandes', *Bulletin de la Faculté des lettres de Strasbourg*, 46 (1968).

BOYCE, ROBERT W. D., 'Business As Usual: The Limits of French Economic Diplomacy, 1926–1933', in id. (ed.), *French Foreign and Defence Policy, 1918–1940: The Decline and Fall of a Great Power* (London, 1998).

CAIRNS, JOHN, 'A Nation of Shopkeepers in Search of a Suitable France, 1919–1940', *American Historical Review*, 79: 3 (1974).

COSTIGLIOLA, F., ' "The Other Side Of Isolation": The Evolution of the First World Bank, 1929–30', *Journal of Economic History*, 59 (1972).

DEIST, WILHELM, 'The Rearmament of the Wehrmacht', in Militärgeschichtliches Forschungsamt (ed.), *Germany and the Second World War. Vol. 1: The Build-up of German Aggression* (Oxford, 1990).

FANNING, RICHARD, 'The Coolidge Conference of 1927: Disarmament in Disarray', in B. J. C. McKercher (ed.), *Arms Limitation and Disarmament: Restraints on War, 1899–1939* (Westport, Conn., 1992).

FERRIS, JOHN, ' "The Greatest Power on Earth": Great Britain in the 1920s', *International History Review*, 13: 4 (1991).

HIDEN, JOHN, 'The Weimar Republic and the Problem of the Auslandsdeutsche', *Journal of Contemporary History*, 12 (1977).

KEETON, EDWARD, 'Economics and Politics in Briand's German Policy, 1925–1931', in Carole Fink, Isabel V. Hull, and MacGregor Knox (eds.), *German Nationalism and the European Response, 1890–1945* (Norman, Okla., 1985).

KRÜGER, P., 'Friedenssicherheit und deutsche Revisionspolitik: die deutsche Außenpolitik und Verhandlungen über den Kellogg–Briand Pakt', *Vierteljahrshefte für Zeitgeschichte*, 22 (1974).

SALEWSKI, MICHAEL, 'Zur deutschen Sicherheitspolitik in der Spätzeit der Weimarer Republik', *Vierteljahrshefte für Zeitgeschichte*, 22 (1974).

SCHRÖDER, HANS-JÜRGEN, 'Deutsche Südosteuropapolitik, 1929–1936', *Geschichte und Gesellschaft*, 2 (1976).

SIEBURG, HEINZ-OTTO, 'Das Gespräch zu Thoiry', in Ernst Schulin (ed.), *Gedenkschrift Martin Göhring* (Weisbaden, 1973).

Survey of International Affairs (volumes released between 1926 and 1930).

TURNER, ARTHUR, 'Anglo-French Financial Relations in the 1920s', *European History Quarterly*, 26: 1 (1996).

WILLIAMSON, PHILIP, 'Safety First: Baldwin, the Conservative Party, and the 1929 General Election', *Historical Journal*, 25 (1982).

WURM, C. A., 'Internationale Kartelle and die deutsch-französischen Beziehungen, 1924–1930: Politik, Wirtschaft, Sicherheit', in S. A. Schuker (ed.) *Duntschland und Frankreich: Von Konflikt zur Aussohnung* (Munich, 2000).

10

Troubled Waters: Uncertainties in Italy, Eastern Europe, and the Soviet Union

Mussolini's Italy

I

'**H**ave faith in the Fascist revolution that will have in 1926 its Napoleonic year', Mussolini proclaimed. 'Have faith in the Italian people that today starts occupying its proper material and moral position in the world.'[1] Such declarations came easily to the boastful Duce, but the fulfilment of such goals was well beyond his grasp. Limited by his country's economic and military weakness and by the remaining checks on his power, he was engaged in a highly complex diplomatic game that ultimately created regional instability but brought few concrete revisionist rewards. The Locarno agreements heralded a Franco–German rapprochement that could block Italian expansion in the Balkans or redirect German attention to Austria and the South Tyrol but Mussolini's participation, however reluctant, increased his prestige (he anticipated a share of the Nobel Peace Prize) and opened up possibilities for manoeuvre. The restless Duce was anxious to start on his 'Napoleonic year'. Given his views about the centrality of violence and war in the creation of the new Italy and the new Italian citizen, neither was ruled out in the search for empire and glory. There was no simple plan or coherent strategy, but a driving ambition for the augmentation and expansion of Italian power. The brutal suppression of opposition at home was paralleled by the increasingly barbaric war against the Senussi in Libya. Mussolini's truculence and bravado found expression in warlike speeches and in a variety of plans for war. In 1925 military preparations were begun for a future invasion of Ethiopia. Between 1924 and 1926, taking advantage of the British clash with

[1] Angelo Del Boca, *Gli italiani in Africa orientale: La conquista dell'impero* (Rome, 1979), ii. 8.

the Turks over Mosul, Mussolini considered an invasion of Turkey. In 1926, in a moment of anger over Yugoslav recalcitrance, Mussolini ordered General Pietro Badoglio to mobilize twenty divisions to attack Yugoslavia, creating war scares in both Belgrade and Paris. The Italian leader's repeated demands that his service chiefs should prepare for a conflict against Yugoslavia, either alone or in partnership with France, aroused apprehension. In January 1928 the army chief of staff resigned and there was a 'quiet revolution' in the general staff. The dictator was warned that Italy could not survive even a defensive war against Yugoslavia, alone, not to speak of a Franco–Yugoslav campaign. The army, already getting the lion's share of the defence appropriations, would need far more funds if it were to contemplate any military action. Increased appropriations could not compensate for Italy's reliance on vital raw-material imports such as coal and oil, or for the many techno-logical deficiencies that plagued its defence industries.

The military chiefs succeeded in reining in their master. There was less opposition from the Palazzo Chigi, whose officials shared Mussolini's revisionism and had no love for the new successor states They would have preferred less risky and more orthodox forms of diplomacy and resented Mussolini's reliance on his nationalist cronies. When, in Janu-ary 1926, Mussolini threatened to cross the Brenner in defence of the Italian possession of the Alto Adige, Secretary-General Contarini, in-censed by this particular piece of bravado, resigned. Only one further appointment was made to the post of secretary-general; after 1927 it was left vacant, and was formally abolished in 1932. Contarini's resignation, like Dino Grandi's appointment as foreign minister in May 1929, did not lead to the anticipated fascist overhaul of the Foreign Ministry. New recruits to the service, the *ventottisti* who came in under the new terms (the old property qualification was dropped) of entry which were intended to attract young fascist party members, were initially posted to the consular service. It was only with time that the fascists gained greater influence in the service. Dino Grandi, whose unexpurgated diary reveals that he was in far greater agreement with Mussolini than his published diary suggests, was given considerable independence only because the Duce was prepared for a temporary pause in his foreign activities while the international situation remained in a state of flux. The new foreign minister (first appointed as under-secretary by Con-tarini because of his supposed malleability) hoped that by acting as mediator and balancer he could gain what had not been won by melodramatic gestures or threats of war. The foreign ministry officials were divided over the best road to revision. Many ex-nationalists felt that only co-operation with Britain or France would pave the way for colonial concessions in Africa and Asia Minor, though they disagreed among themselves about whose friendship was the most profitable. Others, like Raffaele Guariglia, the second most important official at the Palazzo Chigi, favoured the acquisition of colonies only as a means of achieving a much larger role on the continent. Guariglia's directorate was named 'Europe, Levant, and Africa' in order to indicate that his area of competence extended from the entire Mediterranean to the Red Sea and Ethiopia. Others at the foreign ministry were strong Slavophobes, anxious to move against Yugoslavia and establish Italy's place in the Balkans at French expense.

In these years the Duce shuffled his diplomatic cards and took a certain pride in the bewilderment of foreign diplomats, who found it difficult to assess his real intentions. His hatred of the French was one of the most enduring of his prejudices. While his attention was focused on the Balkans, in particular Yugoslavia, the French stood in his way. There was, nonetheless, room for negotiation, and a less ambitious statesman might have gained more if he had played his cards carefully. France was alarmed by Belgrade's militarism and would have preferred to avoid involvement in Yugoslavia's quarrels with Rome. They would have liked the tripartite alliance that Mussolini considered in 1925 but rejected when he was able to conclude his own bargain with Belgrade. Subsequent moves in Albania ended this truce and prompted Yugoslav appeals to the French, who with some reluctance finally agreed to an alliance, signed on 11 November 1927. As with the Franco-Romanian treaty of the previous year, it contained arbitration provisions intended to protect France from involvement in Balkan quarrels and restricted its obligations for consultation to the outbreak of war. The French move was intended not just to deter Italy but to keep the Yugoslavs in check. As Mussolini saw the alliance as a direct challenge to Italy's legitimate expansionist aspirations, it served as a spur to further moves against Yugoslavia. These moves did not mean, however, the end of exchanges with the receptive French.

Briand took up the possibility of new conversations at the start of 1927. The Quai d'Orsay was cautious; Philippe Berthelot, the secretary-general, was opposed to any agreement that might compromise France's relations with 'our most solid clientele', the Little Entente countries. Briand wanted a treaty of arbitration and conciliation and was willing to discuss such disputed questions as Tunisia, where the French wanted to revoke the accords of 1896 and naturalize its large Italian population, and colonial concessions in north-east Africa. During the next months there were moments when Mussolini believed that he could divorce Tunisia, colonies, and other items on the Italian agenda from the contest for influence in the Balkans. Hostile moves on both sides in 1927, including the Italian friendship agreement with Hungary of April 1927 and that of France with Yugoslavia in November, soured the atmosphere. It was not until the spring of 1928 that Briand formally instructed his new ambassador, Count Maurice de Beaumarchais, to approach the Italian leader to reopen talks. Mussolini responded positively, insisting, however, that the resolution of colonial questions must precede any general treaty of friendship and arbitration. Mussolini outlined his demands: the continuation of the 1896 convention on Tunis for another five years; the delineation of the south and western boundaries of Libya; the recognition of Italy's prior claim over Germany to mandates. In August Beaumarchais presented the first draft of the treaty, which Mussolini agreed to study. After prolonged exchanges the French were finally persuaded to offer concessions over Tunisia and the Libyan frontiers, and these, along with the text of the treaty of friendship and arbitration, were officially submitted to the Italians on 21 December 1928. There was no official Italian response for over six months, and when it came the Duce's answer was totally negative and the negotiations came to a halt. Mussolini demanded that the 1896 Tunisian conventions be kept for a minimum of ten years without modification and demanded large increases in the tracts of territory to be ceded along the Libyan frontier. If the French wanted an agreement, they would have to pay the price. Hints regarding the modification of France's support for Yugoslavia or concessions on the question of naval disarmament fell on deaf ears in Paris.

Mussolini's and Briand's priorities were not the same. The French wanted Italian recognition of their predominant influence in the Mediterranean and an assurance of future support against Germany, but would not offer significant concessions to secure them. Nor would they compromise their alliance with Yugoslavia. On the Italian side, the talks were torpedoed by Raffaele Guariglia, who felt that only peripheral questions were being discussed while the real issue was Yugoslavia. His proposal on Libya, claiming most of French Equatorial Africa, was intended to elicit a French refusal. Mussolini found the French annoyingly resistant to his claims to 'legitimate expansion'. Relations between the two governments became increasingly strained over Tunisia and the activities of the anti-fascist émigrés in France. While Briand and Stresemann were trying to negotiate their differences, there was no compelling reason for the French to court the fascist leader and more than a hint of condescension in their treatment of Rome. For Mussolini, France became the very symbol of the decadent liberal state and his propagandists went into overdrive beating the ideological drum.

Mussolini found the British more sympathetic to his cause. He was fortunate in his newly acquired friendship with Chamberlain, who, on the occasion of his first meeting with Mussolini, agreed to abandon any

British political interests in Albania and recognize Italian priority with regard to competing oil claims. Chamberlain was not a naive admirer of the Italian dictator, but, like so many others, welcomed the success of the fascists as the party of order and anti-Bolshevism. He was not, at first, averse to having Italy as a check on French ambitions in the Balkans, nor unduly disturbed by Italian pressure on Turkey at a time when Britain was at odds with Ankara over Mosul. The foreign secretary recognized that Mussolini was a mercurial and unpredictable statesman (there was already talk of a possible 'mad dog' act), and highly sensitive to any slight, but he believed that the Duce's bark was worse than his bite, and if properly handled, he would not disturb the peace of Europe. Chamberlain assumed that population pressure alone would inevitably lead to a programme of expansion, but hoped that Mussolini would look to Asia Minor and Africa rather than to south-eastern Europe for relief. In 1924 the British and Egyptians agreed to cede territory in North Africa; the latter, under considerable British pressure, gave up the oasis of Jarabub on the Libyan frontier. The Foreign Office was willing, moreover, to agree to a division of economic interests in Ethiopia. While willing to tolerate Italian concession-hunting in Egypt, Chamberlain became less conciliatory when the activities of Italian representatives in Egypt and Yemen began to threaten the British position in the Red Sea area and Arabian peninsula. There was a sharp clash in 1928, when the British were having difficulties with the Egyptian nationalists who were backed by the Italians, and when the Italian governor in Eritrea encouraged Yemeni expansionism at the expense of local British allies. Unlike some of his local officials, however, Mussolini was cautious about twisting the lion's tail. In December 1926 he warned the head of the Italian legation in Egypt that 'Political developments in Egypt will not be affected or even influenced by anything we can do. It is childish to challenge Britain in this field [Egypt] and face her hostility.'[2] Whatever his posturings in the Red Sea region, in Arabia, and North Africa, there was not much Mussolini could do against the British. With only about 50,000 Italians actually settled in the existing Italian empire by 1930 and none of the Italian claims to a mandate or to a special position in Palestine recognized, some of Mussolini's advisors felt that he should take up the cause of the local nationalists against the colonial powers. After a brief flirtation with this idea in 1930, it was dropped. An alignment with nationalists overseas lost out to fascist claims for white supremacy in Africa and the moral superiority of Italian rule over other foreign imperialists.

    [2] Haggai Erlich, 'Mussolini in the Middle East in the 1920s', in Uriel Dann (ed.), *The Great Powers in the Middle East, 1919–1939* (New York and London, 1988), 217.

Chamberlain accepted Mussolini's 1926 treaty with Zogu, the crafty Albanian leader, preferring the Italians to the Yugoslavs as underwriters in Albania. There were, however, limits to his willingness to countenance Italian revisionism. Chamberlain's first loyalty was to Briand, and he had no wish to see major conflicts in the Balkans. He took umbrage at the second Treaty of Tirana in 1927 and the reduction of Albania to the status of an Italian protectorate. He came to view Mussolini's intrigues against the Little Entente and his approaches to Romania and Hungary with increasing distrust. He was distinctly alarmed by the Duce's public support for the revision of the Treaty of Trianon, as reported in Lord Rothermere's pro-Hungarian *Daily Mail* in March 1928. Chamberlain's relations with the Duce turned cool. There was an attempted reconciliation between the two men, but Anglo-Italian relations were not restored to their former standing before the Labour victory in London in 1929.

Well before Labour took power, Mussolini began to abandon his policy of joint action in the eastern Mediterranean and the Red Sea. Italy concluded a separate treaty of friendship and arbitration with the Ethiopians in August 1928, winning the right to build a road linking Eritrea and Italian Somaliland. The Duce also took steps to create links with Turkey and Greece, intended to isolate Yugoslavia and to make Italy the chief arbiter of conflicts in the eastern Mediterranean. The turn towards Turkey, though connected with the rapprochement between London and Ankara, was not entirely welcome in London. Once separate Italian agreements were concluded with Turkey in August 1928 and with Greece in September 1928, Mussolini began to work for a settlement between the two countries whose relations were still strained over the forced post-war transfers of populations. Mussolini's inflated hopes to establish Italy as the dominant power in the eastern Mediterranean and to create an Italian-dominated Balkan bloc that would link Turkey, Greece, Bulgaria, and Hungary were soon frustrated. Venizelos, who returned to the premiership of Greece in 1928 and remained in office until 1933, embarked on a series of bilateral agreements that cut right across Mussolini's schemes. The Greek premier concluded a Pact of Friendship with Yugoslavia in March 1929 and the Convention of Ankara with Turkey in October 1930. The Greeks also took the initiative in setting up an annual Balkan conference in 1928 to study questions of common interest, particularly of an economic nature, with the ultimate aim of establishing some kind of regional union. The idea was supported by a variety of Balkan governments, for it allowed them to test possible solutions to contentious problems without officially committing themselves. By the time of its fourth conference in November 1933, Greece, Romania, and

Yugoslavia had moved to turn the meetings into a permanent regional organization. The Balkan pact was signed in Athens in February 1934 by Greece, Romania, Turkey, and Yugoslavia. The new grouping was intended to resist all forms of territorial revisionism. Since it guaranteed existing frontiers, Bulgaria refused to join, considerably weakening its importance. Albania too, which had participated in the conference from 1931, rejected participation.

While there was no love lost between Mussolini and Stresemann, the Duce continued to think that the Germans might become co-partners in the revision of the peace treaties. Notwithstanding their differences, following the conclusion of a German–Italian arbitration pact Stresemann sought Italian support against France in the negotiations over the abolition of the Military Control Commission in the Rhineland. In September 1927 Mussolini played with the idea of an Italian–Hungarian–German combination against the Little Entente states. There were indications, moreover, that he was not above trading opposition to *Anschluss* for a guarantee of Italian possession of the South Tyrol. It may be—though this is pure speculation—that hopes for some future arrangement with Germany over Austria were an additional reason for his unwillingness to come to an agreement with Ignaz Seipel, the Christian Socialist chancellor of Austria (1922–4, 1926–9), despite the latter's promises to move against the irredentist groups in South Tyrol.

In Rome there were conflicting views about the value of a partnership with Germany. Some, like Italo Balbo, the chief of the Italian air force, wanted to cultivate German friendship, but others feared that with its recovery Germany would re-enter the colonial field and prove a successful competitor against the Italians. While Stresemann remained in office any real rapprochement seemed unlikely. The broader European alignments, rather than ideological differences, determined the state of Italo-German relations. Italian overtures to Berlin reflected the state of Franco-Italian hostility, while Stresemann's response was conditioned by the requirements of his western policies. The Germans preferred, wherever possible, to remain neutral in any conflicts between France and Italy. On the whole, Stresemann tried to avoid involvement in the regional politics of the Balkans.

There were continuing secret Italian contacts with German right-wing nationalist groups, including the National Socialists, though the Palazzo Chigi was not prepared to receive Hitler. Cold water was thrown on the upstart Austrian's efforts to contrive a meeting with Mussolini and a deaf ear turned towards Hitler's speeches about shelving the Alto Adige question. Hermann Göring, already one of Hitler's most important lieutenants, paid two visits to Rome, the first in the spring of 1924 and the second in November 1929. In neither case did he actually see Mussolini, but in 1929 he had a number of meetings with the Duce's German-speaking mistress, Margherita Sarfatti. By the time he met Mussolini in May 1931 the Nazis' electoral successes and the efforts of Giuseppe Renzetti, Mussolini's private go-between, had cleared the way for a cordial reception. Göring also met Italo Balbo, the air-force chief, and the two men developed a close personal relationship that withstood their future political differences. An additional and not un-important personal link was established between the fascists and the Nazis through Prince Philip of Hesse. In 1925 Prince Philip, a nephew of Kaiser Wilhelm, married Mafalda of Savoy, the second child of the Italian king. The couple settled in Berlin; the prince joined the Nazi party in 1930. The couple were frequent guests at Carinhall, Göring's sumptuous country residence. Hitler liked Philip, if not his independent wife, and found his social connections of great use in Rome, particularly with the now isolated Italian king, Victor Emanuelle III, who had accepted the establishment of Mussolini's dictatorship and the infringe-ment of his own powers without open protest. A decade later Prince Philip would reappear as Hitler's messenger boy in communicating with the Duce. Italian contacts with the Nazis did not preclude continuing exchanges and support for the Stahlhelm and the DNVP, and the sending of arms to rightist groups in South Germany.

II

Without any realistic hope of finding a great-power backer for his Balkan ambitions, Mussolini advanced his cause by picking on the weakest state in the region while taking all possible steps to isolate Yugoslavia through local alignments. Zogu, in perpetual need of money and faced with an uprising in the north of his country, was prepared to trade Albanian independence for Italian financial support. Britain's withdrawal from Albania left him little choice but to deal with his enemies; Italy offered more than Yugoslavia. The second Treaty of Tirana (November 1927) was a twenty-year defensive alliance that conferred on the Italians an indefinite right to interfere in Albania's internal policies and to take whatever military measures thought necessary to preserve its territorial integrity and political independence. The Italians already controlled Albanian banking and loans; the Italian-financed bridges and roads were constructed with Rome's military needs in mind. The Albanian army came under Italian supervision and a stream of Italian officers and supplies entered the country. With Italian approval, in 1928 Zogu became King Zog I of the Albanians and consolidated his rule over the country. It was a costly affair for the Italians. The economic benefits for Italy were few, and Zog proved an expensive and troublesome client.

Despite vacillations in policy and pressure from those foreign ministry officials who favoured colonial expansion in Africa over a settlement with Yugoslavia, Mussolini's anti-Belgrade sentiments prevailed. Mussolini's moves in Albania, the subsidies to Croatian resistance groups and Macedonian irredentists, and the courting of Romania and Hungary were all part of his offensive against Yugoslavia. Even Mussolini's policy of denationalizing the Slovenes and Croats of Venezia Giulia, inaugurated in the summer of 1927, was intended to show the power of the fascist government in its duel with Belgrade. Typically, Mussolini encouraged discreet negotiations with Belgrade as favoured by the foreign ministry, while doing everything possible to undermine its unity. In June 1928 Stephen Radić, the leader of the opposition Croat Peasant party, was shot and fatally wounded during one of the typically tumultuous sessions of the Skupstina, the Yugoslav parliament. His death in August mobilized all the warring Croatian political parties in a major campaign for separatism and accelerated their search for an outside patron. Mussolini was cautious about fishing in these troubled waters, as he had his own irredentist ambitions in Croatian-populated Macedonia and had the support of only scattered and contending groups of Croatians. When King Alexander imposed his military dictatorship on Yugoslavia in January 1930 and moved in a pro-Serbian direction, the Croat lawyer and leader Ante Pavelić broke with his gradualist allies and fled to Italy. Having abandoned the negotiations with France, mainly because of its unwillingness to give him a free hand in the Balkans, Mussolini decided to give aid and assistance to Pavelić's terrorist organization, the Ustasa, modelled on the terrorist Internal Macedonian Revolutionary Organization (IMRO) in Bulgaria. The Ustasa was sworn to conduct a Holy War against the Serbs by all possible means. For the most part, Italian activity in Yugoslavia consisted of making contacts and gathering information rather than offering actual support for the terrorists, for Mussolini remained somewhat ambivalent. He was far more positive about the anti-Yugoslav IMRO, which had the backing of several key figures in the Bulgarian government. His sponsorship was much disliked by Austen Chamberlain, who wanted Sofia to act against the IMRO. In an endlessly complicated game, the Italians found themselves supporting both factions of IMRO, engaged in a bloody fratricidal war, and subsequently picked the losing side when choosing between them. Much of this covert action, only partly known to the Italian diplomats, turned out to be far more trouble than it was worth and even counter-productive.

Friendless Bulgaria seemed easy prey for the Italians. Under the leadership of Andrei Liapchev (1926–31), a Montenegrin who either would or could not impose controls on IMRO, the Bulgarians, because of the ceaseless action in Macedonia, were in difficulties with both the Greeks and the Yugoslavs. Mussolini's attempts to exploit the situation to Italy's advantage were thwarted by the growing weakness and fractionalization of the Liapchev government; in 1926 nineteen groups were represented in parliament. In 1929 Mussolini visited King Boris of Bulgaria and encouraged him in his designs on Greek-occupied Thrace, hoping to gain an additional bargaining card in Athens. In the following year ties were strengthened when Boris married Princess Giovenna of Savoy, the daughter of the king of Italy. Yet Mussolini's courtship of the king and Liapchev came to nought. Unable to cope with the economic problems created by the worsening depression, Liapchev's government lost the election of 1931.

For a short time it appeared that Mussolini might have some success with the Romanians, who were anxious to take advantage of the Soviet Union's post-Locarno isolation. Mussolini was attracted both by Romania's much-coveted oil deposits and by the possibility of associating Romania with Hungary and Bulgaria in a quadruple pact. He was loath, however, to incur the hostility of the Russians by ratifying the Bessarabian protocol of 1920 recognizing Romanian sovereignty over Bessarabia. The links with Moscow were useful for commercial reasons; the Russians were also possible partners in the Balkans and in Asia Minor. The brief return to power of the anti-Russian General Averescu in Bucharest in early 1926 opened the way for talks. An agreement was reached in September; the Italians recognized the annexation of Bessarabia and accepted a secret clause promising military support in case of either Russian or Hungarian aggression. Mussolini hoped that its secrecy might allow him to avoid offending the Soviet Union. The decision taken to ratify the treaty on 1 February 1927 was connected with Mussolini's need to minimize Romanian opposition to his talks with the Hungarians, with whom the Romanians were in open conflict over Transylvania and over demands for compensation for the Magyar landowners who found themselves on the Romanian side of the border, and whose homes and property were expropriated when they opted to move to Hungary. It quickly became clear that Averescu's Italian orientation was unpopular with the king and the ruling Liberals, the strongest political organization in the country, who suspected that the general hoped to establish a dictatorship. Romania was in no position to move too far from either the anti-Hungarian Little Entente or from France, its chief protector and most important source of investment funds. Nicolae Titulescu, a leading Balkan statesman and an important figure in Geneva (chairman of the League Assembly in 1931) first became foreign minister in June 1927 in the new Liberal government (only 22.6 of the eligible voters went to the polls) under Vintilă Brătianu. At first

Titulescu tried to keep the lines to Rome open, but there was no way that the Romanians could swallow the growing Italian friendship with Hungary. As so often, Mussolini's attempts to cut across the regional disputes in the Balkans in order to isolate Yugoslavia and undermine French influence failed to achieve their purpose. He could not mediate the Romanian–Hungarian dispute or that between Romania and Bulgaria over Dobruja. Titulescu had a successful visit to Belgrade in 1928, and in May 1929 the chiefs of staff of the Little Entente powers agreed to prepare common plans against any foreign threat to the three countries. Mussolini had his greatest success with the Hungarians. Enjoying a relatively calm and prosperous period under Count Bethlen's authoritarian leadership, the Hungarians were anxious to break out of their diplomatic isolation and, with the withdrawal of British interest, were shopping for great-power support. The extremely astute and energetic Hungarian premier approached Grandi at Geneva in 1926. Temporarily rebuffed, he turned instead to Yugoslavia, the least anti-Magyar member of the Little Entente. Mussolini, in response, quickly took up the Hungarian approach and invited Count Bethlen to Rome in April 1927, just at the time when Lord Rothermere was beating the Hungarian revisionist drum in the *Daily Mail*. The grounds for the Italian–Hungarian alliance were narrowly drawn. Bethlen wanted Italian support in his quarrels with Romania over Transylvania and backing for Hungarian claims against Czechoslovakia. Mussolini was willing to support Hungarian revisionism against Yugoslavia but not against Bucharest or Prague. An agreement was signed in April 1927, and the alliance between Mussolini and Bethlen concluded in Milan in April 1928. The two countries decided on a common policy towards Yugoslavia, secret Italian assistance in the rearming of Hungary, and cooperation in finding an Austrian government amenable to their joint direction. Arrangements were made for subsidies to the Austrian Heimwehr, already under the patronage of the Hungarian army. Nothing was said about Transylvania, and Mussolini tried to avoid taking sides on the 'optants' quarrel with the Romanians until the issue was referred to the League Council, when he felt compelled to take the Hungarian side. Austen Chamberlain complained bitterly about the Duce's decision, accusing the Italians of having sold their vote for some indirect and obscure political purpose. Relations with Budapest cooled when Mussolini learned of the pro-German orientation of the Hungarian general staff in 1929. He immediately invited Count Bethlen to send Hungarian air force officers to Italy for training and offered to mediate the question of the 'optants'.

Though anxious to have Hungarian backing against Yugoslavia, Mussolini did not want to become entangled in central European affairs.

The Italians had rejected Beneš's overtures for an eastern Locarno, but with little confidence in either the Slovak or Ruthenian liberation movements, preferred not to underwrite Hungarian aspirations against Czechoslovakia. There were also differences over Austria. Mussolini had little sympathy for the Hungarian Legitimists' programme for a restoration of the Habsburgs or for the revival of the Austro-Hungarian empire. Nor did he have much patience with the pro-*Anschluss*, anti-Habsburg views of the Right Radicals in Hungary. The latter were fervent Hungarian nationalists and intensely loyal to the regent, Admiral Horthy, but like Horthy and Bethlen, were mainly Calvinists who would lose a great deal from a Catholic restoration. They tended to favour a German–Austrian union. Bethlen, who carefully distanced himself from the whole 'king question', was well aware of the doubts among his supporters about the new links with Italy. The bankers, important for Bethlen's economic development plans, opposed any changes that might adversely affect foreign investment; the Legitimists were hostile towards Mussolini and unwilling to accept an alliance with a country still at odds with the papacy, and the left opposition favoured alignment with the Little Entente countries. Though Bethlen moved warily, he pressed forward with the idea of a Hungarian–Italian–German front. With strong Hungarian encouragement, Mussolini further increased his subsidies to the Austrian Heimwehr, hoping for a *coup d'état* and the replacement of the Christian Socialists by this right-wing, anti-socialist movement which began, as did so many such movements, with a core of demobilized soldiers anxious to protect their lands from the dangers of Bolsheviks, Slavs, and Italians.

While supposedly championing Austrian independence, Mussolini was trying, by covert means, to unseat its existing government. He strongly disliked the Christian Socialist chancellor, Ignaz Seipel, who was equally anti-Mussolini, but also despised Seipel's socialist opponents. The Heimwehr was a politically marginal movement, and with a conservative-clerical government in office, its appeal was limited. Its strength lay in the provinces, where Pan-Germanism and South Tyroleon irredentism were strong. When, in the autumn of 1928, the Heimwehr made its move for a 'march on Vienna', Seipel was able to block the projected *putsch*. Thereafter the organization changed its tactics, hoping to solicit broader bourgeois support by taking power through legal means. In April 1929 Seipel, who had modified his anti-Italian position in order to seek support for a renewal of the Austrian loan, suddenly resigned and was replaced by a very weak and short-lived government under Steeruwitz. Already worried by King Alexander's establishment of a dictatorship in Yugoslavia and the election of a Labour government in London in June 1929, Grandi and his officials urged Mussolini to divorce Italy's Austrian policy from Hungarian patronage and conclude a separate agreement with Vienna. Grandi's policy was given further impetus when the existing government fell and was replaced by a 'cabinet of experts' headed by Johannes Schober, the Viennese police chief who had crushed the socialist 'uprising' in the city in 1927. Given Schober's anti-Marxist reputation and known earlier contacts with the Heimwehr, Mussolini gave Grandi a free hand to negotiate a settlement with the new Austrian chancellor.

Mussolini had one great success in 1929, the conclusion of the Lateran agreements on 11 February of that year. It was a striking domestic victory which allowed the Duce to complete his mastery of Italy and tighten his grip on the state. His dictatorship depended on a series of compromises with the traditional institutions of the Italian state, and the Catholic Church was undoubtedly one of the most important of these. There was genuine and widespread popular support for the *Conciliazione*. Mussolini had succeeded where Cavour had failed; he had completed the process of Italian unification. The agreements with the papacy, which established the sovereign state of the Vatican in Rome, provided financial restitution to the Vatican for the Italian seizure of the Papal States in 1870 (making the Church one of the largest holders of Italian state bonds), and recognized the special status of the Catholic Church in Italy, proved to be the Duce's one lasting legacy. The Lateran accords gave his regime international legitimacy and were much applauded abroad, Though there were later differences between the Duce and Pius XI, a determined and autocratic pope, the Vatican connection proved diplomatically useful to the Italians. Otherwise Mussolini had little to show for his ceaseless activity. Even the agreement with Hungary was not an unmixed blessing, as it increased the danger of Hungarian revisionism in central Europe, where Mussolini wanted to maintain the status quo. Neither Bulgaria, Greece, nor Turkey joined the anti-Yugoslav camp and the Little Entente remained intact. Mussolini's policies had alienated the British just as the new Labour government, anti-fascist on principle, had taken office, and relations with France were at a low ebb. Mussolini showed only contempt for Briand's efforts at conciliation and European integration.

By 1929 Mussolini's position at home had become so unassailable that he could afford to give up some of his many offices. In May the portfolio of foreign minister was given to his under-secretary at the Palazzo Chigi, Dino Grandi. The new appointee shared Mussolini's hopes for imperial expansion in the Mediterranean and in Africa. 'The Adriatic is no longer sufficient to defend our independence as the Mediterranean race from the Slavic races', he told the Fascist Grand Council on 5 February 1929. 'It is imperative that beyond the Adriatic and on the Adriatic shores, which is surely a trench that separates East from West, a chain of states must be constituted, from the Channel of Otranto to the Nevoso, each a bridge-head under Italy's control. We have made Albania, we must make Croatia.'[3] Grandi's differences from Mussolini were those of tactics rather than of ends. He preferred to negotiate with the great powers to secure the breathing space Italy needed to build up its armed forces and launch its great campaigns. In December 1929 he convinced his master to *cloroformizzare* the overwrought nerves of Yugoslavia and to again approach the French. The calling of a new naval disarmament conference in London in 1930 gave Grandi the opportunity to negotiate with Paris and to ingratiate himself with the new British government. While believing that there had to be war with France one day, he knew that the Italians would have to make careful preparations before taking action. For Grandi, the preliminary naval talks with the French were of the greatest importance. As he was instructed, however, to insist on naval parity with France, the talks first stalled, and were only resumed because of British pressure and active intervention. For one brief moment, in March 1931, Grandi thought he had won the prize that he wanted, the settlement with France, only to have it snatched away when the French demanded the revision of the key naval clauses undermining the whole arrangement. Believing that France was 'possessed by the fever to be with us', he had boasted to Mussolini, 'it will allow us to be more intransigent about essential matters'.[4] Instead, the Duce had to caution his irate minister against retaliatory action. A warning from Marshal Badoglio, the Italian chief of staff, that Italy was in no position to take on its Alpine neighbour, not to speak of France and Yugoslavia together, only confirmed what Grandi already knew: 'our military forces are and will later be even more in a position to successfully conclude a confrontation with Yugoslavia—however, they are not and will not be so for a confrontation with France. I don't even think about the possibility of both France and Yugoslavia—that would be suicide.'[5] The March talks and Grandi's espousal of the disarmament cause at Geneva considerably improved relations with Arthur Henderson, who visited Rome in early March 1931, and was more inclined to blame France than Italy for the failure of the naval negotiations.

Grandi also initiated a move towards Belgrade. In early January 1929, when King Alexander took command of the government, the way was prepared for the restructuring of the renamed Kingdom of Yugoslavia.

---

[3] H. James Burgwyn, 'Conflict or Rapprochement? Grandi Confronts France and its Protégé, Yugoslavia: 1929–1932', *Storia delle relazioni internazionali* (1987), 75.
[4] Ibid. 83.
[5] Badoglio to Grandi, 28 Mar. 1931, *DDI*, 7th ser., vol. 10, no. 174 (author's translation).

There was still no place for the Croats in the highly centralized state. The Croat separatists again turned to Mussolini but found the Duce reluctant to go beyond the secret subsidies that were under his personal control. Fearing that the French might abandon them, the Yugoslav leaders looked for alternative openings in Rome and in Berlin. In May 1930 Grandi was instructed to 'calm the spirits, but proceed slowly'.[6] Mussolini set the terms for the agreement: the recognition of Italian predominance in Albania and the end of Yugoslavia's military ties with France. Hopes for success were scarcely improved when the Italians executed four captured Slovene terrorists at Trieste after a much-publicized trial. The waves of anti–Italian feeling that swept through parts of Yugoslavia did not prevent King Alexander and his foreign minister from pursuing their new opening. In a letter to Mussolini written on 12 November, and clearly intended to please the Duce, Grandi insisted that: 'A possible accord with Belgrade must always be considered as a transitory and useful device to mark time; and, in practice, to take away from France the initiative of the war (potential or actual) against us, at a moment that is not favourable to us.'[7] Grandi was later to claim that a golden opportunity for settling affairs in the Adriatic and Balkans was lost due to Mussolini's bellicosity and intransigence. The two men, equally inconsistent and changeable in their short-term tactics, often worked at cross purposes. The Duce constantly interfered in Grandi's negotiations while pursuing his own independent line of diplomacy. It is a mistake, nonetheless, to see Grandi, as he depicts himself, as the Machiavellian realist whose attempts to improve Italy's position through careful and pacific diplomacy were ruined by his more impetuous master. There were times when Grandi proved more unyielding than the Duce, and he was certainly no less determined to make the Yugoslavs accept a subordinate place in any relationship with Rome. By the start of 1931 Alexander and his foreign minister were becoming less interested in agreement. The pact with Greece and the successful conclusion of talks for a desperately needed French loan (which included an Italian contribution) strengthened Yugoslavia's diplomatic position. The proposed agreement with Mussolini would have been highly unpopular with the Slovenes and could have damaged Belgrade's revived links with France.

More immediately rewarding was Grandi's rapprochement with the new Austrian chancellor Johannes Schober, the non–party man who was determined to rule free of parliamentary restraints and all other political ties, including those with the Heimwehr, that had helped him to

---

[6] Minute by Grandi, 12 May 1930, *DDI*, 7th ser., vol. 9, no. 29.
[7] Ibid., no. 370.

achieve power. Schober set about trying to improve the parlous state of Austria's finances. He worked to lift the Italian ban on a new international loan while cultivating the Germans. He also managed to satisfy the British and French conditions for financial assistance by disarming the political armies of both right and left. Rather than appease the Hungarians as Mussolini wanted, Grandi successfully argued for an independent approach at Vienna. By the end of the year the Italian veto on the Austrian loan had been withdrawn and Schober, who had agreed to control the irredentist movements in the South Tyrol, announced that his foreign policy would be based on friendship with Italy. Mussolini became more enthusiastic about the new talks once the chancellor asked about the possibility of buying arms from Italy. Schober's visit to Rome was a great success and the new relationship was sealed by an Italo–Austrian treaty signed on 6 February 1930.

The treaty did not prevent Schober from agreeing in principle to the German-proposed customs union when he visited Berlin following his Rome trip. Nor did Mussolini cease to subsidize the Heimwehr, now pledged to end democracy and create a corporate state along fascist lines. Through personal agents, Mussolini also encouraged the ambitions of the Legitimists both in Austria and Hungary in the far-fetched hope that a Habsburg restoration might check growing German influence in the Danube basin. In a curious move, pointing in the opposite direction, Mussolini unsuccessfully set out to convince ex-Empress Zita to renounce Archduke Otto's claim to the Austrian crown in the summer of 1930, though he allowed her to come to live in Italy as a gesture of support. On 30 September Schober resigned and a new Christian Socialist-Heimwehr government, with Karl Vaugoin as chancellor, Ignaz Seipel as minister of foreign affairs, and Count Starhemberg, the Heimwehr leader, as minister of the interior, took office. This cabinet opened the attractive prospect of a greatly expanded Italian role in Vienna. Coupled with the massive rise in the Nazi vote in the September 1930 German elections, Mussolini felt that he was riding the crest of the fascist wave. On 27 October 1930, for the first time in public, Mussolini declared that fascism should be considered a universal principle, and therefore an article for export. Believing that he could mobilize the state apparatus to protect Italy's battered economy from outside deflationary pressures, Mussolini could claim that fascism and corporatism represented the successful middle way between capitalism and Bolshevism in these depression years.

Mussolini and Grandi believed that the European situation favoured Italian revisionism. The increasing fluidity of inter-state relations and the success of authoritarian and right-wing movements suited Mussolini's purposes. The weakness of France could be diplomatically exploited.

With this in mind, and because it was necessary to make cuts in the
Italian defence budgets, Grandi played the peace card at Geneva and
became an advocate of disarmament. He also encouraged the Russians,
agreeing to pave the way for Soviet participation in the European talks
on the Briand plan in May 1931. If Litvinov hoped to expand these
contacts and secure a non-aggression pact with Rome, he was to be
disappointed. Grandi and his officials were prepared to use the Soviet
Union against the French, but like many others in the west, believed
that the country was too weak to assist in the fulfilment of their aims.
Such an agreement would alienate the many states whose co-operation
was essential for successful revisionism.

It was true that in the fragmented Europe of the early 1930s, where
alignments were weak and governments struggling to cope with the
ravages of the depression, a power of the middle rank could exercise an
influence out of proportion to its strength. The danger lay in the Duce's
exaggerated view of Italy's freedom of manoeuvre. Until a major nation
proved willing to back his more grandiose objectives, the rewards even
for the most Machiavellian dictator would prove inadequate. It was
Italy's great misfortune that Mussolini came to believe that Nazi
Germany could provide that extra piece on the chessboard and allow
him to disregard the limits of Italian power.

Uncertainties in Eastern Europe

I

Despite Mussolini's restlessness, there was little change in the position of
the states in south-east Europe in the post-Locarno period. No challenge to the independence of any country, with Albania's exception,
succeeded, and no significant change in the regional balance of power
took place. This was equally true in central Europe. Both Weimar
Germany and the Soviet Union accepted the status quo for the time
being; the former deferred its claims to territorial adjustments and the
latter tried to improve its European position and balance its dependence
on Germany by concluding non-aggression treaties with its neighbours.
The French, with British prompting, took a less positive view of the
links with their Eastern allies in the interests of achieving a modus
vivendi with Germany and an improvement in relations with the
USSR. Many states in eastern Europe continued to suffer from turbulent domestic politics but enjoyed, for a brief period at least, some years
of relative prosperity. Most countries surpassed their pre-war levels of
industrial production, with only Poland seriously lagging behind. The

agricultural picture was less favourable, particularly in the Balkans, where crop production was well below pre-war levels. With the exception of Czechoslovakia and Austria, the east European states continued to depend on agricultural exports to help pay for imports of the raw materials and the industrial goods needed for industrialization. With the bulk of trade directed towards western Europe and the United States, recovery and progress were directly linked to the condition of the world market as well as to the continuing flow of foreign capital to fund the national debt and provide equity capital. Though some bilateral trading agreements were concluded, the absence of any multinational regional system intensified this dependence on world markets. The vulnerability of the mainly agricultural economies was already a subject of concern at the World Economic Conference of 1927, but no agreement on any plan of action was reached before grain prices began their disastrous fall in 1928.

Even during this period of external respite there was a high level of anxiety about borders and minority problems. The regional peace was punctuated by numerous crises, some more real than others, that perpetuated the divisions between the war's winners and losers or kept alive inherited enmities. Poland, the largest of the states in east-central Europe, and Czechoslovakia, the most prosperous, continued their separate efforts to maintain the status quo in what their leaders saw as an increasingly threatening international environment. Both governments believed that the Locarno agreements and the Russo-German treaty of 1926 weakened their security positions; each tried to compensate for their consequences through individual action. Despite having the third largest army in Europe, Poland occupied the more precarious position. Without defensible borders and surrounded by six neighbours (only two of which, Romania and Latvia, were actually friendly), Poland, as Piłsudski told a British visitor in 1920, was 'between the jaws of two colossal powers which by closing them could destroy her'.[8] Count Skrzyński, the Polish foreign minister, who had accepted the Locarno treaties because there was no other alternative, looked for compensatory advantages: the renewal of the Romanian alliance on 26 March 1926, a semi-permanent seat on the Council, which at least salvaged Polish pride, and the unsuccessful efforts to create either a Baltic bloc or a Scandinavian Locarno. The exchange visits and treaties with Czechoslovakia failed to bring the two countries closer together.

Faced with a severe financial crisis and a drop in world prices of Poland's key export products, the relatively long-lasting Grabski

[8] Piotr Wandycz, *Polish Diplomacy 1914–1945: Aims and Achievements* (London, 1988), 18.

government (December 1923 to November 1925) fell from office. Neither the Skrzyński ministry nor its successor could deal with the effects of the deepening depression. The collapse of the zloty, rising unemployment, strikes, and riots provided the background for Marshal Piłsudski's return from 'retirement' to the centre of Polish politics. In three days, and with minimal casualties, the marshal forced the existing cabinet to resign and created a new cabinet of experts under his nominee, Kazimierz Bartel, that took office on 15 May 1926. Piłsudski's authoritarian government had wide popular support; even the illegal Communist party backed it until reprimanded by Stalin and the Comintern. The marshal, who was both commander-in-chief and minister of war, posts which he kept until his death, was the real master of the new pseudo-parliamentary regime, though he left the management of domestic business, with the exception of military matters, in Bartel's hands. Repeated confrontations with the still functioning Sejm, in Piłsudski's words, 'a sterile, jabbering thing that engendered such boredom as made the very flies die of sheer disgust', increased the leader's determination to establish a more authoritarian, honest, and efficient government in Warsaw.[9] A highly secretive man, who surrounded himself with a small group of passionate admirers, Piłsudski remained aloof from politics. He was shrewd enough, however, to create his own party which he hoped would gain the votes to overwhelm the opposition. The left-centre parties were not so easily cowed and Piłsudski's newly formed non-party bloc failed to secure sufficient seats or votes in the 1928 election to assure the triumph of the new regime of 'moral cleansing' (*sanacja*).

Piłsudski lost patience. In 1930 he dissolved parliament and called for new elections in November. On the night of 9/10 September he had most of the leaders of the centre-left parties arrested and imprisoned in a military garrison in Brest-Litovsk where they were humiliated and maltreated. Other arrests and imprisonments followed, though most of the political prisoners were subsequently released. The outcome of the election was never in doubt. Poland was governed arbitrarily rather than despotically. The great majority of the Polish population could hardly have cared less about the subjugation of the Sejm. As in Italy, and indeed in so many eastern European states, the masses proved either apathetic or hostile towards parliamentary forms of government and accepted or welcomed strong leadership. It was the right rather than the left that benefited from the weaknesses of the post-1919 parliamentary regimes, though the terms right and left acquired new meaning as a result of the Great War. While the Jews, who provided a large proportion of the small

    [9] R. J. Crampton, *Eastern Europe in the Twentieth Century* (London and New York, 1994), 48.

middle class, were subjected to all kinds of discriminatory practices, their treatment was more tolerant and humane under Piłsudski than under his successors. The lot of the Ukrainians was less enviable. The Poles were determined on polonization; any opposition to their fierce methods was put down during the so-called pacification movement in 1930. Germans in the towns of western Poland and the German landowners and industrialists in Polish Upper Silesia were under some political pressure but had resources of their own and benefited from German interest and subsidies. Until his death on 12 May 1935 almost everything revolved around Piłsudski, who, nonetheless, remained aloof from the conduct of daily business and who, as his health declined, left Warsaw for increasingly frequent and lengthy vacations.

The 1926 coup was followed by an upswing in the economy. The improvement had begun before Piłsudski took power but his government benefited from the return to relative prosperity in the countryside, where two-thirds of the Polish workforce was employed, and in the cities. The British coal-miners' strike of 1926 helped Polish exports of coal. Grabski's previously planned stabilization programme was put into effect and was crowned by the American-organized stabilization loan of 1927 and Poland's return to the gold standard. From the autumn of 1927 until mid-1928 American capital flowed into Poland, and the exuberant American financial adviser, Charles S. Dewey, who exercised only the most limited supervisory powers over the Polish finances, optimistically planned for ambitious future ventures.

Unlike Beneš, Piłsudski, who was always interested in foreign affairs, had no doctrine of diplomacy but clear ideas as to how best to preserve Polish independence. Professor Piotr Wandycz frequently refers, in his studies of Polish diplomacy, to the marshal's two basic canons, the principle of balance between Germany and Russia and the maintenance of the alliances with France and Romania. As the Polish leader explained to August Zaleski, his relatively young and well-liked foreign minister, who had served previously as minister in Rome, 'Poland must maintain the strictest neutrality between Germany and Russia, so that these two states could be absolutely certain that Poland would not go with one against the other'.[10] In this respect, Piłsudski was fortunate. Both countries were conservatively inclined and, given Stresemann's preoccupation with the western settlements, relations between Germany and the Soviet Union remained too unsettled to allow for a united front against Poland. Convinced that neither the Germans nor the

[10] Piotr S. Wandycz, *The Twilight of French Eastern Alliances, 1926–1936: French–Czechoslovak–Polish Relations from Locarno to the Remilitarization of the Rhineland* (Princeton, 1988), 50.

Russians would be in a position to attack Poland for at least a decade, Piłsudski intended to build up the country's military and economic strength so that it could pursue an independent policy towards both. With regard to France, the situation was more complex. Almost from the time the 1921 treaties were concluded the French regretted certain of their provisions, and already before Locarno had tried to limit France's military obligations to Poland. The 1925 Franco–Polish guarantee treaty linked French intervention on Poland's behalf to League identification of the aggressor in any Polish–German conflict and made no reference to the Soviet Union. Though the subject was obliquely raised in 1927, the Poles knew that the French wanted to bring the 1921 military convention into line with the Locarno accords and to qualify its Soviet clauses to protect France against involvement in any Polish–Soviet conflict. Piłsudski hated the Locarno agreements ('every decent Pole spits when he hears the word [Locarno]') and never forgave Skrzyński for representing the pact as meeting Poland's security needs.[11] He not only refused to consider revision of the 1921 military convention but would try, with little success, to win additional protection for Poland in case of an early evacuation of the Rhineland.

No important diplomatic decision was taken without Piłsudski's concurrence. Among his first moves after the May coup was the calming of Soviet apprehensions raised by his action. He tried to convince the Russians that a distinction should be drawn between his long-range hopes of driving the Soviet Union out of the borderlands and his support for the more immediate and realistic goals embodied in the Treaty of Riga. He showed no interest, however, in Moscow's offer of a bilateral non-aggression pact and took umbrage at the conclusion of the Russo-Lithuanian non-aggression treaty (28 September 1926) and at Moscow's willingness to back the Lithuanian claim to Vilna. This seemingly marginal question soon became a major source of dispute, particularly when a military coup in Lithuania in December 1926 brought to power the fiercely nationalistic and uncompromising Augustus Voldemaras, a man determined to wrest back control over Lithuania's old capital from Poland. Voldemaras was warned that Poland could not indefinitely accept his so-called 'state of war', which was distorting Warsaw's commercial relations with the Baltic states and thwarting attempts to create a northern alliance system.

Much to the concern of the Germans, the Soviets continued to press for an agreement with Poland. Exchanges were interrupted by the assassination of Pyotr Voikov, the Soviet envoy to Poland, in Warsaw

[11] Jan Karski, *The Great Powers and Poland, 1919–1945: From Versailles to Yalta* (Lanham, Md., 1985), 111.

on 7 June 1927 by a Russian émigré. Coming so soon after the break in Anglo-Russian relations, the shooting unleashed a wave of anti-Polish feeling in Moscow.[12] Piłsudski had no wish to antagonize the Russians while his attention was focused on Germany, and he did all he could to defuse the Voikov crisis by offering apologies and monetary compensation. The tension continued as the war scare in Moscow was used in the intra-party struggle between Stalin and his opponents. Briand took alarm, fearing that Piłsudski might take precipitate action. To offset Polish concerns about Franco-German talks for the early evacuation of the Rhineland and demands for some form of compensation, Briand hoped to offer Warsaw an eastern Locarno that would include the Soviet Union and relieve the pressure on Poland. Though the Franco-Soviet negotiations made little progress during the summer and autumn of 1927, Briand tried to keep the door open.

Piłsudski deeply distrusted the Russian leaders and was worried by their negotiations with the French. His major concern was the possibility that the French would agree to some sort of deal with Berlin regarding the German–Polish borders. The year of Locarno was marked by the opening of the German–Polish trade war. With the termination of the 1922 convention obliging the Germans to purchase 6 million tonnes of Upper Silesian coal annually, the Germans cut their coal imports from Poland in half, bringing disaster to Polish Upper Silesia. The Poles retaliated by prohibiting the importation of a wide range of manufactured goods from Germany, and the latter reciprocated by limiting agricultural imports and withdrawing German deposits from Polish banks. Some members of the German foreign ministry thought in 1925–6 that Poland's political and economic difficulties could be exploited in the interests of territorial revision. Though the trade war was more serious for Poland than for Germany, both economies suffered. As it became clear that Poland would survive economically, Stresemann and Schubert developed strong doubts about the use of economic means to secure political goals. German pressure on Poland, moreover, would hardly convince the French to consent to the idea of the change in boundaries that Stresemann intended. It made greater sense to try to normalize relations with Poland and to damp down, so far as was politically possible, agitation for territorial revision. Steps were taken to moderate the trade war and a commercial agreement was signed on 17 March 1930, though the situation was not fully resolved until 1934.

While welcoming these and other modest attempts at de facto normalization, the Polish leaders continued to fear the continuous pressure

[12] For further discussion, see p. 538.

for the return of the annexed territories. They were concerned, too, about the long-term effects of German economic expansion in eastern Europe. In Danzig the German government continued to subsidize the local anti-Polish propaganda campaigns. In 1926 the newly constructed Gydnia port was opened. The Danzigers strongly objected to Polish concessions to shippers who would divert their traffic from Danzig to the Gydnia port; they suffered from the loss of business and called for an increase in German subsidies. The heightened activities of the *Auslandsdeutsche* organizations in Germany were another source of Polish irritation. The secretly funded '*Deutsche Stiftung*' directed much of its attention to the three-quarters-of-a-million Germans living in Poland, who refused to assimilate and felt no loyalty to the Polish state. The sums involved, whether official or private, were far too small to do more than help the German minorities towards self-help. While the Weimar government did not share the views of the extreme nationalists, its support for the German minorities in Poland was of a different order than that for the Baltic or Sudeten Germans. Once Germany entered the League of Nations, extensive use was made of the minorities treaties to publicize Polish violations of the rights of the Germans living in Polish Silesia. The *Volksbund*, a special organization funded from Berlin, kept up a steady stream of petitions to the League Council, some quite trivial. At the time of the sharp public confrontation between Stresemann and Zaleski over the minorities question in 1929, seven of the nine petitions on the Council agenda came from the *Volksbund*. Such conflicts clouded the atmosphere and worked against the establishment of any kind of détente.

Piłsudski assured the new French ambassador to Poland, Jules Laroche, the former political director at the Quai d'Orsay, that the French alliance was the cornerstone of his diplomacy. In Paris, nevertheless, there was considerable apprehension about the marshal's Russophobia and fears that he might come to an agreement with Germany in order to free his hands in the east. Apart from the strains generated by Locarno, considerable ill will was aroused by the financial and commercial links between the two countries. As the French were the second largest group of foreign investors in Poland after the Americans, financial considerations should have cemented the alliance. Instead, they produced friction and confrontation. The French capitalists, who took a narrow commercial view of their investments, were quick to call on the Quai d'Orsay for assistance when the Poles sought to defend their interests. The operations of Skarboferm, the joint company created to administer the former Prussian state mines in Upper Silesia, produced a stream of complaints and there were repeated clashes between the Poles and the Schneider company over the armament works in Starachowice.

Piłsudski was willing to make concessions in the interests of the alliance but the difficulties continued and the condescending attitude of the French made them doubly difficult to resolve. The two economies were not complementary and the Poles found it an uphill battle to correct their large unfavourable trade balance with France. Under pressure, the French agreed to renegotiate the 1924 trade treaty; the negotiations proved long and acrimonious. A more generous protocol was finally accepted in July 1928; the full convention was not adopted until April 1929. The French government proved reluctant to provide the armament loans needed to correct some of the more glaring deficiencies of the Polish army and insisted on attaching conditions more beneficial to France and French industry than to Poland. In an already difficult dialogue, this additional source of friction increased Polish resentment of its ungenerous treatment at the hands of the French.

Much as he needed the alliance with France, Piłsudski came to view the French as 'fair weather friends'. The German arbitration agreement with Poland did not include any territorial guarantees and, accordingly, the bilateral Polish–French treaty guaranteed Polish independence but not its borders. Briand and Berthelot barely disguised their belief, shared by the British, that Germany and Poland would have to work out their territorial differences at some future time. Not even the accession of Poincaré to the premiership in July 1926 and the formation of the National Union cabinet relieved Polish anxieties that French collaboration with Germany might undermine the Polish alliance. The Poles insisted that any move towards an early evacuation of the Rhineland would diminish France's capacity to assist Poland and that further guarantees of Polish security were necessary if Warsaw was to accept such a decision. The abortive Briand–Stresemann conversations at Thiory, despite assurances from both Poincaré and Briand and denials that Poland was discussed, raised the possibility that the French would hand over Danzig or the Corridor as they had Eupen-Malmédy. Though Briand refused to discuss the Rhineland question when pressed by Stresemann in December 1926, Piłsudski was alarmed enough to demand assurances that Poland could count on a long occupation of the Rhineland. He warned that if the French agreed to an earlier evacuation, Poland would demand guarantees equivalent to an eastern Locarno.

During a May 1927 visit to Paris, Zaleski spoke of a German–Polish non-aggression pact guaranteed by France and possibly Britain as a proper return for the shortening of the occupation. Briand insisted that France had the right to take independent decisions with regard to the evacuation and that, in the first instance, it would look for a quid pro quo in the form of German reparations. Despite the evasiveness of the

Quai d'Orsay about common action at Geneva, Polish diplomats continued to assume that Briand would accept the linkage between the evacuation issue and general security problems. Briand, however, made no attempt to raise the question of Polish apprehensions with Stresemann. Though the French were forewarned, it was still a nasty shock when, at the September 1927 League meeting, Zaleski unilaterally proposed a universal non-aggression pact. As Briand anticipated, Chamberlain refused to consider British participation in what was nothing more than a new form of the Geneva Protocol. The Germans saw the proposal as a way of freezing the eastern frontiers—a totally unacceptable proposition. The Czechs liked the idea in principle but thought it impractical. The Russians claimed Zaleski's proposal was specifically directed against the USSR. Briand, after conversations with Stresemann and Chamberlain, introduced reservations that turned the Polish proposal into a meaningless declaration. It was a humiliating experience for the Polish delegation, which expected French support At almost the same time, the Quai d'Orsay decided to send Marshal Louis Franchet d'Esperey to Warsaw to decorate Piłsudski with the prestigious *Medaille Militaire* and to indirectly raise the question of a revised text of the 1921 military convention. The French visitor was subjected to one of Piłsudski's long, rambling monologues, punctuated by numerous anecdotes and illustrations, but the Polish leader never lost sight of the key points at issue. While future talks were not ruled out, Piłsudski would not have the military pact 'locarnized' (his word), nor would he accept any French move to reduce their obligations to Poland in case of a Polish–Soviet conflict. It was a useless mission.

II

Any hopes in Warsaw and Paris that the Czechs would prove more amenable to a political and military arrangement with Poland after Locarno were misplaced. Piłsudski had no love for Beneš and was somewhat jealous of the Czech minister's international reputation and effective propaganda machine. His dislike of the Czechs in general went back to 1919–20 and was shared by many of his countrymen. This mutual distaste, even allowing for the exigencies of the post-war period and the territorial disputes between them, is one of those unpalatable 'facts' of international history that so frustrated the hopes of the peacemakers. When it came to strategic and military matters, notwithstanding his prejudices, Piłsudski was a realist and the military advantages of closer co-operation with Prague and collaboration between the two powers with France were self-evident. This was not Beneš's view, nor that of Masaryk. The Czechs were highly critical of Piłsudski's May coup, with its implications for Polish relations with the Soviet Union. At a time of considerable political difficulty in Prague, some found the successful coup an unfortunate model for their own leadership. Piłsudski's return to power confirmed Beneš's belief that any further engagement with Poland would compromise Czechoslovakia's good standing with Germany and the USSR. He assumed, or at any rate appeared to assume, despite evidence to the contrary, that Germany would treat Czechoslovakia differently from Poland.

There were no quarrels between Prague and Berlin like those that divided Germany and Poland, and Beneš convinced himself that Poland and not Czechoslovakia would be the object of German revisionism. Nor did he want to become involved in Poland's difficulties with the Soviet Union. Whatever his dislike of the Czech Communist party and the strength of the objections of the right-wing parties to granting full recognition to the USSR, Beneš continued to nourish his links with Moscow. Fundamentally, he believed that the collective security system and his network of pacts would guarantee the independence of Czechoslovakia. Unlike Piłsudski, he was far more interested in establishing diplomatic than military ties with France. It was Poland that took the initiative in seeking greater military collaboration between the general staffs and Czechoslovakia which rejected their overtures. This was the case in October 1926 and again in March 1927, when the Polish minister in Prague, Zygmunt Lasocki, was accused of exceeding his instructions in approaching the Czechs and was recalled to Warsaw. He was replaced by Piłsudski's close collaborator Wacław Grzybowski, who insisted that, given Poland's military superiority, it had to be the Czechs who should make the first advances. The only military co-operation between the two countries was of the narrowest technical kind, and French pressure on Prague to foster closer links was notably unsuccessful.

In some respects Beneš's optimism was justified. Relations with France were considerably better than those between Warsaw and Paris. The Czech commitment to democracy and collective security, in contrast to the dictatorial and militaristic Piłsudski, who had no confidence in the League's security system, won widespread support in Paris, particularly in radical and socialist circles. Czechoslovakia enjoyed a good press in France and Beneš was generally respected at the Quai d'Orsay. Admittedly, this was hardly the case in London, where the anti-Czech current was strong and was powerfully reinforced when, in 1930, Sir Joseph Addison, a diplomat known for his Slavo-phobia, was made minister in Prague. The Foreign Office, it should be added, was hardly more sympathetic to Piłsudski, and any Polish illu-sions of enlisting British support for eastern security pacts were soon shattered. In practical terms too, the Czechs made fewer demands on the French than the Poles. In a stronger economic position, Prague could bargain on more equal terms with France, though like the Poles, Czechoslovakia suffered from an adverse balance of trade (Germany and Austria were their main trading partners). The central position of the Schneider conglomerate in Czechoslovakia and its control over the Skoda works was a major asset. As an exporter of arms, there was no need to call on France for stockpiles of equipment. The small Czech army placed a much lighter burden on the Czech government than that carried by Poland. In 1928 Poland was devoting some 30 per cent of its budget to defence expenditure; the comparable Czech figure was 14.7 per cent.

Czechoslovak relations with Germany were far less fraught than those of Warsaw with Berlin. The Reich government, though it took an increasing interest in the Sudeten Germans, refused to intervene in the quarrels between the different Sudeten German factions and blocked any appeals to Berlin. The fact that the post-Versailles border between Germany and the Czech lands followed traditional frontier lines that had remained unchanged for centuries, while the German–Polish border was new and unacceptable to many Germans, further distinguished the relations of each country with Berlin. The Germans continued to favour the 'activists', the Sudeten Germans who campaigned for co-operation with the Czech government, and welcomed the weakening of their opponents. It was the Czech minister in Berlin who first raised the question of the treatment of the Sudeten Germans in early 1926, possibly because, in anticipation of Germany's entrance into the League of Nations, Beneš wanted to forestall any discussion of the minorities issue. Apart from Stresemann's general interest in the German minorities, there were specific groups in Germany promoting Sudeten German self-consciousness. It is true, too, that the Reich government secretly intervened to support Sudeten German financial institutions in order to avoid their bankruptcy or dependence on Czech financial sources. In general, however, the Reich government favoured a low-keyed approach to the question of the Sudeten Germans, and the subject was barely mentioned during talks in Geneva.

In the autumn of 1926 two Sudeten Germans entered the newly formed Švehla government. The Czech and German Social Democratic parties, as well as the Agrarian and Catholic parties, began to work together and there were signs that economic and religious divisions were cutting across the Czech–German nationality divide. The Sudeten German representatives concentrated on behind-the-scenes pressure and avoided public fights over minority questions. The Reich Germans were shocked at their failure to attack Beneš when he opposed

Stresemann's suggestions for strengthening the minorities regime in 1929. The Sudeten Germans identified themselves with the Czechs with regard to the Slovak minority and shared the government's negative view of their more extreme demands. Even in these years of Sudeten German co-operation, Beneš retained private doubts about their ultimate loyalty. In February 1927 the French minister in Prague, François Charles-Roux, admittedly worried about the pro-German influence of the new cabinet ministers, quoted Beneš as saying: 'I am under no illusions about what we can expect from the Germans of Czechoslovakia in the case of difficult circumstances. In no grave threat from abroad will we have them with us. That is beyond doubt, and in a case of this kind, our policy will be to stop [co-operation] and continue without them.'[13] Czechoslovakia was neither the centralized unitary state that Beneš wanted nor the Switzerland that he had held out as a model at the Paris peace conference.

Beneš's difficulties in 1926 and 1927 were of a domestic order. The elections of November 1925 had resulted in an impressive Communist vote and a swing away from the Social Democrats, the traditional pro-Castle party. It was soon apparent that Masaryk would have to deal with the disruption of the five-party coalition. The political climate became tense; there were economic difficulties and extremist demonstrations. Beneš was attacked for his subservience to the great powers and to the League of Nations. In March 1926 the president created a provisional stop gap non-party cabinet of officials that included Beneš. In the political manoeuvring that followed, the extreme nationalist parties turned on Masaryk and Beneš and a small, indigenous 'fascist' movement appeared which was particularly vociferous. More dangerous than these attacks were the negotiations between the Czech and Sudeten German bourgeois parties at the expense of the socialists. It appeared that Beneš's party, the Czechoslovak National Socialist party, would be excluded from any new coalition and the foreign minister would have to resign. Milan Hodža, the leader of the Slovak wing of the Agrarian party and Beneš's chief rival, who had arranged for the entry of the Sudeten Germans into the new government, had prime-ministerial aspirations and began secret manoeuvres in this direction. It was due to Masaryk's unswerving support and insistence that after two months of discussions the embattled Beneš kept his post, though his party was not included in the new centre-right ministry under the veteran Czech agrarian leader, Antonín Švehla, who took office in October 1926. Beneš, his reputation dented and influence curtailed, left Prague during

[13] F. Gregory Campbell, *Confrontation in Central Europe: Weimar Germany and Czechoslovakia* (repr. Chicago, 1978), 172.

the cabinet crisis and did not return until January 1927. The new conservative alliance embraced Czechoslovak, Czech, Slovak, and German parties. Steps were taken to conciliate the Catholic Church and the Slovak populists. The country was reorganized into four provinces (Bohemia, Moravia-Silesia, Slovakia, and Ruthenia), each with its own governor and provincial diet. This far from radical decentralization was accepted by the Slovak leader, Monsignor Hlinka, as a step towards national autonomy, but the more radical nationalists, led by Vojtech Tuka, who was tried for treason in October 1929, were left dissatisfied.

Beneš's authority in the new government was somewhat strengthened when Masaryk was re-elected to the presidency in May 1927 with an overwhelming majority over his Communist opponent. Political conditions, however, remained unsettled, and it was not until the following year that Beneš recovered his self-confidence. While a member of the Švehla government, he initiated moves to create closer economic ties in central Europe in order to offset the danger of *Anschluss*. Despite their expressions of support for the Franco-German accommodation, Beneš and Masaryk were uneasy. The successful German economic offensive in Danubia placed the prospect of *Anschluss* on the agenda, and the Czechs were hardly pleased when the French, as well as the British, appeared unwilling to publicly warn the Germans off moves in this direction. Beneš revived the idea of promoting economic ties between the Little Entente and Austria and Hungary, but his efforts in this direction at the Little Entente meeting in May 1927 evoked little enthusiasm. The representatives reaffirmed their support for Locarno and the French alliances and agreed on a common statement opposing *Anschluss*, but that was the limit of their co-operation. The Little Entente remained what it was at its inception, a series of bilateral agreements containing Hungarian revisionism, and not a Danubian grouping that would protect the economic and political independence of Austria. Without abandoning the possibility of erecting an economic barrier to the continuing German advances in eastern Europe, Beneš began to explore alternative possibilities.

At the March 1927 League Council meeting in Geneva, Masaryk had long conversations with Briand and Stresemann. With the former, he raised his fears about *Anschluss* and the need to create a bloc consisting of Poland, Czechoslovakia, Austria, and Yugoslavia to contain German expansionism. With Stresemann, he talked of the inevitability of changes to the map of Europe and intimated that Czechoslovakia would accept some form of revision of the German–Polish frontier. Having assured the German foreign minister that he did not wish to pull Poland's chestnuts out of the fire of a conflict with Germany, he expressed his hope that conflict could be avoided and the Danzig problem solved. The Czechs and the Poles were each trying to turn the tide of German revisionism against the other. The Germans insisted that there was no basis for Czech concerns about Anschluss. State Secretary Schubert, stopping in Prague on his way to Vienna in May 1927, told Beneš that Anschluss would occur naturally or not at all, but implied that time was obviously on the German side. He did not react to Beneš's vague comments about a Danubian economic confederation, but the latter must have realized that there was no question of Germany accepting any combination from which it was excluded. Nor were the Germans interested in Beneš's feelers for a Czech–German non-aggression pact that offered no real advantages and would annoy the Hungarians. In Berlin the possibility of a special tariff relationship between Czechoslovakia, Germany, and Austria was raised. The idea was received with some sympathy in Sudeten German circles and in Vienna, but Beneš was not interested in a combination that would leave Czechoslovakia economically squeezed in the German–Austrian vice. In early 1928 he considered a non-aggression pact with Hungary, a bilateral treaty with Austria that would lead to a more general regional grouping, or, as was discussed in March with State Secretary Schubert's good friend Max Beer, a 'Vienna or Danzig' formula by which Germany would abandon the idea of *Anschluss*—in any case unacceptable to Europe or to Czechoslovakia—and seek compensation elsewhere. It was a suggestion that Beneš would explore further with entirely negative results, while considerably upsetting the Quai d'Orsay.

III

In the autumn of 1927 Piłsudski took up the cause of the Lithuanian political émigrés. Charges and counter-charges were exchanged over the respective treatment of Poles and Lithuanians. Voldemaras, the Lithuanian dictator, decided to appeal to the League of Nations over the mistreatment of his countrymen and the Polish threat to Lithuanian security; Piłsudski threatened to take military action against the Lithuanian government. The Soviet envoy in Warsaw warned of the consequences of such action. As the crisis escalated Piłsudski announced that he would go to the Geneva meeting in December in order to confront Voldemaras personally. In a secret session of the Council held on 10 December the Polish leader suddenly interrupted his adversary's interminably long speech, struck the table with his open hand, and demanded to know whether Voldemaras wanted war or peace. When the Lithuanian replied 'peace', Piłsudski declared himself satisfied. The Council decided that the 'state of war' between the two countries was over and proceeded to make provision for negotiations between them.

The result was hailed as a triumph for the League and for Briand personally. The Vilna story was far from over. Meetings were held during 1928, but the Lithuanians refused to conclude a treaty with Poland or to reopen the Polish–Lithuanian frontier unless Vilna was handed back, a condition the Poles refused to consider. On a lower key, the conflict continued with pressure from the Russians and Germans on Voldemaras to compromise his differences with Warsaw.

During his two-day stay at Geneva Piłsudski spoke with Briand, Chamberlain, and Stresemann, though the latter talks were general and without political importance. Briand, encouraged by their friendliness as well as by Piłsudski's remarks about the 'indefensible' Corridor, seized the opportunity to launch a diplomatic initiative. Since Locarno he had favoured a Polish retreat from the Corridor in return for an eastern security pact that would include Germany. At Geneva he raised the possibility of a Memel–Danzig exchange with Piłsudski and Stresemann. The Lithuanians should give Memel to Poland, which in turn would abandon Danzig and use Gydnia and Memel as alternative ports. A non-starter from the Polish point of view, the idea was examined at the Quai d'Orsay and the Auswärtiges Amt despite Stresemann's scornful comments on such an exchange. At the Geneva meeting, too, Briand, while warning the Russians not to support Voldemaras's inflated claims against Poland, proposed an eastern Locarno in the form of a non-aggression pact between the Soviet Union, Germany, Poland, the Baltic states, and Romania. Neither Piłsudski nor Stresemann warmed to Briand's proposals. Exchanging parts of the Corridor, which was inhabited mainly by Poles, for Memel would hardly satisfy Poland, while a guarantee of the eastern frontiers in return for minor territorial revisions was not what Stresemann had in mind. The Soviet Union was unlikely to abandon Lithuania and accept Polish possession of Memel. Stresemann pointed out that Poland could not be included in an eastern Locarno until the territorial issues were settled, and that it was most unlikely that Romania would join an eastern pact while the Bessarabian question was unresolved. Briand and Berthelot continued to hint at the utility and feasibility of such exchanges, but their hopes of buying greater security for Poland at reduced cost to France had little chance of success.

The Vilna question dragged on. The Germans and the Soviets tried to restrain Voldemaras, but the stubborn nationalist again and again rejected the Polish terms for settling their differences. There was another storm in the summer of 1928 when it appeared that Piłsudski might make good his threats to march into Lithuania. To considerable French relief, he proved willing to let the League machinery take its course. In August, with all eyes focused on the signing of the Kellogg–

Briand pact, the Vilna conflict dropped out of public sight. In September 1929 Voldemaras was forced to resign the premiership by the Lithuanian president Antana Smetona, and was later tried for high treason. Smetona's new regime was as nationalist and dictatorial as the old but ten years would elapse before Vilna again became front-page news when the Russians, having occupied eastern Poland, ceded Vilna to the Lithuanians as a part of a mutual security pact.

There was no follow-up to the Piłsudski–Stresemann talks and considerable concern in Warsaw about the unsettled relations with the Soviet Union. While Zaleski harboured hopes that the Russians would offer a non-aggression treaty with Poland and its neighbours, there was some anxiety that they might settle separately with France, weakening Poland's negotiating hand. In an effort to assert Poland's diplomatic independence, Zaleski paid a visit to Mussolini in late March 1928. Complaining of insufficient support from France and Romania, and characterizing relations with Prague as 'cold', the Polish visitor spoke warmly of Hungary and the possibility of an eventual rapprochement between Hungary and Romania. The concrete results of the meeting were minimal, but the trip produced an adverse reaction in Paris and in the Little Entente capitals. A year later, in May 1929, Zaleski went to Budapest where the two foreign ministers explored an arms-transit agreement that could be extended to Romania if relations between Hungary and Romania improved. The Hungarians asked Zaleski to be an intermediary between Budapest and Paris. As this trip followed one made by Dino Grandi, Mussolini's under-secretary at the Palazzo Chigi, rumours of concerted action between Rome and Warsaw were widely believed. There was also a later visit to Bucharest, though Piłsudski was known to despise the Romanians, in the hope of reviving a connection that would complement the talks with the Hungarians. Zaleski's trips to Rome and Budapest and the ongoing talks with the Italians gave added point to Beneš's preference for a policy independent of Poland and even at Polish expense.

Zaleski feared an accommodation with Germany at Polish expense throughout 1928. His own attempts to caution the French against any further concessions only aroused anger both in Paris and Berlin. Neither the Poles nor the Czechs were invited to join the discussions in September 1928 that established a committee of experts to discuss reparations and a commission to deal with the Rhineland demilitarization. Beyond verbal assurances, the French did nothing to relieve the Polish distress. As the western powers drew closer to agreement, the distance between Paris and Warsaw increased, but Zaleski had no option but to follow in the wake of France. There was one diplomatic dividend for Poland that eased its eastern position. The Kellogg–Briand pact found little favour in Warsaw, though, as elsewhere, it was hailed as a major contribution to peace. Despite the Vilna affair and difficulties with France and Poland during the preceding autumn, there were new Soviet overtures to both countries. On 19 December 1928 Litvinov proposed a protocol to the Poles that would bring the terms of the Kellogg–Briand pact into operation before its ratification by the original signatories. Most unusually, the Russians accepted the Polish demand that Romania and the Baltic powers be invited to join. The 'Litvinov protocol', signed in February 1929, was part of the general Soviet effort to improve its relations with the outside world at a time of domestic upheaval. This Soviet gesture towards Warsaw seriously alarmed the Germans who, not surprisingly, refused to consider Moscow's offer of a triple arrangement.

The Polish–Soviet breathing space proved to be brief. Relations with both France and Poland deteriorated during 1930, when France replaced Britain as the Soviet *bête noire*. The Polish general staff was instructed to base its planning on the assumption that the Soviet Union was a greater threat to Polish security than Germany. The Poles feared that the Russian political difficulties might result in Soviet military action in eastern Europe. The Soviets, embroiled in a conflict with the French over the 'dumping' of Russian goods and concerned about the Polish–German commercial agreement of 17 March 1930, again discussed the possibility of a Polish preventive war before the Five Year Plan was completed. The Soviet foreign ministry closely followed the debate in Warsaw about the policies to be followed towards Germany. Roman Dmowski, Piłsudski's old right-wing opponent who disliked any move towards Berlin, produced a series of articles claiming that Polish military circles were preparing to attack the Soviet Union. Finally made aware of the mounting unease in Moscow, Zaleski, on 16 April 1930, publicly denied that any such war was being planned and assured the Russians that the talks in Paris had been confined to 'considering commercial measures for meeting certain dangers [i.e. Soviet 'dumping'] . . . Poland needs and wants peace'.[14] There was another shift in Soviet policy towards Poland when difficulties with collectivization and the defeats in China led to renewed offers of a non-aggression pact. This proved to be the beginning of the difficult negotiations that finally led to the Russo-Polish non-aggression pact of 25 July 1932.

The Polish representatives had no say in the decisions that led to the Hague meetings and were not present at the political sessions of the conference in August 1929. The Polish foreign ministry suggested various alternatives to safeguard the country's position, but the French

---

[14] Jonathan Haslam, *Soviet Foreign Policy, 1930–1933: The Impact of the Depression* (London and Basingstoke, 1983), 31.

failed to respond positively to any of Zaleski's overtures which sought to ensure immediate and automatic support for Poland in any conflict with Germany. Worried that their discouraged ally might retreat from the common strategy directed against Germany and turn its full military attention to the eastern front, the French military staff invited their Polish counterparts to Paris in late July 1929. Having prodded the head of the Polish delegation, General Tadeusz Kasprzycki, into admitting that Germany was still Poland's most dangerous enemy, the French went on to explain that after the evacuation of the Rhineland the French would contain any German attack from permanent positions in France and that they could only relieve the Poles, if attacked, by marching up to the Rhine. The Poles, in the interval, would have to stand alone. Though the details of the French defensive strategy (plan B) were not revealed, the Polish representatives probably suspected its contents. They asked that French military equipment be stocked in Poland and steps taken towards collaboration between the two air forces. They also wanted an armament loan of 1.5 billion francs in goods and cash. The French refused to discuss a tripartite Franco-Polish-German pact without the abrogation of the 1925 treaty and a modification of the 1921 military convention, neither of which Piłsudski would accept. It was agreed that any new negotiations would have to wait until after the Hague conference.

At the Hague in January 1930 the Poles were allowed to participate only in the work of the economic commission. Briand agreed to consider their political and military demands in bilateral conversations, but again insisted that there could be no treaty of alliance that would increase France's military obligations towards Poland. Even the grant of an armaments loan was linked to orders for French arms manufacturers financed through a complicated French-devised system. French officials proved even less forthcoming with regard to the creation of military stockpiles in Poland; it was considered too costly and would set a dangerous precedent. Zaleski, though he had achieved little at the Hague, concentrated his efforts on securing what Briand had vaguely offered. Insofar as the Hague conference was a victory for Stresemann and defeat for Briand, Polish security was further weakened. Briand tried to refute the charges made in the Chamber and Senate that France had turned its back on Poland at the Hague and actually claimed that the Polish government had given its approval to the Franco-German rapprochement. As Briand well knew, this was true only in the most figurative sense. The rightist opposition in the Sejm and even some pro-government groups were openly critical, but Zaleski loyally backed Briand and confirmed the essence of his statement. He saw no other possibility but to put his faith in France's continuing loyalty to Poland, while continuing to search for a formula that would provide the automatic and instantaneous assistance that he sought. In Paris the new Tardieu government of 3 November 1929, with Briand still at the Quai d'Orsay, was no more willing to meet Poland's security requirements than its predecessor. The new French premier was a tougher and colder character than Briand and less subtle in his handling of diplomatic issues, but he continued to back the Briand line towards Poland. Tardieu's public assurances of loyalty to allies and friends were sceptically received in Warsaw. The political changes in Berlin that brought Brüning to power raised further Polish apprehensions about future German intentions. Border incidents became more common, and Gottfried Treviranus, a member of the Brüning cabinet, made a series of violent speeches demanding the return of Danzig and the Corridor in the electoral campaign that led up to the disastrous German September 1930 election. It was hardly surprising that, in the autumn of 1930, the Poles were prepared to explore the possibility of a non-aggression pact with the Soviet Union or that Piłsudski, in his customary super-secretive manner, should send an emissary to see Hitler after the Nazi electoral success, suggesting that once Hitler came to power the two men might find a satisfactory arrangement to avoid conflict. The marshal began to think of possibly taking some of the Polish eggs out of the French security basket in favour of a tougher and more independent line. Piłsudski's 'new course' required a far stronger foreign minister than the accommodating Zaleski. On 2 November 1932 Piłsudski's close associate Colonel Józef Beck, already made deputy foreign minister in 1930, was appointed to succeed Zaleski. One of the most disliked and distrusted of the men on the diplomatic circuit, the clever, if arrogant, foreign minister had the task of making bricks out of straw.

Beneš, who had recovered his political position in Prague, viewed the Polish difficulties with a certain sense of detachment. An increasingly confident Beneš took over the leadership of the Czech National Socialists and, with an eye to succeeding Masaryk as president, immersed himself in domestic politics. The political pendulum was swinging in the Masaryk–Beneš direction. In 1929 there was a return to the unified government of the early 1920s, and the new elections of October 1929 freed the government from any dependence on the Slovaks and Sudeten Germans. The broad coalition under František Udržal, very much the Castle's man, included the Czech, Socialist, Agrarian, and Catholic parties. It was due to Masaryk that two Sudeten Germans were included in this all-Czech cabinet.

Beneš still wanted to create some form of central European bloc that would include Austria and Hungary as well as the Little Entente powers. In early 1928 his immediate concern was with Hungary. In January arms smuggled from Italy into Hungary were intercepted at Szentgotthárd on the Austro-Hungarian border. The Italian action set off alarm bells in all the Little Entente capitals but particularly in Prague, where it was believed that the Hungarians were arming the Slovak populists. The case was brought to the League Council, but neither the French nor the British, both courting Mussolini, wanted to make an issue of the matter. Beneš tried to counter Mussolini's encouragement of Hungarian revisionism and the Duce's meddling in Viennese politics by stepping up his efforts to secure a bilateral treaty with the Austrians (the 1921 Treaty of Lány expired in 1926 and was not renewed) and strengthening the Little Entente. Beneš sought to convince the Austrian chancellor, Ignaz Seipel, that he was aiming at a series of bilateral treaties in central Europe that need not involve any abandonment of territorial claims but would be directed at the renunciation of war. His hopes of creating a central European Locarno were stillborn. At a conference in Belgrade in May 1929 the Little Entente states agreed that their treaties should be automatically renewed at the end of each five-year period. They also concluded a tripartite treaty for the peaceful settlement of disputes along League of Nations suggested lines. While not the political union that Beneš wanted, it was an encouraging sign of renewed co-operation. The chiefs of staff of the three governments held the first of a series of meetings to co-ordinate their military planning, in the first instance against Hungary and then in 1930 against a possible Italian attack on Yugoslavia.

In May 1928, after soundings in London, Paris, and Brussels about an enlarged central European regional bloc, Beneš, mainly on his own initiative, paid a private visit to Berlin, the only one he ever made. He saw Chancellor Marx, Julius Curtius, and Schacht the economics minister, and had several conversations with Schubert, deputizing for the ailing Stresemann. The state secretary again assured Beneš that Germany had no immediate intention of annexing Austria, but warned that no German government would stay in office if it opposed eventual Austrian inclusion in the Reich. Beneš spoke of a preferential tariff system to include the Little Entente powers, Austria, Hungary, Bulgaria, and Greece, and parried Schubert's counter-suggestion for a United States of Europe as suggested by Briand, starting with a German–Austrian–Czechoslovak economic unit. Such a proposal, Beneš argued, would be politically provocative and encounter French, British, and Italian opposition. Meanwhile the French concluded a commercial convention with Prague on 2 July 1928, by which France extended most-favoured nation status to most Czech exports in return for lower customs duties. The Quai d'Orsay again pressed for a Czech–Polish military entente, with the usual lack of success. The Polish–Czech military conversations in September 1928 were of a narrow technical nature, confined mainly to intelligence matters.

During the January 1930 Hague talks Beneš met the new German foreign minister, Julius Curtius, and found him more rigid than Stresemann. The French defeat at the Hague brought no reaction from Prague. Nor did it result in a more positive response to French calls for greater military co-operation with Warsaw in the light of the forthcoming withdrawal from the Rhineland. In August, Marshal Pétain attended the Czech army manoeuvres and was considerably impressed by what he saw. He noted, however, that the army was poorly equipped and questioned the loyalty of soldiers of German nationality. He hoped that the Czechoslovak army would not be left alone at the start of hostilities, and urged, yet again, for more solid links between the armies of France, the Little Entente, and, if possible, Poland. There was, however, no role for Poland in Beneš's thinking when he came to reconsider his policy in 1930.

IV

The revival of German revisionism and the sharper nationalist tone of the Brüning government had its counterpart in Czechoslovakia. Four days of anti-Sudeten German and anti-Semitic rioting in Prague while Beneš was in Geneva in 1930 gave Curtius the chance to make political capital of the incident, by preventing the Berlin Philharmonic from fulfilling its engagement in Prague and cancelling further cultural exchanges between the two states. It was only a gesture to counter the nationalist sentiment among the German middle classes that played such an important role in the subsequent German elections. Both the Czechs and Poles were aware of the consequences of the weakened diplomatic position of France and the divisions between Paris and London over the treatment of Germany. Briand's policies of cautious conciliation with Germany came under severe attack from the right in the Chamber; the more sympathetic left-wing parties called for the modification of the Polish alliance in the hope of moving closer to Germany. Zaleski feared that the existing arrangements with Paris were not safe. If Beneš adopted his usual optimistic pose, his reassertion of Prague's continuing solidarity with France, and even its (admittedly less than amicable) relationship with Poland, hardly concealed his concern about the European situation. The Poles pushed forward with negotiations for the promised armaments loan from France. Signed on 18 February 1931, the agreement provided for artillery, naval, and air-force materials totalling 113 million francs. The French agreement, in the face of considerable opposition in Paris, was a pledge of its continuing good faith.

The deepening depression produced a number of proposals to deal with the difficulties of the agricultural states. The Czechs and Poles doubted the feasibility of the Briand plan for a European Union presented in May 1930, and feared that it would compromise the security they already enjoyed. Louis Loucheur's visits to Prague, Bucharest, and Budapest in mid-May 1930, and subsequent French moves in Geneva to consider the question of agricultural surpluses, aroused further apprehension. The Czechs feared that French-inspired moves towards the creation of a Danubian customs area or a union of agricultural states would cut across the Little Entente and challenge Czechoslovakia's primacy in the region. The Little Entente itself was far from solid. Romania, after the sudden return of King Carol to Bucharest in June 1930, was preparing to follow its own line in foreign affairs. In late July the Romanians, Yugoslavs, and Hungarians, meeting in Bucharest, recommended, in response to a request from the League Conference on Concerted Economic Action (February 1930), that the European industrial states admit European cereals at preferential tariff rates, a proposal contravening the most-favoured-nation clauses of existing commercial treaties. In August 1930 Poland organized an agrarian bloc of eight *cordon sanitaire* countries and, despite objections from the two Baltic participants, Latvia and Estonia, agreement was reached on proposals to be forwarded to Geneva. There was a follow-up meeting in Bucharest, without the Baltic states, and the group's preferential tariff recommendations were placed on the League agenda.[15] The Polish action was not well received by Czechoslovakia, France, or Germany which viewed the conferences as political rather than economic. The preferential tariff possibility was discussed in Geneva by various committees during 1930 and 1931. The British, still maintaining free trade in foodstuffs but caught up in their own internal divisions over protection, refused to take any action while the Commonwealth nations opposed the proposal. The French, apart from expressing their dislike for preferential tariff agreements, felt unable to absorb large grain surpluses without hurting their own hard-pressed agricultural sector. In October 1930 the French commerce minister, Pierre-Étienne Flandin, toured the south-eastern capitals and proposed the financing of cereal exports in place of the preferential tariff-rates scheme. In a favourable financial position, the French might have taken more positive action in south-eastern Europe but temporized instead.

---

[15] According to Sally Marks, the bloc formed a permanent organization to explore ways to combat the depression and to strengthen their negotiating hand with regard to the industrial nations. The organization enjoyed a modest success until submerged by the economic and political difficulties of the 1930s. Sally Marks, *The Illusion of Peace: International Relations in Europe, 1918–1933* (2nd edn. Basingstoke, 2003), 101.

The Germans, who had already embarked on negotiations with Romania for a new commercial treaty in early 1930, seized the initiative. The extension of preferential tariff treatment to the states of south-eastern Europe was a way of extending German economic and political influence. Foreign ministry aspirations, however, ran into the opposition of other government departments responding to objections from agrarian interests, and from some leading industrialists who feared the negative effect of preferential tariffs on their overseas markets. Some moves in this direction continued on a bilateral basis, but the process was slow and required international approval if Germany was not to damage trade with some of its major customers. In February 1930 Curtius, taking up one of Schubert's earlier ideas, broached the possibility of some form of customs union with the Austrian chancellor and was encouraged by Johann Schober's favourable response. When considering the German response to Briand's European Union proposals, Bernhard von Bülow, Curtius's state secretary and a far more aggressive nationalist than his predecessor, produced two memoranda for Brüning in July and August 1930. He argued that Germany should become the centre of gravity for the small south-eastern states, and that the union with Austria was the 'most urgent task of German diplomacy'. 'Viewed from the standpoint of the greater future possibilities,' he wrote, 'the solution of the problem of a union with Austria seems even more urgent and important than the question of the Polish Corridor.'[16] After an interruption when the Schober government fell from power, discussions were resumed when Schober returned to office as foreign minister in December 1930. Some in the German foreign ministry may have hoped that other states might join such a union, but Beneš would never accept admission into a German-dominated economic bloc.

The majority of states in eastern Europe, politically stronger but economically stressed, remained sovereign and autonomous. Neither Poland nor Czechoslovakia was at direct risk from either Germany or the USSR, but each was finding it difficult to respond to the changes in post-Locarno Europe. Moves toward co-operative action were limited. The Little Entente remained in existence, held together by the continuing, if diminishing, fear of Hungary. Beneš's efforts to use it as a means of protecting Czechoslovakia against a German move towards Austria failed. Yugoslavia had its treaty with France as protection against Italian revisionism but felt far from safe, while Romania continued to look to Poland for support against the Soviet Union. Another group was

[16] David E. Kaiser, *Economic Diplomacy and the Origins of the Second World War: Germany, Britain, France, and Eastern Europe, 1930–1939* (Princeton, 1980), 16.

emerging in south-east Europe that cut across the Little Entente. Building on the treaties between Greece and Turkey in 1928, and under the Turkish slogan 'The Balkans to the Balkan People', the first Balkan conference was held in Athens on 11–16 October 1930. Its promising start was checked by differences between the ex-enemy state Bulgaria, and Greece, Yugoslavia, and Romania, each of which had benefited from the Bulgarian defeat. The Poles fared no better than the Czechs in their efforts to create regional blocs that would provide additional protection against either Germany or the Soviet Union. Along with Britain and Germany, they opposed the French idea of an 'eastern Locarno', with British, German, and Soviet participation, that Paris hoped would strengthen Polish security and assure the neutrality of the Balkan states in any conflict. The Baltic Union proposal, linking the three Baltic states and either Finland or Poland, as preferred by France, failed to materialize. The Baltic states went their own way, concluding separate economic treaties with Germany and non-aggression treaties with the Soviet Union, though only Lithuania enjoyed cordial relations with Moscow. Finland, strongly anti-Bolshevik and pro-German, sought to ally itself with the Scandinavian rather than the Baltic states.

The most damaging aspect of central European diplomacy remained the failure of Prague and Warsaw to establish an alliance despite the weakening of the French guarantees and the signs of rising German revisionism. All the successor states entered the new decade exposed to any major challenge to the existing distribution of power. The most radical change in eastern Europe was taking place further to the east in the Soviet Union, where Stalin emerged as Lenin's successor and the country entered a period of massive political and economic change. The Stalinist programme of industrialization and forced collectivization, carried out at enormous human cost, was accompanied by renewed efforts to enter the arena of European politics. In 1931 a multilateral department was created in the Narkomindel to deal with multinational affairs in preparation for Soviet participation in a forthcoming series of international conferences. Litvinov's appointment as commissar for foreign affairs in 1930 marked a further stage in the Soviet return to international politics.

The Soviet Union After Locarno

I

In the post-Locarno period, the Soviet Union was in an isolated and exposed position. The Treaty of Berlin, concluded in 1926, only partially reassured its leaders about Germany's future intentions. Chicherin took other steps to secure the country's borders. Neutrality and non-aggression pacts were concluded with the states of Central Asia and the Baltic. The treaties with Turkey (December 1925), Afghanistan (August 1926), and Persia (October 1927) were intended to prevent these countries from being drawn into British-inspired regional pacts directed against the Soviet Union. Chicherin's settlement with Turkey was particularly important, for Ankara held the key to Central Asia. Despite Kemal's successful persecution of the Communist party in Turkey, he was not averse to good relations with Moscow, particularly in view of the Turkish debts still owed to Britain and France which were a constant drain on Turkish finance. When, at the end of the 1920s, the Turks began to face severe financial problems, they looked to Moscow for support and assistance in freeing them from the dictates of their creditors and for underwriting efforts at industrialization. The Soviet Union provided the model for the Turkish five year plan, adopted in 1934, and offered the credits and industrial equipment essential for its success. Along the northern frontiers, after the Soviet failure to come to terms with Poland, treaties were concluded with Lithuania (September 1926), Latvia (July 1927), and Estonia (August 1927). In each case, the form adopted was that used with respect to Turkey. There was no guarantee of borders but provision was made for promises of mutual non-aggression and for neutrality in case of a war with a third party. Each government was pledged not to participate in any kind of coalition hostile to the other. For its part, the Soviet Union agreed to abandon its revolutionary activities in the hope of stabilizing the status quo and promoting bilateral trade agreements. These treaties were all part of the Soviet answer to Locarno, possible because, with the option of a defensive Baltic bloc foreclosed, the Baltic states thought their interests were best served through bilateral settlements with Moscow.

Moscow still hoped to separate France from Britain. Though little progress had been made by French and Soviet experts working on the debt problem, Chicherin came to Paris on 11 December 1925 and, finding Briand cordial (most visitors found Briand friendly), arranged for a future conference that would look at war debts, loans, a trade agreement, and political relations. As the Russians were soon to find, establishing any relationship with the French bristled with difficulty. The Franco-Soviet debt settlement talks opened in February 1926 but soon ran into difficulties. The Soviets would not consider a debt-settlement agreement unless granted loans or credits, and the French, with the Treasury under severe pressure and the country suffering from the depreciation of the franc, refused to consider either. Rakovsky, as in London previously, resorted to personal diplomacy and managed to work out a joint proposal with Albert de Monzie, one of the most sympathetic of the French negotiators. Though Briand and Caillaux, the French finance minister, gave their approval, it is highly doubtful that the draft, which would have forced the large French debt owners to wait for their payments, would have been accepted by the Chamber of Deputies. The whole question became academic when Poincaré, who strongly opposed a settlement with Bolshevik Russia, returned to office as prime minister and finance minister in July 1926.

Britain posed the main threat to the Russians. The hostile Soviet interpretation of Locarno was based on the assumption that it was a British-designed treaty intended to threaten the USSR. The antagonism between the two countries in China mounted with the outbreak and spread of the 30 May 1925 revolutionary movement in Shanghai, and the Moscow agreements in the summer of 1926 to fully support the Kuomintang nationalist offensive. The decision to assist Chiang Kai-shek's Northern Expedition into the Yangtse River basin in central China, where Britain had considerable commercial interests, was taken despite Chiang's anti-Communist coup in March 1926 at the expense of his Soviet advisers and the Chinese Communist Party's (CPC) demand for independence from Chiang and the creation of a separate organization with its own revolutionary programme. The Northern Expedition during the summer and autumn of 1926 was a major success, and in December the Comintern celebrated the progress of 'the world revolutionary process' in China. The CPC was instructed to enter the Nationalist government so that it would be in a position to take over the revolution and establish proletarian rule. The advance into central China, the core of British influence, raised considerable alarm in London, particularly as the Communists specifically channelled anti-foreign and anti-imperialist feeling into attacks on British concessions.

The Soviet attempt to strengthen its position in Europe and pursue a military offensive in China was complicated by the continuing inter-party fights in Moscow. At the same time as the doctrine of 'socialism in one country' was accepted by the party elite, differences emerged during the party congress held in December 1925 over the question of industrialization. Stalin, given his belief in the impending conflict between the Soviet Union and the capitalist states, along with Bukharin, argued that the Soviet Union had to use its own resources to industrialize. Bukharin thought that this could be done within an amended framework of the NEP. Stalin showed little interest in the detailed problems raised by the debate until it became important in the fight against Trotsky. The latter argued that the only way to achieve rapid

industrialization and raise the exceedingly low level of Soviet productivity was to integrate Russia into the capitalist world. This
isolationist–integrationist conflict added further fuel to the Stalin–
Trotsky confrontation. At the start of 1926 it appeared that Stalin had
dealt successfully with the challenge to his authority from Zinoviev and
Kamenev. The reappearance of Trotsky, after almost two years' absence,
at a key party meeting in April 1926 reopened the whole opposition
campaign. In the latter part of May Trotsky came to terms with
Zinoviev and Kamenev, and the 'United Opposition' was formed to
challenge Stalin's tightening grip on the party.

Anglo-Soviet relations deteriorated further during 1926, as domestic
events in Britain heightened anti-Bolshevik feeling in the cabinet and
Soviet paranoia was purposely whipped up by Stalin for political reasons
as the leadership contest in Moscow intensified. Even as the Politburo
was sanctioning the Nationalist offensive and CPC campaign against the
British imperialists in China, Chicherin was trying to normalize relations with the Conservative government. Though Austen Chamberlain
spurned his efforts, the British foreign secretary tried hard to check the
anti-Bolshevik diehards in the Baldwin cabinet (the home secretary, Sir
William Joynson-Hicks, the chancellor of the Exchequer, Winston
Churchill, and Lord Birkenhead, the secretary of state for India), who
were calling for the formation of a diplomatic front against the USSR in
east Asia and a far more aggressive anti-Bolshevik policy at home. While
officially pursuing a policy of 'masterly inactivity', Chamberlain, in the
late winter and spring of 1926, began to make preparations for reopening credit-trade talks. The Foreign Office, reacting to Stalin's victory
over his opponents, actually welcomed the emergence of the 'strong,
stern, silent' Stalin who, it was believed, would rein in the 'fanatical'
Zinoviev and check the dangerous revolutionary movements abroad.
The General Strike in Britain, which began on 3 May 1926, disrupted
the preparations for talks.

Taken completely by surprise when the miners' actions in Britain
escalated into a general strike, the Soviets tried to maintain support for
the strikers while sustaining the momentum towards an Anglo-Russian
détente. As in Germany in 1923, this double effort proved impossible.
The strike brought the doctrinal disagreements among the Bolsheviks to
the forefront of the party battles. The 'dual policy' of negotiating with
the governments of capitalist countries while encouraging 'united front'
alliances with working-class movements came under severe attack. In
the discussions of what was to be done in London, there were conflicts
between the Narkomindel and Comintern, still headed by the disgraced
Zinoviev, and between the Profintern (International Red Labour
Unions) and the Soviet trade-union movement, whose leadership

looked to a united front with the left-wing membership of the British trade unions to advance the Bolshevik aims. In the previous summer the TUC was persuaded to create an Anglo-Russian Joint Advisory Council to act as a bridge between the two trade-union movements. The initiative was hardly welcome to either the Profintern or to the Communist Party of Great Britain, which repeatedly warned of the non-revolutionary and conservative character of the TUC and the futility of moves in this direction.

The Soviet government could not ignore the escalation of the miners' strike but it tried to keep its official distance by using the new contacts between the trade unions. The unwillingness of the TUC to accept 'Red Gold' (£26,000) or to sanction any other form of Soviet intervention in its affairs undermined Moscow's effort to emerge from what was rapidly becoming a no-win situation. Funds collected for the relief of the miners were channelled through the Soviet trade unions to the miners' union. This Soviet tactic, dismissed as pure window-dressing by Sir William Joynson-Hicks, the vehemently anti-Communist home secretary, led to a public outcry against Soviet interference in British affairs and its underwriting of subversive activities. The Joint Advisory Council only continued in existence until the summer of 1927 because of Russian hopes that it might be used to rally British working-class support against an imperialist attack on Russia. It was Trotsky rather than Stalin who took the toughest line, demanding the end of all contacts with non-revolutionary bodies. The Russian experience in the General Strike discredited united-front tactics even before the 1927 disasters in China. The May failure in London was crucially important in the subsequent radicalization of Comintern policy. Collaboration with reformist unions and social democratic parties was abandoned in favour of the struggle of 'class against class', the phrase itself used at the time of the General Strike.

The anti-Bolsheviks in the Conservative cabinet made political capital of Russia's involvement in a strike which the Soviets neither anticipated nor thought would succeed. While the Russian diplomats hoped that the whole affair would fade from view, the Conservative diehards stepped up their campaign for the ending of diplomatic relations with Moscow. Events in Europe magnified Soviet apprehensions of Britain's hostile designs. British influence was detected behind Marshal Piłsudski's coup in Warsaw on 19 May 1926 and his subsequent campaign against the Polish Communists. In the summer of 1926 the Soviets tried, in competition with Piłsudski, to bring the small Baltic countries within their diplomatic orbit as a way of strengthening their position. As so often when the political atmosphere darkened, the Russians again played their commercial card and sent the terminally ill Krasin to

London to seek a new trade agreement. Krasin's reception was decidedly frosty. The Conservative stalwarts pressed their anti-Soviet campaign, using the Russian activities in China as evidence of Soviet ill-will. Few in London, or in Moscow, understood the tangled situation developing in the one country where Soviet hopes for revolutionary success remained high. It was during the winter and spring of 1927 that the divisions between Chiang Kai-shek and his right-wing supporters and the left wing of the Kuomintang, backed by the Chinese Communist party and the Comintern, led to armed battles between the two. After a seesaw struggle, Chiang, backed by the British, who preferred the Nationalists to the Communists, emerged triumphant in April 1927. The Nationalist massacres of Communist and left-wing supporters in Shanghai in mid-April were followed in June by a purge of Communists and the Comintern representatives still in China. The question of Russian tactics in China provoked a considerable debate in Moscow. Though the differences between Stalin and Trotsky were at first minimal, China became another issue dividing the Stalinists and the United Opposition and the contest for power became an ideological struggle over foreign affairs. For their part, the diehards in the Conservative cabinet in London remained convinced that the nationalist movement in China was a Communist front whose successful activities in the Yangtse valley were part of a sustained attack on Britain's imperial position. Even though Chamberlain had considerably improved relations with the Nationalists through direct negotiations, he found it increasingly difficult to control the extremists in his cabinet.

In February 1927 Chamberlain gave way to the anti-Bolsheviks and a warning note was sent to the Soviet chargé d'affaires pointing to a possible diplomatic rupture. The last-minute 12 May raid on the premises of the Soviet trading agency Arcos provided the excuse for the final break in diplomatic relations, though the evidence found hardly justified the peremptory British action. Neither Stalin nor Chicherin had anticipated the London decision. Failing to appreciate the extent of British anger over the activities of the Comintern or the strength of public feeling mobilized by the Conservative diehards, the Soviet leadership overreacted to the diplomatic rupture and indulged in worst-case scenarios. The assassination of Voikov, the Russian representative in Warsaw, by a White Russian émigré on 7 June, attributed to the British intelligence service, was interpreted as a further indication of an elaborate British plot to isolate, weaken, and destroy the Soviet Union. The erosion of Soviet confidence in Stresemann, when he accepted a six-power mandate at the June League Council meeting to warn Moscow against making excessive demands on Poland, made the situation appear even more threatening.

The summer war scare was more than a Stalinist tactic to discredit Trotsky and the United Opposition. The Soviet leadership was genuinely worried by the state of the armed forces and thought that they could not deter a foreign attack or threat, a military failure would threaten authority at home, particularly among the peasantry.[17] The scare, or more accurately the series of scares, was the culmination of a number of Soviet setbacks and difficulties with Britain since 1924. It was the product, too, of the weakening ties with Germany, Russia's one protector against the hostile west. In the background was the old apprehension of Poland, with its army of a quarter-of-a-million men and its links with the Baltic states, Romania, and France. The return of Józef Piłsudski to power revived memories of 1920 and the possible formation of a Polish–Lithuanian–Ukrainian federation. While the party struggle was at its peak, all the political factions in Moscow anticipated the creation of an anti-Russian alliance in Europe and a period of extreme danger for the Soviet Union. Stalin and Bukharin, appropriating the opposition's arguments about a forthcoming conflict for their own political purposes, undoubtedly dwelt on the war danger to discredit the Trotskyists and warned of the dangers of 'factionalism' at a time of national peril. In July 1927, in a statement to the Central Committee that became the official Soviet version of the war scare, Stalin reviewed the series of incidents of the preceding months in Europe and China and highlighted Britain's intrigues and the dangers of its aggression. After the May–June scares, there was another peak of anxiety in September when Brockdorff-Rantzau reported that a 'leading member' of the Narkomindel sketched an imminent situation in which 'Britain would blockade Russia by sea and urge Poland to attack Russia, supported by Romania in the south and Finland in the north'.[18] At one level Soviet anxieties were grounded in the long-held Soviet apprehensions of Britain. Anglo-Russian relations were always more important to Moscow than to London, for the latter was seen as playing the critical role in maintaining the existing balance of power. Any British move against the Soviet Union, whether in Europe or elsewhere, was certain to set Kremlin nerves on edge.

The Soviets sought support in Berlin and Paris, where both Stresemann and Briand were alarmed enough to seek reassurance from London that the Conservative government was not intent on active mobilization against Russia. At another level, the war scare became a

---

[17] For a different view, see David R. Stone, *Hammer and Rifle: The Militarization of the Soviet Union, 1926–1933* (Lawrence, Kan., 2000), 50.

[18] Harvey L. Dyck, 'German–Soviet Relations and the Anglo-Soviet Break, 1927', *Slavic Review*, 25 (1966), 8.

central part of the political battle in Moscow, as the United Opposition mounted its attack on Stalin and Bukharin. Stalin used the crisis to discredit his opponents. He responded to the talk of war by advocating a 'get-tough policy' against Russia's 'enemies' at home and abroad. The OGPU was unleashed, threats were made in Warsaw, and provocative notes dispatched to the European powers. Chicherin was abroad during the early stages of the crisis, seeking treatment for his various illnesses, and Litvinov, left in charge of the foreign ministry, was somewhat more heavy-handed than his chief in carrying out the Politburo orders.

Stresemann, fearful of the effects of the Anglo-Soviet tension on his attempt to balance the two parties, had offered mediation before the Arcos raid but his efforts were overtaken by events. While trying to allay Soviet fears about the British and stressing his absolute loyalty to the Berlin treaty, Stresemann's acceptance of the mandate at Geneva, given Russian concerns that Britain would use Poland as its 'battering ram', shook Soviet confidence in German neutrality. Chicherin, the great defender of Rapallo, returned to Moscow in mid-June and warned the alarmed Brockdorff-Rantzau that his own pro-German policies were coming under attack and his influence declining as a consequence. Chicherin never believed in the danger of British intervention. He openly criticized Stalin's hardline policies and insisted that the Politburo had to decide between executions (the assassination of Voikov had been followed by an OGPU execution of alleged enemy agents, some of whom were accused of working for British intelligence) and foreign investment. In August Chicherin told Brockdorff-Rantzau that the joint goal of 'forcing Poland back to its ethnographical borders' had been compromised and his own relationship with the Politburo jeopardized.[19] The Germans, too, were having second thoughts about their relationship to the USSR: some members of the Auswärtiges Amt believed that Germany could no longer balance between its western and eastern orientation. The fallout was felt in the military sphere. Whereas the Soviets wanted to accelerate the collaboration between the Reichswehr and the Red Army and made proposals for joint weapons production in the spring of 1926, the Germans showed little interest in rearming Russia in the increasingly uncertain international situation. Stresemann and Schubert were acutely aware that the western powers would consider collaboration as a betrayal of trust. Still anxious to continue the collaboration (in mid-August 1927 Stresemann

---

[19] Ingeborg Plettenberg, 'The Soviet Union and the League of Nations', in *The League of Nations in Retrospect: Proceedings of the Symposium Organized by the United Nations Library and the Graduate Institute of International Studies. Geneva, 6–9 November 1980* (Berlin and New York, 1983), 181.

personally and formally sanctioned the establishment of the tank base at Kazan first agreed in March 1926), they took steps to reduce the German commitment and to restrict the government's role to one of intermediary between private German firms and the Soviet organizations. When, in December, the *Manchester Guardian* exposed the arrangements between the Red Army and Reichswehr, already known to the Foreign Office, and Philipp Scheidemann, a Social Democratic deputy, denounced them in the Reichstag, it became imperative to renegotiate the arrangements in order to reduce the political risks involved. Installations for aviation training and tank developments were maintained at Lipetsk and Kazan respectively, and Soviet specialists continued to attend aviation and armour schools, but an effort was made to keep the relationship within politically defensible bounds. Both sides adopted a more cautious view towards their collaboration. It was not until General Werner von Blomberg, the head of the *Truppenamt*, and a small delegation of German officers came on an inspection tour and attended the Red Army manoeuvres in the autumn of 1928 that the Germans initiated moves to improve relations between the two services.

Soviet attempts to bolster their position in France and isolate Britain made little progress. The Poincaré government turned down offers to settle the question of the tsarist debts and to negotiate a non-aggression treaty that might include Poland. The policy of 'buying off France' reached its height in September 1927, when Litvinov made a generous offer to compensate French holders of tsarist bonds and reduced the size of the loan Moscow required. Articles and editorials appeared in the French press condemning Communist subversion in the armed services and Communist activity in China. In late August a vitriolic right-wing press campaign was launched against the Soviet ambassador Rakovsky, who, as a leading member of the United Opposition, had signed a Trotsky opposition statement calling workers and soldiers in capitalist countries to contribute to the defeat of their own governments in case of a war with the USSR. Despite Rakovsky's protestations that party positions had nothing to do with the diplomatic negotiations in Paris, Briand, under strong pressure from Poincaré for actual expulsion, declared him *persona non grata* in mid-October and he had to be recalled. 'The entire affair [the financial negotiations]', observed Chicherin, 'will end as in all tragedy, as vaudeville.'[20] In the middle of October Rakovsky left Paris quietly, and 'unceremoniously' returned to Moscow. Briand, while admitting that Franco-Soviet relations were poor,

[20] Michael Jabara Carley and Richard Kent Debo, 'Always in Need of Credit: The USSR and Franco-German Economic Cooperation, 1926–1929', *French Historical Studies*, 20: 3 (1997), 340.

told Stresemann in Geneva at the end of September that he still hoped for a non-aggression pact with Moscow.

The war danger proved to be a brilliantly effective weapon against the Trotskyists. The struggle continued all through the summer and autumn of 1927 as Stalin and Trotsky clashed over the tactics to be used in China. The vastly expanded United Opposition, supported by senior Soviet diplomats in London, Paris, and Berlin, claimed that Stalin's foreign policy was 'fundamentally wrong' and that the 'united front' tactics which had failed both in Britain and China had brought the world revolutionary process to the brink of disaster. Although the Opposition campaign centred on the Chinese question, it covered the whole range of political and economic policies which Stalin and Bukharin had adopted since the start of 'socialism in one country' and 'temporary capitalist stabilization'. The struggle for power was not without its doctrinal paradoxes. Stalinists pledged to achieving economic autarky supported 'peaceful coexistence' with the capitalist nations, while the members of the Opposition, who favoured integrationist economic policies, insisted on the need to mobilize the working classes against the anti-Soviet activities of their own governments. With Trotsky openly challenging the Stalin–Bukharin leadership, Stalin used the war scare to denounce the Opposition for 'desertion' at a time of national peril. At its summer meeting Stalin carried the Central Com-mittee with him and used the OGPU to check the Opposition. In mid-November Trotsky and Zinoviev were accused of organizing counter-revolutionary demonstrations and expelled from the party. Stalin also convinced the Politburo to agree that the OGPU should be used to deal with all those holding Opposition views. In December 1927 Trotsky was exiled from Moscow and found himself isolated in Alma-Ata, 3,000 kilometres from the capital. Zinoviev and Kamenev gave in to the Stalinists, leaving Trotsky's followers alone in opposition. Rakovsky acted as Opposition spokesmen until he, too, and seventy-five other Trotskyists were expelled from the party.

Even as fears diminished in the absence of any outside hostile action, Stalin continued to use the 'foreign threat' to create the crisis atmos-phere that prevailed during the whole period of the first Five Year Plan. In the autumn of 1927 the condition of the economy deteriorated suddenly as the peasantry, on whom the Soviet economy depended, refused to release their stocks to the state procurement bodies. In early 1928 local officials were sent to coerce the peasantry. Stalin himself spent two weeks in Siberia where he gave fresh orders for the collection of cereals using the old compulsory methods of War Communism. He was convinced that if socialism was to be established in Russia, small, private peasant holdings would have to go. After an avalanche of peasant protest, the grain requisitions were halted, with Stalin temporarily back-tracking and concurring. Still in keeping with NEP policies, attention was again focused on the stalled negotiations with the Americans, French, and Germans as it became essential to secure money and credits abroad. The February 1928 measures led to further prolonged debates over how to handle the worsening economic crisis in general and the massive drop in grain exports in particular, giving Stalin fresh opportunities to consolidate his control over the party and the state.

This was the backdrop to the 'Great Turn' of 1928–9, during which Stalin triumphed over Bukharin and the moderates and turned the country away from the NEP policies to the launching of a programme of rapid industrialization (as Trotsky had recommended), that would create a heavy industrial base and a strong defence industry in the shortest possible time. Believing that the economic crisis could not be solved within the framework of NEP and that the search for foreign credits would not succeed, he intended to overthrow NEP and initiate a 'second revolution' using War Communism's 'orders and command' methods. In November Stalin took the offensive and demanded a comprehensive policy of requisitioning. Proposals, originating from the Urals and Siberia, directed attention to the seizure of grain supplies mainly from the more prosperous peasants, 'kulaks', and it was this method that was applied across the USSR in the winter of 1928–9. Stalin initiated a fresh attack on Bukharin and won the party backing needed to defeat him. In January 1929, the same month that Trotsky was deported, Bukharin and his supporters were charged with heading a 'Right Deviation' (deviation being a loaded word in the Bolshevik vocabulary) from the principles of Marxism-Leninism. In April the Central Committee Plenum, following Stalin's massive attack on Bukharin, the 'half-educated theoretician' who had been his closest colleague, censured Bukharin and gave its backing to the Five Year Plan. Stalin's battle against the right opposition came to an end in November 1929 when the accused produced the confessions of political error he demanded, though the decisive victory had already been won.

It is impossible to separate the leadership battle, the shifts in economic policy, and Soviet foreign policy. There is a strong argument to be made that the formulation of the Five Year Plan in 1928 and its rapid introduction was closely connected with expectations of some future foreign conflict. Stalin had already warned that the period of capitalist stabilization was over and the period of revolutions and wars about to begin. Only by relying on their own resources would the Soviets be able to defend their country and benefit from the divisions among their foes. The Stalinists used both the economic arguments and the international situation to sell the new programme of forced industrialization and collectivization. Recent work on NEP suggests that it would have been possible to reach a level of industrial growth equal or better than that achieved between 1909 and 1913, but hardly that reached by the Soviet Union in the mid-1930s. At the time it seemed to Stalin, who, despite his anti-foreign rhetoric, had favoured seeking foreign capital and technology to assist industrialization, that the crisis could not be resolved within the framework of NEP. The economy was suffering from inflation, industries were dangerously under-capitalized, goods were scarce, and there was a chronic trade deficit. In the eyes of its critics, moreover, NEP was ideologically unsound and its implementation had created a class of internal as well as external bourgeois enemies. There was, from the start, a connection between the demand for rapid and self-generated industrialization and the need to make the USSR impregnable to outside attack. The first Five Year Plan specifically referred to the hostile international environment and the threat of renewed imperialist intervention. It was accepted that, in laying the basis for a modern industrial society, the Soviet Union would be able to enhance its military capabilities. The Red Army leadership, while strongly supporting the case for rapid industrialization, was left dissatisfied by the first Five Year Plan, as it contained no specific defence section. Three months after the first Five Year Plan was approved, on 15 July 1929, the Politburo issued two major policy statements that would encourage the military to 'create a modern military-technical base for defence'.[21] With Stalin's victory over the right, the way was opened for higher military budgets (though not as high as the Red Army wanted) and increasingly more radical mobilization plans. Stalin's new interest in military affairs and his participation in the newly created Defence Committee set up by the Politburo in December 1930 gave a further boost to the army's drive for expansion and for a voice in the direction of the economy. The Manchurian crisis of 1931 would lead to a massive mobilization of the defence industry and a vast projected increase in the production of weaponry, particularly tanks. Mikhail Tukhachevsky, the dynamic ex-chief of staff, who had been exiled to Leningrad for his overambitious plans for expansion, was appointed in June 1931 to the posts of people's commissar for the army and navy and chief of armaments. His appointment confirmed the Soviet intention to dramatically increase its military production, with particular emphasis on the mass production of modern tanks, an industry that had to be started from scratch. In May 1932 Stalin actually apologized to Tukhachevsky for his earlier condemnation of the latter's extremely expensive military-

---

[21] Cited in Stone, *Hammer and Rifle*, 125.

industrial expansion proposals of 1930, that were intended to match the performance achieved by Germany during the First World War.

The ideological foundations for the new course in Soviet policy were laid during 1927 and 1928. Though the 'Great Turn' was premised, in part, on the assumption that the country had to be prepared for imperialist wars and an attack on the Soviet Union, this did not mean the end of 'peaceful coexistence'. The Five Year Plan made it essential both to delay the war threat ('the struggle for peace and disarmament') until the Soviet Union was transformed into a powerful industrial and military state, and to secure the credits and technology needed to assist this transformation. Even Stalin, always suspicious of the capitalist world, recognized the need for outside assistance. A slump in global cereal prices meant that, even with a massive increase in grain exports, there was only a small percentage increase in revenue and short-term credits had to be obtained abroad. Foreign concessions, in any case unpopular with foreign investors, were replaced by technical aid contracts. After a brief period of wavering, Stalin insisted that the foreign trade monopoly system should be maintained despite the opposition it aroused outside the Soviet Union. There was an obvious contradiction between the party-encouraged xenophobia and anti-foreign hysteria of these years and the search for assistance from the west. This was clear at the time of the arrest of the German engineers in 1928 (the Shakhty case), and in 1933 with the arrest of the British Metropolitan-Vickers employees on charges of sabotage and spying—the latter not totally without

TABLE 23. Metropolitan-Vickers Electrical Ltd.: Orders Received from the Soviet Union, 1923–1933

	Value of orders (£)
1923	193,963.00
1924	103,115.00
1925	221,276.00
1926	527,026.00
1927	124,596.00
1928	384,413.00
1929	343,898.00
1930	722,674.00
1931	681,117.00
1932	457,379.00
1933	17,201.00
Total	3,776,658.00

Source: MacDonald Papers: PRO/30/69/6011.

foundation. Soviet needs took precedence over propaganda. Moscow retreated in both instances, at least insofar as the foreigners were concerned. The Soviet Union's need to safeguard its economic position meant that the Narkomindel enjoyed a measure of primacy in establishing the contacts with the capitalist states required for the massive industrialization programme. The Soviets pursued a policy of reconciliation with the west, insofar as was possible, while preparing the USSR for isolation and defence.

II

Litvinov took on the diplomatic tasks set by the 'second revolution'. Chicherin, who had been openly critical of Stalin and Bukharin, was frequently absent from Moscow. Suffering from polyneuritis and dependent on morphine and other drugs for rest, the commissar made the rounds of the central European spas in search of relief. The running of the Narkomindel was left in Litvinov's hands, and Stalin seems to have found him a more congenial head than the increasingly distrusted Chicherin. Litvinov was non-confrontational, well-informed, and efficient. Above all, he had taken no part in the political infighting. Relations between Litvinov and Chicherin were cool. They differed in temperament and work habits, but also in their policies. Chicherin, well-born and highly cultured, was a work-obsessed bachelor. Litvinov was the son of a Jewish bank clerk, married to an Englishwoman who was the daughter of a Jewish university professor. Chicherin was a notoriously inefficient chief, who tried to keep all the work of the commissariat in his own hands; Litvinov was an effective administrator, willing to delegate authority and to encourage and reward initiative and independence. Whereas Chicherin was a revolutionary who remained loyal to the Rapallo connection in order to drive a wedge between Germany and Britain, for which he had a particular rancour, Litvinov, if less intellectually sophisticated, believed that the Soviet Union could only buy safety through some form of integration into the European system. Accepting that his main task was to create a breathing space for the USSR, the chubby, bespectacled deputy commissar seized on the Geneva disarmament talks as a means of underlining Moscow's commitment to 'peaceful coexistence' with the capitalist world. In 1930, not without some opposition, Litvinov replaced Chicherin as commissar, though without the latter's membership in the party Central Committee. Stalin, preoccupied with economic questions, gave Litvinov considerable freedom in directing daily diplomacy. It is true that the Politburo discussed foreign policy on a regular basis, but Stalin determined the outcome of its discussions. Without representation on this body, the members of the Narkomindel were summoned to its meetings only when necessary. Having made their reports, they were dismissed. Nonetheless, Litvinov conducted much of the country's diplomatic business and gradually created his own team of officials in Moscow and in the embassies abroad. The Narkomindel did not escape unscathed from the leadership battles. A number of 'Old Bolsheviks' resigned or defected in the late 1920s, and there was a tightening of discipline and 'cleansing' of staffs in the foreign missions. The commissariat, however, developed along traditional bureaucratic lines. Litvinov's diplomats were mainly men who had lived abroad (some had even studied in foreign universities) as exiles, were fluent linguists, and were familiar with the broad currents of western thought. Unlike the first generation of Soviet diplomats, who had made their names as active revolutionaries, they were professionals who exercised little or no political influence.

The changes that took place in the Comintern structure reinforced Moscow's control and prevented any national deviations from the Stalinist line. As early as November 1926 Bukharin had spoken of the third phase of post-war development stemming from the internal contradictions in the process of capitalist stabilization and leading to greater class antagonism. Many national parties, including the German and British communist parties, were adopting more militant policies before these questions became central to the party conflicts. The Sixth Congress of the Comintern, held in July–September 1928, embraced the fundamental concepts of the 'third period' and the toughened party line advanced by Stalin. Delegates were told that in the new phase of capitalist destabilization and confrontation there would be abundant possibilities for revolutionary action. The call for radical action was accompanied by renewed demands for the centralization and Bolshevization of the national parties that were to be purged of their Trotskyists and Right Deviationists. The Congress called for the end of united-front tactics and the declaration of an all-out war against the social democrats, identified as 'social fascists', and the non-revolutionary trade unions. Bukharin, still head of the Comintern, tried to temper this uncompromising stand, but he was already losing out to the Stalinists. The new Comintern tactics were translated into action during the winter of 1928–9, when the war threat had all but faded. Stalin took no risks, however, that his defeated opponents might find support in the national communist parties. In November 1929 Bukharin lost his Comintern post and was expelled from the Politburo, months after he had been rendered politically harmless. Stalin's new appointee to head the Comintern was the tough and thoroughly loyal Vyacheslav Molotov, who imposed the monolithic rule on the national communist parties that marked their histories in the 1930s. The parties were brought to heel, and all, despite some instances of fierce infighting, adhered to the new ideological line.

There were contradictions between Litvinov's efforts to secure a place on the international stage in order to enhance Soviet prestige and the Comintern's ideologically narrow and exclusive policies. Occasionally, Stalin and the Politburo would chastize Litvinov for ignoring the importance and the strength of the workers' movement, but on the whole they tolerated his efforts without abandoning their belief in the Soviet Union's revolutionary mission and their pride in being 'the number one enemy of the capitalist world'.[22] The radicalization of the international workers' movements, intended to win mass support for the communist parties, proved counter-productive. The isolation and sectarianism of the German Communist party crushed the possibility of a united working-class resistance to Nazism in Germany. The anti-fascist congress and demonstration held in Berlin on 9–10 March 1929 proved to be the last weak gasp of the united-front tactics of the 1920s. The fears expressed in some circles, above all in the French Communist party, about the gains made by the Nazis in Germany and pro-fascist groups elsewhere in Europe were dismissed as exaggerated in Moscow. While the Comintern, highly doubtful about the prospects of success, reined in the more radical elements in the KPD, who thought that the revolution was in sight, the triumph of *realpolitik* in Moscow brought no correction to the self-destructive views of the party. Most of the Soviet leaders, including Stalin, when he took any interest in German affairs, remained complacent about the Nazi threat right up until the eve of Hitler's victory.

III

The vast transformation of the economic structure of the USSR had major political and foreign-policy consequences. The quickened pace of industrialization and the forced collectivization produced violence in the countryside and difficulties in an army mainly recruited from the peasantry. There was a massive drop in agricultural output just when the Soviet Union was dependent on its grain exports to pay for foreign imports of industrial equipment. The state's grain collections rose dramatically between 1928–9 and 1931–2, but in 1932 there was famine in large parts of the highly fertile Ukraine. Industrial workers had to accept cuts in food consumption. It is estimated that some 4–5 million people perished from 'de-kulakization' and the grain seizures of 1932–3. The

[22] Sabine Dallin, 'Les Diplomates soviétiques des années 1930 et leur évaluation de la puissance de l'URSS', *Relations Internationales*, 91 (Autumn, 1997), 343.

overall numbers are undoubtedly higher. The costs were appalling, though hardly revealed to the outside world. Reports did appear in the foreign press and diplomats in Moscow had some awareness of what was happening, but such horrors were hardly of concern to the foreign ministries of Europe. In terms of Stalin's goals, his programmes were paying the demanded dividends. There was an impressive increase in industrial production, above all, in the production of capital goods; the completion of the Five Year Plan, set for September 1933, was announced in December 1932. Trials of real and fictitious malefactors took place in all the major cities of Russia and in the other Soviet republics. The party, itself purged in 1929 and replenished and expanded through a new recruitment campaign launched at the same time, enforced the political loyalties and ideological orthodoxy needed to carry out the new economic policies. By 1932 the military build-up had placed the Red Army on a near wartime footing, though at the cost of adding considerably to the strain on the economy already created by the excessively ambitious economic targets set in 1931. The factories were unable to keep up with programmes set by the defence authorities and both the aircraft and tank

TABLE 24. Soviet Defence Budgets, 1922–1937 (million roubles, current prices)

	Published Defence Budget	NKVM Budget (Davies)	NKVM Budget (Stone)	Total Defence Budget	Overall State Budget
1922–3	230.9				1,460.0
1923–4	402.3		248.2		2,317.6
1924–5	443.8		405.0		2,969.5
1925–6	638.0		602.5		4,050.9
1926–7	633.8		700.0		5,334.6
1927–8	774.6		743.0		6,465.0
1928–9	879.8	850	850.0	1,211.3	8,240.9
1929–30	1,046.0	1,046	995.0	1,685.7	12,335.0
Special quarter	433.7			690.0	5,038.2
1931	1,288.4	1,790	1,810.0	2,976.2	25,097.0
1932	1,296.2	4,308	4,574.0	6,422.9	37,995.1
1933	1,420.7	4,738	4,733.0		42,080.6
1934	5,019.1				5,444.7
1935	8,185.8				73,571.7
1936	14,882.7				92,480.2
1937	17,481.0				106,238.3

Sources: D. R. Stone, Hammer and Rifle: The Militarization of the Soviet Union, 1926–1933 (Lawrence, Kan., 2000), 217; R. W. Davies, The Development of the Soviet Budgeting System (Cambridge, 1958), 65; id., 'Soviet Military Expenditure and the Armaments Industry 1929–1933', Europe-Asia Studies 45 (1993).

industries were in crisis. It was decided at the end of 1932 to cut back the defence programmes to more realistic targets. Nonetheless, great strides had been made in strengthening the country's military arm and defence potential, and the upward trend in defence production would continue, with only a temporary dip in 1935, throughout the 1930s.

The economic revolution in the Soviet Union placed a heavy burden on the Narkomindel, which not only had to prolong the period of peace but cope with the adverse effects of the Soviet 'dumping' of raw materials and agricultural produce on an already severely depressed world market. Litvinov, unlike his predecessor, believed that the way to deal with such difficulties and to prevent the formation of any anti-Soviet coalition was through conventional diplomacy and associating the USSR with any multilateral negotiations promoting peace. In 1928, in one of his last disputes with Chicherin, he successfully argued the case for Soviet adherence to the Kellogg–Briand pact, and though the Americans rejected the idea of Soviet participation in the ceremonies, Russia was the first of the other states to subsequently sign the treaty. In December, in advance of ratification, Litvinov proposed that the USSR and Poland should bring the peace pact into force through a separate treaty. Due to Polish insistence, Latvia, Estonia, and Romania also signed the 'Litvinov protocol' in February 1929, and in April Turkey, Persia, Lithuania, and the Free City of Danzig joined as well. The Soviets had already sent delegates to the World Economic Conference in Geneva in May 1927 (after Swiss restitution for the 1923 assassination of the Soviet delegate sent to the Lausanne conference) to argue the case for the peaceful coexistence between the socialist and capitalist economic systems. In November of the same year Litvinov appeared at the meetings of the preparatory disarmament commission and submitted his proposal for the complete abolition of land, naval, and air forces. Russian views on disarmament, covering a wide spectrum of divergent opinions, changed during the course of the 1920s from Lenin's original proposition that disarmament was impossible under capitalism and a device to delude the working class, to Litvinov's advocacy of total disarmament as the only means of organizing security against war. Stalin, sceptical about the proceedings from the start and embarked on a major rearmament programme of his own, agreed that the disarmament talks might delay war by mobilizing working-class support for peace in the bourgeois states. Litvinov, anxious to identify the USSR with the cause of peace, later claimed that the Soviet purpose at Geneva was to expose the capitalist unwillingness to act, and to push people towards real disarmament. Soviet participation in the preparatory commission's disarmament talks provided ample opportunities for playing on the divisions between the capitalist powers and exposing the hypocrisy of the disarmers, above all the French, with whom relations became particularly difficult during 1930.

Litvinov worked equally hard to improve bilateral relations with Britain and France. Having long been critical of Chicherin's pro-German orientation, he welcomed the approach from the new British Labour government, which took office in June 1929, for the restoration of normal diplomatic relations. Ramsay MacDonald, who had previously been burnt on the recognition issue, was not inclined to be rushed. It was only in the autumn that the British agreed to the Soviet demand that the resumption of political relations, already made dependent on parliamentary approval, had to be the first step in any future negotiations. The Soviets were willing to 'confirm' Article 16 of the unratified 1924 treaty pledging both sides to refrain from propaganda. At the end of December Grigory Sokolnikov, a participant in the United Opposition, was made the first Soviet *polpred* (ambassadorial equivalent) in London and Sir Esmond Ovey became Britain's first ambassador to the USSR. A trade agreement was signed in April 1930. Russian exports to Britain rose dramatically; in the early 1930s Britain was taking almost a third of Russia's exports, and Germany some 16 per cent. The hard-pressed British exporters, however, failed to find the promised markets in Russia, and exports to Russia constituted only about one-fifth of the British purchases. The Soviets spent most of the £18 million in credits provided by Britain under the terms of the 1930 trade agreement in making purchases elsewhere. The diplomatic climate remained cool. As part of the spy and sabotage mania unleashed in Russia, there were public trials with public accusations of capitalist plots and allegations against French and British firms operating in the Soviet Union. The Labour leaders remained suspicious of Russian intentions, and if some sympathetic visitors to the Soviet Union were impressed by the Soviet experiment at a time when capitalism seemed to be in danger of collapse, they were not blind to the costs.

Politicians and officials still knew very little about the country and its people. Few Foreign Office or Quai d'Orsay officials had read Marx or Lenin, and the knowledge of those who knew the old Russia was thought irrelevant. The situation was made worse by the hostility and suspicion with which the Soviet regime regarded all foreigners. British and French diplomats, like others in Moscow, lived in a sealed-off world, and *de jure* recognition made no difference. William Strang, the counsellor of the British embassy from 1930 to 1933, recalled his personal isolation broken only by two private invitations, one for tea with Mrs Ivy Litvinov and the other, along with the ambassador, to a unique, uproarious dinner with Commissar Voroshilov at his dacha outside Moscow. Strang had a general idea of what was happening in the countryside, but any criticism of Stalin's policies would have been totally out of the question and a semblance of normality pervaded the diplomatic correspondence.

There was not much progress in Paris. V. S. Dovgalevsky, an old party member without the political notoriety of his predecessor, arrived in early January 1928, intent on concluding the non-aggression pact that the Russians had suggested earlier as well as new commercial and consular agreements. He quickly concluded that the time was 'extraordinarily unfavourable' for any negotiations, given the state of public opinion and the forthcoming national elections. Some private talks were conducted between the French and Germans on economic co-operation in Russia, encouraged up to a point by Briand and Berthelot, but they did not get very far. Practical considerations and pressure from particular interest groups kept the possibility of agreement on the agenda. French oil imports from the USSR constituted some 15 per cent of all oil imports in 1928 (rising to 29 per cent in 1932), and French officials and commercial representatives, anxious to escape the domination of the 'Anglo-Saxon trusts', Royal Dutch Shell and Standard Oil, whose prices were artificially high, favoured a settlement with Moscow.[23] Nevertheless, given Poincaré's continued opposition to any talks, as well as that of the Finance Ministry and the Bank of France, which vetoed any extension of credit to Soviet trade agencies, the sine qua non of Soviet accommodation, no progress was made either in 1927 or 1928. Jean Herbette, a journalist turned diplomat who was ambassador in Moscow and a warm advocate of rapprochement, became so negative and nervous about Soviet intentions after his home leave in July 1927 that Litvinov became anxious to have him replaced.

Though Poincaré resigned in July 1929, the rapid turnover in cabinets (five during the next seventeen months), bank scandals, and street riots by the anti-parliamentary leagues made it highly unlikely that any French government would embark on negotiations. Political relations were hardly improved by the kidnapping in January 1930, by Soviet agents, of General Alexander Kutepov, the president of the Russian Officers Association in France. The Soviet embassy was accused of being implicated and the right-wing press in Paris pressed for a break in relations with Moscow. Comintern support for an uprising against the French authorities in Indochina was hardly calculated to assist Litvinov's efforts. In February 1930, before the extent of the communist activities in Indochina were known, Litvinov jestingly complained

---

[23] Michael Jabara Carley, 'Five Kopecks for Five Kopecks: Franco-Soviet Trade Negotiations, 1928–1939', *Cahiers du Monde Russe et Soviétique*, 33: 1 (Jan.–Mar. 1992), 26.

about the Comintern in a conversation with the British ambassador in Moscow. 'It's hopeless', he exclaimed. 'Why don't you take the thing. You are a free country. We do not want it here. Do arrange for it to hold its sessions in London.'[24] Press polemics on both sides and trials in Moscow implicating a French embassy official further poisoned the atmosphere, as did the activities of the Soviet trade mission in Paris. In October 1930, a major clash over Soviet 'dumping' led to the imposition of French licences on all Soviet imports and a Soviet embargo on French exports in retaliation. It was a damaging break in relations, for the French encouraged the eastern European states to organize concerted economic action against the USSR, raising the usual Soviet fears about an anti-Soviet front. Pierre-Étienne Flandin, who made a tour of the east European capitals, was nicknamed 'the minister for dumping' by the irate Russians.

It was partly to offset the danger from France that Litvinov decided that the USSR should take part in the disarmament discussions when the preparatory commission was reconvened in November 1930. For this reason, too, he sought to strengthen the Soviet links with fascist Italy and raised the possibility of a non-aggression treaty when he and Grandi met in Milan on 24 November 1930. Litvinov saw the Briand plan of 1930 as part of a French effort to isolate the Soviet Union and insisted that the Soviet Union should make its voice heard in the subsequent League-sponsored talks. Litvinov prevailed over the sceptics in the Politburo and, with Italian assistance, won a half-hearted invitation to join the economic discussions. The commissar for foreign affairs used the occasion of the meeting to propose a pact of economic non-aggression, which would give weight to the Soviet claims that there was a compatibility of economic interest between the USSR and the west European states. The Franco-Soviet trade restrictions were lifted in 1931, and in April, after the announcement of the Austro-German customs union on 21 March, the Quai's secretary-general, Philippe Berthelot, seized the initiative and approached Dovgalevsky, the Soviet *polpred* in Paris, with proposals for the simultaneous negotiations of a non-aggression pact and debt-trade agreement. Months of difficult and interrupted negotiations followed before the talks bore fruit in the Franco-Soviet non-aggression pact of November 1932 and the trade agreement of January 1934.

There was not much joy for the Russians from Germany. Stresemann's slow progress in securing the revision of the Versailles terms precluded any abandonment of the renewed ties with Moscow, but there were increasing doubts at the Auswärtiges Amt, even among

[24] Ibid. 29–30.

the 'easterners', about their worth. The Shakhty case in the spring of 1928, when the OGPU accused fifty engineers, including three Germans, working in the coal-mining industry in the Shakhty region of the north Caucasus of sabotage and treason, froze relations and cut off the trade talks begun in February. At their trial Andrey Vishinsky, the presiding judge, linked the 'saboteurs' to hostile foreign capitalists seeking to undermine the Soviet Union in preparation for the future war of intervention. The 'great leap forward', however, did not permit the disruption of Russia's agreements with Germany, which were still its sole link to a major industrial power. The German engineers were released (their Russian co-defendants were sent to their deaths) and steps taken, mainly due to Litvinov in Chicherin's absence, to reopen the trade negotiations. The Germans felt that they had got very little either from the 1925 trade agreement or the 300 million RM credit of the following year. German trade with the USSR actually fell between October 1926 and October 1927, and the credit was not used to buy German products as was intended. The Deutsche Bank, the bank most involved in Russian business, and various industrialists warned against any further involvement in the disrupted Russian economy. It was mainly the shrinkage of their domestic and export markets that finally drove the Germans back to the Soviet Union in 1931. German industrialists, desperate for markets, secured new export orders from the Soviet authorities. Backed by the Reichsbank and the Brüning government, which, despite its deep financial difficulties, was willing to offer larger and longer lines of credit to Moscow, the industrialists benefited from a large increase in exports. The suppliers of machine tools and electrical goods were the chief beneficiaries. The risks to the financially embattled Reich government were high; if the Soviets had defaulted on the repayment of her credits, the effects on the German finances would have been close to disastrous. The Soviets exploited the depressed conditions in the capitalist world to demand extensive lines of credit in return for orders, forcing even the reluctant British to extend better credit terms than they usually offered. There was no way that the Soviet exports of grain and timber, hardly welcomed abroad, could have paid for the machinery and material needed for the fulfillment of the first Five Year Plan. For a period, during 1931–2, Germany became dependent on Soviet trade to help fill its empty order books.

The most surprising Soviet industrial success in the late 1920s was in the United States, which had long been recognized in Moscow as the most technically advanced nation in the world. American policy towards the Soviet Union was beset with contradictions. While pursuing a non-recognition policy on ideological grounds, and still hoping that the Soviet government would collapse, trade with the USSR was permitted

TABLE 25. Soviet–German Trade, 1929–1934 (000 tons)

Years	The USSR's Export to Germany	The USSR's Import from Germany	Volume of Trade	Balance
1929	425,7	353,9	779,6	71,8
1930	436,3	430,6	866,9	5,7
1931	303,5	762,7	1066,2	−459,2
1932	270,9	625,8	896,7	−354,9
1933	194,1	282,2	476,3	−88,1
1934	233	63,31	286,31	159,7

Source: Sergei Gorlov, *Sovershenno Sekretno: Alians Moskva-Berlin, 1920–1933 gg* (Voenno-politichieskie otnoshenia SSSR-Germania) Moscow (2001), 282, based on archival work in Arkhiv NKVT SSSR (Arkhiv Narkomata Vneshney Torgovli SSSR (Archive of the Peoples Commisariat for Foreign Trade of the USSR), f. osobyi sektor, op. 6066, d.233, 1. 129. German figures identical in H. James, *The Reichsbank and Public Finance in Germany, 1924–1933* (Frankfurt A. M. 1985) 312.

and direct investment and short-term (but not medium- or long-term) loans permitted. In October 1928 General Electric granted to Amtorg, the Soviet Trading Corporation in New York, a $25 million, six-year credit to buy electrical equipment, and renounced its claims for compensation for the nationalization of its Russian firm during the revolution. Over the next two years there were other technical assistance contracts and loans involving RCA (Radio Corporation of America), Standard Oil of New Jersey, and again General Electric, which signed a ten-year contract. In May 1929 the Ford Motor Company agreed to build and finance a 100,000 unit per year factory in Russia.[25] The Americans in 1929–30 temporarily surpassed Germany in exports to Russia and subsequently became the Soviet Union's second most important technological source during the first Five Year Plan.

Though the deepening depression appeared to confirm the Soviet predictions that the capitalist world was on the verge of collapse, this did not lead to any sense of relief or jubilation in Moscow. There were, instead, mounting fears that the economic tension would drive the states to war, and that the war among the imperialists would be accompanied by a war of intervention against the Soviet Union. In 1931, with the first Five Year Plan in full operation, Stalin made the point with unusual directness:

It is sometimes asked whether it is not possible to slow down the tempo somewhat? No, comrades, it is not possible! . . . To slacken the tempo would

[25] Jacobson, *When the Soviet Union Entered World Politics*, 254.

mean falling behind. And those who fall behind are beaten . . . Do you want our socialist fatherland to be beaten and lose its independence? But if you do not want this, you must liquidate its backwardness in the shortest possible time and develop genuine Bolshevik tempo in the matter of constructing its socialist system of economy. There is no other way . . . We are fifty or a hundred years behind the advanced countries. We must make good the distance in ten years. Either we do it, or they crush us.[26]

Though Stalin's 'second revolution', a central part of his drive for personal power, was devised to deal with the procurement crisis of 1928, it intensified the fortress mentality of the Kremlin. The 'foreign threat' and the 'internal class enemy' were used to create social cohesion at home; at some level, the slogans also reflected the Stalinist belief in an inevitable war. Stalin went so far as to argue that military independence would actually ease Soviet relations with other states in the difficult period of turbulence and conflict that would precede confrontation.

In the interests of national security, the Soviet leadership needed a modus vivendi with the capitalist world. There could be no world revolution unless the Soviet Union survived. Always apprehensive of possible coalitions directed against the USSR, by the beginning of the new decade it was France, rather than the economically weakened Britain, which posed the greatest threat. Insofar as such fears were realistic—and neither Chicherin nor Litvinov believed in their reality—they were of course much exaggerated. The British at no time since 1920 were prepared to launch an attack or back an anti-Russian coalition. Nor would they have encouraged Polish irredentism, given Austen Chamberlain's pragmatic attitude towards the eastern frontiers. There was, it is true, an undercurrent of hostility in London that had little to do with the Soviet Union's effective power. After all, even with regard to India, the British were relieved of their recurrent nightmares. Intelligence reports confirmed the military judgement at the end of the 1920s that the Soviet Union was in no position to mount an offensive campaign outside its own territories. The British remained sensitive to the ideological threat posed by the Soviet Union and to the activities of the Comintern, so carefully monitored by the intelligence services. The Russian threat, for immediate purposes, was in the east rather than in Europe. 'Russia is the enemy', and its chief weapon was 'ruthless propaganda all over the world', William Tyrrell, the British permanent under-secretary and future ambassador to France, wrote in the summer of 1926.[27] By 1929 the intelligence services claimed that they had

---

[26] R. Craig Nation, *Black Earth, Red Star: A History of Soviet Security Policy, 1917–1991* (Ithaca, NY, 1992), 65–6.

[27] *DBFP*, ser. Ia, vol. 11, no. 103.

successfully dealt with the threat of communist subversion both in Britain and India, but Bolshevism represented a continuing challenge to the empire. One might go back to the threat from France in 1791 for the nearest historical parallel. The British response was to marginalize and isolate the USSR in Europe and to compromise with nationalist movements (themselves often hostile to communism) elsewhere to consolidate their own position, and to check the spread of any revolutionary virus. The Quai d'Orsay, while equally anti-Bolshevik, regarded the Soviet Union as a secondary danger. There was always the threat of a Russo-German alliance, and the French right made much of the subversive activities of the French Communist party. For France, however, policy towards the USSR could never be divorced from its preoccupation with Germany, and its shifting attitudes towards Moscow had more to do with the state of relations with Berlin than with any form of threat posed by the Soviet Union.

In the early 1920s many westerners thought that the USSR was entering its Thermidorian period and that communism would die a natural death. Lloyd George believed that investment and trade would hasten Russia's return to normality and the abandonment of her unnatural and repugnant economic system. Such hopes began to vanish by the end of the decade, as national interests overrode ideological distaste and political and commercial ties were established with the Soviet Union. Its admission to the comity of nations was a grudging one, and the Soviet Union continued to be treated as a nation of the second rank but still dangerous in a way that most such states were not. 'Russia stands wholly apart from Europe', wrote Owen O'Malley, an official in the Northern Department of the Foreign Office, recommending its recognition in 1922. 'In the consideration of Russian problems,' he added, 'this country can employ neither wisdom drawn from long kinship to other members of the European family, nor experience acquired in relations with savage and tutelary peoples.'[28] The entrance of the Soviet Union into European affairs challenged both the ordering of domestic politics and the traditional concepts of international relations. Soviet activities and those of the national communist parties changed the configurations of the old right and left, dividing the latter and making it more vulnerable to the challenges of the right. On the international stage, whatever may have been its retreat from ideology in the later part of the decade, the Soviet Union remained a revolutionary power. The Soviet government was not strong enough to force its way into the concert of powers, but neither was it so weak as to pay the demanded price for full

---

[28] Owen O'Malley, 'Memorandum on Soviet policy, March 1921–December 1922'. In possession of the author.

admission. The fact that neither Lenin nor Stalin would conclude bargains on capitalist terms nor abandon their revolutionary goals confirmed the western view that the Soviet Union should remain outside the European concert. Though its revolutionary aspirations were subordinated to the more pragmatic interests of the Soviet state, Soviet propaganda, the activities of the Comintern, and communist parties, known or suspected, went beyond the confines of acceptable diplomacy, whether old or new. For many diplomats it was difficult to deal with 'revolutionaries' who were prepared to enlist the international working classes in the defence of the Soviet Union regardless of the cost to their own countries. Practical considerations necessitated contact and even agreement, but many believed that the USSR did not share the basic assumptions that linked the European states, regardless of their forms of government, in some form of loose association.

The cacophony of suspicion and hate that accompanied the industrialization and collectivization programmes magnified this basic distrust. Litvinov's efforts to assure Soviet participation in the deliberations of the capitalist powers were not well received. In his opening statement to the special commission on economic affairs that met in Geneva in May 1931, Litvinov ironically remarked: 'Mr. Chairman, allow me first to express my gratitude for the extremely kind words of welcome addressed to those newly arrived in Europe. The fact of my presence here will certainly inspire great joy in the hearts of all geographers of the world, since this will, if only partly, confirm the hypothesis that the territory of the former Russian empire is still situated in Europe.'[29] Neither the assembled politicians and economists nor even the most talented cartographers could have captured the ambiguities of the Soviet presence in Europe.

Italy, the Balkans, and Central Europe, 1925–1930

Books

Italy

BURGWYN, H. JAMES, *Il revisionismo fascista: la sfida di Mussolini alle grandi potenze nei Balcani e sul Danubio, 1925–1933* (Milan, 1979).

CAROCCI, GIAMPERO, *La politica estera dell'Italia fascista* (Laterza, Bari, 1969).

CASSELS, ALAN, *Mussolini's Early Diplomacy* (Princeton, 1970).

CEVA, LUCIO, *Storia delle forze armate in Italia* (Turin, 1981).

---

[29] Jonathan Haslam, *Soviet Foreign Policy, 1930–1933: The Impact of the Depression* (London and Basingstoke, 1983), 51.

CLARKE, J. CALVITT, *Russia and Italy Against Hitler: The Bolshevik–Fascist Rapprochement of the 1930s* (New York and London, 1991).

DAMIANI, CLAUDIA, *Mussolini e gli stati uniti, 1922–1935* (Bologna, 1980).

D'AMOJA, FULVIO, *La politica estera dell'Impero* (Milan, 1967).

—— *Declino e prima crisi dell'Europa di Versailles: studio sulla diplomazia italiana ed europea, 1931–1933* (Milan, 1967).

DE FELICE, RENZO, *Mussolini il duce: gli anni del consenso, 1929–1936* (Turin, 1974).

—— *Mussolini i Hitler: i rapporti segreti, 1922–1933, con documenti inediti* (Florence, 1975).

DI NOLFO, ENNIO, *Mussolini e la politica estera italiana, 1919–1933* (Padua, 1960).

KENT, PETER, *The Pope and the Duce: The International Impact of the Lateran Agreements* (London, 1981).

KNOX, MACGREGOR, *Mussolini Unleashed, 1939–1941: Politics and Strategy in Fascist Italy's Last War* (New York, 1982).

—— *Common Destiny: Dictatorship, Foreign Policy, and War in Fascist Italy and Nazi Germany* (Cambridge, 2000).

MACK SMITH, DENIS, *Mussolini's Roman Empire* (Harmondsworth, 1979).

PETERSEN, JENS, *Hitler–Mussolini: die Entstehung der Achse Berlin–Rom, 1933–1936* (Tübingen, 1973).

ROCHAT, GIORGIO, *Militari e politici nella preparazione della campagna d'Etiopia: studio e documenti, 1932–1936* (Milan, 1971).

—— *Guerre italiane in Libia e in Etiopia: studi militari, 1921–1939* (Milan, 1991).

—— *L'esercito italiano in pace e in guerra: studi di storia militare* (Paese, 1991).

RUSINOW, DENNISON I., *Italy's Austrian Heritage, 1919–1946* (Oxford, 1969).

SADKOVICH, JAMES J., *Italian Support for Croatian Separatism, 1927–1937* (New York, 1987).

SEGRÉ, CLAUDIO G., *Fourth Shore: The Italian Colonisation of Libya* (Chicago, 1974).

SHORROCK, WILLIAM I., *From Ally to Enemy: The Enigma of Fascist Italy in French Diplomacy, 1920–1940* (Kent, Ohio, 1988).

ZAMBONI, GIOVANNI, *Mussolinis Expansionspolitik auf dem Balkan* (Hamburg, 1970).

The Balkans and Central Europe

CAMPBELL, FENTON GREGORY, *Confrontation in Central Europe: Weimar Germany and Czechoslovakia* (Chicago and London, 1975).

GROMADA, THADDEUS V. (ed.), *Essays on Poland's Foreign Policy, 1918–1939* (New York, 1970).

HIDEN, JOHN and LOIT, ALEKSANDR (eds.), *The Baltic in International Relations Between the Two World Wars: Symposium Organized by the Center for Baltic Studies, November 11–13, 1986, University of Stockholm* (Stockholm, 1988). Esp. article by Romuald J. Misiunas.

HOLTJE, A., *Die Weimarer Republik und das Ost-Locarno Problem, 1919–1934* (Würzburg, 1958).

KLIMEK, ANTONÍN, *Diplomacy at the Crossroads of Europe: Czechoslovak Foreign Policy, 1918–1938*, trans. Libor Trejdl (Prague, 1989).

KORBEL, JOSEF, *Poland Between East and West: Soviet and German Diplomacy Toward Poland, 1919–1933* (Princeton, 1963).

MACARTNEY, C. A., *October Fifteenth: A History of Modern Hungary, 1929–1945*, 2 vols. (Edinburgh, 1961).

ROOS, H., *Polen und Europa: Studien zur polmischen Aussenpolitik, 1931–1939* (Tübingen, 1957).

TONCH, HANS, *Wirtschaft und Politik auf dem Balkan: Untersuchungen zu den deutsch-rumänischen Beziehungen in der Weimarer Republik unter besonderer Berücksichtigung der Weltwirtschaftskrise* (Frankfurt a. M., 1984).

SCHMIDT-HARTMAN, EVA and STANLEY B. WINTERS (eds.) *Grossbütannien, die USA und die Löhmeschen Länder, 1848–1938* (Munich, 1991).

WANDYCZ, PIOTR, *The Twilight of French Eastern Alliances, 1926–1936: French–Czechoslovak–Polish Relations from Locarno to the Remilitarization of the Rhineland* (Princeton, 1988).

WURM, CLEMENS A., *Die französische Sicherheitspolitik in der Phase der Umorientierung, 1924–1926* (Frankfurt a.M., 1979).

Articles

Italy

BURGWYN, H. JAMES, 'Conflict or Rapprochement? Grandi Confronts France and its Protégé Yugoslavia, 1929–1932', *Storia delle relazioni internazionali*, 1 (1987).

CASSELS, ALAN, 'Was There a Fascist Foreign Policy?', *International History Review*, 5: 2 (1983).

CEVA, LUCIO, 'Appunti per una storia dello Stato Maggiore generale fino alla vigilia della "non belligeranza", giugno 1925–luglio 1939', *Storia Contemporanea*, 10: 2 (1979).

—— 'Pianificazione militare e politica estera dell'Italia fascista 1923–1940', *Italiana contemporanea*, 219 (2000).

COHEN, JON S., 'The 1927 Revaluation of the Lira: A Study in Political Economy', *Economic History Review*, 25: 4 (1972).

DE CECCO, MARCELLO and MIGONE, GIAN GIACOMO, 'La collocazione internazionale dell'economia italiana', in J. B. Richard Bosworth and Sergio Romano (eds.), *La politica estera italiana, 1860–1985* (Bologna, 1991).

EDWARDS, P. G., 'The Foreign Office and Fascism, 1924–1929', *Journal of Contemporary History*, 5: 2 (1970).

ERLICH, HAGGAI, 'Mussolini and the Middle East in the 1920s: The Restrained Imperialist', in Uriel Dann (ed.), *The Great Powers in the Middle East, 1919–1939* (New York, 1988).

GUILLEN, PIERRE, 'Franco-Italian Relations in Flux, 1918–1940', in Robert Boyce (ed.), *French Foreign and Defence Policy, 1918–1940: The Decline and Fall of a Great Power* (London, 1988).

—— 'Les Vicissitudes des rapports économiques franco-italiens dans les années vingt', in Enrico Decleva and Pierre Milza (eds.), *La Francia e l'Italia negli anni venti: tra politica e cultura* (Milan, 1996).

KNOX, M., 'The Fascist Regime, its Foreign Policy and its Wars: An "Anti-Anti-Fascist Orthodoxy" ', *Contemporary European History*, 4 (1995).

—— 'Fascism: Ideology, Foreign Policy, and War', in A. Lyttleton (ed.) *Liberal and Fascist Italy* (Oxford, 2002).

LEONCINI, FRANCESECO, '*Italia e Cecoslovacchia 1919–1939*', *Rivista di Studi Politici Internazionali*, 45 (1979).

MIGONE, GIAN GIACOMO, 'La stabilizzazione della lira: la finanza americana e Mussolini', *Rivista di storia contemporanea* (1973).

PETERSEN, JENS, 'Die Außenpolitik des faschistischen Italien als historiographisches Problem', *Vierteljahrshefte für Zeitgeschichte*, 22 (1974).

PETRACCHI, GIORGIO, 'Ideology and Realpolitik: Italo-Soviet Relations, 1917–1933', *Journal of Italian History*, 2: 3 (1979).

SARTI, ROLAND, 'Fascist Modernisation in Italy: Traditional or Revolutionary?', *American Historical Review*, 75: 4 (1970).

—— 'Mussolini and the Italian Industrial Leadership in the Battle of the Lira, 1925–1927', *Past and Present*, 47 (1970).

SEGRÉ, CLAUDIO G., 'Liberal and Fascist Italy in the Middle East, 1919–1939: The Elusive White Stallion', in Uriel Dann (ed.), *The Great Powers and the Middle East, 1919–1939* (New York, 1988).

SHORROCK, W. I., 'France, Italy, and the Eastern Mediterranean in the 1920s', *International History Review*, 8 (1986).

WEBSTER, RICHARD A., 'Una speranza rinviata: l'espansione industriale italiana e il problema del petrolio dopo la prima guerra mondiale', *Storia Contemporanea*, 11: 2 (1980).

The Balkans and Central Europe

BORDIUGOV, G. A. and KOZLOV, V. A., 'La Troika danubiana di Mussolini: Italia, Austria e Ungheria, 1927–1936', *Storia Contemporanea*, 21: 4 (1990).

GASIOROWSKI, ZYGMUNT, 'Stresemann and Poland After Locarno', *Journal of Central European Affairs*, 18 (1958).

KRÜGER, PETER, 'La Politique extérieure allemande et les relations franco-polonaises (1918–1932)', in Georges-Henri Soutou, 'L'Alliance franco-polonaise, 1925–1933: ou comment s'en débarrasser?', *Revue d'Histoire Diplomatique*, 95 (1981).

LIPPETT, HELMUT, 'Zur deutschen Politik gegenüber Polen nach Locarno', *Vierteljahrshefte für Zeitgeschichte*, 19 (1971).

NÖTEL, RUDOLF, 'International Capital Movements and Finance in Eastern Europe, 1919–1949', *Vierteljahrschrift für Sozial-und Wirtschaftsgeschichte*, 61 (1974).

RICCARDI, LUCA, 'Il trattato italo-romano del 16 settembre 1926', *Storia delle relazioni internazionali*, 3 (1987).

ROTHSCHILD, JOSEPH, *East Central Europe between the Two World Wars* (Seattle, 1974).

SCHRÖDER, HANS-JÜRGEN, 'Die deutsche Südosteuropaspolitik und die Reaktion der angelsächsischen Mächte, 1929–1933/34', in Josef Becker and Klaus Hildebrand (eds.), *Internationale Beziehungen in der Weltwirtschaftskrise, 1929–1933: Referate und Diskussionsbeiträge eines Augsburger Symposions, 29. März bis 1. April 1979* (Munich, 1980).

SOUTOU, GEORGES-HENRI, 'L'Alliance franco-polonaise, 1925–1933: ou comment s'en débarrasser?', *Revue d'Histoire Diplomatique*, 95 (1981).

WANDYCZ, PIOTR S., 'La Pologne face à la politique locarnienne de Briand', in Georges-Henri Soutou 'L'Alliance franco-polonaise, 1925–1933: ou comment s'en débarrasser?', *Revue d'Histoire Diplomatique* 95 (1981).

TEICHOVA, ALICE, 'East-Central and South-East Europe', in Peter Mathias and Sidney Pollard (eds.), *The Cambridge Economic History of Europe*, vol. 8 (2nd edn., Cambridge, 1989).

The Soviet Union: Domestic Upheavals and Relations With Europe, 1925–1931

Books

BELOFF, MAX, *The Foreign Policy of Soviet Russia, 1929–1941*, 2 vols. (London, 1949).

CARR, E. H., *Socialism in One Country, 1924–1926*, 3 vols. (London, 1958–64).

——— *The Twilight of the Comintern, 1930–1935* (London, 1982).

——— and DAVIES, R. W., *Foundations of a Planned Economy, 1926–1929*, 3 vols. (New York, 1969–78).

DAVIES, R. W. and WHEATCROFT, S. G. (eds.), *Materials for a Balance of the Soviet National Economy, 1928–1930* (Cambridge, 1985).

DYCK, HARVEY L., *Weimar Germany and Soviet Russia, 1926–1933: A Study in Diplomatic Instability* (London, 1966).

FISCHER, LOUIS, *The Soviets in World Affairs: A History of the Relations between the Soviet Union and the Rest of the World, 1917–1929*, vol. 2 (Princeton, 1951).

GORODETSKY, GABRIEL, *The Precarious Truce: Anglo-Soviet Relations, 1924–1927* (Cambridge, 1977).

HASLAM, JONATHAN, *Soviet Foreign Policy, 1930–1933: The Impact of the Depression* (London and Basingstoke, 1993).

HOFF-WILSON, JOAN, *Ideology and Economics: US Relations with the Soviet Union, 1918–1933* (Columbia, Mo., 1974).

LAMBERT, NICK and RITTERSPORN, GÁBOR T. (eds.), *Stalinism: Its Nature and Aftermath. Essays in Honor of Moshe Lewin* (London, 1992).

McKENZIE, KERMIT, *Comintern and World Revolution, 1928–1943: The Shaping of Doctrine* (London, 1964).

MORRELL, GORDON W., Britain Confronts the Stalin Revolution: Anglo-Soviet Relations and the Metro-Vicks Crisis (Waterloo, Ont., 1995)

NEKRICH, ALEKSANDR, M., *Pariahs, Partners, Predators: German–Soviet Relations, 1922–1941*, ed. and trans. Gregory L. Freeze (New York and Chichester, 1997).

Pons, Silvir, and Andreo Romano (eds.), *Russia in the Age of Wars, 1914–1945* (Milan, 2000).

Reiman, Michal, *Die Geburt des Stalinismus: die UdSSR am Vorabend der 'zweiten Revolution'* (Frankfurt a.M., 1979). English trans., *The Birth of Stalinism: The USSR On the Eve of the 'Second Revolution'*, trans. George Saunders (Bloomington, Ind., 1987).

Salzmann, Stephanie, *Great Britain, Germany and the Soviet Union* (Woodbridge, Suffolk, and Rochester, NY, 2003).

Samuelson, Lennart, *Plans for Stalin's War Machine, Tukhachevskii and Military Economic Planning, 1925–1941* (Basingstoke, 2000).

Stone, D., *Hammer and Rifle: The Militarization of the Soviet Union* (Lawrence, Kan., 2000).

Vigor, Peter Hast, *The Soviet View of War, Peace, and Neutrality* (London, 1975).

Weingartner, Thomas, *Stalin und der Aufstieg Hitlers; die Deutschlandpolitik der Sowjetunion und der Kommunistischen Internationale, 1929–34* (Berlin, 1970).

Williams, Andrew J., *Labour and Russia: The Attitude of the Labour Party to the USSR, 1924–1934* (Manchester, 1989).

—— *Trading with the Bolsheviks: The Politics of East–West Trade, 1920–1939* (Manchester and New York, 1992).

Articles

Bordiugov, G. A. and Kozlov, V. A., 'The Turning Point of 1929 and the Bukharin Alternative', *Soviet Studies in History*, 28 (1990).

Debo, Richard K. and Carley, Michael Jabara, 'Always in Need of Credit: The USSR and Franco-German Economic Cooperation, 1926–1929', *French Historical Studies*, 20: 3 (1997).

Di Biago, Anna, 'Moscow, the Comintern and the War Scare, 1926–28' in Pons, S. and Romano, A. (eds.), *Russia in the age of wars* (Milan, 2000).

Dohan, Michael R., 'The Economic Origins of Soviet Autarky, 1927/8–1934', *Slavic Review*, 35 (1976).

—— 'Foreign Trade', in R. W. Davies (ed.), *From Tsarism to the New Economic Policy: Continuity and Change in the Economy of the USSR* (London, 1990).

Dyck, Harvey, L., 'German–Soviet Relations and the Anglo-Soviet Break, 1927', *Slavic Review*, 25 (1966).

Flory, Harriette, 'The Arcos Raid and the Rupture of Anglo-Soviet Relations, 1927', *Journal of Contemporary History*, 12 (1977).

Gorodetsky, Gabriel, 'The Soviet Union and Britain's General Strike of May 1926', *Cahiers du Monde Russe et Soviétique*, 17 (1976).

Hunter, Holland, 'The Over-ambitious First Soviet Five-Year Plan', *Slavic Review*, 32 (1973).

Jacobsen, Hans-Adolf, 'Primat der Sicherheit, 1928–1938', in Dietrich Geyer (ed.), *Sowjetunion: Aussenpolitik, 1917–1955*, vol. 1 (Cologne, 1972).

Lammers, Donald, N., 'The Second Labour Government and the Restoration of Relations with Soviet Russia, 1929', *Bulletin of the Institute of Historical Research*, 37 (1964).

McDermott, Kevin, 'Stalin and the Comintern During the "Third Period", 1928–1933', *European History Quarterly*, 25: 3 (1995).

Meyer, Alfred G., 'The War Scare of 1927', *Soviet Union/Union Soviétique*, 5 (1978).

Neilson, Keith, 'Pursued by a Bear: British Estimates of Soviet Military Strength and Anglo-Soviet Relations, 1922–1939', *Canadian Journal of History*, 28: 2 (1993).

Simonov, N. S., ' "Strengthen the Defence of the Land of Soviets": The 1927 "War alarm" and the Consequences', *Europe–Asia Studies*, 48, 8 (1996).

Pogge von Strandmann, Hartmut, 'Industrial Primacy in German Foreign Policy? Myths and Realities in German–Russian Relations at the end of the Weimar Republic', in R. Bessel and E. J. Feuchtwanger (eds.), *Social Change and Political Development in Weimar Germany* (London and Totowa, 1981).

Schinness, Roger, 'The Conservative Party and Anglo-Soviet Relations, 1925–1927', *European Studies Review*, 7 (1977).

Uldricks, Teddy, J., 'Russia and Europe: Diplomacy, Revolution and Economic Development in the 1920s', *International History Review*, 1 (1979).

Wheatcroft, S. G., Davies, R. W., and Cooper, J. M., 'Soviet Industrialisation Reconsidered: Some Preliminary Conclusions About Economic Development Between 1926 and 1941', *Economic History Review*, 39 (1986).

11

Faltering Internationalism: Disarmament and Security after Locarno[★]

I

It still looked possible in 1929 that something would be salvaged from the high promise of the Locarno agreements. Winston Churchill told an audience in Montreal that 'the outlook for peace has never been better than for fifty years'.[1] That most divisive and intractable problem, disarmament, was still on the international menu and even the most reluctant statesman had to acknowledge that it would be difficult, if not impossible, to avoid the long-delayed world disarmament conference. The League of Nations was to spend more time and energy on the pursuit of disarmament than on any other enterprise. Four years earlier members of the League of Nations had insisted on taking up what came to be a 'poisoned chalice'. While the Locarno agreements were still being negotiated, the Sixth League Assembly meeting in September 1925 invited the Council to initiate preparatory work for a general and all-inclusive disarmament conference. On 12 December the Council created a Preparatory Commission consisting initially of all ten states on the Council, six other European countries, and three key non-League members: Germany, the Soviet Union (which joined only in 1927 after finally settling a quarrel with the Swiss authorities over the killing of Barzlav Morovsky, a Soviet observer at the Lausanne conference of May 1923), and the United States. The Preparatory Commission held its first meeting in May 1926. Its members were instructed to draw up a draft treaty covering all three spheres of armaments (land, sea, and air), which would then be ratified by a world disarmament conference, expected to be called not later than 1927. The subsequent history of the Preparatory Commission's tortuous progress can best be

---

★For this chapter, see Tables A-7 and A-8 in the Appendix.

[1] Robert Rhodes James (ed.), *Winston S. Churchill: His Complete Speeches 1897–1963* (New York, 1974), v. 4668.

understood in terms of the disagreements between Britain and France and the basic and unresolved Franco-German confrontation. The disparity of views that separated London and Paris was present from the start. Briand, the French statesman most openly identified with the conciliation of Germany and the principles of the League, never abandoned his belief that security had to precede disarmament. Neither the League, the Locarno agreements, nor the 1928 Kellogg–Briand pact outlawing war provided France with the measure of security it needed to consider disarmament. Chamberlain, who ultimately shaped British disarmament policy, assumed that Locarno had settled the security issue and that the French were in a position, as the power with the largest army and air force, to reduce their armed services. He did not acknowledge the need for more extended guarantees as the price for French assent. The Germans, meanwhile, were not yet in a position to make demands, and Stresemann preferred to postpone the issue of equal rights. Nonetheless, Lord Robert Cecil, the main British spokesman for disarmament, made use of the potential German denunciation of the disarmament provisions of the Versailles treaty to push his reluctant colleagues to take action in Geneva. The Germans, after their difficult entrance into the Council, kept a low profile at first, but would emerge later as outspoken critics of the lack of progress.

During 1926–7 the work of the Preparatory Commission was largely of a technical character. The commission was only to discuss methods of limitation; the actual figures would be left to the disarmament conference to decide. Two technical subcommittees surveyed almost every conceivable method of arms limitation and produced exceedingly detailed reports. But each nation's military delegates naturally framed their own analyses in accordance with individual national-security requirements and the final reports were little more than a compendium of different national interests. A certain sense of camaraderie developed among the experts and some areas of agreement emerged. The pace was excruciatingly slow and the Assembly registered its impatience. Urged on by the Council, first the British and then the French presented draft conventions to the third session of the Preparatory Commission, held between 21 March and 26 April 1927. Despite the almost desperate efforts made by Cecil, the British draft reflected the opposition of each of the service departments to any form of effective arms limitation. They stressed the reductions already made, mainly for financial reasons, and claimed that Britain had already disarmed and that it was time for others to act. Except for submarines, no further reductions could be made in the number of ships, the army was already cut to the bare minimum, and the disparity between the British and French air forces had to be corrected in Britain's favour. In Paris, the Conseil Supérieur de la

Défense Nationale, the centre of French strategic decision-making, took a similar line on the impossibility of further arms reduction. Its major concern was to maintain the link between security and disarmament and to safeguard France's future position against Germany. The French army was already facing a further reduction in the period of conscripted service from three years to twelve months, and its leaders demanded the exclusion of reservists from any form of limitation. The French navy, expanding since the Washington Naval Conference, wanted to preserve its free hand in non-capital ship construction, citing both its imperial responsibilities and the Italian threat in the Mediterranean. A technically ageing air force with a fragmented and inefficient industrial base sought strict limitations on all possible rivals or the disarmament of all.

Each of the other participating states proposed its own disarmament scenario. The Italians proved a major obstacle to progress. The country was embarked on a two-year rearmament propaganda campaign, and Mussolini's new naval building programme was already fuelling the Franco-Italian naval race. Poland, the Little Entente countries, and Greece each stressed the need to strengthen the League as an organ of collective security before serious disarmament could begin. The Americans played a minor role in these discussions, supposedly waiting for clearer instructions pending President Coolidge's surprise invitation in 1927 to the five Washington treaty powers to meet at Geneva for another naval conference. The Germans pressed for arms reduction rather than arms limitation. The prospects for a draft convention were hardly promising.

Three key issues divided the land and sea powers and defeated the service experts: the limitation of trained military reserves, the method of naval limitation by overall tonnage or by category, and the degree of supervision and control to be exercised. The British and Americans wanted to limit the number of trained reserves as well as serving soldiers; the French and other continental states with conscription demanded their exclusion. The British, Americans, and Japanese wanted limitations by class of ship; this hardly suited the French and Italians, who wanted to be free to concentrate their resources where they were most useful. There was a continuing battle between the French and the British, backed by the Americans, over the creation of an enforcement agency. The French wanted an effective inspection system, while the British, for whom inspection was anathema, would not agree to any form of institutionalized international control. It was agreed that the limitation of air power should be based on the number and total horsepower of military planes. Due to British intransigence, with American and German support, civil aircraft were exempted from any form of regulation. The British and French drafts at the Preparatory Commission's third session were amalgamated to produce a 'first reading' draft convention. It provided for the limitation and not the reduction of armaments and was little more than a catalogue of Anglo-French differences. The Geneva meetings broke up at the end of April 1927 in an atmosphere of unhappiness and dissatisfaction.

II

The mood of the supporters of League-sponsored disarmament was not improved by the American invitation for naval discussions issued in February 1927. President Calvin Coolidge, anxious to avoid a clash with the 'big navy' group in Congress and seeking the kudos accorded President Harding in 1922 before the forthcoming national elections, had already been thinking of a second Washington conference when the League created the Preparatory Commission. Pressed by the Germans to come to Geneva, and concerned that if they did not join the Preparatory Commission they would be blamed for its anticipated failure, the Americans had reluctantly agreed to join. In the face of the deadlocked situation on the commission, the American president suggested that his conference, which he hoped would extend the Washington ratios to auxiliary ships, should be held in Geneva as an adjunct to the commission's proceedings. The British Admiralty, realizing that the days of relatively generous financial treatment were ending as naval costs rose and demands for general retrenchment increased, turned to arms limitation as a way to cut the costs of its forthcoming large naval building programme scheduled to begin after 1931, when the Washington treaty naval holiday ended. The French and Italians, for different reasons, refused to participate: the French did not want to deal with naval armaments in isolation and feared an extension of the Washington ratios to non-capital ships; the Italians wanted the ratios extended but without sacrificing their parity with France. The League discussions on general disarmament were suspended while the 'private' naval talks went on.

The summer's naval meetings in Geneva, from June to August 1927, were a disaster. It was holiday time, and exceedingly hot in Geneva as well as in Washington, a not unimportant point in the days before air-conditioning. An impasse developed between the American and British naval authorities, with the Japanese unable to mediate their differences, though the latter were saved from their own battle with the Americans over a higher naval ratio. The three naval powers agreed on limiting submarines, destroyers, and other classes of auxiliaries, but the Royal Navy wanted seventy cruisers (fifteen heavy and fifty-five light) while the Americans refused to endorse a cruiser fleet of more than forty-five vessels (twenty-five heavy and twenty light). The Anglo-American debate over cruisers was over both type and numbers. The Americans preferred restricted numbers of heavy cruisers built up to the Washington treaty's limits of 10,000 tons and armed with eight-inch guns for fleet support work. The Admiralty considered light cruisers with six-inch guns or less and weighing around 7,000 tons ideal for both commerce protection and blockade purposes, and wanted to build them with as few restrictions as possible. American needs, according to its delegation, were 'relative': the US navy could be greater or smaller depending on British and Japanese naval strength, so building depended on British action. While not opposing the American right to build up to the British cruiser levels (which it assumed would not happen), the Baldwin government insisted on its 'absolute need' for seventy cruisers to defend the empire and overseas trade, the latter far more important for Britain than for the United States. These 'absolute' requirements, determined by the length of inter-imperial communications, the dependence on overseas oil and food imports, and reliance on the blockade weapon, necessitated special consideration. The Admiralty claims brought an immediate reaction from the Americans. The Anglophobe Admiral Hilary Jones, knowing that neither the president nor Congress would be prepared to build up to the British light-cruiser figures, led the fight against the Royal Navy's 'right' to supremacy.

The clash in Geneva brought to the foreground the conflicting Anglo-American interests but also sparked a fierce domestic debate in London. The British cabinet was divided, torn between those demanding recognition of Britain's global naval supremacy and those anxious to conclude an agreement with the Americans in order to forward the disarmament cause. Cecil, the chief proponent of disarmament, was willing to concede the principle of cruiser parity to the Americans and to negotiate the cruiser question. He had the support of Baldwin, but Chamberlain, preoccupied with European questions, proved indecisive. Leading the cabinet fight to reassert the Royal Navy's naval supremacy and right to seventy cruisers was the highly influential and articulate Churchill, one of the navy's most stalwart defenders. Churchill believed that Britain had to maintain its strategic independence: 'There can really be no parity between a power whose navy is its life and a power whose navy is only for prestige. It always seems to be assumed that it is our duty to humour the United States and minister to their vanity. They do nothing for us in return, but exact their last pound of flesh.'[2] Unable to achieve consensus, Baldwin failed to give the British negotiators at

---

[2] Quoted in Phillips Payson O'Brien, *British and American Naval Power: Politics and Policy, 1900–1937* (Westport, Conn., and London, 1998), 192.

Geneva, Cecil and William Bridgeman, the easily influenced first lord of the Admiralty, any clear direction. At first the British and American negotiators kept matters under control; the former made no difficulty about recognizing the American right to parity in all classes of vessels, and both sides compromised on the question of tonnage level. It was the combative Churchill, strongly seconded by Admiral Beatty, whose highly persuasive invective threw a spanner in the works. With Baldwin on his way to Canada, the cabinet recalled Cecil and Bridgeman, and under Churchill's influence decided that Britain must have its way. Though the British delegates tried to find a way around their own government's one-sided proposals, the cabinet would not compromise. The Geneva conference broke up on 4 August on a rancorous note of mutual hostility.

The collapse of the conference was followed by mutual recriminations. Secretary of State Frank Kellogg accused the British of never intending 'to agree to anything'. The usually mild-mannered Chamberlain called Hugh Gibson, the American delegate, a 'dirty dog'. In disgust at his own government's intransigence and at Churchill's wrecking tactics, Cecil finally made good one of his frequent threats to resign. Herbert Hoover and the British ambassador in Washington discussed the possibility of an Anglo-American war. Yet Churchill's outspoken defence of British naval supremacy did not prevent him from attacking Admiralty plans to lay down three cruisers in both 1927 and 1928. The navy got only one cruiser in 1927 and none the following year. Churchill's anger at the American claims to cruiser parity was undoubtedly fuelled by their 'grasping' attitude towards wartime debts and other financial issues. While attached to the symbols of power, Churchill did not believe that the Americans would spend the money required to engage in a naval race with the British, and so there was no danger in calling their bluff. His intervention, however, spurred the 'big navy' people in Congress to use the Geneva collapse to give substance to their previously unpopular cause. The House of Representatives passed a new naval bill providing for fifteen new cruisers and an aircraft carrier during the next four years, the largest authorization since the end of the war. There remained a strong, if temporarily outmanoeuvred, 'small navy' group in Congress, led by William Borah and Gerald Nye, both Republicans, and William King, a Democrat from Utah, who campaigned against the bill, backed by intense lobbying on the part of peace and church groups. The Senate debate was delayed by the forthcoming elections in November 1928, but the advantage lay with the administration supporters. Nautical tempers ran high, with damning statements on both sides, and the Navy Department refurbished its war plans against Britain and Japan.

III

A misjudged British initiative had given the victory to the 'big navy' faction. During the summer of 1928, hoping to soothe the Americans by restarting the stalled talks in the Preparatory Commission, Chamberlain negotiated an 'armaments compromise' with the French, accepting France's position on trained reservists in return for a division of the cruiser class into two groups, with limitations imposed only on the larger type of cruiser. Gun calibre rather than tonnage was made the primary determinant; countries could have as many 10,000-ton cruisers as they wanted but would be restricted in the number of ships that could carry guns larger than six inches. It may be that Chamberlain took the initiative because of fears of a possible Franco-American deal that would leave the British isolated and cast in the role of villain in Geneva, nevertheless it appears that he expected the Americans to accept the 'compromise'. When the terms of the agreement were prematurely leaked (the official announcement came on 30 July), Berlin, Rome, and particularly Washington each took umbrage. British acceptance of the French demand for unlimited trained army reserves seemed calculated to affront the Germans and underline the strength of the Anglo-French attachment. Like the Americans, the Germans had been neither consulted nor informed about the details of the secret understanding. The Americans, in the middle of a presidential election campaign, made much of the issue. The usually phlegmatic and silent Coolidge exploded at this example of British 'duplicity'. The US navy saw no advantage in building 10,000-ton cruisers and arming them with six-inch guns. After Hoover's victory in the November election, the 'lame duck' Coolidge used his Armistice Day address to castigate the British and issue a call for American naval superiority. On 5 January 1929 the Cruiser Bill was passed in the Senate. It was a tempest in a teapot. Without American participation, no naval limitation agreement had any importance for the British. The Conservative government in London, faced with sharp criticism from both Labour and the Liberals, looked for ways to placate Washington. An ailing Chamberlain, in order to repair his damaged diplomatic fences and in the belief that the blockade issue (the incompatibility of the British doctrine of maritime belligerent rights and the American assertion of freedom of the seas) lay at the bottom of the dispute, accepted a Committee for Imperial Defence subcommittee recommendation to make a secret approach to the White House for an acceptable compromise. Baldwin and Chamberlain were preparing for new discussions in Washington as the British elections approached. For Britain, the Anglo-French deal was dead. The French response to the British initiative had been based, in part, on fears of a German–Russian partnership on the disarmament front. Even more important for Paris, as became clear in the 1929 session of the Preparatory Commission, was the belief that the deal's basic principle, the recognition of the interdependence of armaments, still remained valid.

The Anglo-French summer agreement was little more than an attempt to break the impasse at Geneva through bilateral negotiations, though neither government was anxious to have a disarmament conference at all. With the Preparatory Commission talks stalled, a separate attempt was made to postpone further discussion by again raising the security question. The French hoped that this diversion would postpone the resumption of disarmament talks, or even turn them into a full-scale consideration of security. At their instigation, a Commission on Arbitration and Security (CAS) was created by the Assembly in September 1927 as an adjunct body to the Preparatory Commission. The British went along with the majority, not because of a change of view on security but because they too wanted to postpone the disarmament talks. By late 1929, however, the French no longer cared about the CAS, which had become stuck in the drafting of 'model treaties' providing for the pacific settlement of disputes by compulsory arbitration, by judicial decision, or by conciliation, considered in Paris as an inadequate way of handling the security problem. It would be Henderson, the foreign secretary in the new Labour government, who regarded the work of the CAS as being of genuine benefit to European security, and who in September 1929 revived the pressure to act on its recommendations. In the interim the Germans became increasingly restive at the lack of progress. Less interested in security than in disarmament, they had been promised that discussions would proceed *pari passu*, but this did not happen.

Other diversions also took their toll in lost time. The Soviet Union's appearance at Geneva in 1927 and the dramatic intervention of its delegate, Maxim Litvinov, was the start of an active diplomatic role in the disarmament talks. The Preparatory Commission sessions of November–December 1927 and March 1928 were occupied almost entirely with the introduction and condemnation of Litvinov's proposal for complete and universal disarmament. The British were scathing in their dismissal of what was generally agreed to be an attempt to sow discord and win propaganda points.

One event in the difficult summer of 1928 which lightened the international mood was the conclusion of the Kellogg–Briand pact, or as it was officially known, the 'International Treaty for the Renunciation of War as an Instrument of National Policy'. This had its genesis in an attempt by Briand, in conflict with the Americans over navies, war debts, and tariffs, to draw Washington into a 'solemn declaration' barring war between the two countries. Kellogg answered the French draft only in late December 1927, and managed to convert the French initiative into a multilateral peace pact that rendered Briand's proposal totally innocuous. There was no way that the Americans could be brought into a European security system. A good deal of diplomatic wrangling proceeded the pact's adoption. The pact directed that its signatories renounce war, but provided no means of enforcement. In its final form, the draft was diluted to exclude wars for self-defence and for the fulfilment of existing treaty obligations. At Britain's request, the lesser Locarno powers, the Dominions, India, and Ireland were invited to participate. One American senator contemptuously called the pact an 'international kiss', but this much-quoted description did not reflect the mood of the emotional signing ceremony in Paris. On 27 August at the Quai d'Orsay, in front of numerous reporters and photographers, the representatives of fifteen nations each signed the pact with a special gold pen. This 'pious declaration against sin' proved immensely popular, despite the cynicism of some of the western leaders. The ceremony caught the popular imagination and appeared to revive the flagging Locarno spirit. Stresemann, who had been repeatedly ill during the first six months of the year, suffered his first stroke in August but insisted on coming to Paris for the signing. Chamberlain was too ill to attend the ceremony, but Kellogg himself was present and this appearance by the American secretary of state was hailed as a mark of Washington's concern with European security. Briand, though knowing better, claimed that the United States would join France in any future war. Chamberlain, who had little time for Kellogg or for the new pact, suggested, somewhat more soberly, that if the world thought it probable or even certain that the United States would not assist the treaty-breaker, it would be a 'formidable guarantee' for the maintenance of peace. Thirty-one nations soon followed the original fifteen signatories. It did not escape notice that the Soviet Union, though excluded from the ceremony, was the first to ratify the pact, and that its ratification was followed by overtures to Poland and Lithuania to put it into immediate effect. Poland unexpectedly agreed, asking only that the agreement be extended to include the other Baltic states and Romania. The Soviet approach to Warsaw alarmed Stresemann, but the prompt ratification of the Kellogg–Briand pact by so many other states reduced the importance of the 'Litvinov protocol' of February 1929. In any case, Russian–Polish relations soon deteriorated, much to the German relief.

For most of the watching world 1928 was the year that the Kellogg–Briand pact was signed. Its warm reception encouraged further efforts in Geneva to strengthen the security functions of the League in the interests of preserving the peace. With the disarmament talks suspended until early 1929, the CAS delegates busied themselves during the first half of 1928 with discussing Articles 11 and 16 of the Covenant and related questions. In November 1927 the tireless Fridtjof Nansen had suggested a draft 'model treaty' for compulsory arbitration, open for all states to sign. Another set of draft treaties, following the Locarno pattern, was based on contracts between states renouncing recourse to force and promising mutual assistance in case of violation. There was also a German proposal, backed by France, that states should bind themselves in advance to support any recommendations made by the Council to reduce the danger of war (the 'Model Treaty to Improve the Means of Preventing War') and a Finnish suggestion for providing financial assistance to victims of aggression. Few of these proposals were welcomed by the British, and their doubts were shared by the Canadians and South Americans, who feared the implied extension of their commitments. Though Chamberlain championed the conclusion of 'Locarno model' treaties by other states, he had no intention of offering a British guarantee of any other regional grouping. Nor did he favour the recommendations for facilitating the work of the Council in settling disputes. Britain had not signed the 'Optional Clause' binding states in advance to submit certain classes of international disputes to the Permanent Court of International Justice and agreeing in advance to accept its decisions as binding. Though opened for signature in 1920, only sixteen states had signed it by 1928 (Germany was the one great power). Only the Finnish suggestion of financial assistance won British backing, more as a substitute for Article 16 than, as the initiators intended, an extension of it. The British and the Dominions were not alone in their dislike of sanctions. The Germans were as wary as the British of any attempt to reopen discussion of the contents of the Geneva Protocol which, in their view, would make future treaty revision more difficult. The League discussions were conducted in a piecemeal fashion; agreement always stopped short of the automatic provisions found in the rejected Geneva Protocol. The 1928 debates were little more than a repetition of earlier discussions with lower initial expectations. Three of the drafted model conventions were combined into a 'General Act for the Pacific Settlement of International Disputes' which was approved by the Assembly in September 1928. The British delegation, still dazzled by the glare of the arc-lamps that had illuminated the signing of the Kellogg–Briand pact, could scarcely object. The German and Finnish proposals, unanimously endorsed by the Assembly, were left for future consideration. There was none of the excitement generated by the Protocol; many of the participants felt that these were little more than legalistic exercises.

IV

Given the Anglo-French lack of enthusiasm for the calling of a disarmament conference and their continuing disagreements in the expert committees, it was somewhat surprising that a 'second-reading' draft convention actually emerged from the deliberations of the Preparatory Commission at its sixth session (15 April to 6 May 1929), after a yearlong interruption of its labours and almost two years since the conclusion of the 'first reading' convention. The setbacks of 1928 and the lack of progress had left the major powers in a chastened mood. Prior to the reconvening of the commission, there was a flood of petitions from all parts of the world demanding that progress be made and a date set for the disarmament conference itself. When the delegates assembled in Geneva, conciliation was the order of the day. What conciliation actually meant was the abandonment of the most contested positions. A speech from Hugh Gibson, the American delegate, presented an encouraging message from Hoover accepting a French compromise on naval disarmament. The British and Americans agreed not to demand a limitation of trained reserves. In return the French no longer insisted on budgetary limitations of war material and withdrew from their strongly held position on inspection. Unable to decide how the production of war materials was to be controlled, the commission adopted an American proposal that countries publicize their armament expenditure. In this rather unsatisfactory manner the 'second-reading' draft convention, a set of anodyne technical provisions that hardly advanced the cause of arms limitation, was approved. The German and Soviet representatives pointed out how little had been accomplished and voiced their mutual disappointment over the results. It was somewhat ironical that both these countries were embarking on rearmament programmes. The draft convention, nevertheless, was warmly received by the majority of delegates, and it was rather unfortunate that the Preparatory Commission session was then adjourned so that the main naval powers could resume their private discussions.

Many commentators at the time argued that the quest for general disarmament was not only doomed to failure but counter-productive. There was little hope for real progress in the absence of further security for France, and unsuccessful discussions seemed to produce only ill will. The calling of a disarmament conference would pose even greater dangers, for it would have to deal with the problem of numbers and probably face German claims for equality of treatment. There was much to be said for procrastination. Winston Churchill's 'zoo allegory', contained in a speech to his constituents in October 1928, proved all-too prophetic when the World Disarmament Conference finally met. When the animals in the zoo came together in a disarmament conference, he recounted, first the Rhino argued that teeth were barbarous weapons but horns were strictly defensive, then the Lion defended teeth and claws as honourable means of self-defence, and finally the Bear 'proposed that both teeth and horns should be banned and never used again for fighting by any animal. It would be quite enough if animals were allowed to give each other a good hug when they quarrelled'.[3] In the end, Churchill concluded, they argued so fiercely and became so angry with each other that they had to be persuaded by the keepers to return to their cages. There was a frightening distinction to be made. The difference between the zoo and Geneva was the absence of both zookeeper and cages to which the beasts could be returned. Instead, the chief participants began to rearm, with the most disarmed participant among those proceeding the fastest.

The search for a disarmament agreement continued because the powers could not be seen to fail. The fundamental divisions that prevented progress were disguised. The conflict between German revisionism and French security, and the differing security goals of Paris and London, were left undefined. The British and French governments, when they could, avoided making political choices that would expose the futility of continuing talks. The Conservative government, facing an election in which disarmament would be an issue, felt that the electorate demanded progress. After his resignation Cecil had turned disarmament into a partisan issue; as president of the League of Nations Union, he was able to mobilize the 'dissidents', mainly Liberal or Labour, to campaign for disarmament. Though Baldwin and Chamberlain, planning their trip to Washington, were prepared to take a more positive stance at Geneva, they were tarred with the anti-disarmament brush. In March 1929, on the eve of the new Preparatory Commission meetings, in a somewhat cynical electoral move the Conservative cabinet agreed to accept any disarmament arrangements unanimously adopted in Geneva. The Labour party platform promised the reinvigoration of the League, especially in its arbitration and disarmament goals. Henderson, Cecil, who was brought back to the Foreign Office by Labour as a special adviser on League affairs, Cecil's friend and acolyte Philip Noel-Baker, a Quaker and champion of complete and universal disarmament, and Hugh Dalton, future parliamentary under-secretary at the Foreign Office, took charge of Britain's Geneva policy following Labour's victory in May 1929. There was less public pressure on French ministers. Disarmament as such was not debated in the Chamber of Deputies and

---

[3] Martin Gilbert, *Winston S. Churchill*, Vol. V: *1922–1939* (London, 1976), 305.

there was no equivalent in France to the League of Nations Union. In 1931, when the League of the Rights of Man circulated a ballot in favour of disarmament, they secured only 109,673 signatures. Briand's priorities, security before disarmament, were in accord with public sentiment, and there was little difference between the Quai d'Orsay and the armed services about the line to be followed in Geneva. The able and highly respected René Massigli, head of the Quai's League of Nations section, was concerned not to fall out with the British or to give London and Washington grounds for accusing the French of militarist ambitions. In the United States, because Congress in general and the Senate in particular played such a central part in the foreign-policy process, peace groups could be mobilized and their interventions were highly effective. Particularly before elections, presidential candidates took note. At the very least, in the spring of 1929, no state wished to be singled out and blamed for the lack of progress at Geneva. Governments could not be for war.

There was another consideration that coloured the disarmament talks—money. The hope to cut expenditure on armaments in a period of peace was a major factor in the thinking of many governments, particularly in Britain and the United States. In Washington as in London, an unwillingness to appropriate funds for arms was a powerful incentive to seek some form of agreement. Coolidge, and more productively his successor Hoover, a Quaker with a social conscience and one of the few American presidents to have had extensive experience abroad, genuinely believed that disarmament would promote peace and that money saved on armaments could be used to pay war debts and to restore European prosperity. Congressional unwillingness to fund ship-

TABLE 26. Anglo-French Military Expenditure, 1925–1933 (millions current prices)

	Britain (£)	France (fr.)
1925	114.7	6.524
1926	119.5	7.511
1927	116.7	11.181
1928	117.5	9.778
1929	113.5	13.844
1930	113.1	11.075
1931	110.9	15.915
1932	107.9	13.814
1933	103.9	13.431

Sources: Robert Frankenstein, Le Prix du réarmement français 1935–39 (Sorbonne, 1982), 303; British Parliamentary Papers.

building was paralleled by repeated British Treasury demands for cuts in naval expenditure. When Labour took office in 1929, a year after the 'ten-year rule' was reaffirmed without the need for an annual review, the new chancellor of the Exchequer, Snowden, again cut the service estimates. Army estimates for 1930 were reduced by £605,000; work on the Singapore naval base was suspended and the 1929 naval building programme slashed; the RAF was forced to postpone by three years (until 1938) the completion of its expansion to fifty-two squadrons. It is difficult to judge how far financial limitations were filtered into the estimates, but it was not uncommon to present financial cuts as reductions made to advance the disarmament cause. The service departments used their claims to unilateral disarmament in order to defend themselves against any further reductions in the defence expenditure. By 1930 all three services believed that Britain was under-armed, and that because of financial limitations all the country's forces had to be used for imperial communication and defence and for the air protection of the home islands. The chiefs of staff in 1930 warned: 'This country is in a less favourable position to fulfil the Locarno guarantees than it was, without any written guarantee, to come to the assistance of France and Belgium in 1914.'[4] They argued that Britain's weakened defence posture made it impossible to assume any additional security commitments. The French were not unaware of the financial exigencies that lay behind the British case for arms limitation; Labour prime minister Ramsay MacDonald was concerned that other nations might think that the British pursuit of arms limitation was due mainly to financial weakness. The economic argument was used in London both for and against the case for arms limitation.

The French case against reductions in arms, which the British dismissed with contempt, was based on the claim that France had already cut its armaments to 'the lowest point consistent with national security' as required by the Covenant. In fact, between 1924 and 1930–1 French funding for its defence services increased by 25 per cent, augmented by the additional special credits for the construction of the Maginot Line first included in the budget of 1929–30.[5] The French navy reaped the benefits of this funding, getting over 50 per cent of the defence appropriations between 1924 and 1930. With its eye to the 'German menace', the army felt that the gap between Versailles Germany and France had to be preserved, making it difficult to endorse any arms-limitation

---

[4] Memo by Chiefs of Staff Subcommittee, 'A Review of Imperial Defence, 1930', 29 July 1930, PRO, CAB 4/20, CID paper 1009-B.
[5] Robert Frankenstein, *Le Prix du réarmement français, 1935–1939* (Paris, 1982), 29. See graph on p. 30.

agreements that could reduce it. It was the continuation of this gap, as much as the size and condition of the French army, that provided France with its future military security. The military chiefs made much of the cuts in military service and in the number of effectives to show what France had already done in the way of disarmament. They fought against any further reduction, though the obsolescence of the air force and its qualitative weakness might have encouraged second thoughts. France's need for military supremacy was as great as the British need for naval superiority, and the latter's failure to appreciate the parallel was a constant source of frustration. In the French military view (sometimes shared by the British Admiralty), supremacy and security were one and the same. Though much was made of the German infractions of the Versailles treaty's disarmament clauses, the existing situation was less important than the future, particularly after the Allied withdrawal from the Rhineland. Purely financial considerations become critical only after 1931, when France's new left–centre governments adopted deflationary policies to combat the effects of the depression and administered successive cuts in defence expenditure. In the pre-1930 period, when the nature and siting of the future defensive fortifications were already under discussion and the army chiefs knew they would need major appropriations, the latter rightly felt that the defensive nature of their plans would have wide political and popular appeal, even in those circles sympathetic to disarmament or at least opposed to increases in defence expenditure.

It was primarily the Anglo-French differences and the diversionary Anglo–American naval rivalry that delayed progress on disarmament before 1930, but the Assembly constantly prodded both the Council and the Preparatory Commission to get on with the task. The Germans and Russians, in particular, would not let the issue die. The Germans were in a paradoxical situation, which they exploited to the full. The League was created as part of a treaty intended to constrain them, yet once they joined that body of sovereign states with equal rights and obligations, it was inevitable that they should claim their right to rearm unless all the other League members disarmed to the German levels. With Germany's return to great-power status, symbolized by its presence on the Council of the League, there was a time-bomb ticking in Geneva. The French view was obvious, but the British, too, were wary of raising the armaments question. Some Conservative ministers preferred concentrating on the potential Soviet threat rather than the German danger to the peace. Though he called for the removal of Germany's 'just grievances', Churchill was one of the few consistently arguing that a strong French army was a guarantee of peace. During his lifetime Stresemann did not force the pace. While German domestic opinion was focused on the evacuation of the Rhineland, he preferred to wait. Count Bernstorff, the German disarmament delegate, was instructed to protect Germany's future position and focus the Preparatory Commission's attention on the forthcoming disarmament conference, but to avoid disputation with the French. In the summer of 1928, when the calling of a conference was again postponed, Bernstorff became more outspoken. Stresemann's League policies had to pay larger domestic dividends. The Germans were not the only revisionist power demanding a conference. Soviet security depended on strengthening the state through economic reorganization and the build-up of armaments. Support for disarmament, however, was a way of dividing the capitalist states and forestalling the dangers of capitalist attack. Even if the League served 'imperialist interests', there were practical as well as ideological advantages to be derived from active participation in the Preparatory Commission. After the rejection of his first disarmament proposal, Litvinov reappeared in April 1929 with a second, more promising draft based on a distinction between offensive and defensive weapons: the former were to be massively reduced and eventually abolished. These proposals were revived by the Americans during the course of the disarmament conference itself. In 1929, however, Litvinov's proposal was supported only by Germany, China, and Turkey. The Preparatory Commission decided to proceed to a second reading of its own 1927 draft. Despite the general suspicion with which Litvinov's interventions were greeted, the Soviet delegate mastered the rules and vocabulary of the Geneva game. The adroit, multilingual Russian player identified his country with the pursuit of disarmament and made it difficult to deflect Assembly pressure for the calling of the much-delayed world conference.

Delegates to the Tenth League Assembly, which opened in Geneva in September 1929, the League's anniversary year, were optimistic. In August, at the Hague conference, the reparations conflict had apparently been resolved. The seemingly successful ending of that difficult month-long meeting provided a hopeful setting for the Assembly opening two days later. Diplomats spoke of the 'final liquidation of the war' and anticipated 'new orientations' in European relations. On the disarmament front there were renewed hopes for progress. The inauguration of Herbert Hoover, a known 'internationalist', in March 1929 and the victory of the British Labour party in May 1929 paved the way for a more productive approach to peace. The new American president, even before the onset of the depression, was resolved to cut American defence spending. Prime minister Ramsay MacDonald was as anxious as the president to settle the naval dispute between the two countries, and was set on achieving a general disarmament agreement. Foreign Secretary Arthur Henderson was preparing his new initiatives on international arbitration, intended to reassure the French and advance the disarmament cause. In Paris, the long-serving Aristide Briand (foreign minister in fifteen cabinets, four of which he headed between 1925 and 1932) was both prime minister and foreign secretary from July until October 1929, and remained at the Quai d'Orsay when André Tardieu took office in November. The way seemed open for a rethinking of the European future at a moment when France was financially strong and retained her military edge over Germany. Briand, though accepting that the 'forces profondes' ultimately worked in the German favour and that France had no option but conciliation, had no intention of giving away what remained of French protection without adequate compensation in the form of additional security guarantees.

The British took the initiative, both on the question of disarmament and the promotion of the League's security system. Anxious to move towards a more effective disarmament convention, a British resolution reopened several long-debated issues, such as the dropping of limitations on trained reserves and the weak 'indirect means' adopted to limit war material, supposedly settled at the Preparatory Commission meeting in April. Arguing that there were or would be sufficient security guarantees in place to permit the French to cut their forces, the intention of the new proposals was to increase the pressure on France to assist the cause of disarmament. Cecil, the British representative on the League's Third Committee which handled disarmament, pressed the British views on trained reserves even when it was clear that the French had no wish to reopen the question. Worse still, Cecil's dogmatic approach to disarmament infuriated the French representatives and intensified their suspicions about Anglo-American collusion over naval disarmament. Faced with threats to make difficulties over naval matters unless Britain ceased its 'perpetual attacks' on French land forces, a compromise was found which put off any discussion of the Preparatory Commission's decisions until its next meeting. The French continued to suspect that Britain intended to have its way.

More promising was Henderson's determination to promote the extension of the League system of arbitration and conflict resolution. Unlike his Conservative predecessors, he had great faith in the efforts to strengthen the League's security functions and believed that these would provide a way out of the disarmament–security dilemma without incurring additional British commitments: 'The French would come to trust in arbitration, have a feeling of security, and feel that they could do without calling up all their available man-power every year', he told a British journalist.[6] From the start, the Labour government set its face

⁶ A. L. Kennedy Diary, 18 Sept. 1929, Churchill College, LKEN 1/8.

against a return to the conditions of the Geneva Protocol. Henderson was insistent, however, that Britain should sign the Optional Clause, which was adopted in September 1929 with minor reservations due to Cabinet and Commonwealth fears. Eighteen states had signed before Britain, forty-two soon after its acceptance. Henderson also secured cabinet permission to announce Britain's forthcoming adhesion to the General Act for the Pacific Settlement of International Disputes, with its provisions for conciliation, judicial settlement, and settlement by arbitration. Due to South African opposition, it was not until the Imperial Conference of October 1930 that Britain could go forward, depositing its ratification in May 1931. The cabinet also agreed to accept the Finnish proposal for financial assistance to victims of aggression, though to placate opponents of further commitments to collective security, the agreement was not to come into effect until a disarmament treaty was signed. There was far more dissent about the Model Treaty, subsequently known as the 'Draft General Convention to Strengthen the Means of Preventing War', for it raised the vexed questions of Council direction and the imposition of sanctions. Signatories were to bind themselves in advance, in case of dispute, to carry out any Council directives to reduce the danger of war, including the right to relocate military forces and to appoint supervisory commissioners. In London the Admiralty, backed by MacDonald, objected to this possible limitations on Britain's freedom to move its fleet. It was finally agreed that Britain would obey League directives 'not inconsistent with national safety', but would not accept any extension of sanctions beyond those included in the Covenant. The amended text of the General Convention, adopted by the 1931 Assembly at the time of the Manchurian crisis, gave the Council only limited powers of direction and minimal inspection rights and contained no specific provisions for sanctions.

The French, who felt that the General Convention was generally inferior to the Geneva Protocol, signed mainly because they wanted to demonstrate French co-operation in the search for peace. By the time the World Disarmament Conference opened, twenty-two states had signed the General Convention, including Germany and France but not Britain. MacDonald and Henderson also wanted to bring the Covenant into line with the Kellogg–Briand pact, by eliminating any recourse to war except in self-defence. This particular effort to close the 'gaps' in the Covenant provided the French with a welcome opening to suggest far-reaching amendments (making arbitration obligatory and all sanctions automatic and immediate in their operation) in the direction of the rejected Geneva Protocol. Their amendments, while enlisting the personal support of Cecil, were as unwelcome to the Labour government as the 1924 proposals had been to the Conservatives. The British were willing only to make modest amendments to the Covenant, while the French felt that these, apart from compulsory arbitration, were more dangerous than advantageous for the future security of France. Henderson believed that these various measures and the 'harmonization' of the Covenant and the Kellogg–Briand pact would create a new sense of security in Europe and pave the way for general disarmament. The French feared that the British emphasis on arbitration and disarmament was mainly an attempt to evade the real question of security. French policy-makers dismissed the British attitude, which the CSDN disparagingly summarized as a belief that 'security is above all a question of sentiment, of spiritual detente, sufficiently assured by agreements of a general type such as the Briand–Kellogg pact'.[7] Few in Paris thought that the new recommendations provided the concrete commitments to military intervention or assistance against unprovoked aggression which alone would provide France with security in Europe. While not averse to winning such commitments through the League, they would have preferred, as always, a bilateral agreement with Britain. Whether Labour or Conservative, the British government would not accept commitments that it assumed meant a loss of independence and the dangers of involvement in affairs of no direct interest to Britain. The gap between the French and British concepts of security was as deep as ever.

V

While Henderson continued his futile search for ways to strengthen the League's security system, Briand launched his own alternative direction for European diplomacy. It was on 5 September at the 1929 League Assembly session that the French statesman made his dramatic plea for European economic and political integration by calling for 'some kind of federal bond' in Europe. As so often with this imaginative but frustratingly vague politician, his motivation, like the idea itself, was obscure and ill-defined. Never one to commit his ideas to paper, it has been left to a much later generation of historians, looking at the roots of the federal idea and the present European Community, to use their imagination in reconstructing Briand's intentions. One can only surmise that Briand was trying to regain the diplomatic initiative for France at a time when its policies had become increasingly defensive. It may well be that he was trying to enmesh Germany in a tighter European web than

---

[7] Quoted in Andrew Webster, 'An Argument Without End: Britain, France and the Disarmament Process, 1925–1934,' in Martin S. Alexander and W. J. Philpott (eds.), *Anglo-French Defence Relations Between the Wars, 1919–1939* (Basingstoke and London, 2001), 53.

the League of Nations could provide. There was also an economic motive at work for Briand, an effort to exercise some form of control over Germany's unlimited industrial potential. The French were looking to create a political framework for economic co-ordination and co-operation after the 'final liquidation of the war' and, at the same time, to construct a barrier against American economic domination, so vividly highlighted at the 1927 World Economic Conference. Meeting the visibly ill Stresemann at a session of the League Council in Madrid in early June 1929, Briand argued that France and Germany should form the core of a European grouping aiming at 'political cooperation in order to stabilise the peace, and above anything else, economic cooperation for defence against American superiority'.[8] The one-sided trade relationship with the United States and the discussions leading up to the highly protectionist Hawley–Smoot tariff law gave economic point to Briand's case. He used the anti-American card as a carrot, yet there was almost no possibility of Germany, not to speak of Britain or even France, entering a bloc with an anti-American bias.

Whatever Briand's immediate aims, there existed a wider vision of a federated Europe which would reflect the distinctive identity and the needs of the continental states. In 1927 Briand was made honorary president of the small but influential Pan-European Union founded by Count Coudenhove-Kalergi three years earlier, one of many such groups created in the mid-1920s. Some were concerned with the economic divisions in Europe and the multiplication of borders and tariff barriers; French and German businessmen, industrialists, and bankers were among those promoting either closer Franco-German economic ties (such as cartel agreements) or a more general European solution. Others, responding to the legacies of the recent war, were looking for those common elements of European culture and civilization on which to build a United States of Europe. The European idea was beginning to spread in politically influential circles. Briand's first appeal for a 'federal bond' in Europe was couched in the most general terms. The association would be 'primarily economic', but his speech was more of a rallying-cry than a programme. If the brilliant orator caught the Assembly's ear, the reaction of the chancelleries was more restrained. Stresemann was cautious and called attention to the possible damage to the League. Henderson criticized the proposal's anti-American (and anti-Soviet) intent, while MacDonald was openly dismissive. Qualified support came from the smaller nations. The Quai d'Orsay was called upon to produce a more detailed memorandum to be

---

[8] Quoted in Edward D. Keeton, *Briand's Locarno Diplomacy: French Economics, Politics and Diplomacy, 1925–1929* (New York, 1987), 313.

circulated to interested governments, and to draft a report for the League Assembly of September 1930.

In another speech at the 1929 Assembly, William Graham, the president of the Board of Trade in the second Labour government, offered a 'concrete proposal' for action, a two- or three-year tariff truce in order to provide a breathing space before embarking on a programme of multi-lateral tariff reductions. In February 1930 a 'Preliminary conference with a view to concerted economic action' opened at Geneva attended by thirty countries. More than half were represented by government ministers, an unprecedented development in such League conferences. Only three non-European countries attended, and the Americans sent an observer. The emphasis again was on a tariff truce and a limited agreement on freezing bilateral tariff arrangements for one year was reached. The mood was pessimistic; it was a minimal agreement with few hopes for future tariff reductions. Neither the French bid for a European Union nor the British-backed tariff truce convention of February–March 1930 fulfilled the hopes of their respective initiators. No collective approach to Europe's economic problems emerged.

The Quai's detailed memorandum of May 1930 for the League on European federal union specifically subordinated the economic goal to that of political co-operation. It stressed the need for a prior European system of arbitration, security, and Locarno-like guarantees before the establishment of a common market and integrated economic policies. The cautious political instincts of the French officials prevailed; the economic ministries were not involved. The memo outlined the form the new European Union was to take in loose and opaque terms. The French envisioned a federation based on a moral union between the European states with a conference, executive committee, and secretariat. The new European Union was to exist outside the League but work closely with it. Philippe Berthelot, the Quai's experienced secretary-general, would have nothing to do with this fanciful proposal. He continued to put his faith in France's alliance system and good relations with Britain. The response to the French memorandum was muted, if not hostile. The British Foreign Office had no sympathy with what it deemed the utopian and impractical ideas of European federalism, but was reluctant to undercut Briand's already weakening political position in the Tardieu cabinet. Warnings from William Tyrrell, the British ambassador in Paris, about the fragility of Briand's hold over foreign affairs and the growing support for Franco-German collaboration in the face of the tariff truce conference pierced Foreign Office lethargy. Few took Tyrrell's warnings of a Franco-German settlement seriously; E. H. Carr, a Foreign Office official, minuted that 'hot air is as predominant an element in these Franco-German talks as it was in M. Briand's pan-European claptrap at Geneva'.[9] Henderson and Cecil, seconded by League officials in Geneva, saw some merit in the Briand recommendations if they could be brought within the framework of the League. 'Regionalization within the League' would reduce the danger of the concept without offending its sponsor. The German reaction was cool; the American connection was far too vital to Germany's lifelines to put in peril, and the Germans had their eye on independent action in east-central Europe. Some saw in the circulated memorandum an unwelcome French political move. The Italians and Hungarians returned highly negative reports; in their view, the proposals would confirm French hegemony in Europe. Among the smaller states, apart from Poland and the Little Entente powers, there was caution and considerable scepticism. Almost all the governments referred to the need to include Russia and Turkey, omitted from the original list of participants, and expressed concern about the implied check to the League. Litvinov's reaction to the Soviet exclusion was to view the French move as part of its effort to create an anti-Soviet bloc. The Swiss insisted on the need to preserve their neutrality. It was predictable from the replies to the Quai d'Orsay that only a minimal version of the Briand scheme would survive. Officials cautioned Briand to stick to generalities when he went to Geneva in September 1930.

The line-up suggested that any attempt at political federation would emphasize the divisions between the 'haves' and the 'have-nots', the former victors and vanquished, France's friends and foes. Much depended on Britain's attitude. In the wake of the London Naval Conference talks of early 1930 and the British difficulties in resolving the Franco-Italian dispute over naval parity, relations between London and Paris were strained. British suspicions about France's inflated concerns over its security coloured the Foreign Office response. Despite pervasive hostility to the French initiative which was seen as a means of enforcing the Treaty of Versailles and maintaining the status quo, the Foreign Office officials decided that some show of support for Briand, 'the good European', was necessary. Disregarding the political orientation of the memorandum, officials revived Briand's original emphasis on economic co-operation and agreed to return a friendly, if non-committal, reply underlining the need to bring any such economic discussions within the League framework. It was a check to French hopes for an independent or semi-independent institution.

The situation in Europe was far more worrying in late 1930 than it had been a year earlier. On 14 September Hitler's Nationalist Socialist (Nazi) party won a smashing victory in the German elections, gaining 107 seats

---

[9] Minute by Carr, 9 Jan. 1930, PRO, FO 371/14365, C 230/230/18.

and becoming the second largest party in the Reichstag after the Social Democrats. In a more realistic mood, delegates agreed to sidetrack the Briand proposal to a newly constituted committee, the Commission of Enquiry for European Union (CEEU). As a gesture to its French initiator, Briand was made president by acclamation. The Commission was directed to hold its first regular session in January 1931, and a series of meetings followed. Though its mandate was renewed by the Assembly in September 1931 because of the depression, the talks already had run out of steam. Following careful British attempts to prevent any widening of its focus, the commission's discussions were almost exclusively directed towards economic problems, with the French contributing most of the more constructive ideas, particularly with regard to the relief of the embattled agricultural states of south-eastern Europe. Within the economic context, the British representatives were less hostile to co-operation than some historians have assumed, but their own divisions over tariff policy precluded genuine progress in the numerous committees that the commission spawned. The disasters of 1931 not only struck a heavy blow to *Briandisme* in all its forms, but wreaked havoc with any possibility of achieving European co-operation through the economic route. The Briand initiative failed both in its specific and more general aims. It did not restore the diplomatic initiative to France nor did it further the cause of European co-operation. It provided yet another example of the widening gap between Britain and France at a time when Germany was on the eve of regaining its sovereignty in foreign affairs.

VI

The Briand appeal to the 1929 Assembly had not deflected attention from the question of disarmament. The real action was taking place on the other side of the Atlantic. The Cecil-inspired effort at the Assembly to speed up the Geneva disarmament talks had failed, but by then Anglo-American naval talks had already begun. Hoover and MacDonald, equally anxious for a settlement, prodded their respective naval staffs, and by early September the outlines of a cruiser agreement were already emerging. Hoover and his secretary of state, Henry Stimson, were determined to improve Anglo-American relations. The American 'yardstick' proposal, letting the newer, more powerful American ships count for more than an equal tonnage of older or smaller vessels, proved acceptable to the MacDonald cabinet, where the economizers and disarmers were in the majority and not prepared to press the Admiralty case. The new first lord of the Admiralty was a reformer and strong supporter of the arms-control process. Hoover was greatly aided by the lawsuit brought by one of the 'big navy' lobbyists for fees owed him by the shipbuilders for services rendered at the 1927 Geneva Naval Conference. The subsequent Senate investigation of the 'traffickers in death' provided excellent ammunition for the administration's battles with the 'big navy' group. The psychological breakthrough came with MacDonald's visit to the United States in early October. During this weekend at the presidential rural retreat on the Rapidan River in the Blue Ridge Mountains, the rhetorical socialist and the Quaker businessman–statesman found the basis for compromise. The two men agreed to a limit of eighteen American 10,000-ton, eight-inch gun cruisers (the American navy thought twenty-one an absolute minimum), and Hoover's 'yardstick' proposal was accepted as a way of recognizing American cruiser parity. The visit smoothed the way for the London Naval Conference of 1930, the best prepared of all the naval arms-control conferences. In this case summitry succeeded brilliantly. Not only had the two men achieved a political compromise that downplayed the technical considerations blocking a cruiser settlement, but they inaugurated a period of Anglo-American co-operation on disarmament questions. Invitations for the 1930 conference, issued on 7 October 1929 to the French, Italians, and Japanese, were rapidly accepted.

The all-important Anglo-American preliminary soundings were followed by separate Japanese–American, Franco-Italian, and Anglo-French-Italian conversations. The most immediate problem was the Japanese demand for an increased ratio of 70 per cent in auxiliary vessels, including cruisers, instead of the Washington treaty's 60 per cent ratio. When the Japanese delegation to the conference stopped in Washington on its way to London, Stimson, while refusing to commit himself to any numbers, assured the delegates that steps would be taken to protect the national feeling of the Japanese people. The Americans and British knew that they had to deal with the Japanese demands if the new agreement was to win acceptance in Tokyo. The Franco-Italian exchanges ran into immediate difficulties. Once again, the issue was whether security stood as a precondition to disarmament. The French, who never liked the idea of discussing naval disarmament in isolation, refused to reduce their naval forces unless Italy dropped its claim to naval parity or the British agreed to a 'Mediterranean Locarno' involving automatic sanctions against a violator of the status quo. Neither demand was met. Mussolini was determined on parity as a matter of national prestige, while British cabinet opposition to a Mediterranean security guarantee as 'dangerous and unnecessary' blocked the one possible avenue of compromise. The Foreign Office representative, Sir Robert Craigie, suggested a consultative pact in the Mediterranean, something like the Four Power Pacific treaty of 1921. The Americans held out hope for participation and then retreated to their usual non-involvement stance.

The London naval conference was a glittering occasion, with the participants represented by powerful and well-briefed delegations. Unlike the conference at Geneva in 1927, in London the civilian ministers took control of the proceedings, determined on success. The Labour government abandoned the position so bitterly defended at the abortive 1927 meetings and accepted parity with the Americans in every category of ship. The final treaty included the extension of the building holiday for capital ships for five more years (until 1936), as well as an agreement by the three main naval powers (Britain, America, and Japan) to reduce their battleship fleets from twenty, eighteen, and ten ships to fifteen, fifteen, and nine ships respectively. The three powers also agreed to a 10 : 10 : 7 ratio to cover cruisers and destroyers. The British reduced their earlier minimum requirements from seventy to fifty cruisers; the Americans retreated from their demands for twenty-three heavy cruisers with eight-inch guns and accepted eighteen cruisers instead. The 'yardstick' formula, never expressed in numerical terms, was flexible enough to achieve agreement. It helped that thirty-five of Britain's fifty-nine front-line cruisers would become obsolete within ten years, making a building programme beyond fifty cruisers practically impossible in the short term. The task of negotiating with the Japanese was left mainly to the Americans, another sign of Anglo-American amity. The British, like the Americans, did not want Japan to build any more Washington-class cruisers, and they acted together to force the Japanese to accept a compromise that they knew would be domestically unpopular. The Japanese agreed to a 60 per cent ratio in heavy eight-inch cruisers but otherwise sustained their 70 per cent claim with regard to other categories of ships and won parity in submarines. The Japanese navy fiercely opposed the limitation agreement: the chief of staff of the Imperial Navy resigned. There was a strong nationalist reaction in Tokyo, but Hamaguchi, the Japanese premier subsequently assassinated by xenophobic conservatives, convinced his privy council to ratify the treaty and the civilians in the cabinet and liberal groups in the Diet closed ranks in support. The defeated service officers and their backers prepared for a struggle for the control of future defence policy.

Neither the French nor the Italians signed the new limitation pact. Lengthy and unsuccessful Franco-Italian negotiations, in which the British played a leading part, only reinforced the Anglo-French antagonism. The British, anxious to keep their two-power standard in European waters, were protected from the threat of new building by the inclusion of an 'escalator clause' in the London treaty, but invocation would destroy some of the gains made from the three-power agreement. With no new security arrangement in the Mediterranean, the French refused to budge on their fleet tonnage figures. They further infuriated the British at the conference (who knew through intercepted French telegrams) by attempting to influence the Japanese to reject any restrictions on submarines. MacDonald was particularly angry: he already blamed the Franco-Italian impasse on Paris and now raged against French 'treachery' as well. The British cabinet refused to consider any move to address French security concerns, not even a reaffirmation of action under Article 16 of the Covenant. To the British, French demands for a large fleet seemed totally unreasonable; the French bristled at the condescension manifest in an attitude which showed no appreciation for France's defensive and imperial responsibilities. Basically, the naval treaties were only of secondary interest for the French, as Germany remained their foremost concern. The French, far more than the Italians, insisted on the unity of armaments and the interconnectedness of land, air, and sea defences. Between Paris and Rome the desire for agreement was intermittent at best. In sharp contrast to the high sea powers, the two countries shared a common land border and were colonial rivals in North Africa. Relations, particularly since Mussolini had taken power, were uneasy, if not strained. For the Italians, lagging far behind the French, the navy became more than a status symbol; it would herald the building of the new empire. The French argued that if parity was conceded, the Italians could concentrate their fleet in the Mediterranean and achieve local naval superiority as the French fleet was dispersed through the Mediterranean, Channel, and North Atlantic. The most they would offer was local parity in the Mediterranean, with France accorded extra tonnage for its other responsibilities. There was no meeting of either political or naval minds.

A new phase of the complex negotiations between the British, French, and Italians began after the conclusion of the conference. Eleven months of hard bargaining followed, months that included a brief naval building holiday between Italy and France initiated in the summer of 1930. The Italians, harshly affected by the economic downturn in the autumn of 1930, were forced to raise a loan in Paris and were inclined to compromise. Fears of a renewed naval race between the two Mediterranean states on the eve of the World Disarmament Conference were heightened by the French announcement of a new battle-cruiser to be constructed in reply to the launching of a new German pocket battleship. Again, the diplomats of Britain, France, and Italy conferred and reached a seemingly acceptable 'Bases of Agreement' in March 1931, only to be blocked by a last-minute French veto that ended the possibility of agreement. The compromise collapsed over the question of the replacement of French vessels becoming obsolete before 1936, which had been discussed only in the vaguest terms and was open to different interpretations. Though attempts to resolve the impasse

TABLE 27. Comparative Naval Strength, September 1931

	UK	USA	Japan	France	Italy	Germany
Battleships	15	15	10	9	4	6
Aircraft Carriers	6	4	4	1	0	0
Heavy Cruisers	17	21	14	12	11	0
Cruisers	36	11	24	11	15	6
Destroyers/Torpedo boats	164	256	119	92	86	26
Submarines*	53 + 6	81 + 4	72	61 + 41	75	0
Global Tonnage	1,250,247	1,252,184	850,328	628,603	404,005	125,780

Source: Jane's Fighting Ships for 1931 (London, 1932).
*Second figure is for submarines being built.

would drag on into 1932, the problem never came any closer to solution.

The London Naval Treaty of 1930, with only three signatures to its key provisions, represented the high point of inter-war naval limitation; it could not be extended and would not be maintained. There were unique political reasons that had made compromise possible: American reluctance to translate financial power into naval might; the British decision, already taken by the Conservatives, to cut back on naval construction; the strong commitment of the Anglo-American political leaders not just to agreement but to a breakthrough in the general disarmament talks; and the continuing conservatism of the Hamaguchi government in Tokyo even in the face of the naval revolt.

Basic to the British acceptance of a one-power global standard based on parity was the fundamental assumption that war with the Americans was impossible. Churchill might huff and puff but no one, including Churchill, believed in the reality of the conflict. This was the difference between the pre-1914 Anglo-German naval race and the Anglo-American rivalry of the 1920s. As long as the Americans remained inactive, Britain was 'mistress of the seas'. At the same time, despite their awareness of Japanese xenophobia and military restlessness, most British statesmen believed that Japan was pacifically inclined and, in any case, would not take on both Britain and the United States. At the Imperial Conference of 1930 Australia and New Zealand were forced to accept a further postponement to the completion date of the Singapore base. In June 1931 the 'ten-year rule' was again renewed as the basis for British service estimates. The treaty brought the positive advantages of a steady, long-term building programme. From 1930 until the outbreak of war successive governments never authorized fewer than three cruisers a year. Both Britain and the United States, freed from the distorting effects of the parity question, could concentrate on more vital national or imperial concerns.

The London treaty was a mixed package for Britain. Its effects on the country's immediate naval condition were negligible, but it opened Britain to challenge in the future if no general disarmament agreement was reached. New construction of capital ships would be postponed until 1937. As some 75 per cent of the Royal Navy's warship tonnage would be obsolete by 1936, this would leave Britain weak compared to rivals whose ships were younger (Japan) and, if not bound by the treaty, new and more modern. Moreover, British shipbuilding capacity, already shrinking, would lose half its capacity between 1929 and 1935. This might have happened anyway with the advent of the 'Great Depression', but the extension of the capital-ship building holiday would make it difficult to resume building on a massive scale in 1937. In 1930, however, with disarmament talks still pending, the treaty looked like a good deal for the British. Had an agreement been reached, the cuts in the number of cruisers, the extension of the 'building holiday', and the further erosion of its already shrinking shipbuilding capacity would still have left Britain secure against any naval threat and preserved its quantitative and, in some respects, its qualitative lead over any rival. The government's naval strategy would break down only if multiple threats appeared simultaneously in geographically dispersed areas. It was because no disarmament agreement was reached and the world scene deteriorated so quickly that the London treaty was seen as a major defeat for the Royal Navy.

VII

The work of the Preparatory Commission had been suspended while the naval talks continued. Eighteen months were to elapse between the acceptance of the 'second-reading' draft treaty in May 1929 and the reconvening of the adjourned sixth session of the commission in November 1930. These were the months when the economic situation deteriorated dramatically and attention was focused on the international economy. In its last meeting, from 6 November to 9 December 1930, the Preparatory Commission produced a final draft convention, more in spite of than because of the labours of the previous five years. Neither the British nor the French had changed their basic positions, and so the draft convention consisted of little more than explanations of methods of limitations and blank tables with figures to be decided by the World Disarmament Conference. The effectives of all three services were to be limited but no provision was made for the inclusion of trained reserves. Naval armaments were to be limited by categories, with concessions made to French and Italian demands for flexibility. The principle of budgetary limitation was accepted both for land and naval armaments and for total arms expenditure, but not for air armaments. As the Americans objected to any form of budgetary limitation and would rely only on publicity, British acceptance with regard to naval expenditure was made conditional on eventual American concurrence. Air material was limited by numbers of aircraft in service and in immediate reserve and by limits on total horsepower; the British, Americans, and Germans prevailed and the question of civil aircraft was almost totally ignored. There was to be a Permanent Disarmament Commission to supervise the implementation of the convention, but no provision was made for on-site inspection because of British and American objections. It was agreed to outlaw bacteriological and chemical warfare (manufacture was not prohibited), reaffirming conventions signed in Geneva in 1925, and the only form of arms control to survive into the post-1945 world.

The final denouement exposed the underlying political weakness of the whole enterprise. The high sea powers, concerned with protecting the naval treaties already in existence, supported a French proposal, framed with Part V of the Versailles treaty in mind, to provide for the maintenance of existing disarmament treaty provisions. The Germans denounced this new article, with its unmistakable reference to the hated 1919 settlement. Bernstorff, in an exceedingly bitter speech, condemned the final draft convention which emphasized limitation rather than reduction and left out all the key items on the arms agenda. He was supported by the Soviet representative, though the Russian–German partnership at Geneva was a weak one. Both would attend the forthcoming conference. That any agreement had been obtained at all was mainly due to Cecil's role as head of the British delegation. Forced to recognize that France was not going to surrender its superiority over Germany, he chose to accept partial measures to ensure agreement so that the World Disarmament Conference could at last be summoned. The result was an Anglo-French compromise that was as illusory as it was unexpected. While many criticized the draft convention, it was defended in one crucial respect. As one French newspaper noted: 'Ce document a une grande vertu qui est d'exister.'[10] It was difficult to claim much more. The American delegate, Gibson, voiced the general dissatisfaction felt with a document which, should it be accepted at the conference, hardly provided for that reduction of armaments promised

---

[10] John W. Wheeler-Bennett, *Disarmament and Security Since Locarno, 1925–1931: Being the Political and Technical Background of the General Disarmament Conference, 1932* (London, 1932), 102.

by the Covenant. In January 1931 the Council at last set the date for the long-awaited world conference. The states would meet on 2 February 1932—the year's delay needed (irony of ironies) so that the powers could complete their preparations.

The postponement proved calamitous. Before the ominous events of that disastrous year, and the German government's ever-louder demand for 'equality of status' in armaments, it was generally acknowledged that the key to the situation lay in Paris, and there was no sign that the French were prepared to move. Civilian and military leaders argued that French superiority, whether in military might or in financial strength, was of a transitory nature and disarmament impossible without stronger provisions for security. Would the creation of a collective security system have provided the safety demanded? Or did the French ability to face the visibly changing status quo depend on assurances of British support which London would not offer? Britain's mediating role in Europe was not based on any willingness to defend the 1919 balance of power or to go beyond the Locarno guarantees. In November 1931, in an effort to break the chain that linked the financial and economic crisis with security and disarmament, the Foreign Office suggested that the government accept the principles of the Geneva Protocol in the hope of allaying French misgivings. This proposal was no more success-ful in swaying the British cabinet than any of its predecessors. If some British politicians—and they were few in number—shared the public hope for concrete measures of disarmament, when forced to formulate practical plans for arms limitation there was little to choose between the British and French positions. The creation of a 'national government' in Britain in August 1931 undercut the position and influence of the few real disarmament enthusiasts in London.

The Americans failed to offer any consistent leadership even before the Wall Street crash blunted their power position. Political isolation and absence from the League only served to obscure the security issue even when American naval initiatives encouraged the disarmers. No American leader advocated participation in the European security struc-ture. Some shared the imaginary German fears of French hegemonic ambitions. A majority in both parties believed that any American commitments, unrelated to its own security interests, would only em-broil the United States in age-old European disputes. Even the old Wilsonians had deserted the League's security cause. With the navy, the one formidable arm of the country, already limited, Gibson saw little for the United States to do in Geneva except to exercise a 'helpful influence' from time to time. The most powerful voices favouring disarmament and not just arms limitation were the two most suspect members of the Preparatory Commission, each of whom had started on the road to rearmament. The Nazi victory in the September 1930 election gave a new importance to widespread demands for the ending of reparations and for German equality in arms. Revision of the Versailles treaty disarmament clauses became more imperative in official circles as covert rearmament gathered pace. The great tactical German advantage was the ability to use its weakness in armaments as a source of political strength, while France's quantitative superiority became a diplomatic liability despite the shrinking classes of recruits for the army and its rusting equipment. In the inverted logic of the time, to be weak was by definition to be virtuous. It was a paradox which German policymakers, in their claims for the right to 'equality of rights' (*Gleichberechtigung*), exploited to the full. In Moscow, the announcement of the first Five Year Plan in April 1929 was followed by the inauguration of a five-year military plan intended 'to create a modern military-technical base for defense'.[11] Co-operation between the Red Army and the Reichswehr reached its height between 1928 and 1932. The Soviets had everything to gain both from an alignment with the Germans, however loose, at Geneva and from their mutual support for disarmament. The completion of the Soviet industrialization and militarization programmes depended on a prolonged period of peace. Litvinov's disarmament campaign served not only to divide the capitalist states but was a way to bring the USSR back into the Europe at a time when Moscow could not afford the dangers of total isolation. The Soviet identification with disarmament proved an invaluable asset at a later date, when the Comintern again changed ideological fronts and renewed the united front tactics of the pre-1927 period.

Anglo-French differences over disarmament ultimately came back to the question of Germany. Geography was the determining factor. Britain, protected by the Channel and its naval supremacy, did not conceive of Germany as a security threat. France, with only the demilitarized Rhineland separating it from Germany, could not ignore the danger posed by its neighbour. Committed to changes in the status quo because resistance was impossible, Briand remained uncertain about the degree to which the German leaders would remain faithful to the policies of peaceful and limited revision. He searched for ways to match revisionism with containment. His failure was due, in part, to the unwillingness of the British to go beyond the Locarno guarantees and to the American abstention from any kind of European security arrangement; for only their involvement could have lessened the basic gap between German and French power. Without British underwriting,

[11] Quoted in David R. Stone *Hammer and Rifle: The Militarization of the Soviet Union, 1926–1933* (Lawrence, Kan., 2000), 125.

France had to rely on its superior military power, already recast in a defensive mode, both for its safety and as the necessary precondition for any further concessions to Germany. In 1930 this central problem could not be evaded. It is hardly surprising, however, that neither France nor Britain wanted a disarmament conference that would highlight their differences and bring the German question again to the forefront of European diplomacy. Yet neither government could ignore the mounting public pressures for disarmament. As the international atmosphere darkened, articulate public opinion, particularly on the left, became focused on the disarmament issue. The setting of the date for the World Disarmament Conference fed exaggerated expectations for eventual success. As the League remained the symbolic centre of hopes for peace, the world public came to regard the reduction of armaments as the test of its competence. The opening of the conference unleashed an emotional outpouring that went far beyond the usual chorus of approval. Despite the cracks in the façade of internationalism, there was still considerable optimism that the global regime would hold and that disarmament would further the cause of future peace.

The political failure of the League of Nations was not foreseen in 1929. It was during the Tenth Assembly, on 7 September 1929, that the foundation stone was laid for the Palais de Nations; at the same time the Assembly voted a budget of £1,200,000 without complaint to cover expenses. In ten years Geneva had become part of the diplomatic landscape. It was the 'galleria' of Europe for great and small powers. Aristide Briand found the grand salon of the Palais Wilson wonderfully suited to his oratorical gifts. Gustav Stresemann delighted in the attention of the world press. Even Austen Chamberlain, who at the start of his foreign-secretaryship established his control over League affairs and ended the confusing division of responsibility for British decisions in Geneva, recognized the League's importance and the utility of attendance at its meetings. Though he may have preferred the intimacy of hotel rooms for high-powered decision-making, the League of Nations was an integral part of his foreign policy. Mussolini, who avoided international jamborees, was conscious of the League's influence and quarrelled with the secretary-general, Sir Eric Drummond, over the need to increase Italian representation on the Secretariat. The 'three graces'—Politis of Greece, Beneš of Czechoslovakia, and Titulescu of Romania—attended almost every Assembly meeting and became League fixtures. Non-members began to make more frequent appearances. Unofficial American observers ('something between a guest and a spy') became participants in the League's technical and humanitarian work, and President Hoover made sympathetic noises, reviving hopes for future political links. Unlike Chicherin, Maxim Litvinov, commissar for foreign affairs from July 1930, made a place for himself as the Soviet spokesmen for disarmament. As Stalin pursued his relentless industrialization programme, he was prepared to leave the task of maintaining the peace with the capitalist powers to his adroit diplomatic spokesman. Despite their many divergent interests, almost all the statesmen of Europe had become active participants in the League's affairs.

Security and Disarmament

Books

AHMANN, R., BIRKE, A. M., and HOWARD, M. (eds.), *The Quest for Stability: Problems of West European Security, 1918–1957* (London and Oxford, 1993). Esp. chapters by Keith Robbins, Zara Steiner, Philip Towle, and Maurice Vaïsse.

ANDREWS, E. M., *The Writing on the Wall: The British Commonwealth and Aggression in the East, 1931–1935* (Sydney and London, 1987).

BARROS, JAMES, *Office Without Power: Secretary-General Sir Eric Drummond, 1919–1933* (Oxford, 1979).

BENNETT, EDWARD WELLS, *German Rearmament and the West, 1932–1933* (Princeton, 1979).

BOND, BRIAN, *British Military Policy Between the Two World Wars* (Oxford, 1980).

BOUSSARD, DANIEL, *Un problème de défense nationale: l'aéronautique militaire au parlement, 1928–1940* (Vincennes, 1983).

CARLTON, DAVID, *MacDonald versus Henderson: The Foreign Policy of the Second Labour Government* (London, 1970).

DOBSON, ALAN, *Peaceful Air Warfare: The United States, Britain and the Politics of International Aviation* (Oxford, 1991).

DU REAU, ELISABETH, *L'Idée d'Europe au XX siècle. Des mythes aux réalités* (Brussels, 1996).

FANNING, RICHARD, *Peace and Disarmament: Naval Rivalry and Arms Control, 1922–1933* (Lexington, Ky., 1995).

GEYER, M., *Aufrüstung oder Sicherheit: die Reichswehr in der Krise der Machtpolitik, 1924–1936* (Wiesbaden, 1980).

HALL, CHRISTOPHER, *Britain, America and Arms Control, 1921–1937* (Basingstoke, 1987).

HIGHAM, ROBIN, *Armed Forces in Peacetime: Britain, 1918–1940: A Case Study* (London, 1962).

HOWARD, MICHAEL E., *The Continental Commitment: The Dilemma of British Defence Policy in the Era of the Two World Wars* (London, 1972).

HUGHES, JUDITH, *To the Maginot Line: The Politics of French Military Preparations in the 1920s* (Cambridge, Mass., 1971).

KITCHING, CAROLYN, *Britain and the Problem of International Disarmament, 1919–1934* (London, 1999).

McKERCHER, B. J. C., *The Second Baldwin Government and the United States, 1924–1929: Attitude and Diplomacy* (Cambridge, 1984).

McKercher, B. J. C., (ed.), *Arms Limitation and Disarmament: Restraints on War, 1899–1939* (Westport, Conn., 1992). Esp. chapters by Richard Fanning and B. J. C. McKercher.

—— *Transition of Power: Britain's Loss of Global Preeminence to the United States 1930–1945* (Cambridge, 1999).

Murray, Williamson R. and Millet, Allan R. (eds.), *Military Innovation in the Interwar Period* (Cambridge, 1996).

O'Brien, Phillips Payson, *British and American Naval Power: Politics and Policy, 1900–1936* (London and Westport, Conn., 1998).

O'Connor, Raymond G., *Perilous Equilibrium: The United States and the London Naval Conference of 1930* (Lawrence, Kan. and Westport, Conn., 1962).

Ostrower, Gary B., *Collective Insecurity: The United States and the League of Nations During the Early Thirties* (Lewisburg and London, 1979).

Pegg, Carl H., *Evolution of the European Idea, 1914–1932* (Chapel Hill, NC, 1983).

Richardson, Dick, *The Evolution of British Disarmament Policy in the 1920s* (London and New York, 1989).

Stirk, Peter M. R. (ed.), *European Unity in Context: The Interwar Period* (London, 1989).

Vaïsse, Maurice, *Sécurité d'abord: la politique française en matière de désarmement, 9 decembre 1930–17 avril 1934* (Paris, 1981).

Wheeler-Bennett, John W., *Disarmament and Security Since Locarno, 1925–1931: Being the Political and Technical Background of the General Disarmament Conference, 1932* (London, 1932).

Articles

Alexander, Martin, 'In Defence of the Maginot Line: Security Policy, Domestic Politics and Economic Depression in France', in Robert W. D. Boyce (ed.), *French Foreign and Defence Policy, 1918–1940: The Decline and Fall of a Great Power* (London, 1998).

Babij, Orest M., 'The Second Labour Government and British Maritime Security, 1929–1931', *Diplomacy and Statecraft*, 6: 3 (1995).

Badel, Laurence, 'Trêve douanière, libéralisme et conjoncture, septembre 1929–mars 1930', *Relations internationales*, 82 (1995).

Boyce, Robert W. D., 'Britain's first "No" to Europe: Britain and the Briand Plan, 1929–1930', *European Studies Review*, 10: 1 (1986).

—— 'Was There a "British" Alternative to the Briand Plan?', in Peter Catterall and C. J. Morris (eds.), *Britain and the Threat to Stability in Europe, 1918–1945* (London and New York, 1993).

—— ' "Business as Usual": The Limits of French Economic Diplomacy, 1926–1933', in id. (ed.), *French Foreign and Defence Policy, 1918–1940: The Decline and Fall of a Great Power* (London, 1998).

Carlton, David, 'The Problem of Civil Aviation in British Air Disarmament Policy, 1919–1934', *Journal of the Royal United Services Institute*, 111: 664 (1966).

—— 'The Anglo-French Compromise on Arms Limitation, 1928', *Journal of British Studies*, 8: 2 (1969).

CHRISTIENNE, C. and BUFFOTOT, P., 'L'Aéronautique militaire française entre 1919 et 1939', *Revue d'Histoire Armées*, 2 (1977).

CROZIER, ANDREW J., 'Britain, Germany and the Dishing of the Briand Plan', in P. King and A. Bosco (eds.), *A Constitution for Europe: A Comparative Study of Federal Constitutions and Plans for the United States of Europe* (London, 1991).

DEIST, WILHELM, 'Internationale and nationale Aspekte der Abrüstungsfrage, 1924–1932', in H. Rössler (ed.), *Locarno und die Weltpolitik, 1924–1932* (Göttingen, 1969).

—— 'The Rearmament of the Wehrmacht', in Militärgeschichtliches Forschungsamt (ed.), *Germany and the Second World War*. Vol. I: *The Build-up of German Aggression* (Oxford, 1990).

DOUGHTY, ROBERT, 'The Illusion of Security: France, 1919–1940', in Williamson Murray, MacGregor Knox, and Alvin Bernstein (eds.), *The Making of Strategy: Rulers, States and War* (Cambridge and New York, 1994).

FLEURY, ANTOINE and LUBOR JILEK, (eds.), *Le Plan Briand d'union fédérale européenne: Perspectives nationales et transnationales, avec documents: Actes du colloque international tenu à Genève du 19 au 21 septembre 1991* (Berne, 1998).

KRÜGER, PETER, 'Friedenssicherheit und deutsche Revisionspolitik: die deutsche Außenpolitik und Verhandlungen über den Kellogg–Briand Pakt', *Vierteljahrshefte für Zeitgeschichte*, 22 (1974).

NAVARI, CORNELIA, 'The Origins of the Briand Plan', in Andrea Bosco (ed.), *The Federal Idea*. Vol.1: *The History of Federalism from the Enlightenment to 1945* (London, 1991).

SCHWARTE, CHRISTIANE, 'Le Plan Briand d'union européenne: sa genèse au Quai d'Orsay et la tentative de sa réalisation à la Commission d'étude pour l'Union européene, 1929–1931', in *Mémoire de D.E.A.* (Institut d'Études Politiques de Paris, 1992).

Survey of International Affairs (volumes released between 1926 and 1930).

WEBSTER, ANDREW, 'An Argument Without End: Britain, France and the Disarmament Process, 1925–1934', in Martin S. Alexander and W. J. Philpott (eds.), *Anglo-French Defence Relations Between the Wars, 1919–1939* (Basingstoke and London, 2001).

WHALEY, BARTON, 'Covert Rearmament in Germany, 1919–1939: Deception and Misperception', in John Gooch and Amos Perlmutter (eds.), *Military Deception and Strategic Surprise* (London, 1982).

WHITE, RALPH, 'Cordial Caution: The British Response to the French Proposal for the European Federal Union of 1930', in Andrea Bosco (ed.), *The Federal Idea*. Vol. I: *The History of Federalism from the Enlightenment to 1945* (London, 1991).

—— ' "Through a Glass, Darkly": The Foreign Office Investigation of French Federalism, January–May 1930', in David Dutton (ed.), *Statecraft and Diplomacy in the Twentieth Century* (Liverpool, 1995).

WINKLER, FRED H., 'The War Department and Disarmament, 1926–1935', *The Historian*, 28: 3 (1966).

Theses

TURNER, ARTHUR, 'British Policies Towards France, With Special Reference to Disarmament and Security, 1926–1931', unpubl. D.Phil. thesis, Oxford University (1978).

WEBSTER, ANDREW GOODWIN, 'Anglo-French Relations and the Problems of Disarmament and Security, 1929–1933', unpubl. Ph.D. thesis, Cambridge University, (2001).

Naval Disarmament

Books

DINGMAN, ROGER, *Power in the Pacific: The Origins of Naval Arms Limitation, 1914–1922* (Chicago, 1976).

KAUFMAN, ROBERT GORDON, *Arms Control During the Pre-Nuclear Era: The United States and Naval Limitation Between the Two World Wars* (New York, 1990).

KENNEDY, GREG and NELSON, KEITH (eds.), *Far-flung Lines: Essays on Imperial Defence in Honour of Donald Mackenzie Schurman* (London, 1996). Esp. essays by Ferris, Babig, Kennedy.

LEUTZE, JAMES R., *Bargaining for Supremacy: Anglo-American Naval Collaboration, 1937–1941* (Chapel Hill, NC, 1977).

O'BRIEN, PHILLIPS PAYSON, *British and American Naval Power: Politics and Policy, 1900–1936* (London and Westport, Conn., 1998).

—— (ed.), *Technology and Normal Combat in the Twentieth Century and Beyond* (London, 2001). Esp. essays by Prattie, Rahm, Sumida, and O'Brien.

RANFT, BRIAN (ed.), *Technical Change and British Naval Policy, 1860–1939* (London, 1977).

ROSKILL, STEPHEN, *Naval Policy Between the Wars*, 2 vols. (London, 1968).

Articles

CARLTON, DAVID, 'Great Britain and the Coolidge Naval Conference of 1927', *Political Science Quarterly*, 83: 4 (1968).

DUBAY, ROBERT W., 'The Geneva Naval Conference of 1927: A Study of Battleship Diplomacy', *Southern Quarterly*, 8 (1970).

FANNING, RICHARD W., 'The Coolidge Conference of 1927: Disarmament in Disarray', in B. J. C. McKercher, (ed.), *Arms Limitation and Disarmament: Restraints on War, 1899–1939* (Westport, Conn., 1992).

GIBBS, NORMAN H., 'The Naval Conferences of the Interwar Years: A Study in Anglo-American Relations', *Naval War College Review*, 30 (1977–8).

KENNEDY, GREGORY C., 'Britain's Policy-Making Elite, the Naval Disarmament Puzzle, and Public Opinion, 1927–1932', *Albion*, 26: 4 (1994).

—— 'The 1930 London Naval Conference and Anglo-American Maritime Strength, 1927–1930', in B. J. C. McKercher (ed.), *Arms Limitation and Disarmament: Restraints on War, 1899–1939* (Westport, Conn., 1992).

McKERCHER, B. J. C., 'Belligerent Rights in 1927–1929: Foreign Policy versus Naval Policy in the Second Baldwin Government', *Historical Journal*, 29: 4 (1986).

MURFETT, MALCOLM H., ' "Are We Ready?" The Development of American and British Naval Strategy, 1922–1939', in John B. Hattendorf and Robert S. Jordan (eds.), *Maritime Strategy and the Balance of Power: Britain and America in the Twentieth Century* (New York, 1989).

SUMIDA, JON TETSURO, ' "The Best Laid Plans": The Development of British Battle Fleet Tactics, 1919–1942', *International History Review*, 14: 4 (1992).

—— 'Churchill and British Sea Power, 1908–1929', in R. A. C. Parker (ed.), *Winston Churchill: Studies in Statesmanship* (London, 1995).

TILL, GEOFFREY, 'Perceptions of Naval Power Between the Wars: The British Case', in Philip Towle (ed.), *Estimating Foreign Military Power* (London, 1982).

Part I

Conclusion: Europe Reconstructed?

I

The 1920s must be seen within the context of the aftermath of the Great War and not as the prologue to the 1930s and the outbreak of a new European conflict. It was a post-war and not a pre-war decade. In the ten years that followed the ending of a catastrophic conflict of unexpected length and unimaginable costs, statesmen had to establish new states or adapt traditional structures to the new conditions of the post-war world. They had to rebuild an international state system that had been severely shaken by the years of fighting. The two processes went on simultaneously and interacted with each other. It is impossible to trace the process of European reconstruction without looking at the domestic origins of national foreign policies. Individuals and institutions, as well as the emotional and intellectual constraints within which they operated, left their mark on the decisions taken. The fluidity of post-war relations and the multiplicity of problems forced Europe's statesmen to find new ways of tackling the tasks of rehabilitation, though many continued to think in traditional terms and to prefer the earlier practices that had stood the test of time. During these years the management of international affairs developed a character of its own distinct from that of both its peacetime predecessor and the one that followed. The old and new coexisted in an uneasy relationship.

By the time the decade drew to a close the building-blocks for a reconstructed Europe had been put in place. The states created by the peace treaties retained their political independence and territorial integrity. Among the victor powers, only the pre-war liberal government of Italy proved unable to manage the transition to peacetime, and Mussolini emerged to restore his own brand of order and stability. The Weimar republic, born of defeat, remained an artificial construct unable to attract the active mass support that would have made the task of governing easier. Yet though it moved from crisis to crisis, its constitutional structure held. Almost all the European states had stabilized their currencies and brought inflation under control. Many of the statesmen of Europe proved willing to seek co-operative solutions to solve the political conflicts on the continent and to address its financial and economic ills. The League of Nations was a functioning institution, and the rules and regulations which knit the international community together were being reshaped and augmented. Statesmen were well embarked on the road to a world disarmament conference, a pursuit full of danger but one which many Europeans thought worthwhile. It was mainly in the west and in Czechoslovakia, however, that the democratic forms of government endured. Elsewhere authoritarian governments emerged which challenged or ended the effective power of representative institutions. Under the pressure of mass politics, financial difficulties, and economic and social dislocations, almost all governments became more interventionist than was the customary pattern in pre-war Europe. Though the prevailing fears in governing circles still centred on Bolshevism, a variety of right-wing extremist groups, nationalist, anti-communist, and favouring violence, appeared on the political scene. In the Soviet Union Stalin emerged as the victor in the struggle for Lenin's succession, and was embarking on the vast industrialization programme that confirmed his power and strengthened the totalitarian nature of the Bolshevik regime. Throughout Europe the forces of liberalism, much weakened during the Great War, were on the defensive or in full retreat.

Two fundamentally different currents flowed through the world of international politics, those of nationalism and internationalism. The war and peace settlements had provided a tremendous boost to both, but they pulled in opposite directions. The peace treaties heightened nationalism, strengthened the appeal of statehood, and fuelled national resentments. The creation of the new states inevitably raised the nationalist temperature in eastern Europe. Multi-ethnic states survived because of the power of the dominant nationality, but survival came at the price of the associated negatives: the establishment of centralized and often repressive regimes, hostility towards minorities, and the fierce enmity shown towards neighbouring states. If some governments found it useful to beat the nationalist drum, others found there was little need for such official encouragement. Boundaries—and there were now many more of them—hardly made good neighbours. If the war and peace treaties heightened nationalist sentiments, they also intensified the desire for peace and disarmament. Wilsonian idealism did not vanish with the departure and defeat of the American president. The treaties created the basis for new experiments in international co-operation. The growth of interdependence and the transnational character of so many problems encouraged the development of multilateral diplomacy and the appearance of new international institutions. The latter operated in a world dominated by fiercely independent sovereign states, and growth took place at a slow and uneven pace. It was towards the end of the decade that the clashes between nationalist and internationalist sentiment became increasingly obvious. Against the background of the spreading depression, the stabilization process reached a difficult stage. There were many anxieties about the future, but few predicted the disasters that were soon to follow. It is the argument of this section that there were good reasons for their apparent blindness as well as for the continuing faith in the durability of the emerging international order.

II

The magnitude of the task confronted by the leaders of the victor powers in 1919 staggers the imagination. They faced the unresolved problems of pre-1914 Europe as well as the new situations created by the war. It was not only the reorganization of Europe that was to be discussed, but decisions that would affect many other parts of the world. They met in Paris at a moment of maximum dislocation in the international order, a time of systemic change when it was possible to contemplate a new regime to replace the one that had collapsed so spectacularly. Yet despite the popular hopes roused by Wilson's proclaimed vision of 'liberal internationalism', the treaties of Paris did not represent the victory of principle and morality over national interest. If the treaties incorporated the principles of democracy, collective security, and self-determination, they also reflected the claims of the sovereign states and their often conflicting national requirements. None of the war leaders, now peacemakers, was blind to the changes wrought by the war. Yet the events were too close and the experiences too fresh to assess the full nature of these transformations. The best that could be done was to grapple with their most immediate and pressing consequences. Neither the conditions in Europe nor in Paris were conducive to rational peacemaking, and the chaotic methods of the three main architects of the German treaty, Georges Clemenceau, David Lloyd George, and Woodrow Wilson, did not help. Popular demands in the victor countries for retribution and restitution were at their height. Local wars were still in progress and there were large areas over which the Allies had little or no control. It was only after the terms of the Covenant of the League of Nations were settled that the 'Big Three' could turn to the rest of their overcrowded agenda.

The war had not solved the German problem. Germany was not destroyed and its power was far from irreparably damaged. The German troops were still on French soil when their commanders pressed the imperial government in Berlin to request an armistice. The Germans in 1918 had no radios and knew only what their government told them. The abdication and armistice were major shocks to the body politic.

The high command took pains to spread the idea that a victorious army had been betrayed at home by socialists and Jews: The 'stab in the back' explained the defeat. The majority of Germans could not accept the consequences of the lost war. Hatred of the Treaty of Versailles, and particularly its reparations provisions, though of varying importance during the life of the Weimar republic, was the one political bond that held the deeply divided country together. For the French, the German surrender brought peace but not security. Germany had proved, once again, its military superiority, for France had achieved victory only as a member of a coalition. The country emerged from the fighting more damaged in human and material terms than its defeated enemy, and with much of its adult population suffering from a psychic shock that proved as deep and more long-lasting than the German preoccupation with defeat. French leaders remained obsessed with the fear of German power, for they faced a security problem that neither the British nor the Americans shared. Only France had to live next to Germany. Clemenceau secured as much as possible from his fellow peacemakers to compensate for France's uniquely exposed position and wartime sacrifices. The drastic cuts in Germany's military power and its territorial, financial, and commercial losses gave France a measure of protection and an opportunity, if limited in time, to compensate for the remaining differentials in their industrial potential. Enforcement of the treaty came to be seen as essential for the security of France. The British had secured most of their war aims before the peace conference met, and Lloyd George felt that he was well placed to act as the arbiter between France and Germany. The human and material costs of the war were unexpected and shocking to a nation accustomed to small imperial conflicts. There was a strong feeling both in the cabinet and electorate that the country should never again participate in such a continental conflict. Shorn of its navy and colonies, Germany no longer posed a threat to the security of Britain or its empire. Though Lloyd George favoured containment and wanted restitution, he was convinced that British prosperity depended on a German economic revival and that the peace of Europe depended on Germany's return to grace. He thought that the war had left France too powerful and Germany too weak, misunderstanding the temporary nature of the post-war balance between the two powers. Lloyd George sought a balancing role that would favour the supposedly weaker power at the expense of the strong, in order to create the new equilibrium that would free Britain from the nightmare of military continental interventions. These conflicting views, present at the peace conference but moderated in the presence of Woodrow Wilson and hopes for American participation in European reconstruction, were at the heart of the post-war Anglo-French conflict over the treatment of Germany. It was the latter which benefited from their failure to agree. The Treaty of Versailles was attacked even before it was signed, and has suffered ever since from a highly critical historical press. It was a flawed treaty which left a trail of dissatisfied nations in its wake. It could hardly have been otherwise. Little beyond the common wish to defeat the Germans had kept the war coalition together. There was an even more limited consensus among the treaty's drafters. Apart from a shared belief in Germany's responsibility for the war, each of the negotiators had 'his own agenda, theories, priorities, visions, and prescriptions'.[1] It is no surprise that the Treaty of Versailles was a bundle of compromises. It aimed to solve the almost impossible problem of both punishing and conciliating a country that remained a great power despite the years of fighting. The Versailles treaty was indeed a victor's peace, framed to punish and constrain the Germans. But it was also meant to create a legitimate post-war order that the defeated as well as the victor nations would come to accept. It represented an amalgam of realism and idealism; the traditional means of securing peace after victory were combined with new proposals for managing inter-state relations. Less haste and a more methodical approach might have produced a more consistent treaty, but would not have fundamentally affected its substance with regard to Germany. The Versailles terms, while harsh, were not excessively so. The Reich was not permanently crushed and room was left for its revival. With the disintegration of Austria-Hungary and the fall of tsarist Russia, Germany was actually strategically better placed than in 1914 and the opportunities for advancing its national interests were potentially far greater than those open to the kaiser's government. Due to Woodrow Wilson and Lloyd George, the country's basic unity was preserved and its productive capacity and industrial potential left intact. Reparations did not cripple Germany; despite the sometimes hysterical historical debates that have ensued, the problem of payment was always a political rather than an economic question. It proved politically impossible for the Weimar government to meet the real, as distinct from the nominal, reparation demands of the victors. The Versailles treaty did not solve the German problem, but the traditional view that it was a Carthaginian peace needs to be abandoned.

There were considerable doubts about the adoption of the principle of self-determination, hailed at the time as one of the great achievements of the drafters of the treaties. Wilson was unpleasantly surprised by the number of claimants in Paris and many in the peace delegations were

---

[1] Kalevi J. Holsti, *Peace and War: Armed Conflict and International Order, 1648–1989* (New York, 1991), 178.

highly alarmed by its possible consequences. The makers of the peace had been faced with a fait accompli; the Habsburg Monarchy had disintegrated and could not be resurrected. Wilson believed that national governments based on the consent of the governed were a far better guarantee of peace than the old principles of legitimacy. He had to acknowledge that in eastern Europe popular sovereignty acquired an ethnic dimension and that ethnicity became one of the defining characteristics of the nation-state. In part, the peacemakers were adapting the international system to the realities of the European situation. The national principle, always vaguely defined, had been gaining legitimacy and popularity throughout the previous century. It was now given an international endorsement, and ethnicity and other forms of linguistic, religious, and cultural commonality were recognized as the basis for state-building. This recognition marked one of the seismic shifts in the 1919 international order. While many of the nationalist movements proved ephemeral and some of the newly recognized states enjoyed only the briefest of lives, for the successful ones the peacemakers provided the much-needed stamp of legitimacy. The principle of self-determination, never clearly defined, was selectively applied. The principle was violated or compromised when the strategic interests of the victor powers were engaged, and was not applied to the defeated nations. It was not extended to the new imperial acquisitions or to the older colonies of the victorious European powers. It was much modified in practice when the boundaries of the new states were drawn. It was, nevertheless, true that after 1919 more people lived under governments of their own choosing than at any time earlier or later until 1989. In freeing the old minorities, the makers of the treaties created new ones. Belatedly, they recognized that these new minorities would be in danger. Treaties protecting 'minority rights', a highly sophisticated concept hardly safeguarded in well-established states, were signed by those countries, mainly but not exclusively in eastern Europe, whom the victors thought insufficiently advanced to protect their minorities without some form of oversight. It is true that strident nationalism and anti-Semitism were common features of many of these regimes, but their differential treatment engendered anger and resentment. The attempt to provide some sort of international protection for the civil rights and cultural autonomy of minority groups through the League of Nations, however minimal and inadequate, represented a novel attempt to expand the existing fabric of internationalism. Like so many parts of the treaties, the doctrine of self-determination combined moral principles and the dictates of *realpolitik* at a time when the international system still favoured sovereign states in general and the great powers in particular.

It can be argued that more than pure great-power self-interest was involved in the drafting of the Treaty of Versailles. No such claim can be made about the peace treaties with the other defeated powers, which were far harsher and more vindictive that the one with Germany. The Treaty of Sèvres concluded with the Ottoman Turks was shaped almost entirely by the old adage, 'to the victors go the spoils'. Sèvres was an old-fashioned Allied carve-up of the tottering Ottoman empire, whose demise had long been predicted. It was already clear at the time of its conclusion that the situation in the Middle East (itself a Eurocentric term) was highly volatile and that the enmities among the victor nations precluded a permanent settlement. Sèvres had to be revised. The Treaty of Lausanne, the last and most long-lasting of the peace settlements, was a victory for the new nationalist forces unleashed by the Great War. The new Turkey, however, was confined to its European borders, as had been outlined in the National Covenant. The two main imperial powers, Britain—by far the dominant force in the region—and France nevertheless succeeded in keeping their Arab gains. Though defined as mandates, the checks on the authority of the mandatory powers were limited in scope. The mandate system in the Middle East merely disguised the creation of a new species of imperial expansion.

The treaties with Austria and Hungary were punitive in the extreme. Austria became a shadow of its former self, with nearly a third of its population in Vienna and the rest scattered in its uneconomic Alpine hinterland. It was left in a perilous economic condition and was only rescued from bankruptcy in 1922 by League-organized loans. Hungary, now ethnically homogeneous, was economically viable but so stripped of territories and people as to guarantee its permanent revisionist status. If the Bulgarian peace treaty appeared less severe, this was mainly because of the country's poverty and geographic position rather than from any generosity on the part of the peacemakers. It, too, lost territory to its neighbours and became a land-locked state. Reparations, set at $2\frac{1}{4}$ milliard gold francs (£90 million), have been estimated at constituting one-fourth of its national wealth.[2] It was much easier to impose harsh terms on Germany's weak allies than on a great power, despite warnings of future economic and irredentist consequences, many from advisers in the Allied delegations. The three 'secondary' European peace treaties, primarily of interest to Italy, were based on the political, economic, and territorial ambitions of the victorious nations, both large and small, with scant regard for the principles of self-determination.

    [2] Sally Marks, *The Illusion of Peace* (rev. edn. Basingstoke, 2003), 22.

III

The next ten years were spent trying to cope with the problems of the war and the peace, the problems of reconstruction and stabilization. The multiple effects of the war, quite apart from the situations created by the peace treaties, necessitated a period of intense activity at home and abroad. The 1920s emerge as a period of continuous adaptation and experimentation. Statesmen sought ways to advance their national interests through a revival of the old concert methods, along with the development of new techniques and institutions to address problems no longer suitable for traditional bilateral negotiation. The reconstruction of the European order was left, for the most part, in the hands of the leaders of two and then three European powers, though it could not have been accomplished without American assistance. The necessary but narrowly defined role played by the United States following the American Senate's rejections of the Versailles treaty and Washington's withdrawal from the political affairs of Europe reinforced this continental bias, as did the Soviet Union's continuing exclusion from great-power deliberations. While it may be true that the war accelerated the transfer of power from European to the non-European states, particularly to the United States and Japan, and that the tide was already turning against the European domination of the extra-European world, this was not how Europe's statesmen saw the post-war situation. This was not due to blindness or deliberate oversight, though there was an element of each. The great-power leaders read the warning signs but believed that recovery and stabilization would confirm Europe's world leadership. The failure of the United States to fully exploit its potential power convinced many, particularly in Britain, that it was possible to work out an acceptable modus vivendi with the giant newcomer without losing their own global authority. More worrying was the danger from the Soviet Union, but its threat was contained less through the establishment of the Allied *cordon sanitaire* in Europe, which soon disintegrated, than through the realism of the Soviet leadership and its preoccupation with the survival of the USSR. Japan, as its membership in the League and participation in the Washington naval conference of 1921–2 confirmed, appeared willing to play by western rules, and to confine its strategic ambitions to the western Pacific and its economic expansion in China to what could be achieved without challenging the western powers. As a result, a Eurocentric global regime was established, despite the need for American financial underwriting, by statesmen who still saw Europe as the centre of the world and who shared, in spite of the war and the destruction of long-held moral certainties, common assumptions about European claims to world leadership and political and cultural superiority over other challengers. Even the League of Nations, which Wilson had hoped would institute a global system that would replace the European balance of power and correct the shortcomings of the peace treaties, came to reflect the primacy of European attitudes and concerns.

The war and the peace combined to produce an unusual situation in Europe. There was neither a continental hegemonic power nor a balance of power. The British, who in global terms were still the strongest power and the only rival to the Americans, were ambivalent about the role they wished to take in Europe. Given the high human and material costs of their recent continental commitment, they preferred a balance of power in Europe that would allow Britain to play an arbitral diplomatic role but would restrict her obligations to maintain it. Insofar as British greatness depended on its empire, naval strength, and financial/economic importance, the government had to balance its global and continental interests. Despite the arguments of the isolationists, the imperialists, and the 'Atlanticists' who sought an Anglo-American partnership, it was impossible for Britain to turn its back on Europe. Yet British influence in Europe was based on prestige and potential power rather than on military strength. Its ability to determine the balance of power was repeatedly constrained by imperial interests and an unwillingness to go beyond strictly limited commitments to guarantee the European peace. France, with the largest continental army and air force, sought to preserve the treaty equilibrium, its chief guarantee against the revival of a potentially stronger Germany. During the first half of the decade there were accusations, not without substance, that the French were aiming at a hegemonic role in Europe. All their efforts in this direction had to be abandoned in the light of Anglo-American hostility. The key to French behaviour remained the fear of German power, and its expression was the constant search for 'security', never clearly defined. This fear was, as Briand claimed, a Damoclean sword that hung over the French head and left no action unshadowed by its presence. The preoccupation with the German revival and the bitter imperial quarrels in the Middle East, compounded by clashes of personality between their leaders, drove France and Britain further apart, reducing the possibilities for the joint front against Germany that most French statesmen acknowledged as the essential condition for success. Left in a damaged but hardly destroyed state, Germany concentrated all its diplomatic energies on treaty evasion and revision, particularly with regard to reparations, which could not be collected without its assistance. The reparation issue assumed a central role in the political life of the country. It provided an element of unity, keeping the coalition parties together and preventing their opponents from pressing their opposition too far for fear of provoking foreign reactions. At the same time, it intensified the highly divisive conflicts over who was to pay the costs of the lost war, and allowed the weak Weimar coalitions opportunities for avoiding difficult political solutions that might put the republic at risk. Such evasive action hardly enhanced the power of the government, which had to buy domestic support by offering concessions to the major interest groups.

IV

The Treaty of Versailles set the early parameters for the settlements in Europe. It could have been enforced or revised if the victor nations had held together. Enforcement would have required firm resolution because the Germans refused to accept the 'Versailles *Diktat*' and resisted compliance with its terms. The withdrawal of the Americans and the division of the British and French over interpretation, response, and punishment ensured the failure of this course. Despite France's military superiority, the one attempt in 1923–4 to establish its political and economic pre-eminence in Europe through its own actions ended in failure due to the opposition and intervention of the British and the Americans. The subsequent adjustment of the European equilibrium in the German direction by the Anglo-Americans in 1924 opened possibilities for future revision, though mainly at French expense. Managed revision was certainly possible, for Versailles was not an absolute or doctrinaire treaty but rather an open-ended settlement. None of its drafters suffered from the hubris of thinking that its terms were immutable. As Clemenceau warned the Chamber of Deputies, the treaty was not even 'a beginning but the beginning of a beginning'.[3] But where the French premier called for 'eternal vigilance', Lloyd George spoke of 'remedy', 'repair', and 'redress'. The British contemplated German revival with a sense of economic and financial hope, the French only with political and military dread. Against this background, there could be no agreement about enforcing Versailles or about its revision.

The pace of diplomatic activity quickened. This was due, undoubtedly, to Lloyd George's prodigious energy and his strong belief in the virtues of personal diplomacy. There was a dizzying round of summit meetings and conferences of different durations and fluctuating membership. These gatherings suffered from many of the drawbacks of high-level personal diplomacy. They created and exacerbated tensions between the summiteers and led to both political and administrative complications in home capitals. Ministerial diplomacy, however, was

---

[3] Jean-Bapiste Duroselle, *Clemenceau* (Paris, 1988), 773.

only one of the reasons for the frenetic pace of international negotiation. The vast expansion of the diplomatic map and the importance of the so-called expert, already presaged at the peace conference, brought into the diplomatic arena a host of negotiating agents, whose activities challenged and in some instances dwarfed the role of more traditional diplomats. The importance of financial and economic issues in the post-war world and the centrality of the reparations and war-debts debates to re-establishing the financial order meant that financial and economic departments and private individuals, bankers, businessmen, and economists played forma-tive roles in providing advice and shaping policy. Such changes in diplomatic practices were reinforced by the American interpretation of its diplomatic role, which placed unusual importance on the actions of private individuals and on financial and economic diplomacy. In a period where expert knowledge commanded unusual respect and when it was thought that the principles of scientific management could be applied to a wide range of problems, it was inevitable that the cast of negotiators should be enlarged and that jurisdictional disputes should occur at home and abroad, sometimes muddying the international waters. The experts were supposedly dealing with technical questions and expected to give apolitical advice, but as almost all such issues involved political decisions these distinctions were often meaningless. The lines between domestic and foreign affairs were eroded as so many of the post-war issues had both national and international implications.

Policy-makers were operating in a different climate from their pre-war predecessors. At one end, the breakdown of more traditional barriers between domestic and foreign policy and the new public dimension of so much of the new diplomacy required an often unwel-come awareness of public opinion. Few conferences or meetings of the League of Nations escaped the attention of the world press and photo-graphers. At the other end, there was the increased importance of intelligence, above all signals intelligence, in the conduct of diplomacy. Every major power had diplomatic or military code-breaking bureaus, and these produced more material that was disseminated more widely than in pre-1914 Europe. The reading of coded telegrams and wireless messages permitted a more rapid and often more accurate appraisal of the activities of friends and foes than could be provided by the diplo-mats, though the conclusions drawn were often misleading and some-times wrong. All the major powers, and many of the smaller countries as well, were the beneficiaries and the victims of this 'mutual eavesdrop-ping'.[4] There were still those who considered intelligence operations as

[4] Christopher Andrew, *Secret Service: The Making of the British Intelligence Community* (London, 1985), 261.

something of an embarrassment, and spying, whether overt or covert, an unwelcome addition to their diplomatic armoury, yet almost all accepted intelligence gathering as a normal and unavoidable practice. In this period, when the most powerful nations were the status quo countries and when everyone knew who was powerful or not, intelligence mattered more to diplomacy than to strategy. Intelligence was important mainly with regard to the details of policy rather than to fundamentals. It was most useful during diplomatic negotiations and in dealing with subversion, a new item on the diplomatic agenda. In the case of both the Lausanne and Washington conferences, the bargaining position of the British at the former and the Americans at the latter can only be understood when one knows that each was reading the diplomatic codes of most of its bargaining partners. Intelligence on subversion was more important than before 1914, given the Soviet attempts to destabilize regimes in the west (and Soviet fears of western actions in the USSR), and similar efforts of some of the smaller states in southern and south-eastern Europe against their neighbours. As in earlier and later periods, military intelligence or its interpretation could be misleading (worst-case scenarios), and diplomatic intelligence could suffer from preconceived assumptions and misperceptions. Access to the intercepts embittered Anglo-French relations to the detriment of rational diplomacy. Intelligence sometimes fell short of providing information about the intentions of the main actors; in the case of Mussolini, however, British intelligence proved accurate and explains, in part, why the Duce's threats to the peace could be overlooked. While it is clear that some military and diplomatic decision-makers were far more skilful than others at using intelligence, few could afford to ignore it.

The first years of the decade were particularly turbulent. This was due in part to the number of unresolved problems and the many issues that were left pending. The wars along Russia's European borders did not end until the conclusion of the peace with Poland (Treaty of Riga) in March 1921. The war in the Middle East continued until October 1922, and the Treaty of Lausanne was only concluded in July 1923. Territorial conflicts in central Europe and in the Balkans continued to plague inter-state relations throughout the decade. There were plebiscites to be held and reparations figures to be set. The many commissions created at the peace conference to execute the decisions reached in Paris faced continual difficulties. Their tasks were made no easier by the withdrawal of the Americans, so that membership was often reduced from five to four, increasing the potential for deadlock.

But the real source of instability in western Europe was the impasse in Anglo-French relations and the determination of the Germans to resist the enforcement of the treaty. Their major battles centred on reparations. The French and British could not agree either on the sums to be demanded or the sanctions to be enforced if Germany defaulted on her obligations. The Germans exploited the differences between the two powers and actively cultivated the more sympathetic British. In the background was the successful German propaganda campaign against the Treaty of Versailles which the French failed to counter. Repeatedly thwarted in its efforts to secure reparations, France became more rigid in its defence of the treaty and increasingly viewed German compliance with the reparation clauses as the test for its enforcement. The British had no wish to strengthen France at German expense, and believed that Germany's return to prosperity was more important for British economic recovery than the forced payment of reparations. The Germans made only one full cash payment under the terms of the London Schedule of 1921 until the adoption of the Dawes plan, and repeatedly failed to meet the coal and timber quotas despite their repeated reductions. They not only claimed that the Allied demands could not be met, but also that reparations were the cause of the inflation and hyperinflation that made payment impossible. While neither of the Allies accepted this German reading of the situation, they differed on how the defaulting nation should be treated. More was involved than the debates about sums, deliveries, and sanctions. If Germany, with few foreign wartime debts and a diminishing wartime domestic debt due to inflation, did not pay reparations and the French had to cover their reconstruction costs and war debts from their own resources, the treaty-created economic balance would change to the German advantage. Reparations became the chief way that France could keep German power in check. Neither British nor French efforts to find alternative solutions to the reparations problem met with any success. The French were thrown back on the treaty sanction that the British had always opposed. Poincaré decided to play his Ruhr card. The stakes were high but he expected to win. The French occupation produced a short-term victory and a long-term defeat. Germany was brought to her knees, but France's financial weakness and Anglo-American opposition forced Poincaré to retreat from what seemed a strong position. France lacked the strength and the will to enforce the treaty terms without outside assistance. Poincaré knew that he needed Anglo-American backing to carry through his revisionist policies. He sought to limit the scope of the Dawes inquiry and to secure renewed new Anglo-American guarantees. He tried to revive the powers of the Reparation Commission which would give France a controlling influence over reparation policy. All these efforts would fail in the face of American and British hostility. The need for American loans meant that France would accept an Anglo-American solution to the reparations problem that favoured Germany at French expense. In the summer of 1924, along with the acceptance of the Dawes plan, the new French prime minister, Édouard Herriot, abandoned many of the means of coercing Germany that Clemenceau had secured in 1919. There could be no future Ruhr occupations nor any extension of the occupation of the Rhineland. The Rhineland evacuation clock had begun to move. In addition, France lost the opportunity to conclude a permanent trade agreement with Germany while it still controlled the Ruhr and before some of the Treaty limitations on German economic power ran out. The Dawes plan and London agreements in revising the treaty settlements opened the way for a European settlement on Anglo-American terms. Neither country on its own could have broken the reparations deadlock or established the political conditions that would readjust the treaty balance in Germany's favour. As Stresemann fully understood, American financial underwriting was essential for Germany recovery and for any future bid to regain its great-power status. Financial intervention by itself would have proved insufficient; it was left to the British to translate the American contribution into a politically viable settlement.

V

The mid-decade agreements provided the framework within which Austen Chamberlain, Aristide Briand, and Gustav Stresemann approached the problems of Europe and much else besides during the next four years. The Dawes plan and London agreements made the Locarno treaties possible, and the continued flow of American capital to Europe, and to Germany in particular, was essential for their success. Yet the Locarno treaties were negotiated by the Europeans, and while supported in principle by the Americans, opened the door for a European political settlement with minimal American input. Germany joined the great-power directorate; the concert of Europe was revived. Meeting privately in Geneva hotel rooms, usually on the eve of the League's Council meetings, the three European leaders bargained among themselves to forward the process of revision and stabilization. The smaller powers, rarely invited to join the 'Locarno tea parties' where the major decisions were taken, resented their exclusion but could do little other than protest. By the closing years of the decade it appeared that some progress towards stabilization had been made. There was even some hope that there might be an eastern Locarno and a settlement of the Polish problem, though this had to be postponed to a much later date. It was possible to call 'The Conference on the Final Liquidation of the War' that met at the Hague in early August 1929, and to create a 'Committee on the Liquidation of the Past'. The majority of historians have questioned the reality of this progress. They have categorized the post-1925 period as a time of illusions when the leaders of Europe's democracies, faced with popular demands for the dividends of peace, produced only the façade of a settlement that they could not deliver. A less condemnatory reading of what was attempted before the cracks in the reconstituted order widened to the point of fragmentation would portray the creators of the Locarno settlements as realists and pragmatists who sought to enlarge the diplomatic canvas to meet the challenges of the post-war situation, though their efforts were met with only limited success.

It was at and after Locarno that the three foreign ministers, and their respective ministries, recovered much of their initiatory power in foreign affairs. Their chief advisers played important roles in contributing to the new diplomatic ground rules. The Locarnites revived the concert politics of the past but recognized the utility of using the League of Nations to strengthen positions at home, to deal with the demands of other member states who sought their intervention, and to provide a broader framework for the resolution of transnational problems. The attention of the world press on Geneva had its uses in creating the image of consensus that the Locarnites hoped to project as a necessary part of the peace-building process. Each of three foreign ministers was aware of the limitations on his negotiating freedom. Chamberlain remained a committed globalist, determined to defend Britain's imperial and world-wide interests while focusing most of his energies on Europe. He believed that Britain could and should play the 'honest broker' role in European affairs and intended that Britain's guarantee of France's borders with Germany should encourage the French to offer the concessions needed to reconcile Germany to its constrained position in Europe. He hoped that further confidence-building measures would permit a peaceful readjustment in the relationship between the two neighbouring countries, but always insisted that France had further to go than Germany. The Locarno agreements enhanced British prestige, an important factor in the existing multipolar situation, making it possible to broaden Britain's arbitral role whatever her actual power position. Chamberlain thought in political terms; for this reason, he tended to leave financial questions to the Treasury and Bank of England and was hardly concerned with the absence of the Americans from the security equation. With the British guarantee behind him, Briand could, with reluctance, meet some of Stresemann's demands. Negotiations were possible on the ending of Allied military inspection rights and over the reduction in the number of Allied occupation forces in the Rhineland. He withheld, with Chamberlain's support, the most important of Stresemann's claims, the early evacuation of the Rhineland, in the hope of securing compensation in the form of a final and satisfactory reparation settlement that would cover France's war debts. Germany, readmitted to the concert of Europe and made a permanent member of the Council of the League of Nations, resumed a central position in the management of western European affairs. By retaining his free hand in the east, Stresemann enlarged the room for diplomatic manoeuvre and could forward his plans for future territorial revision. Despite French apprehensions, Germany was, for the moment, militarily impotent. Even with financial stabilization and the removal of some of the Versailles restrictions, the Germans could only achieve revision through peaceful means. Without military forces, the restoration of German power depended on diplomacy and the exploitation of the country's economic strengths, fuelled by the influx of American capital. Necessity as well as a broader vision of Germany's future in Europe lay behind Stresemann's brand of revisionism, whatever may have been his long-term ambitions. Accepting the more positive interpretation of Stresemann's diplomacy, shorn of the embellishments that have turned this conservative nationalist into an enthusiast for European integration, he, like Briand, saw an accommodation between Germany and France and the creation of a stable Europe as the only alternative to a condition of continuing tension that would bring no satisfaction to either.

There were powerful systemic limits to this process of peaceful revision. For France, the problem of the Franco-German power balance involved a shrinking security pie. The German recovery of its great-power status necessarily involved a diminution of French security, and the establishment of what Franz Knipping has called the 'half-hegemonious Bismarkian state' in Europe entailed the acceptance of a subordinate position for France. This was already in evidence in 1928, when Stresemann speeded up the revisionist timetable by demanding the withdrawal of the occupying troops from the Rhineland and a final reparations settlement. The 'economic Locarno' between Germany and France, the cartels and commercial agreements, so important to Stresemann's attempt to reassure the French, could not compensate for France's basic insecurity. Withdrawal from the Rhineland, the delayed fulfilment of Stresemann's goal, became the signal for the revival of French apprehensions. Briand needed reassurances about Germany's future intentions and a strong reaffirmation of British support if the process of accommodation was to continue. Neither was in evidence at the time of the evacuation, and all the signs pointed in the opposite direction. It was, in part, Briand's recognition of the coming impasse that led him to raise the possibility of a European federal union with the deathly ill German foreign minister in the summer of 1929. The equivocal nature of Britain's commitment in Europe was an equally important weakness in the mid-decade stabilization. Britain's real power with regard to France stemmed from its willingness to guarantee France's future security, yet the Locarno guarantees were partial and carefully circumscribed. No British government would engage itself in eastern Europe. British obligations were also restricted in the west and purposely linked to the League's weak and non-binding security system. It was hoped in London that the western guarantees would never need to be honoured. There was no military follow-up to the political arrangements. The memories of the Somme and Passchendaele closed the door to any broader interpretation of Britain's responsibilities in Europe beyond Locarno. It was only after he left office that Chamberlain, highly critical of the anti-French turn in Labour policy, took the unpopular stand that the safety of Britain depended on assuring that of France, Belgium, and Holland. Though Chamberlain genuinely tried to play the 'honest broker' role, he always believed that Briand had taken the greater risks in concluding the Locarno agreements. It was with some justice that Stresemann, who found Chamberlain distant and reserved, never fully trusted his neutrality. The British foreign secretary never grasped the extent of Stresemann's weakness nor the frailty of the Weimar republic. While anxious to see Germany recover, Britain was not prepared to remove the constraints on its power too quickly.

The domestic situations in all three countries presented yet other obstacles to the process of accommodation. Stresemann and Briand, especially the former, cultivated political support, their private negotiations notwithstanding. The successful implementation of any major decisions depended on the backing of the politically and economically influential groups at home. Whenever this support weakened, progress towards accommodations became more difficult. This was the price paid for the democratization of politics and for the increased importance of the domestic roots of decision-making. Stresemann was a cool, calculating realist who believed that revisionism and peace were interdependent, and that both could be achieved through careful diplomacy and economic co-operation. Success depended on his ability to convince the electorate that Germany's return to great-power status, with equal rights, could be achieved through negotiation with France and Britain. The achievements during his lifetime, though considerable, could not compensate, as Stresemann had hoped, for the basic structural weaknesses of the Weimar republic, nor did they satisfy the conservative and nationalist right, the latter seeking the destruction of the republic as well as of the Versailles settlement. Neither foreign-policy success nor the outward signs of economic recovery provided the republic with the lustre required to turn the state into a symbol of German greatness. Stresemann tried to use foreign policy as a way to promote domestic consolidation, but even within his own party he found this an uphill struggle. Believing that the existence of the republic depended on a coalition of the parties of the centre, he intervened in domestic politics to promote and maintain it. The task was becoming increasingly difficult towards the end of his shortened life. Stresemann was rightly alarmed by the growing appeal of the Nazis and the alliance of Hugenberg and Hitler against the Young plan in 1929. This gave a new rallying point for the extreme right and revived the shrill anti-Versailles rhetoric of the earlier years. Stresemann's apprehensions about the visibly rising militant mood were confirmed, after his death, by the widespread jubilation and demands for further concessions when France left the Rhineland in May 1930. Much was made of the liberation of German soil; little was said about the man who had made it possible. Stresemann's posthumous moment of triumph revealed the shallowness of its domestic roots. The weakening of the republic would put his achievements at risk.

There were problems, too, in France. Despite his golden tongue, Briand failed to calm the fears of the French right and centre-right parties about the revival of German power. Under severe pressure after the electoral success of the right in 1928 and the re-emergence of the reparations question, he lost political influence and independence. 'Briandisme' was in retreat in France. Briand's tougher line towards Stresemann made him more dependent on Chamberlain's support, and the Conservative defeat in Britain in 1929 was both a personal and a political blow. Even in Britain, which enjoyed a more solid political structure than either Germany or France, the Labour party seized on Chamberlain's diplomatic difficulties to win an electoral campaign in which foreign policy played a vote-winning part. There followed under Labour, along with a revived interest in the League of Nations, a return to the pre-Locarno view, never fully abandoned, that France rather than Germany posed the greater threat to continental reconciliation and economic recovery. Insofar as the Locarnites intended that their policies should inspire confidence on both sides of the Rhine, they failed to achieve their goals.

VI

The main burden of post-Locarno adjustment rested on only three European states. Though Italy reluctantly became a joint guarantor of the Locarno agreements, Mussolini's regional ambitions threatened the Danubian and Balkan status quo and his relationships with France and Weimar Germany were too disturbed for either to depend on his co-operation. For all Mussolini's rhetoric, Italy remained a minor piece on the European chessboard. For very different reasons, the United States and Soviet Union remained peripheral states, whose interventions in European affairs, however critical in the case of the former, were sporadic and ambiguous in their consequences for the stability of European affairs. Both posed threats, political or economic, to the status quo outside of Europe, mainly affecting Britain, its empire, and trade, but these were checked or absorbed without fundamentally affecting the global balance of power. The Americans sought the stabilization of Europe; the Soviets sought its dissolution. Neither achieved its aims. Given its potentially hegemonic position and its unrivalled financial and economic power, after its successful intervention in co-operation with Britain in 1923–4 America did surprisingly little to advance the process of stabilization during the next five years, and some of its actions proved counter-productive.

It is true that, in the Locarno period, the American contribution to the financial and economic revitalization of Europe, particularly Germany, provided the background for the efforts at political stabilization. Only the United States had the capital needed to stabilize the European currencies, to reconstitute the gold system, and to provide the loans and investment needed for the recovery of German industry. From the start, however, the Republican administrations, backed and prodded by Congress, took a very special and limited view of America's contribution to the reconstruction of Europe. America was to act only as an informal arbiter; its open-door policies and capital flows to the continent would encourage European recovery and promote the continental peace. Washington acted on the assumption that financial and political stabilization could and should be treated in separate categories, and that the American government need take no responsibility for the political consequences of the former. Insofar as possible, financial questions should be depoliticized and settled by financial experts according to non-political criteria. Private investment in Europe was largely uncontrolled; it was left to the investment bankers, whose primary responsibility was to their American investors who naturally were concerned only with profitability. This limited and highly pragmatic conception of the American role, articulated most clearly by the secretary of state, Charles Hughes, was far removed from the repudiated Wilsonian vision of 1918–19. Its successful implementation in 1923–4, when Hughes's main objectives were achieved, convinced both those with a vested interest in European recovery and those opposed to American involvement in Europe's political problems that this was an acceptable form of participation in European affairs.

In many ways, the informal co-operation of government and financiers was an extension of the same Republican principles that were applied to domestic problems. Yet these rules of engagement were too narrowly drawn to promote the stabilization of Europe. Washington did nothing to sustain the Dawes regime; supervision was left in the hands of the independent American reparation agent. Despite his and other warnings of the consequences of the uncontrolled flood of American capital into Germany, the Republican administrations refused to control the amount or direction of private investment, much of which was used for non-productive purposes. American insistence that war debts had to be paid and the refusal to acknowledge the linkage between war debts and reparations reinforced the latter's destabilizing effects on European politics and prevented the very depoliticisation that the United States favoured. It was not until the Hoover moratorium of 1931, and then only for a brief period and without abandoning the principle of separation, that the slate was wiped clean. While the United States was hardly the only culpable party, the failure of the world's leading creditor to offer any radical solution to the reparations–war-debt imbroglio contributed to its ongoing destructive effects. It saddled the new gold system with a burden of indebtedness that reinforced its deflationary consequences and made it more difficult to protect the exchanges from political pressures. Even official participation in the Bank of International Settlement was beyond the limits of government action, though private American banks were permitted to participate. American trade policy hardly accorded with the principles of free trade and the open-door policy and reinforced the protectionist moves of the European powers, with Britain one of the few pre-1932 exceptions. The American objections to direct Franco-German settlements, whether cartels, trade agreements, or the Thiory bargain, as well as its disapproval of Briand's European Union proposals were based on its opposition to closed markets, but the Americans did not practice what they preached.

American self-sufficiency, both in economic and security terms, encouraged a sense of detachment from European affairs. Many Americans felt that they could ignore Europe's difficulties without suffering major damage. While much was expected from financial stabilization and the expansion of trade, successive Republican administrations made it clear that they would take no part in underwriting European security. Without any such interests of its own in Europe, the United States repeatedly refused to join any regional security system; there was no European equivalent to the admittedly limited Washington treaty agreements. Even the limited American participation in the League's disarmament talks did not modify Washington's refusal to associate the United States with League-sponsored actions, nor its unwillingness to join more limited security arrangements. The French bid to bring the Americans into the European equation ended in the non-binding and unenforceable Kellogg–Briand pact, an 'international peace kiss' intended to satisfy American anti-war pressure groups. There could be no European 'buck-passing' to the United States; the latter would not act as an offshore balancer. The security problem was left to the Europeans to solve.

There was little likelihood that the Soviet Union would contribute to the stability of an international regime that its leaders were pledged to destroy. The Soviet role in Europe, however, was very different from that envisioned either by Lenin or Trotsky. Throughout the decade the story of Soviet foreign policy was the changing relationship between its two main strategies, 'revolution' and 'diplomacy'. The 1920s were marked by the movement from the former towards the latter, but without the USSR's abandoning its revolutionary mission. The struggle between the socialist and capitalist worlds could be delayed or indefinitely postponed, but the eventual conflict was inevitable. The failure of world revolution made it imperative to safeguard the revolution at home by opening diplomatic relations with the west and concluding trading agreements with the capitalist powers. During the 1920s the Soviet leadership was more concerned with the security of the USSR than with the pursuit of revolution abroad, despite moments, as in Germany during the autumn of 1923, when it was tempted to play the revolutionary card. Anxious to break out of their diplomatic isolation, the Soviets sought political and economic agreements with all the major western capitalist powers and concluded bilateral non-aggression pacts with neighbours. The triumph of Stalin did not initiate a period of isolation and autarchy. Until the USSR was ready to meet its enemies it needed a period of peace, and the foreign capital and technological assistance required to speed up the process of industrialization and militarization.

What were the leading western powers to make of this revolutionary state that was seeking re-entry into Europe? There was pressure on all three Locarnites to respond to the problems created by the diplomatic practices of the USSR. Britain and France housed both fervent anti-Bolsheviks and those prepared to ignore ideological differences in order to open the vast Russian market for trade and investment. Interaction with the Soviet Union raised ideological problems that exacerbated divisions at home, making it difficult to conclude bilateral or multilateral arrangements based largely on calculations of diplomatic, economic, or strategic gain. Given the suspicion existing on both sides of the capitalist–Bolshevik divide, there was little chance of satisfactory Russian settlements with Britain or France. The threat from Moscow was more often ideological in nature than political or strategic, though the presence of a Communist party in France and the interests of its many holders of tsarist bonds undoubtedly affected political attitudes. The ideological factor, however, did not preclude either Mussolini or Kemal Ataturk, both fiercely anti-Bolshevik at home, from cultivating good relations with Moscow. Nor did the problem of the Communist party in Germany and Stresemann's strong dislike of Bolshevism prevent him from making use of the Soviet card in his foreign policy. The highly conservative German military authorities had few difficulties in promoting military arrangements with Moscow. It was practical politics, rather than any 'community of fate', that dictated the German–Soviet *rapprochement*, the latter limited, however, by Stresemann's decision to align Germany with the western powers. There is little question that dealing with the Soviet Union raised problems of a different dimension than those associated with other capitalist states, regardless of how uncongenial their governments might be to the western democracies. Bolshevism represented a threat to the whole international regime. Moscow refused to accept its rules and conventions; its aim was to subvert the capitalist system and to eliminate the bourgeois class upon which it rested. The 'breathing space', however extended, was still only an interval in the inevitable clash between the two systems. If for practical, and mainly commercial, reasons there had to be an accommodation with Moscow, many westerners felt that they were dealing with a country that stood apart from the civilized world. The Soviet challenge to British interests outside of Europe was a greater source of immediate concern than its activities in Europe, but by the end of the decade it was contained, mainly because of the anti-Bolshevik nature of most nationalist movements. In China and south-east Asia, however, Russia was still considered the chief menace to British interests obscuring the threat of Japanese expansion. Apart from exacerbating relations, as in the case of Britain and France or France and Italy, extra-European conflicts did not affect the continental distribution of power. At the same time there was less room for mediating European quarrels by directing attention to the extra-European world, as had been done in the late nineteenth century.

VII

Even as the European leaders revived the concert system, they recognized the importance and usefulness of the League of Nations, which became an integral part of the international regime. It was not, of course, the Wilsonian League, quite apart from the absence of the Americans. In ways that President Wilson might have considered ancillary, or even diversionary, to the League's main purpose, the League of Nations became the centre of international diplomacy and injected a new multinational dimension to the practice of traditional negotiation.

Attendance at League meetings became almost mandatory after 1925, when the foreign secretaries of the Locarno powers were almost always present. The middle-sized and small states found a public platform for their grievances and demands; their representatives, despite their loss of influence in the Council, continued to play important parts in the proceedings of the Assembly and the League's committees. Those outside the League, like the United States, found it useful to attend League-sponsored conferences and to associate themselves with some of its expanded activities. Without exaggerating the importance of the League's political work, the Geneva institution developed useful ways to handle inter-state disputes. The Council, proceeding pragmatically, and without any progression in its success rate, dealt with inter-state conflicts either in areas for which it had special responsibility or in cases that were brought to its attention. It may be true that the institutional-ization of collective action added little to the actual co-operation be-tween the great powers, the sine qua non of successful intervention; but the shift of responsibility to Geneva and the working out of modes of procedure that provided the basis for acceptable solutions explain why governments felt it worth bringing their disputes to the Council table. For the most part, the League handled the 'small change of diplomacy', but a great deal of international negotiation actually passed through its hands. The Geneva system was not a substitute for great-power diplo-macy, as Wilson had intended. It was an adjunct, but one that contrib-uted to the more effective handling of international politics.

Slowly, and with many setbacks, the League's functional activities gradually moved the boundaries between the sovereignty of the state and the claims of the international community. Some of the ground-work had been laid earlier, but much of the League activity was new. If its efforts appeared limited and inadequate for the demands placed on the system, it must be remembered that these were innovative begin-nings in a rocky and unmapped terrain. The weaknesses of the Inter-national Labour Organization and such League-centred operations as the minorities-protection system and the even more modest mandate system were all too obvious. They depended on a 'naming and shaming' approach which left redress in the hands of the offending state. None-theless, these efforts to inscribe group guarantees into international law were part of an attempt to create international institutions that would give social groups some form of protection against the state, if only through the mobilization of international opinion. The League, through its Secretariat, tackled a vast range of humanitarian problems, extending from the unexpectedly continuing refugee problem to such older con-cerns as the abuse of women and children, drugs, and epidemic controls. Private individuals and institutions, working alongside the League, were able to mobilize national and international opinion in order to create new possibilities for investigation, intervention, and assistance. The League provided the mantle of international legitimacy which convinced reluctant governments to co-operate. Operating on shoestring budgets, and constantly badgering member states to subsidize its efforts, the League extended the rules and conventions of the international regime. It was a weak edifice, under constant threat, and dependent on creating networks of support for even limited international action, but it had its place in the international order.

During the 1920s the collective security system had not yet been put to the test. Only confirmed internationalists in Geneva, like Lord Robert Cecil and the representatives of some of the smaller powers without practical alternatives, took an overly optimistic view of its future. If the general public, above all in Britain, was ill-informed about the doubts of its leaders, this was due mainly to the latter's unwillingness to face the political consequences of disappointing popular expectations. While the French sought to tighten and expand the League's security regime, the British—though Labour was more sympathetic than the Conservatives—drew back from supporting automatic and compulsory measures and from any increase in Britain's League obligations. The most ambitious, and ultimately the most disastrous, attempt at international co-operation was the search for a disarmament agreement. Few causes enlisted more public sympathy across the European continent. From 1920 until the calling of a world disarmament conference in 1932, with some success but more often failure, the member states of the League wrestled with the problem. Constantly prodded by the Assembly, the pursuit of disarmament continued, despite the conflicts between Britain and France over security questions and arms-limitation methods and the disputes between the main naval powers over the extension of the Washington treaty, the one actual disarmament treaty of the period, which was negotiated outside of Geneva. The search for a disarmament formula went on throughout the decade because millions of people believed that peace could be achieved if only—or only if—the nations would disarm. The 1920s ended on a note of optimism; the new leaders of Britain and the United States were known to favour a naval treaty, and there were high hopes in the Preparatory Commission when it resumed its labours in 1929 that agreement would be reached on a general draft treaty and the date set for the World Disarmament Conference. By this time the League was fully identified with the disarmament cause.

The enthusiasm for internationalism and international institutions was illustrated by initiatives in the realm of financial management. With the re-establishment of the gold standard, the financial experts intentionally revived a global mechanism that was intended to allow large flows of capital to take place without interference from national states. The advantage of the system was that it supposedly worked automatically to correct imbalances and to maintain equilibrium. The bankers hoped to remove the control of national fiscal policies from the hands of ignorant politicians, necessarily influenced by their electorates, and to allow the central bankers to oversee the proper functioning of the system. In the early 1920s Montagu Norman established contacts with other central bankers (but not the head of the Bank of France) and, in partnership with Benjamin Strong, sought to promote their co-operation in the stabilization of the European currencies. Working through the League of Nation's Financial Committee, there were some notable successes. The weaknesses of the revived gold standard began to emerge towards the end of the decade, but faith in its operations remained unshaken. The central bankers' inability to counteract its deflationary effects or to handle the massive accumulation of gold in the United States and France revealed the clash of interest between the interests of the states and the health of the world system. The stabilization efforts of 1927–8 put a considerable strain on central bank co-operation, as the Bank of France demanded a role equal to that of the Bank of England, and Benjamin Strong came to distrust Norman. The weakness of sterling cast doubts on the viability of the gold–exchange system that had made London, alongside New York and later Paris, so important for the management of international finance. The American and French central bankers urged a return to the classic gold standard which they believed (wrongly) would not need co-ordinated international management, and which would leave each country free to manage its own domestic financial affairs. Banker hopes for international co-operation lay behind the establishment of the Bank of International Settlement in November 1929. Responsible for the reception and distribution of the Dawes payments, it was also intended to act as an instrument of central bank co-operation in an effort to make the international money markets less volatile. It was unfortunate in the date of its establishment, on the eve of a series of bank crises that were to shake the very foundations of the gold standard. Efforts were also made, usually through the medium of League-organized international conferences, to promote common action on tariffs and other hindrances to world trade. The optimism among the delegates to the World Economic Conference of 1927 that their recommendations for stemming the protectionist tide would be adopted by the European governments was dissipated by the end of the decade. The collective action that was taken, after much discussion and with many reservations, proved too weak to reverse the global trend towards protectionism. The beliefs—'part hopes, part illusions—in the restoration of one market driven world by means of international institutional engineering were destroyed by the experience of the Great Depression'.[5] Such beliefs were characteristic of men who thought that a return to the more peaceful and secure world of pre-war Europe could be achieved through the signing of international treaties and the creation of new international institutions.

VIII

The division of Europe into east and west long pre-dated the Great War and the peace settlements, but little that was done after 1919 bridged the gap and in some ways the distance increased as average incomes in eastern Europe fell further behind those of the west by 1930. The Locarno treaties further underlined the lines of division between west and east. Yet, for all it distinctiveness in terms of politics, economic, social, and intellectual life, eastern Europe was part of the broader European continent. There was, of course, not one east European story; each country in the region had its own history. Many, nevertheless, responded and contributed to the same political and economic currents found in the west. The nationalist virus was not confined to the eastern states, nor were the fears of domestic Bolshevik disruption, or the hopes invested in the new international institutions. Some statesmen on both sides of the divide recognized the dangers of this belt of small, individual, and fiercely independent states for the future peace of Europe, but such anxieties were not sufficiently pressing for effective defensive action to be taken.

The basis of recovery was precarious. Many countries continued to suffer from chronic political instability and resorts to violence. Land reform failed to solve the problem of agricultural poverty, which was aggravated by high population growth. Almost all nations, with Czechoslovakia the exception, suffered from high foreign indebtedness. Many governments, before the effects of the depression were felt, suffered from an aggressive nationalism that expressed itself in hostility to minorities and 'beggar-my-neighbour policies'. Despite the absence of war, each country harboured fears about its national security. If some of these anxieties resulted from the peace settlements, others were created or heightened by the actions of those in power. All the east-central and Balkan states had at least one hostile neighbour, and Poland, with five neighbours, had three. This would have mattered less had the political elites and parties not used nationalist or irredentist activity as a way of confirming political control or as a means of courting popularity

---

[5] Harold James, *The End of Globalization: Lessons from the Great Depression* (Cambridge, Mass. and London, 2001), 25.

among various segments of their respective populations. There were no wars, but there was no peace.

It may well be that strong and authoritarian governments were necessary in countries where there was no previous experience of democratic government, and where neither their histories nor cultural inheritance favoured democratic practices. Few of the hopes of the peacemakers of 1919 were fulfilled. Self-determination proved no more successful in promoting democracy than the displaced imperial rule. If the successor states maintained their independence and outward unity, they often did so at the expense of democratic politics. It was primarily in Czechoslovakia, the country whose degree of industrialization, social structure, and high literacy rates most closely approximated those of the west, that democracy took root, and even here much was owed to the ability of its president, Jan Masaryk, to keep the multitude of parties working together. Throughout, political fragmentation, often the result of ethnic divisions, resulted in rapid turnovers in government and the discrediting of democratic institutions. Even more illusory were the 1919 hopes for the assimilation and toleration of minorities. Assimilation was rare, and restricted mainly to the old-established minorities for whom the new frontiers brought few changes. In most of the multi-ethnic states the dominant nationalities imposed their authority through discriminatory legislation or violence. While some minorities were more successful than others in improving their positions, the ratio between the satisfied and dissatisfied hardly changed over the course of the decade. The minority treaties failed to fulfil their promise, and the specially crafted protection clauses for the Jewish minority did little to prevent the imposition of restrictive and discriminatory legislation. As the Jews were not a nationality and lacked even 'surrogate' spokesmen, most abandoned hope of relief through the League's protective system.

Exaggerated nationalism and particularism not only contributed to the overriding sense of insecurity in the region but prevented the regional co-operation that would have benefited national economies and strengthened regional security. Protectionist policies in eastern Europe tended to be more severe against neighbours than against the western states. The massive shift from the common market of the old Habsburg empire to western Europe and the United States was, in part, economically motivated but also reflected the overriding importance of nationalist sentiment. It was only as the agricultural depression spread that Czechoslovakia and Poland launched initiatives to create defensive economic blocs. The French and British, despite their recognition of the need for regional co-operation, failed in their competitive efforts to establish them. Britain, France, and the United States provided the much-needed import capital to most of the states of eastern Europe, with the exception of Czechoslovakia. France lacked the financial means to carry out wartime plans to create an exclusive sphere of influence in these regions, while British and Americans investors had more attractive areas in which to invest their funds. Though important in many countries because of the lack of domestic alternatives, foreign investment was insufficient to alter the economic balance in these predominately agricultural nations. Much of this foreign capital was used unproductively, and the high interest rates led to heavy burdens of debt which were financed by yet more loans or by the selling off of industrial and raw-material assets to foreign investors with their own interests in mind. Germany was already emerging as the region's most important trader, offering the complementary markets that the French lacked. Italy became Yugoslavia's main customer. Borrowing and trading practices, essential for prosperity, increased the economic dependence of the eastern states on the west.

Regional security pacts were weak. The Little Entente was based on the mutual enmity of the three members towards Hungary. Apart from Hungary, each state had a different potential enemy, and efforts to enlarge the Little Entente or to redirect its attention towards other revisionist powers ended in failure. Poland had bilateral alliances but could not create northern blocs against the Soviet Union. The Baltic states failed to conclude regional pacts either with Poland or with Sweden and Finland, and made only limited progress towards the creation of a smaller Baltic alliance. The states in 'the other Europe' did not join together because they had different security interests. As a consequence, they were left exposed to aggressive action should any great power choose to act. For Poland and Czechoslovakia, as well as the other two members of the Little Entente, the French alliance system remained their main defence against such action. Yet the French were unable to get the Poles and Czechs to bury their differences, and the absence of a Czech–Polish alliance remained a serious strategic weakness for all three powers. After Locarno, France increasingly viewed her eastern obligations as a burden, one that the British refused to share and thought inimical to the European peace process. The alliances were kept and periodically refurbished, but the Poles undoubtedly harboured doubts about putting all their eggs in the French security basket. It was natural that many states, in the Baltic, east-central Europe, and the Balkans, should look to the League of Nations to provide some form of security through collective action or disarmament and were strong advocates of the Geneva system. No leader, not even the ever-optimistic Beneš, thought that the League was the sole answer to their security concerns, but many hoped that collective action through the League would strengthen the position of the smaller states. Most of these countries, however poor, were building up their military forces and using foreign loans for this purpose. Poland, hardly an enthusiast for the League, was one of the highest spenders. Few of the revisionist powers could have thought that their treaty-restricted armies could challenge the status quo. Nor did many of the victor states believe that small and ill-equipped forces would provide adequate protection against any one, or two, revisionist great-power neighbours should they start to rearm. However powerful the internationalist impulse behind the disarmament movement might have been—and Beneš spent more time in Geneva than in Prague—idealism and realism went hand in hand. The security predicament of the eastern European states resided partly in the structural problems created by the peace treaties, but even more in the failure of policy-makers to take advantage of the respite of peace during the later 1920s to find some means of working together effectively. The continuing fragmentation and internal divisions of the region at the end of the decade were often troubles of its own making.

IX

The 1920s were a rich and innovative period, as different in many ways from the past as the peace of 1919 was from that of 1815. It is the combination of great-power politics and the experiments in international co-operation that makes this decade so distinctive. The variety of international problems and the altered base of domestic politics required the adoption of new diplomatic methods. The altered relationship between governments and people, whether in the democracies or in the authoritarian governments that developed during the decade, had its impact on the way states managed their foreign affairs. The traditional and the experimental coexisted in an often uneasy relationship. Governments used the old concert and balance-of-power mechanisms to survive in an anarchical international society, but they also contributed, to a greater or lesser degree, to the building of a more diversified international regime. These early attempts at co-operative international action were made despite the semi-absence of the United States and the extreme hostility of the Soviet Union. If the leaders of the democratic powers presented their policies in ways which encouraged hopes for a new order while continuing to run their affairs in the traditional manner, they were also forced to extend the possibilities for European co-operation. The broadening of the diplomatic map produced new responses, often weak and hesitant, from statesmen who grasped how multinational negotiation could further national interests. This was a period when more doors were opened than shut.

This was not an age of illusions; it was a time of hope. Illusions are built upon nothing; hopes may have real foundations, however fragile or temporary. This was the case with the post-war decade. Though the fundamental problems resulting from the Great War remained unsolved, some of the great-power leaders believed that with patient effort the present difficulties could be overcome. Having survived the devastating and traumatic experience of war, the majority of Europeans sought peaceful and prosperous futures. Some genuinely believed that progress had been made. 'The Conference for the Final Liquidation of the War' was not so named out of blithe optimism or cynical irony, but rather out of the conviction that healing the war's destructive legacy was a manageable problem to which practical and realizable solutions could be found. The western European leaders were neither cynics nor idealists, but realists and pragmatists. Even the Bolsheviks, without abandoning their ideological goals, moved in the direction of practical international politics. Admittedly, statesmen sought solutions that would meet the requirements of the moment rather than more imaginative and far-seeing possibilities for the longer term. A few at intervals—Lloyd George at Genoa, Briand, and Stresemann towards the end of the decade—attempted to extend the boundaries of the possible, but never succeeded in changing the existing context within which their decisions had to be reached.

The bases of Europe's reconstruction were real but they did not prove lasting. The treaties were revised but the distinctions between the status quo and revisionist nations remained in place. Domestic reconstruction was aided by international action but also encouraged antagonistic nationalist claims at the expense of co-operative action. Foreign policies were used to buttress domestic structures, as in Germany, with the result that internal conflicts were not resolved. The international order was far too weak to shoulder the burdens of national adjustment. No single state or group of states stepped forward to guarantee the status quo; France, the power with most at stake, was unable to act alone, and neither the British nor the Americans were prepared to underwrite her efforts. The British attempted a difficult, if not impossible, balancing act: to allow the Germans to unravel the equilibrium established in 1919 while keeping some of the treaty restraints in place. With the triumph of Labour in 1929, the British changed tactics and returned to the Anglo-American policies of 1924, but with a singular lack of success. Time was running out both for the survival of constitutionalism in Germany and for an international approach to the problems of depression and disarmament.

There were no wars. The memories of the past upheavals were still too fresh, and no country, either in western or eastern Europe, was in a position to challenge the status quo by force. The international system created during the course of the decade was still functioning in 1929, and few anticipated its collapse. Locarno had provided a window of opportunity that was closing. The cracks in the reconstructed system began to open during the last phase of reconstruction. The death of Stresemann, Chamberlain's loss of office, and Briand's diminished influence removed from the scene the three men most anxious to translate the 'Locarno spirit' (or *esprit* or *Geist*, the latter translated as 'spirit' or 'ghost') into something more concrete. Looking back at the history of the period, it is possible to see both how far the three statesmen had succeeded in rebuilding the European edifice, and what weaknesses in their reconstructions blocked further progress even before the depression became the 'Great Depression' and altered the strategic landscape. The Hague conferences on 'the final liquidation of the war' ended the discussion of the main issues that could be solved through the existing process of negotiation. They brought to the surface the problems that remained and the great-power tensions that would make their resolution so difficult.

As the 'hinge years' of the inter-war period began, those trends which we have identified as 'post-war' began to overlap with the ominous 'pre-war' trends of the 1930s. The next section of this book deals with these years of transition, years dominated by a depression that was global in its reach and in its consequences. The line from 1919 to 1939, via 1929 and 1933, was not a straight one. It was not the Treaty of Versailles that brought down the Weimar republic, nor was the opposition to its terms the decisive factor in Hitler's capture of power. Versailles did not make Hitler's victory inevitable. This form of reductionist thinking, which attributes the disasters of the 1930s to the peace settlements of 1919, still found in too many accounts of the inter-war period, serves only to distort our understanding of the road to disaster. The 'hinge years' were one of the major twists in that crooked path to the new Armageddon.

PART II

The Hinge Years, 1929–1933

12

The Diplomacy of the Depression: The Triumph of Economic Nationalism*

I

The years between 1929 and 1933 represent the hinge connecting the two decades of the inter-war period, the decade of reconstruction and the decade of disintegration. A time of great fluidity and unease in international relations, the cracks that had opened in the European state system by the late 1920s now began to gape even wider. The chief feature of the period, dominant in all historical discussions, was that of economic crisis. It is important to realize that while the 'Great Depression' altered the European landscape for the rest of the decade, it was not solely responsible for the decline of internationalism that followed. The problems that faced Europe existed before 1929; efforts had been made to solve them and some progress made, but they had not vanished and the stresses of economic depression and uncertainty about national security made their solution much more difficult. The irony was that the culmination of two of the key quests of the 1920s to promote European stability, the end of reparations and the calling of a world disarmament conference, occurred in circumstances which turned many hopes to ash. The actions taken during this hinge period would unleash the full force of nationalism and give greater importance and influence to the more dynamic revisionist countries, Japan, Italy, and Germany, once Adolf Hitler and the National Socialists 'captured' power in January 1933. The search for solutions to the old problems of European stability and security continued but in a very different global context, as states opted for highly nationalist solutions to the problems of economic recovery and armaments.

At the centre of these 'hinge years' lies 1931, the *annus terribilis*, to borrow Arnold Toynbee's memorable phrase. 'The year 1931 was distinguished from previous years by one outstanding feature', wrote

*For this chapter, see Tables A-3 to A-6 in the Appendix.

Toynbee. 'In 1931, men and women all over the world were seriously contemplating and frankly discussing the possibility that the Western system of society might break down and cease to work.'[1] It was a year when the compromises which had raised hopes for a new beginning in European affairs began to unravel, and those subterranean but powerful forces destructive of the attempted stabilization came to the surface. It was a transitional period during which the problems of peacemaking shifted to more immediate and pressing concerns, which contained within them the origins of many of the dislocations of the international order that followed. A triple predicament confronted European policy-makers: a financial crisis to accompany the ongoing economic depression; security anxieties, as disarmament unavoidably came to the fore in circumstances favouring German revisionism; and a challenge to internationalism and extra-European co-operation arising from Japan's expansionist policies in the Far East.

The year was dominated by a deepening depression that engulfed almost all of the European continent, the United States, and much of the rest of the globe. Financial flows propagated the international spread of deflation and depression. Banking and financial crises swept through Europe, leading to the British abandonment of the gold-exchange standard in September and the virtual destruction of the mid-1920s world financial system. The banking crises formed the 'fulcrum of the Great Depression', and their systemic effects undermined the institutions of global exchange.[2] The consequences of the depression for the European economies and for the machinery of multilateral trade and payments were felt throughout the continent. Only a few states, such as Spain, managed to escape comparatively unscathed. Commodity prices plummeted, manufacturing production dropped, and international trade contracted. The number of business failures increased, the net income of corporations decreased, per-capita incomes diminished, and unemployment figures soared. Among the west European nations, Germany suffered most in terms both of industrial production and unemployment rates, while France remained relatively unaffected until the following year. The states of eastern Europe were particularly hard hit. Agricultural prices fell and new lending stopped; the continued absence of the latter meant that prices fell further. Countries chronically short of capital were now cut off from the foreign capital imports that had covered the gaps in their external accounts and financed their heavy debt burdens. The chiefly agricultural states, Bulgaria, Romania, and Yugoslavia, were

[1] Arnold Toynbee, *Survey of International Affairs, 1931* (London, 1932), 1.
[2] Patricia Clavin, *The Great Depression in Europe, 1929–1939* (Basingstoke, 2000), 111.

in considerable difficulty but the depression was ultimately more prolonged in semi-industrialized Poland and in industrialized Austria and
Czechoslovakia. The banking and financial crises began in central
Europe: Austria and Hungary were the first victims in the summer of
1931, followed by Germany. There were numerous bank failures elsewhere in Europe and in the non-European countries as well. By the end
of 1931 some nations had followed Britain and abandoned gold. Those
who refused to depreciate their currency instituted defensive measures
to avoid financial and economic collapse. Most statesmen opted for
nationally oriented recovery programmes, often at the expense of their
neighbours, rather than co-operative action in dealing with the deflationary pressures on the world economy.

Hopes for disarmament, bright at the start of 1931, dimmed as the
Brüning government in Berlin, struggling with an unpopular deflationary policy and a resurgent Nazi nationalist movement, pushed for
'equality of status' (Gleichberechtigung) as a means of restoring public
confidence. The German position was made clear to the other powers:
there would be no agreed disarmament treaty unless the claim to
equality was granted in advance. The secret Groener–Schleicher plans
for the expansion and reorganization of the Reichswehr were first
implemented under Brüning. For France it was a particularly disappointing year. Despite its dominant military and a strong financial
position, the Paris government found itself neither able to create a
common front against the Germans, mainly because of the British and
the Americans, nor to come to direct arrangements with Berlin. The
Franco-German clash of interests surfaced before the long-postponed
World Disarmament Conference actually opened in Geneva on 2 February 1932, as did the gap between the French and the British concepts
of security. The British would have happily postponed the conference
even further for fear of inevitable failure, but domestic as well as
international pressure made retreat impossible. With elections pending
in France, Germany, and the United States in 1932 and a 'national
government' in power in Britain, disarmament became a political issue
that could not be settled behind closed doors. It proved to be the
'poisoned chalice' from which all the statesmen were forced to drink.

The difficulties in the Far East provided a troubling backdrop for the
disarmament discussions. On 18 September 1931 skirmishes between
Japanese troops and Chinese forces developed into a major conflict, and
a Chinese appeal to the United States under the Kellogg–Briand pact
and to the League of Nations under Article 11 of the Covenant internationalized the conflict. While the Council called for a Japanese
withdrawal and prepared to send a five-man investigating commission
to the Far East, Japanese military activity continued. By the time the

League commission reached Tokyo at the end of February 1932 the Japanese were in virtual control of Manchuria. While Britain, the United States, and the Soviet Union were the most interested outside parties, the involvement of the League posed a challenge to its competence at the very moment when the disarmament question at Geneva reached the public stage. The speed and completeness of the Japanese victory led to a loss of confidence in an international system already under pressure. The weakness of the system was further exposed in March 1933 with the Japanese decision to leave the League. 'The Japanese eagle retired to its eyrie,' Professor Ian Nish, the British historian of Japan, recounts, 'proud, self-righteous and disdainful.'[3] The rumbles from the Far East were clearly heard in London and in Moscow as well as Geneva. Their difficulties in the Pacific only reinforced American doubts about co-operation with the League, and opened questions about the troubled Anglo-American partnership.

The *annus terribilis* began and ended in gloom and despondency. Around it, the 'hinge years' were marked by a pervasive slide from optimism to pessimism about the lasting prospects of European reconstruction. The overlapping themes of depression, Far Eastern crisis, and disarmament dominated international politics. In 1929 economic reconstruction seemed to be in some measure underway; the disarmament process, though with few tangible successes, was moving forward, and the League of Nations had achieved some degree of authority. By 1933 economic nationalism had triumphed, the disarmament talks were near collapse, and first Japan and then Germany were to leave the League.

II

From 1929 the world economy stumbled and then fell into an unprecedented slump. Signs of the spreading economic malaise were noted early. In order to combat the difficult world trading conditions, a number of initiatives were launched, ranging from the British-inspired year-long tariff truce of 1930–1 to the French attempts to translate Briand's proposals for a federated Europe into practical recommendations. The French sponsored, too, a series of cereals conferences attended by the east European states. The opposition between the British free-trade approach and France's regional efforts blocked effective relief to the countries most adversely affected by price deflation and the contraction of world trade. It was not only agriculture that was in difficulty. Demand for industrial products began to fall in Germany

---

[3] Ian Nish, *Japan's Struggle with Internationalism: Japan, China and the League of Nations, 1931–3* (London, 1993), 239.

during April 1929, in the United State during June, and in Britain, where production was already sluggish, during July. It failed to revive in 1930 or 1931. In October 1929 the Wall Street stock-market crash sent shock waves through the international community. The actual amount of money lost was relatively small, but the psychological impact was considerable. American lending collapsed and then temporarily revived during 1930, mainly to Germany and to the less developed world. The respite proved short. By the spring of 1930 the renewed decline in world prices made overseas investment unattractive. There was, simultaneously, a sharp contraction in American import demand, adding to Europe's difficulties. By mid-1930 most countries were engulfed in depression and, during the second half of the year, agricultural and industrial prices fell further. In Germany industrial production fell nearly 30 per cent from their 1929 figures. Unemployment figures rose almost everywhere. France was still the outstanding exception; at the end of

TABLE 28. Unemployment, 1921–1933 (000)

	USA	Germany	France	Italy	UK
1921	4,918	346	13		
1922	2,859	215	28		
1923	1,049	818	10		1,251
1924	2,190	927	10		1,113
1925	1,453	700	12	110	1,228
1926	801	2,100	11	114	1,385
1927	1,519	1,300	47	278	1,109
1928	1,982	1,400	16	324	1,246
1929	1,550	1,899	10	301	1,240
1930	4,340	3,076	13	425	1,954
1931	8,020	4,520	64	734	2,647
1932	12,060	5,574	301	1,006	2,745
1933	12,830	4,804	305	1,019	2,521

Sources: Germany: D. Abraham, The Collapse of the Weimar Republic (Berlin, 1986); Walter G. Hoffmann, Das Wachstum der deutschen Wirtschaft, (Berlin, 1965); G. Bry, Wages In Germany 1871–1945 (Princeton, 1960); L. Preller, Sozialpolitik in der Weimarer Republik (Stuttgart, 1949); Statistisches Jahrbuch für das Deutsche Reich, 1939 (Berlin, 1940), 389. France and Italy: B. R. Mitchell European Historical Statistics (London, 1981), 174–80. UK: G. C. Peden, British Rearmament and the Treasury (Edinburgh, 1979), Appendix B; M. Thomas, 'Labour Market Structure and the Nature of Unemployment in Interwar Britain' in B. Eichengreen and T. J. Hatton (eds.), Interwar Unemployment in International Perspective (London, 1988). USA: US Historical Statistics, Colonial Times to 1970, Series D8–10 (Washington, DC 1975).

1930 her industrial production had only slipped 7 per cent from its 1929 average and there were only 10,000 registered unemployed. Most people expected that conditions would improve; instead they grew steadily worse during 1931. Governments feared inflation, while their countries slipped further and further into deep depression.

In Germany, the continuing budgetary difficulties of the Brüning government and the ever-increasing number of unemployed intensified the pressure on the chancellor to produce results. Efforts to improve Germany's export performance and achieve a balanced budget through an austerity programme weakened Brüning's support on the right and left. The chancellor failed to persuade management and labour to compromise their differences in order to reach agreement on a common economic programme. There has been an ongoing dispute among historians about Brüning's economic and political policies, and whether his period in power represented the first stage in the dissolution of the republic or a last attempt to save its parliamentary regime.[4] The terms of the debate were radically altered by Professor Knut Borchardt's arguments that Brüning had no real alternative to the deflationary programme adopted in March 1930, given the structural problems of the Weimar economy that he had inherited and the domestic and foreign restraints within which he had to operate.[5] Professor Borchardt and his supporters believe that it would have been almost impossible to finance any expansionary programme when it was finally realized in mid-1931 that this was not an ordinary depression. Public-works proposals on a substantial scale, such as the Woytinsky, Tarnow, Baade plan of December 1931, were neither politically acceptable nor financially viable. The demands of Germany's foreign creditors (and the state was particularly dependent on external funding) and the domestic limitations on credit expansion restricted Brüning's room for manoeuvre. Throughout the winter and spring of 1932 Brüning held to his conviction that little

---

[4] See Hans Mommsen, *From Weimar to Auschwitz: Essays in German History* (Cambridge, 1991), and his textbook, *The Rise and Fall of Weimar Democracy* (Chapel Hill, NC and London, 1996), esp. chs. 10 and 11. For a general defence of Brüning's policies, see William L. Patch, Jr., *Heinrich Brüning and the Dissolution of the Weimar Republic* (Cambridge, 1998).

[5] Knut Borchardt, 'Constraints and Room for Manoeuvre in the Great Depression of the Early Thirties', and 'Economic Causes of the Collapse of the Weimar Republic', published in English translation in Knut Borchardt, *Perspectives on Modern German Economic History and Policy* (Cambridge, 1991). See Borchardt's 'Noch Niemals: Alternativen zu Brünings Wirtschaftspolitik?', *Historische Zeitschrift*, 237 (1983), discussed in Ian Kershaw (ed.), *Weimar: Why did German Democracy Fail?* (London, 1990). See also Borchardt, 'A Decade of Debate About Brüning's Economic Policy', in J. von Kruedener (ed.), *Economic Crisis and Political Collapse: The Weimar Republic 1924–1933* (Oxford, 1990).

could be done to relieve the effects of the depression until the latter had 'bottomed out' and Germany was freed from reparations. Even more contentious are the arguments that Brüning actually tried to save the parliamentary regime and did not, as his own autobiography suggested, work for the establishment of a constitutional monarchy. According to William Patch, Brüning's efforts, as the Catholic leader of the Centre party, to rally conservative Protestants and moderate Social Democrats to the defence of the republic were undermined by President Hindenburg and his circle of reactionary landowners and army generals, who played the central role in the ultimate collapse of the Weimar state.[6]

Whatever defence might be made of Brüning's deflationary economic policies and high-risk political strategies, it is apparent that the withdrawn chancellor never fully grasped the extreme importance of courting the public nor did he appreciate the devastating psychological and political effects of prolonged unemployment during his last months in office when he focused on the ending of reparations. A skilled back-room tactician, he lacked the flair and the charisma so badly needed at a time of extreme atomization and politicisation. Even allowing for his age and post-war disillusionment, those who attended Brüning's post-1945 seminars at Harvard (including the author) will recall his inability to engage and excite his listeners. Depending on a small group of advisers, a dozen or so trusted colleagues, including the state secretary of the foreign ministry, Bernhard von Bülow, Brüning's concept of 'civic virtue' and service to the nation was of limited relevance to the existing state of German politics. His alignment with those favouring an authoritarian restructuring of the republic hardly augured well for its future. The view of Brüning as a moderate, holding the extremists at bay, enlisted contemporary foreign support. The perceptive British ambassador in Berlin, Horace Rumbold, who came to respect Brüning without minimizing his political weakness, predicted an interregnum in the domain of foreign policy as the German government wrestled with its economic and financial problems. The far less sympathetic French ambassador, André François-Poncet, who disliked and distrusted the chancellor (the feelings were mutual), preferred the aristocratic Kurt von Schleicher and accepted his view that a dictatorship, or at least a coalition extending from the Centre to the Nazi party, was needed.

Brüning's main hope in 1930 was to bring cartel prices and wages under control and to attack the welfare subsidies and civil service pay that were inflating the Reich's expenditure. Dependent on the middle-class parties and the passive consent of the Social Democrats, and

---

[6] Patch, *Heinrich Brüning*, see ch. 5, 'Brüning's Fall', and ch. 6, 'The Destruction of the Rule of Law'.

criticized by both right and left, he found it impossible to govern when the Reichstag was in session. In July 1930 the SPD, DNVP, and DVP combined with the Nazis and Communists to vote against the chancellor's budget. Brüning resorted to the Hindenburg card, as General Schleicher and the president's other intimates had been urging. Using the presidential powers under Article 48 of the Weimar Constitution, Brüning dissolved the Reichstag (two years before the expiry of its full term) and ruled by decree. His rejected fiscal programme was then implemented with only minor alterations. The new elections, held in September 1930, resulted in the dramatic rise in the Nazi vote, from 810,000 in 1928 to 6.4 million in 1930, making it the second largest party (107 seats) after the Socialists in the Reichstag and a major political force for the first time in its history. There was also an impressive (from fifty-four to seventy-seven seats) though less spectacular gain for the KPD, intensifying fears across the whole political spectrum of a possible Bolshevik coup. With a much-shrunken political base, and relying on the sufferance of the Social Democrats, Brüning proceeded to apply by decree the deflationary medicine that he felt was needed to cure the sick German patient. The Reich-chancellor's office derived its legitimacy from the president; government by experts replaced government by parties. The conservative right and the moderate left acquiesced in Brüning's rule by decree as the preferable alternative to Hitler. The turn away from parliamentary rule marked a new stage in the slide towards an authoritarian state

The September election results led to the loss of 1 million RM in gold and foreign currency as Germans and foreigners deserted the mark. Once again the Reich government bought time by resorting to foreign bankers, in this instance a consortium of American banks led by the Boston investment house Lee Higginson, a less reputable firm than J. P. Morgan's, which had decided that Germany was a poor risk. Despite the credit, the budgetary difficulties of the Reich continued. With memories of 1922–3 still sharp, German investors were not interested in taking up long-term government bonds. As the government and the Reichstag were forced to resort to short-term borrowing, investor confidence, both domestic and foreign, diminished and there were further losses of gold and foreign exchange. There was talk in Paris at the end of 1930 of extending French credits to non-exporting German firms and of joint Franco-German projects in south-east Europe and in Russia. No action resulted and Brüning appeared indifferent, suspecting that a political price would be demanded.

It was natural, given the precariousness of Brüning's position, that his government should seek a foreign-policy success. The chancellor shared the general view that reparations played a large part in the Reich's economic difficulties and that only cancellation would enable the country to properly reorganize its finances. He feared, however, that any proposal to revise the Young plan barely six months after its ratification would shock the international community and lead to a withdrawal of the short-term loans on which Germany was so heavily dependent. He hoped that by renouncing heavy borrowing and paying reparations from Germany's own resources via a massive export campaign, he could underscore the country's financial weakness and convince its creditors, above all the British, of the need for reparation revision. At the end of 1930 Germany enjoyed a trade surplus, achieved through a decrease in imports (partly due to the new programme of agricultural protectionism) rather than an increase in exports. Unemployment continued to rise and German living standards visibly declined. In mid-December 1930 Brüning told his intimates that the political situation would make it necessary to raise the reparation question. Foreign Minister Curtius suggested a new approach: 'If the whole world becomes calm, then it would be hard to raise the issue of reparations. Therefore [we should take] some political initiative alongside reparations. Disarmament and the eastern question [i.e. the Polish border] would be suitable. They could give an economic rationale. Can we not solve the reparations problem by raising the issue of disarmament?'[7] Brüning took soundings in Washington and London. The Americans showed little interest in the chancellor's proposal for a world conference to discuss disarmament, reparations, and war debts. Financiers in New York were more intent on stabilizing the existing situation so that German commercial debts would be paid. The main Washington concern was to discourage talk of a German moratorium for fear that the debtor countries would demand war-debt reductions. The British had no wish to take up reparations without the possibility of a war-debt settlement. The Foreign Office, where the foreign secretary, Arthur Henderson, was preoccupied with disarmament, dismissed the Berlin feelers and warned Curtius that the Britain would join with France in opposing renegotiation or a moratorium on reparations.

However attractive reparation revision might appear, foreign reactions and the opposition of some of his advisers made Brüning cautious. As no way could be found to deal with the continuing budgetary difficulties undermining confidence at home, he told colleagues in February 1931 that the subject of reparations would have to be raised no later than the summer of 1932. Early in March 1931 the chancellor decided a further dose of deflation (increases in taxation and reductions in Reich expenditure) and an attack on reparations were both politically

---

[7] Patch, *Brüning*, 15.

and economically necessary. The worried British ambassador in Berlin suggested that Brüning be invited to Chequers, the British prime minister's official residence, to improve his domestic standing. Henderson, forewarned that the Germans would raise the question of reparations, cautioned the chancellor that the visit was only 'to serve as a gesture of friendship and equality; which might strengthen the Brüning government vis-à-vis its own public'.[8]

Before the Germans came to Chequers, however, the Austro-German customs union bombshell exploded. Since 1928 the Auswärtiges Amt had been promoting Germany's economic and political interests in central and south-eastern Europe. Wherever possible, the Germans tried to meet the demands of the depression-hit states for preferential customs regulations to assist agricultural exports. The French, unable to offer such advantages because of their own producers, wrestled unsuccessfully with various alternatives: distribution centres, agrarian credits, and bilateral treaties within a pan-European framework. Bülow and some of his subordinates agreed that the moment was ripe for a new German move towards Austria. Preliminary talks were held in Berlin in February 1930, when the Austrian premier, Johann Schober (26 September 1929–28 September 1930), after a visit to Rome, discussed the possibility with Foreign Minister Curtius. Nothing concrete emerged; a conventional Austro-German trade treaty, signed two months later, did not even contain the preferential tariffs wanted by the Austrians. The Austrian export trade was hard hit by the increased tariffs on industrial products throughout Europe. At the same time, the Vienna government was faced with mounting budgetary difficulties as tax revenues were considerably less than expected. The government was warned of an incipient banking and credit crisis stemming from Vienna's continuing role in borrowing money from the west and financing industrial developments in central and south-eastern Europe. The Creditanstalt, Austria's largest bank, was central to these transactions. Foreign funds flowed into the bank, where the last scion of the Viennese Rothschilds, Louis von Rothschild, a man more interested in hunting and his artistic and philanthropic affairs than in banking, was president. This was not a private matter. The Austrian government had encouraged the bank to extend credit to shaky firms at a time of crumbling business confidence and activity. In 1929 the bank was forced to take over the bankrupt Bodencreditanstalt whose illiquidity had resulted primarily from its frozen industrial accounts. The Austrian central bank, the Nationalbank, was aware of the Creditanstalt's overextended position and tried to sweeten the pill through an elaborate system of

---

[8] Henderson to Rumbold, PRO, FO 371/15214, C2695/11/18.

cross-deposits by which money deposited in American and British banks was transferred to the Creditantstalt, a backhand and costly transfer of funds. These transactions tied up a good portion of the Nationalbank's foreign exchange, making its own position far weaker than was assumed. The Creditantstalt was unable to conceal the extent of its continuing losses, for as a giant industrial holding company (over 60 per cent of Austrian industry was dependent on the bank), it was bound to feel the icy winds of the industrial depression.

Schober, now Austria's foreign minister (3 December 1930–11 May 1932), in a desperate attempt to bolster the country's economy visited Rome, Paris, and Berlin in search of assistance. The Germans seized their opportunity. Early in January 1931 the Austrians were presented with a draft agreement for a customs union. Curtius, Bülow, and Karl Ritter, chief of the economic department at the German foreign ministry, were the main instigators; Brüning's reluctant approval of the talks was kept secret both from cabinet colleagues and the Austrians, in case they failed. For the chancellor, the question of timing was all important as he prepared to launch his reparations campaign. Curtius hoped that such a diplomatic coup would steal the nationalists' thunder at home and provide a 'unifying focus for German politics'.[9] As a meeting of the Committee of Enquiry for European Union was scheduled for 24 March, to which Henderson was coming, Curtius decided on an earlier announcement to forestall any European action and French interference. Elaborate precautions were taken to avoid inciting European indignation, but the joint Austro-German efforts failed to prevent the outcry from Czechoslovakia and France. The former appealed to France for assistance and warned the Austrians of a trade war if the project was not dropped. The French, taken by surprise, saw the initiative as a direct threat; the move was compared to the 1911 German challenge at Agadir. Not only did the project revive French fears of *Anschluss* and a German *Mitteleuropa*, but it was personally embarrassing for Briand, who only one week earlier had assured the French Chamber that *Anschluss* was a diminishing threat. The German ambassador in Paris was warned that his country's action was an 'amazing imprudence', calculated to injure the development of Franco-German relations. Bitter at his public humiliation, Briand tried to organize a joint *démarche* in Paris, London, Rome, and Prague. After some initial hesitations the Poles agreed, but Piłsudski, detecting some wavering in Paris, considered whether acceptance of the customs union could not be linked to German recognition of the Polish frontiers. On

[9] Harold James, 'Economic Reasons for the Collapse of the Weimar Republic', in Kershaw (ed.), *Weimar*, 53.

13 May Briand suffered a massive defeat in the French presidential elections, though he remained as foreign minister.

However critical of Curtius's failure to consult the other powers, the British were unwilling to join the joint *démarche* by the guarantors of the Geneva protocol of 1922 safeguarding Austrian economic independence. From Berlin, Rumbold warned that an aggressive French reaction would undercut Brüning's political standing and lead to an explosion in Germany. Any German illusions that the British would actually condone the Austrian–German action were ill-founded. Henderson's interest in a Franco-Italian naval limitation agreement and his fears that the German move would negatively rebound on the forthcoming Geneva disarmament talks led to efforts to defuse the quarrel. Henderson's plan was to delay the Austro-German talks (the details were still unsettled) by seeking a legal judgement from the Permanent Court of Justice on the compatibility of the customs union with the 1922 Geneva protocol. With the issue now in the international arena, Brüning became a staunch defender of Curtius's actions. The talks with Austria were to continue even if the Germans conceded that the Court could pass judgement on the legality of the project. The Austrians, on the contrary, caught between the Germans and French, from whom they were seeking a second tranche of a loan, were clearly frightened. When French counter-proposals, worked out with Beneš, for economic assistance to east-central Europe with special preferential treatment for Austrian products were vetoed by the British and Germans, Laval agreed to Henderson's proposal. The British resolution, seconded by Grandi and Briand, received the unanimous assent of the League Council.

It was while Henderson was acting as an intermediary in the affair that the banking difficulties in Austria and Germany reached crisis proportions. The collapse of the Creditanstalt in May came as a shock. The news of the customs union had increased general nervousness, but there was no significant withdrawal of foreign short-term credits. On the night of 11–12 May, however, after having announced a delay in publishing its accounts, the Creditanstalt publicly revealed losses of 140 million shillings (the sum was considerably higher), which it blamed on the costs of absorbing the Bodencreditanstalt. Depositors lost confidence and withdrew funds. Once the run on the shilling began, the exchange was threatened and the Austrian government appealed for international assistance. The run began with the Creditanstalt revelations and not, as charged by the Germans and British, with French action to force an Austrian repudiation of the customs union. It was only at the next stage that the French would use their financial muscle to increase the pressure on the exchange and to demand the abandonment of the customs union as the price for financial assistance.[10] The Schober government, fearing that the collapse of the Creditanstalt would bring down the entire Austrian economy, intervened to save the bank from bankruptcy. Its action further increased the government's budgetary deficit; the problems of the government and those of the bank became intertwined. As withdrawals continued, the state, already under severe financial pressure, became the Creditanstalt's main shareholder and creditor, assuming debts that it could not cover.

The Austrians secured a BIS loan and a 'standstill agreement' by which the foreign banks agreed not to withdraw deposits in return for promises of favourable future treatment. The loan was too little and too late. In the process of arranging for further international assistance and in the midst of discussions with the French, the Austrian situation deteriorated sharply. The Nationalbank told the Schober government to start preparations for a moratorium and the introduction of exchange controls. On 16 June the French government demanded that, in return for its financial assistance, the Austrians should submit their finances to League control and surrender the customs union. The Schober ministry rejected the 'ultimatum', although the decision to drop the customs union was already taken, and fell from office. On the same day as the French demand, Montagu Norman, without consulting the Foreign Office, offered the Austrians a short-term loan covering the credit the Austrians sought from the BIS. The loan was renewed each week until August, when, with the pound under pressure and the League of Nations involved, the Bank of England was forced to request repayment. The British and French actions provoked intense irritation in their respective capitals. After difficult talks, a second BIS loan was arranged—again too small to make a difference.

As the payment of the 1923 League loan was threatened, the League's financial committee intervened to appoint a representative to supervise the Austrian budget and introduce stringent measures of control. Even these measures were insufficient and the Austrians stopped the servicing of the League loan. Foreign creditors agreed to accept a new agreement that included both a conversion loan and Austrian acceptance of a strict, League-enforced austerity programme. A further standstill agreement, freezing creditor accounts, was concluded. The final arrangements for the League loan were made at the Lausanne conference in June–July 1932. The long delay was due to arranging the state guarantee for the liabilities of the Creditanstalt and the drawn-out discussions with the

---

[10] For evidence see Iago Gil Aguado, 'The Creditanstalt Crisis of 1931 and the Failure of the Austro-German Customs Union Project', *Historical Journal*, 44: 1 (2001), 214–15.

bank's foreign creditors. The bank was reconstituted under a new Dutch general director, with another Dutchman appointed to oversee the budget and austerity measures demanded by the League's financial committee. By 1936 the Creditanstalt had become an Austrian national bank without any international interests and operating mainly under government control. The Austrian government also took steps to stem the loss of foreign exchange from the Nationalbank. On 9 October 1931 the central bank introduced exchange controls that directed the amounts and destination of any gold and foreign currency leaving Austria. These developed into a very complicated system of bilateral payment agreements organized on a country-by-country basis. Though officially still on the gold standard, the government was able to control its impact on the domestic economy. Such exchange controls became one of the commonest ways for the eastern European states to manage their foreign payments.

Norman's fears of foreign contagion were justified. On 11 May, the same day that the Creditantstalt situation became public, Hungary was faced with a rapid loss of foreign exchange from the National Bank. As in the case of Austria, the government came to the assistance of its largest banks, though with a greater degree of success. Loans from the BIS were too small to cover the government's indebtedness and failed to restore confidence. Foreign creditors, mainly American and British, negotiated a standstill agreement that froze their loans inside Hungary; it became the model for the subsequent Austrian and German accords. Gyula Karolyi, Bethlen's nominee and successor as minister president, accepted a renewal of League oversight and the imposition of an austerity programme. As in Austria, the Hungarian government imposed exchange controls to block the outflow of gold and foreign currency.

III

The most extensive and most important banking crisis in central Europe occurred in Germany. As elsewhere, unbalanced budgets and a weak and overextended banking system lay behind the loss of domestic and foreign confidence. Between 1927 and 1930 a renewed outflow of short- and long-term capital took place and a number of small German banks collapsed in 1929. After the Creditanstalt crisis (German financial involvement was negligible), German banks began to lose funds more rapidly, with the less reputable banks losing a considerable percentage of their deposits. More ominously, the German government's budgetary problems remained unsolved. The government deficit grew, as tax yields fell and state spending, particularly on unemployment relief, rose.[11] Unable to raise the necessary funds domestically, the Brüning government became ever more dependent on external funding. The failure to negotiate a new Lee Higginson loan and the collapse of talks with the French cut off possible escape routes, while the worsening world financial situation precluded new long-term foreign loans. Anticipating a deficit of 800 million marks (smaller than the deficit in Britain or the United States) in the 1931–2 budget, Brüning decided on a new, draconian emergency decree. To counter the fierce political debate that would inevitably follow, the chancellor and his cabinet decided to move on the reparations front. The reparations manifesto, issued on 6 June 1931 when Brüning and Curtius were already at Chequers, noted that 'the limit of the privations we can impose on our people has been reached', and that Germany's 'precarious economic and financial situation' required the relief of its 'unbearable reparation obligations'.[12] However politically necessary, it proved a maladroit move at a time of receding foreign confidence and when the Germans were trying to negotiate a new international loan under the Young plan.

In the four days between 6 and 10 June the Reichsbank lost 400 million marks of its gold and foreign-exchange reserves. The Germans were primarily responsible for the domestic panic. Foreign banks were growing nervous, but it was only much later that the loss of foreign confidence played a significant part in the banking crisis. The Chequers meeting on 6–7 June, intended by the British as a friendly gesture towards Brüning, turned into a discussion of reparations. Having reopened the question, the Germans immediately retreated. The British

TABLE 29. German Foreign Indebtedness, 1931–1934 (millards RM at current exchange rates)

	Short-term standstill	Other	Total	Long-term	Total
July 1931	6.3	6.8	13.1	10.7	23.8
Feb. 1932	5.0	5.1	10.1	10.5	20.6
Sept. 1932	4.3	5.0	9.3	10.2	19.5
Feb. 1933	4.1	4.6	8.7	10.3	19.0
Sept. 1933	3.0	4.4	7.4	7.4	14.8
Feb. 1934	2.8	3.9	6.7	7.2	13.9

Source: Steven Schuker, *American Reparations to Germany*, Princeton Studies in International Finance, 61 (1988), 72.

[11] Spending on unemployment relief rose from 1.2 billion RM in 1928 to 3.2 billion RM in 1931. See Harold James, 'Economic Reasons for the Collapse of the Weimar Republic', in Kershaw (ed.), *Weimar*, 41.

[12] Patch, *Heinrich Brüning*, 160.

were assured that the *Tributaufruf* (reparations decree) was intended for domestic purposes only and was not an appeal for immediate cancellation, though Brüning warned that payments could not be continued after November. MacDonald, while dampening hopes of revising the Young plan, expressed some optimism about the forthcoming summer visit of American secretary of state Henry Stimson as a prelude to future reparations–war-debt discussions. Not for the first time in this overlong reparation saga, the Europeans waited for the Americans to act.

The immediate effect of this inconclusive summit and Brüning's attempt to smother the reparations fire was to add to his multiple political and financial difficulties. This led to a further withdrawal of funds from the German banks, mainly by Germans and other Europeans and later by the Americans. On his return the chancellor faced demands that either the Reichstag or the budget committee be recalled to discuss the new emergency decrees. The ensuing political stalemate in mid-June was accompanied by new and heavy Reichsbank losses of gold and foreign exchange, despite a rise in the discount rate from 5 per cent to 7 per cent on 13 June. As the financial difficulties continued, the agitation against reparations swelled. Through a mixture of threats of resignation and concessions, the chancellor temporarily defused the political crisis and put his amended emergency decree into effect, but he was unable to calm the financial waters. Foreign central bankers remained convinced that the Reichsbank could do far more to restrict the capital flight and that the Germans should deal with their own difficulties. The Reich government knew that the volume of this short-term debt posed a dangerous threat to the stability of the currency, and pressed Hans Luther, who replaced Schacht as head of the Reichsbank in 1930, to open a line of credit with the other central banks or the BIS. Luther opposed such an appeal, hoping to make the government reform the financial system. His hand was forced when the financial haemorrhaging of gold and foreign exchange on 18–19 June reduced the gold reserves of the Reichsbank to close to the legal minimum reserve of 40 per cent of note issue. The general preoccupation with the government's insolvency and the publication on 17 June of the accounts of the giant Nordwolle textile concern, which was heavily committed to the Danat Bank, a major bank already under pressure, further undermined domestic confidence. Luther appealed to the central bankers and the BIS, and secured their agreement on 24 June to a $100 million credit on condition that the Reichsbank make capital flight more difficult by restricting discounts.

There was also action in Washington. Stimson had alerted President Hoover to the seriousness of the central European crisis in late May. The president decided that some kind of action was necessary to restore confidence, and began to consider the possibility of a general, but temporary, moratorium on all inter-governmental debts. Wall Street financiers, as well as midwestern and New England bankers, were worried about the large American private investment in Germany. Hoover wavered, anxious about any association between war debts and reparations, and fearing the response of Congress and the American taxpayer to the loss of war-debt payments. He finally responded to the mounting political pressure and the need to counteract the depressed financial mood. He was concerned, too, that Germany would invoke the suspension provisions of the Young plan and initiate a new round of reparation–war-debt talks. On 20 June Hoover publicly called for a one-year moratorium on all intergovernmental debts, including both principal and interest. The French were informed only twelve hours before the announcement and took umbrage at the president's pre-emptory initiative.

The news of the moratorium gave the Brüning government imme-diate, if brief, relief. As Hoover had been warned, on the previous day Brüning and Luther had agreed to an appeal for the suspension of Germany's reparation payments within the next few days. The president had been advised to consult with the French, who, after the Americans, had the most to lose from the moratorium. Already angered by Norman's Austrian intervention, which was seen as an anti-French move, the latter suspected yet another Anglo-American deal with Germany at their expense. The Americans and British had huge commercial credits tied up in Germany; the French banks had pulled out their far more limited funds. Laval and his finance minister, Pierre-Étienne Flandin, insisted that France was being asked to forgo reparation payments solely for the benefit of Germany and the American and British private investors. Under strong domestic pressure, the French ministers refused to accept the moratorium without winning counter-concessions. It would take two weeks of difficult negotiations before they came into line. In a not untypical comment, the British prime minister noted in his diary: 'France has been playing its usual small minded and selfish game over the Hoover proposal. Germany cracks whilst France bargains.'[13]

Laval had little choice; political pressure meant that he had to demand concessions in return for accepting the moratorium. The Americans could not be allowed to dictate terms, nor the Germans left totally free from their obligations. Laval insisted that the Reich should continue to pay its unconditional Young annuities (which the Germans had expected to pay) during the moratorium year, making it more possible to renew reparations afterwards, but suggested that the money should be

---

[13] David Marquand, *Ramsay MacDonald* (London, 1977), 605.

lent back to the BIS. The Americans, anxious to conclude the matter, conceded the French demand on the understanding that the funds remitted to the BIS would be immediately reloaned to Germany. Hoover, who kept tight control over the talks, was sympathetic to the view that Germany's budgetary savings should not be used for increased arms expenditure. It was finally agreed that the reloaned funds should be earmarked for the state-owned German railways. Laval again tried to secure political concessions from Germany, such as the renunciation of the customs union and a promise to refrain from building a second pocket battleship. The American response was cautious; the president still needed Congressional approval of the Hoover moratorium. Any signs of interference in Austro-German affairs would make this more difficult. Backed by the British, he asked the Germans to make a 'voluntary concession' on the battleship. Brüning reluctantly agreed not to increase the military budget during the moratorium period and to postpone the construction of a third, as yet unauthorized, battleship. The chancellor was too dependent on Hindenburg and the Reichswehr to go further. French efforts to redirect a part of the German unconditional annuity to the states of central Europe also proved unavailing. It was decided instead to create a special fund with the backing of the three major central banks and the BIS to help underwrite their financial stability. Throughout these negotiations, British and American 'Gallophobia' intensified, though they failed to agree on what to do about Germany once the Hoover moratorium lapsed. Norman believed that if

TABLE 30. Financial Effect of the Hoover Moratorium (£000)

	Suspended receipts	Suspended payments	Net loss or gain
USA	53,600		−53,600
UK	42,500	32,800	−9,700
Canada	900		−900
Australia	800	3,900	3,100
New Zealand	330	1,750	1,420
South Africa	110		−110
France	39,700	26,300	−16,000
Italy	9,200	7,400	−1,800
Belgium	5,100	2,700	−2,400
Germany		77,000	77,000
Hungary		350	350
Austria		300	300
Bulgaria	150	400	250

Source: Barry Eichengreen: Golden Fetters (1992), 278.

the German situation became desperate enough, France would have to agree to reparations cancellation and that Britain would get the reparation–war-debt solution that he wanted. Hoover had no intention of walking down that road. The French gave way, trying only to keep in operation current contracts for deliveries in kind which they hoped would encourage Franco-German economic integration. It took three weeks to negotiate the moratorium. The delay robbed the president's initiative of its desired psychological impact, as awareness of the shortcomings of the one-year moratorium spread. The period of remission was too short to restore financial confidence, and the spectre of the renewal of the whole system of government indebtedness remained in place.

The Hoover moratorium did nothing to stop the German bank crisis. It was not reparations that were fuelling the crisis. On 3 July, three days before the French accepted Hoover's proposal, Nordwolle filed a bankruptcy petition putting its major creditors, the Darmstädter and Dresdner banks, under serious strain. The Reichsbank took no action, fearing that foreign, mainly British, creditors would spread the panic. With the other private banks unwilling to assist the Darmstädter, Luther used an emergency decree to set up a syndicate of industry and Berlin banks to guarantee the bank, and in effect made a commitment to take on bills from the guaranteeing enterprises, a risky procedure in view of the Reichsbank's own very narrow safety margin. The Reichsbank and the Reich government were now directly involved in maintaining German stability. German and international withdrawals continued, the latter becoming a significant factor. The Reichsbank's reserves of gold and foreign exchange dipped below the 40 per cent limit, the minimum level necessary to maintain the gold standard. Given the haunting spectre of the 1922–3 inflation, neither the politicians, the bankers, nor the German people would contemplate the devaluation of the mark. The government acted not just to save the Danat Bank but to avoid the collapse of the entire banking system. Luther took to the air, flying—at a time when this was still a dramatic gesture—to London and then on to Paris and Basle, only to find the financial doors closed. Montagu Norman sent out conflicting signals, first supporting and then opposing a joint central bank credit, the latter on the grounds that the credits would be used later to pay reparations to France. He claimed that Britain was already overexposed because of its credits to Austria, and finally confessed that he had no money to lend. The situation in London was beginning to unnerve the highly strung Norman, who was already showing signs of his breakdown in late July. George Harrison of the FRBNY set out an extensive list of financial and economic conditions, almost all of which required further credit restrictions (just what was not needed), before he would consider additional credits for Germany. Arguments that, without a foreign loan, Brüning would fall and the Nazis or Bolsheviks take power only confirmed the central banker's low opinion of the Germans. The French bankers referred Luther to Finance Minister Flandin, who, in return for a loan, demanded a moratorium on German actions against France, the dropping of cruiser construction, cancellation of the customs union, and the abandonment of hopes for the revision of the Polish border. Brüning would never consider such terms. Luther's mission was a total failure.

The measures taken by the Reich government and Reichsbank to prop up the credit structure failed to restore banking confidence. Over the weekend of 11–12 June it was decided that the Reichsbank's restrictions on discounts demanded by Harrison and Norman should cease. Another effort was made to secure foreign loans. When the central bankers gathered in Basle for their scheduled BIS board meeting on 13 July, Luther put the German case for a loan, arguing that the economy was essentially sound but warning that the banking crisis was so severe that there had to be a moratorium on all debts within forty-eight hours. Little was accomplished; the Germans were left without a loan. The bankers dispersed having concluded that the world's problems were too complex for the central banks to solve and would have to be left to their respective governments. On the same day, 13 July, the German government ordered all private banks to close. Future payments were restricted to sums required for taxes, wages, and unemployment insurance. Foreign credits in Germany were frozen and all foreign-exchange transactions were concentrated in the hands of the Reichsbank.

The German actions were paralleled by numerous futile international efforts to tackle the German problem. Both Stimson, the American secretary of state, and Henderson, the British foreign secretary, were in the French capital, the latter to discuss disarmament questions. The statesmen could reach no agreement on what should be done. Laval proposed a joint loan and a conference in Paris to discuss terms. Henderson reported that Norman was overextended and trying to reduce his foreign commitments. The French suggested the granting of a £125 million credit to Germany, with Dawes-like controls over the Reichsbank's use of the foreign funds. At the same time, they pressed Brüning to come to Paris to negotiate a financial-political deal on a bilateral basis. With American backing, Henderson suggested a seven-power conference to meet in London on 20 July, winning Laval's reluctant consent to attend if the Germans would first consult with the French. Neither the Americans nor the British wanted to offer Brüning a guaranteed loan; their focus was the immediate banking crisis. They did not trust Laval, whose main concern was future relations with

Germany. Norman, more virulently Francophobe than usual, and MacDonald and Snowden, both suspicious of Laval's intentions, turned on Henderson and poured cold water on the idea of a separate Franco-German meeting. The three men were at one in believing that France posed the principal threat to European stability and would try to hold Germany to ransom. All these somewhat frantic exchanges, conducted in three capitals and involving politicians, diplomats, and central and private bankers, were taking place against the background of the deteriorating British financial and banking situation and Montagu Norman's increasingly panicky reactions. To complicate the scenario further, the central bankers who had encouraged their statesmen to intervene found themselves at odds with their own politicians. Telephonic summitry made matters worse, contributing to the panic and shortening the time for reflection. A heatwave in Washington took its toll on American tempers.

Two summit meetings were arranged. MacDonald, furious with Henderson, with whom relations were always difficult, feared that the Paris summit would make the London meeting superfluous. It was, nevertheless, Henderson's diplomacy which ensured that the London meeting took place with the French present. Brüning and Curtius came to Paris en route to London hoping to get a short-term credit for the Reichsbank. The German chancellor was more inclined to bargain than his cabinet was told. Meetings were held with the French, the Americans, and with all the Young plan signatories. The Americans offered nothing but a halt to the withdrawal of American credit. When Laval and Flandin met privately with Brüning, the chancellor refused to give the public recognition of the political status quo that the French demanded in return for credits. Neither side thought that this would end negotiations. Laval assumed that Germany's need for financial help would force Brüning to make political concessions.

The London conference (20–3 July) proved to be an inconclusive affair and hardly, as *The Times* predicted, the most important financial gathering since the war. MacDonald concentrated attention on the question of Germany's immediate needs and, together with Stimson, set the agenda. The idea of a loan for Germany faded from sight. The June central bank credit of $100 million was renewed for ninety days and the volume of credits already extended to Germany was to be maintained. The Germans, but also the central bankers and private debtors who had quickly organized themselves into separate committees on both sides of the Atlantic, pressed for a standstill agreement, the former in order to prevent a German credit collapse and the impoverishment of international trade, and the latter to gain protection for their funds and some kind of guarantee for future repayment. The terms of the standstill agreement were to be arranged by a committee in Basle. The conference also agreed to a BIS inquiry (the Wiggin–Layton committee) into Germany's long-term credit requirements. The Germans hoped that this committee of bankers would look into its capacity to pay reparations, but its brief was narrowly drawn in London and the continuing disputes between powers precluded any radical reconsideration of Germany's external obligations.

Both the standstill committee and the Wiggin–Layton committee met in Basle in August. On 13 August the foreign-creditor representatives from eleven countries drew up a six-month standstill agreement, which was formalized on 19 September. The foreign credits were frozen on their original terms but service was guaranteed. The provisions covered all credit lines open on 31 July, amounting to approximately £300 million. Of this total, British institutions had extended some £65 million, of which £46 million went to the German banks and about £19 million to commerce and industry.[14] The standstill covered only a portion of Germany's foreign debt, and even that only partially. Three-quarters of the standstill-protected loans had been used for fixed investments or for the maintenance of stocks and not, as was assumed by both sides, for financing international trade. It proved extremely difficult to unfreeze this large illiquid debt, further reducing the prospect of Germany securing new credits abroad. On 22 January 1932 the standstill agreement was renewed for a further year, despite disagreements among the creditors and the failure to include the short-term debts of the Länder and municipalities (a separate standstill agreement was made in April 1932). The standstill provided Germany with important advantages. Relieved from the prospect of a sudden withdrawal of foreign loans, the Germans could manage their monetary problems without unduly worrying about the international consequences. Germany's creditors, moreover, would have to pay a price to free funds that were always in danger. The Germans had acquired a valuable political weapon, used in the first instance to soften up the Americans and British over the reparation issue at the Lausanne conference in June–July 1932. The Wiggin–Layton committee, focusing on Germany's short-term credit crisis, recommended a further six-month renewal of German credit if the central bank credits were renewed at the same time. The committee went no further on reparations than to issue a warning that Germany's international payments had to be adjusted if it was to secure long-term loans. The reparation ball was returned to the politicians' court.

[14] Neil Forbes, *Doing Business With the Nazis: Britain's Economic and Financial Relations with Germany, 1931–1939* (London and Portland, Oreg., 2000), 36.

In Berlin, Brüning moved to save the banking system. The cabinet advanced money to a consortium of industrialists who would purchase the Darmstädter Bank. Funds were given to the larger Dresdener Bank in exchange for 75 per cent ownership by the Reich. Luther, who was generally blamed at home for the banking debacle, set up a new institution on 28 July, the Acceptance and Guarantee Bank, which by providing an additional signature to make bills eligible for discounting by the Reichsbank opened the way for a more liberal discount policy. The new bank gave acceptance credit to the Darmstädter and to the savings banks that had made long-term loans to the municipalities and small savers. Along with temporary Reich support, the new institution was effective enough for the banks to reopen for business on 5 August. The savings banks opened three days later. Highly suspicious of the bankers, whom he felt had misled the government, Brüning initiated a radical reform of the whole banking structure. He insisted that the Reich should take direct control of both the Darmstädter and Dresdner banks, and appointed provincial businessmen to take the place of the former directors 'who were burdened with the guilt of the collapse'.[15] The other big banks were also affected by the Brüning diktat and many of their directors were sacked and replaced. With state participation in the new capitalization of the banks, enormous losses could be written off. By 1932 91 per cent of the Dresdner's capital, 70 per cent of the Commerz Bank's, and 35 per cent of the Deutsche Bank's was in public ownership.[16] Other public institutions were formed to take over and write off bad assets and to manage long-term industrial participations. Through the newly created Acceptance and Guarantee Bank, the Reichsbank used the system of rationing non-monetary credit to influence the restoration of private industry while safeguarding the interests of the state. Exchange controls were used to allocate foreign exchange to industry. The government also offered subsidies to exporters in order to compensate for the overvaluation of the mark after the British and American devaluations and, through the subsidy system, closely monitored their business transactions with foreigners. In 1932, after cancelling its most-favoured-nation agreements, the Germans negotiated bilateral clearing agreements with Bulgaria, Estonia, Greece, Romania, and Yugoslavia. Preferential tariffs were set for specified quantities of imported wheat and the surpluses used for debt repayments. This practice would be extended under Schacht's leadership in September 1934 with the adoption of the New Plan.

[15] Harold James, *The German Slump: Politics and Economics 1924–1936* (Oxford, 1986), 317.

[16] Harold James, *The End of Globalization: Lessons From the Great Depression* (Cambridge, Mass., 2001), 63.

Responding to the strong anti-capitalist mood and hoping to undermine communist support, Brüning made a series of speeches about the evils of capitalism and warned that the government might be forced to dissolve all cartels and syndicates and redirect the investment decisions of the big banks. In fact, the measures introduced by Brüning and Luther propped up the capitalist system but altered the relationship between government, bankers, and industrialists. The Reich reduced its internal and foreign debt on highly advantageous terms and used its credit and exchange controls to prevent damage to the balance of trade. The Reichsbank discreetly permitted its gold reserves to drop from 40 per cent in relation to the notes in circulation to 10 per cent, allowing the Germans to refloat their economy without abandoning the gold standard. While publicly identified with orthodoxy and deflation, the Reichsbank, through its credit-expansion schemes, exchange controls, and export subsidies, instituted an unheralded reflationary policy which, along with Brüning's wage cuts, began to stimulate recovery during the first half of 1932, admittedly at a slow and uneven pace. Contrary to expectations, the Germans did not have to appeal again for foreign loans. The Reichsbank interventions set the pattern for the dirigiste techniques that Schacht was to exploit when he replaced Luther as president of the Reichsbank under Hitler.

IV

Even at the London conference, attention was shifting to the deteriorating financial situation in Britain, particularly at risk as one of the world's major short-term debtors. Britain's financial problems were not new; throughout 1930 Norman had wrestled with the pressure on the exchanges, and a 1931 winter run on sterling did not end until April. D. E. Moggridge, the British economic historian, has argued that 'the underlying trend of Britain's balance of payments would probably have forced sterling off gold at some stage during 1931–32', and that the political events during the summer of 1931 only hastened the onset of the crisis.[17] Norman was pessimistic in view of what he took to be the Labour government's incompetence, but offered no financial solutions to the exchange crisis. While the Macmillan committee (the Committee on Finance and Industry appointed in October 1929) heard extensive evidence on how to reform the monetary system (John Maynard Keynes was one of its star witnesses), the MacDonald government, faced with massive unemployment and an already unbalanced budget, followed 'a

[17] D. E. Moggridge, 'The 1931 Financial Crisis: A New View', in Barry Eichengreen (ed.), *Monetary Regime Transformations* (Aldershot, 1992), 315.

policy of drift with the rudder jammed'. Though there was some unease in banking circles, it was only in July that a real sense of alarm began to spread as the pound came under pressure and the Bank of England had to defend sterling's parity with its gold and currency reserves. Not only was the budget in current deficit but larger deficits were predicted for the coming year. The country already faced a negative balance of payments, due in part to the rundown of London balances by institutions whose countries were facing financial difficulties and to the movement of British and foreign capital to more secure financial markets. British banks were heavily involved in both the Austrian and German banking crises. With the standstill agreement arranged at the London conference, their assets in Germany were frozen and funds could not be withdrawn without damaging the whole financial settlement. In the knowledge that the banks were dangerously exposed, the Bank of England tried to protect them from sliding into illiquidity.

There was a heavy run on sterling during the weekend of 12–13 July, blamed on the French, to whom Labour leaders attributed the most Machiavellian intentions. Pressure came from commercial banks in the smaller countries of Europe, hurt through the blocking of the German credits, who retained large sterling reserves in London. On 13 July, the same day the German banks suspended payment, the Macmillan committee released its estimates of Britain's short-term external obligations, exposing the thinness of the Bank's gold cover. The politicians, nevertheless, were unprepared for the crisis that began two days later, believing that the London conference would relieve the pressure on sterling. There were few such illusions at the Bank of England. Over the next few weeks London became the principal victim of the general loss of confidence. As so often, and without real foundation, the British accused the French of orchestrating the movement of gold from London. A number of private banks found themselves in difficulty; Lazards was secretly rescued by the Bank of England. The latter, too, was under pressure. Norman hesitated to raise the bank rate yet higher, partly out of concern for the depressed state of industry, but also worried about the effects on depositor confidence. He appealed to George Harrison of the FRBNY. More willing to assist the Bank of England than the Reichsbank, Harrison agreed to buy pounds while the Bank of England would sell dollars. Norman waited for the impending visit of J. P. Morgan to seek a private American support credit for the pound. There was also American activity in Paris, where Stimson found Laval willing to use his influence to stop any further French withdrawals of gold. President Hoover refused to become involved in the British situation. Not only did its position appear less perilous than that of Germany, but with far less American capital invested in Britain, fewer

Americans were at risk. In any case, Hoover had to deal with the more pressing problem of the deepening depression in the United States. A *New York Times* cartoon on 26 July depicted a preoccupied father Hoover talking on the telephone to Europe, trying to ignore his crying children, the farmers, the miners, and the railroads.

The Norman–Morgan meeting produced no promise of an American credit; the two men agreed that the Labour government should take steps to balance the budget to restore confidence before seeking assistance abroad. The French, too, were approached for a credit, even before the FRBNY credit had been arranged, and on 25 July Sir Robert Kindersely, a director of the Bank of England, was sent to Paris for consultations with the Bank of France. The two central banks extended a £50 million credit to the British. Clément Moret, governor of the Bank of France (1930–5), repeatedly offered to arrange a long-term loan, but Norman ignored the offer. By this time Norman was reaching the end of his emotional resources. His last full day at the Bank of England was 29 July; barring one brief visit on 3 August, he did not return to Threadneedle Street until the end of September, by which time Britain had left gold. Norman's deputy and replacement, Sir Ernest Harvey, asked the French for a repeat of the dollar–franc swap that had worked quite effectively in February. The discount rate was raised to 4 per cent at the end of July and discussions for a French credit continued in Paris. Still the Bank of England spokesmen were reluctant to move in this direction, believing that the real difficulty lay in Britain's unbalanced budget and the cabinet's unwillingness to make the necessary cuts in expenditure. The May Committee on National Expenditure report published on 1 August, with its recommendations for balancing the budget, predicted a budget deficit of £120 million, well above the anticipated figures though in fact an underestimation. Committee members urged that taxes be raised and wasteful expenditure cut, mainly unemployment insurance. The publication of the May report created a major public uproar, seriously undermining domestic and foreign confidence.

Ramsay MacDonald was in deep political difficulty; he felt it was absolutely necessary to reassure financial opinion by tackling the budget. Talk of a 'national government' revived but, at first, there was little enthusiasm among opposition leaders. The Bank of England, having lost almost half its international reserves, looked for budgetary action. As parliament dispersed for its summer recess, the American and French central banks agreed to extend credits, two-and-a-half times larger than those offered the Reichsbank, on a three-month basis to be repaid in gold and with the understanding that the credit could be twice renewed. Instead of restoring world confidence in sterling, a new attack on sterling began after the Bank Holiday weekend. Gold was massively withdrawn on 5 August and the pound fell below the gold specie export point against both the dollar and the franc. To the irritation of the Americans and the French, the Bank of England did not use its traditional banking weapons nor fully employ its reserves to defend sterling during August. The Bank of England did nothing because of its concerns for the stability of the British banks. Raising the bank rate to 6 per cent would have signalled that the pound was under strain and encouraged depositors to get out of sterling. It was feared, too, that higher interest rates would send up the unemployment figures, encouraging a further speculative attack on the pound. There was little point in using the Bank of England's reserves 'just to allow British banks to make payments and thus slide into illiquidity'.[18] The Bank of England's confusing behaviour was intended to put pressure on the Labour leaders. MacDonald responded. Conferring with the chancellor of the exchequer, he agreed on large tax increases to meet half the budget deficit and expenditure cuts, including on unemployment insurance, to meet the other half. Conversations were opened with the Conservative and Liberal leaders. MacDonald authorized the Bank and Treasury officials to see whether the Americans would raise a loan to support sterling until parliament met on 1 September. The Americans warned that the banks would not act until convinced that a 'strong budget program' would be adopted.

Home investors were deserting sterling. The Germans, who had bought sterling in June and July, moved into other currencies. French private investors continued to sell their pounds. On 18 August the Wiggin–Layton report revealed how much (15 per cent) of Germany's long-term debt was in British hands. By recommending the continuation of the standstill arrangements, it ensured that much of the debt would remain illiquid. All the monetary authorities stressed that action on the budget deficit was essential for the return of market confidence. With his experts in agreement about what had to be done, MacDonald had to carry his proposals in a divided cabinet and secure Liberal and Conservative co-operation. The cabinet, told of an even higher budget deficit than predicted in the May report, accepted the need for tax increases and economies but resisted the recommended cuts in benefits. The issue was narrowed, both in terms of divisions within the Labour party and in the negotiations with the Conservative and Liberal leaders, to the question of reductions in unemployment insurance. While the political manoeuvring continued, it became clear that the Labour cabinet would split and that a 'national government' was becoming a

---

[18] James, *The End of Globalization*, 73.

realistic alternative. The Bank of England was asked to act as an intermediary between the cabinet and potential lenders in New York and Paris. The final appeal for a private bankers' credit (any public loan would depend on parliamentary approval of a balanced budget) on terms outlined by the politicians elicited equivocal assent from J. P. Morgan in New York. The latter informed Morgan Grenfell in London that the investing and banking public in the USA 'looks upon the whole European situation as in a bad mess and will not be too ready to undertake to bail out any one part of the situation'.[19] The partners wanted assurances that the proposed budget had the support of the Bank of England and the City and asked that the French provide an equivalent loan. Armed with the Morgan cable, MacDonald faced his divided cabinet on 23 August. The Labour government resigned on the following day and was succeeded by a National Government of Conservatives, Liberals, and the rump of Labour under Ramsay MacDonald. Most of the Labour party, including Arthur Henderson, went into opposition.

The new cabinet quickly agreed to the proposed austerity budget, with labour arguably hit hardest. Charges of a 'bankers ramp' were particularly resented by Morgan's, though it is probably true that the Bank of England and Morgan's told the Labour leaders what had to be done. Even as the National Government was being formed, revelations in *The Times* that the central bank credits were 'approaching exhaustion' resulted in a massive one-day run on sterling. Bank of England officials pressed the new government for rapid decisions and reassuring comments, even while efforts were made to secure the new foreign loans. Both the Americans and the French set conditions which the British had to accept. It says a good deal about the prestige of Morgan's and the importance of sterling that the American credit, the largest of Morgan's inter-war credit operations, was successfully floated at a moment when significant numbers of American banks were failing and the massive American involvement in Germany had turned investors against European adventures. The loans, amounting to $200 million each from New York and Paris, were given on 28 August. Even with agreement on a slashed budget and the fresh foreign credits, the withdrawal of foreign exchange and gold continued. Once the budget and retrenchment measures were announced, public debate became intense and the parties in the National Government considered the possibility of an immediate election. On 15 September the naval crews on the Atlantic fleet docked at Invergordon refused duty and demonstrated against cuts in lower-deck pay. The fleet sailed but the Board of Admiralty had to promise

[19] Diane B. Kunz, *The Battle for Britain's Gold Standard in 1931* (London, New York, and Sydney, 1987), 104.

revisions. The more extreme cuts were subsequently reduced. At the same time, the Indian financial crisis and a flight from the rupee resulted in a war of nerves between the Indian and British governments, a conflict which the latter won after a very difficult struggle.

The Netherlands and the French and Swiss central banks lost considerable funds, as each was operating on the gold-exchange standard and maintained large sterling reserves in London. Their nationals pulled their funds out from London, adding to the flood of withdrawals. The Bank of England insisted that world distrust of sterling was due to a lack of political confidence; officials warned that an election campaign would only increase this uneasiness. There seemed little point in engaging in a protracted struggle. The bankers supported devaluation. On 18 September, when the flight from sterling reached new heights, the Bank of England directors abandoned their defence of the gold standard. They dismissed American advice to use the bank rate and exchange controls. On the contrary, the exchange rate was allowed to fall and gold reserves were lost so as to confirm the so-called inevitability of the decision. Depreciation was not forced on the Bank of England; it still had sufficient resources to continue the struggle. The final steps were taken during the weekend of 19–20 September, with the Bank taking the lead in the decision-making process. When the markets opened on 21 September the pound was a floating currency. The decision was unexpected and the Americans taken by surprise. Despite strong pleas from the Americans and the French, whose high sterling reserves were at risk, there was no retreat. The National Government survived with its political reputation intact, but the Bank of England's efforts to present devaluation as an action forced on the country did not go unchallenged. The official announcement that: 'It is one thing to go off the gold standard with an unbalanced budget and uncontrolled inflation; it is quite another thing to take this measure, not because of internal financial difficulties, but because of excessive withdrawals of borrowed capital', hardly impressed foreign observers. The domestic reaction was calm. An election, held on 27 October, resulted in the greatest political victory of the inter-war period; the National Government coalition won 554 of 615 contested seats. It was a Conservative triumph, nonetheless, taking 470 seats and establishing a governmental dominance that would endure throughout the following decade.

It is hard to exaggerate the general sense of world shock at the British action. The pound was identified with the maintenance of the gold standard and confidence in sterling was at the heart of the gold-exchange system. Denmark and Sweden immediately went off gold; within four weeks eighteen countries followed. It was the 1925 story in reverse. The United States lost $180 million-worth of gold during the subsequent week, much of the drain originating in Paris where the French, after losing millions of francs on their sterling deposits, converted dollars into gold. Other investors sought reassurance about the soundness of the dollar. Despite a favourable balance of trade, the Americans were now at risk. Large gold outflows and currency withdrawals resulted in a new wave of American bank failures, over 800 in September and October alone. October 1931 was the worst month of all. The failure of central bank co-operation either to ameliorate the German crisis or to protect the gold-linked pound was a double blow to the international financial system established in the second half of the 1920s. It is highly doubtful whether the central banks could have handled the crises of 1931, which were both budgetary and financial. 'The credibility crises that destroyed the gold standard', Kenneth Mouré has argued, 'needed resolution in the province of politics, not central banking.'[20] There were recriminations on both sides of the Atlantic and Channel. Snowden blamed the United States and France for 'sterilizing' three-quarters of the world's gold. The Bank of France took umbrage at the barrage of British criticism. Having worked assiduously to support the Bank of England, it was faced with heavy losses on sterling. Countries like the Netherlands which had put their faith in Britain's continued loyalty to the gold standard were left wounded and vulnerable. German concerns about a flood of cheap British exports led to the imposition of further protective measures.

In London, devaluation halted the deposit losses. There were fears that the pound might depreciate too much or too little to restore the balance of trade but, after a sharp drop, the pound stabilized and recovered. By the end of December the pound reached a low of $3.25, 30 per cent below par, involving a 40 per cent appreciation of those currencies that did not immediately follow sterling off gold. Investor confidence was restored and funds were left in London. The trade deficit did not begin to fall until January 1932. By that time, despite much talk of a return to the gold standard, it was clear that Britain had gained a good deal from its action and would shape its future monetary policies with domestic goals in mind. The departure from the gold standard had a liberating effect on the British economy. Uncoupled from gold, the authorities could reduce interest and bank rates and intervene in the foreign-exchange market to keep the exchange rate depressed. Between January and June 1932 the bank rate was reduced from 6 per cent to 2 per cent and kept at this level until the outbreak of the war. The government's 'cheap money' policy was one of the factors

---

[20] Kenneth Mouré, *The Gold Standard Illusion: France, the Bank of France, and the International Gold Standard, 1914–1939* (Oxford, 2002), 266.

in the housing boom that became the chief carrier of Britain's industrial recovery from the Great Depression. Devaluation temporarily increased the competitiveness of British goods abroad, though the advantage was cut as other countries devalued and imposed trade barriers.

Though the consequences were not immediately clear, the British action marked the end of the international gold standard. All of the Dominions (Canada had already left before the British devaluation) and most of the empire countries with currencies pegged to sterling left the gold standard early. The parallel sterling–rupee depreciation in India actually made it profitable for Indians to export gold to London, building up the Bank of England's depleted gold reserves. The Scandinavian countries, Latvia, Estonia, and Japan followed Britain off gold during the next few months. Whereas at its height, in 1931, forty-seven countries had been on gold, by the end of 1932 among the major countries only Belgium, France, Italy, the Netherlands, Poland, Switzerland, and the United States were still operating on the gold standard.[21] Those that left gold recovered more quickly than those that battled on. The difficulty was that countries devalued their currencies at different times, and their staggered and competitive actions were often characterized by 'beggar-thy-neighbour' policies that intensified international tensions. With the destruction of the gold standard, no other framework for international co-operation emerged.

Unexpectedly—for there was no planning for the new financial era—a 'sterling bloc' came into being by the end of 1931 with currencies pegged to the pound rather than to gold. The countries concerned could buy currency freely, whether inside or outside the sterling area, and buy gold, though not at any fixed price. Convertibility made the pound an attractive reserve, particularly as the National Government was seen to follow 'sensible' fiscal and monetary policies. The empire and Commonwealth constituted the heart of the sterling bloc, but other nations too chose to peg their currencies to the pound. The British government hoped to reclaim its position as a global financial centre, though the bloc had no organization or formal agreements between its participants, who were free to enter and leave when they wished. The Treasury and Bank of England used the newly created Exchange Equalization Account, under the latter's control, to keep the pound steady and low in the interest of the British balance of trade. Countries within the empire were encouraged to keep their exchanges stable with regard to one another. Elsewhere, the Exchange Equalization Account was bitterly resented, for it appeared to institutionalize the depreciation of the pound, providing Britain with a major trading advantage. While Britain

---

[21] Eichengreen, *Golden Fetters*, 298–9.

undoubtedly gained by coming off gold, the depreciation of her currency intensified the deflationary pressures on those countries that remained on the gold standard. Currencies that were once undervalued on gold, like the French and Belgian franc, became overvalued as the depression continued.

One effect of the financial crises in Germany and Britain, and later in the United States and France after the franc was finally devalued in 1936, was to strengthen the power of governments at the expense of the central banks. The latter lost their dominant roles in the management of monetary policy, as financial and fiscal policies became part of broader state political and economic strategies. The central bankers came to be blamed for the woes of the times by such diverse politicians as Brüning, MacDonald, Hoover, Roosevelt, and Hitler. It was not that ministers knew more (or less) about the workings of finance than the bankers. Few of the participants in these extraordinary events understood what was happening, and many were surprised by the consequences of their own actions. But the crises of 1931–2 were so overwhelming and so decisive for the future of the state that the politicians assumed and retained their control over monetary affairs. The brief experiment in central-bank management of the gold-exchange standard was over. The British Treasury, working with and through the Bank of England, which shared many of its aims, took charge of Britain's monetary policies and developed its own programme to underwrite the government's broader objectives. Central bankers still played a role in financial diplomacy and consultations between central bankers continued, but within narrowly defined limits. The Bank of International Settlements, a meeting place for the central bankers and responsible for handling specified problems, became a centre for economic research and analysis and for the collection of statistics about the world economy.

Britain's abandonment of gold was followed by the adoption of protection, a radical departure from the trade policies that had been followed since 1846. Immediately after leaving the gold standard, despite the protective covering provided by exchange depreciation, the government introduced a number of 'emergency measures' to protect home markets. Such short-term tactics soon became a permanent feature of the British scene. The chancellor of the Exchequer, Neville Chamberlain, son of the politician who had made protection an electoral issue, announced that a tariff was needed to improve Britain's adverse balance of trade and to provide an insurance against hyperinflation. The Abnormal Importation Act (November 1931) was followed by the Import Duties Act (March 1932), a measure that raised duties on a long line of finished goods from 10 per cent to 20 per cent, with even higher duties on some particular industrial products. For the moment empire goods escaped, as did raw materials and almost all foodstuffs. With the budget still in deficit (the service estimates in the April 1932 budget were the lowest of the inter-war period), Chamberlain hoped the tariffs would bring in new revenue and help to balance the budget. His father's linkage between tariffs and imperial unity was soon revived. The new tariffs became the basis for the imperial preference agreements negotiated at the Imperial Economic Conference in Ottawa between 21 July and 20 August 1932. These consisted of a series of bilateral mutual agreements between Britain and the individual Dominions, accompanied by the maintenance or creation of higher trade barriers against foreigners. As the empire countries were largely exempted from the original 1932 tariff, the only way Britain could offer preferential treatment to the Dominions was to raise restrictions (through tariffs and even quantitative restrictions) against foreign imports, including new or additional 'Ottawa duties' levied mainly on foodstuffs. The British also promised not to reduce certain preferential margins and certain duties on foreign goods during the five-year term of the agreement, and for three years would put no duties or quota controls on specified empire agricultural products (mainly eggs, poultry, and milk products). Special provision was made to protect Canada from Soviet competition in the British market. In return, the British won some minor tariff concessions and preferences for British goods, mainly resulting from increases of Dominion tariffs on foreign goods.

The Ottawa agreements led to an increase in the proportion of British trade with the empire. Between 1930 and 1938 British exports to the empire rose from 43.5 per cent to 49.9 per cent of its total exports; imports increased from 29.1 per cent to 40.4 per cent of the total.[22] As Britain remained the world's largest importer, the shift in trade towards the British empire and to the sterling area was bound to effect other nations. Over the period 1929–38 the share of countries which were neither in the empire nor in the European sterling group fell from 63 per cent to 49 per cent.[23] The establishment of a sheltered domestic market and an imperial economic bloc that would maintain barriers against outsiders signalled that Britain's main interests were domestic and imperial, and that trade with foreign countries came a poor third. Bilateral agreements were concluded with the Scandinavian countries and

---

[22] Derek H. Aldcroft, *The British Economy* (Brighton, 1986), i. 81. For other figures, making the same point, but covering the period 1929–38, see C. H. Feinstein, P. Temin, and G. Toniolo, *The European Economy Between the Wars*, (Oxford, 1997), 153–4.

[23] Feinstein, Temin, and Toniolo, *European Economy*, 153. See, however, Ian M. Drummond, *British Economic Policy and the Empire, 1919–1939* (London, 1972), 102–3, for comments on the limited effects of the Ottawa agreements on British trade with other nations.

Argentina, where Britain was in a powerful negotiating position, and subsequently with other nations. The British drove hard bargains with the smaller primary exporters, who gained, in return, access to secure and important markets. The remaining multilateralists in London, mainly at the Foreign Office and Board of Trade, would have an uphill struggle to make their voices heard. The Foreign Office warned of the political consequence of protectionism in a memorandum of November 1931: 'a high protective tariff, combined with empire preference, implies a measure of dissociation from Europe [and] a corresponding diminution of our influence over European affairs.'[24] Britain had abandoned its long fight against discriminatory regional and bilateral schemes for salvaging European and world trade. Her new financial and trade policies would encourage the development of the contending regional blocs that characterized the later 1930s and fuelled the rivalries between the so-called 'have' and 'have not' nations. The year 1931 was a decisive break in Britain's inter-war history. The departure from gold and the adoption of protection marked a radical retreat from Britain's traditional role as the supporter of the liberal international order. If, as some historians have argued, Britain was 'too internationalist' for its own good in the 1920s, it now moved decisively in the opposite direction.

V

The impact of the depression was worse in eastern than in western Europe. As the countries of the region were (with but few exceptions) primary commodity producers, the massive fall in agricultural prices hit the peasants and farmers particularly hard. The price scissors gap—that is, the disparity between agricultural and industrial prices—compounded their difficulties. By 1932–3 many peasants were on the verge of bankruptcy or actually lost their land. With Czechoslovakia's exception, moreover, the east European countries were heavily dependent on foreign capital imports, both short- and long-term, to cover the gaps in external accounts and to pay the interest on foreign loans. The sudden withdrawal of foreign short-term capital and the drying up of longer-term capital proved catastrophic. Governments had to act swiftly if they were to avoid international insolvency. Most temporarily closed their banks, imposed foreign-exchange controls, raised tariffs, and introduced import and export controls. Governments, though anxious to check the immediate capital outflow during the 1931 summer crisis, were unwilling to depreciate their currencies for fear of returning to the inflationary situations of

---

[24] FO memorandum, 'Changing Conditions in British Foreign Policy', 26 Nov. 1931, PRO, CAB 24/225.

the early 1920s. They relied instead on exchange controls and trade restriction to stop the haemorrhaging of gold and foreign exchange and to reduce the imports that they could no longer afford. Most governments postponed or suspended the payment of foreign debts. Poland, in contrast to most of its neighbours, pursued a policy of unrestricted foreign payments and stayed on gold in the hope of restoring foreign confidence and encouraging investment, but by the summer of 1936, close to complete ruin, the Poles finally suspended foreign payments, went off gold, and issued strict exchange and import–export decrees.

Exchange controls and trade restrictions appeared to succeed in the short run. Capital outflows were checked and trade balances improved. But the net long-term effect of these defensive measures was a lower level of income and trade than might have resulted had governments depreciated their currencies. Exchange controls tended to raise domestic prices and overvalued currencies made exporting more difficult. The need to conserve foreign exchange encouraged the negotiation of bilateral clearing agreements. Already suggested by the president of the Austrian Nationalbank at a meeting of national banks in Prague in 1931 as a purely technical device, it became a widely adopted means of saving foreign exchange. Trade could be financed through clearing accounts in which the value of exports and imports could be balanced without

TABLE 31. Index of East European Trade, 1929–1934 (1928=100)

	1929	1930	1931	1932	1933	1934
Exports						
Bulgaria	126.0	70.0	47.0	35.0	41.0	39.0
Czechoslovakia	99.6	102.9	96.1	70.0	n/a	n/a
Hungary	95.1	97.7	75.9	64.2	54.2	60.5
Poland	109.0	104.0	82.0	65.0	59.0	55.0
Romania	89.0	68.0	48.0	40.0	35.0	34.0
Yugoslavia	104.4	100.6	101.5	83.1	63.1	58.3
Imports						
Bulgaria	83.0	73.0	80.0	68.0	48.0	46.0
Czechoslovakia	97.0	89.3	67.9	65.0	n/a	n/a
Hugary	86.7	92.5	88.0	85.3	97.2	78.9
Poland	95.0	97.0	77.0	74.0	54.0	48.0
Romania	81.0	87.0	89.0	81.0	81.0	76.0
Yugoslavia	90.7	91.8	84.6	59.5	56.6	60.9

Note: Value of exports and imports per ton.
Source: Adapted from M. Kaser and E. A. Radic, *The Economic History of Eastern Europe 1919/1975*. Vol. II. *Interwar Policy, the War and Reconstruction* (Oxford, 1986), 217, 233. Figures for Czechoslovakia, Hungary, Yugoslavia compiled by M. Loko from *Statistical Yearbook, League of Nations, Geneva* (1934), tables 101, 104; 1936, Table 117, 118, 119.

TABLE 32. German Share of East European Trade, 1929–1938 (%)

	Exports to Germany				Imports from Germany			
	1929	1932	1937	1938	1929	1932	1937	1938
Bulgaria	22.9	26.0	43.1	59.0	22.2	25.9	54.8	52.0
Czechoslovakia	22.1	19.6	13.7	20.1	24.9	22.9	15.5	19.1
Hungary	11.7	15.2	24.0	40.0	20.0	22.5	25.9	40.9
Poland	34.2	16.2	14.5	24.1	26.9	29.1	14.5	23.0
Romania	27.4	12.5	22.3	26.5	24.1	23.6	28.9	40.0
Yugoslavia	8.5	11.3	21.7	42.0	15.6	17.7	32.4	39.4

Source: D. H. Aldcroft and S. Morewood, *Economic Change in Eastern Europe Since 1918* (Aldershot, 1995), 67.

transferring cash payments from one state to another. Foreign exchange would be used only to cover any liabilities that resulted. The result was a further shift away from multilateral to bilateral trade, both between the countries of south-eastern Europe and with Germany and Italy. In time, extensive German purchases resulted in the accumulation of the large frozen balances owed by Germany to the exporting countries and increasing German domination of east European trade. In the absence of capital inflows and in the interest of promoting autarchical systems, many countries took over the direction or ownership of industrial enterprises. Poland and Romania had the highest incidence of state ownership, Czechoslovakia the lowest. Later on, public works and defence contracts increased the states' control over the economy.

The result of these measures and the moves towards autarchy was to considerably expand the powers of political elites and bureaucracies at a time when economic difficulties were exacerbating existing internal divisions, whether political, social, ethnic, or religious. Almost everywhere in the region (and in some western countries as well) the 'other' became objects of suspicion or hatred. Jews and gypsies (or Roma) became obvious scapegoats. The depression not only discredited liberal democracy in many ruling circles, it gave a new *raison d'être* to the development of authoritarian governments in countries where the democratic impulse had always been weak. Poland in 1930, Romania and Yugoslavia in 1931, and Hungary in 1932 were among the first to embark on this right-wing dictatorial road. The waves of xenophobic nationalism, anti-parliamentary feeling, and isolationist sentiment unleashed by the depression were to feed even more radical movements on the right in the years that followed.

Mussolini claimed that fascism provided the third way between the failed democratic states and Bolshevik Russia. There were banking difficulties in Italy in 1930 and 1931, but they were swiftly and secretly solved by the government. By the end of 1930 the withdrawal of foreign lines of credit had forced many of the so-called mixed banks (banks financing industrial ventures) to secure advances from the Bank of Italy. Rather than let the major banks face bankruptcy, the government intervened. Agreements were made between the Ministry of Finance and the Bank of Italy and the Credito Italiano (February 1931) and Banca Commerciale (October 1931) by which the latter two banks sold all their industrial and similar securities to two separate holding companies. The Bank of Italy made sufficient advances to the holding companies to cover the first instalment of the sums that they would pay to the banks as the price of their industrial portfolios. The sums were calculated not on the market price of the securities but at a level that would restore liquidity to the banks. In return, the banks agreed not to undertake any long-term credit operations in the future or to hold industrial securities in their portfolios. The state's actions solved the liquidity problems of the banks; there were no suspension of payments, bank holidays, or panics as happened elsewhere. In order to help the major industrial firms cut off from their traditional sources of long-term credit, the government established in January 1933 the Instituto per la Riconstruzione Industriale (IRI), a state-owned holding company which received all the industrial equities held by the two holding companies. The IRI was allowed to issue state-guaranteed long-term bonds at good interest rates which made them highly attractive to investors. Through the IRI, the Italian government became actively involved in the management of a large share of Italy's steel, shipping, electric power, and communications industries. Italy stayed on gold until 1936 and used exchange-rate controls and wage cuts in vain efforts to stimulate recovery. Unemployment remained high until Mussolini's Ethiopian adventure changed the industrial scene.

No state tried to reproduce the Soviet model of total control. Russia's immunity from the world depression proved a powerful propaganda weapon, but even those few countries, like Turkey, that introduced Soviet-inspired five year plans did not follow the Soviet model. Between 1930 and 1931 there was almost a tenfold increase in the value of Soviet grain exports. The peasantry paid heavily, more heavily than could be imagined, for this export surplus needed to finance the machinery imports required for industrialization. In 1931, the peak year of Soviet imports, Russia took 27.5 per cent of American industrial exports (for some industries the percentage was far higher) and four-fifths of Germany's engineering exports. Thereafter imports dropped sharply; collapsing grain prices meant that massive grain exports were needed to pay for machinery at a time of acute shortage and peasant disturbances.

In 1932–3 the urban workers as well as the peasants were going hungry. Yet forced collectivization continued, as did the industrialization and militarization of the state. If the level of agricultural output did not reach the levels achieved before the Great War until the mid-1950s, even sceptical estimates put the annual expansion of industrial output between 1928 and 1941 at 10 per cent and the production of capital goods probably grew at twice the rate of consumer goods during the Five Year Plan.[25] The Soviet Union was set to achieve Stalin's goals, an autarchic, industrialized state with the peasants supplying both the labour force and the food supplies needed to achieve these ends. The leap forward in industrial and military terms was impressive; the human costs horrendous.

Whereas for many states the depression became the 'Great Depression' during 1931, there were good reasons why the French should have thought that they would escape the 'economic blizzard' that struck central Europe and Britain. It was only during the latter half of the year that the French economy began to feel the cold economic winds, and even then France remained in a relatively privileged position. In contrast to Britain, Germany, and the United States, the level of French industrial production was as high in 1930 as in 1929 and the decline in 1931 was only 10 per cent as opposed to 25 per cent and more in the three other countries. Unemployment figures, though rising during 1931, were low compared to those in Germany and Britain, and the Laval government was taken by surprise when queried about the high number (92,000) of *chomeurs secourus* (those receiving unemployment assistance) in December 1931.[26] France's monetary position was strong and the franc one of the strongest currencies in the world. Gold continued to flow into the country, due to the repatriation of capital by individual Frenchmen and banks and the purchase of francs by foreigners moving out of the stricken capital markets elsewhere. When sterling went off gold, the Bank of France took steps to protect itself from further losses on foreign exchange and began to convert its dollar holdings into gold, adding to its already considerable holdings. The French were convinced that their strong monetary position resulted from their orthodox financial and monetary policies. They believed that the origins and spread of the depression resulted from the failure of other nations to operate the gold standard according to the rules (not deflating when they should have done), and that, because of the overvaluation of sterling, prices had been allowed to rise well above

---

[25] Figures in Robert Service, A *History of Twentieth Century Russia* (paperback edn., London, 1998), 182.

[26] Julian Jackson, *The Politics of Depression in France, 1932–1936* (Cambridge, 1985), 23–30.

TABLE 33. Bank of France Accounts, March 1929–Dec.
1932 (million francs)

	Gold reserves	Foreign exchange	Reserve ratio (%)
Mar. 1929	34,186	28,910	41.29
June	36,625	25,732	44.11
Sept.	39,411	25,814	45.71
Dec.	41,668	25,914	47.26
Mar. 1930	42,557	25,635	49.29
June	44,052	25,602	50.19
Sept.	48,431	25,570	52.45
Dec.	53,578	26,147	53.17
Mar. 1931	56,116	26,278	54.90
June	56,426	26,187	56.07
Sept.	59,346	22,706	57.02
Dec.	68,863	20,211	60.51
Mar. 1932	76,831	12,425	69.67
June	82,100	6,068	75.90
Sept.	82,681	4,716	77.02
Dec.	83,017	4,222	77.29

Source: Kenneth Mouré, *Managing the Franc Poincaré: Economic Understanding and Political Constraint in French Monetary Policy, 1928–1936* (Cambridge, 1991), 55–6.

their justified level. French industry had not overproduced (thought to be one of the causes of the depression), and France's financial policies had been wise and prudent as the healthy state of the franc showed. The flow of gold into France and America would cease, and indeed reverse, when conditions abroad improved and the system produced its own correctives. French financiers, economists, and politicians argued that the world would recover only if governments did not intervene to distort the workings of the self-regulating gold standard and ceased to sustain high prices through a variety of state-sponsored devices. Assumptions about how the world financial structure worked, as well as fears of runaway inflation coloured the thinking of the financial and political establishments even after the American devaluation in 1933. There was one major concern in 1931: the growth of the budget deficit, not a major item in 1930–1 but a repeated problem through and after 1931–2. Reductions in tax revenues and the growth in government spending meant that government receipts fell short of the estimates. Tax cuts, losses during the Hoover moratorium year, and money lent to Hungary and Yugoslavia added to the problems generated by the world depression. The large budget surpluses that had accumulated after the stabilization of the franc in 1926–8 and been used to support Tardieu's 'prosperity plan' (a five-year programme of public spending introduced

TABLE 34. French Budgets 1926–1933 (million francs)

	Receipts	Expenditure	Balance
1926	43,064	41,976	1,088
1927	46,086	45,869	217
1928	48,177	44,248	3,929
1929–30*	64,268	59,334	4,934
1930–1	50,794	55,712	−4,918
1931–2	47,944	53,428	−5,484
1932	36,038	40,666	−4,628
1933	43,436	54,945	−11,509

*Note:** 15-month budget.
Source: Alfred Sauvy (with Anita Hirsch), *Histoire économique de la France entre les deux guerres* (Paris, 1984), iii. 379.

in November 1929) disappeared entirely, and political attention focused on a deficit that could not be concealed. The memories and lessons learned from the Poincaré stabilization shadowed official thinking. An unbalanced budget meant inflation, currency depreciation, loss of confidence in the franc, and social chaos. If the franc was not to be devalued (all parties were agreed on this), the budget had to be balanced. The government was prepared to adopt deflationary policies, but needed to appease the powerful agricultural bloc, and protect the 'small men', the artisans and peasants, who were the backbone of the Radical party which held the balance of power in the Chamber of Deputies. The French adopted protective tariffs and import quotas while pledged to maintaining the franc.

There were a series of inconclusive moves in eastern Europe, where the Quai d'Orsay noted with anxiety signs of closer German–Russian co-operation. In the spring of 1931 the two Rapallo countries concluded a new economic arrangement, the Piatakov agreement, that provided for further German deliveries of goods to Russia worth 300 million RM in addition to the regular annual exports of the same amount. Though massively in debt to the Germans, the Russians were able to buy up the German machinery needed for the Five Year Plan at much-reduced prices. In June 1931 the Berlin treaty between the two countries was renewed. French exporters who, like the Germans, looked to the Soviet Union as a potential market pressed for government support. The Quai d'Orsay, under Berthelot's guidance, took up the Russian proposals for a non-aggression pact to be complemented by a parallel treaty between Warsaw and Moscow.[27] With considerable

[27] See discussion on pp. 526 and 553.

doubts on both sides, the treaty was initialled in June 1931. The Russians, worried about the Japanese, were anxious to stabilize their western frontiers, including those with Poland and Romania. Non-aggression pacts remained a favourite device for neutralizing foreign threats without entering the League security system. Piłsudski moved cautiously, wanting to preserve his independence from France through separate negotiations with Moscow, but also anxious that the new accords with Russia should not devalue the Franco–Polish treaty. The Poles dropped demands for simultaneous Soviet non-aggression pacts with all their neighbours. In turn, the Soviets concluded bilateral treaties with Finland and Latvia in January and February 1932 and Piłsudski had to move faster than he wanted. The Soviet–Polish treaty was initialled in January 1932; its signing was delayed until July because of Romanian procrastination in the absence of any settlement of the Bessarabian question.

In the interval the French blew hot and cold over the new treaties, leaving the Poles in a state of irritation and confusion over their ally's intentions. It was to the French advantage to drive a wedge between Moscow and Berlin. Laval hoped that Russia would remain neutral in any Franco-German conflict and that Poland would be deterred from aggressive action against the Soviets. But André Tardieu, who replaced Laval in February 1932, had strong doubts about the Russians and, to the fury of the Poles, refused to prod the Romanians any further. After repeated ultimata at Bucharest, Warsaw went ahead in July with a vague promise not to ratify the new pact until Romania concluded its own negotiations. Acting independently, Piłsudski secured a promise of Russian neutrality in case of a third-party attack. He was now in a position to turn to Berlin for similar assurances to implement his old policy of balance. The French, whose bungled diplomacy was partly to blame for Piłsudski's mounting irritation, were deeply annoyed at this demonstration of Polish independence. Other differences during 1932 over financial, commercial, and military (the French military and naval missions in Warsaw were both abruptly terminated) matters further soured relations. Piłsudski's nursing of the French alliance was linked to the absence of an alternative. He had little trust in an uncertain ally who might strike a bargain with the Germans at Polish expense.

After protracted negotiations the Czechs secured an important loan from France in 1931, part of which was to be used to cover Skoda's debt to Schneider's Union Européene. The loan was tied more openly than usual to the purchase of French industrial exports. Yet Beneš's various proposals to create an agrarian bloc in south-eastern Europe proved unacceptable to the French. When the Germans began to offer special bilateral arrangements, France proposed unilateral preferences in their own markets despite strong opposition from the farm organizations. Neither the loans to Romania and Yugoslavia nor the preferential treaties concluded with Hungary, Yugoslavia, and Romania between September 1931 and January 1932 eased the situation in these countries. In the spring of 1932 André Tardieu, who for a brief period became premier and foreign minister (March–May 1932), tried to counter German ambitions in the region by promoting a Danubian confederation (Czechoslovakia, Romania, Yugoslavia, Hungary, and Austria) with outside financial and economic assistance. Tardieu proposed a system of mutual tariff reductions with special treatment by outside states of the three agricultural countries whose products could not be absorbed by Austria and Czechoslovakia. The project, supported with some reservations by the Little Entente, was blocked by the British, Italians, and Germans when their representatives met in London on 6–8 April 1932. Britain, thinking in terms of its own imperial agricultural agreements, refused to back France on financial aid to the region. The Italians saw the proposal as a Prague-sponsored manoeuvre to gain influence over Austria and Hungary; in March 1932 Mussolini concluded his own preferential treaties with Vienna and Budapest. The Germans, fighting off what they saw as a French challenge, argued that the proposal would not solve the problems of the agrarian states. At the Lausanne conference in June 1932 a special committee was created to consider the impact of indebtedness in central (excluding Germany) and eastern Europe. Fourteen nations took part in the Stresa conference in September. Memoranda prepared by the participants and by the League of Nations on the problems of indebtedness and agricultural exports were to be submitted to the League's Commission of Enquiry for European Union (CEEU). No agreement on common action could be reached. Objections from Britain, having just concluded the Ottawa agreements, and from Germany and Italy blocked plans for an internationally sponsored loan, and no concrete action was taken. Two kilograms of memoranda were forwarded to the preparatory meetings of the World Economic Conference planned for 1933, but none of the smaller powers were invited to participate in the pre-conference talks. The main result was the growing frustration of the smaller powers with their neighbours in the west. The so-called 'Tardieu plan' was buried and no new French initiative followed. Even the Little Entente states that were anxious for more generous French financial assistance did not wish to estrange either Italy or Germany. One more promising sign was the conclusion of the Ouchy convention, by the Netherlands, Belgium, and Luxembourg in June 1932, calling for an immediate 10 per cent reduction in import duties and a 50 per cent cut in duties over five years. British and German opposition prevented the adhesion of the Scandinavian states, the other original signatories of the Oslo convention, the earlier and weaker response of the low tariff countries to the breakdown of the Geneva tariff conference of 1930. No extended liberalized trade zones emerged in Europe.

VI

Given their situation during 1930–1, the French should have regained the diplomatic initiative in European affairs, This was, however, 'l'année des occasions perdues', Maurice Vaisse's descriptive term of French disarmament policy in 1931 which covers other aspects of its diplomacy as well. Some of these failures can be attributed to its leadership. Policy was indecisive, with too many goals pursued simultaneously; Briand, Laval, and Flandin each had his own diplomatic strategy. With Briand's eclipse and the reduction in the Quai d'Orsay's influence, the international perspective was lost and the way opened for the more narrow-minded and nationalistic deputies in the Chamber of Deputies to make their voices heard. Under political pressure, Laval's policy became more inflexible, as over reparations, despite the changed external situation. French financiers were unwilling to take risks either with regard to Germany or east-central Europe, and the need to protect French agricultural producers limited what could be done with regard to imports. Much of the French failure, however, resulted from German resistance to their political demands and the American and British unwillingness to back alternative strategies.

The reparations question still remained at the top of the diplomatic agenda. At the time of the Hoover moratorium negotiations, and again at the London conference in July 1931, the French sought without success some form of political quid pro quo from the Germans for financial assistance. They had to prepare themselves instead for Brüning's demand for the abolition of reparations backed by the British, and for the latter's proposed world conference on reparations, war debts, gold, credits, and tariffs which might leave France isolated. The coalition parties exercised a veto on cabinet decisions. They would not sanction any initiative on reparations without major concessions on war debts. Unable to conclude bargains with the Americans or the Germans, Laval and Flandin were under continual pressure to preserve the framework of the Young plan and assure the priority of reparation payments over private commercial debts. This meant a clash with the British, who feared that the continued payment of reparations would threaten Britain's commercial loans to Germany. While the Americans went along with the British with regard to reparations, they were far less sympathetic to the latter's hopes for the abolition of war debts. It was the British, still reeling from the September crisis, and not the French who started talks in Paris, Berlin, and Washington in preparation for what

MacDonald called 'a big bold lead in the world', a new world financial and economic conference.[28]

The French made many proposals. In September 1931 the new French ambassador in Berlin and former Chamber spokesman for the Comité des Forges, the witty and voluble André François-Poncet, spoke of an alliance between French and German industry in his first press conference in Berlin. As author of the main French counter-offer to the Austro-German custom union proposal, the ambassador favoured closer French economic ties with German industry and renewed cartel arrangements (the international steel cartel had collapsed in 1931 as a result of a quarrel over quotas) between the two countries. Prime Minister Laval and Foreign Secretary Briand visited Berlin in October 1931 and took the lead in establishing a Franco-German commission to further economic collaboration. The objective was an eventual customs union that would serve as the core of a broader European union. A number of Franco-German agreements on specific products were eventually negotiated, but none covered a major industry and neither side was committed to the commission. The Auswärtiges Amt remained sceptical about the political rewards of the negotiations and the German Finance Ministry was dubious about the economic benefits. Talks about a possible Franco-German debt-repayment bargain were left in the hands of private bankers and industrialists, but were soon abandoned as the Germans elected to use their foreign debts as future bargaining chips. Even at an economic low point, the Germans would not accept French terms.

In late October 1931, the French premier invited himself to Washington. Originally planned to soothe ruffled feathers over the Hoover moratorium, at the meeting Laval and Hoover and their respective Treasury officials focused on the reparations issue but also discussed security questions. The Polish ambassador had warned the Americans that the Polish–German conflict was reaching crisis point and that conflict was imminent. Though Laval told Secretary of State Stimson that the Polish Corridor was a 'monstrosity', he insisted that the Poles would fight rather than accept any territorial modifications and that the question was not one for negotiation. For his part, Laval unsuccessfully sought to bring the Americans into a consultative security pact in anticipation of the forthcoming disarmament conference, only to find that neither Stimson nor the president was interested. The two Americans believed that the French were aiming for a hegemonic position in Europe and that their 'attitudes' with regard to the Polish

[28] Patricia Clavin, *The Failure of Economic Diplomacy: Britain, Germany, France and the United States, 1931–1936* (Basingstoke, 1996), 24.

question, disarmament, and reparations were thoroughly reprehensible. The president disliked and distrusted Laval and blamed him for the massive gold withdrawals from American banks that had followed the British devaluation. Preoccupied with his own country's financial and banking problems, Hoover was in no mood to make further 'sacrifices' for the sake of selfish Europeans. 'We had started with a hundred fifty years of isolation from Europe', the president told Laval. 'Fifteen years ago we were dragged by Europe into the war for the first time.' He summed up the results of the following fifteen years: 'it had cost the lives of some 75,000 men and disabled over 200,000 more.' The United States had spent in loans or war payments something like $400 billion, and yet 'Europe was now more unstable than it was in 1914'.[29] Both statesmen wished to see the gold standard maintained and sought a return to exchange stability. They agreed that the Germans should be advised to activate the Young plan's Special Advisory Committee which Hoover hoped would recommend far-reaching changes in Germany's obligations, conditional and unconditional. Laval, on the contrary, wanted to narrow the competence of the experts' study and to avoid radical changes in the Young plan regime. Hoover promised that if the European governments approved the advisory committee's recommendations, he would ask Congress to re-establish the World Disarmament Conference and reconsider war-debt repayments. Any French optimism on war debts soon vanished. The debate on the Hoover moratorium in Congress in December 1931–January 1932 revealed the legislators' extreme hostility towards any form of debt reduction, as well as their deep suspicion of Wall Street 'internationalism'. In the face of this barrage Hoover retreated into his domestic shell, hoping that reforms in the credit system and an expansion of the construction industry would improve the American economy. The Europeans would have to sort out their own difficulties at the forthcoming Lausanne conference without American participation. In fact, it was only at the very last moment that an American delegation was actually put together for the World Disarmament Conference, despite the president's abiding interest in arms reduction.

Brüning made his appeal to the advisory committee on 20 November 1931. In presenting an exhaustive account of the country's current financial situation, the German delegation hoped to lay the basis for the subsequent cancellation of all German reparations. Brüning wanted the Lausanne conference postponed for domestic reasons, but also in the hope that the Laval ministry would be replaced by a more

---

[29] Stimson Diaries, 23 Oct. 1931, quoted in Kunz, *The Battle for Britain's Gold Standard*, 153–3.

accommodating government in the May elections. If economic conditions improved after a reparations settlement in January, he would lose the argument for total abolition. The French, too, played for time. Stimson's declaration that American participation was 'impossible and undesirable' strengthened Laval's unwillingness to countenance a long-term moratorium on German payments or a general discussion of reparation revision. Mounting budgetary difficulties hardly encouraged French enthusiasm for a final solution to the reparations question. The British, still hoping for a settlement of the war-debts and reparations question, proposed that the January meeting be postponed until June. Though Laval (prime minister of three ministries from January 1931 to February 1932) was willing to try various alternatives, including approaches to Berlin, this political juggler of the right was too shrewd a politician to move far from the prevailing consensus that it was useless and dangerous to pursue co-operation with Germany while Hitler waited in the wings. The effort to attach political conditions to loans or credits aroused the anger of the British and the Americans. The French were again pushed into a defensive policy, unable to act in open opposition to the Anglo-Saxon powers.

The radical right parties in the Chamber of Deputies were unlikely to support imaginative policies in foreign affairs. It was not only a question of the checks on the policies of the 'new men' of the right like Tardieu and Laval, who, despite the changes of ministries, dominated French politics in these years. Neither the Tardieu plan nor French proposals for an international security force at the Geneva disarmament conference won the backing of the British or the Americans. The swing to the left in the May 1932 elections and the return of Herriot to office, though it marked a change in French attitudes, only intensified the defensive character of French diplomacy. Mindful of the lessons of 1924–5, when his policies had encountered the opposition of the so-called *mur d'argent*, Herriot appointed the orthodox technician Louis Germain-Martin as minister of finance. The new minister reduced civil service salaries, cut expenditure, and proposed tax increases that were reduced in the Chamber. The budget remained in deficit.

Continued German resistance to the French proposals was one reason for the latter's failure. During the autumn months of 1931 Brüning picked up the financial pieces resulting from the summer crises without winning new popular support. On 5 September 1931 the Hague Tribunal ruled that the proposed Austro-German customs union was incompatible with the Geneva protocol. Well before this, the Austrians had abandoned the union in return for a League loan. Foreign Minister Curtius paid the price for failure and resigned on 3 October. Identified with a more aggressive foreign policy, he had failed to improve

Brüning's political ratings. 'We are living not by the hour,' Curtius was quoted as saying, 'but by the minute hand of the clock.' Without a foreign-policy success to balance the unpopular deflationary measures, Brüning looked to the abolition of reparations for both political and economic relief. Brüning's new ministry, reconstituted after Curtius's resignation, was even weaker than its predecessor. His power depended on the old president's support and the highly uncertain loyalty of Hindenburg's intimate circle. While the chancellor tried to balance between the opposing aims of the most powerful economic interest groups, Hitler's popularity increased. The anticipated disarmament and reparation conferences provided fresh grist to the Nazi mills. The Reichsbank's modest reflationary policies began to pay dividends during the first half of 1932, but recovery was slow and uneven. The nadir of the German depression was not reached until the summer of 1932. Despite widespread demands for more decisive action to deal with unemployment, the Brüning government believed that any major 'pump-priming' policies would increase the budget deficits and set off a further round of financial panics and bank collapses. Only a very modest programme was put into effect. It was argued that the adoption of openly inflationary programmes would revive the traumas of 1923–4 and totally shatter public confidence in the government. As a result, no attempt was made to use the Reichsbank's reflationary policies as political carrots. On the contrary, Brüning and Luther disguised what they were doing behind a heavy veil. The public at large, viewing the massive extent of state aid to the banks, became increasingly antagonistic towards the banks, the financial system, and the existing political structure.

TABLE 35. German Unemployment and Welfare Recipients, 1925–1932 (conservative annual averages)

	Unemployed (millions)	% Unionized	Welfare Recipients (millions)
1925	0.7	6.5	
1926	2.1	18.4	
1927	1.3	8.8	1.571
1928	1.4	8.6	
1929	1.9	13.3	
1930	3.3	22.8	1.983
1931	4.6	34.4	
1932	5.6	44.2	4.608

Sources: David Crew, *Germans on Welfare* (Oxford, 1998), and other sources. See Table 28, p. 639.

Unemployment figures continued to rise, production fell further, and disinvestment continued. Despite the standstill agreement and a temporary trade surplus, the Germans claimed that the Reichsbank's gold and foreign-exchange reserves were rapidly falling. A new emergency decree announced on 8 December 1931 contained a 10 to 15 per cent reduction in salaries and wages and other deflationary measures. The unemployed, some without work for more than two years, responded in various ways, ranging from total despair (suicide rates went up) and apathy to brawling and street action. While most citizens were only onlookers, the violence in the street escalated, sparked mainly by the paramilitary organizations of both Nazis and Communists. The two extreme groups engaged in verbal duels at mass meetings and in open and bloody street battles. They held in common their denunciation of the Social Democratic Party and attacks on the Weimar republic. The Stalinist-directed underground groups, assisted by funds from Moscow and GPU agents assigned to a 'special tasks' office in the Berlin embassy, covertly prepared for the forthcoming 'German revolution'. In February 1932 Ernst Thälmann, the Communist leader, warned the KPD Central Committee that 'nothing would be more disastrous than an opportunistic overestimation of Hitler-fascism'.[30] The panicked flight to political extremes was confirmed by the gains of both the KPD and the NSDAP. In a deeply fragmented culture, where the many small political and economic interest groups had already turned against the republic, Hitler's siren songs became more persuasive. He and his party held out the prospect of a national people's community that would embrace all classes and interest groups. It did not matter that the charismatic leader of the NSDAP had no prescription for economic recovery. He projected an image of action and hope that contrasted sharply with the unpopular policies of the Brüning government. Paul Schmidt, the chief interpreter at the Auswärtiges Amt, recalled that the chancellor travelled in railway carriages with the blinds drawn so that he should not see what Germany and Germans really looked like. Already the parties of the right looked to the inclusion of the Nazis in some future government.

In December 1931 Brüning announced that Germany could no longer fulfil its obligations and requested a meeting to revise the Young plan, though privately he claimed that Germany did not expect outright cancellation. In January he told the British and French ambassadors that Germany would announce at the forthcoming Lausanne conference that it could not pay reparations either at present or in the

---

[30] Michael Burleigh, *The Third Reich* (paperback edn., Basingstoke and Oxford, 2000), 136.

foreseeable future. There was no consensus among Germany's creditors about what action should be taken. The British, anxious to free their frozen funds in Germany and hoping to reduce the burden of world indebtedness, wanted the end of the whole reparations–war-debt regime. The French and Americans, for different reasons, opposed cancellation. During the early months of 1932, as German gold and foreign-currency reserves began to drop again, its creditors feared a moratorium on German foreign payments. In Britain the bankers warned the Treasury of the dire economic and political consequences of a German collapse and pressed for the cancellation of reparations with one final German payment to the BIS. Brüning sought to buy time until world economic recovery and diplomatic success would bring the electorate back to its senses. The German presidential elections in March–April 1932 (a not entirely convincing victory by Hindenburg over Hitler) and the defeat of the Social Democrats in Prussia revealed the strength of Hitler's appeal and exposed the full weakness of the chancellor's position. There was no reward for Brüning's active and successful campaign for Hindenburg's re-election. The chancellor desperately needed a victory at the Geneva disarmament conference and the promise of the abolition of reparations at Lausanne if he was to survive. Neither seemed forthcoming in the spring of 1932.

The immediate prospects for abolition were not encouraging. The British tried to appease the French, by intentionally misleading them into believing that Britain might return to gold if Germany was again solvent and British assets in Germany unfrozen. The Americans insisted that the reparations problem would have to be solved without any consideration of war debts. Without progress on war debts, the French would not move on reparations. The Germans feared that the issue could not be resolved until after the US presidential elections in November, and that if Hoover was defeated it could run until well into 1933. Still, Brüning offered only the continuation of existing policies. Meanwhile, the pressure from President Hindenburg, prompted by General Kurt von Schleicher and others, to bring the Nazis into the Prussian and Reich governments intensified, as did the campaign to discredit Brüning. Forced to summon the Reichstag to request authorization for further government borrowing on the basis of the emergency decrees, Brüning portrayed himself on 11 May, on the eve of the delayed Lausanne conference, as a long-distance runner now in 'the last hundred meters before the finishing line'.[31] He would not enjoy the victory. The banning of the SA (an indignant Goebbels complained that the Berlin police had left him stranded by confiscating his chauffeur-driven car) led to the forced

---

[31] Patch, *Heinrich Brüning*, 255.

resignation of Wilhelm Groener from his interior ministry office. Brüning offered Groener's other office, minister of defence, to the arch-intriguer Schleicher, the head of the ministerial office in the Reichswehr ministry and a close companion of Hindenburg's son, Oskar. The offer was rejected; Schleicher was conspiring with Hitler to win Nazi support for a rightist presidential cabinet to follow Brüning's fall. The chancellor resigned on 30 May, undone by Schleicher and his small cabal who had the 85-year-old president's ear. It was a commentary on the almost total atrophy of democratic politics that power was now concentrated in a small and unrepresentative clique determined to replace the republic with a right-wing authoritarian state.

The new chancellor, who would represent Germany at Lausanne, Franz von Papen, was an ex-general staff officer and wartime military attaché in the United States who, through incredible and repeated incompetence, had revealed the activities of a German sabotage ring operating in neutral America and was declared persona non grata. A Centre party deputy in the Prussian state parliament, he was originally picked by Schleicher to pacify Brüning's party. A man of little substance, with strong anti-Bolshevik and anti-parliamentary views, Papen led a cabinet of mainly noblemen recruited from Hindenburg's social and military milieu. Schleicher took the defence portfolio; among the three bourgeois members of the cabinet, two were from the boards of I. G. Farben and Krupp. Without either party or popular support, Papen looked to the international conferences in Lausanne and Geneva for the successes that he needed. There was little sympathy for the 'old Prussian clique' in London, and even less when MacDonald met von Papen. Nonetheless, the British leaders sought to bridge the gap between France and Germany over reparations. Appealing to Neurath, the German ambassador in London, about to become foreign minister in the Papen cabinet, the British foreign secretary, Sir John Simon, revived the idea of a pledge of appeasement in Europe extending over a substantial period of time as the quid pro quo for the abolition of reparations. It was an idea that surfaced again during the course of the Lausanne talks but which served only to muddy the financial waters.

Britain was the driving force behind the search for international action. It was thought in London that a European agreement on reparations could be used as the basis for a bargain with the United States on war debts. Herriot's victory in the May elections encouraged British optimism about a change in French policy. At the least Herriot supported the conference idea, if not the total abrogation of reparations. On the eve of the Lausanne conference, French and German financiers met to see if some kind of compromise could be reached; either a lump payment of 3 million Reichsmarks or a lien on railway profits in return for the ending of reparations. It may have been that both sides, despite official comments to the contrary, realized that concessions were necessary if the Lausanne conference was not to fail. The State Department made clear that nothing decided at Lausanne should imperil war-debt payments to the United States. The American attitude particularly annoyed the chancellor of the Exchequer, Neville Chamberlain, who would have liked to dispense with the conference altogether and proceed through an agreement with France. He convinced the cabinet to dismiss MacDonald's misgivings about antagonizing Washington and to go ahead as planned. To remind the French that more was at stake than a deal over reparations, Piłsudski sent a Polish destroyer into Danzig harbour on the eve of the conference in order to demonstrate Poland's right to use the free city as a *port d'attaché* for her navy.

The Lausanne conference opened on 16 June under MacDonald's chairmanship. There were conciliatory speeches by Papen (in French) and Herriot, but these diplomatic courtesies hardly disguised their differences. Papen denounced reparations as unrealizable, harmful, and destructive; Herriot reminded his audience of the economic potential of Germany and the sacrifices being demanded of France without compensation. At first the major diplomatic activity was between the two main adversaries, with the British acting as intermediaries. Prompted by the British, Papen spoke of a four-power treaty to secure peace in Europe, future contacts between the chiefs of staff of the two countries, and a Franco–German consultative pact in return for complete cancellation. He became less precise but more lyrical during a 'tête-à-tête' with Herriot on 24 June; the French prime minister was impressed enough to persuade his cabinet to consider an exchange. After a weekend in Berlin, where the political realities pointed in a different direction, the German chancellor retreated, paring down the offer which Herriot in turn rejected. The French were further angered by a strong Italian declaration in favour of cancelling both reparations and war debts and by the appearance of an Italo–German front at Geneva where the disarmament talks were being conducted simultaneously. The reparations conference arrived at an impasse; MacDonald, who had deliberately imposed a tight timetable on the representatives to secure agreement, had to return to London before 13 July when the British delegation would set out for Ottawa.

After an unfortunate attempt by MacDonald to again link disarmament and reparations, the British proposed returning to the idea of a *forfait*, a final lump-sum payment that would cancel out all German obligations under the Dawes and Young plans, beyond servicing the two loans already issued to the public. After considerable wrangling over the nominal value of what was in fact an imaginary figure, a compromise sum of 3 billion marks was accepted. MacDonald again suggested political compensations for the Germans, encouraging Papen to demand even further concessions (including the retraction of the war-guilt clause and a commitment to equality of armaments) that led to a bitter confrontation with Herriot. Through promises to both parties, the British brought this difficult and frustrating conference to what they considered a successful end. The Lausanne agreements, finally concluded on 9 July, were a victory for the Germans, and Papen anticipated a warm reception when he returned to Berlin. After 1 July 1932 Germany would no longer have to raise money for reparation payments. The Young plan payments were abolished. The Germans would pay a maximum of 3 billion marks, constituting the obligations of the Hoover moratorium years and a contribution to European reconstruction. This would be in the form of 5 per cent bonds deposited with the BIS which would not be offered for sale until the Young plan loan rose above 90 per cent of its nominal value. In other words, the bonds would not be issued until the German economic equilibrium was completely restored. If not issued, the bonds would be destroyed fifteen years after the ratification of the Lausanne convention. They were actually burnt in 1948. The conditions attached to the new agreement underlined its illusory character. To secure French agreement to the reparations settlement, the British and French concluded a secret 'gentlemen's agreement' that postponed ratification of the Lausanne agreement until a settlement was reached between the reparation powers and the United States on war debts. The existing moratorium on both payments would continue until the Lausanne convention went into effect. Subsidiary agreements extended the moratorium on non-German reparations until December and established a committee to work out an agreement in the interim. Yet another special committee was created to tackle the financial and economic problems of central and eastern Europe. The seemingly important Stresa conference held in September produced reams of paper but no concrete results.

When news of the supposedly secret 'gentlemen's agreement' reached Washington there was a chorus of dismay. American bankers had pressed the State Department to give positive, if unofficial, support to the Lausanne agreements, but political tempers were raised. The president and Congress were incensed at the European decision, in Hoover's words, 'to gang up against the United States'.[32] In part to conciliate the Americans, the Europeans had agreed at Lausanne to a world economic and financial conference to restore international co-operation in order to raise world prices. The British hoped to keep the Americans

[32] Clavin, *The Great Depression in Europe, 1929–1939*, 152.

involved in the European crisis and to secure the cancellation of war debts. While unwilling to discuss war debts, the US Treasury and Federal Reserve Bank, along with the French, intended to use the conference to persuade Britain to return to the gold standard. Herbert Feis, the impressive economic adviser at the Department of State, harboured the admittedly utopian hope that there might be proposals for co-ordinated currency depreciation to stimulate world recovery. He could not have been more wrong.

'No more reparations. They have gone. No more attempting in a blind and thoughtless way to heap burdens and burdens on anyone's shoulders', Ramsay MacDonald told his listeners at the last plenary session of the Lausanne conference. 'Those great payments of sums which represent no transfer of goods have not been a punishment upon one nation, they have been an affliction on all nations, and it is from this transfer of sums which upset the world's economy that the whole world is suffering so much today.'[33] Many shared MacDonald's sentiments. The abolition of reparations was viewed on both sides of the Atlantic as one of the necessary prerequisites for economic recovery. The French, once again, found themselves on the losing side. The political implications were far more disturbing than the financial ones. Insistence on the final forfeit had been little more than a face-saving device. The French knew the Germans had succeeded yet again in chipping away at the already enfeebled Versailles system. There was no Franco-German political bargain; Herriot rightly declined the worthless carrots that Papen offered. The British promised a bilateral Anglo-French consultative pact to be announced at the end of the Lausanne conference. What this would mean in terms of co-operation at the Geneva disarmament talks was uncertain for, with the projected ending of reparations, disarmament would take centre stage in the Franco-German conflict. The Lausanne agreement was followed by German domestic actions to reduce its remaining external debt, helped considerably by the British and later the American departures from the gold standard. The Germans had won a victory, but it was not to have the effects that Brüning had intended. Papen failed to gain any political clout from the conference. He returned to an empty station platform and a chorus of hostile press comments. The Nazis and right-wing parties made much of the failure to cancel all German payments or to win the equality of arms and the abolition of the war-guilt clause they demanded. The parties of the left were determined not to be saddled with acceptance of any new reparation agreement, though the Social

[33] Bruce Kent, *Spoils of War: The Politics, Economics, and Diplomacy of Reparations, 1918–1932* (Oxford, 1989), 371–2.

Democrats actually approved of Papen's action. Dr Schacht sent a congratulatory message to the chancellor and then hedged his bets to preserve his new Nazi links. The Lausanne agreements were used as ammunition by the nationalist right in the July elections, when the depression reached its nadir point and the Nazis doubled their representation in the Reichstag.

Reparations were quietly buried; there was no purpose in calling the conference promised in the 'gentlemen's agreement' if the Lausanne convention was not ratified. The Germans were freed from the 'foreign shackles' on which they blamed their difficulties. In all, the Germans had paid about 19.1 milliard gold marks in reparations, less than a third of it in cash and nowhere in sight of the 50 milliard gold marks of the original London Schedule of Payments.[34] To the very end, because the Hoover moratorium was only a short-term measure, reparations and war debts continued to shake the stability of the international capital markets. Reparations had intensified the domestic and foreign pressures on the Reich government. Their disappearance had little effect on the German situation, except as a potent reminder of Germany's unjust treatment by its wartime enemies. Brüning had wanted to keep Germany attached to the international economic system. He did not wish, as did many of his right-wing critics, to repudiate her international loans and follow a policy of autarchy. He had hoped that once reparations were abolished, massive foreign lending would resume. Once the Nazis took power and Schacht returned as head of the Reichsbank, he used and expanded financial procedures already in place to reduce or default on Germany's long- and short-term debts and to encourage autarchic trade practices.

Reparations were gone but war debts still had to be paid. The American situation made matters no easier. Once the British left gold, the financial pressures had shifted to the United States. Hoover was facing a far more difficult crisis in 1932 than he had encountered the previous year, when he had taken vigorous action to stimulate the economy, including expansionary fiscal measures. He now moved into a defensive position. Attention, as had happened in Europe, was focused on the federal budgetary deficit: the 1932 deficit of $2.7 billion

[34] See discussion in Ch. 4: 'The Primacy of Economics: Reconstruction in Western Europe, 1919–1924'. The Germans probably paid between 20.5 milliard gold marks to 22.9 milliard marks, nowhere near the 50 milliard marks of the original London Schedule of payments. If the latter sum was unrealistic, the low sums paid were hardly worth the damage done to Germany, her creditors, and the international economy. See Niall Ferguson, *The Pity of War* (London, 1999),   417 and Stephen Schuker, 'American "Reparations" to Germany, 1919–1933', in Gerald D. Feldman et al. (eds.), *Die Nachwirkungen der Inflation auf die deutsche Geschichte, 1924–1933* (Munich, 1985), 364, 371. Also Sally Marks, *The Illusion of Peace* (rev. edn., Basingstoke, 2003), 143.

was the highest peacetime deficit up to that time.[35] By early 1932 there were over 10 million people unemployed, about 20 per cent of the workforce, and almost one-third of those in employment were working part-time. The social misery was palpable; the popular reaction was one of apathy and despair. The president's reputation reached an all-time low. Nominated in June 1932 by a listless Republican convention, Hoover seemed overwhelmed by events. The autumn election campaign was all about the depression. The Democratic candidate, Franklin D. Roosevelt, blamed the situation on Hoover, but neither side offered concrete recommendations. On 8 November Roosevelt won a smashing victory, taking all but six states (with 472 to 59 electoral college votes).

In November 1932 the British and French ambassadors in Washington, in a joint action, asked for a review of the war-debts settlements and the postponement of the 15 December payments. Hoover was conciliatory but powerless; the president-elect refused to commit himself until after he took office. The British Treasury knew that Britain could pay, but claimed that the conditions of the global depression and the depreciation of sterling made this impossible. It was mainly for political reasons that the cabinet, spurred by Neville Chamberlain and the Treasury, rejected an American offer to have an independent commission determine the capacity of its debtors to pay. The Treasury considered defaulting on the 15 December payment, but the Foreign Office, fearing a crisis in Anglo-American relations, intervened. When it became clear that the Americans would not consider renegotiation or abandonment, the Treasury was forced to capitulate and an exceedingly reluctant Chamberlain agreed to make the payment ($95 million) in full, hoping that this would give Britain the moral advantage at the forthcoming World Economic Conference. Chamberlain's failure to move the Americans and Roosevelt's actions at the conference left the chancellor of the Exchequer and future prime minister with an abiding distrust of the Americans and their 'dark-horse' president that remained with him throughout his premiership. The British made two token payments in 1933 and, after learning that they would be classified as defaulters and excluded from future access to American capital markets under the Johnson Bill pending in Congress, decided to make no further payments at all to 'this untrustworthy race'.[36] The Herriot government

---

[35] Figures from David M. Kennedy, *Freedom from Fear: The American People in Depression and War, 1929–1945* (Oxford, 1999), 79.

[36] Both quotations, the first from Vansittart and the second from Alexander Cadogan, in Robert Boyce, 'World Depression, World War: Some Economic Origins of the Second World War', in Robert Boyce and E. M. Robertson (eds.), *Paths to War: New Essays on the Origins of the Second World War* (London, 1989), 85.

fared no better in Washington. The Americans pointed out that French gold withdrawals from the Federal Reserve would cover its debt obligations until 1942, and showed little interest in French claims that a war-debt settlement would improve the European political atmosphere and encourage further moves like the recent Franco-German economic and financial accords and their proposed joint preparations for the World Economic Conference. The Herriot government, unable to retain the support of the left while pursuing the deflationary fiscal policies demanded by the right, was already doomed. Conscious of the need for American support on security issues, Herriot chose to 'fall honourably' by asking the Chamber to sanction payment of the December 1932 instalment ($19 million). France defaulted as Herriot was defeated on 12 December. The question was mainly one of principle; no Chamber would sanction payments to the United States, particularly at a time when the budget was in deficit. The Americans retaliated. The Johnson Act of 11 January 1934 prohibited making loans to governments in default on obligations to the United States. It was to prove a major barrier to American assistance to Britain and France in 1939. Both countries were on the long list of defaulters.[37] Germany, like all those owing large amounts in commercial loans, was not.

VII

The World Economic and Monetary Conference opened on 12 June 1933 in London's newly opened Geological Museum, with sixty-five countries and six international organizations in attendance. The gathering, which unlike Genoa (1922) or Geneva (1927) was intended to be dominated by the political authorities and not the economic experts, was to deal with current problems such as the collapse of economic confidence and prices, the operation of the gold standard, and the spread of protectionism and other barriers to trade. By the time the conference opened the new cast of political leaders was in place. Although the now-ailing Ramsay MacDonald was still prime minister in Britain and was made chairman of the conference, the massive Conservative majority within the National Government following the October 1931 elections meant that Stanley Baldwin, the Conservative leader, and Neville Chamberlain, the already influential chancellor of the exchequer, were the dominating figures in the cabinet. In France, the Radical leader, Édouard Daladier, assumed the premiership on 31 January and stayed in office until 24 October 1933. In a sequence of events described

[37] They included, besides Britain and France, Belgium, Czechoslovakia, Estonia, Hungary, Italy, Latvia, Lithuania, Poland, Romania, and Yugoslavia.

in Chapter 14, Adolf Hitler became chancellor of Germany on 30 January 1933, the head of a coalition cabinet of National Socialists and Nationalists. In Washington, Franklin Roosevelt took office on 4 March 1933. The changes in leadership made it unlikely that the depression governments would succeed in finding common solutions to the world's financial and economic ills. All these leaders were committed, first and foremost, to national economic programmes as against international co-operation. None was prepared to take a leadership role in stimulating international recovery through co-operative action.

The divisions between the leading powers were already clear in the preliminary pre-conference meetings convened in Geneva in November 1932 and January 1933. Britain's main interest was war-debt abolition, despite its exclusion from the conference agenda because of American objections. Her representatives hoped to promote the cheap-money policy that was already benefiting the home economy. Though the main instigator of the conference, Britain found itself practically isolated at Geneva because of the floating pound, which France and the gold-standard nations blamed for the current blockages to world trade. The French, who had long dragged their feet over the calling of a conference, were interested only in a return to orthodox gold-standard practices. They were convinced that there could be little progress without a British lead on stabilization. On the gold issue the Americans tended to support the French, but Hoover and then Roosevelt wanted progress made towards reducing restrictions on international trade. The new Democratic administration had secured a tariff truce for the period of the World Economic Conference, and Cordell Hull, Roosevelt's secretary of state, even before entering office tried to use this as the basis for a bilateral reciprocal tariff agreement (RTA) with the British. It was hoped that this might lead to multilateral tariff negotiations throughout the world through the operation of unconditional most-favoured-nation agreements. Chamberlain was not interested; Britain's £70 million trading deficit with the United States, as well as her new protectionist and imperial orientation, hardly favoured moves towards freer trade. Hull's proposals aroused considerable discomfort in Germany and in many of the east European countries, which feared that an Anglo-Saxon alliance would destroy their newly created protective fences.

No one quite knew what to expect from the new American president. Neither Roosevelt's statements during Hoover's lame-duck interregnum or during the former's meeting with the outgoing president gave any indication of what might follow. The president-elect was an extraordinary man who continues to elude his historians. A patrician, educated at Groton and Harvard, in a manner common only to the highest and most exclusive social circles in America, he had set his sights on the White House very early in his legal career. He was both progressive and conservative, without a fixed programme or any discernable principles. Gifted with an uncanny talent for communicating with voters of all backgrounds, his optimism and good cheer were infectious. An attack of poliomyelitis in 1921 left him partially crippled and condemned to wear heavy steel braces on his legs whenever he stood or 'walked'. Though he led the public campaign for research and relief, he carefully avoided being photographed either in a wheelchair or being carried. While marked by his four-year struggle for rehabilitation, the gains in inner strength, compassion, and humility did not alter Roosevelt the politician. He remained the great pragmatist, the consummate political trimmer, and the master reconciler. Hoover believed that the depression stemmed from international causes which had to be addressed. Roosevelt and his advisers were convinced that the problems and the solutions to the economic crisis were domestic. Roosevelt campaigned on promises of fiscal orthodoxy, cuts in federal expenditure, and a balanced budget, but Hoover suspected that Roosevelt's domestic priorities would lead to the abandonment of the gold standard, dollar deflation, and the introduction of inflationary policies. This was not yet, but would become, Roosevelt's agenda. Almost immediately on taking office the new president called Congress into special session, halted all transactions in gold, and declared a four-day national banking holiday that was later extended. When the banks reopened deposits and gold began to flow back into the banking system.

The Americans were not forced off gold; the dollar was purposely floated in order to raise domestic prices. Roosevelt's unexpected suspension of dollar convertability on 19 April, while the British and French representatives, MacDonald and Herriot, were on their way to Washington for pre-conference talks, destroyed French apathy. Gold exports from America ceased, and instead of a Franco-American partnership that would persuade Britain to return to gold, France was faced with the prospect of financial isolation. Roosevelt's unprecedented action in taking the dollar off gold to raise prices changed the international financial landscape. The pre-conference talks with Roosevelt were wide-ranging but inconclusive. The president gave no indication of what he expected to do with the dollar. No one knew whether he would go for depreciation to raise the American price level or support central-bank co-operation in an effort to stabilize world currencies. The president was not impressed by his European visitors, who expressed a variety of conflicting views on currency and trade questions but showed no inclination to compromise their existing positions. There was little enthusiasm for reducing tariffs, even should the president support his secretary of state's internationalist approach to trade questions and convince the Congress to follow Hull's lead. Schacht, the Nazi-appointed president of the Reichsbank (1933–9), in his May talks with Roosevelt (whom he thought quite similar to Hitler!) threatened a default on American commercial debts frozen under the standstill agreements. The subsequent news that Schacht and Norman had renewed the Anglo-German standstill agreement only increased the president's suspicions and anger at European duplicity. As the dollar fell on the international exchanges, Roosevelt became less interested in any stabilization agreement. In the final days of May, however, he joined Daladier and MacDonald in backing a temporary stabilization agreement for the duration of the conference, in the hope that such an agreement, after weeks of inconclusive talks between the central bankers, would halt speculation over currency issues and allow delegates to get on with other financial and trade questions.

Unfortunately for Roosevelt's hopes, public attention was almost entirely focused, even after the World Economic Conference opened, on the talks between the treasury representatives and central bankers at the British Treasury and Bank of England. The supposedly secret deliberations were held in the full glare of press publicity. Although the French initiated the tripartite financial talks, they were 'remarkably passive, and grudging',[38] and offered nothing concrete beyond a warning that no progress could be made on economic matters without at least the temporary stabilization of the dollar and pound. It hardly helped that, fearing a more radical turn in American policy, the French began to press for a permanent stabilization agreement. The American delegates had come without instructions. They, like the delegates to the conference, represented the internationalist side of Roosevelt's diplomacy at a moment when mainly short-term developments were pushing the president in a nationalist direction.[39] The British were torn between wanting to avoid competitive depreciation and inflationary chaos in Europe and keeping the advantages of the depreciated pound and the sterling bloc. Despite all the difficulties, the central bankers succeeded in working out technical agreements limiting exchange-rate fluctuations between the three currencies. The Anglo-American bankers, moreover, agreed to a declaration cautiously promising a future return to gold under 'proper conditions'. The final arrangements, as the central bankers knew, were not in their hands. News of the agreement leaked,

[38] Kenneth Mouré, *Managing the Franc Poincaré: Economic Understanding and Political Constraint in French Monetary Policy, 1928–1936* (Cambridge, 1991), 105.
[39] Patricia Clavin, 'The Fetishes of So-Called International Bankers: Central Bank Co-operation for the World Economic Conference, 1932–3', *Contemporary European History*, 1: 3 (1992), 300.

the exchange markets firmed, and American commodity and stock markets declined. There was an immediate American reaction. Roosevelt not only rejected the stabilization rate ($4.00 to the pound) as too low, but in a series of cables made clear his objections to any programme that would limit his right to control fluctuations in the value of the dollar.

With the announcement of Roosevelt's rejection on 22 June, rumours circulated that the conference would collapse. The French and the nations on gold pressed Britain for a firm commitment to monetary stabilization, warning of monetary chaos in Europe. The British would go no further than a currency declaration; Chamberlain rejected Dominion and Indian pressure to align the pound with the dollar, but he would not lead an anti-American European bloc. On 28 June Britain and the gold-bloc nations agreed on an innocuous declaration, further weakened at British insistence so that the Americans could join, calling for a return to monetary stability as quickly as practicable and recognizing that all countries desired an eventual return to the gold standard 'under proper conditions'.[40] The draft declaration was sent, via Washington, to the president, who had begun a ten-day sailing holiday. On 1 July Roosevelt sent Hull a detailed rejection of the stabilization agreement. The next day he cabled his 'bombshell message' for release to the conference on 3 July. 'The world will not long be lulled by the specious fallacy of achieving a temporary and probably an artificial stability in foreign exchange on the part of a few large countries only', Roosevelt wrote. 'The sound internal economic situation of a nation is a greater factor in its well-being than the price of its currency.'[41] Dismissing the 'old fetishes of so-called international bankers', Roosevelt promised their replacement by a dollar which would keep its same purchasing and debt-paying power for a generation. Told of the anger of the five gold countries and MacDonald's despair, Roosevelt explained to Hull that he had purposely used harsh language because he felt that the conference was concerned only with the temporary stabilization talks and was ignoring its main objectives. Mainly due to the efforts of the Americans, who did not want Roosevelt blamed for the demise of the conference, the committees continued to meet for another three weeks, but the heart had gone out of the talks. No progress was made with regard to tariff reductions or production controls or with the implementation of the recommendations for helping the Danubian nations. The president's blunt rejection of the temporary stabilization agreement, marked by its extreme hostility towards the

[40] Calvin, 'Fetishes', 300.
[41] Robert Dallek, *Franklin D. Roosevelt and American Foreign Policy, 1932–1945* (New York, 1979), 54.

European participants, had brought the conference to an effective end, and it limped morosely to a close on 27 July.

Though Roosevelt's 'bombshell message' had led to the spectacular collapse of the stabilization talks, ultimate responsibility for the demise of the conference was not his alone. The conditions for international economic co-operation did not exist in 1933. Even the three major players, Britain, the United States, and France, who supposedly shared common liberal values, found it difficult to reach agreements that would bridge their financial and commercial differences. Neither the Americans nor the British were prepared to lead a co-ordinated move towards currency depreciation. Contrary to the hopes of the European gold countries, however, Britain had no intention of returning to gold. Nor would she retreat from her new protective policies. Though a temporary stabilization agreement would have been helpful (and Roosevelt's stated reasons for veto were open to question), the French were intent on permanent stabilization and showed little interest in the conference agenda. A return to gold-standard orthodoxies, contrary to French beliefs, was hardly the way to bring about recovery. The other powers, including Germany, which was pleased not to be blamed for the collapse of the conference, drew their own conclusions from the behaviour of the big three. The Germans seized the opportunity to play on the differences between Washington and London in order to prevent the creation of a common front against the National Socialist regime. The Nazis believed that they could 'wait to heap the odium of the failure on to others, while ensuring that Germany reaped the benefits'.[42] The conference ended in a chorus of mutual recriminations.

Rather than the international chaos predicted by the French, a hybrid system of currency and trading blocs, each around a major power, emerged in the international arena. The sterling bloc was the first to appear on the scene. While Roosevelt experimented with the value of the dollar in an effort to raise prices and the Americans discouraged pegging, Britain supported nations that voluntarily joined the sterling bloc. To quiet fears that Britain might join the gold-bloc nations during the conference, the British Commonwealth Declaration was signed on 27 July 1933, resolving to raise prices, to ease credit and money without monetizing government deficits, to eventually return to the gold standard, and to keep exchange rates stable within the sterling area. The prospect of stable exchange rates encouraged Sweden, Denmark, and Argentina to join the bloc (Norway was already officially pegged to sterling). During the pre-conference Geneva talks, and in London, a second bloc emerged made up of those states which stayed on the gold

---

[42] Quoted in Clavin, *The Great Depression in Europe, 1929–1939*, 165.

standard. France, Belgium, Czechoslovakia, the Netherlands, Poland, Italy, and Switzerland worked together in a very loose combination in order to protect their existing parities on gold. They were able to check the speculation against the Dutch florin and Swiss franc that had persisted all through the conference, but with little cohesion and no organization could not agree on other common policies beyond maintaining gold parities. Their central banks failed to co-operate and no trading bloc was formed. Even bilateral negotiations were circumscribed by the high prices resulting from overvalued currencies and by a general unwillingness to open domestic markets to others. As the only group of countries following harsh deflationary regimes, they remained mired in the depression even when recovery began elsewhere. Czechoslovakia devalued in 1934, and though Mussolini boasted about the stability of the lira, exchange-rate controls were soon adopted in Italy. The remaining countries continued to pursue deflationary policies, but each was subsequently forced (France in 1936 after a long battle) to devalue its currency. A third bloc of nations, the so-called 'exchange control countries', Germany, Hungary, and most of the east European states, though nominally on gold, acted individually to end convertibility into other currencies or gold. All tightened controls over foreign exchange and embarked on centrally directed economic policies. Bilateral clearing agreements became the norm in managing external trade, allowing Nazi Germany to greatly expand its economic influence throughout the region.

The depression and financial crisis were further blows to the weak political base of the Weimar republic, which had shouldered the burden of defeat, the Versailles treaty, inflation and hyperinflation, and a stabilization that had alienated many of those most needed to assure the republic's survival. 'It would have taken a very strong democratic tradition and commitment', Gerald Feldman has written, 'to withstand these objective circumstances, and these were obviously absent.'[43] A depression of unusual depth underscored the existing fragmentation of Weimar's political culture and the growth of anti-democratic sentiments among various interest groups across the political spectrum. The depression opened the way for the right-wing, nationalist, anti-republican elite to take power and to create, as they had always wanted, an authoritarian regime. It was these 'right-wing gravediggers of the Republic' who made Hitler chancellor in January 1933. The Nazi authorities, building on the modest expansionary programmes of Papen and Schleicher, capitalized on the cyclical upswing of 1933–4. The highly

[43] G. R. Feldman, 'Hitler's Rise to Power and the Political Culture', *German Politics and Society*, 14 (Spring, 1996), 99.

successful attack on unemployment paid economic and political dividends. If, as Harold James has argued, during the first years of Hitler's rule 'there was little that was specifically Nazi about the German economy', Nazi activity, energy, and propaganda raised expectations and hopes that fed the revival and increased the regime's popularity.[44] While opposition existed, terror enforced compliance. A pragmatist like Roosevelt, Hitler took power without any specific economic programme, but his political purposes were of an entirely different and avowedly revolutionary order. While not imposing Soviet-like controls over the economy (the Five Year Plans and Soviet methods were studied closely), Hitler would aim at the creation of an autarchic state with expansionist aims in mind.

Many economic historians, with some notable exceptions, have accepted the Eichengreen–Temin thesis that the gold standard itself was the 'primary transmission mechanism' of the Great Depression, and that only its abandonment and the adoption of reflationary policies would have brought it to an end.[45] Those states which abandoned gold recovered the fastest; those that stayed on gold and pursued deflationary policies suffered the longest; and those countries that remained on gold but introduced a battery of defensive measures, including exchange controls, fell somewhere in between. Successive unilateral devaluations and the haphazard way in which they took place increased the balance-of-payments pressures on those still on gold. The 'beggar-thy-neighbour' effects of the British and American devaluations hit Belgium and France with particular severity. Countries in eastern Europe, too, found their currencies overvalued by some 60 per cent by the end of 1933, with a corresponding drop in their export receipts. Almost everywhere trade barriers went up, effectively cutting or channelling trade into the newly created trading blocs or into bilateral clearings.

Recovery from the depth of the depression, in 1933 and 1934, except for the gold bloc, was slow and uneven, and associated with home rather than international markets. World trade actually diminished in the course of the 1930s, though the European share remained constant at about 29 per cent. Trade was diverted rather than increased. There was no return to the capital flows and international investments of the previous decade. The direction of capital flows changed dramatically, large amounts of short-term capital went from the debtor to the creditor

[44] Harold James, 'Innovation and Conservatism in Economic Recovery: The Alleged 'Nazi Recovery' of the 1930s', in W. R. Garside (ed.), *Capitalism in Crisis: International Responses to the Great Depression* (London, 1993).

[45] Kenneth Mouré, *The Gold Standard Allusion*; M. Flandreau, C.-L. Holtfrerich, and H. James (eds.), *International Financial History in the Twentieth Century: System and Anarchy* (Cambridge, 2003). See essays by K. Mouré and S. Schuker.

TABLE 36. Growth of Industrial Production, 1929–1934 (%)

Countries/Regions	1929–32	1929–33	1929–34
Gold bloc	−28.17	−22.60	−21.84
Exchange control	−33.50	−31.70	−21.24
Sterling area	−8.75	−2.53	8.88
Other countries with depreciated currencies	−17.48	−1.63	3.26

Note: Figures are calculated as unweighted averages of country data. Gold bloc: Belgium, France, Netherlands, Poland, Switzerland; Exchange control: Austria, Czechoslovakia, Germany, Hungary, Italy; Sterling area: Denmark, Finland, Norway, Sweden, UK; Other depreciators: Brazil, Colombia, Chile, Mexico, Costa Rica, Guatemala, Nicaragua, El Salvador, USA.

Source: Barry Eichengreen, Golden Fetters: The Gold Standard and the Great Depression 1919–1939 (Oxford, 1992), 351.

TABLE 37. Indices of World Trade (1929 = 100)

	1932	1933	1934	1935	1936	1937
Value at current prices	39	35	34	35	38	46
Volume	75	75	78	82	86	96
Price	52	47	44	42	44	48

Source: C. H. Feinstein, P. Temin, and G. Toniolo, The European Economy Between the Wars (Oxford, 1997), 170.

nations as asset-holders tried to preserve their investments in the face of currency depreciation and widespread fears of inflation. Speculators fuelled the flow of 'hot money'. As Americans eschewed investment in Europe, and neither political nor economic developments favoured a revival of tourism, the inflow of capital, mainly from Europe, and the American trade surplus resulted in a massive increase in American gold holdings by 1938. Long-term investment remained relatively stable; Britain, the United States, and France retained important external assets, and the British, with more than half (58.7 per cent) of their portfolio concentrated within the empire, suffered far less than the Americans from the national defaults that took place elsewhere. Those without empires looked on with envy.

The depression left in its wake a fragmented global economy. The preoccupation with national revival fanned existing antagonisms between the states. Recovery in Britain and the United States increased commercial enmities as well as their shared distrust of France. The crises of 1931–3 had shown that France was too weak to stabilize the international monetary system on its own, but the British and Americans believed that French actions had encouraged its destabilization. As France entered a period of prolonged depression and political instability, neither country offered much in the way of assistance. In eastern Europe the trend towards greater state intervention and the adoption of autarchic policies gave added importance to the traditional nationalisms of the region. Dangerously for all those who sought a respite from the upheavals of the Great Depression, Germany and Japan each embarked on policies of self-renewal that put further strains on the surviving international structure. The World Economic Conference proved to be the last of the international efforts to promote financial and economic co-operation. Its failure convinced the participants that there was little to be gained from co-operative action and confirmed the movement away from internationalism, and towards the adoption of individual recovery agendas dictated by exclusively national political and economic objectives. The more forward-looking hopes of the 1920s had been abandoned. Was it not significant that the 1933 World Economic Conference, called to promote international co-operation, was housed among the relics in a geological museum?

Books

AUBOIN, ROGER, *The Bank for International Settlements, 1930–1955*, Essays in International Finance, no. 22 (Princeton, 1955).

BARBER, WILLIAM J., *From New Era to New Deal: Herbert Hoover, the Economists and American Economic Policy, 1921–1933* (Cambridge, 1985).

BECKER, JOSEF and HILDEBRAND, KLAUS (eds.), *Internationale Beziehungen in der Weltwirtschaftskrise, 1929–1933: Referate und Diskussionsbeiträge eines Augsburger Symposiums, 28. März bis 1. April 1979* (Munich, 1980).

BENNETT, EDWARD W., *Germany and the Diplomacy of the Financial Crisis, 1931* (Cambridge, Mass., 1962).

—— *German Rearmament and the West, 1932–1933* (Princeton, 1979).

BERNSTEIN, MICHAEL A., *The Great Depression: Delayed Recovery and Economic Change in America, 1929–1939* (Cambridge, 1987).

BOND, BRIAN, *British Military Policy Between the Two World Wars* (Oxford, 1980).

BORCHARDT, KNUT, *Perspectives on Modern German Economic History and Policy*, trans. Peter Lambert (Cambridge, 1991). Esp. chapter 9: 'Constraints and Room for Manoeuvre in the Great Depression of the Early Thirties: Towards a Revision of the Received Historical Picture'.

BORDO, MICHAEL D., GOLDIN, CLAUDIA, and WHITE, EUGENE N. (eds.), *The Defining Moment: The Great Depression and the American Economy in the Twentieth Century* (Chicago and London, 1998).

CAIRNCROSS, ALEC and EICHENGREEN, BARRY, *Sterling in Decline: The Devaluations of 1931, 1949 and 1967* (Oxford, 1983).

CAPIE, FORREST, *Depression and Protectionism: Britain Between the Wars* (London, 1983).

—— and WOOD, GEOFFREY E. (eds.), *Financial Crises and the World Banking System* (London, 1986).

CLARK, IAN, *Globalization and Fragmentation: International Relations in the Twentieth Century* (Oxford, 1997).

CLARKE, PETER, *The Keynesian Revolution in the Making, 1924–1936* (Oxford, 1988).

CLAVIN, PATRICIA, *The Failure of Economic Diplomacy: Britain, Germany, France and the United States, 1931–1936* (Basingstoke, 1996).

—— *The Great Depression in Europe, 1929–1939* (Basingstoke, 2000).

COTTRELL, P. L. and MOGGRIDGE, D. E. (eds.), *Money and Power: Essays in Honour of L. S. Pressnell* (Basingstoke, 1988).

DRUMMOND, IAN M., *British Economic Policy and the Empire, 1919–1939* (London, 1972).

—— *Imperial Economic Policy, 1917–1939* (London, 1974).

—— *The Floating Pound and the Sterling Area, 1931–1939* (Cambridge, 1981).

EICHENGREEN, BARRY, *Golden Fetters: The Gold Standard and the Great Depression, 1929–1939* (New York, 1992).

—— and LINDERT, PETER H. (eds.), *The International Debt Crisis in Historical Perspective* (Cambridge, Mass. and London, 1989).

FERRELL, R. H., *American Diplomacy in the Great Depression* (New Haven, Conn., 1957).

FORBES, NEIL, *Doing Business With the Nazis: Britain's Economic and Financial Relations with Germany, 1931–1939* (London and Portland, Oreg., 2000).

FRIEDMAN, M. and SCHWARTZ, A. J., *Monetary History of the U.S., 1867–1960* (Princeton, 1963).

GALBRAITH, JOHN K., *The Great Crash, 1929* (Boston, 1955).

GARSIDE, W. R. (ed.), *Capitalism in Crisis: International Responses to the Great Depression* (London, 1993).

GORLOV, SERGEI, *Sovershenno Sekretno: Alians Moskva—Berlin, 1920–1933 gg (Voenno-politichieskie otnoshenia SSSR–Germania)* [Top Secret: The Moscow–Berlin Alliance, 1920–1933 (Military-Political Relations, USSR–Germany)] (Moscow, 2001).

HOLLAND, R. F., *Britain and the Commonwealth Alliance, 1918–1939* (London, 1981).

HOWSON, SUSAN, *Sterling's Managed Float: The Operations of the Exchange Equalization Account, 1932–1939* (Princeton, 1980).

JACKSON, JULIAN, *The Politics of Depression in France, 1932–1936* (Cambridge, 1985).

JAMES, HAROLD, *The Reichsbank and Public Finance in Germany 1924–1933: A Study of the Politics of Economics During the Great Depression* (Frankfurt a.M., 1983).

—— *The German Slump: Politics and Economics, 1924–1936* (Oxford, 1986).

—— *The End of Globalization: Lessons From the Great Depression* (Cambridge, Mass., 2001).

JOHNSON, H. CLARK, *Gold, France, and the Great Depression, 1919–1932* (New Haven, Conn., 1997).

JONES, LARRY EUGENE, *German Liberation and the Dissolution of the Weimar Party System, 1918–1933* (Chapel Hill, NC, 1988).

KENNEDY, DAVID M., *Freedom From Fear: The American People in Depression and War, 1929–1945* (Oxford, 1999).

KINDLEBERGER, CHARLES, *The World in Depression, 1929–1939* (London, New York and Sydney, 1973).

KRUEDENER, JÜRGEN BARON VON (ed.), *Economic Crisis and Political Collapse: The Weimar Republic, 1924–1933* (Oxford, 1990).

KUNZ, DIANE B., *The Battle for Britain's Gold Standard in 1931* (London, New York and Sydney 1987).

LINK, W., *Die amerikanische Stabilisierunqspolitik in Deutschland 1921–1932. Die Vereinigten Staaten von Amerika der Wiederaufstieg Deutschlands und der Erste Weltkrieg* (Düsseldorf, 1970).

McMURRY, DEAN SCOTT, *Deutschland und die Sowjetunion 1933–1936: Ideologie, Machtpolitik und Wirtschaftsbeziehungen* (Cologne, 1979).

MEYER, F. V., *Britain, the Sterling Area and Europe* (Cambridge, 1952).

MIDDLETON, ROGER, *Towards the Managed Economy: Keynes, the Treasury and the Fiscal Policy Debate of the 1930s* (London, 1985).

MOURÉ, KENNETH, *Managing the Franc Poincaré: Economic Understanding and Political Constraint in French Monetary Policy, 1928–1936* (Cambridge, 1991).

—— *The Gold Standard Illusion: France, the Bank of France, and the International Gold Standard, 1914–1939* (Oxford, 2002).

MURRAY, WILLIAMSON, KNOX, MACGREGOR, and BERNSTEIN, ALVIN (eds.), *The Making of Strategy: Rulers, States and War* (Cambridge and New York, 1994).

NASH, G. D., *The Crucial Era: Great Depression and World War II, 1929–1945* (2nd edn., New York, 1992).

PATCH, JR., WILLIAM L., *Heinrich Brüning and the Dissolution of the Weimar Republic* (Cambridge, 1998).

POLLARD, SIDNEY, *The Development of the British Economy: 1914–1990* (4th edn., London, 1992).

SCHULZ, GERHARD, *Zwischen Demokratie und Diktatur: Verfassungspolitik und Reichsreform in der Weimarer Republik* (Berlin, 1963, 1992).

—— *Aufstieg des Nationalsozialismus: Krise und Revolution in Deutschland* (Frankfurt a.M. Berlin Vienna, 1975).

—— *Von Brüning zu Hitler: der Wandel des politischen Systems in Deutschland 1930–1933* (Berlin, 1992).

SKIDELSKY, ROBERT, *Politicians and the Slump* (Oxford, 1967).

STIEFEL, DIETER, *Die große Krise in einem kleinen Land: Österreichische Finanz- und Wirtschaftspolitik, 1929–1938* (Vienna, 1988).

SVENNILSON, INGVAR, *Growth and Stagnation in the European Economy* (Geneva, 1954).

TEICHOVA, ALICE, *An Economic Background to Munich: International Business and Czechoslovakia, 1918–1938* (London and New York, 1974).

—— *Kleinstaaten im Spannungsfeld der Großmächte: Wirtschaft und Politik in Mittel-und Südosteuropa in der Zwischenkriegszeit* (Munich, 1988).

TEICHOVA, ALICE, and COTTRELL, P. L. (eds.), *International Business and Central Europe, 1918–1939* (Leicester, 1983).

TEMIN, PETER, *Lessons From the Great Depression* (Cambridge, Mass. and London, 1989).

TONIOLO, GIANNI, *L'economia dell'Italia fascista* (Rome, 1980).

WÄCHTER, DETLEF, *Von Stresemann zu Hitler: Deutschland 1928 bis 1933 im Spiegel der Berichte des englischen Botschafters Sir Horace Rumbold* (Frankfurt a.M., 1997).

WILLIAMSON, PHILIP, *National Crisis and National Government: British Politics, the Economy and Empire, 1926–1932* (Cambridge, 1992).

WILSON, J. H., *American Business and Foreign Policy, 1920–1933* (Lexington, Ky., 1971).

WURM, CLEMENS A., *Business, Politics and International Relations: Steel, Cotton and International Cartels in British Politics, 1924–1939* (Cambridge, 1993).

Articles

AGUADO, IAGO GIL, 'The Creditanstalt Crisis of 1931 and the Failure of the Austro-German Customs Union Project', *Historical Journal*, 44: 1 (2001).

AUBOIN, R., 'The Bank of International Settlement, 1930–1933', *Studies in International Finance*, 22 (1985).

BALDERSTON, THEO, 'The Origins of Economic Instability in Germany, 1924–1930: Market Forces versus Economic Policy', *Vierteljahresschrift für Sozial- und Wirtschaftsgeschichte*, 69 (1982).

BERNACKE, B. and JAMES, H., 'The Gold Standard, Deflation and Financial Crisis in the Great Depression: An International Comparison', in R. G. Hubbard (ed.), *Financial Markets and Financial Crises* (Chicago, 1991).

BESSEL, RICHARD, 'Why Did the Weimar Republic Collapse?', in Ian Kershaw (ed.), *Weimar: Why Did German Democracy Fail?* (London, 1990).

BOOTH, ALAN, 'The British Reaction to the Economic Crisis', in W. R. Garside (ed.), *Capitalism in Crisis: International Responses to the Great Depression* (London, 1993).

BORCHARDT, KNUT, 'Could and Should Germany Have Followed Great Britain in Leaving the Gold Standard?', *Journal of European Economic History*, 13 (1984).

—— 'A Decade of Debate About Brüning's Economic Policy', in Jürger Baron von Krüdener (ed.), *Economic Crisis and Political Collapse: The Weimar Republic, 1924–1933* (New York and Oxford, 1990).

BOUVIER, JEAN, 'The French Banks, Inflation and the Economic Crisis, 1919–1939', *Journal of Economic History*, 2 (1984).

BOYCE, ROBERT, 'World Depression, World War: Some Economic Origins of the Second World War', in id. and Esmonde M. Robertson, (eds.), *Paths to War: New Essays on the Origins of the Second World War* (London, 1989).

—— 'Economics and the Crisis of British Foreign Policy Management, 1914–1945', in Dick Richardson and Glyn Stone (eds.), *Decisions and Diplomacy: Essays in Twentieth-Century International History in Memory of George Grun and Esmonde Robertson* (London, 1995).

—— 'Business As Usual: The Limits of French Economic Diplomacy, 1926–1933', in id. (ed.), *French Foreign and Defence Policy, 1918–1940* (London, 1998).

CAIN, P. J. and HOPKINS, A. G., 'Gentlemanly Capitalism and British Expansion Overseas: II. New Imperialism, 1850–1945', *Economic History Review*, 40 (1987).

CIOCCA, PIERLUIGI and TONIOLO, GIANNI, 'Industry and Finance in Italy, 1918–1940', *Journal of European Economic History*, 13: 2 (1984).

CLAVIN, PATRICIA, 'The World Economic Conference of 1933: The Failure of Political Internationalism', *Journal of European Economic History*, 20: 3 (1991).

—— ' "The Fetishes of So-Called International Bankers": Central Bank Co-operation for the World Economic Conference, 1932–3', *Contemporary European History*, 1: 3 (1992).

EICHENGREEN, BARRY, 'The Origins and Nature of the Great Slump Revisited', *Economic History Review*, 45: 2 (1992).

—— and UZAN, M., 'The World Economic Conference as an Instance of Failed Economic Cooperation', Berkeley Department of Economics, Working Paper 90–149 (Berkeley, Cal., 1990).

FERDERER, J. PETER and ZALEWSKI, DAVID A., 'To Raise the Golden Anchor? Financial Crises and Uncertainty During the Great Depression', *Journal of Economic History*, 59: 3 (1999).

GARSIDE, W. R., 'Party Politics, Political Economy and British Protectionism, 1919–1932', *History*, 83 (1998).

—— and GREAVES, J. J., 'Rationalisation and Britain's Industrial Malaise: The Interwar Years Revisited', *Journal of European Economic History*, 26: 1 (1997).

GOLDINGER, WALTER, 'Das Projekt einer deutsch-österreichischen Zollunion von 1931', in *Österreich und Europa* (Graz, 1965).

HEINEMAN, JOHN, L. 'Constantin von Neurath and German Policy at the London Economic Conference of 1933: Backgrounds to the Resignation of Alfred Hugenberg', *Journal of Modern History*, 41, 2 (1969).

HEYDE, PHILIPP, 'Frankreich und das Ende der Reparationen: das Scheitern der französischen Stabilisierungskonzepte in der Weltwirtschaftskrise 1930–1932', *Vierteljahrshefte für Zeitgeschichte*, 48 (2000).

JAMES, HAROLD, 'The Causes of the German Banking Crisis in 1931', *Economic History Review*, 37 (1984).

—— 'Economic Reasons for the Collapse of the Weimar Republic', in Ian Kershaw (ed.), *Weimar: Why Did German Democracy Fail?* (London, 1990).

—— 'Financial Flows Across Frontiers During the Inter-war Depression' *Economic History Review*, 45: 3 (1992).

—— 'Innovation and Conservatism in Economic Recovery: The Alleged "Nazi Recovery of the 1930s', in W. R. Garside (ed.), *Capitalism in Crisis: International Responses to the Great Depression* (London, 1993).

MAIER, CHARLES, 'The Economies of Fascism and Nazism', in id. (ed.), *In Search of Political Stability: Explorations in Historical Political Economy* (Cambridge, 1987).

MOGGRIDGE, D. E., 'The Gold Standard and National Financial Policies, 1913–39', in Peter Mathias and Sidney Pollard (eds.), *The Cambridge Economic History of Europe*. Vol. 8: *The Industrial Economies: The Development of Economic and Social Policies* (Cambridge, 1989).

MOURÉ, KENNETH, ' "Une éventualité absolument exclue": French Reluctance to Devalue, 1933–1936', *French Historical Studies*, 15: 3 (1988).

ORDE, ANNE, 'The Origins of the German–Austrian Customs Union Affair of 1931', *Central European History*, 13 (1980).

POGGE VON STRANDMANN, HARTMUT, 'Industrial Primacy in German Foreign Relations? Myths and Realities in Russian–German Relations at the End of the Weimar Republic', in Richard Bessel and Ernst J. Feuchtwanger (eds.), *Social Change and Political Development in Weimar Germany* (London and Ottawa, 1981).

REDISH, ANGELA, 'British Financial Imperialism after the First World War' in Raymond E. Dumett (ed.) *Gentlemanly Capitalism and British Imperialism: The New Debate on Empire* (London, 1999).

SCHWARZ, L. D., 'Searching for Recovery: Unbalanced Budgets, Deflation and Rearmament in France during the 1930s', in W. R. Garside (ed.), *Capitalism in Crisis: International Responses to the Great Depression* (London, 1993).

TEMIN, PETER, 'Transmission of the Great Depression', *Journal of Economic Perspectives*, 7: 2 (1993).

TÜRKES, MUSTAFA, 'The Balkan Pact and its Immediate Implications for the Balkan States, 1930–1934', *Middle Eastern Studies*, 30: 1 (1994).

WILLIAMSON, PHILIP, 'A "Banker's Ramp"? Financiers and the British Political Crisis of August 1931', *English Historical Review*, 99 (1984).

Eastern Europe and the Depression

Books

ALDCROFT, DEREK H. and MOREWOOD, STEPHEN, *Economic Change in Eastern Europe Since 1918* (Aldershot, 1995).

BARLAS, DILEK, *Étatism and Diplomacy in Turkey: Economic and Foreign Policy Strategies in an Uncertain World, 1929–1939* (Leiden, New York, and Cologne, 1998).

BEREND, I. T. and RÁNKI, GYÖRGY, *Economic Development in East Central Europe in the 19th and 20th Centuries* (New York, 1974).

COTTRELL, PHILIP LEONARD (ed.), *Rebuilding the Financial System in Central and Eastern Europe, 1918–1994* (Aldershot, 1997).

KAISER, D. E., *Economic Diplomacy and the Origins of the Second World War: Germany, Britain, France and Eastern Europe, 1930–1939* (Princeton, 1980).

KASER, M. C. and RADICE E. A. (eds.), *The Economic History of Eastern Europe 1919–1975*. Vol. 1: *Economic Structure and Performance Between the Wars* (Oxford, 1985).

—— *The Economic History of Eastern Europe 1919–1975*. Vol. II: *Interwar Policy, the War and Reconstruction* (Oxford, 1986).

LAMPE, J. R. and JACKSON, M. R., *Balkan Economic History, 1550–1950* (Bloomington, Ind., 1982).

RÁNKI, GYÖRGY, *Economy and Foreign Policy: The Struggle of the Great Powers for Hegemony in the Danube Valley, 1919–1939* (Boulder, Col., 1983).

Articles

ALDCROFT, D. H., 'Eastern Europe in an Age of Turbulence, 1919–1950', *Economic History Review*, 41 (1988).

—— 'Depression and Recovery: The Eastern European Experience', in W. R. Garside (ed.), *Capitalism in Crisis: International Responses to the Great Depression* (London, 1993).

BEREND, I. T., 'Agriculture', in M. C. KASER and E. A. RADICE (eds.), *The Economic History of Eastern Europe 1919–1975*. Vol. 1: *Economic Structure and Performance Between the Wars* (Oxford, 1985).

COTTRELL, P. L., 'Aspects of Western Equity Investment in the Banking Systems of East Central Europe', in Alice Teichova and P. L. Cottrell (eds.), *International Business and Central Europe, 1918–1939* (Leicester, 1983).

DAVIES, R. W., 'Economic and Social Policy in the USSR, 1917–41', in Peter Mathias and Sidney Pollard (eds.), *The Cambridge Economic History of Europe.* Vol. 8: *The Industrial Economies: The Development of Economic and Social Policies* (Cambridge, 1989).

DRABEK, Z., 'Foreign Trade Performance and Policy', in M. C. Kaser and E. A. Radice (eds.), *The Economic History of Eastern Europe 1919–1975*. Vol. 1: *Economic Structure and Performance Between the Wars* (Oxford, 1985).

FISCHER-GALATI, S., 'Eastern Europe in the Twentieth Century: "Old Wine in New Bottles" ', in J. Held (ed.), *The Columbia History of Eastern Europe in the Twentieth Century* (New York, 1992).

KOFMAN, J., 'Economic Nationalism in East-Central Europe in the Interwar Period', in H. Szlajfer (ed.), *Economic Nationalism in East-Central Europe and South America* (Geneva, 1990).

NÖTEL, RUDOLF, 'International Capital Movements and Finance in Eastern Europe, 1919–1949', *Vierteljahresschrift für Sozial- und Wirtschaftsgeschichte*, 61 (1974).

—— 'Money, Banking and Industry in Prewar Austria and Hungary', *Journal of European Economic History*, 13 (1984).

—— 'International Credit and Finance', in M. C. Kaser and E. A. Radice (eds.), *The Economic History of Eastern Europe 1919–1975*. Vol. II: *Interwar Policy, the War and Reconstruction* (Oxford, 1986).

RÁNKI, GYÖRGY and TOMASZEWSKI, J., 'The Role of the State in Industry, Banking and Trade', in M. C. Kaser and E. A. Radice (eds.), *The Economic History of Eastern Europe 1919–1975*. Vol. II: *Interwar Policy, the War and Reconstruction* (Oxford, 1986).

RAUPACH, H., 'The Impact of the Great Depression in Eastern Europe', *Journal of Contemporary History*, 4 (1969).

Roon, Ger van, *Small States in Years of Depression: The Oslo Alliance 1930–1940* (Assen and Maastricht, 1989).

Salmon, Patrick, *Scandinavia and the Great Powers, 1890–1940* (Cambridge, 1997).

Stambrook, F. G., 'A British Proposal for the Danubian States: The Customs Union Project of 1932', *Slavonic and Eastern European Review*, 42 (1963).

Teichova, Alice, 'Structural Changes and Industrialisation in Interwar Central-East Europe', in P. Bairoch and M. Levy-Leboyer (eds.), *Disparities in Economic Development Since the Industrial Revolution* (London, 1981).

Teichova, Alice, 'Industry', in M. C. Kaser and E. A. Radice, (eds.), *The Economic History of Eastern Europe 1919–1975*. Vol. 1: *Economic Structure and Performance Between the Wars* (Oxford, 1985).

—— 'East-Central and South-East Europe 1919–39', in Peter Mathias and Sidney Pollard (eds.), *The Cambridge Economic History of Europe*. Vol. 8: *The Industrial Economies: The Development of Economic and Social Policies* (Cambridge, 1989).

—— 'Eastern Europe in Transition: Economic Development During the Interwar and Postwar Period', in id. (ed.), *Central Europe in the Twentieth Century: An Economic History Perspective* (Aldershot, 1997).

Zauberman, A., 'Russia and Eastern Europe, 1920–1970', in C. M. Cipolla (ed.), *The Fontana Economic History of Europle*, Vol. 6., Part 2: *Contemporary Economies* (London, 1976).

13

The Manchurian Crisis: The European Powers and the Far East

I

At 10:20 a.m. on 18 September 1931, in the suburb of Mukden, a bomb exploded on the Southern Manchurian railway. The damage was minimal but a Japanese patrol claimed they had been fired upon by Chinese soldiers and were forced to retaliate. By the following morning the Japanese had breached the walls of Mukden and occupied the city. It was a premeditated action, expected, albeit scarcely sanctioned, by the commander of the Kwantung army and by the military authorities in Tokyo. In the words of the Lytton Commission's later report on the incident, the Japanese executed their contingency plan 'with swiftness and precision' against Chinese opponents who were surprised and disorganized. So began the so-called 'Manchurian incident', which led ultimately to the creation of a Japanese puppet state, Manchukuo, and to Japan's withdrawal from the League of Nations, the first great power to desert Geneva. The Japanese move signalled the disappearance of what was left of the Washington agreements on China and posed a successful challenge to the League's peacekeeping functions. It was the failure of the League, coinciding with the collapse of the disarmament talks, which made a complex, confused, and remote dispute of considerable importance to the Europeans.

Japan's successful action in Manchuria has come to be seen as part of a nationalist upsurge against a western-created form of internationalism. The origins of the crisis can be traced to post-war nationalist movements in China and Japan, intent on change at home and the assertion of the full independence of their respective countries. For the Chinese this meant, beyond crushing the power of the contending warlords, the elimination of all forms of western privilege that compromised their sovereignty. In Tokyo, the conquest of Manchuria by force and without regard to foreign opinion demonstrated a rejection of the internationalist policies symbolized by participation in the League of Nations and in the so-called Washington system. The crisis did not lead immediately to war between Japan and China. It was far from obvious that

Japan would follow up its actions in Manchuria with further inroads into Chinese territory. Nor did the Japanese action carry with it the threat of conflict with Britain, the United States, or the Soviet Union, though individual Japanese spoke of an inevitable clash with one of the latter two. The withdrawal from the League was a voluntary act in accordance with the terms of the Covenant. Japan was condemned at Geneva for its actions in Manchuria but was not subjected to sanctions. It was far from clear in 1933 how far she would retreat into isolation. These events, nonetheless, marked a change in Japan's policy and in western perceptions of her intentions. They revealed, too, weaknesses in the international structure that had been created during the 1920s that called into question some of the fundamental principles on which it was based.

During the 1920s the Washington treaties of 1921–2 had provided the framework for great-power diplomacy in East Asia. The Soviet Union was the major absentee; it was neither invited to the Washington conference nor was it a party to any of the Washington treaties. Apart from the Five Power naval treaty, the Four Power and Nine Power treaties constituted the heart of the post-war political settlement in the Pacific (see discussion on pages 375–8). In the Four Power treaty the United States, Britain, France, and Japan agreed to respect the status quo and confer should any external threat or dispute between them threaten their insular possessions in the Pacific. The Nine Power treaty specifically mentioned China; signatories were to respect China's sovereignty, independence, territorial and administrative integrity, and to maintain the principle of equal opportunity for commerce and industry (the 'open door' principle) for all. China was to be given every opportunity to develop 'an effective and stable government'. It was awarded an immediate customs revenue increase to an effective 5 per cent and promised a future conference to prepare for Chinese tariff autonomy. It was these treaties that led to the use of the phrase 'Washington structure' or 'Washington system', though the terminology is not found in either the British or French sources.[1] It is highly questionable whether they actually constituted a 'system'. Each of the signatories could and did interpret the agreements as best fitted its own national interests during the 1920s. The treaties attempted to regulate relations between the imperial powers, but did not put an end to the empires themselves. There were no sanction clauses should any country embark on policies contrary to the 'Washington spirit'. In this sense the treaties were parchment arrangements, intended to maintain the regional status

---

[1] Ian Nish, *Japanese Foreign Policy, 1869–1942: Kasumigaseki to Miyakezaka* (London, 1977), 141.

Map 14. Nationalist China, 1930–33: Japanese incursions.

quo but to allow for the peaceful and gradual change acceptable to the participating states. The 'new internationalism' had been extended from Europe to the Pacific, with the important difference that the Americans were active participants in the Washington settlements.

The treaties reflected the changes that the war had brought to East Asia and recognized the new shifts in national influence. The British acknowledged the new position of the United States in accepting parity in capital ships with the Americans and in allowing the Anglo-Japanese treaty to lapse. Its replacement, the Four Power pact, was a broader but far looser security arrangement than the 1902 alliance. The Japanese, too, accommodated the Americans, though there were reservations in Tokyo both about the naval ratios and the political agreements. Many Japanese were dismayed by the ending of the popular British alliance that had been negotiated on the basis of full equality. Whatever its limitations on Japan's freedom of action, it had allowed the Japanese to pursue an imperial policy before and during the Great War. Japan, like Britain, joined the weaker Four Power pact—'We have discarded whiskey and accepted water'[2]—seen by its critics, however erroneously, as the product of Anglo-American collusion at Japan's expense. In renouncing its wartime policy of obtaining concessions in China, modifying some of its earlier demands on China, and accepting the 'open door' pledge for the future, opponents of the treaty argued that Japan had lost much and gained little. The treaty negotiators insisted that Japan had considerably improved relations with the United States and with China and had won recognition as an equal partner in shaping the post-war order in the Pacific. They rightly claimed that Japanese security had been enhanced and that it had much to gain, economically as well as politically, from a policy of conciliating China and co-operating with the British and Americans. The international policies Japan had adopted at the Versailles conference were now extended to the Far East.

The Chinese negotiators were given a warmer welcome on their return than their Japanese counterparts, mainly because Japan had agreed to leave Shantung. Admittedly, some members of the Chinese intelligentsia expressed strong reservations about the inferior status accorded China under the new agreements. Spurred by the doctrines of self-determination and by the Marxists winds, those who joined the ranks of Sun Yat-sen's nationalist movement, the Kuomintang, wanted faster and more radical changes than the gradual amelioration of China's subordinate status promised in the Nine Power treaty. Once political unity was achieved, would the imperial powers accept the abrogation of the unequal treaties and the abandonment of their special rights? Though at the time of the Washington conference China was weak and without a real central government, the seeds of a national revival had already been sown. It was the emergence of Chinese nationalism

---

[2] An unnamed Japanese diplomat in Richard Storry, *Japan and the Decline of the West in Asia, 1894–1943* (London, 1979).

that challenged the assumptions behind the Washington settlements and directly affected the positions of the excluded Russians as well as the British, the Americans, and Japanese. After thirteen years of civil anarchy Chiang Kai-shek in 1928 succeeded in uniting a major part of the country and created a Kuomintang government at Nanking. From 1923 until Chiang's purges of the Communists and Kuomintang leftists in 1927–8, the Bolsheviks and their Chinese supporters were one of the main driving forces behind the nationalists' military victories. Chiang's bloody purges were a stunning blow to Comintern hopes in China and had a critical impact both on the local situation and on the doctrinal debates and leadership quarrels in Moscow (see page 538). Admittedly, a core of Chinese Communists survived. An independent movement led by Chu The and Mao Tse-tung established itself in the rural border areas of south-east China and massed a considerable and well-disciplined guerrilla army, able repeatedly to defeat Chiang's German-trained troops. It was only at the end of 1934, with his fifth campaign, that Chiang succeeded in bottling up the Red Army in north-west China after its epochal 'Long March' of some 6,000 miles from its south-east China base.

In 1929 Chiang Kai-shek tried to evict the Russians from the co-managed Chinese Eastern Railway in northern China (see Map 14). Direct talks failed and the Soviets massed troops and attacked the Chinese forces, seizing the railway. Chiang was forced to retreat, and a truce was arranged restoring the previous joint Russo-Chinese administration of the railway. The final discussions were not concluded until late 1931, by which time the Soviet possession of the Chinese Eastern Railway posed a major problem in its relations with Japan. The Soviets were left with an important but exposed strategic outpost in Manchuria. In the early 1930s, Moscow was faced with an anti-Communist Chinese nationalist movement under Chiang Kai-shek's leadership and a revival of the traditional Russo-Japanese conflict along its Far Eastern borders.

While the troubled alliance between the Kuomintang and the Bolsheviks remained in place, the British became the main victims of the anti-foreign demonstrations that accompanied the Northern Expedition. An incident in Shanghai on 30 May 1925 resulted in a wave of anti-British sentiment and an effective boycott of British and other foreign goods in southern China and in Hong Kong. As the Northern Expedition moved into central China, the British concessions in the Yangtse Valley were explicitly targeted by Michael Borodin, the Comintern representative in China, and his Communist supporters. Chinese crowds overran the British concessions at Hankow and Kiukiang, which were surrendered to the Nationalists. The threat to the

International Concession at Shanghai provoked a more robust British reaction. In January 1927 a battalion of Indian troops was dispatched from Hong Kong and plans were made to send further forces to defend the foreign inhabitants of the international concessions. Neither the Americans nor the Japanese, though their assistance was requested, joined in this military riposte, which was a powerful demonstration of British strength. In March 1927 the Nationalists attacked Nanking; the British, American, and Japanese consulates were ravaged and three British subjects killed. In this case, Britain did not react, partly because no effective military response was possible. There was no way that the British could turn back the Nationalist tide by military means. The Foreign Office had already embarked on an alternative policy, which was pursued despite the Nationalist assaults. The leading Foreign Office expert on the Far East, Sir Victor Wellesley, advised that only a policy of conciliation and the restoration of China's sovereign rights and tariff autonomy would preserve British prestige and its commercial stake in China. Though the decision was reached before the open split between Chiang Kai-shek and the leftists, it was hoped in London that the Kuomintang would purge itself of its Communist allies and that negotiations with the moderates would be possible. The new line won further support in London with the failure of the special tariff conference called by the official Chinese government in 1925 to fulfil the promises made at the Washington conference. It was the last time that the three Washington treaty powers met together with the Chinese. By the time the conference ended in April 1926 China was engulfed in a civil war and the British, American, and Japanese delegates were hopelessly at odds with one another over the tariff question.

The British, who were blamed by the others for the conference's failure, reconsidered their policy during the summer and decided to act unilaterally. On 18 December 1926, in a public memorandum, the British declared their willingness to grant China unconditional tariff autonomy, to free all her revenues from foreign control, and to implement recommendations made for the improvement of the Chinese judicial system that would open the way to the future abolition of extraterritorial rights. There were assurances, too, that the British concessions would ultimately revert to Chinese control. Austen Chamberlain's 'Christmas message' was given a poor reception by the Americans and Japanese, but proved to be more than just 'solemn words'. Eugene Chen, the Nationalist minister for foreign affairs, and Owen O'Malley, the counsellor of the British Legation in Peking, concluded an agreement on 19 February 1927 effectively granting the Chinese control over the Hankow and Kiukiang concessions, with special safeguards for British subjects and trade. After Chiang's successes and break with the

Communists, the British opened talks with the Nationalists at Nanking along the lines of the Chamberlain message. The difficulty was that Chiang was not master in his own house. A new series of wars and factional disputes broke out; by the end of 1931 there were two Chinese governments, one at Nanking and the other at Canton. In the same year devastating floods had swept through the central provinces, drowning or leaving homeless hundreds of thousands of people, leading to appeals to the League for assistance. In January 1932 a British Foreign Office official noted: 'there is virtually no Chinese Government in existence; the nominal Government at Nanking is without power and on the point of collapse.'[3]

Japan was the third country most directly and fatally concerned with Chiang Kai-shek's campaigns. The resumption of the Northern March in 1928 threatened the position in Manchuria that had been established after the Japanese victory in the Russo-Japanese War of 1904–5. Chiang's moves northwards brought about the direct confrontation that had been avoided in the earlier stages of the Nationalist advance. Japan had a greater stake in China than either the British or the Americans, and its interests in Manchuria were of far more importance than those of Britain in central China. Seven out of every ten foreigners living in China were Japanese, the overwhelming majority in Manchuria. Before 1931 Japan's exports to China constituted 25 per cent of her total trade, as compared to Britain's 5 per cent. China absorbed nearly 80 per cent of Japan's foreign investments, as compared to less than 6 per cent of Britain's and less than 1.5 per cent of those of the United States.[4] At the end of 1930 about 35 per cent of all foreign investments in China were Japanese. These were mostly concentrated in Manchuria, in the many commercial and industrial enterprises connected with the South Manchurian Railway, the southern spur of the Chinese Eastern Railway that the Japanese took over, along with the Russian lease on Kwantung, after their victory over Russia in 1905. A Japanese agreement with China in 1915, which still exercised legal suzerainty over the area, extended the leases from twenty-five to ninety-nine years and guaranteed Japanese rights of priority for railway and other loans in South Manchuria and Eastern Inner Mongolia. Japan came to dominate the political and economic life of the railway zone; all its subjects in the rest of South Manchuria had the right to live, lease land, and trade there. The Chinese Eastern Railway was patrolled by Japanese guards backed

---

[3] Ian Nish (ed.), *Anglo-Japanese Alienation, 1919–1952: Papers of the Anglo-Japanese Conference on the History of the Second World War* (Cambridge, 1982), 38.

[4] Margaret Lamb and Nicholas Tarling, *From Versailles to Pearl Harbor: The Origins of the Second World War in Europe and Asia* (Basingstoke, 2001), 63.

TABLE 38. China's Trade with the UK, USA, and Japan, 1920–1931

	EXPORTS (%) 5-year Av.			IMPORTS (%) 5-year Av.			BALANCE OF TRADE 5-Year Av. (Mil. HKT & USD)					
	USA	JAPAN	UK*	USA	JAPAN	UK*	USA (HK Ta^)	($)	JAPAN (HK Ta)	($)	UK (HK Ta)	($)
1916–20	15.948	27.262	7.124	14.386	31.514	9.486	−2.9	−3.3	−75.6	−86.34	−35.8	−40.9
1921–25	15.948	25.892	5.882	16.54	24.996	10.098	−55.9	−45.72	−53.9	−43.15	−84.9	−68.6
1926–30	14.352	23.948	6.65	15.83	25.506	7.886	−70.9	−46.1	−95.6	−62.1	−46.1	−29.9
1931	13.22	29.13	6.65	18.73	23.78	7.83	−201.1	−68.3	−307.8	104.6	−55.4	−18.8

Note: *Excludes Hong Kong and British India.

Sources: Chen Tasi M.A and Kwan-Wai Chan D.C.S, Trend and Character of China's Foreign Trade 1912–1931, China Institute of Pacific Relations (Shanghai, 1933), 40–44, 52–53. Hsiao Liang-Lin, China's Foreign Trade Statistics (Harvard, 1965) 22–44, 148–50, 163–172, 191–2.

^ US balance of trade was negative during WW1, then moved into a positive balance in 1919, the 5-year average understates the true picture.

by the Kwantung army, which was responsible for the protection of Japanese subjects and enterprises in the railway zone and leased territory. The Kwantung army became the chief channel for directing Japanese policy in Manchuria. Officered by some of the most radical and expansionist elements in the Japanese army, it enjoyed a considerable degree of independence in its Manchurian activities. Korean peasants, forced off their own land by the Japanese occupation of Korea, had come to settle in considerable numbers, as had masses of Chinese attracted by the new economic opportunities in the railway zone. With abundant room for expansion and development, many in Tokyo, as well as in the Kwantung army, felt that Manchuria and Mongolia could be used to syphon off some of Japan's excess population and to supply the raw materials and foodstuffs needed to fuel the industrialization essential to Japanese existence and growth. 'Japan has been caught unawares within three unsurmountable walls: the tariff wall, the migration wall and the peace wall. The first wall excludes Japan's manufactured goods from other countries. The second cuts off the migration of her people. And the third prohibits the readjustment of the unequal distribution of territories among nations with different density of population.'[5]

It was to be expected that Japan would vigorously defend its interests in Manchuria, and both the British and the Americans accepted its right to protect its own citizens and enterprises against the assertive and nationally minded Kuomintang government. The Anglo-Americans took a somewhat sanguine view of possible Japanese action in Manchuria. Japanese anti-Bolshevism had united the Washington powers when a Soviet victory in China seemed possible, and as long as relations with the Soviet Union remained unsettled, if not hostile, the Japanese presence in north China was highly welcome. Through most of the 1920s, moreover, the Japanese had acted within the confines of the Washington treaties, and in some instances, over tariff autonomy and during the Shanghai riots, had proved more conciliatory towards the Chinese Nationalists than had the British. The policies followed by Shidehara Kijuro (foreign minister, 1924–7, 1929–31), and intermittently by his critic and political opponent, General Tanaka Giichi (premier and foreign minister, 1927–9), pointed towards a policy of future conciliation with China as long as Japan's special interests in Manchuria were recognized. Both men, while seeking to avoid entanglement in China's civil wars, watched Chiang Kai-shek's northern campaigns with considerable alarm as Japanese interests were threatened. Shidehara, though indentified

---

[5] Y. Tsurumi, 'Japan in the Modern World', *Foreign Affairs*, 9: 2 (Jan. 1931), 252, quoted in Sandra Wilson, 'The Manchurian Crisis and Moderate Japanese Intellectuals: The Japan Council of the Institute of Pacific Relations', *Modern Asian Studies*, 26: 3 (1992).

with the multilateralism of the Washington treaties, was willing to use force to defend the Japanese position but was unwilling to assist the British in their battles with the Nationalists between 1925 and 1927. He repeatedly turned down British requests for assistance, preferring to act on his own as he did in Hankow. Tanaka, who replaced the unpopular Shidehara in 1927 was dedicated to a more 'positive policy' which found expression in two military interventions in Shantung, first in 1927 and then in April 1928, when Japanese troops engaged the Kuomintang forces in a bloody encounter at Tsinan, the capital of Shantung, followed by a harsh, year-long occupation of the city. Tanaka's military interventions failed to stop the Nationalists' advance, and each was followed by highly effective anti-Japanese boycotts that seriously damaged Japanese trade. Sino-Japanese talks made no headway; nor was any progress made on the tariff question, which the other foreign powers had settled through negotiation.

   The British, at first, had welcomed Tanaka's 'positive policy', for unlike Shidehara, he appeared willing to move Japanese troops into northern China and hopefully might take a more active interest in the defense of Pekin and Tientsin. Their own position, however, began to improve as the new links with Chiang Kai-shek produced dividends and British trade in the Yangtse valley started to revive. It was Tanaka, who, in the summer of 1928, solicited British cooperation and whose efforts were met with a cool response in London. With the British and Americans already engaged in negotiations with Nanking over recognition and extraterritorial rights, the Japanese changed tack, and in talks with the Nationalists in 1929 arrived at a satisfactory tariff settlement and an acceptable compromise over Tsinan. The Japanese recognized the Kuomintang government on 3 June 1929. With less success, Tanaka tried to re-establish a common front with the British and Americans at a time when factional disputes had interrupted the westerners' talks with the Nationalists. While pressing on with the negotiations in Nanking, Tanaka also began to court the 'Old Marshal', Chang Tso-lin, Chiang Kai-shek's rival and the strongest Chinese warlord in Manchuria. With half-a-million fighting men at Pekin, the much-coveted capital of China, Chang was preparing to challenge Chiang Kai-shek for the control of north China. Tanaka saw Chang as a possible ally in Manchuria, but he did not want to sanction a new war in the north that might spill over into the northern provinces, damaging Japanese property and disrupting trade. His desires for negotiations were doomed to disappointment. A Kwantung army officer blew up the train taking Chang to Mukden, killing him in the misplaced hope that in the ensuing chaos the army leaders would seize Manchuria. In the meantime, Kuomintang officials encouraged local anti-Japanese feeling in

Manchuria and pressed on with the construction of their own railway lines to contest the monopoly of the Japanese-controlled South Manchurian Railway. The failure of his Chinese policies brought Tanaka down, and a new cabinet took office in July 1929 under Hamaguchi Osachi, with Shidehara again at the foreign ministry. Shidehara sought an overall diplomatic settlement with Nanking in line with the other two Washington treaty powers, but proved as tenacious as Tanaka in his defence of Japan's interests in Manchuria, seeking some form of Chinese recognition of Japan's rights in the province and objecting to their plans to build a rival railway system. Though he failed to move the Chinese, Shidahara's policies ominously provoked continued domestic criticism in military quarters and opposition circles.

II

Just at the time the Hamaguchi cabinet took office in 1929, Japan began to feel the effects of the world depression. The imposition of the harsh fiscal and financial policies needed to strengthen the yen against the dollar plunged the economy into deep distress. Swept by the same winds that were unleashed in Europe, all the tensions created by the political changes of the previous decade and the instability of Japan's economic growth came to the surface. Though formally a constitutional monarchy with a special place for the emperor, Japan's highly complicated governmental machinery operated with considerable difficulty, and corruption and bribery were rife throughout the system. The depression hit Japan with particular ferocity. The price of silk, Japan's most important export, fell dramatically and the volume of Japan's export trade dropped by more than 40 per cent between 1929 and 1930. Conditions were worst in the rural areas, where prices of rice and other agricultural crops fell some 30–40 per cent, and the drastic cutbacks in American imports of raw silk led to widespread impoverishment. The economic hardships and social dislocations in the countryside provided the dry timber for the nationalist cause. It was the militarists who took up the twin demands for an aggressive foreign policy and major political and social changes at home. The leaders of the Kwantung army, now a powerful and semi-autonomous force in Manchuria, and their supporters in Tokyo had actively propagandized in the late 1920s for the annexation of Manchuria and Mongolia. The region was to be the resource base for Japan's future role as the leading nation in East Asia, and its occupation the necessary prelude to that final and total war of mankind between Japan and the United States which Colonel Ishiwara, the doctrine's leading propagandist, believed inevitable. In Tokyo the Kwantung army found its main support among the China specialists on the general staff. Some were linked to a larger group of middle-rank officers who, strongly critical of the willingness of their seniors (such as General Tanaka) to take part in corrupt civilian governments, were attracted to the idea of a reform of the whole political system under army leadership and supported ultra-nationalist calls for a 'national restoration'. Fiercely anti-Bolshevik and conscious of the deep despair among the peasants, many believed that the greed of the capitalists and the corrupt party system would drive the rural and urban poor into the communist camp. Demands for a more aggressive foreign policy and a political and social revolution were popular rallying cries at a moment when the political structure was weak, the ruling party divided, and the economic situation disastrous. If there was little unanimity among the rebel groups in Tokyo, almost all were united in their criticism of Shidehara's diplomacy, and during 1930–1 the clashes between the militarists and the civilian cabinet gave the opposition (Seiyukai) party the opportunity to whip up popular discontent.

The first public confrontation came not with the army but with the naval staff over the London naval treaty. The Japanese won a 70 percent ratio in capital ships but had to accept a 10 : 6 ratio in heavy cruisers, though the Americans agreed to defer the later stages of their cruiser-building programme which would be completed only in 1936. Until that time the Japanese would enjoy a de facto 70 per-cent ratio. The compromise, negotiated between the Americans and Japanese, did not satisfy the navalists or the members of the opposition party. The ratification proceedings provoked a constitutional crisis over the 'right of supreme command' which the civilians won only by the narrowest of margins. Behind the constitutional debate was the critical question of who had the right to determine issues of national security, the civilian cabinet or the naval and military authorities. The cabinet triumphed and the treaty was ratified in February 1931, but it proved a pyrrhic victory for the government. Nationalist unrest increased; general-staff opposition to Shidehara's diplomacy intensified, and an assassination attempt made on Hamaguchi in November 1930 resulted in his death six months later. Shidehara, mauled in the Diet during the ratification debate, took over as temporary prime minister. The navy showed its strength by winning the promise of support for an additional building programme which the financially pressed government could ill afford. Henceforth, neither the navy nor the army was prepared, as in the past, to accept new budgetary restraints imposed by civilian governments. The British and Americans watched the anti-treaty backlash in Tokyo with considerable anxiety, but continued to believe that the naval treaties were safe until 1936 when they would come up for revision.

There was talk in the traditionally anti-Japanese American Navy Department of some future war in the Pacific, but no real alarm. British attention was focused on the French and Italians, who could not settle their naval differences, rather than on Japan. Both Washington and London still believed that Japan would continue to honour the agreements and that Shidehara would seek an understanding with the Nationalists in China as both the western powers had done.

While the debates over the naval treaty continued, Japanese army officers voiced their dissatisfaction with Shidehara's China policies. The new prime minister, Wakatsuki Reijiro, and Shidehara favoured participation in the World Disarmament Conference, but the military, hoping to avoid any reductions in its budgets, demanded control over policy-making at Geneva. The military malcontents in the capital were still divided in their views, with some favouring a coup in Tokyo and others preferring prior action in Manchuria. There was, however, general agreement about a forward policy in the Chinese province. In a policy guide for the general staff prepared in August 1931, the drafters recommended that steps should be taken to bring about 'a general understanding within Japan and abroad of the necessity to use force in Manchuria'.[6] The spring of 1932 was picked as the target date for action. Under pressure, Shidehara secured some concessions from the Chinese Nationalists in Nanking, and in return was prepared to consider the abrogation of the unequal treaties. He would not compromise, however, on Japanese railway rights in southern Manchuria. Relations in the northern provinces were becoming increasingly tense and small incidents took on major significance. The assassination of a Kwantung army intelligence officer, Captain Nakamura Shiaro, by Chang Hsueh-liang's troops while on a mission in northern Manchuria set off a massive anti-Chinese campaign among Japanese residents in South Manchuria and in Japan itself. Public support for action in Manchuria increased. The two governments discussed possible lines of settlement of the incident, but neither was in full control of its nationals. The Kwantung army was already preparing to seize Manchuria, with the general staff loosely informed. Colonels Ishiwara and Itagaki now implemented their well-laid plans. The conspirators were able to act before they could be stopped by the military authorities in Tokyo. The bomb set off on 18 September in the suburb of Mukden provided the necessary pretext for action. The moment was well chosen. The Soviet Union was in no position to mount a military response; it had scant forces in the Far East and had just begun a major military expansion plan. The British were

---

[6] James B. Crowley, *Japan's Quest for Autonomy: National Security and Foreign Policy 1930–1938* (Princeton, 1966), 84.

facing a major financial crisis: two days after the Manchurian crisis erupted London went off gold, a world-shaking event which left officials in a state of shock. The Americans, too, were engulfed in financial and economic problems and unprepared to give much attention to events in the Pacific. Chiang Kai-shek was engaged in a political struggle with the Cantonese leaders, and in July had renewed his campaign against the Communists. It was unlikely that he would reinforce the 'Young Marshal', who had chosen to provide support for the Nationalists.

The Kwantung army gamble paid off. Within twelve hours Mukden was in Japanese hands. The general staff was in favour of the action and the war ministry unwilling to oppose it. Shidehara argued against the aggressive approach, and the prime minister ruled that the crisis should be localized and promptly settled. His instructions were undermined by the army's invocation of the right of supreme command and the dispatch of vague discretionary orders to Manchuria. The Japanese public response was enthusiastic, the international response less so.

The Chinese, advised by the experienced diplomat Wellington Koo, appealed on 21 September to the League of Nations under Article 11, which did not automatically require League action, and to the United States as a signatory to the Kellogg–Briand pact. Suddenly Manchuria was an international issue. This shrewd Chinese move, strongly opposed by the Japanese, paved the way for a highly successful diplomatic and propaganda campaign in Geneva. The Mukden action was discussed in the Council, where the Chinese had just taken their non-permanent seat. Both sides were called upon and agreed to withdraw their troops, the Japanese as soon as conditions permitted. There was considerable optimism expressed in the low-powered committee of five handling the Council's business, particularly when Secretary of State Henry Stimson offered his 'whole-hearted sympathy' for the League's endeavours. On 7 October, however, Japanese planes attacked Chinchow, the Chinese administrative capital to the north of the Great Wall where Chang Hsueh-liang had quartered his troops after fleeing from Mukden. There was a sharp foreign reaction to the Chinchow bombings in Geneva and in Washington. The Council reconvened and, notwithstanding the Japanese dissent, invited the Americans to join its deliberations. The American consul-general in Berne, Prentiss Gilbert, took his seat at the council table, reaffirming American moral support for the League but rapidly distancing the United States from its actions. The high hopes of American co-operation soon collapsed. Gilbert was instructed to withdraw from the proceedings, and on 16 November when the council met in Paris (to accommodate the ailing Briand) the American ambassador, Charles Dawes, was brought from London to set up shop at the Ritz Hotel but instructed not to attend Council meetings. For the moment the Council restricted its efforts to encouraging direct Sino-Japanese talks. While Shidehara set out his conditions for such negotiations, the Kwantung army expanded its operations. The unfortunate Japanese representative at Geneva, arguing in good faith that his country intended to withdraw its troops, found himself repeatedly outflanked by events in Manchuria.

On 24 October the Council, meeting under Briand's chairmanship, called on the Japanese to withdraw their troops by 16 November, the date of the next Council meeting. The Japanese opposed the deadline, arguing that since unanimity was necessary, the resolution carried no weight. While there was no agreement on this constitutional point, Briand insisted on the moral force of the recommendation and it went forward. The authority of the League was now engaged, to its ultimate disadvantage. News of the attack in the north on Tsitsihar by a local Chinese commander, financed by the Japanese, and an advance on Chinchow stirred the Council to further action. In public sessions on 9 and 10 December it reaffirmed its earlier resolution for the speedy withdrawal of the Japanese troops and unanimously agreed to send an investigating commission of five members (a British chairman, later named as Lord Lytton, with French, German, Italian, and American representatives), together with a Chinese and a Japanese assessor, to Manchuria. Operating under Article 11, the Council instructed the commission to report and not to mediate or recommend the basis for a settlement. Acceptance of the inquiry, the Japanese delegate warned, would not preclude action against 'bandits'. The very able Chinese representative, Alfred Sze, immediately pointed out the dangers of this exception. There was, nevertheless, relief among the delegates that some positive action had been taken. Time was won for calmer heads to prevail and for the League's somewhat slow and cumbersome machinery to function. Some delegates shared Sze's concerns about the Japanese exception, and a small group from Spain, Guatemala, Peru, Panama, and Poland unsuccessfully pressed for a reaffirmation of the basic principles of collective security. The creation of the 'Lytton Commission', as it was generally known, was as far as the Council was prepared to go. It was one of Briand's last initiatives on behalf of the League, and warm tributes were paid to the chairman before the Council dispersed to wait for the commission's findings. It would be a long wait.

The civilians in Tokyo won a temporary reprieve. The protests of the League Council and expressions of Stimson's displeasure strengthened the moderates' hand and allowed the general staff to assert its authority using the emperor's name. Senior officers in Tokyo, worried about the

Kwantung army's independent actions and the danger of provoking the Russians, stopped the actions against Tsitsihar and Chinchow. However, nothing prevented the Kwantung army leaders from laying plans, first proposed by Japanese residents in Manchuria, for an autonomous, multiracial state under Japan's control, with Pu-Yi, the last Ching emperor, possibly installed as a symbolic head. Shidehara had an opportunity to settle directly with the Chinese. The intensification of diplomatic activity between Tokyo and Nanking proved fruitless, however, though it was the Chinese who brought the dialogue to an end. Chiang Kai-shek would neither opt for all-out negotiations nor authorize his armies to engage the Japanese. In mid-December 1931 he would be forced, along with his colleagues, to resign all his offices amidst violent student demonstrations against him. His policies of 'non-resistance, non-compromise, and non-direct negotiations' weakened the position of the moderates in the Wakatsuki cabinet and allowed the Kwantung army to extend its jurisdiction in Manchuria at minimal human cost. With the collapse of the bilateral exchanges the fate of the cabinet was sealed. It was impossible both to co-operate with the western powers in Geneva (Shidehara had persuaded the cabinet to accept the League inquiry) and to satisfy the demands of the Kwantung army. The cabinet resigned on 12 December and Inukai Ki, a member but not the leader of the Seiyukai opposition, took office. More moderate than many, he reopened talks with the Chinese that would preserve the fiction of Chinese sovereignty over Manchuria while permitting the reinforcement of the army in Manchuria. By late February he had to abandon his plans. The Kwantung army moved into Chinchow, taking the city on 3 January 1932. The last remnant of Chinese administration in Manchuria was removed and the Kwantung army could proceed to put in place the apparatus of the new state.

III

In Europe there was at first a confused response to events in the Far East, partly for lack of information. The League of Nations was intensely Eurocentric in its concerns, and for most of its predominantly European membership Manchuria was very far away indeed. Of the three major outside powers involved in the Sino-Japanese dispute, only Britain was a member of the League and the United States and Soviet Union both viewed the Geneva system with varying degrees of suspicion. The Dutch and French were sympathetic towards the Japanese. The Dutch Indies were rich in war materials, including oil, and although the Netherlands, as one of the small powers, was among the natural supporters of the League's authority, its all-important colonial interests pointed in the Japanese direction. The Netherlands had secured identical notes in 1922 from the signatories of the Four Power treaty declaring their intention to respect the island possessions of Holland in the Pacific region, but they overcame their wartime fears of a Japanese invasion and actually encouraged extensive Japanese investment in the Dutch Indies as a counterweight to American and British investment. The Dutch found a stable Japan a far more attractive prospect than a nationalist and revolutionary China, and saw the Japanese as an important check on indigenous nationalist movements in their colony. The French, too, kept a low profile in Geneva. They had investments in China and a number of concessions, including a sizeable one at Shanghai, but their total commercial stake in China was small and not to be compared in importance to their investments in Indochina. A Communist-supported uprising in Indochina in 1930, the agitation of the Communist party in the colony, and the infiltration of revolutionary men and ideas from southern China underlined the importance of Japan as a source of stability in the region. France's chief interests lay in Europe and, faced with the concurrent problems of reparations and disarmament, hopes for Japanese support on these issues were balanced against the greater need to avoid offending the Americans or the British. Throughout 1932 there were rumours of secret understandings between France and Japan, yet beyond the wish to keep its lines open, the Quai d'Orsay would not risk breaking Council ranks. When, in the summer of 1932, the Japanese offered the French a treaty based on mutual guarantees against Russia and support for the security of IndoChina, their proposal was rejected. Herriot was far too anxious for American backing on war debts to anger Stimson with a positive reply. Nor, with the League of Nations involved and her allies demanding action against Japan, could France risk undermining its authority. The Quai d'Orsay favoured the most limited form of intervention possible, and repeatedly assured the Japanese of France's continuing friendship.

Both the Germans and Italians were even more circumspect in their behaviour at Geneva. Individuals and interest groups in Germany responded in different ways to the Sino-Japanese dispute; there were military and economic links with China, but also economic and diplomatic advantages to be secured through German–Japanese co-operation. As matters stood, the Germans walked a fine line at Geneva, anxious not to offend China but unwilling to be drawn into any anti-Japanese front. There was no break in the Wilhelmstrasse's policies during the domestic upheavals of 1932 or when Hitler took power. By this time the German diplomats were already beginning to lose interest in the League, but were not yet prepared to see its authority discarded. The Italians also took a back seat in the proceedings, despite a concession in Shanghai and representation on the Lytton Commission. Beyond admitting that Manchuria was a 'hard nut to crack', Mussolini saw no real advantage to be gained from going beyond the defence of the limited Italian interests in China. The weakness of the Geneva system did not escape his attention.

Because none of the permanent members of the Council favoured intervention in what was obviously a highly complex and geographically remote dispute which the League was singularly ill-prepared to handle, the great-power delegates used their influence to restrict the scope of the League's involvement and to avoid any adverse judgement of Japan that might result in the application of sanctions. It would be the smaller nations at Geneva, namely Czechoslovakia, the Scandinavian states, Spain, Greece, Colombia, Bolivia, Ireland, and South Africa, which would make the defence of China a test of the League's prestige and a challenge to the great powers' unwillingness to defend the rights of the weak against the strong.

The real function of European membership in the united front will be to grant to Russia, Great Britain and the United States a reasonably free hand to concentrate their energies on the settlement of the Far Eastern crisis... Whether this may prove possible will depend to a great extent on the degree to which the three Powers—Russia, Great Britain and the United States—can adjust their mutual difficulties and harmonize their interests in Eastern Asia.[7]

It was these three states, Britain, the United States, and the Soviet Union, and not the League that would determine the international response to the Japanese assault on Manchuria. Though they did not work together, their policies were basically the same. None of them thought it to be in its national interest to challenge Japan over Manchuria.

League members expected that Britain, by virtue of its interests in the Far East and its influence in the Council, would take the international lead over Manchuria. It was not the role that Sir John Simon, the foreign secretary, wanted. If trade, despite its drastic reduction in recent years, and investment (5.9 per cent of Britain's foreign total) as well as commercial hopes for the future pointed in the Chinese direction, Britain's strategic interests in East Asia favoured support for Japan. 'We should have more to lose than any other Power,' minuted Wellesley, head of the Far Eastern department, 'as the whole of our policy in the Far East rests very much on Japanese goodwill.'[8] Notwithstanding

---

[7] Memorandum by John Franklin Carter (State Department), 19 Feb. 1932, in Justus D. Doenecke, *The Diplomacy of Frustration: The Manchurian Crisis of 1931–1933* (Stanford, Calif., 1981), document no. 41.

[8] Quoted in Christopher Thorne, *The Limits of Foreign Policy: The West, the League and the Far-Eastern Crisis, 1931–1933* (London, 1972), 191.

Chamberlain's 'Christmas memorandum' and negotiations with the Nationalists, the Foreign Office believed that Japan had a strong case in Manchuria. 'There exists a wide-spread feeling which I believe to be justified, that although Japan has undoubtedly acted in a way contrary to the principles of the Covenant,' Simon told his cabinet colleagues, 'she has a real grievance against China . . . This is not a case where the armed forces of one country have crossed the frontiers of another in circumstances where they had no right to be on the other's soil.'[9] The cabinet, beset by its financial and economic concerns, left the Manchurian problem to the Foreign Office. MacDonald was having difficulties with his eyes, and his interventions in foreign affairs were sporadic. Simon was free to chart his own course. The foreign secretary would have preferred to treat the Manchurian question as a Sino-Japanese dispute, and favoured from the start direct negotiations between Tokyo and Nanking. He foresaw only difficulties for Britain should the League become involved. But once the Chinese saw how the League could be used, in Wellesley's words, to 'bamboozle foreign governments about the real state of China', Simon had to take an active part in the League's deliberations.[10] His main anxiety was the fear that the member states might overreact and depart from a position of strict neutrality. In no case, he argued, should the Council open the doors to sanctions. Even Lord Robert Cecil and the leaders of the League of Nations Union agreed that they were difficult to apply and inappropriate in this instance. Sir Miles Lampson, minister at Nanking, warned that any pressure on the Chinese would prove counter-productive and disastrous for both the British and the League. Sir Francis Lindley, the newly appointed ambassador in Tokyo, insisted that most Japanese backed the government and would ignore any threat, even if endorsed by the Americans. While the Foreign Office came to reject Lindley's overly optimistic view of Japanese motives, it agreed that only a continuing Japanese presence in Manchuria would avoid chaos in the provinces and dangerous disorder at home. Simon arrived at the uncomfortable conclusion, guaranteed to expose Britain to criticism, that the authority of the League should be upheld but that Japan should not be censored.

This highly equivocal position, well in keeping with Simon's predilection for fence-sitting (Lloyd George quipped that he had 'sat on the fence so long that the iron had entered his soul'), was further weakened by the generally held assumption that whatever Britain did in East Asia would depend on American power. The British had accommodated themselves to the growth of American influence at the Washington

[9] DBFP, ser. II, vol. 8, no. 76.
[10] Victor Wellesley, in DBFP, ser. II, vol. 9, no. 239.

conference. It was now argued that there could be no economic sanctions without US participation, nor could Britain take any risk of war unless the Americans were willing to fight. 'We are incapable of checking Japan in any way if she really means business and has sized us up, as she certainly had done', minuted Robert Vansittart, the permanent under-secretary at the Foreign Office. 'Therefore we must eventually be done for in the Far East unless the United States are eventually prepared to use force . . . By ourselves we must eventually swallow any and every humiliation in the Far East. If there is some limit to American submissiveness, this is not necessarily so.'[11] There were those who contested this pessimistic reading of British capabilities, but at a time when British self-confidence had been severely shaken and the chiefs of staff were preparing briefs for the Disarmament Conference, many officials took a gloomy view of what Britain could do alone. Almost any British action appeared either to invite Japanese hostility or to raise the prospect of a war which Britain had no intention of fighting. Manchuria was hardly a vital British interest and, with no fleet east of Malta, words could not be backed by deeds. As the British assumed, correctly enough, that however sharply Stimson might rebuke the Japanese the Americans would not support sanctions, the Foreign Office was determined to walk warily lest Britain be dragged in Stimson's wake and be left to clear up the 'resultant mess'. At the same time, Simon could not afford to disassociate Britain from the Americans, whose partnership in the Far East was thought essential for future British security. It has been claimed, with some justice, that British policy in the Far East had as much if not more to do with the United States than with Japan. By underlining its dependence on the unpredictable Americans, the Foreign Office found additional reasons for following a circumspect policy in the Far East. The reluctance to take any risks, even when there was no threat to peace in Europe, suggests the degree to which 'crisis avoidance' was becoming the dominant note in British diplomacy.

In regional terms, the events of 1931–2 confirmed the symbolic transfer of power signalled at Washington in 1922. If much was hoped from the United States, little was expected. In almost every sense, it had less at stake in the Far East than Britain. Nonetheless, America had taken the lead in negotiating the Nine Power treaty of 1922 and the final form of the Kellogg–Briand pact. It was in the Far East that the 'open door' policies had been forged and that American internationalism, those self-denying ordinances sanctioned not by force but by the 'moral reprobation of the world', was tested. President Hoover, preoccupied with the

---

[11] *DBFP*, ser. II, vol. 9, pp. 282–3.

country's economic difficulties, left the initiative to Stimson, but kept a restraining hand on his secretary of state. Like Simon, Stimson believed that the Japanese had a good case and that no simple judgement of right and wrong was possible. 'The peace treaties of modern Europe made out by the Western nations of the world', he wrote in his diary on 7 October, 'no more fit the three great races of Russia, Japan, and China, who are meeting in Manchuria, than, as I put it to the Cabinet, a stovepipe hat would fit an African savage. Nevertheless they are parties to these treaties and the whole world looks on to see whether the treaties are good for anything or not.'[12] A personal friend and admirer of Shidehara's, Stimson's first impulse was to avoid American involvement and give the Japanese minister the time needed to bring the army under control. During September 1932 Stimson therefore refused to invoke either the Nine Power treaty or the Kellogg–Briand pact, and rejected pressing invitations to join the Council's deliberations. Behind his statesman-like façade, however, there lurked a highly volatile and impulsive personality. He soon found the public policy of neutrality as irritating as it was non-productive. Reacting sharply to the Japanese bombing of Chinchow, he declared it was time 'to take a firm ground and aggressive stand toward Japan', without having any specific plans in mind.[13] Stimson pressed Eric Drummond, the League's secretary-general, to invoke the obligations of the Nine Power treaty and Kellogg–Briand pact, and with Hoover's approval showed some indication of working with the League. But the appointment of Gilbert was intended only to signal American displeasure at the Chinchow bombing while shifting the responsibility of responding from Washington to Geneva. Neither Stimson nor the president, who was even more anxious about any League connection than his secretary of state, was prepared to ignore the strong anti-League feeling at home. Presidential caution increased as the date for the reassembly of Congress grew closer. In mid-October the president condemned Japanese behaviour as outrageous and a moral affront to the United States, but warned: 'Neither our obligations to China, nor our own interest, nor our dignity require us to go to war over these questions. These acts do not imperil the freedom of the American people, the economic or moral future of our people ... We will not go along on war or any of the sanctions, either economic or military, for those are the roads to war.'[14] If Stimson was prepared to take greater risks than the president, at no point did he

---

[12] Henry L. Stimson and McGeorge Bundy, *On Active Service in Peace and War* (New York, 1948), 233.
[13] Stimson Diaries, 8 Oct. 1932.
[14] Quoted in Thorne, *The Limits of Foreign Policy*, 162.

contemplate going beyond these prescribed limits. The problem would be to find some other way of influencing Japanese behaviour.

Stimson's uncertainties over American policy did not preclude strong words at Tokyo despite his minister's advice to the contrary. But the policies he followed during 1931–2 reflected the ambiguities and contradictions in his thinking. He continued to hope that Shidehara would regain control over Japanese policy, while writing in his diary in November that Japan was 'in the hands of virtually mad dogs'.[15] He avoided associating the United States with the Council's three-week deadline set for the withdrawal of Japanese troops because it was an un-neutral act, while simultaneously pressing Shidehara to evacuate Manchuria and begin talks with the Chinese. Stimson's signs of displeasure at Tokyo were not without effect. Combined with Briand's pleas on behalf of the Council, the secretary's admonitions gave some weight to the 'internationalists' in their attempt to slow the Kwantung army's advance. To Stimson's great indignation, this proved to be only a temporary check, soon to be abandoned. He was still searching for a policy when the Council on 10 December decided to send its investigating commission to Manchuria. He welcomed the decision and agreed to American participation. With no sign of a Japanese withdrawal, and the collapse of the Wakatsuki ministry, Stimson's attitude hardened. Within hours of the fall of Chinchow on 3 January the secretary of state prepared the first draft of his famous non-recognition doctrine. In notes sent to China and Japan on 7 January Stimson declared America's intention 'not to recognize any situation, treaty or agreement' that 'may impair the treaty rights of the United States or of its citizens in China'. Nor would the Americans recognize any treaty or change 'brought about by means contrary to the Pact of Paris', a threat pregnant with possibilities that were never tested. The 'open door' policy was also invoked.[16] The 'Stimson doctrine' (Hoover took some umbrage at the omission of his name) won considerable acclaim in the United States. The fact that a stand had been made on the sanctity of treaties and not on America's material interests attracted idealists without unduly upsetting the isolationists. While no one in Washington believed that any American interest in China was of sufficient importance to justify sanctions or the threat of war, all could welcome the maintenance of international law.

Hostile voices were raised. Such statements would hardly stop Japan and could only increase tension in the Pacific, it was argued. Realist critics, writing after 1945, have argued that by tying American policy to

---

[15] Stimson Diaries, 19 Nov. 1932.
[16] Dept. of State, *Foreign Relations of the United States, 1932*, vol. 3 (Washington, DC, 1948), 8. Henceforth cited as *FRUS*.

an outmoded treaty structure instead of the protection of specific interests, the Stimson doctrine made inevitable treaty revision more difficult and placed the United States and Japan on a collision course. This overly deterministic view minimizes the importance of the domestic roots of Japanese foreign policy, but rightly calls attention both to the futility and the negative consequences of the gesture, one that would soon be adopted by the League to conceal its own impotence. The Stimson doctrine postponed any clear definition of American interests in the Pacific. The Americans had ranged themselves with the status-quo powers in the Pacific without being willing to do anything to sustain that position. Like the Kellogg–Briand pact, non-recognition represented a retreat from commitment. There was less enthusiasm for the Stimson doctrine abroad. The Japanese returned a somewhat ironic reply, expressing gratitude over America's continued sensitivity to the 'exigencies of Far Eastern questions', but insisting that conditions had changed since the Washington treaties were signed. Stimson tried hard for many weeks to associate London with his initiative, but the British were content with an assurance from Tokyo that Japan would respect the open door in Manchuria. Baldwin announced that the government would wait for the Lytton report and avoid embroiling itself with either side. When a new and far more frightening situation developed in Shanghai in January 1932, the British saw the collective policy of the League as a way of conciliating Stimson, who wanted to warn off the Japanese and reinforce the Anglo-American forces there, without antagonizing Japan. It proved to be a flawed approach that was ultimately as ineffective as Stimson's.

The third outside player in China, the Soviet Union, was the most directly threatened by the Japanese seizure of Manchuria. Given the military circumstances in the Far East, Stalin was condemned to passivity. Able to read the Japanese army ciphers, the Russians learned in March 1931 from an intercepted telegram sent by the Japanese military attaché in Moscow of an inevitable clash between the two countries 'sooner or later'.[17] It is probable, too, that Richard Sorge, the brilliant Soviet military agent in Shanghai, provided confirming intelligence. The Russians feared that the Mukden incident might result in a general Far Eastern conflict, not immediately but possibly in a few months time. Steps were rapidly taken to strengthen the newly formed Special Red-Banner Far Eastern Army, and submarines were to be sent to the Far East. As the implications of the Manchurian occupation were absorbed during the winter of 1931–2, a decision was taken to sanction

---

[17] For text and also that of intercepted telegram from Hirota, the ambassador in Moscow, see David R. Stone, *Hammer and Rifle*, 186.

both the mechanization of the Soviet army for which Stalin's deputy chief of staff, Mikhail Tukhachevsky, had been agitating, and to expand the military mobilization programmes. In the first few weeks of 1932 the military equipment order-and-procurement budget nearly doubled, with the tank programme given the most drastic increases. This vast military reorganization put an enormous strain on an already overtaxed economy.[18] The Soviet Far East could not supply the food needed, and wheat and livestock had to be requisitioned from European Russia and from the Ukraine at a time when both were in short supply. Apart from the enormous difficulties created by the collectivization programme, there was the need for massive grain exports to pay for industrial re-equipment. The good harvest of 1930 was followed by a poor one in 1931 and the shortage of food led to famine and to widespread peasant discontent, far worse in the Far East than elsewhere because much of the land was farmed by individuals resistant to any form of collectivization. Concessions had to be made and measures instituted to improve the regional situation. The forced requisitions from European Russia and from the Ukraine, one of the worst-affected areas, continued throughout 1932, despite another poor harvest. Apart from the disastrous effects of the famine on the country as a whole, disaffection and low morale spread through the armed services. Just as the Japanese war scare reached its height in the spring of 1932, the Soviets were having increasing difficulties in keeping to existing production schedules. The Kwantung army had good intelligence; the Soviet Union was not in a position to contest its Manchurian challenge.

While building up its military might, the Russians embarked on a public policy of appeasing the Japanese. In December 1931 Litvinov made the first of repeated offers of a non-aggression pact, only to be rebuffed by Tokyo. Tension mounted as the Kwantung army advanced up the Soviet-controlled Chinese Eastern Railway. On 5 February the Japanese occupied Harbin, the key Soviet railway junction in Manchuria; there was no Russian reaction. Occasionally the Soviets assisted some anti-Japanese leader in the Vladivostok area, but for the most part they tried to avoid being drawn into the local struggle. Russian protests about the use of the Chinese Eastern Railway to transport Japanese troops were disregarded, and the Japanese merely seized the sections that they needed. By mid-April 1932 the Russians had all but lost control over the line. The main challenge to the Kwantung army came not from the Soviet Union but from 'bandits', small bands of Chinese using highly effective guerrilla tactics.

[18] See Table 24, p. 549 for Soviet military spending, 1922–1937.

IV

In late January 1932 the Shanghai crisis erupted. The city, made up of three boroughs, the Chinese Chapei, the French concession, and the International Settlement (itself divided into Japanese, British, American, and Italian sections) was the greatest port in Asia and the centre of international life in China. Of these, though the Japanese section was the most populous, the British was the wealthiest and the most important, the focus of their investment and trade in China. Tensions in Shanghai between the Chinese and Japanese had long been high, and Chinese residents had boycotted Japanese shops and goods with devastating results. After an incident at a Chinese towel factory in Chapei on 18 January when workers assaulted five Japanese, including two priests, the Japanese residents retaliated, burning the factory and attacking a nearby police station. What began as rioting and street fighting became a major confrontation as the local Japanese naval commander sent in the marines. When Commander Shiozawa's young and inexperienced forces proved unable to establish control, the Tokyo government, though shocked by the officer's precipitate action (the mayor of Shanghai was one of the least anti-Japanese Nationalist politicians), agreed to send additional ships and army reinforcements. Forced to face the tough, left-wing, and fiercely anti-Japanese 19th Route Army, the conflict escalated. The shelling and air bombardment of Chapei, viewed by foreign residents of the International Settlement and recorded by Western journalists and newsreel cameramen, shocked their worldwide audience. In those more innocent days such pictures had an enormous impact on readers and viewers, and world opinion shifted in the Chinese direction. These accounts created or reinforced stereotyped images of oriental savagery and barbarism that were to persist long after Manchuria had vanished from the headlines.

On 1 February a Japanese destroyer fired on Nanking, and both the British and Americans feared that similar actions were planned in other major ports as part of a general assault on China's independence. More Japanese ships and troops arrived in Shanghai as new assaults were met with fierce resistance. For some five weeks a 'war in everything but name' raged in the city and its environs. While authorizing reinforcements, the Tokyo government insisted that its troops were being sent only to protect the International Settlement, and that there was no wish to expand hostilities. A request was made for the good offices of Britain and the United States, and a special representative was sent to assist with the peacemaking. On 19 January, in the face of Japanese objections, the Chinese delegate successfully appealed to the League Council under Articles 10 and 15. The secretary-general set up an investigating committee in the city composed of the consuls of six European states, with the United States added later. On 12 February the Chinese asked the Council to refer the dispute to the full Assembly under Article 15, and a special session of the Assembly was summoned for 3 March. The date became an important deadline for the Inukai government, which wanted to end the crisis before the Assembly could interfere.

The Americans and British, especially the former, were in a state of considerable alarm, fearing for the safety of their own citizens and property in the International Settlement as well as the protection of their rights. Talks initiated by their local consuls-general were blocked by Japanese military action. Ships were ordered to Shanghai; protests, in which the Italians joined, were made about the Japanese use of harbours in the International Settlement for landing troops and about acts of barbarity towards the Chinese population. Different intermediaries tried to arrange truce talks. Stimson, angered by the Japanese rejection of Anglo-American conditions for their good offices at Shanghai, became increasingly agitated. Though President Hoover was opposed to threats, which could produce a strong reaction, he shared Stimson's sense of outrage. As the possibility of intervention was mooted in the American press, public anti-war feeling surfaced. There was some relief at the State Department when the news of the Lindbergh baby kidnapping diverted attention from Shanghai. Simon, in Geneva for the disarmament talks, was cautious and indecisive, anxious to keep close to Stimson but wanting to distinguish between the Shanghai and Manchurian crises and to concentrate Anglo-American efforts on mediation in the former. He wanted, moreover, to avoid any threatening gestures towards Japan that would make this more difficult. On 5 February Admiral Howard Kelly, the British commander-in-chief (China Station), reached Shanghai and further naval reinforcements followed. Japanese, British, American, and Italian ships were all anchored in the harbour, presenting a formidable display of naval strength. Apart from the Japanese warships naval involvement was minimal, but the representatives of the foreign communities felt they had made their point. Admiral Kelly tried his hand at truce talks, but without success. On 9 February Stimson broached the idea of a strong démarche on the basis of the Nine Power treaty of 1922 and the extension of the non-recognition doctrine to Shanghai. He approached both the British and French, warning the former, whose co-operation he wanted, that if 'absolutely necessary' he would move alone. The British procrastinated and the French sent no reply. The British and American ministers in China, Sir Miles Lampson and Nelson Johnson, arrived in Shanghai on 12 February and tried, again unsuccessfully, to bring the two sides together. Instead, the Japanese commanders demanded that the Chinese withdraw their troops 20 kilometres from the city, and when their ultimatum was rejected, launched an all-out attack. Lampson reported to London that conciliation had failed and placed the blame upon the intransigence of the Japanese military authorities.

Simon still sought to avoid Stimson's 'very strong indictment of Japan', and in a series of static-ridden transatlantic telephone conversations returned equivocal replies to the secretary's importunings. Even his so-called refusal to act on 15 February was somewhat ambiguous, feeding Stimson's hopes and making the American's subsequent disillusionment that much more bitter. Conferring with colleagues in MacDonald's hospital room, Simon opted for what he thought was the much safer course of working with the League. A draft was prepared for a League resolution, with references to the Kellogg–Briand pact and Nine Power treaty and acceptance of the non-recognition principle. On 16 February the twelve neutral members of the Council issued an appeal to Japan to exercise restraint by virtue of her position as a great power and Council member. The Japanese delegate was assured that no censure of Japan was intended. Stimson felt that Britain had 'let America down'. In an open letter to Senator Borah, dated 23 February, he restated America's non-recognition policy in forceful terms, indirectly warning the Japanese that if adopted by others, non-recognition 'will eventually lead to the restoration of rights and titles of which she [China] may have been deprived'.[19] If the Japanese disregarded the Nine Power treaty, he threatened, the United States would reconsider the military agreements made at the same time. No further American action followed, despite continued murmurings about British pusillanimity. What transpired in February became the subject of a bitter debate between the two ministers, each reinterpreting the events of 1932 to cast himself in the best light. In fact neither country was prepared to challenge Japan, the strongest military power in East Asia. The American secretary of state was less forthright and clear-minded than he later claimed. There was no request for joint action 'to stop Japan' in February 1932, nor any call for a Nine Power treaty conference. Simon was far more vacillating and indecisive in his dealings with Washington than his autobiography suggests. The foreign secretary, advised by Lindley, the ambassador in Tokyo, thought that a démarche would weaken the position of the already powerless moderates. He feared, too, that the Americans would desert at the first signs of Japanese anger, leaving the British

[19] *FRUS, Japan, 1931–1941*, vol. 1, 83.

alone to pick up the pieces. Quite apart from Simon's inept handling of Stimson, the London–Geneva–Washington telephone conversations added to the two men's mutual incomprehension. It seems likely that the Foreign Office had not really taken Stimson's initiative seriously, thinking it was primarily intended to alert the American public to the dangers of isolationism.

The contrasts in personality between Stimson and Simon were reflected in their diplomacy. Stimson was impulsive, impatient, and restless. He was more unsettled in his private views than his public declarations as aversion to professional advice suggested. He shared the sense of American exceptionalism that has left such an enduring mark on American diplomacy. Believing that the United States should stand for the sanctity of treaties, he was unprepared for Japan's unilateral disregard of their contents. It was not for American trade or the 'open door' that Stimson took the high moral road, but as a demonstration of American rectitude. Having taken a strong stand, he soon had second thoughts about its wisdom. Simon was cautious to a fault, inclined, like the well-trained lawyer that he was, to weigh all the possibilities before acting. He neither understood nor responded to the bursts of emotion that carried Stimson along. By temperament alone he preferred 'trimming to crusading'. Torn between those who looked back with nostalgia on the Anglo–Japanese alliance and those who believed strongly in the League of Nations, Simon sought the middle course. British commercial interests in China had to be balanced against those in Japan, the balancing act made no easier by the smouldering resentment of British residents in China against the boycotts of the past. The fear of joining Stimson, knowing that neither the secretary of state nor the president intended to go beyond lecturing the Japanese, had to be weighed against the need to preserve the future Anglo-American partnership in the Pacific. Simon felt that he could not afford to move too far from the Americans, even though Britain's regional interests pointed to a policy of conciliating Japan. Here was a juggling act worthy of the 'iron chancellor', but Simon was no Bismarck. Anglo-American differences left a bitter taste on both sides of the ocean. In the corridors of power suspicion and distrust complicated future relations. State Department officials were convinced that the British were cowardly and looked to others to fight their battles. Stimson, a strong Anglophile before this crisis, would not forget the extent of his disillusionment. British unhappiness was just as strong. 'You will get nothing out of Washington but words', Baldwin complained. 'Big words but only words.'[20] Others echoed Baldwin's

---

[20] Quoted in Keith Middlemas and John Barnes, *Baldwin: A Biography* (London, 1969), 729.

complaint, and in 1937 Neville Chamberlain would return to the same refrain. In retrospect, one can see that the two countries were not very far apart in their handling of Japan. Such detachment was impossible at the time, particularly as neither man achieved his goal. Simon's subsequent actions at Geneva, intended to pacify Stimson without alienating Japan, hardly improved his reputation. His manoeuvrings and equivocations not only raised tempers in Washington but earned him the opprobrium of League enthusiasts. It would be hard to argue that a joint démarche in February 1932 would have changed either the Shanghai or Manchuria situations.

The Japanese government, if not the Kwantung army, had to consider the international reaction to what was happening in Shanghai and Manchuria. The Wakatsuki cabinet had resigned on 12 December 1931. The new cabinet, under the 76-year-old Inukài, faced with domestic turmoil at home and the fighting in Shanghai, was not in a strong position to control its war hawks. In the early months of 1932 a small group of fanatical young naval and army officers, more interested in domestic reform than foreign policy, initiated a series of political assassinations that continued until the premier himself became a victim in May. Even as Inukai struggled to keep the lines open to China, the Kwantung army went its own way. The occupation of Harbin closed, in the army's view, the whole Manchurian question. Neither Anglo-American declarations nor League admonitions could have prevented the formal inauguration of the new puppet state of Manchukuo, with Henry Pu-Yi as regent, on 9 March. The only problems were differences over the form of the new state and its headship, as some Kwantung army leaders saw an opportunity to inaugurate some of their more radical ideas. The Inukai ministry lacked the political clout to delay the army's announcement until after the Assembly session in Geneva. It managed to withhold recognition, in part to deflect international criticism but also as a protest against the military's action. The general staff gave its blessing to the creation of the new state.

Attention now shifted to Geneva. For different reasons, both the Chinese and the British wanted to make use of the League. The political situation in China was so unstable that Simon was quoted as asking whether China was a country or a geographical phrase. Apart from the 19th Route Army, whose resistance made a good impression on the Americans, the Chinese had shown little stomach for military action. Though the Cantonese government was more anti-Japanese than Chiang, the Nationalists looked to Geneva for eventual relief. The Chinese delegates to the League knew that the Assembly, meeting in special session for only the second time in its history (the first was to discuss the admission of Germany), would be more sympathetic to China's cause than the Council. The Assembly resolution of 4 March called for a ceasefire in Shanghai, negotiations between Japan and China, assisted by the foreign representatives on the spot, and for the withdrawal of Japanese troops. By this date the Japanese armies in Shanghai had forced the Chinese forces to withdraw to an acceptable distance from the city. Admiral Kelly, in Lampson's absence, acted as the intermediary between the Japanese and Chinese representatives, and was already on the way to achieving an agreement on the eve of the Assembly's resolution. The Japanese generals announced a ceasefire for 3 March; the Chinese had yet to agree. Both countries' representatives voted for the League resolution of 4 March. The League achievement in imposing a truce was hailed as a triumph for internationalism. The tensions between the opponents in Shanghai were so great that it was impossible to get them to sit down together until 24 March. Even then progress was so agonizingly slow that the Chinese asked for the matter to be transferred to Geneva, only to have the question referred back to the four-power representatives in Shanghai.

The special Assembly turned from Shanghai to the question of Manchuria. Speaker after speaker, led by Guiseppe Motta, the president of Switzerland, and Beneš of Czechoslovakia, blamed the great powers but particularly Britain for the temporizing procedures of the Council and the failure to protect China. The principles of the Covenant and the reputation of the League, they argued, had been tarnished and brought into disrepute. Simon, accused of shielding Japan, responded by reaffirming Britain's loyalty to the Covenant. He took an active part in framing the Assembly resolution of 11 March, passed two days after the inauguration of Manchukuo. The resolution declared that Japan's actions in China were contrary to the Covenant and Pact of Paris, and delegates endorsed the doctrine of non-recognition in Stimsonian terms. A committee of nineteen was set up to enforce and monitor the League's past and present resolutions. There was relief that the League had taken action (Washington gave its approval) and vindicated its honour. At last something had been done. The 11 March resolution provided Simon with a way 'to marry' the League and the United States. He explained the difficulties of supporting the League and co-operating with the United States:

[C]o-ordinating these two efforts has tended to expose the United Kingdom at Geneva to the reproach that we were either (a) working behind the back of the League, or (b) failing to show ourselves as vigorous as the United States of America were prepared to be. There is no justification for either of these criticisms but Geneva is a place where the United Kingdom has not only got to take the lead, but to take the blame for everything that is done.[21]

In combining the old and new methods of diplomacy, the foreign secretary hoped to disarm his internationalist critics without sacrificing British interests in the Far East. This meant avoiding joint action with a 'reckless' Stimson, and upholding the League without permitting resolutions that would outrage Japan. Simon and almost all his advisers were unduly obsessed with the fear of the 'burden of resentment' and the possibility of war. It made them ultra-cautious in Geneva as well as in Tokyo.

The ceasefire in Shanghai proved to be only the start of long and tedious negotiations. The differences between the Chinese and Japanese were only resolved after prodigious efforts on the part of Sir Miles Lampson, with the assistance of his American, French, and Italian colleagues. Conversations were repeatedly interrupted by exchanges of fire between the two armies. Ugly incidents in the city could have ended the truce negotiations. But the Tokyo government, as well as its local representatives, wanted to proceed. Japan's Shanghai offensive was distinct from what happened in Manchuria. The naval commander who began it probably wanted glory for his service and thought it would be a limited engagement. Given the mood in Japan and the power of the naval and military leaders, the government had to uphold the prestige of its forces. Yet, worried about the effects of the fighting on Anglo-American attitudes and, even more concretely, on the value of the yen in London and New York, the cabinet wanted to get its troops home. The disruption of Japanese activities in Greater Shanghai made the fighting a doubly costly affair. Once national pride was satisfied, the troops could be withdrawn. The cabinet internationalists had no wish to challenge the status quo in Shanghai, and the actions of the international community, the naval demonstrations, financial pressure, and attempts at mediation, assisted the effort to bring the unwanted crisis to an end. The truce was finally signed on 5 May 1932. The agreement, with some modifications, restored the pre-crisis status quo. Chinese troops would remain 20 kilometres away from the International Settlement, while Japanese troops would leave Shanghai. A commission of friendly powers, not a League commission, would monitor the withdrawals. By the end of the month almost all the Japanese forces were gone. There was considerable relief both in London and Washington. The expected 'round table conference' to settle residual difficulties never happened. Discussions between the local Chinese authorities and the

---

[21] *DBFP*, ser. II, vol. 9, no. 636.

members of the International Settlement's Municipal Council soon stalled, mainly due to Japanese intransigence.

The Shanghai crisis led to sharpened perceptions of the Japanese threat. Unease in the Foreign Office about Japan's future intentions appeared to make it imperative to keep Japan in the League and avoid her ostracism and isolation. The crisis, too, dramatically illustrated the gap between Britain's interests and its power to defend them. On 22 February a committee created by the chiefs of staff reported on the Far Eastern situation should Japan become hostile. It was pointed out that Singapore, Hong Kong, and Trincomalee, situated off the southern tip of India, could not in their present condition be defended pending the arrival of the main British fleet, which would take thirty-eight days to reach Singapore.[22] On 23 March the cabinet agreed to abandon the 'ten year rule' first adopted in 1922. Defence estimates would no longer be framed on the assumption that there would be no major war for the next ten years. For a time the country's defensive needs in the Pacific—above all, work on the Singapore base which had been repeatedly slowed down, deferred, and in 1929 stopped altogether by the Labour government—were given priority in planning. Only Britain and the United States possessed the necessary resources to check the Japanese, but neither their respective fleets nor their base facilities were adequate for a war in the Far East. British navalists thought the Americans 'jealous, unreliable and indifferent to Britain's security', while the Americans suspected that the British were unwilling to recognize their new place on the world's oceans.[23] The World Disarmament Conference and the economic climate (in 1931 defence expenditure took 2.5 per cent of the country's budget) hardly encouraged high British defence spending. Few guessed in 1932 how short the period of grace would be. The Americans, too, reconsidered their defence policies in the light of the Japanese challenge. The secretary of state and some of his official advisers came to share the assumption of senior naval officers that a future conflict between Japan and the United States was inevitable. Responding to American naval weakness in the Pacific (it had more battleships than Japan but fewer cruisers, one less aircraft carrier, and far longer supply lines), Stimson began to press for an immediate naval build-up to treaty limits. President Hoover reacted differently; American unpreparedness provided for him one more reason for diplomatic caution and general disarmament. Responsive to anti-war feeling in the country and looking for cuts in expenditure, Hoover was not going to back a major naval building programme.

[22] CAB 4/21, Imperial Defence Policy, Annual Review for 1932 by the Chief of Staff Subcommittee, CID 1082-B, COS, 23 Feb. 1932.
[23] Thorne, *The Limits of Foreign Policy*, 75.

V

With the ceasefire in Shanghai and the League resolution of 11 March, the Far East faded from public view and the League sat back to wait for the Lytton Commission findings. The commission only arrived in Japan on 29 February 1932, and soon embarked on its extensive travels in China and Manchuria, overwhelmed at the start of the journeys by lavish entertainment and a mass of partisan documentation. At Shanghai, where its members were allowed no part in the local negotiations, Lord Lytton queried Matsuoka, the Japanese special representative, about a durable solution to the Manchuria–Mongolia problem that would meet Japan's legitimate demands but save China's face. The diplomat-politician replied that 'this task is beyond my intelligence'.[24] Private letters from Lytton were written in a similarly pessimistic vein. 'Manchuria simply bristles with difficulties which at present seem to be insoluble', he told his wife. 'Conditions are going to be too difficult for League machinery.'[25] Despite their lack of linguistic skills and local Japanese obstruction, the commissioners did a conscientious and thorough job in Manchuria and returned again to Tokyo on 4 July in a conciliatory mood, anxious to discuss what they knew to be a highly complex situation. Uchida Yosuya, the ex-president of the South Manchurian Railway and the new foreign minister in the Saito cabinet, informed Lytton, in rather brusque and offensive terms, that Japan would deal with the question of recognition without concern for the signatories of the Nine Power pact or the members of the League.

The decision to recognize Manchukuo was announced in the Diet on 25 August. Uchida, after giving a reasoned and dignified explanation of the Japanese action, answered an interpellation from Mori Kaku, the most outspoken Seiyukai nationalist, by assuring his interrogator that the Japanese people would not 'cede a foot, even if the country turned to scorched earth'.[26] His belligerent words made the headlines, but the cabinet decision did not carry the threat of a challenge to the occidental nations. There was no expectation that the western powers or the Soviet Union would contest the Japanese action. On the contrary, conscious of their diplomatic isolation, the Japanese tried for a pact with France and, despite some clashes in Heilungkiang, the barren and mountainous but strategically important province, took no decision to challenge the Soviet Union. Throughout these months the Soviet card was in full

---

[24] Ian Nish, *Japan's Struggle with Internationalism: Japan, China and the League of Nations, 1931–1933* (London, 1993), 113.
[25] Ibid. 114.
[26] Thorne, *The Limits of Foreign Policy*, 275.

diplomatic play. The Chinese had already concluded a pact with Moscow; the French signed a non-aggression treaty with the Soviets in November 1932, and Stimson and Borah led a short but abortive campaign for recognizing the Soviet Union as an anti-Japanese gesture. While some Japanese officers were talking about a 'preventative war' against Russia, the foreign ministry was seriously considering the Soviet offer of a non-aggression pact. The question was discussed by the Japanese ambassador in Moscow in 1932, and further pursued by Matsuoka on his way to Geneva for the Lytton report debate. It was only in December that the Japanese refused to sanction formal negotiations. Contact ceased when Tokyo took umbrage at Russian demands to publish the exchange of notes in a Soviet bid to win western approval. Recognition of Manchukuo represented a victory for the Kwantung army, but prime minister Saito still hoped to make an arrangement with the Chinese Nationalists. Others, like Uchida and General Araki, the war minister, argued that the other powers would be forced to accept what could not be undone. Recognition was followed by steps to establish the independent character of the new regime. With both the Canton and Nanking governments in disarray, the Chinese were hardly in a position to riposte. There was little support from the western states. The Americans, whatever Stimson's declared sympathies for China, produced neither loans nor military assistance, and the British, more bluntly, refused all aid until a more stable government was established. As the whole question of resisting Japan was a source of contention among the rival Chinese Nationalist factions and British economic interests had to be considered, there was little incentive for Britain to go beyond a policy of neutrality. On 15 September Japan gave formal recognition to the new state of Manchukuo, in open defiance of the League's resolutions and in anticipation of the Lytton Commission's findings.

The Lytton Commission's report, 139 foolscap pages finished in Peking in early September, was published in Switzerland on 10 October 1932. The commissioners were unanimous in their conclusions. The differences between the chairman, Lord Lytton, who wanted a stronger section on Manchuria, and the French member, General Henri Claudel, who was prepared to accept the Japanese position in Manchukuo with some constitutional safeguards, were bridged through the moderating influence of the American and Italian representatives. Having personally concluded that nothing could make Manchuria anything but Chinese, Lytton hoped that if Japan was left alone circumstances would prove too strong for it and liberal opinion would reassert itself. By stating the facts without pillorying Japan, the commissioners intentionally left the door open for further negotiations. The report was even-handed in its discussion of the background to the crisis. The Kuomintang government was castigated for the lawlessness, insecurity, and boycotts in China and Manchuria. The Kwantung army was held only partly to blame for what happened at Mukden. Japan was given credit for the remarkable growth of the Manchurian economy, though the role of China was not neglected. Manchuria was a divided community and a region where many races met, the commissioners insisted, so no simple solution would prove workable. In the key paragraphs, however, the report contested the Japanese version of the Manchurian story. The Manchukuo government had been imposed and 'cannot be considered to have been called into existence by a genuine and spontaneous independence movement'. There was 'no general Chinese support for the Manchukuo Government which is regarded by local Chinese as an instrument of the Japanese'.[27] For that non-existent 'thoughtful and impartial reader', the recommendations were moderate and sensible but hardly realistic. New Sino-Japanese treaties would be necessary, the commission suggested, and Japanese rights in Manchuria recognized. The Manchurian government should enjoy a large measure of autonomy, exercised in a manner consistent with Chinese sovereignty and administrative integrity. If acceptable to the Chinese with reservations, the report suited neither the Saito cabinet nor the overwhelming majority of its Japanese audience. Those caught up in the highly charged nationalist atmosphere were prepared to reject the League, its western bias and the assumptions of oriental inferiority on which the Covenant was based, but on this point the cabinet was still divided. The government asked for six weeks to consider the report and produce its own rejoinder. Some ministers thought that, if discussions were delayed long enough, international interest in Manchuria would fade and Manchukuo would be accepted as a fait accompli. The Japanese objections, detailed in a document as long as the original report, were reviewed at the League Council's meetings in late November and were stridently presented by Matsuoka at the plenary session of the League on 6 December. Evoking the image of a 'crucified Japan', Matsuoka opposed the League's acceptance of the Lytton report and rejected any possible revocation of the Japanese recognition of Manchukuo. He warned the delegates that if Japan were condemned it would leave the League, an eventuality he privately hoped could be avoided.

Some of the delegates from the smaller states, led by Beneš, infuriated by the dilatory tactics of the Council and Japanese, demanded positive action, but there was little agreement about what action should be taken.

---

[27] League of Nations, *Appeal by the Chinese Government: Report of the Commission of Enquiry* [Lytton Report] (Geneva, 1932), 97, 111.

To condemn Japan, as Beneš recommended, and expel her from the League would only advertise the League's impotence. To do nothing was even more intolerable, and would seriously damage the League's reputation. Small-power indignation reached its peak with Sir John Simon's speech at the plenary session. In a misguided attempt to stem the anti-Japanese tide, the British foreign secretary recalled the Lytton Commission's criticism of both China and Japan, and emphasized the need for conciliation as opposed to condemnation. Simon later defended himself, claiming with some justice that the French, Italian, and German delegates had made similar speeches without attracting condemnation. Whatever their anger with Simon, the delegates drew back from condemning Japan. The Assembly resolved only that the committee of nineteen should study the Lytton report and the Japanese observations on it and draw up proposals for a settlement. These endless discussions, prolonged by the slowness of the Japanese, continued into the new year. There was an intensification of the anti-Japanese mood when the Kwantung army seized Shanhaikuan, a city on the Chinese–Manchurian border that was the gateway to Jehol province, on 1 January 1933. The renewal of military action had the same effect on international opinion as the bombing of Chinchow a year earlier. Nonetheless, the committee of nineteen continued with its fruitless search for an acceptable formula. The British, clinging to an illusion derived from reading the Japanese diplomatic codes, believed that Matsuoka was more intransigent than his government and tried a direct intervention in Tokyo. The League's secretary-general, Eric Drummond, along with the highly respected and most senior Japanese official on the Secretariat, Sugimura Yotaro, made their own recommendations, only to have their efforts torpedoed by publicity in the anti-Japanese press. There was a storm of criticism against Drummond for his singular behaviour that may well have precipitated his decision to resign from his League position. Unlike his United Nations counterpart today, the secretary-general had no mandate to negotiate with one party to the dispute. Matsuoka and some of his colleagues, unwilling to accept the confrontation that rejection of the Drummond–Sugimara compromise would bring, also tried a last-minute intervention that failed. On 21 January 1933, faced with further Japanese reservations to their recommendations, the exhausted members of the committee of nineteen abandoned their efforts and prepared their draft report for the Assembly.

The Saito cabinet was fully committed to a position of no compromise on Manchukuo, but had not decided on a course of action should the Assembly accept the Lytton report. The moderates lost ground when the Kwantung army decided to proceed with the subjugation of Jehol, where Chang Hsueh-liang had gathered a large army in anticipation of the Japanese attack. On 17 February the cabinet decided both to oppose the committee of nineteen's draft report and to sanction the Jehol advance. An ultimatum was sent on 23 February, and by 4 March the army took possession of Jehol city, putting the numerically superior Chinese army to flight. A temporary lull in the fighting followed as the Chinese forces regrouped in the passes through the Great Wall. The timing of the Japanese action, probably dictated by the melting of the snows, suggests that the dispositions of the League were no longer of importance. Despite a Chinese appeal the League powers refused to take up the Jehol dispute, fearing to further complicate the task of peace-making. They were hesitant, too, about intervention in a region whose revenues, used to support Chang Hsueh-liang, were based on the opium trade and whose inhabitants, mainly Mongols, had appealed to the League against Chinese misrule. The Jehol advance, as anticipated in Tokyo, dimmed the prospect of gathering support in the Assembly. As so often, the efforts made by Prime Minister Saito, the naval chiefs, the court party, and the emperor failed to restrain the army. On 22 February, the day before the Assembly met in extraordinary session, the privy council endorsed the cabinet's decision to leave Geneva unless the draft resolution was substantially altered. The question of resignation from the League was left undecided.

It was a foregone conclusion that the Assembly, where the anti-Japanese current ran strong, would take a tougher line than the Council. The committee of nineteen's recommendations, incorporating the first eight chapters of the Lytton report, insisted on the withdrawal of Japanese troops into the railway zone and Japanese recognition of China's sovereignty in Manchuria. But while concluding that 'a large part of Chinese territory has been forcibly seized and occupied by Japanese troops and that, in consequence of this operation, it has been separated from and declared independent of the rest of China', there was still no outright condemnation of Japan, no appeal to Article 16, and the door again left open for future negotiations with the assistance of a newly created advisory committee.[28] On 24 February 1933 the committee's report was adopted by forty-two votes to one, with Siam (a new government trying to assert its independence from Japan) abstaining. Japan stood alone, internationally isolated. After a speech made more in sorrow than in anger and, for the first time, sympathetically received by the delegates, Matsuoka left the chamber. The exit of the Japanese delegation was caught by the newsreel cameras. The film still conveys the sense of drama that marked the occasion.

---

[28] *League of Nations Official Journal*, Special Supplement, no. 112.

VI

In Geneva, there was a moment of euphoria. While some delegates might have preferred a more censorious report, most believed that the facts of the situation had been stated and the League was seen by the world to have stood by its principles. The full English text of the League's report was broadcast in Morse code from its wireless station. All who wanted to listen were well informed. There could be no complaints from those who sought to mobilize world opinion as an arbiter in international disputes. The United States and the Soviet Union were invited to join the new advisory committee; the earlier Japanese veto on their participation in the deliberations of the committee of nineteen could now be ignored. President Roosevelt agreed but the Soviets declined, pointing to the hostile attitude of so many of its members towards the USSR. The Russians intended to keep their hands free vis-à-vis Japan. The League members had accepted the doctrine of non-recognition out of a sense of helplessness.

In one sense at least the effort succeeded. With but a few exceptions (San Salvador in 1934), all the member nations kept to the pledge of non-recognition, despite Japanese offers of a quid pro quo in the form of an 'open door' for trade. The Soviet Union, as a result of the Chinese Eastern Railway agreement concluded with Japan in March 1935, was the first major power to break ranks. Even among those states that subsequently left the League, the diplomatic boycott continued until Germany in 1936 and Italy in 1937 extended official recognition. Manchukuo continued to exist in the face of the world's displeasure until 1945. Life in the new state proved less attractive than early enthusiasts anticipated. Order was not restored, for the army failed to quell the hordes of local bandits (the term 'bandit' often synonymous with anti-Japanese guerrillas) that had long plagued the provinces. The hoped-for Japanese migration never materialized and Manchukuo's resources could not meet the demands of the massive rearmament programme that inevitably followed the army's successful challenge to civilian rule. There was still the question of the League to be resolved. In the Geneva delegation, Matsuoka and some of his colleagues wanted Japan to remain, but the military members, highly critical of the disarmament discussions, were anxious to cut the ties with the international body. The decision was made on 24 February in Tokyo, where Araki and Uchida led the successful campaign for withdrawal. The emperor and the court party tried to soften the parting through the careful wording of the documents used to initiate the divorce. The pro-League party, mainly academics and some businessmen, many of whom had espoused the government's case for Manchukuo, proved totally ineffective. Matsuoka was given a hero's welcome on his return via Britain and the United States, the way prepared by an officially orchestrated campaign depicting his efforts as a triumph for Japanese independence.

Once the Shanghai problem had been solved, the Foreign Office had been content to 'wait for Lytton' while trying to maintain its distance and independence from the Lytton Commission itself. There was plenty to occupy the government departments; the disarmament negotiations and the Lausanne and Ottawa conferences all took place during the summer of 1932. Miles Lampson, home on leave, complained bitterly to Nelson Johnson, the American minister at Peking, about 'the complete indifference of everyone towards China and Chinese affairs. No one here cares a twopenny d——n about it.'[29] Manchuria was an unfortunate distraction from the real business at hand. Yet the difficulties in the Far East and the weakness of the League were not without importance for the conduct of European affairs. Britain, in particular, began to reassess its security position. Simon outlined his contradictory desiderata:

I had a conversation with Senator Reed... —he is in Mr. Stimson's confidence—and gained the impression that Mr. S. is not nearly so eager for vehement denunciations as he was when the crisis was further off. For ourselves, the controlling considerations must be (1) be faithful to the League and act with the main body if possible (2) do not take the lead in an attitude which, while necessarily futile, will antagonise Japan seriously (3) be fair to both China and Japan (4) work to keep Japan in the League.[30]

Too shrewd to believe that world opinion would force Tokyo to reverse her policies, Simon shared the view that the financial costs of the occupation and Chinese resentment might eventually bring about a change. The British did not react to the Japanese recognition of Manchukuo, preferring to leave the question to the League. The Lytton report was warmly received in London and Simon became its strongest advocate. The report 'goes far to exonerate Japan,' a Foreign Office official noted, 'although she must expect some blame for her methods of precipitating the crisis and for the exaggerated political aims which she has pursued'.[31] British efforts were focused on conciliation. Simon even briefly considered creating a small body for the purpose, hoping that Lampson might repeat in Geneva his successful role in Shanghai. The foreign secretary, as he admitted to Baldwin, had gone as far as he could

[29] Lampson to Johnson, 30 June 1932, Johnson Papers, quoted in Thorne, *The Limits of Foreign Policy*, 290.

[30] Minute by Simon, 17 Sept. 1932, *DBFP*, ser. II, vol. 10, no. 674.

[31] Memo by Orde, 12 Oct. 1932, *DBFP*, ser. II, vol. 10, no. 746.

to conciliate Japan without risking permanent damage to Britain's relations with China. Simon used all his influence in the committee of nineteen to win time for Japan and to block any form of censure. Once the Japanese rejected all the League's efforts and departed, the British made no effort to recall them. As one official wrote: 'I would of course prefer that Japan should be reasonable and stay in the League but if—or as—she won't, why worry too much?'[32] Simon argued that though the League stood for moral principles which Britain shared, it was not an institution intended to maintain peace by coercion. Japan was too great a nation to respond to mere threats, as had Bulgaria and Greece in 1925. As it was clearly against Britain's interests that the League should proceed to sanctions, Simon was content to escape with nothing more forceful than the moral condemnation of Japan which Stimson had proposed in an unacceptable form more than a year earlier. Public sentiments in Britain shifted during 1932, and Japan was increasingly seen as the aggressor nation. Criticisms of Simon's policies mounted but, with few exceptions, there was no demand for sanctions. The actualities of war gave new substance to the nightmares of pacifists, further reducing the possibility of intervention. Simon's complicated diplomatic game could hardly be judged a success. Japan left the League; Manchukuo continued to exist; Britain, temporarily at least, was blamed for Japan's isolation; and the image of 'perfidious Albion' was revived in Geneva. Anglo-American relations were marked by bitterness and recriminations. By exposing Britain's dependence on the United States, Simon had tied British policy to the vagaries of American diplomacy. The hunt for a more independent policy that would protect Britain's more important strategic interests in the Far East without offending the United States preoccupied both the Foreign Office and the Treasury in the post-crises months. Finally, the British sense of the vulnerability of their empire, so important for the mother country, was intensified. Coming after the financial debacle of 1931 and the turn to protection, Britain became singularly unwilling to face any foreign challenges that could disturb the peace.

The Manchurian issue faded from public attention in the United States, which was now fully preoccupied with the depression and the forthcoming election. The State Department waited for and welcomed the Lytton report. There was no support for the idea of a Nine Power treaty conference. It is true that the gap between Hoover and his secretary of state widened during the summer of 1932 as the president took to the campaign trail. Stimson took a more sympathetic approach as a consequence of the Manchurian crisis towards French efforts to

---

[32] Quoted in Nish, *Japan's Struggle with Internationalism*, 227.

sustain the status quo; he dismissed the president's dramatic disarmament initiative as 'something from Alice in Wonderland'. Hoover, on the contrary, became more insistent on the payment of war debts and a change in the French position on disarmament. Though it paid no electoral dividends, Hoover had correctly judged the public mood. Most Americans took pride in the Stimson doctrine but rejected any further intervention in Pacific affairs. Commercial interest groups were divided, depending on the location of their Far Eastern markets, but there were no war hawks among their ranks. The Far East dropped out of public concern as the number of bankruptcies increased, unemployment soared, and apple lines were seen on the streets of New York.

Neither Britain nor the United States was prepared to use economic or naval power to stop Japan. Its actions in Manchuria did not threaten the national interests of either country, and its position in East Asia was too strong to be attacked with impunity. For both Simon and Stimson, Japan's methods were more repugnant than her goals. Stimson's interventions in the Far East fanned anti-American feeling in Japan without defining or advancing America's real interests, while President Roosevelt's subsequent endorsement of the non-recognition formula was given without any real consideration of its practical consequences. The United States declared its interest in preserving the outdated Washington treaties without any clear intention of forcing Japan to keep them. Simon's policies were equally unsatisfactory, whether with regard to China, Japan, the United States, or the League. In the conditions of the depression, neither government was willing to use its economic power to stop the Japanese seizure of Manchuria. The forces behind the nationalist movements, unleashed by the impact of the economic crisis on Japan, were too strong to have been checked by international diplomacy, whether of the old or new variety. An early Anglo-American warning to Japan might have been more useful to the moderates than Simon's attempts at neutrality and the slow mobilization of the League. Would the Japanese have reacted as negatively as Anglo-American diplomats predicted if she had been publicly rebuked, or were the risks exaggerated? In the end, the western powers neither checked Japan nor brokered a Sino-Japanese agreement. They did nothing to show their disapproval of Japanese actions beyond refusing to 'recognize' their consequences. 'Non-recognition' may have made future Sino-Japanese reconciliation more difficult. It was clearly a barrier to the fulfilment of the hopes of Japanese moderates that Britain and the United States would come to accept Manchukuo as a fait accompli. There were other ways of handling the Manchurian dispute. The western countries might have recognized the exceptional nature of the Manchurian case and accepted Japan's alteration of the status quo in the provinces. Some British politicians and the French would have preferred such a course, but Japanese behaviour, Stimson's invocation of the non-recognition principle, and the internationalization of the crisis ruled out such a solution. Some, Lord Lytton for one, believed that some future agreement between the two antagonists was possible and that bridges for accommodation could be built. This was an over-optimistic view of the situation in Japan, given the new position of the military and the spread of nationalist sentiment. The continuing weakness of the Nationalist government in China added to the volatility of the situation but hardly encouraged regional peacemaking.

In fact the Japanese would not accept compromise solutions. Opportunities for settlement were deliberately rejected. Japan might have stayed in the League, but those who favoured 'going it alone' triumphed. Many of the 'Old Liberals', who believed Japan's future development was identified with the international order created by the industrialized west, came to accept the justice and wisdom of the Manchurian action. Because it was successful, the army's challenge enhanced its reputation and gave the militarists a greater say in the making of foreign policy than before the onset of the crisis. The military began and ended the Manchurian incident. The economic arguments made in London that the occupation would be too costly proved illusory. By going off gold in response to the effects of the British devoluation, letting the yen depreciate, and increasing exports to easier markets, Takahashi Korekiyo, the veteran finance minister between 1931 and 1936, pulled Japan out of the depression. Rising military expenditure seems to have stimulated the domestic economy, and recovery was well under way by 1933. Japan entered a boom period. In the latter half of 1935 Takahashi, concerned about the costs of high inflation, wanted to reverse course and the military took fright. In February 1936 the 81-year-old finance minister was assassinated by an extremist group of army officers. There would be no cuts in defence expenditure. The Tangku truce of 31 May 1933 was concluded between the Japanese and Chinese generals on the spot without outside intervention. Both forces were exhausted, as Chinese resistance intensified as the fighting moved closer to Tientsin. Both sides agreed to a demilitarized zone 30–40 miles wide south of the Great Wall. Chiang Kai-shek, who returned to power in Nanking during March, was preparing for a summer campaign against the communists. Beyond denouncing the terms of the truce in a letter to the League, he did nothing. Though the truce was never formalized, the fighting stopped. Less than a year later, faced with a possible British loan to China, the Japanese asserted that they had the sole responsibility for preserving peace in East Asia. Other countries were warned off giving military

TABLE 39. Percentage of Japanese Trade in East Asian Sphere of Influence

Trade of	Share of	Imports (%)				Exports (%)			
		1929	1932	1935	1938	1929	1932	1935	1938
Japan	Korea and Formosa	12.3	26.2	24.1	30.0	16.8	21.6	23.4	32.9
	Kwantung	6.0	4.0	0.8	1.6	4.8	6.8	9.2	13.7
	Manchuria	1.9	2.7	5.9	9.0	2.5	1.5	3.9	8.1
	Rest of China	5.8	4.0	4.1	4.4	10.9	7.3	4.6	8.0
	Totals	26.0	36.9	34.9	45.0	35.0	37.2	41.1	62.7

Source: League of Nations, Review of Trade 1938 (Geneva, 1939), 35.

aid or financial assistance to China that could be used against Japan. The Amau declaration of 17 April 1934 was more than a declaration of independence; it was the Japanese equivalent of the American Monroe Doctrine.

The Soviets did not recover from the Manchurian shock. The build-up of the Special Red-Banner Far Eastern Army continued, as did the implementation of the Red Army's vastly increased military production programme. The crash military build-up added to the general economic crisis resulting from the excessively ambitious targets set under the Five Year Plan. Planning for 1933 showed significant cuts in production schedules. There was no purge of those who failed to fulfil their schedules. In the spring of 1933 Litvinov, who was pressing for a policy of accommodation with Japan, secured the upper hand and won Stalin's backing. At the commissar's behest, after an approach from the Japanese minister in Moscow, the Russians agreed to sell the Chinese Eastern Railway (CER) to Japan. If, theoretically, the railway gave the Soviets a forward base in Manchuria, in practice the CER represented a likely cause of conflict and war. During the course of the negotiations over the price to be paid for the railway the Soviet position suddenly stiffened, and the Japanese arrest of six Soviet CER employees was used as an excuse for temporarily breaking off the talks. Russian self-confidence was returning, restored by a good harvest, the reinforcement of the armies in the Far East, and diplomatic recognition by the United States on 16 November 1933. When, at the end of 1933, rumours began to spread about a possible Japanese invasion, Stalin felt he could take a strong stand. In a clear reference to Japan, the Soviet leader told the delegates to the Seventeenth Party Congress, convened on 26 January 1934, that 'those who try to attack our country will receive a crushing repulse to teach them in future not to poke their pig snouts into our

Soviet garden (*thunderous applause*)'.[33] As it soon became clear that the Japanese war threat was more apparent than real, the Russians, still anxious to resolve the railway issue and to conclude a good financial bargain, returned to Litvinov's policy of appeasement and resumed the talks. The CER sale was brought to a successful end in March 1935, but uneasiness about the future still remained. Stalin believed that the Soviet Union would have to face the Japanese alone. Until Russia could build up its forces to fight a two-front war and force the Japanese to bargain on equal terms, he had little choice but to support Litvinov's accommodationist line.

In retrospect, it is clear that the Manchurian episode was a turning point in Japanese foreign policy and in great-power perceptions of Japanese intentions. There was no predictability or inevitability about what might follow, but there could be no return to the assumptions of the 1920s. Japan's leaders had rejected the internationalist path in favour of a military solution to the Manchurian problem. The importance of these events went beyond the regional conflict. The Japanese actions were seen not only as a challenge to the Nine Power treaty but to the Covenant of the League and to the Kellogg–Briand pact as well. The League's 'failure' in Manchuria administered a blow to the Geneva system. If in London the government found its many doubts about the exaggerated claims of the League's more enthusiastic supporters confirmed, the representatives of many of the smaller nations drew their own conclusions about the unwillingness of the great powers to use the Geneva security system against one of their own number. As there had been no appeal to Article 16 (the Chinese feared that if war was 'declared' most of the other states would have opted for neutrality, cutting China off from supplies or credits), the League's collective security provisions were not actually brought into operation. Confidence in those provisions was shaken but not yet destroyed. Various interpretations of the check to internationalism were offered at the time. Some argued that the Covenant was not really designed with the Far East in mind, and that its failure in Manchuria was not a test of its peacekeeping provisions. Others decided, mainly in retrospect, that Article 16 should have been invoked and that a real opportunity to check aggression had been missed. There were ambiguities in the Manchurian case; as with later examples of aggression, it was not a black-and-white issue. This was clearly the view of the Lytton Commission. Japan's actions in Manchuria were not 'a simple case of the violation of the frontier of one country by the armed forces of a neighbouring country, because in Manchuria there are many features without

---

[33] Jonathon Haslam, *The Soviet Union and the Threat from the East: Moscow, Tokyo and the Prelude to the Pacific War* (Basingstoke and London, 1992), 37.

any exact parallel in other parts of the world'.[34] It was argued by some that the Assembly had acted despite the reservations of the great powers, and that the response had been appropriate to the Japanese action. Others were less sanguine. In Britain and France, the advocates of non-violence were convinced that the League ultimately would have to rely on the use of force to maintain the peace. They turned away from Geneva to more extreme forms of pacifism and isolationism. The Manchurian crisis overlapped with the World Disarmament Conference. The latter's collapse was to prove an even more resounding blow to the prestige of the League and to the hopes of its supporters. Expectations were so high that the disappointment was deep and ultimately dangerous. Those who continued to believe that international action could check aggression found it difficult to come to terms with the new rearmament era. The blows to internationalism were coming from every direction.

Books

BAMBA, NOBUYA, *Japanese Diplomacy in a Dilemma: New Light on Japan's China Policy, 1924–1929* (Kyoto, 1972).

BARNHART, MICHAEL A., *Japan Prepares for Total War: The Search for Economic Security, 1919–1941* (Ithaca, NY and London, 1987).

BEASLEY, W. G., *Japanese Imperialism, 1894–1945* (Oxford, 1987).

BELL, PETER, *Chamberlain, Germany and Japan, 1933–1934* (London, 1996).

BEST, ANTHONY, *British Intelligence and the Japanese Challenge in Asia, 1914–1941* (Basingstoke, 2002).

BORG, DOROTHY and OKAMOTO, SHUMPEI (eds.), *Pearl Harbor as History: Japanese–American Relations, 1931–1941* (New York and London, 1973).

BURNS, RICHARD DEAN and BENNETT, EDWARD M. (eds.), *Diplomats in Crisis: United States–Chinese–Japanese Relations, 1919–1941* (Santa Barbara, Cal., 1974).

COBLE, PARKS M., *Facing Japan: Chinese Politics and Japanese Imperialism, 1931–1937* (Cambridge, Mass. and London, 1991).

COOX, ALVIN and CONROY, HILARY (eds.), *China and Japan: Search for Balance Since World War I* (Santa Barbara, Cal., and Oxford, 1978).

CROWLEY, JAMES B., *Japan's Quest for Autonomy: National Security and Foreign Policy, 1930–1938* (Princeton, 1966).

DORE, RONALD and RADHA, SINHA (eds.), *Japan and World Depression: Then and Now. Essays in Memory of E. F. Penrose* (Basingstoke, 1987).

DREIFORT, JOHN E., *Myopic Grandeur: The Ambivalence of French Foreign Policy toward the Far East, 1919–1945* (Kent, Ohio, 1991).

DUUS, PETER, MYERS, RAMON H., and PEATTIE, MARK R. (eds.), *The Japanese Informal Empire in China, 1895–1937* (Princeton, 1989).

FERRELL, R., *American Diplomacy in the Great Depression: Hoover–Stimson Foreign Policy, 1929–1933* (New Haven, Conn., 1957).

---

[34] Quoted in Crowley, *Japan's Quest for Autonomy*, 185.

Fox, John P., *Germany and the Far Eastern Crisis, 1931–1938: A Study in Diplomacy and Ideology* (Oxford, 1982).

Fraser, T. G. and Lowe, Peter (eds.), *Conflict and Amity in East Asia: Essays in Honour of Ian Nish* (Basingstoke, 1992).

Fung, E. S. K., *The Diplomacy of Imperial Retreat: Britain's South China Policy* (Oxford, 1991).

Gittings, J., *The World and China, 1922–72* (London, 1974).

Haggie, Paul, *Britannia at Bay: The Defence of the British Empire Against Japan, 1931–1941* (Oxford, 1981).

Hagihara, Nobutoshi et al. (eds.), *Experiencing the Twentieth Century* (Tokyo, 1985).

Haslam, Jonathan, *The Soviet Union and the Threat from the East: Moscow, Tokyo and the Prelude to the Pacific War* (Basingstoke and London, 1992).

Hata, Ikuhiko, *Reality and Illusion: The Hidden Crisis Between Japan and the U.S.S.R., 1932–1934* (New York, 1967).

Hornbeck, Stanley K., *The Diplomacy of Frustration: The Manchurian Crisis of 1931–1933 as Revealed in the Papers of Stanley K. Hornbeck*, compiled and with an introduction by Justice D. Doenecke (Stanford, Cal., 1981).

Hsu, I. C. Y., *The Rise of Modern China* (New York, 1970).

Iriye, Akira, *After Imperialism: The Search for a New Order in the Far East, 1921– 1931* (Cambridge, Mass., 1965).

—— *The Origins of the Second World War in Asia and the Pacific* (London and New York, 1987).

Jordan, Donald A., *Chinese Boycotts versus Japanese Bombs: The Failure of China's 'revolutionary diplomacy,' 1931–32* (Ann Arbor, Mich., 1991).

Kataoka, Tetsuya, *Resistance and Revolution in China: The Communists and the Second United Front* (Berkeley, Cal., 1974).

Kennedy, Malcolm D., *The Estrangement of Great Britain and Japan, 1917– 1935* (Manchester and Berkeley, Cal., 1969).

Kirby, William C., *Germany and Republican China* (Stanford, Cal., 1984).

Lamb, Margaret and Tarling, Nicholas, *From Versailles to Pearl Harbor: The Origins of the Second World War in Europe and Asia* (Basingstoke, 2001).

Large, Stephen S., *Emperor Hirohito and Showa Japan: A Political Biography* (London, 1992).

Lensen, G., *The Damned Inheritance: The Soviet Union and the Manchurian Crises, 1924–1935* (Tallahassee, Fl., 1974).

Louis, William R., *British Strategy in the Far East, 1919–1939* (Oxford, 1971).

Lowe, Peter, *Great Britain and the Origins of the Pacific War: A Study of British Policy in East Asia, 1937–1941* (Oxford, 1987).

McKercher, B. J. C., *Transition of Power: Britain's Loss of Global Pre-eminence to the United States, 1930–1945* (Cambridge, 1999).

Matsusaka, Yoshihisa Tak, *The Making of Japanese Manchuria, 1904–1932* (Cambridge, Mass., 2001).

Mitter, Rana, *The Manchurian Myth: Nationalism, Resistance, and Collaboration in Modern China* (Berkeley, Cal., 2000).

Morley, James William *The Fateful Choice: Japan's Advance into Southeast Asia, 1939–1941* (New York, 1980).

—— (ed.), *Japan Erupts: The London Naval Conference and the Manchurian Incident, 1928–1932: Selected Translations from Taiheiyo senso e no michi, kaisen gaiko shi* (New York, 1984).

MORTON, WILLIAM FITCH, *Tanaka Giichi and Japan's China Policy* (Folkestone and New York, 1980).

MUHLE, ROBERT, *Frankreich und Hitler. Die Französische Deutschland-und Außenpolitik, 1933–1935* (Paderborn, 1995).

NEIDPATH, JAMES, *The Singapore Naval Base and the Defence of Britain's Eastern Empire, 1919–1941* (Oxford, 1981).

NISH, IAN H., *Japanese Foreign Policy, 1919–1942: Kasumigaseki to Miyakezaka* (London and Boston, 1977).

—— *Japan's Struggle with Internationalism: Japan, China and the League of Nations, 1931–1933* (London, 1993).

—— *Japanese Foreign Policy in the Interwar Period* (London, 2002).

—— (ed.), *Anglo-Japanese Alienation, 1919–1952: Papers of the Anglo-Japanese Conference on the History of the Second World War* (Cambridge, 1982).

—— (ed.), *Some Foreign Attitudes to Republican China* (London, 1984).

OGATA, SADAKO N., *Defiance in Manchuria: The Making of Japanese Foreign Policy, 1931–1932* (Berkeley, Cal., 1964).

OSTROWER, GARY B., *Collective Insecurity: The United States and the League of Nations During the Early Thirties* (Lewisburg and London, 1979).

PANTSOV, ALEKSANDR VADIMOVICH, *The Bolsheviks and the Chinese Revolution 1919-1927* (Richmond, Va., 2000).

PRITCHARD, JOHN, *Far Eastern Influences upon British Policy Towards the Great Powers, 1937–1939* (New York and London, 1987).

SPENCE, JONATHON D., *The Search for Modern China: A Documentary Collection* (New York, 1999).

STIMSON, H. L. and BUNDY, MCGEORGE, *On Active Service in Peace and War* (New York, 1948).

STOREY, R., *Japan and the Dedline of the West in Asia, 1894–1943* (London, 1979).

SUN, YOULI, *China and the Origins of the Pacific War, 1931–1941* (Basingstoke and New York, 1993).

TETSUYA, KATAOKA, *Resistance and Revolution in China: The Communists and the Second United Front* (Berkeley, Cal., 1974).

THORNE, CHRISTOPHER, *The Limits of Foreign Policy: The West, the League and the Far Eastern Crisis of 1931–1933* (London, 1972).

WALDRON, ARTHUR, *From War to Nationalism: China's Turning Point, 1924–1925* (Cambridge, 1995).

YOUNG, LOUISE, *Japan's Total Empire: Manchuria and the Culture of Wartime Imperialism* (Berkeley, Cal., 1998).

Articles

BERND, MARTIN, 'Die deutsch-japanischen Beziehungen während des Dritten Reiches', in Manfred Funke (ed.), *Hitler, Deutschland und die Mächte: Materialien zur Außenpolitik des Dritten Reiches* (Düsseldorf, 1976).

BEST, A, 'Constructing an Image: British Intelligence and Whitehall's Perception', *Intelligence and National Security*, 12 (1997).

CH´EN, JEROME, 'The Chinese Communist Movement 1927–1937', in John K. Fairbank and Albert Feuerwerker (eds.), *The Cambridge History of China*. Vol. 13, Part II: *Republican China, 1912–1949* (Cambridge, 1986).

FERRIS, JOHN, 'Worthy of Some Better Enemy? The British Estimate of the Imperial Japanese Army, 1919–41, and the Fall of Singapore', *Canadian Journal of History*, 28 (1993).

FUNG, EDMUND S. K., 'The Sino-British Rapprochement, 1927–1931', *Modern Asian Studies*, 17 (1983).

HARUM, GOTO-SHIBATA, 'Anglo-Japanese Co-operation in China in the 1920s', in Nish, J., Kibata, Yoichi (eds.), *The History of Anglo-Japanese Relations*, vol. 1: *The Political-Diplomatic Dimension, 1600–1930* (Basingstoke and New York, 2000).

IRIYE, AKIRA, 'Japanese Aggression and China's International Position, 1931–1949', in John K. Fairbank and Albert Feuerwerker (eds.), *The Cambridge History of China*. Vol. 13, Part II: *Republican China, 1912–1949* (Cambridge, 1986).

—— 'The Manchurian Incident: Japan's Revisionist Militarism, 1931–1932', in John K. Fairbank and Albert Feuerwerker (eds.), *The Cambridge History of China*. Vol. 13, Part II: *Republican China, 1912–1949* (Cambridge, 1986).

—— 'The Search for a New Order', in id., *Japan and the Wider World: From the Mid-nineteenth Century to the Present* (Edinburgh, 1997).

—— 'Japanese Diplomacy in Transition', in id., *Japan and the Wider World: From the Mid-nineteenth Century to the Present* (Edinburgh, 1997).

MCKERCHER, B. J. C., 'A Sane and Sensible Diplomacy: Austen Chamberlain, Japan, and the Naval Balance of Power in the Pacific Ocean, 1924–29', *Canadian Journal of History*, 21 (1986).

NISH, IAN, 'Some Thoughts on Japanese Expansion', in Wolfgang J. Mommsen and Jürgen Osterhammel (eds.), *Imperialism and After* (London, 1986).

—— 'Jousting with Authority: The Tokyo Embassy of Sir Francis Lindley, 1931–1934', *Proceedings of the Japan Society of London*, 105 (Dec. 1986).

—— 'European Images of Japan: Some Thoughts on Modern European–Japanese Relations', *Japan Foundation Newsletter*, 20: 3 (1992).

—— 'Intelligence and the Lytton Commission, 1931–1933', in Dick Richardson and Glyn Stone (eds.), *Decisions and Diplomacy: Essays in Twentieth Century International History in Memory of George Grun and Esmonde Robertson* (London, 1995).

—— 'Echoes of Alliance, 1920–30', in Nish and Kibata, vol 1: *The Political-Diplomatic Dimension, 1600–1930* (Basingstoke and New York, 2000).

PRITCHARD, JOHN, 'The Greater East Asia and the Pacific Conflict', in Peter Calvocoressi, John Pritchard, and Guy Wint (eds.), *Total War: The Causes and Courses of the Second World War* (revised edn., Harmondsworth, 1979).

THORNE, CHRISTOPHER, 'Viscount Cecil, the Government and the Far Eastern Crisis of 1931', *Historical Journal*, 14 (1971).

TSURUMI, YUSUKE, 'Japan in the Modern World', *Foreign Affairs*, 9: 2 (1931).

WILSON, SANDRA, 'The Manchurian Crisis and Moderate Japanese Intellectuals: The Japan Council of the Institute of Pacific Relations', *Modern Asian Studies*, 26: 3 (1992).

14

The Poisoned Chalice:
The Pursuit of Disarmament

I

The World Disarmament Conference opened in Geneva on 2 February 1932. Sixty-four states were invited; fifty-nine were actually represented, including all the major powers. Millions of petitions arrived from all over the world expressing the signers' hopes for peace. Special prayers were said in churches for the success of the conference. Ominously, though it had been almost seven years in the making, there was an additional hour-long delay to the conference's formal opening as members of the League Council met in special session to consider the dangerous situation in Shanghai. A considerable debate took place in political circles over whether the times were auspicious for such a disarmament gathering at all. Statesmen in Britain and in France would have welcomed the further postponement of a conference they

TABLE 40. Size of Armed Forces: Figures Prepared for the World Disarmament Conference, 1932

	Army		Navy	Air	
	Home	Overseas		Home	Overseas
UK	114,745	29,777	96,042	23,038	6,889
France	362,167	246,103	57,129	32,110	8,398
Germany	100,500	—	15,000	—	—
Italy	462,281	29,137	51,326	21,418	775
USA	106,426	20,501	77,187	25,680	1,519
Japan	252,360	—	78,322	16,821	—

Note: Includes all effectives but not reservists. British overseas forces do not include the Indian Army or the Dominions. French overseas includes all French colonies and mandates. Italian home army includes 260,000 men serving 18 months plus short-term conscripts. US overseas forces includes the Philippines, the Panama Canal, Nicaragua, and China.

Sources: League of Nations, *Armaments Yearbook*, vol. 8 (1932); Special Edition, *Conference for the Reduction and Limitation of Armaments* (Geneva, 1932).

feared would create new discords among the nations. The Brüning government would not accept any further postponement in the proceedings. The Preparatory Commission had completed its task in December 1930; in January 1931 the Council set the date for the conference. The additional year's wait ironically was considered necessary for there to be adequate 'preparation', but with pressure relieved by the conclusion of the formal preparatory process, this was where practical progress ceased (see Table 40). Preoccupied with financial and political crises, there were no meaningful private negotiations between the main states over disarmament. In their absence, attention at the League Assembly in September instead turned to a minor Italian initiative for a year-long 'armaments truce' to freeze current levels of armaments while the disarmament conference was in session. The idea caught public attention, and from 1 November 1931 the member states of the League and those attending the conference agreed to such a truce in arms programmes, particularly welcome for those feeling the cold winds of depression. Still, there were fears in London and Paris that the truce might be made permanent and so jeopardize their armaments development and replacement schedules. There would be no simple solutions to even the most apparently straightforward problems of disarmament.

To many contemporaries the Geneva gathering was of critical importance. It came at a moment when fears of future wars were mounting but before the wave of public optimism created by Locarno and the Kellogg–Briand pact had fully receded. The prospect of aerial bombardment and gas warfare added a new dimension of horror to the ongoing debate. Statesmen were fully aware of the expectations of large numbers of people, and in the functioning democracies politicians had to consider the electoral costs of failure. Why the enormous attention paid in the world press to yet another League effort to limit arms? In the background was the rediscovery, some ten years after the armistice, of the Great War. The events of 1914–18 were re-created between roughly 1928 and 1933 in prose, poetry, and film; there was an outpouring of revisionist histories and political and military memoirs. The men of the *generazione bruciata* (the Italian term more evocative than the English 'lost generation') were intent on disinterring the war from the official monuments and gravestones commemorating the dead. There was a general European assault on the collective amnesia of the mid-1920s, with Italy one of the few exceptions. To be sure, the message conveyed was often ambivalent and even contradictory; wartime examples of leadership, heroism, and camaraderie transcended the horror and purposelessness of the carnage. For some the war was a time of personal liberation and supreme fulfilment, and yet also an example of waste, futility, and horror. To many writers, the purpose was to portray a lost world of combat whose survivors were left homeless. The anti-war message was also taken up by the film-makers, earliest in the United States where *What Price Glory?* appeared in 1926, but also in Germany. Whatever the intent, the re-creation of the war experience was not that of the wars of the pre-1914 period. The war generation had lost its innocence.

Erich Maria Remarque's *Im Westen nichts Neues* (*All Quiet on the Western Front*), published in Germany in 1929, was the most popularly acclaimed of the German 'war boom' novels. By the end of 1930 the book had sold almost 1 million copies in Germany and another million in Britain, France, and the United States. Remarque denied he had written an anti-war novel: 'I merely wanted to awaken understanding for a generation that more than all others has found it difficult to make its way back from the four years of death, struggle and terror, to the peaceful fields of work and progress.'[1] The book's popularity at home infuriated the German nationalists and the Weimar veterans' organizations. The military deplored Remarque's influence; the communists denounced his bourgeois decadence. The film version's first viewing in December 1930 was disrupted by violent demonstrations, mainly by National Socialists. Such was the public impact that the censor's office in Berlin, with Brüning's full approval, banned any further showings. Remarque, though the best-known and most widely read of the German writers, did not stand alone. Ludwig Renn, Fritz von Unruh, Arnold Zweig, and the anonymous *Schlump* were sold in Germany and translated abroad. The French realist vision of the war was shaped by writers such as Henry Barbusse, Romain Rolland, Jules Romains, Georges Duhamel, Maurice Genevoix, and André Maurois. Barbusse and Rolland became the leaders of the new pacifist movements created in the early 1930s. The works of several of these authors came out during or immediately after the war. Their impact on the wider reading public outside French borders was considerably delayed. Some soldier-writers took longer to digest their experience. The young Céline (Louis-Ferdinand Destouches), who was wounded after three months at the front in 1914 and invalided out of the army, only wrote about his soul-searing experience in *Voyage au bout de la nuit*, published in 1932. 'I'll never get over it, that is a truth I pass on to you yet again, one shared by a few of us. It's all there. The tragedy, our misery, it's most of our contemporaries' ability to forget. What a rabble.'[2] The appearance of Remarque's work in France, literally

---

[1] Erich Maria Remarque to General Sir Ian Hamilton, 1 June 1929.
[2] Destouches to Joseph Garcin, Sept. 1931, in Frederic Vitoux, *Céline: A Biography* (American edn., New York, 1992), 192.

translated as *À l'ouest rien de nouveau*, opened the way to a stream of other German war stories.

In Britain, above all, the causes and course of the war were re-examined and the nation's politicians and military leaders, more often than not, found wanting. Studies by Winston Churchill, Lloyd George, and the influential military journalist Captain Basil Liddell Hart initiated a public debate about the way the war was fought and the high price paid for military incompetence. It was at this time, too, that British ex-servicemen began to publish memoirs of 'their war', often in fictional form; accounts they believed to be more 'real' and 'honest' than those of the wartime propagandists and government spokesmen. Writing for a growing audience, Richard Aldington, Edmund Blunden, Guy Chapman, Robert Graves, Frederick Manning, Siegfried Sassoon, and R. C. Sheriff, among many others of varying talent, highlighted the human cost and destructiveness of combat while paying high tribute to the comradeship of men in battle and the classlessness of trench warfare. Sheriff's *Journey's End* played to capacity audiences in London and became an international stage hit. Many of the British novels were translated into German.

There is, without doubt, a connection between the revival of war memories, whatever their ambiguities, and the appearance of the new pacifism of the 1930s. The feeling that no war was worth fighting intensified as the sense of some impending apocalypse grew. In terms of influence the pacifist groups were marginal rather than mainstream organizations, yet their meetings, rallies, and propaganda reached a wider audience than at any previous time. Pacifist movements represent only a small minority of people in any country at any time. Far more important and numerous in the 1930s were the national and international peace movements, diverse in their membership, goals, and programmes, some dating from before 1914 but all anti-war in some measure. The calling of the disarmament conference mobilized these groups and their adherents.

In Britain the League of Nations Union (LNU), the most numerous and important of these bodies, sought to enlist a million members, threw its full weight behind the disarmament movement, organizing meetings, rallies, and petitions. The LNU's most memorable effort came after the collapse of the conference. In its 'peace ballot' campaign of 1935 (parodied by one pacifist as 'a questionnaire on temperance organised by the liquor trade') 11,640,066 people cast their vote in favour of collective security. The overwhelming majority were for international agreements on arms reduction and a ban on the production of arms for private profit. Such public manifestations in favour of peace could be variously interpreted. For most LNU members, backing for collective security meant League action that would prevent war. Theirs was not a vote for a resort to arms by Britain. Far more balloteers supported economic than military sanctions in the hope that the former alone would check aggression. Only extreme pacifists argued that a vote for sanctions in any form—the heart of the League's collective security system—was a vote for war. Confusions in the public mind over what League action actually meant left the government with a large measure of latitude when it began to consider rearmament. The peace ballot was merely a later confirmation of what the national politicians already knew on the eve of the Geneva talks: Britain had to be seen to support the cause of disarmament. Those service chiefs, cabinet ministers, and backbenchers who were more concerned about Britain's defences than disarmament had to put their case carefully in public. Few would openly risk the danger of being called 'warmongers'. The government had to avoid a disaster at Geneva.

Demonstrations of support for disarmament and the League made their impact on the National governments of MacDonald and Baldwin, as did a series of by-elections in 1933–4 in which Labour played the 'peace card' with some measure of success. Some indication of the climate of opinion in 'establishment' circles can be found in the controversy engendered by the 'King and Country' debate at the Oxford Union on 9 February 1933. In no way different from the usual Thursday-night meetings of the student union, generally ignored by those outside Oxford, the very phrasing of the motion: 'That this House will in no circumstances fight for its King and Country', evoked memories of wartime jingoism. The victory of the proposers was, in many ways, a backward-looking protest. But the widespread press and public reaction to the 'Oxford pledge' suggests that the debate raised unsettling questions with a wider political resonance than could have been anticipated. The subject was widely discussed in the American press, where the vote was usually cited as an example of the weakness and decadence of the British ruling classes.

The most important British pacifist organization, the Peace Pledge Union, was formally instituted only in 1936, but its roots lay in the debates occasioned by the proceedings and collapse of the World Disarmament Conference. Started by Canon Dick Sheppard, the PPU attracted a cross-section of men and women, churchmen, academics, and writers, including Storm Jameson and Vera Brittain, many politicized by the domestic events of 1931 and then stirred to action by the rising fear of a new war. The 'never again' mood engendered both a pacifist and isolationist response. The PPU was larger (at its height, it had 136,000 members), more intellectually distinguished, and more publicly known than any previous pacifist group in Britain. Many members of the League of Nations Union and other peace societies found a more congenial home within its ranks. It was paradoxical, if understandable, that as the real war-clouds gathered, the PPU became more absolute in its 'pacificism'.

In France, disarmament became a major political issue dividing the parties of the right and left. The former were united in their belief that Germany posed a threat to the security of France and that strong defensive measures, above all a well-equipped army and modernized navy, were necessary; those on the left supported the cause of disarmament and welcomed the forthcoming disarmament conference. On either side of the divide, however, there was a wide spectrum of opinion, and the differences between them were sharper in opposition than when in office. Both the radical and socialist parties were split on the road to be followed, as was intellectual Catholic opinion. For the radicals, as became clear at their annual conference in early November 1931, Édouard Herriot gave far more weight to security than disarmament, while Édouard Daladier and Pierre Cot placed disarmament first in their order of priorities. A majority of socialists followed Léon Blum, who argued that it was incumbent on France to disarm even without supplementary guarantees for its security. He later became one of Herriot's most persistent critics. There were other socialists, as well as radicals, however, who held to the Briand triad of 'arbitration, security, disarmament', without making any distinction about their relative importance. The communists went their own way. At the meeting of the 'Amsterdam Congress against Imperialist War', convened in August 1932 by Rolland and Barbusse, even the 'integralists' exempted war for the defence of the Soviet Union from their rejection of all military action. In the May 1932 parliamentary elections a surprisingly large number of candidates addressed the disarmament question, given the usual preoccupation of the electorate with domestic issues. The number of successful candidates opposing or supporting disarmament was about equal (geography was a key factor), but the overwhelming majority, like most Frenchmen, wanted to have both security and disarmament. While no government wished to incur the stigma of failure at Geneva, France's statesmen had considerable room for manoeuvre as they sought to preserve the country's defences without openly challenging sections of the electorate.

Until the elections the public initiative lay with the disarmers. The peace groups mobilized their forces in the winter and spring of 1931–2; newspapers and journals joined the campaign to inform the public and propagandize for the disarmament cause. There was a multiplicity of initiatives reflecting the diversity of societies and views so characteristic of the French peace movement. *The Comité d'Action pour la SDN,*

Conciliation Internationale, Centre Européen de la Dotation Carnegie, Association de la Paix par le Droit, and the *Ligue des Droits de l'Homme* were only some of the active organizations. Hopes of creating a single voice for peace with the prestige of the British LNU were doomed to failure. Each French group had its own scenario. A massive international Congress of Disarmament at the Trocadero in Paris in November 1931, with over a thousand delegates, brought out many committed supporters but also attracted nationalist counter-demonstrators, leading to an 'exchange of invectives and even of blows'.[3] In January the Socialist Party and the CGT organized a massive pro-disarmament meeting; in April the Ligue des Droits de l'Homme and the peace cartels held a well-attended conference in Paris. At no other time were these movements so active or so well supported.

French pacifist campaigners were also active. Between 1930, when it was founded, and 1934, when it reached the apogee of its influence, the French Ligue Internationale des Combattants de la Paix (LICP) successfully challenged the notions of pre-war peace advocates with its espousal of a complete renunciation of war. Created as a 'haven for all forms of absolute pacifism', the LICP preached the doctrine of total pacifism.[4] It recruited socialists and anarchists (communists rejected imperialist conflicts but hailed the class war), and reached into the provinces and to Algeria. In the winter of 1931–2 and again in 1932–3 there were massive propaganda campaigns across the whole country. Victor Méric, the leader of the organization, claimed a membership of 20,000, while many thousands more heard LICP speakers. The movement's spread, fed by the increasing distrust felt towards the politicians in Paris and Geneva, was cut short by the death of Méric and the internal quarrels between pro-and anti-communist factions that gathered force after 1934. In France, as in Britain and the United States, women were in the forefront of the 'integral pacifist' groups. The French section of the International League of Women for Peace and Liberty (LIFPL), though smaller than its equivalent in Britain, Denmark, or Germany, grew from 500 women in 1925 to a claimed membership of 4,500 in the early 1930s. The French feminist interest in disarmament reached its height during the World Disarmament Conference, when a massive effort was made to preach the message to a wider if frustratingly apathetic female audience. As with the non-feminist groups, the increasingly Marxist and communist orientation of some sections of the LIFPL led to its isolation

---

[3] Maurice Vaïsse, *Sécurité d'abord: la politique Française en matière de désarmement, 9 décembre 1930–17 avril 1934* (Paris, 1981), 157.

[4] Norman Ingram, *The Politics of Dissent: Pacifism in France, 1919–1939* (Oxford, 1991), 146.

and impotence well before the rise of Hitler posed new ideological problems. The situation was somewhat different in Germany, where pacifist groups in the early 1930s were rendered impotent by losing their links to the mainstream political parties. It was the Great War and defeat that had made their message popular, though it was soon to be muffled by the widespread 'war guilt' debate. A mass meeting organized in Berlin in 1919 under the slogan '*Nie wieder Krieg*' ('no more war') attracted between 100,000 and 200,000 people, and the subsequent movement of the same name drew strong backing from the SPD and the trade unions. By 1928, however, rivalries among the leaders virtually destroyed the unity of the organization, and the subsequent fragmentation and weakening of the centre and socialist parties undermined its mass appeal. The largest German pacifist organization, the *Deutsches Friedenskartell*, with a membership of over 50,000 in 1925, was torn by quarrels between moderates and radicals, and with the victory of the latter the moderates withdrew. By 1932 the organization, with only a few thousand members left, was no longer playing any part in Weimar politics. Small pacifist bodies were still active in the years before Hitler came to power, but they remained undersized and were vulnerable to attack by both the 'nationalist opposition' and the communists engaged in their struggle against the 'social fascists'. The Brüning administration showed little sympathy with the anti-war campaigns or the people who sponsored them. The case for pacifism was kept alive only through the writings of some left-wing intellectuals. The cause itself lost political credibility.

Public opinion remained polarized along political lines. In contrast to the anti-war novels and films mentioned earlier, there was in Germany also a new vogue for the works of 'soldierly nationalism' written in the early 1920s, which were republished in large editions and sold in tens of thousands during the last years of the republic. The writers, almost all ex-soldiers, had eschewed party politics in the 1920s, when their positive image of war appealed to the parties of the right and the ex-servicemen's associations. Out of fashion during the stabilization period, these writings acquired a new popularity. The view of war as an ennobling and meaningful, even an aesthetic experience, and the message that war alone provided the means by which nations became unified and rejuvenated, took on a new significance in the circumstances of 1931–2. The existence of the Stahlhelm, the Free Corps, and the other paramilitary bodies of the right and left meant that organized violence was an integral part of Weimar political life well before the SA showed its strength. From 1927 onwards, moreover, many German university teachers and students began to accept and preach extreme nationalist views. Even without an active Nazi recruitment campaign,

National Socialist student groups appeared in many German universities. Far too young to have served in the Great War, this generation of students proved highly receptive to the message of 'soldierly nationalism'. University students became active participants in the *Wehrsport* activities organized by German military leaders looking to the creation of a future militia.

One must distinguish between the weakening of the German pacifist movements and the spread of nationalism and even militarism and violence, on the one hand, and public attitudes towards war, on the other. Even where disillusioned and frightened by the polarization and radicalization of politics, large sections of the German bourgeoisie and working classes remained pacifically inclined. This was particularly true of the older generation that reacted with bewilderment to the cult of youth, the breakdown of traditional social restraints, and the resurgence of violence in the cities. For many citizens the demand for 'equal rights' (*Gleichberechtigung*) was identified only with the restoration of German pride and prestige, and not with war. Trade unions in Germany, as in other countries, set about mobilizing public opinion on the eve of the World Disarmament Conference. Petitions prepared by the two largest German international unions were endorsed in meetings organized by the SPD. More than 600,000 people attended these rallies. Relatively little attention, except among a few pacifists, was paid to Hitler's glorification of force or his foreign-policy aims as stated in *Mein Kampf*. Ernst Thälmann, the KPD candidate for the Reich presidency in 1932, argued that 'A vote for Hitler is a vote for war', but he was referring to the threat of future imperialist conflicts between capitalist states and not specifically to Nazi doctrines. It was the promise of national renewal and relief on the domestic front that brought voters into the National Socialist camp, and not demands for *Lebensraum*. Both before and after his ascent to power Hitler represented himself as a 'man of peace'. His use of the vocabulary of violence, force, and struggle was directed towards Germany's internal struggle for regeneration. Germans as well as foreigners were assured that 'nobody wanted peace and tranquillity more than himself and Germany'.[5] This shrewd observer of the public mood shaped his rhetoric to suit his audience, domestic as well as foreign.

II

If world public opinion meant anything in 1932, the World Disarmament Conference should have been a great success. Instead, it was

[5] Norman H. Baynes, *The Speeches of Adolf Hitler, April 1922–August 1939* (New York, 1969), ii. 1003.

clear from the start that any progress towards disarmament would require a massive diplomatic effort. The Germans would set the terms of the disarmament debate. It is worth noting that by 1932 Britain, France, and the United States had undertaken several sustained years of unilateral cuts to their military budgets. This was in stark contrast to the claims of Germany, where initial steps of programmatic secret rearmament had begun in 1928. The pulpit available to German policy-makers afforded by being 'officially disarmed' via the Treaty of Versailles, however, gave them enormous political leverage. With the reparation question settled from July 1932, the earlier German claim for equality of rights came to the forefront of European diplomacy. 'The counter-part of the obligations assumed by Germany in 1919 is a formal undertaking on the part of the other states that disarmament by Germany should be simply a prelude to general disarmament by the other powers', Julius Curtius, Brüning's foreign minister, reminded the Assembly in September 1931.[6] The implicit threat, which played most strongly in the minds of British policy-makers, was that unless the Germans received satisfaction they would claim the unilateral right to rearm. Stresemann, despite his healthy respect for military might, had avoided grasping this particular nettle. His efforts had been directed at using the diplomatic and economic means at Germany's disposal to restore the country to its great-power position. Neither the violations of the Versailles restrictions nor the links with the Soviet Union, which he sanctioned, were of a kind to provide the Germans with a credible army. The change came under Brüning, and the new factor was the Reichswehr decision to raise and equip a force that would enable the state to determine its own future. The origins of this decision can be traced back to the changes in the leadership of the Reichswehr that began with the forced resignation of General von Seeckt in 1926 and his eventual replacement as minister of defence by General Wilhelm Groener in January 1928. Unlike Seeckt, who liked to work in secrecy and isolation, Groener believed in co-operation with the politicians in pursuit of the army's goals. The Reichswehr would accept civilian political control in return for the funds and backing it needed. Groener, moreover, had different ambitions for the Reichswehr than his predecessor. He wished to create an integrated military force capable of fulfilling Germany's revisionist goals in the foreseeable future. Eminently practical in his thinking, Groener balanced the continuing need to work with foreign powers to open the way for rearmament while trying, at the same time, to rationalize and improve the existing

---

[6] Speech by Curtius, 12 Sept. 1931, *League of Nations Official Journal*, Special Supplement no. 93 (Geneva, 1931), 88–92.

Reichswehr structure which he believed to be the guarantee of Germany's independence and great-power status.

Groener concentrated on what the Reichswehr could do under existing conditions and how it could be equipped to perform its defensive tasks. Whereas the aloof Seeckt had been convinced that the day of mass armies was over and that rapid technological changes made the accumulation of large reserves of weapons unnecessary and counterproductive, the new Reichswehr leaders were convinced that Germany needed a mass army with modern weapons to defend itself properly. They sought from the state the necessary political and financial support to expand and equip (including tanks and aircraft) the professional army, and to give Germany's youth the pre-military training required to build up reserves from which to recruit a future militia. Both actions were forbidden by the Versailles treaty. In 1928 Groener obtained cabinet approval for a five-year army armaments programme, as well as funds for the construction of the first 'pocket battleship' as a means to gain naval support, for he did not believe the new and expensive ships were necessary. With 1928 accepted as the 'normal year' for military budgeting, the Reichswehr was able to limit the cabinet's freedom to restrict expenditure and so was able, for the most part, to avoid major cuts in defence appropriations during the depression years. A more ambitious 'second armaments programme' (to cover the years 1933–8) was already being discussed during 1930, but was not adopted by the Reichswehr or given cabinet approval until 1932. This aimed at the creation of a well-equipped twenty-one-division field army, with minimum stocks for a period of six weeks, by 1938. The plans for 1933–8 required additional funding and radical changes in the structure and equipping of the existing army that could not be implemented within the Versailles structure. It would depend, too, given the shortage of experienced recruits available in the relevant groups, on finding ways to train young men who could be mobilized for any future conflict. This would be accomplished through the creation of a new 'militia', using youths who had engaged in *Wehrsport* activities (recreational exercises such as marching, map-reading, callisthenics, and target shooting), and who would then be given three months' training in units of the regular army; some of the militia would be retained after training. Meanwhile, the idea would have to be sold to the Allies. The major source for past recruitment for the *Wehrsport* had been such paramilitary groups as the Stahlhelm and its affiliates. After 1930 the Nazi SA was clearly the most promising source, despite the strong antipathy of the military establishment towards Hitler and his cohorts.

The Reichswehr moved with caution as it laid its plans, always fearful that a new disarmament convention might curtail its programme.

Brüning's first priority was to deal with reparations, and the chancellor was anxious to avoid any additional cause for confrontation with France. The financial crisis of 1931 also limited what the army could do. In their planning for 1933–8, the most modest programme considered (the so-called 'six week programme') would cost just under 100 million marks each year. This would have to be raised from over-appropriations for the Reichswehr and from other ministry budgets already subject to scrutiny and strain. An alternative, the larger 'Billion Programme' linked to work-creation schemes and still considered inadequate by the army leadership, was put forward and rejected by the cabinet. The Reichswehr opted for a modified version of its minimum plan. For these reasons, the army chiefs agreed to Brüning's demand that the reparations question be settled before making a major push on the disarmament front. Every effort would be made to disguise the intention to rearm and to postpone a clash with France. The diplomatic spotlight in Geneva would be on getting other states to disarm to German levels. Even within this framework, divisions occurred between the Reichswehr and the Auswärtiges Amt. Groener's proposals for Geneva in March 1931 included the abolition of Part V of the Versailles treaty and the granting of parity in forces with France at whatever level would be established for the French metropolitan army. State Secretary von Bülow, the chief civilian adviser on disarmament, argued that these were excessive and dangerous demands that would alert other negotiators to the German intention to rearm and foreclose the possibility of concessions. It would be wiser, he believed, to accept an initial disarmament convention that would last for five years, after which Germany would be free to do as she wished. As there was no money to spare for extensive rearmament, it was unnecessary to demand the recognition of Germany's full equality of rights as a precondition for negotiation. These differences were not resolved before the opening of the disarmament conference, but a sufficient measure of agreement was reached to present a united front at Geneva and to launch a campaign at home for a disarmament agreement that would include the ending of special restrictions on Germany. The message was endorsed by an impressive list of academics, many of whom would be among Hitler's first exiles. In Geneva, the army temporarily gave way to the diplomats.

At home, during the autumn of 1931, the Reichswehr began to recruit from the SA for its enlarged *Wehrsport* programme and in January Nazis were permitted to enlist in the Reichswehr itself. But the involvement of the SA in street fighting and fears of right-wing putsches before the coming elections led the *Länder* governments to demand a ban on the SA which Groener, as minister of the interior, somewhat reluctantly imposed. Behind the army's policy towards the SA were more fundamental political questions. Though Groener and his protégé, General Kurt von Schleicher, head of the Reichswehr's Ministerial Office since its creation in March 1929, had pressed Brüning's candidature on Hindenburg and welcomed the transition to presidential government, the strong Nazi showing in the September 1930 elections alerted Schleicher to their importance. This highly political general—a 'cardinal in politics', as Groener described Schleicher—thought he could use the SA without paying Hitler's price. Schleicher was convinced that Hitler could be manipulated like one of the glass animals on his otherwise barren desk. In the winter and spring of 1932 he was intriguing against both Groener and Brüning, using his friendship with Hindenburg's son, Oskar, to undermine the president's confidence in their continuing leadership. Hindenburg was re-elected to a second term on the second ballot of the presidential elections on 10 April, but Hitler's 15 million votes underlined his expanding popular appeal. Groener was forced out on 13 May over the decision to lift the ban on the SA; Brüning followed on 30 May. In both cases, Schleicher played the leading part.

The diplomatic outlook from Paris during 1931–2 seemed increasingly worrying on many fronts. In particular, French policy-makers viewed the forthcoming disarmament conference with mounting apprehension. Well-informed by their own and the Polish intelligence services, they suspected or knew that the Germans were preparing rearmament plans. The War Ministry's intelligence arm, the Deuxième Bureau, had no doubts about German violations of the Versailles restrictions, the state of its current military preparedness, or its intentions to demand continual concessions over armaments after any initial success. The Deuxième Bureau was convinced that the Germans wanted to increase the size of their army and win the right to equip it with the war materials forbidden by Versailles. While overestimating Germany's existing military and industrial strength, the French military chiefs repeatedly warned of the fatal consequences of the gap between 1918-vintage French and modern German armaments. Whatever may have been the subsequent disagreements between the Quai d'Orsay and the War Ministry over the policy to be followed at Geneva, both agreed that Germany had to be held to the treaty restrictions. France's forces were numerically superior, but policy-makers doubted whether in practice they could successfully defend the status quo, either by threat or military action. The thinking of the general staff centred on the protection of the frontiers and the overseas territories from foreign attack. The building of the Maginot fortifications, begun in 1930, and a strategy based on a citizen army defensively deployed, had strong public backing. There could be no repetition of the losses of 1914–18 or the destruction caused by fighting on French territory. The defence chiefs argued that France had already disarmed to the lowest level possible given the absence of any guarantees of its security. The War Ministry, which believed that France had nothing to gain and everything to lose from the forthcoming disarmament conference, refused to consider any concessions at all. The politicians chose to pursue a different strategy, a reasoned defence of the French position and the creation of a diplomatic front with the other great powers, above all Britain, to maintain the Treaty of Versailles safeguards. This was the battle that was lost at Geneva.

Viewed from abroad, France appeared as the most powerful military nation on the continent and, as such, the main obstacle to disarmament. This appearance of overwhelming strength was deceptive. Apart from the Soviet army, the French ground forces were the largest in Europe, but this was an army in crisis, badly organized, with a divided command, too many senior officers, low morale, and outdated equipment. The high command was wedded to a Great War strategy sanctified by association with the great Marshal Pétain and therefore difficult to challenge, as the young Colonel Charles de Gaulle was soon to discover. General Weygand, Marshal Foch's brilliant ex-chief of staff, became chief of the general staff in 1930; his appointment initiated a period of sharp conflict between the military and the politicians. Always a controversial figure, Weygand, ultra-conservative and Catholic ('Up to his neck in priests, naturally', was Clemenceau's comment), was deeply distrusted by the left. His second-in-command, Maurice Gamelin, thought to be more republican in his sympathies, was specifically appointed as a political counterweight. Weygand constantly complained about the state of his forces and their poor equipment, run down during the colonial campaigns in Morocco and the Levant and not subsequently replaced. Every defence budget between 1928 and 1931 caused a crisis; no funds were available for modernization, since the building of the frontier fortifications took up the major part of the army's appropriations. Both Weygand and Gamelin argued that France's military strength had been cut to dangerously low levels of manpower. With the introduction of a one-year service term in March 1928, the army had been reduced from thirty-two to twenty-five divisions, the absolute minimal number consistent with national security.

The navy was in far better shape than the army. After the Washington Naval Conference it was reconstituted and enlarged; though capital ships were now tightly restricted, the number of light cruisers and submarines was multiplied to guard the routes between France and her African colonies. Growing in confidence, the admirals repeatedly blocked the efforts made in 1931 and 1932 to conclude an agreement with Italy, seen as France's most immediate naval threat. The rejection of the Franco-Italian naval accord finally pieced together in March 1931, the Bases of Agreement, proved to be the critical moment, despite repeated British efforts to breathe new life into subsequent talks. Captain (later Admiral) Darlan argued that the moment for concessions to Italy had passed; Admiral Violette, chief of the naval staff, indulged in outbursts of wild Anglophobia. Berthelot and the Quai d'Orsay, thought to be strongly anti-Italian, were nonetheless acutely conscious of the dangers and costs of isolation at Geneva. They were, however, unable to convince the naval chiefs to accept any form of compromise. The price of their failure in 1931 was Italian hostility, British anger, and American irritation. There was talk in naval circles of an '*attaque brusque*' by the Italian navy and air force, the former expanded under Mussolini's naval building programme and the latter improved due to the efforts of Italo Balbo, the chief of the Italian air force. News of Brüning's visit to Rome and Dino Grandi's to Berlin in October 1931 fanned apprehensions at the Quai d'Orsay of what could be expected at Geneva. France had no independent air force; control was shared between the army and navy. What existed was more remarkable for its quantity than quality. Bombers were notable by their absence. This may explain why the diplomats of the Quai's League of Nations section, who took the leading part in shaping the French disarmament proposals, pushed the idea of internationalizing civilian aircraft and prohibiting bombers, much against the will of the air minister, Jean-Louis Dumesnil. All three services, as in every country, pointed to their individual inadequacies and demanded increased funding. In the autumn of 1931, on the eve of the disarmament conference, the service chiefs in France won their fight for increased estimates, though they did not get the total sums demanded. A quarter of the 1932 budget was to be devoted to national defence; total expenditure rose from 14,252 (1931–2) to 15365 million francs in 1932. Weygand was still arguing in May 1932 that the army had 'sunk to the lowest level consistent with the security of France in the present state of Europe'.[7]

A French memorandum to the League of 15 July 1931 provided a very clear exposition of France's stand on disarmament and security. Its preparation had revealed major differences, both substantive and tactical, between the military, who opposed any concessions on armaments and rejected the idea of 'equality', and the diplomats, who were anxious to avoid the impression of implacable hostility towards any form of disarmament which could only result in French diplomatic isolation.

[7] P. C. F. Bankwitz, *Maxime Weygand and Civil–Military Relations in Modern France* (Cambridge, Mass., 1967), 85.

The Quai d'Orsay succeeded in toning down the War Ministry's uncompromising draft, but the more diplomatically phrased final document still retained the essential elements of the French position. Three
general points were made. First of all, France would stand by the arms
restrictions imposed on the defeated powers by the peace treaties.
Second, the country had already made large reductions in its armaments
on a voluntary basis and had reached the lowest point consistent with its
national security in the present condition of Europe and the world.
Finally, the French argued that disarmament was a political question that
required political solutions along the lines of the abortive Geneva
Protocol, the Treaty of Locarno, and the General Act. It was only
when every state was guaranteed against aggression by assistance that
was 'mutual, effective, and prompt' that the simultaneous reduction of
armaments could take place. Issued in the middle of the summer
financial crisis in Germany, the French memorandum appeared far less
conciliatory and flexible than the Quai had intended, and provoked a
strong hostile reaction both in Berlin and in London. The specific
numbers on effectives, material, and expenditure requested by the
League were maximized in order to cover the French requirements
during the disarmament treaty period and until a security regime was put
in place.

Although under Pierre Laval the French were enjoying a period of
relative political stability, and until the last months of 1931 appeared to
have escaped the ravages of the depression, they found it difficult to
capitalize on their existing military and financial strength. Though
Briand stayed at the Quai d'Orsay during 1931, he lost ground during
the summer and autumn and never recovered from the double shock of
the Austro-German customs union and the débâcle of his defeat in the
French presidential elections in May. It was Laval who had to defend
what was left of 'la politique Briand' against the criticism of the right in
the Chamber, and who took command of French diplomacy even
before he assumed control of the Quai d'Orsay in January 1932. Briand's
physical deterioration was obvious, though he was still conducting some
business in Paris until the end of the year. 'He cut a pathetic figure. He
could hardly speak', recorded Alexander Werth, the French journalist.
'He was like the dying symbol of forlorn hopes.'[8] Laval had the invent-
iveness, dexterity, and drive which should have led to a marked improvement in France's diplomatic position, yet none of his efforts paid
the expected dividends.

---

[8] Alexander Werth, *The Twilight of France, 1933–1940: A Journalist's Chronicle* (London, 1942), 8.

As the date for the opening of the disarmament conference drew nearer, the French found their allies difficult, their friends cool, and the Germans elusive. There were tensions with both the Belgians and the Poles. The Belgian king, Albert I, was highly critical of the Versailles system and apprehensive of French intransigence. Politicians, diplomats, and the military leaders in Brussels had deep misgivings about arrangements that exposed Belgium to the possibility of independent French action without consultation with Brussels. Fears about their subordinate role were compounded by French condescension. Anxious that the disarmament conference should be a success, the Belgians feared that French inflexibility would block any progress at Geneva. In Poland, Piłsudski was already considering a more independent line towards Paris. Faced with the deteriorating European situation and the growing spirit of *révanche* in Germany, he was determined to keep himself free to move in whatever direction was necessary or even to strike out on his own course of action. The difficulties implicit in the Franco–Polish relationship were apparent in the separate French and Polish negotiations with the Soviet Union during 1931–2.

France's financial strength did not produce the *rapprochement* with Germany that Laval had thought possible and made a central part of his policy. The disparities between French wealth and German poverty, moreover, only generated Anglo-American sympathy for the Germans and intensified their pressure on France to make concessions to Berlin. Laval was prepared to make some compromises, but he was reined in both by his more cautious Quai advisers and by his own cabinet hardliners, above all, André Tardieu. As long as Brüning was concentrating on the ending of reparations, he preferred to exploit the differences between France and the Anglo-American powers than to come to an arrangement with France. He risked very little in turning down French offers. Approaches from the German military offering a political entente in return for French recognition of the German claim to equality of rights in arms were made in November 1931 and again during 1932. For the most part, however, the French response, particularly on the military side, was distinctly cool. Given the dangerous and unsettled political situation in Germany, this was not the time to remove the restraints on German military power or to consider cuts in French armaments.

After his visit to Berlin in September 1931, Laval went off the following month to Washington, this time without Briand but with a powerful financial team and his 20-year-old daughter, who had a more successful visit than her father. Paul Claudel, the French ambassador in Washington, summed up the situation: 'As long as the United States can offer nothing to us, it is obvious that they have no right to demand

anything from us.'[9] Laval went with hopes for future war-debt negotiations and also for some kind of American involvement in the underwriting of European security. There was some indication of a future
accord on financial matters, but little progress on disarmament and
security (see pp. 678–9). During their meetings Hoover vaguely suggested that, the Europeans had settled the reparations question, something might be done on war debts. On disarmament and security
questions there was no meeting of minds. Laval pressed for a ten-year
moratorium on Versailles treaty revision and a consultative pact. He got
neither. The Americans insisted that nothing could be expected from
the United States with regard to French security. Hoover, who disliked
and distrusted the French, shared the common view that they were
aiming at the 'hegemony' of Europe and were misusing their position of
power. Even the more sympathetic officials at the State Department
argued that the United States could only offer additional strategic
guarantees to France if it would reverse its attitude towards Germany,
meet the latter's grievances, and take some steps towards arms limitation.
Though the premier appeared well satisfied with the results of his
American visit and was named 'man of the year' by *Time* magazine,
the trip brought no concrete advantages for France and left behind
mixed impressions of Laval. The French leader had hoped to finish
the year with a voyage to Rome, but the strong anti-Italian sentiments
of the French navy and the failure of the naval talks torpedoed that idea.

The most striking weakness in the French diplomatic armoury was
the inability to come to terms with Britain before the disarmament
conference met. If the Franco-German problem was at the heart of
the failure to achieve a European settlement, France's search for a British
guarantee and the latter's reluctance to provide one was the fatal leit-
motiv of the disarmament talks, and more broadly of the whole inter-
war European security problem. Neither the Labour nor National
governments would go beyond the Locarno guarantees, which defined
the limits of Britain's involvement in France's security concerns. Even
while separate discussions on this fundamental issue were proceeding in
each capital, new sources of tension between France and Britain made it
highly unlikely that they would join in a common policy at Geneva.
The French were anxious for joint conversations before the disarmament conference opened; the British rejected the offer of a meeting.
Anglo-French differences over reparations and Europe's financial
troubles shadowed their relationship during the opening stages of the
disarmament conference. France's apparent military superiority, like its
financial strength, was the subject of recurrent criticism in London,

---

[9] Quoted in Jean-Paul Contet, *Pierre Laval* (Paris, 1993), 111.

particularly when compared to German weakness. The French were determined not to sacrifice their national interests in order to placate the British, but nonetheless it was a somewhat strange situation that the more militarily powerful country should be the wooer rather than the wooed.

Against this difficult diplomatic background, which exposed the extent of French isolation, policy-makers in Paris worked on the details of the programme to be presented to the disarmament conference. Many issues had been settled at the time of the 15 July memorandum, but debates continued over specific security and technical arms-limitation proposals. The diplomats, looking for flexibility and grounds for compromise, clashed with the service chiefs over the idea of a permanent international military force and over various suggestions for regional security pacts along the lines of Locarno. The Air Ministry fought a continuing battle against the proposed abolition of bombers and the internationalization of civil aviation. It was the energetic Tardieu, replacing André Maginot as minister of war in January 1932 after the latter's sudden death from food poisoning, who transformed the somewhat confused recommendations considered by the CSDN into a coherent and aggressive plan that could be presented at Geneva. By taking the initiative, Tardieu intended to have the first and hopefully last word at the forthcoming conference. The French would set the agenda and others would have to respond. The French programme for enhanced security would become the focus of international debate rather than the German claim for equality of rights. Both in its minimum and maximum versions, the 'Tardieu plan' was intended to preserve the status quo in armaments and deflect attention from arms reduction to considerations of security. The French plan, in the minimum form accepted by generals Weygand and Gamelin, concentrated on the 'organization of peace'. The stress was upon expanding the League's power to act, through some combination of expanded arbitration, effective supervision of any agreement, and the creation of a League-supervised international military force composed of contingents from each nation which alone would possess the most powerful weapons (particularly military aircraft). Tardieu thus went to Geneva with a plan of action in hand. Admittedly, it highlighted the long-held demand that security precede disarmament, but it did offer room for compromise if France's basic requirements were met. Whether a more open-ended approach to the security question would have advanced the French position (Maurice Vaïsse, the foremost authority on French disarmament, claims that 1931 was a 'year of missed opportunities' for France)[10] is open to question when

---

[10] Vaïsse, *Sécurité d'abord*, 78.

one looks at the British side of the ledger and sees how little room there was for compromise between two opposing definitions of national security. The British were reasonably quick to take up the question of disarmament policy but were impossibly slow in their unsuccessful attempt to answer it. A 'Three Party committee' had met during the first half of 1931 but reached only conclusions of numbing generality. Preoccupied with the financial and economic crisis, it was not until after the October elections that officials and ministers determinedly took up the problem. Even then there was a marked reluctance on the part of the latter to take any decision on the key political questions that were at the heart of the disarmament question. Everyone agreed that France held the key to the European situation and that it would demand a price in terms of enhanced security for any reduction in its armaments. Was Britain willing to pay this price in any form that would allow negotiations to go forward? French behaviour over disarmament questions stoked British distrust and dislike not just in the cabinet and the City but also in parliament and the press. France was the subject of persistent criticism. Unless the French reduced their armaments, it was stated bluntly, there could be no successful outcome of the disarmament talks. France, rather than Italy, was held responsible for the difficulties over the extension of the London Naval Treaty, and the anti-French fallout from the unsuccessful efforts at British mediation was already poisoning relations before the disarmament conference met. The permanent under-secretary Robert Vansittart summed up the British view: 'We desire disarmament—or the end of over-armament—and we do not desire a perpetual [French] hegemony. This is recognised not only by the Cabinet, but by an overwhelming majority in the public opinion of this country.'[11] The other side of the British coin, particularly disturbing for the French, was a considerable sympathy for Germany and respect for Brüning in London circles. The former arose, in part, from financial self-interest, but there is little doubt that many, regardless of their political affiliation, believed that the Versailles treaty imposed impossible and unjust conditions on Germany which had to be removed if the Weimar republic was to survive. The deteriorating German domestic situation fuelled British appeasement; Brüning was seen as one of the last bulwarks against the rising tide of political extremism and the collapse of parliamentary government. In London, as in Paris, there was no lack of information about the growing political influence of the Reichswehr or about German infractions of the disarmament

---

[11] Memo by Vansittart, 'The United Kingdom and Europe', 1 Jan. 1932, PRO, CAB 24/227, CP 4(32).

clauses of the Treaty of Versailles. The reports of the British military attaché in Berlin were, nonetheless, reassuring, and British ministers, unlike their French counterparts, were willing to accept German assurances that they sought only the principle of equality and not actual equality in the size of their armed forces. Insofar as it was acknowledged that Germany was rearming, this was thought to be a way to bring pressure on Poland in the interests of territorial revision which the British viewed as inevitable, rather than any indication of wider aggressive intentions. Contrary to the French, who viewed German infringements of the Versailles restrictions as the first step towards a military challenge to the peace settlement, the British argued that Germany was far too weak in every sense to pose any danger to an over-mighty France.

At the request of Lord Reading, the foreign secretary under the interim National Government (August–October 1931), the Foreign Office considered the question of European security. Reacting to the multiple crises of the summer, senior officials argued that a major initiative was necessary if a solution was to be found to the interlocking problems of European 'confidence' that included monetary, war-debt and reparations questions, disarmament and security, the territorial status quo of Europe, and the revision of the peace settlements. In an unusually wide-ranging policy memorandum, printed on 26 November 1931, officials recommended that in order to break this chain of insecurity Britain would have to engage itself further in Europe and offer guarantees similar to those in the rejected Geneva Protocol of 1925, much of which had already been adopted in a piecemeal fashion. The Foreign Office presented its case elegantly and concisely: 'World recovery (the aim of our policy) depends on European recovery; European recovery on German recovery; German recovery on France's consent; France's consent on security (for all time) against attack.'[12] In return for its commitment, at a minimum Britain could demand concessions on war debts and reparations, a full measure of disarmament, and an examination of the rectification of the European frontiers. The disarmament conference, where Britain could play the pivotal role, would provide the opportunity for dealing with all the different but interrelated aspects of the single problem of stabilizing the peace. Not all officials, to be sure, thought that a greater British continental commitment was the best way to revive European confidence. Vansittart, who had not participated in the drafting of the memorandum, believed that

---

[12] Foreign Office memorandum, 'Changing Conditions in British Foreign Policy, With Reference to the Disarmament Conference, a Possible Reparations Conference, and Other Contingent Problems', 26 Nov. 1931, PRO, CAB 24/225, CP 301(31).

there was far too much public and political opposition to any such commitment, as well as Dominion hostility, to make acceptance possible. None of the various Foreign Office alternative proposals won cabinet acceptance. On 15 December 1931 the cabinet made it clear that it would have nothing to do with a revived Geneva Protocol. Ministers not only recorded their refusal to go beyond Locarno, they stated their conviction that Germany had 'strong moral backing for her claim to the principle of equality'.[13] The cabinet's only positive recommendation was to suggest a further study of a 'Mediterranean Locarno', and even this possibility was subsequently rejected. To the deep frustration of the Foreign Office, the government would not grapple with the question of any positive programme for the World Disarmament Conference. The new foreign secretary from November 1931, Sir John Simon, admitted that 'I do not see any daylight at present on disarmament policy at all'.[14] He lacked the decisiveness, resolution, and political courage needed to force his colleagues to face the prospect of the Franco-German clash that everyone thought was inevitable, and to decide on a viable way to postpone or handle this conflict. Every attempt to fashion a more positive plan of action failed to achieve its purpose.

Nor was there any progress on technical proposals that might be offered at the conference, such as prohibiting or limiting the use of 'aggressive' weapons. The Dominion representatives at their January 1932 meeting repeated the British arguments that their respective states were already dangerously disarmed, and that the abolition or limitation of almost any weapon would adversely affect some Dominion's national interest. In London there were prolonged quarrels between the service departments and the Foreign Office over what types of weapons might be prohibited. The War Office refused to consider the abolition of tanks, 'definitely a life-saving weapon'. The Air Ministry engaged in a prolonged battle with the Foreign Office over the abolition of military and naval aviation and the international control of civil aircraft. The British delegation consequently went to Geneva without any specific programme in mind. Its members would underline the steps Britain had already taken in reducing its armaments and try to mediate between France and Germany on an *ad hoc* basis. Faced with rising public demands for a positive outcome of the disarmament conference, the government would be forced to demonstrate its positive intentions, but given its strong political position and the primacy of financial and economic problems, it was thought that this could be handled as a public-relations exercise without in any way compromising British security. Britain's case at the conference 'might be lacking in positive new proposals', MacDonald told the cabinet, 'but the sentiment and the intention behind it were excellent. . . . Whether other nations believed us or not was not very material, provided that the whole case were put and reached our own public.'[15] Far from being the active leader—as had been the hope of many across Europe when the Labour government's foreign secretary, Arthur Henderson, had been appointed president for the disarmament conference in May 1931—the British seemed set to do little more than sit on the sidelines.

III

Tardieu introduced the French plan to the World Disarmament Conference on 5 February 1932 by unexpectedly circulating it at the end of a preliminary procedural session and before the scheduled opening speech by Simon three days later. His tactics failed to achieve their purpose. Neither the Americans nor the British favoured the French idea of enhanced security. Neither liked the idea of an international police force, and both pressured the French delegation to show more sympathy towards German demands for treaty revision. The British, having ruled out the one positive contribution that might have advanced the cause of disarmament, had little more in mind than to act as the 'honest broker' between France and Germany. At best, the Foreign Office sought to avoid discussion of the Tardieu plan, and would try to shift the blame for delays at Geneva to others until some better alternative emerged. In his opening speech, Simon raised the possibility of qualitative disarmament, that is, the reduction or abolition of certain categories of weapons such as submarines and land guns above a certain calibre. He referred to the need to strengthen defence at the expense of attack by dealing with 'offensive' weapons. Tardieu's intervention did not lead to the public debate on security that the French wanted. To the immense relief of the British, the new premier (Laval fell from office on 16 February and was quickly replaced by Tardieu) was dissuaded from presenting a dossier he constantly threatened to produce on Germany's illegal rearmament, which might have altered the mood at Geneva. Instead, Rudolf Nadolny, the German spokesman, took a moderate line in public and private and won considerable sympathy in Anglo-American circles. He correctly judged that there was nothing to be gained from confrontation and much to lose from a public airing of German misdemeanours. During March the German generals and von Bülow again approached

---

[15] Cabinet 3(32), 14 Jan. 1932, PRO, CAB 23/70.

François-Poncet, the French ambassador in Berlin, suggesting a dialogue on the basis of the Tardieu plan. Repeatedly warned about the power of the military in Berlin, the French premier was hardly tempted to follow up approaches based on French recognition of German claims to equality.

The conference's proceedings in February and March, concerned primarily with procedural matters and generally running second in importance to the special League Assembly in early March on the Sino-Japanese conflict, produced no major upsets. The French efforts to build a united front against the Germans made no headway. Massigli tried in vain to break the impasse with Italy over the Mediterranean naval talks, warning the French naval chiefs of the damage being done to the country's bargaining position at the conference. There was no comfort from the British. The unwell Ramsay MacDonald, bothered by eye operations, remained the Francophobe he had always been. Tardieu, he recorded in his diary, incarnated all of France's worst qualities: 'how foolish it is to be crooked and dishonest.'[16] Simon insisted that the Germans had a moral right to equality, while warning Tardieu not to expect Britain to take on new international obligations. The conference was soon adjourned until 11 April for its Easter recess.

During the break in proceedings Simon pondered. While hardly the man to do battle with the service chiefs, he possessed a surfeit of legalistic ingenuity. He proposed to the cabinet that the existing limitations on German armaments be taken out of Part V of Versailles and transferred to a new disarmament convention that would leave Germany tied to the same restrictions as every other state and for the same limited period of time. Disregarding the inevitable French objection to such an arrangement, Simon pressed for whatever qualitative restrictions on offensive weapons the service departments would tolerate: the scrapping of tanks and artillery of specified weights and calibre, and the abolition of submarines, an old goal always resisted by France and Italy. Due to strong objections from the Air Ministry, nothing was decided on the air arm and the question of bombers and bombing was referred to the delegation at Geneva. In essence, the British were not offering enough to start the ball rolling at the conference. In March, faced with the crisis in Manchuria, the British cabinet, on the recommendations of the chiefs of staff, agreed to abandon the 'ten year rule' and to take steps to improve Britain's defensive position in the Far East. The Treasury did not object if due regard was paid to 'the serious financial and economic situation that still obtains'. This may explain why the suggested figures

---

[16] MacDonald Diary, 1 May 1932, quoted in David Marquand, *Ramsay MacDonald* (London, 1977), 718.

for inclusion in any new disarmament convention provided for an increase of almost 50 per cent over the 1932 estimates (£104 million to £150 million), and why the service chiefs ruled out budgetary disarmament at Geneva.

By the time the delegates reassembled in April, Brüning was running out of time and the French parliamentary election campaign had opened. It was generally expected and even hoped at Geneva that Tardieu would be replaced by the less hard-line Anglophile Herriot. There was no lack of diplomatic action at Geneva. The American delegate, Hugh Gibson, anxious to get the conference moving, suggested the abolition of the most aggressive arms of war, a recommendation supported by the British, Germans, and Italians but vigorously criticized by Tardieu and the French chiefs of staff. They felt it disregarded the French plan of 5 February, with its provisions for supervision and sanctions; instead, they advocated putting the most powerful weapons in the hands of the League, not abolishing them. Simon's simplified version of the recommendation for the prohibition of 'offensive' weapons brought Tardieu racing back from the election trail to keep open the possibility of retaining such weapons under international control. The conference's technical commissions were given the thankless and ultimately hopeless task of distinguishing between 'offensive' and 'defensive' weapons. The purpose of the Anglo-American exercise was, in part, a successful attempt to divert attention from the Tardieu programme in anticipation of a victory for the left in Paris.

Secretary of State Henry Stimson, sent to reinforce the American team as well as to confer with the British over the Far Eastern crisis, met with Brüning and MacDonald at Bessinge, the American's villa near Geneva, on 26 April. Tardieu was absent electioneering, though he had promised to return. This was the background to what the commentator John Wheeler-Bennett called the 'April tragedy', following Brüning's own misleading *post hoc* recollections of his 'success in putting across all the demands of the Reichswehr one hundred percent with all the great powers excepting France'.[17] The American and German accounts of the meetings differ on points of interpretation as to what was said and accepted. Brüning, arguing that the budgetary crisis foreclosed the possibility of massive rearmament, outlined the *Umbau* ('rebuilding') proposal accepted by the army high command in April. According to his account, he asked for the reduction of military service from ten to six years, the right to raise a 'militia on the Swiss model', and the right to fortify the German frontiers. The German chancellor explained that the

[17] Heinrich Brüning, *Memoiren, 1918–1934* (Stuttgart, 1970), 563.

Germans would renounce heavy offensive weapons if other governments agreed, but would need defensive arms. There is some doubt
whether the German chancellor actually put forward Groener's idea of a
100,000-man, 'Swiss style' militia with very short terms of service that
would have allowed for a considerable expansion of the pool of trained
reserves without any major outlay of funds. If he did put this proposal
forward, his British and American colleagues failed to understand its true
import. There is no doubt that the German chancellor made a good
impression at Bessinge, where, according to their accounts, he placed
most of his emphasis on French disarmament. MacDonald and Stimson
neither accepted nor declined Brüning's more detailed demands, all
having agreed that the discussions were informal and that no decisions
could be taken in the French absence. Tardieu had delayed his return to
Geneva, staying in Paris recovering from laryngitis and flu. Though
genuinely ill, he certainly did not relish a four-power meeting in which
France would stand alone. It may be, too, that he was given warnings of
Brüning's impending fall and the strengthening of the military influence
in Berlin. Brüning greatly exaggerated his espousal of the nationalists'
goals in his memoirs and the level of Anglo-American support, but the
real check to German ambitions came not from his fall but from French
opposition to the demand for 'equality of rights'. There was nothing in
the Bessinge conversations to encourage French acceptance, and so no
missed opportunity was cut short by Brüning's dismissal from office.

Nor were further efforts made by either the Americans or British to
promote an agreement when Tardieu was replaced as premier, following the victory of the left in the elections during the first week of May,
by the supposedly more sympathetic Herriot. The latter did not actually
form a government until 7 June, due to the turmoil following the
assassination of French president Paul Doumer on 7 May. Tardieu
continued to serve as interim premier in the meantime, setting back
all significant discussions on disarmament for a month. A genial lunch
between the gourmand premier-elect and the American negotiators,
Norman Davis and Hugh Wilson, produced only a vague promise to
hold pre-Lausanne reparations conference talks on disarmament.
Herriot's main interest was to smooth relations with London and
Washington, not to come to an arms agreement with the Germans.
Though the left parties were highly critical of the military and
demanded cuts in military expenditure, once elected Herriot would
prove as determined as his predecessor to win additional safeguards for
France before conceding equal rights to Germany. The concurrent
publication of the Stresemann letters, revealing the extent of the late
German foreign minister's irredentism (Herriot was described as a
'jellyfish'), hardly encouraged French confidence in further conciliation.

For somewhat different reasons, mainly arising from their mutual concerns over the outcome of the reparation talks at Lausanne, both the British and French favoured private conversations without the Germans during the early summer of 1932. The Geneva talks were stalled. Herriot summed up the proceedings of the technical commissions: 'Do you know what was their conclusion after six months of work? That the offensive character of a weapon depends upon the intention of the one who employs it.'[18] Winston Churchill's zoo fable of 1928, where the horns and teeth of each animal seemed perfectly natural to its owner yet threatening and aggressive to others, was about to become a reality. Only the special committee concerned with chemical and bacteriological warfare went forward.

The tripartite conversations between the British, French, and American foreign secretaries concentrated on specific measures of qualitative disarmament along the lines suggested by Simon. These discussions were disrupted by the sudden announcement on 22 June of a new version of President Hoover's disarmament proposal. The American delegates Gibson and Davis had been pressing for an American initiative since holding conversations with Stanley Baldwin, the acting prime minister, in London and with Tardieu and Herriot in Paris in May, but had been checked by Stimson and by opposition from the navy and the army, neither of which found the Tardieu proposals acceptable. In late May, however, Hoover, alarmed by the worsening economic situation and the budget deficit, and anxious to reduce military expenditure, intervened in the conflict between the American delegation in Geneva and the navy, army, and State Department. Hoover was genuinely anxious for a success at Geneva, but his dramatic intervention was also a move intended to influence the American presidential campaign, with elections approaching in November. MacDonald and Herriot were told of the 'Hoover plan' while they were at Lausanne; their governments urged postponement as unofficial conversations were already underway at Geneva and these hopefully promising talks would be undermined by the introduction of the presidential proposal. With the Democratic convention scheduled for the last week of June, Hoover had to act if he were not to be accused of political expediency. The president proposed cutting the number of battleships by half, the number of cruisers and aircraft carriers by one-fourth, and of defence contingents by one-third. Tanks, large mobile guns, and most kinds of military aircraft were to be abolished and there was to be a ban on chemical warfare. Hoover and Stimson apparently hoped for a quick resolution approving the principles of the plan, followed by a six-month adjournment.

[18] Quoted in Vaïsse, *Securité d'abord*, 238.

The Hoover plan was enthusiastically acclaimed by disarmers in Britain and France (Léon Blum was one of its most enthusiastic endorsers), and was well received by the Italians. It was seen by Litvinov as coming close to the Soviet recommendations. Many of the delegations from the smaller nations were enthusiastic. Paul-Boncour, now the French minister of war, ironically commented on its simplicity and irrelevance to French concerns for the organization of peace. There were detailed criticisms of the proposals from Paris: the absence of budgetary limitations, the naval clauses that would reduce France's existing naval superiority over Italy, the disregard of demographic criteria in the provisions relating to military effectives, and above all, the absence of any inspection system and enforcement machinery. The French again put the case for regional security guarantees and a consultative agreement with the United States. The British reaction was even more hostile. Simon was furious at this unexpected intervention, which interrupted his private tripartite discussions but also highlighted his own unpreparedness; the Admiralty took umbrage at the proposed cuts in cruisers, which casually threw over the careful balance established at the 1930 London conference; the Air Ministry would not consider the scrapping of military aircraft. It was now essential to find a policy, a task made no easier by Simon's habitual unwillingness to take a stand and the continuing resistance of the Admiralty and War Office to Foreign Office demands for a substantive demonstration of British goodwill. The weak counter-scheme, announced by Stanley Baldwin, who was already taking an active interest in the disarmament debate, was intended to convince the home and foreign public of Britain's commitment to disarmament. It was a poor effort, and the parliamentary opposition made excellent use of the disparity between the American and British alternatives. Despite widespread support for the Hoover plan among the smaller nations, British and French opposition was enough to deprive the Americans of their hoped-for breakthrough.

As the Geneva powers began to debate the contents of some face-saving adjournment motion, the Germans prepared their challenge. Following Brüning's dismissal as chancellor at the end of May, Hindenburg appointed Franz von Papen, a political lightweight aligned with the extreme right of the Catholic Centre party, in his stead. Schleicher anticipated being able to dominate von Papen and so to control the new government's policy. As defence minister, Schleicher was able to dictate the course of the Reichswehr's rearmament policies. After the reparations issue was settled at Lausanne, nothing and nobody could prevent him from pressing Germany's claim to equal rights. He was unconcerned about courting international approval and saw from the start how *Gleichberechtigung* could be used to build support at home.

The Germans had kept a low profile in the opening sessions at Geneva; Schleicher's success in Berlin heralded a more aggressive stand. Schleicher brushed aside Auswärtiges Amt reservations and demanded a showdown if German demands were not met. Bülow, a strong revisionist but a realist, acutely aware of Germany's continued military weakness and the advantages of Anglo-American backing, described the Reichswehr's nine objectives, outlined in 'The Hidden German Goal at the Disarmament Conference' (14 June 1932), as a 'Christmas List'.[19] He was strongly opposed to making the demand for equality of rights the basis of an ultimatum. Nadolny, too, warned against 'breaking the china' at Geneva. Unsuccessful efforts made at Lausanne and Geneva to draw the Herriot government into bilateral discussions strengthened Schleicher's hand. In Berlin, Constantin von Neurath, the former ambassador in London and new foreign minister in the von Papen cabinet, proved unable to keep the disarmament talks under his control. On 12 July the full cabinet agreed to the Reichswehr's rearmament programme regardless of what happened at Geneva, and opened the possibility of a showdown at the disarmament conference. Schleicher was determined on the annulment of Part V of the Treaty of Versailles which so restricted German military power. While the Americans, British, and French struggled to produce an acceptable adjournment motion, Schleicher and Neurath agreed to warn delegates that Germany would not return to the conference unless given satisfaction on the principle of equality during the adjournment.

The German 'ultimatum' proved to be the most significant result of the first Geneva session. The final resolution was prepared by Beneš, assisted by Simon, who had given the Czech statesman this unenviable assignment to avoid taking on himself the responsibility of failure. There were agreements on the prohibition of chemical, bacteriological, and incendiary warfare and of air attacks on civil populations. Delegates accepted a conditional prohibition on all air bombing (opposed by the British Air Ministry) and recommendations that bombers should be put under an international regime. Limitations were to be placed on heavy artillery. The 'armaments truce' was extended for an additional four months. It was little enough to show after six months of work. Herriot conceded as much when he commented in his closing speech to the conference that 'there have been times when we may have wondered whether the verb "to disarm" was not in every language an irregular verb, with no first person, and only conjugated in the future tense'.[20]

[19] Edward Bennett, *German Rearmament and the West, 1932–1933* (Princeton, 1979), 181.
[20] Speech by Herriot, 22 July 1932, *Records of the Conference for the Reduction and Limitation of Armaments, series B: Minutes of the General Commission*, i. pp. 186–8.

The Germans did not get the recognition of equal rights they sought. The Wilhelmstrasse might have accepted what they believed to be only a postponement of the German claims to equal rights, but Schleicher and the Reichswehr chiefs were impatient. Von Papen and Schleicher tried, unsuccessfully, to arrange a modus vivendi with Hitler. The defence minister was anxious to recruit the SA for an expanded *Wehrsport* programme, and ultimately wanted to incorporate the Nazi paramilitary organization into a reorganized Reichswehr. The ban on the SA was lifted and the Reichstag dissolved for new elections. In late July a successful coup d'état was carried out in Prussia, where the Social Democrats still held power despite losing their electoral majority. Prussia was now brought under the Berlin government's control and the police organized to support an authoritarian and repressive local regime. The army would have no more difficulties with the 'Prussian bulwark' as in the past. Neither would Hitler. Pleas for caution at Geneva were disregarded. On 22 July Nadolny presented the German statement, with the definite threat, drafted by Neurath personally, not to return to the conference unless the German demand for the principle of equality was conceded. The next day both the German and Soviet governments voted against the adjournment resolution.

IV

On 31 July 1932 the Nazis increased their representation in the Reichstag from 107 to 230 seats out of 608. This proved to be the high point of their electoral popularity and the highest result of any single party in free Weimar elections. Though still without the majority needed to form a government, Hitler immediately claimed the chancellorship and key ministries for his party, only to be publicly rejected and humiliated by Hindenburg. Efforts to bring Hitler into the cabinet failed on 13 August. Schleicher, in radio speeches and communications to the French, left no doubt about the German intention to rearm if their demands were not met. There would be no progress at Geneva unless the German claim to equality of rights was conceded in advance. Just as the German tone became more threatening, the Berlin authorities launched a new campaign for a settlement with France. Frustrated by the lack of response from Herriot, Schleicher tried to force the pace. In a secret memorandum sent to Paris on 29 August the Germans detailed their terms. Germany should have the same rights to security as other nations. A new disarmament convention placing the same restrictions on Germany and for the same duration of time as for others would prepare the way for the 'necessary adjustment of armaments'. The Germans claimed the right to reduce the length of service in the professional army from twelve to six years, and to raise a militia amounting to 40,000 men who would be given three months' training. Weapons permitted to others should not be prohibited to the Germans, though in the first instance they would require only 'samples' of these weapons. In return, the Germans would consider the French security proposals and accept such limitation measures as agreed to by all the other states. The Reichswehr's real plans were of far more ambitious scope, an expansion of almost four times the Versailles treaty numbers of soldiers. This was only disclosed to the Auswärtiges Amt in October 1932. The German diplomats believed the second armaments programme was well beyond the country's financial means, and argued that the new naval building plans posed a direct and unnecessary challenge to the Anglo–Americans. But their disapproval had no effect on the Reichswehr, and the decision on the reorganization and expansion of the army was given cabinet approval at the beginning of November.

There were some, including André François-Poncet, the French ambassador in Berlin, officials at the Quai d'Orsay (though not Alexis Léger, the influential director of political affairs), and a large section of the French Socialist party, taking its lead from Blum, who argued for the opening of talks in Berlin. There were warnings that the von Papen cabinet might well be replaced by an even more uncompromising ministry. Herriot's immediate advisers, however, including Joseph Paul-Boncour in Geneva and, most important of all, the army chiefs, generals Weygand, Gamelin, and Pétain, strongly opposed any settlement with Berlin. In the end Herriot refused to be bullied by Schleicher. The French premier was particularly intent on implementing the recent Lausanne agreement with the British to consult together whenever Germany approached either government about the Versailles treaty terms. In a note to Berlin on 11 September that neither accepted nor rejected the bid for equality, the French dismissed the proposal of bilateral talks and demanded that the question of German rearmament be submitted to the Council of the League. The response of the other powers and France's eastern allies encouraged some degree of optimism in Paris. Neither the Americans nor the British accepted the German version of what was conceded at Bessinge, and both particularly disliked Schleicher's attempt to settle matters directly with the French. Even the Italians, who had previously mounted a barrage of critical comment about the League, counselled caution at Berlin. The Poles and Czechs welcomed Herriot's strong stand. The Quai d'Orsay thought it possible to build a diplomatic front on the commonly expressed opposition to any form of German rearmament. The French were under no illusions about the nature of the German menace. Herriot told his military heads in October:

I am convinced that Germany wishes to rearm . . . We are at a turning point in history. Until now Germany has practised a policy of submission, not of resignation certainly, but a negative policy; now she is beginning a positive policy. Tomorrow it will be a policy of territorial demands with a formidable means of intimidation: her army. The instinctive reaction is to say that we will suppress not one man, not one gun.[21]

The French premier, however, did not follow his instincts. He argued that France was too weak to risk such a response, and sought instead an accommodation with the Americans and British lest France be blamed for intransigence and the failure of the conference. The country risked, he argued, not only present but future isolation at a time when she might have to face the challenge of a rearmed Germany. Herriot urged his generals to accept some limitation on French arms along the lines of the Hoover proposals, and to seek security commitments that Britain and the United States would accept.

There was not much assistance from the Americans or the British. The American position can only be understood in terms of the run-up to the election of November 1932. While Hoover and Stimson supported the German claim for juridical equality, they wanted French disarmament and not German rearmament. The political changes in Germany revived Hoover's abiding distrust of Prussian militarism. During the summer of 1932 gestures were made to reassure the French about American intentions. In his nomination acceptance speech at the Republican convention in August, Hoover spoke of America's willingness to consult 'in times of emergency to promote world peace', reiterating a pledge made a few weeks earlier by his secretary of state. But when Stimson prepared a strong aide-memoire to express American disapproval, Hoover objected, insisting that the American public favoured Germany's demand for equality and would not countenance the break-up of the disarmament conference. In the midst of a political campaign, the president could not risk coming to Herriot's assistance. The revision of the disarmament clauses of Versailles was a European problem that had to be settled without American involvement.

Faced with the need to respond to the German offensive, it was decided in London that Britain should champion German equal treatment in terms of the legal definitions to be included within a new disarmament treaty, but retain the limitations on German armaments in Part V of the Treaty of Versailles. The British insisted that the disarmament conference was the only place where future modifications could be made. MacDonald and Simon had accepted von Neurath's assurances that the Germans wanted the recognition of their rights and

---

[21] *Documents Diplomatiques Français, 1932–1939*, série I, vol. 1, no. 250.

not rearmament, though aware of Schleicher's intention to break free of Part V and to reorganize the Reichswehr. For the Foreign Office, Germany's presence and co-operation at the conference remained the most essential goal of British diplomacy. If Germany refused to attend or the conference failed, it would be in a position to rearm at will and would then become a real danger to peace; in the words of the British ambassador in Berlin, 'a Dämmerung of this old Europe if not an "Untergang" '.[22] The British cabinet would not consider making any further commitments to the French beyond the Covenant and Locarno. The British public reply to the German demands, which appeared in the press on 19 September but was circulated to the other powers on the previous day, was well received by the Americans and French but shocked the Papen government. It proposed that the arms clauses of the Versailles treaty, unless modified by common agreement, be included in a new convention, while conceding the German claim, on moral rather than juridical grounds, to equality of status and treatment. At the same time, the Germans were warned against rearmament and told that questions of status should be settled by 'patient discussion' and not by 'pre-emptory challenge'.[23] If the disarmament conference failed, it was agreed at the Foreign Office, Germany had to remain bound by her Versailles obligations. The statement, applauded in Paris, caused an uproar in Germany. Much to Simon's surprise, the German press took umbrage at both its contents and tone. Having been repeatedly assured by their own leaders that only the French blocked the claim to equality, the public 'reprimand' from London came as a disagreeable shock. Great pains were taken on the French side to co-ordinate policies with London. The British, on the contrary, sought to detach themselves from the promises made at Lausanne for co-operative action with regard to Germany, and searched for ways to reopen the dialogue with the Germans.

In difficulty with the Liberals in the National Government over the Ottawa preferential tariffs, it was doubly important that the cabinet respond positively to the appeals of the League of Nations Union as well as other church, feminist, and anti-war groups agitating for a new initiative to break the deadlock at Geneva. The cabinet, without any ideas of its own, looked to its foreign secretary for a lead. Simon discovered, to his dismay, that the Admiralty and Air Ministry were unwilling to sanction cuts that would allow him to act at Geneva. Simon found himself defending departmental policies he disliked. Unlike their

---

[22] Horace to Anthony Rumbold, 13 Dec. 1932, Rumbold Papers, Add. V, box 5, Bodleian Library, Oxford.
[23] *DBFP*, ser. II, vol. 4, no. 92.

French colleagues, the British chiefs of staff were willing to countenance a measure of German rearmament. They did not believe that Germany was capable of fighting a successful defensive war against Poland in 1932, and predicted that it would not pose a threat to the peace until after 1938. They assumed, with a continued blinkered assessment of French capabilities, that France would maintain its military superiority and that British security interests were not engaged. The services did not take the full measure of the Reichswehr's 'Umbau' plans in 1932 and dismissed French warnings as exaggerated.

Herriot, whose political position was already weakening because of the government's budgetary difficulties, underestimated Britain's willingness to conciliate the Germans in order to rescue the Geneva talks. He also misinterpreted the sympathetic noises from Washington on war debts and security. Equally illusory were Quai d'Orsay hopes for a *rapprochement* with Rome. There was a resumption of Franco-Italian naval talks in November, but the new exchanges soon collapsed when the French naval authorities, a law unto themselves, refused to accept a building truce that left open the possibility of parity in the Mediterranean. It was against this background of qualified optimism, but also out of fears of French isolation, that, after unproductive Belgian and Czech efforts in the same direction, Joseph Paul-Boncour, the French defence minister, prepared in October a new version of Tardieu's 'maximum' plan. Departing from the 1931 scenario, the French accepted the German claim to equality of rights and agreed to a measure of French disarmament. At the heart of this 'constructive plan' was the proposal that virtually all national forces (troops used for colonial purposes were exempted) would be placed at the disposal of the League, leaving only militias for the use of individual states. Military and naval planes would come under League control and civilian aircraft would be 'internationalized'. To satisfy the Americans and British, there would be a three-tier approach to the question of security: a consultative pact which all nations could join, a pact for the non-continental League members, and a European pact of mutual assistance that would provide the kind of guarantees sought in the old Geneva Protocol. Even after modifications, Weygand was bitterly opposed to the new initiative; it meant the destruction of the French army and the reduction of the country's defensive strength. Gamelin, who found Weygand too unbending and obstructive in his dealings with the politicians, was less strident but no less hostile to the idea of an international force and national militias. Overruled in the cabinet, Weygand warned Herriot that the premier's faith in the Anglo-Saxons was misplaced and ultimately dangerous. The French high command was not prepared, however, to engage in a public battle they would certainly lose, and the right-wing press, fearful that Weygand might be dismissed, was less openly hostile than predicted. The government's radical–socialist supporters applauded the new effort. It accorded well with the need for economy; Weygand was forced to accept a 5–10 per cent cut in defence appropriations as part of the government's effort to balance the budget. There was strong popular support for disarmament, and the plan matched the left's traditional prejudices against professional armies. If, as Herriot expected, the Germans rejected the 'constructive plan', it was believed that other states would recognize the German intent to rearm and come on to the side of France. The new proposal was presented to the Bureau of the Conference on 4 November (two days before the German elections) and made public on 14 November.

By this time the British had decided on an initiative of their own to avoid a showdown between Germany and France. MacDonald, feeling that Simon had lost the initiative in the negotiations, pushed for a more assertive British role. With Hoover's defeat by Roosevelt in the November presidential election and American concentration on war debts, MacDonald believed that Britain would have to act alone. After acrimonious debates with the service departments, Simon finally produced a disarmament formula recognizing the German claim to equality and recommending measures of qualitative disarmament by stages that would not lead to an increase in any country's (that is, German) armed strength. The new arms convention, binding on all signatories to the disarmament treaty, would replace Part V of the Versailles treaty. It would give the Germans the same rights as other nations to all categories of arms, but in smaller quantities. These anodyne suggestions, announced in parliament on 10 November and presented to the bureau of the conference a week later, contained no reference at all to the French plan or French security demands. The announcement was intended to assure the British public that the government was determined on disarmament and would set the pace at Geneva. Simon had first to achieve a compromise that would allow the talks to resume. Out of 'deference to MacDonald', the much-perturbed Herriot, who had no wish to smooth the way for the Germans, hurried to London for consultations, hoping to prevent a pre-Geneva great-power meeting. Aware of mounting public hostility to his position and afraid to cross the British, the Frenchman retreated, virtually agreeing both to the four-power gathering and to the formal acceptance of German equality, Berlin's minimum demand for participation. Herriot's only small victory was the transfer of the meeting's venue from London to Geneva. Though Neurath and Bülow rejected Simon's attempt to get an immediate 'no use of force' declaration as a gesture of German goodwill, they signalled their willingness to participate in the great-power conclave.

The Reichswehr, for its part, was unenthusiastic. The final orders for the implementation of the new rearmament programme were given on 7 November, and the army was quite prepared to abandon the diplomatic game.

Internal politics provided the backdrop for the army's rearmament plans. Not even Hindenburg's backing could save the Papen government, which had no Reichstag majority. After a massive Reichstag vote against his 'cabinet of barons', parliament was again dissolved and new elections held on 6 November. Though the Nazi vote fell by about 2 million and the party was now in financial difficulties, the NSDAP was still the largest party with 196 seats, and Hitler prepared to gamble on an 'all or nothing' strategy. It was at this point that Schleicher moved. After weeks of intrigue he convinced the reluctant Hindenburg to dismiss von Papen, who resigned on 17 November. Schleicher took on the chancellorship on 2 December. He offered a cabinet seat to Gregor Strasser, Hitler's second-in-command, in the hope of pressuring Hitler to come to the negotiating table. Instead, Hitler won the intra-party battle and Strasser was forced to resign all his party offices and go on 'vacation'. Schleicher had underestimated Hitler's political power; the following month he would disastrously do so again.

The British seem to have disregarded Schleicher's role in the dumping of von Papen and to have taken little notice of his central role in promoting Reichswehr aims. Horace Rumbold, the ambassador in Berlin, claimed that Schleicher was 'no Machiavellian intriguer', and held out hope that the threat from Hitler would be contained. The unsettled conditions in Germany only convinced MacDonald and Simon that it was essential to get talks going before it was too late, an argument to be rehearsed many times in the years that followed. Ignoring the belated warnings from their military attaché in Berlin that additional German demands for forbidden weapons actually implied rearmament, MacDonald and Simon set about convincing von Neurath to come to the pre-conference meeting. Their efforts were seconded by the American representative Norman Davis, who, hoping for an appointment as secretary of state in Franklin Roosevelt's new administration, sought 'to give a Christmas present to the world' in the form of a preliminary convention to suspend all rearmament for three years. Baron Aloisi, the secretary-general of the Consulta who replaced Grandi at Geneva, warmly supported full American participation in the great-power talks.

In the face of the strongest opposition from the right and right-centre, led by Flandin and Tardieu respectively, Herriot gave way, knowing that the Americans, British, and Italians had decided on the recognition of *Gleichberechtigung* without conceding France's demands for security.

Davis warned him at the end of November that the United States would not adhere to the new French proposals. The repetition of Herriot's 1924 defeat at MacDonald's hands suggests that the Radical leader was far too trusting in dealings with his less scrupulous counterpart. It is true that the 'constructive plan' waiting to be discussed at Geneva implied French recognition of the German claims, but Herriot's premature concession could only weaken his bargaining hand. At the Geneva talks (6–11 December), apart from avoiding isolation and the breakdown of the negotiations, neither Herriot nor Paul-Boncour, the main French participants, won any substantive gains for France. Assisted by Aloisi, Simon led the search for a formula acceptable to the equally stubborn French and German negotiators. Neurath and Bülow might have compromised, but Schleicher insisted on the unconditional and irrevocable concession of equality as the price for the German return. Davis, anxious for a breakthrough, added to the representatives' difficulties by pressing for his own interim plan, which no one actually wanted (Herriot was the one temporary exception) and which the Germans finally vetoed. The final short statement of 11 December, based on Herriot's draft, defined rather than solved the fundamental problem. The four powers agreed that 'one of the principles that should guide the Conference on Disarmament should be the grant to Germany, and to the other disarmed Powers, of equality of rights in a system which would provide security for all nations'.[24] The announcement was rendered even more innocuous by leaving all details of arms limitation for the disarmament conference to decide. On this basis, Germany rejoined the official talks.

On 14 December, about to fall from office over the issue of the payment of war debts to America, Herriot, despite great bitterness about the Anglo-American desertion, spoke of the 'unity of the free' and likened himself to Socrates as the advocate of obedience even to unjust laws. His policy of concessions to the Anglo-Saxons had proved a failure. MacDonald had disappointed and deceived him. The British prime minister, by contrast, basked in his newly won plaudits. He had broken the deadlock at Geneva and reaped the rewards of personal success, the victory made sweeter by the obligatory applause of his old rival, Arthur Henderson, reduced to playing a spectator's role despite his presidency of the disarmament conference. The British had achieved their principal objectives. MacDonald and Simon represented the views of an electorate that was both revisionist and isolationist in temper. The majority pressing for disarmament also wanted a minimum of European entanglements. Even Winston Churchill, an anti-disarmer and unusual

---

[24] Bennett, *German Rearmament and the West*, 267.

among politicians (he was no longer in the cabinet) in sharing the French view of German intentions, supported treaty revision. The Germans were not, he argued, after equality of status. 'They are looking for weapons, and, when they have the weapons, believe me they will ask for the return . . . of lost territories.' Strongly opposed to any equalization of German and French armaments, he nevertheless told his fellow MP's: 'The removal of the just grievances of the vanquished ought to precede the disarmament of the victors. To bring about anything like equality of armaments . . . while those grievances remain unredressed, would be almost to appoint the day for another European war.'[25] There was little encouragement here for France.

At the end of 1932 the French were more isolated than they had been at the start of the year. They were being forced to accept the prospect of German rearmament without having won any new guarantees of security. They had missed opportunities to strengthen their hand in 1931, too concerned with future dangers to take advantage of current strength. Tardieu and Herriot had each tried to seize the initiative; both had failed. French diplomacy, like its strategy, would become increasingly defensive. The British, on the contrary, after a temporary loss of confidence in the autumn of 1931, again appeared ready to set the diplomatic pace. The return of Germany to Geneva was seen as their triumph; the calling of the World Economic Conference, to be held in London on 12 June 1933, was due to their initiative. This shift of activity from Paris to London was accentuated by the American depression and the increased detachment of the Americans from European affairs. The real gainers, of course, were the Germans, who, thanks to the British, were being courted and could set their terms.

This was not good news for France's allies. The smaller nations resented the great-power conversations in Geneva. In Warsaw it was believed that France was abandoning the anti-revisionist cause and would accept German rearmament. Prospects for future Franco-Polish co-operation were further dimmed by the resignation of Zaleski, to the regret of both the French and Czechs, and his replacement by Piłsudski's closest confidante, Colonel Josef Beck, a dynamic, ambitious, and tough negotiator, thought at the Quai d'Orsay to be untrustworthy and anti-French. Beck sought to reassure Herriot and Paul-Boncour (briefly premier in December 1932–January 1933), but he was nonetheless openly critical of the 11 December declaration and warned that Poland would not be bound by decisions taken without its participation. Continuing fears that the French would seek a bargain over the 'Polish

[25] Churchill speech to Commons, 23 Nov. 1932, quoted in Martin Gilbert, *Churchill: A Life* (London, 1991), 511.

Corridor' confirmed Piłsudski's (and Beck's) intention to look beyond Paris for protection. The members of the Little Entente, too, particularly the Czechs, were alarmed at the French capitulation and the prospect of German rearmament at a time when Mussolini was making bellicose noises in the Balkans and speaking of a great-power European directorate that would undercut the League. In the face of this double threat, the Little Entente powers met at Belgrade on 18–19 December 1932. A new Organizational Pact, signed at Geneva on 16 February 1933, created a single administrative structure for three-power co-operation and included a permanent secretariat sitting at Geneva. The new joint council of foreign ministers would have to approve any 'unilateral act changing the actual situation of one of the States of the Little Entente in regard to an outside State'.[26] The pact was open to the accession of others. Beneš, as always when under pressure, made friendly noises in Warsaw, but the Romanians, currently engaged in a diplomatic duel with the Poles (there was little love lost between their respective foreign ministers) and moving in opposite directions with regard to the Soviet Union, blocked this move. The tightening of the Little Entente links, though hardly the revolutionary move intended by Beneš, arose out of Mussolini's threats and later Hitler's accession to power, but was also a response to French weakness. The Quai d'Orsay tried to put a positive gloss on developments in which it played no part, but officials could not disguise from themselves that this was a negative verdict on their recent diplomacy.

V

The death throes of the Weimar republic had little, if any, effect on the determination of the Reichswehr to rearm and to control disarmament policy at Geneva. In the short-lived Schleicher cabinet (December 1932–January 1933) the new chancellor worked closely with General von Hammerstein, the army commander-in-chief. The army proceeded with the first stages of its November plans. More questionably, Schleicher called on the Reichswehr to assist in the implementation of the domestic policies he had devised to enlarge his extra-parliamentary base. The programmes instituted by the so-called 'socialist in military boots' to attract trade unionists and unemployed youth served only to alienate the industrial and agricultural elites without winning the support of the SPD or gaining adherents among the nationalists. For their

---

[26] Piotr S. Wandycz, *The Twilight of French Eastern Alliances, 1926–1936: French–Czechoslovak–Polish Relations from Locarno to the Remilitarisation of the Rhineland* (Princeton, 1988), 250.

part, the army officers became increasingly restive about Schleicher's methods and particularly uneasy about the heavy involvement of the army in essentially political tasks. A convergence of interests prepared the way for the destruction of the republic. Schleicher had insufficient popular backing to carry through his programme and would need presidential support to rule by decree. The large industrialists, still in 1932 subsidizing the parties of the right, could not offer any realistic political alternative. The agrarian leaders close to Hindenburg and some of the anti-Schleicher industrialists urged the president to reinstate von Papen's authoritarian government buttressed by an alliance with Hitler. The NSDAP, fearing that it had reached the limits of its electoral appeal, was ready for a bargain. Most important of all in practical terms, the presidential clique again became active. Von Papen, smarting from his recent defeat and anxious to revenge himself on Schleicher, re-emerged as the key player. Still the president's favourite, he became the chief intermediary between the Hitler group, the DNVP leaders, and the presidential palace where Hindenburg's son, Oskar, lent his support to the idea of a von Papen–Hitler combination. Believing that Hitler could be 'fenced in' by appointing a majority of reliable right-wing politicians, von Papen was prepared to offer him the chancellorship and two cabinet posts which Hitler demanded for Göring and Frick. In mid-January 1933, the still-reluctant Junker field marshal, who despised the uncouth 'Austrian corporal', authorized von Papen to proceed. The latter was able to resurrect the Harzburg front of rightist nationalists, enlisting Alfred Hugenberg and the Stahlhelm leader, Franz Seldte, for his 'national front'. Blomberg, an old enemy of Schleicher's and a general known to Hindenburg, replaced Schleicher at the Defence Ministry. Already favourably disposed towards the Nazis, Blomberg proved to be a crucial ally for Hitler. The cabal was already at work when Hindenburg rejected Schleicher's request for a dissolution of the Reichstag and the grant of emergency powers. Schleicher resigned on 28 January.

At 11:30 a.m. on Monday, 30 January 1933, a new chapter began in the history of the inter-war period. Quite unexpectedly to outside observers, the chaotic political situation in Germany was resolved with the appointment of Adolf Hitler as chancellor. Pressed separately by both von Papen and Schleicher, the latter anxious to ensure that the former did not himself return to the chancellorship, Hindenburg overcame his personal distaste and duly swore Hitler in. Von Papen was confident that he would succeed where Brüning and Schleicher had failed. Few men have been so disastrously wrong. The timing and means by which Hitler came to be chancellor made a working partnership with the existing military and diplomatic establishments possible. Hitler operated from within the political system, using the existing rules of the game to overthrow them. In his first months, still without that monopoly of power which was the necessary first step to all that would follow, Hitler was particularly careful in his relations with the Reichswehr, even to the point of recognizing its historic claim to an independent existence within the state. He was, no doubt, assisted by the Reichswehr's disillusionment with the Schleicher experiment and Blomberg's willingness to renounce the army's responsibilities for keeping domestic order. To underline the Reichswehr's renewed non-political role, the new defence minister was sworn in before Hitler and the rest of the cabinet took office. Co-operation was not difficult. Hitler recognized the Reichswehr as the 'most important institution of the state', and limits were placed on those Nazis who hoped to use it as an instrument of party rule along with the SA. The army would stay 'unpolitical and impartial'; this would mean, in effect, condoning any action taken by Nazi organizations in carrying out the 'revolution'. The army heads knew that Hitler would endorse their programme of comprehensive rearmament. This meant, given unified, strong, and stable government, the necessary funding for the second armaments programme and possibly more. 'The conformity between Hitler's goals and those of the military leaders was one of the main guarantees of the stability of the regime in the following years', Wilhelm Deist has written. 'For the Reichswehr this "alliance" represented primarily a domestic guarantee of its unchanged military and armaments objectives.'[27]

In a dinner speech to district army commanders on 3 February, four days after his appointment, Hitler called for a 'clean sweep' in home affairs: 'Adjustment of youth and of the whole people to the idea that only a struggle can save us and that everything else must be subordinated to this idea.... Training of youth and strengthening of the will to fight with all means.' He was suitably vague about future goals: 'How should political power be used when it has been gained? That is impossible to say yet. Perhaps fighting for new export possibilities, perhaps—and probably better—the conquest of new living space in the east and its ruthless Germanization. Certain that only through political power and struggle can the present economic circumstances be changed.' There was little here to alarm the military and much to applaud. Revisionist aims could still be pursued; anything more radical was far in the future. Hitler called attention to the weakness of the German state during the period of rearmament. 'It will show whether or not France has *statesmen*; if so, she will not leave us time but will attack us (presumably with

[27] Wilhelm Deist, 'The Rearmament of the Wehrmacht', in Deist *et al.*, *Germany and the Second World War*. Vol. I: *The Build-Up of German Aggression* (Oxford, 1990), 401.

eastern satellites).'[28] Hitler's capture of power would not affect Germany's position at the disarmament conference; the negotiations were left in the hands of Blomberg and Neurath.

The disarmament conference had already been hanging by a thread in December 1932. The deal done in Geneva to bring Germany back to the conference table had not solved anything, but merely highlighted again the need to confront the fundamental underlying problem of European security: how to balance French fears with German revisionism. But the luxury of time had run out. Brüning was gone, for what he was worth, and the governments of Papen and Schleicher endorsed policies well beyond the essentially co-operative revisionism of Stresemann. The government of Hitler posed threats of an entirely different character. It was the final cut of the disarmament conference's thread, though this was not immediately apparent. Hitler would initially be afraid to move too radically on the international stage, as he consolidated his power at home. But when he did move, ten months later in October 1933, it would be to pull Germany out of the disarmament conference and out of the League of Nations itself. This would be the end of the inter-war movement to disarm.

Contemporary Accounts

Survey of International Affairs (London, volumes for 1931–4).

TEMPERLEY, A. C., *The Whispering Gallery of Europe* (London, 1938).

WHEELER-BENNETT, JOHN, *The Pipe Dream of Peace: The Story of the Collapse of Disarmament* (London, 1935).

—— *Disarmament and Security Since Locarno, 1925–1931: Being the Political and Technical Background of the General Disarmament Conference, 1932* (London, 1932).

Books

BELL, PETER, *Chamberlain, Germany and Japan, 1933–1934* (London, 1996).

BENNETT, EDWARD, *German Rearmament and the West, 1932–1933* (Princeton, 1979).

BIALER, URI, *The Shadow of the Bomber: The Fear of Air Attack and British Politics, 1932–1939* (London, 1980). Esp. chs. 1–2.

BONGIORNO, JOSEPH, *Fascist Italy and the Disarmament Question, 1928–1934* (New York and London, 1991).

BOUSSARD, DANIEL, *Un problème de défense nationale: l'aéronautique militaire au parlement, 1928–1940* (Vincennes, 1983).

---

[28] Notes by General Liebmann, in J. Noakes and G. Pridham (eds.), *Nazism, 1919–1945: A Documentary Reader*. Vol. 3: *Foreign Policy, War and Racial Extermination* (Exeter, 1998), 628–9 (emphasis in original).

CASTELLAN, GEORGES, *Le Réarmament clandestin du Reich, 1930–1935: vu par le Deuxième Bureau de l'État-Major Français* (Paris, 1954).

FRANKENSTEIN, ROBERT, *Le Prix du réarmament français, 1935–1939* (Paris, 1982). Esp. the first chapter.

HALL, CHRISTOPHER, *Britain, America and Arms Control, 1921–1937* (Basingstoke, 1987).

HIGHAM, ROBIN, *Armed Forces in Peacetime: Britain, 1918–1940: A Case Study* (London, 1962).

JACKSON, PETER, *France and the Nazi Menace: Intelligence and Policy-Making, 1933–1939* (Oxford, 2001).

KITCHING, CAROLYN, *Britain and the Problem of International Disarmament, 1919–1934* (London, 1999). Chs. 7 and 8.

McKERCHER, B. J. C., *Transition of Power: Britain's Loss of Global Pre-eminence to the United States, 1930–1945* (Cambridge, 1999). Chs. 3 to 5.

NADOLNY, STEN, *Abrüstungsdiplomatie 1932–1933: Deutschland auf der Genfer Konferenz im Übergang von Weimar zu Hitler* (Munich, 1978).

NOEL BAKER, PHILIP, *Disarmament and the World Disarmament Conference, 1932–1933, and Why It Failed* (Oxford, 1979).

PATCH, Jr., WILLIAM, *Heinrich Brüning and the Dissolution of the Weimar Republic* (Cambridge, 1998). Esp. the final chapter.

ROSTOW, NICHOLAS, *Anglo-French Relations, 1934–1936* (London, 1984). Chs. 1 and 2.

VAÏSSE, MAURICE, *Sécurité d'abord: la politique française en matière de désarmement, 9 decembre 1930–17 avril 1934* (Paris, 1981).

Articles

MARTIN, A. and W. J. PHILPOTT, 'The Entente Cordiale and the Next War: Anglo-French Views on Future Military Cooperation, 1928–1939', in Martin Alexander (ed), *Knowing Your Friends: Intelligence Inside Alliances and Coalitions from 1914 to the Cold War* (London, 1998).

ANDERSON, DAVID G., 'British Rearmament and the "Merchants of Death": The 1935–1936 Royal Commission on the Manufacture of and Trade in Armaments', *Journal of Contemporary History*, 29: 1 (1994).

DEIST, WILHELM, 'Brüning, Herriot und die Abrüstungsgespräche von Bessinge, 1932', *Vierteljahrshefte für Zeitgeschichte*, 5 (1957).

—— 'Schleicher und die deutsche Abrüstungspolitik im Juni/Juli 1932', *Vierteljahrshefte für Zeitgeschichte*, 7 (1959).

—— 'The Rearmament of the Wehrmacht', in W. Deust et al (ed.), *Germany and the Second World War*. Vol. I: *The Build-Up of German Aggression* (Oxford, 1990).

DUTTON, DAVID, 'Simon and Eden at the Foreign Office, 1931–1935', *Review of International Studies*, 20: 1 (1994).

JACKSON, PETER, 'French Intelligence and Hitler's Rise to Power', *Historical Journal*, 41: 3 (1998).

LEE, MARSHALL, 'Disarmament and Security: The German Security Proposals in the League of Nations, 1926–1930: A Study in Revisionist Aims in an International Organization', *Militärgeschichtliche Mitteilungen*, 1 (1979).

McKercher, B. J. C., 'Of Horns and Teeth: The Preparatory Commission and the World Disarmament Conference, 1926–1934', in id. (ed.), *Arms Limitation and Disarmament: Restraints on War, 1899–1939* (Westport, Conn., 1992).

Richardson, Dick, 'Process and Progress in Disarmament: Some Lessons of History', in Vilho Harle and Pekka Sivonen (eds.), *Europe in Transition: Politics and Nuclear Security* (London, 1989).

—— 'The Geneva Disarmament Conference, 1932–1934', in id. and Glyn Stone (eds.), *Decisions and Diplomacy: Essays in Twentieth Century International History in Memory of George Grun and Esmonde Robertson* (London, 1995).

—— and Kitching, Carolyn, 'Britain and the World Disarmament Conference', in Peter Catterall and C. J. Morris (eds.), *Britain and the Threat to Stability in Europe, 1918–1945* (London and New York, 1993).

Schroeder, Paul, 'Historical Reality vs. Neo-Realist Theory', *International Security* (1994).

Thompson, J. A. 'Lord Cecil and the Pacifists in the League of Nations Union', *Historical Journal* 20, 4 (1973).

Vaïsse, Maurice, 'Continuité et descontinuité dans la politique française en matière de désarmement, février 1932–juin 1933: l'exemple du contrôle', in *La France et l'Alemagne, 1932–1936: communications présentées au colloque franco-allemand tenu à Paris (Palais du Luxembourg, salle Medicis) du 10 au 12 mars 1977* (Paris, 1980).

—— 'Security and Disarmament: Problems in the Development of the Disarmament Debates, 1919–1934', in R. Ahmann, A. M. Birke, and M. Howard (eds.), *The Quest for Stability: Problems of West European Security, 1918–1957* (Oxford, 1993).

Whaley, Barton, 'Covert Rearmament in Germany, 1919–1939: Deception and Mis-representation' in John Gooch and Amos Perlmutter (eds.), *Military Deception and Strategic Surprise* (London, 1982).

Winkler, Fred H., 'The War Department and Disarmament, 1926–1935', *Historian*, 28: 3 (1966).

Theses

Underwood, J. J., 'The Roots and Reality of British Disarmament Policy, 1932–1934', unpubl. Ph.D. thesis, Leeds University (1977).

Webster, Andrew, 'Anglo-French Relations and the Problems of Disarmament and Security, 1929–1933', Unpubl. Ph.D. thesis, University of Cambridge (2001).

Pacifism and Anti-War Groups

Books

Birn, Donald S., *The League of Nations Union, 1918–1945* (London, 1981).

Ceadel, Martin, *Pacifism in Britain, 1914–1945: The Defining of a Faith* (Oxford, 1980).

CHATFIELD, CHARLES, *For Peace and Justice: Pacifism in America, 1914–1941* (Knoxville, Tenn., 1971).

HOLL, KARL and WETTE, WOLFRAM (eds.), *Pazifismus in der Weimarer Republik: Beitrage zur historischen Friedensforschung* (Paderborn, 1981).

INGRAM, NORMAN, *The Politics of Dissent: Pacifism in France, 1919–1939* (Oxford, 1991).

KYBA, PATRICK, *Covenants Without the Sword: Public Opinion and British Defence Policy, 1931–1935* (Waterloo, Ont., 1983).

MOSSE, GEORGE L., *Fallen Soldiers: Reshaping the Memory of the World Wars* (New York and Oxford, 1990).

PROST, ANTOINE, *Les Anciens Combattants, 1914–1939* (Paris, 1977).

VAÏSSE, MAURICE (ed.), *Le Pacifisme en Europe: des années 1920 aux années 1950* (Brussels, 1993).

Articles

BARTOV, OMER, 'Martyrs' Vengeance: Memory, Trauma, and Fear of War in France, 1918–1940', in Joel Blatt (ed.), *The French Defeat of 1940: Reassessments* (Providence, RI and Oxford, 1998).

BIRN, DONALD S., 'The League of Nations Union and Collective Security', *Journal of Contemporary History*, 9: 3 (1974).

BRAMSTEAD, ERNEST, 'Apostles of Collective Security: The LNU and its Functions', *Australian Journal of Politics and History*, 13 (1962).

CEADEL, MARTIN, 'The "King and Country" Debate, 1933: Student Politics, Pacifism and the Dictators', *Historical Journal*, 22: 2 (1979).

—— 'The Peace Movements between the Wars: Problems of Definition' in Richard Taylor and Nigel Young (eds.), *Campaigns for Peace: British Peace Movements in the Twentieth Century* (Manchester, 1987).

EKSTEINS, MODRIS, 'The Fate of the Film "All Quiet on the Western Front" ', *Central European History*, 13 (1980).

LUKOWITZ, DAVID C., 'British Pacifists and Appeasement: The Peace Pledge Union', *Journal of Contemporary History*, 9: 1 (1974).

PUGH, MICHAEL, 'Pacifism and Politics in Britain, 1931–1935', *Historical Journal*, 23: 3 (1980).

THOMPSON, J. A., 'Lord Cecil and the Pacifists in the LNU', *Historical Journal*, 20: 4 (1977).

VAÏSSE, MAURICE, 'Le Pacifisme française dans les années trente', *Relations Internationales*, 53 (1988).

WETTE, WOLFRAM, 'Ideology, Propaganda and Internal Politics As Preconditions of the War Policy of the Third Reich', in Deist et al. (ed.), *Germany and the Second World War*, vol. I: *The Build-Up of German Aggression* (Oxford, 1990).

Part II

Conclusion:
The Hinge Years, 1929–1933

I

The 'hinge years' of 1929–33 witnessed the threat to the hopes and institutions nurtured during the previous decade and the collapse of many of them. They saw the revival of those destructive nationalistic strains, strengthened by the Great Depression, the motor force of these years, which would shape the following period until the outbreak of war in 1939. The *annus terribilis*, 1931, was the watershed year that unleashed a systemic crisis of unexpected depth and severity, but these years need to be seen as a whole, the creaking hinge that was attached both to the 1920s and 1930s. The competing but irreconcilable demands of national and international interests came to define this transitional period, with the former clearly in the ascendant. The claims and the powers of the state expanded and those of the international community contracted. While there was no single moment when the road to a new war began, one chapter in the history of international relations ended and a new one began. The European mood was visibly darkening. The strains of the world crisis hastened the collapse of the Weimar republic but did not in themselves make the triumph of Hitler inevitable. His appointment to the chancellorship on 30 January 1933, nevertheless, would alter the contours of both German history and European international affairs.

The three chapters in Part II are interconnected: each records a major failure in international co-operation. Their combined effect was to destroy much of the international fabric that had been so painfully woven during the preceding decade. By 1933 depression policies, the 'shooting war' in the Far East, and the failure of the disarmament talks created a whole set of problems only indirectly connected with the enforcement or revision of the peace treaties. The results were seen at the national and international level. Democratic countries became more interventionist in dealing with domestic policies as governments acquired expanded powers; elsewhere, authoritarian governments emerged. Reparations were ended at Lausanne and the debtor nations soon ceased to pay their war debts, but the effects of the depression were to heighten the politicization of financial and commercial policy and lead to the development of national strategies of recovery that were antipathetic to international co-operation. Because Japan was a major power and the Sino-Japanese dispute in Manchuria had been internationalized, its unchecked resort to military action and departure from the League of Nations were major blows to the latter's reputation and prestige. The Japanese rejection of their more internationally oriented policies raised disturbing questions about the general efficacy of collective action in maintaining peace. Though its importance as a turning point in Pacific relations should not be exaggerated, the Japanese action in Manchuria had repercussions beyond its geographic location. It represented a check to the influence of the League of Nations and posed a threat to the already weakened institutional framework for international co-operation. The simultaneous opening and subsequent collapse of the World Disarmament Conference talks, before Hitler took power, proved even more damaging to the confidence of the internationalists, in part because hopes were so high. The profound effects of the Great War had left most policy-makers desperate to avoid its repetition yet anxious to be prepared should another conflict threaten. Urged on by vocal elements in their electorates and by the representatives of the smaller powers, the spokesmen for the great powers tried to find ways to bridge the differences between such ideas as disarmament and collective security on the one hand, and the other certainties about the need to ensure national defence and military security on the other. In disarmament, as in the economic and financial spheres and in the playing-out of events in the Far East, it was becoming clear that the hopes of 1920s internationalism had seen their heyday come and go; national considerations would now dominate.

II

The spreading and intensifying global depression was the key reason for the darkening mood between 1929 and 1933. The mid-decade stabilization and the renewed attempts to solve the reparations–war-debt impasse depended on assumptions of continuing economic prosperity and a flow of American capital to Europe, particularly to Germany. Statesmen and officials alike assumed that the growth of world trade and the re-establishment of the gold standard would promote prosperity and peace. Yet, by 1930, with but few important exceptions, almost all the European countries, and the United States and Japan as well, were feeling the cold economic winds. Though the timing and severity of the depression varied from country to country, it was a global phenomenon which began with a drop in the prices of agricultural goods and primary products, but which spread from the agricultural to the industrial sectors and affected industrial as well as agricultural states. Contemporaries were slow to recognize that this depression was different in magnitude and consequences from any previous downturn in the business cycle. Both statesmen and experts found it difficult to respond to its massive impact and the rise in unemployment beyond the application of orthodox financial remedies. The leaders of the already heavily indebted agricultural states of eastern Europe tried to avoid devaluing their currencies for fear of a return to the inflationary and socially chaotic conditions of the immediate post-war period. Instead, they introduced deflationary measures to balance their budgets and protect their currencies even as their countries were plunging deeper into depression. Most governments resorted to higher tariffs and, later, to import and exchange controls in order to protect home markets and to avoid national bankruptcy. They either reneged on their foreign debts (Poland was one of the exceptions) or renegotiated payment terms. Bilateral trading agreements became commonplace, and clearings were used as a way of avoiding the loss of gold and foreign exchange.

Necessity, the absence of foreign assistance, and the discrediting of liberal capitalism encouraged governments to take active steps to assist their debt-ridden agricultural sectors. Despite the lack of foreign capital, efforts were made to speed up industrialization in the hope of creating more self-sufficient economies. Governments in eastern Europe assumed direction or control over major industries, particularly those of strategic importance, and took over firms formerly under foreign domination. The drive for industrialization, increasingly directed towards rearmament, was only partially successful, and the prosperity of most of the region still depended on comparatively backward agricultural production. Insofar as the right-wing governments of the 1930s were able to avert economic and financial disaster, they did so through state intervention, buttressed, unfortunately, by appeals to nationalist sentiments revived by the economic hardships of the farmers and peasants.

The western industrialized states, faced with shrinking markets and a contraction of foreign lending, similarly struggled with unbalanced budgets, rising unemployment, and losses of both domestic and foreign confidence. Convinced by their experiences in the early 1920s that liberal credit policies would bring inflation and social chaos, their leaders, too, instituted or adopted more stringent deflationary policies in order to avoid being pushed off gold. The timing and depth of the depression varied from state to state. Germany was an early victim; the roots of its troubles were mainly domestic, and there were already signs of economic difficulties in 1928. The French, whose problems were at first budgetary, did not feel the full impact of the depression until after the British and American devaluations. The United States, mainly for domestic reasons but also as a result of contracting foreign markets, suffered a sharp economic contraction before the end of the decade. It was, however, the drying up of American lending in 1929, despite a temporary revival in 1930, that so adversely affected the European economies and made the situation in Germany considerably worse. The Reich government, chronically short of domestic sources of credit, depended on American loans to underwrite its budget deficits, while German industry had come to rely on American capital inflows for development and expansion. The search for short-term funding to cover Germany's budgetary deficits undermined creditor confidence; German as well as foreign asset-holders moved their capital out of the country. With neither bankers nor industrialists able to raise new funds, bankers called in their loans and industrialists cut production. Unemployment figures, already high, continued to rise, putting severe pressure on the underfunded Reich unemployment schemes and budgets. Disputes over levels of taxation and spending intensified Germany's political turmoil and further exacerbated its economic malaise.

Because the 'peace process' in the later 1920s depended, in part, on American capital underwriting, its restrictive monetary practices contributed to the worsening of the European situation. The Federal Reserve Board had raised the discount rate in August 1929 in order to cool the speculative fever of the American stock market. The results were to trigger the Wall Street crash of 24 October 1929 and, though the amount of wealth lost was in fact small, confidence was severely shaken and American optimism and faith in limitless bounty collapsed. The prospects in Europe hardly favoured further American investment. The drop in American primary prices was reflected in price-falls throughout the globe, and the contraction of its market for primary products had an immediate and devastating effect on exporters elsewhere. The European reaction to the tightening of American monetary policy made it difficult to contain the American deflationary shock. Fearful of initiating a financial crisis that would devalue their currencies and set off an inflationary spiral that would drive their currencies off gold, most European policy-makers in gold-standard countries followed the American example and raised their discount and interest rates. It was through the 'mechanics' of the gold standard that the deflationary impulse was transmitted from the United States to Europe, making the situation even worse. The widely held belief in the benefits of the gold standard and the fears of inflation checked the adoption of expansionary policies that might have allowed nations to absorb the shock.

While implementing orthodox gold-standard policies, European governments also adopted new measures of trade protection. The hopes of the delegates to the World Economic Conference of 1927 that the protectionist trend might be reversed remained unfulfilled. Few of the subsequent meetings and conferences called to address the agricultural problems of the eastern European economies resulted in constructive action. The French and British continued to differ on what should be done, while the German–Austrian customs union initiative in March 1931, in part politically motivated, raised the spectre of *Anschluss* and alarmed the French and the Czechs. Farmers in northern and western Europe, also suffering from the global price-drops, feared the consequences of dumping as the Soviets as well as the eastern Europeans sought markets for their agricultural products. Farmers in France, Belgium, and Holland won higher tariffs and the introduction of quota systems. All the political parties in the Weimar republic courted the rural vote and offered protective measures to their agricultural producers. Well-organized peasant parties in eastern Europe grew in influence, while nationalist sentiment reinforced the protectionist mood. In the United States, the Smoot–Hawley tariff, which went into operation in 1930, began with a presidential initiative to deal with farmer discontent and was extended through Congressional action to cover a wide range of industrial imports as well. Its implementation, though far from the only cause, set off a new wave of European protectionist legislation. The shrinkage of trade was accompanied by increased levels of hostility between neighbouring states.

It was the banking crises of the summer of 1931 that actually plunged Europe into the depths of an unprecedented structural crisis that fundamentally altered the financial and economic landscape for the rest of the decade. The bank failures that started in Austria and Hungary and spread elsewhere turned the depression into 'the Great Depression', with far-reaching political as well as economic and financial consequences. The mechanisms of financial co-operation proved inadequate as international efforts, whether through the central banks or the Bank of International Settlement, failed to stop the acceleration of the crisis. Apart from the political obstacles to co-operation, central bank action proved too slow and too limited to stop the runs on the exchanges. The bankers, who were often blamed for the catastrophe, felt that the problems were beyond their capacity to solve and looked to the politicians to save the situation. In most cases, in order to relieve the pressure on the exchanges, the afflicted governments, even when given international assistance, imposed exchange controls to direct the amount and destination of gold and foreign currency leaving the country. The German banking crisis was the most serious and severe of the summer panics. The government introduced a series of measures which protected the country from the consequences of staying on the gold standard. As adequate foreign loans were not forthcoming, and the Hoover moratorium on reparations and war debts was only a temporary measure, Reich intervention became essential if the whole banking structure was not to collapse. Though the Brüning government still hoped that its austerity programme and the end of reparations would restore the country's financial and economic independence and pave the way for Germany's re-entry into the international economy, it acted to help the commercial banks; standstill agreements were negotiated to prevent foreigners from removing their funds, and exchange and trade controls were instituted. The government secretly allowed the Reichsbank to introduce modest reflationary measures. Germany remained on gold, but the Reichsbank was no longer playing by gold-standard rules.

More important internationally, the British financial crisis of July–September 1931 resulted in the devaluation of the pound on 21 September and the beginning of a worldwide retreat from the gold standard. Along with the United States, Britain was the world's major short-term lender; it was bound to feel the effects of the summer crises, quite apart from its already existing balance-of-payments problems on both its current and capital account. Britain's short-term liabilities were more than double her gold-exchange and liquid assets. The government's budgetary difficulties greatly accelerated the loss of confidence in the pound. Along with the dollar, the pound was a world currency, and many countries, including France, kept their reserves in London. Intended to be only a temporary measure to avoid adopting more resolute, if economically and politically damaging, policies to defend the pound, the British devaluation marked the beginning of the end of the world gold standard. By the time of the British action, seven other countries had already abandoned the gold standard; another twenty-four nations rapidly followed its example. The devaluation saved threatened British banks, and due to the post-devaluation stability of the pound many foreign investors felt confident enough to leave their funds in London. The subsequent introduction of a cheap money policy set the stage for domestic recovery by encouraging spending on housing and consumer durables. The Americans nailed down the gold coffin after President Roosevelt's unitary decision to float the dollar on 19 April 1933, taken for the sake of the domestic economy and in order to raise commodity prices and stimulate economic activity. The Americans were under no market compulsion to devalue; it was a national decision taken without any international consultation. The dollar's subsequent depreciation further increased the deflationary pressures on those countries that remained on gold. The latter, including France, were soon engaged in economically and politically damaging struggles to keep their currencies pegged to gold. It was a struggle that could not be sustained. Czechoslovakia in 1934, Belgium in 1935, France, Switzerland, and the Netherlands in 1936—all were forced to devalue their currencies. Cutting the so-called golden chains was not sufficient to foster domestic recovery: expansionary measures had to be introduced. The departure from the gold standard was a major shock to those who took this radical step, but the fears of disaster proved unfounded and neither the British nor later the Americans saw any reason to return to gold. Admittedly, neither fully exploited its new-found freedom. The beliefs in balanced budgets and limited spending that could be covered by taxation persisted long after the abandonment of the gold standard.

Many economic historians believe that only the abandonment of the gold standard allowed the adoption of the monetary policies needed to encourage economic recovery and growth. Unfortunately, the decisions to devalue were uncoordinated and taken without regard to their effects on other countries. Neither the British nor the Americans were prepared to assume a leadership role, and neither devaluation became the basis for international co-operation. The new monetary policies were accompanied by the adoption of yet more protectionist measures. Even Britain, the flag-bearer of free trade, during the winter of 1931–2 and at the Ottawa conference in July 1932 abandoned its traditional policies. As a result, British trade was further oriented towards her empire. Throughout Europe, and elsewhere as well, tariffs were raised, followed by a general move towards the introduction of quota systems and the creation of import monopolies along Soviet lines. Quotas and the use of exchange controls led to the linking of trade and debt policies. Bilateral trade and payment arrangements became commonplace, particularly in central and south-eastern Europe. The Germans, under the Nazis, expanded the system already begun under Brüning, turning away from the industrialized nations in favour of trade with nations of the 'Reichsmark bloc' (Bulgaria, Greece, Hungary, Romania, Turkey, and Yugoslavia), as well as with countries in South America. The British, too, concluded bilateral trading agreements with states outside the Ottawa system and made arrangements with debtor nations in which a proportion of their payments for exports was used to pay off debts. There were some counter-moves in northern Europe, and an initiative from Cordell Hull, the American secretary of state, who attempted to start a worldwide cut in tariff levels soon after Roosevelt's electoral victory. His proposals for an extended trade truce and a bilateral trade agreement with the British found little support, either in London or in the many countries depending on protective measures to insulate themselves from the adverse world conditions. In June 1934, mainly because of Hull's tireless campaign against the evils of protection, Congress passed the Reciprocal Trade Agreement Act, which, though dependent on bilateral negotiations, marked the first partial reversal of America's traditional tariff policy.

The World Economic Conference of 1933 was the last attempt at international co-operation over finance and trade before the outbreak of the European war. Neither the United States nor Britain was willing, either individually or jointly, to assume the leadership of a co-ordinated reflationary movement. Few of the participating nations, least of all Nazi Germany, were willing to abandon measures that, while remaining on gold, allowed them the freedom to act without considering the foreign consequences. It was at this conference, too, that the Americans detached themselves from Europe. Convinced that the causes of the depression were domestic, Roosevelt sought remedies that precluded international solutions. His predecessor, Herbert Hoover, admittedly with some reluctance, had engaged the United States more directly than previous Republican presidents in international financial matters, even to the point of suggesting further concessions on war debts and had actively intervened in the Geneva disarmament talks. Though always working within self-imposed limits and with a sharp eye on Congress, he had cooperated with Ramsay MacDonald on a whole range of problems during his first years in office. During 1932–3 this partnership began to unravel as differences over war debts, disarmament questions, and the Manchurian crisis drove the two countries apart. Once Roosevelt took office, the gulf between the Americans and the Europeans appeared to widen. The president was singularly unimpressed by the European leadership; his meetings with the British, French, and German representatives before the meetings of the World Economic Conference confirmed his belief that they were not interested in international co-operation but only with the promotion of their own narrow national interests. Roosevelt and Neville Chamberlain developed a strong antipathy towards each other which persisted even after the latter's ascent to the prime-ministership in 1937. It was under Franklin Roosevelt that American economic and political isolationism would reach a new peak.

The abandonment of the gold standard did not lead to the collapse of the world economy, but governments found no alternative basis for co-operation. A number of often competitive currency and trade blocs emerged. Governments increasingly took control over trade policy; bilateral and barter trading practices both restricted and redirected world trade, making it almost impossible to restore a liberal world economy. The differences between the blocs and between the so-called 'have' and 'have-not' nations took on a new importance, as nations looked to their empires or would-be empires and spheres of influence to strengthen their economies. Some governments tried to achieve greater self-sufficiency and greater independence from the world markets, but few were successful. The Soviet Union was the great exception. By the mid-1930s it was well on the path to 'armed autarky'. After 1931, a peak year for imports (mainly foreign machinery) paid for by forced grain collections and widespread famine, foreign trade contracted and Soviet imports fell dramatically. Through a system of control and terror, and barter arrangements, Soviet industrialization was achieved without foreign assistance. Economic decision-making took place in a vacuum, without any concern for world prices, and was increasingly dictated by political rather than economic considerations. At terrible cost to the Russian workforce, and above all to the peasantry, Stalin moved to fulfill his goal of creating 'socialism in one country'.

World recovery began in 1933; it was slow, erratic, and incomplete, and nationally rather than internationally focused. Global markets remained depressed and world trade did not revive. There was some recovery in the volume of world exports and imports, but they failed to reach the 1929 level. Prices continued to fall until 1935. With the breakdown of the world's capital markets, there was no way to sustain unbalanced trade (outside the clearing agreements), and so countries sought to balance their trade by reducing the overall level. There was no revival of the capital flows of the past. In time, capital began to move from the debtor to the creditor nations as investors, fearing currency depreciation and political uncertainties, sought safer havens for their capital, mainly in Britain and the United States. The depression and the official measures taken to encourage recovery accentuated divisons in many European countries. Financial policy became part of a more general economic recovery strategy dictated by the political head of the states. Bankers, Jews, gypsies, and foreigners were blamed for economic difficulties. Economic turbulence exacerbated political instability and exposed economic, social, and ethnic tensions. The ravages of the depression did much to discredit not only the capitalist system but also liberal democratic practices. Centrally directed government recovery programmes gave a new *raison d'être* to the imposition of authoritarian governments in many parts of Europe. The powers of the state were strengthened as the degree of its intervention in the economy increased, though no government approximated to the all-embracing role of the Soviet authorities. Almost everywhere politics became increasingly polarized, and the remaining middle parties either lost votes and influence or were crushed. It was the far right rather than the left who were the main beneficiaries. National communist parties, partly because of their own and Comintern misjudgements, were rarely able to capitalize on the failures of political and economic liberalism. The communist campaign against the 'social fascists' fatally divided the left without initiating red revolutions. The Soviet Union, mired in its own ideo-logical preconceptions, failed to take the full measure of the ideology of the radical right.

The connection between the conditions of depression and the rise of dictatorships was not a simple one. Countries where democratic forms of government were new or poorly rooted were obviously at far greater risk than such well-established democratic states as Britain and the United States. Though the effects of the depression in the United States were as devastating and demoralizing as those in Germany, and President Roosevelt exercised executive powers on a scale never before seen in peacetime, there was no real danger of a dictatorship in Washington—despite later Republican charges—and no radical shift to the very small extremist parties. Important political changes took place in both Britain and France, and the French government came under severe pressure after 1933, but in both cases the existing consti-tutional forms survived. It was the military defeat in 1940 and not the depression that brought the Third Republic to an end. The economic crisis in Germany, however, acted as a trigger for the final collapse of the democratic experiment. Some have argued that the Weimar republic was a gamble at best, and one unlikely to succeed given its uncertain beginnings and the number of economic blows it had suffered in its very short life: inflation, hyperinflation, stabilization at high domestic cost, and economic stagnation. The so-called golden years of the republic in the late 1920s were marked by 'the crisis before the crisis', that is, unresolved economic difficulties and a growing disillusionment with republicanism. Even before the collapse of the Müller coalition cabinet in March 1930, Weimar's political culture was dangerously fragmented. The traditional parties of the centre and right were already in decline, and the number of special-interest groups and local associations seeking authoritarian solutions multiplying. The republic was facing a crisis of political legitimacy before the full impact of the depression was felt. Yet it had survived previous crises, and it can be argued that a majority of Germans remained loyal to the republic during these difficult years, though without any strong emotional attachment to its survival. There had been too little time between its inception and the onset of an unusually severe economic crisis to create the loyalties required for political legitimacy.

The effects of the depression created the conditions under which Weimar ultimately collapsed. The very severity of the crisis and the impact of Brüning's deflationary policies intensified the sense of despair about the future and the search for alternative political solutions in many parts of the electorate. As disillusionment spread, it fanned that search for deliverance that allowed the Nazis to attract adherents from across the whole electoral spectrum. If it had not been for the depression, it is doubtful whether the Nazis, whatever their political dynamism, could have attracted over one-third of the German electorate in 1932. The depression, too, provided the opportunity for the traditional right-wing elite to gain power. It set out to destroy the Weimar constitutional order and restore the old authoritarian system that it had long favoured. The shift towards presidential government, begun under Brüning, had by 1932 closed off the possibility of a return to parliamentary politics and opened the way for the final 'gravediggers of the republic' to take office. Given the high degree of politicalization and the clashes in the streets between rival militias, chancellors Papen and Schleicher needed mass followings to survive. Hitler could offer what they lacked. By the end of 1932 the Nazi party was popular and broad-based, but it seemed to have reached the limits of its electoral potential. Its stalling momentum left it ripe for exploitation. Hitler, with uncanny political cunning, elected to wait until the conservatives made their bid for his participation in their government. The Nazis could not have finished the republic off on their own; such action was not necessary. Hindenburg and his circle of advisers invited them to share power and brought Hitler to the chancellorship. It proved to be their fatal mistake.

III

Events in the Far East resulted in a further attack on the international structure created during the 1920s. Admittedly, the 'Washington system' was hardly a system. Quite apart from the absence of the USSR, the rise of Chinese nationalism and the decisions of each of the Washington treaty signatories to go their own way had already altered the bases of the treaties. Japan ratified the naval agreement of 1930, but its stormy reception and political aftermath showed the extent of the opposition to the 'internationalist policies' of the government. As elsewhere, the depression put a severe strain on a political structure already under nationalist attack. The sharp contraction of Japan's export markets radicalized sections of the rural population and provided popular backing for those military elements that wanted both a return to a purer form of political life and a more positive foreign policy. The military action in Manchuria, a victory for the Kwantung Army and their supporters in Tokyo, represented a break in Japanese foreign policy. Any future solution of Sino-Japanese problems would take place outside the Washington treaties, the Kellogg–Briand pact, and the League of Nations. It was not at all clear how far the reforming officers were prepared to go either at home or abroad, but it was predictable that the military nationalists would have a far greater say in the making of

Japanese foreign policy than in earlier years. The Amu declaration of 1934, the Japanese 'Monroe doctrine', warned the Chinese and other foreign governments that Japan would not tolerate any military assistance or foreign loans to China. The Japanese would settle their own affairs without outside interference. There were still those in Tokyo who looked for a settlement with Chiang and the Kuomintang; a confrontation with the Chinese would not be a simple matter. The future was still uncertain.

The Chinese appeal to the League of Nations internationalized a regional issue. As a result, the League's dependence on great-power action was graphically revealed, as was the importance of non-League members, the United States and the Soviet Union, to any successful intervention. The Japanese success in Manchuria was reassuring for any future revisionist states but unsettling for the smaller status-quo powers, which had led the fight for League intervention. The failure to check Japan was a blow to the League's reputation, but the picture was not entirely black. Distinctions were drawn between events in the Far East and in Europe. Because sanctions were not actually invoked, and because Japan left the League in accordance with the provisions of the Covenant, delegates remained hopeful about the League's future peacekeeping role. The Assembly had condemned the Japanese action, and at least one great power, Britain, had been forced to take that body's demands into consideration. Yet the League's adoption of the doctrine of non-recognition was a demonstration of its impotence. Many of the delegates in Geneva, after the establishment of Manchukuo, had doubts about the practicability of the League's peace-keeping functions.

It may be true that the adoption of the non-recognition principle made it more difficult to achieve a future negotiated settlement. The Lytton report had suggested that Manchuria was something of a special case, and the members of the commission were careful not to condemn Japan outright. Some even hoped that, with time and the recovery from Japan's sense of wounded pride, the Japanese would consider a compromise over Manchuria. Anglo-American hopes that Japan was too economically fragile to pursue a forward policy in China in the interim were misplaced. In 1931 the Japanese went off the gold standard, adopted only in early 1930, and allowed the yen to depreciate. The undervalued yen and a major export drive inaugurated a period of Japanese prosperity. Military spending boosted the home economy, leading to full employment by 1936. Western tariffs, quotas, and preferences, many aimed at Japan, intensified the search for yen-bloc autarky. Economic success increased the militarists' appetite for further territorial expansion.

Neither the Anglo-Americans nor the League attempted to stop Japan, but neither did they suggest a new basis for settling the Sino-Japanese dispute. The Japanese aggression in Manchuria (signals intelligence alerted the British to the premeditated nature of Japan's actions at Mukden) and Shanghai gave greater substance to Admiralty demands for building up Britain's naval defences in the Far East and for the ending of the ten-year rule. Though the Shanghai dispute was satisfactorily contained, neither Britain nor the United States emerged from the Manchurian affair with credit, as each blamed the other for the failure to check Japanese aggression. In fact, neither government was prepared to defend the so-called Washington system. Many at the Foreign Office believed that Britain could not act alone in the Far East, but bridled at its dependence on American support. Whatever the contrary views held by Neville Chamberlain and the Treasury, any British initiative in the Far East had to consider the American reaction. The crisis also underlined the critical importance of the Soviet Union's role. In part, the Japanese action in Manchuria resulted from a perception of Soviet interest in north Manchuria and Inner Mongolia. There was a faction in Tokyo already thinking in terms of a war with the USSR. Russian policy in the Far East, torn between conciliation and confrontation, posed problems for the British and Americans. It was difficult to know what future part the USSR would play in China, and how this would affect the Far Eastern and European balances of power. In this sense, too, the Manchurian affair had international implications that were still unclear.

IV

The disarmament story was a Greek tragedy in its predetermined end. Though often tedious in its seemingly endless repetitions, its importance, so often overlooked, should not be underestimated for it provides one of the clearest examples of the attempt and failure to achieve multilateral international agreement. During their fourteen-year search for a way to promote general disarmament, both the disarmers and their opponents perpetuated illusions that ultimately benefited only the destroyers of the peace. Policy-makers were unable to bridge the gap between internationalist ideals and demands of national security. Disarmament was a political and not a technical process. The cause of failure, which pre-dated Hitler's coming to power and Germany's final departure from the conference, underscored the fault-lines of the Locarno stabilization. The basic Franco-German conflict over security, British preference for a limited liability security system, and America's ultimate lack of interest in any collective security system blocked all possibilities for progress. The Geneva talks began to undermine the existing distribution of power well before the military balance was actually changed.

German goals at Geneva evolved as the demand for an end to reparations was supplanted in 1932 by the demand for equality in armaments. The rhetoric of 'equality', however, was never more than a tactic. It provided a potent propaganda weapon against the other major powers, for it emphasized Germany's status as the only officially disarmed major power. The logic of the disarmament process meant the burden of responsibility for progress lay in the hands of the former Allies; German delegates therefore simply rejected all proposals which did not lead to increases in German armaments. More importantly, concessions on armaments were required in Berlin in order to provide cover for the secret programmes of illegal rearmament which had been ongoing since the late 1920s and had accelerated under Papen and Schleicher. A revision of the Versailles treaty restrictions was vital. Many observers in Britain and the United States agreed, though for somewhat different reasons, that European stabilization could only come from a new agreement on armaments to which Germany voluntarily subscribed. This would mean a relative decrease in the gap between the armed forces of Germany and France, something which appeared acceptable to those in both countries who continued to view France as over-armed, militarist, and possibly possessing hegemonic ambitions on the continent.

The French understood the nature of the German challenge, but could not find the means to contain it. Their major concern was to secure British backing for France in advance of further German rearmament. An ever-present and enervating fear of a more powerful Germany, and some deep-rooted weariness that precluded independent action, were at the root of the French failures at Geneva. To these must be added an abhorrence of war that permeated wide sections of the French public, including many of the ex-servicemen of the Great War. Most French believed that 'arbitration, security, and disarmament' was the right policy for the government to pursue. If leaders such as Tardieu and Herriot put security first, neither thought that this could be achieved through French military preparedness. Dependent on finding allies or, at the least, building up diplomatic fences to keep Germany disarmed, France could not use her military margin to regain the diplomatic initiative at Geneva.

Much of the blame for the French failure must rest with the British and Americans. There were serious errors of judgement on the British side; some understandable given the assumption that the Germans could not be treated as second-class citizens in a weak European system without threatening its very existence. It was believed in London that, given some kind of inducement, the Germans would agree to accept some form of revised Versailles armaments agreement that would not, in practice, leave Germany free to rearm. The British fruitlessly sought a formula that would hold out the promise of equality in arms to Germany without actually ceding it. It was thought necessary, too, to find a way to strengthen the existing Reich government for fear of what might come next. Cabinet ministers thought that Britain could act as an umpire between France and Germany without any further input on the security side beyond what was given at Locarno. Other factors contributed to their defensive cast of mind. The Manchurian crisis had underlined Britain's vulnerabilities as a world power and exposed the frailty of the Far Eastern security system. Japanese action in China and the unpredictability of the American response posed practical problems that reinforced the government's unwillingness to take on new continental engagements. The 1931 crisis also contributed to the retreat from Europe. British prosperity was no longer dependent, as it was during the 1920s, on European recovery. The creation of the sterling bloc and the turn to imperial protection provided satisfactory alternatives. A National Government whose major interests were domestic rather than international recovery, and a relatively inexperienced foreign secretary allergic to any form of risk, had good reasons to prefer a policy of limited continental commitment.

The British could not opt for isolation; the Americans could. American participation in the World Disarmament Conference was linked to the widespread view that the arms race was the principle cause of the Great War. There was also the belief that money saved on armaments could be used more productively, for instance, for the payment of war debts to the benefit of the American taxpayer. In military circles there was some sympathy for German revisionist goals, given the apparent margin of French military superiority. Neither the military nor the politicians, however, believed that European differences fundamentally affected American security. The failure to take up the Hoover proposals, like the arguments over war debts and trade, only served to reinforce Congressional suspicion of Europeans in general and the French in particular. Even the disarmament impulse was to turn isolationist. The deepening depression accentuated the American retreat from Europe and stifled the nascent internationalism of the Hoover administration. As the domestic problems of the depression took precedence over all other issues, the economic and financial benefits to be achieved through international collaboration were judged too inconsequential to be weighed against the protection of the home economy. For the president-elect, the political advantages of independent action were overwhelming, quite apart from the so-called effectiveness of his often disastrous trial-and-error approach. Roosevelt had far too much on his political plate to take an active role in Geneva. It was hardly surprising that, during 1933, the American role became increasingly peripheral.

When the World Disarmament Conference finally met, the main protagonists had to face the gap between what was being said at Geneva and what was occurring at home, where military advisers strongly opposed arms-limitation agreements or thought them only appropriate for others. Was support for the ideals of disarmament and the League of Nations really compatible with doctrines of national interest and 'absolute needs' in armaments? Questions that had been postponed or had been obscured by more immediate concerns in the 1920s now came to the forefront of the Geneva discussions. Neither the Franco-German clash over arms nor the Anglo-French conflict over security could be papered over with drafts and resolutions. The failure to find a modus vivendi between France and Germany before Hitler came to power accelerated that turn to extreme nationalism that the new German chancellor so brilliantly exploited by offering the vision of a revived Germany. Further attempts made in 1933 to bridge the gap between Berlin and Paris and to revive the links between Paris and London did not encourage much optimism about the future. Hopes in Geneva for a new arms agreement faded as Europe's statesmen looked for more practical ways to achieve peace, security, and prosperity. And already there were some who were willing to chance the fortunes of war.

V

At the Hague in August 1929 only a few questioned the appropriateness of a conference to mark 'the final liquidation of the war'. By the beginning of 1933 talk of future war had become common currency. The meetings of statesmen and experts had been unable to prevent or solve the problems of the deepening depression, nor had they produced an acceptable arms-control programme. Despite the truce in China, there was little confidence in a permanent Far Eastern peace. Statesmen took over where the experts failed, looking for solutions that would bring relief and protection. These would not come from Geneva. The collapse of the World Economic Conference and the World Disarmament Conference were symbolic of the failure of the promise of internationalism. So was the Japanese departure from the League, though perfectly legal within the terms of the Covenant. The three chief architects of Locarno, or at least the memory of them, became unpopular in influential political circles. Briand and Stresemann, after their deaths, were bitterly criticized by many of their own countrymen, and Austen Chamberlain, very much an elder statesman, was excluded from the National governments. The Locarno spirit had temporarily survived their passing from the scene, but the pace of disintegration visibly quickened as the depression deepened and brought about radical economic and political change. In the post-depression world, national strategies of survival left only limited room for international co-operation.

Dates may be little more than markers of convenience, but the importance of 30 January 1933 cannot be overestimated. A new and tragic chapter in Europe's history began with Hitler's appointment to the chancellorship of Germany and his subsequent seizure of complete power. It marked both an ending and a beginning. The lights of the 1920s—reconstruction, internationalism, multilateralism, disarmament—were dimmed. The following years would see the gathering shadows of disintegration, nationalism, autarky, and rearmament. The theme of the book shifts from the attempted reconstruction of Europe after the Great War to the preparations for a new power struggle in Europe. Unlike the 1920s, when the many different national and international threads make it difficult to impose a narrative pattern on events, the post-1933 period has a central theme that places Hitler and Nazi Germany at the centre of European developments. There are lines of continuity between the two periods, both in western and eastern Europe. Not all of the previous international fabric was destroyed by the upheavals of the hinge years. More striking, however, are the altered patterns of international politics in the post-1933 period, as almost all the European statesmen came to terms with the challenge posed by Hitler and the Third Reich. It is an appropriate moment to leave this account of the post-war period for the more ominous story of the pre-war years.

APPENDIX A
STATISTICAL TABLES

TABLE A-1. US$ Conversion Tables, 1918–1941

	$/GBP	GBP/$	Fr./$	RM/$	Lira/$	Yen/$	Swiss Fr./$	Rouble/$
1918	4.77	0.21	5.45	8.37	6.33	1.89	4.85	3.37
1919	3.81	0.26	10.82	47.62	13.08	1.98	5.38	
1920	3.49	0.20	10.82	72.99	28.58	1.99	6.49	
1921	4.16	0.24	12.75	190.19	22.70	2.09	5.15	
1922	4.61	0.22	13.83	7,352.94	19.88	2.05	5.28	
1923	4.36	0.23	19.05	*na	23.04	2.13	5.72	
1924	4.70	0.21	18.52	4.20	23.25	2.60	5.16	
1925	4.85	0.21	26.77	4.20	24.81	2.32	5.18	
1926	4.85	0.21	25.32	4.20	22.55	2.04	5.18	
1927	4.88	0.20	25.38	4.19	18.59	2.17	5.18	
1928	4.85	0.21	25.58	4.20	19.10	2.18	5.19	1.94
1929	4.88	0.20	25.39	4.18	19.10	2.04	5.14	1.94
1930	4.86	0.21	25.24	4.19	19.09	2.02	5.16	1.94
1931	3.37	0.30	25.49	4.23	19.57	2.23	5.13	1.90
1932	3.28	0.30	25.62	4.20	19.57	4.82	5.20	1.93
1933	5.12	0.20	16.34	2.68	12.16	3.25	3.30	1.93
1934	4.95	0.20	15.16	2.47	11.71	3.47	3.09	†4.96
1935	4.93	0.20	15.15	2.47	12.38	3.48	3.08	5.04
1936	4.91	0.20	21.42	2.46	19.01	3.51	4.35	5.90
1937	5.00	0.20	29.46	2.48	19.01	3.44	4.32	5.29
1938	4.67	0.21	37.99	2.47	19.01	3.68	4.42	5.30
1939	3.93	0.25	44.90	2.49	37.25	4.27	4.46	5.30
1940	4.04	0.25	49.19	2.49	43.18	4.27	4.31	5.30
1941	4.04	0.25	44.94	2.50	52.78	4.27	4.31	5.30

Notes: Official exchange rates, not black-market rates. *The Rentenmark replaced old Reichmark at 1bn. to 1 in 1924. †Linked to French franc in gold bloc.

Source: 'Global Financial Data', database; R. L. Bidwell, Currency Tables (London, 1970).

TABLE A-2. Purchasing Power of £ and $
(current values)

	£	$	£ = (current $)
1918	24.42	11.70	37.85
1919	27.05	10.20	41.93
1920	23.52	8.83	36.46
1921	29.76	9.90	46.13
1922	36.47	10.50	56.53
1923	35.30	10.30	54.72
1924	35.04	10.30	54.31
1925	35.68	10.00	55.30
1926	38.66	10.00	59.92
1927	40.73	10.10	63.13
1928	41.05	10.30	63.63
1929	40.34	10.30	62.53
1930	47.82	10.50	74.12
1931	53.20	11.60	82.46
1932	57.20	12.90	88.66
1933	55.10	13.60	85.41
1934	55.56	13.20	86.12
1935	53.08	12.90	82.27
1936	50.31	12.70	77.98
1937	47.82	12.30	74.12
1938	47.82	12.50	74.12
1939	50.42	12.70	78.15
1940	55.56	12.60	86.12

Source: Samuel H. Williamson, 'What Is the Relative Value?', *Economic History Service* (16 Apr. 2003). *http://www.eh.net/hmit/compare.*

TABLE A-3. Ethno-Linguistic Composition of South-Central Europe before 1931

	(000)						(% age)					
	Poland	Czechoslovakia	Yugoslavia	Albania	Bulgaria	Greece	Poland	Czechoslovakia	Yugoslavia	Albania	Bulgaria	Greece
Poles	21,993,000	82,000					68.9	0.6				
Ukrainians	4,442,000		28,000				13.9		0.2			
Germans	741,000	3,232,000	500,000		4,000		2.3	22.3	3.6		0.1	
Jews	2,733,000	187,000	18,000		47,000	63,000	8.6	1.3	0.1		0.9	1.1
Russians	139,000	549,000	36,000		20,000		0.4	3.8	0.3		0.4	
Czechs	38,000	7,406,000	53,000				0.1	51.1	0.4			
Greeks				50,000	11,000	5,760,000				4.3	0.2	92.8
Bulgars					4,455,000	17,000					81.3	0.2
Pomaks					102,000						1.9	
Gypsies		32,000	70,000	10,000	135,000	5,000			0.5	0.9	2.5	0.1
Belorussians	1,697,000						5.3					
Albanians			505,000	983,000		19,000			3.6	92.4		0.3
Macedonians				10,000		82,000				0.9		1.3
Magyars		692,000	468,000					4.8	3.3			
Lithuanians	83,000						0.3					
Slovaks		2,282,000	76,000					15.8	0.5			
Romanians		13,000	138,000		69,000			0.1	1.0		1.3	
Bosnian Muslim												
Serbo-Croats			10,731,000						77.0			
Slovenes		3,000	1,135,000						8.1			
Turks			133,000		578,000	191,000			0.9		10.3	3.2
Italians			9,000						0.1			
Valacs				10,000	1,500	20,000				0.9		0.3
Montenegrins				7,000						0.6		
Armenians					27,000	34,000					0.5	0.5
Tatars					6,000						0.1	
Gagauz					4,000						0.1	
Others	50,000	2,000	34,000		19,000	13,000	0.2	0.2	0.4		0.4	0.2
Total	31,916,000	14,480,000	13,934,000	1,070,000	5,478,500	6,204,000						

Source: Paul Robert Magocsi, *Historical Atlas of East Central Europe* (Washington, DC, 1993), 125–50. Compiled with cited primary sources.

TABLE A-4. Consolidated Current Expenditure Accounts for all Levels of Governments in Germany, 1925–1932 (milliard RM)

	1925	1926	1927	1928	1929	1930	1931	1932
Purchases of goods and services	7.9	8.3	8.7	9.6	10.0	8.7	7.8	6.9
Defence expenditure[†]	0.6	0.7	0.8	0.8	0.7	0.7	0.6	0.6
Interest on public debts	0.2	0.6	0.7	0.8	1.0	1.2	1.3	1.2
Transfers to households	3.2	4.6	4.7	5.5	6.2	7.0	7.2	6.7
Reparations[*]	1.1	1.2	1.6	2.0	2.3	1.7	1.0	0.2
Public investment and reconciliation of capital account	2.0	2.3	4.0	3.5	2.7	3.1	1.4	0.7
TOTAL	15.0	17.7	20.5	22.2	22.9	22.4	19.3	16.3
% of national income at market prices	22.3	27.0	25.5	26.4	28.8	31.2	33.0	32.1

Notes: *Reich govt. accounting; † does not include secret rearmament.
Source: Steven Schuker, American 'Reparations to Germany', Princeton Studies in International Finance, 61 (1988), 33.

TABLE A-5a. Imports, Exports, and Index of Trade, 1920–1940

(a) Imports and exports

	Italy (Lira m.)		France (Franc m.)		UK (£ m.)			Germany (RM m.)	
	Imports	Exports	Imports	Exports	Imports	Direct exports	Re-exports	Imports	Exports
1920	26,822	11,628	49,905	26,894	1,933	1,334	223	3,929★	3,709★
1921	16,914	8,043	22,754	19,772	1,086	703	107	5,732★	2,976★
1922	15,741	9,160	24,275	21,379	1,003	720	104	6,301★	6,188★
1923	17,157	10,950	32,859	30,867	1,096	767	119	6,150★	6,102★
1924	19,373	14,270	40,163	42,396	1,277	801	140	9,132	6,674
1925	26,200	18,170	44,095	45,755	1,321	773	154	12,429	9,284
1926	25,879	18,544	59,598	59,678	1,241	653	125	9,984	10,415
1927	20,375	15,519	53,050	54,925	1,218	709	123	14,114	10,801
1928	21,920	14,444	53,436	51,375	1,916	724	120	13,931	12,055
1929	21,303	14,767	58,221	50,139	1,221	729	110	13,359	13,486
1930	17,347	12,119	52,511	42,835	1,044	571	87	10,349	12,036
1931	11,643	10,210	42,206	30,436	861	391	64	6,713	9,592
1932	8,268	6,812	29,808	19,705	702	365	51	4,653	5,741
1933	7,432	5,991	28,431	18,474	675	368	49	4,199	4,872
1934	7,675	5,224	23,097	17,850	731	396	51	4,448	4,178
1935	7,790	5,238	20,974	15,496	756	426	55	4,156	4,270
1936	6,039	5,542	25,414	15,492	848	441	61	4,228	4,778
1937	13,943	10,444	42,391	23,939	1,028	521	75	5,495	5,919
1938	11,273	10,497	46,065	30,590	920	471	62	4,449	5,264
1939	10,309	10,823	43,785	31,590	886	440	46	5,207	5,653
1940	13,220	11,519	45,770	17,511	1,152	441	26	5,012	4,868

★ all figures are given in current values with the exception of those in 1913 values which are starred.

(Continued)

TABLE A-5a. (Continued)
(b) World Trade

	Exports	Imports	Index (1929 = 100)
1913	19,800	20,800	74.0
1920	31,600	34,200	53.5
1921	19,700	22,100	55.0
1922	21,700	23,600	59.0
1923	23,800	25,900	65.5
1924	27,850	28,980	75.7
1925	31,550	33,150	83.2
1926	29,920	32,120	85.2
1927	31,520	33,760	91.9
1928	32,730	34,650	95.2
1929	33,024	35,595	100.0
1930	26,480	29,080	93.0
1931	18,910	20,800	85.5
1932	12,885	13,970	74.5
1933	11,710	12,460	75.4
1934	11,300	12,000	72.8
1935	11,600	12,200	78.2
1936	12,600	13,100	81.8
1937	15,000	16,100	96.5
1938	13,400	14,300	89.0

Sources: B. R. Mitchell, *European Historical Statistics*, 4th edn. (London, 1998); Woytinski, *World Commerce and Governments: Trends and Outlook* (New York, 1955): Table 14, p. 39.

TABLE A-5b United States Trade, 1920–1940

	Exports						Imports						(%) GNP		
	Total $m.	Europe	UK	France	Germany	Other	Total $m.	Europe	UK	France	Germany	Other	Exports	Gen. Imports	Farm exports, Farm income
1920	8,228	4,466	1,825	676	311	1,654	5,278	1,228	514	166	89	459	9.3	5.9	27.3
1921	4,485	2,364	942	225	372	825	2,509	765	239	142	80	304	6.1	3.4	26.2
1922	3,832	2,038	856	267	316	644	3,113	991	357	143	117	374	5.2	4.2	21.9
1923	4,167	2,093	882	272	317	622	3,792	1,157	404	150	161	442	4.8	4.4	19.1
1924	4,591	2,445	983	282	440	740	3,610	1,096	366	148	139	443	5.2	4.1	20.7
1925	4,910	2,064	1,034	280	470	820	4,227	1,239	413	157	164	505	5.4	4.6	19.4
1926	4,809	2,310	973	264	364	709	4,431	1,278	383	152	198	545	4.9	4.5	17.2
1927	4,865	2,314	840	229	482	763	4,185	1,265	358	168	201	538	5.1	4.3	17.6
1928	5,128	2,375	847	241	467	820	4,091	1,249	349	159	222	519	5.2	4.2	17.0
1929	5,241	2,341	848	266	410	817	4,399	1,334	330	171	255	578	5.0	4.2	15.0
1930	3,843	1,838	678	224	278	658	3,061	911	210	114	177	410	4.2	3.4	13.3
1931	2,424	1,187	456	122	166	443	2,091	641	135	79	127	300	3.2	2.7	12.9
1932	1,611	784	288	112	134	250	1,323	390	75	45	74	196	2.8	2.3	14.0
1933	1,675	850	312	122	140	276	1,450	463	111	50	78	224	3.0	2.6	13.1
1934	2,133	950	383	116	109	342	1,655	490	115	61	69	245	3.3	2.5	11.6
1935	2,283	1,029	433	117	92	387	2,047	599	155	58	78	308	3.1	2.8	10.6
1936	2,456	1,043	440	129	102	372	2,432	718	200	65	80	373	3.0	2.9	8.5
1937	3,349	1,360	536	165	126	533	3,084	843	203	76	92	472	3.7	3.4	9.0
1938	3,094	1,326	521	134	107	564	1,960	567	118	54	65	330	3.6	2.3	10.7
1939	3,177	1,290	505	182	46	557	2,318	617	149	62	52	354	3.5	2.5	8.4
1940	4,021	1,645	1,011	252		382	2,625	390	155	37	5	193	4.0	2.6	6.2

Source: Dept. of Commerce, *US Historical Statistics from Colonial Times to 1957* (1963).

TABLE A-6. East European trade, 1920–1933: inter-, intra-, and world balance of trade ($m.)

	Albania			Bulgaria			Czechoslovakia			Hungary			Poland			Romania			Yugoslavia			
	Intra-	Inter-	World	Intra-	Inter-	World	Intra-	Inter-	World	Intra-	Inter-	World	Intra-	Inter-	World	Intra-	Inter-	World	Intra-	Inter-	World	
1920		-3.4	-5.3	4.4	-18.4	-15.9	58.6	-61.5	59.4	-19.1	-18.2	-87.3				-1.6	-117.9	-117.7	-19.3	-63.6	-107.2	1920
1921	-0.1	-4.2	-5.2	-0.5	-21.0	-12.1	67.1	59.4	60.4	-38.5	-25.2	-92.0				4.0	-84.0	-82.5	-33.5	-21.3	-66.7	1921
1922	-0.2	-2.3	-3.0	-3.0	-6.3	3.4	67.4	3.2	205.4	-25.7	-31.8	-72.2	18.5	-54.3	-62.2	13.8	-17.4	20.3	-25.9	-15.3	-62.4	1922
1923	-0.6	-3.0	-5.0	-6.4	-27.1	-23.6	43.6	-49.6	110.1	-30.2	-16.8	-29.3	48.0	-26.9	25.8	4.0	-21.9	42.0	-13.8	-9.5	-4.7	1923
1924	-0.1	-2.3	-2.6	-4.8	-13.1	-9.6	38.8	-86.1	58.2	-28.2	-28.0	-44.1	24.5	-54.3	-69.4	19.9	-52.3	17.7	-0.5	-3.5	28.5	1924
1925	-0.1	-1.3	-1.5	-12.0	-25.1	-27.1	21.9	-42.6	60.1	-6.1	-30.1	-13.6	22.6	-96.5	-107.7	8.8	-53.4	-6.4	8.4	-19.3	4.4	1925
1926	-0.5	-3.8	-4.2	-2.8	-13.0	0.4	5.4	59.6	123.5	-42.2	-32.1	-54.2	40.0	42.2	134.8	-5.3	-51.5	8.8	-2.5	-2.6	5.6	1926
1927	-0.9	-3.6	-4.5	-5.9	-11.7	6.1	46.2	56.4	108.9	-62.7	-55.3	-102.4	22.1	-88.1	-72	9.3	-36.9	43.4	-25.5	-9.9	-27.5	1927
1928	-1.5	-3.6	-5.7	-7.1	-12.8	-9.9	57.2	16.4	101.1	-59.9	-66.0	-113.8	20.4	-143.1	162.1	4.1	-61.9	-47.6	-30.6	-9.3	-41.4	1928
1929	-1.8	-5.1	-7.8	-10.1	-16.3	-23.5	55.2	-16.0	25.6	-40.0	-32.5	-7.4	25.2	-69.5	-56.4	-6.0	-13.8	-6.9	0.2	1.7	9.7	1929
1930	-1.6	-4.8	-6.8	3.9	0.7	19.8	-46.0	1.3	87.8	-23.0	-9.7	26.2	17.9	-12.6	35.6	21.2	18.8	55.9	-24.3	5.2	-5.4	1930
1931	-1.9	-4.7	-7.2	0.6	-3.5	15.6	-6.3	14.5	67.6	-28.5	-2.7	9.2	17.0	25.6	78	14.6	0.3	65.8	-3.6	-2.0		1931
1932	-1.2	-3.4	-6.0	-2.9	-7.3	-1.1	-5.8	-23.1	-3.6	-18.6	-4.8	1.8	12.7	7.3	42.1	13.0	8.6	48.2	-3.4	-3.3	4.5	1932
1933	-1.1	-1.8	-3.3	-0.8	0.4	7.9	-2.4	1.1	2.2	-3.8	-1.2	23.1	3.5	11.6	25.2	-0.8	-0.1	24.8	-0.6	-2.3	11.5	1933

Source: Adapted from M. Kaser, *Economic History of Eastern Europe* (1985).

'Intra': Eastern Europe

'Inter': Western Europe, US, and USSR

'World': Aggregate trade of all countries

TABLE A-7. European Military Personnel, 1919–33
(All types on active service, 000s)

	France	UK	Germany	Italy
1919	2,364	1,333	114	301
1920	1,457	596	114	1,350
1921	547	448	114	841
1922	545	368	114	291
1923	511	337	114	311
1924	479	337	114	380
1925	475	342	114	299
1926	471	341	114	317
1927	494	338	114	318
1928	469	330	114	317
1929	411	325	114	315
1930	411	318	114	315
1931	441	319	114	322
1932	422	317	114	322
1933	449	316	118	330

Source: Peter Flora et al., State, Economy and Society in Western Europe, 1815–1975. Vol 1. The Growth of Mass Democracies and Welfare States, (London 1983) 248.

TABLE A-8. Military Expenditure, 1919–41 (Current US $000)

	UK	France	Germany	Italy	Russia	USA
1919	745,209	634,729	80,023	273,088	1,417,699	11,217,796
1920	1,475,661	361,910	79,025	305,619	1,813,426	1,657,118
1921	824,711	318,474	74,696	490,890	1,337,524	1,116,342
1922	549,008	476,084	27,754	384,911	1,646,534	860,853
1923	584,227	418,297	866,282	186,033	885,597	678,256
1924	584,242	261,851	118,739	175,163	835,358	570,142
1925	580,411	324,761	147,858	160,126	1,447,885	589,706
1926	562,657	281,326	156,632	174,453	1,724,660	558,004
1927	567,952	452,194	169,185	296,251	2,044,459	596,501
1928	542,969	381,380	183,045	258,203	2,372,196	678,100
1929	534,694	377,983	164,457	259,732	2,798,721	701,300
1930	512,181	498,642	162,783	266,243	3,519,631	699,200
1931	489,350	495,306	146,845	298,244	3,509,380	698,900
1932	326,642	543,528	149,553	282,783	2,228,018	641,600
1933	333,267	524,231	452,198	351,603	2,363,450	570,400
1934	540,015	707,568	709,088	455,733	3,479,651	803,100
1935	646,350	867,102	1,607,587	513,379	5,517,537	806,400
1936	892,341	995,347	2,332,782	1,149,686	2,933,657	932,600
1937	1,245,603	890,526	3,298,869	1,235,503	3,446,172	1,032,900
1938	1,836,997	919,284	7,415,163	746,050	5,429,984	131,499
1939	7,895,671	1,023,651	12,000,000	669,412	5,849,123	980,000
1940	9,948,329	5,707,762	21,200,000	606,523	6,145,214	1,657,000
1941	11,280,839	605,022	28,900,000	541,238	6,884,227	6,301,000

Source: J. David Singer and Melvin Small, Correlates of War Project, Internet based database: National Material Capabilities Data Codebook, url: http://www.umich.edu/cowproj/capabilities.html accessed 29 May 2004.

APPENDIX B
PRIME MINISTERS AND FOREIGN
MINISTERS OF SELECTED EUROPEAN
POWERS

Czechoslovakia

Prime Minister	Period of Office
Karel Kramář	14 Nov. 1918–10 July 1919
Vlastimil Tusar	10 July 1919–15 Sept. 1920
Jan Černý	15 Oct. 1920–2 Sept. 1921
Edvard Beneš	26 Sept. 1921–7 Oct. 1922
Antonin Švehla	7 Oct. 1922–17 Mar. 1926
Jan Černý	18 Mar. 1926–12 Oct. 1926
Antonin Švehla	12 Oct. 1926–1 Feb. 1929
František Udržal	1 Feb. 1929–21 Oct. 1932
Jan Malypetr	31 Oct. 1932–6 Nov. 1935
Milan Hodža	9 Nov. 1935–22 Sept. 1938
Jan Syrový	22 Sept. 1938–1 Feb. 1939
Rudolf Beran	1 Feb. 1939–13 Mar. 1939
Alois Eliáš	27 Apr. 1939–28 Sept. 1941

Period of Office	Foreign Minister
16 Nov. 1918–1935	Edvard Beneš
18 Dec. 1935–1936	Milan Hodža
28 Feb. 1936–1938	Kamil Krofta
4 Oct. 1938–1939	Frantisek Chvalkovský

France

Prime Minister	Period of Office	Foreign Minister
Georges Clemenceau	16 Nov. 1917–18 Jan. 1920	Stéphen Pichon
Alexandre Millerand	20 Jan. 1920–18 Feb. 1920	Alexandre Millerand
Alexandre Millerand	18 Feb. 1920–23 Sept. 1920	Alexandre Millerand
Georges Leygues	24 Sept. 1920–12 Jan. 1921	Georges Leygues
Aristide Briand	16 Jan. 1921–12 Jan. 1922	Aristide Briand
Raymond Poincaré	15 Jan. 1922–26 Mar. 1924	Raymond Poincaré
Raymond Poincaré	29 Mar. 1924–1 June 1924	Raymond Poincaré
Frédéric François-Marsal	9 June 1924–10 June 1924	Edmond Lefebvre du Prey (9–14 June 1924)
Édouard Herriot	14 June 1924–10 Apr. 1925	Édouard Herriot
Paul Painlevé	17 Apr. 1925–27 Oct. 1925	Aristide Briand
Paul Painlevé	29 Oct. 1925–22 Nov. 1925	Aristide Briand
Aristide Briand	28 Nov. 1925–6 Mar. 1926	Aristide Briand
Aristide Briand	9 Mar. 1926–15 June 1926	Aristide Briand
Aristide Briand	24 June 1926–17 July 1926	Aristide Briand (to 18 July 1926)
Édouard Herriot	19 July 1926–21 July 1926	Édouard Herriot (to 23 July 1926)
Raymond Poincaré	23 July 1926–6 Nov. 1928	Aristide Briand
Raymond Poincaré	11 Nov. 1928–27 July 1929	Aristide Briand
Aristide Briand	29 July 1929–22 Oct. 1929	Aristide Briand
André Tardieu	7 Nov. 1929–17 Feb. 1930	Aristide Briand
Camille Chautemps	21 Feb. 1930–25 Feb. 1930	Aristide Briand
André Tardieu	5 Mar. 1930–4 Dec. 1930	Aristide Briand
Théodore Steeg	18 Dec. 1930–22 Jan. 1931	Aristide Briand
Pierre Laval	30 Jan. 1931–13 June 1931	Aristide Briand
Pierre Laval	13 June 1931–12 Jan. 1932	Aristide Briand
Pierre Laval	14 Jan. 1932–16 Feb. 1932	Pierre Laval (from 13 Jan. 1932)
André Tardieu	20 Feb. 1932–10 May 1932	André Tardieu (to 2 June 1932)
Édouard Herriot	3 June 1932–14 Dec. 1932	Édouard Herriot
Joseph Paul-Boncour	18 Dec. 1932–28 Jan. 1933	Joseph Paul-Boncour (from 31 Dec. 1932 to 27 Jan. 1933)
Édouard Daladier	31 Jan. 1933–24 Oct. 1933	Édouard Daladier (from 30 Jan. 1933)
Albert Sarraut	26 Oct. 1933–23 Nov. 1933	Édouard Daladier
Camille Chautemps	26 Nov. 1933–27 Jan. 1934	Édouard Daladier
Édouard Daladier	30 Jan. 1934–7 Feb. 1934	Édouard Daladier
Gaston Doumergue	9 Feb. 1934–8 Nov. 1934	Louis Barthou (to 9 Oct. 1934) Pierre Laval (from 13 Oct. 1934)

France

Prime Minister	Period of Office	Foreign Minister
Pierre-Étienne Flandin	8 Nov. 1934–31 May 1935	Pierre Laval
Fernand Bouisson	1 June 1935–4 June 1935	Pierre Laval
Pierre Laval	7 June 1935–22 Jan. 1936	Pierre Laval
Albert Sarraut	24 Jan. 1936–4 June 1936	Pierre-Étienne Flandin
Léon Blum	4 June 1936–21 June 1937	Yvon Delbos
Camille Chautemps	22 June 1937–14 Jan. 1938	Yvon Delbos
Camille Chautemps	18 Jan. 1938–10 Mar. 1938	Yvon Delbos
Léon Blum	13 Mar. 1938–8 Apr. 1938	Joseph Paul-Boncour
Édouard Daladier	10 Apr. 1938–20 Mar. 1940	Georges Bonnet (10 Apr. 1938–13 Sept. 1939 Édouard Daladier (from 13 Sept. 1939)
Paul Reynaud	21 Mar. 1940–16 June 1940	Paul Reynaud (to 18 May 1940) Édouard Daladier (from 18 May 1940 to 5 June 1940) Paul Reynaud (5–16 June 1940)
Philippe Pétain	16 June 1940–12 July 1940	Paul Baudoin

Germany

Reichskanzler	Period of Office	Foreign Minister
Philipp Scheidemann	13 Feb. 1919–21 June 1919	Ulrich Graf von Brockdorff-Rantzau
Gustav Bauer	21 June 1919–27 Mar. 1920	Hermann Müller
Hermann Müller	27 Mar. 1920–21 June 1920	Adolf Köster
Constantin Fehrenbach	21 June 1920–10 May 1921	Walter Simons
Joseph Wirth	10 May 1921–26 Oct. 1921	Friedrich Rosen
Joseph Wirth	26 Oct. 1921–22 Nov. 1922	Joseph Wirth 21 Jan.–24 June 1922; Walther Rathenau 21 Jan.–24 June
Wilhelm Cuno	22 Nov. 1922–13 Aug. 1923	Frederic Hans von Rosenberg

Germany

Reichskanzler	Period of Office	Foreign Minister
Gustav Stresemann	13 Aug. 1923–30 Nov. 1923	Gustav Stresemann
Wilhelm Marx	30 Nov. 1923–15 Jan. 1925	Gustav Stresemann
Hans Luther	15 Jan. 1925–16 May 1926	Gustav Stresemann
Wilhelm Marx	16 May 1926–28 June 1928	Gustav Stresemann
Hermann Müller	28 June 1928–30 Mar. 1930	Gustav Stresemann (to 4 Oct. 1929) Julius Curtius
Heinrich Brüning	30 Mar. 1930–9 Oct. 1931	Julius Curtius
Heinrich Brüning	9 Oct. 1931–1 June 1932	Heinrich Brüning
Franz van Papen	1 June 1932–3 Dec. 1932	Konstantin Freiherr von Neurath
Kurt von Schleicher	3 Dec. 1932–30 Jan. 1933	Konstantin Freiherr von Neurath
Adolf Hitler	30 Jan. 1933–30 Apr. 1945	Konstantin Freiherr von Neurath to 4 Feb. 1938

Italy

Period of Office	Prime Minister	Foreign Minister
30 Oct. 1917–23 June 1919	Vittorio Emanuele Orlando	Barone Sidney Sonnino
23 June 1919–16 June 1920	Francesco Saverio Nitti	Tommaso Tittoni (to Nov. 1919); Vittorio Scialoja (from Nov. 1919)
16 June 1920–4 June 1921	Giovanni Giolitti	Conte Carlo Sforza
4 July 1921–25 Feb. 1922	Ivanoe Bonomi	Pietro Paolo Tommasi Marchese della Torretta
23 Feb. 1922–31 Oct. 1922	Luigi Facta	Carlo Schanzer
31 Oct. 1922–25 July 1943	Benito Mussolini	Benito Mussolini (to June 1924); Luigi Federzoni (June 1924– Nov. 1926); Benito Mussolini (from Nov. 1926)

Poland

Prime Minister	Period of Office
Jędrzej Moraczewski	17 Sept. 1918–16 Jan. 1919
Ignacy Jan Paderewski	16 Jan. 1919–27 Nov. 1919
Leopold Skulski	13 Dec. 1919–9 June 1920
Władysław Grabski	23 June 1920–24 July 1920
Wincenty Witos	24 July 1920–13 Sept. 1921
Antoni Ponikowski	19 Sept. 1921–6 June 1922
Artur Śliwiński	28 June 1922–7 July 1922
Julian Ignacy Nowak	31 July 1922–14 Dec. 1922
Władysław Sikorski	16 Dec. 1922–26 May 1923
Wincenty Witos	28 May 1923–14 Dec. 1923
Władysław Grabski	19 Dec. 1923–13 Nov. 1925
Aleksander Skrzyński	20 Nov. 1925–5 May 1926
Wincenty Witos	10 May 1926–14 May 1926
Kazimierz Bartel	15 May 1926–30 Sept. 1926
Józef Piłsudski	2 Oct. 1926–27 June 1928
Kazimierz Bartel	27 June 1928–13 Apr. 1929
Kazimierz Świtalski	14 Apr. 1929–7 Dec. 1929
Kazimierz Bartel	29 Dec. 1929–17 Mar. 1930
Walery Sławek	29 Mar. 1930–23 Aug. 1930
Józef Piłsudski	25 Aug. 1930–4 Dec. 1930
Walery Sławek	4 Dec. 1930–26 May 1931
Aleksander Prystor	27 May 1931–9 May 1933
Janusz Jędrzejewicz	10 May 1933–13 May 1934
Leon Kozłowski	15 May 1934–28 Mar. 1935
Walery Sławek	28 Mar. 1935–12 Oct. 1935
Marian Zyndram-Kościałkowski	13 Oct. 1935–15 May 1936
Felicjan Sławoj-Składkowski	15 May 1936–30 Sept. 1939
Ignacy Jan Paderewski	19 Jan. 1919–15 Dec. 1919
Stanisław Patek	15 Dec. 1919–9 June 1920
Eustach Katejan Władisław	24 June 1920–26 May 1921
Konstanty Skirmunt	11 June 1921–6 June 1922
Aleksander Skrzyński	26 June 1922–8 July 1922
Konstanty Skirmunt	16 July 1922–29 July 1922
Gabriel Narutowicz	31 July 1922–9 Dec. 1922
Aleksander Skrzyński	17 Dec. 1922–26 May 1923
Marian Seyda	29 May 1923–28 Oct. 1923
Roman Dmowski	28 Oct. 1923–13 Dec. 1923
Aleksander Skrzyński	19 Dec. 1923–1924
Maurycy Klement Zamoyski	7 Jan. 1924–25 July 1924
Aleksander Skrzyński	25 July 1924–5 May 1926
Gaetan Dzierzykraj-Morawski	10 May 1926–17 May 1926
August Zaleski	17 May 1926–1932
Józef Beck	2 Nov. 1932–17 Nov. 1939

Soviet Russia/Union of Soviet Socialist Republics

Chairman of the All-Russian Central Executive Committee
30 Mar. 1919–15 July 1938   Mikhail Kalinin

Chairman of the Council of People's Commissars

8 Nov. 1917–21 Jan. 1924	Vladimir Ilich Lenin
2 Feb. 1924–19 Dec. 1930	Aleksey Rykov
19 Dec. 1930–6 May 1941	Vyacheslav Molotov
6 May 1941–5 Mar. 1953	Joseph Stalin

Secretary-General of the Communist Party
3 Apr. 1922–5 Mar. 1953   Joseph Stalin

Foreign Ministers

27 Oct. 1917–30 May 1918	Leon Trotsky (expelled from the Soviet Union, 31 Jan. 1929)
30 May 1918–21 June 1930	Georgy Chicherin
27 July 1930–3 May 1939	Maksim Litvinov
3 May 1939–1949	Vyacheslav Molotov

United Kingdom (Britain)

Prime Minister	Period of Office	Foreign Secretary
David Lloyd George	7 Dec. 1916–19 Oct. 1922	Arthur James Balfour
		George Nathaniel, Earl Curzon (from Oct. 1919). Created Marquis in 1921
Andrew Bonar Law	23 Oct. 1922–20 May 1923	George Nathaniel, Marquis Curzon
Stanley Baldwin	22 May 1923–22 Jan. 1924	George Nathaniel, Marquis Curzon
James Ramsay MacDonald	22 Jan. 1924–4 Nov. 1924	James Ramsay MacDonald
Stanley Baldwin	6 Nov. 1924–4 June 1929	Austen Chamberlain
James Ramsay MacDonald	5 June 1929–26 Aug. 1931	Arthur Henderson
James Ramsay MacDonald	26 Aug. 1931–5 Nov. 1931	Rufus Daniel Isaacs, Marquis of Reading
James Ramsay MacDonald	5 Nov. 1931–7 June 1935	Sir John Simon
Stanley Baldwin	7 June 1935–28 May 1937	Sir Samuel Hoare, Anthony Eden (from Dec. 1935)

United Kingdom (Britain)

Prime Minister	Period of Office	Foreign Secretary
Neville Chamberlain	28 May 1937–10 May 1940	Anthony Eden, Edward Frederick Wood, Viscount Halifax (from Feb. 1938)

United States of America

Presidents	Period of Office
Woodrow Wilson	4 Mar. 1913–4 Mar. 1921
Warren Harding	4 Mar. 1921–2 Aug. 1923
Calvin Coolidge	3 Aug. 1923–4 Mar. 1929
Herbert Hoover	4 Mar. 1929–4 Mar. 1933
Franklin Delano Roosevelt	4 Mar. 1933–12 Apr. 1945

Secretary of State	Period of Office
Robert Lansing	24 June 1915–13 Feb. 1920
Bainbridge Colby	23 Mar. 1920–4 Mar. 1921
Charles Evans Hughes	5 Mar. 1921–4 Mar. 1925
Frank B. Kellogg	5 Mar. 1925–28 Mar. 1929
Henry Lewis Stimson	28 Mar. 1929–4 Mar. 1933
Cordell Hull	4 Mar. 1933–30 Nov. 1944

APPENDIX C
CHRONOLOGY OF
INTERNATIONAL EVENTS, 1918–1933

1918

5 Jan.	Lloyd George speech on Allied peace aims
8 Jan.	Wilson's 'Fourteen Points'
1 Mar.	Treaty between Finland and Soviet Russia
6 Mar.	Soviet–German Treaty of Brest-Litovsk
	British troops land at Murmansk
5 Apr.	Japanese occupy Vladivostock
7 May	Treaty of Bucharest between Romania and the Central Powers
10 July	Constitution as Russian Soviet Federated Socialist Republic adopted
29 Sept.	German Army High Command calls for armistice
	Armistice between Bulgaria and the Allied powers
4 Oct.	Germany requests armistice
28 Oct.	Germany: mutiny of the High Seas Fleet at Kiel
30 Oct.	Armistice of Mudros: Turkish unconditional surrender
3 Nov.	Austria–Hungary agrees armistice
5 Nov.	'Lansing Note' released
	Independent Polish state proclaimed
9 Nov.	Proclamation of the German republic
	Romania re-enters war on side of Allied powers
11 Nov.	German armistice
12 Nov.	Austrian republic proclaimed
14 Nov.	Czechoslovak republic proclaimed
16 Nov.	Hungarian republic proclaimed
4 Dec.	Formation of Kingdom of Serbs, Croats, and Slovenes
13 Dec.	President Wilson arrives in France
18 Dec.	French-led Allied forces land at Odessa

1919

4 Jan.	'Red Army' captures Riga
18 Jan.	Paris Peace Conference opens
8 Feb.	Lloyd George returns to Britain (until 14 March)

15 Feb.	Wilson returns to USA (until 14 March)
19 Feb.	Attempted assassination of Clemenceau
2–6 Mar.	First Congress of the Communist International (Third International; Comintern founded), Moscow
21 Mar.–	
1 Aug.	Soviet republic created in Hungary (Béla Kun)
24 Mar.	Council of Four begins deliberations
25 Mar.	Lloyd George's 'Fontainebleau memorandum'
28 Mar.	Hungary invades Slovakia
29 Mar.	China leaves peace conference
10 Apr.	Romania invades Hungary
24 Apr.	Italy leaves peace conference
7 May	Versailles Treaty presented to Germany
15 May	Greek forces occupy Smyrna
6 June	Finland declares war on Soviet Russia
21 June	German fleet scuttled at Scapa Flow
28 June	Treaty of Versailles signed
	Polish minorities treaty signed
4 Aug.–	
13 Nov.	Romanian forces occupy Budapest
11 Aug.	Germany: Weimar constitution comes into force
10 Sept.	Treaty of St-Germain-en-Laye with Austria
	Czechoslovak and Serb-Croat-Slovene Kingdom minorities treaties signed
12 Sept.	D'Annunzio seizes Fiume
27 Sept.	British troops withdrawn from Archangel
12 Oct.	British evacuate Murmansk
19 Nov.	US Senate fails to ratify Treaty of Versailles
27 Nov.	Treaty of Neuilly with Bulgaria
9 Dec.	Romanian minorities treaty signed

1920

8–16 Jan.	Paris conference: Britain, France, Italy (discuss Fiume, trade with Russia)
10 Jan.	Treaty of Versailles comes into force
15–22 Jan.	Helsingfors conference: Poland, Finland, Estonia, Latvia, Lithuania discuss common policy towards Soviet Russia
15 Jan.	Allies formally demand surrender of ex-kaiser (Dutch refusal received 27 January)
16 Jan.	League of Nations: first meeting of the Council, Paris
18 Jan.	French government takes control of Saar mines
21 Jan.	Paris peace conference officially closes: last meeting of Supreme Council and formal empowerment of the Conference of Ambassadors
2 Feb.	Soviet–Estonian peace treaty of Tartu (Dorpat)
9 Feb.	Allied troops enter Danzig

10 Feb.	Voting in first plebiscite zone in Schlesvig (result in favour of Denmark)
12–23 Feb.	London conference in London: Britain, France, Italy, Greece (discuss Near East, Fiume)
15 Feb.	Allies take over Memel
2 Mar.	Armistice between Romania and Soviet Russia
14 Mar.	Voting in second plebiscite zone in Schlesvig (result in favour of Germany)
16 Mar.	Allies occupy Constantinople
19 Mar.	Second and final US Senate rejection of the Treaty of Versailles
6 Apr.– 17 May	French occupation of Frankfurt and Darmstadt
19–26 Apr.	San Remo conference: Britain, France, Italy, Belgium, Japan, Greece (discuss Near East, mandates, German disarmament)
25 Apr.	Polish offensive against Soviet Russia
5 May	Supreme Council assigns 'A' mandates: Syria to France; Mesopotamia and Palestine to Britain
15–17 May	Hythe conference: Britain, France (discuss reparations)
4 June	Peace Treaty of Trianon with Hungary
11 June	Soviet Red Army takes Kiev
19–20 June	Hythe conference: Britain, France, Greece (discuss Near East)
21–2 June	Boulogne conference: Britain, France, Italy, Belgium, Japan, Greece (discuss disarmament, reparations)
2–3 July	Brussels conference: Britain, France, Italy, Belgium, Japan (discuss reparations)
5–16 July	Spa conference: Britain, France, Italy, Belgium, Japan, Poland, and Germany (discuss reparations, disarmament, Near East, Russo-Polish war)
6 July	Soviet Russian offensive against Poland begins
11 July	Plebiscites in Allenstein and Marienwerder (in favour of union with Germany)
12 July	Soviet Russian–Lithuanian peace treaty
16 July	Spa Protocol on reparations
8 Aug.	Hythe conference: Britain, France (discuss Russo-Polish war)
10 Aug.	Treaty of Sèvres with Sultanate Turkey
	Greek and Armenian minorities treaties signed
11 Aug.	Soviet Russian–Latvian peace treaty of Riga
14–16 Aug.	Poles defeat Soviet Russians at Warsaw
14 Aug.	Czech–Yugoslav alliance
1–8 Sept.	Baku Congress of the Peoples of the East
7 Sept.	Franco-Belgian military convention
20 Sept.	Council assigns Eupen and Malmédy to Belgium
24 Sept.– 8 Oct.	International Financial Conference, Brussels: 39 states attend
9 Oct.	Poland seizes Vilna
12 Oct.	Soviet Russian–Polish armistice
14 Oct.	Soviet Russian–Finnish peace treaty of Tartu (Dorpat)

27 Oct.	League of Nations headquarters established in Geneva
28 Oct.	Bessarabian accord—French recognition of Romanian sovereignty
12 Nov.	Italo-Yugoslav Treaty of Rapallo
15 Nov.–	
18 Dec.	League of Nations: first meeting of the Assembly in Geneva
15 Nov.	Danzig formally becomes a 'Free City'
2 Dec.	Treaty of Aleksandropol between Turkey and Armenia
10 Dec.	Nobel Peace Prizes awarded to Wilson (1919) and Bourgeois (1920)
15 Dec.	Austria admitted to League of Nations
16 Dec.	Statute of the Permanent Court of International Justice opened for signature at Geneva
	Bulgaria admitted to League of Nations

1921

24–30 Jan.	Paris conference: Britain, France, Italy, Belgium, Japan (discuss reparations, disarmament, Austrian reconstruction, Near East)
26 Jan.	Independence of Estonia and Latvia recognized by Allied powers
19 Feb.	Franco-Polish treaty of mutual assistance
21 Feb.–	
14 Mar.	London conference: Britain, France, Italy, Belgium, Japan, Greece and Turkey, Germany (discuss Near East, reparations)
26 Feb.	Soviet Russian–Persian treaty
28 Feb.	Soviet Russian–Afghanistan treaty
1 Mar.	Montenegro joins the Serb-Croat-Slovene Kingdom
3 Mar.	Polish–Romanian defensive alliance against Russia
8 Mar.–	
30 Sept.	Allied troops occupy Duisburt, Ruhrort, and Düsseldorf
8–16 Mar.	Soviet Russia: Congress of the Communist Party adopts New Economic Policy
16 Mar.	Anglo-Soviet trade agreement
	Soviet Russian–Turkish treaty
18 Mar.	Polish–Soviet Treaty of Riga
20 Mar.	Upper Silesian plebiscite
27 Mar.	Failed Habsburg coup in Hungary
23–4 Apr.	Lympne conference: Britain, France (discuss reparations)
23 Apr.	Czechoslovak–Romanian alliance
27 Apr.	Reparations Commission fixes total German debts at 132 billion gold marks
29 Apr.–	
5 May	London conference: Britain, France, Italy, Belgium, Japan, and Germany (discuss reparations)
5 May	London schedule of reparations payments and Allied ultimatum to Germany

11 May	German government accepts 'London Schedule'
7 June	Romanian–Yugoslav alliance
19 June	Paris conference: Britain, France, Italy (discuss Near East)
16–19 July	League of Nations: first session of Temporary Mixed Commission (disarmament)
8–13 Aug.	Paris conference: Britain, France, Italy, Belgium, Japan (discuss Upper Silesia, Near East, disarmament)
22 Aug.	League of Nations: Nansen appointed high commissioner for refugees
24 Aug.	US peace treaty with Austria
25 Aug.	US peace treaty with Germany
29 Aug.	US peace treaty with Hungary
7 Oct.	Wiesbaden agreements between Loucheur and Rathenau regarding deliveries in kind
12 Oct.	League Council partitions Upper Silesia between Germany and Poland
13 Oct.	Treaty of Kars between Russia, Turkey, and the Bolshevik governments of Armenia, Azerbaijan, and Georgia
20 Oct.	Peace of Ankara between France and Turkey
5 Nov.	Soviet Russia–Mongolia treaty
12 Nov.– 6 Feb.	Washington Naval Conference: USA, Britain, Japan, France, Italy
12 Nov.	Independence of Albania recognized by Allied powers
6 Dec.	Anglo-Irish peace agreement
18–22 Dec.	London conference: Britain, France (discuss reparations, security, reconstruction)
21 Dec.	Turco-Soviet Treaty of Friendship

1922

6–13 Jan.	Cannes conference: Britain, France, Italy, Belgium, Japan, and Germany (discuss reparations, Anglo-French pact, agenda for general conference on European reconstruction)
6 Feb.	Washington treaties signed: Five Power treaty on naval limitation; Nine Power treaty on China; supplementary Four Power Pacific treaty
15 Feb.	Opening of the Permanent Court of International Justice at the Hague
25 Feb.	Boulogne conference: Britain, France (discuss conditions for Genoa conference)
12 Mar.	Communist republics of Georgia, Armenia, and Azerbaijan combine to form the Transcaucasian Soviet Republic
15 Mar.	Soviet–German military agreement
22–6 Mar.	Paris conference: Britain, France, Italy (discuss Near East)

10 Apr.–	
19 May	Genoa conference: 29 European states (European reconstruction, relations with Soviet Russia)
16 Apr.	Soviet–German Treaty of Rapallo
22 May	Italo-Russian trade agreement
26 May	Lenin suffers his first stroke
24 June	Germany: Rathenau murdered
26 June–	
20 July	Experts' Conference at the Hague (discuss relations with Russia)
30 June	Lithuania recognized by Allied powers
1 Aug.	Balfour note on war debts
7–14 Aug.	Allied powers conference in London: Britain, France, Italy, Belgium (discuss reparations)
10 Sept.	British–Soviet Russian trade agreement
18 Sept.	League of Nations: Hungary admitted as member of League French and Italian governments order withdrawal of troops from Chanak
4 Oct.	League of Nations: Geneva protocols for financial reconstruction of Austria adopted
8–9 Oct.	Conference at Reval: Finland, Estonia, Latvia, Poland (discuss Russian non-aggression proposal)
11 Oct.	Mudanya armistice between Allied powers and Ankara government ends Chanak crisis
19 Oct.	Britain: dissolution of Lloyd George coalition
23 Oct.	Britain: Conservative government formed by Bonar Law
25 Oct.	Japanese evacuate Vladivostok
28 Oct.	Italy: 'march on Rome' by Mussolini's fascists
30 Oct.	Italy: Mussolini appointed prime minister
22 Nov.	Germany: Cuno (non-party) cabinet formed
17 Nov.	Britain: Conservatives win general election; Bonar Law remains prime minister
20 Nov.–	
4 Feb.	Lausanne conference on peace with Turkey (first part)
2–12 Dec.	Moscow conference on disarmament: Soviet Union, Finland, Estonia, Latvia, Poland, Lithuania
9–11 Dec.	Allied powers conference in London: Britain, France, Italy, Belgium (discuss reparations)
10 Dec.	Formation of the USSR
26 Dec.	Reparations Commission declares Germany in timber default
30 Dec.	Union of Soviet Socialist Republics constituted by Treaty of Federation signed in Moscow (Russia, Belarus, Ukraine, Transcaucasian Federation)

1923

1 Jan.	USSR officially established.
2–4 Jan.	Allied powers conference in Paris: Britain, France, Italy, Belgium (discuss reparations)
9 Jan.	Reparations Commission declares Germany in coal default
10 Jan.	Lithuanians invade Memel territory
11 Jan.	French and Belgian troops begin occupation of the Ruhr
30 Jan.	Greek–Turkish convention on exchange of populations
4 Feb.	Lausanne conference breaks down as Turkish delegation rejects draft peace terms
16 Feb.	Conference of Ambassadors assigns Memel to Lithuania
14 Mar.	Allies recognize Vilna and East Galicia as Polish
16 Mar.	German government issues ordnance in support of 'passive resistance'
23 Apr.– 24 July	Lausanne conference on peace with Turkey (second part)
22 May	Britain: Baldwin succeeds Bonar Law as Conservative prime minister
9 June	*Coup d'état* in Bulgaria (overthrow of premier Stamboliiski)
18 June	Anglo-American war debt agreement
24 July	Treaty of Lausanne between Allied powers and Turkey
3 Aug.	USA: Coolidge (Republican) becomes president following death of Harding
13 Aug.	Germany: Stresemann (DVP), first 'Great Coalition' cabinet formed
31 Aug.	Italy occupies Corfu
3–29 Sept.	League of Nations: fourth meeting of the Assembly, Geneva
13 Sept.	Spain: military dictatorship imposed by Primo de Rivera
22 Sept.	League of Nations: Council submits Corfu dispute to Committee of Jurists
27 Sept.	Ruhr: 'Passive resistance' called off by German presidential decree
28 Sept.	League of Nations: Ethiopia admitted to League
29 Sept.	League of Nations: Assembly adopts the draft Treaty of Mutual Assistance
6 Oct.	Germany: Stresemann second cabinet formed
21–6 Oct.	Rhineland separatists seize public buildings in Aachen, Coblenz, Bonn, Wiesbaden, Mainz
29 Oct.	Turkey: proclamation of the republic; Atatürk (Mustapha Kemal) elected first president
8–11 Nov.	Germany: abortive Nazi (Hitler and Ludendorff) 'beer hall' putsch in Munich
15 Nov.	Germany: Rentenmark introduced to end inflation
30 Nov.	Germany: Marx (Centre) first cabinet formed
	Experts' Committee on reparations established by Reparations Commission (Dawes appointed chairman on 21 December)

6 Dec.	Britain: general election, with Conservative losses and a Labour minority
16 Dec.	Greece: large majority for republicans (Venizelists) in general election
20 Dec.	League Council adopts scheme for financial reconstruction of Hungary

1924

14 Jan.	Reparations: first meeting of the Dawes Committee
21 Jan.	Death of Lenin
22 Jan.	Britain: Ramsay MacDonald forms Labour government
24 Jan.	Franco-Czechoslovak treaty of alliance signed in Paris
27 Jan.	'Adriatic treaty' between Italy and Serb-Croat-Slovene Kingdom signed in Rome
1 Feb.	Britain gives diplomatic recognition to Soviet Union
7 Feb.	Italy gives diplomatic recognition to Soviet Union
14–25 Feb.	League of Nations: Conference of Naval Experts on the extension of the Washington naval treaty, in Rome
25 Mar.	Greece proclaimed a republic (confirmed by plebiscite on 13 April)
9 Apr.	Reparations: presentation of Dawes Committee report on German reparations payments ('Dawes plan')
16 Apr.	German government accepts Dawes plan
25 Apr.	Acceptances of Dawes plan received by Reparations Commission from Britain, France, Belgium
4 May	Germany: Reichstag elections with gains for nationalist and leftist parties
11 May	France: elections to Chamber. Victory for 'Cartel des gauches'
17 May	Memel statute adopted
31 May	Soviet–Chinese diplomatic relations established
3 June	Germany: Marx (Centre) second cabinet formed
10 June	France: Millerand resigns as president
13 June	France: Doumergue elected president by parliament
15 June	France: formation of Herriot ministry
20–2 June	Herriot–MacDonald meetings at Chequers
5 July	League of Nations: British Labour government rejects draft Treaty of Mutual Assistance
	Italy and Czechoslovakia sign pact of cordial collaboration in Rome
16 July–16 Aug.	London conference on reparations
16 Aug.	Final protocol of the London conference signed: Dawes plan adopted
18 Aug.	Evacuation of Allied troops from Ruhr begins (completed on 18 November)
29 Aug.	Germany: Dawes legislation approved by Reichstag

1 Sept.–	
2 Oct.	League of Nations: fifth meeting of the Assembly, Geneva
13 Sept.	Parker Gilbert appointed agent-general for reparations
20 Sept.	League of Nations: Britain submits Mosul question for League determination
2 Oct.	League of Nations: 'Geneva Protocol for the Pacific Settlement of International Disputes' adopted by Assembly
8 Oct.	Britain: Labour government defeated and elections called
25 Oct.	Britain: publication of Zinoviev letter
28 Oct.	France gives diplomatic recognition to Soviet Union
29 Oct.	Britain: Conservatives win large majority in general election
31 Oct.	Dawes plan comes into force
4 Nov.	USA: Coolidge (Republican) elected president
6 Nov.	Britain: Conservative government formed under Baldwin
7 Dec.	Germany: Reichstag elections, with losses by extremist parties

1925

5 Jan.	Allies postpone evacuation of first Rhineland zone (Cologne), due on 10 January
15 Jan.	Germany: Luther (non-party) first cabinet formed
21 Jan.	Japanese *de jure* recognition of Soviet Union
18 Feb.	Final report of the Inter-Allied Military Control Commission
28 Feb.	Germany: death of Reich-President Ebert
12 Mar.	British government formally rejects the Geneva Protocol
17 Apr.	France: formation of Painlevé ministry
23 Apr.	Czechoslovak–Polish treaty for conciliation and arbitration
26 Apr.	Germany: election of Hindenburg as Reich-President
28 Apr.	Britain returns to gold standard
4 May– 17 June	League of Nations: Conference for the Control of the International Trade in Arms, Munitions and Implements of War, Geneva: 44 states attending
18 July	Germany: publication of *Mein Kampf*
5–16 Oct.	Locarno conference: Treaty of Locarno initialled on 16 October
12 Oct.	Soviet–German commercial treaty
16 Oct.	French mutual guarantee treaties with Poland and Czechoslovakia
19–29 Oct.	Greek–Bulgarian frontier incident
27 Nov.	Germany: Reichstag approves Locarno treaties
28 Nov.	France: formation of Briand ministry
1 Dec.	Treaty of Locarno signed in London
	Evacuation of first Rhineland zone (Cologne) begins (completed 31 January 1926)
10 Dec.	Dawes and Chamberlain awarded Nobel Peace Prize
14 Dec.	League Council delivers judgement on Greek–Bulgarian frontier dispute

| 17 Dec. | Turco-Soviet Pact of Non-Aggression and Neutrality |

1926

20 Jan.	Germany: Luther (non-party) second cabinet formed
10 Feb.	Germany applies for admission to League of Nations
8–17 Mar.	League of Nations: special session of Assembly on admission of Germany
9 Mar.	France: Briand reforms ministry
17 Mar.	League of Nations: Brazil blocks German entry to League
26 Mar.	Polish–Romanian guarantee treaty signed at Bucharest
24 Apr.	German–Soviet Treaty of Neutrality and Friendship ('Berlin treaty')
29 Apr.	French–American provisional war-debt agreement (Bérenger–Mellon)
3–12 May	Britain: General Strike
12–15 May	Poland: Marshal Piłsudski carries out *coup d'état*
16 May	Germany: Marx (Centre) third cabinet formed
18–26 May	League of Nations: first session of Preparatory Commission for the World Disarmament Conference, Geneva
10 June	Franco-Romanian friendship and arbitration treaty signed in Paris
14 June	League of Nations: Brazil withdraws from the League
24 June	France: Briand again reforms ministry
30 June	League of Nations control withdrawn from Austria and Hungary
12 July	French–British war-debt agreement (Caillaux–Churchill)
23 July	France: formation of Poincaré ministry
3 Aug.	France: Chamber votes on fiscal stabilization measures demanded by Poincaré
17 Aug.	Greece and Serb-Croat-Slovene Kingdom (Yugoslavia) treaty of Friendship signed in Athens
31 Aug.	Soviet–Afghan Pact of Neutrality and Non-Aggression
8 Sept.	League of Nations: Germany admitted to the Assembly and becomes a permanent member of the Council
11 Sept.	League of Nations: Spain withdraws from the League
16 Sept.	Italo-Romanian friendship treaty signed in Rome
17 Sept.	Briand and Stresemann hold discussions at Thoiry
22–7 Sept.	League of Nations: second session of Preparatory Commission for the World Disarmament Conference, Geneva
28 Sept.	Lithuanian–Soviet Agreement on Non-Aggression and Neutrality
30 Sept.	International Steel Agreement between France, Germany, Belgium, Luxembourg
3–6 Oct.	First Pan-European Congress, Vienna
6 Oct.	Germany: General von Seeckt dismissed as chief of army command

| 27 Nov. | Italo-Albanian treaty of friendship signed in Tirana |
| 10 Dec. | Stresemann and Briand awarded Nobel Peace Prize |

1927

29 Jan.	Germany: Marx (Centre) fourth cabinet formed
31 Jan.	Inter-Allied Military Control Commission withdrawn from Germany
21 Mar.–	
26 Apr.	League of Nations: third session of Preparatory Commission for the World Disarmament Conference, Geneva
5 Apr.	Italo-Hungarian friendship treaty
4–23 May	League of Nations: World Economic Conference, Geneva: 50 states attending
13–15 May	Little Entente: conference of foreign ministers at Joachimstal
27 May	Britain breaks off relations with Soviet Union after ARCOS raid
20 June–	
4 Aug.	Geneva Naval Conference: USA, Britain, Japan
17 Aug.	Franco-German commercial treaty
28 Sept.	USSR–Lithuanian treaty of non-aggression signed in Moscow
1 Oct.	Soviet–Persian non-aggression pact
11 Nov.	France and Serb-Croat-Slovene Kingdom sign treaty of understanding in Paris
22 Nov.	Italian–Albanian treaty signed at Tirana
30 Nov.–	
3 Dec.	League of Nations: fourth session of Preparatory Commission for the World Disarmament Conference, Geneva
1–2 Dec.	League of Nations: first session of Committee on Arbitration and Security
10 Dec.	Polish–Lithuanian state of war ends

1928

20 Feb.–	
7 Mar.	League of Nations: second session of Committee on Arbitration and Security, Geneva
15–24 Mar.	League of Nations: fifth session of Preparatory Commission for the World Disarmament Conference, Geneva
29 Apr.	France: elections to Chamber
20 May	Germany: Reichstag elections, with gains by left and losses by middle-ground parties
7 June	France: Poincaré reforms his ministry
24–5 June	France: official stabilization of the franc
27 June–	
4 July	League of Nations: third session of Committee on Arbitration and Security, Geneva
28 June	British proposals presented to French for an 'armaments compromise'

28 June	Germany: Müller (SPD) second cabinet formed ('Great coalition')
2 Aug.	Friendship treaty between Italy and Ethiopia signed at Addis Ababa
27 Aug.	Signing of Kellogg–Briand pact outlawing war ('Paris Peace Pact')
1 Sept.	Albania proclaimed a kingdom, President Zogu becoming King Zog
16 Sept.	Geneva agreement regarding reparations and Rhineland evacuation
26 Sept.	League of Nations: Assembly adopts the General Act
1 Oct.	First Soviet Five Year Plan
7 Nov.	USA: Hoover (Republican) wins presidential elections

1929

10 Jan.	Reparation Commission formally appoints experts nominated by Belgium, France, Britain, Italy and Japan (also Germany and USA)
9 Feb.	'Litvinov Protocol': non-aggression pacts linking USSR, Romania, Poland, Latvia, and Estonia (27 Feb., Turkey; 3 Apr., Persia; 5 Apr., Lithuania)
11 Feb.	Lateran Accords between Italy and the Holy See. Reparations: Committee of Experts ('Young Committee') holds first formal meeting, Paris (until 7 June)
24 Mar.	Italy: parliamentary election (single list) produces plebiscitary acceptance of fascist regime
15 Apr.– 6 May	League of Nations: sixth session (first part) of Preparatory Commission for the World Disarmament Conference, Geneva
29 May	Britain: general election with large gains for Labour
5 June	Britain: Ramsay MacDonald forms Labour government
7 June	Reparations: Young Committee report signed by experts
27 June	Germany: Reichstag votes funds for construction of 'Cruiser A' (pocket battleship).
20 July	France: Chamber approves ratification of war-debt agreements with USA and Britain
31 July	France: Briand takes on premiership of Poincaré ministry
6–31 Aug.	Hague conference on reparations and Rhineland evacuation
30 Aug.	Hague conference: agreement reached on Rhineland evacuation
31 Aug.	Hague conference: final protocol signed recording acceptance in principle of Young plan
2–25 Sept.	League of Nations: tenth meeting of the Assembly, Geneva
5 Sept.	Briand speech to Assembly introducing idea of European federal union
14 Sept.	Withdrawal of British troops from Rhineland begins (completed on 13 December)

19 Sept.	Britain and France sign the 'Optional Clause' of the statute of the Permanent Court of International Justice
1 Oct.	Britain re-establishes diplomatic relations with the Soviet Union
3 Oct.	Death of Stresemann
	Diplomatic relations restored between Britain and Soviet Union
	Kingdom of the Serbs, Croats, and Slovenes, renamed 'Yugoslavia'
29 Oct.	New York stock exchange crash
7 Nov.	France: formation of Tardieu ministry
13 Nov.	Bank for International Settlements established
30 Nov.	Evacuation of second (Coblenz) zone of Rhineland by French and Belgian troops completed
10 Dec.	Kellogg awarded Nobel Peace Prize
21 Dec.	USSR: Stalin's fiftieth birthday celebrations; beginning of 'personality cult'
22 Dec.	Germany: failure of nationalist plebiscite to reject Young plan
28 Dec.	France: Chamber votes credits for beginning construction of frontier fortifications ('Maginot line')

1930

3–20 Jan.	Second Hague conference on the Young plan
21 Jan.–22 Apr.	London Naval Conference: USA, Britain, Japan, France, Italy
17 Feb.–24 Mar.	Preliminary Conference for Concerted Economic Action, Geneva ('tariff truce conference'): 26 European and 3 non-European states
5 Mar.	France: Tardieu forms new ministry
7 Mar.	Germany: Schacht resigns as President of Reichsbank; succeeded by Luther
12 Mar.	Germany: Reichstag ratifies Young plan
29 Mar.	France: Chamber approves Hague accords
30 Mar.	Germany: Brüning (Centre) cabinet formed
22 Apr.	London Naval Treaty signed
28 Apr.–9 May	League of Nations: fourth session of Committee on Arbitration and Security, Geneva
17 May	Reparations: Young plan comes into force
	French memorandum on proposed European federal union ('Briand plan')
17 June	USA: Hoover signs Smoot–Hawley tariff bill
26 June–3 July	USSR: 'Five Year Plan in Four Years' approved

30 June	Allied occupation of Rhineland ended: Inter-Allied High Commission leaves Wiesbaden and last French troops leave third zone (Mainz)
18 July	Germany: Reichstag dissolved by President Hindenburg
14 Sept.	Germany: Reichstag elections; Brüning government remains in office, but large gains for National Socialists and Communists
23 Sept.	League of Nations: meeting of European states on Briand plan creates Commission of Enquiry for European Union (CEEU)
5–12 Oct.	First Balkan conference in Athens: Albania, Bulgaria, Greece, Yugoslavia, Romania, Turkey
6 Nov.– 9 Dec.	League of Nations: sixth session (second part) of Preparatory Commission for the World Disarmament Conference, Geneva (draft disarmament convention adopted)
17–28 Nov.	League of Nations: Second Conference for Concerted Economic Action, Geneva (first session)
18 Dec.	France: Steeg forms ministry

1931

19–24 Jan.	League of Nations: 62nd session of League Council, Geneva, summons the World Disarmament Conference for 2 February 1932
30 Jan.	France: Laval forms ministry
1 Mar.	'Bases of Agreement' reached on Franco-Italian naval disarmament
16–18 Mar.	League of Nations: Second Conference for Concerted Economic Action, Geneva (second session)
20 Mar.	Germany: Reichstag approves appropriations for 'Cruiser B' (pocket battleship)
21 Mar.	Austro-German customs union proposal announced (concluded on 19 March)
14 Apr.	Spain: fall of monarchy and proclamation of the republic
6 May	Soviet–Lithuanian treaty of 1926 renewed for five-year period
11 May	Failure of Austrian Kreditanstalt
13 May	France: Doumer defeats Briand in presidential election
19 May	Germany: pocket battleship Deutschland ('cruiser A') launched
21 May	League of Nations: Britain and France accede to the General Act
5–9 June	Brüning and Curtius visit Britain for conversations at Chequers
6 June	Germany: Brüning government issues reparations 'manifesto'
15 June	Soviet–Polish Treaty of Friendship and Commerce
20 June	'Hoover moratorium' on all intergovernmental debts for one year
23 June	Germany and Britain accept Hoover proposal
24 June	Soviet–Afghan Treaty of Neutrality and Non-Aggression

Soviet–German Treaty of Friendship and Neutrality renewed for three years.

25 June   Banks of England, France, the Federal Reserve Bank of New York, and the BIS grant Reichsbank credit of $100 million

1 July   German banking crisis resumes (with foreign withdrawals peaking on 6 July)

13 July   Germany: collapse of Darmstädter und Nationalbank ('Danat' bank)

Britain: Macmillan report on finance and industry published

20–3 July   London Financial Conference

31 July   Britain: May report on national expenditure published

8–18 Aug.   International Bankers Committee convened in Basle to study German economic situation: 'Standstill agreement' initialled on 19 August

10 Aug.   French–Soviet non-aggression pact initialled

26 Aug.   Britain: National Government formed

2–19 Sept.   Financial crisis in London

3 Sept.   Austria and Germany withdraw their proposed customs union

15 Sept.   Royal Navy sailors at Invergordon 'mutiny' against pay cuts

18 Sept.   'Mukden incident': Japan begins military operations in Manchuria

21 Sept.   Britain: decision announced to abandon gold standard

China appeals to League Council, under Article 11 of the Covenant

27 Sept.   General Convention to Improve the Means of Preventing War opened for signature

9 Oct.   Germany: Brüning forms new cabinet, taking over foreign affairs ministry himself

27 Oct.   Britain: National Government wins large majority in general elections

29 Oct.   Japanese forces attack Shanghai

31 Oct.   Soviet–Turkish treaty renewed for five-year period

16 Nov.–
10 Dec.   League of Nations: 65th session of Council resumes, in Paris, for meetings on Manchurian crisis

19 Nov.   German government asks Bank of International Settlement to convene Young plan advisory committee

3 Dec.   Statute of Westminster passed

10 Dec.   League of Nations: Council unanimously adopts resolution on a Committee of Inquiry for Manchurian crisis (Lytton Commission)

11 Dec.   Britain: Statute of Westminster grants full self-government to Dominions

1932

7 Jan.   USA: Stimson note on non-recognition of changes in China

14 Jan.	France: Laval reforms ministry, removing Briand from Quai d'Orsay
18 Jan.	Original date set for Reparations Conference at Lausanne (postponed until 16 June)
21 Jan.	Soviet–Finnish non-aggression pact
22 Jan.	USSR: Second Five Year Plan
25 Jan.	Soviet–Polish non-aggression pact
28 Jan.	Sino-Japanese clash at Shanghai
30 Jan.–4 Feb.	XVII Congress of the Communist Party of the USSR (second Five Year Plan)
2 Feb.	League of Nations: World Disarmament Conference opens in Geneva, with 59 states attending
3 Feb.	Soviet–Lithuanian non-aggression pact (three-year period)
4 Feb.	Soviet–Estonian non-aggression pact (three-year period)
5 Feb.	World Disarmament Conference: 'Tardieu plan' presented by France
	Soviet-Latvian non-aggression pact
8–24 Feb.	World Disarmament Conference Open.
20 Feb.	France: Tardieu forms his third ministry
3–11 Mar.	League of Nations: Special Session of Assembly on Sino-Japanese crisis
7 Mar.	Death of Briand
9 Mar.	Japanese creation of puppet state of Manchukuo
11 Mar.	League adopts principle of non-recognition of Manchukuo
13 Mar.	Germany: Hindenburg leads in presidential elections, but strong showing by Hitler forces a second ballot
23 Mar.	Britain: Cabinet abandons 'ten-year rule' on defence planning
3 Apr.	Armistice in Shanghai
10 Apr.	Germany: Hindenburg wins on second ballot of presidential election
13 Apr.	Germany: Brüning government imposes decree banning Nazi SA
24 Apr.	Germany: state elections (Prussia, Bavaria, Württemberg) with large gains by Nazis
26 Apr.	World Disarmament Conference: General Commission suspends sittings, to allow technical commissions to work and 'private conversations' to take place
	World Disarmament Conference: MacDonald, Stimson, and Brüning meet at Bessinge
7 May	France: President Doumer assassinated
8 May	France: elections for Chamber, with swing to parties of left
10–12 May	Germany: Reichstag re-convenes; Groener forced to resign, but Brüning wins vote of confidence on 12 May
20 May	France: Lebrun elected by parliament as new president, Austria: Dolfuss government installed
1 June	Germany: von Papen cabinet formed, with Schleicher as defence minister

3 June	France: Herriot forms ministry
16 June– 9 July	Lausanne Conference on German reparations
16 June	Germany: von Papen government lifts ban on Nazi SA
22 June	World Disarmament Conference: 'Hoover plan' presented to General Commission
13 July	Anglo-French declaration on political consultation
20 July	Germany: von Papen deposes Prussian state government
21 July– 20 Aug.	Imperial Economic Conference, Ottawa
23 July	World Disarmament Conference: General Commission passes 'Beneš resolution' then adjourns; Germany and USSR alone vote against resolution
25 July	Soviet–Polish non-aggression pact
31 July	Germany: Reichstag elections: Nazis become largest party
7 Sept.	World Disarmament Conference: German government withdraws from disarmament conference until principle of 'equality' recognized
12 Sept.	Germany: von Papen dissolves Reichstag after suffering humiliating defeat (512 votes to 42) in vote of no-confidence
21–6 Sept.	World Disarmament Conference: Bureau of conference resumes meetings, without Germany
1 Oct.	League of Nations: Lytton report on Manchuria published
4 Nov.	World Disarmament Conference: Paul-Boncour presents French 'constructive plan' to Bureau
6 Nov.	Germany: Reichstag elections, with Nazis losing seats but remaining largest party
17 Nov.	Germany: von Papen resigns as chancellor
29 Nov.	Franco-Soviet non-aggression pact
3 Dec.	Germany: von Schleicher cabinet formed
11 Dec.	World Disarmament Conference: British, French, Italian, US, and German delegates agree on 'five-power formula' for Germany's return to disarmament conference
15 Dec.	Expiry of Hoover moratorium French default on war debt payment to USA
18 Dec.	France: Paul-Boncour forms ministry
31 Dec.	USSR: Announcement of completion of the first Five Year Plan in four years and three months.

1933

12 Jan.	Japanese cross Chinese frontier into Jehol province
23–31 Jan.	World Disarmament Conference: Bureau resumes meetings, with Germany attending
28 Jan.	Germany: Resignation of Schleicher as chancellor
30 Jan.	Germany: Hitler appointed chancellor
31 Jan.	France: Daladier forms ministry

1 Feb.	Germany: Reichstag dissolved for new elections
2 Feb.	World Disarmament Conference: General Commission reconvenes, after adjournment since 23 July 1932
16 Feb.	Little Entente Pact of Organization
24 Feb.	League adopts Lytton report
27 Mar.	Japan: Japan leaves League
5 May	Soviet–German treaties renewed
31 May	Sino-Japanese truce of Tangku
12 June– 25 July	World Economic Conference, London
15 July	Four Power Pact signed at Rome
14 Oct.	Germany leaves League and Disarmament Conference
17 Nov.	US recognition of the USSR

GENERAL BIBLIOGRAPHY*
Volume 1

Manuscript and Primary Sources

Work in these archives has been highly selective. For the most part, private collections have been seen in their entirety. Only general categories of Foreign Office and Ministry papers have been cited, except when used in the text.

Britain

Private Papers

Lord d'Abernon	Public Record Office, Kew
Lord Avon (Anthony Eden)	Birmingham University Library
Earl Baldwin (Stanley Baldwin)	Cambridge University Library
Earl Balfour (Arthur J. Balfour)	British Museum
Sir Alexander Cadogan	Churchill College, Cambridge: ACAD and Public Record Office, Kew: FO 800/ 293
Viscount Cecil of Chelwood (Lord Robert Cecil)	British Library, London
Lord Robert Cecil	British Library, London
Austen Chamberlain	Birmingham University Library: AC and Public Record Office, Kew: FO 800/263
Neville Chamberlain	Birmingham University Library: NC
Winston S. Churchill	Churchill College, Cambridge: CHAR
Marquis Curzon of Kadlestone (George Nathaniel Curzon)	India Office Library, London
Lord Hankey (Maurice Hankey)	Churchill College, Cambridge: HNKY
Lord Harding of Penshurst (Charles Harding)	Cambridge University Library
Arthur Henderson	Public Record, Kew: FO 800/280/4

*An annotated, selective bibliography of secondary works will appear at the end of volume II as well as a list of biographies arranged according to country.

Sir Hugh Knatchbull-Hugessen	Churchill College, Cambridge: KNAT
David Lloyd George	House of Lords Library
James Ramsay MacDonald	Public Record Office, Kew: PRO 30/69
Harold Nicholson MSS	Sissinghurst, now Balliol College, Oxford
Philip Noel-Baker	Churchill College, Cambridge: NBKR
Owen O'Malley	Private Collection
Sir Eric Phipps	Churchill College, Cambridge: PHPP, Public Record Office, Kew: FO 794/16
Sir Horace Rumboldt	Bodleian Library, Oxford: MS. Rumbold
Sir Orme Sargent	Public Record Office, Kew: FO 800/272-9
Sir John Simon	Bodleian Library, Oxford: MSS. Simon and Public Record Office, Kew: FO 800/285-91
Lord Strang (William Strang)	Churchill College, Cambridge: STRN
Lord Templewood (Samuel Hoare)	Cambridge University Library
Lord Vansittart (Robert Vansittart)	Churchill College, Cambridge, VNST, I and II

Public Record Office, Kew

Cabinet Office: CAB (Cabinet, Committees, Secretariat),
Including CAB 29/Peace Conference and Other International Conferences
Prime Minister's Office

Foreign Office: General Correspondence, Political: FO 371
Czechoslovakia
France
Germany
Italy
Poland
USA
USSR
Yugoslavia

Foreign Office: Private Collections, ministers and officials: FO 800

France

Private Papers

Papiers d'Agents-Archives Privées dans les Archives du Ministère des Affaires étrangères, Paris:

Robert Coulondre
Édouard Herriot

Henri Hoppenot
René Massigli
Alexandre Millerand
Joseph Paul-Boncour
André Tardieu

Papiers 1940:
Georges Bonnet
Édouard Daladier
Henri Hoppenot
Alexis Léger

Archives Nationales, Paris

Série AP (Archives Privées)
Édouard Daladier   496 AP
Alexandre Millerand   470 AP

Archives du Ministère des Affaires étrangères, Paris
Série à Paix, 1914–1920
Correspondence politique et commerciale, 1918–1940

Série Y, Internationale
Société des Nations, service français
Société des Nations, désarmement

Série Z, Europe, 1918–1940
Allegmagne
Grande-Bretagne

Italie

Germany

Personal Papers (Nachlässe)
Ulrich v. Brockdorff-Rantzau
Erich Kordt
Gustav Stresemann

Bundesarchiv Koblenz

Nachlass Bernahrd von Bülow

Politisches Archiv des Auswärtigen Amtes, Bonn

Büro Reichsminister
Büro Staatssekretär
Abteilung II F-M (Militär und Marine)
Geheimakten, 1920–1936

Länder III England
Länder IV Randstaaten
Länder IV Russland
Abteilung II F – Abrüstung

Wirtschafts-Reparationen
Abteilung III England
Abteilung III Wirtschaft
Politische Abteilung IV Russland
Abteilung IV Wirtschaft
Wirtschaft Sonderreferat
Parlamentarischer Untersuchungsausschuss

Deutsche Botschaft London
Deutsche Botschaft Moskau
Deutsche Botschaft Paris

League of Nations

Archives de la Société des Nations, Geneva
Conférence du désarmement   I.I.
Union Euopéenne   V

Printed Official Sources

Belgium

Documents diplomatiques belges, 1920–1940
   Tome 1: période 1920–1924 (Brussels, 1964)
   Tome 2: période 1925–1931 (Brussels, 1964)
   Tome 3: période 1931–1936 (Brussels, 1964)

Britain

Documents on British Foreign Policy, 1919–1939
   Series I: *1919–1925*, 27 vols. (London, 1947–85)
   Series IA: *1925–1930*, 7 vols. (London, 1966–75)
   Series II: *1929–1938*, 21 vols. (London, 1946–84)
British Documents on Foreign Affairs: Reports and Papers from the Foreign Office Confidential Print, Part II: From the First to the Second World War
   Series A: *The Soviet Union, 1917–1939*, 17 vols. (Frederick, Md., 1984–92)
   Series B: *Turkey, Iran and the Middle East, 1918–1939*, 35 vols. (Frederick, Md., 1985–97)
   Series C: *North America, 1919–1939*, 25 vols. (Frederick, Md., 1986–95)
   Series F: *Europe, 1919–1939*, 67 vols. (Bethseda, Md., 1990–6)

Series J: *The League of Nations, 1918–1941*, 10 vols. (Frederick, Md., 1992–5)
Series K: *Economic Affairs, Cultural Propaganda, and the Reform of the Foreign Office, 1910–1939*, 4 vols. (Bethseda, Md., 1997).
Parliamentary Debates
Parliamentary Debates (Official Reports)
House of Commons: Fifth Series, vols. 110–284: 15 Oct. 1918–21 Dec. 1933
House of Lords: Fifth Series, vols. 21–90: 29 July 1918–1 Mar. 1934

China

BRANDT, C., SCHWARZ, B., and FAIRBANK, J. K. (eds.), *Documentary History of Chinese Communism* (Cambridge, Mass., 1953).
DANIELS, ROBERT V., *A Documentary History of Communism*, 2nd edn., 2 vols. (London, 1987).

France

Chambre des Députés, Débats Parlementaires Journal officiel de la République française
    12ᵉ législature (1919–24)
    13ᵉ législature (1924–8)
    14ᵉ législature (1928–32)
Sénat, Débats Parlementaires
Journal officiel de la République française
    12ᵉ législature (1919–24)
    13ᵉ législature (1924–8)
    14ᵉ législature (1928–32)
Documents diplomatiques français, 1932–1939
    1ère série: *1932–1935*, 13 vols. (Paris, 1964–84)
    Série 1920–1932 (publication continuing)
    Tome 1: *10 janvier 1920–18 mai 1920* (Paris, 1999)

Germany

Akten der Reichskanzlei: Weimarer Republik
    Das Kabinett Scheidemann: Feb–Juni 1919 (1971)
    Das Kabinett Bauer: 21. Juni 1919 bis 27. März 1920 (1980)
    Das Kabinett Müller I: März–Juni 1920 (1971)
    Das Kabinett Fehrenbach: Juni 1920–März 1921 (1972)
    Die Kabinette Wirth I und II (1973)
    Das Kabinett Cuno (1968)
    Die Kabinette Stresemann I und II: 13. August bis 6. Oktober 1923, 6. Oktober bis 30. November 1923 (1978)
    Die Kabinette Marx I und II: 30. November 1923 bis 3. Juni 1924, 3. Juni 1924 bis 15. Januar 1925 (1973)
    Die Kabinette Luther I und II: 1925–6, 2 vols. (1977).
    Die Kabinette Marx III und IV: 17. Mai 1926 bis 29. Januar 1927, 29. Januar 1927 bis 29. Juni 1928 (1988)

Das Kabinett Müller II: Juni 1928–März 1930, 2 vols. (1970)
Die Kabinette Brüning I und II: 30. März 1930 bis 10. Oktober 1931, 10. Oktober 1931 bis 1. Juni 1932, 2 vols. (1982)
Das Kabinett von Papen: 1. Juni bis 3. Dezember 1932 (1989)
Das Kabinett von Schleicher: 3. Dezember 1932 bis 30. Januar 1933 (1986)
Akten zur Deutschen Auswärtigen Politik, 1918–1945
  Serie A: *1918–1925*, 13 vols. (Göttingen, 1982–95)
  Serie B: *1925–1933*, 23 vols. (Göttingen, 1966–83).

Italy

I documenti diplomatici italiani
  Sesta serie: *1918–1922*, 2 vols. (Rome, 1956–80)
  Settima serie: *1922–1935*, 16 vols. (Rome, 1953–90)
MUSSOLINI, BENITO, *Opera Omnia*, ed. Susmel, Edoardo and Duilio vols. 14–26: *14 Sep 1919–18 Dec. 1934* (Rome, 1954–8).

Switzerland

Commission Nationale pour la Publication de Document diplomatiques Suisses, Nationale Kommission für die Veröffentlichung diplomatischer Dokumente der Schweiz
  Documents diplomatiques suisses—Diplomatische Dokumente der Schweiz—Documenti diplomatici svizeri, vols. 7–10: *11 Nov. 1918–31 Dec. 1933* (Bern, 1979–82).

USA

Department of State, *Papers Relating to the Foreign Relations of the United States*, vols. for 1919–1933 (Washington, DC, 1934–52).
Papers of Woodrow Wilson, ed. A. S. Link, vols. 45–8 (Princeton, 1965–85).

USSR

Dokumenty vneshnei politiki SSSR
  7 noiabria 1917 g.–31 dekabria 1938 g., 21 vols. (Moscow, 1957–77).
Royal Institute of International Affairs, *Soviet Documents on Foreign Policy, 1917–1941*, ed. Jane Degras, 3 vols. (London, 1951–3).
DEGRAS, JANE (ed.), *The Communist International 1919–1943: Documents and Commentary*, 3 vols. (London, 1956–65).
League of Nations *Official Journal*

Memoirs, Diaries, and Autobiographies

ALOISI, BARON POMPEO, *Journal: 25 juillet 1932–14 juin 1936*, trans. Maurice Vaussard (Paris, 1957).
AMERY, LEOPOLD C. M. S., *My Political Life*, 3 vols. (London, 1953–5).

AMERY, LEOPOLD C. M. S., *The Leo Amery Diaries*, ed. John Barnes and David Nicholson (London, 1980).

APPONYI, ALBERT, *The Memoirs of Count Apponyi* (London, Toronto, 1935).

AVON, LORD (ANTHONY EDEN), *The Eden Memoirs*, 3 vols. (London, 1960–5).

BAINVILLE, JACQUES, *Journal, 1919–1926* (Paris, 1949).

BECK, COLONEL JOZEF, *Dernier report: politique polonaise, 1926–1939* (Neuchâtel, 1951).

BENEŠ, EDVARD, *The Struggle for Collective Security in Europe and the Italo-Abyssinian War* (Prague, 1935).

—— *Czechoslovakia's Struggle for Freedom* (Halifax, NS, 1941).

BLONDEL, JULES-FRANÇOIS, *Ce que mes yeux ont vu de 1900 à 1950: récit d'un diplomate*, 2 vols. (Arras, n.d.).

—— *Au fil de la carrière: récit d'un diplomate, 1911–1938* (Paris, 1960).

BONNET, GEORGES E., *Vingt ans de vie politique, 1918–1938* (Paris, 1969).

BRINON, FERNAND DE, *Mémoires* (Paris, 1949).

BRÜNING, HEINRICH, *Memoiren* (Stuttgart, 1970).

—— *Briefe und Gespräche, 1934–1945: ein historisches Dokument und 'Selbstbildnis' des umstrittenen Reichskanzlers*, ed. Claire Nix and Reginald Phelps (Stuttgart, 1974).

BRUNS, CARL GEORG, *Gesammelte Schriften zur Minderheitenfrage* (Berlin, 1934).

BULLITT, WILLIAM C., *The Bullitt Mission to Russia* (New York, 1919).

CAILLAUX, J., *Mes mémoires*, 3 vols.: *III. Clairvoyance et force d'ame dans les épreuves 1912–1930* (Paris, 1942–7).

CAMBON, PAUL and CAMBON, H. (eds.), *Correspondence, 1870–1924*, 3 vols. (Paris, 1940–6).

CECIL, LORD ROBERT, *A Great Experiment* (London, 1941).

—— *All the Way* (London, 1949).

CERUTTI, ELISABETTA, *Vista de vicino* (Milan, 1951); English trans., *Ambassador's Wife* (London, 1952).

CHAMBERLAIN, SIR AUSTEN, *Down the Years* (London, 1935).

CHARLES-ROUX, FRANÇOIS, *Souvenirs diplomatiques: Rome–Quirinal, février 1916–février 1919* (Paris, 1958).

—— *Une grande ambassade à Rome, 1919–1925* (Paris, 1961).

CHURCHILL, WINSTON SPENCER, *Complete Speeches, 1897–1963*, 8 vols., ed. Robert James Rhodes (London, 1974).

CLAUDEL, PAUL, *Claudel aux États-Unis, 1927–1933* (Paris, 1982).

CLEMENCEAU, GEORGES, *Grandeur and the Misery of Victory* (London, 1930).

CLÉMENTEL, ÉTIENNE, *La France et la politique économique interalliée* (Paris, 1931).

CURTIS, JULIUS, *Sechs Jahre Minister der deutschen Republik* (Heidelberg, 1948).

D'ABERNON, LORD, *Ambassador of Peace: Pages from the Diary of Viscount D'Abernon*, 3 vols. (London, 1929–30).

DALTON, HUGH, *Call Back Yesterday: Memoirs, 1887–1945* (London, 1953–7).

DAWES, CHARLES GATES, *Journal as Ambassador to Great Britain, 1929–1933* (New York, 1939).

DE GAULLE, CHARLES, *Lettres, notes et carnets, 1919–1940: Charles de Gaulle à Paul Reynaud*, vol. II: *1919–juin 1940* (Paris, 1980).

DIRKSEN, H. VON, *Moskau, Tokio, London: Erinnerungen und Betrachtungen zu 20 Jahren deutscher Aussenpolitik, 1919–1939* (Stuttgart, 1949).

ERDMANN, KARL DIETRICH, *Kurt Riezler: Tagebücher, Aufsätze, Dokumente* (Göttingen, 1972).

FEIS, HERBERT, *Three International Episodes: Seen From E.A.* (New York, 1966).

FLANDIN, PIERRE-ÉTIENNE, *Politique française, 1919–1940* (Paris, 1947).

FOCH, F., *Mémoires*, 2 vols. (Paris, 1931).

FRANÇOIS-PONCET, ANDRÉ, *Souvenirs d'une ambassade à Berlin: septembre 1931–octobre 1938* (Paris, 1946).

—— 'France and the Rhine', *Spectator* (Mar. 1946), 267–8.

—— 'France and the Ruhr', *Economist* (Apr. 1946), 570–2.

GAMELIN, GÉNÉRAL MAURICE, *Servir*, 3 vols.: *II. Le Prologue du drame 1930–août 1939* (Paris, 1946–7).

GILBERT, MARTIN S. *Companion Volumes. Volume IV. Part I Documents January 1917–June 1919* (London, 1977).

Part 2 Documents July 1919–March 1921 (London, 1977).

Part 3 Documents April 1921–November 1922 (London, 1977).

Volume V. 'The Exchequer Years' 1923–1929 (London, 1979).

'The Wilderness Years' 1929–1935 (London, 1981).

GLADWYN, BARON (HUBERT MILES GLADWYN JEBB), *The Memoirs of Lord Gladwyn* (London, 1972).

GRAZZI, EMANUELE, *Il principe della fine: L'impresa di Grecia* (Rome, 1945).

GREGORY, JOHN DUNCAN, *On the Edge of Diplomacy: Rambles and Reflections, 1902–1928* (London, 1929).

GREW, JOSEPH C., *Turbulent Era: A Diplomatic Record of Forty Years, 1904–1945*, ed. Walter Johnson, 2 vols. (Boston, 1952).

GREY, VISCOUNT, *Twenty Five Years* (New York, 1925).

GUARIGLIA, RAFFAELE, *Ricordi, 1922–1946* (Naples, 1950).

HANKEY, MAURICE, *Diplomacy By Conference: Studies in Public Affairs, 1920–1946* (New York, 1946).

HARDINGE, LORD, of Penshurst (CHARLES HARDINGE), *The Old Diplomacy: The Reminiscences of Lord Hardinge of Penshurst* (London, 1947).

HEADLAM, CUTHBERT, *Parliament and Politics in the Age of Baldwin and MacDonald: The Headlam Diaries, 1923–1935*, ed. Stuart Ball (London, 1992).

HEADLAM-MORLEY, Sir JAMES, *A Memoir of the Paris Peace Conference 1919*, ed. Agnes Headlam-Morley, Russell Bryant, and Anna Cienciala (London, 1972).

HENDERSON, NEVILLE, *Water Under the Bridges* (London, 1945).

HENOT, EDOUARD, *Jadis*, vol 2: D'une guerre à l'autre, 1914–1936 (Paris, 1952).

HILGER, GUSTAV, *Wir und der Kreml: Deutsch–soujetische Beziehungen, 1918–1941*, 2nd edn. (Frankfurt-am-Main, 1986).

HITLER, ADOLF, *Mein Kampf* (Munich, 1940).

—— *Hitler's Second Book: A Document from the Year 1928*, introduction by Telford Taylor; trans. Salvator Attanusio (New York, 1962).

HOHLER, Sir THOMAS BEAUMONT, *Diplomatic Petrel* (London, 1942).

HOOKER, NANCY (ed.), *The Moffat Papers: Selections from the Diplomatic Papers of Jay Pierrepont Moffat, 1919–1943* (Cambridge, Mass.: 1956).

HOOVER, HERBERT, *The Memoirs of Herbert Hoover*, vol. II: *1929–1933* (New York, 1952).

—— *Memoirs of Herbert Hoover: The Cabinet and the Presidency, 1920–1933* (New York, 1952)

HORTHY, MIKLÓS, *Ein Leben für Ungarn* (Bonn, 1953).

HORTHY, NICHOLAS, *Memoirs* (London, 1956).

HOUSE, EDWARD MANDELL, *The Intimate Papers of Colonel House*, ed. Charles Seymour (Boston, 1928).

HULL, CORDELL, *Memoirs of Cordell Hull*, 2 vols. (New York, 1948).

HYMANS, PAUL, *Mémoires*, 2 vols. (Brussels, 1958).

JÁSZI, OSCAR, *Revolution and Counter-revolution in Hungary* (London, 1924).

KÁROLYI, MIHÁLY, *Fighting the World: The Struggle for Peace* (London, 1924).

—— *Count Karolyi and Hungary: From Defeat to Victory* (London, 1945).

KESSLER, C. (ed.), *The Diaries of a Cosmopolitan: Count Harry Kessler, 1918–1937* (London, 1971).

KEYNES, JOHN MAYNARD, *Two Memoirs* (London, 1949).

KNATCHBULL-HUGESSON, HUGH, *Diplomat in Peace and War* (London, 1949).

LANSBURY, GEORGE, *My Life* (London, 1928).

LARGADELLE, HUBERT, *Mission à Rome: Mussolini* (Paris, 1955).

LOUCHEUR, LOUIS, *Carnets Secrets 1908–1932* (Bussels and Paris, 1962).

LAROCHE, JULES, *La Pologne de Piłsudski: souvenirs d'une ambassade, 1926–1935* (Paris, 1953).

—— *Au Quai d'Orsay avec Briand et Poincaré, 1914–1926* (Paris, 1957).

LEE, 1st Viscount of Fareham (ARTHUR HAMILTON LEE), *A Good Innings: The Private Papers of Viscount Lee of Fareham*, ed. Alan Clark (London, 1974).

LEITH-ROSS, Sir FREDERICK, *Money Talks: Fifty Years of International Finance* (London, 1968).

LENIN, V. I., *Collected Works*, vols. 26–47 (Moscow, 1964–80).

LLOYD-GEORGE, DAVID, *The Truth About the Peace Treaties*, 2 vols. (London, 1938).

—— *Memoirs of the Peace Conference*, 2 vols. (London, 1939).

LOCKHART, ROBERT HAMILTON BRUCE, *Retreat From Glory* (London, 1934).

—— *Friends, Foes and Foreigners* (London, 1957).

—— *The Diaries of Sir Robert Bruce Lockhart*, ed. Young, Kenneth (London, 1973).

LONDONDERRY, Marquiss of, *Wings of Destiny* (London 1943).

LOUCHEUR, LOUIS and DE LAUNAY, JACQUES (eds.), *Carnets secrets, 1908–1932* (Paris, 1962).

MADRIAGA, SALVADOR DE, *Morning Without Noon: Memoirs* (Farnborough, 1974).

MANTOUX, PAUL, *Les Délibérations du Conseil des Quatre, 24 mars–28 juin 1919: notes de l'officier interprete Paul Mantoux*, 2 vols. (Paris, 1955).

MOREAU, ÉMILE, *Souvenirs d'un gouverneur de la Banque de France: l'histoire de la stabilisation de la France, 1926–1928* (Paris, 1954).

MORGAN, GENERAL J. H., *Assize of Arms: Being the Story of the Disarmament of Germany and Her Rearmament, 1919–1939* (London, 1945).

NADOLNY, RUDOLF, *Mein Beitrag: Erinnerungen eines Botschafters des Deutschen Reiches*, ed. Günter Wollstein (Cologne, 1985).

NICOLSON, HAROLD, *Diaries and Letters*, vol. I: *1930–1939* (New York).

—— *Peacemaking, 1919* (London, 1933).

NITTI, FRANCESCO SAVEIO, *Rivelaziono, dramatis personae* (Bari, 1963).

NOËL, LÉON, *Les Illusions de Stresa: l'Italie abandonnée à Hitler* (Paris, 1975).

OSUSKÝ, STEFAN, *Le Calvaire de la Tchécoslovaquie: vues sur l'Europe nouvelle* (Tours, 1940).

PAPEN, FRANZ VON, *Memoirs*, trans. Brian Connell (London, 1952).

PAUL-BONCOUR, JOSEPH, *Entre deux guerres*, vol. *Les Lendemains de la victoire, 1919–1934* (Paris, 1945–6).

PRINCARÉ, Raymond, *Au service de la France. Neuf années de souvenirs*, 10 vols (Paris, 1926–1933).

POGGE VON STRANDMANN, HARTMUT (ed.), *Walther Rathenau: Industrialist, Banker, Intellectual and Politician. Notes and Diaries 1907–1922* (Oxford, 1985).

PRITTWITZ UND GAFFRON, FRIEDRICH VON, *Zwischen Petersburg und Washington: Ein Diplomatenleben* (Munich, 1952).

REYNAUD, PAUL, *Mémoires*, 2 vols.: *I Venu de me montagne* (Paris, 1960).

ROOSEVELT, FRANKLIN D., *The Public Papers and Addresses of Franklin D. Roosevelt*, compiled by Samuel I. Rosenman: Vol. 2. *The Year of Crisis, 1933* (New York, 1938–50).

ROSEN, FRIEDRICH, *Aus einem diplomatischen Wanderleben*, vols 3 and 4 (Wiesbaden, 1959).

SAINT-AULAIRE, COMTE AUGUSTE FÉLIX CHARLES DE BEAUPOIL, *Confession d'un vieux diplomat* (Paris, 1953).

SALANDRA, A., *Memorie politiche 1916–25* (Milan, 1951).

SALTER, BARON (Sir JAMES ARTHUR SALTER), *Memoirs of a Public Servant* (London, 1961).

SCHMIDT, PAUL, *Statist auf diplomatischer Bühne, 1923–45* (Bonn, 1950).

SELF, ROBERT C. (ed.), *The Austen Chamberlain Diary Letters: The Correspondence of Sir Austen Chamberlain With his Sisters Hilda and Ida, 1916–1937* (Cambridge, 1995).

SEYDOUX, FRANÇOIS, *Mémoires d'Outre Rhin* (Paris, 1975).

SEYDOUX, JACQUES, *De Versailles au plan Young; réparations, dettes interalliées, reconstruction européene* (Paris, 1932).

SIMON, JOHN, *Retrospect* (London, 1952).

SNOWDEN, 1st Viscount (PHILIP SNOWDEN), *An Autobiography*, 2 vols. (London, 1934).

STRANG, BARON (WILLIAM STRANG), *Home and Abroad* (London, 1956).

STRESEMANN, GUSTAV, *Vermàchtmis. Der Nachlass in drei Bänden*, ed. H. Bernhard, 3 vols. (Berlin, 1932–3).

—— *His Diaries, Letters and Papers*, ed. Eric Sutton, vol. 3 (London, 1940).

SZINAI, MIKLÓS and SZUCS, LÁSZLÓ (eds.), *The Confidential Papers of Admiral Horthy* (Budapest, 1965).

TABOUIS, GENEVIÈVE, *They Called Me Cassandra* (New York, 1942).

—— *Vingt ans de 'suspense' diplomatique* (Paris, 1958).

TIRARD, PAUL, *La France sur le Rhin; douze années d'occupation rhénane* (Paris, 1930).
TITULESCU, NICOLAE, *Romania's Foreign Policy (1937)* (Bucharest, 1994).
TARDIEU, ANDRÉ, *La paix* (Paris, 1921).
VANSITTART, BARON (ROBERT GILBERT VANSITTART), *The Mist Procession: Lessons of My Life* (London, 1958).
VARÈ, DANIELE, *Laughing Diplomat* (London, 1938).
WEYGAND, General Maxime, *Mirages et réalité*, vol. 2 (Paris, 1957).
WINDISCHGRAETZ, LUDWIG PRINCE, *My Adventures and Misadventures*, ed. and trans. Charles Kassler (London, 1967).

Biographies

BOYLE, ANDREW, *Montagu Norman: A Biography* (London, 1967).
BULLOCK, ALAN, *Hitler: A Study in Tyranny* (London, 1952; rev. edn. 1962).
—— *Hitler and Stalin: Parallel Lives* (London 1991).
BURNS, JAMES MACGREGOR, *Roosevelt: The Lion and the Fox* (New York, 1956).
BUSCH, BRITON COOPER, *Hardinge of Penshurst: A Study of the Old Diplomacy* (Hamden, Conn., 1980).
CAMERON, ELIZABETH R., 'Alexis Saint-Léger Léger', in Gordon A. Craig and Felix Gilbert (eds.), *The Diplomats, 1919–1939* (Princeton, 1963).
CHALLENER, RICHARD D., 'The French Foreign Office: The Era of Philippe Berthelot', in Gordon A. Craig and Felix Gilbert (eds.), *The Diplomats, 1919–1939* (Princeton, 1963).
CHOSSUDOWSKY, E. M., *Chicherin and the Evolution of Soviet Foreign Policy and Diplomacy* (Geneva, 1973).
CLAY, Sir HENRY, *Lord Norman* (London, 1957).
COHEN, STEPHEN F., *Bukharin and the Bolshevik Revolution: A Political Biography, 1888–1938* (London, 1974).
COINTET, JEAN-PAUL, *Pierre Laval* (Paris, 1993).
COLTON, JOEL, *Léon Blum: Humanist in Politics* (New York, 1986).
CONTE, FRANCIS, *Christian Rakovski (1873–1941): A Political Biography* (Boulder, Col., 1989).
CRAIG, GORDON A. and GILBERT, FELIX (eds.), *The Diplomats, 1919–1939* (Princeton, 1963).
DEBO, RICHARD K., 'Litvinov and Kamenev—Ambassadors Extraordinary: The Problem of Soviet Representation Abroad' *Slavic Review*, 34 (1975), 463–82.
DESTREMAU, BERNARD, *Weygand* (Paris, 1989).
DEUTSCHER, ISAAC, *Trotsky*, 3 vols. (New York, 1954–63).
—— *Stalin: A Political Biography*, 2nd edn. (New York, 1960).
DILKS, DAVID, *Neville Chamberlain*, Vol. 1: *Pioneering and Reform, 1870–1929* (Cambridge, 1984).
DOß, KURT, *Zwischen Weimar and Warschau: Ulrich Rauscher, Deutscher Gesandter in Polen 1922–1930. Eine politische Biographie* (Düsseldorf, 1984).
DU RÉAU, ÉLISABETH, *Édouard Daladier, 1884–1970* (Paris, 1993).
DUROSELLE, J. B., *Clemenceau* (Paris, 1988).

EPSTEIN, KLAUS, *Matthias Erzberger and the Dilemma of German Democracy* (Princeton, 1959).

FAUSOLD, M. L and MAZUZAN, G. T., *The Hoover Presidency: A Reappraisal* (New York, 1974).

FARRAR, MARJORIE MILBANK, *Principled Pragmatist: The Political Career of Alexandre Millerand* (Leamington Spa, 1990).

FEILING, KEITH GRAHAME, *The Life of Neville Chamberlain* (London, 1946).

FELDMAN, GERALD D., *Hugo Stinnes. Biographie eines Industriellen 1870–1924* (Munich, 1998).

FERRELL, R. H., KELLOGG, FRANK, B., and HENRY, L., *Stimson* (New York, 1963).

FERRO, MARC, *Pétain* (Paris, 1987).

FEST, JOACHIM C., *Hitler*, trans. Richard and Clara Winston (Harmondsworth, 1977).

FORD, FRANKLIN L., 'Three Observers in Berlin: Rumbold, Dodd and François-Poncet', in Gordon A. Craig and Felix Gilbert (eds.), *The Diplomats, 1919–1939* (Princeton, 1963).

FREIDEL, FRANK, *Franklin D. Roosevelt: A Rendezvous With Destiny* (Boston, 1990).

GILBERT, MARTIN, *Sir Horace Rumbold: Portrait of a Diplomat, 1869–1941* (London, 1973).

GOLDBACH, MARIE-LUISE, *Karl Radek und die deutsch–sowjetischen Beziehungen, 1918–1923* (Bonn, 1973).

HAMILTON, MARY AGNES, *Arthur Henderson: A Biography* (London, 1938).

HAWLEY, E. W. (ed.), *Herbert Hoover as Secretary of Commerce* (Iowa City, 1981).

HECKSCHER, AUGUST, *Woodrow Wilson* (New York, 1991).

HÜRTER, JOHANNES, *Wilhelm Groener: Reichswehrminister am Ende der Weimarer Republik 1928–1932* (Munich, 1993).

JACOBS, DAN NORMAN, *Borodin: Stalin's Man in China* (Cambridge, Mass. 1981).

JAMES, ROBERT RHODES, *Churchill: A Study in Failure, 1900–1939* (London, 1970).

JEANNENEY, JEAN-NOEL, *François de Wendel en république: l'argent et le pouvoir, 1914–1940*, 3 vols. (Lille, 1976).

—— *Georges Mandel. L'homme qu'on attendait* (Paris, 1991).

JENKINS, ROY, *Churchill* (London, 2001).

JOLL, JAMES, *Intellectuals in Politics: Léon Blum, Walter Rathenau and F. T. Marinetti: Three Biographical Essays* (London, 1960).

JUDD, DENIS, *Lord Reading: Rufus Isaacs, First Marquess of Reading, Lord Chief Justice and Viceroy of India, 1860–1935* (London, 1982).

KEIGER, JOHN F. V., *Raymond Poincaré* (Cambridge, 1997).

KERSHAW, IAN, *Hitler: 1889–1936: Hubris* (London, 1998).

KEYNES, JOHN MAYNARD, *Essays in Biography* (London, 1933).

KUPFERMAN, FRED, *Pierre Laval, 1883–1945* (Paris, 1976).

KÜPPERS, HEINRICH, *Joseph Wirth. Parlamentarier, Minister und Kanzler der Weimarer Republik* (Stuttgart, 1997).

LACOUTURE, JEAN, *De Gaulle*, vol. I: *Le Rebelle, 1890–1944* (Paris, 1984–6).

LÉGER, ALEXIS SAINT-, *Briand* (New York, 1943).

LINK, ARTHUR S., *Woodrow Wilson: Revolution, War, and Peace* (Arlington Heights, Ill., 1979).

MARQUAND, DAVID, *Ramsay MacDonald* (London, 1977).

MICHALKA, WOLFGANG and LEE, MARSHALL M. (eds.), *Gustav Stresemann* (Darmstadt, 1982).

NAMIER, JULIA, *Lewis Namier: A Biography* (Oxford, 1971).

O'CONNOR, TIMOTHY EDWARD, *Diplomacy and Revolution: G. V. Chicherin and Soviet Foreign Affairs, 1918–1930* (Ames, Ind., 1988).

OUDIN, BERNARD, *Aristide Briand: la paix, une idée neuve en Europe* (Paris, 1987).

PELLING, HENRY, *Winston Churchill* (London, 1974).

PETRIE, CHARLES, *The Life and Letters of the Right Hon. Sir Austen Chamberlain*, 2 vols. (London, 1939–40)

PHILLIPS, HUGH D., *Between the Revolution and the West: A Political Biography of Maxim M. Litvinov* (Boulder, Co., 1992).

PUSAY, M. J. *Charles Evans Hughes*, 2 vols. (New York, 1951).

RÖDDER, ANDREAS, *Stresemanns Erbe. Julius Curtius and die deutsche Außenpolitik 1929–1931* (Paderborn, 1996).

ROSKILL, STEPHEN W., *Hankey: Man of Secrets*, 3 vols. (London, 1970–4).

SCHEIDEAMM, CHRISTIANE, *Ulrich Graf Brockdorff-Rantzau (1869–1928). Eine politische Biographie* (Frankfurt-am-Main, 1998).

SCHWARTZ, HANS-PETER, *Konrad Adenauer: German Politician and Statesman in a Period of War, Revolution, and Reconstruction*, trans Louise Willmot, vol. I: *From the German Empire to the Federal Republic, 1876–1952* (English edn., Oxford, 1995).

SEBAG-MONTEFIORE, SIMON, *Stalin: The Court of the Red Tsar* (London, 2003).

SERVICE, ROBERT, *Lenin: A Biography* (London, 2002).

SHEPHERD, JOHN, *George Lansbury: At the Heart of Old Labour* (Oxford, 2002).

SIEBERT, FERDINAND, *Aristide Briand 1862–1932: Ein Staatsmann zwischen Frankreich und Europa* (Zurich, 1973).

SKIDELSKY, ROBERT JACOB ALEXANDER, *John Maynard Keynes: A Biography*, vol. I: *Hopes Betrayed, 1883–1920;* vol. II: *The Economist as Saviour, 1920–1937* (London, 1983–2000).

STEVENSON, FRANCES, *Lloyd George: A Diary* (New York, 1971).

SUAREZ, GEORGE, *Briand, sa vie, son oeuvre*, vol. VI: *L'Artisan de la paix, 1923–1932* (Paris, 1952).

THOMPSON, JOHN A., *Woodrow Wilson* (London, 2002)

TUCKER, ROBERT CHARLES, *Stalin as Revolutionary, 1879–1929: A Study in History and Personality* (London, 1974).

—— *Stalin in Power: The Revolution from Above, 1928–1941* (New York, 1990).

ULAM, ADAM BRUNO, *Stalin: The Man and His Era* (New York, 1973).

VOLKOGONOV, DIMITRI, *Lenin: Life and Legacy*, trans. and ed. Harold Shukman (London, 1994).

WANDEL, ECKARD, *Hans Schäffer: Steuermann in wirtschaftlichen und politischen Krisen* (Stuttgart, 1974).

WATSON, DAVID, *Georges Clemenceau: A Political Biography* (London, 1968).

WILLIAMSON, JOHN GRANT, *Karl Helfferich, 1872–1924, Economist, Financier, Politician* (Princeton, 1971).

WILSON, JOAN HOFF, *Herbert Hoover: A Forgotten Progressive* (Boston, 1975).

WRIGHT, JONATHON, *Gustav Stresemann: Weimar's Greatest Statesman* (Oxford, 2002).

WRIGLEY, CHRIS, *Arthur Henderson* (Cardiff, 1990).

YOUNG, ROBERT J., *Power and Pleasure: Louis Barthou and the Third French Republic* (Montreal and London, 1991).

INDEX

Note:
Bold entries refer to maps and tables.
Treaties, agreements, conventions and pacts are indexed under the heading 'treaties, agreements, conventions and pacts'.